The ACT Prep Black Book

"The Most Effective ACT Strategies Ever Published"

Second Edition

By Mike Barrett and Patrick Barrett

I attribute my success to this—I never gave or took any excuse.
Florence Nightingale

Dedication

This book, like all of our books, is dedicated to students who want to improve their odds of success in college and beyond, and to the adults who mentor them through this critical time in their lives. We thank our family, friends, clients, and readers all over the world for the support and feedback that made this second edition of the *ACT Prep Black Book* possible.

We count ourselves very lucky that our Black Books have allowed us to connect with people in ways we never imagined when we started writing them. We put a lot of ourselves into this book, and we hope you find it helpful.

Check Us Out Online

All you need to prepare for the ACT is this Black Book, and some official ACT practice tests. You can get official ACT practice tests in the Red Book, which is our affectionate name for *The Official ACT Prep Guide*, published by ACT, Inc. See page 22 for more.

But if you'd like more from me—including sample videos and updates related to test preparation, admissions, and the college experience—please connect with me on the following channels:

ACTprepVideos.com

This is where you can sign up for my e-mail newsletter and check out sample videos of question walkthroughs to see how I think through real ACT practice questions in real time.

YouTube.com/TestingIsEasy

This is my YouTube channel, where you can find sample videos from my online video courses, as well as videos about other aspects of test prep and admissions.

Facebook.com/TestingIsEasy

This is my Facebook page, the primary place where I keep in touch with my students, and also a place to share updates, interesting articles, commentary, and the occasional gif of a goat riding a dirt bike through a mall. This feed is also posted on Instagram.com/TestingIsEasy and Twitter.com/TestingIsEasy, if you prefer to follow it there.

TestingIsEasy.com

This is my main website and blog where you can find videos and articles about many different aspects of test preparation and college admissions.

And look for more soon—including a podcast . . .

Table of Contents

PLEASE Read This First!!!! (Getting the Most out of *The ACT Prep Black Book, Second Edition*)

Hi!

As you've probably noticed, this book is pretty long. It had to be, in order for us to include everything we wanted to say about the ACT.

The good news is that you don't need to read every page in this Black Book in order to raise your score significantly—but there's a part of this book that addresses any problem an ACT-taker is likely to have. Everything from time management (page 36) to testing anxiety (page 41) to language barriers (page 578) and more is covered, not to mention detailed strategies for every section of the test and full walkthroughs for three official full-length ACT tests from ACT, Inc., so you can model the ideal test-taking thought process directly. This lets you focus your energies on your problem areas. And if you want a detailed and thorough understanding of every aspect of the test, then, by all means, enjoy all 500+ pages :)

One way or another, the goal is to show you how the ACT actually works, and how you can strategically exploit the limitations of the test in order to raise your score as much as possible in as little time as possible. Toward that end, we've drawn on our decades of experience with standardized testing and feedback from clients, readers, and students all over the world to present this edition of the Black Book. We hope you like it.

What's in this Black Book

Our discussion of the ACT will include the following main parts:

- A Note to Concerned Parents
- Part 1: Secrets of the ACT
- Part 2: When To Use Official ACT, Inc., Materials, And When Not To
- Part 3: Goals and Training
- Part 4: Time Management
- Part 5: Key Techniques for the Whole ACT
- Part 6: Reading Test Training and Walkthroughs
- Part 7: Math Test Training and Walkthroughs
- Part 8: Science Test Training and Walkthroughs
- Part 9: English Test Training and Walkthroughs
- Part 10: Writing Test Training
- Part 11: Closing Thoughts

As you can see, Parts 1-5 cover ideas that are more general and foundational, while Parts 6-10 cover training for specific sections of the ACT. Part 11 addresses ideas and situations that would be harder to cover without the background provided in the rest of this Black Book, such as how to prepare if your goal is to make a perfect score, what to do when a question seems like it doesn't follow the rules you've learned, and how to modify your training if you're not a native speaker of English.

You may be tempted to skip or skim the earlier parts of this book, and dive straight into the parts that you think are most relevant to your needs as you currently understand them. Of course, it's your right to do that if you feel like it, but I'd strongly recommend that you read Parts 1-5 instead of skipping them (after all, that's why we wrote them :)). They lay an important foundation that will help you understand why the strategies in the rest of the ACT Prep Black Book work, which will help you apply them more effectively and consistently as you learn them.

The parts of this Black Book that cover section-specific training for the ACT will start out by describing the following key information:

- the big secret behind the relevant section of the ACT
- the necessary background information (such as math formulas, grammar rules, or aspects of experimental design)
- unwritten, ACT-specific rules and patterns
- a step-by-step process for attacking questions in the section
- any other relevant notes or special techniques

After that, each section will demonstrate all of the above training in action against real ACT questions published by ACT, Inc., in *The Official ACT Prep Guide* (which I'll affectionately refer to as the "Red Book," because it's red, and it's a book). That way, you'll be able to see my techniques in action against three full official tests, which will help you master the strategies you'll learn in this Black Book.

(As we'll see in "Part 2: When To Use Official ACT, Inc., Materials, And When Not To," starting on page 20, you'll need a copy of the Red Book in order to get the full benefit from the question walkthroughs in this Black Book, because we're not allowed to re-print ACT questions from the Red Book. And see "(But Wait—which Red Book!?)" on page 22 of this Black Book for more on the differences among the several versions of the Red Book currently available.)

Two Notes On The Walkthroughs

One of the most valuable things about this book is that it contains more than 600 detailed walkthroughs of real ACT test questions from ACT, Inc. (you'll learn more about why that's so important in Parts 1 and 2 of this Black Book). Here are two important ideas to help you get the most out of these walkthroughs.

Read the Entire Walkthrough!

If you're going to look up a walkthrough in this book for a particular real ACT question, be sure to read the whole thing, including any introductory text explaining the key concepts involved in the question, and any notes at the end of the walkthrough! If you just read part of the walkthrough, you may not notice many of the key details of the question that will actually be useful to you on test day.

My Walkthroughs are More Thorough Than You'll Need to be on Test Day!

My walkthroughs often go into a lot of detail, but that doesn't mean that applying these techniques on test day should take you a long time! Remember that the point of my walkthrough is to show you everything of importance that's going on in the question, so you can understand how the ACT really works—but even though the description of a particular question might go on for pages, we could often have chosen the correct answer in 10 seconds or less on test day, and pretty much always in 30 seconds or less, if our only goal were to answer the question and not thoroughly dissect it as part of our training.

Remember that, on test day, you don't have to explain to someone every single aspect of what's going on in each question the way we do in this book; you just have to find the right answer in the way that's quickest and most comfortable for you. In the Math walkthroughs, for example, we might look at 2 or 3 different ways to answer one question—but you won't need to find multiple solutions to these questions on test day. We're just looking at a lot of different ways to show you that multiple approaches can be successful, so you can find which one works best for you.

My purpose in this Black Book is to communicate the ideal thought process when encountering a new ACT question, so I often need to go into some detail, and focus on aspects of a question that may not seem important to an untrained test-taker. In time, you'll find that a lot of the thoughts I spell out on the page in a walkthrough become second-nature for you, so that you don't even consciously register them for more than a split second as you work through a question.

About My Writing Style . . .

You may have already noticed that I use an informal, conversational writing style in this Black Book. I do this because my students and readers tend to find that style much easier to read and digest than a formal "textbook" style.

This means I might do a few things your English teacher wouldn't love, such as starting sentences with conjunctions like "and" or "but." Most teachers will tell you not to do that in formal writing, even though famous and respected authors have written that way for centuries. Even E. B. White, that eminent arbiter of grammar and style, once wrote this:

> Life's meaning has always eluded me and I guess it always will. But I love it just the same.

You'll also find that many of my sentences would be unacceptable if they appeared on the ACT English section. Don't worry about that, though; as we'll discuss in the training for that section, you'll find that most modern writers don't follow all the rules of that section in real life. (In fact, most or all of the passages on the ACT Reading section—and many of the prompts and answer choices that make up the rest of the ACT itself—violate rules that the ACT English section requires you to follow as a test-taker.)

So I don't think of my Black Books as examples of formal writing, and I hope you don't, either. I prefer to have more of a conversation, while still making my meaning as clear as possible. In my experience, readers find this approach much more engaging and ultimately much more effective, which is the whole point.

A Note to Concerned Parents

If you are truly serious about preparing your child for the future, don't teach him to subtract—teach him to deduct.
Fran Lebowitz

Every so often, I get an e-mail from a parent who is concerned about my method of preparing for standardized tests. Basically, the parent is worried that approaching the test in the way I recommend somehow corrupts the purpose of the test as a learning experience for his child. Let me take a minute to address this concern in the beginning, so we're all on the same page for the rest of this book and for the rest of your preparation.

As I've already mentioned, and as I'll continue to mention throughout this Black Book, standardized tests like the ACT have very little in common with the tests you might take in school. In school, tests have a lot to do with your ability to memorize a lot of information ahead of time, and then recall that material on test day. But doing well on the ACT is much more about being able to understand a set of standardized rules and patterns, and then recognizing those patterns and rules in action and responding accordingly on test day, in a highly repetitive way.

In other words, preparing for (and doing well on) the ACT isn't a learning experience in the way you might think it should be. The skills that you need to do well on the ACT simply aren't the same skills you've developed in school, for the most part.

Let me be very clear here: I think learning is extremely important. I think it's a very big deal for students to be passionate about learning and understanding new material. It's essential for all of us to read novels, and learn history, and study science, and to develop and grow intellectually—not just in high school or college, but for our whole lives.

But if a high school student is trying to do her best on the ACT, then developing and growing in those ways simply isn't going to help much, because the ACT doesn't actually reward that kind of growth. So when I say things like "don't worry about exactly what this word means," or "there's no point in learning advanced math formulas for this kind of situation," it's absolutely not because I'm against learning stuff in general. It's only because the point of this Black Book is to help my readers get the best scores on the ACT that they possibly can, and doing that requires them to know how the test actually works—even if it seems like we're avoiding an opportunity to learn something.

If that's a surprise to you, bear with me, and we'll address all those issues more specifically in the coming sections.

Even though it might seem like preparing for a test as important as the ACT should necessarily involve sharpening the skills one would traditionally associate with being a "good student," it's probably best if you don't look at it this way. It's much better if we understand that doing well on the ACT requires a different set of skills from those required to do well in school, so that we can focus on developing those skills. The ACT is simply an obstacle we have to overcome so we can move on to the next step in the educational process.

Again, I'm a firm believer in doing well in school, reading widely, learning new words, and studying math and science . . .

. . . but if I told my readers to do those things *in order to improve their ACT scores,* I'd be wasting their time.

Since our only goal here is to get the highest score we can, and since that involves following all the rules of the ACT, we'll focus on learning and exploiting those rules for the duration of this Black Book.

Okay! Glad we covered that. If some of it didn't make sense, it'll probably be cleared up after you read Part 1 of this Black Book, which starts on the next page. In that Part, we'll discuss how everybody *thinks* the ACT works, and how it *actually* works.

Part 1: Secrets of the ACT

This part of the Black Book will cover the most important aspects of effective ACT preparation. Unfortunately, these are things that most untrained test-takers never realize, so they spend more time than necessary on their ACT preparation . . . and end up with very little to show for all that effort.

The rest of this Black Book will build on these fundamental concepts; you'll see them at work in all of my training and walkthroughs. In this part of the Black Book, you'll learn the following:

- why it's absolutely necessary to practice with questions that follow the same rules as the questions you'll see on test day
- why the ACT isn't designed like a regular high school test
- how ACT, Inc. is able to create difficult questions using relatively simple concepts
- why some people do better in school than they do on the ACT, or vice-versa
- why there must be only one valid answer for each ACT question
- how common classroom experiences can set you up with the wrong expectations on test day
- the ACT's biggest design weakness
- how different wrong answer choices can make a question much easier or harder
- what to do when it seems like a question has more than one good answer
- key differences between classroom discussions and the mindset you'll need for the ACT
- the best way to use answer choice patterns
- and more . . .

What You Must Understand about the ACT

Human beings, who are almost unique in having the ability to learn from the experience of others, are also remarkable for their apparent disinclination to do so.
Douglas Adams

Millions of students worry over the ACT every year. They spend countless hours (and dollars) trying to cram scientific theories and obscure trig formulas into their heads so they can get the best possible score—and most of them just end up frustrated and unhappy with their results, despite all their work. If you're reading this Black Book, it's probably because you're also unhappy with your performance so far on the ACT. (If you were happy with your score, you wouldn't need to keep preparing, right?)

Because so many people have such a tough time with the ACT (and with other standardized tests like it), the test has developed a reputation for being a difficult obstacle to overcome. A lot of people will tell you that the only way to "prepare" for the ACT is to read novels, study advanced math, take AP science classes, watch the Discovery Channel between practice essays, and do all kinds of other pointlessly rigorous things.

But those people are wrong.

Not Hard—Just Unusual

The ACT isn't hard because it's advanced. It's hard because it tests the *basics*—but in very strange ways. It's designed according to rules that are actually pretty simple, even though they're also pretty different from the rules that govern tests in high school and college.

That's a very important idea, so make sure you never forget it: the ACT is only challenging because it's a weird test of basic skills, not because it's an advanced test that rewards you for being a genius!

If you want to beat the ACT in the most effective, efficient way possible, you'll need to understand it in a way that most test-takers never do. That level of understanding requires us to take a step back and look at why and how the test was designed. That way, we can understand the limitations of the test, how it tries to make up for those limitations, and how we can take full advantage of the situation.

The Purpose of the ACT

Why are there standardized tests like the ACT? One simple answer might be that they provide a standard measure that allows schools to compare one student to another. When a college or university has applicants from different backgrounds with completely different educational experiences, it can be hard to compare their GPAs in a meaningful way, since those GPAs will reflect different classes taken at different schools. But if all the applicants take a test that's "standardized," so that the results of the test can be reliably compared to each other even when students take the test on different days in different places, then colleges can have some way to measure students against one consistent standard, which can (at least in theory) give us some idea about which students might be better suited to a particular college.

Let's think about that—just about every school considers both your GPA and your ACT (or SAT) score when you apply. This suggests (and many other details confirm) that schools consider your GPA and your standardized test scores to be measurements of *two different things*. If they both measured the same thing, there would be no need to track both of them, right?

So the first important thing to remember about the ACT is that it's a tool used by schools in the admissions process. Except in certain situations that might require a student to get a certain score to be considered for a scholarship or other award, the only reason people take the ACT is because they're applying to a college.

This evidence strongly supports something I've already said and will continue to mention throughout this book:

1. Doing well on the ACT and doing well in school are two different things.

Simply put, the skills that get rewarded on the ACT are not the same as the skills that get rewarded in the classroom.

This is why we all know people with awesome grades in advanced classes who simply can't figure out how to score well on the ACT, not to mention other students who struggle in the classroom but who can get elite standardized test scores without really seeming to try very hard.

It's also why students who spend dozens of hours on the sorts of activities that might get rewarded in a classroom—like memorizing formulas, reading novels, and so on—often end up with scores that are no better than they were before all that work. For this reason, as previously discussed, we won't be spending our time on that kind of preparation.

(There is, of course, some overlap between the skills used in high school and the skills used on the test, but it's important for us to clarify early on that the most important skills needed in each scenario are actually very different.)

So we've established that the skills required to get a good score on the ACT aren't the same as the skills required to get good grades in high school. Now we need to figure out exactly how they're different, so we know what kinds of skills to practice in order to do well on the test.

A Real-Life Example

Let's begin by imagining you're in a typical high school classroom, and your teacher is going over a multiple-choice test he's just handed back to the class.

When the teacher mentions the answer for one particular question, half the students in the class raise their hands. It turns out that the wording of the question confused them, and many ended up marking a wrong answer choice that seemed to be right because they misread the question. One student in particular stands up and explains why she chose that answer, and why she believes it should be considered right based on the wording of the question. The teacher sees that the question was a little ambiguous, and decides to give credit for both answer choices, or even decides to give everybody credit because, in retrospect, the question was confusing.

This sort of thing happens every day in schools all across the country, and it's quite understandable. More often than not, high school teachers are overworked. They teach multiple classes, and—in addition to grading homework and projects—they have to make their own tests for each class. So you can see how an overworked teacher might occasionally make an error in the creation of a test question, especially since he probably doesn't have as much time to proofread as he would like.

This sort of thing DOES NOT happen on the ACT. (I know that a question on the test does get challenged and overturned every once in a while, but that's so unusual that it may as well never happen for our purposes.)

The ACT isn't a test that one busy person wrote to use in one high school class. Instead, it's a product created by many people over a long period of time, and one of the most important elements of the test is that the right answer choice for each question must be completely, 100% certain—the term I like to use is "airtight." On every real ACT question, the ACT can point to concrete, consistent reasons why the correct answer choice is correct, and why every other answer choice for that question is wrong, and literally nobody can argue with those reasons. (Trust me on this—I know it may not seem to be true at this point in your training.)

Why is this so important? Well, think about what the ACT is. It's the backbone of an entire company whose purpose is, basically, to make the ACT. The company that makes the ACT (which is creatively called "ACT, Inc.") is a non-profit, but it still employs a lot of people, and those people's jobs depend on the test being relevant and useful to the college admissions process.

Well, how relevant or useful would the ACT be if the answers weren't airtight? If the questions were subjective, or if they frequently had more than one valid answer but only gave credit for one arbitrary choice, then there would be no correlation between ACT scores and college performance. If that were to happen, colleges would quickly realize that the ACT wasn't a reliable tool for evaluating students, and they'd stop accepting ACT scores on applications. That means people would stop taking the ACT, which would be bad news for everybody who works at ACT, Inc.

This is why ACT, Inc. has people whose job is to make sure that the questions on the test are airtight. So here's our next important fact to remember:

2. The ACT's very existence depends on each question being airtight. Every question must have exactly one predictably correct answer, or the ACT would have no reason to exist.

To explore further the inner workings of the ACT, let's think a little more about what it means for a test to be standardized. For one thing, it means that two people can take the ACT hundreds of miles apart, on different days, and their scores can still be reliably compared to one another.

How is that possible?

ACT, Inc. obviously can't administer the exact same test, every single time, with the exact same questions word for word. If it did that, pretty soon everybody would know those questions, and everybody would get a perfect score, and the ACT would be useless.

That means the challenge for ACT, Inc. is to make a *new* test with completely *different* questions (on the surface) for each test date—but the scores for each new test must still be consistently and meaningfully comparable to each other.

So how does ACT, Inc., do that?

Well, to start with, the basic structure for the ACT has to be consistent—it has to have the same number of answer choices for each given question type from test to test, the same amount of time for breaks in between sections, the same number of sections with the same number of questions on each section, and so on.

But that isn't enough by itself. After all, just answering any group of 60 math questions in 60 minutes isn't automatically the same thing as answering any other set of 60 math questions in 60 minutes. The questions in each batch must test the *same concepts* in the *same ways*, without actually repeating each other. For that matter, the wrong answer choices themselves must be *wrong* in similar ways—if you made two versions of a test, both asking the exact same questions, but one test used wrong answer choices that were very tricky, and one only used wrong answer choices that were clearly wrong, then one test would be much harder than the other, *just because the answer choices were different*. (See "The ACT's Biggest Weakness," on page 17 of this Black Book, for more on this.)

You can probably see where I'm going here: every official ACT on every test date must test the same things in the same ways, with the same types of right answers and the same types of wrong answers, or else the results from different test dates couldn't be reliably compared to one another. Of course, the exact questions themselves have to be different on each test, as do the exact passages on the English, Reading, and Science sections ... *but the questions always have to follow the same rules and patterns, in the exact same ways, on every test.*

Some of those rules and patterns are very obvious, like the number of questions in a section. The other standards are more subtle. They aren't directly stated in any official materials from ACT, Inc.; instead, they're the sort of thing you have to look for very carefully (or learn from this Black Book :)). If these other standards were too easy to figure out, then everybody would realize exactly how to beat the test. All of this leads up to our next important ACT fact ...

3. The ACT must be exactly the same in every important way every time it's given. It must always yield to the same strategies. If you know those strategies, you can beat the test.

The standardization of the ACT means that if a set of strategies can beat the official tests that have been released in sources like the Red Book, then those strategies must be able to beat the test every time, because, again, the test has to be fundamentally the same each time it's given, or else there's no point in giving it.

So if we can come up with strategies that always beat real practice ACT questions, then we know we can use those strategies to beat the real ACT on test day, so we can get the score we want, and move on with our lives.

Of course, I've already come up with those strategies, and this Black Book will teach them to you.

(I keep driving this point home because, at some point in their preparation, my students often say something like,

> Okay Mike, I know your strategies usually work, but I found an official ACT practice question where they just don't. This question must just be different.

Literally every single time this happens, it's because the student has overlooked or misunderstood an important part of the question, or forgotten an important part of the strategy. Once we identify the mistake, it becomes apparent that the question is just another standardized question that we can beat using the strategies in this Black Book. See "Understand Your Mistakes" on page 34 of this Black Book and "When Things Go Wrong" on page 576 for more.)

As you can see, much of the proper approach to the ACT relies on a deep understanding of the test's design. And that leads us to our next major point.

4. We should only practice for the ACT with real ACT questions written by ACT, Inc., and not with fake questions written by any other company.

Because of the subtle standards that ACT, Inc. uses to design the ACT, we must only ever work with real ACT questions created by ACT, Inc. when we prepare! Fake ACT questions made by third-party companies don't follow all the important rules and standards we just discussed, so you should never use them to prepare for the ACT. We'll come back to this critical idea repeatedly throughout this Black Book, and we'll discuss some different sources of these real ACT questions in more detail in Part 2 of this Black Book, starting on page 20.

Summary

Okay! Let's quickly recap what we've learned so far:

1. Doing well on the ACT isn't the same as doing well on a normal high school test.
2. Every question on the ACT must be airtight.
3. The ACT has to be the same in all the ways that matter every time it's administered.
4. You must always and only use real practice ACT questions to prepare for the ACT.

If you've understood the above points, you're now armed with a better grasp of the ACT than probably 90% of the people who take the test—and we haven't even started talking about actual test items yet. Good for you! Keep it up :)

The ACT's Biggest Weakness

All men can see these tactics whereby I conquer, but what none can see is the strategy out of which victory is evolved.
Sun Tzu

While we're talking about the key things that make the ACT unique (and uniquely beatable), we should address the test's single biggest weakness, which is probably the fact that it has to use the multiple-choice format. This format causes a lot of problems for the test-maker, and trained test-takers can take advantage of those problems if we use the right strategies.

Why is the ACT Multiple-Choice?

Let's take a second to discuss one of the most important (and also most easily overlooked) attributes of the ACT: except for the essay, every single question uses the multiple-choice format. Why is that? (We'll talk about the essay later in this Black Book.)

Think about it. If you were face-to-face with someone, and you really wanted to test whether she knew something, would you ask her a multiple-choice question? Or would you just ask a regular, open-ended question without providing answer choices, and force her to demonstrate her knowledge by coming up with her own answer?

Of course, you'd just ask an open-ended question. That would be the best way to know if the student really grasped the material. That's why it's much harder to fake your way past an oral exam or an essay question on a high school test than it is to get lucky and answer a multiple-choice question correctly.

But the ACT is full of multiple-choice questions. (There's an optional ACT Writing test with one essay question, of course. We'll cover it in "Part 10: Writing Test Training (The ACT Essay)" on page 554 of this Black Book.)

Why can't the ACT just ask us tons of open-ended questions and let us fill in the blanks with our own answers? Because it would be pretty hard to grade millions of tests every year *using the exact same standards of grading for every test-taker* if people could just write down whatever random answers they wanted. Having to read and consider every single answer individually would be impossibly time-consuming and expensive. It would also require a looser grading structure, because different test-takers would write about different things in response to the same questions, and those responses would have to be evaluated by different graders. (This is why standardized tests with open-ended questions can only use broad grading scales like $1 - 5$ or $1 - 6$, while multiple-choice standardized tests can be much more precise in their grading scales.)

Instead, the ACT needs a format that allows it to grade tests efficiently and with a high degree of accuracy. It also needs a format that allows it to apply the exact same standards to every single test-taker, so each test-taker's results can be reliably compared to the results of every other test-taker with a high degree of precision.

These goals can only be achieved if the test provides a set of answers to choose from.

Multiple-choice tests are obviously easier and more efficient to grade than free-response tests. They also allow a much higher degree of precision when it comes to applying standards: in addition to writing the question prompts according to particular standards, the testing company can sculpt right answers and wrong answers to follow certain standards as well.

That's a major benefit to you as a test-taker, because it means that every single ACT question has to put the correct answer right in front of your face.

It also changes your job as a test-taker. Instead of needing to know the actual answer to a question on your own, all you need to do is select the right answer from four or five choices that are provided for you. That difference might not sound like a big deal, but it definitely can be. We'll come back to this idea over and over again.

The Importance of Answer Choices

In this Black Book, we're going to do everything we can to take advantage of the information provided to us by the ACT in the test itself. We're going to pull Reading answers right out of the provided text, without interpretation or subjectivity. We're going to see through strange presentations of Math problems and use basic formulas (if we even need formulas at all) to find the right answers. We're going to take in all the scientific information built right into Science questions so we can find the correct answers to questions on scientific topics we've never heard of. And so on.

Still, it's easy to forget that there's an extremely important source of information sitting right in front of us on every multiple-choice question: the answer choices themselves.

This is why I emphasize that students must always, ALWAYS read each ACT question completely, including the answer choices, before they start to figure out the answer. Too many people just read the question prompt (the part that doesn't include the answer choices), then stop and try to solve the problem on their own. Afterwards, they check to see if their answer is reflected in the choices. This approach, though typical, will make life harder for you and cause you to miss hints and clues that are basically staring you in the face once you know how to look for them.

Of course, we'll talk more about those clues as we look at each question type specifically. For now, I just want you to get used to this idea right from the beginning.

So how can answer choices make a question easier? Let's take a look at an extreme example that I'll make up right now, just to illustrate the point. Imagine that you were taking a history test in school, and you saw this question:

Who was the King of Prussia during the Franco-Prussian War?

Unless you're a Prussian history buff, you'd probably start to sweat a little if you saw this question. (Of course, it could never appear on the actual ACT. Again, I'm just using it to illustrate a point.)

Now let's imagine that you see this on a test, instead:

Who was the King of Prussia during the Franco-Prussian War?

A. Wilhelm I

B. Purple

C. Wednesday

D. The Cleveland Browns

If we use our powers of deduction, we can probably pick choice (A) with confidence. Why is that? Well, it doesn't take much thought to realize that neither purple, nor Wednesday, nor the Cleveland Browns could ever be the king of something.

So even though we probably never would've been able to come up with "Wilhelm I" as an answer on our own, almost anyone could pick the right answer out of those four choices.

(Also note that if you had just read the question, realized you didn't know the answer, and then skipped on to the next question without taking a look at the answer choices, you'd be missing out on easy points.)

That was a ridiculous example, of course, but this exercise illustrates the way answer choices can hint at the correct answer when considered in the context of the original question.

Let's look at a slightly trickier version of the same question:

Who was the King of Prussia during the Franco-Prussian War?

A. Wilhelm I

B. Haloti Ngata

C. Thomas Jefferson

D. Nelson Mandela

In this version, all of the incorrect answer choices are people's names. This makes a strategic guess a little more difficult than it was the last time around. Let's consider each answer choice as though we don't already know the answer.

(A) sounds plausible. At the very least, there's no obvious reason to eliminate it. The name sounds like it could be Prussian, and a lot of names of kings have a Roman numeral after them.

(B) seems like it's probably wrong. We may have an idea that Prussia was a country in Europe, and this name doesn't sound European.

We probably know that (C) is someone from American history who was probably never the King of Prussia, since he kept pretty busy in America.

We may have heard of the person in answer choice (D) before, and, if so, we probably know he was a more recent figure in world history. If we know that the Franco-Prussian war didn't happen too recently, we can be pretty certain that (D) isn't right.

Taking all of that into consideration, we can be pretty certain that (A) is correct. (Even if we haven't heard of (D) before, the Roman numeral after the name kind of helps sell (A) in this case.)

Do you see what happened there? Even though we didn't necessarily know anything about kings of Prussia or about the Franco-Prussian war, and even though all four choices were people's names, we were able to apply some basic reasoning to the answer choices to come up with a pretty solid idea of which one was correct.

Hopefully, you begin to get the idea. The answer choices can contain valuable hints and clues that can keep you on your game throughout the test, and if you don't take the time to read them for every question, you're making things harder on yourself. You won't find clues on every single question, but getting into this habit will certainly pay off on most of them. (We'll discuss this more in "Always Consider Every Answer Choice!" on page 42 of this Black Book.)

Wrong-Answer Choices are Standardized, Too!

As we just learned, using different types of wrong-answer choices can have a huge impact on the difficulty of a question, even if the question prompt and the right answer are the same. For this reason, if ACT, Inc. wants its scores to be consistent and useful for colleges, it needs to keep its wrong-answer choices as standardized as the rest of the test.

Knowing that the wrong answer choices are standardized can be extremely helpful. The ACT tries to use wrong answer choices to lure you off track, and if you know in advance what kinds of tactics the test will use, you're much less likely to fall for them. And if you keep these wrong answer types in mind while you practice, you'll get better and better at spotting them, which will make you even more efficient.

This doesn't mean you'll have to classify every single wrong answer choice you see if you want to do well on this test, or even that it would be possible to do so if you wanted to. Not every single choice will fit one of the patterns we're going to talk about. But as we learn about each question type, we'll discuss the major answer-choice patterns you can expect to see on real ACT practice questions. If you keep these in mind while you practice, you'll be surprised at how obvious these wrong answer choices will start to become.

Using Answer-Choice Patterns

Later in this Black Book, we'll talk about specific answer-choice patterns as part of our discussion of each section of the test. Those patterns can be extremely helpful, but it's very important that we understand the proper way to use them. It can be tempting to rely on them too heavily, but doing that is much more likely to hurt your score than it is to help it.

So the point of understanding the design of the answer choices isn't that they'll just tell you the correct answer if you know how to decode them. Instead, understanding how the ACT uses wrong-answer patterns will help you in two main ways:

1. If you look at a question and you're not sure what to do, the answer choices can often point you in the right direction, because they include concepts that the test thinks are relevant to the question.

2. Once you've found an answer choice that you like, the answer-choice patterns can help you confirm that you're probably correct—or they can help you catch a mistake if you were wrong.

This is a big deal, because it helps to prevent two of the main things that the ACT tries to do: it tries to present concepts in bizarre ways so we're not sure what to do, and it tries to get us to make simple mistakes without noticing them. So appreciating the value of answer choices can be a great weapon against the test.

We'll look at all of this in more detail when we talk about the different sections of the ACT, of course. I just want to make sure from the beginning that you understand how useful the answer choices can be. They won't always tell you the correct answer outright, but they can often point you in the right direction, and help keep you from making small mistakes that cost you points for no reason.

Part 2: When To Use Official ACT, Inc., Materials, And When Not To

In this part of the Black Book, I'll explain why it's so important to work with real ACT questions from ACT, Inc.... but it's also important to ignore ACT, Inc.'s own "explanations" of those real ACT questions (you'll see why I put the word "explanations" in quotation marks like that, too). We'll also talk about all the different readily available real ACT practice tests, and what your options are if you've already exhausted that supply—which really shouldn't be an issue for most readers.

Among other things, you'll learn the following:

- where we can find real test questions from ACT, Inc.
- why practicing with "harder" questions than you'll see on test day isn't a good strategy
- why ACT, Inc.'s "explanations" are often unhelpful for most test-takers who need them
- the elements of a good explanation for an official ACT question
- the most important part of using real ACT questions in your training
- why your review and analysis of any ACT question should always be directed at diagnosing similar situations on test day
- how ACT, Inc.'s "explanations" of Math questions often ignore the techniques that high-scorers actually use
- how ACT, Inc.'s "explanations" of Reading questions often use circular reasoning and appeals to outside knowledge to avoid revealing too much
- how ACT, Inc.'s "explanations" of English questions often rely on vague, undefined terms like "clearest" and "understandable" instead of spelling out the technical aspects of an answer choice that make it right or wrong
- how ACT, Inc.'s "explanations" of Science questions often deliberately give the false impression that we need a lot of scientific knowledge to do well on a question
- why ACT, Inc.'s available practice materials should be plenty for you, if you prepare wisely
- which other practice materials to use—and which to avoid—if you do feel like you need more practice questions
- and more . . .

Using the Official ACT Prep Guide (the "Red Book")

> Whatever you would make habitual, practice it; and if you would not make a thing habitual, do not practice it, but accustom yourself to something else.
>
> Epictetus

As we saw in "What You Must Understand about the ACT" on page 14 of this Black Book, training with real ACT questions is essential, because those questions are the only ones that are guaranteed to follow the same rules and patterns you'll see on test day. The most commonly used source of these questions is *The Official ACT Prep Guide,* which is published by ACT, Inc. We'll call this "the Red Book."

And before we get too much further into our discussion of the ACT, I want to discuss the Red Book in a little more detail.

First, let's talk about this book from the perspective of the test-maker: ACT, Inc. That company's job is to create and administer the ACT, and to make sure the ACT is relevant and useful for colleges. Part of that usefulness is making sure the test creates a spectrum of results—if everybody who took the ACT got roughly the same score, the test wouldn't help colleges rank their applicants.

In other words, it's not in the interest of the good people who make the ACT to tell us exactly how their test works so we can all ace it!

In fact, it's in their best interest to keep most of the standards and patterns in the test as secret as possible, so that test-takers who know those standards or patterns will do well, and other test-takers will struggle, and the whole test-taking population will get a nice range of scores that colleges will find useful in their admissions processes.

So while *The Official ACT Prep Guide* is extremely valuable as a source of real ACT practice tests—which you MUST have if you hope to do well on this test!—we'll find that the ACT prep advice in that book is often less than helpful. You can read it if you like, of course, but I wouldn't recommend following it in most cases. The real ACT practice tests in the Red Book are what matters.

In addition to general test preparation advice, the Red Book also contains official explanations for its own official practice questions. But you have to be careful about putting too much stock in those explanations . . .

Why do We Bother Explaining Questions from the Red Book?

This Black Book contains full walkthroughs for every question in the first three practice tests in *most* editions of the Red Book—more on that in a moment—and the Red Book also contains explanations of its own questions.

You may be asking yourself why we'd bother writing out a ton of in-depth explanations for test items that are already described in the Red Book. It's an important question to ask, and it has a very important answer.

If you've read Part 1 of this Black Book, you're probably getting the idea that we're going to approach the ACT very differently from the way most people approach this test. The approach you'll learn from me is certainly different from the way ACT, Inc., wants you to approach the test, because the ACT wouldn't be useful to colleges if every person who took the test did very well on it.

We've already talked about how the ACT wants you to see its questions in a way that's different from the way they really are. Among other things, the test doesn't want you to realize how the right answer choices are objectively right, and the wrong ones are objectively wrong. The ACT seems to want you to think there's some kind of gray area on the test, probably because that makes the test more challenging.

Unfortunately, this apparent desire to seem mysterious often comes through in the Red Book's answer explanations. For example, most Red Book explanations (all but the ones for Math questions) start by saying something like this (emphasis mine):

> Question 17. The *best* answer is (A).

When the Red Book addresses the other choices, it introduces them by saying,

> The best answer is NOT

Did you catch the subtle implication in those phrases? When the Red Book talks about a "best" answer, instead of talking about "right" or "wrong" answers, most readers will naturally make the mistake of assuming that more than one answer to an ACT question might be pretty good, but one of the choices is subjectively "best," and it's our job as test-takers to guess which choice the ACT is going to reward. But, in reality, only one answer for each question can possibly be right if we know the ACT's rules, and the others are all inarguably wrong.

You might think I'm harping on this too much, because it might seem like a minor point right now. But people who don't embrace it have a much harder time improving on the ACT—almost an impossible time, actually. So if you do look at the answer explanations in *The Official ACT Prep Guide,* it's very important that you don't fall for the ACT's trick of the "best" answer. For every question, there's one correct answer choice, and the rest are wrong, without exception. Don't ever get distracted from that fact.

And this is only one example of the kinds of problems you might run into with the Red Book's explanations of its own questions. At best, the Red Book explanations are frequently adequate. They'll generally point out the major issues involved in a question, and they'll occasionally point out something of value about a wrong answer choice. At worst, the Red Book explanations can be unclear and even misleading. Sometimes they can even be wrong . . .

How can the Red Book's Explanations of its Own Questions be "Wrong?"

When I say that some explanations from the Red Book are "wrong," I don't mean that they support the wrong answer for the question being explained. Instead, what I mean is that the explanation uses unreliable *reasoning* to try to justify why a choice is right or wrong. We can tell the Red Book's reasoning is unreliable—and wrong—if it might lead a test-taker to choose a wrong answer for other questions.

In other words, the *real* reasoning behind all real ACT questions must be consistent, since the test is standardized, as we've established. If a proposed explanation for a real ACT question could lead to wrong answers on other real ACT questions, then the proposed explanation is wrong, and there must be some other reason that the right answer is right.

One example of this kind of issue appears in the explanation for question 13 from the Reading section of practice test 1 in the Red Book (test 2 in the 2020-2021 Red Book). The Red Book's "explanation" of the right answer requires us to know which parts of a car "most people would consider essential." The explanation also talks about "the point" of a part of the passage, which indicates that a test-taker should try to interpret what an author intended to say, instead of relying on what's actually said. But as we'll see in Part 6 of this Black Book, when we talk about strategies for ACT Reading, the kind of interpretation and "common sense" outside knowledge of the subject matter that's referred to in this Red Book explanation will lead most people to wrong answers if they try to apply it on test day. As it turns out, the easiest way (and, more importantly, the most consistent way) to answer this question with certainty is to know that unattributed quotation marks in an ACT Reading passage are always a sign that the author doesn't agree with the normal meaning of the quoted term, much like when a friend might use "air quotes" to emphasize that they don't personally agree with a term. (We'll discuss this more in the ACT Reading section training later in this Black Book; for more on this question in particular, see its walkthrough on page 68 of this Black Book). This exact logic will let a test-taker identify the right answers to future questions that also involve unattributed quotation marks—but, again, the Red Book never gives its readers this simple, direct explanation. Instead, the Red Book strongly suggests that we should use outside knowledge and common sense when we try to answer future ACT questions, which is a really bad idea, as we'll learn later in this Black Book.

In addition to using unreliable reasoning, the Red Book will also fail to point out the most direct and efficient ways to answer questions, particularly on the ACT Math section. A brief example of this can be found in the Red Book's explanation for question 44 from the Math section of practice test 3 in the Red Book (form 16MC3 if you have the 2020-2021 Red Book—more on that later in this section): that explanation uses "the angle-angle similarity property" to work out the answer in multiple steps, the way a geometry teacher would reward in school. But our walkthrough, which appears on page 312 of this Black Book, also points out that you can answer the question in seconds just by considering the scale of the provided diagram—something the Red Book doesn't tell you.

Further, the Red Book's explanation for Science questions are often unnecessarily formal, which can give the false impression that test-takers need sophisticated scientific knowledge to find the right answer. Consider ACT, Inc.'s explanation for question 13 from the Science section of practice test 1 in the Red Book (test 2 in the 2020-2021 Red Book). That explanation uses the terms "stoichiometry," "hydroxide ions," and "monohydrate," even though a test-taker doesn't need to know any of those terms to answer the question! (See our walkthrough for that question on page 353 of this Black Book for an approach to this question that doesn't rely on knowing those terms.)

The Red Book's English explanations are no better. For example, ACT Inc.'s explanation for question 31 from the English section of practice test 2 in the Red Book (test 3 in the 2020-2021 Red Book) says that the right answer "creates the clearest and most understandable sentence," which implies that other answer choices also create clear and understandable sentences, but they just aren't as clear and understandable as the right answer. The explanation goes on to say that every other choice is "unnecessary and confusing," without providing any useful information about how to figure out what makes something "unnecessary and confusing" according to the ACT—which may seem especially strange to a lot of readers when they realize that every answer choice in the question uses the same three words in the same exact order! So this explanation basically leaves the reader with the impression that it's her job to figure out what's "clear" and "understandable," and avoid what's "unnecessary" and "confusing," with almost no concrete guidance on how to do that. (Our walkthrough of this question, which appears on page 496, explains which answer is right by referring to the specific rules for comma usage that the ACT requires us to follow, so test-takers will know how to respond to similar situations on test day.)

(Of course, those four Red Book explanations aren't the only ones that we take issue with. They're just singled out here because they have flaws that are relatively easy to understand without getting into the details of how different types of ACT questions actually work yet.)

Don't get us wrong—some of ACT, Inc.'s explanations are decent. The problem is that many of them aren't.

On the other hand, the walkthroughs in this Black Book will tell you definitively and objectively why the right answers to Red Book questions are right, and why the wrong answers are wrong, and you'll be able to take what you learn from each of our walkthroughs and apply it to future real ACT questions, which is the whole point of training in the first place.

You'll see that the approach we teach in this Black Book works on all the questions in the Red Book, as well as on any real ACT questions you'll see in the future, including on test day. Our explanations will also tell you which errors might lead you to certain wrong answers, and they'll often show you multiple approaches per question, so you can decide which suits you best.

(But Wait—which Red Book!?)

For some reason, ACT, Inc. has decided to release very similar editions of *The Official ACT Prep Guide* –the Red Book—almost every year for several years. This can create confusion for readers who want to ensure they have the right edition of the Red Book to work with the question walkthroughs in this Black Book. The good news is that you can basically use any one of those editions of the Red Book with this Black Book, because they're so similar. Before we get into more detail, let me recap a few ideas to keep in mind for the sake of this discussion:

- This Black Book contains walkthroughs for all the questions on three real entire practice ACT tests, and you'll need the Red Book so you can have copies of those tests.

- All you need from the Red Book is the practice tests; the rest of the information in the Red Book isn't really useful.
- All practice tests for the current version of the ACT are equally valid. A more recent practice test isn't more valid or useful than a less recent practice test as long as they're both for the current version of the ACT, because all practice tests for the current version of the ACT are written using the same standards. All of the practice tests in the editions of the Red Book that we discuss below are for the current version of the ACT, and they're all equally valid and useful for ACT preparation.

With that in mind, if you have any of the following versions of the Red Book, then the first three practice tests in your Red Book are the ones that correspond to the question walkthroughs in this Black Book for practice tests 1, 2, and 3, and you're all set to use this Black Book with your edition of the Red Book:

- The Official ACT Prep Guide 2016-2017 (ISBN: 978-1119225416)
- The Official ACT Prep Guide 2018 (ISBN: 978-1119386896)
- The Official ACT Prep Guide 2018-2019 (ISBN: 978-1119508069)
- The Official ACT Prep Guide 2019-2020 (ISBN: 978-1119580508)

Note that the 2016-2017 and 2018 editions above contain only the three tests that correspond to the walkthroughs in this book. The 2018-2019 edition has those three tests, plus one more, and the 2019-2020 edition has the four tests from the 2018-2019 edition, plus one more, for a total of five.

If you don't have a copy of the Red Book, we recommend you get the 2019-2020 edition, because it has all three tests corresponding to the walkthroughs in this book, plus two more practice tests. But, again, any of the above editions will work fine with this Black Book.

So if you have one of the above books, you're set, and when we refer to Practice Test 1, 2, or 3 in this Black Book, you can match those up to Practice Tests 1, 2, or 3 in your Red Book. (Bear in mind that the first practice test in the Red Book appears near the front of the Red Book, and the remaining practice tests appear near the back of the Red Book. So if you skip to the back of the Red Book to find the practice tests, then you're overlooking the first practice test, which starts in the first 50 pages or so!)

The 2020-2021 Red Book (ISBN 978-1119685760)
The only other current version of the Red Book at the time of this writing is the 2020-2021 edition, which is a little more confusing for our purposes. When ACT, Inc., released the 2020-2021 edition of the Red Book, they decided to change the order of the practice tests in the Red Book for the first time. They added a new practice test to the beginning of the book, which caused the old Practice Test 1 to become Practice Test 2 in the 2020-2021 edition, and old Practice Test 2 to become Practice Test 3. They also removed the test that used to be Practice Test 3 in the earlier editions, and left Practice Tests 4 and 5 from the previous edition in place.

So if you already have the 2020-2021 version of the Red Book, then you'll need to remember a few things when using this Black Book:

1. When we mention "Practice Test 1," we're talking about the *second* practice test that appears in your Red Book.
2. When we talk about "Practice Test 2," we're talking about the *third* practice test that appears in your copy of the Red Book.
3. When we talk about Practice Test 3 in this Black Book, we're referring to an ACT practice test that isn't in your copy of the Red Book. You can look online for that missing practice test by searching for ACT test form 16MC3, which is the official name for the test that appears as Practice Test 3 in other editions of the Red Book, but is missing from the 2020-2021 edition.

The Official ACT Prep Pack(s)
There's also another version of *each* of these recent editions of the Red Book, called *The Official ACT Prep Pack*, even though the book doesn't come bundled in a special way. Each "Prep Pack" is exactly the same as its corresponding Red Book, except that it costs more, has a different cover, and comes with a code that grants you access to more online practice tests and some online training from ACT, Inc. You can feel free to buy the Prep Pack version of the Red Book if you like, but we don't really recommend it, because there are other real ACT practice tests that you can access easily in printed form (as we discuss on the next page), and ACT, Inc.'s preparation advice isn't great.

So here's the bottom line . . .
If you don't have a copy of the Red Book already, then we recommend you get the 2019-2020 version (ISBN 978-1119580508). It has the three practice tests that correspond to the walkthroughs in this book, plus two more practice tests.

If you have a copy of any Red Book listed above, other than the 2020-2021 Red Book, then you still have the three practice tests that correspond to the walkthroughs in this Black Book, in the same order we refer to them in this book—so you've got what you need to prepare.

If you have the 2020-2021 version of the Red Book (ISBN 978-1119685760), then you also still have what you need to prepare! You just need to remember that when we mention "Practice Test 1," that's Practice Test 2 in your edition of the Red Book, and when we mention "Practice Test 2," we're talking about Practice Test 3 in your Red Book. Also, when we mention "Practice Test 3" in this Black Book, we're talking about a test that ACT, Inc., removed from the 2020-2021 edition of the Red Book, but you can search for that practice test online as ACT test form 16MC3.

Also, PLEASE REMEMBER that the first practice test in any edition of the Red Book is about 50 pages into the book, separate from the other practice tests, which appear towards the end of the Red Book.

That's pretty much it—remember, the most important reason to have the Red Book is the official ACT practice tests in that book. The walkthroughs later in this Black Book will help you understand those official practice tests in a way that most test-takers never will.

"But What if I Run out of Practice Materials?!"

At the time of this writing, each current edition of *The Official ACT Prep Guide* contains at least three official ACT practice tests, as we just discussed in "Using the Official ACT Prep Guide (the "Red Book")" on page 21 of this Black Book.

Really, these three tests on their own should be enough practice for most test-takers who prepare for the ACT according to the ideas in this Black Book, assuming they review their practice as we discuss in "How to Train for the ACT—Mastering the Ideas in this Book" on page 29.

Some more recent editions of the Red Book have even more practice tests in addition to the three that are analyzed in this Black Book. But I sometimes hear from readers who want more real tests to practice with, whether because they've already used all the tests in the Red Book before reading this book, or because they just want the security of knowing more practice materials are available for them. So fear not—there are other real ACT practice tests out there, available from ACT, Inc., itself. But there are also some practice materials from other sources that I wouldn't use if I were you. Keep reading for information on additional real practice tests from ACT, Inc. that can help you in your preparation.

Sample Tests from ACT.org

Every couple of years, ACT.org (the official website of the ACT) releases a PDF of a test in the current format that you can print out. We've collected a number of these PDFs for you, and you can find them by going to testingiseasy.com/practice and scrolling down to the section with ACT practice tests.

And Five More ACT Practice Tests!

As it turns out, the version of the Red Book from before the last test update in 2016—that is, the third edition of the Red Book, called *The Real ACT Prep Guide, 3rd Edition* (ISBN: 978-0768934403)—contains five practice tests in the previous format of the ACT. There are only two differences between the tests in the third edition of the Red Book and the current version of the ACT, and they're both minor:

1. The ACT Writing section (also known as the ACT Essay) has a different format now (but there's a good chance that you don't have to take the ACT Writing test anyway, as we'll discuss in Part 10 of this Black Book).
2. The current ACT includes one ACT Reading passage that actually involves two passages (but the strategies for approaching these "paired passage" questions on the ACT are no different from the strategies for approaching other kinds of ACT Reading passages, as we'll discuss on page 58 of this Black Book).

Other than that, you can consider the practice tests in the third edition of the Red Book to be just as valuable and useful as the practice tests in the current Red Book.

So if you're looking for more practice tests that are essentially the same as the current version of the test, the third edition of the Red Book is another good option. You can usually find a decent used copy online for under $10.

Still Not Satisfied?

Between the different editions of the Red Book and the official questions from ACT.org, you have more than a dozen different official ACT Practice Tests you can use to prepare, which should be plenty for anybody who prepares using the methods in this Black Book.

If you've already gone through all the ACT practice tests we just talked about, and you still want more, my first bit of advice for you is to go back through those same practice tests again. Take a second look (and maybe a third and fourth look) at all those questions (especially the ones you missed on your first attempt!) and really re-analyze each one. Think about what makes the right answer right, what makes the wrong answers wrong, what you need to know to choose the correct answer, how you could find that information quickly, and so on—basically all the stuff we'll talk about in "Drills and Exercises" on page 30 of this Black Book, and "Understand Your Mistakes" on page 34 of this Black Book.

After that, if you *insist* on using other practice materials—which, again, really shouldn't be necessary for just about anybody, and, again, isn't really something I recommend—then here's a list of your various practice material options, and the pros and cons of each one, listed in order from most acceptable to least acceptable.

SAT Practice Tests

The ACT and SAT are definitely not identical tests, but they're pretty similar in a lot of ways.

- **Pros:** The ACT Reading section is pretty similar to the SAT Reading section, the ACT Math section is pretty similar to the SAT Math section, and the ACT English section is pretty similar to the SAT Writing and Language section. If you practice with those materials, you'll be using questions written by a creator of a nationally standardized test—just not ACT, Inc. Many individual questions that you see on the SAT could have appeared on the ACT, and vice versa.
- **Cons:** The SAT is a different test from the ACT, made by a different organization. The standards on the two tests overlap somewhat, but they aren't exactly the same. You may pick up some habits that work well against SAT questions but that aren't as effective against ACT questions. Every SAT section includes questions that are actually more similar to ACT Science questions than a lot of people realize, but the SAT still doesn't include anything that directly corresponds to the ACT Science section.

Third-Party Practice Tests

These are potentially the worst practice questions you could use, because the companies that write them don't necessarily understand the way the real ACT is designed, and they have no incentive to develop questions that consistently adhere to ACT, Inc.'s rules and standards.

- **Pros:** None to speak of.
- **Cons:** These tests may seem to imitate the real ACT on the surface, especially to untrained test-takers, which can make it even harder for them to realize the important differences that can exist between these tests and the real ACT. I would strongly advise you to stay far away from practice materials written by third-party companies. In theory, I suppose it's conceivable that a third-party company could create practice questions that followed the same rules as the actual ACT, but I've never seen it done.

What about harder practice questions?

Some test prep companies have a reputation for making fake ACT practice questions that are supposedly harder than the real thing. Some test-takers think it's a good idea to practice with these questions, because they think that practicing with something that's harder than the real thing will make the real thing seem easy by comparison.

But the same basic problem with all third-party practice materials still exists: these are fake practice questions that aren't necessarily made according to the real standards of the ACT. If they don't challenge you *in the same ways that actual ACT questions would challenge you*, then it doesn't matter how challenging they are in other ways.

Imagine that you wanted to learn to make a grilled cheese sandwich. Would it help you to learn how to make your own cheese first? Probably not, even though making your own cheese is much harder than making a grilled cheese sandwich, and the two activities sound like they're kind of related. The bottom line is that learning to make cheese is a waste of time if your actual goal is to make a sandwich.

Similarly, any time you spend working on fake ACT practice questions, no matter how hard they are, is time you're not pursuing your actual goal of getting better at real ACT questions, because those fake questions could be breaking the ACT's rules if they require you to know and do things that the real test will never require you to know or do.

So if you want to improve your performance on the ACT, you need to work exclusively with real ACT practice questions written by ACT, Inc.

Conclusion

So now you've read about the real ACT practice tests that are easiest to find, and you also know my take on the most common alternatives to real ACT practice materials. I want to make it absolutely clear, one more time, that *I don't recommend using any practice materials other than the official materials from ACT, Inc.* The real, official, full-length ACT tests available from ACT, Inc., which we described above, should be more than enough for almost anyone.

Again, if you've already done all of those practice tests, you can still review them, using some of the drills and exercises that I described in "How to Train for the ACT—Mastering the Ideas in this Book" on page 29. The key to doing your absolute best on the ACT isn't to churn out as many hours of mindless practice as you can; it's to review your practice until you understand every mistake you've ever made from ACT, Inc.'s perspective, so you can avoid those issues in the future.

Part 3: Goals and Training

Now we'll talk about the right way to set goals during your ACT training, and then we'll arm you with a bunch of ideas for scheduling your time, and creative exercises that are far more effective than just taking practice tests over and over again.

In this part of the Black Book, you'll learn the following:

- the key abilities required for a perfect ACT score (or any other score you want)
- what you actually have to do to improve on the ACT
- how to set goals that make progress easier to achieve and track
- the approach I recommend for mastering the ideas in this Black Book
- how to focus on the critical step that usually comes before you stop making mistakes
- what to fix *before* you start worrying about time management on test day
- the best order of attack for most people to use against the different sections of the ACT
- why not to attack your weak areas first, especially if you're aiming for a specific target score
- why mindlessly taking practice tests doesn't help people as much as they expect
- some unusual drills and exercises that will help you understand how the ACT really works
- how to arrange your preparation schedule—if you even need a schedule in the first place
- and more . . .

"How Well can I do on the ACT?"

Your present circumstances don't determine where you can go; they merely determine where you start.
Nido Qubein

Sooner or later, almost every client I work with will ask me this question in one form or another:

"How well can I do on the ACT?"

Often they'll include their best score to date on a practice (or real) test, and then mention a target score:

"If I've already scored a 23, would it be possible for me to get a 31?"

There's a pretty good chance you've asked someone this question, or at least thought it to yourself. It's understandable—the ACT is a big deal, and it can have a big impact on where you'll end up going to college, not to mention how much you might pay for your education.

Concentrating on this kind of question probably isn't a good use of your time, but here's the most complete answer I can give you without knowing you personally:

If you have the following skills, then you have all of the basic tools that you need to get any score on the ACT, including a 36:

- speaking and reading American English without much trouble
- having a reasonable understanding of the basic principles of arithmetic, geometry, algebra, and trigonometry
- knowing some basic science (like how to identify the control group in an experiment, or the idea that ice is frozen water)

This is true because finding the correct answer to every question on the ACT requires nothing more than the correct application of these skills, or of some combination thereof.

Notice that I said these are the "basic tools" you need to get any score—simply having the tools isn't the same thing as knowing how to use them properly, which will be the real focus of this Black Book. As it turns out, most people who take the ACT have the necessary knowledge to score significantly higher on the test than they actually do, but they approach it the wrong way. The proper technique makes a much bigger difference than most untrained test-takers ever realize.

"Really, though, how well can *I* do on the ACT?"

You might feel like I haven't *really* addressed the question of how well you, in particular, can do on the ACT. Well, here's another way to look at the answer to that question: the only real way to know how well you can do is to prepare for the test correctly, take it, and then find out what the results are. All that matters here is the actual score you get—not what some tutor or diagnostic test says you *should* get. Anything else is just talk.

Besides, whether someone tells you that you should be able to get a 25 or a 35, you're still going to have to learn the right way to beat the test, and then practice those methods until you get them right. So knowing the score you "should" get (which is just speculation anyway) doesn't have any impact on the way you'll prepare for the test, which is what you should really be focusing on.

Anyone with the basic skills mentioned above has what it takes to score a 36. Really. The challenge everybody faces is that the ACT is very different from the tests you take in high school. The ACT rewards you for figuring out the answers to weird questions about basic concepts, and for paying careful attention to small details. Neither of those skills requires any advanced knowledge.

What they do require is that you make some deliberate effort—that you really work to get a better understanding of how the test works, and change the way you think about it. It means carefully reviewing your practice to see exactly what's stopping you from answering the questions you find challenging.

But what if you already know that you need to hit a specific target score in order to get into a particular program, or be guaranteed a scholarship, and you don't care about scoring any higher than your target? In that case, there are specific tactics that may help you reach that point faster.

Hitting a Target Score

Some students who prepare for the ACT have a target score in mind, typically either for a scholarship program or for a certain school they'd like to attend. People in this situation tend to work hard on their "problem" areas—for example, if Science is your lowest score, then you might spend a lot of time trying to improve that section, since it has the most room for improvement.

That might seem logical, and it might work for some people, but let me propose an alternative: if you're trying to hit a target score and you're not *too* far off, you might want to start by taking your strongest area and getting even better at that. This can be very effective for a few different reasons.

First of all, it's your strongest area, so you must be reasonably comfortable with the material, which means that improving your performance on it could be less stressful and more effective than trying to improve in a section you find difficult.

But there's another important angle to consider, and it has to do with the way the test is scored. When you take a section of the test—the English section for example—you end up with a certain number of questions answered correctly; on an English section, that number is somewhere from 0 to 75, since there are 75 questions on the English section.

Of course, your final score for the section is somewhere from 1 to 36, so that raw score from 0 to 75 must be converted to a final score from 1 to 36—and the payoff for each additional correct answer isn't constant.

The closer you get to the top of the scoring scale, the more each individual correct answer tends to contribute to your score. To see what I mean, take out your copy of *The Official ACT Prep Guide*, and find the section with the "Scale Score Conversion Table" for practice test 1 (test 2 in the 2020-2021 Red Book). In the second column of that table, under "English," you can see the number of questions you have to get right to earn the scaled score in the first column on the left, under "Scale Score." So let's say you got 39 English questions right—that would correspond to a scaled score of 19. You could get 4 more questions right (for a total of 43), and you'd still only have a scaled score of 20—that's a 1-point improvement for 4 more correct answers.

Now, let's imagine you're higher up on the chart, and you've answered 67 questions correctly. That corresponds to a scaled score of 31 on this test. In this case, if you get 4 more questions right (for a total of 71 questions answered correctly), you'll have a scaled score of 35—that's 4 more points on your final score for that section, for only 4 more correct answers. At this end of the scale, almost every additional correct answer gets you another scaled point, whereas in the middle of the scale you could answer several more questions right and only raise your scaled score for that section by a point or so.

Not every ACT has this exact conversion scale, because the conversion will vary slightly each time the test is administered, for reasons we don't need to address now. Still, we'll generally find that there's less payoff for each individual additional correct answer in the middle of the scale than there is toward the top of the scale.

So if you can improve on sections where you're already near the upper end of the scoring scale, you'll get a bigger payoff for each new right answer, instead of struggling on a section you're less comfortable with and getting a smaller payoff per question.

One more thought: if you happen to be getting a perfect score on your strongest section (good job, by the way!) then you can just move on to your next best section, and so on, as needed.

What if I have to Improve on a Particular Section?

If your target score requires you to improve on a specific section, and you can't just pick which section you want to improve on, then you won't necessarily benefit from the scoring issue we just discussed, but you can still focus on the question types within that section that you do best on.

For example, if you need to improve your Reading score, and you do best on the questions with line citations, then you can work on line citation questions until you can reliably answer every single one of them correctly. If you need to improve your English score, and you're better at the English questions that have to do with punctuation, you can start by getting even better at those. And so on.

What if I Need a Significant Improvement in my Score?

If you need to increase your score by a large margin in order to hit your target score, it probably won't be enough just to work on your strongest areas. Instead, you'll likely have to improve in several areas. Still, you can start your preparation by working on your strongest section first, then move on to the next strongest one, and so on. As you continue to hone your skills on each successive section, the odds are good that your overall understanding of the test will develop in such a way that the other areas of the test that used to give you trouble may become easier. If you do have a lot of time, then I'd recommend you consider following the "order of attack" that I discuss in "How to Train for the ACT—Mastering the Ideas in this Book" on page 29 of this Black Book.

How to Train for the ACT—Mastering the Ideas in this Book

> *The essence of training is to allow error without consequence.*
> Orson Scott Card

It's very important for you to read this Black Book and learn all the strategies for each question type. But it's every bit as important that you actually apply that knowledge to real ACT practice questions in your training. After all, it's one thing to read along as I walk you through a solution to a problem, pointing out all the things to watch out for and be careful about . . . and it's something entirely different to answer questions on your own without any guidance, which is what you'll have to do on test day.

So you MUST learn to do these things on your own.

After questions about specific question types, the most common question I hear comes down to this: "How should I train for the test?" That question is usually followed by a string of questions about different specific training strategies and schedules. Because I hear these questions so often, I thought it would be a good idea to address them in the beginning of this Black Book, before we even get into the specific training for each section.

The bottom line is that there's no single training schedule or approach that works best for everybody. Every student has her own strengths, weaknesses, goals, attention span, scheduling issues, and so on. So instead of trying to put together a one-size-fits-all approach, I'll give you some general guidelines, and then I'll advise you on how to tweak them to fit you personally.

How to Use the Walkthroughs in this Book

This book contains walkthroughs for every real ACT practice question in three real practice tests from the Red Book. (Remember that the first practice test in the Red Book is usually found about 50 pages into the Red Book, separate from the other practice tests near the end of the book! Also, see page 23 of this Black Book if you have the 2020-2021 Red Book.) The best way to use those walkthroughs is to read the training in this book, and then read and analyze enough of the corresponding walkthroughs so that you feel comfortable with applying the training in this book to real ACT practice questions on your own. After that, you can use the remaining walkthroughs as a reference for any questions that give you trouble in your practice—and you can always just read (even reread) walkthroughs for practice questions you've already done to help you get very comfortable and familiar with the mechanics of the ACT, so you're ready for anything that appears on test day.

The Recommended Training Progression

Most people track their progress by looking at practice test scores, but I wouldn't recommend that, at least not in the beginning. The score on test day is what ultimately matters, of course, but evaluating yourself based only on that number isn't going to be very helpful at this stage.

Instead, my recommendation is that you track your progress based on your understanding of the test. This is more subjective, but more useful at this point in your training.

The first thing you want to do is develop a general understanding of each section of the test. You can do that by reading this Black Book and taking a look at the sample solutions until you feel like you understand how the different question types work.

Next, you want to develop the ability to recognize and understand your mistakes. Notice that we're not even trying to fix those mistakes yet; we're just trying to learn to *recognize* them. That means you need to be able to do some practice work, then take a second look at the questions you missed and figure out where you went wrong. You need to identify what you misunderstood or overlooked that stopped you from answering the question correctly, and what you could have done to avoid the mistake and get the question right.

After you know why you're making mistakes, you need to train yourself to fix them. This is extremely important. Take the knowledge you've gained so far and apply it in your practice, either to avoid errors in the first place, or to recognize them and resolve them once you've made them. Your goal at this point in your training is to avoid careless mistakes, so that the only time you miss a question is when it involves a concept you're not familiar with.

Once students train themselves to stop making careless errors, they're typically scoring in a range that they're quite happy with. If you get to this point and you still need to increase your score, then you'll need to take a look at what's stopping you from answering the remaining questions. Be careful, though—too often, students conclude that they're missing Math questions because they don't know some obscure formula, or missing Science questions because they don't know enough physics or chemistry. In almost every case, the real issue has to do with a failure to understand some principle or idea related to the structure of that question type. Take a close look and try to identify the real issue, so you can work on it.

(Also, if you're having performance issues related to timing, be sure to take a look at "Part 4: Time Management," starting on page 36 of this Black Book. Remember that when you're trying to work on your timing, your goal isn't to do the same thing more quickly—it's to find a *different approach* to the test in the first place, which is faster and simpler.)

Order of Attack

A lot of students like to start their preparation by focusing on the section of the ACT they have the most trouble with. That's understandable. If you've got the time, though, I'd definitely recommend you prepare for each section in the order laid out in this book. That way, you'll be able to build on the skills learned in each section as you progress through the training.

I almost always start students off on the Reading section, for a few reasons. The first reason is that careful, precise reading is the most important skill on the entire ACT (yes, even on the Math and Science sections), so it makes sense to start developing that skill directly, right from the beginning. The second reason is that it's usually easier to see how predictable and repetitive the Math, Science, and English questions are if we've already seen how predictable and repetitive the ACT Reading questions are.

The only two situations I can think of in which I wouldn't recommend that you start with ACT Reading would be the following:

1. You literally never miss any ACT Reading practice questions, or
2. You have very little time before test day, and you feel you need to spend that time working on other sections.

Unless one of these applies to you, I would definitely say that you should start your training with the ACT Reading section.

After you feel comfortable with the Reading section, I find it's usually best to work on ACT Math. As we'll discuss in the Math training section, excelling at ACT Math essentially comes down to being able to read a question, figure out which basic math concepts need to be applied to find the answer, and then apply them. Typically, the bigger challenge is just figuring out which math concepts to use; the actual math you do on most problems is pretty simple (but you still need to look out for careless errors at all times).

Because ACT Math problems appear on the surface to vary more than the questions in other sections, it might take a little more time for you to get comfortable with the approach to the ACT Math section, which is why I usually like to introduce it as soon as possible after the Reading training.

After that, I'd recommend that you take a look at the Science section. The skills you need to do well on the Science section are basically the same as the ones you will have learned for Reading and Math. Mostly, you'll be using the careful reading we'll talk about in the Reading section, only now it'll be applied to charts, graphs, and scientific texts. You may also need a little bit of basic math thrown in there, and a tiny bit of basic science, which is so minimal that it's almost irrelevant. We'll talk more about that in the Science training section.

Next you'll want to look at the ACT English section. Some of these question types will require skills that are similar to the ones from the Reading section, and of course we'll also talk about how to attack the other question types.

Last, we'll talk about the optional ACT Writing Test, also known as the ACT Essay. Before you spend any time on ACT Writing, you should find out if your target schools even ask for an ACT Writing score, because many schools don't—and if your target schools don't require you to take the ACT Writing test, then there's no reason to take it or prepare for it. Just visit the schools' websites or call their admissions departments directly to find out.

Drills and Exercises

What do you do to prepare for a test in school? You probably gather together all the notes and materials you've covered leading up to the test, and you sit down and memorize those specific concepts, because you know they'll show up on test day. This works pretty well for most people in a high school environment.

Well, many students try to do something similar when they prepare for the ACT. They review a lot of school material, and then they take the test—and they typically find that all their preparation has very little positive impact on their ACT performance, and they wonder what to do next.

Once you read the training sections of this Black Book that explain the proper approach to each question type, you'll see why the typical style of preparation isn't very effective. Preparing for the ACT isn't about memorization. There will be some limited amount of memorization as you internalize the material, but mostly you'll be learning and practicing skills that you can apply to real ACT questions.

In each training section of this book, you'll develop an understanding of how a particular part of the test works, and you'll learn about the standards and patterns that appear on each question type. Once you've learned that, you can read through the question walkthroughs in this book, and then spend some time working with real ACT practice questions on your own, possibly by doing some of the drills we'll discuss in just a moment. Eventually your goal is to be able to apply the correct techniques to real ACT questions without any help.

Let me reiterate that you shouldn't actually do the following drills until you've studied the training materials in this book; I'm just discussing them here because I often get asked about this when I first start working with a student.

With that in mind, here are my four favorite drills and exercises you can do with real ACT practice questions, when the time comes. These will help you develop the skills you'll need on test day.

(I've gone ahead and given them weird names so they'll be easy to remember.)

1. Semi-Structured Stare-and-Ponder

This is a great, low-pressure way to begin to apply your knowledge to practice questions, and it can also be a good option as you progress in your preparation if you feel like you need to spend some time on a relatively unstructured exercise.

All you need to do is flip through your copy of *The Official ACT Prep Guide* (the "Red Book") until you find a question you'd like to work on (any question will do).

Then, you just take all the time you need to read and think about the question, the answer choices, and any associated passage, diagram, chart, graph, or anything else.

Of course, you probably want to think about what the right answer is at some point, but, beyond that, you just want to think about everything else that could possibly be going on in this question. Your goal is to understand exactly what the writers and editors of the question were thinking about when they created it. Why is the question worded the way it is? Why was each wrong answer choice included—what kind of mistakes is the question trying to get you to make? How could somebody miss this question? Can you predict any common mistakes that test-takers might make when they attempt this question? Which specific design rules does the question follow? How could the elements of this question appear in future questions?

The things you could choose to ponder go on and on, though some ACT questions definitely give us more to ponder than others do. The point here is just to spend as much as time you need in order to think about every possible aspect of the question based on what you've learned from this Black Book. If you happen to get the answer wrong, then of course you'll want to think about why you got it wrong, what you missed or misunderstood in the question, and how you could avoid that mistake in the future—reading that question's corresponding walkthrough in this Black Book will be helpful in that process, of course. But the goal of this exercise isn't simply to get the question right—the goal is just to understand how the question was built, in terms of the concepts from this Black Book.

After you've thought about every aspect of a particular ACT question, just move on to another question and ponder it in the same way you pondered the first one. When you're done, move on to another question and repeat the process again. And so on and so on, for as long as you care to sit and ponder.

Of course, you don't want to try to look at a question this way on test day. On test day, your goal is to be efficient, accurate, and purposeful, because you're working with a time limit.

This exercise is very effective because it helps you to look at any given ACT question and then start to pull it apart and think about it effectively. That way, it'll be much easier for you to separate right answers from wrong answers, and it'll be much harder for the ACT to trick you.

2. Practice-and-a-Postie

In the title for this drill, the word "postie" stands for "post-mortem," and I included it in the title of the drill to make it very clear that simply doing a practice section or test isn't enough by itself if you want to see improvement. It's *absolutely essential* that you thoroughly review all of your practice work before you move on and do more practice work.

Let me be clear—when I talk about reviewing all of your practice work, I don't just mean checking the answer key to see what you missed. I mean going back over every single question you missed or were unsure about, and trying to figure out what was going on in each question that stopped you from being certain about the correct answer. That way you'll know how to overcome similar issues on test day.

Typically, the process of reviewing your work should take about as much time as the original practice takes (at least until you hit a point where you don't miss any questions at all). In other words, if you spend 30 minutes doing practice questions, you'll probably spend about 30 minutes doing a thorough review of everything you got wrong. It might take you even longer, especially in the beginning. Give it as much time as it takes to do a thorough job.

I just want to make sure we're very clear on the importance of the review. It's the most important part of this drill—and the most important part of all your training—because it's the part where you see what you did wrong and you figure out how to fix it in the future. Most people who try to prep for the ACT just take practice test after practice test without doing any real review at all, and they never figure out why they're not improving. You simply must review your work, or you'll never realize what you're consistently doing wrong!

So you'll do a practice section, or a whole practice test if you feel like it, and then thoroughly review your work afterward. You can do the practice timed, or untimed—it's not so important to work with a time limit in the beginning, but the real thing will be timed, of course, so you'll need to get comfortable with that as you get closer to the test date.

As with the other drills, don't bother doing this until you've digested the training material later in this book, because you'll just get frustrated otherwise, and you won't have much to go on when you try to review your mistakes. Above all, don't bother doing practice sections if you aren't going to review the outcome once you're done so you can figure out what's causing your mistakes.

3. The "Shortcut" Search

The "Shortcut" Search can be a drill on its own, or it can be part of the review you do in the previous exercise. Either way, in this drill you need to know the answers to the questions you're working with ahead of time. So this drill is something you should do with questions that you've already tried to answer for some other drill. That way, you don't burn through the limited number of real ACT practice questions available from ACT, Inc.

In this drill, your goal is to take as much time as you need to try to figure out any and all "shortcuts" you might have been able to use to arrive at the correct answer in the least amount of time possible. I'm putting the word "shortcuts" in quotation marks because I take issue with the idea that approaching questions in this way is lazy. Actually, it requires more creativity and training than any other approach, and the whole point of this Black Book is to get you to be able to identify and exploit those "shortcuts" as often as possible. There's nothing wrong with approaching the test in the most efficient and reliable way possible, even if that approach differs from the way we approach things in school.

For example, on a Math question, you might realize that some pattern in the answer choices gives you a hint at how to set up the problem. On a Science question, you might realize that several of the values in the answer choices are far too small or large to be possible answers, so they could be eliminated right away. On a Reading question, you might figure out which exact word or phrase makes the right answer right, and then you could think about the fastest way you could have figured that out. On an English question, you might realize that the phrase before the one you're being asked about has the same structure as one of the answer choices . . . and so on. The training sections and the walkthroughs in this Black Book will show you how to look for these kinds of solutions reliably and confidently.

When you practice looking for these alternative solutions in this kind of drill, you should feel free to take as much time as necessary to try to find solutions that could have been worked out in seconds if you had noticed them right away. In other words, if it takes you 10 minutes (or even longer) of thinking about a question to figure out a solution that would have taken 30 seconds, there's nothing wrong with that at this point. Of course, you probably won't have the luxury of staring at an individual question for 10 whole minutes on test day, but doing this kind of drill now, as part of your preparation, will help you identify these kinds of super-efficient solutions more quickly when it counts.

As with the other drills, you should wait to do this one until you're familiar with the training material, and then you'll know what to look for.

4. What would Make it Right?

In this drill, you'll look at wrong answer choices and ask yourself, "What would make it right?"

For example, in a Science question that asks you about a value in Table 1, you might see a wrong answer choice that incorrectly uses the corresponding value from Table 2. In that case, the answer to "What would make it right?" would be "If the question asked about Table 2 instead of Table 1, then this answer choice would be right."

For another example, if a Reading question asks for the meaning of a certain phrase in the text, and one of the wrong answers gives a correct meaning for another phrase later in the text, the answer to "What would make it right?" would be "If the question had asked about the other phrase in the text, that would make it right."

As you'll learn later in this Black Book, the ACT will frequently offer wrong answer choices that are still relevant to the passage or problem—just not in the way that the question requires. Thinking about how the question could be changed to make wrong answer choices correct gives you another opportunity to think about how the test is designed from the standpoint of ACT, Inc., and it will also help you to identify wrong answers more quickly and reliably on test day.

Figuring out your Schedule

As I mentioned above, I've found that there's no single training schedule that works best for every student. So instead of trying to come up with one that would only work for some people, I'm laying out some ideas you should think about to determine the best approach for you.

Do you Need an Early Start?

When a teacher assigns a big project that's due in several weeks, some people rush home and begin right away, while others prefer to wait until the day or two before to get started. Neither approach is necessarily better, as long as you're happy with the results that you get.

The methods that I teach for the ACT can really be taught and learned in less than a week. But not everybody is comfortable with that, and if you aren't, then you should allow yourself more time—probably at least a month or two.

If you're used to doing work at the last minute, then you might feel okay with a lot less preparation time. I've seen both approaches work quite well, as long as the person in question felt comfortable with the approach he chose.

What's your Attention Span?

Some people can't stand to work on their preparation for more than 20 minutes or so at a time, while others can go for a couple of hours or more and still be productive. If you're the sort of person with low test prep stamina, you're going to need to study more frequently to make up for it; if you can spend more time on each individual prep session, then you won't need to have so many sessions. This is something you need to be realistic about as you try to map out the time you'll spend preparing.

How Much of a Score Increase are you Shooting For?

As you might imagine, students who need larger score increases should probably plan to allow themselves more time to prepare than students who need smaller score increases.

How Much will you Improve after each Practice Session, on Average?

Unfortunately, there's no universal answer to this question: some students can take 20 practice tests and still not improve much (usually because they aren't trained well and they don't review their work sufficiently), while other people really take to the material quickly and make noticeable improvement in their first practice session. It will depend a lot on your confidence, and on how well you take direction. If you read this Black Book but don't make a conscious effort to implement what you learn, your improvement will be slower. If you make a wholehearted effort to implement the right approach, though, you'll probably progress more quickly, even if it's frustrating at first.

What determines your level of progress will be the quality of your practice, not the quantity, so don't go into it thinking that you just need to get through a certain number of practice tests in order to get the score you want. Instead, be prepared to go through as many practice questions as necessary in order to feel comfortable applying the correct strategies for each part of the test. This typically takes fewer practice sessions than people expect. But whether it's more or fewer doesn't really matter, as long as you make sure to focus on the quality of your practice. Make sure you pay attention to what you're doing, and make sure you really digest the information in this Black Book, and try to change the way you see the test accordingly.

Do you Really Even Need a Schedule?

Most people like the idea of mapping out a schedule, because it feels comfortable and productive. Even so, I would like to put the idea out there that maybe you don't need to try to establish any kind of rigid schedule for your preparation. Allow me to explain.

Because preparing for a standardized test like the ACT is so different from preparing for a normal high school test, it's hard to make an accurate prediction of exactly how much prep time you'll actually need. That means students who try to lay out a schedule might quickly find that some aspects of preparation take a lot more or a lot less time than they anticipated, which can throw off the whole idea of a schedule, and possibly create a stressful situation.

Here's what I would do instead, if I were in your shoes: start prepping (in some way) as early as you can—which is to say, now. The prep you do doesn't necessarily have to be torturous and mind-numbing.

If you're short on time, you'll probably want to get in as much preparation as you can between now and test day anyway. If you're not short on time, then starting now will let you prepare in a low-pressure environment without strict time limits. Just take an active interest in your progress, read through this book, and start trying to apply the strategies to real ACT practice questions in your copy of *The Official ACT Prep Guide*. Use these drills and exercises to practice in ways you find to be mentally engaging, and take breaks when you get bored or lose focus. Above all, after any work with real ACT practice questions, always thoroughly review any mistakes and/or issues you encounter in those questions.

If you notice that you're making good progress relative to your target score and your test date, then keep it up. If you feel like you're not making enough progress, then try to increase the amount of focus and energy you bring to your prep sessions; if that still doesn't work, then consider making more time to prepare.

It really is that simple—just stay motivated and keep at it.

Understand Your Mistakes

Failure is the key to success; each mistake teaches us something.
Morihei Ueshiba

A vital step in your improvement on the ACT is developing the ability to recognize and understand your mistakes and weaknesses so you can do what's necessary to avoid the mistakes and strengthen the weaknesses—and, ultimately, to improve your score.

But, as we've already discussed (and will continue to discuss in more detail), the ACT tests different types of skills from the skills tested in the classroom, and it does so in a highly structured and standardized way that's very unfamiliar to most students. This results in a lot of test-takers missing questions, but not understanding exactly why they're missing those questions.

This means that if you aren't careful when you try to figure out your weak points, you might end up focusing on skills that are irrelevant to the mistakes you're making, which can cause you to waste time without improving your score.

An Example from ACT Math

Let's say you miss a trig question while you're working on the ACT Math section. A lot of people might decide to respond to this by learning more trigonometry so their scores would improve. They might go to a math teacher and ask for help, or go online and find some trigonometry videos. Some people in this situation might spend hours, or days, or even weeks making time to study trig in the hopes of improving their performance on the ACT.

But hold on a minute—what if you take a closer look at the way you approached the trig question that started all of this? You might notice that you cross-multiplied incorrectly, or even that you misread the question, or had your calculator in the wrong mode, or bubbled an answer incorrectly.

In other words, just missing a trig question on the ACT doesn't necessarily indicate that you need to learn more trig! One of the most important skills in ACT Math (whatever the specific subject matter) is the ability to execute simple mathematical operations consistently and correctly; in my experience, much of the aggravation that people experience on the ACT comes from a failure to do that. The simple fact is that most people just aren't used to being as careful with basic math as the ACT Math section requires them to be.

In this example, that means you could end up spending days or weeks on trigonometry when, in reality, you might just need to read more carefully, think more about the answer choices in the question, or even just remember to carry a 1 correctly.

An Example from ACT Reading

In the context of the ACT Reading section, you might miss a question that involves an unfamiliar word, and then decide you need to learn what that word means. But closer inspection of the question often reveals that the meaning of the unknown word isn't directly relevant to finding the correct answer, and that a more careful application of the strategies in this book would have led you to the right answer anyway.

An Example from ACT Science

You may miss a question on the ACT Science section that mentions some biological concept. If you missed a question like that on a high school science test, you'd probably expect that you needed to learn more biology. But on the ACT Science section, missing that question would almost definitely mean that you just didn't read a line of text or a label on a diagram closely enough, because the passage contains enough information to answer the large majority of questions on any ACT Science section. If you review the question you missed, you'll probably find there was a key phrase in the passage you overlooked, which would have given you the right answer with no outside science knowledge at all.

An Example from ACT English

If you're pretty confident in your knowledge of American English grammar, and you keep missing ACT English questions with no prompt whose choices don't seem to have any grammatical errors, then you might decide that you need a better understanding of "good writing style." You might decide to read literature by more classic authors of American English, like Mark Twain or Laura Ingalls Wilder. (That's a great thing to do in real life, by the way, but it won't help you on the ACT English section.) But "good style" on the ACT English section isn't identical to what might be called "good style" in a Literature class. Instead, the ACT English section consistently rewards answer choices that follow a strict set of rules, and those rules are never really taught in school (of course, you can learn them from the ACT English Toolbox on page 418 of this Black Book).

Identify What Actually Went Wrong!

So whether you're evaluating your own practice, or you're looking at a diagnostic test from a tutor or test prep company (or even from ACT, Inc. itself), be careful. You might be told that you need to learn more math, grammar, or science—or who knows what else—but it's much more likely that your problem is related to executing some relatively basic skill in a consistent manner. Standardized tests like the ACT require a higher degree of precision and consistency (especially in executing basic skills) than normal classroom tests do, and this is the most common difficulty for most students.

When you look at a question you've missed, go back through your work so you can figure out exactly how you made your mistake. It might not have anything to do with subject matter. In fact, most test-takers can probably safely start with the assumption that they know enough subject matter to answer almost all (or even all) the questions on a real ACT.

Once you know the real issue that caused you to miss a question, you can work to fix it. It might take a little bit more time in the beginning, but it can save you a ton of time in the long run if it means you're not wasting energy trying to strengthen an area that isn't actually a weakness, or working to avoid a type of mistake you aren't actually making in the first place.

As we noted above, one very common kind of mistake for most test-takers is the mistake of not paying full attention to the task at hand, which can show up in a wide variety of ways, costing you points in ways that you may not even realize.

Remember that Carelessness will Cost You!

In "What You Must Understand about the ACT" on page 14 of this Black Book, we discussed the idea that the ACT is fundamentally different from the kinds of tests and evaluations found in high school and college. One of the most important and far-reaching differences is the way the ACT punishes carelessness.

In school, for instance, math teachers may give you partial credit on a test question if they can see that you tried to apply the correct formula, even though you made a small calculation mistake and arrived at the wrong answer.

But what happens if you set up an ACT Math problem correctly and do almost everything right, and then make a small calculation error on the last step and choose a wrong answer?

Here's what happens: you get no credit on that question whatsoever. It's exactly the same as it would have been if you'd just left the question blank and done no work at all.

Or imagine you're in a discussion in English class about a character in a book who was very unhappy, and you describe that character as being "desperate." Your English teacher probably wouldn't think twice about this small discrepancy; she'd see that you clearly had a general understanding of the mental state of the character, and she'd appreciate that you were sharing your perspective on the book.

But on an ACT Reading question, you can't describe an unhappy character as "desperate" unless there's something in the text that specifically describes how that character was in a difficult situation and was feeling totally hopeless, because that's what the word "desperate" literally means. A lot of desperate people are probably unhappy, but not every unhappy person is desperate, so if you chose an ACT answer that described someone as "desperate" without something in the text that specifically supported that word, you'd be *completely wrong*. No partial credit for the question, no consideration for your other thoughts about the character—on the ACT, you're just wrong, exactly as though you'd left the question blank.

Noticing these details and avoiding carelessness is so important that most students could probably hit their target scores simply by training themselves to eliminate careless errors. Yes, really—it's that big of a deal.

So how do we Avoid these Careless Errors?

As we said above, it's important to understand how many of the questions you miss in your practice sessions are actually due to carelessness, rather than a lack of outside knowledge.

The biggest thing you need to do to avoid careless errors is to realize that this test demands a different mindset from the one that most high school students have in the classroom. The ACT doesn't care about the big picture, or about advanced material. It's about simple ideas and simple tasks done exactly the right way . . . over and over and over again. If you let yourself make minor mistakes in that process, it'll hurt your score, *even if you fully understand the major concepts involved.*

Embrace this different mindset when you're preparing for the ACT (and performing on test day). Review your practice carefully as described in "Drills and Exercises" on page 30 of this Black Book, and pay attention to the specific mistakes you make so you can avoid them in the future.

Part 4: Time Management

This part of the Black Book will focus on the best way to manage your time on test day. We'll start with the general plan for attacking a section on test day, and then we'll have a broader discussion about using your time in the most effective way possible.

In this part of the Black Book, you'll learn:

- why just marking your best guess for every question isn't a good strategy
- why you should never forget your training (even when a question seems impossible)
- why you shouldn't worry about being stumped a few times on test day
- how the ACT is specifically designed to take advantage of most people's guessing instincts
- the right way to think about guessing, so it can help your score instead of getting in the way
- how quickly a trained test-taker can generally answer a real ACT question
- why and how you should approach each section of the ACT in multiple passes
- easily overlooked test-taking mistakes that can cost you points and undo your hard work
- and more . . .

The General Game Plan for Attacking a Section of the ACT on Test Day

> We cannot make events. Our business is wisely to improve them.
> Samuel Adams

In a few pages, we'll discuss specific strategies for dealing with time-management issues on the ACT. Before we do that, though, I want to make sure we're on the same page when it comes to the best way to attack a multiple-choice section of the ACT when the clock is running, because I've learned over the years that most test-takers have never learned how to do that.

The optimal basic approach to a section of the ACT relies on remembering three important things at all times:

1. Every question on a given section of the ACT is worth one raw point on that section, no matter how hard or easy the question is for you.
2. Every real ACT question is carefully designed so that it follows certain rules. The answer to a real ACT question is never arbitrary or unpredictable if we know the ACT's rules, and if we read and understand every word in the question. (See "What You Must Understand about the ACT" on page 14 of this Black Book for more on that.)
3. You should answer every question before time runs out, because there's no penalty for marking a wrong answer.

The Reason to Make Multiple Passes on a Section

For these reasons, the best approach to a section of the ACT involves making multiple passes through the section, so that you maximize the possibility of investing your time and energy in the questions that will seem easiest for you, and minimize the amount of time and energy you spend on questions that you'll just have to guess on anyway. (Of course, as you continue to improve your understanding of the ACT and your execution of the ideas in this Black Book, the number of questions you have to guess on will drop, until it ideally reaches zero.) As you near the end of the allotted time for the section, you should start thinking more about checking over your work and guessing on any questions you haven't answered yet.

The First Pass

On the first pass, you look at each question in order, and decide whether to answer it or skip it for the moment:

- If you understand the question and you can answer it relatively quickly and easily, then you go ahead and answer it.
- If you think you understand the question, but that it might take you a relatively long time to figure out the answer, then you skip it. You'll save it for a later pass. If you want, you can mark that question in your test booklet in a way that lets you know you decided to skip it because you thought it would take a little too long to answer, not because you thought you wouldn't be able to answer it at all.
- If you don't think you can figure out the answer to the question, then you skip it. Again, if you want, you can mark the question with a quick symbol in your test booklet that indicates you thought the question was too hard the first time you saw it. If time permits, you'll come back to these questions later.

At the end of your first pass through the section, you will have answered all the questions that seemed fairly quick and easy for you. You will also have looked through every question in the section, and you'll have a pretty solid idea of which questions seemed like ones you would have been able to answer if you were willing to spend more time on them, and which questions seemed too hard for you to answer with certainty no matter how much time you were willing to spend on them.

(It takes some practice to figure out how aggressive you should be with skipping questions during the first pass. Some people like to skip a question as soon as they come to a word or a concept they're not familiar with; this saves time, but it might cause you to skip questions in the first pass that you could have answered correctly if you'd finished reading them. Other people prefer to read a whole question before deciding whether to skip it; this gives them a better idea of the question, but it can also take up more time. Play with different approaches during your practice and see what works best for you. Also bear in mind that your ability to answer questions quickly and correctly will improve as you practice the concepts in this Black Book on real ACT questions from the Red Book. So will your ability to spot questions that are going to be challenging for you.)

When the first pass is over, you immediately flip back through the section and begin the second pass.

The Second Pass

In the second pass, you attack the questions that seemed like ones you could answer with certainty if you spent a little more time. Ideally, you should try to attack the easiest of these questions first, and then the next easiest one after that, and so on. But don't worry too much about observing a strict order—the time you waste trying to figure out exactly which question is the next easiest for you is time you could be spending on answering questions.

If you come across a question during the second pass that seems a little harder than you thought, you can skip it again and save it for the third pass.

At the end of the second pass, you will have answered all the questions that seemed like ones you could figure out with certainty, whether those answers came to you pretty easily or you had to work a little harder for them.

The Third Pass

At this point, if you have enough time left, you should make a third pass through the section and reconsider the questions you've been avoiding so far. You may find you actually can answer some of them now, because you realize what you'd previously overlooked or misunderstood. You may also decide those questions really are too challenging for you to answer, and you'll have to guess on them.

If you don't have enough time for a third pass, then you should shift your focus to guessing on the questions you haven't answered yet, and/or re-checking the questions you've already answered. (You may be wondering how much time is "enough time" for a third pass. The answer will depend on you, because different test-takers will work at different speeds and decide to skip different numbers of questions in the first two passes. You'll develop a sense of how much time you need as you keep practicing with real ACT questions.)

Let's spend a little time talking about guessing and re-checking on the ACT, because they're very important skills that most test-takers ignore.

Guessing on the ACT

The ACT has no wrong-answer penalty. In other words, the ACT doesn't take any points away from you if you answer a question incorrectly (as opposed to leaving it blank). With that in mind, there's never a reason to leave a question blank on the ACT; you should always at least mark something, even if you're just randomly choosing an answer in under a second. It can't hurt you, and there's a small chance that it could help.

But guessing on ACT questions shouldn't be your default response!

Notice I'm not suggesting that you guess on any questions until you've gone through at least two passes in a section and answered the questions you could handle with certainty.

In contrast, most untrained test-takers just kind of float through the entire ACT without ever actually being certain about the answers they're choosing. These test-takers are basically guessing on every single question. They don't know how the ACT works, they don't have a game plan, and they suffer for it.

So you need to maintain a disciplined approach to every real ACT question you encounter, because that's the only way to make sure you attack each question using the principles in this Black Book. The guessing mindset is a dangerous trap to fall into, and it harms a lot of ACT-takers.

Remember that every question on the ACT must be airtight, and that there's always exactly one correct answer, and that correct answer is undeniably right, according to the ACT's rules—no matter how strange it might seem to an untrained test-taker.

It's absolutely important that you remember this at all times. If you don't, you may end up facing a challenging question that you can't quite figure out right away, and you may forget that every question has one clearly correct answer. You might decide that this one question is the exception, and that really two or three of the answer choices are all equally valid. Then you might start to deviate from the strategies you've learned from this Black Book as you go through the rest of the test, and you might end up with a much worse score than you could have achieved if you had just remembered the rules.

This is especially dangerous because ACT, Inc. goes out of its way to include wrong answer choices that would be acceptable in a classroom setting, and to use misleading phrasing that makes it sound like you need to make a judgment call to find the right answer. This is done to trick untrained test-takers into answering based on their undisciplined hunches, instead of using consistent, repeatable, dependable strategies like the ones we'll discuss later in this Black Book. Don't fall for it! We'll see more about how the test tries to do this for each specific question type in the training for each section of the ACT, which is found in Parts 6, 7, 8, and 9 of this Black Book.

Of course, you're probably going to run into ACT questions on test day that challenge you so much that you skip them in your first two passes. In those cases, you should still mark the answer choice that seems most likely to be correct (either because of the content of the answer choice, or because it fits an answer-choice pattern that you've learned in this Black Book).

But if you do find yourself guessing on a particular question, you have to remember that it's not because the question can't be answered with certainty, and it's not because the strategies you've learned in this Black Book don't work. It's because there's something about this question that you just aren't seeing. It might be a word you don't really know, or it might be a math concept that you're overlooking, or a complicated sentence you don't quite understand, or it might just be that you're getting flustered and forgetting something about how the questions work.

That's fine. You can be totally stumped a few times on test day and still get a great score. The point is not to beat yourself up about it, and not to lose faith in your ACT training simply because you're unable to execute that training sometimes. (See "When Things Go Wrong" on page 576 of this Black Book for ideas on what to do when you can't figure out how to handle a question.)

Again, if you've got no other options, you should guess on a question before time runs out rather than leave it blank. But guessing shouldn't be your game plan! Understanding the test and paying attention to the right details should be your game plan, and that's what you'll learn to do in this Black Book.

Re-Checking your Answers

One of the major themes of this Black Book is that the ACT is a very detail-oriented test of relatively basic concepts. This means that a lot of test-takers cost themselves a lot of points just because they don't pay enough attention to what they're doing, not because they don't know enough to answer a question.

So it should come as no surprise that I highly recommend re-checking your answers on a section if you have time. (You should be constantly re-checking your work and your assumptions as you go through each question in the first place. You should also be using the knowledge of the ACT's design that you get from this Black Book to make sure you can account for each part of a question as you answer it, because that's another good way to make sure you haven't made a small mistake somewhere.)

But the issue is whether you should re-check your answers or guess on the questions you've skipped, if you don't have enough time to do both.

Again, the answer comes down to your personal style and tendencies. If you do a good, careful job of checking your answers as you go, then you may not find any mistakes in your re-checking. On the other hand, you may also find that you're not very good at guessing correctly on the ACT, in which case it might make more sense to shift more of your energy towards re-checking the questions you actually understand. If you notice that you usually *do* find errors when you re-check your work, then you definitely want to make an effort to have time for that.

The only way to know which activity is more likely to result in extra points for you is to experiment with both of them in your practice sessions. Of course, the most ideal scenario is one in which you have enough time to do both.

The Bottom Line

So here's the best general way to approach a section of the ACT. You'll notice that it bears little resemblance to what most people do on the test, which is simply to mark their best guess on each question as they encounter it.

1. Start by answering all the questions that seem relatively simple and easy for you. Skip the ones that seem too hard or too time-consuming for now.

2. After you've made your first pass through the section, go back and do the questions that seemed like they would be time-consuming but still possible to figure out. Try to approach them in order from easiest to hardest, but don't obsess over getting the order exactly right. Skip any questions that turn out to be too hard to answer for now.

3. After the second pass, go back and revisit the questions you've skipped so far. You may find that you can actually figure some of them out after all. If so, go ahead and answer them. Save the remaining questions for guessing.

4. Remember that a small mistake on a question can be all it takes to cost you that question! (See "Understand Your Mistakes" on page 34 for more.) Depending on the results you obtain in your practice sessions, consider leaving yourself enough time to re-check the questions you felt you could answer with certainty.

5. Be sure to guess on all remaining unanswered questions before time runs out.

Attacking a section of the ACT in this kind of disciplined, focused way will allow you to make sure you answer as many questions as possible with total certainty. It will also ensure that you spend your time and energy where it will do you the most good.

One Final Note

This probably goes without saying, but make sure you bubble in your answer sheet correctly as you're going through each pass! It would be a shame to work through the section correctly and still lose a lot of points because you didn't pay attention to the numbering on the answer sheet.

Timing Issues

Time is what we want most, but what we use worst.
William Penn

Most of the students I work with are at least a little concerned about the timing aspect of the ACT before we start working together. When you keep running out of time before you've finished a practice section, it's understandable that you might get a little worried. Often, students who have this problem try to solve it by timing themselves as they do a bunch of practice sections, hoping to improve their time management without really doing anything in particular to change their approach. They're basically trying to do what they've always done, and just hoping they'll somehow get it done faster.

But in most cases, even students with major timing problems are best served by putting those issues aside temporarily and focusing on mastering the concepts presented in this book. If you can do that, you'll often find that your timing issues resolve themselves.

Let me elaborate on that a little.

Any single ACT question can be approached in a number of different ways. Some approaches will result in wrong answers, and some in right answers; some take a long time, and some take only a matter of seconds. Not surprisingly, people with timing issues on the ACT usually approach questions in ways that are more time-consuming and complicated than necessary, instead of attacking questions in the easiest and most direct ways.

But the solution to this problem isn't to train yourself to do the complicated, time-consuming approaches more quickly, as though you were hitting fast-forward on a video! Instead, the solution is to learn a completely different approach—one that's better because it's less complicated and can naturally be completed in less time.

Usually, the more "academic" approach to an ACT question—the one that feels more like a solution to a normal high school test item—is the most comfortable and familiar approach for most test-takers. Unfortunately, it's also the approach that usually takes a lot more time than necessary.

Since most people don't appreciate the important differences between the ACT and a normal high school test, they also don't realize that this academic approach is unnecessarily slow and complicated when applied to most real ACT questions.

Students without timing issues usually aren't just doing the normal "academic" approach at super speeds. Instead, they're using an entirely different approach that simply doesn't take as much time.

To illustrate this idea, let's imagine that two people each have to chop an onion. One person uses a knife and a cutting board and takes five minutes to get the job done. The other person uses a food processor and takes 10 seconds.

Is the second person better at chopping onions than the first person? Of course not. She just knows how to use the food processor; she'd probably take just as long as the first person if she only had a knife and cutting board. Similarly, the first person could probably also chop the onion in ten seconds if he knew about the food processor.

So if you're worried about time management, your first step should be just to learn the most efficient ways to attack the ACT, which is what we'll cover in this Black Book, instead of trying to get faster at the approach you're already using. The odds are good that your time-management problems will no longer exist once you learn to attack each question the way a trained test-taker would. You'll be using the food processor instead of the knife, so to speak.

This is one of the reasons that people who excel on standardized tests like the ACT often finish sections with a ton of extra time. It's not because they're superhuman; it's because understanding the test goes hand-in-hand with answering questions more quickly—when you work on your understanding of the test, the average time you need per question will naturally go down considerably, even without special training to increase your speed.

All the same, there are a few little tips and strategies that might be helpful for some students, so let's talk about them here.

30 Seconds or Less

When approached correctly, every single ACT question can be answered in 30 seconds or less, and many can be answered in less than 10 seconds. Again, this doesn't involve actually going through a bunch of complicated steps at lightning speed. It means using an approach with fewer, quicker steps in the first place.

When I talk about how it's possible to complete all real ACT questions in less than 30 seconds, I don't mean that you have to do each problem in less than 30 seconds in order to be successful. Even the best test-takers run into questions they just have a hard time figuring out at first, and even the quickest students get stuck occasionally. By the time you've got the right techniques down, though, you should be doing enough of the questions quickly enough that you aren't hurt by the ones that take a little more time.

Read a Little Faster

This one might seem a little obvious, but it helps. There are all kinds of speed-reading courses and related schools of thought out there, but most people can noticeably increase their reading speed by just making a point of reading faster. I like to compare it to walking: most people could walk faster than they normally do without much extra effort. They just don't, unless they think about it.

So, whether you're reading for pleasure, for school, or for test prep, just consciously think about doing it a little faster than normal. If you keep it up, you should be able to start automatically reading more quickly.

In general, if you can read fast enough to keep up with your classes in school, then you shouldn't have anything to worry about on the ACT, but you might as well try this strategy out and see if it helps.

One more thing: if you have a serious issue with reading speed that's been diagnosed by a professional, you should look into contacting ACT, Inc., to request extra time on test day.

Dealing with Anxiety

Anxiety can be a big problem for a lot of students, and it can manifest itself in different ways. Some students freeze up, get confused, or second-guess themselves in practice or on test day because of it.

There are two main ways to deal with this issue that I like to recommend to my students. The first way is to make a conscious effort to channel this nervous energy into something productive. When you start to feel restless or nervous during practice, switch to a less-structured drill, like the Semi-Structured Stare-And-Ponder (which we talked about in "Drills and Exercises" on page 30 of this Black Book).

Even taking a little break from training to take a walk and get some fresh air can be productive, if it means you're able to relax and focus on the test when you get back.

The other way of dealing with anxiety is to take the time to understand where it comes from, and then explore those issues.

In the vast majority of cases in my experience, anxiety over the ACT comes from the fact that it's an important test that will have an impact on the college you attend, and most people aren't sure how to do well on it.

Let's address those ideas.

First of all, I should point out that your ultimate happiness and success in life will depend on a lot more than your ACT score. This single thing isn't going to make or break you, no matter how much it might feel like that's the case right now.

Secondly, if you plan to go to college, you're probably going to have to take this test (or the SAT). There's basically no way around it, so you may as well just commit to doing the best you can, and then see how it goes.

Finally, the test can also seem challenging because most test-takers and tutors don't understand how it really works. The odds are good that a lot of the advice you've received about the ACT isn't actually helpful, and may even be harmful. In that case, the best thing to do is just to start from square one and use the material in this book. You'll probably find that performing on the test will become much less stressful than it used to be.

Go Through Multiple Passes on Each Section

Approaching each section of the ACT in multiple passes will allow you to minimize the amount of time you waste on questions that you find more challenging. For a detailed discussion of this important strategy, see "The General Game Plan for Attacking a Section of the ACT on Test Day" on page 37 of this Black Book.

Summary

Every student is different, but most time management issues come down to the things we discussed in this section. In my experience, the best way for almost anyone to deal with this problem is to learn and practice the techniques in this book, because most students will find that using the optimal techniques will allow them to answer questions much more quickly than they do on their own.

Part 5: Key Techniques for the Whole ACT

Before we discuss more specific training for the different kinds of ACT questions, we'll briefly discuss two concepts that you'll be able to use many times throughout the test.

In this part of the Black Book, you'll learn the following:

- how most people look at a set of answer choices, and why it holds them back
- the importance of always considering every answer choice on an ACT question
- why we must think of every ACT question as a system of ideas
- a habit that will help you catch your mistakes (and answer questions more effectively in the first place)
- how a question's answer choices can often reveal ACT-specific shortcuts that untrained test-takers don't notice
- what the vertical scan is, why it's so useful on the ACT, and how to execute it on every section of the test
- and more . . .

Always Consider Every Answer Choice!

When untrained test-takers think they've found the right answer to a question, they typically mark it immediately and then move on to the next question—even if the choice they've selected is the very first one in the set, and they haven't looked at the others at all. This is a very common way to go through the test, but it's a terrible habit to get into!

As we've seen repeatedly by now, ACT, Inc., deliberately creates wrong answers on the ACT so they'll appeal to people who've made a mistake in addressing the question—whether through misreading, miscalculating, or even just being nervous.

So as trained test-takers, we always want to make sure that we're giving ourselves every opportunity to assess what's really going on in a question . . . and to catch any mistakes we might make so we can correct them and get the high scores we deserve.

Catching Your Mistakes

One of the best ways to catch your mistakes on the ACT is to check *every* answer choice whenever you answer a question.

When you read through the whole set of answer choices, you're giving yourself access to more information about the question, which is always helpful for a trained test-taker who understands how ACT questions are constructed. You might end up realizing that more than one of the choices seems like a valid answer at first, in which case you know that you need to revisit the question and keep your training in mind so you can figure out which choice really is correct. Or you might realize that some of the other choices fit hidden patterns that suggest the choice you like really is correct, in which case you can have even more confidence that you've answered the question correctly. These are advantages that other test-takers won't have.

Finding the Easiest Approach to Any Question

And as we'll see throughout this Black Book, trained test-takers can almost always use the relationships among a set of answer choices to help them diagnose what's going on in a question before they even start thinking about which answer is likely to be correct:

- On the Reading and Science sections, being aware of the options in the answer choices can help you zero in on the parts of the passage that might be relevant to a question, allowing you to focus your energies effectively.

- On the English section, noticing the similarities and differences among the answer choices can help you realize which grammatical concepts are actually being tested by a question, while untrained test-takers might incorrectly focus on ideas that aren't relevant to finding the right answer at all.

- On the Math section, being aware of the relationships among a set of answer choices can help you identify solutions that might take less than 10 seconds and not even require a calculation, while untrained test-takers waste unnecessary time on a formal solution that will involve more steps and a greater potential for errors and frustration.

Every ACT Question is a System of Ideas

You'll see throughout this Black Book that we try to understand each question as a whole system of ideas—and that system includes all of the answer choices! When you read each answer choice, you're in a better position to see what's going on in the whole question: what kinds of mistakes ACT, Inc. hopes you'll make, what you need to focus on to find the correct answer in the most efficient way, and so on.

So remember to check every answer choice, even if you're sure you've found the right answer after the first choice or two! You'll understand questions better in the first place, which will allow you to attack them more quickly and more successfully; when you do make a mistake, you'll have a much better chance of catching it and correcting it.

On the next page, we'll explore one specialized way of considering every answer choice: the vertical scan.

The Vertical Scan: A Key Tactic for Trained Test-Takers

Before we start discussing the details of the different kinds of questions you'll encounter on test day in a few pages, I want to discuss a special technique that will often come in handy on the ACT (and, indeed, on most standardized multiple-choice tests). I call this technique the "vertical scan," and it can help you notice the similarities, differences, and other relationships within a set of answer choices more easily, and keep them clear in your head with less effort.

An Important Note before we Get Started!

The vertical scan is just one way to get a quick, accurate impression of the similarities and differences among a set of answer choices. It doesn't have to be the only way you read the answer choices for a question, and you don't have to use it on every question! You'll probably run into a few situations in which the vertical scan gives you enough information to be able to answer a question with total certainty, but there will also be lots of times when you decide to scan the answer choices vertically *and* read them horizontally as well. I'm not suggesting that you never read horizontally on test day! I'm just giving you another tool for evaluating answer choices that a lot of untrained test-takers never think of.

How to Execute the Vertical Scan

Performing the vertical scan is relatively easy: we just mentally divide a set of answer choices into a few "columns" based on the similarities and differences that initially leap out at us, and then we proceed to read *down* each column, instead of reading or skimming *across* each choice as a separate row, which is what most untrained test-takers do when they read a set of answer choices.

An Example from the English Section

See the diagram below for a general demonstration of the difference between the way an untrained test-taker looks at a set of answer choices, and the way we analyze those answer choices with a vertical scan. These choices are taken from question 45 in the English section of practice test 2 in the Red Book (test 3 in the 2020-2021 Red Book):

Normal Horizontal Reading and the Vertical Scan
(dashed arrows indicate reading direction)

Untrained / horizontal-only reading approach
A) astronomer peering through
B) astronomer, peering through,
C) astronomer: peering through
D) astronomer peering through,

Trained / vertical scanning approach
A) astronomer peering through
B) astronomer, peering through,
C) astronomer: peering through
D) astronomer peering through,

On the left side, we can see the answer choices more or less as they appear in the test booklet. Most untrained test-takers will just read them in sequence from left to right, and try to remember each item separately afterward. Their inner monologue while reading might be something like this: "Okay, the choices are astronomer-peering-through, astronomer-comma-peering-through-comma, astronomer-colon-peering-through, and astronomer-peering-through-comma."

On the right side, we can see the same answer choices visualized as five rough "columns." When we scan down the columns, it's easier to note several things:

- In the first "column," we can see quickly that every choice uses the word "astronomer" (that is, no choice uses a word like the possessive noun "astronomer's," nor the plural "astronomers," as the first word in the choice).
- The second "column" shows us the following:
  - One choice includes a comma after "astronomer."
  - One choice includes a colon in that position.
  - Two choices have no punctuation at all in that position.
- The third "column" shows us that each choice uses the word "peering," instead of some other form of the verb "to peer."
- The fourth "column" shows us that the last word in every choice is "through."
- The fifth "column" shows us that two choices have a comma after "through," and two choices have no punctuation in that position.

Our inner monologue while we do a vertical scan on this question might sound something like this: "It looks like every choice starts with 'astronomer,' and then two choices have no punctuation after that, but one choice has a comma after 'astronomer' and one choice has a colon there. Every choice also has 'peering' and 'through,' and then two choices end with a comma, and two have no punctuation at the end."

When we use the vertical scan to look at the choices in this way, it becomes easier to realize which options the question is actually presenting to us. For example, in this question, we can see that we should focus on the ACT's rules for comma usage and colon usage, since the presence or absence of commas and colons are the only differences among the choices. This also means we don't have to worry about the grammatical forms of any words. (For a complete discussion of that question, take a look at the corresponding walkthrough in the ACT English section of this Black Book, on page 503.)

An Example from the Math Section

Now let's look at an example from ACT Math. The following choices are taken from question 29 in the Math section of practice test 1 in the Red Book (test 2 in the 2020-2021 Red Book):

Normal Horizontal Reading and the Vertical Scan
(dashed arrows indicate reading direction)

Untrained / horizontal-only reading approach	Trained / vertical scanning approach
A) $x < -4y + 2$	A) $x < -4y + 2$
B) $x > -4y + 2$	B) $x > -4y + 2$
C) $x < 2y + 2$	C) $x < 2y + 2$
D) $x < 4y + 2$	D) $x < 4y + 2$
E) $x > 4y + 2$	E) $x > 4y + 2$

Again, on the left side we see the answer choices as they appear in the test booklet. Most untrained test-takers will simply read the choices from left to right, as they're presented.

But on the right side we can see the same choices visually divided into columns. When we make a quick vertical scan of those columns, we can note the following things more easily:

- Every choice begins with x.
- Three choices say that x is less than the right-hand side of the expression, and two choices say x is greater than the right-hand side of the expression.
- Two choices involve a negative y-term, and three choices involve a positive y-term.
- Four choices involve multiplying the y-term by 4, and one choice involves multiplying it by 2.
- Every choice involves adding 2 to the y-term.

This can be helpful, because it lets us know that we should focus our attention on the following issues:

1. Which direction the inequality symbol should face.
2. Whether the y-term should be positive or negative.
3. Whether the coefficient of the y-term should be 4 or 2.

Zeroing in on these issues can often help us figure out how to attack the question in the most efficient, effective way possible. (For a complete discussion of this question, take a look at its walkthrough in the ACT Math section of this Black Book, on page 191.)

An Example from the Reading Section

ACT Reading questions are structured in a way that often makes it harder to apply the vertical scan in an obvious way—although you'll probably notice opportunities to use the technique on that section as you get further into your training. For now, we'll look at question 2 in the Reading section of practice test 2 in the Red Book (test 3 in the 2020-2021 Red Book) for an example of how this approach might be used on ACT Reading (note that the columns are easier to notice if we pay more attention to (B), (C), and (D) than to (A)):

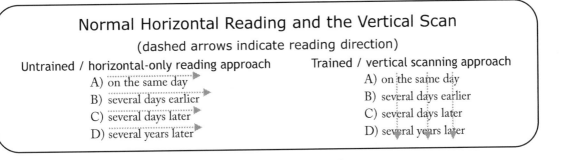

Normal Horizontal Reading and the Vertical Scan
(dashed arrows indicate reading direction)

Untrained / horizontal-only reading approach	Trained / vertical scanning approach
A) on the same day	A) on the same day
B) several days earlier	B) several days earlier
C) several days later	C) several days later
D) several years later	D) several years later

In this case, the vertical scan makes the following issues in the question obvious:

- One choice would let us say that something happens "on the same day," while the other choices all involve things happening at some other time.
- Of the three choices that mention something happening on a different day . . .
  - . . . two choices mention a difference of days, while one choice mentions a difference of years.

• ...one choice mentions something happening earlier, and the other two choices mention it happening later.

Recognizing these distinctions would help us find the key phrases in the passage that tell us which choice is correct. It would also alert us that the ACT wants test-takers to make mistakes about the order of two events, and whether those events will be separated by days or years (if they don't occur on the same day), according to the relevant passage. Being aware of these specific pitfalls would make it easier for us to verify that we're picking the right answer, rather than accidentally picking (D) instead of (C) because they both begin with "several" and end with "later," for example.

(For a full explanation of this question, see its walkthrough in the ACT Reading section of this Black Book, on page 79.)

An Example from the Science Section

Finally, we'll consider a brief example from the ACT Science section. The vertical scan can be successfully applied to many sets of answer choices on this section, even when individual choices span multiple lines of text, as we'll see in the walkthroughs for the ACT Science section later in this Black Book. For now, we'll look at a set of shorter choices, from question 1 in the Science section of practice test 3 in the Red Book (form 16MC3 if you have the 2020-2021 Red Book):

```
          Normal Horizontal Reading and the Vertical Scan
                  (dashed arrows indicate reading direction)
      Untrained / horizontal-only reading approach    Trained / vertical scanning approach
              A) Day 1 at Site 1                              A) Day 1 at Site 1
              B) Day 30 at Site 1                             B) Day 30 at Site 1
              C) Day 1 at Site 2                              C) Day 1 at Site 2
              D) Day 30 at Site 2                             D) Day 30 at Site 2
```

Here, we can see clearly that the ACT is presenting us with every possible combination of the following elements:

- Either Day 1 or Day 30
- Either Site 1 or Site 2

Recognizing these limited options allows us to identify the relevant parts of the presented data and quickly determine the right answer, without wasting time considering parts of the passage that don't affect the answer to the question. (For more on this question, take a look at its walkthrough on page 387 of this Black Book.)

When to Use the Vertical Scan

We can use the vertical scan whenever we notice that the answer choices in a question are highly similar to each other, or whenever we want to reconsider the relationships among the answer choices in light of the answer-choice patterns we've been trained to notice on a particular type of question. (We'll discuss specific answer-choice patterns later, in the parts of this Black Book devoted to the different types of questions you'll see on test day.)

As noted above, we'll generally find that sets of answer choices on the English, Math, and Science sections of the ACT are the most vulnerable to the vertical scan, but we'll sometimes find that Reading questions can also be successfully attacked with a vertical scan. This is because those three sections use more question types with answer choices that imitate each other visually, while questions on the Reading section tend to have answer choices that are less visually similar to each other.

Now that we've seen how to perform vertical scans, let's discuss some more ways they can help you ...

Benefits of the Vertical Scan

We've already mentioned that vertical scans can help you note and keep track of the differences among a set of answer choices. But why is that a big deal in the first place?

Once you understand how the ACT actually works (which you'll learn as you go through this Black Book), you'll find that one of the major challenges on test day is simply keeping track of all the relevant details in a question and making sure you never fall for the test's repeated tricks.

The vertical scan can help you overcome this challenge in several important ways:

- It can give you a simple way to notice all the options being presented to you, since you're directly comparing the answer choices to each other instead of evaluating each choice individually.
- It can help alert you to the mistakes the ACT is hoping you'll make, by calling your attention to the relationships among the answer choices.
- It can make some answer choice patterns more obvious. (We'll discuss the answer choice patterns for each question type in the corresponding training later in this book.)
- It can help you pinpoint the type of question you're dealing with, because your training will make you aware of the types of

choices that are featured in different question types. Knowing the rules and patterns of the question you're working on can help you limit your thinking to the kinds of issues that can be relevant to a given question.

The vertical scan can also help you figure out what a prompt is even asking in the first place, which may not always be obvious when you first encounter a question. This is often possible because the vertical scan makes it easier to notice relationships among the ideas represented in each answer choice in a set. For example, if the differences in a set of answer choices for an English question all relate to whether particular words are singular or plural, then you know that the question could be testing your understanding of things like subject-verb agreement (see page 420 of this Black Book) or pronoun ambiguity (see page 419), which might not have been obvious when you first read the relevant sentence. If the answer choices to a Math question all differ from each other by a factor of 10, then you know that multiplying or dividing by 10 is probably a key element of the ideal approach to the question, which may not have been obvious from the prompt. Finally, if the choices for a Science question all refer to numbers that appear in only one Figure, then you know that Figure is relevant to the question, even if that wasn't clear before.

Conclusion

By now, you can probably tell that the vertical scan is a very powerful tool in a lot of situations, whether as a stand-alone reading method in some questions, or in combination with the normal line-by-line method of reading answer choices for most questions. Keep it in mind as you continue your training. You'll see many more examples of its use in the question walkthroughs throughout this Black Book.

Part 6: Reading Test Training and Walkthroughs

In this part, we'll finally start tackling a specific test on the ACT, applying all of the training concepts we've discussed so far. Remember that prepping for the ACT Reading test is the best way to lay the foundation for the rest of the ACT: reading carefully and paying attention to details that other people will overlook are key skills throughout the test.

In this part of the Black Book, you'll learn the following:

- the single most important secret of doing well on the ACT Reading section
- why ACT, Inc. had to design ACT Reading questions the way they're designed
- the key role that literal reading plays throughout the ACT
- how ACT, Inc. tries to trick us into thinking subjectively instead of objectively
- why it's so important to consider the precise meaning of each word we encounter
- the key patterns that account for all wrong answers on the ACT Reading section
- the different approaches to reading the passages on test day, and how to find the one that suits you best
- why you shouldn't take notes when you read a passage on test day
- the recommended process for answering ACT Reading questions
- how to answer "Vocabulary in Context" questions
- why questions about the author's "attitude" still require us to think objectively, and how to do that
- how to remain objective when answering questions about the "main idea" of a passage
- what constitutes "humor" on the ACT
- how to attack questions about paired passages and why they don't differ much from other Reading questions
- how to apply all of these ideas to every Reading question in three official ACT practice tests
- and more . . .

ACT Reading

> *Tell me* how *you are searching, and I will tell you* what *you are searching for.*

Ludwig Wittgenstein

Overview and Important Reminders for ACT Reading Questions

ACT Reading is tough for a lot of students, and it kind of embodies a central complaint many people have about this test: how can you pick *one* right answer to a question about a passage? How can a student be sure she's chosen the right answer, when anything a person reads might be interpreted in several different ways that are equally valid?

Don't worry. This is one of the many aspects of the ACT that are nothing like their apparent counterparts in a normal high school situation. We're going to learn exactly how the ACT can design Reading questions with correct answers that are just as certain and inarguable as correct answers on the ACT Math section.

After all, we've already learned that these questions and answers MUST be "airtight"—regardless of the subject matter—or else the ACT would be worthless to colleges.

In fact, the ACT Reading section is the best place to start understanding how the test really works. Once you see the standardization at work here, it'll help you understand the rest of the test.

The other reason that I always like to discuss the Reading section first is that the secret skill required to beat the ACT Reading section is the single most important skill on the entire test. If you can really, truly understand and master this skill, then you'll be able to get a great score across the board, in every section.

The Big Secret of ACT Reading

What is this secret skill that you need to beat the ACT Reading section?

Pssst—don't tell anybody else:

You have to be able to read.

That's really it. Well, to be more specific, you have to be able to read *carefully* and *precisely*. In other words, you have to hone the skill of reading exactly what's on a page, and taking in everything that's stated directly in the text, without taking in anything that's not.

That probably seems like it should be pretty straightforward. So why is this part of the ACT such a challenge?

Well, it turns out that the kind of reading you need to do on the ACT is almost the exact opposite of the kind of reading students are trained to do in high school. I'll show you what I mean.

A real-life example

Let's imagine a typical discussion in a typical English class in a typical high school or college, and then consider how the skills developed during such a discussion might be incorrectly applied to a Reading question on the ACT.

Imagine you're in an English class, talking about a passage from a book you're currently reading. In this passage, the main character is very upset. She's just learned that her cousin has a serious illness, and the passage describes how worried and concerned she is for his health. Your teacher asks the class for their opinions on the main character's emotional state.

You raise your hand and say something like, "I think the main character seems troubled and conflicted." Your teacher asks, "Conflicted? Why do you say conflicted?" You then go on to explain that you were in a position like this once and you remember feeling conflicted, so you think the character probably feels conflicted, too. Your teacher thanks you for your contribution, and probably agrees that, yes, it's possible the main character in this passage might feel conflicted.

This sort of open interpretation is often encouraged in a classroom, but it'll cause you to miss a lot of questions on the ACT.

We've talked about the idea that all ACT questions have to be "airtight" and objective in order for the test to serve its function in the admissions process. The only way for a correct answer on an ACT Reading question to satisfy this requirement is to avoid any kind of interpretation, because interpretation is always subjective.

And the only way for a correct answer choice to refer to a passage without interpreting it is to restate some element of the passage exactly, or to have the passage provide a literal demonstration of the idea in the answer choice. Any other description of the text would necessarily involve interpretation, and then the correct answer wouldn't be objectively correct anymore.

So if the same hypothetical passage we were just talking about appeared on an ACT test, and you chose an answer saying that the main character felt "conflicted," you'd get the question wrong, even though your English teacher would probably accept that analysis.

If an ACT passage describes someone in a difficult spot as upset, worried, and concerned, then we can choose any answer that means exactly the same thing as "upset," "worried," or "concerned" . . . but we can't pick a word like "conflicted" unless the text specifically states that a character feels two different emotions at the same time, and that those emotions seem to go against each other, because that's what the word "conflicted" literally means.

So if the passage said something like

> I was worried about my cousin's illness, but I was also optimistic that he would be lucky enough to overcome it.

then you could pick a choice that described the character as "conflicted," because being "worried" and "optimistic" are two conflicting emotions. Further, the ideas of those emotions would be connected by the word "but," which literally demonstrates that the speaker considers them to be conflicting ideas. See how that works?

On the ACT, it's not enough that being worried or upset is a negative thing, and that feeling conflicted is typically a negative thing that could kind of go along with the idea of being upset and worried. It doesn't matter that *you* might feel conflicted if you were in the position described in the text, or that you think you could defend your reasoning in a classroom discussion.

The only thing that matters in ACT Reading is that the answer you choose is restated or demonstrated directly and specifically in the text, in a way that requires no interpretation. If an answer choice is supported by the text in this way, then it's right. If not, then it's wrong.

That's such an important concept that I'll say it again, with exclamation points:

The only thing that matters in an ACT Reading question is that the answer you choose is restated or demonstrated literally and specifically in the text, without interpretation! If it is, then it's right! If it's not, then it's wrong!

Just Trust Me—At Least until you Read the Walkthroughs

It might not seem like what I'm saying is right. I'm sure that you're thinking, even now, of times when you've seen an ACT Reading question that seemed to require interpretation of the text.

But the reason you feel like you should be interpreting the text is that you've always been trained to do that in other situations, and because the ACT wants you to think that it's like a regular school test. The test specifically designs answer choices that are supposed to take advantage of your habit of interpreting everything you read in your own way, instead of just reading exactly what the passage says and nothing more.

This is why a lot of people might read a passage about a character who feels "upset," "worried," or "concerned," and then wrongly mark an answer choice that says the character felt "conflicted." Students are taught to think of words in a passage as approximations that can be twisted and turned to accommodate a lot of different meanings. On the ACT, though, words can only mean exactly what they mean—nothing more, and nothing less.

This is what I'm talking about when I say that the only skill you need on the ACT Reading section is to be able to read carefully. Really, if someone reads about a character who feels "upset," "worried," or "concerned," and then decides that the character must feel "conflicted," that person hasn't actually read the passage carefully, at least not as far as the ACT is concerned. Instead, that person has read a passage that contained some information, and then assumed that some other information must also be true, even though the passage never said it was.

So this is what I mean when I talk about careful, precise, effective reading: I mean that you must train yourself to take in all the information in the text, without missing anything, and without adding in any of your own assumptions. Just because someone is "happy," you can't assume that person is "energetic." Just because someone is "sad," that doesn't mean the person is "anxious." We might think of these terms as being similar to each other in a certain context, but they aren't actually synonyms.

On the ACT we must get used to the idea that a word means only exactly what it says, and nothing more. Wrong answer choices will often try to get you to equate two different words that seem sort of related so that you'll make the kind of assumption you might make in an English class, and then get the question wrong.

Remember: wrong answer choices will try to exploit your English class instincts! Stay on your guard, and don't fall for their tricks.

Careful Reading at Work against a Real Question

With that in mind, let's take a look at an official Reading question published by ACT, Inc. We'll look at question 3 from the Reading section of practice test 1 in *The Official ACT Prep Guide*, which is test 2 in the 2020-2021 Red Book. (As we discussed in "Part 2: When To Use Official ACT, Inc., Materials, And When Not To" on page 20 of this Black Book, you'll need a copy of the Red Book as you prepare for the ACT, because it's the only book that contains real practice ACT tests from the company that makes the test.)

We're going to walk through the prompt and the answer choices, and you'll be able to see a lot of the concepts in play that we've been discussing so far.

I'm going to take more time going through this first question than I will with other examples later, just to give you a thorough introduction to these concepts. Don't be intimidated by how long the explanation is, and don't think that you'll have to go through every detail of every answer choice on test day the way I'm going to do it right now.

Now, let's jump in.

One of the first things to notice is that the prompt for this question includes the phrase "can best be described as." This is a perfect example of how the ACT will often phrase its concrete, black-and-white, 100% objective questions in terms that make them sound like a classic open-ended kind of question that might come up in a discussion in English class.

If it weren't trying to trick you, the test could have replaced that entire phrase with the word "was," because, really, that's what the ACT is going to reward—a straightforward statement (literally restated or demonstrated by the text) of what "Mama's reaction" *actually was*. But, instead, the test asks us how her reaction "can best be described."

Do you see how sneaky that is? The ACT is trying to put you in the position of making a judgment call about which choice seems "best" to you. They want you to ask yourself something like, "How could I possibly know which description is best? Isn't Mama the only one who knows how she really feels?" But you have to remember that ACT questions can never be subjective or unpredictable. If they were, the test wouldn't be standardized. So there must be a concrete reason in the text that one answer choice is right and the others are wrong.

When you see this kind of wording in the prompt of an ACT Reading question, you have to get used to reading it as though it said something like "Which of the following is a plain, direct description, based on the passage, of Mama's reaction when she learned the name Baba gave the baby?" Now you're in the right mindset. You're not venturing your best guess—you're searching for concrete evidence to support a correct answer and to eliminate 3 incorrect answers, so you can reach a logical conclusion that nobody could possibly argue with.

(Sorry to go on about that. It's just really important that you learn to catch these things.)

Now let's look at the first answer choice. It says Mama's reaction was "disapproval followed by resignation." This idea is directly, literally demonstrated in the text by the phrase "Mama must not have fought long" (line 54), and the phrase "because I still have my name" (lines 67-68):

- If Mama "must not have fought long," then that means she *did* fight for some period of time, even if that time was short. If she fought the name, then she must have disapproved of it, because people only fight against something they don't like.
- Since Mama didn't fight "long," and since the author "still ha[s the] name" given by Baba, we know that Mama must have given up her fight without getting what she wanted. Giving up on a fight means literally the same thing as resigning, or "resignation," as we see in (A).

So every word in (A) is fully and directly restated or demonstrated by the text, which is why (A) is correct.

Now let's check out the other answer choices, to see how they differ from (A), and why they'll attract untrained test-takers.

Choice (B) could tempt an untrained test-taker for a few reasons. First of all, we just saw evidence in our discussion of (A) that Mama fought against the name, so some test-takers might think this shows "annoyance." (It can be argued that fighting something isn't necessarily the same as being annoyed by it—annoyance is usually caused by a more minor incident than something that would provoke a fight, and most people who fight things would probably say that their feelings are stronger than "annoyance"—but, for the sake of this discussion, let's say that a test-taker wasn't sure whether the word "annoyance" was an appropriate word for Mama's reaction.)

Secondly, an untrained test-taker might subjectively believe that what happens in lines 34-43 is amusing, especially because it ends with the phrase "three weeks' worth of laughter" (42-43). (Of course, if we read carefully, we see that *Baba's* reaction is described in lines 34-43, not Mama's reaction, as the prompt requires. We also see that the "laughter" is enjoyed by "the staff," and not by Mama—nor even by Baba, for that matter.)

Beyond that, some test-takers might also be tempted to describe the events from lines 48-53 as amusing, because they think that the image of Mama walking down the hallway while Baba pleads with her is amusing. But this inclination is wrong on the ACT. The text never literally states or demonstrates that Mama thinks anything is amusing: the incident isn't described with any word like "funny" or "hilarious" relating to Mama's perspective, nor does it mention that Mama laughed or chuckled or giggled, or anything like that. So, even if the test-taker is personally amused by what's described in lines 48-53, that doesn't matter—because the *text* never says *Mama* was amused, and we can only pick an answer that's literally demonstrated or restated in the relevant text.

(Let me take a little timeout here to point out that we're being far more nitpicky than just about any high school English teacher would be about this passage—*which is exactly my point.* This is how we must read passages on the ACT! We can't make assumptions about things that aren't stated in the text, and we can't decide that one phrase means "basically" the same thing as another phrase unless we think carefully about the two phrases and determine that they actually do mean the same thing as each other.)

So even if we thought that Mama was annoyed—which isn't really supported by the text in the first place—we definitely can't conclude that she reacted with "amusement," as (B) would require. So we know that (B) is definitely wrong.

But a lot of untrained test-takers won't look at (B) in this way. Instead, they'll vaguely remember that Mama seemed annoyed, and that something around the time of Mama hearing the name might have seemed kind of funny to them, and they'll think that (B) might be a decent response to the prompt, just as it would probably be an acceptable thing to say in an English class.

If you can understand why a lot of untrained test-takers might choose (B), and you can also understand how (B) must be 100% wrong according to the standards of the ACT, then you're well on your way to grasping the critical importance of careful reading on the ACT.

Now let's consider (C). Some untrained test-takers might assume that Mama is embarrassed, possibly because they themselves might be embarrassed to find out that their child had a name they didn't like, or because they might think it would be embarrassing to walk around a hospital while someone was "screaming" (line 51) at them. *But the text never says or demonstrates that Mama is embarrassed:* it never says that she's ashamed, or that she couldn't stand to show her face to people, or anything else like that. So, as trained test-takers, we already know that (C) can't be right.

Beyond that, (C) says Mama reacted with "outrage," which is an extreme version of anger. In order for us to say that Mama felt "outrage," the text would have to say something like "Mama was furious" or "Mama was so angry she couldn't see straight." But nothing like that appears in the text, so "outrage" can't be acceptable here on the ACT—still, some untrained test-takers will imagine that a new mother might be outraged over her child being given a name she didn't like, so they'll assume that (C) is plausible, even though the text never literally states or demonstrates that Mama is outraged.

Finally, (D) is also wrong because it isn't literally restated or demonstrated in the text. In fact, (D) is a perfect example of a type of choice that untrained test-takers will often fall for, because it reflects the way they think *they* might feel if they were in the situation described in the passage—after all, most people would assume that they would play a role in naming their own baby, right? Most people would also assume that someone in this situation would feel resentment toward the person who gave their baby a name they didn't like. So (D) would look like a pretty attractive option to these people, and it would probably also reflect the kind of character analysis that would be acceptable in a literature class—but it's still wrong on the ACT, because it doesn't follow the standards for this section of the test:

- "Shock" means something like "extreme surprise," but the text doesn't literally state that Mama experiences any level of surprise at all.
- "Resentment" means something like "ongoing bitterness at having been treated poorly," but the text doesn't describe Mama's ongoing feelings about Baba's naming decision—the text only says that Mama didn't change the name. It doesn't provide any further information about Mama's feelings toward Baba regarding the naming of the baby. (Lines 85 and 86 do mention "a reality that filled [Mama] with great sadness," but that part of the text isn't talking about the episode of Baba naming the baby. And, even if it were, "sadness" and "resentment" aren't technically the same thing either: resenting someone means that we blame them for something that makes us feel bad, but the text doesn't specifically say that Mama blames anyone, even in lines 85 and 86.)

Remember: all that matters is exactly what's stated in the text. So if you read the text about Mama and Baba, and you read question 3, and you read the answer choices, then you can only conclude that (A) is absolutely the right answer, because it's directly restated and demonstrated in the text. Choices (B), (C), and (D) are absolutely, 100% wrong according to the ACT, because they differ from the text. There's no arguing, there are no gray areas, there's no valid difference of opinions. One choice is right, and the rest are wrong. (For my walkthrough of this question, please see page 64 of this Black Book.)

You MUST intentionally develop this black-and-white mindset about ACT Reading—and about the rest of the ACT—if you want to do your best on the test. As part of developing this mindset, it will be helpful to be aware of the standardized ways that the ACT constructs wrong answers to ACT Reading questions. We'll get into those now.

ACT Reading Wrong Answer Patterns

Let's consider some of the different answer-choice patterns in ACT Reading questions.

ACT Reading Answer-Choice Pattern 1: Confused Relationships

This type of answer will mention one or more concepts taken directly from the passage, but it will confuse the way those concepts originally relate to each other in the text. So, for example, if the text says that a student learned an important lesson from a teacher, then a choice following this pattern might say the teacher learned an important lesson from the student. If the passage describes an applicant who's nervous about a job interview, then this kind of wrong answer might mention that the interviewer is nervous about talking to the applicant, and so on.

A real-life example of this kind of wrong answer occurs in the second half of choice (B) from the question we just looked at, question 3 from the Reading section of practice test 1 in the Red Book (test 2 in the 2020-2021 Red Book). That part of the choice says Mama reacted with "amusement" when she learned the name that Baba gave the baby. Lines 34-43 *do* include the phrase "three weeks' worth of laughter," which might seem to justify the use of the word "amusement"—but it's "the staff" (42) that enjoys the laughter, not Mama. So, even though this choice mentions the concept of amusement, and the prompt mentions the concept of Mama, and both of those concepts appear in the passage, the choice is wrong because it confuses the *relationship* of the amusement to other concepts in the passage and the prompt. The passage never actually says *Mama* is amused. (Again, you can see my full walkthrough for that question on page 64 of this Black Book.)

Test-takers might choose this type of wrong answer either because they're reading too carelessly and they don't take the time to realize their mistake, or because they aren't sure what's going on in the question, but they vaguely remember something like this from the passage, so they go with it.

Remember: if you see a concept from the text mentioned in an answer choice, you still have to make sure the choice accurately reflects the relationships among the relevant concepts in a way that's consistent with what appears in the text. Don't be careless.

ACT Reading Answer-Choice Pattern 2: Barely Relevant

You'll also frequently see wrong answer choices that are almost completely irrelevant—just kind of random thoughts that get stuck in with the other choices.

The ACT probably includes these almost irrelevant choices because it knows that lots of untrained test-takers will read the passage subjectively and try to give credit to any interpretation that they encounter, just like they're taught to do in English class.

Of course, as trained test-takers, we know better than to wonder if a barely relevant choice might contain a valid interpretation of a text, because we know that the ACT doesn't reward those interpretations—which is why they're irrelevant and wrong on the ACT. It's not enough for the text not to contradict an answer choice; the text must specifically restate or demonstrate what the answer choice says in order for that choice to be right. But a lot of people who take the ACT don't know that, and many people will pick an irrelevant choice because they can't see anything obviously wrong with it, and it never occurs to them to think about the test in a literal way. Don't make this mistake!

A real-life example of this kind of wrong answer is choice (C) from question 5 in the Reading section of practice test 1 in the Red Book (test 2 in the 2020-2021 Red Book), which says, "Mama had a tendency to change her mind quickly." There's no mention in the passage of Mama tending to change her mind or not, which makes this choice irrelevant to the plain text of the passage. (See this question's walkthrough on page 65 of this Black Book for more.)

So don't be surprised when you see irrelevant choices on test day, and don't waste your time or energy wondering why the test would include a choice that's obviously not related to the passage!

ACT Reading Answer-Choice Pattern 3: Direct Contradiction

This is an interesting type of wrong answer choice that comes up a lot, which surprises many people when they first hear about it. You can probably guess how it works from the name: basically, the ACT just sticks in an answer choice that's exactly the opposite of what's stated in the text.

Why would the ACT offer a choice that's such an obvious contradiction of the passage? It's probably because this is the sort of thing that might fluster an untrained test-taker, who wouldn't expect to see an answer choice that said exactly the opposite of what the text says. Those people will likely get confused and wonder whether they misread the passage, the prompt, or the answer choice, and then go back and carefully read everything all over again—doubting themselves and wondering what they're overlooking the whole time. Another possible reason is that a choice that contradicts the text can often seem to restate the text if a test-taker just overlooks or misreads a single negating word. For example, if the passage says, "Chris was not always happy," and the choice says, "Chris was constantly happy," then the choice would seem to be restating the passage exactly if someone simply overlooked the word "not" when reading the passage.

A real-life example of this type of wrong answer choice is (F) from question 14 in the Reading section of practice test 1 in the Red Book (test 2 in the 2020-2021 Red Book). This choice says something happened "gradually" and was "unnoticed at the time by the public," which directly contradicts both the relevant part of the passage and the right answer (which says that the event "occurred swiftly" and was a "public event of sorts"). For more on this question, see its walkthrough on page 68 of this Black Book.

So don't automatically assume that you've misread something if you think an answer choice is exactly the opposite of what the text says. Instead, be on the lookout for these contradictory answer choices, and make sure you don't overlook negating words like "not," "can't," or "never!"

ACT Reading Answer-Choice Pattern 4: Reasonable Statement not in the Text

This is one of the most dangerous wrong answer choice types. Basically, this type of wrong answer makes a statement related to the text that sounds reasonable to an untrained test-taker. These statements generally take one of the following forms:

- a statement of fact that many readers would agree with, such as a statement providing extra historical or scientific context for an idea from the passage
- a literary interpretation of a character, event, or setting, which would be acceptable in most English classes, but which isn't actually restated or demonstrated anywhere in the text

An example of this type of wrong answer choice is choice (D) from the question we looked at a few pages ago (that is, question 3 from the Reading section of practice test 1 in the Red Book, which is test 2 in the 2020-2021 Red Book). It makes a statement about a mother's reaction that might seem like a completely reasonable character analysis to many readers, but that isn't actually stated in the text. That means (D) reflects some kind of assumption by the reader, so it's wrong on the ACT. It doesn't matter whether we might think the assumption could be defended with a strong argument in a discussion. (Again, for the full walkthrough of this question, see page 64 of this Black Book.)

So remember: an answer choice is wrong if it makes an assumption that isn't literally restated or demonstrated by the relevant part of the text, even if that assumption would seem reasonable in a discussion.

ACT Reading Answer-Choice Pattern 5: Off by One or Two Words

This might be one of the most dangerous and sneaky types of wrong answer when it comes to trapping test-takers who know how the test works. For this type of wrong answer, the ACT provides a phrase that mirrors the passage exactly—except for one or two words. Even when test-takers know they have to find answer choices that are restated or demonstrated by the passage, they can still fall for these kinds of wrong answers if they're not in the habit of constantly attacking every single word they read, or if they just misread or overlook one or two words on the page.

An extreme example of this type of wrong answer is choice (A) on question 21, from the Reading section of practice test 1 in the Red Book (test 2 in the 2020-2021 Red Book). This choice mentions "an artist's most famous painting and the experience that inspired it," and the choice is wrong because the passage talks about multiple *paintings* (plural!) and the *experiences* (plural!) that inspired them. Many untrained test-takers will pick this choice because they correctly note that the passage does talk about an artist's paintings and the experiences that led to them, but don't realize that a difference as small as the difference between "painting" and "paintings" can be enough to make an answer wrong on the ACT. (For my full walkthrough of this question, see page 71 in this Black Book.)

So remember, on test day, that you have to pay attention to every word in each answer choice! If one word differs from the relevant text, then the whole choice is wrong—even though most English teachers wouldn't be so precise in school.

ACT Reading Answer-Choice Pattern 6: Wrong Part of the Passage

Some ACT Reading questions will cite a specific line or paragraph from the text. This is because the ACT knows that many untrained test-takers won't bother to go back to the original text to verify an answer choice before they pick it, so it's easy to trick them by presenting an answer choice that's accurately restated or demonstrated by a part of the passage that's not cited in the prompt.

Many untrained test-takers will see a wrong answer like this, vaguely remember that they saw the same idea in the passage, and then pick the choice without ever realizing that the prompt requires them to look elsewhere in the passage. As trained test-takers, we always need to make sure that we're looking at the part of the passage that's relevant to the prompt when we pick an answer choice. This is especially true if we think that two choices both seem to restate the passage accurately—it may well be that one of them is restating the wrong part of the text, which still makes it a wrong answer. (Question 13 from the Reading section of practice test 3 in the Red Book—form 16MC3 online if you have the 2020-2021 Red Book—demonstrates this pattern. You can see our walkthrough of that question on page 99 of this Black Book.)

Conclusion

By now, it should be clear that careful reading is the backbone of the ACT Reading section: all the right answers are restated or demonstrated by the text in a way that becomes clear with careful reading, and all the wrong answers are deliberately created by the ACT to attract untrained test-takers who don't know how the test works or who don't read carefully enough. On page 57 we'll start talking about a step-by-step way to attack ACT Reading questions, but, before we do that, we'll cover some general tactics for reading ACT passages in the next section.

How to Read Passages on The ACT Reading Section

One of the most common questions I get is about how test-takers should read passages on the ACT Reading section. (Is it better to skim the passage before reading it carefully? Is it better to look at the questions before reading the passage? Is reading the passage even necessary?)

Another popular question is how to take notes on the passages. (Which kinds of words should be underlined, circled, or starred? How should a student note the main idea of a paragraph while reading it?)

So let's talk about those things. My answers are pretty simple, really:

1. You can read or skim the passage in any way you want, as long as it leaves you enough time to finish the section and mark answers with certainty. You can even skip reading the passage if you prefer, and then just refer back to portions of the text on a question-by-question basis. (We'll discuss this more below.)

2. You shouldn't take notes on the passage(!)

Like most good ACT advice, those two tactics contradict most of what you may have heard from teachers, tutors, and prep books, so let's explore them a little. (If you haven't already read my previous remarks on what separates right answers from wrong answers on ACT Reading questions, I'd recommend you go back to pages 49-54 and do that before proceeding.)

When I talked about correct answer choices for ACT Reading questions, I indicated that they're always literally restated or demonstrated by elements of the relevant portion of the original passage. This is necessary because ACT, Inc., needs to have an objective, legitimate reason to say that one choice is right and the others are wrong, and the only real way to do that is to have the correct answer be the only choice that's directly restated or demonstrated by the passage.

This means there are always specific words and phrases in the passage that correspond to the correct answer. It also means that, technically, the only portion of the text you would need to read for any question is the specific portion that contains the words restated in the correct answer choice for that question.

So, *in theory*, if it were somehow possible to know in advance which portions of the passage were going to contain the key phrases restated in the right answer, then we could avoid reading the rest of the passage without harming our score.

In other words, there's literally no benefit whatsoever in trying to get an overall impression of the passage, because there will never be a real ACT question that requires us to do that—even when a question seems to ask about broader concepts or large portions of the passage, there will always be certain specific phrases that make the right answer right.

(To be sure, there are some people who try to draw inferences from the entire text and still have some success, but it's not the most efficient or reliable approach, and it's never *necessary*. We can always find the answer for every question spelled out somewhere in the passage according to the ACT's unwritten rules, even when the question asks about the main idea of a paragraph or passage.)

For this reason, it doesn't really matter which specific method you use to read the text. All that matters is that you can locate the relevant portion of the text and figure out which answer choice restates it as quickly as possible, without sacrificing accuracy.

General Approaches to Reading Passages

Broadly speaking, there are three ways to read ACT Reading passages, and I recommend you play around with them to see what works best for you. Again, you can mix, match, or modify these approaches as you see fit, so long as you come up with a system that lets you find the relevant portion of the text quickly enough to allow you to complete the entire section within the time limit.

Read the passage, then the questions.

The first approach is the old standard of simply reading the entire passage before attempting the questions. This is by far the most widely used approach. It can definitely work, as long as you don't read too slowly to finish the section before time is called. One note, though—if you read the passage first, don't worry about trying to understand it as an organic whole. Definitely don't take notes on it, for reasons we'll get into in a moment. Just give it a thorough once-over. You're going to have to come back to specific parts of it later to verify which answer choices are correct anyway, so just read it once and move on to the questions.

Skip the passage and go straight to the questions.

The second-most popular approach is to skip reading the passage and just move straight to the questions. Then, you start with the questions that have specific line citations. For each citation question, you go back to the relevant portion of the text, read that portion, and then consider the answer choices. When you've finished all the citation questions, you'll generally have a good idea of how the passage is structured. Then you move on to the questions with no citations. Many of those questions will mention key concepts that you'll recall from the citation questions, so you'll know where to go back in the passage and locate those portions of the text again. When a question has no citation and also doesn't refer to something that you've already read, you can simply skim the portions of the text that you haven't read yet to find the relevant key terms, and proceed accordingly.

Skim the passage, then answer the questions.

That brings us to the third type of approach, which simply involves lightly skimming the passage before approaching the questions, in order to construct a rough mental map of where different terms and concepts appear in the passage. I want to stress that, so I'll say it again: in this type of skimming, you're just moving your eyes through the passage quickly, NOT trying to understand the text, but trying to get a rough idea of where various concepts appear on the page so you can use your "roadmap" later. This way, if a question lacks a citation, you can look at the concepts in the question and in the answer choices and recall those concepts from your skimming, which allows you to zero-in on the relevant part of the text and then find your answers. Of course, you can always re-skim if you need to.

Paired passages aren't special

Once per test, the ACT presents us with a "paired passage," which consists of two shorter passages (called "Passage A" and "Passage B") on a common subject, instead of one normal-sized passage. The questions for the paired passage will be split into three groups, usually consisting of three or four questions each, presented in the following order:

1. questions about Passage A only
2. questions about Passage B only
3. questions about both passages together

Some people are intimidated by paired passages, but we don't need a special approach for reading paired passages, and the questions about them really aren't any different from questions about single passages (as we'll discuss in "What about Paired Passages?" on page 58 of this Black Book). Depending on your preference, you can mix and match any of the following strategies for reading paired passages—you'll notice these are basically the same strategies we discussed for reading single passages above:

- read both of the paired passages in a row before answering any of the questions
- read Passage A and use it to answer the questions about Passage A, then read Passage B and answer the questions on Passage B and on both passages together
- skip reading both passages at first, and only refer back to them as required by the questions
- skim both passages to get an idea of where different concepts appear within them, and then use that "roadmap" of the passages to answer the questions

(Again, you can see "What about Paired Passages?" on page 58 of this Black Book for more on the process of answering questions about paired passages.)

Experimentation is key.

It's important to be aware of the different approaches discussed above, and to be ready and willing to play around with them during your practice sessions, so you can figure out what works best for you personally. If my experience told me that one approach was best for everybody, then I would recommend that approach to everybody—instead, my experience has repeatedly shown me that different students will prefer different reading approaches based on their personalities and skills.

I'll say it one more time: there is no single best approach to reading passages that's guaranteed to work best for everybody. If you're wondering which approach is best for you, then just try the different approaches in practice and see which one feels most comfortable and allows you to get the most questions right in the allotted time.

Why you shouldn't take notes

You may be wondering why I'm opposed to the idea of taking notes on ACT passages. The reason is simple, actually: taking notes involves interpreting the text, and interpreting the text isn't helpful on the ACT. As we keep discussing, the correct answer to every single question is spelled out somewhere on the page, so there's no need for you to interpret what you're reading. If all you're worried about is exactly what the text says, what's the point of taking a note? It'll either be an interpretation of the text, which we don't want, or else it will exactly restate the text, which is pointless, because then you're just copying down what the text already says.

Instead of developing some kind of note-taking system for ACT passages, it's much better to develop the habit of making sure that every choice you pick on test day is literally restated or demonstrated directly on the page somewhere.

Conclusion

Now that we've discussed the key concepts you'll need to know for the ACT Reading section—everything from the underlying philosophy and design of the section to some different ways to read the passages on test day—we'll start putting all of these ideas into an actionable, step-by-step plan that you can use against real test questions, starting on the next page.

The General Process for Answering ACT Reading Questions

Most ACT Reading questions can be answered with a fairly simple process, which we'll discuss now. Later, I'll show you how to answer other types of ACT Reading questions that might seem a bit harder—although the process we'll use for all ACT Reading questions is basically the same, with a few very minor, very occasional modifications.

For right now, let's assume that we're talking about questions with specific line citations.

1. Read or skim the passage if you want to.

There are a lot of ways to approach reading the actual passage, as we discussed on page 55. Pick whichever approach works for you, whether it's one of the ones I explained or your own approach.

2. Read the question, noting the citation. Then read the citation.

Find the citation in the text that the question is referring to. Read it. If the cited line picks up in the middle of a sentence, go back up to the beginning of that sentence and start there. It may also help to read the sentence before or after the sentences in the citation, but this often isn't necessary.

(For questions that don't have citations, see "What about Questions without Citations?" on page 57 of this Black Book.)

3. Find three wrong answers.

It's generally easiest to find wrong answers first. For one thing, there are three of them in every question, as opposed to just the one right answer. For another, it's usually easier to identify ways that answer choices differ from the text than it is to feel confident that a choice says exactly the same thing as the text. Expect that most (and very possibly all) of the wrong answers you find on any one question will fit into one of the types we talked about earlier, on pages 53-54.

If you end up not being able to eliminate 3 choices, then you're making some kind of mistake. It might be that you've misread the text or the question, or didn't read enough of the surrounding text. It might be that your understanding of one of the words you read is slightly (or very) inaccurate. It's often the case that people who are left with 2 or 3 answer choices that seem to restate the text probably aren't being picky enough about sticking to exactly what each word means to ensure an accurate restatement.

If you end up eliminating all 4 answer choices from consideration, then, again, you've definitely made some kind of mistake, but it might be a different kind of mistake. You may have been referring to the wrong part of the passage, for instance. You might also have misread or misunderstood one or more words.

4. Confirm the remaining answer choice.

See if the remaining answer choice fits the right answer pattern (in other words, see if it's literally restated or demonstrated in the relevant portion of the passage, without contradicting the text). If it does, that's great. You've found the right answer.

If you still can't identify one choice that clearly restates the passage and three choices that don't restate the passage, you should consider moving on and coming back to this question later. If you come back later and still can't come up with an answer, and/or if time is running out, you should just mark your best guess, since there's no penalty for wrong answers on the ACT—but remember that you're only guessing because you were unable to execute some part of the proper approach to ACT Reading questions, not because this question was just different somehow. It's very important that you maintain your awareness that every ACT Reading question must follow the same rules, even if you end up having to guess on some of them. (See "The General Game Plan for Attacking a Section of the ACT on Test Day" on page 37 of this Black Book for more on this.)

And that's it, believe it or not—the process for ACT Reading questions typically isn't as complex as the processes for other question types can be. As I noted above, the simple process we just went through works on all line-citation questions exactly as described. In a broader sense, it also works on all other ACT Reading questions. But we'll discuss some more specific considerations for other kinds of questions and situations below.

Some Small Modifications to this General Process

Let's look at some small adjustments we might make if the question isn't exactly a classic line-citation question.

What about Paragraph Citations?

Sometimes a question asks about a whole paragraph, rather than asking about a specific line in a passage. These questions work the same way as line citation questions, except that you should go ahead and read the whole cited paragraph. See question 34 from the Reading section of practice test 2 in the Red Book (test 3 in the 2020-2021 Red Book) for an example of a question that cites a paragraph, and see its walkthrough on page 92 for an example of how such a question can be approached successfully.

What about Questions without Citations?

When a question has no citation, very little actually changes in our approach to it. The answer is still going to be spelled out somewhere on the page, but now it might be anywhere in the passage, instead of being near a specific line mentioned in the prompt.

Let me say that again: even though there's no specific citation, the answer is still going to be spelled out somewhere! You should NOT try to answer a question like this by making a broad inference from the overall passage that isn't directly restated or demonstrated by actual phrases from the text.

I often recommend saving any general, non-citation questions for last. In other words, you can skip around and do all the citation questions for a passage first, then come back and answer the questions without citations. This can be helpful because answering the citation questions can cause you to go back through a lot of the passage if you're not familiar with it, and you'll often find that the answers to general, non-citation questions are right there in the citations for other questions. That way, you can save some time and energy by doing the citation questions first.

Even if answering the citation questions doesn't actually cause you to read the part of the text that contains the answer to a general question, you still haven't lost any time by saving the non-citation questions—you've just failed to *save* some extra time, that's all. Plus, it's still helpful to know that the answer to the general question isn't in the citations for the other questions, because then you know you don't need to re-read or skim those areas of the text when you go back through to try to find the answers.

Sometimes the prompt for a non-citation question will still contain a clear reference to a part of the passage, even if it's not a line citation or a paragraph citation. For example, question 5 from the Reading section of practice test 1 in *The Official ACT Prep Guide* (test 2 in the 2020-2021 Red Book) asks why "Mama didn't go to the office of the City of Boston clerk." Even though it doesn't say which line this refers to, someone who has read the passage would know this question is asking about a certain moment in the narrative from the essay, and if we've already answered some other questions and read some pieces of the passage then we might be able to use this detail to find the relevant text pretty quickly. (Further, in this case, if we hadn't read the whole passage before encountering this question, we could still find the relevant part of the text by skimming for the capital letters in the phrase "City of Boston." See my walkthrough for this question on page 65 for more.)

Again, the critical thing to remember with non-citation questions is that the answer is always clearly restated or demonstrated somewhere within the passage, even though the question lacks a line citation. There is literally never a moment on a real ACT in which the only way to answer a Reading question is to draw a general inference from your overall "feeling" of the text. If ACT questions required those kinds of inferences, the test's reliability would disappear.

What about Main Purpose, Main Idea, Best Description Questions?

Sometimes, an ACT Reading question will ask about something like the "main purpose" or "main idea" of a passage, or will ask how some aspect of the passage can "best be described." These questions can be frustrating because they sound like they require the test-taker to make an interpretation or judgment call. But, as trained test-takers, we know that the ACT Reading section never rewards that kind of subjectivity. As it turns out, these questions actually function just like any other ACT Reading question: the right answer will be literally restated or demonstrated somewhere in the relevant text. We'll frequently see this idea at work in the walkthroughs starting on page 62 of this Black Book.

There's one very unusual exception to this rule—in fact it doesn't even show up a single time on most ACT tests. But, every once in a while, we'll find that one of these "main idea" questions has more than one answer choice that's directly restated or demonstrated by the relevant text! When that happens, the right answer will be the one that's restated or demonstrated more times than the other choice. So if (A) contains an idea that appears once in the relevant text, and (B) contains an idea that appears three times in the relevant text, then (B) will be the right answer.

What about Paired Passages?

One of the four "passages" in each ACT Reading section will be a "paired passage," meaning it will involve two different texts on related subjects, often by different authors. The ACT will sometimes ask questions about areas of agreement or disagreement between the two passages. When this happens, untrained test-takers often worry that they need to read the authors' minds, which, of course, seems very subjective and unfair.

But we have to remember that every answer to a Reading question is spelled out somewhere in the text, and these questions are no exception.

Whenever the ACT asks a question about two passages at once, it must always be the case that the right answer is directly restated or demonstrated by phrases within one or both of the passages. Really, the situation isn't much different from what we see in any other ACT Reading question; it's just that we might have to find the text supporting the right answer by searching within two smaller passages, rather than one regular-sized passage.

This might sound a little complicated, but it's actually not that difficult in practice. You can find a couple of questions that ask about areas of agreement among multiple authors in questions 28 and 29 from the Reading section of practice test 2 in the Red Book (test 3 in the 2020-2021 Red Book); my walkthroughs for those questions start on page 89 of this Black Book.

As we noted in "How to Read Passages on The ACT Reading Section" on page 55 of this Black Book, you don't need to read paired passages in any special way or particular order. You can choose to read them right in a row before answering the questions, or just go straight to the questions and refer back to parts of the paired passages when necessary, or use any other approach you like, as long as you keep in mind that the right answer will always be stated or demonstrated in the relevant text, just as it will on single-passage questions.

What about "EXCEPT" Questions?

Some questions take the normal question-answering process and turn it on its head, often by using the word "EXCEPT" or "NOT" in all capital letters. Such a question might say something like "all of the following are found in the passage EXCEPT . . ." For a question like this, we're still going to read the relevant portion of the text carefully, but now the correct answer is going to be the only choice that does NOT appear in the passage.

It's always important to make sure you read all four answer choices for every question (it helps you catch mistakes). It's ESPECIALLY important on these "EXCEPT" questions, because test-takers often accidentally forget about the word "EXCEPT" and just choose the first answer they see that appears in the text—and they get the question wrong as a result. If you accidentally overlook the word "EXCEPT" but still read all four answer choices, you'll have a better chance of noticing your mistake, because you might notice that more than one choice seems to be right. That should make you re-evaluate the situation. (Question 15 from the Reading section of practice test 3 in the Red Book—form 16MC3 online if you have the 2020-2021 Red Book—is a good example of an "EXCEPT" question. Its walkthrough is on page 100 of this Black Book.)

What about "Vocabulary in Context" Questions?

Some questions ask you how a word is used in the passage. They often read something like this: "As it is used in line 33, the word *illumination* most nearly means . . ."

For these questions, we're not just looking for an answer choice that's a synonym of the original word in the prompt, because most or all of the wrong answers will also be synonyms of that word in one sense or another. The right answer will be the only choice that's literally restated or demonstrated in the part of the passage surrounding the key word from the prompt.

As an example, consider question 15 from the Reading section of practice test 2 in the Red Book (test 3 in the 2020-2021 Red Book). It asks about the word "finest," and the wrong answers are the "fairest," "thinnest," and "greatest." In various contexts, each of those words could be a synonym for "finest:"

- In an archaic sense, "fairest" and "finest" could both describe an attractive person or a well-made instrument.
- The finest hairs on someone's head are the thinnest hairs.
- The finest musician could also be called the greatest musician.

So how do we know that all of those choices are wrong, and "slightest" is the right answer? We can figure it out because the text in the passage surrounding the word "finest" uses the word "but" to create a contrast between the phrase "finest finger adjustments" and the idea of something so "enormous" that it has to be turned by "two workmen." This contrast demonstrates that "finest" is being used in the passage as an antonym for the idea of something heavy and difficult, and the phrase "slightest fingertip adjustments" is the only option that reflects that demonstrated contrast. (Note that the word "fingertip" in the text also demonstrates the idea of something on a very small scale.) The complete walkthrough for this question is on page 84 of this Black Book.

Once more, then, we see that the ACT Reading section rewards us for thinking in terms of careful reading, restatement, and demonstration. You'll see more examples of this concept in our walkthroughs starting on page 62 of this Black Book.

What about Unattributed Quotations ("Scare Quotes")?

Occasionally—maybe once per test—you'll encounter an ACT Reading passage with words or phrases in quotation marks that aren't attributed to any speaker. If quotation marks are used in an ACT passage without the quote being attributed to a specific source, then they show that the author doesn't agree with the use of that word or phrase. (Unattributed quotation marks are often called "scare quotes" in English class.)

Think of these quotation marks like the "air-quotes" that people sometimes make with their fingers while they're speaking, to show that they're using a word or phrase in a way that they might not personally agree with or think is appropriate. If your friend says she went to a "great party," and puts air-quotes around "great party," then you know she didn't really think it was a great party.

Question 13 from the Reading section of practice test 1 in the Red Book (test 2 in the 2020-2021 Red Book) is a good example of a question that involves unattributed quotations. Its walkthrough is on page 68 of this Black Book.

What about "Idiomatic Expressions?"

Once in a while, a prompt or answer choice on the ACT Reading section will involve the word "idiomatic" or "idiom," which can confuse untrained test-takers who aren't familiar with this term. On the ACT Reading section, we can think of an idiom or idiomatic expression as a phrase whose meaning differs from the literal meanings of the words involved in the phrase.

Consider question 32 from the Reading section of practice test 2 in the Red Book (test 3 in the 2020-2021 Red Book) for an example of this idea. The right answer is the phrase "idiomatic expressions," which is demonstrated by phrases in the passage like "ants have made bank" (line 73) and "ants flash chemical badges" (line 78). Again, these phrases are "idiomatic," according to the ACT's rules, because they can't be taken literally: the ants haven't really made a bank, and they don't really flash any badges. (For more on this question, see its walkthrough on page 91 of this book.)

(Note that the technical definition of an "idiom" is a bit more complex than this, but this definition is all we need to know to be able to answer an ACT Reading question that mentions this concept.)

What about "Irony?"

Some ACT questions will ask about irony, which is a more technical literary term than we tend to encounter on this test. For ACT purposes, all we need to remember is that irony involves some kind of unexpected contrast or contradiction.

This concept comes up very rarely on the ACT. In fact, one instance in the Red Book technically appears in an ACT English question that's based on reading comprehension principles. That example is question 59 from the English section of practice test 1 in the Red Book (test 2 in the 2020-2021 Red Book), which asks for the choice that "completes the irony that is set up in the first part of the sentence." The first part of the sentence mentions "a wall that once protected the future capital of one of the ancient world's most famous empires." The right answer is (C), which tells us that the wall is now "within a fast-food restaurant." For ACT purposes, we know that (C) "completes the irony," as the prompt requires, by providing unexpected information about the location of the wall—most people wouldn't expect an ancient and important piece of history to be inside something as modern and ordinary as a fast food place. (For a full walkthrough of this reading-based ACT English question, see page 474 of this Black Book.)

(Note that, as we also saw in our discussion of idiomatic expressions, the technical definition of "irony" is a bit more complex than the definition we use to answer ACT questions.)

What about "Humor," "Amusement," etc.?

Roughly once per test, an ACT Reading question might involve use a term like "humorous," "amusing." These questions often frustrate untrained test-takers, because they seem to require us to judge subjectively whether something is funny—what if we don't have the same sense of humor as the writers of the ACT? Of course, as trained test-takers, we know that there must be an objective, consistent strategy that will allow us to answer these questions correctly, or else they couldn't appear on the ACT.

As it turns out, all we need to know in order to answer these questions is that the ACT uses the idea of humor in very particular ways that don't reflect their use in everyday life: whether the ACT describes a phrase as "humorous" has nothing to do with whether it makes you laugh. There are two main situations we need to look out for when the test mentions something being funny, and each one gets handled in its own way:

1. If the question asks whether *a character in the passage* thinks something is amusing or humorous, then we can only say this is the case if the text specifically demonstrates that the character felt that way. For example, the text would have to say, "this idea made Maria chuckle to herself," or, "it always seemed funny to him that [blah blah blah]."

2. If the question just mentions the idea of something being amusing or humorous in general, without mentioning any character's point of view, then we can only say a phrase or situation is humorous if it involves a statement that can't literally be taken as true, or that involves something unexpected or unusual. (You may notice that this sort of overlaps with other ideas we've discussed in this section, but don't worry—the ACT won't ask you to make a judgment call between calling something "idiomatic" and calling it "humorous.") Consider question 32 from the Reading section of practice test 2 in the Red Book (test 3 in the 2020-2021 Red Book) for an example of this idea. That question asks which choice "the author makes repeated use of," and (H) says, "humorous quotations." We know that we can call a quotation "humorous" if it can't be literally true, or it involves something unexpected or unusual. But the quotations that appear in the passage are basically one- or two-word technical terms, so they don't fit this description. That means we can't call them "humorous" on the ACT, and (H) is wrong. See our walkthrough of this question on page 91 of this Black Book for more.

What about "Attitude" Questions?

Sometimes the ACT asks about the author's attitude, or about how a passage might be characterized, and so on. Untrained test-takers are usually tempted to answer these kinds of questions in the same way they would in a literature class: they usually just read the passage and make a subjective assessment of how it makes them feel, and then look for an answer choice that describes their feelings.

But, as we've mentioned repeatedly, the ACT wouldn't be a reliable test if it were based on subjectivity and inference.

So, even for "attitude" questions, the correct answer is going to be literally restated or demonstrated in the text. For example, if the right answer is that the author's attitude is "optimistic," then the text will have to say that the author always expected good things to happen, or that she was "hopeful," or something like that.

ACT Reading Quick Summary

This is a one-page summary of the major relevant concepts. Use it to evaluate your comprehension or jog your memory. For a more in-depth treatment of these ideas, see the rest of this section.

The Big Secret: The answer to every question comes directly from what's on the page, without any interpretation or subjectivity.

The actual rules for attacking ACT Reading questions are simple. The hard part is making sure you follow them carefully all the time. Here they are:

- Correct answers are always directly supported in the text through restatement or demonstration.
- Details make the difference—this is not like reading in high school. One word (or even the difference between the singular and plural versions of a word!) can make an answer choice wrong.
- There is always one—and only one—inarguably correct answer per question.

Here are the most common wrong-answer patterns you'll see:

- Wrong answers might mention concepts from the text but confuse the relationship between those ideas.
- Wrong answers might be barely relevant to the text.
- Wrong answers might directly contradict what the text says.
- Wrong answers might make a reasonable statement that isn't in the text.
- Wrongs answers might restate the text exactly except for one or two words.
- Wrong answers might accurately restate the wrong part of the text.

Here's the general ACT Reading process:

- Skim, read, or skip the passage (experiment to find the method you prefer).
- Read the question, and note any citation.
- Read the relevant portion of the text (the citation if there is one, or the part of the text that involves similar concepts to those mentioned in the question).
- Find three wrong answer choices (make use of wrong answer patterns).
- Confirm the remaining answer choice.
- Mark the correct answer.
- Save general passage questions and more difficult questions for the end, and use the knowledge of the text you've gotten from answering the other questions to make these less challenging.

Note that some questions—like EXCEPT questions, and questions related to humor, irony, author's attitude, etc.—involve minor modifications to this process, but each of these question types is likely to appear once (or not at all) on any given test, and they all still rely on a plain, direct reading of the text. See the relevant training earlier in this section for more on those modifications.

Go back through the ACT Reading walkthroughs and follow along in your copy of *The Official ACT Prep Guide* to see demonstrations of these ideas.

Reading Question Walkthroughs

We'll now see the ACT Reading process in action against every real ACT question from three practice tests in the Red Book. (Remember, I recommend that you only prepare with official practice questions, because those are the only questions that are guaranteed to play by the rules of the real test. For more on that, see "Using the Official ACT Prep Guide (the "Red Book")" on page 21 of this Black Book.)

IMPORTANT NOTE: If you have the 2020-2021 edition of the Red Book (ISBN: 978-1119685760), then "Test 1" in this Black Book refers to Practice Test 2 in your edition of the Red Book, and "Test 2" in this Black Book refers to Practice Test 3 in your Red Book. What we refer to as "Test 3" in this Black Book has been removed from the 2020-2021 edition of the Red Book, but it can be found online as ACT test form 16MC3. (See **The 2020-2021 Red Book** on page 23 of this Black Book for more.)

Before we start working through those questions, I'd like to take a second to explain how my walkthroughs for this section are set up. (By the way, if you'd like to see some video demonstrations of these ideas, go to www.ACTprepVideos.com for a selection of demonstration videos that are free to readers of this book.)

Sample Reading Walkthrough

The question walkthroughs in this book are laid out in a way that allows us to do the following:

- capture the ideal thought process for attacking individual questions, from initial assessment of the question through consideration of each answer choice
- make it easier to pick and choose specific pieces of information in the walkthrough, while also allowing you to read the entire walkthrough easily
- present the walkthroughs so they can stand on their own, while still making it easy to refer back to the relevant parts of the training for more details on key ideas if you want a refresher
- demonstrate how mechanical and repetitive real ACT questions are

Here's a diagram of an example walkthrough, with the elements of the walkthrough explained on the next page:

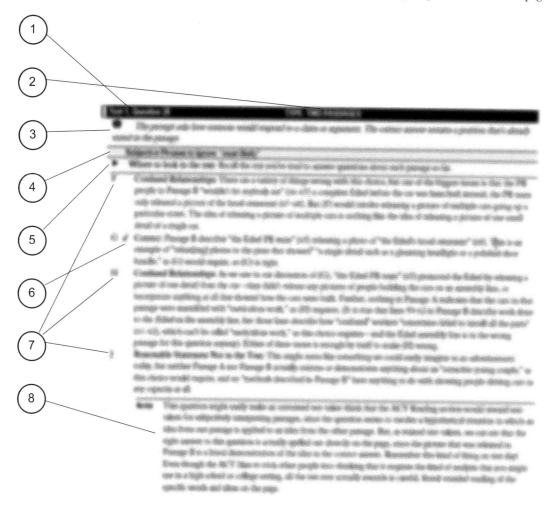

Explanation of Walkthrough Elements

The elements of the walkthrough are presented in a way that reflects the ideal mental process for approaching an ACT Reading question. First, we quickly get a general impression of what's going on in the question, then we remind ourselves of what the question wants us to do, and finally we consider each answer choice and figure out which common ACT pattern it reflects. Here's an explanation of the individual elements reflecting this general process:

1. This shows the test number and question number of the question being analyzed in the walkthrough. You can use this information to locate the relevant question in the Red Book.

2. This indicates the type of question, according to our rough classification system. I've deliberately avoided discussing the idea of classifying the questions in detail during your training, because I don't want you to think that classifying a question is a particularly important step in the process of answering that question. At the same time, as you work with more and more official ACT questions, you'll naturally begin to notice that some questions are extremely similar to others, and the questions will sort of automatically organize themselves into "types" in your mind, even if you're not trying to categorize them deliberately. So I've included general classifications of each question in the walkthroughs to help show you what kinds of associations a trained test-taker might initially make on reading the prompt for a question. Don't worry if your idea of a question's type doesn't always match exactly with mine! The classification isn't what really matters—all that really matters is that you stay in the habit of answering every question based on a literal reading of the words and figures on the page, and that you pick an answer choice that's restated or demonstrated by the text. Item 3 will tell you more about each type.

3. This italicized text is a quick reminder of the specific issues that are likely to come up in the question and how you should expect to tackle them, based on the "type" identified in Item 2. See the description of Item 2 above for more.

4. This Item reminds us that we can ignore the kinds of subjective wording that the ACT often uses to try to fool untrained test-takers into interpreting the text. Remember that we should never try to interpret the text or read it subjectively, even though the test frequently uses phrases like "it can most reasonably be inferred" and "primarily."

5. This part of the walkthrough will give you suggestions for finding the relevant part of the passage, based on the prompt and on parts of the passage you may have already encountered when answering other questions.

6. The correct answer will be noted with a checkmark icon, and the corresponding explanation will show exactly how the correct answer is restated or demonstrated by the relevant part of the passage.

7. The descriptions of the wrong answers will begin with a brief mention of the overall pattern being followed by the wrong answer, and then a lengthier explanation showing how the answer choice fits that pattern. (Remember to see "ACT Reading Wrong Answer Patterns" starting on page 53 of this Black Book for an explanation of these patterns.) Please keep in mind that you can still answer a question correctly without classifying or interpreting the wrong answers exactly the same way I do! Ultimately, all that matters is that you realize the wrong answers aren't restated or demonstrated in the relevant part of the text. If I decided to classify something as an example of the "confused relationships" pattern and you think it's a better example of the "off by one or two words" pattern, that's fine. I've just indicated these patterns to help you see how I'm structuring my thinking as I approach a question.

8. If I feel that something is noteworthy about the question but I can't fit it in the rest of the walkthrough, then I'll note that at the end of the walkthrough. Be sure to pay attention to these notes when they appear, as they'll often contain useful information about what a particular question can teach us generally about future ACT questions.

Note that some walkthroughs are missing some of the Items in this list! If one of the Items above isn't relevant to a particular question, then it's omitted.

Remember that the ultimate goal of these walkthroughs is to help you see how I attack each question, and how I recommend you do the same. But, in the end, what matters most is that you develop an approach for ACT Reading questions that allows you to identify the one correct answer choice that's directly restated or demonstrated on the page, and the three wrong answers that aren't. Feel free to modify my approach as you see fit, as long as your modifications still bring you the results you want within the time limit.

TEST 1 (TEST 2 IN 2020-2021 RED BOOK)

ⓘ　　*The prompt often mentions describing the passage without a line citation. The answer must still be restated or demonstrated by some specific part of the text. (See "What about Questions without Citations?" on p. 57.)*

> **Subjective Phrases to Ignore: "best described as"**

▶　**Where to look in the text:** Since the answer choices mention the difference between different kinds of narration, scan for words like "I," "my," "he," "she," and so on, which will help indicate what kind of narration the passage uses.

A　**Direct Contradiction:** This choice says the events of the story "happened before the narrator was born," but the narrator says in line 3 that the story happened "the day I was born," and line 7 says the action in the story that takes place in the hospital begins "seconds after [the narrator's] birth."

B ✓　**Correct:** The narrator refers to herself as "I" as early as the first sentence, demonstrating that she's a "first person narrator," as the prompt requires. The narrator also "offers insight into characters' thoughts" a number of times, as the prompt further requires: for example, lines 9-10 ("Baba realized that he didn't know my sex for sure…") and line 32 ("…Mama said, thinking he meant me"). Finally, we know the author is speaking about "a time she was too young to remember," as the prompt requires, because she begins the passage by saying, "I don't remember how I came to know this story," which demonstrates that she doesn't remember the events of the day herself, and that she must have heard or read them from some other source. She also says the story takes place on "the day I was born" (3), which demonstrates that she was too young to remember the events herself. Since every part of this choice is literally restated or demonstrated in the text, it must be right.

C　**Off by One or Two Words:** The narrator uses "I" to refer to herself, so she's a first person narrator, and not a third person narrator, as (C) would require. (A third person narrator would only use pronouns like "he," "she," "it," and "they.")

D　**Barely Relevant:** Nearly every part of this choice is wrong, for the reasons we mentioned in our analysis of the other choices.

ⓘ　　*The prompt asks about the purpose or role of a part of the text. The answer must be accurately restated or demonstrated by the relevant text, with no interpretation. (See "What about Main Purpose, Main Idea, Best Description Questions?," p. 58.)*

> **Subjective Phrases to Ignore: "primarily"**

▶　**Where to look in the text:** Skim for "piece of lint" or "flake of dandruff" from prompt, or "grandfather" from two of the answer choices.

F　**Confused Relationships:** This choice might be tempting, but it has multiple issues. First, this choice says the narrator's *grandfather* doesn't value family traditions, but the text talks in lines 15-21 about *Baba* not following a tradition in naming his child (this will trap a lot of untrained test-takers who might assume that "Baba" is a nickname for a grandfather without consulting the text closely enough). Second, the text only says that Baba seems not to value the specific tradition of naming his son after the narrator's grandfather, but that isn't the same thing as saying Baba doesn't value family traditions in general, as this choice would require.

G　**Confused Relationships:** The phrase involving the lint and the dandruff says Baba "brushed off" an "onus" (19-20). But a person can't literally brush off an onus, since an onus isn't a physical object, which means this is a figurative description, so it can't describe any literal movement Baba made.

H　**Direct Contradiction:** The phrase involving the lint and the dandruff says Baba "brushed off" the "onus" (19-20). That is, Baba *didn't* name his child after the child's grandfather. It doesn't make sense to say that Baba *not* following the tradition of naming the baby after the baby's grandfather emphasizes how important that tradition is, as this choice would require.

J ✓　**Correct:** The text says the name that Baba gave his child "was not my grandfather's name" (15), so we know that Baba didn't follow the tradition of giving the grandfather's name to the child, which means he "ignored" it, as this choice requires. The text says that the responsibility to name a son after the child's grandfather was an "onus" (18), and that Baba brushed off that onus "unceremoniously" (20), which restates the idea that he ignored the tradition in a "casual way," as the choice also requires. This answer choice is fully supported by the text, so it's correct.

ⓘ　　*The prompt often mentions describing the passage without a line citation. The answer must still be restated or demonstrated by some specific part of the text. (See "What about Questions without Citations?" on p. 57.)*

> **Subjective Phrases to Ignore: "best"**

▶　**Where to look in the text:** Skim for "Mama" and "Baba" and mention of the baby's name.

A ✓　**Correct:** The text says, "Mama must not have fought long" (54) against the name, which means she *did* fight the name, even if not for long. Since Mama fought the name, we know she "disapprov[ed]" of it, as (A) requires. The text also describes how Mama got out of bed before she should have right after hearing the baby's name (48-53), and that she "ignor[ed]" (50) Baba as he "scream[ed]" (51) about the name being "beautiful" (51) and "so unique" (51), all of which also demonstrates that she disapproved of the name. We also know that the narrator says, "I still have my name" (67-68), which means that Mama must have given up her fight without succeeding in changing the narrator's name. Since giving up and accepting something you don't like is the definition of the term "resignation" in (A), we can see that the text demonstrates Mama's resignation, as (A) also requires. Since every part of (A) is directly restated or demonstrated in the text, we know (A) is right.

B   **Confused Relationships:** This choice might tempt some untrained test-takers because Mama's reaction might arguably be described as "annoyance," and we might think, subjectively, that the action described in lines 34-43 is amusing to us—but there's a difference between a situation involving Mama that seems amusing to us or to the "staff" (42), and a situation in which *Mama herself* reacts with "amusement," as (B) and the prompt actually require. Since the question asks what Mama's reaction was, and the text never explicitly says or demonstrates that Mama was amused, we know (B) can't be right.

C   **Reasonable Statement Not in the Text:** We might imagine that Mama would feel embarrassed or outraged about her daughter having a name that Mama doesn't like, or about having someone "screaming" (51) to her, but the text doesn't actually say or show that Mama felt either of these emotions. (Note that Mama didn't like the name, as we saw in the explanation for (A), but for a word like "outrage" to be appropriate, the text would have to make clear that Mama was extremely angry, which it doesn't do—and, even if it did, the text still wouldn't restate or demonstrate the idea of embarrassment, which would be enough by itself to make (C) wrong.)

D   **Reasonable Statement Not in the Text:** A reader might subjectively imagine that Mama would feel "shock" and "resentment" about her daughter having a name that Mama doesn't like, and a statement like (D) would probably be a welcome analysis of Mama's motivations in a literature class. But (D) is wrong on the ACT because the text doesn't literally restate or demonstrate either of these emotions—the text never says Mama was surprised, or that she was always angry at Baba afterward for what he'd done, which is what the terms "shock" and "resentment" would require.

Test 1, Question 4 (Test 2 in the 2020-2021 Red Book—see page 23 for more)   **TYPE: CITATION QUESTION**

ℹ️   *The question includes a citation from the text. The answer must be directly restated or demonstrated in the cited text, or in the text closely surrounding the cited text. (See "The General Process for Answering ACT Reading Questions," p. 57.)*

Subjective Phrases to Ignore: "best"

F   **Confused Relationships:** The text describes how "Mama would have to go to the office of the City of Boston clerk" (57-58), but the phrase "would have" means she never actually went there. Further, the narrator is the one speaking, so we can't call this text "Baba's account." Either issue by itself would be enough to make this choice wrong. (Note that the following paragraph does mention that Baba "liked to" "embellish[]" (71), but nothing in the text restates or demonstrates the idea that the cited text is an example of Baba embellishing, as this choice would require.)

G ✓ **Correct:** The narrator describes a series of events using phrases like "who knows" (54), "must have" (54, 64, 65) and "maybe" (55, 56, 60) repeatedly, which supports the idea that the narrator doesn't know whether these things happened, but she thinks they may have happened, just as this choice requires.

H   **Barely Relevant:** This paragraph is told from the narrator's point of view, not from Mama's. And it doesn't tell how Nidali originally got her name; instead, it points out that Mama never changed Nidali's name from the name that Baba gave her, and it imagines reasons for not changing the name.

J   **Barely Relevant:** As we saw in the discussion of (G), this text isn't talking about a memory. Instead, it mentions some events that the narrator thinks may have happened. Further, nothing in this paragraph informs us about the narrator's personality, since all of the hypothetical actions discussed in the paragraph would have been Mama's actions if they really did happen.

Test 1, Question 5 (Test 2 in the 2020-2021 Red Book—see page 23 for more)   **TYPE: DESCRIBE THE PASSAGE**

ℹ️   *The prompt often mentions describing the passage without a line citation. The answer must still be restated or demonstrated by some specific part of the text. (See "What about Questions without Citations?" on p. 57.)*

▶   **Where to look in the text:** Skim for "Mama" or "City of Boston." You may also have encountered the relevant text when you answered question 4.

A   **Barely Relevant:** The text indicates that it was *Mama* (not Baba, as (A) requires) who might think the process of going to the clerk could bring a bad outcome, but not because of *when* the change would happen. The text tells us Mama thought it would be unlucky to go to a place where "people went to fill out death certificates" (64-65) to change the baby's name. Since nearly every part of this choice differs from the text, we know it must be wrong.

B   **Barely Relevant:** The text doesn't say anything about any winter storm, so this choice can't be right. In fact, the text mentions that the story took place "on August 2" (3), and that Mama didn't want to take the baby "through the heat" (63), so a "winter storm" seems to be the opposite of what Mama might be worried about.

C   **Barely Relevant:** The text doesn't say anything about Mama having a tendency to change her mind, so (C) can't be right.

D ✓ **Correct:** The text speculates that when Mama considered going to the clerk to change the baby's name, "she must've further imagined that going on such a trip…would surely bring about my death—because I still have my name" (65-68). The phrase

---

"because I still have my name" indicates that the narrator is basing her conclusion about what Mama "must've" done on the fact that her name is still Nidali, just as this choice requires.

Test 1, Question 6 (Test 2 in the 2020-2021 Red Book—see page 23 for more)   TYPE: CITATION QUESTION

ⓘ   *The question includes a citation from the text. The answer must be directly restated or demonstrated in the cited text, or in the text closely surrounding the cited text. (See "The General Process for Answering ACT Reading Questions," p. 57.)*

Subjective Phrases to Ignore: "most nearly"

F   **Off by One or Two Words:** The text only presents one description of the events surrounding the origin of Nidali's name, so we can't pick a choice that says there are "conflicting stories" about the origin of her name.

G   **Confused Relationships:** The text says the apartment was filled with "blueprints and plastic models of houses *instead of* notebooks and poetry" (76-77) (emphasis added). So the notebooks and poetry that the narrator mentions are things that Baba doesn't actually have, which means the phrase "these stories" can't refer to "Baba's notebooks and poetry," as (G) would require.

H ✓ **Correct:** The narrator says Baba "…must have embellished. Baba liked to do that: tell stories that were impossible but true all at once…" (71-73). This restates the idea that "Baba liked to tell" embellished tales, as (H) requires. Line 78 tells us that "Baba put…sadness into these stories." Since Baba is the one putting emotions into the stories, we know the phrase "these stories" (78) must refer back to those embellished stories that Baba told, and not to anyone else's stories. So the phrase "these stories" at the end of the paragraph refers back to Baba's embellished stories, as (H) requires.

J   **Confused Relationships:** As we saw for (H), lines 71-72 tell us that "Baba liked to…tell stories," and the phrase "these stories" in line 78 refers back to the stories mentioned in line 72. In other words, the cited phrase refers to *Baba's* stories, not to the narrator's stories, as (J) would require, which means (J) must be wrong.

Test 1, Question 7 (Test 2 in the 2020-2021 Red Book—see page 23 for more)   TYPE: DESCRIBE THE PASSAGE

ⓘ   *The prompt often mentions describing the passage without a line citation. The answer must still be restated or demonstrated by some specific part of the text. (See "What about Questions without Citations?" on p. 57.)*

▶   **Where to look in the text:** Skim for "Mama" or "Baba" and mention of either one working. Also, if you've read most of the passage and haven't yet encountered the relevant text, focus on the parts of the passage you haven't read yet.

A   **Barely Relevant:** This choice might be tempting to an untrained test-taker, because the narrator uses phrases like "movie star" (70-71) and "rock star" (74, 81) to describe Baba and Mama. But those phrases don't specifically indicate that Baba and Mama were actually famous for their artistic abilities—and, even if the phrases did have that meaning, we couldn't know for sure that Baba and Mama were proud of their work, as (A) would require. The paragraphs that actually describe the professional lives of Baba and Mama (lines 69-86) never say that either was proud of his or her professional life, so (A) is wrong.

B   **Reasonable Statement Not in the Text:** We might subjectively imagine that Baba and Mama feel anxiety over the fact that each has a passion that he or she doesn't follow, but this idea isn't specifically restated or demonstrated by the text—so, as trained test-takers, we know this choice must be wrong.

C ✓ **Correct:** The text says that Baba "used to be a writer and was now an architect" (74-75), which is a statement about his professional life. Then the text directly states that Baba's house was filled with objects related to architecture ("blueprints and plastic models of houses") instead of objects related to writing ("notebooks and poetry"), and that this "filled him with great sadness" (76-78). The text also says that Mama was "a musician who no longer played music" (81-82), which is a statement about her profession, and that the fact that the house was filled with many thing "instead of a piano" "filled her with great sadness" (85-86). So we can see that both Baba and Mama are directly described as having "great sadness" related to their professional lives, just as this choice requires.

D   **Direct Contradiction:** As we saw in the explanation for (C), Baba and Mama both felt sadness about their professional lives, not contentment.

Test 1, Question 8 (Test 2 in the 2020-2021 Red Book—see page 23 for more)   TYPE: DESCRIBE THE PASSAGE

ⓘ   *The prompt often mentions describing the passage without a line citation. The answer must still be restated or demonstrated by some specific part of the text. (See "What about Questions without Citations?" on p. 57.)*

▶   **Where to look in the text:** Skim for "superstitious" from the prompt. Also skim for "Mama," "Baba," "Nidali," or "Rhonda" from the answer choices, and see which ones are described as superstitious. You may also have encountered the relevant text when you answered questions 4 and 5.

F ✓ **Correct:** The narrator describes Mama as "the most superstitious of all humans" (60-61). Since all the characters in the story are humans, we know the narrator must consider Mama the most superstitious character.

G   **Confused Relationships:** In line 61, the narrator says Mama is "even more" superstitious than Baba, so (G) must be wrong. This choice might attract someone who misread and reversed the relationship between Baba's level of superstition and Mama's, or who only recalled that the passage mentioned Baba was very superstitious, without remembering that the passage says Mama is "even more" (61) superstitious than he is.

H   **Barely Relevant:** The text doesn't say anything about Nidali being superstitious.

J   **Barely Relevant:** The text doesn't say anything about Rhonda being superstitious.

ℹ️   *The prompt often mentions describing the passage without a line citation. The answer must still be restated or demonstrated by some specific part of the text. (See "What about Questions without Citations?" on p. 57.)*

Subjective Phrases to Ignore: "most strongly suggests"

▶   **Where to look in the text:** Skim for "Mama" or "Baba" and the idea of telling stories. Also, if you've read most of the passage and haven't yet encountered the relevant text, focus on the parts of the passage you haven't read yet.

A   **Reasonable Statement Not in the Text:** We might subjectively imagine that someone would react this way to hearing embellished stories all the time, but the text doesn't actually say that Mama would yawn or roll her eyes in these situations, so (A) is wrong.

B   **Reasonable Statement Not in the Text:** As with (A), we might imagine that someone would react this way to hearing embellished stories all the time, but the text doesn't actually say that Mama ignores Baba when he tells his stories.

C   **Direct Contradiction:** As we see in the explanation for (D), Mama doesn't chime in with more exaggerations—instead, she exposes Baba's exaggerations.

D ✓   **Correct:** The text says that Baba liked to "tell stories that were impossible but true all at once" (72-73), and that Mama "liked to expose him when he told such stories," (79-80) and that she was his "story-cop" (80). The idea of Mama "exposing" Baba when he was telling impossible stories, like something a cop might do, restates the idea that she "correct[ed] him about the accuracy of details," as this choice requires.

ℹ️   *The prompt often mentions describing the passage without a line citation. The answer must still be restated or demonstrated by some specific part of the text. (See "What about Questions without Citations?" on p. 57.)*

▶   **Where to look in the text:** Skim for long words and capitalized letters from the answer choices, like "embellished," "Mama," "Baba," "musician," "architect", and "imagination." Also remember that ideas from (G), (H), and (J) like "rock star," "musician," and "architect" were in the text when we answered question 7. Also, if you've read most of the passage and haven't yet encountered the relevant text, focus on the parts of the passage you haven't read yet.

F ✓   **Correct:** The last paragraph of the text says, "home meant embellishing, and that's why I loved school…they taught us facts based on reality" (87-89). This idea is directly restated in (F), so (F) is right.

G   **Off by One or Two Words:** The text does say that Mama is a "true rock star" (81), but the idea that Baba is an "amateur musician" never appears in the passage.

H   **Direct Contradiction:** The text says that Baba's house was filled with objects related to architecture ("blueprints and plastic models of houses") instead of objects related to writing ("notebooks and poetry"), and this "filled him with great sadness" (76-78). (H) expresses the opposite of this idea by saying that Baba was happy as an architect.

J   **Reasonable Statement Not in the Text:** We might subjectively imagine that "writing requires great imagination" and "playing music requires great skill," as this choice would require, but the text never discusses the requirements for writing or playing music.

ℹ️   *The prompt often mentions describing the passage without a line citation. The answer must still be restated or demonstrated by some specific part of the text. (See "What about Questions without Citations?" on p. 57.)*

Subjective Phrases to Ignore: "best"

▶   **Where to look in the text:** Skim for "San Francisco" and "1903" in Passage A.

A   **Direct Contradiction:** The text *does* say automobiles were "unpopular" in several places, but it doesn't say they were "affordable for the average citizen," as (A) would require. Instead, the text tells us that the "cheapest automobile" cost "twice the $500 annual salary of the average citizen" (26-27).

B   **Barely Relevant:** The text does mention San Francisco "banning automobiles from all tourist areas" (22-23), which may seem connected to the idea of "tourists" in (B) at first, but the passage doesn't actually say anything about the vehicles themselves being "used…by tourists" as opposed to being used for "practical purposes," as (B) would require. (Note that "picnic parties" (36) don't necessarily have to involve "sightseeing" and aren't necessarily attended by "tourists," as (B) would require—the passage doesn't specifically say that the drivers or users of the car are tourists, nor whether they live in areas local to where they're driving, etc.) So the text doesn't restate or demonstrate the ideas in (B).

C   **Barely Relevant:** The text mentions that the debut of the automobile in San Francisco was an "unmitigated disaster[]" (3), but nothing in the text restates the idea of the automobile failing "to capture the public imagination." And Passage A doesn't mention any "public relations efforts," as (C) would require—Passage B is the one that talks about hype and marketing.

D ✓   **Correct:** The text calls the automobile a "civic menace, belching out exhaust, kicking up storms of dust,…and tying up horse traffic" (9-12), which demonstrates that the automobile was "a public nuisance," as this choice requires. The rest of the second paragraph further demonstrates that several city and state governments disliked cars so much that they came up with special laws that made using cars more difficult. The text also mentions "drivers" (35) having "'picnic parties' held out of the view of angry townsfolk" (36-37), which demonstrates that there were still some people who used cars, as (D) requires.

Test 1, Question 12 (Test 2 in the 2020-2021 Red Book—see page 23 for more)   TYPE: CITATION QUESTION

ⓘ   *The question includes a citation from the text. The answer must be directly restated or demonstrated in the cited text, or in the text closely surrounding the cited text. (See "The General Process for Answering ACT Reading Questions," p. 57.)*

▶   **Where to look in the text:** Look at the line number that each choice refers to.

F   **Confused Relationships:** The surrounding text mentions "exhaust" and "storms of dust" (10), and describes cars being "mired" (11) and "tying up horse traffic" (12), all of which indicates that the text is describing cars getting stuck in literal puddles. So we can't say "puddles" is being used "figuratively," as this choice would require.

G ✓   **Correct:** Line 13 mentions "monuments to legislative creativity" made by "local lawmakers" (12). The rest of the paragraph describes the unusual laws of different governments relating to the use of automobiles. So the text is calling these laws "monuments," but a law isn't literally a monument: a law is a rule people follow, and a monument is a physical structure whose purpose is to remind people of something. The word "monuments" can't be taken literally here, so (G) must be right.

H   **Confused Relationships:** The text describes how the "bells" would "ring" (18) when the wheels revolved. The idea of the bells actually ringing (18-19) demonstrates that the law would have required real, literal bells, so (H) can't be right.

J   **Confused Relationships:** The cars had "little power" (39), so it makes sense that they'd have difficulty climbing literal "hills" (39). The text even describes "automobiles straining for the top" of a specific steep road, "Nineteenth Avenue" (40-42). In context, it's clear that the text describes actual "hills," not figurative ones, so (J) can't be right.

Test 1, Question 13 (Test 2 in the 2020-2021 Red Book—see page 23 for more)   TYPE: PURPOSE OF CITED TEXT

ⓘ   *The prompt asks about the purpose or role of a part of the text. The correct answer must be accurately restated or described by the relevant text, with no interpretation. (See "What about Main Purpose, Main Idea, Best Description Questions?," p. 58.)*

    Subjective Phrases to Ignore: "most likely"

A ✓   **Correct:** As trained test-takers, we know that unattributed quotation marks indicate that the author disagrees with the normal usage of the term in quotes (see "What about Unattributed Quotations ("Scare Quotes")?" on page 59 of this Black Book for more). In this case, then, the author is saying that "bumpers, carburetors, and headlights" (30) aren't actually accessories; since an "essential" is the opposite of an "accessory" in this context, we know (A) is right. This directly demonstrates the idea that "the features were actually essentials," as (A) requires.

B   **Barely Relevant:** The previous paragraph discusses various laws related to automobiles, but this portion of this paragraph discusses the costs associated with owning an automobile, and makes no mention of documents of any kind.

C   **Barely Relevant:** The passage never says anything about whether people understood this term properly, so this choice isn't restated or demonstrated anywhere on the page.

D   **Direct Contradiction:** The text specifically tells us that the "cheapest automobile" cost "twice the $500 annual salary of the average citizen" (26-27), which means they weren't "inexpensive," as this choice would require. And the author never says that "bumpers, carburetors, and headlights" (30) are luxurious—or even mentions the idea of "luxury" at all—as this choice would also require. Either issue on its own would be enough to make this choice wrong.

Test 1, Question 14 (Test 2 in the 2020-2021 Red Book—see page 23 for more)   TYPE: DESCRIBE THE PASSAGE

ⓘ   *The prompt often mentions describing the passage without a line citation. The answer must still be restated or demonstrated by some specific part of the text. (See "What about Questions without Citations?" on p. 57.)*

    Subjective Phrases to Ignore: "best"

▶   **Where to look in the text:** Skim for "Edsel" in Passage B.

F   **Direct Contradiction:** The text says when the Edsel was released, "nearly 3 million Americans flocked to showrooms to see the Edsel," but "very few of them bought the Edsel" (71-73), and that people "just didn't like the car" (75). If few people bought the car right from the beginning, then the phrase "happened gradually" in the answer choice isn't restated or demonstrated by the text. Further, if millions of people saw the car in the showroom but didn't buy it, then the phrase "went unnoticed…by the public" is also contradicted by the text.

G   **Direct Contradiction:** The text makes no mention of "promising initial sales," as this choice would require. In fact, the automaker "promised to sell 200,000 cars the first year," but only sold "63,110" (87-89). Then "Ford pulled the plug" (90-91) only a few years later. Since the car didn't even come close to meeting the first year's projected sales, we can't say the car had "promising initial sales," and this choice must be wrong.

H ✓   **Correct:** As we saw in the discussion of (F), millions of people came to see the car right away, which demonstrates the idea that the failure "was on a huge scale," as this choice requires. And as we saw for (G), the car came nowhere close to its first year sales projections, and then Ford "pulled the plug" (90-91) not long after, which supports the idea that the failure "occurred swiftly." Further, we're told that the "hype" (65) from the PR team "worked perfectly" (64-65), and that "hundreds of publications" (69) even printed a picture of the hood ornament. All of that publicity, and the millions of people who "flocked to showrooms" (71-72) demonstrate that the failure "was a public event of sorts," as the choice also requires. Since every part of this choice is directly demonstrated by Passage B, we know it's right.

J   **Direct Contradiction:** The text says that the car was launched shortly after "a stock market plunge" (85) and that "sales of all premium cars plummeted" (85-86) around the time the Edsel launched, directly contradicting the idea that "other automakers were doing well" at that time, as this choice would require.

Test 1, Question 15 (Test 2 in the 2020-2021 Red Book—see page 23 for more)   TYPE: CITATION QUESTION

ⓘ   *The question includes a citation from the text. The answer must be directly restated or demonstrated in the cited text, or in the text closely surrounding the cited text. (See "The General Process for Answering ACT Reading Questions," p. 57.)*

Subjective Phrases to Ignore: "is typical of Passage B in the way it"

A   **Barely Relevant:** The text mentions different "varieties of Edsel" (44), but doesn't say anything about "other cars of the 1950s," as this choice would require, which means it can't possibly contrast data about different cars of the 1950s.

B   **Barely Relevant:** The cited text doesn't say anything about "Ford executives," nor about "consumers" being involved in "the design of the Edsel," as this choice would require. Either issue by itself would be enough to make this choice wrong.

C   **Barely Relevant:** The cited text never restates or demonstrates anything about a "typical consumer," including what the perspective of such a consumer would be, so this choice must be wrong.

D ✓   **Correct:** The phrase "not one, not two, but 18 varieties" (44) demonstrates and emphasizes the idea that 18 is a lot of varieties to have according to the author; having a lot of something demonstrates the idea of being "marked by extremes," as this choice requires, so it's right.

> **Note**   Some untrained test-takers might get hung up on the phrase "typical of Passage B" from the prompt, and spend a lot of time trying to decide how the given statement is echoed or imitated in other parts of Passage B. But if we just consider each answer choice, we find that three of them describe ideas that don't appear anywhere in the passage, while only the right answer actually describes an idea that appears anywhere in Passage B at all. This is another great example of how the ACT likes to include questions that seem to require literary analysis or interpretation of an entire passage, but that really just depend on carefully reading the relevant text with no interpretation at all.

Test 1, Question 16 (Test 2 in the 2020-2021 Red Book—see page 23 for more)   TYPE: DESCRIBE THE PASSAGE

ⓘ   *The prompt often mentions describing the passage without a line citation. The answer must still be restated or demonstrated by some specific part of the text. (See "What about Questions without Citations?" on p. 57.)*

▶   **Where to look in the text:** Skim for "E-day," "45,000," or "2,846" in Passage B.

F   **Confused Relationships:** E-day was the day the Edsel was launched, but lines 84-85 tell us that "Edsel" was "launched a couple months after a stock market plunge." So E-day came after the plunge, which means it didn't come first chronologically, since (G) refers to the plunge.

G ✓   **Correct:** As we discussed in the explanation for (F), the stock market plunge came two months before "E-day," according to lines 84 and 85. Further, the sales figures in the other two choices occurred after the car was launched: (H) occurred in "the second year" (89) after the car was launched, and the sales figures in (J) happened in "1960" (90). (Note that the text says E-Day was "September 4, 1957" (70).) Since (H) and (J) happened after E-day, which happened after the stock market plunge, the plunge must have happened first out of all of the choices.

H   **Confused Relationships:** As we saw in the explanation for (G), "sales dropped below 45,000" after the Edsel was launched on E-day, which was after the stock market plunge, so this event didn't occur first chronologically

J   **Confused Relationships:** As we saw in the explanation for (G), "sales reached 2,846" after the Edsel was launched, and after the stock market plunge. Some test-takers may choose this wrong answer because it occurred *last* chronologically, and they misread or misremembered the prompt. Remember that we always need to look out for those kinds of small mistakes, which can cost us a question even when we understand all the concepts involved!

Test 1, Question 17 (Test 2 in the 2020-2021 Red Book—see page 23 for more)   TYPE: CITATION QUESTION

ⓘ   *The question includes a citation from the text. The answer must be directly restated or demonstrated in the cited text, or in the text closely surrounding the cited text. (See "The General Process for Answering ACT Reading Questions," p. 57.)*

Subjective Phrases to Ignore: "primarily"

A   **Barely Relevant:** The text doesn't discuss Edsels in the present day, and doesn't discuss antique cars. (The text talks about cars from the 1950s, but it does so *in the time period of the 1950s.* In other words, in 1957, a car from 1957 isn't an antique.) Further, the text certainly never says that anyone found the Edsel valuable at any time.

B   **Barely Relevant:** The text doesn't describe the makers of the Edsel "ushering in" any "type of car," as this choice would require—in order for this choice to be acceptable on the ACT, the text would have to say something like "the term 'premium car' was invented to describe the Edsel and other cars like it," but no idea like that occurs anywhere in the text.

C ✓ **Correct:** The text calls the Edsel an "upscale car" (84), and "upscale" means the same thing as "premium" (86). Also, the text says a "major problem" (84) was the Edsel having bad sales because it was "launched a couple months after a stock market plunge" (84-85) when "sales of all premium cars plummeted" (85-86). This demonstrates that the Edsel "belong[s] to" the group "premium cars," as (C) requires. So we know (C) must be right.

D **Confused Relationships:** The two paragraphs before the citation describe people not liking the Edsel for various reasons, and include a sarcastic "joke[]" (81) about what the word "Edsel" stands for (81-82). But the citation doesn't connect the idea of a "premium car[]" (86) to any of those issues—in fact, the paragraph with the citation begins with the phrase "another major problem" (83), indicating that the problem in the citation is a different problem from the one in lines 80-82.

Test 1, Question 18 (Test 2 in the 2020-2021 Red Book—see page 23 for more)　　　**TYPE: TWO PASSAGES**

ⓘ *May ask about agreement or disagreement between passages, or how an idea from one passage applies to the other, etc. The answer is still literally restated or demonstrated. (See "Paired passages aren't special," p. 56; "What about Paired Passages?" p. 58.)*

▶ **Where to look in the text:** Always remember to read the introductory text at the very beginning of each passage! In this case, the information in that text is required in order for you to find the right answer.

F ✓ **Correct:** The first passage describes events that took place in 1903, and we know from the intro that the passage was taken from a book published in 2001. The second passage describes events in the 1950s, and was taken from an article published in 2007. So both articles were written about events that took place decades earlier, just as (F) requires.

G **Barely Relevant:** Neither article contains any information about the author's background.

H **Barely Relevant:** Both articles describe problems related to automobiles—Passage A describes how the automobile was seen as a "civic menace" (9) when it first appeared, and Passage B describes the failed launch of a specific car, the Edsel. But neither article discusses the overall contribution the automobile has made to society in general, as (H) would require.

J **Confused Relationships:** Passage A mentions "puddles" (11) in the street, and "horse traffic" (12), and the idea that "road signs were only just being erected" (32-33), all of which are "information about traffic and road conditions," as (J) mentions. But that passage doesn't discuss "automobile design," which is also part of (J). Conversely, Passage B mentions the Edsel's "push-button transmission…in the middle of the steering wheel" (47-48), and the "vertical chrome oval" in the Edsel's grill (50-51), which is "a discussion of automobile design" as described in (J). But Passage B doesn't discuss "traffic and road conditions," as (J) also requires. So each passage discusses one of the topics from choice (J), but neither discusses both, which means (J) is wrong. Untrained test-takers who misread the prompt or this answer choice might be attracted to it, because the choice seems to combine elements of both passages—but we were asked to find *one* answer choice whose statements describe *both* passages, not a choice that describes separate, different elements of each passage.

Test 1, Question 19 (Test 2 in the 2020-2021 Red Book—see page 23 for more)　　　**TYPE: TWO PASSAGES**

ⓘ *May ask about agreement or disagreement between passages, or how an idea from one passage applies to the other, etc. The answer is still literally restated or demonstrated. (See "Paired passages aren't special," p. 56; "What about Paired Passages?" p. 58.)*

▶ **Where to look in the text:** Recall the text you've read to answer questions about each passage so far.

A ✓ **Correct:** The second paragraph of Passage A discusses a number of laws related to automobiles, but Passage B never discusses any laws.

B **Direct Contradiction:** Both passages discuss public opinion. Among other things, Passage A says that "consumers were staying away from the 'devilish contraption' in droves" (4-5), and Passage B says of people at the time that "they just didn't like the car" (75). This choice will attract untrained test-takers who misread the prompt and think they should find an answer choice that reflects something common to both passages.

C **Direct Contradiction:** Both passages discuss economics. Passage A discusses the price of a car relative to an average person's annual salary in lines 25-31, and Passage B discusses the impact of the stock market on car sales in lines 83-86. Like (B), this choice will attract some test-takers who misread the prompt.

D **Direct Contradiction:** Only Passage B includes quotations from specific people in the automobile industry when it quotes Jim Arnold in lines 53-56 and C. Gayle Warnock in lines 73-76. Passage A doesn't have any quotations from industry experts. This choice will appeal to untrained test-takers who misread the prompt, and incorrectly think that it asked for an element of Passage B that didn't appear in Passage A.

Test 1, Question 20 (Test 2 in the 2020-2021 Red Book—see page 23 for more)　　　**TYPE: TWO PASSAGES**

ⓘ *May ask about agreement or disagreement between passages, or how an idea from one passage applies to the other, etc. The answer is still literally restated or demonstrated. (See "Paired passages aren't special," p. 56; "What about Paired Passages?" p. 58.)*

Subjective Phrases to Ignore: "most likely"

▶ **Where to look in the text:** Recall the text you've read to answer questions about each passage so far.

F **Confused Relationships:** There are a variety of things wrong with this choice, but one of the biggest issues is that the PR people in Passage B "wouldn't let anybody see" (66-67) a complete Edsel before the car was launched; instead, the PR team only released a picture of the hood ornament (67-68). But (F) would involve releasing a picture of multiple cars going up a particular street. The idea of releasing a picture of multiple cars is nothing like the idea of releasing a picture of one small detail of a single car.

G ✓ **Correct:** Passage B describes "the Edsel PR team" (65) releasing a photo of "the Edsel's hood ornament" (68). This is an example of "releas[ing] photos to the press that showed" "a single detail such as a gleaming headlight or a polished door handle," as (G) would require in combination with the prompt, so (G) is right.

H **Confused Relationships:** As we saw in our discussion of (G), "the Edsel PR team" (65) promoted the Edsel by releasing a picture of one detail from the car—they didn't release any pictures of people building the cars on an assembly line, or incorporate anything at all that showed how the cars were built. Further, nothing in Passage A indicates that the cars in that passage were assembled with "meticulous work," as (H) requires. (It is true that lines 59-62 in Passage B describe work done to the *Edsel* on the assembly line, but those lines describe how "confused" (61) workers "sometimes failed to install all the parts" (61-62), which can't be called "meticulous work," as this choice requires—and the Edsel assembly line is in the wrong passage for this question anyway). Either of these issues is enough by itself to make (H) wrong.

J **Reasonable Statement Not in the Text:** This might seem like something we could easily imagine in an advertisement today, but neither Passage A nor Passage B actually restates or demonstrates anything about an "attractive young couple," as (J) would require, and no "methods described in Passage B" have anything to do with showing people driving cars in any capacity at all.

Note This question might easily make an untrained test-taker think that the ACT Reading section would reward test-takers for subjectively interpreting passages, since the question seems to involve a hypothetical situation in which an idea from one passage is applied to an idea from the other passage. But, as trained test-takers, we can see that the right answer to this question is actually spelled out directly on the page, since the picture that was released in Passage B is a literal demonstration of the idea in the correct answer. Remember this on test day! Even though the ACT likes to trick other people into trying the kind of analysis that you might use in high school or college, all the test ever actually rewards is careful, literal-minded reading of the specific words on the page. (See "Paired passages aren't special" on page 56 of this Black Book and "What about Paired Passages?" on page 58 for more.)

Test 1, Question 21 (Test 2 in the 2020-2021 Red Book—see page 23 for more)   **TYPE: DESCRIBE THE PASSAGE**

ⓘ *The prompt often mentions describing the passage without a line citation. The answer must still be restated or demonstrated by some specific part of the text. (See "What about Questions without Citations?" on p. 57.)*

A **Off by One or Two Words:** This choice will attract a lot of untrained test-takers, but it's wrong because the words "painting," "experience" and "it" are all *singular*. The passage never mentions a single work as the "artist's most famous painting," as this choice would require, though it does mention "his greatest *paintings*" (69-70) (emphasis added), plural. (The passage doesn't focus on any one painting. In fact, the only sentence that mentions a specific painting at all actually mentions two paintings, "Eastern Point and Cannon Rock" (76-77).) Similarly, the passage mentions a variety of experiences that shaped the artist's career, but it doesn't focus on a single "experience," as this choice would require. This is a great example of the kind of thing that would be a perfectly welcome remark in a classroom discussion, but a completely wrong answer on the ACT. Remember to look out for these kinds of small details on test day.

B **Reasonable Statement Not in the Text:** The passage does discuss a few specific landscapes and their influence on one particular painter, but it doesn't "explore" the "relationship" between the entire "natural world" and all of the "fine arts," as this choice would require. So, among other issues, we can't say the passage is about "the fine arts" because only one art—painting—is discussed in the passage. For this choice to be right, the text would need to make some kind of generalizing statement saying that Homer's evolution as a painter was typical of the way many artists in a variety of disciplines reacted to their own natural environments, or something along those lines; as we can see, the text never makes any kind of statement like that. This choice might be an acceptable observation in a humanities class, but it's wrong on the ACT.

C ✓ **Correct:** We can see that the passage demonstrates the idea of "an overview of an artist's career" because the passage tells us about much of Winslow Homer's life as a painter, from 1867 when "two of Homer's canvases were chosen to hang at the Great Exposition in Paris" (10-11), to Homer's "summer at the town of Tynemouth" (29), to his time "on the coast of Maine for the last 25 years of his life" (53-54). We can also see that the passage demonstrates the idea of "important influences" on Homer's work, because of the discussion of "the influence of Japanese art on Homer's painting" (17-18), the way that what Homer saw in Tynemouth "would occupy [him] for many years to come" (48-49), and how, once in Maine, "the sea outside his window now inspired the artist to create what came to be known as his greatest paintings" (68-70). Since every part of this choice is demonstrated in the passage in a literal way, we know it's the right answer.

D **Barely Relevant:** (D) must be wrong because the passage discusses the work of Winslow Homer, and doesn't mention any other "artists" who dealt with a "peculiarly American" world, as this choice would require. (The second paragraph discusses some Japanese prints, but no particular artist is mentioned, and we have no reason to believe the Japanese artwork would "epitomize a peculiarly American nineteenth-century world.")

Note Each of the wrong answers for this question is the kind of academic-sounding comment that would probably be acceptable in a classroom setting. Check the discussions of those choices above and make sure you understand why those choices are wrong on the ACT.

Test 1, Question 22 (Test 2 in the 2020-2021 Red Book—see page 23 for more)   **TYPE: DESCRIBE THE PASSAGE**

ⓘ   *The prompt often mentions describing the passage without a line citation. The answer must still be restated or demonstrated by some specific part of the text. (See "What about Questions without Citations?" on p. 57.)*

> **Subjective Phrases to Ignore: "reasonably" "most likely"**

▶   **Where to look in the text:** The passage describes events in roughly chronological order, so skim for references to Homer's work toward the end of the passage.

F   **Confused Relationships:** The passage says Homer painted scenes of "Atlantic City" (37) before he even went to Tynemouth, which was before he lived in Maine near the end of his life. This choice might attract untrained test-takers who misread or misremember the prompt and think it's asking about the beginning of Homer's career, not the end of it.

G ✓ **Correct:** The text says that Homer lived "on the coast of Maine for the last 25 years of his life" (53-54) where "the sea outside his window now inspired the artist" (68), and that the sea there was "prone to monstrous gales" (70-71) and "screaming winds" (72), which are ideas restated by the phrase "pitched about on a stormy ocean" from the answer choice. So the text directly demonstrates the idea that "a painting created by Homer late in his life" as mentioned in the prompt would be of a boat "violently pitched about on a stormy ocean," as this choice requires.

H   **Confused Relationships:** The text says that Homer painted scenes of "farm life" (25) in the 1870s, before he traveled to Tynemouth or Maine; as we saw for (G), Maine is where Homer spent the later part of his life.

J   **Barely Relevant:** The only mention of Paris comes early in the beginning of the second paragraph, before Homer went to Tynemouth or Maine, and the text never says that Homer painted Parisian scenes. This choice will attract untrained test-takers who don't read the text carefully and simply assume that painters who go to Paris will naturally want to paint scenes of Parisian life.

Test 1, Question 23 (Test 2 in the 2020-2021 Red Book—see page 23 for more)   **TYPE: DESCRIBE THE PASSAGE**

ⓘ   *The prompt often mentions describing the passage without a line citation. The answer must still be restated or demonstrated by some specific part of the text. (See "What about Questions without Citations?" on p. 57.)*

> **Subjective Phrases to Ignore: "best"**

▶   **Where to look in the text:** Skim for "shapes" and any of the adjectives from the answer choices.

A ✓ **Correct:** Lines 20-22 describe how the "weakness of earlier compositions" was "replaced by a boldness…in which simple shapes are massed into powerful designs." Since the words "weak" and "powerful" in (A) are directly restated by the relevant parts of the text, we know (A) is right.

B   **Barely Relevant:** The text doesn't discuss the sharpness or roundness of shapes in Homer's paintings.

C   **Confused Relationships:** The text mentions that Homer spent time in Tynemouth, and that the light there was "gloomier and more dramatic than that of the Jersey coast" (38-39). But that isn't the same thing as saying the "shapes" in Homer's paintings used to be dark, and later became light, as this choice would require. (In fact, if anything, the text describes a shift from a lighter setting to a darker setting when Homer moved to Tynemouth—but, again, the change in Homer's settings isn't the same thing as the change in the way he "depicted shapes," which is what the prompt actually asked about.)

D   **Confused Relationships:** The text says that Homer's "later paintings" showed a world with a "melancholy atmosphere" (8-9), but the text never says the "shapes" in his paintings were melancholy, nor that the "shapes" were ever "uplifting" before being melancholy.

Test 1, Question 24 (Test 2 in the 2020-2021 Red Book—see page 23 for more)   **TYPE: DESCRIBE THE PASSAGE**

ⓘ   *The prompt often mentions describing the passage without a line citation. The answer must still be restated or demonstrated by some specific part of the text. (See "What about Questions without Citations?" on p. 57.)*

▶   **Where to look in the text:** Skim for "Tynemouth."

F   **Direct Contradiction:** The text says that in Tynemouth, Homer "became enthralled by the dramas of the people who make their living from the ocean" (39-41), and that what he saw there "would occupy Homer for many years to come" (48-49). Also, the last paragraph describes how Homer continued to paint ocean scenes in Maine later in life. So the text directly contradicts the idea that what Homer saw at Tynemouth only inspired him "for a short time," and it also directly contradicts the idea that "Homer soon abandoned" the scenes he encountered at Tynemouth for his previous subjects.

G   **Barely Relevant:** We saw in the explanation for (F) that Homer continued to be inspired by what he saw in Tynemouth for years to come, not for a "short time." Further, the text makes no specific mention of Homer's "commercial success," nor of Homer having "little" of that success; any of these issues by itself would be enough to make this choice wrong. (The text does mention paintings being "successful back home" (32-33), but it doesn't necessarily say that this success was commercial in nature, nor does it ever say that any of the paintings were less successful than other paintings.)

H   **Barely Relevant:** We saw in the explanation for (F) that Homer was inspired by what he saw at Tynemouth for a long time, so the first part of this choice is properly reflected in the text. But the text never says that he returned to Tynemouth, so the second component of this choice has nothing to do with the text.

J ✓ **Correct:** As we saw in the explanation for (F), Homer "continued to be inspired by what he saw [in Tynemouth] for years," just as this choice requires.

ⓘ   *The prompt often mentions describing the passage without a line citation. The answer must still be restated or demonstrated by some specific part of the text. (See "What about Questions without Citations?" on p. 57.)*

Subjective Phrases to Ignore: "mainly"

▶   **Where to look in the text:** Skim for "Tynemouth." Also bear in mind that this question is related to the subject matter from question 24.

A   **Confused Relationships:** The text says that Homer painted "tourist scenes" (25) in the 1870s, before he went to Tynemouth in "1881" (26). This choice will attract a lot of test-takers who don't read the text carefully enough to notice that it doesn't specifically mention tourist scenes being painted at Tynemouth, even though it does mention the phrases "tourist scenes" and "Tynemouth" in close proximity to each other.

B ✓ **Correct:** The text says that in Tynemouth, Homer "became enthralled by the dramas of the people who make their living from the ocean: the fisherman's wives staring out to sea as they wait for their men, the launch of the lifeboat to rescue sailors from a foundering ship, the agonizingly fragile fishing boats being tossed on angry waves" (39-44). This directly demonstrates the idea of "the interplay between the sea and the lives of fishermen and their families" from this choice.

C   **Off by One or Two Words:** The text mentions "farm life" (25) in the same paragraph that discusses what Homer saw in Tynemouth, but as we saw in our discussion of (B), the "dynamic struggle" with the "forces of nature" is a struggle with the sea by *the fishermen and their communities*, not by "farmers," as this choice would require.

D   **Barely Relevant:** The text does say that Tynemouth was on the "North Sea" (35), as (D) requires, but it calls the waters there "dangerous and unpredictable" (35), not "soothing." Also, as we saw in the explanation for (B), Homer was captivated by the dramatic lives of the fisherman, not just the "beauty of the North Sea."

ⓘ   *The prompt often mentions describing the passage without a line citation. The answer must still be restated or demonstrated by some specific part of the text. (See "What about Questions without Citations?" on p. 57.)*

Subjective Phrases to Ignore: "most strongly"

▶   **Where to look in the text:** Skim for text related to "Great Exposition," "Caribbean," and "melancholy" from the answer choices. Also bear in mind that this question is related to the subject matter from questions 24 and 25.

F ✓ **Correct:** The text says, "it wasn't until 1881, however, that [Homer] found the subject matter that would inspire him most" (25-27). After describing Homer's time observing fishing life in Tynemouth, the text says, "here at last was a subject matter that matched the artist's deepest feelings" (44-46), and that what Homer saw there "would occupy him for many years to come" (48-49). All of this demonstrates that Homer's "discovery of [this] subject matter...profoundly inspired him," just as (F) requires.

G   **Reasonable Statement Not in the Text:** The text does mention that Homer had two paintings "at the Great Exposition in Paris" (11), and some untrained test-takers may assume that this was a great honor that would transform an artist's life. But the text never actually mentions any "sense of accomplishment" connected to having those paintings on display at the Exposition, as (G) would require—so (G) is wrong.

H   **Reasonable Statement Not in the Text:** The text does say that Homer spent "parts of the winter in the Caribbean" (63-64), but the text never specifically says that Homer was "inspired" there, as this choice would require. Some untrained test-takers will assume that Homer's time in a tropical environment would impact his painting, and pick this choice even though it's not literally restated or demonstrated in the text.

J   **Barely Relevant:** The text mentions that Homer's later paintings depicted a world with "a stark and melancholy atmosphere" (9), but that doesn't mean that Homer rejects the belief "that the world was stark and melancholy," as (J) would require. (If anything, it would suggest that he *embraces* the idea that the world is stark and melancholy, but even this idea doesn't actually appear in the text.)

Note   Many untrained test-takers will get hung up on the fact that the prompt mentions "the main turning point in [Homer's] development," and spend a lot of mental energy trying to figure out which of the changes in the text should be counted as the "main" one: the Japanese influence, the discovery of new subject matter, the time in Maine, et cetera. But, as trained test-takers, we know that we never need to analyze the text subjectively, as we might need to in a classroom setting, because we know that the right answer will be the only choice that's literally restated or demonstrated by the prompt. In this case, only (F) actually reflects what's on the page in a literal way, so it must be right; all the other choices add extra ideas to what appeared in the text, so they must be wrong no matter which aspects of Homer's life they might also mention. Remember this on test day! Don't let the ACT fool you into thinking you need to make subjective judgments on the test. All you need to do is find the choice that's literally restated or demonstrated by the passage.

ⓘ   *The prompt often mentions describing the passage without a line citation. The answer must still be restated or demonstrated by some specific part of the text. (See "What about Questions without Citations?" on p. 57.)*

▶   **Where to look in the text:** Skim for "Paris." Also bear in mind that this question is related to the subject matter from questions 21 and 23.

A   **Direct Contradiction:** The text says that Homer encountered "Japanese art" (18) in Paris, and that the "influence" on "Homer's painting was immediately apparent" (17-19), which is the opposite of "subtle" in this choice. Also, the text says that, after Paris, Homer "replaced" (21) elements of his former style with "simple shapes…massed into powerful designs" (21-22), which means he wasn't using those kinds of shapes before. But (A) uses the word "continued," which would contradict the text by indicating that Homer was already painting shapes this way. Finally, (A) mentions a change in Homer's use of color after his experience in Paris, but the text only mentions a change in the way Homer used shapes, as we just discussed. Any of these issues on its own would make (A) wrong.

B ✓   **Correct:** As we saw in the explanation for (A), Homer's experience in Paris "made a deep impression on the artist" (17) and its effect was "immediately apparent" (19): he "replaced" (21) his weak compositions with "boldness and lucidity" (21). The terms "deep," "immediately," "weakness," and "boldness" are all extreme terms that demonstrate the notion of a "dramatic" effect, as (B) requires. Further, the text's statement about the "weakness" (20) of earlier work being replaced by "boldness and lucidity" (21) is restated by the phrase "became bolder and clearer." Since every part of (B) is directly restated or demonstrated by the passage, (B) is right.

C   **Direct Contradiction:** As we saw in the explanations for (A) and (B), the impact of Homer's experience in Paris was "immediately apparent" (19), not "imperceptible." This choice may appeal to some untrained test-takers who only remember that Homer had another major change later in his life when he moved to Maine, and who don't bother to go back to the text and verify their selection before picking an answer choice.

D   **Direct Contradiction:** The first part of this choice seems to work with the text: the phrases we considered above for (B) would also demonstrate a "significant" effect, since "significant" and "dramatic" are synonyms in this context. But the text says Homer still "continued to paint his genre subjects" (24) after his time in Paris. The word "continued" tells us that he was painting the same thing he used to paint, which is the opposite of "abandon[ing] the subjects he'd been painting before his time in Paris," as (D) would require.

ⓘ   *The question includes a citation from the text. The answer must be directly restated or demonstrated in the cited text, or in the text closely surrounding the cited text. (See "The General Process for Answering ACT Reading Questions," p. 57.)*

Subjective Phrases to Ignore: "main"

F ✓   **Correct:** The text says that, in Maine, Homer created "his greatest paintings" (69-70). This demonstrates the idea that those paintings are "the culmination of his artistic skills," because a "culmination" is the fullest realization of something. (See the note below for a discussion of the word "culmination.")

G   **Reasonable Statement Not in the Text:** An untrained test-taker might think this is a good subjective analysis of the kind of painting described in the passage, but the last paragraph never actually says anything about "the human spirit," as this choice would require (in fact, it never even mentions Homer's personal spirit). (See the note below for ideas on working around the word "grandeur.")

H   **Confused Relationships:** The text does say that Homer used "graphic shapes and…directional lines" (78-79) to depict the sea, but the text never says this is the "most effective way to depict water," as (H) would require. (No part of the passage mentions whether any painting technique is "effective," or even what it would mean for a technique to be "effective.")

J   **Confused Relationships:** The author does talk about Homer's "greatest paintings" (69-70) involving the "sea" (74), and he also mentions two specific paintings, *Eastern Point* and *Cannon Rock* (76-77), as evidence of the "lasting effect" (80) that *Japanese printmaking* had on *Homer's work*—not that *viewing Homer's paintings* had on the *author*. So most of the individual concepts from (J) are present somewhere in the text: "two [paintings]," "famous paintings," "paintings of the sea," and a "lasting effect." But the relationships of those concepts in (J) has nothing in common with their relationships in the passage, so (J) is wrong. Beyond that, the last paragraph never mentions the author, or anything having any effect on the author, in any way. This is a classic example of the kind of wrong answer that confuses concepts from the passage in the hopes of trapping an untrained test-taker who hasn't read carefully enough.

Note   Many people won't know the words "culmination" and "grandeur" before answering this question, but it's still possible to tell that (F) must be correct. One way to arrive at this conclusion is to start by realizing that (G), (H), and (J) must all be wrong for the reasons noted above (note that (G) must be wrong no matter what "grandeur" means, because nothing in the last paragraph discusses the human spirit). We could also recognize that the word "culmination" is attached to the phrase "artistic skills" by the preposition "of," which means that (F) can be right if "culmination" goes along with the ideas of "great[ness]" (69) and "fam[e]" (85) from the passage. Since we can see that it's possible for (F) to be right but impossible for the other choices to be right, we know that (F) is the answer, even if we don't know the words "culmination" and "grandeur."

ⓘ   *The prompt often mentions describing the passage without a line citation. The answer must still be restated or demonstrated by some specific part of the text. (See "What about Questions without Citations?" on p. 57.)*

▶   **Where to look in the text:** Skim for "Tynemouth." Also, if you've read most of the passage and haven't yet encountered the relevant text, focus on the parts of the passage you haven't read yet.

A   **Barely Relevant:** The text never says that Tynemouth originally inspired Homer to be a painter, nor that Homer had ever been to Tynemouth before.

B   **Reasonable Statement Not in the Text:** An untrained test-taker might naturally assume that a city like Paris could be distracting for an artist, but the text never actually says that Homer found Paris distracting, nor that he went to Tynemouth to escape distraction. Either of these issues is enough to make (B) wrong.

C   **Reasonable Statement Not in the Text:** An untrained test-taker might imagine the Jersey coast could be crowded (especially if he watched MTV in elementary school—does anybody still do that? the authors of this book don't know because they're old now). But the text never actually says the coast was crowded, nor that Homer wanted a break from the Jersey coast. As with (B), either issue would be enough by itself to make this choice wrong.

D ✓ **Correct:** The text says, "it is possible that [Homer] was searching for a town filled with the type of tourists and bathers that made his paintings of the Jersey shore successful back home" (30-33), which directly restates the idea that he "hoped to find the kinds of subjects he had depicted in some of his earlier popular paintings" as (D) requires: "hoped to find" restates "was searching for," "kinds" restates "types," "subjects" restates "tourists and bathers," and "popular" restates "successful."

Note   The phrases "speculates" and "may have" in the prompt aren't subjective here, even though they would be subjective in the prompts of most ACT Reading questions. This is because the third paragraph does involve the author literally speculating about why Homer went to Tynemouth: the author says Homer's reasons are "unknown" (28) and that it's "possible" (30) the decision was motivated by the subject matter of his work. (This is a very nit-picky distinction to make when discussing the design of this question, and most test-takers wouldn't notice that we didn't point out the phrases "speculates" and "may have" as words that could be ignored when approaching this question. But we wanted to point it out for the benefit of those readers who are interested in a complete and accurate understanding of all aspects of the ACT.)

ⓘ   *The prompt often mentions describing the passage without a line citation. The answer must still be restated or demonstrated by some specific part of the text. (See "What about Questions without Citations?" on p. 57.)*

▶   **Where to look in the text:** Skim for "Prouts Neck." Also, if you've read most of the passage and haven't yet encountered the relevant text, focus on the parts of the passage you haven't read yet.

F   **Reasonable Statement Not in the Text:** An untrained test-taker might assume that poor sales would make a painter "irritable," as (F) requires, but the text never discusses how well Homer's paintings sold, so this choice can't be right. (Even terms like "successful" (32-33) and "famous" (85) don't literally indicate that the paintings sold well—they may have simply been successful with critics and famous among other artists, without ever selling well.)

G   **Reasonable Statement Not in the Text:** An untrained test-taker might imagine this would make a painter of outdoor scenes "irritable," but the text doesn't discuss storms stopping Homer from painting; it doesn't even say that he painted outdoors (in fact, line 58 says he "built a studio with an ocean view" rather than painting outside).

H   **Confused Relationships:** The text describes Homer's fascination with the sea, and with fisherman and their families using boats, but it never actually mentions the idea of Homer himself going boating—let alone the idea of rough seas preventing him from doing so—which means this choice isn't restated or demonstrated by the text.

J ✓ **Correct:** The text explicitly says, "when [Homer] was working...he could be extremely short-tempered when interrupted" (65-67), and we know from the passage that Homer's work was "painting," as (J) requires. This literally restates the idea that "Homer could be irritable when he was interrupted while painting," as reflected in the prompt and (J), so (J) is right.

ⓘ   *The prompt often mentions describing the passage without a line citation. The answer must still be restated or demonstrated by some specific part of the text. (See "What about Questions without Citations?" on p. 57.)*

Subjective Phrases to Ignore: "best"

A   **Barely Relevant:** The text doesn't debate the existence of exoplanets, or mention anything about the possibility of exoplanets not existing; instead, it states in the first paragraph that many such planets have already been identified, and never mentions anyone doubting that possibility, or any evidence contradicting it.

B ✓ **Correct:** The text starts by saying that "new worlds are being discovered every week" (3-4), and then describes several examples of these newly-discovered planets in the first paragraph. Then the text mentions that scientists want to find "planets resembling Earth" (19), and discusses whether the "Doppler technique" (38) can be used to find "an Earth" (43) at a distance to its star that's similar to the distance between Earth and the Sun. In the last paragraph, the text mentions the idea of "discover[ing] a rocky planet roughly the size of Earth orbiting in the habitable zone" (81-82). So we can see that the passage demonstrates exactly the organization described in (B): it first discusses the "search for planets" in general, and then focuses "on the search for planets like our own."

C **Barely Relevant:** The text never "defines" what planets are in any way, as this choice would require, so it's wrong.

D **Barely Relevant:** This choice may be tempting to an untrained test-taker if she knew that "Icarus" (6) was a figure from Greek mythology, or that "Saturn" (7) and "Jupiter" (10) were figures from Roman mythology. But the question of whether a "refer[ence] to mythology" appears in the text doesn't actually matter, because the text never describes "exoplanets the size of Earth or smaller," as (D) would require; the smallest exoplanet whose size is mentioned in the text is still "70% larger than Earth" (59). So we know (D) is wrong.

▌ Test 1, Question 32 (Test 2 in the 2020-2021 Red Book—see page 23 for more)　　　TYPE: DESCRIBE THE PASSAGE

ⓘ　　*The prompt often mentions describing the passage without a line citation. The answer must still be restated or demonstrated by some specific part of the text. (See "What about Questions without Citations?" on p. 57.)*

▶ **Where to look in the text:** Skim for quotation marks, question marks, or any other typography that might suggest a rhetorical question or excerpt.

F **Barely Relevant:** We can tell that the text doesn't contain any questions at all, since there are no question marks in the passage. This means it can't possibly contain any rhetorical questions.

G ✓ **Correct:** The text demonstrates the use of figurative language when it compares searching for an Earth-like planet to "trying to see a firefly in a fireworks display" (24-25), and measuring that planet's gravitational pull to "listening for a cricket in a tornado" (26-27). We know these phrases aren't literal because the universe isn't a fireworks display or a tornado, so the process of looking for an Earth-like planet can't literally involve dealing with a fireworks display or a tornado.

H **Barely Relevant:** Any excerpts from other writings would have to include quotation marks, or be set off with special margins, or be indicated in some other way by the typography on the page. The only thing like that in the passage are the quotation marks around the terms "exoplanets" (5), "hot Saturn" (7), "hot Jupiter" (10), and "floaters" (17). The passage doesn't say that those terms were excerpts from anyone else's writings, let alone from "the writings of astronauts," as (H) would require.

J **Direct Contradiction:** This choice has the same basic problem as (H): the passage doesn't indicate a source for any of the quoted phrases in the text, so this choice can't be right, since it mentions a source for those phrases.

▌ Test 1, Question 33 (Test 2 in the 2020-2021 Red Book—see page 23 for more)　　　TYPE: CITATION QUESTION

ⓘ　　*The question includes a citation from the text. The answer must be directly restated or demonstrated in the cited text, or in the text closely surrounding the cited text. (See "The General Process for Answering ACT Reading Questions," p. 57.)*

A **Barely Relevant:** It's true that the passage discusses "equipment used to locate previously unidentified planets," as we see in (A), and some test-takers might think those pieces of equipment could be called "exotica." But the word "such" (18) must refer to an idea that has already appeared in the text, and the notion of "sophisticated equipment" from (A) doesn't show up in the passage until the phrase "pushing technology to the limits" in line 27. The word "such" from line 18 can't refer to an idea that hasn't been introduced yet, which means (A) must be wrong. See the discussion of (D) for more.

B **Confused Relationships:** An untrained test-taker may accidentally think that the phrases "hot Saturn" (7) and "hot Jupiter" (10) are references to planets in "our own solar system," as (B) requires, but the passage makes it clear that "hot Saturn" is "whirling around its [own] parent star" (7-8), and "hot Jupiter" is "circling another star" (9). So the text never specifically mentions the Jupiter and Saturn in our own solar system, as (B) would require.

C **Off by One or Two Words:** The text leading up to line 18 does include "claims about planets far from Earth," as (C) would require, but the author never says anything to indicate that these claims are "overblown." This single word that isn't literally restated or demonstrated by the text is enough to make (C) wrong.

D ✓ **Correct:** As we saw in our discussion of (A), the word "such" (18) must refer to an idea that has already appeared in the text, or that appears in the same sentence as the word "such" itself. The text before line 18 mentions a planet where a year "lasts less than three days" (8-9), a planet "whose upper atmosphere is being blasted off to form a gigantic, comet-like tail" (10-12), and "three benighted planets…orbiting…a once mighty star…the size of a city" (12-15). These phrases appear before the term "such exotica" and demonstrate the idea of "planets and solar systems vastly unlike Earth and its solar system," as (D) requires, so (D) is right. See the note below for more.

Note　Some untrained test-takers will feel like they're unable to answer this question because they don't know the word "exotica." But we never actually need to know the word "exotica" in order to answer this question! Instead, all we need to do is identify the only choice that's literally restated or demonstrated by the part of the text before line 18. When test day

---

comes, don't worry if you can't immediately identify the meanings of every word on the page, because you'll often find that you can still identify the right answer with total certainty anyway.

Test 1, Question 34 (Test 2 in the 2020-2021 Red Book—see page 23 for more)   **TYPE: CITATION QUESTION**

ⓘ   *The question includes a citation from the text. The answer must be directly restated or demonstrated in the cited text, or in the text closely surrounding the cited text. (See "The General Process for Answering ACT Reading Questions," p. 57.)*

Subjective Phrases to Ignore: "main"

F   **Reasonable Statement Not in the Text:** An untrained test-taker might assume that scientists would be disappointed by their inability to find life on an exoplanet, but the paragraph never actually says that anything has "disappointed scientists," as (F) would require.

G   **Confused Relationships:** The second paragraph mentions "planets...orbiting their stars" (19-20), but it never says that any exoplanets themselves were once suspected of being stars, as this choice requires.

H   **Barely Relevant:** The second paragraph never says anything at all about planets spinning at the same speed as Earth, as this choice would require—in fact, it never mentions spinning at all. (This choice may attract untrained test-takers who assume that "orbiting...at just the right distance" (19-20) is the same thing as spinning at the same rate that Earth spins, but there's no reason to make that assumption: orbiting and spinning are different concepts, and distance isn't the same thing as the rate at which an object spins.)

J   ✓   **Correct:** The second paragraph says that planets like Earth are "inconspicuous" (23), which literally restates the idea of being "extremely hard to detect" from (J). But even if we didn't know the word "inconspicuous," we could still see that the author says our planet is "dim" (23) and that trying to find it would be like "trying to see a firefly in a fireworks display" (24-25) or "like listening for a cricket in a tornado" (26-27), which demonstrates the idea of being "extremely hard to detect."

Test 1, Question 35 (Test 2 in the 2020-2021 Red Book—see page 23 for more)   **TYPE: DESCRIBE THE PASSAGE**

ⓘ   *The prompt often mentions describing the passage without a line citation. The answer must still be restated or demonstrated by some specific part of the text. (See "What about Questions without Citations?" on p. 57.)*

▶   **Where to look in the text:** Skim for "Doppler" and "spectroscopic."

A   **Confused Relationships:** The text says the Doppler technique analyzes starlight "for evidence...[of] the gravitational pull of [the star's] planets" (35-37). (A) does mention "light," but it describes the "intensity" of that light reaching Earth. Since the text doesn't mention the *intensity* of light in connection with the Doppler technique, the passage fails to restate or demonstrate (A) exactly, which means (A) is wrong.

B   ✓   **Correct:** As we saw in the explanation for (A), the text tells us that the Doppler technique uses light to detect "evidence...[of] the gravitational pull" (35-37) of a planet on its sun, exactly as restated in (B).

C   **Barely Relevant:** The passage never mentions anything about the speed of rotation of any planet. (The passage does mention the speed of orbits, as in lines 7-9, but this isn't the same as rotation on an axis.)

D   **Barely Relevant:** This choice's idea of an exoplanet's "former sun" seems to restate an idea from earlier in the passage that has nothing to do with the Doppler technique described in line 34. (That idea appears in lines 15-17: "untold numbers of worlds have...been flung out of their systems to become "floaters" that wander in eternal darkness.") The discussion of the spectroscopic Doppler technique doesn't mention anything about any "former sun," so (D) can't be the right answer to this question

---

Test 1, Question 36 (Test 2 in the 2020-2021 Red Book—see page 23 for more)   **TYPE: DESCRIBE THE PASSAGE**

ⓘ   *The prompt often mentions describing the passage without a line citation. The answer must still be restated or demonstrated by some specific part of the text. (See "What about Questions without Citations?" on p. 57.)*

▶   **Where to look in the text:** Skim for "Kepler." If you've read some of the passage already and haven't found the relevant text, look in the parts of the passage you haven't read yet.

F   **Barely Relevant:** The idea of water not being "baked away" or "frozen into ice" appears in lines 83-84, but the passage never makes any connection between the state of water on a planet and the "Kepler method" from the prompt.

G   **Direct Contradiction:** The text says that the Kepler method involves detecting "the slight dimming [of starlight] that could signal the transit of a planet" (69-70). But (G) talks about "uninterrupted light," which is the opposite of light that's dimmed. (G) also mentions "light from the supposed planet," not the "light of...stars" (65-66).

H   **Direct Contradiction:** The text says that the scientists look for "slight dimming" (69) in the light, not "identical results" in the images as (H) requires. Further, the text says that the Kepler method involves taking pictures "every 30 minutes" (65), not "24 hours apart" as (H) requires.

J   ✓   **Correct:** The text says that the Kepler method involves looking for "slight dimming" (69) in the light coming from stars, because that dimming "could signal the transit of a planet" (69-70). The text further states that "scientists won't announce the presence of a planet until they have seen it transit at least three times" (74-76). This literally restates the idea that there must be "three occurrences of a slight dimming in a star" to indicate the presence of a planet, as (J) requires.

ⓘ   *The prompt often mentions describing the passage without a line citation. The answer must still be restated or demonstrated by some specific part of the text. (See "What about Questions without Citations?" on p. 57.)*

▶   **Where to look in the text:** Skim for one of the numbers from the answer choices. You may also have encountered the relevant text when you answered question 35.

A   **Off by One or Two Words:** The text says that "370 'exoplanets'" (5) have been "identified" (4), but it doesn't say that each of these planets has been photographed, which is what the prompt specifically asked about.

B   **Confused Relationships:** The text says that the Kepler satellite includes a camera with a ".95 meter aperture and a 95-megapixel detector" (63-64), but the text never mentions the idea of 95 *planets* being photographed, as (B) requires.

C ✓   **Correct:** The text says that "only 11 exoplanets…have as yet had their pictures taken" (31-33), which matches (C) exactly.

D   **Direct Contradiction:** As we saw in the explanation for (C), 11 exoplanets have had their picture taken. This choice might have been tempting for untrained test-takers who failed to find a reference in the passage to planets being photographed, and who then assumed the number must be zero—but in order for (D) to be correct according to the ACT's rules of literal-minded restatement and demonstration, the text would specifically need to state that zero exoplanets had been photographed, which it doesn't do!

ⓘ   *The prompt often mentions describing the passage without a line citation. The answer must still be restated or demonstrated by some specific part of the text. (See "What about Questions without Citations?" on p. 57.)*

▶   **Where to look in the text:** Skim for "Kepler," "100,000," and "150." Also, if you've read most of the passage and haven't yet encountered the relevant text, focus on the parts of the passage you haven't read yet.

F ✓   **Correct:** The text specifically says that the Kepler "captur[es] the light of more than 100,000 stars in a single patch of sky" (65-66), which is a literal restatement of (F).

G   **Barely Relevant:** The text only says the Kepler can "detect the slight dimming" (69) of a star; the text never connects the idea of this dimming to the idea of "determin[ing] distance," as (G) would require.

H   **Confused Relationships:** The first paragraph does mention a "star 150 light-years out" (9-10), but the passage never describes the Kepler (or anything else) traveling that distance away from Earth, so (H) isn't restated or demonstrated by the passage.

J   **Confused Relationships:** The last paragraph mentions the idea of water being present on other planets, but the passage never actually says that the Kepler can detect the presence of water, so (J) isn't restated or demonstrated by the passage.

ⓘ   *The prompt often mentions describing the passage without a line citation. The answer must still be restated or demonstrated by some specific part of the text. (See "What about Questions without Citations?" on p. 57.)*

▶   **Where to look in the text:** Skim for "Deneb," "Vega," and "70." You may also have encountered the relevant text when you answered question 38.

A ✓   **Correct:** The text says that the Kepler examines an area of the sky "between the bright stars Deneb and Vega" (66-67). If the area of the sky examined by Kepler is between those two stars, then those two stars must literally be "at the edges of the area," just as (A) requires.

B   **Confused Relationships:** The previous paragraph does mention a planet "only 70 percent larger than Earth" (59), but Deneb and Vega themselves are described as "bright stars" (67), not planets, so (B) must be wrong.

C   **Barely Relevant:** Deneb and Vega are described as "bright stars" (67), not scientists.

D   **Reasonable Statement Not in the Text:** Deneb and Vega are described as "bright stars" (67). Nothing on the page indicates that they aren't stars anymore. (Some test-takers may know that light takes a long time to reach Earth from stars in other solar systems, and that it's possible that Deneb and Vega may not exist anymore even though we can still see the light coming from them—but, as trained test-takers, we know that outside scientific knowledge isn't relevant on the ACT Reading section, and we always answer ACT Reading questions based only on the words that are printed on the page.)

ⓘ   *The prompt often mentions describing the passage without a line citation. The answer must still be restated or demonstrated by some specific part of the text. (See "What about Questions without Citations?" on p. 57.)*

▶   **Where to look in the text:** Skim for "Kepler" and "Doppler" close to each other. You may also have encountered the relevant text when you answered questions 31 and 36.

F   **Barely Relevant:** The length of a particular planet's year is mentioned in lines 8-9, but the discussion of "combining Kepler results with Doppler observations" (78-79) isn't mentioned in connection with the length of any planet's year.

G   **Confused Relationships:** The text does mention the idea of a planet being in the "habitable zone" (82), which is related to a planet's distance from its star. But the text never actually says that "combining Kepler results with Doppler observations" (78-79) provides any information about distance, so (G) can't be right.

H ✓ **Correct:** The text specifically says that "combining Kepler results with Doppler observations" (78-79) might allow scientists "to determine the diameters and masses of transiting planets" (79-80), which directly restates the ideas from (H) in combination with the prompt.

J **Barely Relevant:** The passage mentions the distances of a few different objects from Earth. But the passage never says that "combining Kepler results with Doppler observations" (78-79) provides any information about that distance, so (J) is wrong.

TEST 2 (TEST 3 IN 2020-2021 RED BOOK)

Test 2, Question 1 (Test 3 in the 2020-2021 Red Book—see page 23 for more)   **TYPE: DESCRIBE THE PASSAGE**

ⓘ *The prompt often mentions describing the passage without a line citation. The answer must still be restated or demonstrated by some specific part of the text. (See "What about Questions without Citations?" on p. 57.)*

▶ **Where to look in the text:** Skim for "Crown."

A ✓ **Correct:** The text demonstrates that Crown was "tidy," as the stereotype requires, when it describes the care he takes in his appearance (he "kept [his hair] shining" (14), his mustache "showed careful attention" (16-17), etc.) and his devotion to the concept of order (21), which is a synonym for tidiness. The text restates the idea that Crown was "meticulous," as the stereotype requires, when it talks about his devotion to "accuracy" (24). Finally, the text restates the idea that Crown was "industrious," as the stereotype also requires, when it talks about his "cheerful acceptance…of hard work" (79-80), and when it says that the idea of "industry" (86-87) being necessary in order to reap a "reward" (87) was "in him deeper than the marrow of his bones" (90-91). Since Crown exhibits all the characteristics of the stereotype in the prompt, (A) is right to say that the description of Crown "firmly reinforces the stereotype."

B **Confused Relationships:** As discussed in the explanation for (A), the passage reinforces the stereotype throughout; it never says anything that would contradict or weaken the stereotype, as (B) would require.

C **Barely Relevant:** As we saw for (A) and for (B), the passage reinforces the aspects of the stereotype related to tidiness and industriousness—not just the meticulous aspect—and the passage never says anything to weaken the idea that any part of the stereotype applies to Crown.

D **Barely Relevant:** The text never indicates who keeps Crown's office clean, so, based on the passage, there's no way to say whether Crown "expects others to do the tidying up," as (D) would require.

Test 2, Question 2 (Test 3 in the 2020-2021 Red Book—see page 23 for more)   **TYPE: CITATION QUESTION**

ⓘ *The question includes a citation from the text. The answer must be directly restated or demonstrated in the cited text, or in the text closely surrounding the cited text. (See "The General Process for Answering ACT Reading Questions," p. 57.)*

Subjective Phrases to Ignore: "reasonably be inferred"

F **Confused Relationships:** The text says the appointment in the third paragraph is "at twelve" (17). In normal English, the phrase "at twelve" indicates something is happening at twelve o'clock on the same day the phrase "at twelve" is being said (as long as no other day is mentioned in connection with the phrase, which is the case here). The text says the meeting in the first paragraph is "this Friday" (5). In normal English, "this Friday" means the soonest upcoming Friday—a day in the future. So the "appointment" is happening on the same day that Crown is "work[ing] in his office" (8), and the meeting is happening on the next Friday, which is some day in the near future. That means (F) can't be right.

G **Direct Contradiction:** As we saw in the explanation for (F), the text says the meeting is happening a few days after the appointment, not the other way around. This choice will attract a lot of test-takers who don't read the passage carefully enough, or who misremember the prompt and think it's asking us to describe when the *appointment* happens in relation to the *meeting*, rather than the other way around.

H ✓ **Correct:** As we saw for (F), the text clearly says that the meeting is happening a few days in the future—that is, on the soonest Friday after Crown is "work[ing] in his office" (8)—and the appointment is happening on the same day that Crown is "work[ing] in his office" (8). This means the meeting must happen some number of days after the appointment, and (J) is the only choice that allows for that possibility.

J **Barely Relevant:** As we saw in the explanation for (F) and (H), the text says clearly that the meeting is happening after the appointment—but the text never indicates that "years" will pass before the meeting happens, which would contradict the use of the word "this" in the phrase "this Friday" (5).

> **Note**   It's not possible to know the specific number of days until the meeting on Friday (4-5): for all we know from the text, "this Friday" might be up to 6 days away. But only (H) allows for the possibility of "this Friday" occurring at some point in the future that's closer than the passing of multiple years, so (H) must be right.

ⓘ   *The prompt often mentions describing the passage without a line citation. The answer must still be restated or demonstrated by some specific part of the text. (See "What about Questions without Citations?" on p. 57.)*

▶   **Where to look in the text:** Skim for "Zwick" and "Crown."

A   **Reasonable Statement Not in the Text:** The text describes Crown as a serious businessman who believes in "order" (21), "accuracy" (24), and "modernity" (47). If this were a classroom discussion, we might easily imagine that Crown and his "chief clerk, Stefan Zwick" (60-61) would both be "fastidious about meeting a deadline," as this choice requires... but this is the ACT Reading section, and the idea of meeting a deadline isn't actually discussed anywhere in the text, which means this choice must be wrong.

B ✓   **Correct:** The text says that Crown "was always searching for the newest methods" (50-51) to improve his business. When Crown suggested Zwick learn to use a typewriter, Zwick replied "a quill pen suits me perfectly" (64), and Crown objected that a quill pen would "make[] Crown's look old-fashioned" (66-67). So the text clearly demonstrates that Crown likes modern equipment and doesn't like to be old-fashioned, while Zwick initially prefers his quill pen to the new typewriter. This shows clearly that Zwick is "less inclined to embrace new technology" than Crown, just as (B) requires.

C   **Off by One or Two Words:** In the text, Zwick does "state[s] his preferences to his superiors," as (C) describes, by telling Crown he'd rather not use a typewriter in lines 63-64. But the text never mentions Crown interacting with anyone superior to himself, so we have no basis for comparing the two characters in that way. (By the way, the passage does mention Crown begging the owner of another business to teach him to use an abacus in lines 36-38, but the text never says the owner was in charge of Crown, or that Crown worked in the laundry—and, even if Crown had worked in the laundry for the owner, the text still doesn't say anything about Crown being "afraid to state his preferences" to his superiors.)

D   **Confused Relationships:** The text does demonstrate that Crown is "concerned with the company's public image" when he says it "doesn't suit [Crown]" (66) for his business to look "old-fashioned" (67). But the text never says whether Zwick cares about how people see the company, so we have no literal basis for comparing Zwick to Crown in this regard, as (D) would require. (Some untrained test-takers may subjectively interpret Zwick's resistance to the typewriter as a sign that Zwick doesn't care about the company's image, but the text only says that Crown views the typewriter as a reflection of the company—it's very possible from the text that Zwick never thought of the typewriter as a reflection on the company, and simply didn't want to learn to use a new technology. Further, even if Zwick had viewed the typewriter as a reflection on the company, this choice would still be wrong because it says Zwick is *more* concerned, and the misreading we just described would make Zwick seem *less* concerned.)

ⓘ   *The question includes a citation from the text. The answer must be directly restated or demonstrated in the cited text, or in the text closely surrounding the cited text. (See "The General Process for Answering ACT Reading Questions," p. 57.)*

▶   **Where to look in the text:** Look in the context immediately surrounding line 72. We may also have encountered the relevant text for this question in finding the relevant text for question 3.

F ✓   **Correct:** The text uses the word "blanched" in line 72 to describe Zwick's reaction. In this context, "blanched" refers to the idea of going pale because you're shocked or upset by something, so the word "blanched" literally demonstrates that Zwick is indignant over what Crown proposes. (Even if we didn't know the word "blanched," we could still see that Zwick must be upset by Crown's proposal of hiring a woman in lines 69-71 because, after Zwick blanches, Crown says that Zwick "leave[s] him no choice," which indicates that Crown is proposing something that Zwick doesn't want. See the note below for more.)

G   **Confused Relationships:** If we didn't read the surrounding text of line 72, we might incorrectly conclude that Zwick was reacting to an actual woman being in his office when he wasn't expecting one. But when we read the lines before and after 72, we can see that Crown has instructed Zwick to "hire one of those young women" (69), because Zwick is "leav[ing] [Crown] no choice" (73) but to do so. So the surrounding text makes it clear that no actual person has shown up at the office unannounced; instead, Crown threatens Zwick with the possibility of a new employee that Zwick doesn't want.

H   **Confused Relationships:** As we saw in the explanation for (G), Zwick is reacting to the *possibility* of a woman being hired. There's never actually a "new employee" in the passage that Zwick could be excited to meet, as (H) would require.

J   **Confused Relationships:** As we saw for (G) and (H), Zwick is reacting to the *possibility* of a woman being hired, so we have no literal textual basis for referring to a "recently hired female coworker," as (J) would require.

Note   As we noted for (F), some test-takers won't be familiar with the word "blanched," so they might be frustrated when they first read the citation for this question. But, as trained test-takers, we know that we can often work around challenging words on the ACT; in this case, it turns out that we can still tell (F) must be right as long as we realize that Crown and Zwick are talking about the proposed possibility of hiring a new person, because (F) is the only choice that reflects the idea of a hypothetical person, as opposed to an actual person who has been hired or come to the office. All of the wrong answers discuss a new, actual, physical person being present in the office, whether as a "surprise visitor," "new employee," or "coworker." If we can read carefully enough to realize that the "woman" in line 72 is never actually present in the office, then we can determine that (F) must be right without knowing the word "blanched." Keep this kind of thing in mind on test day, and don't give up on a question just because it mentions a word you're not familiar with!

Test 2, Question 5 (Test 3 in the 2020-2021 Red Book—see page 23 for more)   **TYPE: CITATION QUESTION**

ⓘ   *The question includes a citation from the text. The answer must be directly restated or demonstrated in the cited text, or in the text closely surrounding the cited text. (See "The General Process for Answering ACT Reading Questions," p. 57.)*

A   **Barely Relevant:** The text does tell us that Crown's "weekly trim" is happening relatively soon—at "twelve" (17), in fact—but the prompt asks about "the passage's opening," and the "weekly trim" isn't mentioned until the third paragraph, in lines 17-18. So (A) can't be relevant to the question. (Furthermore, the passage never says Crown is preoccupied with being on time for the trim anyway, so (A) would also have to be wrong for that reason, even if the trim were mentioned in the part of the passage described in the prompt.)

B   **Confused Relationships:** The text says that Crown "hadn't hesitated to install expensive pasteurization equipment" (52-53). So Crown has already installed that equipment before the passage begins, which means he can't be worried about "whether to install" it at the start of the passage, as (B) would require. Further, the question asks about "the passage's opening," but the installation of the equipment isn't mentioned until lines 52-53—and, as we see in lines 50-54, Crown was never worried about installing the equipment in the first place, because he always uses modern technology. Any of these issues by itself would be enough to make (B) wrong.

C   **Barely Relevant:** The question asks about "the passage's opening," but Zwick isn't even mentioned until line 61. Further, the text doesn't indicate that Zwick demonstrates "impertinent behavior" at any point—in fact, the first time Zwick is quoted, he specifically speaks "respectfully" (63). Any of these issues would be enough by itself to make this choice wrong.

D ✓   **Correct:** In the "passage's opening," which the prompt refers to, we see that Crown's "most immediate" (3) worry was "a civic responsibility" (3-4), which restates (D) exactly.

Test 2, Question 6 (Test 3 in the 2020-2021 Red Book—see page 23 for more)   **TYPE: DESCRIBE THE PASSAGE**

ⓘ   *The prompt often mentions describing the passage without a line citation. The answer must still be restated or demonstrated by some specific part of the text. (See "What about Questions without Citations?" on p. 57.)*

▶   **Where to look in the text:** Skim for "Crown," as well as words related to "student" from the prompt or "ciphering" and "success" from the answer choices

F   **Direct Contradiction:** The text calls Crown a "mediocre student" (33), which is the opposite of being "exceptionally gifted," so (F) is wrong.

G ✓   **Correct:** The text says Crown was a "mediocre student" (33), but "at ciphering he was a prodigy" (34). This exactly restates (G), so (G) is right.

H   **Reasonable Statement Not in the Text:** As we saw in the discussion of (G), Crown *was* a better student in some areas than others, but the text doesn't say that Crown applied himself in some areas of study more than he did in other areas of study, so this choice has no textual basis, even if some untrained test-takers will automatically assume that students do better in areas where they apply themselves. (The text does mention Crown begging someone to teach him to use an abacus in lines 37-38, but that happened when Crown was "in America" (37), which was after his education "in Germany" (32), meaning Crown was no longer a student at that time. And, even if Crown had been a student, the incident with the abacus would only show that Crown was passionate about learning the abacus; the text still never mentions Crown doing poorly in some area of study where he didn't apply himself, which (H) would require.)

J   **Barely Relevant:** As we saw for (H), the text *does* mention Crown acquiring a "counting aid" as described in the prompt, when he learned to use an abacus "in America" (37). But, when Crown was a student, he was still "in Germany" (32), so the abacus didn't have an impact on his performance as a student. On top of that, the text says Crown was always a "prodigy" (34) with numbers and could "do calculations in his head, with astonishing speed" (35-36), which contradicts the idea that a counting aid would have helped him anyway. Any of these issues is enough to make (J) wrong.

Test 2, Question 7 (Test 3 in the 2020-2021 Red Book—see page 23 for more)   **TYPE: DESCRIBE THE PASSAGE**

ⓘ   *The prompt often mentions describing the passage without a line citation. The answer must still be restated or demonstrated by some specific part of the text. (See "What about Questions without Citations?" on p. 57.)*

Subjective Phrases to Ignore: "most" "typically"

▶   **Where to look in the text:** Skim for question marks.

A   **Reasonable Statement Not in the Text:** An untrained test-taker might imagine that a boss would ask an employee a question like this, but no statement in the text literally restates or demonstrates the idea that Crown asked his employees about their weekends, so (A) can't be correct.

B   **Reasonable Statement Not in the Text:** This choice has the same problem as (A): the text never restates or demonstrates the idea that Crown asked about repairing equipment like typewriters, so (B) must be wrong, even if this question might sound reasonable to an untrained test-taker.

C ✓ **Correct:** The text says that "questions [Crown] asked of his employees often involved numbers" (42-43). It then provides examples of Crown's questions about things like temperatures, populations, amounts of things, costs, etc.—that is, questions whose answers would involve numbers (43-46). This choice, which asks about the "figure" by which sales might increase, is the only choice that involves numbers, so it's the right answer.

D **Reasonable Statement Not in the Text:** This choice has the same problem as (A) and (B): it sounds like the kind of thing that a boss might ask in the real world, but no part of the text indicates that Crown ever asks this kind of question, so (D) is wrong.

Test 2, Question 8 (Test 3 in the 2020-2021 Red Book—see page 23 for more)   **TYPE: DESCRIBE THE PASSAGE**

ⓘ   *The prompt often mentions describing the passage without a line citation. The answer must still be restated or demonstrated by some specific part of the text. (See "What about Questions without Citations?" on p. 57.)*

▶ **Where to look in the text:** Skim for the words in the answer choices. Also, we may have encountered the relevant text for this question in finding the relevant text for question 3.

F **Direct Contradiction:** The text indicates that Crown thinks a quill pen looks "old-fashioned" (67), and he wants Zwick to learn to use a typewriter instead. The text never restates or demonstrates the idea that Crown thinks a *typewriter* is "increasingly obsolete," as the prompt requires.

G **Direct Contradiction:** The text says Crown "insisted that modern machines be used in the office" (56-57), and goes on to say that Crown "could hear the pleasing ratchet noise of a mechanical adding machine" (57-58). The ideas of Crown liking modern machines in his office, and being pleased by the sound of an adding machine in his office, demonstrate that Crown thinks adding machines are modern, not "increasingly obsolete" as the prompt requires.

H ✓ **Correct:** The text indicates that Crown thinks a quill pen "makes Crown's look old-fashioned" (66-67). Since "old-fashioned" is a synonym for "obsolete," (H) is directly restated in the text, and must be the right answer.

J **Reasonable Statement Not in the Text:** The text says Crown learned to use an abacus when he first came to America (36-38), and line 58 refers to a mechanical adding machine in Crown's office, so some untrained test-takers may assume that Crown thinks the usefulness of the abacus has been exceeded by the usefulness of the mechanical adding machine, which would make the abacus obsolete in Crown's eyes. But, as trained test-takers, we know that the answer needs to be literally demonstrated or restated in the passage, and the passage never actually says Crown thinks the abacus is "increasingly obsolete," as the prompt requires, so (J) is wrong. (The text does say the abacus is "ancient" (39), but a technology can exist for a long time without being obsolete, like the wheel or the lever; for (J) to be correct, the text would specifically need to state that Crown thinks the abacus should no longer be used, which it never does.)

> **Note** Many untrained test-takers will be confused by the fact that all of the technologies in the answer choices are obsolete by today's standards. But as trained test-takers, we know that we only need to focus on the literal meaning of the text, and ignore our own ideas about the passage. When we do that, it becomes clear that Crown only refers to one object as "old-fashioned," which means (H) must be right.

Test 2, Question 9 (Test 3 in the 2020-2021 Red Book—see page 23 for more)   **TYPE: DESCRIBE THE PASSAGE**

ⓘ   *The prompt often mentions describing the passage without a line citation. The answer must still be restated or demonstrated by some specific part of the text. (See "What about Questions without Citations?" on p. 57.)*

Subjective Phrases to Ignore: "primarily"

▶ **Where to look in the text:** Skim for "principle" from the prompt, and/or for any term related to the disciplines in the answer choices. Also, if we've seen most of the passage at this point but haven't encountered the relevant text for this question, we'll probably find that text in one of the few places we haven't yet looked, which is likely to include the right place—the last paragraph.

A ✓ **Correct:** The text says that "every solid house or building was supported by a strong foundation; and so there was a foundation on which Joe Crown's three principles rested" (76-78). Terms like "solid house," "building," and "foundation" are related to architecture, just as (A) requires.

B **Confused Relationships:** This choice will attract a lot of untrained test-takers, since the passage repeatedly mentions Crown's business and career, and even says that the three principles "ruled Joe Crown's business and personal life" (20-21). But the question asks about "the metaphor" that "describe[s]" the principles, and the "imagery" used in that description; the passage never uses any kind of image or metaphor from the world of business to describe the principles, even though the principles themselves are related to Crown's career. This wrong answer demonstrates, once again, the extreme importance of reading everything very carefully on test day; otherwise, you might not catch the difference between the metaphor used to illustrate the principles, and the thing that the principles are related to, which is the key to realizing why (B) is wrong.

C **Barely Relevant:** The passage never mentions anything related to astronomy, stars, or anything else connected to (C), so (C) must be wrong.

D **Confused Relationships:** The text mentions Crown's literal time in school in lines 32-36. But the passage never says that education is related to Crown's "three principles" (20), and no "metaphor[ical]…image[ry]" from the "discipline" of education appears in the passage, as the prompt would require.

Test 2, Question 10 (Test 3 in the 2020-2021 Red Book—see page 23 for more)   **TYPE: DESCRIBE THE PASSAGE**

ℹ   *The prompt often mentions describing the passage without a line citation. The answer must still be restated or demonstrated by some specific part of the text. (See "What about Questions without Citations?" on p. 57.)*

▶   **Where to look in the text:** Skim for terms related to the words "refrigerators," "cross-stitch," "photographs," and/or "bells" from the answer choices. Also, we may have encountered the relevant text for this question in finding the relevant text for question 9.

F   **Confused Relationships:** The passage mentions Crown "invest[ing] heavily in refrigerated freight cars" (55-56), but never mentions any "outdated refrigerators," so (F) has no literal textual support, and must be wrong.

G   **Confused Relationships:** The text mentions "a small framed motto which [Crown's] wife had…cross-stitch[ed]" (83-84). But the text never tells us the object is "newly hung," as (G) requires; even if it did, whether the object was "newly hung" wouldn't indicate anything about how long "Crown has been in the brewery business," as the prompt requires. Crown could have been in the business for any period of time and still have only chosen to hang the motto recently. Any of these issues by itself would be enough to make (G) wrong.

H ✓   **Correct:** The "photographs" referred to in this choice are described as "fading" (81). The process of a photograph "fading" takes time, so, if Crown has a fading picture of a company picnic, then he must have had his company long enough for the photograph to fade, which means the phrase "fading brown photographs of annual brewery picnics" (81-82) literally demonstrates something about the length of time Crown has had his brewery business, just as the prompt requires.

J   **Barely Relevant:** A bell on a typewriter is mentioned in line 59, but the passage never describes a bell that marked the beginning of Crown's workday "for the last twenty years," as described in this answer choice, so (J) is wrong.

Test 2, Question 11 (Test 3 in the 2020-2021 Red Book—see page 23 for more)   **TYPE: DESCRIBE THE PASSAGE**

ℹ   *The prompt often mentions describing the passage without a line citation. The answer must still be restated or demonstrated by some specific part of the text. (See "What about Questions without Citations?" on p. 57.)*

     Subjective Phrases to Ignore: "best"

▶   **Where to look in the text:** Skim for "William," "Caroline," and/or "comet."

A   **Reasonable Statement Not in the Text:** Some untrained test-takers might assume that William would feel the way that (A) describes if they were going to analyze his character subjectively, as they might in a classroom discussion. But the text never actually mentions any response from William to "Caroline's discovery of a comet" as described in the prompt, so (A) must be wrong since it's not literally reflected in the text.

B   **Confused Relationships:** The text mentions "the verification of Caroline's comet" (89) but never specifically says who verified it. Some untrained test-takers may assume that William did the verification, since the text indicates that Caroline was William's assistant (17-18), but, as trained test-takers, we know that we can't simply assume (B) is right if it's not literally restated or demonstrated in the passage.

C   **Reasonable Statement Not in the Text:** As with (A), some untrained test-takers might imagine that William would resent the recognition of Caroline's discovery. But the text doesn't say that he felt that way, so (C) can't be right.

D ✓   **Correct:** As we saw in the explanations for the other choices, the text never tells us "how William felt about Caroline's discovery," exactly as (D) describes. So (D) is right.

Test 2, Question 12 (Test 3 in the 2020-2021 Red Book—see page 23 for more)   **TYPE: DESCRIBE THE PASSAGE**

ℹ   *The prompt often mentions describing the passage without a line citation. The answer must still be restated or demonstrated by some specific part of the text. (See "What about Questions without Citations?" on p. 57.)*

▶   **Where to look in the text:** Skim for "octagon," or any description of the telescope or discussion of the size of the telescope (which may include numbers).

F   **Confused Relationships:** The text does mention "a series of ladders" (15-16), but it doesn't "compar[e]" anything to that series of ladders, as the prompt requires.

G   **Confused Relationships:** This choice has basically the same issue as (F): the text does mentions "an enormous wooden gantry" (9-10), but it doesn't "compar[e]" anything to that wooden gantry, as the prompt requires, so (G) must be wrong. (G) will attract a lot of untrained test-takers because the word "enormous" is used to describe the gantry, and that may seem to go along with the phrase "emphasizes the large size" in the prompt. But, again, the prompt specifically mentions "comparing the tube's height" to something, and nothing is compared to the gantry, so (G) is wrong.

H   **Confused Relationships:** As we saw with (F) and (G), the text mentions "a series of haylofts" (33-34), but it doesn't compare anything to that series of haylofts.

J ✓   **Correct:** The text says the "telescope" mentioned in the prompt would have an "octagon tube 40 foot long" (6); the text also says, "the forty-foot would be higher than a house" (14). We know the phrase "forty-foot" must describe the octagon tube, because the octagon tube is the only thing in the text described as "40 foot long," which means the author directly compares the "forty-foot" "octagon tube" to a "house," just as (J) and the prompt require.

Test 2, Question 13 (Test 3 in the 2020-2021 Red Book—see page 23 for more)   **TYPE: PURPOSE OF CITED TEXT**

ⓘ *The prompt asks about the purpose or role of a part of the text. The answer must be accurately restated or demonstrated by the relevant text, with no interpretation. (See "What about Main Purpose, Main Idea, Best Description Questions?," p. 58.)*

Subjective Phrases to Ignore: "primary"

A   **Confused Relationships:** The fifth paragraph does say that Caroline "hoped to carry out her comet 'sweeps'" (37), but it never actually describes any "methods" that she uses to do this, as (A) would require.

B ✓ **Correct:** The first four paragraphs mention William a number of times and describe his construction of the telescope, which demonstrates the idea of "William's project" as mentioned in (B). Then this paragraph and much of the remaining passage focuses on "Caroline's own astronomical work," as (B) also requires.

C   **Confused Relationships:** The fifth paragraph does mention that "sheds and stables were...converted into workshops and laboratories" (31-33), and that haylofts above the stables "could be converted into a separate apartment" (34-35). But it never mentions that Caroline herself made any renovations to the stables as (C) says, nor that the renovations were intended "to accommodate William's telescope," as (C) also says. Either issue by itself would be enough to make (C) wrong.

D   **Barely Relevant:** The passage never even mentions William's observation techniques, so there's no literal basis for saying that the text compares Caroline's observation techniques to William's, as (D) would require.

Test 2, Question 14 (Test 3 in the 2020-2021 Red Book—see page 23 for more)   **TYPE: DESCRIBE THE PASSAGE**

ⓘ *The prompt often mentions describing the passage without a line citation. The answer must still be restated or demonstrated by some specific part of the text. (See "What about Questions without Citations?" on p. 57.)*

Subjective Phrases to Ignore: "primarily"

▶   **Where to look in the text:** Skim for "Book of Work Done," and also for an excerpt from a book, which would probably have different formatting from the formatting in the rest of the passage, and/or be surrounded by quotation marks.

F   **Reasonable Statement Not in the Text:** We might imagine that the notes Caroline took would include information about how she determined that her finding was a comet, but the relevant excerpt in lines 81-88 doesn't mention that process, so (F) isn't literally demonstrated in the text, which means it's wrong.

G   **Confused Relationships:** The notes in lines 81-88 use the word "I" several times to describe things that Caroline has done, and the only "observation" mentioned in those lines is "I saw...a comet" (82-84), which is clearly Caroline's observation, not William's—so we can't call these "observation notes...for William," as (G) would require. (The text does refer to Caroline as William's assistant in lines 17-18, but that passing reference has nothing to do with the excerpt referred to in the prompt.)

H ✓ **Correct:** The text just before the excerpt says Caroline's notes convey "her growing excitement" (80), which directly restates the phrase "growing sense of excitement" in (H). The excerpt itself demonstrates no obvious excitement in the entry for August 1st; it then uses all capital letters in the entry for August 2nd to say that the object "IS A COMET" (85), and mentions in the entry for August 3rd that Caroline "did not go to rest" (85-86) until she had written to people to announce the comet. So the excerpt clearly demonstrates Caroline's growing excitement. Either of these things (the restatement in 80 or the demonstration in 81-88) would be enough to establish that (H) is right.

J   **Barely Relevant:** The excerpt mentions "Dr. Blagden" and "Mr. Aubert" (86-87), but it never specifically says those two people played any role "in verifying Caroline's discovery," as (J) would require.

Test 2, Question 15 (Test 3 in the 2020-2021 Red Book—see page 23 for more)   **TYPE: VOCABULARY IN CONTEXT**

ⓘ *The prompt asks about the specific meaning of a word in the passage. The right answer must still be directly restated or demonstrated in the text surrounding the cited word. (See "What about "Vocabulary in Context" Questions?" on p. 59.)*

Subjective Phrases to Ignore: "most nearly"

A ✓ **Correct:** The word "slightest" means something like "very small." The word "finest" in the passage describes "fingertip adjustments" (12), which are contrasted (through the word "but" (11)) to the "enormous wooden gantry" (10) that would need to be turned by "two workmen" (11). Something must be small if it's on the scale of a fingertip, and if it's unlike something so enormous it requires two workmen to be turned. So "slightest" is directly demonstrated by the text, and (A) is right.

B   **Reasonable Statement Not in the Text:** In some other context, the word "finest" might mean something like "most beautiful," which could go along with a word like "fairest." But the passage never mentions anything related to beauty, so (B) can't be right.

C   **Reasonable Statement Not in the Text:** Nothing in the relevant text restates or demonstrates the idea of something being thin, as (C) would require, so it's wrong. Some test-takers might be drawn to this choice because they assume that a finger could be a common example of something long and thin, but this thought process is flawed for at least two reasons. First, the word "finest" in the passage is followed by the word "fingertip," not the word "finger," and fingertips aren't particularly known for being thin. Second, the complete phrase in the prompt being described by the word "finest" is "finest fingertip adjustments," as we noted for (A).

Nothing about the surrounding text demonstrates the idea of a "thin adjustment"—in fact, it's difficult to imagine how the phrase "thin adjustment" could have any real meaning, and it certainly doesn't have any relevance to the passage. So (C) can't be right.

D   **Reasonable Statement Not in the Text:** In another context, the word "finest" could mean something like "best," which would go along with a word like "greatest." But the relevant text doesn't restate or demonstrate the idea of the "fingertip adjustments" being particularly better than other fingertip adjustments, as (D) would require, so it's wrong.

ⓘ   *The prompt often mentions describing the passage without a line citation. The answer must still be restated or demonstrated by some specific part of the text. (See "What about Questions without Citations?" on p. 57.)*

Subjective Phrases to Ignore: "most strongly suggests"

▶   **Where to look in the text:** Skim for "William" and "Caroline" in close proximity to each other. Also, we may have come across the text relevant to this question in answering question 12.

F   **Confused Relationships:** The text doesn't restate or demonstrate the idea that Caroline was communicating with workmen while she was in her booth. The only mention of Caroline communicating with anyone from the booth indicates that she'd be communicating with William: "Astronomer and assistant would be...shouting commands and replies...eventually connected by a metal speaking-tube" (21-24).

G   **Confused Relationships:** The only mentions of Caroline doing calculations say that "she would check over the calculations of William's nebulae by day" (38-39), and that she was "unable to calculate the mathematical coordinates of the [comet]" (73-74). Neither of these statements restates or demonstrates the idea that Caroline "preferred seclusion" when doing the calculations, as (G) requires—or even that she actually did the calculations in the "special booth" (18-19) in the first place.

H   **Barely Relevant:** The text never indicates anything about the size of the "viewing platform" (16), so there's no literal basis for (H).

J ✓ **Correct:** The text mentions that Caroline "would have to be shut in a...booth...to avoid light pollution" (18-19), and that she would have her "lamp,...clocks, and...journals" (20-21) for working. This demonstrates that they wanted to avoid "pollution" (19), or "interfer[ence]" as described in (J), from Caroline's lamp while William used the telescope, just as (J) describes.

ⓘ   *The prompt often mentions describing the passage without a line citation. The answer must still be restated or demonstrated by some specific part of the text. (See "What about Questions without Citations?" on p. 57.)*

Subjective Phrases to Ignore: "most"

▶   **Where to look in the text:** Scan for "The Grove" and "Royal Society." We may also have read the lines relevant to this question's correct answer in answering questions 13 and 16.

A   **Barely Relevant:** The text never discusses the idea of William (or anyone else) being inspired by anything.

B ✓ **Correct:** The text says William's "project required a new house with larger grounds for...the telescope" (25-27), and that they moved to "The Grove" for that purpose. Since the answer to (B) appears in the text in lines 25-27, it's the right answer.

C   **Barely Relevant:** The text does say in lines 73-74 that Caroline was "unable to calculate the mathematical coordinates of the object," but it never says why she was unable to do that, as (C) would require.

D   **Barely Relevant:** The text says in lines 89-91 that the "verification of Caroline's comet was achieved much more rapidly than William's discovery of the planet Uranus had been," but it never says how long that actually took, as (D) would require.

Note   Untrained test-takers might be frustrated by the idea of trying to figure out which question is "most directly answered" in the text, as the prompt seems to require. But, as trained test-takers, we know—as soon as we read the prompt!—that only one of the choices will be answered at all. On test day, remember that the ACT Reading section will never require you to pick between two choices that are arguably equally good answers to the prompt. Don't let the ACT fool you when it deliberately tries to mislead test-takers with phrases like "most directly."

ⓘ   *The prompt often mentions describing the passage without a line citation. The answer must still be restated or demonstrated by some specific part of the text. (See "What about Questions without Citations?" on p. 57.)*

Subjective Phrases to Ignore: "most reasonably"

▶   **Where to look in the text:** Skim for "two-foot" or "Newtonian." Also, we may have come across the text relevant to this question in answering question 13.

F ✓ **Correct:** The text says that the reflector William built appeared "much fatter, heavier, and stubbier than normal reflectors of this type," and that this difference was "because of its large aperture" (42-44). If the large aperture is what makes it look different from "normal telescopes," then William's reflector must have a larger aperture than "normal telescopes" have, exactly as (F) requires.

G   **Barely Relevant:** The text does say that the telescope was "suspended from...the box-frame" (44-45), but it doesn't say that this box-frame was smaller than normal, as (G) would require.

H   **Direct Contradiction:** The text says, "the magnification was comparatively low at twenty-four times" (51-52), so William's telescope actually had less magnifying power than "normal telescopes of its type." This choice will attract untrained test-takers who don't read carefully enough to realize that they're getting the relationship between William's two-foot reflector and "normal telescopes of its type" exactly backwards.

J   **Direct Contradiction:** The text says the telescope had "huge light-gathering power" (50), and nothing in the text indicates that the telescope had "less light-gathering power" than "normal telescopes," as (J) would require.

▌ **Test 2, Question 19 (Test 3 in the 2020-2021 Red Book—see page 23 for more)**   **TYPE: DESCRIBE THE PASSAGE**

ⓘ   *The prompt often mentions describing the passage without a line citation. The answer must still be restated or demonstrated by some specific part of the text. (See "What about Questions without Citations?" on p. 57.)*

▶   **Where to look in the text:** Skim for "Caroline," "Coma Berenices," "Big Dipper," "Ursa Major," and "Pole Star." Also, if we've looked at most of the passage and still haven't come across the relevant text, we could look for that text in the remaining parts of the passage.

A   **Confused Relationships:** The text describes the object "moving through Ursa Major...towards a triangulation of stars in...Coma Berenices" (63-66). So we're told that the object is moving "*towards*...Coma Berenices" (emphasis added), not "*through* Coma Berenices" (emphasis added), as (A) would require. Further, the text doesn't mention the comet's movement in relation to the Pole star, as (A) would also require.

B   **Confused Relationships:** As we saw in the explanation for (A), Caroline saw something moving *towards* Coma Berenices, not *through* it and towards something else, as (B) would require.

C ✓ **Correct:** As we saw in the explanation for (A), Caroline saw something moving *towards* stars in Coma Berenices, so we already know the second half of this choice is directly restated in the text. We also saw for (A) that the object was moving "*through* Ursa Major" (63), as the first half of this choice says. Since (C) is exactly restated in the text, it must be right.

D   **Confused Relationships:** The text says Caroline saw an object moving "*towards* a triangulation of stars in...Coma Berenices" (65-66, emphasis added), not "*through* a triangulation of stars" (emphasis added), as (D) would require. Further, the text doesn't say that triangulation of stars included the Pole Star.

> **Note**   The structure of this question will confuse a lot of untrained test-takers because of its frequent re-use of the words "toward" and "through," which can easily be confused for each other, and its use of exotic astronomical terms like "Coma Berenices" and "Ursa Major." But, as trained test-takers, we realize that we can answer the question pretty quickly and with total confidence once we zero-in on the specific elements of the answer choices that make them different from each other. When we do that, we see that we need to identify whether the text says the object moved *through* Coma Berenices (as in (A) and (B)), Ursa Major (as in (C)), or a triangulation of stars (as in (D)), and we may need to identify whether the object moved *toward* the Pole Star (as in (A)), the Big Dipper (as in (B)), or Coma Berenices (as in (C) and (D)).

▌ **Test 2, Question 20 (Test 3 in the 2020-2021 Red Book—see page 23 for more)**   **TYPE: DESCRIBE THE PASSAGE**

ⓘ   *The prompt often mentions describing the passage without a line citation. The answer must still be restated or demonstrated by some specific part of the text. (See "What about Questions without Citations?" on p. 57.)*

▶   **Where to look in the text:** Skim for "Caroline" and "stargazers." Also, we may have come across the text relevant to this question in answering question 19.

F ✓ **Correct:** The text says Caroline was "cauti[ous], but also...certain[]" (71-72) about finding "something so quickly" (67), which restates the phrase "found the comet quickly" from (F). The text also says this area of the sky was "familiar" (67) because it was "the first stop of every amateur stargazer" (68-69), which restates the idea that the area was "familiar to astronomers and stargazers," just as (F) also requires. Since every part of this choice is restated in the relevant part of the passage, we know it must be right.

G   **Barely Relevant:** The text doesn't make any statement comparing Caroline's knowledge of nebulae and her knowledge of comets.

H   **Reasonable Statement Not in the Text:** The text mentions "William's discovery of the plant Uranus" (90-91), but it doesn't actually say that Caroline played any role in that discovery. An untrained test-taker might assume that Caroline played a role in all of William's work, since she's referred to as his "assistant" (17) for the operation of the forty-foot telescope mentioned in the first few paragraphs of the passage—but, as trained test-takers, we know that we can only pick an answer choice if it's actually restated or demonstrated in the text, so we can't assume that Caroline played any part in the discovery of Uranus if the passage doesn't explicitly say she did.

J   **Reasonable Statement Not in the Text:** The text does mention that Caroline was "unable to calculate the mathematical coordinates of the object" (73-74) that turned out to be a comet, so many untrained test-takers will assume that she was unable to do the calculation because she lacked experience, as (J) says. But the text doesn't actually say anything about Caroline's level of experience with those calculations, so (J) can't be right. (For example, it's possible from the text that Caroline has a lot of experience with those calculations but just isn't good at them, or that she normally has access to a reference work that she couldn't access while observing the new comet, or that the atmospheric conditions during her observation made the calculations impossible because she couldn't see certain other objects for reference, or who knows what—there are a lot of possible reasons why somebody might be unable to complete a calculation that have nothing to do with her amount of experience.)

ⓘ *The prompt asks about the purpose or role of a part of the text. The answer must be accurately restated or demonstrated by the relevant text, with no interpretation. (See "What about Main Purpose, Main Idea, Best Description Questions?," p. 58.)*

Subjective Phrases to Ignore: "main"

A **Reasonable Statement Not in the Text:** This choice will attract a lot of untrained test-takers because it might seem like it would be a valid interpretation of the author's motivations if we were discussing the essay in a literature class. But, as trained test-takers, we can see that there are several problems with (A). Among other things, the first two paragraphs don't directly restate or demonstrate any "popularity" of the book, as (A) would require: it's possible for an author to give a reading from a book that few people like, and it's possible for an author to attend a party for a reason other than the popularity of her book. Another issue is that the people described in the first two paragraphs don't specifically say they want to meet the author, as (A) requires: the woman in lines 3 and 4 asks if it's possible to take a walk with someone who isn't the author, and the woman quoted in the second paragraph doesn't actually say she wanted to meet the author—only that she had expected the author to be different. Since (A) isn't literally restated or demonstrated by the text, it's wrong.

B ✓ **Correct:** At the end of the first paragraph the narrator says that her "mother" (6) and "the woman in the book...were not exactly the same" (6-7), which directly demonstrates the idea in (B). At the end of the second paragraph, the narrator says that herself and "the narrator of the book" (15) again, were "not exactly the same" (16), which demonstrates the concept in (B) a second time.

C **Confused Relationships:** Some untrained test-takers might imagine that Gornick could be frustrated with her readers, because the first two paragraphs mention encounters with readers who don't seem to understand something about Gornick's book. But neither paragraph restates or demonstrates the idea that Gornick is "frustrat[ed]," as (C) would require—so (C) is wrong. The second paragraph mentions a woman who expresses "disappointment" (10) in meeting Gornick, but (C) describes *Gornick* being *frustrated*, rather than a *reader* being *disappointed*, and (C) pluralizes "readers" even though only one reader is described as disappointed—any of these differences from the text is enough by itself to make (C) wrong.

D **Wrong Part of the Passage:** This choice will attract untrained test-takers who don't pay careful attention to the part of the text mentioned in the prompt, because Gornick does discuss the proper classification of her memoir (and all memoirs) in lines 42-29. But (D) is wrong because the prompt refers us to lines 1-16, which don't say anything about classifying Gornick's writing.

ⓘ *The prompt often mentions describing the passage without a line citation. The answer must still be restated or demonstrated by some specific part of the text. (See "What about Questions without Citations?" on p. 57.)*

Subjective Phrases to Ignore: "most directly"

▶ **Where to look in the text:** Skim Passage A for "*Fierce Attachments*," then check each line citation in the answer choices. We also encountered "the party guest's disappointment" described in the prompt when we were answering question 21.

F ✓ **Correct:** "The party guest's disappointment upon meeting the author of *Fierce Attachments*," as mentioned in the prompt, refers to the moment when "one of the guests blurted out in a voice filled with disappointment, 'Why, you're nothing like the woman who wrote *Fierce Attachments*!'" (9-12). So the guest is upset that the actual author of the book doesn't seem like the woman who corresponds to the author in the author's memoir. This idea of a difference between the author herself and the person who corresponds to the author in the memoir is restated by the phrase in (F), which says that the real people aren't the same as the versions of those people depicted in the memoir. (The phrase "rough draft" conveys an idea that one version of a person is sort of a preparation for another version of the person, but that aspect of the phrase isn't really important here—all that matters for this question is that a rough draft is inherently different from the real thing, just as the author seems different from the version of the author that the guest encountered in the memoir.)

G **Confused Relationships:** As we discussed in (F), "the party guest's disappointment" mentioned in the prompt has to do with finding out that the author of the memoir wasn't the same as the version of herself depicted in the memoir. That idea isn't related to the author "becom[ing her] mother" as we see in (G)—in fact, we find out in lines 31-41 that the author's realization she had become her own mother is "trace[d] out" (34) in the memoir. So the guest can't be disappointed by the author becoming her own mother, since the guest is disappointed about a difference between the author and the memoir, and we see now that the memoir reflected the idea of the author becoming her own mother. If the guest thought the author had become her own mother, as this choice indicates, that would mean the author was similar to what the guest encountered in the book, which would contradict the text we saw in our discussion of (F). (If that doesn't make sense, it may help to re-read this explanation a couple of times—we made it as clear as we could :))

H **Confused Relationships:** The "complicated insight" referred to in this choice is the author's realization that she had become her mother, which we explored in (G), so (H) must be wrong for the same reasons that (G) is wrong. (In fact, as trained test-takers, we also know that (G) and (H) must both be wrong simply because they refer to the same idea, and we know that each real ACT question can only have one valid answer, so both of these answers can't be right.)

J   **Barely Relevant:** As we discussed for (F) and (G), "the party guest's disappointment" is related to the author's failure to live up to the guest's expectations of how the author should seem in person. The phrase in this choice has nothing to do with that expectation.

Test 2, Question 23 (Test 3 in the 2020-2021 Red Book—see page 23 for more)   **TYPE: DESCRIBE THE PASSAGE**

ⓘ   *The prompt often mentions describing the passage without a line citation. The answer must still be restated or demonstrated by some specific part of the text. (See "What about Questions without Citations?" on p. 57.)*

▶   **Where to look in the text:** Skim Passage A for phrases related to the phrase "heart of her memoir" from the prompt. We also encountered the text relevant to this question when we were checking the answer choices from question 22.

A   **Confused Relationships:** The text says that the book includes "walks taken in Manhattan in the 1980s" (36-37), and that the walks are part of "the situation" (37) in the book. But the author never says Gornick thought of these walks, or of "the situation," as "the heart of her memoir," as (A) would require.

B ✓   **Correct:** Lines 31 and 32 literally say that the "revelation…[that]I had become my mother" (31-32) is "at the heart of [the] memoir." This literally restates (B) in connection with the prompt, so it's right.

C   **Confused Relationships:** (C) has the same issue that (A) had: the passage says that "our life in the Bronx in the 1950s" (35-36) is part of "the situation" (37) of the book, but it never says that period, or "the situation," is "the heart of her memoir," as the prompt requires.

D   **Barely Relevant:** The text never actually refers to a "shared history," as (D) would require; the closest it arguably comes is the reference to "our life" (35), which is described as part of the same "situation" (37) we mentioned in our analysis of (A) and (C) above. Gornick never says that any "shared history" was "the heart of her memoir," as (D) requires, so (D) is wrong.

Test 2, Question 24 (Test 3 in the 2020-2021 Red Book—see page 23 for more)   **TYPE: DESCRIBE THE PASSAGE**

ⓘ   *The prompt often mentions describing the passage without a line citation. The answer must still be restated or demonstrated by some specific part of the text. (See "What about Questions without Citations?" on p. 57.)*

▶   **Where to look in the text:** Skim Passage A for the words in the answer choices. Also, if we've read most of Passage A and haven't yet found the text relevant to this question, we should look for that text in the remaining unread parts of Passage A.

F   **Direct Contradiction:** The text explicitly says that "memoirs belong to the category of literature, not of journalism" (42-43). This choice will attract a lot of untrained test-takers who don't read carefully enough, and only remember that the passage mentioned memoirs and journalism in the same sentence.

G   **Reasonable Statement Not in the Text:** A personal diary might be called a memoir in real life, but the question specifically asks what "Gornick believes." Since the passage never says anything about "personal diaries," (G) can't be restated or demonstrated in the passage, which means it's wrong.

H   **Direct Contradiction:** The issue with (H) is similar to what we saw for (F): the text specifically describes a difference between "memoir" and "historical narrative" in lines 43-46 , which means Gornick sees memoirs and historical narratives as different things, and (H) can't be right.

J ✓   **Correct:** As we saw in the explanation for (F), the text literally says that "memoirs belong to the category of literature" (42), exactly as (J) requires.

Test 2, Question 25 (Test 3 in the 2020-2021 Red Book—see page 23 for more)   **TYPE: DESCRIBE THE PASSAGE**

ⓘ   *The prompt often mentions describing the passage without a line citation. The answer must still be restated or demonstrated by some specific part of the text. (See "What about Questions without Citations?" on p. 57.)*

▶   **Where to look in the text:** Skim Passage B for "Hemingway."

A   **Reasonable Statement Not in the Text:** The text never actually mentions Hemingway's friends. It does mention *A Moveable Feast* being autobiographical, and it does mention "settl[ing] old scores" (64-65), his "portrayal…of others" (65-66), his "personal relationships" (69), and his "contemporaries" (74-75)—but none of those phrases necessarily restates or demonstrates that Hemingway was ever friendly with anybody! Untrained test-takers who are familiar with Hemingway or with autobiographies in general might assume that a famous writer would use "composites" of his "friends" in his writing, and this choice might trick them for that reason. But, as trained test-takers, we know this choice isn't restated or demonstrated in the text, so it can't be right.

B   **Reasonable Statement Not in the Text:** This choice has the same problems we just saw in (A): none of the phrases on the page actually literally indicate that Hemingway even had a family, much less that he wrote about them. Some untrained test-takers might imagine that an author like Hemingway could base his protagonists on family members, but the text doesn't restate or demonstrate this idea, so (B) is wrong.

C ✓   **Correct:** The text explicitly says that "[Hemingway's] protagonists are often conscious projections and explorations of the self" (55-56), which is a literal restatement of (C) in combination with the prompt.

D   **Direct Contradiction:** The text says that Hemingway's fiction "contains numerous autobiographical elements" (54-55), and that his protagonists are "often conscious projections…of the self" (55-56). So we can't say his characters are "completely made-up," as (D)

---

would require, which makes (D) wrong.

ⓘ   *The prompt often mentions describing the passage without a line citation. The answer must still be restated or demonstrated by some specific part of the text. (See "What about Questions without Citations?" on p. 57.)*

▶   **Where to look in the text:** Skim Passage B for the italicized phrase "*A Moveable Feast.*"

F ✓   **Correct:** The text says Hemingway wanted to use *A Moveable Feast* "to leave to the world a flattering self-portrait" (72-73), which restates the idea of leaving a particular kind of portrait from (F). The text also calls the book "his portrayal of self and others" (65-66) and says that the book portrays "its author and his contemporaries" (74-75), which restates the phrase "of himself and his contemporaries" in (F). Since every part of (F) is restated in the passage, (F) is right.

G   **Off by One or Two Words:** The text does say that Hemingway "felt that he had been unfairly portrayed by some of his contemporaries" (67-68), as (G) would require, but it doesn't say those contemporaries were also writing memoirs "during the same time period," as (G) would also require. That difference from the passage is enough to make (G) wrong.

H   **Barely Relevant:** The passage never mentions whether Hemingway could produce any kind of document for any purpose, so (H) can't be right.

J   **Barely Relevant:** The passage never says anything about how good Hemingway's memory was, so (J) must be wrong.

Note   As will always be the case on the ACT Reading section, the right answer to this question is the only choice that's literally restated or demonstrated by the relevant part of the passage; we never actually need to figure out if the idea in (F) is relevant to the difficulty in determining the accuracy of *A Moveable Feast*, as the prompt mentions. Many untrained test-takers will waste their time trying to figure out if (F) is a good reason for the idea in the prompt, instead of simply noting that (F) must be right because none of the other choices literally reflect ideas from Passage B. Keep this in mind on test day and don't let yourself get distracted when the ACT deliberately tries to make its questions seem more sophisticated than they are.

ⓘ   *The prompt often mentions describing the passage without a line citation. The answer must still be restated or demonstrated by some specific part of the text. (See "What about Questions without Citations?" on p. 57.)*

Subjective Phrases to Ignore: "best" "seems"

▶   **Where to look in the text:** Skim Passage B for "*A Moveable Feast.*"

A   **Reasonable Statement Not in the Text:** An untrained test-taker might assume the author would have a positive view of *A Moveable Feast*, since she bothered to write about it, and since many untrained test-takers incorrectly assume that passages on the ACT will always portray their subjects positively. But, as trained test-takers, we see that the author never literally describes *A Moveable Feast* as one of Hemingway's "best works," as (A) would require.

B ✓   **Correct:** The author describes *A Moveable Feast* as "particularly complex" (61), which literally restates the phrase "complex example of a book" from (B). Further, the author says the book is "in many ways, just as fictional" (59-60) as Hemingway's fiction, that the "accuracy of the anecdotes [in the book]...can never be entirely resolved" (75-76). She also says that Hemingway "lied relatively seldom about pure facts" (79-80). All of these statements demonstrate that *A Moveable Feast* "combines fact and fiction," as (B) requires. Since every part of (B) is literally restated or demonstrated in the passage, (B) is right.

C   **Off by One or Two Words:** The author specifically says that the "accuracy of the anecdotes [in the book]...can never be entirely resolved" (75-76), which means that the author isn't sure whether the book is "accurate," as (C) would require. This single word is enough to make (C) wrong, even though the rest of the choice is reflected in the passage.

D   **Reasonable Statement Not in the Text:** Many untrained test-takers will assume that the author would want us to read *A Moveable Feast* "with other books from the same time period," as (D) would require, simply because that's how groups of books are often assigned to be read in high school or college literature classes. But, as trained test-takers, we know (D) must be wrong because the passage never mentions the idea of reading *A Moveable Feast* in connection with any other book.

ⓘ   *May ask about agreement or disagreement between passages, or how an idea from one passage applies to the other, etc. The answer is still literally restated or demonstrated. (See "Paired passages aren't special," p. 56; "What about Paired Passages?" p. 58.)*

▶   **Where to look in the text:** Skim for "I" in Passage A (since that passage was written by Gornick) and "Hemingway" in Passage B. Also, we may have come across the relevant text from Passage A in answering questions 22 and 23.

F   **Off by One or Two Words:** Neither passage mentions "*wholly* fictional situations" (emphasis added), as (F) would require. Gornick does say that the "literalness of the situation" (38-39) wasn't that important to her, but this isn't the same thing as saying her writing involves completely fictional situations, as (F) describes. And Passage B says *A Moveable Feast* features "relative factual accuracy" (87-88), which also contradicts the idea of a completely fictional situation as described in (F). Since the prompt requires us to find an answer that's reflected in both passages, either of these issues would be enough by itself to make (F) wrong.

G   **Wrong Part of the Passage:** Passage B does say that Hemingway wanted "to leave to the world a flattering self-portrait" (72-73), as (G) describes. But the prompt requires us to find a choice that's literally restated or demonstrated in *both* passages, and Passage A doesn't say that Gornick wanted to portray herself "in a flattering way," as (G) would require.

H   **Wrong Part of the Passage:** This choice has the same issue as (G): Passage B says that Hemingway "settled old scores" (64-65) and wanted "to present his own version of personal relationships" (68-69), just as (H) describes. But Passage A doesn't say Gornick also used this approach, and the prompt requires us to find a choice that's restated or demonstrated by both passages, so (H) is wrong.

J ✓   **Correct:** Gornick refers to "the history [she] wanted badly to trace out" (33-34) in her memoir, which restates the idea of having a story she wanted to tell, as (J) requires. She says this story was the process by which she "had become [her] mother" (32), which demonstrates the idea of using material from her own life, as (J) also requires. Similarly, Passage B calls *A Moveable Feast* "openly autobiographical" (57), which restates the idea of using material from the author's life, as (J) requires; Passage B also describes a number of desires that motivated Hemingway's writing of *A Moveable Feast* in lines 63-73. Passage B also says Hemingway "generally selected...episodes so that they would show him as innocent, honest, dedicated, and thoroughly enjoying life" (84-86), which demonstrates the idea of having a particular story he wanted to tell, as (J) also requires. Since every part of (J) is literally restated or demonstrated in both passages, (J) is right.

Test 2, Question 29 (Test 3 in the 2020-2021 Red Book—see page 23 for more)   **TYPE: TWO PASSAGES**

ⓘ   *May ask about agreement or disagreement between passages, or how an idea from one passage applies to the other, etc. The answer is still literally restated or demonstrated. (See "Paired passages aren't special," p. 56; "What about Paired Passages?" p. 58.)*

    Subjective Phrases to Ignore: "most reasonably" "would"

▶   **Where to look in the text:** We may have encountered the relevant text from Passage A when we answered question 24, and the relevant text from Passage B when we answered question 27.

A   **Confused Relationships:** Among other issues, the author of Passage B does call *A Moveable Feast* "in many ways, just as fictional" (59-60) as Hemingway's fiction—but the author of Passage B isn't Hemingway himself, and the prompt asked us for a statement that *Hemingway* would agree with. That, by itself, is enough to make (A) wrong.

B   **Barely Relevant:** Neither passage ever addresses the issue of the exactness of a memory of an event, so there's no literal basis for an answer choice that mentions this concept at all, which means (B) must be wrong.

C ✓   **Correct:** Gornick says that her writing "belong[s] to the category of literature, not of journalism" (42-43), which demonstrates the idea that the writing is "artistic" as described in (C), since literature is a type of art; this idea is further demonstrated when Gornick says her job is to "get to the bottom of the tale" (48-49), since a tale is a type of artistic work. And Gornick demonstrates that she considers "only facts" to be less important than a memoirist's art, as (C) also requires, when she says that "what mattered most...was not the literalness of the situation" (38-39), and that she doesn't owe a reader a "record of literal accuracy that is owed in newspaper reporting or historical narrative" (45-46). Similarly, Passage B says that Hemingway sometimes lied about "pure facts...in order to reinforce...an idealized self-portrayal" (80-83). Lying about "facts" to reinforce a "portrayal" directly restates the idea of valuing "an artistic whole" over "only facts," since the "portrayal" (83) being reinforced is the memoir, which Passage B calls "literary" (63) and a "self-portrait" (73), indicating that it's a work of art, as (C) requires. Since every part of (C) is literally restated or demonstrated in both passages, (C) must be right.

D   **Barely Relevant:** The issue with (D) is similar to the one we identified for (B): neither passage discusses the idea of "documented evidence" at any point, so no choice that makes a statement about "documented evidence" can be right.

Test 2, Question 30 (Test 3 in the 2020-2021 Red Book—see page 23 for more)   **TYPE: TWO PASSAGES**

ⓘ   *May ask about agreement or disagreement between passages, or how an idea from one passage applies to the other, etc. The answer is still literally restated or demonstrated. (See "Paired passages aren't special," p. 56; "What about Paired Passages?" p. 58.)*

    Subjective Phrases to Ignore: "most closely"

▶   **Where to look in the text:** We may have encountered the relevant text when we answered questions 24 and 29.

F   **Confused Relationships:** Passage A *does* describe a meeting in which one person doesn't live up to the other's expectations in lines 9-12, but the idea of meeting someone who doesn't live up to your expectations doesn't literally restate or demonstrate anything from the quote in the prompt, so (F) is wrong.

G ✓   **Correct:** Passage A explicitly says that "what actually happened is only raw material; what matters is what the memoirist makes of what happened" (39-41). This is essentially a phrase-by-phrase restatement of (G), and it refers directly to the idea that there's a difference between "real life" and the "story" of a "memoir," as the prompt says. So (G) is right.

H   **Confused Relationships:** Passage B *does* say that Hemingway "was...conscious that [*A Moveable Feast*] would be his literary testament" (62-63), but the idea of being aware of your literary testament doesn't restate or demonstrate the difference between "story" and "history" as described in the quote in the prompt, so (H) is wrong.

J   **Confused Relationships:** The problem with this choice is similar to what we saw in (H): Passage B *does* say that Hemingway "lied relatively seldom about pure facts" (79-80), but that idea doesn't demonstrate the difference between "story" and "history" as we see in the quote from the prompt, so (J) can't be right.

ℹ️   *The prompt often mentions describing the passage without a line citation. The answer must still be restated or demonstrated by some specific part of the text. (See "What about Questions without Citations?" on p. 57.)*

Subjective Phrases to Ignore: "main"

A   **Confused Relationships:** The text refers to "Argentine ants" (15, 38-39, etc.) many times, and the text refers to discoveries of concepts like "supercolonies" (61-62, 75) that are related to ants, but it doesn't actually mention the discovery of Argentine ants in the United States, as (A) would require. (A) will attract a lot of test-takers who don't read the passage carefully enough to notice the difference between discovering facts related to ants, and discovering the ants themselves.

B   **Confused Relationships:** The text does say that Argentine ants are "squishy, small, stingless wimps, as ants go" (52-53), but the text never says anything about specific physical differences between Argentine ants and other insects. In order for this choice to be right, the text would need to say something like "some other insects have translucent wings, but Argentine ants have no wings at all," or otherwise refer to the biological structures of ants *and* other insects.

C   **Barely Relevant:** The text mentions "the size" of some "supercolonies," as referred to in (C), but it doesn't actually say anything about any "technology" used to investigate that size, as (C) would require, so (C) is wrong.

D ✓ **Correct:** The very first sentence describes how a biologist "struggled for years with the question of which colonizing organisms fail and which succeed" (1-3). The passage goes on to refer repeatedly to "factors that contribute to....success as an invasive species," as (D) requires. For example, lines 39-40 ask if that success is "just a consequence of the number of tries," and "lack of aggression" (64-65) is mentioned as something that might help a species "compete with other species" (66). Finally, lines 75-77 observe that "supercolonies...look to be common among invasive ants." All of these quotes from the passage, among others, demonstrate the idea of the discussion mentioned in (D), so (D) is right.

ℹ️   *The prompt often mentions describing the passage without a line citation. The answer must still be restated or demonstrated by some specific part of the text. (See "What about Questions without Citations?" on p. 57.)*

▶   **Where to look in the text:** Skim for quotation marks.

F   **Barely Relevant:** A personal anecdote is a story told by an author about his own experiences. But the author never uses words like "I" or "my," nor does he refer to himself in any other way, so (F) can't be right. (See the note below for more.)

G ✓ **Correct:** As we saw in "What about "Idiomatic Expressions?"" on page 59 of this Black Book, the ACT Reading section uses the word "idiomatic" to describe a phrase whose meaning differs from the literal meanings of the words involved. (This often overlaps with what we might call "slang"—and many English teachers teach it that way—although it's not exactly the same idea.) In this essay, phrases like "made bank" (73), "ants flash chemical badges" (78), and "the term...becomes fuzzy" (83) all involve commonly understood usage of a phrase that doesn't literally line up with the meanings of the individual words in the phrase: the ants don't really make a bank, they don't literally have badges, the term doesn't actually have fuzz, and so on. Since (G) is the only choice that's demonstrated by the passage, it's right. Note that the term "idiomatic" is a little more technical than what we tend to encounter in ACT Reading questions, but—as we saw in our discussion of the other answer choices—we could pretty easily rule out all the other choices, which makes this question a lot less challenging than it might seem to be for test-takers who get distracted by the word "idiomatic." (See the note below for more.)

H   **Off by One or Two Words:** Quotation marks do appear throughout the passage, but none of those quotations can be called "humorous" according to the ACT, as (H) would require—so (H) must be wrong. (Remember that the ACT considers something to be humorous if it can't be taken literally—see the training on page 59 in this Black Book for more on that.)

J   **Barely Relevant:** As we saw in the discussion of (F), the author never even refers to himself, so he can't be critical of himself, as (J) would require. (See the note below for more.)

Note   Some untrained test-takers might read this prompt and wonder which concept from the answer choices would "establish" a "somewhat casual tone." But if we check each answer choice, we find that three of the choices mention ideas that don't actually appear anywhere in the passage, as we just saw in our analysis, and only one choice mentions something that does actually appear in the passage—so we could answer this question by just choosing the only answer that accurately describes any aspect of the passage, and we never need to think about the idea of "establish[ing]" a "casual tone," as the prompt says.

ℹ️   *The prompt often mentions describing the passage without a line citation. The answer must still be restated or demonstrated by some specific part of the text. (See "What about Questions without Citations?" on p. 57.)*

▶   **Where to look in the text:** Skim for "Case," "Holway," "Suarez," "Argentine," and "Ward."

A   **Confused Relationships:** Case joins Holway and Suarez in line 63, which is after Suarez recruited Holway and Ward in lines 25-

27. And all of that happened after Suarez found the samples of Argentine ants in the Smithsonian in lines 14-15. So the event in (A) can't be the first thing to occur, as the prompt requires. See the note below for more on the order of events in the passage.

B   **Direct Contradiction:** The text says that workers from three colonies were brought together "in 2009" (86). Among other things, we know this must be after Suarez found ant samples in the Smithsonian in "1999" (4-5). (This choice may attract some untrained test-takers who misread the prompt and think they should be looking for the choice that occurred last chronologically, not first.)

C ✓   **Correct:** The text says that Suarez found the Argentine ant samples at the Smithsonian in "1999" (4-5), which was before Suarez "solicited the help of...Holway...and...Ward" (25-27), before "Ted Case joined forces with Holway and Suarez" (63-64), and before three workers from separate colonies "were put together" (87-88) "in 2009" (86). Since no other choice can happen before this choice, (C) must be right.

D   **Confused Relationships:** Holway and Ward weren't "recruited by Suarez to assist with his research" until lines 25-27, which was after Suarez found the Argentine ants in the Smithsonian collection in lines 4-5.

Note   The events in this passage happen to be described in chronological order. If we've already read most or all of this passage before attacking this question, then knowing that the passage is in chronological order will help us to find the answer. But it's worth pointing out that not every ACT Reading passage will describe events in chronological order, so, on test day, you shouldn't assume that a passage is presented in any particular order.

▌ Test 2, Question 34 (Test 3 in the 2020-2021 Red Book—see page 23 for more)   **TYPE: PURPOSE OF CITED TEXT**

ⓘ   *The prompt asks about the purpose or role of a part of the text. The answer must be accurately restated or demonstrated by the relevant text, with no interpretation. (See "What about Main Purpose, Main Idea, Best Description Questions?," p. 58.)*

Subjective Phrases to Ignore: "main"

F   **Wrong Part of the Passage:** This choice may appeal to some untrained test-takers who don't realize that the prompt focuses on only the fifth paragraph, and not the entire passage. But the fifth paragraph never refers to Argentine ants specifically—it only discusses the possible outcomes whenever any species invades a new area.

G ✓   **Correct:** The phrase "pioneering group" (41) restates the idea of a "pioneering species" in (G), and the text says one such group "might be wiped out...a second might survive...yet another...might thrive" (43-45); these different possibilities demonstrate the different "possible outcomes" mentioned in (G). The fifth paragraph also says, "relatively few invasive species truly prevail" (49), which literally demonstrates the idea of "stress[ing] the improbability that the species will thrive," as (G) also requires.

H   **Barely Relevant:** The fifth paragraph mentions "invasive species" (49) in general, but never explains what that term means, nor mentions ants directly, as (H) would require.

J   **Barely Relevant:** The fifth paragraph doesn't mention Argentine ants at all, and it doesn't mention any other pioneering species that's "more successful" than Argentine ants, as (J) would require.

▌ Test 2, Question 35 (Test 3 in the 2020-2021 Red Book—see page 23 for more)   **TYPE: CITATION QUESTION**

ⓘ   *The question includes a citation from the text. The answer must be directly restated or demonstrated in the cited text, or in the text closely surrounding the cited text. (See "The General Process for Answering ACT Reading Questions," p. 57.)*

A   **Barely Relevant:** The prompt refers to "ant behavior described in lines 56-58;" those lines describe two Argentine ants from different colonies being put together and "accept[ing] each other" (58). The information in (A) has nothing to do with the behavior mentioned in the lines from the prompt, so (A) can't be right.

B   **Barely Relevant:** As we saw in the discussion of (A), the lines referred to in the prompt describe two Argentine ants from different colonies being put together and "accept[ing] each other" (58). This choice compares the aggressiveness of different types of Argentine ants, but the text doesn't say anything about whether California's Argentine ants are more or less aggressive than other ants, so (B) can't be right.

C   **Barely Relevant:** This choice has an issue similar to what we saw in (A) and (B): it introduces an idea ("California's ecosystem") that has nothing to do with the behavior mentioned in the lines from the prompt.

D ✓   **Correct:** As we saw in the discussions of (A) and (B), the lines from the prompt describe ants from different colonies "accept[ing] each other" (58). If this mutual acceptance is "unusual," as the prompt describes, then the usual behavior must be something besides acceptance. This choice says that "ants from different colonies typically fight one another," so it directly states the condition that would make the lines in the prompt "unusual."

Note   The prompt for this question will make most untrained test-takers assume that they need to analyze the author's reasoning in order to uncover his assumptions, just as we might need to do when analyzing literature in a classroom setting. But, as trained test-takers, we can tell that (D) is the only choice that limits itself to ideas that are directly relevant to the citation in the prompt—that is, how ants react when put together—which means it's the only choice that can possibly be correct on the ACT. Remember this kind of thing on test day, and don't let the ACT fool you into thinking you have to read an author's mind to find the right answer!

ⓘ *The prompt often mentions describing the passage without a line citation. The answer must still be restated or demonstrated by some specific part of the text. (See "What about Questions without Citations?" on p. 57.)*

▶ **Where to look in the text:** Skim for the terms "Suarez," "Smithsonian," and "1999" from the answer choices.

F ✓ **Correct:** The passage says, "like many biologists...Suarez struggled for years with the question of which colonizing organisms fail and which succeed" (1-3). The idea that Suarez "struggled for years" with this question restates the idea of studying this question "for a number of years," as (F) requires. The phrase "like many biologists" (1) is a restatement of "many biologists" from (F). Since every part of (F) is literally restated in the passage, (F) is right.

G **Direct Contradiction:** The text says that Suarez "studied [this question] the hard way...until 1999" (3-4). This means that Suarez was already studying this question *before* 1999, which directly contradicts the statement in (G) that such studies began in 1999.

H **Confused Relationships:** The text does mention the Smithsonian, but it never says only the Smithsonian was studying any particular question, as (H) would require.

J **Direct Contradiction:** As we saw for (F), the passage says, "many biologists" (1) studied the question in the prompt, which means that Suarez didn't study it "exclusively," as (J) would require.

ⓘ *The prompt often mentions describing the passage without a line citation. The answer must still be restated or demonstrated by some specific part of the text. (See "What about Questions without Citations?" on p. 57.)*

▶ **Where to look in the text:** Skim for "Suarez" and "Smithsonian."

A **Direct Contradiction:** The text says that when Suarez looked through the jars he "found relatively few samples of Argentine ants" (14-15); since "relatively few" (14) contradicts the word "most" from (A), (A) is wrong.

B **Confused Relationships:** The text does mention that Suarez eventually asked for "the help of...Holway...and...Ward" (25-27), but it never says that Holway and Ward were the ones who collected the samples, or that the samples were part of a "larger study" as described in (B).

C **Barely Relevant:** The third paragraph is the one that describes the results of looking at the samples, and it never says anything about any of the species being "previously undiscovered," as (C) would require.

D ✓ **Correct:** The text says that what Suarez found "far more interesting" was "vials of ants collected at ports of entry in the eastern U.S. from 1927 to 1985" (16-18). The phrase "far more interesting" (16) restates the idea that he was "most interested" from (D); "vials of ants" (17) restates the idea of "samples" from (D); and "collected at ports of entry in the eastern U.S. from 1927 to 1985" (17-18) restates the phrase "collected at eastern US ports of entry" in (D).

ⓘ *The prompt often mentions describing the passage without a line citation. The answer must still be restated or demonstrated by some specific part of the text. (See "What about Questions without Citations?" on p. 57.)*

▶ **Where to look in the text:** Skim for "Argentine." We also may have skimmed the relevant text in answering question 34.

F ✓ **Correct:** The text says Argentine ants are "stingless wimps" (52).

G **Off by One or Two Words:** The text says Argentine ants are "ecologically dominant" (51-52), not "physically dominant." This choice will attract a lot of untrained test-takers who vaguely remember reading something about the ants being dominant, but don't go back to the passage to verify that every word of (G) is literally reflected there.

H **Confused Relationships:** The text says that Suarez found samples of Argentine ants (in a museum) that were "collected in the United States" (8), but it never says Suarez was actually the *first* to *discover* Argentine ants, as (H) would require.

J **Direct Contradiction:** The text mentions "a third [colony of Argentine ants] from Japan" (87), which contradicts the idea that the ants failed to thrive in Japan, as (J) would require.

ⓘ *The prompt often mentions describing the passage without a line citation. The answer must still be restated or demonstrated by some specific part of the text. (See "What about Questions without Citations?" on p. 57.)*

▶ **Where to look in the text:** Skim for "aggressive" and "peaceful." Also, if you've read most of the passage and haven't yet encountered the relevant text, focus on the parts of the passage you haven't read yet.

A **Confused Relationships:** The text says that Argentine ants have a "lack of aggression" (64-65) and live in huge colonies called "supercolonies" (61-62). The text never specifies the size of colony that "aggressive ants" live in, as (A) would require. This choice will attract a lot of untrained test-takers who don't read carefully, and incorrectly assume that Argentine ants must be more aggressive since they've spread across so much of the globe.

B ✓ **Correct:** The text says that peaceful Argentine ants "wasted less energy" (68); in contrast, it says the "aggressive ants wasted energy...and so gathered less food" (70-71). These lines directly indicate that the aggressive ants spend less time gathering food, as

(B) requires.

C   **Barely Relevant:** The text never discusses the likelihood of any particular ant living in a colony—in fact, it never mentions the possibility of an ant not living in a colony.

D   **Confused Relationships:** The idea of a "survivor species" is brought up in line 36, before the discussion of "aggressive ants," and the text never talks about the likelihood that aggressive ants can be a "survivor species." Like (A), this choice will attract a lot of untrained test-takers who simply assume that aggressive animals will be more likely to survive, instead of basing their answers on the plain language of the text.

Test 2, Question 40 (Test 3 in the 2020-2021 Red Book—see page 23 for more)	**TYPE: DESCRIBE THE PASSAGE**

ⓘ   *The prompt often mentions describing the passage without a line citation. The answer must still be restated or demonstrated by some specific part of the text. (See "What about Questions without Citations?" on p. 57.)*

> **Subjective Phrases to Ignore: "most clearly"**

▶   **Where to look in the text:** If you've read most of the passage and haven't yet encountered the relevant text, focus on the parts of the passage you haven't read yet.

F   **Confused Relationships:** The text mentions "supercolonies" (61-62) and "chemical badges" (78), but it says the "chemical badges identify[] [the ants'] home nest" (78-79); the text never says anything about chemical badges being "identical" across a whole supercolony, as (F) would require. (In fact, the text seems to say that supercolonies are possible when the badges are absent, because "without such markers" (79), "the clarity of 'us versus them' breaks down" (80-81), which seems to be the condition that allows the Argentine ants to form supercolonies. But we don't have to notice any of this to realize that (F) must be wrong—all we have to realize is that the text never says anything about identical chemical badges.)

G ✓   **Correct:** The text says, "ants flash chemical badges identifying their home nest" (78-79), which restates this answer choice almost exactly.

H   **Confused Relationships:** The text refers to "different nests swap[ping] workers and queens" (82) when "peace breaks out among colonies of *an ant species*" (81-82) (emphasis added). So the text describes nests within *one species* swapping workers and queens—not "ant colonies from *different* species" (emphasis added) doing the swapping, as (H) would require. This choice will attract a lot of untrained test-takers who don't notice the difference between the singular phrase "an ant species" (81-82) and the plural phrase "different species" in (H).

J   **Confused Relationships:** The text mentions a "conglomeration" (84) of ants "from Italy to Portugal" (85-86), but it never goes as far as saying that conglomeration is "the largest supercolony of ants in the world," as (J) would require. (Among other things, the passage leaves open the possibility that supercolonies of other species of ants could exist, because lines 74-77 say it isn't "just...the Argentine ant" that exhibits the behavior in the passage, and "supercolonies...look to be common among invasive ants.") Many untrained test-takers will be drawn to this choice because the supercolony from Italy to Portugal involves the names of two separate countries, while the other supercolonies referred to in the passage are only described as occupying one place ("California" (85) and "Japan" (87)). But the passage never says anything about ranking the sizes of the supercolonies, nor about whether the methodology for trying to do so would be based on the geographic area occupied by members of the supercolony, or anything at all about the idea of a "largest supercolony," so there's no way (J) can be right.

TEST 3 (FORM 16MC3—SEE PAGE 23)

Test 3, Question 1 (Form 16MC3 if you have the 2020-2021 Red Book—see page 23 for more)	**TYPE: DESCRIBE THE PASSAGE**

ⓘ   *The prompt often mentions describing the passage without a line citation. The answer must still be restated or demonstrated by some specific part of the text. (See "What about Questions without Citations?" on p. 57.)*

> **Subjective Phrases to Ignore: "reasonably be inferred"**

▶   **Where to look in the text:** Skim for "Shades Bowen" from the prompt, and "Everett Payne" and "Sonny Boy Blue" from the answer choices.

A ✓   **Correct:** The text says that "Shades Bowen" sat in "the bullpen" (5-6), where "young locals gathered...hoping for a chance to perform" (9-10). Then the text says, "the custom was to invite one or two [young locals]" (11-12) to play, but "Everett Payne...was the one being invited to sit in" (14-15). Since Everett Payne is "the one" (15) who gets invited to play, we know the other musicians in the bullpen, including Shades Bowen, didn't get to play with the band. This means Shades Bowen "did not accompany Everett Payne as he played 'Sonny Boy Blue,'" exactly as (A) describes. (The word "accompany" in this context means something like "play music with," but, even if we don't know that word in this context, we can still tell that (A) refers to the idea of doing something with Everett Payne as he played, and we can still tell from the passage that Shades Bowen didn't do anything with Everett Payne "as he played 'Sonny Boy Blue,'" as (A) would require.)

B   **Barely Relevant:** The text says that Everett Payne was "not long out of the army" (14-15), but it never says that Shades Bowen had been in the army with Everett Payne—or even that Shades Bowen was ever in the army at all.

C   **Barely Relevant:** The text says that "young locals gathered" (9) in the bullpen, which is the only reference to anyone's age in the whole passage. The text never says that Shades Bowen is older or younger than anyone else in the passage.

D   **Confused Relationships:** The text says that Shades Bowen was one of the "local musicians...in what was called the bullpen" (6-8), and that "one or two" (11) of those musicians would get "a chance to perform" (10) with the band if they were invited by the band. So the text says that Shades Bowen is somebody who hopes to be allowed to play with the band—not somebody who gets to decide if other people can play in the band, as (D) would require.

| Test 3, Question 2 (Form 16MC3 if you have the 2020-2021 Red Book—see page 23 for more)   TYPE: CITATION QUESTION

ⓘ   *The question includes a citation from the text. The answer must be directly restated or demonstrated in the cited text, or in the text closely surrounding the cited text. (See "The General Process for Answering ACT Reading Questions," p. 57.)*

    Subjective Phrases to Ignore: "main"

F   **Confused Relationships:** At this point in the text, Everett has already been performing for a while, since he has "played the song straight through as written" (38-39), including the "rather long introduction" (39); we're even told he's been playing all of this music "at a slower tempo" (41) than other people would. So the reaction in line 62, which comes after all the playing in lines 38-43, can't be related to how the audience "initially" felt, as (F) would require. Beyond that, the text never mentions that the audience had any particular expectations for Everett Payne's performance—it may seem that Hattie has some expectation related to Everett Payne, but even if she does, Hattie is just one person, not the whole "audience." So (F) must be wrong.

G ✓ **Correct:** As we started to see with (F), the preceding several paragraphs describe Everett Payne playing a lot of music on the piano: after playing the song through once in lines 38-43, he then plays the tune again in his own way in lines 48-61. Then the statement in line 62 tells us what everyone in the club did after Everett played for a while. This statement clearly demonstrates "the audience's reaction to Everett Payne's performance," just as (G) says.

H   **Barely Relevant:** This choice might tempt some test-takers, because the statement in line 62 comes right after the description of Everett Payne's performance, and it might seem to make sense that something that "counteract[s]" something else would come right after the thing it's counteracting. But "counteract" means something like "cancel out," or "neutralize," or "work against," or something along those lines—and there's no reason to think that the "collective in-suck of breath" in line 62 does any of those things to the description of Everett Payne's performance. In order for this choice to be right, there would have to be some phrase to describe how the "in-suck of breath" somehow undid the description of the performance, or canceled its effect, or something along those lines, and no such idea appears in the text.

J   **Barely Relevant:** The text never discusses whether anyone in the audience besides Hattie knew Everett Payne. There can be "a collective in-suck of breath throughout the club" (62) whether people in the club know who a musician is or not. Since this choice has nothing to do with the literal meanings of the words in the passage, it must be wrong.

| Test 3, Question 3 (Form 16MC3 if you have the 2020-2021 Red Book—see page 23 for more)   TYPE: DESCRIBE THE PASSAGE

ⓘ   *The prompt often mentions describing the passage without a line citation. The answer must still be restated or demonstrated by some specific part of the text. (See "What about Questions without Citations?" on p. 57.)*

    Subjective Phrases to Ignore: "most strongly suggests"

▶   **Where to look in the text:** Skim for "second set." We may also recall reading the relevant text when we answered question 1.

A ✓ **Correct:** The first paragraph says that Everett Payne was invited onstage "nearing the end of the second set" (1). Later, we're told that a musician is customarily invited up "toward the end of the final set" (10-11). So the "second set" in line 1 and the "final set" in line 11 must be the same set, since the text only describes the possibility of musicians being invited up at one point in the performance.

B   **Reasonable Statement Not in the Text:** The description of Everett Payne's playing certainly sounds like it would take a long time, so a lot of untrained test-takers will be drawn to this choice. But, as trained test-takers, we notice that the text never explicitly says how long either set actually lasts. Since there's no literal way to know the length of either set, there's no way to compare their lengths, which means there's no literal basis for (B) in the text.

C   **Direct Contradiction:** The text says there are only two sets, as we saw for choice (A): Everett Payne is invited up "near[] the end of the second set" (1), which is also "the final set" (11).

D   **Direct Contradiction:** The text describes "invit[ing] one or two of [the bullpen musicians] to sit in with the band" (11-12) "toward the end of the final set" (10-11). The word "with" (12) specifically indicates that the invited bullpen musicians played *along with the band*, which means they weren't performing by themselves, as (D) would require. The phrase "toward the end of the final set" also indicates the invited musicians played for only part of the set, instead of playing for the whole set, as (D) would also require. Either of these issues would be enough by itself to make (D) totally wrong.

| Test 3, Question 4 (Form 16MC3 if you have the 2020-2021 Red Book—see page 23 for more)   TYPE: DESCRIBE THE PASSAGE

ⓘ   *The prompt often mentions describing the passage without a line citation. The answer must still be restated or demonstrated by*

---

some specific part of the text. (See "What about Questions without Citations?" on p. 57.)

▶ **Where to look in the text:** Skim for the beginning of the description of Payne playing the song he chose.

F **Confused Relationships:** The passage does mention the audience being silent after the performance, when it says "everyone...could only sit there as if they were in church and weren't supposed to clap" (81-83). But the passage asks about how people "initially reacted" to the "choice of music," and the silence in lines 81-83 is a reaction to the *performance* of the music—not the *choice* of the music, as (F) would require—which means it isn't relevant to this question.

G **Confused Relationships:** This choice has the same basic problem as (F). The "collective in-suck of breath throughout the club" (62) happens in the middle of the performance, which means it's not how "the audience initially reacted to Everett Payne's choice of music," since they'd been hearing the music for a while—and already knew what his "choice of music" was for a while—when the "in-suck of breath" happened.

H ✓ **Correct:** After Everett Payne played "the opening bars of 'Sonny Boy Blue'" (33), we're told that "the purists...slouched deeper in their chairs in open disgust" (35-37). Since the purists are reacting to "the opening bars" (33) of the song, we know that they're "initially react[ing]," as the prompt requires. And since a slouch is a kind of "posture," as (H) requires, and disgust can be a kind of reaction, as the prompt requires, we can see that every part of (H) is directly restated or demonstrated in the relevant part of the text.

J **Confused Relationships:** This choice has the same issue as (F) and (G): the passage does tell us that "the purists...stood up" (87-89), but it tells us this happened *at the end of the performance*, not when the purists "initially" heard "Everett Payne's choice of music," as the prompt specifies.

Test 3, Question 5 (Form 16MC3 if you have the 2020-2021 Red Book—see page 23 for more)　　　**TYPE: DESCRIBE THE PASSAGE**

ⓘ *The prompt often mentions describing the passage without a line citation. The answer must still be restated or demonstrated by some specific part of the text. (See "What about Questions without Citations?" on p. 57.)*

▶ **Where to look in the text:** Skim for "Sonny Boy Blue," "Hattie," and "Everett Payne." Also, recall that the text relevant to question 4 had to do with the very beginning of Payne playing "Sonny Boy Blue," so skim the text before that description.

A **Direct Contradiction:** The text says, "Hattie watched [Everett Payne]...taking his time, moving with what almost seemed a deliberate pause between each step" (16-19). Taking his time and pausing between each step are the exact opposite of "mov[ing] quickly," as (A) would require.

B **Direct Contradiction:** The text says Everett Payne's thoughts are "on something other than his surroundings" (22), and also that he sits down to play "without...acknowledging the audience" (30). These ideas demonstrate the opposite of "study[ing] the audience around him," as (B) says.

C ✓ **Correct:** The text says "[Hattie] watched now as [Everett Payne]...conferred with the bassist and drummer" (26-27), which directly restates (C).

D **Direct Contradiction:** The text specifically says Everett Payne sat down to play "without announcing the name of the tune he intended playing" (28-29), so (D) is exactly contradicted by the passage.

Test 3, Question 6 (Form 16MC3 if you have the 2020-2021 Red Book—see page 23 for more)　　　**TYPE: DESCRIBE THE PASSAGE**

ⓘ *The prompt often mentions describing the passage without a line citation. The answer must still be restated or demonstrated by some specific part of the text. (See "What about Questions without Citations?" on p. 57.)*

　　Subjective Phrases to Ignore: "most nearly"

▶ **Where to look in the text:** Skim for "purists." Also recall that we saw discussion of the "purists" in the text relevant to question 4.

F **Direct Contradiction:** We know the purists aren't "open minded," as (F) would require, because we can see that they showed "open disgust" (37) after only a few chords of music, which means they reacted without giving Everett Payne a chance to show what he wanted to do.

G ✓ **Correct:** We see that the purists are snobbish in line 88, which says that they "normally refused to applaud even genius." We see that they're intolerant when they show "open disgust" (37) at the first few bars that Everett Payne plays. Since both parts of this choice are literally demonstrated in the passage, we know (G) is right.

H **Reasonable Statement Not in the Text:** Untrained test-takers might expect people who care a lot about jazz to be "well educated," but the text doesn't literally restate or demonstrate anything at all about their education, so (H) can't be right.

J **Barely Relevant:** Nothing in the passage restates or demonstrates anything about the experience level of the purists, one way or the other, so (J) can't be right.

Test 3, Question 7 (Form 16MC3 if you have the 2020-2021 Red Book—see page 23 for more)　　　**TYPE: DESCRIBE THE PASSAGE**

ⓘ *The prompt often mentions describing the passage without a line citation. The answer must still be restated or demonstrated by some specific part of the text. (See "What about Questions without Citations?" on p. 57.)*

　　Subjective Phrases to Ignore: "reasonably be inferred"

▶ **Where to look in the text:** Skim for "Bach." Also, if we've read most of the passage and haven't encountered the relevant text, we should focus on the parts of the passage we haven't read yet.

A   **Barely Relevant:** The text says Hattie "speculated" (65) that one of Everett Payne's ears was "trained on the bedrock that for him was Bach and the blues" (76-77), so it mentions the idea that "Bach and the blues" are "influences," as (A) would require. But the text never mentions Everett Payne trying to "avoid representing" those influences, as (A) would require.

B ✓ **Correct:** As we saw for (A), Hattie thinks Everett Payne is partially focused on "the bedrock that for him was Bach and the blues" (76-77). The word "bedrock" means something like "foundation," just as (B) requires. We also see that Hattie refers to Everett Payne's "dazzling array of ideas" (63-64) while he's playing, which demonstrates that his playing is "inventive," as (B) also requires.

C   **Confused Relationships:** This choice will attract a lot of untrained test-takers because the text does say that one of Everett's ears was "directed skyward" (68), toward "heaven" (67), listening to "the true music of the spheres, of the maelstrom up there" (72-73). But the text says Everett Payne's "*other* ear" (75) (emphasis added) is the one that "remained earthbound, trained on...Bach and the blues" (76-77). So the ear that's devoted to "Bach and the blues," as described in the prompt, isn't the ear that's devoted to "the true music of the heavens," so we can't conclude that "Bach and the blues" is "the true music of the heavens," as (C) would require.

D   **Confused Relationships:** The text does say that "Sonny Boy Blue" is a "Tin Pan Alley tune" (42), but it never says that Everett Payne can only play Tin Pan Alley tunes, which is what the word "limited" in (D) would require. Further, the text never makes any connection between "Bach and the blues" and Tin Pan Alley tunes, as (D) would also require. Either of these issues is enough by itself to make (D) wrong.

❚ Test 3, Question 8 (Form 16MC3 if you have the 2020-2021 Red Book—see page 23 for more)   **TYPE: DESCRIBE THE PASSAGE**

ⓘ   *The prompt often mentions describing the passage without a line citation. The answer must still be restated or demonstrated by some specific part of the text. (See "What about Questions without Citations?" on p. 57.)*

▶   **Where to look in the text:** Skim for "Sonny Boy Blue" and the description of the beginning of Payne's performance.

F ✓ **Correct:** The text says, "at first...he played the song straight through...at a slower tempo than was called for" (38-41). The phrase "at first" (38) indicates that this part of the text is relevant to when "Everett Payne first played," as the prompt requires. The phrase "at a slower tempo" (41) restates "more slowly" from (F). The phrase "than was called for" (41) restates "intended by the composer" in (F). Since every part of (F) is directly restated in the relevant part of the passage, we know (F) is right.

G   **Confused Relationships:** The text says Abe Kaiser "call[ed] Everett Payne's name" (3) to play with the band, but it never says Abe Kaiser suggested that Payne play "Sonny Boy Blue," so (G) isn't restated or demonstrated in the relevant text, which means it's wrong.

H   **Barely Relevant:** The text says that Everett Payne "conferred with the bassist and drummer" (27) before he played, and that the two of them "also treat[ed] the original as if it were a serious piece of music" (46-47), just as Everett Payne did. The text never says the bassist or drummer didn't want Payne to play "Sonny Boy Blue," so (H) isn't restated or demonstrated in the passage.

J   **Confused Relationships:** Many untrained test-takers will pick this choice because the text does say that Everett Payne plays his own version with "a dazzling pyrotechnic of chords...polyrhythms, [and] seemingly unrelated harmonies" (53-55), which means he's not playing the song the way it was originally written at that point. But, as trained test-takers, we see that the prompt asks how "Everett Payne first played" the song, and the text says, "at first...[Everett Payne] played the song straight through as written" (38-39), which contradicts the idea that he initially followed anything besides the original tune, as (J) would require. In other words, the passage clearly says that Everett Payne *first* plays the song all the way through as it was originally written, and only starts playing his own version after doing that.

❚ Test 3, Question 9 (Form 16MC3 if you have the 2020-2021 Red Book—see page 23 for more)   **TYPE: DESCRIBE THE PASSAGE**

ⓘ   *The prompt often mentions describing the passage without a line citation. The answer must still be restated or demonstrated by some specific part of the text. (See "What about Questions without Citations?" on p. 57.)*

▶   **Where to look in the text:** Skim for "Hattie" or "Sonny Boy Blue."

A ✓ **Correct:** The text says that Hattie "speculated" (65) that "the source" (65) of Everett Payne's "array of ideas and wealth of feeling" (64) had to do "with the way he held his head...tilted" (66-67). These quoted phrases in lines 64-67 literally restate the ideas from (A) and the prompt, so we know (A) is right.

B   **Confused Relationships:** The text does describe "Sonny Boy Blue" as a "little simpleminded tune" (59-60), but it never refers to the "the simplemindedness of the song" as the source for Everett Payne's "ideas and feelings," as (B) would require in connection with the prompt.

C   **Confused Relationships:** The text does say Everett Payne played "Sonny Boy Blue" "at first...with...formality" (38-42). But the passage never refers to "his ability to play with great formality" as the source of his "ideas and feelings," as (C) would require in connection with the prompt, so (C) is wrong.

D   **Reasonable Statement Not in the Text:** An untrained test-taker who wanted to analyze this passage as though she were in a literature class instead of an ACT testing session might assume that Everett Payne had a connection to the audience, and that this connection could inspire him to play the piano in beautiful and challenging ways. But the passage never literally mentions anything about any kind of "connection" between Everett Payne and "the silent audience," as (D) would require, nor does it say that Hattie thought such a connection was the source of the "musical ideas and feelings" mentioned in the prompt. So (D) can't be right.

ⓘ   *The prompt often mentions describing the passage without a line citation. The answer must still be restated or demonstrated by some specific part of the text. (See "What about Questions without Citations?" on p. 57.)*

▶   **Where to look in the text:** Skim for "Hattie." Also, if we've read most of the passage and haven't encountered the relevant text, we should focus on the parts of the passage we haven't read yet.

F   **Off by One or Two Words:** The text does say that part of Everett Payne's playing is "at a slower tempo" (41) and "with a formality" (41-42), but it never says that Hattie thinks Everett Payne is playing *too* slowly, which is what the word "overly" in this choice would require. This small, one-word difference from the text is enough to make (F) completely wrong. (See the note below for more on the issue of Hattie's perspective.)

G   **Confused Relationships:** The text does describe Everett Payne's actions as "deliberate" (18), and it does say he moves "absentmindedly" (21). But these words are descriptions of Everett's way of walking, not his performance—and the prompt asks how Payne's *performance* seemed to Hattie, not what she may have thought about the way he walked. (See the note below for more on the issue of Hattie's perspective.)

H   **Confused Relationships:** The passage mentions people sitting like they "were in church and weren't supposed to clap" (82-83), but that isn't literally the same thing as saying that Hattie thought Everett's performance itself was "like a song played in a church," as (H) requires. (See the note below for more on the issue of Hattie's perspective.)

J ✓ **Correct:** The text tells us that "it seemed to Hattie" (79) that "[Everett Payne] took them on a...roller coaster of a ride" (78-79). The phrase "it seemed to Hattie" (79) literally restates that we're reading Hattie's opinion, as the prompt requires. The phrase "roller coaster of a ride" (79) is repeated word-for-word in (J). (See the note below for more on the issue of Hattie's perspective.)

Note   From a literary standpoint, it's not totally clear whether the entire passage is written from Hattie's perspective, as the prompt for this question requires, or if only certain parts of the passage are presented from Hattie's perspective. But, as trained test-takers, we know that we don't have to worry about that distinction for two reasons. The first reason is that we know the passage must literally restate or demonstrate things in a way that doesn't require us to use literary analysis, because that's how the ACT Reading section works. The second reason is that, as it turns out, only one choice accurately restates ideas directly from the passage, so it must be the right choice whether we know whose perspective the other parts of the text are written from or not. (In other words, for example, it doesn't matter whether Hattie's perspective or the narrator's perspective would be the source of the observation that Everett Payne played slowly and formally in lines 38-43, because the text never restates the word "overly" in (F) anyway. The same kind of analysis can be applied to the other wrong answers.) It's also worth noting that the right answer is the only one that uses a phrase like "it seemed to Hattie" (79)—but even if that phrase hadn't appeared, we would still know that only (J) accurately restates the text, so (J) has to be right. On test day, remember not to get bogged down in the possible literary aspects of a passage! Instead, focus on the literal meaning of the text and remember your training.

ⓘ   *The prompt often mentions describing the passage without a line citation. The answer must still be restated or demonstrated by some specific part of the text. (See "What about Questions without Citations?" on p. 57.)*

Subjective Phrases to Ignore: "principal" "best"

A ✓ **Correct:** The use of the word "should" in the last paragraph ("our communities should be shaped by choice, not by chance" (80-81), "the goal should be an integrated system" (87-88), "we should demand land-use planning" (90)) literally demonstrates that the author is trying to convince the reader to have the same opinion as the one expressed in the passage. This is what "persuasive" means, so this choice is correct.

B   **Confused Relationships:** As we saw in our discussion of (A), the use of the word "should" in the passage demonstrates that the author wants to persuade the reader to believe something. If this were an explanatory passage, it would simply teach the reader about what sprawl is, rather than trying to convince the reader that sprawl is bad and should be avoided.

C   **Confused Relationships:** As we saw in our discussion of (A), this passage is persuasive, because its use of the word "should" indicates that it wants the reader to agree that steps should be taken to avoid sprawl. If this were a descriptive passage, it would just provide basic information about the concept of sprawl, rather than trying to convince the reader to agree with a certain position.

D   **Confused Relationships:** As we saw in our discussion of (A), this passage is persuasive. If this were a narrative passage, it would tell a story, rather than trying to convince the reader that sprawl should be avoided.

Note   We were able to answer this question by focusing on the use of a specific word ("should"), rather than trying to develop a generalized, overall sense of the text. This literal-minded, detail-oriented approach is exactly how a trained test-taker should always respond to a question on the ACT, no matter how much a prompt seems to be inviting us to consider the passage in a less objective way.

ℹ️   *The prompt often mentions describing the passage without a line citation. The answer must still be restated or demonstrated by some specific part of the text. (See "What about Questions without Citations?" on p. 57.)*

Subjective Phrases to Ignore: "best"

▶   **Where to look in the text:** Check the line citation for each answer choice.

F   **Direct Contradiction:** The author calls sprawl "a destructive, soulless, ugly mess" (9-10). Each of those words is strongly negative, so we know the author wouldn't want to create "incentives for sprawl," as (F) would require. In fact, if we look at the context of the citation from (F), we can see that the text says, "too many government entities have adopted laws and policies that constitute powerful incentives for sprawl" (20-22), which literally means the author wants fewer of these "laws and policies."

G   **Direct Contradiction:** According to the author, the quote from (G) is supported by "grim evidence" (33) and relates to "corroding" (36) a "sense of community" (36). The words "grim" and "corroding" are very negative, and demonstrate that the author doesn't like the idea in (G). So we know that he wouldn't "like to see it happen," as the prompt requires.

H   **Direct Contradiction:** After mentioning the "'affordable'" (53) housing, the author asks, "'affordable' for whom?" (54) He goes on to explain that this housing results in "higher taxes" (59) that "we all [pay for]" (59). In short, nothing in the passage shows that the author wants this "'affordable' housing on the edge of town"—or even that he agrees it's actually affordable in the first place (see "What about Unattributed Quotations ("Scare Quotes")?" on page 59 of this Black Book).

J ✓ **Correct:** The narrator clearly refers to the quote in (J) as "the goal" (87), which demonstrates that he wants to see it happen, just as the prompt requires.

ℹ️   *The question includes a citation from the text. The answer must be directly restated or demonstrated in the cited text, or in the text closely surrounding the cited text. (See "The General Process for Answering ACT Reading Questions," p. 57.)*

A   **Direct Contradiction:** The author asks a question and answers it in the *first* paragraph; he doesn't ask any questions at all in the *last* paragraph. Many untrained test-takers will pick this choice because they misread or misremember the prompt in a way that causes them to get the desired relationship between the paragraphs exactly backwards.

B   **Wrong Part of the Passage:** The author does cite statistics in the *next-to-last* paragraph, but this question asks about the *last* paragraph, which doesn't mention statistics at all. Some untrained test-takers will pick this choice because they'll vaguely remember some statistics being cited near the end of the passage, but they won't bother to go back to the text to verify whether those statistics were in the last paragraph.

C   **Direct Contradiction:** The author uses emotional language, like the word "frustrated" (8), in the *first* paragraph, but doesn't do so in the *last* paragraph—not the other way around. This wrong answer will trap a lot of untrained test-takers for the same reason (A) will.

D ✓ **Correct:** In the first paragraph the author describes the problem of "communities drowning in a destructive, soulless, ugly mess called sprawl" (9-10), without saying what can be done to solve the problem. In contrast, the entire last paragraph is essentially a list of solutions to the problem introduced in the first paragraph.

ℹ️   *The prompt often mentions describing the passage without a line citation. The answer must still be restated or demonstrated by some specific part of the text. (See "What about Questions without Citations?" on p. 57.)*

▶   **Where to look in the text:** Scan for longer words from the answer choices, like "development," "synonymous," "automobiles," and "communities."

F ✓ **Correct:** The author does say a lot about sprawl, but he never actually says how long it's been happening in U.S. cities. (Since this is an "EXCEPT" question, the right answer is the only one that's NOT directly restated or demonstrated in the relevant text. See "What about "EXCEPT" Questions?" on page 58 for more.)

G   **Direct Contradiction:** The author says specifically, in lines 17 and 18, that "development that destroys communities isn't progress." This means there can be some types of development that aren't examples of progress in the author's opinion, which answers the question in (G).

H   **Direct Contradiction:** Lines 67 through 72 describe zoning laws and codes, and then lines 73 and 74 say the codes are "a major reason why 82 percent of all trips in the United States are taken by car." This directly answers the question asked in (H), so (H) is wrong.

J   **Direct Contradiction:** The author offers an answer to this question in the final paragraph, though we have to read carefully to see it. The paragraph says, "one of the most effective ways to reach this goal" (81-82) is "sensible land-use planning" (82). The paragraph also refers to the idea of shaping communities "by choice, not by chance" (80-81), and the idea of making choices that encourage "alternatives to the automobile" (84). He ends by saying people "should demand land-use planning…in favor of…communities" (90-

91). All of these suggestions are ways that the "communities" mentioned in (J) can "combat sprawl," as (J) requires. We know this because the rest of the passage equates sprawl with unplanned, chaotic development (9-10), and also with widespread reliance on cars for transportation 73-77), among other, similar ideas. So we know that the steps in this paragraph that could be taken to fight bad development and the use of cars are also steps that would fight sprawl, according to the author. That means the answer to (J) does appear in the passage, so (J) is wrong.

Test 3, Question 15 (Form 16MC3 if you have the 2020-2021 Red Book—see page 23 for more)   **TYPE: DESCRIBE THE PASSAGE**

ⓘ   *The prompt often mentions describing the passage without a line citation. The answer must still be restated or demonstrated by some specific part of the text. (See "What about Questions without Citations?" on p. 57.)*

▶   **Where to look in the text:** Skim for "superstore" and "downtown."

A   **Direct Contradiction:** The text says that "a single new superstore may have more retail space than the entire downtown business district" (43-44), which literally restates (A) in combination with the prompt. But this is an "EXCEPT" question, so the right answer will be the only choice that's NOT literally restated or demonstrated in the text, and (A) is wrong.

B ✓   **Correct:** The text never says anything about "serious downtown renovations" as reflected in (B), let alone that such renovations could be caused by a superstore. Since this is the only choice that's not literally restated or demonstrated in the relevant text, it's the right answer to this "EXCEPT" question.

C   **Direct Contradiction:** Like (A), this choice directly restates a part of the passage, so it's a wrong answer on an "EXCEPT" question. (In this case, (C) restates the following sentence: "when a store like that opens...downtown becomes a ghost town" (44-47).)

D   **Direct Contradiction:** Like (A) and (C), this choice is wrong because it restates a part of the text exactly. (The text says of a new superstore that "when a store like that opens, the retail center of gravity shifts away from Main Street" (44-46).)

Test 3, Question 16 (Form 16MC3 if you have the 2020-2021 Red Book—see page 23 for more)   **TYPE: CITATION QUESTION**

ⓘ   *The question includes a citation from the text. The answer must be directly restated or demonstrated in the cited text, or in the text closely surrounding the cited text. (See "The General Process for Answering ACT Reading Questions," p. 57.)*

F   **Barely Relevant:** The tenth paragraph never mentions "environmental destruction," as (F) would require. The word "environment" (71) appears, but only in reference to the surrounding area where a person lives; nothing in the paragraph mentions the idea of destroying that environment, nor of destroying anything else.

G   **Direct Contradiction:** The text says that "current zoning laws make it impossible...to create...[a] compact walkable environment" (69-71), which directly contradicts (G).

H ✓   **Correct:** The text says that the "land-use regulations" mentioned in (H) "are a major reason why 82 percent of all trips in the United States are taken by car" (73-74), and that transportation costs, "most of which are auto-related," now account for "more than 18 percent" (75-77) of the average American household budget, which is "more than it spends for food and...health care" (77-79). These statistics demonstrate that people are forced to drive more now, and that they're paying a relatively large portion of their budget to do that, just as (H) says.

J   **Confused Relationships:** The text mentions that the average household spends more on transportation "than it spends for food and three times more than it spends for health care" (77-79). But the text never says that Americans should spend less of their budgets on food and healthcare, as the phrase "too much" in (J) would require.

Test 3, Question 17 (Form 16MC3 if you have the 2020-2021 Red Book—see page 23 for more)   **TYPE: DESCRIBE THE PASSAGE**

ⓘ   *The prompt often mentions describing the passage without a line citation. The answer must still be restated or demonstrated by some specific part of the text. (See "What about Questions without Citations?" on p. 57.)*

▶   **Where to look in the text:** Skim for "retail development." We also may have seen the relevant text when we were answering question 15.

A   **Barely Relevant:** The author never specifically mentions any kind of development that's immediately next to the existing downtown areas, as (A) requires.

B   **Direct Contradiction:** The text says that sprawl "leav[es] historic buildings...underused" (26-27), which is the opposite of utilizing historic buildings, as (B) would require.

C ✓   **Correct:** The text refers to "retail development that transforms roads into strip malls" (38-39) (which restates (C) exactly) as "one form of sprawl" (38), which exactly restates the phrase "one form of sprawl" from the prompt.

D   **Direct Contradiction:** The text says that the effects of sprawl are "corroding the...sense of community" (36), which directly contradicts the statement in (D).

Test 3, Question 18 (Form 16MC3 if you have the 2020-2021 Red Book—see page 23 for more)   **TYPE: VOCABULARY IN CONTEXT**

ⓘ   *The prompt asks about the specific meaning of a word in the passage. The right answer must still be directly restated or demonstrated in the text surrounding the cited word. (See "What about "Vocabulary in Context" Questions?" on p. 59.)*

Subjective Phrases to Ignore: "most nearly"

F   **Reasonable Statement Not in the Text:** In some other context, "detached" could mean "objective," because both words can describe someone who isn't influenced by personal feelings. But the passage doesn't say anything about this meaning of "objective," or about ignoring personal feelings, or about the difference between subjectivity and objectivity, etc., so (F) isn't literally restated or demonstrated in the relevant part of the passage, which means it's wrong.

G ✓   **Correct:** The word "detached" is used in line 51, in the phrase "a detached home in the middle of a grassy lawn." If the home is "in the middle of a grassy lawn," then, by definition, it must be "set apart" from other houses, just as (G) requires, since there's a grassy lawn all around it.

H   **Reasonable Statement Not in the Text:** In another context, "detached" could mean "broken apart," because both terms can describe two things that were once connected, but have been physically separated. But the text doesn't restate or demonstrate the idea of houses being together and then "broken apart" as (H) would require, so (H) is wrong.

J   **Barely Relevant:** The phrase "taken away" could only fit if the "home in the middle of a grassy lawn" (51-52) had been physically taken from one place to another, or the home had been taken from one person and given to another person, which isn't restated or demonstrated in the relevant text.

❚ Test 3, Question 19 (Form 16MC3 if you have the 2020-2021 Red Book—see page 23 for more)   TYPE: CITATION QUESTION

ⓘ   *The question includes a citation from the text. The answer must be directly restated or demonstrated in the cited text, or in the text closely surrounding the cited text. (See "The General Process for Answering ACT Reading Questions," p. 57.)*

    Subjective Phrases to Ignore: "most nearly"

A   **Confused Relationships:** The text does mention "needless duplication of services" (60), but that idea occurs in a separate paragraph from the quotation mentioned in the question, and nothing in the text indicates that the "duplication of services" (60) is related to the idea of a "level field" (64).

B   **Barely Relevant:** The text mentions the idea of "higher taxes" (59) as a way to pay for the "needless duplication of services" (60) we just discussed for (A), but it never says the higher taxes only apply to "some people," as (B) would require. Nor does the text actually say that higher taxes make anyone's lives "more difficult," as (B) would also require—and none of this connects to the idea of a "level field" (64) from the prompt.

C   **Direct Contradiction:** The text says, "people who say that sprawl is merely the natural product of marketplace forces at work fail to recognize that the game isn't being played on a level field" (62-64). When we break that sentence down, we see that the author is saying that people who think sprawl is an example of "marketplace forces" don't realize that the playing field isn't level—in other words, the absence of "a level field" is why it's *wrong* to say that "marketplace forces are at work." So (C) says the opposite of what the relevant text says.

D ✓   **Correct:** As we saw for (C), the idea that "the game isn't being played on a level field" (64) is something that isn't realized by people who think "sprawl is... the natural product of marketplace forces" (62-63), according to the author. The author then immediately explains that "government...is riddled with policies that...encourage sprawl" (64-66). Taken together, these lines explicitly say that sprawl isn't actually a natural result of marketplace forces—instead, it's the result of marketplace forces that have been changed by decisions made by governments. This is exactly what (D) says, so (D) is right.

❚ Test 3, Question 20 (Form 16MC3 if you have the 2020-2021 Red Book—see page 23 for more)   TYPE: CITATION QUESTION

ⓘ   *The question includes a citation from the text. The answer must be directly restated or demonstrated in the cited text, or in the text closely surrounding the cited text. (See "The General Process for Answering ACT Reading Questions," p. 57.)*

    Subjective Phrases to Ignore: "most likely"

F   **Direct Contradiction:** The text refers to the idea of "prohibiting mixed uses and mandating inordinate amounts of parking" (67-68). Since "prohibiting" and "mandating" are opposite ideas, the text is directly saying that "mixed uses" and "parking" are opposite ideas in context, which means (F) must be wrong.

G   **Off by One or Two Words:** The text says that "prohibiting mixed uses" (67) "makes it impossible... to create the sort of compact walkable environment that attracts us to older neighborhoods and historic communities" (69-72). So the text says that "prohibiting mixed uses" gets in the way of *creating an environment* that is *like* a historic neighborhood—this isn't the same thing as saying that "mixed uses" *preserve existing* historic neighborhoods, as (G) would require. Instead, "mixed uses" are being described as things that lead to a situation *like* the ones found in older neighborhoods and historic communities.

H   **Confused Relationships:** The text talks about having a "walkable environment" (71) and mentions that "82 percent of all trips...are taken by car" (73-74), so a lot of untrained test-takers will be attracted to this choice. But, as trained test-takers, we realize that the text never actually discusses the idea of actively stopping cars from being driven to local businesses, as (H) would require. There's a difference between working towards a walkable environment that doesn't require as much driving, which is what the author discusses, and "ensuring that automobiles" cannot be driven in an area, which is what (H) says.

J ✓   **Correct:** This choice is a bit unusual for an ACT Reading question, but it still follows all the test's rules for a right answer, of course. In order to find the part of the text that directly demonstrates the right answer in a literal way, we need to notice that the text also uses the phrase "mixed-use" in line 85, where it explains that "mixed-use zoning...reduce[s] the distances...between home and work"

(85-87). Since "home" and "work" are two different "types of development" as described in (J), and "mixed-use zoning" brings these two different types of development closer together, we see that the text literally demonstrates the idea of combining more than one kind of development in a given area, as (J) requires.

ⓘ *The prompt often mentions describing the passage without a line citation. The answer must still be restated or demonstrated by some specific part of the text. (See "What about Questions without Citations?" on p. 57.)*

Subjective Phrases to Ignore: "best"

A ✓ **Correct:** The passage literally demonstrates the author's "developing interest," just as (A) requires. The first line says "it started" when she was a teenager (we find out over the course of the passage that the word "it" refers to the author's interest in flowers, plants, and related areas of science), the day she "went on a nature walk" (2) and first saw a copy of the field guide (14-24). The author says that "by...the next summer" (67) she had "fully discovered the joy of the hunt" (67-68) and viewed "data" (69) about each species as a "trophy" (69), which demonstrates an increased level of interest from the beginning of the passage. Finally, the closing paragraph demonstrates that the author came to know more about the world around her because of her interest in individual plants when she says, among other things, that her knowledge of "plant communities" (86-87) led her to "travel" (91) down a "road" (90) that included areas of science like "quaternary geology, biogeography, evolutionary biology" (89-90), which are all different disciplines related to the study of the natural world. So the passage begins by describing how "it [the narrator's interest in flowers] started," then goes on to describe her experience identifying more flowers, and finally says that this pursuit led her to "the grand schemes of things" (87) and other studies of the natural world. This demonstrates the ideas from (A), so (A) is right.

B **Off by One or Two Words:** The author does begin by describing an event that led to a lifelong fascination, but as we discussed in (A), this fascination is originally with flowers in general, then with plants, and finally with other areas of science—not a lifelong fascination with *asters* in particular, as (B) would require. (It's true that the first flower she takes notice of is an aster (6, 8), but the rest of the passage clearly indicates that the author becomes interested in a wide array of subjects as a result of her initial interest in a single aster.)

C **Confused Relationships:** This choice is wrong for a few reasons. One reason is that the passage doesn't "review" any relationships, as (C) would require; it only mentions a few other people in passing, without discussing any details of the author's relationships to those people. Beyond that, "identify[ing]...plants" (81) in general isn't the same thing as "sharing an interest in flowers," specifically, as (C) would require—the text never says that Julie, or any other person other than the narrator, is specifically interested in flowers. Any of these issues by itself would be enough to make (C) wrong.

D **Reasonable Statement Not in the Text:** Some untrained test-takers might assume that someone with such a passion for plants and the natural world might pursue a related career—but the text never specifically demonstrates or restates the idea that the author makes money from anything, as the word "profitable" would require, nor that she decided to pursue any topic professionally, as the word "career" would require. So (D) must be wrong.

ⓘ *The prompt often mentions describing the passage without a line citation. The answer must still be restated or demonstrated by some specific part of the text. (See "What about Questions without Citations?" on p. 57.)*

Subjective Phrases to Ignore: "best"

▶ **Where to look in the text:** Skim for a question mark and quotation marks to locate the question and response referred to in the prompt.

F **Barely Relevant:** Nothing in the relevant text literally demonstrates or restates the idea of acceptance, so (F) must be wrong.

G **Barely Relevant:** As we saw with (F), nothing in the relevant text literally demonstrates or restates the idea of surprise, so (G) must be wrong, too.

H ✓ **Correct:** The young man's use of the word "just'" (6) demonstrates that he doesn't think the question is challenging or important. Further, the author says the young man might have "sniff[ed] as he turned away" (7) after answering the question; both sniffing and turning away from someone literally demonstrate a lack of interest in a topic or a lack of concern for it. And when the author echoes the young man's phrase "just an aster" (8) and continues by saying "and I was just a total ignoramus" (8-9), she's expressing that the *young man* seemed to think she was an ignoramus. Each of these elements of the text, even considered separately, demonstrates literally that, "as portrayed by the author," the young man showed he had no respect for the question and didn't consider it important, which is essentially the definition of "condescension." (See the note below if you had difficulty with the words "ignoramus" and/or "condescension.")

J **Barely Relevant:** We discussed the relevant text and what it literally indicates in (H); (J) has the same problem as (F) and (G), which is that nothing in the passage literally demonstrates or restates the idea of anger.

Note Some test-takers may not know the word "condescension" from the right answer, or the word "ignoramus" from the relevant text. But, as will often be the case with difficult words on the ACT, it's still possible for us to know with certainty that (H) must be right even if we don't know one or both of those words. First, it's clear that (F), (G), and (J) aren't literally present in the text about the young man, as we saw above. Since we know that the one right answer for each question has to be literally demonstrated or restated in the text, we'd know for sure that (H) must be right as soon as we determined the other choices were all wrong. Further, if we knew the word "condescension" but didn't know the word "ignoramus," we'd be able to find the right answer by noting that the sniff combined with the use of the word "just" are both literal demonstrations of condescension, no matter what the word "ignoramus" meant. Remember this kind of thing on test day, and don't give up on a question just because it includes a few words you may not feel sure of!

Test 3, Question 23 (Form 16MC3 if you have the 2020-2021 Red Book—see page 23 for more)   TYPE: DESCRIBE THE PASSAGE

ⓘ   *The prompt often mentions describing the passage without a line citation. The answer must still be restated or demonstrated by some specific part of the text. (See "What about Questions without Citations?" on p. 57.)*

▶   Where to look in the text: Skim for the flower names in the answer choices.

A   **Confused Relationships:** The author never actually gives a name for the flower she's looking at during the mountain hike, which is discussed in lines 31-51. She does list the names of other plants that are similar to the one she's looking at in lines 50-51—including each of the flowers in the answer choices—as examples of other "five-petaled yellow flowers" (50) that are "packed" (49) into the "six more pages" (49) she still has to consider in trying to find the name of the flower she sees on the hike, but she never definitively states that any of those names is appropriate for the flower she's looking at.

B   **Confused Relationships:** This choice has the same problem as (A): it's listed as one example of a flower in the field guide in lines 50-51, but it isn't specifically identified as the flower the author was looking at.

C   **Confused Relationships:** This choice has the same problem as (A): it's listed as one example of a flower in the field guide in lines 50-51, but it isn't specifically identified as the flower the author was looking at.

D ✓   **Correct:** As we saw in the discussion for (A), the author never specifically names the flower she's looking at on the mountain hike in lines 31-51.

Test 3, Question 24 (Form 16MC3 if you have the 2020-2021 Red Book—see page 23 for more)   TYPE: DESCRIBE THE PASSAGE

ⓘ   *The prompt often mentions describing the passage without a line citation. The answer must still be restated or demonstrated by some specific part of the text. (See "What about Questions without Citations?" on p. 57.)*

Subjective Phrases to Ignore: "most strongly implies"

▶   Where to look in the text: Skim for "Peterson's."

F ✓   **Correct:** We know the author found the book "daunting at first," as (F) requires, because when she first starts using the book, she says that becoming familiar with the book "wasn't going to be an easy affair" (28-29), and she calls the book "stubborn" (54). The words "stubborn" and "not easy" are both synonyms for "daunting" in this context. And we know the author thought the Peterson's was "preferable to either a more or a less complete guide," as (F) also requires, because she says "a less complete guide would have been...more frustrating in the end" 58-60), but "a more complete book would have been impossible for me to use" (60-61). Since every part of (F) is literally restated in the passage, we know (F) is right.

G   **Confused Relationships:** The author says, "*a less complete guide* [than the Peterson's guide] would have been easier to start with, but more frustrating in the end" (58-60) (emphasis added). So the author does say that one kind of guide would have been "easy" at first but "frustrating" later, as (G) would require—but the prompt asked us about "the Peterson's guide," which isn't the same as the hypothetical "less complete guide" being discussed in lines 58-60, so (G) is wrong.

H   **Reasonable Statement Not in the Text:** An untrained test-taker might reasonably imagine that pairing a difficult book "with a different guide written for beginners," as described in (H), would make the learning process easier. But, as trained test-takers, we know that the ACT Reading section doesn't care about what we could reasonably imagine; it only cares about what's literally restated or demonstrated on the page. The author never mentions pairing one kind of book with another, so (H) can't be right.

J   **Barely Relevant:** The author never mentions any dissatisfaction with the illustrations in the Peterson's, as (J) would require.

Test 3, Question 25 (Form 16MC3 if you have the 2020-2021 Red Book—see page 23 for more)   TYPE: CITATION QUESTION

ⓘ   *The question includes a citation from the text. The answer must be directly restated or demonstrated in the cited text, or in the text closely surrounding the cited text. (See "The General Process for Answering ACT Reading Questions," p. 57.)*

Subjective Phrases to Ignore: "most nearly"

A   **Reasonable Statement Not in the Text:** In some other context, the phrase "get in" might describe the process of arriving at a physical location, as (A) would require. But the author uses the phrase "get in" in the context of a discussion about a "book" (54) and a "landscape" (56), with nothing in the text demonstrating or restating the idea of arriving anywhere, so (A) can't be right.

B   **Reasonable Statement Not in the Text:** As we saw with (A), it's possible to imagine some kind of context where "get in" could refer to becoming a member of a group, as (B) would require. But the author never mentions becoming a member of anything, which means the text isn't restating or demonstrating anything from (B), so (B) can't be right.

C ✓   **Correct:** The text surrounding the phrase from the prompt describes the author "consulting [the] crowded pages" (52-53) of a reference book, and says the "book led [the author] to the particulars, and that's what [she] wanted" (57-58); she finally says that after "wrestling with the [book]" (61-62), she was able to start seeing plants as "individuals" (63). All of these quotes demonstrate that the author was learning more and more about the subject of plant life by working with the book, just as (C) requires.

D   **Reasonable Statement Not in the Text:** As with (A) and (B), this choice could reflect a possible meaning of the phrase "get in" in some other context, but the text surrounding the quote in the prompt never discusses "be[ing] friendly with someone," as (D) would require, so (D) must be wrong.

Test 3, Question 26 (Form 16MC3 if you have the 2020-2021 Red Book—see page 23 for more)   **TYPE: DESCRIBE THE PASSAGE**

ⓘ   *The prompt often mentions describing the passage without a line citation. The answer must still be restated or demonstrated by some specific part of the text. (See "What about Questions without Citations?" on p. 57.)*

Subjective Phrases to Ignore: "best"

▶   **Where to look in the text:** Skim for "Julie." We also may have encountered some of the relevant text in answering question 21.

F   **Barely Relevant:** The text does say that the author and her "friend Julie...identified individual plants in [their] rambles" (81-82), but it never says anything about which person has more experience with anything, as (F) would require.

G   **Barely Relevant:** The text does mention "bogs" (83) and "montane forests" (83-84), but it never explicitly says anything about where anyone lives in relation to those environments, or about Julie owning a house, as (G) would require.

H ✓   **Correct:** In the last paragraph, which discusses how the narrator and Julie "identified...plants in [their] rambles" (81-82) and learned about "plant communities" (86-87) together, the passage says, "bogs held one community, montane forests held another" (83-84), and the plants in these communities "were clues to intricate dramas" (85). Then the passage says that other areas of study Julie and the narrator encountered "arrived rooted in real place and personal experience" (88-89) because of this knowledge of "plant communities" (86-87). In other words, the narrator is describing in these lines the valuable knowledge she and Julie acquired as a result of their understanding of "various communities of plants" as mentioned in (H), which means she "sees value" in that understanding, as (H) also requires. Beyond that, the fact that Julie spends time and energy on identifying plants demonstrates that she finds it worthwhile to do that, and the use of the term "clues" indicates that the plant identifications provided valuable information for the purpose of understanding some larger set of ideas; all of these concepts demonstrate that Julie "sees value", as the prompt requires. So (H) must be right.

J   **Barely Relevant:** The text never mentions anyone who stops using the Peterson's, so (J) can't be right.

Test 3, Question 27 (Form 16MC3 if you have the 2020-2021 Red Book—see page 23 for more)   **TYPE: DESCRIBE THE PASSAGE**

ⓘ   *The prompt often mentions describing the passage without a line citation. The answer must still be restated or demonstrated by some specific part of the text. (See "What about Questions without Citations?" on p. 57.)*

▶   **Where to look in the text:** Skim for "Peterson's."

A   **Confused Relationships:** Line 31 mentions an event that happened when the author had had the book "for about a week," so some untrained test-takers might assume the right answer should be a time period measured in days or weeks, if they don't read carefully. But, as trained test-takers, we see that the event in line 31 isn't discussed in connection with the book "[becoming] her closest companion," as the prompt requires.

B   **Confused Relationships:** This choice has the same problem as (A): the phrase "for about a week" (31) doesn't appear in the passage in connection with the idea of the book becoming the author's closest companion, as the prompt requires.

C   **Confused Relationships:** Line 67 refers to "the time the next summer came," which does refer to a time period measured in months. But that phrase refers to how long it took the author to "discover[] the joy of the hunt" (67-68), which isn't something she discusses in connection with the book becoming her closest companion, as the prompt requires.

D ✓   **Correct:** The text says that the Peterson's guide became her "closest companion" (26), just as the prompt requires, "over the next several years" (line 25), which is exactly restated by (D).

Test 3, Question 28 (Form 16MC3 if you have the 2020-2021 Red Book—see page 23 for more)   **TYPE: CITATION QUESTION**

ⓘ   *The question includes a citation from the text. The answer must be directly restated or demonstrated in the cited text, or in the text closely surrounding the cited text. (See "The General Process for Answering ACT Reading Questions," p. 57.)*

Subjective Phrases to Ignore: "most nearly"

F   **Confused Relationships:** The author does mention the word "landscape" (56) in the statement from the prompt, but she doesn't say anything about "understand[ing] landscapes" themselves, as (F) would require. She also says that she "wanted" (58) the "particulars" (57), which was why she read the book; that desire for "particulars" contradicts the idea of not looking at "details" in (F). Any of these issues by itself would be enough to make (F) wrong.

G   **Reasonable Statement Not in the Text:** Some untrained test-takers who approach the ACT Reading section as though it were a discussion in a literature class will be drawn to this choice because they might think it would make sense for a landscape to lose its appeal if it were analyzed, just as (G) indicates. But the author never directly demonstrates or restates the idea of landscapes "los[ing] their appeal" under any conditions, so (G) can't be right.

H   Barely Relevant: No part of the passage mentions the author painting anything.

J   ✓ Correct: In the text that's mentioned in the prompt, the author specifically says that she "wanted" (58) to learn the "particulars" (57) of a landscape from her field guide, as a way to "*get in*" (56) (emphasis in original). The phrase "particulars" (57) restates the idea of "individual parts" from this choice. The phrase "get in" (56) restates the idea of "[seeking] a deeper knowledge" from (J). (If you're not clear on the meaning of the phrase "get in" in this context, please go take a look at our analysis of choice (C) from question 25 earlier in this section.)

Test 3, Question 29 (Form 16MC3 if you have the 2020-2021 Red Book—see page 23 for more)   **TYPE: CITATION QUESTION**

ℹ️   *The question includes a citation from the text. The answer must be directly restated or demonstrated in the cited text, or in the text closely surrounding the cited text. (See "The General Process for Answering ACT Reading Questions," p. 57.)*

Subjective Phrases to Ignore: "primarily" "suggest"

A   Reasonable Statement Not in the Text: The text never mentions a publishing company, nor says anything about the book being made cheaply or shoddily, as (A) would require. This choice will attract a lot of untrained test-takers who don't read carefully and assume that the only reason a book would change over time is that it was made poorly...even though the author refers to "annotations" (66), which can't be the result of simple wear and tear because they involve someone writing in the book.

B   ✓ Correct: The author says, "the book changed: its cover was stained...the spine grew invitingly lax, and some of the margins sprouted cryptic annotations" (64-66). These changes—especially the annotations, which have to be written by someone—demonstrate that the book physically changed as she kept using it, just as (B) requires.

C   Confused Relationships: The text does mentions "cryptic annotations" (66) in the margins of the book. But annotations in the margin that appear (or "sprout[]" (66)) over time are something that a reader *adds* to a book, not something *already in* the book that a reader would "encounter[]," as (C) requires. Further, nothing in the passage indicates how frequently the annotations appear (that is, how many annotations there are in a given number of pages), so (C)'s use of "often" isn't restated or demonstrated in the passage.

D   Reasonable Statement Not in the Text: The text mentions that the book became "stained by water and snack food" (64-65), which might seem to reflect carelessness, and could be something the author might reasonably regret, if we were trying to analyze the text like a piece of literature. But, as trained test-takers, we see that the author never explicitly says anything about regretting treating the book in a particular way, so (D) must be wrong.

Test 3, Question 30 (Form 16MC3 if you have the 2020-2021 Red Book—see page 23 for more)   **TYPE: DESCRIBE THE PASSAGE**

ℹ️   *The prompt often mentions describing the passage without a line citation. The answer must still be restated or demonstrated by some specific part of the text. (See "What about Questions without Citations?" on p. 57.)*

▶   **Where to look in the text:** Skim for the italicized phrase "*Solidago hispida.*"

F   Confused Relationships: The author has difficulty identifying a yellow flower in lines 33-51, but "*Solidago hispida*" isn't that flower. Instead, "*Solidago hispida*" appears in line 72, and the author never says she had trouble identifying it.

G   Direct Contradiction: The author mentions "*Solidago hispida*" as an example of a flower she had "found...before" (70) and "was happy to see...again" (70-71), which means she has seen it at least twice. This contradicts the idea that she "hopes to finally come across" it, as (G) would require.

H   ✓ Correct: As we saw in the explanation for (G), the author uses "*Solidago hispida*" as an example of a flower she had "found...before" (70) and "was happy to see...again" (70-71), which directly restates the idea that she "was pleased to encounter [it] again," as (H) requires. We also know that she "had learned to identify" the flower, as (H) requires, because she calls it by name (71-72).

J   Barely Relevant: The author never offers an opinion on whether "*Solidago hispida*" is "an appropriate name," as (J) would require—if anything, the author says that the whole naming system for plants "makes such delightful sense" (79-80), which would contradict the idea that a name for a particular plant might not make sense.

Test 3, Question 31 (Form 16MC3 if you have the 2020-2021 Red Book—see page 23 for more)   **TYPE: DESCRIBE THE PASSAGE**

ℹ️   *The prompt often mentions describing the passage without a line citation. The answer must still be restated or demonstrated by some specific part of the text. (See "What about Questions without Citations?" on p. 57.)*

Subjective Phrases to Ignore: "reasonably be inferred"

A   Reasonable Statement Not in the Text: The passage does describe various scientists communicating with each other, and some untrained test-takers may assume that (A) is right because it seems reasonable to think that communication is important in science. But the text never specifically says or demonstrates that "communication among scientists" is "important," or "critical," or "vital," or any other word that would make (A) right on the ACT.

B   Incorrect: This choice could attract some test-takers because the text does say that the "shape" (19) of a snow crystal depends on its "facets" (19), and later tells us that "the size and shape of the snow crystals" (64-65) has an impact on the "amount[] of snowpack water" (63). But the passage never tells us *how* those facets influence snowpack, as (B) would require, so (B) can't be right. (In other words, the text never says that differences in snow crystal facets cause the crystals to stack or move in different ways, or absorb or deflect light differently, or stay colder longer, or anything like that--these could be examples of *how* the facets influence snowpack, but no such idea appears in the text.)

C   **Confused Relationships:** The passage mentions two different uses of the scanning electron microscope: to "look at biological problems relating to agriculture" (36-37), and "to image snow crystals" (45) (this same idea of imaging snow appears again in the last paragraph). But making two brief mentions of using a scanning electron microscope isn't the same as "showcase[ing] the varied uses of the scanning electron microscope." For a word like "varied" to be appropriate, the text would have to say something like "the scanning electron microscope can be used in many different situations for many different purposes" or "the scanning electron microscope can be useful in a wide variety of ways," or something along those lines. No such idea is restated or demonstrated in the text, so (C) must be wrong. (It's true that the text does describe the scanning electron microscope being used two different ways, and does say that "it was the first time anyone had attempted to image snow crystals with scanning electron microscopy" (44-46). But demonstrating two different uses of the microscope isn't the same as "showcase[ing] the varied uses" of the microscope, especially since the text doesn't go into much detail about the first use—"look[ing] at biological problems related to agriculture" (36-37)—so we don't really know how different it is from the second use—"imag[ing] snow crystals" (45)—and demonstrating a difference is necessary to justify a word like "varied," as (C) would require. Also, the fact that "it was the first time anyone had attempted to image snow crystals with scanning electron microscopy" (44-46) doesn't necessarily mean that doing so was very different from other uses of the scanning electron microscope—for example, the text even says that both uses involved looking at things that are frozen: "frozen" "tissue" (39-40) and "snowflakes" (43).)

D ✓   **Correct:** The second paragraph says "information about...snow crystals...has practical applications in...diverse areas" (11-13), which restates the idea of "practical applications of the study of snow crystals" from (D), and alludes to a wide range of such applications. Later, the passage discusses using information about snow crystals to "predict the amount of water available in a winter snowpack" (55-56), to impact "climate change predictions" (74-75), and also in the fields of "predicting avalanches, designing artificial snow, and...examining air pollution" (85-87). These mentions "demonstrate some of the practical applications" from lines 11-13. Since the concepts in (D) are demonstrated several times in the passage, (D) is right.

■ **Test 3, Question 32 (Form 16MC3 if you have the 2020-2021 Red Book—see page 23 for more)**   **TYPE: DESCRIBE THE PASSAGE**

ⓘ   *The prompt often mentions describing the passage without a line citation. The answer must still be restated or demonstrated by some specific part of the text. (See "What about Questions without Citations?" on p. 57.)*

▶   **Where to look in the text:** Skim for "scanning electron microscopy," "Colorado," "Montana," "Utah," "Wyoming," and "75 percent."

F   **Confused Relationships:** There are a lot of things wrong with (F). One of the most obvious ones is that the passage never refers to the idea of anyone "encouraging scientists," as (F) would require. Further, many of the other phrases in (F) are demonstrated or restated by different parts of the passage, but they aren't tied together in a way that reflects the relationships in (F). The passage mentions "making estimates" as part of the "Snowmelt Runoff Model" (54-55), but those are estimates of the amount of water that will be generated by the snowmelt, not estimates of "water requirements," as (F) would require. The passage does mention "water...demand" (81), but not as a quantity being estimated, as (F) would require. And the only thing being discussed in the passage that's arguably "far into the future," as (F) would also require, is the "warming up" (77) that Rango expects to "happen by 2100" (76). And none of the ideas we've mentioned so far for (F) relate directly to the idea of "sav[ing] money," as described in the prompt.

G ✓   **Correct:** Lines 71-72 say that "improving the prediction by 1 percent would save $38 million." When we look earlier in the text to see what "the prediction" could refer to, we see the phrase "the forecasted amounts of snowpack water" (63), which are found by "employing the scanning electron microscopy results" (62-63). So the text says literally that using the scanning electron microscope can allow the amounts of snowpack water to be forecasted more accurately, and that those more accurate forecasts could save tens of millions of dollars for every 1% improvement in the forecast. Since (G) literally restates the relevant information from the text, we know it's correct.

H   **Barely Relevant:** The text never mentions anything related to the process of "identifying biological problems," as (H) would require (it does mention two people working on "biological problems related to agriculture" (36-37), but it doesn't discuss how those problems were originally identified). And the text certainly never connects the idea of biological problems to the idea of saving money, as the prompt would require.

J   **Confused Relationships:** The text does say that snowmelt accounts for "about 75 percent of the annual water supply" (57-58) of those states, but that's the only time the text mentions the figure of 75%. The text never discusses "increasing the water supply...by 75 percent," as (J) would require.

■ **Test 3, Question 33 (Form 16MC3 if you have the 2020-2021 Red Book—see page 23 for more)**   **TYPE: CITATION QUESTION**

ⓘ   *The question includes a citation from the text. The answer must be directly restated or demonstrated in the cited text, or in the text closely surrounding the cited text. (See "The General Process for Answering ACT Reading Questions," p. 57.)*

  Subjective Phrases to Ignore: "reasonably be inferred"

A   **Confused Relationships:** Temperature and humidity are mentioned in line 29, but not in connection with the phrase "metamorphosed conditions" from lines 47-48.

B   **Confused Relationships:** This has an issue similar to what we saw for (A): the text mentions dust in line 19, but not in connection with the phrase "metamorphosed conditions" from lines 47-48.

C ✓ **Correct:** The phrase "metamorphosed conditions" is immediately followed by an explanation: "crystals often change once on the ground" (48-49). This is exactly what (C) says, so (C) is right.

D **Confused Relationships:** Again, we see the same problem that (A) and (B) had: the text mentions changing environmental conditions in lines 74-83, but not in connection with the phrase "metamorphosed conditions" in lines 47-48.

▌ Test 3, Question 34 (Form 16MC3 if you have the 2020-2021 Red Book—see page 23 for more)   TYPE: DESCRIBE THE PASSAGE

ⓘ   *The prompt often mentions describing the passage without a line citation. The answer must still be restated or demonstrated by some specific part of the text. (See "What about Questions without Citations?" on p. 57.)*

▶   **Where to look in the text:** Skim for "Snowmelt Runoff Model."

F **Confused Relationships:** The passage says that scientists use "microwave satellite data" (54) *along with* "electron microscopy data" (53) in the Snowmelt Runoff Model. So we can see that the satellite data and the scanning electron microscopy data are both separate parts of the model, not that one form of data "allows...the model to include...predictions...about" the other form, which is what the prompt requires.

G ✓ **Correct:** The text says, "before employing the scanning electron microscopy results, the forecast[s]...were inaccurate whenever the size and shape of the snow crystals varied much from the norm" (62-65). So the predictions must have been more accurate "whenever...the snow crystals varied...from the norm" *after* the scanning electron microscopy results were considered. This means that the scanning electron microscopy results must have provided information about "structural variations of snow crystals," as (G) requires, because "size and shape" are synonymous with "structure" in this context.

H **Barely Relevant:** The passage does say that some "western states" (56) get 75 percent of their annual water supply from snowmelt. But this isn't the same thing as saying that those areas get "the most snowfall," as (H) would require. And the text never mentions scanning electron microscopy data, in itself, providing information about which places have the most snowfall. Either of these issues by itself is enough to make (H) wrong.

J **Confused Relationships:** The passage does say that two scientists "were using scanning electron microscopy to look at biological problems relating to agriculture" (35-37). But their work isn't described as being related to the Snowmelt Runoff Model, as described in the prompt; they were just the first two people who happened to "image[] some snowflakes" (43).

▌ Test 3, Question 35 (Form 16MC3 if you have the 2020-2021 Red Book—see page 23 for more)   TYPE: DESCRIBE THE PASSAGE

ⓘ   *The prompt often mentions describing the passage without a line citation. The answer must still be restated or demonstrated by some specific part of the text. (See "What about Questions without Citations?" on p. 57.)*

▶   **Where to look in the text:** Skim for "Rango" and "2100."

A **Confused Relationships:** The last paragraph mentions the idea of finding pollution in snowflakes, but that idea isn't discussed in connection with "what will happen by 2100" (76), which is what the prompt tells us to consider.

B **Confused Relationships:** The idea of "more accurate predictions of the water supply" is discussed in lines 62-73, but, as we saw with (A), that idea isn't mentioned in connection with "what will happen by 2100" (76), as the prompt requires.

C **Confused Relationships:** Just as with (A) and (B), we see that the idea of snowflakes containing "sulfur and nitrogen" is mentioned in line 89, but that idea isn't connected to "what will happen by 2100" (76), which is what the prompt is telling us to consider.

D ✓ **Correct:** Lines 74-83 mention "climate change predictions" (74-75), and say that "by 2100" (76), the "overall snow accumulation [will] decrease[]...greatly increasing water's economic value" (78-82). We can see that the phrase "greatly increasing water's economic value" (82) corresponds to the phrase "water's economic value is likely to increase" in the prompt, which indicates that we're looking at the part of the passage that's relevant to the prompt. We can also see that the phrase "overall snow accumulation [will] decrease[]" (78-79) directly restates the phrase "will reduce overall snow accumulation" from (D). Since every part of (D) and the prompt is literally restated by the relevant part of the text, we know (D) is right.

▌ Test 3, Question 36 (Form 16MC3 if you have the 2020-2021 Red Book—see page 23 for more)   TYPE: DESCRIBE THE PASSAGE

ⓘ   *The prompt often mentions describing the passage without a line citation. The answer must still be restated or demonstrated by some specific part of the text. (See "What about Questions without Citations?" on p. 57.)*

▶   **Where to look in the text:** If we've read most of the passage and haven't encountered the relevant text, we should focus on the parts of the passage we haven't read yet.

F **Confused Relationships:** The text does say that each year "1 septillion" (2) snowflakes fall worldwide, but it doesn't say that such a large number of snowflakes is the thing that gives those snowflakes "infinite variety," as (F) would require in combination with the prompt.

G ✓ **Correct:** The text says, "as the crystals fall, they encounter different atmospheric conditions that produce flakes with unique attributes" (3-5). The phrase "different atmospheric conditions" (4) directly restates "varied atmospheric conditions" from (G). The phrase "unique attributes" (5) demonstrates the reason for the "infinite variety" mentioned in the prompt: if every snowflake has unique attributes from all other snowflakes, then the variation among snowflakes must be infinite.

H   **Barely Relevant:** The passage never mentions the *rate* at which snowflakes fall, as (H) would require.

J   **Barely Relevant:** The text does refer to "complex…conditions" (5-6), but it doesn't say that those complexities "slow" anything, as (J) would require, so (J) can't be right. In fact, the text doesn't refer to the process of forming crystals being faster or slower under any particular conditions at all.

Test 3, Question 37 (Form 16MC3 if you have the 2020-2021 Red Book—see page 23 for more)   TYPE: DESCRIBE THE PASSAGE

ⓘ   *The prompt often mentions describing the passage without a line citation. The answer must still be restated or demonstrated by some specific part of the text. (See "What about Questions without Citations?" on p. 57.)*

▶   **Where to look in the text:** Skim for "snowflakes." Also, if we've read most of the passage and haven't encountered the relevant text, we should focus on the parts of the passage we haven't read yet.

A   **Direct Contradiction:** It's true that lines 18-19 refer to something forming around "a nucleus of dust"…but that something is a snow "crystal" (18), not a snowflake, and the prompt asks us to find an attribute of *snowflakes* that isn't shared by *snow crystals*, not the other way around. This choice will confuse a lot of untrained test-takers who don't read the prompt carefully enough to notice that (A) is exactly backwards from what the prompt asked us to find.

B   **Direct Contradiction:** The text says that "*snowflakes* are collections of two or more snow *crystals*" (16-17) (emphasis added), which reverses the relationship between snowflakes and snow crystals described in (B). As we saw with (A), a lot of untrained test-takers won't pay close enough attention to catch this reversal, and will end up picking (B).

C   **Confused Relationships:** This choice restates an idea from line 20, but that idea relates to snow crystals—not snowflakes, as the prompt asked. As with (A) and (B), this statement about snow *crystals* will fool a lot of untrained test-takers who don't read carefully enough, or try hard enough to remember what the prompt was actually asking for, and forget to look for a choice that makes a statement about snow*flakes*.

D ✓ **Correct:** As we saw in the explanation for (B), the text says that "snowflakes are collections of two or more snow crystals" (16-17), just as (D) requires.

Test 3, Question 38 (Form 16MC3 if you have the 2020-2021 Red Book—see page 23 for more)   TYPE: CITATION QUESTION

ⓘ   *The question includes a citation from the text. The answer must be directly restated or demonstrated in the cited text, or in the text closely surrounding the cited text. (See "The General Process for Answering ACT Reading Questions," p. 57.)*

F   **Confused Relationships:** The text does say that snowflakes have "unique attributes" (5), but the text never connects that idea with the term "'designer' snowflakes" (32).

G ✓ **Correct:** The text says "Libbrecht creates "designer" snowflakes in his lab" (31-32), which is a direct restatement of (G), so (G) must be right.

H   **Barely Relevant:** An untrained test-taker might see the word "design" and think this choice could be relevant to the idea of "designer" snowflakes…but, as trained test-takers, we notice that the phrase "grand design of nature" isn't demonstrated or restated anywhere in the text, so (H) can't be right.

J   **Reasonable Statement Not in the Text:** An untrained test-taker might assume the word "designer" would have to do with how aesthetically pleasing the snowflakes are, because of phrases like "designer clothing" in everyday speech. But, as trained test-takers, we know this idea can't be right because it isn't stated anywhere in the text.

Test 3, Question 39 (Form 16MC3 if you have the 2020-2021 Red Book—see page 23 for more)   TYPE: VOCABULARY IN CONTEXT

ⓘ   *The prompt asks about the specific meaning of a word in the passage. The right answer must still be directly restated or demonstrated in the text surrounding the cited word. (See "What about "Vocabulary in Context" Questions?" on p. 59.)*

Subjective Phrases to Ignore: "most nearly"

A   **Reasonable Statement Not in the Text:** In another context, "critical" could mean something like "evaluative," because being "critical" of something can mean evaluating that thing. But the text surrounding the word "critical" doesn't demonstrate or restate the idea of evaluating anything, so (A) can't be right.

B   **Reasonable Statement Not in the Text:** "Critical" could mean something like "faultfinding" in some other context. But the text surrounding the word "critical" doesn't mention anyone identifying any kind of flaw, mistake, or anything else that could be considered a fault, so (B) must be wrong, since it isn't literally restated or demonstrated in the passage.

C ✓ **Correct:** The text says that, for some states, "75 percent of the annual water supply comes from snowmelt" (57-58). Then the text says, "snowmelt water is critical to crop irrigation and hydroelectric power, as well as recreation and domestic water supplies, fisheries management and flood control" (58-61). If most of the annual water supply in these places comes from snowmelt, then it must be the case that the snowmelt water is "vital" to all the things in the list that require water ("crop irrigation," "hydroelectric power," "domestic water supplies," etc.). Since (C) is directly demonstrated in the text, it's right.

D   **Confused Relationships:** In some other situation, "critical" could mean something like "acute," just as it could also mean the same thing as the words we saw in (A) and (B). But the surrounding text doesn't demonstrate or restate the idea of anything being acute. so (D) can't be right. Some untrained test-takers will think that if something is vital, then a shortage of that vital thing could lead to

Page 108   Facebook.com/TestingIsEasy   Youtube.com/TestingIsEasy an acute emergency, which will lead them to pick (D). But we need to avoid that kind of undisciplined thinking: the word "critical" (59) is used to describe the water itself, not the possibility of a shortage in that water, so "acute" can't be right.

🛈   *The prompt often mentions describing the passage without a line citation. The answer must still be restated or demonstrated by some specific part of the text. (See "What about Questions without Citations?" on p. 57.)*

▶   **Where to look in the text:** Scan for longer words from the answer choices, like "pollutants," "snowmelt," "artificial," and "avalanches."

F ✓   **Correct:** The text mentions that you can look at snow in a scanning electron microscope to "examin[e] air pollution" (87), but it never actually mentions a way to "extract pollutants from snow," as (F) describes.

G   **Direct Contradiction:** Lines 53-56 mention that "research about snow" helps scientists to "gauge snowmelt," exactly as described in (G). This same idea is also restated exactly in lines 84-85. Since this is an "EXCEPT" question, that makes (G) wrong.

H   **Direct Contradiction:** Lines 84-86 mention that "research about snow" helps scientists to "design[] artificial snow," which is essentially the exact phrase from (H)—making (H) the wrong answer to this "EXCEPT" question.

J   **Direct Contradiction:** Just as we saw with (G) and (H), line 85 mentions that "research about snow" helps scientists to "predict[] avalanches," which makes (J) the wrong answer.

Part 7: Math Test Training and Walkthroughs

In part 6, we just saw how to attack the ACT Reading section by relying on literal reading and objectivity, and by remembering the important differences between the ACT and a normal test or discussion in a high school setting. Now, we'll build on this foundation in order to address the ACT Math section. You'll see how we combine our awareness of the test's unique design with our existing math knowledge and our reading skills, allowing us to find correct answers quickly and efficiently.

In this part, you'll learn the following:

- why the ACT Math section is unlike the math tests you take in high school
- the single biggest secret of the design of the ACT Math section
- the two critical components of success on the ACT Math section
- all of the basic math ideas that you'll need on test day
- what backsolving is, why it helps some test-takers a lot, and how to apply it in ways most people aren't aware of
- why it's so important to consider every answer choice on the ACT Math section—and how it can save you time
- the unwritten rules of the ACT Math section
- why formulas matter much less on test day than most people would expect
- why every real ACT Math question can potentially be answered in under 30 seconds
- the hidden patterns of the ACT Math section, and how they can help you attack and check questions efficiently
- the 3 major types of approaches to an ACT Math question, along with the advantages and drawbacks of each
- the recommended 7-step "Math Path" for attacking questions quickly and effectively on test day
- how the ACT's provided diagrams can sometimes be used to answer questions with total certainty at a glance
- why it can be important not to think about "showing your work" on test day
- how to apply these concepts to every Math question from three official ACT practice tests
- and more . . .

ACT Math

In mathematics the art of proposing questions is more valuable than solving them.

Georg Cantor

Overview and Important Reminders for ACT Math Questions

We just covered in some detail how the right way to handle the ACT Reading section isn't at all like the right way to handle a typical English class. In an English class, we get credit for being open-minded and imaginative, and for seeing multiple possible meanings in a passage. On the ACT Reading section, we must interpret the text to mean only and exactly what it directly says—no more, and no less.

In the same way that being successful on the ACT Reading section means we have to recognize it as different from the kind of reading we'd do in school, doing well on ACT Math means appreciating how very different ACT Math is from school math. (You'll also see this pattern repeated when we talk about ACT Science and ACT English.)

But, for now, let's take a minute to think about what the ACT Math section is and how it has to work. Then, we'll be in a better position to understand how to beat it.

The ACT is given to around 2 million American high school students each year. Those students go to lots of different schools with thousands of different teachers, and take lots of different kinds of math classes, like algebra, geometry, trigonometry, calculus, and statistics.

Some students go far into calculus and statistics, while others don't get past basic algebra. Some students have the choice to take advanced math, and others go to schools where those classes aren't even offered.

How would you test such a large, diverse group of test-takers, if you were in charge of the ACT?

If you came up with a very advanced test (with calculus, and statistics, and advanced trigonometry), the students who hadn't taken those subjects would have almost no chance at a good score—even if they were very good in the math classes they'd taken, they wouldn't know how to handle an ACT Math section loaded with advanced math they'd never seen before.

On the other hand, it seems that if you made a math test that just covered all the basic topics like simple algebra, geometry, and a little trigonometry, then everybody's scores would be too high. Simple math like that wouldn't be much of a challenge for most high school students, and a test that everybody scored well on wouldn't be of much use to colleges trying to rank their applicants.

So it seems like the test should only ask about relatively basic high school math . . . while still being hard enough that not everybody would do well on it. How could a test accomplish that?

Well, one way would be to test simple math ideas, but to present those simple math ideas in unusual ways that students aren't used to seeing. If the questions ask about basic math ideas in unexpected ways, then the test can simultaneously accomplish both goals: any student with a basic level of math knowledge could potentially answer the questions, since the questions would stick to a certain set of relatively simple math concepts, but the unusual presentation would cause difficulties for a lot of students, so scores wouldn't be high across the board.

As it turns out, that's exactly how the ACT Math section works.

That's why you'll find some students who get straight A's in advanced math courses but can't figure out ACT Math, while other students who've only ever done relatively basic stuff in math classes can do surprisingly well on the ACT. It's a different kind of test from what you'd expect in a normal high school math class, and it requires a different approach if you want to succeed.

The Big Secret of ACT Math

At this point, you might not be convinced. You might ask yourself, "If the math really is so simple, how come so many people think it's so challenging?"

I would first respond by pointing out that many people think ACT Reading is impossible to master, and we've already discussed at length how the only thing you need to do to answer every question is just to read carefully and find the answer choice that directly restates the text. That's simple enough to do, but many people struggle because they don't know they're supposed to do it.

This is the same type of situation we see with ACT Math. Students don't know how to handle this kind of test, so they want to approach it like they approach high school math tests, which won't work. You're probably starting to understand why that approach fails—let's go into it a little bit more.

Think about the period of time leading up to a typical high school math test. Imagine that your math class is starting a new unit, which probably focuses on a handful of closely related mathematical ideas. For several days or weeks, you'll study those ideas. You'll get homework assignments in which you might do a few dozen problems at a time that all have you repeat basically the same solution with different numbers, over and over again.

Once you've done enough drilling and practicing of those concepts, you'll take a test. That test will ask you to do a few different types of questions—all the things you've been practicing and drilling for weeks. If you've been doing your homework, and paying attention in class, then the material on the classroom test will all be stuff you've seen a lot of times before, and every question will be basically the same thing over and over again. When the test is over, you'll start a new unit on a new topic and go through the whole process again with new material.

The ACT Math section is nothing like that. ACT Math questions will all seem different from each other. When you look at an ACT Math question, it may not be immediately obvious what you're even supposed to do, let alone how you should go about doing it. If you're good at following the format of a normal math test in school, then some ACT Math questions might feel completely foreign to you.

If you're like a lot of untrained test-takers, you'll get frustrated. You may even panic, and you'll probably conclude that ACT Math is way harder than normal math—which is exactly what the people who make the ACT want you to think. But people only think that because nobody has ever told them how the ACT Math section really works.

The Two Critical Components of ACT Math Success

We've learned that ACT Math is all about relatively basic math ideas being presented in unusual ways. That means there are two things we need in order to do well on this section:

- We need basic knowledge of the kinds of math that can appear on the ACT (arithmetic, algebra, geometry, and a tiny bit of trigonometry).
- We need an understanding of the ACT's unwritten rules, patterns, and standards that govern the way ACT Math questions can operate.

Once we're comfortable with the basic math concepts that can appear on the ACT, and we're familiar with the various ways those basic concepts can be presented, we've got everything we need to answer any ACT Math question we'll ever see, even if the question throws us when we first look at it.

We'll start off by covering all of the basic math ideas that can appear in ACT Math questions in the next section, the ACT Math Toolbox.

ACT Math Toolbox

In the coming pages, we'll be discussing the best way to approach ACT Math. We'll talk about that in terms of patterns and strategies and standards, as we do with the other sections.

But before we do that, we need to be sure that we're familiar with all the math concepts that are allowed to appear in the ACT Math section—most of the math is pretty basic by high school and college standards, but we still need to go over it to make sure we're properly prepared.

The goal of this section is to review each important concept quickly and efficiently. If you need more of an explanation for any given topic, consider asking your math teacher for additional guidance.

You might notice that the material in this review actually seems to be easier than the questions you see in real ACT Math questions. That's because the challenge in the majority of ACT Math questions isn't the actual math you need to do; it's figuring out the proper way to set up the solution. Once you do that, the math is often quite simple (as we'll see in this Toolbox and in the walkthroughs).

Remember that you don't have to be an expert on every one of these concepts. You just need to be able to understand them, and to have an idea of how to work with them in order to be ready for this section of the test. Also, bear in mind that some of this material might seem unfamiliar when you first look at it—if that's the case, I strongly recommend you read through the whole Toolbox twice. Most students are more comfortable with the concepts on the second read-through.

This list is based on the mathematical concepts that appear in the math sections of currently available, up-to-date real ACT practice tests.

Again, this section isn't about learning the strategic approach to the ACT Math section—that will come later. First, you just have to make sure you're familiar with a relatively dry, boring list of math ideas, and the best way to do that is to go over each one as completely (but quickly) as possible. Let's get started.

Number lines

A number line is a simple diagram that arranges numbers from least to greatest value on a line.

The positions on a number line can be labeled with actual numbers, or with variables.

> This number line shows all the integers from -6 to 4:

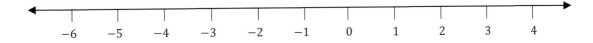

Absolute value

A number's absolute value is that number's distance from zero on the number line.

> -4 and 4 both have an absolute value of 4. We signify the absolute value of a number with vertical lines on either side of the number: $|-4| = |4| = 4$.

We can create equations using absolute values and one or more variables.

> $|x| = 4$
> $x = 4$ or $x = -4$

Properties of integers

Any number that can be expressed without a fraction, decimal, or special symbol is an integer.

Integers can be negative or positive.

Zero is an integer.

> These numbers are integers: $-45, -2, 0, 11, 432$
>
> These numbers are NOT integers: $\pi, 12.1, \frac{2}{3}$

Integers can be even or odd.

Only integers can be odd or even—a fraction or symbolic number is neither odd nor even.

Even integers can be divided by 2 with nothing left over.

Odd integers have a remainder of 1 when they're divided by 2.

> These are even integers: $-14, 8, 38$
>
> These are odd integers: $-11, 47, 603$

An even number plus an even number results in an even number.

An odd number plus an odd number results in an even number.

An odd number plus an even number results in an odd number.

An even number multiplied by an even number results in an even number.

An even number multiplied by an odd number results in an even number.

An odd number multiplied by an odd number results in an odd number.

Some integers have special properties related to addition and multiplication:

- When you multiply or divide any number by 1, the number is unchanged.
- When you multiply any number by 0, the result is 0.
- It's impossible to divide a number by 0 on the ACT Math section.
- Adding or subtracting 0 to or from any number leaves that number unchanged.

Digits

A digit is the individual number character used to write a number.

These are one-digit numbers: 3, 7, 2

These are two-digit numbers: 93, 28, 11

Special characters are not digits.

These numbers don't involve digits: π, i

We can refer to digits by the order they appear in the number, starting from the left.

The third digit in the number 3,920 is 2.

The first digit after the decimal in the number 5.19 is 1.

We can also refer to digits by the values they represent.

4,319.72

In the number above:

4 is the thousands digit.

3 is the hundreds digit.

1 is the tens digit.

9 is the units digit.

7 is the tenths digit.

2 is the hundredths digit.

Rational numbers versus irrational numbers

A rational number is any number that can be expressed as a ratio of two integers.

4 is rational because it's equal to $\frac{4}{1}$.

3.9 is rational because it's equal to $\frac{39}{10}$.

0.428 is rational because it's equal to $\frac{428}{1000}$.

Irrational numbers cannot be expressed as a ratio of two integers.

Examples of irrational numbers:

$\sqrt{5}, \pi$

Basic operations

You'll have to do basic operations (addition, subtraction, multiplication, division) with integers, fractions, and decimals.

These are examples of basic operations on integers:

$3 + 4 = 7$
$5 - 2 = 3$
$3 \times 7 = 21$
$8 \div 4 = 2$

These are examples of basic operations on fractions:

$$\frac{1}{2} + \frac{3}{2} = 2$$

$$\frac{4}{3} - \frac{2}{3} = \frac{2}{3}$$

$$\frac{3}{2} \times \frac{1}{2} = \frac{3}{4}$$

$$\frac{7}{4} \div \frac{1}{4} = 7$$

(These are discussed in more detail in the "Fractions" section on page 116 of this Black Book.)

These are examples of basic operations on decimals:

$2.3 + 3.19 = 5.49$

$9.3 - 6.3 = 3$

$1.24 \times 3.5 = 4.34$

$8.7 \div 10 = 0.87$

Multiples

A "multiple" of an integer is a number that can be reached when the integer is multiplied by another integer.

21 is a multiple of 7 because $7 \times 3 = 21$, and 3 is an integer.

The multiples of 7 are 7, 14, 21, 28, 35, 42, and so on.

Every integer is the smallest multiple of itself.

The "least common multiple" of a set of numbers is the smallest multiple common to each member of the set.

The least common multiple of 4, 5, and 6 is 60, because 60 is the smallest number that's a multiple of 4, 5, and 6.

Factors

A "factor" of an integer is an integer that can be multiplied by another integer to arrive at the original integer.

7 is a factor of 21, because $7 \times 3 = 21$, and 7 and 3 are integers.

The factors of 21 are 1, 3, 7, and 21.

The "greatest common factor" of a set of numbers is the largest factor common to each member of the set.

The greatest common factor of 24, 60, and 72 is 12, because 12 is the largest number that's a factor of 24, 60, and 72.

1 is a factor of every integer.

Every integer is its own greatest factor.

A "prime number" is an integer with only two factors: itself, and 1.

1 is not a prime number.

Order of Operations (PEMDAS)

When an expression involves multiple types of operations, the rules of math require us to perform them in a certain order, called the order of operations. Many students learn the proper order by memorizing the acronym **PEMDAS**, which stands for **P**arentheses, **E**xponents, **M**ultiplication, **D**ivision, **A**ddition, **S**ubtraction.

This is the order in which we must perform the operations in an expression. Any PEMDAS operations that don't appear in an expression are omitted when we evaluate that expression.

$1 + (9 - 3) \times 7 - 6^2 \div 2$

First we do the operation within the **P**arentheses:

$1 + 6 \times 7 - 6^2 \div 2$

Next, we address the **E**xponent expression:

$1 + 6 \times 7 - 36 \div 2$

Then we do any **M**ultiplication in the equation:

$1 + 42 - 36 \div 2$

Then we do the **D**ivision:

$1 + 42 - 18$

Next we do any **A**ddition:

$43 - 18$

Finally, we do any Subtraction that might be in the equation:

25

That gives us the simplified value of the expression:

Word problems

In general, ACT word problems are descriptions of either real-life situations or abstract concepts.

Example of a word problem about a real-life situation:

"Ann buys two sandwiches for four dollars each. She also buys a few bottles of water. Each bottle of water costs seventy-five cents. Ann pays with fifteen dollars and gets four dollars and seventy-five cents in change. How many bottles of water did she buy?"

Example of a word problem about an abstract concept:

"If y is the arithmetic mean of 5 consecutive even numbers, what is the median of those 5 consecutive even numbers, in terms of y?"

In order to solve ACT word problems, we have to turn them into math problems.

To do that, we note all the numbers given in the problem, and write them down on scratch paper. Then, we identify key phrases and turn them into mathematical symbols for operations and variables. Finally, we use these to relate the numbers we wrote down in the first place.

In the phrase "two sandwiches for four dollars each," the word *each* tells us we have to *multiply* the two sandwiches by the four dollars so that we can find out how much money was spent on the two sandwiches: $2 \times 4 = 8$. Eight dollars were spent on the two sandwiches if they cost four dollars each.

If Ann paid with 15 dollars and got back $4.75, we know that the total cost of the sandwiches and water was $15.00 − $4.75, or $10.25. If we know that the sandwiches cost $8.00, that means the three water bottles cost $10.25 − $8.00, or $2.25.

If the cost of the water bottles was $2.25, and we know that each water bottle is $0.75, then we can find the number of water bottles by dividing the total cost by the cost of each one: $2.25 / $0.75. Seventy-five cents goes into $2.25 three times, so we know that Ann bought three water bottles.

As you can see, once we've converted the word problem into a math problem, we can solve it like any other question. We'll talk more about the general approach to ACT Math questions in our discussion of the "The Math Path" on page 155 of this Black Book.

Fractions

A fraction is a number that represents parts of a whole.

Fractions look like this:

$$\frac{\text{number of parts represented in the fraction}}{\text{number of parts the whole is divided into}}$$

Peter and Jane are sharing a pack of gum. There are 8 sticks of gum in the pack, and Peter takes 3 of them.

Since Peter has 3 of the 8 sticks in the pack of gum, he has $\frac{3}{8}$ of the pack of gum.

The number above the fraction bar is the *numerator*.

The number under the fraction bar is the *denominator*.

If the value of the numerator is less than the value of the denominator, the value of the fraction is less than 1.

If a fraction's numerator is greater than its denominator, then the value of the fraction is greater than 1.

$\frac{2}{5}$ is the same as two fifths, which is less than 1.

$\frac{8}{2}$ is equal to 4, which is more than 1.

Any integer can be seen as having the denominator 1 underneath it.

9 is the same as $\frac{9}{1}$.

The "reciprocal" of a fraction is what we get if we switch the numerator and denominator of the fraction.

The reciprocal of $\frac{2}{9}$ is $\frac{9}{2}$. The reciprocal of 4 is $\frac{1}{4}$. (Remember that all integers can be thought of as having the denominator 1.)

Multiplying fractions requires two steps. First, we multiply the numerators to find the numerator in the product fraction. Second, we multiply the denominators to find the denominator in the product fraction.

$$\frac{3}{8} \times \frac{5}{7} = \frac{?}{?}$$

In step 1, we multiply the numerators to determine the product numerator. In this case, $3 \times 5 = 15$. So we write 15 as the numerator of the new fraction.

$$\frac{3}{8} \times \frac{5}{7} = \frac{15}{?}$$

In step 2, we multiply the denominators to determine the product denominator. In this case, $8 \times 7 = 56$. So 56 is the denominator of the product.

$$\frac{3}{8} \times \frac{5}{7} = \frac{15}{56}$$

To divide one fraction by another, we simply multiply the first fraction by the RECIPROCAL of the second fraction.

$$\frac{3}{10} \div \frac{2}{3} = \frac{3}{10} \times \frac{3}{2} = \frac{9}{20}$$

Notice that, to divide $\frac{3}{10}$ by $\frac{2}{3}$, we multiplied $\frac{3}{10}$ by the reciprocal of $\frac{2}{3}$, which is $\frac{3}{2}$.

If you multiply a non-zero integer by a fraction that's smaller than 1, the result will have a smaller absolute value than the original number did.

$$4 \times \frac{3}{7} = \frac{12}{7}, \text{ and } \frac{12}{7} \text{ is closer to 0 than 4 is.}$$

$$-9 \times \frac{1}{5} = -\frac{9}{5}, \text{ and } -\frac{9}{5} \text{ is closer to 0 than } -9 \text{ is.}$$

Fraction a is equal to fraction b if you could multiply the numerator and denominator of fraction a by the same number to get the numerator and denominator of fraction b.

$$\frac{2}{3} \text{ is equal to } \frac{24}{36}, \text{ because } \frac{2}{3} \times \frac{12}{12} = \frac{24}{36}$$

Since $\frac{12}{12}$ is the same as 1, and we can multiply $\frac{2}{3}$ by $\frac{12}{12}$ in order to get $\frac{24}{36}$, we know that $\frac{2}{3}$ is equal to $\frac{24}{36}$.

"Simplifying" or "reducing" a fraction is the process of dividing the numerator and denominator of the fraction by their greatest common factor.

$$\frac{15}{20} \text{ is equal to } \frac{3}{4}.$$ The greatest common factor of 15 and 20 is 5; when we divide both the numerator and the denominator by 5, we're left with $\frac{3}{4}$.

In order to add or subtract fractions, they must have the same denominator. That means we have to find the "least common denominator" of the fractions, and then convert the fractions so they all have the least common denominator as their denominators. The least common denominator of two or more fractions is the least common multiple of their denominators. That might sound confusing, so let's look at an example.

$$\frac{1}{2} + \frac{1}{3}$$

We can't add one half and one third in these terms, because they have different denominators.

What's the least common denominator of these two fractions? It's 6, because the least common multiple of 2 and 3 is 6.

We need to put both fractions in terms of sixths in order to be able to add them.

One half is the same as three sixths, and one third is the same as two sixths.

Now our expression looks like this:

$$\frac{3}{6} + \frac{2}{6}$$

Once both numbers have the same denominator, we just add the numerators, keep the same denominator, and we're done:

$$\frac{3}{6} + \frac{2}{6} = \frac{5}{6}$$

Now let's look at an example involving subtraction.

$$\frac{5}{6} - \frac{1}{4}$$

In this case, we can put both numbers in terms of twelfths, which looks like this:

$$\frac{10}{12} - \frac{3}{12}$$

Now we just subtract the second numerator from the first, and keep the same denominator:

$$\frac{10}{12} - \frac{3}{12} = \frac{7}{12}$$

Exponents

When we multiply a number by itself a certain number of times, the result is an exponent of that number.

y^4 is an example of an exponential expression. It's equal to $y \times y \times y \times y$. In this example, the y is called the "base," and the 4 is the exponent.

Exponents can be either positive or negative.

To evaluate a positive exponent, we multiply the base by itself as many times as the exponent tells us to.

We evaluate a negative exponent the same way we evaluate a positive exponent, except that we take the reciprocal of the end result.

$$y^4 = y \times y \times y \times y$$
$$y^{-4} = \frac{1}{y \times y \times y \times y}$$

We can multiply exponent expressions if they have the same base. In that situation, we just add the exponents.

$$(n^3)(n^4) =$$
$$(n \times n \times n)(n \times n \times n \times n) =$$
$$n \times n \times n \times n \times n \times n \times n =$$
$$n^7$$

It's also possible to divide exponent expressions with the same base by subtracting the bottom exponent from the top exponent.

$$\frac{n^5}{n^2} =$$
$$\frac{n \times n \times n \times n \times n}{n \times n} =$$
$$n \times n \times n =$$
$$n^3$$

We can also raise an exponential expression to another exponent by multiplying the two exponents:

$$(n^4)^5 =$$
$$(n^4)(n^4)(n^4)(n^4)(n^4) =$$
$$n^{20}$$

Raising any number to an exponent of zero results in the number 1:

$$n^0 = 1$$

Logarithms

A logarithm is an expression that tells us how many times we multiply one number by itself to get another number. The expression $\log_x y = z$ means that if you multiply x by itself z times, the result is y. In that expression, we would call x the "base" of the logarithm, as in "the logarithm of y with base x is z." Let's look at an example with real numbers.

$\log_2 32 = 5$, because we would have to multiply 2 by itself 5 times to get 32: $2 \times 2 \times 2 \times 2 \times 2 = 32$

Logarithms don't come up often on the ACT, but they do show up sometimes, so we need to make sure we understand them.

Squares and square roots

The square of a number is that number multiplied by itself.

Four squared is equal to 4×4, or 16.

The square root of a number is the amount that must be multiplied by itself to result in that number.

The square root of 16 is the number that results in 16 when multiplied by itself. That number is 4, so the square root of 16 is 4.

Squared numbers are always positive. This is true because a positive number multiplied by a positive number has a positive result, and a negative number multiplied by a negative number also has a positive result.

Keep in mind that you can easily find the square or the square root of a number with your calculator if necessary.

Ratios, proportions, and percentages

We can express a relationship between two numbers using ratios, proportions, and percentages.

A ratio is expressed as a pair of numbers with a colon between them.

If you walk 4 miles for every 1 mile Jake walks, then the ratio of *the distance you travel* to *the distance Jake travels* is 4 : 1.

A proportion is typically written as a fraction.

If you walk 4 miles for every 1 mile Jake walks, then you can compare the distance you travel to the distance Jake travels with the proportion $\frac{4}{1}$. (Also, the proportion to compare how far Jake walks to how far you walk would be $\frac{1}{4}$.)

A percentage is a type of proportion that compares one number to 100.

To find a percentage, first create a proportion or fraction. Then, divide the numerator by the denominator and multiply the result by 100.

If Jake walks 1 mile for every 4 miles you walk, then the proportion that compares the distance Jake travels to the distance you travel is $\frac{1}{4}$. If we divide 1 by 4 and multiply by 100, we see that Jake walks 25% as far as you walk.

Ratios can be set equal to each other and "cross-multiplied." (Don't worry if you don't already know how to do this—it's just an algebraic shortcut, and you don't specifically have to know how to do it for the ACT.)

If two quantities have a relationship such that increasing one quantity causes a consistent, predictable, proportional increase in the other quantity, we say those two quantities "vary directly" or are "directly proportional."

Imagine that you're driving a car that can go 20 miles on one gallon of gas. If you have one gallon of gas, you can drive 20 miles. If you have 3 gallons, you can drive 60 miles. If you have 10 gallons, you can drive 200 miles. The distance you can travel "varies directly with" or is "directly proportional to" the amount of gas you have, since every additional gallon of gas increases the distance you can drive in a predictable way.

If x and y vary directly, then their relationship can be expressed by the equation $x = vy$, where v is a constant.

If x and y vary directly and x is 60 when y is 3, then $x = 20y$. We can see that increasing either variable automatically increases the other variable. For example, we see that x is 200 if y is 10.

If two quantities have a relationship such that increasing one causes a consistent, proportional decrease in the other, we say those two quantities "vary indirectly" or are "inversely proportional."

Imagine that you are riding your bike for a distance of 20 miles. If you ride your bike at 5 miles per hour, you will cover the distance in 4 hours—4 hours of traveling at 5 miles per hour means you cover 20 miles. However, if you speed up to 10 miles per hour, you will cover the same distance in 2 hours—2 hours of traveling at 10 miles per hour means you cover 20 miles. When you double your speed, you cut the travel time in half. We can say that speed and travel time "vary indirectly" or are "inversely proportional," since increasing one value causes the other value to decrease in a consistent, predictable way.

If x and y are inversely proportional, then $xy = v$, where v is some constant.

If x and y vary indirectly and x is 4 when y is 5, then we know $xy = 20$. Increasing either variable creates a decrease in the other; for example, x is 10 if y is 2.

Simple probability

The probability of a possible event tells us how likely that event is to happen. It's expressed as a fraction with a value between 0 and 1. The closer a probability fraction is to 1, the more likely the event is to happen; the closer a fraction is to zero, the less likely the event is to happen.

To create a probability fraction, you first figure out the total number of possible outcomes and make that number the denominator of the fraction. Then, you figure out the number of desired outcomes that satisfy the requirements of that event, and you make this number the numerator of the fraction.

What's the probability of a flipped penny landing tails-side up? There are 2 possible outcomes when the penny is flipped: heads or tails. So 2 goes in the denominator of the fraction. Out of those 2 outcomes, we're only interested in one (tails), so 1 goes in the numerator of the fraction. That means the probability of the coin landing tails-up is $\frac{1}{2}$.

To find the probability of two or more events happening in a row, we just multiply the probability of the first event by the probability of the second event.

What's the probability of a penny landing tails-side up twice in a row? We know that the probability of a penny landing tails-side up one time is $\frac{1}{2}$. That means the probability of a penny landing tails-side up twice in a row is $\frac{1}{2} \times \frac{1}{2}$, or $\frac{1}{4}$.

Probability fractions can be manipulated just like any other fractions—for example, a probability of $\frac{2}{8}$ is equivalent to a probability of $\frac{1}{4}$.

Probability Distribution

On the ACT, we tend to see a probability distribution presented as a table. The table will have two columns; the first column lists different possible outcomes, and the second column lists the corresponding probability for each outcome. For example, imagine that people who play a game of chance get a certain score from 1 to 5, and that there is a certain probability that any given player will get each score from the table. The probability distribution for those scores might look like this:

Score	Probability
1	0.2
2	0.4
3	0.2
4	0.1
5	0.1

So if we read the table above, we can see that the probability of getting a 1 is 0.2, and the probability of getting a 3 is 0.2, and so on. We can also add the probabilities of two outcomes to find the probability of either outcome happening. For example, the probability of scoring either a 4 or 5 is 0.2, because 0.1 + 0.1 = 0.2.

We can also find the expected value of a random player's score by multiplying each score by its probability, and then adding all the results, like this:

$$1 \times 0.2 = 0.2$$
$$2 \times 0.4 = 0.8$$
$$3 \times 0.2 = 0.6$$
$$4 \times 0.1 = 0.4$$
$$5 \times 0.1 = 0.5$$

$$0.2 + 0.8 + 0.6 + 0.4 + 0.5 = 2.5$$

So we can see that the expected value of a random player's score would be 2.5.

"Counting problems"

What I call a "counting problem" on the ACT is a question that asks you to figure out the total number of ways that two or more events could happen.

You may have studied these problems in math class; if so, you probably called them "permutation and combination" problems.

Here's the general rule for these problems: if the first of two events could happen in any one of x ways, and the second of two events could happen in any one of y ways, then the total number of ways that the events could happen together is given by xy.

That might sound a little complicated, so let's do an example and you'll see how it works.

Imagine you have to buy one fruit and one vegetable. There are 4 kinds of fruit and 5 kinds of vegetables. How many possible combinations of one fruit and one vegetable can you pick?

Well, there are 4 kinds of fruit, so there are 4 possibilities for the first event (choosing a fruit). There are 5 kinds of vegetables, so there are 5 options for the second event (picking a vegetable).

So the total number of possible combinations of one fruit and one vegetable is 4×5, which is 20.

Often, the biggest challenge in this type of question is making sure you correctly count the number of possible outcomes for each event.

Imagine three horses are running a race. In how many different orders can these horses finish the race in 1st, 2nd, and 3rd place? We must start by figuring out how many possible outcomes there are for each event.

First place has 3 possible outcomes, because there are 3 horses and any horse could finish first. Second place has only 2 possible outcomes--because one horse has already finished first, leaving only 2 that could be in second place (remember, the same horse can't finish in both 1st and 2nd place). Finally, 3rd place has 1 possible outcome, because we've already picked a horse for 1st place and another for 2nd place, leaving only 1 possibility (out of the 3 horses) for 3rd place. When we multiply these numbers we get 3×2×1=6, so the answer is 6.

Charts, tables, and graphs

Charts, tables, and graphs are three ways to represent data. To use charts, tables, and graphs, we simply read the labels of each section to find the information we need. The following chart shows the number of days spent on vacation of three different age groups for five different months.

Facebook.com/TestingIsEasy   Youtube.com/TestingIsEasy

Average Number Of Days Spent On Vacation

AGE	March	April	May	June	July
21 − 25	2	3	4	3	4
26 − 30	1	1	3	1	1
31 − 35	2	4	3	2	2

From this chart, we can see that people 21 − 25 years of age spend an average of 4 days on vacation in May, and people 31 − 35 years of age spend an average of 2 days on vacation in June, and so on.

The following table shows the scores of Student 1 on four different math tests.

Student 1's Math Test Scores

Test Number	Score
1	79
2	78
3	86
4	90

From this table, we can see that Student 1 scored an 86 on math test 3, and a 79 on math test 1, and so on.

The following graph shows the average number of siblings of students in 4 classes:

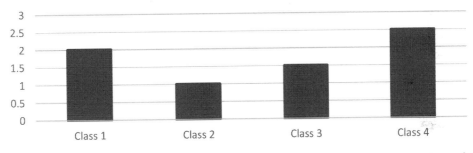

Average Number Of Siblings

From this table, we can see that the average number of siblings for students in Class 2 was 1, and the average number of siblings for students in Class 3 was 1.5, and so on.

Simple statistics

There are three main concepts you'll need to be familiar with when it comes to statistics on the ACT: average (arithmetic mean), median, and mode.

The arithmetic mean of a set of numbers is what you get when you add the numbers together and then divide the result by the number of things that you added together. (This is also called the "average" of the set of numbers.)

The mean of $\{7, 18, 23\}$ is 16, because $\frac{7 + 18 + 23}{3} = 16$.

The median of a set of numbers is the number in the middle of the set when all the numbers in that set are ordered from least to greatest.

The median of $\{7, 18, 23\}$ is 18, because when those numbers are ordered from least to greatest, 18 is in the middle.

If the set has an even number of elements, then the median of that set is the average of the two numbers that end up in the middle of the set when the elements of the set are ordered from least to greatest.

The median of $\{7, 12, 18, 23\}$ is 15, because there's an even number of elements in the set, and 15 is the arithmetic mean of the two numbers in the middle of the set when the numbers are ordered from least to greatest (12 and 18).

The mode of a set of numbers is the number that appears in the set more frequently than any other.

The mode of $\{16, 17, 18, 19, 24, 24, 95\}$ is 24, because 24 appears more often than any other number in the set.

The **range** of a set of numbers is the difference between the highest number in the set and the lowest number in the set.

> The range of $\{7, 7, 23, 44\}$ is 37, because 44 is the largest number in the set, 7 is the smallest, and $44 - 7 = 37$.

On a graph that shows a set of data points, the line of best fit is a line that demonstrates the trend in the data. In the sample figure below, the points represent actual data, while the dashed line demonstrates the *trend* in the data:

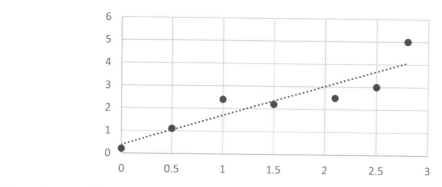

On the ACT, you'll never have to calculate a line of best fit on your own, but you will need to understand that the line of best fit shows us the overall trend in the data—it doesn't represent *actual* data.

Expressing relationships with variables

You can use variables to express a relationship between two quantities.

> If one quantity is equal to three times another quantity, we can represent them with x and y respectively, and write this: $x = 3y$.

If you have a value for y, you can plug it in to find a corresponding value for x.

> If $x = 3y$, and we know $y = 4$, then we can write $x = 3(4)$, so $x = 12$ when $y = 4$.

Equations

On the ACT, an equation is a statement with an equals sign and at least one algebraic expression.

> $3y = 15$ is an equation, because it has an algebraic expression ($3y$) and an equals sign.

When we solve an equation for a variable, we find the value of the variable in that equation. We do this just as you've learned in your high school math classes—by carrying out the same operations on both sides of the equation until the variable is alone on one side of the equals sign, and its value is on the other side.

> $3y = 15$ (given equation)
>
> $\dfrac{3y}{3} = \dfrac{15}{3}$ (divide both sides by 3)
>
> $y = 5$ (simplify)

If an equation has multiple variables, we can solve the equation "in terms of" one particular variable. To do this, we just isolate the target variable on one side of the equation.

> Solve this expression in terms of z.
>
> $2z + 5y = 3x$ (given equation)
>
> $2z = 3x - 5y$ (subtract $5y$ from both sides)
>
> $z = \dfrac{3x - 5y}{2}$ (divide both sides by 2)

A system of equations is a group of two or more equations that have the same variables.

> This is a system of equations:
>
> $a - b = 3$
>
> $4a + b = 27$

Solving a system of equations means identifying the values of the variables in the equations. One way to do this is to solve one of the equations in terms of a particular variable, like we did in the last example. Then, we substitute that value into the other equation and obtain a numerical value for the other variable.

> To solve the system of equations above, we'll begin by isolating the a in the first equation.
>
> $a - b = 3$ (first equation)
>
> $a = 3 + b$ (add b to both sides)

Now that we know a is equal to $3 + b$, we can plug that in to the other equation:

$4a + b = 27$	(second equation)
$4(3 + b) + b = 27$	(substitute $3 + b$ for a)
$12 + 4b + b = 27$	(distribute the 4)
$12 + 5b = 27$	(simplify)
$5b = 15$	(subtract 12 from each side)
$b = 3$	(divide both sides by 5)

Since we know b equals 3, we just plug that back into the first equation, and solve for a:

$a - (3) = 3$	(substitute 3 for b)
$a = 3 + 3$	(add 3 to both sides)
$a = 6$	(simplify)

So in the given system of equations, $a = 6$ and $b = 3$.

Operations on polynomials

A polynomial is an expression that includes multiple terms, at least one of which contains a variable.

$5x + 3$
$x^2 - 2x + 9$
$4ab^2 + 5a$

When we write a polynomial, we list the terms in decreasing order of the exponent of the variable. That sounds complicated, so let's look at an example.

$x^4 + 3x^3 + 5x^2 - 2x + 4$

We started with the x-term raised to the fourth power, then followed with the one raised to the third power, then the one that was squared, then the x-term without an exponent (which is the same as x^1), then the constant with no x-term (which is the same as an x^0 term, since any number raised to the power of zero is equal to 1).

Polynomials can be added, subtracted, multiplied, and divided, but sometimes there are special considerations.

When we add or subtract polynomials, we simply combine like terms.

Let's add the polynomials $5x + 3$ and $x^2 - 2x + 9$:

$5x + 3 + x^2 - 2x + 9$	(original expression)
$x^2 + (5x - 2x) + (9 + 3)$	(group like terms)
$x^2 + 3x + 12$	(simplify)

As you can see, we combined the x^2 terms (there was only one, in this case), the x terms ($5x$ and $-2x$), and the constants (3 and 9). Notice that you can only add or subtract like terms during this process.

Let's add the polynomials $2x^3 + 4x^2$ and $x + 7$:

$2x^3 + 4x^2 + x + 7$

In this case, nothing can be combined, because there are no like terms. So we just write the sum as shown above.

We can multiply a polynomial by another quantity by multiplying each term in the polynomial by that term.

$3y(5x + 6)$	
$(3y \times 5x) + (3y \times 6)$	(distribute the $3y$)
$15xy + 18y$	(multiply)

A binomial is a polynomial with two terms.

We can multiply one binomial by another binomial using the FOIL technique, which you've probably encountered in your math classes. Here's how it works:

Let's multiply $2x + 5$ by $x - 1$:

$(2x + 5)(x - 1)$

First, we multiply the first two terms of each polynomial together (the "F" in FOIL stands for "first"). That gives us $2x(x)$, or $2x^2$.

Next, we multiply the outer two terms together (the "O" in FOIL stands for "outer"). That gives us $2x(-1)$, or $-2x$.

Next, we multiply the two inner terms together (the "I" in FOIL stands for "inner"). That gives us $5(x)$, or

$5x$.

Last, we multiply the last two terms of each polynomial together (the "L" in FOIL stands for "last"). That gives us $5(-1)$, or -5.

Now that we have all the terms, we simply add them together (combing like terms, as always):

$$2x^2 + (-2x) + 5x + (-5)$$
$$2x^2 + 3x - 5$$

On the ACT, we can also divide a polynomial by another quantity if each term of the polynomial has a factor in common with the quantity we're dividing by. Simply divide each term of the polynomial individually.

If we divide $14ab + 2b$ by $2b$, we recognize that $14ab$ and $2b$ are both divisible by $2b$, and that the result of dividing both terms by $2b$ is $7a + 1$:

$$\frac{14ab + 2b}{2b}$$
$$\frac{14ab}{2b} + \frac{2b}{2b}$$
$$7a + 1$$

Factoring polynomials

On the ACT, factoring polynomials means taking a polynomial and breaking it into two expressions that can be multiplied together to get the original polynomial.

On the ACT, there are three possible factoring situations you'll need to be able to recognize:

1. common factors

2. "FOIL" in reverse

3. difference of squares

Recognizing common factors comes down to noticing that each term in a polynomial shares a factor that can be factored out.

If we have a polynomial like $(3x + 9)$, we can see that both $3x$ and 9 are divisible by 3. That means we can divide a three out of each term in the polynomial and end up with the factors 3 and $(x + 3)$, because $3(x + 3) = 3x + 9$.

Factoring polynomials can also mean doing the steps of FOIL backwards. It can be a little intimidating, but it's easier than it looks when you get used to it.

Suppose we're asked to factor the trinomial $6x^2 - 7x - 3$ into two binomials.

We'll need to reverse-FOIL the trinomial. We can see the product of the first terms of each polynomial will have to be $6x^2$. So we'll just pick two x terms to try out, like $3x$ and $2x$:

$(3x+?)(2x+?)$

We also know the last terms will have to multiply together to equal -3, so they must be either -1 and 3 or 1 and -3. We'll just try one pair (reverse-FOILing often involves some trial and error).

$(3x + 1)(2x - 3)$

Then we multiply out our binomials to see if we've reverse-FOILed correctly:

$(3x + 1)(2x - 3)$	(our guess for the factorization)
$6x^2 - 9x + 2x - 3$	(FOIL the two binomials)
$6x^2 - 7x - 3$	(simplify)

In this case, we got it on the first try; if you don't, of course, you can look at what didn't work and try other pairs of factors. Problems like this on the ACT aren't too common, and the factors usually aren't too hard to figure out. This gets a lot easier with a little bit of practice.

There's a special case in factoring binomials called a "difference of squares." You can recognize a difference of squares because both terms in the binomial will be squares, and the second term will be subtracted from the first (this is why it's called a "difference" of squares; this special factoring shortcut doesn't work when the squares are added together). When we see this situation, the two factors are the following:

- the square root of the first term *plus* the square root of the second term
- the square root of the first term *minus* the square root of the second term

$4x^2 - 25 = (2x + 5)(2x - 5)$

Remember that 1 is a square, and that x^2 is the same as $1x^2$. That means something like $x^2 - 9$ is a difference of squares as well, with factors of $(x + 3)$ and $(x - 3)$.

Simple quadratic equations

A quadratic equation involves three terms. On the ACT, the three terms are usually the following:

4. a variable expression raised to the power of 2, like x^2.

5. a variable expression not raised to any power, like $6x$.

6. a constant (a regular number with no variable), like -5.

> $x^2 + 6x = -5$ is a quadratic equation because it involves a term with x squared, a term with x, and a constant.

On the ACT we solve quadratic equations by factoring, as discussed in the previous section on factoring polynomials. To do that, we have to set one side of the equation equal to zero first.

$x^2 + 6x = -5$	(original equation)
$x^2 + 6x + 5 = 0$	(add 5 to both sides)

Once we have the equation equal to zero, we factor the polynomial.

$x^2 + 6x + 5 = 0$	(original equation with one side set equal to 0)
$(x + 5)(x + 1) = 0$	(reverse FOIL)

Since the product of the two factors is zero, we know that one of the factors must be equal to zero, but we don't know which one. So solving a quadratic equation usually results in two possible values for the variable: one value causes one of the factors to equal zero, and the other value causes the other factor to equal zero.

$(x + 5) = 0$	or	$(x + 1) = 0$
$x = -5$	or	$x = -1$

If we want to test our solutions, we just plug them back into the original equation to see that they work:

$x^2 + 6x = -5$

$(-5)^2 + 6(-5) = -5$	$(-1)^2 + 6(-1) = -5$
$25 - 30 = -5$	$1 - 6 = -5$

Inequalities

An inequality is a statement that tells us that two quantities are not equal. An inequality makes use of one of the following signs:

- $<$ means "less than."
- $>$ means "greater than."
- $\leq$ means "less than or equal to."
- $\geq$ means "greater than or equal to."

Inequalities are solved the same way that equations are solved, with one important difference: when you multiply by -1 to solve for a variable, you also have to switch the direction of the inequality symbol.

$-\dfrac{x}{3} = 4$	$-\dfrac{x}{3} \leq 4$	
$-x = 4(3)$	$-x \leq 4(3)$	(multiply both sides by 3)
$-x = 12$	$-x \leq 12$	(simplify)
$x = -12$	$x \geq -12$	(multiply both sides by -1)

Some inequalities involve only one variable:

> $x > 3$
> $y \leq 1.2$

Some inequalities involve more than one variable:

> $y \geq x - 19$
> $n < 14r + 2$

Inequalities can be solved for a particular variable, just like equations can.

> Let's solve $3y - 11 > 9x + 4$ for y:

$3y - 11 > 9x + 4$	(original inequality)
$3y > 9x + 15$	(add 11 to both sides)
$y > 3x + 5$	(divide both sides by 3)

We can also represent an inequality on the coordinate plane by shading in the region of the graph that satisfies the inequality.

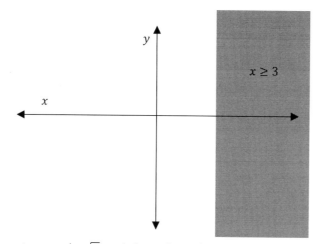

Radicals

A radical expression uses the $\sqrt{\ }$ symbol to indicate the square root of a given number.

$\sqrt{2}$ is equal to the square root of 2.

Radical expressions can be multiplied together.

$\sqrt{2} \times \sqrt{7} = \sqrt{14}$

Radical expressions can also be factored.

$\sqrt{12} = \sqrt{4 \times 3} = \sqrt{4} \times \sqrt{3} = 2\sqrt{3}$

Radical expressions on the ACT are always positive.

Imaginary numbers

Imaginary numbers involve the imaginary quantity i. The quantity i represents the square root of -1.

$\sqrt{-25} = \sqrt{-1 \times 25} = \sqrt{-1} \times \sqrt{25} = i \times 5 = 5i$

Complex numbers

A complex number involves a real number and an imaginary number. On the ACT, a real number is any number that doesn't involve i or the square root of a negative number, and an imaginary number is any number that does involve i or the square root of a negative number.

Examples of real numbers:

$\sqrt{5}, 19, \pi, -4$

Examples of imaginary numbers:

$\sqrt{-7}, 14i, i$

Examples of complex numbers:

$4 + i$
$6 - 3i$

To do operations involving i, just treat i like its own variable, except that any time you get an i^2, it becomes a -1.

$3i(2 + i)$
$6i + 3(i^2)$
$6i + 3(-1)$
$6i - 3$

Complex Conjugates

On page 124 of this toolbox, we talked about something called a difference of squares. A related idea that may appear on the ACT—rarely—is the complex conjugate. On the ACT, this idea might come up when a complex number appears in the denominator of a fraction, like this:

$\dfrac{7}{4-i}$

When a complex number appears in a denominator, we can get rid of the imaginary term in the denominator if we multiply the numerator and denominator by the complex conjugate of the denominator. The complex conjugate will just be the same complex number that appears in the denominator originally, *with the sign between the two terms changed.* In this example, the original denominator is $4 - i$, so we'd multiply the numerator and denominator by $4 + i$:

$$\frac{7}{4-i} \times \frac{4+i}{4+i}$$ (multiply original expression by complex conjugate of denominator)

$$\frac{28+7i}{16-i^2}$$ (simplify)

$$\frac{28+7i}{16-(-1)}$$ (substitute $i^2 = -1$)

$$\frac{28+7i}{17}$$ (simplify)

(Notice that this process got rid of the i-term in the denominator.)

Sequences

A sequence is a series of numbers that follows a rule, so that if you know any number in the sequence, and you know the rule that governs the sequence, you can figure out any other number in the sequence.

Typically, a sequence on the ACT will depend either on addition/subtraction or multiplication/division.

A sequence that relies on addition or subtraction to generate the next term is called an arithmetic sequence.

Example of an arithmetic sequence:

$2, 7, 12, 17, 22 \ldots$ (each term is 5 more than the term before it)

A sequence that relies on multiplication or division to generate the next term is called a geometric sequence.

Example of a geometric sequence:

$3, 12, 48, 192, 768 \ldots$ (each term is 4 times the term before it)

You may have studied "series" in your math classes. ACT questions about sequences aren't as complicated as a high school math question about a series can be. For example, there's no sigma notation on the ACT. (If you've never heard of sigma notation, or you've never studied formal mathematical series, don't worry about it.)

Sequences on the ACT can either go on forever or stop at some point, depending on the setup of the question.

The ACT Math section might ask you to figure out any of the following:

- The sum of a certain set of terms in a sequence.
- The average of a certain set of terms in a sequence.
- The value of a particular term in a sequence.

Common difference and common ratio

The "common difference" of an arithmetic sequence is the difference between two consecutive terms.

In this sequence, the common difference is 9, because the difference between each term and the term before it is 9: $5, 14, 23, 32, 41, 50, 59$

The "common ratio" of a geometric sequence is the ratio of any one term to the term before it.

In this sequence, the common ratio is 5, because each term is 5 times the term that comes before it.

$1, 5, 25, 125, 625 \ldots$

Matrices

A matrix is a set of numbers displayed in a grid format. (The plural of "matrix" is "matrices.") Matrix questions are rare on the ACT, and tend to be relatively simple.

Examples of matrices:

$$\begin{bmatrix} 3 \\ -1 \end{bmatrix} \quad \begin{bmatrix} 25 & -2 & 16 \\ 8 & 5 & 7 \end{bmatrix} \quad [87 \quad 4]$$

You can add or subtract matrices of the same size by adding or subtracting corresponding elements (add the first terms to get the first term in the answer, the second terms to get the second term in the answer, and so on):

$$[6 \quad 3 \quad -5] + [-2 \quad 2 \quad 4] = [4 \quad 5 \quad -1]$$

You can multiply one matrix by another only when the number of columns in the first matrix is equal to the number of rows in the second. The result will have as many rows as the first matrix and as many columns as the second matrix.

$$\begin{bmatrix} a \\ b \\ c \end{bmatrix} \times \begin{bmatrix} x & y & z \end{bmatrix} = \begin{bmatrix} ax & ay & az \\ bx & by & bz \\ cx & cy & cz \end{bmatrix}$$

You can also multiply a matrix by a number. To do that, just multiply each element by that number.

$$4\begin{bmatrix} 3 & 1 \\ 7 & 2 \end{bmatrix} = \begin{bmatrix} 12 & 4 \\ 28 & 8 \end{bmatrix}$$

Geometric notation

The ACT likes to use the following notation to describe lines, rays, angles, and so on. You've probably seen this notation in your classes, but don't worry if you haven't—it's not hard to learn.

AB describes the distance from A to B.

$\overleftrightarrow{AB}$ describes the line that goes through points A and B (the arrows indicate an infinite extension into space in both directions).

$\overline{AB}$ describes the line segment with endpoints A and B (the lack of arrowheads on the symbol indicates that the given segment doesn't continue on to infinity).

$\overrightarrow{AB}$ describes the ray with endpoint A that goes through B and then continues on infinitely.

$\overrightarrow{BA}$ describes the ray with B for an endpoint that goes through A and continues on infinitely.

$\angle ABC$ describes the angle with point B as a vertex that has point A on one leg and point C on the other.

$\angle ABC = 60°$ indicates that the measure of the angle with point B as a vertex and with point A on one leg and point C on the other is 60 degrees.

$\triangle ABC$ describes the triangle with vertices A, B, and C.

$\square ABCD$ describes the parallelogram with vertices A, B, C, and D.

$\overline{AB} \perp \overline{BC}$ indicates that the line segments $\overline{AB}$ and $\overline{BC}$ are perpendicular to each other.

$\overline{AB} \parallel \overline{BC}$ indicates that the line segments $\overline{AB}$ and $\overline{BC}$ are parallel to each other.

Angles in a plane

Degrees are the units that we use to measure angles.

The measure of this angle is 45 degrees:

This angle is 90 degrees, also called a "right angle:"

This is a 180-degree angle, which is the same thing as a straight line:

Congruent angles are just angles with the same measures. So if one angle has a measure of 30° and another angle has a measure of 30°, those two angles are congruent.

Sometimes angles have special relationships. Three types of special relationships that appear often on the ACT are vertical angles, supplementary angles, and complementary angles.

Vertical angles are the pairs of angles that lie across from each other when two lines intersect. In a pair of vertical angles, the two angles have the same degree measurements as each other.

Angles $\angle ABC$ and $\angle DBE$ are a pair of vertical angles, so they have the same degree measurements as each other. Angles $\angle ABD$ and $\angle CBE$ are also a pair of vertical angles, so they have the same measurements as each other as well.

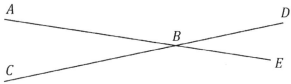

Supplementary angles are pairs of angles whose measurements add up to 180 degrees. When supplementary angles are next to each other, they form a straight line.

$\angle ABC$ and $\angle ABD$ are a pair of supplementary angles, because their measurements together add up to 180 degrees—together, they form the straight line CD.

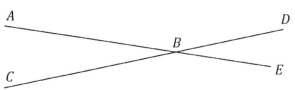

Complementary angles describe angles who measures add up to 90°.

In the figure below, $\angle AXB$ and $\angle BXC$ are complementary, because the sum of the measures of the two angles is 90°.

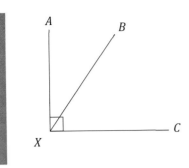

Triangles

A triangle is a three-sided figure. Triangles show up frequently on the ACT Math section.

The measures of the three angles in any triangle add up to 180 degrees.

The height of a triangle, also known as its "altitude," is the length of a line segment from one point of the triangle that would intercept the line containing the opposite side of the triangle at 90°.

The area of a triangle is equal to one half of the base times its height, or $\frac{1}{2}bh$.

This diagram shows how base and height are determined so they can be used to find the area of a triangle in the formula $\frac{1}{2}bh$:

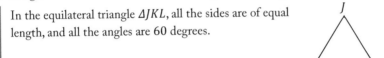

The longest side of any triangle is always opposite the biggest angle, and the shortest side of any triangle is always opposite the smallest angle.

An "equilateral" triangle has sides that are all the same length, and its angles measure 60 degrees each.

In the equilateral triangle $\triangle JKL$, all the sides are of equal length, and all the angles are 60 degrees.

An "isosceles" triangle has two sides that are the same length as each other, and two angles that are the same size as each other.

In the isosceles triangle $\triangle XYZ$, side $\overline{XY}$ is the same length as side $\overline{XZ}$. Also, $\angle XYZ$ and $\angle XZY$ have equal measurements:

A "right" triangle includes a ninety-degree angle as one of its three angles.

There's a special relationship involving the measurements of the sides of a right triangle: If you square the lengths of the two shorter sides, and then add those two squares together, the result is the square of the length of the longest side, or hypotenuse.

In this right triangle, $a^2 + b^2 = c^2$:

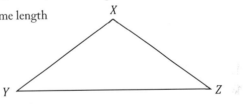

This formula, $a^2 + b^2 = c^2$, is called the "Pythagorean Theorem," and it comes up a lot on the ACT.

We call a set of numbers that satisfies this formula a "Pythagorean Triple." There are four of these in particular that you'll want to know on the ACT:

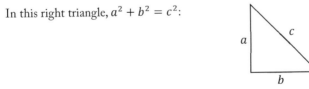

$\{3, 4, 5\}$ is a Pythagorean triple because $3^2 + 4^2 = 5^2$

$\{1, 1, \sqrt{2}\}$ is a Pythagorean triple because $1^2 + 1^2 = \sqrt{2}^2$

$\{1, \sqrt{3}, 2\}$ is a Pythagorean triple because $1^2 + \sqrt{3}^2 = 2^2$

$\{5, 12, 13\}$ is a Pythagorean triple because $5^2 + 12^2 = 13^2$

When we multiply each number in a Pythagorean triple by the same number, we get another Pythagorean triple.

If we know $\{3, 4, 5\}$ is a Pythagorean triple, then we also know $\{6, 8, 10\}$ is a Pythagorean triple, because $\{6, 8, 10\}$ is what we get when we multiply every number in $\{3, 4, 5\}$ by 2.

In a $\{1, 1, \sqrt{2}\}$ right triangle, the angle measurements are 45°, 45°, 90°.

In a $\{1, \sqrt{3}, 2\}$ right triangle, the angle measurements are 30°, 60°, 90°.

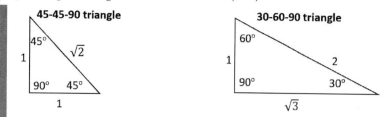

Two triangles are **similar triangles** if they have all the same angle measurements.

Between two similar triangles, the relationship between any two corresponding sides is the same as between any other two corresponding sides.

Triangles ΔABC and ΔDEF below are similar. Side $\overline{AB}$ has length 8, and side $\overline{DE}$ has length 24, so every side measurement in ΔDEF must be three times the corresponding side in ΔABC:

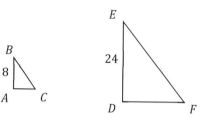

In every triangle, the length of each side must be less than the sum of the lengths of the other sides. (Otherwise, the triangle wouldn't be able to "close," because the longest side would be too long for the other two sides to touch.)

You can see in this diagram that the longest side is longer than the two shorter sides combined, which means the two shorter sides are too far apart to connect and "close" the triangle:

Parallelograms

A parallelogram is a four-sided figure with two pairs of parallel sides. Each side is parallel to its opposite side. In a parallelogram the measures of all four angles add up to 360°, and opposite angles are equal.

In $\square STUV$, the sum of the interior angles is 360°, and opposite angles have equal measurements.

Rectangles

Rectangles are parallelograms whose internal angles each measure 90°.
The area of a rectangle is equal to its length times its width.

This rectangle has a length of 24 and a width of 10. That means the area is 24 × 10, or 240.

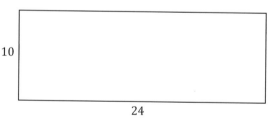

If you know the lengths of a rectangle's sides, then you can use the Pythagorean Theorem to figure out the length from one corner to the opposite corner, which is called the "diagonal."

In this rectangle, the Pythagorean Theorem tells us that diagonal $\overline{EG}$ must have a length of 26, since $10^2 + 24^2 = 26^2$.

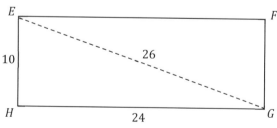

Squares

A square is a special kind of rectangle with sides of equal length. Like a rectangle's area, a square's area can be found by multiplying its width by its height. Since all the sides are the same length, this is the same as squaring the length of any side of the square.

This square has sides of length 4. To find its area, we simply square the length of a side, which gives us 16.

Trapezoids

A trapezoid is a four-sided figure with one pair of opposite sides that are parallel. In a trapezoid, all the internal angles add up to 360. The area can be found by averaging the lengths of the parallel sides and multiplying the result by the height. This formula is given as $\frac{a+b}{2}h$, where a and b are the lengths of the parallel sides and h is the height.

In this trapezoid, the parallel sides are of length 8 and 10, and the height is 3. That means the area is $\frac{8+10}{2} \times 3$, or 27.

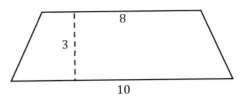

Perimeter

The perimeter of any non-circle object on the ACT can be found by adding up the lengths of all its sides.

In this rectangle, there are two sides of length 10, and two sides of length 3. That means the perimeter is $10 + 10 + 3 + 3$, or 26.

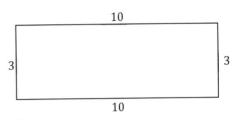

Circles (diameter, radius, arc, tangents, circumference, area)

A circle is defined as the set of points in a plane that are all equidistant from a single point, called the center. A circle has the same name as its center point.

Circle C consists of all the points in one plane that are 7 units away from the center, point C:

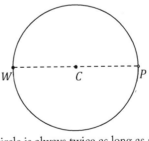

A radius is a line segment drawn from the center of a circle to the edge of that circle.

In circle C above, the line segment $\overline{CP}$ is a radius of circle C because it stretches from the center of the circle (C) to the edge of the circle (in this case, point P).

All points on the edge of a circle are the same distance from the center point, so all radii of a circle have the same length.

A diameter is a line segment that starts at one edge of a circle, passes through the center, and continues all the way across to the opposite edge of that circle.

$\overline{WP}$ is a diameter of circle C because it starts at one edge of the circle, passes through the center of the circle, and stops at the far edge of the circle.

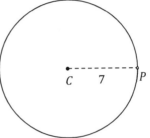

A diameter is basically made up of two opposite radii, so a diameter of a circle is always twice as long as a radius of that circle.

A diameter of a circle is the longest line segment that can be drawn through the circle without extending outside the circle.

A line is "tangent" to a circle when it lies in the same plane as the circle and intersects the circle at only one point. A tangent line is perpendicular to the radius of the circle that ends at the point shared by the tangent line and the circle.

Circle C has a tangent line $\overleftrightarrow{OQ}$ that intersects the circle at point P, and is perpendicular to radius $\overline{CP}$.

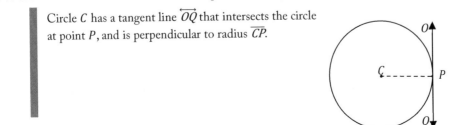

An arc is a portion of a circle. We can measure an arc by drawing one radius to each of the endpoints of the arc, and then measuring the angle formed by those radii at the center of the circle.

Circle C has a 90° arc $\overparen{BD}$. The measure of that arc is the same as the measure of the angle formed by radius $\overline{BC}$ and radius $\overline{CD}$.

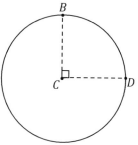

The length around a circle is its circumference; this is similar to the perimeter of a polygon.

You can find the circumference of a circle by multiplying π by the diameter. Since the diameter is two times the radius, the circumference can also be expressed as two times π times the radius, or $2\pi r$.

$\overline{CP}$ is a radius of circle C with a length of 3. The circumference of circle C is equal to $2\pi(3)$, or 6π.

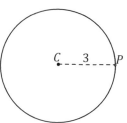

The area of a circle is equal to π times the square of the radius, or πr^2.

$\overline{CP}$ is a radius of circle C with a length of 3. The area of circle C is equal to $\pi(3)^2$, or 9π.

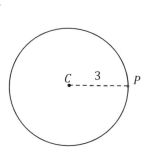

Translations, rotations, and reflections

The words "translation," "rotation," and "reflection" all describe ways that an object can be moved in a plane.

If an object is translated, that means it's sliding from one place to another. It doesn't spin, flip, or rotate.

In this diagram, the letter "B" is being translated in the direction indicated by the arrow. Notice that it doesn't spin, flip, or rotate.

If an object is rotated, then it's turned, or spun. We have to know what point it is being turned with reference to, and we say that it's being rotated "about" that point.

In this diagram, the letter "B" is being rotated about the given point:

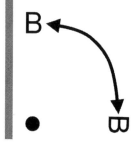

If an object is reflected across a line, then the object is flipped so that it appears as a mirror-image on the other side of that line.

In the following diagram, the letter "B" is reflected across the dashed line.

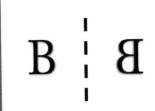

Three-dimensional geometry

You might occasionally encounter an ACT Math question that involves finding the volume of a three-dimensional object. Finding that volume will be a simple matter of knowing and applying the volume formula for that type of object, so let's take a look at those here.

The volume of a rectangular prism can be found by multiplying its length times its width times its height: $V = lwh$

The rectangular prism below has a length of 8, a width of 3, and a height of 4. That means its volume is equal to $8 \times 3 \times 4$, or 96.

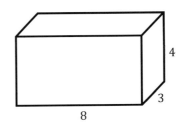

A cube is just a rectangular prism whose height, length, and width are all equal. We can find the volume of a cube by cubing the length of any side of the cube.

Each side of the cube below is 5 units long. That means its volume is equal to $5 \times 5 \times 5$, or 5^3, or 125.

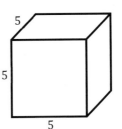

The volume of a cylinder is equal to the area of the circular face of the cylinder multiplied by its height. Since the area of the circular face is equal to πr^2, the volume is equal to $\pi r^2 h$.

The circular face of the cylinder below has a radius of 2, and the cylinder has a height of 6. That means its volume is equal to $\pi(2)^2(6)$, or 24π.

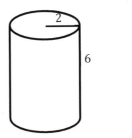

The volume of a sphere is equal to $\frac{4}{3}\pi r^3$.

The radius of the sphere below is 4. That means its volume is equal to $\frac{4}{3}\pi(4)^3$, or $\frac{256}{3}\pi$.

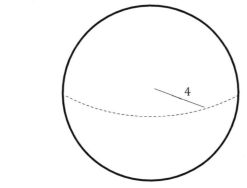

Points and lines in a plane

Any two points in a plane can be connected by a unique line.

Given any two points in a plane, there is a midpoint halfway between them.

Any set of three or more points may or may not lie on the same line. If they're on the same line, we say the points are "collinear."

The xy-coordinate plane has 4 quadrants numbered $I, II, II,$ and IV:

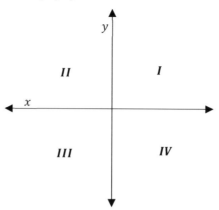

The origin is the point where the x-axis and y-axis intersect. The coordinate pair that corresponds to the origin is $(0, 0)$.

A point can be plotted on the xy-coordinate plane in (x, y) notation if we make the x-value the horizontal separation between the point (x, y) and the origin $(0, 0)$, and then we make the y-value the vertical separation between (x, y) and $(0, 0)$. In other words, we can graph a point on a coordinate plane by finding the intersection of the vertical line corresponding to its x-coordinate and the horizontal line corresponding to its y-coordinate.

The point $(3, 2)$ is located at the intersection of the vertical line $x = 3$ and the horizontal line $y = 2$:

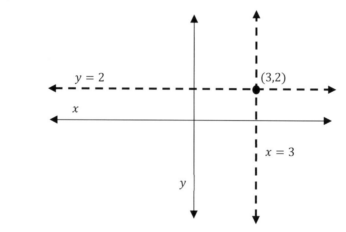

We can graph a line by connecting all the points whose (x, y) coordinates are solutions for the equation of that line:

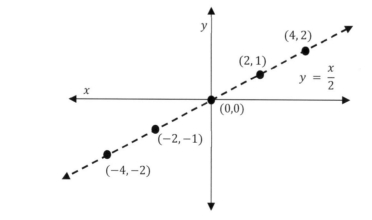

You can find the distance between two points in a coordinate plane by creating a right triangle on the plane with the distance between the two points as the hypotenuse (this is essentially an application of the Pythagorean Theorem, or the distance formula).

Let's find the distance between the points $(-1, -3)$ and $(3, 2)$. We'll begin by plotting them and then constructing a right triangle whose hypotenuse will be the distance between the points.

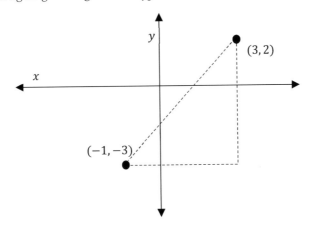

The length of the horizontal leg is the distance between the two x coordinates, and the length of the vertical leg is the distance between the two y coordinates.

In this case, the horizontal length is $3 - (-1)$, or 4, and the vertical length is $2 - (-3)$, or 5. Once you have the lengths of the two legs, you can plug them in to the Pythagorean Theorem and solve for the hypotenuse.

$a^2 + b^2 = c^2$ (Pythagorean Theorem)

$4^2 + 5^2 = c^2$ (substitute lengths of legs)

$16 + 25 = c^2$ (square 4 and 5)

$41 = c^2$ (add 16 and 25)

$\sqrt{41} = c$ (take square root of each side)

So the distance between $(3, 2)$ and $(-1, -3)$ is equal to $\sqrt{41}$.

The midpoint between two points in a coordinate plane is the coordinate pair whose x coordinate is the average of the x coordinates of the two points, and whose y coordinate is the average of their y coordinates.

The midpoint between $(-2, 4)$ and $(3, 7)$ is $\left(\frac{-2 + 3}{2}, \frac{4 + 7}{2}\right)$, or $\left(\frac{1}{2}, 5\frac{1}{2}\right)$

Polar coordinates

Earlier in this section we discussed coordinate pairs in the xy-coordinate plane. Most students have encountered this concept in their math classes. A less common way to plot points is by using polar coordinates.

(This concept comes up rarely on the ACT, and the odds are good that you won't see it on test day—but it does come up every once in a while and most students have never heard of it, so let's take a minute to discuss it.)

Like the more common coordinate pairs we already discussed, polar coordinates use a pair of numbers to designate the location of a point in the coordinate plane. The first number represents the distance of the point from the origin. The second number represents the measure of the angle created by drawing a line from the point to the origin, and connecting that line with the positive portion of the x-axis.

The point in the example diagram is 5 units away from the origin. When you draw a line from that point to the origin, it creates a 135° angle with the positive portion of the x-axis. (Note that in the figure I bolded the lines making the 135° angle to illustrate this concept.) Also notice in the example above that the angle measure is positive, to represent and angle opening upward from the positive portion of the x-axis. A negative angle measure would represent an angle opening downward from the same position.

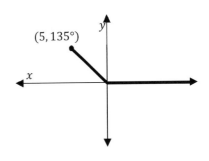

Functions

A function can be thought of as a formula that tells you how to start with one value and generate another value. Functions are often written in $f(x)$ notation, also called "function notation."

$f(x) = 2x^2 + 1$ is a function written in function notation.

This notation can be written with other variables besides f and x (like $h(j)$, $y(z)$, and so on).

Be sure not to confuse $f(x)$ with an expression like $(f)(x)$ or fx, which would mean "f times x"!

To find the value of a function for a certain x, we plug the x into the function and solve for $f(x)$. In other words, we insert our value for x everywhere the function has an x, and then we do the math described in the function.

In the function $f(x) = 2x^2 + 1$, we can find the value of $f(x)$ where $x = 3$ like this:

$$f(x) = 2x^2 + 1 \qquad \text{(original function)}$$
$$f(3) = 2(3)^2 + 1 \qquad \text{(substitute } x = 3\text{)}$$
$$f(3) = 2(9) + 1 \qquad \text{(square 3)}$$
$$f(3) = 18 + 1 \qquad \text{(multiply 2 by 9)}$$
$$f(3) = 19 \qquad \text{(simplify)}$$

So in this function, when x equals 3, we see that $f(x)$ equals 19. In other words, $f(3) = 19$ for this function.

Every function has a "domain" and a "range."

The domain of a function is the set of the numbers on a number line that generate a defined value when they're plugged into the function for x.

In the function $f(x) = 2x^2 + 1$, the domain is all the numbers on the number line, because we can plug in any value for x and get a valid result for $f(x)$.

In the function $f(x) = \dfrac{9}{x-5}$, the domain is all numbers except 5, because when $x = 5$, the denominator is equal to zero, and dividing by zero gives an undefined result.

The "range" of a function is the set of numbers that $f(x)$ can possibly equal.

The function $f(x) = x^3 - 3$ has a range of negative infinity to positive infinity, because it's possible to get any number for $f(x)$ when we plug in all possible x values.

The function $f(x) = x^2$ has a range from zero to positive infinity, because any value we use for x can result in any non-negative value for $f(x)$, but cannot result in a negative value for $f(x)$.

For every x value in a function, there can be no more than 1 corresponding y value. If an equation yields multiple y values for the same x value, then that equation isn't a function.

We can check the graph of an expression to see if it's a function by using something called "the vertical line test."

In order for the graph of a function to pass the vertical line test, we must be able to draw a vertical line anywhere on the graph of the function without crossing the function more than once.

Here's the graph of a linear function:

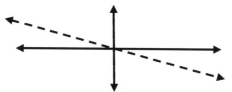

We see that the function represented by the dashed line passes the vertical line test because we could draw a vertical line anywhere on the graph and never cross the dashed line more than once with each vertical line:

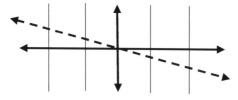

Here's an example of a graph of an expression that *fails* the vertical line test, so it's not a function:

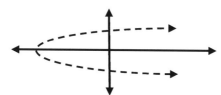

As we can see, there are a number of places where we can draw in vertical lines that would cross the graph of the expression more than once:

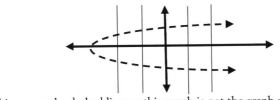

Again, this means the dashed line on this graph is not the graph of a function.

Even though one x-value of a function can't have multiple corresponding y-values, one y-value can be shared by multiple corresponding x-values in the same function—in other words, there is no "horizontal line test" that we need to worry about.

Linear equations with one variable

On the (x, y) coordinate plane, a vertical or horizontal line can be expressed as a linear equation with one variable.

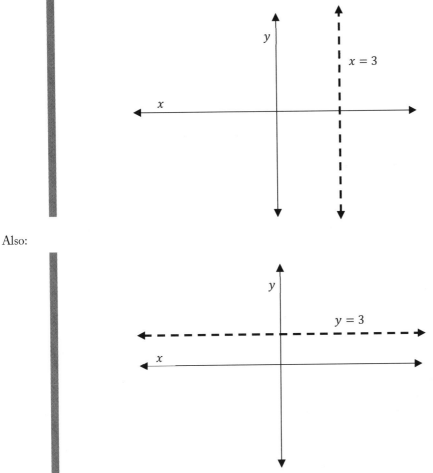

Also:

Linear functions

A linear function is a function such that all the (x, y) value pairings form a straight line when they're plotted as points on a graph.

$f(x) = x - 1$ is linear, because all the (x, y) pairings that it generates form a straight line when plotted on a graph.

Here are some (x, y) pairings for the function $f(x) = x - 1$:

x	y
-2	-3
-1	-2
0	-1
1	0
2	1
3	2

When we plot the (x, y) pairings from a linear function, we can see they fall in a straight line:

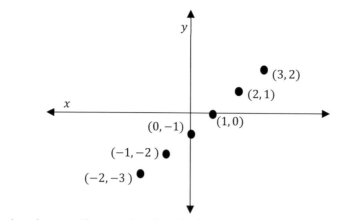

As you can see, we've only plotted six specific points based on the (x, y) coordinates we got for six specific values of x. But we can see that the domain for $f(x) = x - 1$ must be all numbers from negative infinity to infinity, because any x value we plug in will result in a defined y value. So we can draw a line connecting these plotted points, and the line will represent all possible (x, y) pairs that satisfy $f(x) = x - 1$.

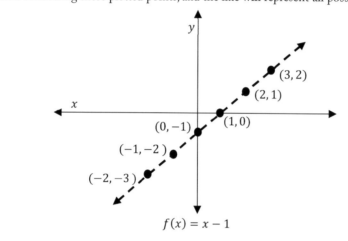

The slope of a linear function is a measure of how much the graph of the function rises or falls as it moves from left to right. A positive slope means that the line rises as it moves from left to right, and a negative slope means that the line descends as it moves from left to right.

The slope of a line is expressed as a fraction. The numerator of the fraction is the vertical separation of a pair of points on the line, and the denominator is the horizontal separation of the points. This ratio is always constant for any two points on a given line.

One way to calculate the slope of the linear function $f(x) = x - 1$ is to choose two points on the line and compare their vertical and horizontal separation. We'll use the points $(1, 0)$ and $(3, 2)$.

The numerator of the slope fraction will be the vertical separation between the two points. The y coordinates of these points are 0 and 2. Since $0 - 2 = -2$, the vertical separation is -2.

After we know the vertical separation between the two points, we put that value in the numerator of the fraction that describes the slope of the line, like this:

$$\frac{-2}{?}$$

Now we have to find the denominator of the slope. That number is the horizontal separation between the two points, which is the same as the difference between the x coordinates.

The x-coordinates of these points are 1 and 3. So the horizontal separation between them is also -2, because $1 - 3$ is -2.

Now we put this value for the horizontal separation in the denominator, to get our slope fraction:

$$\frac{-2}{-2}$$

So the slope of the line $f(x) = x - 1$, which contains points $(1, 0)$ and $(3, 2)$, is $\frac{-2}{-2}$, which is the same as 1.

(Note that it doesn't matter which order we subtract the x and y values in, as long as we use the same order for both calculations. In this example, we subtracted the $(3, 2)$ values from the $(1, 0)$ values both times.)

You'll often see linear functions written in something called "slope-intercept form," which looks like this: $y = mx + b$. (Remember that $f(x)$ is the same as y in this context.)

This $y = mx + b$ form is called "slope-intercept form" because it lets us easily determine two things about a given line:

- Its slope.
- Its y-intercept (that is, the y-value at which the line crosses the y-axis).

In slope-intercept form, m corresponds to the slope fraction, and b is the y-intercept.

> The function $f(x) = x - 1$ is in $y = mx + b$ form.
>
> According to $y = mx + b$ form:
>
> - y represents the $f(x)$ value.
>
> - m represents the slope, which is the coefficient of x. In the case of $f(x) = x - 1$, the coefficient of x is 1, which means the slope is $\frac{1}{1}$. In other words, from any given point on the line, moving one unit up and one unit to the right will leave us at another point on the line.
>
> - x represents the x value.
>
> - b represents the y-intercept, which in this case is equal to -1. We saw on the graph of the function on the previous page that the line does indeed cross the y-axis at $y = -1$.

Another example:

> $f(x) = \frac{x}{3} + 17$
>
> In this function, the slope, or m, is equal to $\frac{1}{3}$. (Remember that $\frac{x}{3}$ is the same as $\frac{1}{3}x$.)
>
> The y-intercept, b, is equal to 17.

Another example:

> $f(x) = -3x + 4$
>
> In this function, the slope is equal to -3.
>
> The y-intercept is equal to 4.

Two linear functions with the same slope and different y-intercepts are parallel.

Two lines are perpendicular when their slopes are the negative reciprocals of one another (for example, 2 and $-\frac{1}{2}$).

You'll never have to graph a linear function on the ACT. Instead, you might have to use your understanding of graphs to figure out a value, or to pick one graph out of several others as the correct graph of a particular function. (Your calculator may come in handy for that—see "Using a Calculator" on page 158 of this Black Book for more.)

Graphing quadratic functions

In a quadratic function, the x term is squared when the function is expressed in its most simplified form.

> $y = x^2$ is a quadratic function.

Quadratic functions are NEVER linear—instead, they're represented by a curved line on the xy-coordinate plane.

You'll never have to draw the graph of a quadratic function on the ACT. You'll only have to use provided graphs to answer questions, or choose which graph is correct for a given function. (Again, your calculator may be useful in those situations. See "Using a Calculator" on page 158 of this Black Book for more.)

Quadratic functions on the ACT can extend infinitely up or down.

> The graph of $y = x^2$ extends "up" infinitely. It looks like this:
>
>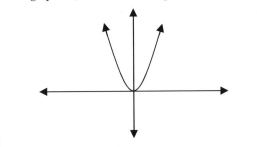
>
> The graph of $y = -x^2$ extends "down" infinitely. It looks like this:

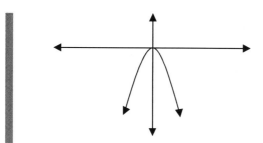

You can also think of the "direction" of the graph of a quadratic equation in terms of its range. When the range extends to negative infinity, the graph "opens down." When the range extends to positive infinity, the graph "opens up."

The highest point of a quadratic function that "opens down" is the (x, y) pair that has the greatest y value.

The lowest point of a quadratic function that "opens up" is the (x, y) pair that has the lowest y value.

The "zeroes" of a quadratic function are the points where the graph of the function touches or crosses the x-axis. To find the zeroes, set $f(x)$ equal to zero, then solve the resulting equation.

To find the zeroes of $f(x) = 2x^2 - 8$, we set $f(x)$ equal to zero and then solve for x:

$0 = 2x^2 - 8$	(substitute 0 for $f(x)$)
$8 = 2x^2$	(add 8 to both sides)
$4 = x^2$	(divide both sides by 2)
$x = 2 \ \ \text{or} \ \ x = -2$	(take square root of both sides)

So the zeroes of $f(x) = 2x^2 - 8$ are 2 and -2.

Asymptotes

For our purposes on the ACT, an asymptote is a line that the graph of a curve approaches but doesn't touch as the graph goes off to infinity. On the ACT, we need to be able to recognize vertical asymptotes and horizontal asymptotes. The quickest, easiest, and most reliable way to find the asymptotes of an equation is to look at the graph of that equation on your calculator, and see if there is a line that the graph approaches but doesn't touch as the graph goes off to positive and negative infinity. If that's a little confusing, it should be more clear after we look at an example.

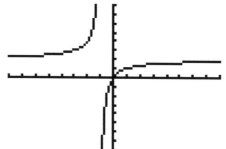

Above is the graph of $y = \dfrac{2x}{x+1}$. We can see that the equation has a vertical asymptote at $x = -1$ and a horizontal asymptote at $y = 2$, because the graph approaches those lines but doesn't touch them as the curves go off to infinity. Here's another version of the above graph, with the asymptotes drawn in as dashed lines:

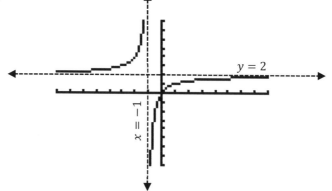

Trigonometry

The trigonometry that you need on the ACT is relatively basic and limited. The most important things you need to know are the three basic trigonometric ratios and their inverses.

You've probably learned the three basic ratios in math class with the acronym "**SOHCAHTOA**."

"**SOH**" stands for **S**ine = **O**pposite / **H**ypotenuse

---

Facebook.com/TestingIsEasy Youtube.com/TestingIsEasy

"CAH" stands for Cosine = Adjacent / Hypotenuse

"TOA" stands for Tangent = Opposite / Adjacent

Given a right triangle:

The "hypotenuse" is the side that's opposite the right angle.

The "opposite" side is the one across from the angle whose sine, cosine, or tangent we're evaluating.

The "adjacent" side is the side that's next to the angle we're evaluating (the one that isn't the hypotenuse).

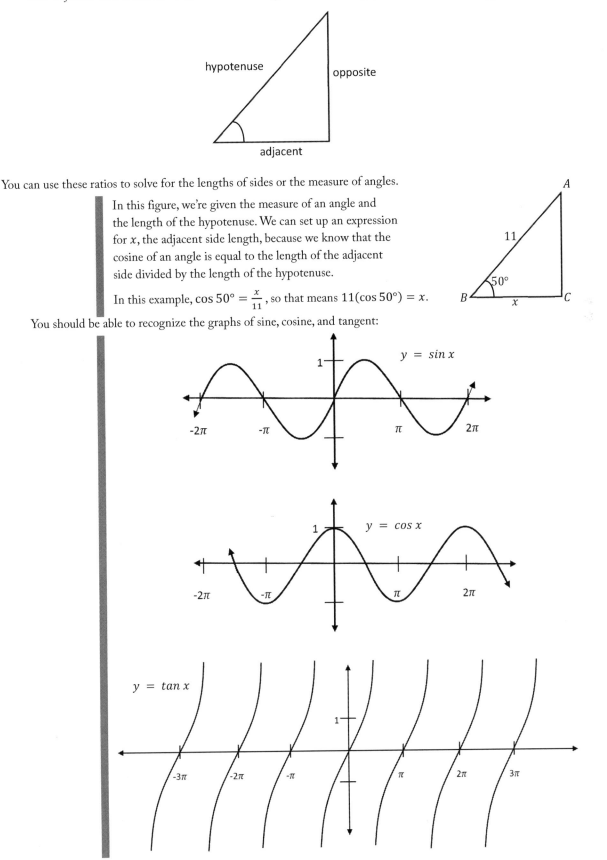

You can use these ratios to solve for the lengths of sides or the measure of angles.

In this figure, we're given the measure of an angle and the length of the hypotenuse. We can set up an expression for x, the adjacent side length, because we know that the cosine of an angle is equal to the length of the adjacent side divided by the length of the hypotenuse.

In this example, $\cos 50° = \frac{x}{11}$, so that means $11(\cos 50°) = x$.

You should be able to recognize the graphs of sine, cosine, and tangent:

$y = \sin x$

$y = \cos x$

$y = \tan x$

The period of a graph is the smallest section of the graph that you could "copy and paste" over and over again to make the graph.

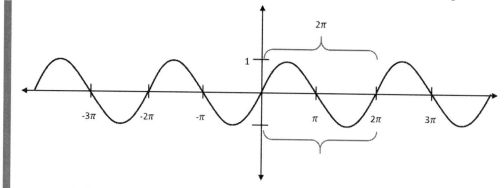

The period of $y = \sin x$ is 2π, because the graph repeats itself every 2π units.

NOTE: If you've studied trigonometry in school, you may be familiar with the idea of trigonometric identities. Although the ACT sometimes designs questions in a way that makes untrained test-takers think they need to understand how to use these trig identities, you never actually need to know them for the ACT. See "ACT Math Rule 2: No Advanced Formulas" on page 146 of this Black Book for more. (If you've never heard of trig identities, or if you don't remember any of them, don't worry—they're not something you need to know for the ACT).

Vectors

The ACT will occasionally ask you about vectors, and those questions will often involve unit vector notation. For the purposes of ACT Math, vectors are lines that have a magnitude and a direction; positive vectors point up or to the right, while negative vectors point down or to the left. When a vector is in unit vector notation, it's basically broken down into its vertical and horizontal components; the vertical component of the vector is expressed with the bold, lower-case letter **j**, while the horizontal component is expressed with the bold, lower-case letter **i**. Essentially, **i** represents a 1-unit perfectly horizontal vector, and **j** represents a 1-unit perfectly vertical vector, and this notation expresses any vector as a combination of these 1-unit vectors. For example, a vector in this notation might be expressed as 4**i** + 3**j**, or 2**i** − 7**j**, or −10**i** + 9**j**. That probably sounds a little weird if you're not already familiar with this notation, so let's look at an example.

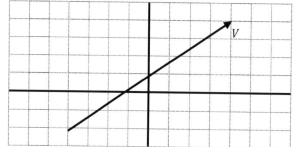

If we wanted to describe vector $\overrightarrow{UV}$ above using unit vector notation, we would first need to determine the number of horizontal units and vertical units that the vector covers. We can do that by basically figuring out the horizontal distance between point U and point V, and then figuring out the vertical distance between point U and point V. The horizontal distance becomes the coefficient of the **i**, the vertical distance becomes the coefficient of the **j**:

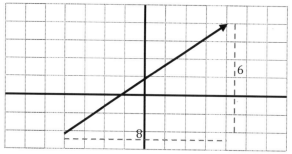

We can see that the vector above spans 8 horizontal units and 6 vertical units, so the unit vector notation for vector $\overrightarrow{UV}$ would be 8**i** + 6**j**. Notice that both values are positive because the vector goes up and to the right.

We can add vectors by just adding their **i** components and their **j** components separately. So the sum of 2**i** − 3**j** and 4**i** + 7**j** is (2**i** + 4**i**) + (−3**j** + 7**j**), or 6**i** + 4**j**.

The ACT might also ask about the component form of vectors. This form is really very similar to the unit notation, for our purposes. We still break down the vector into a horizontal distance and a vertical distance, and a positive value still indicates a vector that goes up or right while a negative value still indicates a vector that goes down or left.

The difference is that instead of using **i** and **j**, we just make the horizontal and vertical component into a coordinate pair with weird pointy brackets, like this: $\langle 7,4 \rangle$. So $\langle 7,4 \rangle$ would represent a vector that spans seven units to the right and 4 units up. Again, we can add vectors in this form by adding the horizontal and vertical values separately, like this: $\langle 1,2 \rangle + \langle -5,3 \rangle = \langle (1-5),(2+3) \rangle = \langle -4,5 \rangle$. We can also multiply the vector like this: $2\langle 3,5 \rangle = \langle 6,10 \rangle$.

The ACT sometimes refers to vectors as a single lowercase bold letter, like **c** or **k**, and other times as two points in a plane with an arrow above them, like $\overrightarrow{BC}$ or $\overrightarrow{ST}$. Either way, though, if the problem is about vectors, the ACT will specifically call it a vector.

Conclusion

If you're familiar with all the concepts in this toolbox, then you have the basic math knowledge necessary to answer any real ACT Math question. Of course, it's important to remember that simply knowing these concepts isn't enough to guarantee a good ACT Math score. It's equally important—perhaps *more* important—to focus on the design of the ACT Math section and to learn how to take apart challenging questions.

After all, the difference between people who score high on the ACT Math section and people who don't usually has very little to do with math knowledge. Generally speaking, people who score higher on the ACT Math section have a better understanding of how the test works, and pay more attention to small details—*that's* what actually sets them apart from the average test-taker.

On the next page, we'll start talking about the tactics that trained test-takers use when they apply their math knowledge to the ACT . . .

Special Technique: Backsolving

In "The ACT's Biggest Weakness" on page 17 of this Black Book, we discussed how the weaknesses of the multiple-choice format can be used to our advantage on the ACT. In the ACT Math section, we can often exploit the multiple-choice format in even more ways than we can on the rest of the test, because we can sometimes test values from the answer choices instead of having to solve a math question on our own.

There are two general types of situations on the ACT Math section in which you can find the correct answer by testing values in a variable expression:

1. If a question asks us to solve for a variable and the answer choices don't involve variables, we can often just plug each answer choice back into the expression from the question.

2. If a question has a variable (or variables) in the answer choices, we can often assign an arbitrary value to that variable (or those variables) and then evaluate each expression in the prompt and the answer choices.

Both of these concepts might make a lot more sense once we consider some examples. We'll look at both of them now, starting with the easier one:

Plugging values from the answer choices into an expression from the question

Sometimes you'll see a question that presents some kind of expression with a single variable, and then asks you for the number that makes that expression true.

If such a question only has numbers in the answer choices, then the most straightforward (and fastest) approach is sometimes just to plug each answer choice into the variable expression to see which one works. Let's look at question 15 from the Math section of practice test 1 in the Red Book (test 2 in the 2020-2021 Red Book) to see this idea in action. (Remember that the first practice test in each edition of the Red Book is usually found about 50 pages into the Red Book, separate from the other practice tests near the end of the book!)

This question asks us which value "is a solution to the equation $x^2 - 36x = 0$." Then it gives us five numbers to choose from.

Some test-takers will start trying to factor out the equation to find a solution, as though they were taking an algebra test in high school. This approach will work if you do it correctly, but a lot of people don't like to factor expressions with variables. Since we know that one of the values in the answer choices must be a solution for the equation, we can just plug each choice into the equation and use a calculator to see which one causes the $x^2 - 36x = 0$ equation to be true, like this:

(A) $(72)^2 - 36(72)$ $5184 - 2592 = 2592$
(B) $(36)^2 - 36(36)$ $1296 - 1296 = 0$
(C) $(18)^2 - 36(18)$ $324 - 648 = -324$
(D) $(6)^2 - 36(6)$ $36 - 216 = -180$
(E) $(-6)^2 - 36(-6)$ $36 + 216 = 252$

When we plug each answer choice into the equation from the prompt, we can see that only one of them results in a value of zero, as required. That means we know the correct answer is (B), 36. (For a full walkthrough of this question, including other ways to solve it, see page 176 of this Black Book.)

Now let's talk about a slightly more advanced way to answer an ACT Math question by testing values.

Using arbitrary values to test answer choices containing variables

If the choices for a question involve a variable, then we can sometimes solve the question by assigning a value to the variable and then evaluating the expressions provided in the prompt and in the answer choices.

I know that might sound a little confusing, so let's check out a real-life example of this technique in action by looking at question 47 from the Math section of practice test 1 in the Red Book, which is test 2 in the 2020-2021 Red Book (again, remember that the first practice test is near the front of the Red Book).

This question asks us which answer choice is equivalent to $\frac{12x^6 - 9x^2}{3x^2}$ for all nonzero values of x. All of the answer choices are expressions that involve one term being subtracted from a term involving an exponent of x.

To apply this technique to the question, we would just choose some value for x, and then plug that x-value into each expression in the prompt and in the answer choices. The right answer will be the choice that comes out to the same value as the expression in the prompt.

So let's give it a try. We'll arbitrarily pick $x = 2$ and see what happens. (Note that the prompt says that x can't be zero, so we MUST pick a nonzero value for this question.)

When we plug $x = 2$ into the expression from the prompt, we get $\frac{12(2)^6 - 9(2)^2}{3(2)^2}$, which reduces to $\frac{732}{12}$, or 61.

Now let's plug $x = 2$ into each answer choice and see what we get:

(A) $4x^3 - 3x = 4(2)^3 - 3(2) = 26$

(B) $4x^3 - 3 = 4(2)^3 - 3 = 29$

(C) $4x^4 - 9x^2 = 4(2)^4 - 9(2)^2 = 28$

(D) $4x^4 - 3x = 4(2)^4 - 3(2) = 58$

(E) $4x^4 - 3 = 4(2)^4 - 3 = 61$

We can see that only (E) can be correct, since it's the only choice that equals our target value, 61.

(Of course, some people would prefer to approach the specific question by manipulating the expression in the prompt without substituting any actual numbers. That's fine, of course—for a full breakdown of this question, see its walkthrough on page 206 of this Black Book. Just keep in mind that this type of question gives us the option of attacking it in a more concrete way like this if we want to. This can be very useful on more complicated questions.)

Important notes

There are some very important things to be aware of when you use this technique.

For one thing, it's important to make sure that any arbitrary values you pick still meet the requirements in the prompt, if there are any. For example, if the prompt says that it's only talking about negative numbers, then you can't arbitrarily pick a positive number to use for backsolving.

It's possible, through sheer chance, that you might pick variables that result in more than one answer choice coincidentally matching the expression from the question. If that ever happens, just pick new values for the variables and re-evaluate everything. It's extremely unlikely that such a coincidence will happen on the second try as well, so there should only be one choice left that satisfies the question.

You can decrease the likelihood of this kind of coincidence by avoiding certain values when you make your substitution. I'd advise you not to choose the values 0, 1, or -1 for any question, because of their unique properties; I also try to avoid picking any values that already appear in the prompt.

It's also important to keep in mind that you don't have to use this approach if you don't want to. There are always other ways to approach a question, but it can sometimes be helpful to remember that this option exists if you can't figure out a quick algebraic solution to the question.

You'll see this approach in action against other real ACT practice questions as you go through the ACT Math walkthroughs later in this section.

Unwritten Test Design Rules of ACT Math

Now that we've talked a little bit about how ACT Math works, and we've covered the concepts that can appear in ACT Math questions, let's talk about the unwritten rules of ACT Math.

ACT Math Rule 1: You Usually Have to Know the Words and Symbols

In the walkthroughs we looked at for the ACT Reading section, it was often possible to find a correct answer choice for a question even if we didn't know a few words in the question or in the relevant portion of the text. But it will usually be difficult to work around unknown terms on the ACT Math section: if an ACT Math question asks about the greatest common factor of two numbers, you have little chance of getting that question right if you don't know the definition of the term "greatest common factor."

Fortunately, you shouldn't have a problem with math terminology on the ACT if you're comfortable with the concepts from the Math Toolbox in this Black Book. Just remember that you need to get familiar with any unknown math terms you might run into while you're preparing. It's possible that you'll see those terms again on test day. (Of course, it occasionally happens that you can figure out the right answer to an ACT Math question even if you don't recognize all the words and symbols in the question. For example, if you were unfamiliar with the term "greatest common factor," you might still be able to use your knowledge of the individual terms "greatest," "common," and "factor" to find the answer, especially if you could also take the answer choices into consideration as you worked on the question. But, the vast majority of the time, you'll find that it's hard to determine the right answer to an ACT Math question with total confidence unless you know the terms and notation in the question.)

ACT Math Rule 2: No Advanced Formulas

You'll need to use some formulas on the ACT, but the formulas will be relatively simple and largely repetitive. The real challenge is usually figuring out exactly what the question is asking, and then deciding which simple formulas to apply.

Don't spend any practice time studying advanced math concepts like trig identities or statistical regression, because they won't help you on this test. Instead, familiarize yourself with the ideas in the ACT Math Toolbox in this Black Book, and, once you've read all the training, start working through the ACT Math walkthroughs later in this section.

(By the way, roughly once per test you'll run into a math question I call the "note" question. The note question is usually a trig question that seems fairly advanced at first, but then provides a note that explains the formula or conversion necessary to answer the question. These questions often intimidate test-takers who don't read the note, because the questions seem to require prior knowledge of advanced math if we don't realize that those formulas have been provided for us in the question. If we do read the question carefully, we can see that these questions actually just require us to read the provided formula and substitute the provided values in the appropriate places—a relatively basic math skill. The Red Book contains the following note questions with trig formulas:

- Question 59 from the Math section of practice test 1 in the Red Book (test 2 in the 2020-2021 Red Book); my walkthrough is on page 219 of this Black Book
- Question 35 from the Math section of practice test 2 in the Red Book (test 3 in the 2020-2021 Red Book); my walkthrough is on page 251 of this Black Book
- Question 56 from the Math section of practice test 3 in the Red Book (form 16MC3 online if you have the 2020-2021 Red Book); my walkthrough is on page 323 of this Black Book

ACT Math Rule 3: Calculations are Relatively Simple

As you work through real ACT Math practice questions, you'll find that the calculations you'll do are relatively easy. The real challenge is often in knowing how to set the problem up—the final calculation you'll need to do will frequently be along the lines of "4 + 7" or "2 − 0" or something like that.

In fact, if you find yourself writing out a very complex expression while trying to solve a question, that can often be a warning sign that you're on the wrong track. You'll see this idea in action once we start going through the ACT Math question walkthroughs.

ACT Math Rule 4: Limited Subject Matter

As we've discussed, there's a set group of math concepts that can come up in ACT Math questions, and those concepts are discussed in the ACT Math Toolbox in this book. Once you feel good about those concepts, you know the math ideas you need to know for the ACT Math section. All that's left is to learn how to deal with the unusual presentation of those ideas in real questions.

This is important because most untrained test-takers will panic when they see a challenging ACT Math question, because they assume they don't know the math involved. But trained test-takers are confident they know all the math necessary to answer any question on the ACT, so they don't panic when they see a strange question. Instead, they remain calm and follow the "Math Path," which is a rough outline for solving challenging ACT Math questions that we'll discuss on page 155 of this Black Book.

ACT Math Rule 5: 30 Seconds or Less

This is an important concept, and it may seem hard to believe right now: every ACT Math question can technically be solved in 30 seconds or less if you find the most efficient approach to it.

But this doesn't mean that your answer must be wrong if it takes you longer than 30 seconds to find it!

As we'll see in the ACT Math walkthroughs in a few pages, we can always find multiple valid approaches to every ACT Math question. An approach that takes longer than 30 seconds isn't necessarily any worse than one that takes less than 30 seconds, as long as you still have enough time overall to finish the ACT Math section and get the score you need.

But it's very important to understand, strategically, that every question *can* be answered in less than 30 seconds. This is important because the ACT likes to make simple things seem complicated so that untrained test-takers won't know what to do. The test will go out of its way to make you think that some questions require 2 or 3 minutes of complicated calculations—but if you remember that every real ACT Math question can actually be answered in less than 30 seconds, you'll be motivated to try to view the questions in simpler terms.

These under-30-second solutions often involve unorthodox ways of looking at questions; in many cases, they'll involve techniques your teacher wouldn't let you use in a math class. For example, you might have to rely on the scale of a diagram or realize that some value can be factored out of an expression—we'll talk about these techniques, and others, over the coming pages.

ACT Math Rule 6: All Necessary Information

Unless there's an answer choice that says the correct answer can't be determined from the given information, every single question must provide all the information you need to find the answer. Sometimes it might seem like a question is leaving something out—if it seems that way, then you're forgetting some math idea, or overlooking something. In this case, we have to try to look at all the information in the problem in a different way and generate a solution. We'll expand on this idea when we talk about the general process for answering ACT Math questions, and when we do the math walkthroughs in a few pages.

ACT Math Rule 7: Scale is Pretty Much Always Accurate

The ACT says that "figures are NOT necessarily drawn to scale" (emphasis in original) on the ACT Math section . . .

. . . but literally every single diagram I've ever seen in a real ACT Math section has been drawn to scale. That means their angle measurements are consistent with what the question describes, and the relative lengths of lines are accurate, as well. (For example, if one side of a rectangle is labeled 6 units long and another side is labeled 3 units, then the ACT's diagram will accurately show the longer side being twice as long as the shorter side.)

This can be very helpful, because the ACT often provides us with wrong answer choices that are much too large or too small to be correct when we consider them in terms of the diagram's scale, leaving the correct answer as the only choice that seems plausible relative to the scale. For an example of this idea in action, look at question 43 from the Math section of practice test 2 in the Red Book (test 3 in the 2020-2021 Red Book). That question asks for "the degree measure of the smaller of the 2 angles" in the diagram. When we look at the diagram, we can see that the angle in question is clearly larger than 45°. Only choice (D) is larger than 45° (in fact, the next largest option is 29°, which is obviously much too small given the scale of the diagram), so we know (D) must be right. (For a more complete explanation of this question, see the walkthrough on page 260 of this Black Book.)

So keep your eyes open for opportunities to use ACT Math diagrams to your advantage like this. They don't come up on every single question, of course, but when you do encounter them they can often get you quick, easy points. It's not uncommon for a real ACT Math section to offer us 3 or 4 opportunities to answer questions this way.

(One important note: even though I've never seen an ACT Math diagram that wasn't to scale, I always double-check that a diagram seems to be to scale before I rely on the scale to choose my answer. I usually do this by making a rough comparison of two labeled lengths on the diagram, to confirm that their relative lengths seem consistent with the labels.)

ACT Math Rule 8: Answer Choices are Important!

The choices for each ACT Math question aren't randomly generated—they're constructed as carefully as the rest of the question.

Let's think about this—imagine that you're doing an ACT Math question and you find an answer of 10, but 10 isn't an answer choice. In that scenario, you'd be getting a free shot to try to do the problem again, because you would know you'd made a mistake.

The ACT doesn't want that to happen, so it tries to provide wrong answers that anticipate the mistakes it thinks you're likely to make. That way, if you make one of those mistakes, you'll find an answer choice that reflects it, and you'll be likely to choose that wrong answer without realizing you're wrong.

These cleverly positioned wrong-answer choices might seem like they would make it harder to get ACT Math questions right, but they can actually work to our advantage if we know how to exploit them. Depending on the context of the question, we can use a set of answer choices to give us hints about which concepts are involved in the solution to the question, or even about which answer choice is likely to be correct.

We'll talk more about this in the section called "ACT Math Answer-Choice Patterns" on the next page, and you'll see these concepts in action in the ACT Math section walkthroughs.

ACT Math Answer-Choice Patterns

Earlier in this Black Book, we discussed the importance of answer choices in general. We've also talked about different types of answer choices on the ACT Reading section. Now, let's take a look at some of the answer-choice patterns you'll see on the ACT Math section.

You know by now that wrong-answer choices can contain valuable information if we know how to exploit them. Well, some of the special characteristics of answer choices on the Math section can be particularly useful.

Now, I should point out that some people sort of intuitively just "get" some of the concepts that we're about to talk about. But, even if you feel like you already know some of this stuff, I still recommend that you read this section carefully. It can be very valuable to see these strategies spelled out in black and white—and you may also discover some tactics you've never thought about before.

In order to understand how the sets of answer choices on the ACT Math section are designed, let's imagine we're actually in charge of writing a math question that's going to be used on the ACT. We've got the beginning of the question all ready to go, but we need to add in some wrong-answer choices to complete it.

Our main goal is to provide choices that might trap someone who made a mistake in solving the question, or who didn't understand the question in the first place and just wanted to take a guess.

As we discussed in "The ACT's Biggest Weakness" on page 17 of this Black Book, if the wrong-answer choices are unrelated to the question, then it'll be too easy for test-takers to identify the right answer without understanding the question. So we might try to provide "decoy" answers that a confused person could accidentally pick. Let's look at a fake sample question to illustrate this concept (of course, this question is too simple to be an ACT Math question, but we're just using it to illustrate a basic concept):

> $176 \times 4{,}673 = y$
> What is the value of y?

Now, that's not something most test-takers can do in their heads. But most test-takers could pick out the correct answer in just a few seconds if these were the choices:

> (A) 1
>
> (B) 0
>
> (C) −11,395
>
> (D) 822,448
>
> (E) $\frac{1}{12}$

These answer choices make the correct answer instantly obvious. The only number that's remotely large enough is choice (D), and (D) is the correct answer. Beyond that,

- (A) is obviously too small.
- (B) is impossible since we're multiplying two numbers and neither number is zero.
- (C) is impossible since it's negative and neither of the two numbers being multiplied is negative.
- (E) is impossible since it's a fraction and we're multiplying two whole numbers.

In other words, the wrong answers make this fake question very easy for any test-taker who knows the basics of multiplication and who bothers to read the answer choices.

This is an extreme and unrealistic example that I designed to illustrate a point, but you see what I mean. Coming up with some plausible incorrect answer choices is every bit as important as any other part of the design of the question.

Now, let's think a little more about how we might try to come up with incorrect answer choices if we were trying to write an ACT Math question.

Imagine the question we're creating involves solving for x in this equation:

> $2x^2 = 50$

and then plugging x into this equation to solve for y:

> $y = 3x + 2$

For the first step, a test-taker on the right track would figure out that $x = 5$, because $2(5)^2 = 50$. Then she'd plug x into the second equation, and get $y = 17$, because $17 = 3(5) + 2$.

You can probably see that one really good wrong-answer choice for us to include would be 5. Some test-takers might figure out that $x = 5$ in the first part of the problem, and then forget that we actually asked them to solve for y, and they have another step left.

So we'd definitely want to include 5 as a wrong-answer choice. That way, we'd catch anybody who managed to do the first part of the question correctly, but who lost track of what the question actually asked for, and failed to finish it.

Another good wrong-answer choice for us to include might be 77. Some test-takers might realize that $2x^2 = 50$, but then accidentally plug x^2 into the second equation instead of x. Really, x is 5, but x^2 is 25; if a test-taker accidentally plugged $x = 25$ into the expression $y = 3x + 2$, he'd end up with 77 as the answer, because $77 = 3(25) + 2$.

Still another tricky wrong-answer choice might be 1. This is the result when a test-taker correctly finds the value of x in the first equation—but then accidentally plugs that value in for y in the second equation and solves for x, instead of the other way around. That test-taker would find that $5 = 3(1) + 2$, and would think that the correct answer was 1.

There are other set patterns the ACT often uses to generate wrong-answer choices on the Math section, and we'll discuss them below. For now, though, you get the idea: the ACT puts a lot of thought into the wrong-answer choices for each question.

It's very clever of the test to include these tricky wrong answers in order to catch as many people in their mistakes as possible. But, if we're paying attention, we can use these patterns to our advantage.

If the ACT has to include wrong answers that are closely related to things going on in the question, and if we know how to look for those relationships in the answer choices, then the set of answer choices can become like a set of clues to help us realize which math concepts are related to the question—in some cases, the answer choices can even offer strong hints about which answer choice is likely to be correct.

Not every single question will have answer choice clues exactly like that, but almost every real ACT Math question will have something in the answer choices that can help us out if we know to look for it. With that in mind, let's discuss a few of the most common wrong answer types in real ACT Math questions. (Of course, you'll see ample demonstrations of all of these concepts in use against real ACT questions when we do the math walkthroughs in a few pages.)

You'll find that some of the answer-choice patterns on an ACT Math question can be easily identified before you start working on a question, such as the "Halves and Doubles" pattern . On the other hand, some patterns can only be identified after you've started working on a question, such as the "Right Approach, Wrong Step" pattern. We'll discuss the pre-solution patterns first, and then tackle the post-solution patterns.

Pre-Solution Patterns

These patterns reflect relationships in the answer choices that we can notice before we've even tried to attack the question.

Hidden Pattern 1: Halves and Doubles

There are many ACT Math questions that involve multiplying or dividing by two. For whatever reason, it's just some arbitrary pattern the ACT likes to follow sometimes, even when it doesn't seem particularly relevant to a specific question that incorporates it.

At any rate, you'll often see incorrect answer choices on the ACT Math section that are half of the right answer, or double the right answer.

For a real-life example, look at question 15 from the Math section of practice test 1 in the Red Book (test 2 in the 2020-2021 Red Book). The correct answer is (B), 36. Choices (A) and (C) are 72 and 18, respectively—one is double the correct answer, and the other is half as much as the correct answer.

(Notice that this pattern could appear in a question where finding half or double the correct answer could result from a likely mistake, or it might appear in a question where the idea of multiplying or dividing by two has nothing to do with finding an answer to the question. We'll see examples of this in the walkthroughs later in this section.)

So this is another important pattern to remember: if you see two answer choices, and one is twice the other, or even if you see three or more in a series that keeps multiplying or dividing by two, then one of those choices is disproportionately likely to be correct—not *guaranteed* to be correct, by any means, but likely to be.

Hidden Pattern 2: "Opposites"

You'll sometimes encounter answer choices that are opposites of other choices for the same question. For example, a question might have choices like 5 and -5, or $\frac{2}{7}$ and $-\frac{2}{7}$.

Untrained test-takers commonly lose track of negative signs when they're doing their calculations, which can cause them to come up with an answer that's the opposite of the correct answer. So you'll commonly see two answer choices that are opposites of one another, and the correct answer is slightly more likely to be one of those two choices than it is to be an answer choice whose opposite isn't present in the other choices.

But these types of opposites aren't the only "opposites" that you should look out for on test day! You might also see any of the following kinds of opposites:

- a pair of choices that are reciprocals of one another, such as $\frac{x}{y}$ and $\frac{y}{x}$
- a pair of choices that include commonly confused concepts, such as sine and cosine
- a pair of choices that could be thought of as complements or supplements of one another, such as 20° and 70°, or 60% and 40%

For the purposes of this pattern, any pair of choices like this can be thought of as "opposites," because they all reflect an attempt by the ACT to get us to confuse two concepts that might seem easily interchangeable if we aren't paying close enough attention.

If you see this pattern in a set of answer choices, you should be especially careful to double-check your work for any mistake that could result in choosing the "opposite" of the correct answer. Such mistakes could involve things like multiplying an expression by -1 instead of 1, or confusing the numerator and denominator of a fraction, and so on.

We find an example of this pattern in question 12 from the Math section of practice test 2 in the Red Book (test 3 in the 2020-2021

Red Book). In that question, the right answer is (K), -20. One of the wrong answers is 20. The prompt for the question involves an algebraic equation with negative numbers, so the ACT seems to be anticipating that some test-takers will make mistakes in dealing with the negative numbers and end up with the opposite of the right answer. (For a full walkthrough of this question, see page 228 of this Black Book.)

As with any pattern in the answer choices, seeing a pair of opposites doesn't guarantee that one of the opposites is correct, but noticing this pattern can often help alert you to potential mistakes that you'll want to avoid while you figure out your solution. You'll see several examples of how this pattern can influence our thinking in the walkthroughs later in this Black Book.

Hidden Pattern 3: Wrong Answers Try to Imitate Right Answers

The basic idea behind this pattern is that the ACT likes to incorporate some elements of the correct answer into the incorrect answers, so that test-takers who can only figure out part of a complicated question will still see more than one choice that seems like it might be right.

That abstract description probably sounds a little strange, so let's look at a concrete example of this concept. Please check out question 5 from the Math section of practice test 2 in the Red Book (test 3 in the 2020-2021 Red Book).

You can see that all the answer choices for that question share a few obvious characteristics:

- They all have a fraction on the left side of the equals sign.
  - The numerator in that fraction is either 429 or $s + 429$.
  - The denominator in that fraction is either 5 or 6.
- They all have either 85 or $\frac{85}{100}$ on the right side of the equals sign.

On a question like this, the ACT seems to want the wrong answers to share as many features as possible with the right answer. That way, for instance, a test-taker who correctly figured out that the denominator in the fraction on the left should be 6 would still have to figure out whether (B), (D), or (E) were correct. On top of that, even if a test-taker correctly determined that the right answer was $\frac{s+429}{6} = 85$, he might still misread the answer choices if he were in a hurry, and accidentally bubble the wrong letter anyway. (Untrained test-takers do that kind of thing all the time. It's one of the reasons people often feel like the ACT is going well when they're taking it, only to be disappointed when they get their results.)

For these kinds of reasons, we'll often find that the ACT uses wrong answers that include many elements of the right answer, whenever the correct answer to a question is complicated enough to make these kinds of wrong answers possible.

This pattern can make us aware of the specific issues we need to look out for when approaching a question. For example, in the question we just analyzed, we can tell that we need to pay close attention to the issue of whether the denominator should be 5 or 6, because the ACT is clearly indicating that it thinks some test-takers will make a specific mistake that causes them to end up with the wrong value in the denominator (instead of offering five different values for the denominator in the five answer choices, which would indicate that the ACT thought there were a variety of mistakes that test-takers were likely to make when it came to the denominator).

This pattern can also provide hints that help us find non-traditional solutions to a question. If we have no idea where to start on a question, we might see if any patterns in the answer choices suggest that certain elements are likely to be part of the correct answer, and then try to work backwards from there.

You'll see several examples of these kinds of tactics discussed in the walkthroughs in a few pages. (For more on the significance of the answer choices in question 5 from the Math section of practice test 2 in the Red Book—test 3 in the 2020-2021 Red Book—see "Hidden Pattern 6: Most Like the Others (or *Almost* Like the Others)" below.)

Hidden Pattern 4: Be Aware of Series

The ACT often creates a set of answer choices that include a mathematical series. In these cases, the common difference or common ratio among the choices in the series can give you clues to important concepts in the question.

For example, you might see a series of three choices in which each choice increases by a set quantity—like the series 10, 17, 24. This might give you a clue that adding or subtracting 7 is a key part of finding the right answer. You might also see choices forming a series that involves multiplying by a certain number—like 0.89, 8.9, 89, 890. That might tell you that multiplying or dividing by ten is likely to be part of finding the right answer.

You can see a real-life example of this pattern in question 18 from the Math section of practice test 2 in your copy of *The Official ACT Prep Guide* (test 3 in the 2020-2021 Red Book). The choices include 10, 20, 40, and 80. In this series, each term is twice as much as the term before it. The question involves two different rates, with one rate being half as fast as the other rate. The series in the answer choices makes it very clear to a trained test-taker that the ACT expects some people to make a mistake in their reading or algebra that causes them to be off by a factor of two, so we know that we need to pay particular attention to that possibility as we proceed to answer the question. (For a full walkthrough of this question, including a variety of ways to approach it, see page 233 of this Black Book.)

Let me stress that a series isn't enough, on its own, to determine a right or wrong answer with complete certainty! When you see a series in a set of answer choices, you should consider whether the difference among those choices is relevant to the situation in the question, and you should make sure that you're not making a mistake that causes you to pick one of the wrong choices in the series.

Post-Solution Patterns

These patterns are just as useful for trained test-takers as the pre-solution patterns are, but they can usually only be identified after we've done some calculations for a particular question. (We should also note that, on some questions, any of the pre-solution patterns we just discussed might only really be noticeable after you've finished the solution, so they can all be thought of as potential post-solution patterns too, depending on the circumstances.)

Hidden Pattern 5: Easy Calculation Mistake

As you can imagine, an extremely common type of wrong answer simply involves making small, predictable calculation mistakes.

This sort of thing might involve multiplying when we're supposed to divide, or finding the area of a figure instead of the perimeter. It might reflect forgetting how to do FOIL or add fractions correctly. Basically, the ACT likes to give you chances to make tiny mistakes in the execution of a solution—this way, you can still arrive at a wrong answer even if you figure out the correct overall approach to the question.

A real-life example of this type of wrong answer can be found in choice (G) of question 4 from the Math section of practice test 3 in *The Official ACT Prep Guide* (form 16MC3 online if you have the 2020-2021 Red Book). This question asks us to find the total distance run by Kaya in two days, which requires us to add $1\frac{2}{5}$ and $2\frac{1}{3}$.

To do this correctly, of course, we'd need to find a common denominator so that both fractions could be added together. (Incidentally, we'd do this by converting both fractions to fifteenths, which would give us the numbers $1\frac{6}{15}$ and $2\frac{5}{15}$. Adding them together would give us $3\frac{11}{15}$).

But if a test-taker forgot how fractions worked, he might just try to add the corresponding parts of the expressions $1\frac{2}{5}$ and $2\frac{1}{3}$:

- 1 plus 2 to result in 3 for the whole number
- 2 (in the first numerator) plus 1 (in the second numerator) to give 3 for the numerator
- 5 (in the first denominator) plus 3 (in the second denominator) to give 8 for the denominator

That would give us an incorrect result of $3\frac{3}{8}$, which is choice (G).

We'll see many more wrong-answer choices that give us the opportunity to make these kinds of mistakes in the walkthroughs.

Hidden Pattern 6: Most Like the Others (or *Almost* Like the Others)

Being aware of this pattern can give us a significant advantage on the ACT, but we should take care not to rely on it too much.

You should never select an answer choice based purely on this pattern alone—unless you've given up all hope of understanding the question, and you're just marking an answer as a best guess. (For more on this, see "Guessing on the ACT" on page 38 of this Black Book.)

In "Hidden Pattern 3: Wrong Answers Try to Imitate Right Answers," we talked about the way the ACT often incorporates elements of the right answer for a question when creating the wrong answers for that question. Because the goal of this tactic is to present test-takers with a lot of options that include parts of the right answer, we'll often (but not always!) find that the right answer will be the choice that has the most characteristics in common with the other choices.

With that in mind, let's return to the choices in question 5 from the Math section of practice test 2 in the Red Book (test 3 in the 2020-2021 Red Book), and see if we can figure out which choice has the most in common with the other choices.

All of the choices have a fraction to the left of the equals sign, so we know the right answer will have that feature.

Next, we see that 2 choices have 429 as the numerator of a fraction, while 3 choices have $s + 429$ as the numerator. So, according to this pattern, we might expect $s + 429$ to be the numerator of the fraction in the right answer, because it appears most frequently in the choices.

After that, we see that 2 choices have a 5 as the denominator of that fraction, while 3 have a 6 as the denominator. So we'd expect the right answer to have a 6 as the denominator according to this pattern, because the majority of the choices have a 6 there.

Finally, we see that 4 of the choices end with the number 85, while 1 choice has $\frac{85}{100}$. So, according to this pattern, we'd expect the right answer to have 85 in this position, in order to side with the majority.

Taking into account all of the most common features in the choices, we'd expect the right answer to be $\frac{s+429}{6} = 85$ according to this pattern . . . and it is.

But before you get too excited over this kind of approach, I want to stress that this approach is NOT, under ANY circumstances, the only thing that I would recommend you rely on when answering an ACT Math question! (For a full walkthrough of this particular question, detailing other things you should consider when approaching it, see page 223 of this Black Book.)

You shouldn't rely exclusively on this pattern because it doesn't work 100% of the time. Sometimes a set of answer choices seems like it's set up to follow this pattern, and the right answer ends up not being the one that this pattern would predict. In fact, sometimes the right answer is the one with the most common characteristics *in all but one* place—almost as though the ACT knew we were wise to them!

We can call this related pattern the "*Almost* Like The Others" pattern.

You can see this answer-choice pattern in question number 29 from the Math section of practice test 1 in the Red Book (test 2 in the 2020-2021 Red Book). For this question, you might expect the right answer to have the following elements:

- a first term of x (since 5 out of 5 choices have x in this position), then

- a less-than sign (since 3 out of 5 choices have a less-than sign), then
- no negative sign (since 3 out of 5 choices have no negative sign in this position), then
- a $4y$ term (since 4 out of 5 choices have a $4y$ term in this position)

This analysis might lead us to predict that (D) was the right answer, if we made the mistake of blindly following the "Most Like The Others" pattern. But the right answer is actually (A), $x < -4y + 2$, which sides with the majority of the other answer choices in every area *except* that it includes a negative sign. It's *almost* like most of the other choices, but it includes the less common option for that negative sign. (For a full explanation of this question, see its walkthrough on page 191 of this Black Book.)

As I said, this kind of thing can happen on the ACT. So if our goal is to answer every question correctly, we have to consider other things in addition to these patterns. The point of being aware of these patterns is NOT to depend exclusively on them—the point is to use them as guides, and as tools for evaluating a given question from multiple perspectives.

Hidden Pattern 7: Right Approach, Wrong Step

This is one of the things we talked about in our fake example above. Sometimes you'll see a wrong answer choice with a number that you need to find in order to answer the question, but that number itself isn't the right answer.

You can see a real-life example of this wrong answer type in choice (A) of question 3 from the Math section of practice test 1 in *The Official ACT Prep Guide* (test 2 in the 2020-2021 Red Book). This question asks for the value of $x^2 - 4$, given that $x^2 + 4 = 29$. (Before I go any farther, I'll note that there are several ways to answer this question, but that for the sake of discussing this answer-choice pattern, we'll approach this question the way most test-takers do, which is the way most students would approach a question like this in a math class.)

Most people will solve this question by first figuring out the value of x. When we do that, we find that $x = 5$. Some untrained test-takers will stop here, because they've found the value of x. Those test-takers will notice that choice (A) is 5, and they'll pick (A) and move on, not realizing that they didn't actually answer the question that was asked in the prompt!

The question doesn't ask for the value of x. Instead, it asks for the value of $x^2 - 4$. Since $x = 5$, we know that $x^2 - 4 = 21$, which means (C) is correct. (Notice that (D) is 25, which is the value of x^2. Many approaches to this question will involve finding the value of x^2, so (D) is another "right approach, wrong step" answer choice that will catch untrained test-takers who forgot what the question was actually asking for. For other ways to solve this problem, see its walkthrough on page 166 in this Black Book.)

This type of wrong-answer choice shows up frequently. So, before you select an answer, always check to make sure you've done the whole problem, and that the answer you're about to select is actually the answer to the question being asked, and not just a number you need to find along the way. Don't make the mistake of thinking that you must be right just because you arrived at a number that appears in one of the answer choices!

Understanding the Major Types of Approaches to ACT Math Questions

As we'll see repeatedly in the various walkthroughs in this Black Book, one of the most important aspects of approaching the ACT like a trained test-taker is the realization that the ACT doesn't really test the same skills and knowledge that get tested in high school and college, which means that we'll often find that the most effective way to approach an ACT question is very different from the kinds of approaches you can use on questions in school.

This idea is perhaps most important on the Math section of the ACT, because we'll often find that the types of formulas and techniques we might use in a math class can't be applied at all to an ACT Math question. In fact, we'll see that most ACT Math questions can be successfully approached in more than one way, and some of the most effective approaches for a particular question might include some combination of trial and error, graphing something on your calculator, noting the scale on a diagram, or even just remembering the definition of a term, and so on.

There are three general types of ways to approach ACT Math questions, and you should be aware of all of them, even though you'll only need to come up with one successful approach per question on test day. The general types of approaches are the following:

1. concrete approaches
2. abstract approaches
3. test-smart approaches

Concrete Approaches

Generally speaking, concrete approaches to an ACT Math question involve the idea of actually testing out or observing specific mathematical situations that are described in a question, and then picking the answer choice that fits with what you've observed in your test. Concrete approaches can include things like the following, which we'll discuss in more detail below:

- backsolving
- trial and error
- calculator graphing

Using a concrete approach can often allow you to find a correct answer to an ACT Math question even if you don't completely remember or understand all the details of the math concepts that appear in the question.

One reason that ACT Math questions often lend themselves to concrete approaches is that the test's format means that nobody can check your work in the way that a teacher might check it in class—your answer sheet only reflects your final answer to a question, not the process that you used to get there. So, for example, if a question asks you to find the length of a line in a diagram, the ACT has no way of knowing whether you found the answer through formal geometry, or by knowing the diagram was drawn to scale and eye-balling the diagram and comparing the line to the answer choices, which is much faster for most people. So when you're trying to decide how to attack a question, remember that the test doesn't expect you to follow the rules you might have to follow in math class.

Many test-takers find it easier to check whether a given choice could be correct than to go through the mental work of finding a correct answer completely on their own. So, for example, if a multiple-choice question asks us to find the possible solutions to an algebraic equation, it's often easier to plug in the values from each choice to find the one that works, rather than formally working out the algebra, as you'd have to do in a math class.

For these reasons, concrete approaches to ACT Math questions are often attractive to test-takers who prefer to avoid more abstract or conceptual math. But there's a potential drawback to concrete approaches: they generally take longer than other kinds of approaches, because they typically involve working through every single answer choice to make sure we've identified the correct one with no false positives (see the article "Special Technique: Backsolving" on page 144 of this Black Book for more details on this idea). Concrete solutions also tend to require a test-taker to do more calculations than the other approaches require, even if the calculations we use for concrete approaches are less advanced than the math ideas we'd apply in abstract or test-smart solutions.

With that in mind, let's discuss the three major types of concrete approaches in a little more detail.

Backsolving

Backsolving is the process of testing concrete values against an algebraic expression in a question's prompt, which allows us to identify the correct answer choice without actually going through a formal algebraic solution. (Backsolving is probably one of the most well-known "tricks" for ACT Math questions, but most test-takers don't realize all the ways backsolving can be applied, or all the ways it can go wrong if you're not careful. The best-known form of backsolving is probably the process of plugging a number from each answer choice back into an algebraic expression from the prompt to see which choice results in a valid statement, instead of formally solving that algebraic expression. But we can also sometimes use backsolving even when the answer choices are all algebraic expressions themselves. That's why I included an entire article on how to backsolve correctly on page 144. I recommend you read it.)

Trial and error

Trial and error (which is also sometimes called the "guess-and-check" approach) is similar to backsolving, but we use it in situations where we can't just test out answer choices to identify the correct one. Instead, we make up our own values to test against the prompt, and then adjust our next guess up or down based on the results of testing out the previous guess; we repeat this process until we make a guess that checks out to be the correct answer to the question.

Calculator graphing
Many questions on the ACT Math section address topics like the x- and y-intercepts of functions, or other aspects of a function that can be easily read off the screen of a graphing calculator if we input the function from the prompt.

Abstract
Abstract approaches to ACT Math questions involve applying generalized mathematical reasoning, rather than working out specific instances of a given situation, as we'd do in a concrete approach. Abstract approaches usually require less time to execute than concrete approaches do—in fact, we'll sometimes find that we can apply an abstract approach without actually writing down any calculations at all. The trade-off for this speed improvement over concrete approaches is that abstract approaches generally require a test-taker to be a little more comfortable with math as an academic subject.

Sometimes the key to approaching a question in an abstract way lies in the specific definitions or attributes of a mathematical concept, and keeping these definitions and attributes in mind allows us to see the right answer right away, often without picking up our pencils or calculators.

Test-Smart
A test-smart approach to an ACT Math question is one in which we combine our knowledge of math (and possibly some basic calculations) with an awareness of the limitations of the ACT's design and patterns. This can sometimes let us see quickly that the correct answer to a question must have a particular type of appearance (such as including an x-term with a negative coefficient) or be in a particular range of the number line, and that only one choice fits that requirement, which means it must be correct. Some test-smart solutions are so quick that we can't even really list out steps for them, because the act of noticing the possibility of the test-smart solution reveals the answer to the question.

Now that we've discussed the major types of approaches to ACT Math questions, let's consider an example of a real ACT question from the Red Book that can be approached in each of these three ways.

An Example of an Official ACT Question that Allows all 3 Types of Approaches: Question 43 from the Math Section of Practice Test 2 in the Red Book (Test 3 in the 2020-2021 Red Book)
This question asks for the measure of an angle in a diagram. My walkthrough for this question starts on page 260 of this book.

- The first solution in my walkthrough is a concrete one, in which we plug the values from the answer choices into the diagram to see which one causes the measurements of the angles to add up to 180°.
- My second solution is abstract: we use algebra to create an equation, and then solve for x in that equation and use that x-value to find the answer.
- Finally, in my third solution, we rely on the scale of the diagram, and realize that only one choice can possibly reflect a large enough number to be the size of the angle in the diagram. This approach is only possible because the ACT drew the diagram to scale and chose the set of answer choices in a way that allowed us to recognize a key difference among those choices.

Conclusion and Progression
As you may have noticed in the example we just saw, I generally tend to organize my walkthroughs for ACT Math questions so that concrete approaches are presented before abstract approaches, and test-smart approaches are presented last of all. To be clear, it's not that every question lends itself easily to all three types of solutions; it's just that, in general, I present the more concrete solutions first, and then transition into more abstract solutions last.

I do this because I want my readers to have the best chance of understanding each approach and how they relate to each other. Concrete approaches are generally the easiest types of approaches for most people to understand; abstract approaches basically involve realizing in a general way what the concrete approaches are showing us in specific instances. Finally, test-smart approaches represent a level of applied abstract thinking that combines math principles with the design of the test. By generally handling more concrete approaches for a given question earlier than more abstract approaches, the walkthroughs can help test-takers who don't feel comfortable with the higher-level approaches develop the kind of confident understanding of the test that allows them to come up with faster solutions on test day.

The General Process for Answering ACT Math Questions

I've said before that the ACT is basically one big reading test, and that's as true on the Math section as it is anywhere else. If you can train yourself to read carefully and precisely—just like you do in the Reading section—you'll be able to "decode" what's going on in any ACT Math question, so you can see through the unusual presentation to the simple math concept underneath.

How do we do that? We follow something I call the "Math Path!" (I just call it that because it rhymes. Unfortunately—or maybe fortunately—I haven't been able to come up with good rhyming names for anything else in this Black Book . . .)

The Math Path

The Math Path is what I call the steps you should take when you're confronted with a challenging ACT Math question:

1. Read the prompt carefully and note what it's asking for.
2. Consider diagrams, if there are any.
3. Read and analyze the answer choices.
4. Think about which areas of ACT Math might be involved.
5. Try to figure out a 30-second solution.
6. Carry out your solution.
7. Check everything! Consider using a different approach to re-solve the problem or confirm your solution.

Before I explain these steps in more detail, I just want to point out that you are, of course, free to modify them as you see fit—as long as your method consistently yields correct answers and allows you to complete the section within the time limit. You should also feel free to ignore these steps completely on easier questions if you see what to do right away. The Math Path is simply one way to organize your thoughts when you can't figure out how to attack a question.

Now, let's look at each step in turn.

1. Read the prompt carefully and note what it's asking for.

As I've said repeatedly, the entire ACT is a reading test, and reading accurately will do wonders for your score on every section, including this one. The first step in solving any math question is to read the prompt carefully, paying attention to the specific math terms and concepts that appear.

In school, you usually don't need to read math questions so carefully, because school tests ask us to use the same math techniques over and over again in questions that are basically identical to one another. But ACT Math doesn't work like that. We never know precisely which combination of basic math concepts will appear in a particular question, so we have to pay attention to each question from the very beginning.

2. Consider diagrams, if there are any.

As trained test-takers, we know that ACT Math diagrams are drawn to scale, even though the ACT test booklet tells us not to assume that they are. So, when a question involves a diagram, we can sometimes (but not always!) answer the question just by looking at the diagram itself and using its scale to eliminate choices that are obviously too large or too small. As one example of this situation, consider question 10 from the Math section of practice test 2 in the Red Book (test 3 in the 2020-2021 Red Book). We can tell from the scale of the diagram that (F) must be right. (For more, see our walkthrough on page 226. We'll also see this idea at work in other real ACT Math questions.)

3. Read and analyze the answer choices.

Most untrained test-takers will read the prompt of an ACT Math question, then try to answer the question on their own. When they have a solution they like, they'll see if it matches one of the answer choices; if it does, they pick it and move on without another thought.

That approach *can* lead to a great score—as long as the test-taker is good at figuring out what every ACT Math question wants her to do, and as long as she never makes a mistake in reading the question or performing her calculations. Few people fall into that category.

We trained test-takers know that it's much smarter and easier to consider the answer choices along with the prompt from the very beginning. We know the answer choices can contain clues and useful information, just like the question prompt does.

Concepts that appear in the answer choices can show you what the ACT expects test-takers to think about when they approach the question. If all of the answer choices include π, that's a clue that circles or radians are probably involved. If there are a lot of square roots in the answer choices, then you might be dealing with right triangles, or possibly with exponents, or with taking the square root of something for another reason. If the answer choices involve lots of numbers with unique properties like 0 and 1, or if two choices have quantities that are reciprocals or opposites of each other, then the question might be focusing on other specific mathematical concepts or properties. And so on—we'll see these ideas at work against real ACT questions in the math walkthroughs in a few pages.

You might also be able to identify relationships among the answer choices that fit some of the patterns we discussed in "ACT Math Answer-Choice Patterns" on page 148 of this Black Book. Noticing those patterns can give you insight into which choices might be likely to be correct.

4. Think about which areas of ACT Math might be involved.

Now that you've read the question stem and answer choices, think about what areas of math might possibly be related to the question. Sometimes, when untrained test-takers come across a question they can't answer right away, they have an instinct to try to throw all their math knowledge at it just to see what happens. This usually just gets confusing and wastes time, leaving them more frustrated than they were before.

So in this step, instead of panicking and thinking in broad terms about all the math you know, you want to narrow your focus to the areas of math that are directly related to the question.

How do you do that? By thinking about the terms, concepts, and relationships you've identified so far.

Remember that the ACT Math section can only test you on a certain limited inventory of math concepts—that's an inherent limitation of its standardization.

If you understand the math concepts from the Math Toolbox in this Black Book (which starts on page 113), then you technically know enough math to answer every ACT Math question you'll ever see, as long as you can figure out how to combine those relatively basic math concepts in different ways to solve the ACT's questions.

Toward that end, it's important to remember that math always proceeds logically, by small steps—not just on the ACT, but everywhere. This means the correct approach to the question must be closely related to the concepts and relationships that are included in the prompt and the answer choices (and the diagram, if there is one).

For example, key concepts in the question and the answer choices will let you know what kind of math you need to think about. If you see words like "radius" and "diameter," you know the question is related to circles, which means you need to look for opportunities to apply the few circle-related ideas the ACT allows itself to test (radius, tangent, arc length, circumference, area, and so on). If a question mentions sine, then it's obviously related to basic trig, and you may need to start thinking about right triangles, "opposite over hypotenuse," and so on.

If necessary, identify the "bridge" concepts that connect what the prompt is asking for to the ideas in the question.

In some situations, the math concepts that you've noticed in the question may not directly address what the prompt asked you to find in the first place. For example, the prompt may have described a situation changing over the course of an hour and then asked you to describe the rate of change in terms of minutes, without explicitly reminding you that there are 60 minutes in one hour. In this scenario, the "bridge" concept would be the idea of converting between hours and minutes: coming up with an effective solution to the question requires you to remember the bridge concept and realize that it's relevant.

If we wanted to be really technical, we could say that every single ACT Math question involves a bridge concept in the sense that solving every question requires us to realize something that's not directly spelled out on the page. But in many cases, the bridge concept is fairly obvious. For example, if a question gives us an algebraic equation and asks us to solve for a variable, then the bridge concept is the idea that we can transform the equation in a series of steps that all involve modifying both sides of the equation in the same way, until the variable is isolated on one side of the equation. Most test-takers don't need to be reminded of a bridge concept like that, because they automatically know that they can solve for a variable in that way.

But we'll sometimes find that the bridge concepts are less obvious, and we may need to spend a few seconds trying to identify the concept that relates the ideas in the prompt (and/or the diagram) to the answer choices.

Note things to look out for before you start your solution!

As trained test-takers, we know that one of the most important aspects of maximizing our score on a standardized test is the idea of avoiding mistakes (or catching them and correcting them after we've made them).

The Math sections of the ACT will provide us with a lot of opportunities to make small mistakes like the following:

- confusing the numerator and denominator of a fraction
- solving for the wrong variable in a question that involves more than one variable
- simplifying a fraction incorrectly
- . . . and so on.

These kinds of mistakes can easily cause us to miss questions even when we fully understand what they're asking us to do.

So one of the easiest and most straightforward ways to improve your ACT Math score is to get in the habit of identifying the aspects of a question that might cause you to make a mistake . . . *before* you make the mistake, so you can avoid it in the first place.

Again, one of the best ways to do this is to pay attention to answer choice patterns. For example, if you notice that two choices are opposites, then there's a good chance that some untrained test-takers might misunderstand the question in a way that causes them to pick the opposite of the right answer. You can also notice potential pitfalls in a question when you read the prompt—for example, if a question mentions more than one variable, then you know that it's important to keep the variables separate in your mind, and to remember which variable (if any) the prompt is asking you about, because some untrained test-takers will make the mistake of finding the wrong variable.

5. Try to figure out a 30-second solution.

Once you've taken note of the concepts and relationships in the question and thought about what types of math are related to the question, it's time to try to fit all of those puzzle pieces together into a solution.

Remember that all ACT Math questions can be answered in 30 seconds or less, and many can be answered in less than 10 seconds. (If you don't believe me now, you'll see what I mean later, when we walk through some real ACT Math practice questions from the Red Book.)

As I mentioned in "Unwritten Test Design Rules of ACT Math" on page 146 of this Black Book, your solutions can still be perfectly valid even if they take longer than 30 seconds. But I still encourage you to look for a 30-second solution to each ACT Math question you encounter, because looking for those kinds of solutions will encourage you to approach the section in non-traditional ways.

These non-traditional approaches will vary depending on the subject matter of the question, as you'll see when we do the walkthroughs in a few pages. But here are some general ideas for discovering these simplified, quick solutions:

- Look out for the answer choice patterns we discussed in "ACT Math Answer-Choice Patterns" on page 148 of this Black Book. They can often help you pinpoint the key concepts to address in a given question.
- Look for expressions from the prompt that are equivalent, or that cancel each other out.
- Look for ways you might plug answer choices into an expression, or use a calculator, or eliminate choices that are much too small or much too large.
- In general, don't rely on formulas. (The ACT Math section does occasionally test your knowledge of a formula directly, but you'll find that most real ACT Math questions don't have formulaic solutions.)
- In general, look for the solution to be simple, and don't feel limited by the things your math teacher would accept.

The ability to identify fast, efficient solutions to ACT Math questions is a skill you'll have to develop with practice. Going through the walkthroughs that appear in a few pages will be a big, big help with that. If you read and understand all of this material, and you work with real ACT Math questions, and you stick with it even when it's frustrating, you'll learn to cut through the bizarre, unpredictable presentations of the questions so you can see the predictably simple math concepts that are hidden underneath.

For more on the general types of solutions you can apply to ACT Math questions, see "Understanding the Major Types of Approaches to ACT Math Questions" on page 153 of this Black Book.

6. Carry out your solution.

Now that you've read the question and the answer choices, focused on the relevant math domains that are allowed to appear on the ACT, and thought of the most efficient solution you can, your job is just to execute the solution.

Obviously, it's important not to make any small mistakes at this point, so be sure you guard against any small miscalculation or misreading.

Notice that actually doing the calculation is one of the *last* steps in properly approaching a challenging ACT Math question. It's much more important to spend a few seconds in the beginning reading carefully, observing relationships among the concepts present in the question, and then thinking deliberately about the most efficient approach you can come up with. If you do those things well, then the calculation itself becomes a lot easier to do—sometimes, you'll find you can answer the question without even doing a calculation at all!

7. Check everything! Consider using a different approach to re-solve the problem or confirm your solution.

This is the last step, and perhaps the most important.

Once you've done everything else, you MUST take a moment to re-evaluate your solution.

There are a lot of different ways to do this—but, as usual, the normal ways of doing it aren't really that reliable.

What I would NOT recommend would be to go back through everything you just did, and see if you can catch any mistakes. Most people who do this will find that they just re-make the same mistakes they made a few seconds before, since no real time has passed after their initial solutions, and they haven't given themselves a chance to see the question differently.

Instead, I like to evaluate the question from a fresh perspective. This will be more likely to help me identify any mistakes I might have just made, because I'm not just rushing back through the same steps I just did.

The easiest way to evaluate the question from a fresh perspective is to look at the answer choices and try to figure out why the ACT included them in the question, since most wrong-answer choices reflect mistakes that could have been made in solving the question. It's not necessary to find an explanation for every single answer choice, but we'll often see that some of the wrong answer choices will point to errors we might have made in our solution.

I also look to see if I can observe any common ACT patterns among the answer choices, and whether those patterns indicate that the answer choice I like is probably correct. Both of these approaches to the question allow me to see it from another perspective, which gives me a better chance of catching any small mistakes I might have made.

You'll see several examples of these ideas in action during the walkthroughs in the next few pages.

ACT Math Path Conclusion

It may seem like this Math Path is a little complicated, especially when I've told you that all real ACT Math questions can be answered in 30 seconds or less. But if we think about it, we'll see the first four steps of the process are just reading the whole question and the answers, and matching up what you find to math ideas and test-design concepts you know from your training. This is something that can be done very quickly, with practice. The remaining three steps are coming up with a solution, executing that solution, and then checking your work. These steps can also be done quickly if you practice looking for efficient solutions to ACT Math questions.

You don't have to consciously map out each step, and slowly do them one-by-one. I just recommend that you get in the habit of considering these seven points if you want to answer questions as quickly and effectively as possible. Thinking about the problems in this way will keep you focused and help you work through the test, while still giving you a good opportunity to catch your mistakes, which is vital to getting a good score.

Now that we've discussed the general approach I recommend for challenging questions on the ACT Math section, let's take a look at some other issues that might come up on specific types of questions.

ACT Math Closing Thoughts

We've covered all the main issues that are generally related to the ACT Math section. In this section, we'll explore a few concepts that apply more to certain sub-types of ACT Math questions. After that, we'll put these strategies to the test against real practice ACT Math questions in the walkthroughs.

Using a Calculator

Calculators can definitely come in handy on the ACT Math section—but not as often as many untrained test-takers might expect. The trick is to know when to use the calculator, and when not to.

Most of the difficulty in *most* ACT Math questions involves simply understanding a question in the first place and setting it up correctly. As I've said repeatedly in this Black Book, the entire ACT is primarily a reading test, and that includes the Math section. You'll see a lot of questions that combine basic concepts in ways you've never thought of before, and the major challenge with those questions will involve close reading and careful thinking.

Of course, calculators aren't much help when it comes to reading questions and setting up solutions to them.

But there are four situations you could encounter on the ACT in which you may find a calculator useful:

- Simple calculations
- Evaluating more advanced numerical expressions
- Generating graphs for some questions about functions
- Evaluating expressions with variables

Simple calculations

Some test-takers just aren't confident doing any math in their head at all—either because they dislike math in general, or because the ACT Math section in particular makes them nervous. For them, the calculator can be a welcome crutch. They might even feel the need to use it on almost every question, because they don't trust themselves to add or subtract single-digit numbers.

There's nothing wrong with using a calculator on every question, of course, as long as it works for you in your practice sessions. You should do whatever you have to do on test day to make sure that you don't make any careless mistakes, and if a calculator helps you prevent those mistakes, then you should use it.

But you still have to be careful! Certain kinds of mistakes are arguably *more* likely to be made on a calculator, and many test-takers are less likely to check their work carefully if they use a calculator on a question. When you use a calculator, you might accidentally press the wrong button, causing you to execute the wrong operation at the wrong time, or possibly even execute an operation on the wrong numbers in the first place. Some questions will include wrong answer choices that reflect those mistakes, which means that a lot of untrained test-takers will never realize they might have used their calculators incorrectly. (This is more likely to happen with mistakes that involve executing the wrong operations, or executing the right operations in the wrong order.)

So don't let your guard down on a question just because you decide to use a calculator when you answer it. You still have to check back over every question by reviewing the steps you followed, and you still need to evaluate the rest of the answer choices to see if you can figure out what kinds of mistakes in the solution might have led to those choices, as we discussed in the Math Path on page 155 of this Black Book.

Evaluating more advanced numerical expressions

The ACT occasionally asks us questions that reward us for evaluating numerical expressions that involve things like exponents, radical signs, or fraction bars. When this happens, it can be useful to enter the expression into a calculator, and let the calculator give you back a simplified numerical value for the expression. In some cases, simply entering the expression into your calculator will be enough to find the answer to the question, but not always. For walkthroughs of such questions, check out the following:

- my walkthrough for question 6 from the Math section of practice test 1 in the Red Book (test 2 in the 2020-2021 Red Book), which is on page 168 of this Black Book
- my walkthrough for question 8 from the Math section of practice test 2 in the Red Book (test 3 in the 2020-2021 Red Book), which is on page 225 of this Black Book
- my walkthrough for question 49 from the Math section of practice test 3 in the Red Book (form 16MC3 online if you have the 2020-2021 Red Book), which is on page 317 of this Black Book

Outside of these questions, very few Red Book questions actually reward us for using a calculator to evaluate a numerical expression, without doing any other work. This is a good indication of how rarely you should expect this kind of thing on test day.

Generating graphs for some questions about functions

Some graph-related questions on the ACT Math section can be successfully attacked with graphing calculators, especially the ones that ask us to identify which answer choice contains an accurate graph of a given function, or that ask us to describe the graph of a given function.

In these kinds of situations, it can be helpful to enter the function in your graphing calculator so you can see what it actually looks like—sometimes, that's all you have to do in order to figure out the correct answer. (Of course, you still have to make sure you read the question carefully and enter the function correctly.)

These kinds of questions don't come up very often on the ACT, and the Red Book explanations for these questions are unlikely to mention that they can be solved with graphing calculators in a matter of seconds.

But I'll be happy to tell you when graphing a function on your calculator would be the easiest way to solve a question, of course. For an example of a calculator-based solution to a Red Book question that asks us to identify the correct graph of a function, see this Black Book's walkthrough for question 54 from the Math section of practice test 2 in the Red Book (test 3 in the 2020-2021 Red Book), which is on page 270 of this Black book. For an example of a calculator-based solution to a Red Book question about the behavior of a graph, see this Black Book's explanation for question 39 from the Math section of practice test 1 in the Red Book (test 2 in the 2020-2021 Red Book), which appears on page 199 of this Black Book.

In each of those walkthroughs, you'll notice that I still go through the rest of the Math Path, even though I show you how to answer the question with a calculator. You'll also notice that I discuss other solutions to the questions that don't rely on calculators, so you can see how questions can still be solved without a calculator if you prefer.

Finally, don't be surprised if you don't see tons of questions on test day that allow you to do this—but, on the other hand, if you do see some, make sure you seize the easy opportunity to get them right!

Evaluating expressions with variables

The calculator can also occasionally come in handy when an ACT question asks us to evaluate expressions with variables, especially when the question is asking us to find the value of a particular variable.

(We already discussed this general idea in the section called "Special Technique: Backsolving" on page 144 of this Black Book, but I want to re-visit this concept because a calculator can sometimes make this approach easier to use.)

There are two general ways in which this can be done:

- If the choices for a question don't have any variables, then we may be able to use the calculator to plug each choice into an expression from the question and determine which one is correct. For an example of this kind of question, see my walkthrough of question 15 from the Math section of practice test 1 in the Red Book (test 2 in the 2020-2021 Red Book), which appears on page 176 of this Black Book.

- If some of the answer choices include variables, then we may be able to assign arbitrary values to the variables and then use our calculators to evaluate each answer choice and see which one expresses an amount equal to the expression in the original question. (That might sound a little complicated, but it will probably make a lot more sense once you see me do it in the walkthroughs in a few pages.) For an example of this kind of question, see my walkthrough for question 1 from the Math section of practice test 1 in the Red Book (test 2 in the 2020-2021 Red Book), which appears on page 164 of this Black Book.

Keep all of these possible uses for calculators in mind as you read through the walkthroughs in this Black Book, and as you do your own practice on real ACT Math questions—but remember that you can't rely on a calculator to answer real ACT Math questions for you, and you still need to be careful not to make mistakes when you use one.

Finding the Areas of Odd-Looking Shapes

Some ACT Math questions will ask us to find the area of a figure. This can be particularly challenging when the figure doesn't look like any of the familiar shapes whose area formulas we know.

But if the ACT asks us to find the area of an odd-looking shape, then that odd-looking shape must consist of some combination of "normal" shapes like rectangles, triangles, circles, and trapezoids. We can find the area of the odd-looking shape by finding the individual areas of the "normal" shapes and combining them.

For two examples of this concept, see the following walkthroughs in this Black Book:

- the walkthrough for question 30 from the Math section of practice test 2 in the Red Book (test 3 in the 2020-2021 Red Book), which appears on page 248 of this Black Book

- the walkthrough for question 24 from the Math section of practice test 3 in the Red Book (form 16MC3 online if you have the 2020-2021 Red Book), which appears on page 296 of this Black Book

Let this be one more reminder that the best thing to do when you're confronted with an unfamiliar situation on the ACT Math section is to keep a level head and remember that ACT Math questions can always be solved relatively quickly, using only the concepts from the ACT Math Toolbox, which starts on page 113 of this Black Book. Instead of panicking like an untrained test-taker would, your job is to figure out which concepts from the Toolbox are relevant, and how to combine them to answer the question.

"NOT" and "EXCEPT" Questions

The ACT loves to use "NOT" and "EXCEPT" questions to get you to choose wrong answers. We see this across every section of the test. In many of these questions, there will be four answer choices that *do* satisfy whatever the question is asking about, and one that doesn't. The people who make the ACT are hoping you'll overlook the word "NOT" or "EXCEPT" in the prompt. That way, you can notice one of the four answer choices that seem to satisfy what the question is asking about, and then choose that answer without realizing you were supposed to find the one choice that *doesn't* satisfy whatever the question is talking about.

(This is one more reason why it's so important to review all the answer choices in a question before you move on to the next question. If you overlook the word "NOT" or "EXCEPT" and choose the first answer choice that seems valid, you can still catch your mistake if you look at the other answer choices, because you'll notice that several of them seem to be equally valid. This gives you the chance to go back over the question and realize that you misread it.)

We can see an example of this type of trap by looking at question 19 from the Math section of practice test 2 in the Red Book (test 3 in the 2020-2021 Red Book). The prompt asks which choice "does NOT represent a line." If we accidentally overlook the word NOT, we might think we're looking for the one answer choice that DOES contain the equation of a line. A lot of test-takers in that position would just choose (A) and move on. But if we read carefully, we know that we need to find the only choice that is NOT the equation of a line, which means (E) is correct.

The ACT always puts the words "NOT" and "EXCEPT" in capital letters on these kinds of questions, but you'd be surprised how often people completely overlook those words. Always consider all your answer choices, and always read carefully!

Your Work doesn't Matter

This is another example of how ACT Math differs from school math: your work doesn't matter on the ACT, in the sense that nobody is going to know or care how you arrived at your answers. A lot of test-takers lose a lot of time on the ACT Math section because school has conditioned them to do math in a very formal way.

But there's no need to approach math formally on the ACT! In fact, we'll often run into situations in which the formal approach makes answering an ACT Math question harder and more time-consuming.

Of course, if you prefer to use formal math for some reason, and if you can do it quickly enough to finish the section in the time allotted (and you get the questions right), then there's nothing inherently wrong with that. But if you have trouble with the ACT Math section, then you shouldn't feel obligated to approach it in a way that would please your high school math teacher. As I've mentioned repeatedly, and as you'll see when we go through the walkthroughs, the easiest and fastest solutions to many ACT Math questions involve tactics that are only possible because of the standardized, multiple-choice nature of the test. Don't be afraid to embrace that. (See "Understanding the Major Types of Approaches to ACT Math Questions" on page 153 of this Black Book for more on different ways to attack ACT Math questions.)

Don't Think about the "Order of Difficulty"

A lot of untrained test-takers believe they'll see harder ACT Math problems towards the end of a section, and easier problems toward the beginning. Even though there might be some general truth to this concept (depending on how we define the words "harder" and "easier"), I'd strongly advise you to ignore this idea, because it doesn't actually help you on the ACT Math section.

First of all, what's difficult for you isn't necessarily the same thing as what's difficult for other test-takers—even if everybody else who takes the ACT struggles with question 55 on test day, that doesn't mean you will, too. Different people can come up with different, equally valid solutions to the same ACT Math question, and those equally valid solutions can involve different levels of complexity and challenge. So the notion that each individual ACT question has an objective amount of "difficulty" that will be constant for all test-takers is ridiculous.

Secondly, regardless of any general, overall "difficulty" trend, you can still encounter questions that seem relatively difficult for you near the beginning of a section, and questions that seem relatively easy for you near the end of a section, especially as you improve your understanding of how the test works.

My major concern here is that I don't want you to make any assumptions about how hard an ACT Math question is likely to be until you've actually read it and thought about it a little. It's also important to remember that questions can pose different types of challenges, and any of those challenges might lead you to miss a question. Some questions seem pretty simple, but offer a lot of opportunities to make careless mistakes; others might seem very challenging at first, but then offer a very simple solution to a trained test-taker who knows how to spot it.

Just approach each ACT Math question with an open mind. Some will take more time and energy, and others will take less. It doesn't do any good to think about whether a question is supposed to be easy or hard for other people, or whether a question is easier or harder than the ones before or after it. Either way, our job is always to look at each question, read it carefully, try to figure out the most efficient solution we can, implement that solution, and check for mistakes. When we do the walkthroughs in a few pages, you'll see several examples of questions that appear earlier in a section but can still be very tricky, and questions that appear later in a section but can still be answered in a few seconds by a trained test-taker.

ACT Math Quick Summary

This is a one-page summary of the major relevant concepts. Use it to evaluate your comprehension or jog your memory. For a more in-depth treatment of these ideas, see the rest of the section.

The Big Secret: The ACT Math section tests relatively simple math ideas in unusual ways. We need to get used to reading the problems carefully so we know what exactly we're being asked to do.

The concepts tested in ACT Math questions are limited. Those concepts can be found in the ACT Math Toolbox in this book.

ACT Math questions can all be done in 30 seconds or less. (Of course, that doesn't mean you'll be wrong if you take longer.) Remember that the most efficient solutions to ACT Math questions often involve non-traditional techniques like finding expressions that cancel out, noticing factors, considering the scale of a diagram, and so on. Paying attention to answer choices from the beginning will often help you find these efficient solutions.

Wrong answer choices contain valuable information. They're just as important as any other part of the question, so read them carefully. Think about concepts they might involve, and how quantities in different answer choices might relate to one another, and to the process of solving the problem.

Here are some of the most common answer choice patterns you'll see:

- A wrong answer choice is half or double the correct answer choice.
- A wrong answer is in some way the opposite of the right answer.
- A wrong answer choice is the result of an easy calculation mistake a test-taker might make when solving the problem.
- A wrong answer choice contains a "Right Approach, Wrong Step" answer that's involved in the solution to the problem, but isn't the solution itself.
- A correct answer choice has characteristics that are similar to most or many of the wrong answer choices.
- A correct answer choice is part of a series with other answer choices.

Here's an abbreviated version of the general ACT Math process, or "Math Path," recommended for use against challenging questions:

1. Read the prompt carefully and consider the specific words that are used.
2. Consider any diagrams that appear.
3. Read and consider the answer choices. Note concepts and relationships.
4. Think about what areas of math are involved based on characteristics of the question and the answer choices.
5. Try to think of a solution to the problem that will take 30 seconds or less. The best ACT Math solutions are often unorthodox. They might involve testing the answer choices, graphing something on a calculator, observing patterns in the answer choices, and so on.
6. Do the solution you came up with in the previous step.
7. Check your work, preferably by trying to identify the ACT's reasoning behind the wrong answer choices. Remember that high-scorers can't typically avoid all mistakes; they're just able to catch their mistakes after they make them.

Go back through the ACT Math walkthroughs and follow along in your copy of the Red Book to see demonstrations of these ideas.

Math Question Walkthroughs

Now that we've thoroughly discussed the right approach to the ACT Math section in general terms, we'll go through all the ACT Math questions in three practice tests from the Red Book, so you can see the approach in action against official ACT questions. (See "Using the Official ACT Prep Guide (the "Red Book")" on page 21 of this Black Book for details on why official questions are so important.) And if you'd like to see some video demonstrations of these ideas, go to www.ACTprepVideos.com for a selection of demonstration videos that are free to readers of this book.)

IMPORTANT NOTE: If you have the 2020-2021 edition of the Red Book (ISBN: 978-1119685760), then "Test 1" in this Black Book refers to Practice Test 2 in your edition of the Red Book, and "Test 2" in this Black Book refers to Practice Test 3 in your Red Book. What we refer to as "Test 3" in this Black Book has been removed from the 2020-2021 edition of the Red Book, but it can be found online as ACT test form 16MC3. (See **The 2020-2021 Red Book** on page 23 of this Black Book for more.)

Sample Math Walkthrough

My ACT Math walkthroughs are roughly similar to the ACT Reading walkthroughs we saw earlier in this Black Book, though the Math ones have a few more components. As with the Reading walkthroughs, you don't need to worry about copying my approach exactly when you attack a question on your own. Instead, the walkthroughs are presented in a format that lets us do the following:

- show the ideal thought process for attacking a question, from the initial assessment, through one or more solutions, ending with checking the result and observing any relevant post-solution patterns in the answer choices (but remember that you only need to find one solution on test day! I just show multiple solutions to help you understand that ACT Math questions can be attacked in a variety of ways)
- allow you to focus on the specific information you're interested in for a particular question, while also letting you read through the entire walkthrough easily if you prefer
- present each walkthrough so it can stand on its own as a full explanation of the question, while still making it easy to refer back to relevant parts of the training for more details if you want a refresher
- show how simple the reasoning and calculations are for most ACT Math questions, and how important it is to avoid small mistakes

Here's a diagram of a sample walkthrough, with the key elements of the walkthrough explained on the next page:

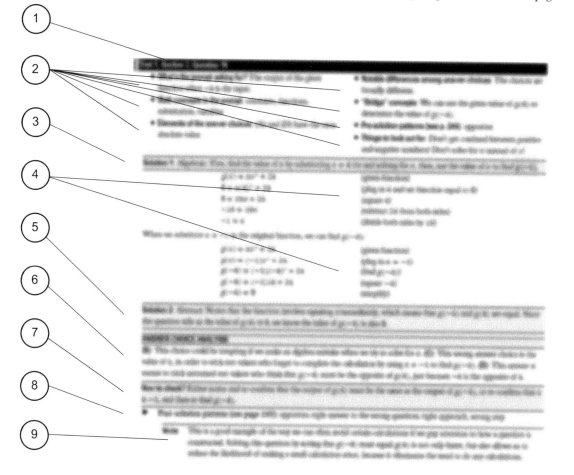

Explanation of Walkthrough Elements

The elements of the walkthrough are presented in an order that reflects the "Math Path" from page 155 of this Black Book:

1. This shows the test number and question number of the question being analyzed in the walkthrough. You can use this information to locate the relevant question in the Red Book.

2. This area of the walkthrough reflects steps 1-4 of the "Math Path" on page 155 of this Black Book; in other words, this part of the walkthrough shows the kinds of things that a trained test-taker might notice initially, while she was deciding on the best way to attack the question. This part of the walkthrough reflects the following ideas:

   - the specific thing that the prompt is actually asking for

   - the math concepts in the prompt, diagram, and/or answer choices

   - the notable differences among the answer choices (you could choose to use a vertical scan to pick these out, as described on page 42 of this Black Book)

   - the patterns in the answer choices that might be observable before we attempt a solution

   - a list of potential mistakes and pitfalls to look out for before we begin our solution

3. This Item reflects step 5 in the "Math Path" on page 155 of this Black Book. It names the first solution that the walkthrough will explore. It begins with a simple one- or two-word description of the type of solution that's being discussed (such as "backsolving" or "graphing"), and then proceeds to a one- or two-sentence description of the steps that would be taken for the solution. As you become more comfortable with ACT Math, you may be able to understand the entire solution just from this Item. (In Item 4, this simple description will be fleshed out at length.)

4. In this Item, which reflects step 6 in the "Math Path" on page 155 of this Black Book, we spell out the specific steps for the solution in Item 3. These steps allow you to follow along with the exact process that would lead to the answer to the question according to the approach in Item 3.

5. Here you'll find a different potential solution to the question from the one in Item 3, also reflecting step 5 in the "Math Path" on page 155 of this Black Book. Just like the description in Item 3, this description will begin with a one- or two-word rough classification of the type of solution being proposed (such as "abstract" or "test-smart"), followed by a one- or two-sentence description of the solution. If necessary, this Item will be followed by another set of relevant steps, just as Item 4 provides the steps for the solution in Item 3. Note that you only need to find one solution on test day! We just go through multiple solutions in the walkthroughs so you can come to understand how each question can be attacked in multiple ways.

6. After all the possible solutions are presented, along with their various steps, Item 6 discusses the wrong answer choices, and indicates likely errors that might have led to some of them.

7. This Item provides a quick indication of a way to check over our work in order to catch any mistakes we might have made.

8. This Item notes any answer choice patterns that might only be noticeable after we've executed a solution. (Items 6, 7, and 8 all reflect Step 7 in the "Math Path" on page 155 of this Black Book.)

9. If I feel that something is noteworthy about the question but I can't fit it in the rest of the walkthrough, then I'll note that at the end of the walkthrough. Be sure to pay attention to these notes when they appear, as they'll often contain useful information about what a particular question can teach us generally about future ACT questions.

Note that some walkthroughs are missing some of the items in this list! If one of the Items above isn't relevant to a particular question, then it's omitted.

Remember that the ultimate goal of these walkthroughs is to help you see multiple ways that I might attack each question, and how I recommend you do the same. Also notice that the walkthroughs always begin by pointing out all the key details of the question that will help you figure out the most efficient solution to apply—this is very important to keep in mind on test day!

As always, feel free to modify my approach as you see fit, as long as your modifications still bring you the results you want.

TEST 1 (TEST 2 IN 2020-2021 RED BOOK)

Test 1, Question 1 (Test 2 in the 2020-2021 Red Book—see page 23 for more)

- **What's the prompt asking for?** The choice that's equivalent to the expression in the prompt.
- **Math concepts in the prompt:** addition, algebraic expressions, multiplication, negative numbers, PEMDAS
- **Notable differences among choices:** (A) and (B) begin with $-2a$, while (C) and (D) begin with $-a^2$, and (E) begins with $-2a^3$. (A), (C), and (E) all end with -35, while (B) and (D) end with 7. (C) and (D) both include

$-a$, while the other choices each only include 2 terms.
- **Concepts in the choices:** addition, binomials, cubing, multiplication, negative numbers, squaring, subtraction, trinomials, variables
- **Pre-solution patterns (see p. 149):** wrong answers try to imitate right answers
- **Things to look out for:** Don't make any small mistakes with PEMDAS, or with any other aspect of your calculations! Don't overlook any negative signs!

Solution 1: Calculator/Backsolving: Pick an arbitrary value for a and use it to determine the numerical value of the expression in the prompt. Then use the same a-value to find numerical values for each answer choice, and pick the choice whose numerical value matches the numerical value of the expression in the prompt. Use a calculator to evaluate the expressions if you prefer.

Let's plug $a = 3$ into the expression in the prompt.

$a(4 - a) - 5(a + 7)$	(original expression)
$(3)(4 - (3)) - 5((3) + 7)$	(plug in $a = 3$)
$(3)(1) - 5(10)$	(combine like terms in parentheses)
$3 - 50$	(multiply)
-47	(simplify)

So when $a = 3$, the expression in the prompt is equal to -47. Now we can plug $a = 3$ into the expressions from the answer choices to see which one equals -47.

$-2a - 35$	(expression from (A))
$-2(3) - 35$	(plug in $a = 3$)
-41	(simplify)

The expression in (A) isn't equal to -47 when we plug in $a = 3$, so (A) can't be correct. Let's try (B).

$-2a + 7$	(expression from (B))
$-2(3) + 7$	(plug in $a = 3$)
1	(simplify)

The expression in (B) isn't equal to -47 when we plug in $a = 3$, so (B) can't be correct. Let's try (C).

$-a^2 - a - 35$	(expression from (C))
$-(3)^2 - (3) - 35$	(plug in $a = 3$)
$-9 - 3 - 35$	(simplify)
-47	(simplify)

The expression in (C) is equal to -47 when we plug in $a = 3$, so (C) looks like it might be right. Let's try the remaining choices to make sure we haven't made any mistakes.

$-a^2 - a + 7$	(expression from (D))
$-(3)^2 - (3) + 7$	(plug in $a = 3$)
$-9 - 3 + 7$	(simplify)
-5	(simplify)

The expression in (D) isn't equal to -47 when we plug in $a = 3$, so (D) can't be correct. Finally, let's try (E).

$-2a^3 - 35$	(expression from (E))
$-2(3)^3 - 35$	(plug in $a = 3$)
$-54 - 35$	(simplify)
-89	(simplify)

The expression in (E) isn't equal to -47 when we plug in $a = 3$, so (E) can't be correct.

After considering each choice, we can be confident that (C) is right.

Solution 2: Abstract/Algebra: Simplify the expression in the prompt and pick the choice that matches your simplified expression.

$a(4 - a) - 5(a + 7)$	(original expression)

Page 164   Facebook.com/TestingIsEasy   Youtube.com/TestingIsEasy

$$4a - a^2 - 5a - 35 \qquad \text{(distribute } a \text{ and 5)}$$

$$-a^2 - a - 35 \qquad \text{(simplify)}$$

This matches the expression in (C), so (C) is right.

Solution 3: Test-smart: Note that the right answer must include a^2 and 35, and pick the only choice that does.

When we realize that we need to distribute the a and the -5, we might notice that the right answer will have to include both an a^2 term and -35. Only (C) has both of these characteristics, so (C) must be right.

ANSWER CHOICE ANALYSIS

(A): This could reflect the mistake of trying Solution 2 above and failing to multiply a by a correctly in the first parenthetical expression. **(B):** This combines the mistake in (A) with the mistake of forgetting to multiply -5 by 7. **(D):** This reflects the idea of forgetting to multiply -5 by 7 when simplifying the second parenthetical expression. **(E):** Somewhat like (A), this choice reflects another possible mistake when distributing the a-term in the prompt. There's no way to arrive at a^3 correctly, since simplifying the expression in the prompt will never involve multiplying a by a^2, or multiplying three a-terms together.

How to check? Try an alternate approach above. Pay special attention to the highest possible degree of a in the right answer, and to determining the correct constant, since both of those issues seem to be areas where the ACT expects untrained test-takers to make mistakes, if we judge from the answer choices.

> **Note** Most math teachers would require students to approach this question in math class using an approach like the one in Solution 2. But as trained test-takers, we know that we can use other approaches to solve questions on the ACT, like the approaches in Solutions 1 and 3 above. Keep this in mind throughout your training.

Test 1, Question 2 (Test 2 in the 2020-2021 Red Book—see page 23 for more)

- **What's the prompt asking for?** The choice that accurately orders the numbers in the prompt from least to greatest.
- **Math concepts in the prompt:** decimal points, fractions, inequalities, ordering
- **Elements of the choices:** Each choice is an inequality statement that includes the three numbers in the prompt joined by two less-than signs.
- **Notable differences among choices:** (G) and (H) both begin with 0.03, (J) and (K) both begin with $\frac{1}{4}$, and (F) is the only choice that begins with 0.2. (F) and (G) both end with $\frac{1}{4}$, (H) and (J) both end with 0.2, and (K) is the only choice that ends with 0.03. (F) and (J) both have 0.03 in the middle, (G) and (K) both have 0.2 in the middle, and (H) is the only choice with $\frac{1}{4}$ in the middle. (F) is the reverse of (J), and (G) is the reverse of (K).

- **Concepts in the choices:** decimal points, fractions, inequalities
- **Pre-solution patterns (see p. 149):** wrong answers try to imitate right answers; opposites
- **Things to look out for:** Don't make any small mistakes in reading the numbers or assessing their relative sizes! If you use a calculator, don't mis-key anything! Don't assume this question will be easy just because the concepts involved seem simple!

Solution 1: Calculator/Abstract: Convert each choice to a decimal expression and use your knowledge of the properties of decimals to order the numbers correctly.

$\frac{1}{4} = 0.25$, so the three numbers in decimal form are 0.2, 0.03, and 0.25. The smallest number must be 0.03, the next largest number must be 0.2, and the largest is 0.25. so (G) is right. (Note that it may be helpful to think of 0.2 as the equivalent form 0.20 when you order the numbers.)

Solution 2: Test-smart: Identify the number that must be highest and the number that must be lowest. Pick the appropriate choice.

Once we realize that $\frac{1}{4}$ is the largest number, we can eliminate (H), (J), and (K). After we realize that 0.03 is the smallest number, we can also eliminate (F). The only remaining choice is (G), the correct answer.

ANSWER CHOICE ANALYSIS

(F): This could reflect the mistake of ordering the numbers according to the nonzero digits that appear in each number: 2, 3, and 4. **(H):** This choice might reflect a mistake in determining the decimal equivalent of $\frac{1}{4}$. **(J):** This combines the mistakes in (F) and (K): incorrectly assuming that the value of the numbers is reflected solely in the values of their nonzero digits, and ordering the numbers from (perceived) greatest to least in spite of the less-than signs. **(K):** This is the reverse of the right answer. It will attract a lot of untrained test-takers who accurately understand the ideas in the question but rush their approach because they're nervous about getting to answer all the questions on the rest of the test in time.

How to check? Try an alternate approach above. Be especially careful that you're not making a small mistake in comparing any of these numbers, since the choices are clearly set up to encourage you to do that!

▶ Post-solution patterns (see p. 151): most like the other choices; opposites

Test 1, Question 3 (Test 2 in the 2020-2021 Red Book—see page 23 for more)

- **What's the prompt asking for?** The value of $x^2 - 4$ according to the prompt.
- **Math concepts in the prompt:** addition, equations, squaring, subtraction, variables
- **Notable differences among choices:** (A) is the square root of (D), and (B) is the square root of (C). (D) is 4 more than (C)—this may be relevant because the prompt involves adding and subtracting 4.
- **Concepts in the choices:** adding 4, square roots
- **Things to look out for:** Don't accidentally pick an answer that's equal to x—remember what the prompt asked you to find! Don't make any small mistakes in your reading or calculations!

Solution 1: Algebra: Find x, and use the value of x to find $x^2 - 4$.

$x^2 + 4 = 29$	(first expression from the prompt)
$x^2 = 25$	(subtract 4 from both sides)
$x = 5$	(take square root of both sides)

Now we can plug $x = 5$ into the second equation.

$x^2 - 4$	(second expression from the prompt)
$(5)^2 - 4$	(plug in $x = 5$)
$25 - 4$	(simplify)
21	(simplify)

So the answer is (C).

Solution 2: Algebra: Find $x^2 - 4$ directly from the value of $x^2 + 4$, without isolating x first.

We can subtract 8 from $x^2 + 4$ to get $x^2 - 4$, so we can subtract 8 from both sides of the given equation to find the value of $x^2 - 4$:

$x^2 + 4 = 29$	(first expression from the prompt)
$x^2 - 4 = 21$	(subtract 8 from both sides)

So again, the answer is (C).

Solution 3: Test-smart: Realize that the value the prompt asks for must be 8 less than the given value, so $x^2 - 4$ must be 8 less than 29, and (C) must be right.

In a sense, the prompt asks us to compare $x^2 + 4$ and $x^2 - 4$. Both of those expressions involve x^2; the only difference between them is that one expression adds 4 to the starting point of x^2, and one expression subtracts 4 from that starting point. That means one expression must be 8 more than the other, since $4 + 4 = 8$. So the right answer must be 8 less than 29, which means (C) is right.

ANSWER CHOICE ANALYSIS

(A): This is x itself. As trained test-takers, we should expect to find a choice with the value of x, to attract untrained test-takers who try Solution 1 above but forget what the prompt actually asked them to find. **(B):** This is the square root of $x^2 - 4$, but the prompt never asks us to find the square root of that number—in fact, it never really asks us to find the square root of any number, since we can answer the question without identifying the value of x, as shown in Solutions 2 and 3 above. **(D):** This is x^2, which is an example of a "right approach, wrong step" answer to finding $x^2 - 4$ if we follow Solution 1 above. Some untrained test-takers will pick this choice because they don't remember what the prompt asked them to find. **(E):** This is $x^2 + 8$. It might attract some untrained test-takers who try Solution 2 above but make a mistake when they try to subtract 8 from $x^2 + 4$ to find $x^2 - 4$, and end up adding 8 to x^2 instead.

How to check? Try an alternate approach above. The fact that we seem to be able to identify x itself, and to tell which thought processes would lead to the wrong answers, strongly suggests that we've found the right answer.

▶ Post-solution patterns (see p. 151): right approach, wrong step; right answer to the wrong question

Test 1, Question 4 (Test 2 in the 2020-2021 Red Book—see page 23 for more)

- **What's the prompt asking for?** The percentage of the rectangle in the prompt that lies in Quadrant III.
- **Math concepts in the prompt:** area, percentages, plotting points in the xy-coordinate plane, quadrants, rectangles, vertices
- **Math concepts in the diagram:** quadrants, the xy-coordinate plane
- **Elements of the choices:** Each choice is a percentage below 50%.
- **Notable differences among choices:** (H) is the only

choice that involves a decimal point. (G) is 50% larger than (F), and (K) is 50% larger than (J).

- **Concepts in the choices:** 50% increases, decimal points, percentages

- **Things to look out for:** Don't confuse the quadrants! Don't plot the points from the prompt in the wrong positions on the graph! Don't make any small mistakes in your calculations! (Especially look out for any opportunity to make a mistake and be off by 50%, since the answer choices seem to be anticipating that kind of mistake!)

Solution 1: Geometry: Plot the points from the prompt on the provided graph. Determine the area of the resulting rectangle, and then determine the portion of that rectangle that's in Quadrant III.

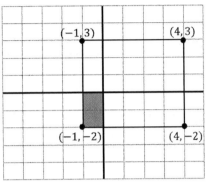

We can see that the area of this rectangle is 25 units, either from noticing that the length and width of the rectangle are both 5, and then multiplying 5 × 5 to get an area of 25 (because the area of a rectangle is equal to its length multiplied by its width), or just by counting the squares in the rectangle. We can also see that 2 square units in the plane lie in Quadrant III (those are the two gray squares in the diagram above).

We can find the percentage of the area of the rectangle that lies in Quadrant III by dividing the number of the rectangle's square units that lie in Quadrant III by the area of the entire rectangle:

$$\frac{2}{25} = 0.08 = 8\%$$

So the answer is (F).

ANSWER CHOICE ANALYSIS

(G): This is the percentage of the rectangle in Quadrant II, so this choice could attract test-takers who don't know which Quadrant is which, or who simply misread the question in the prompt. **(H):** This choice could reflect a mistake in determining a percentage, since the correct approach requires us to convert $\frac{2}{25}$ to a percentage, and this choice is $\frac{25}{2}$ with a percent sign after it. **(J):** This is the percentage of the rectangle in Quadrant IV. Like (G), this choice could trick someone who didn't know which Quadrant was which, or who misread the prompt. **(K):** This is the percentage of the rectangle in Quadrant I, so it's similar to (G) and (J) from the standpoint of test design.

How to check? Carefully re-check your reading and your work. Be especially careful about making sure you've considered the right Quadrant!

▶ **Post-solution patterns (see p. 151):** right answer to the wrong question

Test 1, Question 5 (Test 2 in the 2020-2021 Red Book—see page 23 for more)

- **What's the prompt asking for?** The cost of the clothing in 1991, given the conditions in the prompt.

- **Math concepts in the prompt:** linear relationships, prices, rates

- **Elements of the choices:** Each choice is a number of dollars between $750 and $1000.

- **Notable differences among choices:** (B), (D), and (E) form a series in which each choice is $38 less than the choice before it.

- **Concepts in the choices:** adding 38

- **Pre-solution patterns (see p. 149):** be aware of series

- **Things to look out for:** Don't make any small mistakes in your reading or calculations!

Solution 1: Arithmetic: Determine the average increase per year according to the prompt, and use that to find the price in 1991.

In 10 years, the cost of clothing increased by $1,000 − $620, or $380. So the average increase per year must have been $\frac{\$380}{10}$, or $38. In other words, the cost of clothing went up by $38 per year during this period.

1991 was 6 years after 1985, so the cost of clothing must have increased by 6 × $38, or $228. The cost in 1985 was $620, so the cost in 1991 must have been $620 + $228, or $848. So (B) is correct.

Solution 2: Arithmetic: Subtract $620 from $1000, and multiply the result by 0.6 to find the price increase after the 6-year period from 1985 to 1991. Add the result to $620 to find the price in 1991.

We can find the increase over the given 10 year period by subtracting $620 from $1000, which gives us $380. The prompt asks about the price in 1991, which is 6 years after the starting point of 1985. So $\frac{6}{10}$, or 0.6 of the price increase must have happened over that 6 year period. We can find the price increase over 6 years by multiplying $380 by 0.6, which gives us $228. When we add that to the starting amount we get $620 + $228, or $848. Again, we can see that (B) is right.

ANSWER CHOICE ANALYSIS

(A): This reflects the arithmetic mistake of thinking that the difference between $1000 and $620 is $480, instead of $380, and then correctly executing the other steps of either Solution 1 or Solution 2. **(C):** This reflects the arithmetic mistake of thinking that the difference between $1000 and $620 is $320, instead of $380, and then correctly executing the other steps of either Solution 1 or Solution 2. **(D):** This is the cost in 1990, which isn't what the prompt asked for. Some untrained test-takers might pick (D) because they mis-count the number of years between 1985 and 1991. **(E):** This is the cost in 1989, which reflects a mistake similar to the one in (D).

How to check? Try an alternate approach above. The fact that some wrong answers seem to reflect the cost in other years should reassure us that we've correctly identified the annual rate of increase, but we still need to make sure we've read carefully and found the cost for the correct year.

Test 1, Question 6 (Test 2 in the 2020-2021 Red Book—see page 23 for more)

- **What's the prompt asking for?** The choice whose range includes the square of 9.2371.
- **Math concepts in the prompt:** ranges, square roots, squaring
- **Elements of the choices:** Each choice is a range.
- **Notable differences among choices:** (F), (G), (H) and (J) all have ranges of 1, while (K) spans a range of 18.
- **Things to look out for:** Don't make any mistakes in your reading or calculations!

Solution 1: Calculator: Use your calculator to find the square of 9.2371 and pick the choice that contains the result.

$9.2371^2 \approx 85.324$, and ≈ 85.324 is between 81 and 99, so (K) must be correct.

Solution 2: Calculator/Backsolve: Find the square roots of the numbers in each choice. Pick the choice that results in a range containing 9.2371.

We don't even have to do the math for (F), (G), or (H), because all of these numbers are themselves less than 9.2371 (except for 10, which is only a little more than 9.2371), and their square roots will definitely be less than 9.2371. Let's find the square root of the numbers in (J):

$\sqrt{18} \approx 4.24$ and $\sqrt{19} \approx 4.36$

9.2371 isn't between 4.24 and 4.36, so (J) can't be right. Let's check (K):

$\sqrt{81} = 9$ and $\sqrt{99} \approx 9.95$

9.2371 is between 9 and 9.95. After considering the answer choices, we know that (K) is right.

Solution 3: Test-smart: Realize that the square of 9.2371 must be more than the square of 9 (which is 81). Only (K) contains numbers greater than 81, so (K) must be right.

ANSWER CHOICE ANALYSIS

(F): The numbers in this choice are both less than 9.2371, so they must both be less than the square of 9.2371. **(G):** This choice has the same problem as (F). **(H):** This choice does contain one number that's greater than 9.2371, but we can still tell that the square of 9.2371 must be greater than 10. **(J):** The square root of 19 is approximately 4.36, so the square of 9.2371 must be greater than 19.

How to check? Carefully recheck your reading and your calculations, especially with respect to the possibility of confusing the idea of squaring a number with the idea of finding the square root of that number.

Test 1, Question 7 (Test 2 in the 2020-2021 Red Book—see page 23 for more)

- **What's the prompt asking for?** The probability that a randomly chosen candy is NOT grape-flavored, according to the prompt.
- **Math concepts in the prompt:** probability, random selection
- **Elements of the choices:** Each choice is a fraction less than 1.
- **Notable differences among choices:** (A) and (E) both have 5 in the denominator, while (B) and (D) both have 4, and (C) is the only choice with 2 in the denominator. (A), (B), and (C) all have 1 in the numerator, while (D) has 3 and (E) has 4. 4 is the only number that appears in both the numerator and denominator of different choices. (A) and (E) are complements of each other, and (B) and (D) are complements of each other. (B), (C), and (D) form a series in which each choice is $\frac{1}{4}$ more

than the choice before it.
- **Concepts in the choices:** complements, fractions
- **Pre-solution patterns (see p. 149):** opposites

- **Things to look out for:** Make sure you don't accidentally pick the answer that reflects the probability of picking a grape-flavored candy! Make sure you don't confuse the numbers of pieces of candy available in different flavors!

Solution 1: Probability: Construct a probability fraction reflecting the number of non-grape-flavored candies in the bag, and simplify it.

The numerator of the probability fraction is the number of desired outcomes. In this case, that's the number of pieces of candy that aren't grape flavored: that's 4 lemon, 3 strawberry, and 1 cherry, or 8 total pieces of candy that aren't grape flavored.

The denominator of the probability fraction is the number of possible outcomes. In this case, that's the total number of pieces of candy, which the prompt tells us is 10 pieces.

So the probability fraction is $\frac{8}{10}$. This option doesn't appear in the answer choices, but $\frac{8}{10}$ can be reduced to $\frac{4}{5}$, so (E) is correct.

Solution 2: Test-smart: Note that the right answer must be greater than $\frac{1}{2}$ (because most of the candies aren't grape flavored) and must have a factor of 10 as the denominator (because there are 10 candies in the bag). Only (E) satisfies those requirements, so (E) must be right.

ANSWER CHOICE ANALYSIS

(A): This is the complement of the right answer—it represents the probability of choosing a grape-flavored candy, which is the opposite of what the prompt asked for. It will attract a lot of untrained test-takers who don't read the prompt carefully enough. **(B):** This choice combines the mistakes in (A) and (D): finding the probability of picking the grape candy instead of the non-grape candy, and forgetting to include the number of pieces of grape candy in the denominator of the probability fraction. **(C):** This choice may attract test-takers who just assume that the chance of doing something is equal to the chance of not doing it, no matter what the activity is. **(D):** This reflects the mistake of not including the number of pieces of grape candy in the denominator of the fraction—as trained test-takers, we know that the denominator of a probability fraction must include every possible outcome, including the outcomes that we're finding the probability for.

How to check? Try an alternate approach above. Make sure you haven't confused the numbers of the different kinds of candies, or forgotten to include the right things in the numerator and denominator of the fraction.

Test 1, Question 8 (Test 2 in the 2020-2021 Red Book—see page 23 for more)
- **What's the prompt asking for?** The coordinates of A under the conditions in the prompt.
- **Math concepts in the prompt:** midpoint, plotting points in the xy-coordinate plane
- **Math concepts in the diagram:** the origin, the xy-coordinate plane
- **Elements of the choices:** Each choice is a pair of single-digit coordinates.

- **Notable differences among choices:** The x-coordinates of (F), (G), (H), and (J) are all negative, while all the other coordinates in the choices are positive
- **Concepts in the choices:** coordinates, negative numbers, positive numbers
- **Things to look out for:** Don't confuse any of the coordinates in the prompt! Don't make any small mistakes in your reading or calculations!

Solution 1: Geometry/Backsolving: Plot B and the midpoint from the prompt in the given coordinate plane, and then plot each point from the answer choices. Pick the choice that makes sense given the position of B and the midpoint from the prompt.

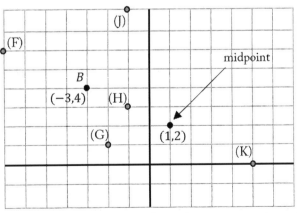

When we plot each point, we can see that (K) is the only point that makes sense given the position of B and the midpoint.

Solution 2: Graphing: Plot point B and the midpoint on the graph, and use their relative positions to find the coordinates of A.

For free sample video demonstrations, go to www.ACTprepVideos.com

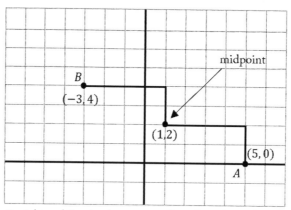

We can see that we have to travel 4 units right and 2 units down to get from B to the midpoint, so it must be the case that we have to travel 4 more units right and 2 more units down to get from the midpoint to A. That brings us to $(5,0)$, so (K) is right.

Solution 3: Test-smart: Note that the x-coordinate of A must be positive, and pick the only choice that satisfies that requirement.

The x-coordinate of B is negative, and the x-coordinate of the midpoint is positive. The midpoint is between B and A, so point A must be even farther to the right than the midpoint, which means the x-coordinate of A must be positive as well. Only (K) has a positive x-coordinate, so (K) must be right.

ANSWER CHOICE ANALYSIS

(F): This choice would seem to be right if we misread the prompt and think that B is at $(1, 2)$ and the midpoint is at $(-3, 4)$, instead of the other way around, as the prompt says. **(G):** This choice combines the mistakes involved in (H) and (J): finding the midpoint of the two points in the prompt, and using the wrong signs when applying the midpoint formula. **(H):** This choice is the midpoint between the two points whose coordinates appear in the prompt, but that isn't what the prompt asked us to find—instead, we were supposed to find the point that makes $(1, 2)$ the midpoint of a line segment with one end at $(-3, 4)$. This choice will attract a lot of untrained test-takers who are good at math but who don't pay enough attention when they read the prompt. **(J):** This choice could be the result of trying to solve this question using the midpoint formula but making a mistake with respect to the signs of the numbers in the formula.

How to check? Try an alternate approach above. Make sure that you pay close attention to the coordinates associated with A, B, and the midpoint in the prompt.

▶ **Post-solution patterns (see p. 151):** right answer to the wrong question

Note This question is a great example of the way the ACT often "punishes" untrained test-takers for using formal approaches to questions. In this case, using the midpoint formula would be the formal approach that a math teacher would usually require in school, but the three solutions we just covered are much faster and easier to use, and they offer fewer opportunities to make mistakes. Keep this in mind as you continue your preparation.

▌ Test 1, Question 9 (Test 2 in the 2020-2021 Red Book—see page 23 for more)

- **What's the prompt asking for?** The number of customers that the company had one year ago.
- **Math concepts in the prompt:** adding 8, doubling
- **Elements of the choices:** Each choice is an even number from 50 to 100 inclusive.
- **Notable differences among choices:** (A) is half of (E), which may be relevant because the prompt mentions the idea of doubling the number of customers. The difference between (A) and (B) is 4, which is also the difference between (C) and (D);

this may be relevant because the prompt mentions the ideas of 8 and the idea of doubling, and 8 is the result when we double 4.

- **Concepts in the choices:** adding four, doubling
- **Pre-solution patterns (see p. 149):** halves and doubles
- **Things to look out for:** Don't confuse the roles of the numbers 116, 8, and 2! Don't make any other small mistakes in your reading or calculations!

Solution 1: Concrete/Backsolving: Try each answer choice as the number of customers from one year ago, and pick the choice that results in 116 customers now, according to the conditions in the prompt.

We can test each answer choice by multiplying that choice by 2 and then adding 8 to the result. The correct answer will produce a value of 116, Andrea's current number of customers.

(A): $50 \times 2 + 8 = 108$ (result if Andrea had 50 customers 1 year ago)

(B): $54 \times 2 + 8 = 116$ (result if Andrea had 54 customers 1 year ago)

(C): $62 \times 2 + 8 = 132$ (result if Andrea had 62 customers 1 year ago)

(D): $66 \times 2 + 8 = 140$ (result if Andrea had 66 customers 1 year ago)

(E): $100 \times 2 + 8 = 208$ (result if Andrea had 100 customers 1 year ago)

We can see that only (B) produces a result of 116 customers, so (B) is right.

Solution 2: Algebra: Create an equation that relates the number of customers from one year ago to the numbers in the prompt. Solve your equation to find the answer to the question.

Let x equal the number of customers Andrea's company had 1 year ago. The prompt says that 116 is 8 more than twice the number of customers Andrea's company had 1 year ago. Twice the number of customers Andrea's company had 1 year ago would be $2x$, and 8 more than that would be $2x + 8$. So it must be true that $116 = 2x + 8$.

$$116 = 2x + 8 \qquad \text{(equation based on prompt)}$$
$$108 = 2x \qquad \text{(subtract 8 from both sides)}$$
$$54 = x \qquad \text{(divide both sides by 2)}$$

Again, we can see that (B) is right.

Solution 3: Mental math: Reason that if 116 is 8 more than double a number, then 108 must be double the number. If 108 is double the number, then the original number was 54. So (B) is right.

ANSWER CHOICE ANALYSIS

(A): This choice reflects the mistake of finding half of 116 and then subtracting 8, rather than subtracting 8 and then finding half of the resulting number. **(C):** This reflects a misreading of the prompt that would cause us to think that 116 was eight *less* than double the number of customers from the previous year, which would lead someone to think that 124 was double the number of customers from the previous year. **(D):** This choice combines the mistakes of (A) and (C): it reverses the order of dividing by 2 and subtracting 8, and then it *adds* the 8 instead of subtracting it. **(E):** This choice is the result of simply doubling 8 and subtracting the result from 116, without taking into account any kind of doubling of the number of customers from the previous year, as the prompt requires.

How to check? Try an alternate approach above. Make sure that you carefully read and understand the sequence of doubling numbers and then adding 8 to them.

▶ **Post-solution patterns (see p. 151):** easy calculation mistake

Test 1, Question 10 (Test 2 in the 2020-2021 Red Book—see page 23 for more)

- **What's the prompt asking for?** The amount per foot that Joseph must pay after he pays the $500 fee.
- **Math concepts in the prompt:** base fees, prices, rates
- **Elements of the choices:** Each choice is a price in dollars.
- **Notable differences among choices:** (F) and (J) end in .00, while (H) and (K) end in .50 and (G) ends in .80.

(F) and (G) both begin with 4.

- **Things to look out for:** Don't forget to subtract the $500 fee from the estimate when finding the cost per foot! Don't confuse the numbers involved in the 200 foot fence and the $2200 estimate! Don't make any small mistakes in your calculation!

Solution 1: Arithmetic: Subtract the base fee from $2200. Divide the remaining amount of money by 200 to find the cost per foot.

$500 less than the $2,200 estimate is $1700, so we can divide $1700 by 200 feet to find the cost per foot. The result is $\frac{\$1700}{200}$, which is equal to $8.50 per foot. So (H) is right.

Solution 2: Algebra: Create an equation that relates the cost per foot to the numbers in the prompt. Solve the equation to find the answer.

The prompt says that the fence company charges a $500 fee, and also a certain cost per foot of fence, which we'll call x. Joseph's fence will be 200 feet long. So the total cost for Joseph's fence will be $500, plus the length of the fence in feet multiplied by the cost per foot of the fence. That's the same as $500 + 200x$. The prompt tells us that this cost is $2,200, so we can set the expression equal to $2,200. The result is $2,200 = \$500 + 200x$. We can solve that equation for x to find the cost per foot of the fence.

$$\$2,200 = \$500 + 200x \qquad \text{(equation based on prompt)}$$
$$\$1,700 = 200x \qquad \text{(subtract \$500 from both sides)}$$
$$\$8.5 = x \qquad \text{(divide both sides by 200)}$$

So $8.50 is the cost per foot of the fence, and (H) is right.

Solution 3: Test-smart: Note that the answer must be between $5.00 and $10.00. Pick the choice that satisfies those requirements.

If the cost per foot were $5 or less, then the total cost would be no more than $1,500, because $1,000 + \$500 = \$1,500$. So (F) and (G) must be wrong. If the cost per foot were $10 or more, then the total cost would be at least $2,500, because $2,000 + \$500 = \$2,500$. So (J) and (K) must also be wrong. That only leaves (H), the correct answer.

ANSWER CHOICE ANALYSIS

(F): This is the result of accidentally subtracting 200 from 2200 and then dividing by 500, rather than subtracting 500 from 2200 and then dividing by 200. In other words, this choice would be right if the fee were $200 and the fence were 500 feet long, instead of the other way around. If you picked this choice, you may want to make sure that you read more carefully in the future. **(G):** This is the result of accidentally adding 200 to 2200 and then dividing by 500, but nothing in the prompt indicates that we should add anything to 2200. **(J):** This is the result of ignoring the $500 fee that's included in the estimate, and simply dividing 2200 by 200. This choice may attract untrained test-takers who are good at math but who read this question too quickly. **(K):** This is the result of adding $500 to the cost of the estimate before dividing by the length of the fence, but the prompt tells us that the estimate already includes the $500 fixed cost, so we need to *subtract* $500 from the estimate before dividing.

How to check? Try an alternate approach above. Make sure that you have accurately understood which number represents the length of the fence, which number represents the estimate, and which number represents the fixed cost.

Test 1, Question 11 (Test 2 in the 2020-2021 Red Book—see page 23 for more)

- **What's the prompt asking for?** The dimensions of Karla's living room in feet.
- **Math concepts in the prompt:** area, dimensions, perimeter
- **Elements of the choices:** Each choice is a pair of dimensions.
- **Notable differences among choices:** The first numbers in (B), (C), (D), and (E) form a series in which each number is 2 more than the choice before it. The second numbers in (C), (D), and (E) form a series in which each number is 2 less than the one before it.

- **Pre-solution patterns (see p. 149):** be aware of series
- **Things to look out for:** Don't forget that the perimeter of a rectangle is twice the sum of its dimensions! Don't make any small mistakes in your reading or calculations!

Solution 1: Concrete/Backsolving: Try each answer choice as the dimensions of Karla's living room, and pick the choice that results in an area of 180 and perimeter of 54.

The area of a rectangular room is the length of the room multiplied by its width. The perimeter of a room is twice the length of the room plus twice its width. We can calculate the area and perimeter that results from each of the possible sets of dimensions in the answer choices to see which one has an area of 180 and a perimeter of 54.

(A) $Area = 9 \times 20 = 180$ $Perimeter = 2(9) + 2(20) = 58$

(B) $Area = 10 \times 18 = 180$ $Perimeter = 2(10) + 2(18) = 56$

(C) $Area = 12 \times 15 = 180$ $Perimeter = 2(12) + 2(15) = 54$

(D) $Area = 14 \times 13 = 182$ $Perimeter = 2(14) + 2(13) = 54$

(E) $Area = 16 \times 11 = 176$ $Perimeter = 2(16) + 2(11) = 54$

Only the dimensions in (C) correspond to a room with an area of 180 and a perimeter of 54, so (C) is correct.

Solution 2: Algebra/Geometry: Write an equation that relates the area of Karla's living room to its perimeter, and pick the choice that reflects the solution to your equation.

We know that the area of a rectangle can be found with the equation $A = lw$, where A is the area of the rectangle, l is the length of the rectangle, and w is the width of the rectangle. We also know that the area of the room is 180, so we can plug in $A = 180$. That gives us this equation: $lw = 180$

We know that the perimeter of a rectangle is equal to the sum of the 4 sides of the rectangle, which is the same as twice the width of the rectangle added to twice the length of the rectangle. We can represent that with $2l + 2w = P$, where P is the perimeter of the rectangle. We also know that the perimeter of the room is 54, so we can plug in $P = 54$. That gives us this equation: $2l + 2w = 54$

We can solve for either variable in one equation, then solve for the result in the other equation.

$2l + 2w = 54$ (second equation)

$2l = 54 - 2w$ (subtract $2w$ from both sides)

$l = 27 - w$ (divide both sides by 2)

Now we can plug $l = 27 - w$ into the first equation and solve for w.

$lw = 180$ (first equation)

$(27 - w)w = 180$ (plug in $l = 27 - w$)

$27w - w^2 = 180$ (distribute w)

Let's make this into a more recognizable quadratic equation so it's easier to work with.

$27w - w^2 - 180 = 0$ (subtract 180 from both sides)

$-w^2 + 27w - 180 = 0$ (reorder the terms so the squared term is first)

$w^2 - 27w + 180 = 0$ (multiply both sides by -1)

$$(w - 15)(w - 12) = 0 \qquad \text{(reverse FOIL)}$$

So the equation is true when $w = 15$ or when $w = 12$. Let's plug those values into either of the original equations and solve for l. We'll use the area equation for no particular reason.

$$lw = 180 \qquad \text{(area equation)}$$

$$l(15) = 180 \qquad \text{(plug in } w = 15\text{)}$$

$$l = 12 \qquad \text{(divide both sides by 15)}$$

So when $w = 15$, $l = 12$. We can also see that plugging in $w = 12$ will give us $l = 15$, which makes sense, because it doesn't matter which side of a rectangle we call the length and which side we call the width; the area will still be the two dimensions multiplied together. So the values are interchangeable here. We can see that (C) is the right answer.

Solution 3: Test-smart: Realize that the perimeter is twice the length plus twice the width, so half the perimeter is just the sum of the length and the width. That means the length plus the width is half of 54 feet, which is 27 feet. The dimensions must be two numbers that add up to 27 and have a product of 180. Only (C) meets this requirement, so (C) is right.

ANSWER CHOICE ANALYSIS

(A): This choice may attract a lot of untrained test takers who don't check their work carefully, because it results in an area of 180, but a perimeter of 58. Many untrained test takers who are working quickly won't catch the discrepancy between 58 and 54. **(B):** Like (A), this choice will attract a lot of people who don't notice that its dimensions create a perimeter that's slightly off from 54 (in this case, 56). **(D):** This choice describes a room with the proper perimeter, but we can tell right away that it won't create an area of 180 because multiplying these numbers won't produce a number that ends in a 0, as we would need in order to have an area of 180. **(E):** This choice has the same problem as (D): it correctly creates a perimeter of 54, but it can't produce an area that ends in 0.

How to check? Try an alternate approach above. Be very careful when you add the dimensions together, because some of the wrong answers are clearly set up to create perimeters that are close to 54.

Test 1, Question 12 (Test 2 in the 2020-2021 Red Book—see page 23 for more)

- **What's the prompt asking for?** The number of quarters that Jeremy would have left after buying a box of 25 candies at Tamika's shop.
- **Math concepts in the prompt:** linear relationships, prices, reading data from a table
- **Math concepts in the diagram:** prices, reading data from a table
- **Elements of the choices:** Each choice is a two-digit number.
- **Notable differences among choices:** (F) and (K) add up to 40, and (G) and (J) also add up to 40. This may be relevant because the prompt tells us Jeremy has $10.00 in quarters, which means he has 40 quarters.
- **Concepts in the choices:** complements
- **Pre-solution patterns (see p. 149):** opposites
- **Things to look out for:** Don't read the data for the wrong shop! Don't forget that $10.00 is equal to 40 quarters! Don't make any other small mistakes in your reading or calculations!

Solution 1: Arithmetic: Use the table to determine the amount of change Jeremy should have, and then divide that amount by $0.25 to find the number of quarters.

Tamika's shop sells a box of 25 candies for $4.25. If Jeremy uses $10.00 to buy a box of 25 candies for $4.25, he'll have $10.00 − $4.25, or $5.75 left over. In quarters, that amount is $\frac{\$5.75}{\$0.25}$, or 23. So (J) is right.

Solution 2: Arithmetic: Determine the number of quarters necessary to pay for 25 candies at Tamika's shop, and subtract that number from 40 to find the right answer.

$10.00 is 40 quarters, because $0.25 × 40 = $10.00. A box of 25 candies from Tamika's shop is $4.25, which is the same as 17 quarters, because $\frac{\$4.25}{\$0.25} = 17$. If Jeremy has 40 quarters and spends 17 quarters, then he has 23 quarters left over. So (J) is right.

Solution 3: Test-smart: We know that Jeremy starts out with an even number of quarters, and that he spends an odd number of quarters (because a box of 25 candies from Tamika's shop costs $4.25), so he must have an odd number of quarters left over. That eliminates (F), (H), and (K). We also know that he spent less than half his money, and he started out with 40 quarters. So he must have more than 20 quarters left over, which eliminates (G). Only (J) remains, so (J) must be right.

ANSWER CHOICE ANALYSIS

(F): This is how many quarters you would have to spend on a box of 10 candies from Carrie's shop, but that isn't what the prompt asks for.
(G): This "right approach, wrong step" answer is the number of quarters necessary to buy the 25 candies at Tamika's shop, but the prompt asked us to find the number of quarters that Jeremy has left after buying the candies, not the number of quarters necessary to buy the

candies themselves. **(H):** This choice is similar to (G) because it's the number of quarters necessary to buy 25 candies at Carrie's shop, rather than Tamika's, so it reflects two mistakes in approaching the question. **(K):** This is how many quarters you would have left over under the conditions in the prompt if you bought a box of 10 candies from Carrie's shop, but the question asks how many you would have left over after buying a box of 25 candies from Tamika's shop.

How to check? Try an alternate approach above. Be especially careful about making sure you've read the data from the correct column and row, and remember that there are four quarters in a dollar.

▶ **Post-solution patterns (see p. 151):** right answer to the wrong question

Test 1, Question 13 (Test 2 in the 2020-2021 Red Book—see page 23 for more)

- **What's the prompt asking for?** The average price per candy in a box of 20 candies at Tamika's shop.
- **Math concepts in the prompt:** linear relationships, prices, reading data from a table
- **Math concepts in the diagram:** prices, reading data from a table
- **Elements of the choices:** Each choice is an amount of money

below $0.50.

- **Notable differences among choices:** (A), (B), and (D) form a series in which each choice is $0.11 more than the choice before it.
- **Things to look out for:** Don't read data from the wrong part of the table! Don't make any small mistakes in your calculations!

Solution 1: Arithmetic: Find the price of 20 candies at Tamika's sweet shop, and divide it by 20 to find the average price per candy.

The table tells us that a box of 20 candies from Tamika's treat shop costs $3.75. We can divide that number by 20 to find the cost per piece of candy, which gives us $\frac{\$3.75}{20} = \$0.1875$, which rounds to approximately $0.19. So (B) is right.

Solution 2: Test-smart: We can mentally multiply each answer choice by 20 to find which result is closest to the cost of a box of 20 candies from Tamika's shop, which is $3.75. The value in (A) gives us $1.60, (B) gives us $3.80, (C) gives us $4.60, (D) gives us $6.00, and (E) gives us $9.00. Choice (B) is closest to the actual cost, so (B) is right. (Notice that we know approximation is okay here because the prompt asks for the answer "to the nearest $0.01.")

ANSWER CHOICE ANALYSIS

(A): This is the result when we figure out the increase in the cost of 20 candies as compared to 5 candies at Tamika's shop, and then divide that increase by 20—but the prompt doesn't say anything about comparing the cost of 20 candies to the cost of 5 candies; it only says that we need to find the unit cost of 20 candies bought from Tamika's shop. **(C):** This is the unit price of candies if someone buys 20 candies from Carrie's shop, rather than from Tamika's shop. **(D):** This is the unit price of 5 candies at Carrie's shop. So this choice essentially combines the mistakes in (C) and (E): assuming that the unit price is the same for all numbers of candies, and reading the data for Carrie's shop instead of Tamika's. **(E):** This is the average cost per candy when someone buys five candies at Tamika's shop, but the question asks for the average cost per candy when someone buys 20 candies there. This choice may attract untrained test-takers who check the price per candy on the first row of the table because they assume that the price per unit must be constant (since the prompt says there's a linear relationship between the price and the number of candies). But it's possible for the unit price to change when different quantities are purchased even though the relationship between the price of the candies and the number of candies purchased is linear.

How to check? Carefully reconsider your reading and your calculation. Be especially careful about making sure you take the data from the right row and column.

Test 1, Question 14 (Test 2 in the 2020-2021 Red Book—see page 23 for more)

- **What's the prompt asking for?** The equation that accurately portrays the relationship between c and n in the table.
- **Math concepts in the prompt:** linear relationships, prices, reading data from a table
- **Math concepts in the diagram:** prices, reading data from a table
- **Elements of the choices:** Each choice is an equation with c isolated on the left-hand side and an n-term immediately after the equals sign.
- **Notable differences among choices:** (F) and (H) involve adding a constant, while (J) and (K) involve subtracting a constant and

(G) has no constant. (F), (G), and (H) all have coefficients of n that are less than 1, while (K) has a coefficient for n that's greater than 1, and (J) has a coefficient for n that's exactly 1.

- **Concepts in the choices:** coefficients, constants, decimal points, linear equations
- **Things to look out for:** Make sure that the answer you pick accurately reflects all the prices for Carrie's shop, not just some of them! Make sure you work with the data from Carrie's shop, rather than Tamika's!

Solution 1: Concrete: Try (n, c) pairings from the provided table in the equations from each choice. Pick the choice whose equation is valid for all (n, c) pairings.

Let's start by trying the equation in (F) with the values from the table until we get one that doesn't create a true statement.

$$1.50 = 0.2(5) + 0.5 \quad \text{(equation from (F) with the first row of } n \text{ and } c \text{ values plugged in)}$$

$$1.50 = 1.50 \qquad \text{(simplify)}$$

The first row worked; let's try the next row.

$$2.50 = 0.2(10) + 0.5 \qquad \text{(equation from (F) with the second row of } n \text{ and } c \text{ values plugged in)}$$

$$2.50 = 2.50 \qquad \text{(simplify)}$$

The second row worked; let's try the next row.

$$3.50 = 0.2(15) + 0.5 \qquad \text{(equation from (F) with the third row of } n \text{ and } c \text{ values plugged in)}$$

$$3.50 = 3.50 \qquad \text{(simplify)}$$

The third row worked; let's try the next row.

$$4.50 = 0.2(20) + 0.5 \qquad \text{(equation from (F) with the fourth row of } n \text{ and } c \text{ values plugged in)}$$

$$4.50 = 4.50 \qquad \text{(simplify)}$$

The fourth row worked; let's try the next row.

$$5.50 = 0.2(25) + 0.5 \qquad \text{(equation from (F) with the fifth row of } n \text{ and } c \text{ values plugged in)}$$

$$5.50 = 5.50 \qquad \text{(simplify)}$$

The fifth row worked; let's try the last row.

$$6.50 = 0.2(30) + 0.5 \qquad \text{(equation from (F) with the sixth row of } n \text{ and } c \text{ values plugged in)}$$

$$6.50 = 6.50 \qquad \text{(simplify)}$$

We can see that the numbers from every row worked for this equation, so (F) appears to be right. Let's check the other choices to make sure we didn't make a mistake.

$$1.50 = 0.3(5) \qquad \text{(equation from (G) with the first row of } n \text{ and } c \text{ values plugged in)}$$

$$1.50 = 1.50 \qquad \text{(simplify)}$$

The first row worked; let's try the next row.

$$2.50 = 0.3(10) \qquad \text{(equation from (G) with the second row of } n \text{ and } c \text{ values plugged in)}$$

$$2.50 = 3.00 \qquad \text{(simplify)}$$

The second row didn't work, so this choice must be wrong. Let's look at the equation from (H).

$$1.50 = 0.5(5) + 1.5 \qquad \text{(equation from (H) with the first row of } n \text{ and } c \text{ values plugged in)}$$

$$1.50 = 4.00 \qquad \text{(simplify)}$$

The first row didn't work, so this choice must be wrong. Let's look at the equation from (J).

$$1.50 = 5 - 3.5 \qquad \text{(equation from (J) with the first row of } n \text{ and } c \text{ values plugged in)}$$

$$1.50 = 1.50 \qquad \text{(simplify)}$$

The first row worked; let's try the next row.

$$2.50 = 10 - 3.5 \qquad \text{(equation from (J) with the second row of } n \text{ and } c \text{ values plugged in)}$$

$$2.50 = 6.50 \qquad \text{(simplify)}$$

The second row didn't work, so this choice must be wrong. Finally, let's look at the equation from (K).

$$1.50 = 1.4(5) - 5.5 \qquad \text{(equation from (K) with the first row of } n \text{ and } c \text{ values plugged in)}$$

$$1.50 = 1.50 \qquad \text{(simplify)}$$

The first row worked; let's try the next row.

$$2.50 = 1.4(10) - 5.5 \qquad \text{(equation from (K) with the second row of } n \text{ and } c \text{ values plugged in)}$$

$$2.50 = 8.50 \qquad \text{(simplify)}$$

The second row didn't work, so this choice must be wrong. After checking each answer choice, we can see that only (F) produced a valid statement for each row of the table, so (F) must be right.

Solution 2: Graphing: Graph each choice and pick the choice that goes through the appropriate (n, c) coordinates (remember that n will correspond to the x-axis on your calculator, and c will correspond to the y-axis).

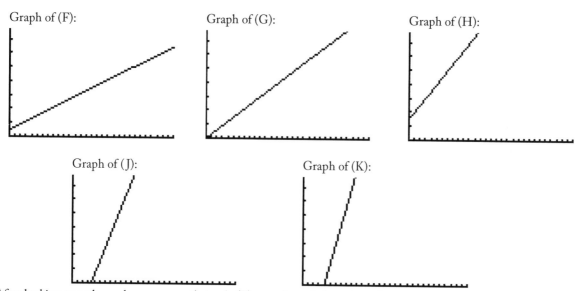

Graph of (F):   Graph of (G):   Graph of (H):

Graph of (J):   Graph of (K):

After looking at each graph, we can see that only (F) goes through the points that correspond to the n and c values from the table. This is most obvious when we look at the points on the right side of each graph where the n-values are in the $20-30$ range; the corresponding c-values in the wrong answer choices get up to 7, 8, or even significantly higher and off the visible part of the graph entirely, while the values in the table don't go any higher than $6.50 (for an n-value of 30). So (F) must be right.

Solution 3: Test-smart: Note that the coefficient of n must be 0.2, and pick the only choice that satisfies that requirement.

When we look at the table we can see that c increases by 1 as n increases by 5. So the coefficient of n must be $\frac{1}{5}$, or 0.2. Only (F) has 0.2 for a coefficient of n, so (F) must be right.

ANSWER CHOICE ANALYSIS

(G): This choice works for the price of 5 candies at Carrie's shop, but it doesn't work for the other prices at Carrie's shop. A lot of test-takers who try Solution 1 above will fall for this choice because they don't bother to test the other prices before moving on to the next question. **(J):** Like (G), this choice accurately describes the price of 5 candies at Carrie's shop, but it doesn't work for any of the other prices in the table. **(K):** This choice is like (G) and (J) in the sense that it only accurately relates n to c when $n = 5$, but the prompt told us to find an equation that relates n to c for all the prices at Carrie's shop.

How to check? Try an alternate approach above. Make sure you consider all of the prices at Carrie's shop, instead of only considering one price!

Test 1, Question 15 (Test 2 in the 2020-2021 Red Book—see page 23 for more)

- **What's the prompt asking for?** The choice that makes the equation in the prompt true.
- **Math concepts in the prompt:** equations, exponents, subtraction, variables, zero
- **Elements of the choices:** Choices are multiples of 6.
- **Notable differences among choices:** (E) is the only negative number, and it's the opposite of (D). (A), (B), and (C) form a series in which each choice is half as much as the choice before

it. (B) is the square of (D) and (E), which may be relevant because the question includes x^2.

- **Concepts in the choices:** multiplying by six, multiplying by two, negative numbers, positive numbers, squaring
- **Pre-solution patterns (see p. 149):** halves and doubles; opposites
- **Things to look out for:** Don't make any small mistakes in your reading or calculations!

Solution 1: Backsolving/Concrete: Use your calculator to test each choice as x. Pick the choice that makes the original equation true.

$x^2 - 36x = 0$	(original equation)
$(72)^2 - 36(72) = 0$	(plug in $x = 72$ from (A))
$5,184 - 2,592 = 0$	(simplify)
$2,592 = 0$	(simplify)

This choice results in an invalid statement, so (A) can't be correct. Let's try (B).

$x^2 - 36x = 0$	(original equation)
$(36)^2 - 36(36) = 0$	(plug in $x = 36$ from (B))
$1,296 - 1,296 = 0$	(simplify)
$0 = 0$	(simplify)

This choice results in a valid statement, so (B) appears to be correct. Let's look at the remaining choices to make sure we haven't made a mistake.

$$x^2 - 36x = 0 \qquad \text{(original equation)}$$
$$(18)^2 - 36(18) = 0 \qquad \text{(plug in } x = 18 \text{ from (C))}$$
$$324 - 648 = 0 \qquad \text{(simplify)}$$
$$-324 = 0 \qquad \text{(simplify)}$$

This choice results in an invalid statement, so (C) can't be correct. Let's try (D).

$$x^2 - 36x = 0 \qquad \text{(original equation)}$$
$$(6)^2 - 36(6) = 0 \qquad \text{(plug in } x = 6 \text{ from (D))}$$
$$36 - 216 = 0 \qquad \text{(simplify)}$$
$$-180 = 0 \qquad \text{(simplify)}$$

This choice results in an invalid statement, so (D) can't be correct. Let's try (E).

$$x^2 - 36x = 0 \qquad \text{(original equation)}$$
$$(-6)^2 - 36(-6) = 0 \qquad \text{(plug in } x = -6 \text{ from (E))}$$
$$36 + 216 = 0 \qquad \text{(simplify)}$$
$$252 = 0 \qquad \text{(simplify)}$$

This choice results in an invalid statement, so (E) can't be correct. After considering each choice, we know that (B) is right.

Solution 2: Algebra: Isolate x on one side of the equation to find the right answer.

$$x^2 - 36x = 0 \qquad \text{(original equation)}$$
$$x^2 = 36x \qquad \text{(add } 36x \text{ to both sides)}$$
$$x = 36 \qquad \text{(divide both sides by } x)$$

So (B) is right.

Solution 3: Graphing: Graph $y = x^2 - 36x$ and find the x-coordinate that corresponds to a y-coordinate of zero.

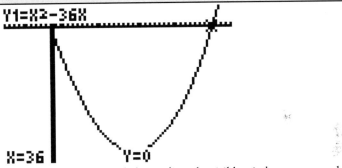

We can see that $y = 0$ when $x = 36$. So (B) is right. (Notice that it may help to adjust the visible window on your calculator so you can have a better idea of what the graph is doing.)

ANSWER CHOICE ANALYSIS

(A): This choice is probably present because it's twice as much as the correct answer, which fits a common pattern on the ACT Math section. **(C):** Like (A), this choice is probably here because it's half as much as the right answer, in keeping with a common pattern on the ACT Math section. **(D):** This choice and (E) would both seem to be valid for x if an untrained test-taker misread the equation in the prompt as $x^2 - 36 = 0$. **(E):** See the explanation for (D).

How to check? Try an alternate approach above. Make sure you've read the original equation correctly, and that there's no reason to multiply or divide 36 by 2, since the answer choices seem to expect some test-takers to try that.

Note If we did happen to misread the original equation as $x^2 - 36 = 0$, our habit of considering every answer choice before moving on to the next question (see page 42 of this Black Book) would help us realize we must have made a mistake, since both (D) and (E) would be valid answers according to our misreading—and, as trained test-takers, we know that an ACT Math question can't have more than one valid answer. This would make us realize that we must have misunderstood something in the question, and we could then go back and fix it. This is a great example of why it's so important to be disciplined and stick to your training on test day!

Test 1, Question 16 (Test 2 in the 2020-2021 Red Book—see page 23 for more)

- **What's the prompt asking for?** The measure of $\angle DEF$ according to the prompt.

- **Math concepts in the prompt:** angles, collinear points, degrees, triangles, vertices

- **Math concepts in the diagram:** angles, collinear points, degrees, triangles, vertices
- **Elements of the choices:** Each choice is a number of degrees.
- **Notable differences among choices:** (F) and (J) add up to 180, which may be relevant because the sum of the degrees in the angles of a triangle is 180, and because a straight line corresponds to 180 degrees of arc.

- **Concepts in the choices:** 180 degrees, angle measurements, supplementary angles
- **Pre-solution patterns (see p. 149):** opposites
- **Things to look out for:** Don't make any small mistakes in your reading or calculations! Don't confuse the labels of the two angles in the diagram!

Solution 1: Geometry: Use the given information to determine the measures of ∠EDF and ∠EFD. Then use those angle measurements to find ∠DEF.

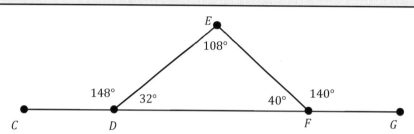

∠EDC and ∠EDF combine to form a straight line, which means they add up to 180°, so the measure of ∠EDF must be 180° − 148°, or 32°. ∠EFG and ∠EFD also form a straight line, so the measure of ∠EFD must be 180° − 140°, or 40°. The sum of the measures of the three angles of a triangle must be 180°, so the measure of ∠DEF must be 180° − 32° − 40°, or 108°. That means (J) is right.

ANSWER CHOICE ANALYSIS

(F): This is a "right approach, wrong step" answer because we need to find that the sum of ∠EDF and ∠EFD is 72° before we can find the measure of ∠DEF—but this sum is not what the prompt asked us to find. **(G):** This could be the result of making a mistake while trying to subtract 72 from 180, causing you to be off by 10. **(H):** This would be correct if the two unlabeled angles in the diagram were both 140°, but only one of them is actually 140°, so this choice is wrong. **(K):** This reflects a misreading similar to the misreading we saw in (H): it would be the right answer if both labeled angles in the diagram were 148°, but only the angle on the left is 148°, so this choice is wrong.

How to check? Carefully reconsider your reading and your calculations. The fact that the angle which is supplementary to the right answer is present in the wrong answers should help reassure us that we've probably answered correctly, since this question deals with supplementary angles and we can expect that many untrained test-takers will accidentally pick the supplement of the right answer.

▶ Post-solution patterns (see p. 151): right approach, wrong step

---

Test 1, Question 17 (Test 2 in the 2020-2021 Red Book—see page 23 for more)

- **What's the prompt asking for?** The maximum number of notepads that can fit in a closed box according to the prompt.
- **Math concepts in the prompt:** cubes, rectangular prisms, volume
- **Elements of the choices:** The choices are all positive two-digit numbers.
- **Notable differences among choices:** (A), (B), and (C) form a series in which each choice is one more than the choice before it. (D) is twice as much as (B). (E) is three times as much as

(C), which may be relevant because the prompt involves multiples of 3.
- **Concepts in the choices:** adding one, multiplying by 2, multiplying by 3
- **Pre-solution patterns (see p. 149):** halves and doubles
- **Things to look out for:** Don't confuse any of the dimensions in the prompt! Don't make any small mistakes in your reading or calculations!

Solution 1: Geometry/Concrete: Sketch out the shapes described in the prompt, and determine how many notepads could fit along each dimension of the box. Use that information to determine the total number of notepads that can fit in the box.

The prompt says that each notepad is a cube with an edge length of 3, which would look roughly like this:

The prompt also says the notepads ship in a box that's 9 inches long, 9 inches wide, and 12 inches tall, which could look like this:

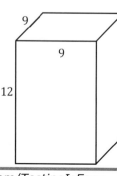

Based on this information, we can see that 3 notepads would fit along the length and width of the box (since the edge of each notepad is 3 inches, and the length and width of the box are each 9 inches), and 4 notepads would fit along the height of the box (since the edge of each notepad is 3 inches, and the height of the box is 12 inches).

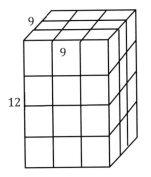

So we can calculate the number of notepads in the box by multiplying the number of notepads that can fit along each dimension. The result is 3 notepads × 3 notepads × 4 notepads = 36 notepads, so the answer is (E).

Solution 2: Geometry/Abstract: Calculate the volume of the box and the volume of each notepad. Divide the larger number by the smaller number to find the number of notepads that can fit in the box.

We can divide the volume of the box by the volume of one notepad to find how many notepads can possibly fit in the box. The total volume of the box is given by multiplying the length, width, and height of the box together; the total volume of a notepad is given by multiplying the notepad's length, width, and height together. So our calculation is $\frac{9 \times 9 \times 12}{3 \times 3 \times 3} = \frac{972}{27} = 36$. Again, we can see that (E) is right.

Solution 3: Test-smart: Note that the right answer must be a multiple of 12 and must be larger than 12, and pick the only choice that satisfies those requirements.

Once you realize that 4 notepads fit into the 12-inch height of the box described in the prompt, and 3 notepads fit into the 9-inch width of that box—and there is still another dimension to account for—you know that the answer must be greater than 12, and it must also be a multiple of 12. Only (E) meets this requirement, so (E) must be right.

ANSWER CHOICE ANALYSIS

(A): This is the result of attempting Solution 1, but adding the numbers 3, 3, and 4, instead of multiplying them. **(B):** This choice reflects the mistake of determining the total surface area of the faces of the box and dividing it by the total surface area of the faces of a notepad, rather than dividing the volume of the box by the volume of the notepad. **(C):** This choice could reflect the mistake of misreading the dimensions of the box as 3 × 9 × 12 rather than 9 × 9 × 12, or the mistake of attempting Solution 1 but forgetting one of the dimensions and only multiplying 3 and 4 at the end, instead of 3, 3, and 4. **(D):** This choice reflects the error of attempting Solution 2 above but using the total surface area of all the faces of the box instead of the volume of the box in your calculation.

How to check? Try an alternate approach above. Be especially careful to make sure that you don't misread the dimensions in the prompt.

▶ **Post-solution patterns (see p. 151):** right approach, wrong step

Test 1, Question 18 (Test 2 in the 2020-2021 Red Book—see page 23 for more)

- **What's the prompt asking for?** The value of the function in the prompt when x equals -4.
- **Math concepts in the prompt:** exponents, functions, negative numbers, PEMDAS, variables
- **Elements of the choices:** Each choice is a multiple of 16.
- **Notable differences among choices:** (F) is the opposite of (K) and (G) is the opposite of (J).

- **Concepts in the choices:** multiplying by 16, negative numbers, opposites, positive numbers
- **Pre-solution patterns (see p. 149):** opposites
- **Things to look out for:** Don't make any mistakes related to PEMDAS! Don't overlook the negative signs in the prompt! Don't key anything into your calculator incorrectly! Don't make any other mistakes related to reading or calculations!

Solution 1: Concrete/Calculator: Use your knowledge of PEMDAS or your calculator to evaluate $-4(-4)^3 - 4(-4)^2$ and pick the corresponding answer choice.

$f(x) = -4x^3 - 4x^2$	(given function)
$f(-4) = -4(-4)^3 - 4(-4)^2$	(plug in $x = -4$ to find $f(-4)$)
$f(-4) = -4(-64) - 4(16)$	(exponents)
$f(-4) = 256 - 64$	(multiplication)
$f(-4) = 192$	(subtraction)

So (J) is right. Note that we could also just enter $-4(-4)^3 - 4(-4)^2$ into a calculator and find the answer that way.

Solution 2: Calculator/Graphing: Use your calculator to graph the function in the prompt, and pick the choice that represents the y-value when x equals -4.

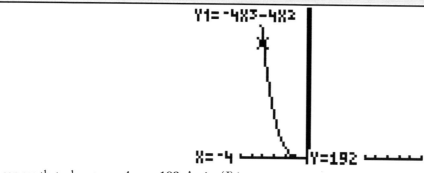

We can see that when $x = -4, y = 192$. Again, (J) is correct.

ANSWER CHOICE ANALYSIS

(F): This is the result if we accidentally overlook the negative sign on the first 4 in the equation: $4(-4)^3 - 4(-4)^2 = -320$. **(G):** This is the result of accidentally ignoring both negative signs in the original equation: $4(-4)^3 + 4(-4)^2 = -192$. **(H):** This choice is equal to $(-4)^2$. There are a lot of ways an untrained test-taker could make a mistake on the question and arrive at this answer through a combination of misreading the page and/or mis-keying information into the calculator. **(K):** This reflects the mistake of ignoring the second minus sign in the equation, resulting in $-4(-4)^3 + 4(-4)^2 = 320$.

How to check? Try an alternate approach above. Be especially careful when it comes to negative signs, since the answer choices make it very clear that the ACT expects untrained test takers to make mistakes when handling the negative numbers in the prompt.

Test 1, Question 19 (Test 2 in the 2020-2021 Red Book—see page 23 for more)

- **What's the prompt asking for?** The choice with an (x, y) pair that satisfies both equations in the prompt.
- **Math concepts in the prompt:** (x, y) pairs, negative numbers, positive numbers, systems of equations
- **Elements of the choices:** Each choice is a pair of numbers separated by a comma.
- **Notable differences among choices:** (A) and (B) are the only choices that involve negative numbers. (B) and (C) are the only choices that involve decimals. (E) is the only choice that involves zero. Each of the negative x-values in (A) and (B) has its opposite in another choice. 1 is the only number that appears in the choices as both a possible value for x (in choice (C)) and a possible value for y (in choice (D)).
- **Concepts in the choices:** (x, y) pairs, decimal points, negative numbers, one, zero
- **Pre-solution patterns (see p. 149):** opposites
- **Things to look out for:** Don't confuse any parts of the equations with each other! Don't overlook any negative signs in the equations! Don't make any other small mistakes in your reading or algebra!

Solution 1: Concrete: Try each answer choice in both equations. Pick the choice that makes both equations true.

$x + 2y = 4$	(first equation)
$-2 + 2(3) = 4$	(plug in $(-2, 3)$ from (A))
$4 = 4$	(simplify)

Plugging the ordered pair from (A) into the first equation yields a valid statement. Let's check the same ordered pair in the second equation:

$-2x + y = 7$	(second equation)
$-2(-2) + 3 = 7$	(plug in $(-2, 3)$ from (A))
$7 = 7$	(simplify)

Plugging the ordered pair from (A) into the second equation also yields a valid statement. Choice (A) appears to be correct, but let's check the other answer choices to make sure we haven't made a mistake:

$x + 2y = 4$	(first equation)
$-1 + 2(2.5) = 4$	(plug in $(-1, 2.5)$ from (B))
$4 = 4$	(simplify)

Plugging the ordered pair from (B) into the first equation yields a valid statement. Let's check the same ordered pair in the second equation:

$$-2x + y = 7 \qquad \text{(second equation)}$$
$$-2(-1) + 2.5 = 7 \qquad \text{(plug in } (-1, 2.5) \text{ from (B))}$$
$$4.5 = 7 \qquad \text{(simplify)}$$

Plugging the ordered pair from (B) into the second equation yields an invalid statement, so (B) can't be right. Let's try (C):

$$x + 2y = 4 \qquad \text{(first equation)}$$
$$1 + 2(1.5) = 4 \qquad \text{(plug in } (1, 1.5) \text{ from (C))}$$
$$4 = 4 \qquad \text{(simplify)}$$

Plugging the ordered pair from (C) into the first equation yields a valid statement. Let's check the same ordered pair in the second equation:

$$-2x + y = 7 \qquad \text{(second equation)}$$
$$-2(1) + 1.5 = 7 \qquad \text{(plug in } (1, 1.5) \text{ from (C))}$$
$$-0.5 = 7 \qquad \text{(simplify)}$$

Plugging the ordered pair from (C) into the second equation yields an invalid statement, so (C) can't be correct. Let's try (D):

$$x + 2y = 4 \qquad \text{(first equation)}$$
$$2 + 2(1) = 4 \qquad \text{(plug in } (2, 1) \text{ from (D))}$$
$$4 = 4 \qquad \text{(simplify)}$$

Plugging the ordered pair from (D) into the first equation yields a valid statement. Let's check the same ordered pair in the second equation:

$$-2x + y = 7 \qquad \text{(second equation)}$$
$$-2(2) + 1 = 7 \qquad \text{(plug in } (2, 1) \text{ from (D))}$$
$$-3 = 7 \qquad \text{(simplify)}$$

Plugging the ordered pair from (D) into the second equation yields an invalid statement, so (D) is wrong. Finally, let's try (E):

$$x + 2y = 4 \qquad \text{(first equation)}$$
$$4 + 2(0) = 4 \qquad \text{(plug in } (4, 0) \text{ from (E))}$$
$$4 = 4 \qquad \text{(simplify)}$$

Plugging the ordered pair from (E) into the first equation yields a valid statement. Let's check the same ordered pair in the second equation:

$$-2x + y = 7 \qquad \text{(second equation)}$$
$$-2(4) + 0 = 7 \qquad \text{(plug in } (4, 0) \text{ from (E))}$$
$$-8 = 7 \qquad \text{(simplify)}$$

Plugging the ordered pair from (E) into the second equation yields an invalid statement, so (E) can't be correct. After considering each choice, we can conclude that (A) is right.

Solution 2: Algebra: Isolate one of the variables in one of the equations, and use the result in the other equation to solve for the other variable. Plug that value into either equation to find the value of the first variable. Pick the choice that corresponds to the coordinate pair you find.

$$x + 2y = 4 \qquad \text{(first equation)}$$
$$x = 4 - 2y \qquad \text{(subtract } 2y \text{ from both sides)}$$

Now we can plug $x = 4 - 2y$ into the second equation and solve for y.

$$-2x + y = 7 \qquad \text{(second equation)}$$
$$-2(4 - 2y) + y = 7 \qquad \text{(plug in } x = 4 - 2y)$$
$$-8 + 4y + y = 7 \qquad \text{(distribute the } -2)$$
$$5y = 15 \qquad \text{(add 8 to both sides and combine like terms)}$$
$$y = 3 \qquad \text{(divide both sides by 5)}$$

Now we can plug $y = 3$ into either equation and solve for x. We'll use the first equation, for no particular reason.

$$x + 2y = 4 \qquad \text{(first equation)}$$
$$x + 2(3) = 4 \qquad \text{(plug in } y = 3)$$
$$x + 6 = 4 \qquad \text{(simplify)}$$

$$x = -2 \qquad \text{(subtract 6 from both sides)}$$

We found that $x = -2$ and $y = 3$, so the solution for the given system of equations is $(-2, 3)$, and (A) is right.

Solution 3: Graphing: Graph both equations on your calculator, and pick the choice with the (x, y) coordinates of the point of intersection on the graph.

The easiest way to graph these equations on your calculator is to solve each one for y.

$$x + 2y = 4 \qquad \text{(first equation)}$$
$$2y = 4 - x \qquad \text{(subtract } x \text{ from both sides)}$$
$$y = \frac{4-x}{2} \qquad \text{(divide both sides by 2)}$$

So the first equation is equal to $y = \frac{4-x}{2}$. Let's solve the second equation for y.

$$-2x + y = 7 \qquad \text{(first equation)}$$
$$y = 7 + 2x \qquad \text{(add } 2x \text{ to both sides)}$$

So the second equation is equal to $y = 7 + 2x$.

When we graph $y = \frac{4-x}{2}$ and $y = 7 + 2x$, the point of intersection will be the answer to this question:

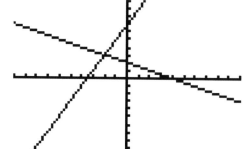

We can see that the equations intersect at the point $(-2, 3)$, so (A) is right.

Solution 4: Algebra: Combine the equations, solve for one of the variables, and then plug that value into either equation to solve for the other variable.

We can multiply the first equation by 2 and then add the two equations together.

$$\begin{aligned} 2x + 4y &= 8 \\ + \quad -2x + y &= 7 \\ \hline 5y &= 15 \end{aligned}$$

When we divide both sides of the result by 5, we see that $y = 3$. We can plug $y = 3$ into either equation to solve for x. We plugged $y = 3$ into the first equation in a previous solution; let's plug it into the second equation just to show that this process will work with either equation.

$$-2x + y = 7 \qquad \text{(second equation)}$$
$$-2x + 3 = 7 \qquad \text{(plug in } y = 3\text{)}$$
$$-2x = 4 \qquad \text{(subtract 3 from both sides)}$$
$$x = -2 \qquad \text{(divide both sides by } -2\text{)}$$

Again, the solution for the given system of equations is $(-2, 3)$, and (A) is right.

ANSWER CHOICE ANALYSIS

(B): This choice is valid in the first equation, but not in the second. The right answer needs to be valid in both equations. **(C):** This choice has the same problem as (B). **(D):** This has the same problem as (B) and (C). **(E):** Again, this has the same issue that we see in the other wrong answers.

How to check? Try an alternate approach above.

▶ Post-solution patterns (see p. 151): right approach, wrong step

▎Test 1, Question 20 (Test 2 in the 2020-2021 Red Book—see page 23 for more)

- **What's the prompt asking for?** The value of x that makes the equation in the prompt true.
- **Math concepts in the prompt:** log, variables

- **Elements of the choices:** Each choice is an even number.
- **Notable differences among choices:** (F), (G), and (H) form a series in which each choice is 2 more than the choice before it.

(F), (H), and (J) form a series in which each choice is twice as much as the choice before it.

- **Concepts in the choices:** adding 2, multiplying by 2
- **Pre-solution patterns (see p. 149):** halves and doubles

- **Things to look out for:** Don't make any small mistakes with your calculator! Don't make any mistakes when squaring the answer choices! Don't confuse log with multiplication or addition!

Solution 1: Calculator/Concrete: Evaluate each choice as x in the original equation. Pick the choice that results in a value of 2, as the prompt requires.

$\text{Log}_4\ 36 \approx 2.58$	(value from (F) plugged into the given expression)
$\text{Log}_6\ 36 = 2$	(value from (G) plugged into the given expression)
$\text{Log}_8\ 36 \approx 1.72$	(value from (H) plugged into the given expression)
$\text{Log}_{16}\ 36 \approx 1.29$	(value from (J) plugged into the given expression)
$\text{Log}_{18}\ 36 \approx 1.24$	(value from (K) plugged into the given expression)

Only the value from (G) matches the expression in the prompt, so (G) is right.

Solution 2: Calculator/Graphing: Graph the equation $y = \log_x 36$ and find the x-coordinate whose y-value is 2.

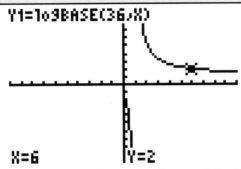

When we graph the expression from the prompt, we can see that $x = 6$ when $y = 2$. So the answer is 6, and (G) is right.

Solution 3: Abstract/Algebra: Recognize that the equation is asking for the number that can be squared to produce 36, and pick the appropriate choice.

If we understand logarithms, we know we can read the expression $\log_x 36 = 2$ as though it says "what number x, raised to the 2nd power, is equal to 36?" In other words, "what number can we square to get 36?" $6^2 = 36$, so the answer is 6, and (G) is right.

ANSWER CHOICE ANALYSIS

(F): This choice could be the result of misreading the original equation as $\log_x 16 = 2$. **(H):** This choice may be present to complete the series that includes (F) and (G). It could also reflect the result of combining the mistakes in (F) and (K): misreading the equation as $\log_x 16 = 2$, and assuming incorrectly that log is related to division rather than exponents. **(J):** This choice may attract test takers who correctly realize that the answer to the question is 6, and then misread this answer choice as 6 instead of 16. **(K):** This could reflect the mistake of confusing the idea of finding the square root with the idea of dividing by 2.

How to check? Try an alternate approach above.

▶   **Post-solution patterns (see p. 151):** right answer to the wrong question

---

Test 1, Question 21 (Test 2 in the 2020-2021 Red Book—see page 23 for more)

- **What's the prompt asking for?** The area of the photograph that was cut away to make it fit in the frame.
- **Math concepts in the prompt:** area, multiplication
- **Notable differences among choices:** (C) is the only odd number. (B), (C), and (D) form a series in which each choice is one more than the choice before it. (D) is half of (E). (D) is also the sum of (A) and (B).

- **Concepts in the choices:** addition, even numbers, multiplication, odd numbers
- **Pre-solution patterns (see p. 149):** halves and doubles
- **Things to look out for:** Don't confuse the two sets of dimensions! Don't make any small mistakes in your reading or calculations!

Solution 1: Geometry/Concrete: Sketch a 5×7 rectangle to represent the photograph, and then sketch a 4×6 rectangle inside it to represent the frame. Sketch in a line segment to divide the excess area into two rectangles. Find the area of each rectangle in the excess region, and add those areas to find the excess area of the photograph.

We can make a diagram of the picture and the size of the frame, like this:

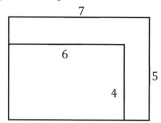

(Note that this is easier if we sketch the diagram so the rectangles share a corner, instead of centering one rectangle in the other.)

We can now find the area of the part of the photograph that was cut off. We'll draw in a dashed line to divide the part that was cut off into two rectangles, and then we'll add in the dimensions we know based on the information in the prompt.

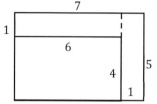

So we need to add the areas of a 1×5 rectangle (on the right side of the diagram) and a 1×6 rectangle (on the top of the diagram). (We know that the missing dimensions of these rectangles are both 1 because the difference between 6 and 7 is one and the difference between 4 and 5 is one.) That gives us $5 + 6$, or 11, so (C) is correct.

Solution 2: Geometry/Abstract: Determine the area of the smaller rectangle and subtract it from the area of the larger rectangle.

This question is essentially asking for the difference in area between the smaller rectangle and the larger rectangle. The area of the smaller rectangle will be 4×6, and the area of the larger rectangle will be 5×7. Subtracting the smaller area from the larger area gives us $(5 \times 7) - (4 \times 6) = 35 - 24 = 11$. So (C) is right.

Solution 3: Test-smart: Recognize that the right answer must be an odd number, and pick the only choice that's an odd number.

Once we know that we have to subtract one area from the other, and that one area will be odd and one area will be even, we know the result will be an odd number. Only (C) is odd, so (C) must be right.

ANSWER CHOICE ANALYSIS

(A): This is the difference between the sums of the dimensions for each rectangle, but the question asks us to consider the areas of the two rectangles; in order to do that, we have to multiply the width of each rectangle by its height, rather than adding those dimensions to each other. **(B):** This choice could be the result of trying Solution 1 above but forgetting about the 1-square-inch region in the upper right-hand corner of the sketch. **(D):** This could be the result of trying Solution 1 and accidentally counting the 1-square-inch region in the upper-right hand corner of the sketch twice—that is, counting it once when considering the horizontal strip of the picture that was cut away, and then accidentally counting it again when considering the vertical strip of the picture that was cut away. **(E):** This is the area of the frame itself, which means it's the area of the part of the picture that isn't cut away in the prompt. It could be here as a "right approach, wrong step" answer choice, or it could be meant to attract untrained test-takers who try a solution like 1 or 2 above and somehow get confused about which part of the picture is discarded and which part is kept.

How to check? Try an alternate approach above. Make sure you haven't misread the prompt or counted any portion of the picture the wrong number of times.

▶ **Post-solution patterns (see p. 151):** opposites; right approach, wrong step; right answer to the wrong question

Test 1, Question 22 (Test 2 in the 2020-2021 Red Book—see page 23 for more)

- **What's the prompt asking for?** The choice that must be true given the conditions in the prompt.

- **Math concepts in the prompt:** inequalities, lines, ordering, points

- **Elements of the choices:** Each choice is an inequality statement that says the length of the line segment on the left is shorter than the length of the one on the right.

- **Notable differences among choices:** AB only appears on the right-hand side of inequalities in the choices; (F), (G), and (J) all include it. (H) and (K) both have line segments on the right-hand side that also appear on the left-hand side in other

choices (CD and BC, respectively). BD only appears on the left-hand side of the inequalities; (G) and (H) both include it. CD appears on the left-hand side of the inequalities in (J) and (K), and on the right-hand side of (H).

- **Concepts in the choices:** inequalities, line segments

- **Pre-solution patterns (see p. 149):** wrong answers try to imitate right answers

- **Things to look out for:** Don't confuse the orders of the points! Don't assume that B must be the midpoint of AC just because the prompt says B is between A and C! Don't assume that D

must be the midpoint of BC just because D is between B and C! Remember that the right answer must be true in all configurations that satisfy the prompt—don't pick a choice just because it can sometimes be true! Don't misread the order of the points in the prompt, and don't misread the letters in the answer choices!

Solution 1: Geometry/Concrete: Sketch a variety of possible configurations of A, B, C, and D that conform to the prompt. Pick the only choice that accurately describes all of the configurations you've sketched.

Here's one possible orientation of the points described in the prompt:

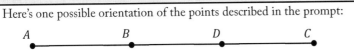

Let's see if we can eliminate any of the answer choices based on our sketch. (Remember that the distances between the points aren't mentioned in the prompt, only certain details about their order—so any distance between points in the diagram could be made larger or smaller as long as the information in the prompt about the order of the points isn't contradicted. Also, remember that the right answer is a statement that *must* be true, so if we can think of any situation that makes an answer choice not true without contradicting the information in the prompt, we can eliminate that answer choice.)

We can eliminate (F), because in our diagram we can clearly see that $\overline{BC}$ is larger than $\overline{AB}$. We can also eliminate (G), because we know that the prompt doesn't provide any details about the distance between different points. In our diagram, $\overline{BD}$ and $\overline{AB}$ look roughly equal, but we know that point B could appear to the right of its current position, in which case $\overline{AB}$ would be greater than $\overline{BD}$, or it could appear to the left of its current position, in which case $\overline{BD}$ would be greater than $\overline{AB}$. For example, the diagram could look like this:

Choice (H) has pretty much the same issue as (G). Point D could appear more to the left (closer to B) or more to the right (closer to C), which means this statement isn't necessarily true. The diagram could look like this without contradicting the prompt:

We can eliminate (J) as well, because the prompt doesn't provide any information about the distance between points C and D as compared to the distance between points A and B. The diagram could look like this, for example:

But the statement in choice (K) must be true. We can see in our diagram (which is based on information in the prompt) that point D appears between B and C. So no matter what the distance is between B and D as compared to the distance between D and C, $\overline{BC}$ must be longer than $\overline{CD}$ because $\overline{BC}$ *contains* $\overline{CD}$, plus the distance between B and D. After considering our diagram and each answer choice, we can be confident that (K) is right.

Solution 2: Geometry/Abstract: Think about the properties of the line segments referred to in the answer choices (AB, BC, BD, and CD). Pick the choice that reflects an unchangeable relationship among two of those four segments.

Three of the four line segments that appear in the answer choices ($\overline{AB}$, $\overline{BD}$, and $\overline{CD}$) consist of 2 points with no points between them, and only one ($\overline{BC}$) consists of 2 points with another point (D) between them. If we think about these different choices, and the fact that the prompt never provides any information about the distances between any points, the only one of the line segments in the answer choices that could be larger than another choice would be $\overline{BC}$, because it contains segments $\overline{BD}$ and $\overline{CD}$, and therefore must be larger than either of those segments individually. Choice (K) says that $\overline{CD}$ is smaller than $\overline{BC}$, so (K) must be right.

ANSWER CHOICE ANALYSIS

(F): This choice compares line segments formed by B and two points on either side of B, and there's no way for us to know from the prompt whether one of the points on either side of B is closer to B than the other. **(G):** This choice has an issue similar to the one we saw in (F): it compares two line segments that are defined by a single point (B) and by two points on either side of that point, so it's impossible to say that one segment must always be shorter or longer than the other according to the information in the prompt. **(H):** This choice has the same problem we see in (F) and (G), assuming that we've accurately read the prompt and placed the points in the order $ABDC$. But if we misread the prompt and/or assume that the points appear in the order $ABCD$, then that misreading could cause us to conclude that (H) was right (assuming we also misread the direction of the inequality in (H)). **(J):** This choice compares two line segments that don't overlap each other or have any endpoints in common; the prompt doesn't provide information that allows us to compare the lengths of these segments.

How to check? Try an alternate approach above. Also, since it would clearly be easy to misread the prompt or the answer choices and arrive at a wrong answer, make sure you've read everything accurately—both in the prompt and in the answer choices.

Note   Many untrained test-takers have a hard time with this question because they assume that the points must appear on the line in alphabetical order, even though the prompt says that D comes between B and C. This is one more great example of the extreme importance of critical reading skills across the entire ACT, including here on the math section. On test day, if it feels like a question just doesn't have a right answer (or if it seems to have more than one right answer), then you should get in the habit of re-reading everything to make sure you haven't misunderstood some key detail, no matter which section of the test you're working on.

Test 1, Question 23 (Test 2 in the 2020-2021 Red Book—see page 23 for more)

- **What's the prompt asking for?** The choice that could possibly be equal to y, according to the prompt.
- **Math concepts in the prompt:** cubing, greatest common factor, integers, positive numbers, squaring, variables
- **Notable differences among choices:** (A) is the product of (B) and (E), and it's also the product of (C) and (D). (B) is the product of (D) and (E). (D) and (E) are the only prime numbers in the answer choices. (C) is the only square number in the choices. (A), (B), and (D) form a series in which each choice is one-third of the choice before it.
- **Concepts in the choices:** multiplication, prime numbers, squaring
- **Pre-solution patterns (see p. 149):** be aware of series
- **Things to look out for:** Don't accidentally find the value of x! Don't accidentally find the value of either of the algebraic expressions in the prompt! Don't make any other small mistakes in your reading and calculations!

Solution 1: Concrete/Backsolving: Try each answer choice as the value of y under the conditions in the prompt. Pick the only choice that makes the situation in the prompt possible.

The greatest common factor of x^2y^2 and xy^3 is xy^2, so according to the prompt, $xy^2 = 45$. If one of the answer choices could be equal to y, then that means we could square that answer choice and multiply it by x to get 45. (Remember that the prompt says x is a positive integer.) Let's take a look at each answer choice.

(A) $45^2 = 2025$. We can't multiply 2025 by a positive integer to get 45, so (A) is wrong.

(B) $15^2 = 225$. We can't multiply 225 by a positive integer to get 45, so (B) is wrong.

(C) $9^2 = 81$. We can't multiply 81 by a positive integer to get 45, so (C) is wrong.

(D) $5^2 = 25$. We can't multiply 25 by a positive integer to get 45, so (D) is wrong.

(E) $3^2 = 9$. We _can_ multiply 9 by a positive integer to get 45, because $9 \times 5 = 45$, and 5 is a positive integer.

So (E) is the right answer.

Solution 2: Abstract/Algebra: Determine how to express 45 in terms of x and y, and use that information to find y.

As we saw in the previous solution, the greatest common factor of x^2y^2 and xy^3 is xy^2, so $xy^2 = 45$. In other words, it must be possible to multiply x by y^2 to get 45. If we think of some squares, like 1, 4, 9, 16, 25, and so on, we can see that one square that we could multiply by a positive integer to get 45 would be 9, because $9 \times 5 = 45$.

So y^2 can equal 9, which means y could equal 3. That means (E) is right.

(Note that y could also equal 1, according to the information in the prompt—but 1 doesn't appear in the answer choices, so we don't really need to consider it.)

ANSWER CHOICE ANALYSIS

(A): This choice will be tempting to test-takers who thought the greatest common factor was y, but as we discussed above, the greatest common factor is xy^2. **(B):** This is the value of xy, which might attract some test-takers who misread the prompt. It could also attract test-takers who mistakenly think that xy is the greatest common factor, and see this as a possible value for y. **(C):** This is y^2, which is a number that you might find on the way to identifying y itself. This choice will attract a lot of untrained test-takers who correctly understand the concepts in the question but don't pay attention to what the prompt actually asks them for. **(D):** This is the value of x when $y = 3$. It will attract untrained test-takers who misread the prompt, or who confuse x and y at some point while they're working on the question.

How to check? Try an alternate approach above. Since each choice represents some number that's clearly relevant to the concepts and expressions in the prompt, double-check your answer to make sure it's what the prompt is asking you to find.

▶ **Post-solution patterns (see p. 151):** right answer to the wrong question

Test 1, Question 24 (Test 2 in the 2020-2021 Red Book—see page 23 for more)

- **What's the prompt asking for?** The choice that accurately describes the scenario in the prompt.
- **Math concepts in the prompt:** bias, control groups, placebo, ranges, testing
- **Elements of the choices:** Each choice consists entirely of text.
- **Notable differences among choices:** (F), (G), and (J) involve the word "randomized," while (H) and (K) both involve the word "nonrandomized." (G) and (H) use the word "experiment," while (J) and (K) use the phrase "sample survey," and (F) is the only choice that uses the word "census."
- **Concepts in the choices:** censuses, experiments, randomness, sampling, surveys

- **Pre-solution patterns (see p. 149):** wrong answers try to imitate right answers
- **Things to look out for:** Don't misread any of the text in the prompt or the answer choices!

Solution 1: Reading comprehension: Carefully read the prompt and the answer choices, and pick the choice whose words are demonstrated in the prompt, just as you would for a Reading, English, or Science question.

Every choice begins with the word "randomized" or "nonrandomized." The prompt says that 150 balls were chosen out of 300 balls "without bias." The phrase "without bias" in this context means the same thing as saying the balls were chosen randomly, so we know the right answer should begin with the word "randomized." That eliminates (H) and (K).

The remaining choices end with the word "census," "experiment," or "survey." The prompt describes how 150 people were given a drug, another 150 people were given a placebo, and then 2 weeks later, the two groups were compared. This is a description of an experiment, as described in (G), so (G) is right. Note that "census" and "survey" both describe a process involving asking people questions, which isn't described in the prompt. Also note that we don't need to know what a "placebo" is to be able to answer the question; we can tell from context that a placebo is something different from a drug, which is enough for us to recognize the description of an experiment.

ANSWER CHOICE ANALYSIS

(F): The word "census" makes this choice wrong, because a census is a specialized kind of survey in which the members of a population are counted, and detailed information is gathered about some of them. The prompt doesn't describe this kind of process, so (F) can't be right.
(H): The word "nonrandomized" makes this choice wrong because the prompt clearly describes half of the volunteers being chosen by a computer simulation "without bias," which means the process is randomized. **(J):** This choice is wrong because of the word "survey," which would describe a process in which members of a population provide information about themselves. But in the prompt, the volunteers are only described as taking medicine or a placebo—the prompt doesn't describe them answering questions. **(K):** This choice combines the issues in (H) and (J).

How to check? Carefully re-read the entire question, paying strict attention the meanings of the terms in the answer choices.

Note This question is an extreme example of the way the ACT often likes to ask math questions that don't involve any kind of calculation or formulas. Keep this in mind on test day! You won't always use the same kinds of math techniques on the ACT that you'd use in a classroom setting!

Test 1, Question 25 (Test 2 in the 2020-2021 Red Book—see page 23 for more)

- **What's the prompt asking for?** The number of seconds until the two signs flash at the same time again.
- **Math concepts in the prompt:** multiples of 10, multiples of 4
- **Notable differences among choices:** (C) is twice as much as (B), and (E) is twice as much as (D).
- **Concepts in the choices:** multiplying by 2

- **Pre-solution patterns (see p. 149):** halves and doubles
- **Things to look out for:** Make sure that you find the amount of time until the very next moment when the lights flash at the same time, instead of just any amount of time after which they'll flash at the same time again! Don't make any small mistakes in your reading or calculations!

Solution 1: Concrete/Diagram: Make a timeline showing the numbers of seconds at which each light will flash, and use it to determine the first time at which both lights will flash together.

We'll call the "certain instant" when the signs flash at the same time 0 seconds, and we'll make an "X" on the timelines each time one of the lights flashes:

0	1	2	3	4	5	6	7	8	9	10	11	12	13	14	15	16	17	18	19	20	21	22	23
X				X				X				X				X				X			
X										X										X			

We can see that the first time after 0 seconds that both lights flash at the same time is at 20 seconds, so (D) is right.

Solution 2: Concrete/Arithmetic: List out the number of seconds at which each light will flash, and use that information to determine the first time at which both lights will flash together.

Let's call the "certain instant" when the signs flash at the same time 0 seconds. The sign that flashes every 4 seconds will flash at 0, 4, 8, 12, 16, 20, 24, 28, 32, 36, and 40 seconds (and more, but we'll stop there and see if that's enough). The sign that flashes every 10 seconds will flash at 0, 10, 20, 30, and 40 seconds, and so on. We can see that the next time after 0 seconds that they will flash at the same time will be at 20 seconds. So (D) is right.

Solution 3: Abstract/Arithmetic: Pick the choice that reflects the least common multiple of 4 and 10.

We know that the right answer will have to be a multiple of both 4 and 10, so we can eliminate (A), (B), and (C). We also know that the prompt asks for the "next time" that the signs flash at the same time, so we need to pick the smallest number that's a multiple of 4 and 10. That's 20, so (D) is right.

ANSWER CHOICE ANALYSIS

(A): This is the difference between the numbers of seconds after which each light will flash, but that isn't relevant to what the question asked us to find. This choice could reflect the fundamental misunderstanding or misreading of the prompt. **(B):** This is the average of the lengths of time between flashes of each light, so it may tempt untrained test-takers who try to set up some kind of algebraic expression for this question. But neither light will be flashing 7 seconds after the first time the two lights flash simultaneously, because 7 isn't a multiple of 4 or 10. **(C):** This choice is the sum of the two lengths of time described in the prompt, but it's not a time when either light will be flashing, so it can't be the right answer to the question. **(E):** This choice does represent a number of seconds at which both lights will flash, but it's not the *next* time the lights will flash, which is what the prompt requires. This will trap a lot of untrained test-takers who don't realize that the lights will also flash simultaneously after only 20 seconds.

How to check? Try an alternate approach above. Be especially careful to make sure that your answer reflects a time when both lights will flash, and that there are no choices with lower numbers that also reflect a time when both lights will flash.

Test 1, Question 26 (Test 2 in the 2020-2021 Red Book—see page 23 for more)

- **What's the prompt asking for?** The choice that always produces a negative value no matter which nonzero values of a and b are used.

- **Math concepts in the prompt:** negative numbers, nonzero numbers, variables

- **Elements of the choices:** Each choice is an algebraic expression that uses a once and b once.

- **Notable differences among choices:** (H), (J), and (K) involve absolute value brackets, while (F) and (G) don't. (H) involves adding the b-term, while the other choices involve subtracting

it. (G) and (K) involve negative signs with the a-term, while the other choices don't.

- **Concepts in the choices:** absolute value, addition, negative numbers, subtraction

- **Pre-solution patterns (see p. 149):** wrong answers try to imitate right answers; opposites

- **Things to look out for:** Don't forget that the prompt allows for values of a and b that can be either positive or negative! Don't misread any of the answer choices, even though they're similar to one another!

Solution 1: Concrete/Backsolving: Pick an array of arbitrary values for a and b, and test them in the answer choices until only one choice produces negative values for all of your test pairs.

Let $a = 2$ and $b = 3$.

$a - b$	(expression from (F))
$2 - 3$	(plug in $a = 2$ and $b = 3$)
-1	(simplify)

So the statement in (F) is negative when $a = 2$ and $b = 3$. But we need to find an answer choice that is *always* negative, and we don't know yet if the statement in (F) is *always* negative. Let's check the other choices.

$-a - b$	(expression from (G))
$-2 - 3$	(plug in $a = 2$ and $b = 3$)
-5	(simplify)

The statement in (G) is also negative when $a = 2$ and $b = 3$. Let's check the remaining answer choices.

$|a| + |b|$	(expression from (H))
$|2| + |3|$	(plug in $a = 2$ and $b = 3$)
5	(simplify)

The statement in (H) is positive when $a = 2$ and $b = 3$, so (H) can't be correct.

$|a| - |b|$	(expression from (J))
$|2| - |3|$	(plug in $a = 2$ and $b = 3$)
-1	(simplify)

The statement in (J) is negative when $a = 2$ and $b = 3$.

$-|a| - |b|$	(expression from (K))
$-|2| - |3|$	(plug in $a = 2$ and $b = 3$)
-5	(simplify)

The statement in (K) is negative when $a = 2$ and $b = 3$.

So the statements in (F), (G), (J), and (K) were all negative when $a = 2$ and $b = 3$. We need to pick new values for a and b. Let's try an a value that's bigger than the b value, since we can see that this will at least rule out choice (F).

(Bear in mind that we don't need to check choice (H) because we've already ruled it out.)

Let $a = 6$ and $b = 4$.

$a - b$	(expression from (F))
$6 - 4$	(plug in $a = 6$ and $b = 4$)
2	(simplify)

The statement in (F) is positive when $a = 6$ and $b = 4$, so we can rule this choice out. Let's look at (G).

$-a - b$	(expression from (G))
$-6 - 4$	(plug in $a = 6$ and $b = 4$)
-10	(simplify)

The statement in (G) is negative when $a = 6$ and $b = 4$. Let's check (J).

$|a| - |b|$	(expression from (J))
$|6| - |4|$	(plug in $a = 6$ and $b = 4$)
2	(simplify)

The statement in (J) is positive when $a = 6$ and $b = 4$. We can rule this choice out, too. Let's check (K).

$-|a| - |b|$	(expression from (K))
$-|6| - |4|$	(plug in $a = 6$ and $b = 4$)
-10	(simplify)

The statement in (K) is negative when $a = 6$ and $b = 4$.

Now we've narrowed it down to (G) and (K). We haven't tried any negative numbers yet, so let's try $a = -2$ and $b = -3$.

$-a - b$	(expression from (G))
$-(-2) - (-3)$	(plug in $a = -2$ and $b = -3$)
5	(simplify)

The statement in (G) is positive when $a = -2$ and $b = -3$. We can rule out (G).

$-|a| - |b|$	(expression from (K))
$-|-2| - |-3|$	(plug in $a = -2$ and $b = -3$)
-5	(simplify)

The statement in (K) is negative when $a = -2$ and $b = -3$.

We found values that make (F), (G), (H), and (J) positive, so (K) must be the right answer.

Solution 2: Abstract/Algebra: Consider the attributes of the concepts in the answer choices and identify the choice that must always produce negative numbers.

(F): This will only produce negative numbers when b is a larger number than a, but the prompt requires us to pick the choice that would produce negative values for *all* nonzero values of a and b, so this choice is wrong.

(G): This choice will produce negative numbers when a and b are both positive, or when a is positive and b is negative and the absolute value of b is less than the absolute value of a. But the prompt requires us to find the choice that produces a negative value for *all* nonzero values of a and b—even when, for example, a and b are both negative numbers.

(H): This choice will always produce a positive number, because it involves adding two nonzero absolute-value quantities, which must be positive by definition. An untrained test-taker might pick this choice if she accidentally thought the prompt was asking for the expression that would produce a *positive* number no matter what, instead of the one that would produce a *negative* number no matter what.

(J): This choice will only produce a negative number when the absolute value of b is greater than the absolute value of a, but, as we saw with (F), the prompt requires an expression that will produce only negative numbers for *all* nonzero values of a and b, even when their absolute values are equal, or when the absolute value of a is greater than the absolute value of b.

(K): This choice will always produce negative numbers, because it starts by taking the absolute value of a—which must be a positive value—then taking the opposite of that positive value—which must be a negative value. Then the expression subtracts the absolute value of b. In other words, this expression will always result in subtracting a positive value from an already negative number, which must always be negative. So (K) is right.

ANSWER CHOICE ANALYSIS

See Solution 2 above.

How to check? Try an alternate approach above. Carefully re-check your assumptions and/or calculations with respect to positivity and negativity, and make sure you've considered every possible combination of a-values and b-values, as the prompt requires.

Test 1, Question 27 (Test 2 in the 2020-2021 Red Book—see page 23 for more)

- **What's the prompt asking for?** The number of points of intersection of the two figures described in the prompt.

- **Math concepts in the prompt:** axis of symmetry, center of a circle, circles, graphing in the xy-coordinate plane, intersection, parabolas, radii, vertex of a parabola

- **Elements of the choices:** The choices form a series

of integers from 0 to 4 inclusive.

- **Concepts in the choices:** one, zero

- **Pre-solution patterns (see p. 149):** halves and doubles

- **Things to look out for:** Don't confuse the details of the circle with the details of the parabola! Don't misread any of the coordinates in the prompt! Don't miscount the point of intersection!

Solution 1: Graphing: Sketch the figures described in the prompt and determine the number of points of intersection.

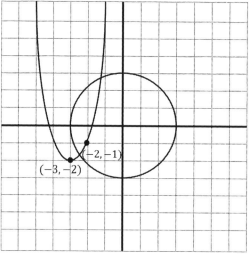

We can see that the circle and parabola intersect at 2 points, so (C) is right.

ANSWER CHOICE ANALYSIS

(A): This could reflect a somewhat large mistake in graphing that might cause an untrained test-taker to graph the two figures so they're too far apart from each other, such as misreading the prompt and thinking the circle had a radius of 1, which would lead to the conclusion that the two figures don't intersect. **(B):** This choice could be the result of accidentally overlooking one of the points of intersection while you were counting, or of not seeing one of the points of intersection because you didn't fully sketch out the entire circle or a large enough portion of the parabola.

How to check? Carefully reconsider your reading, your assumptions, your graphing, and your counting, since the answer choices make it clear that the ACT expects that some test-takers will miscount by one or two points.

Note   Many untrained test-takers who see this question will assume incorrectly that they need to figure out the equations for the two figures described in the prompt, because most high school math questions about the intersections of two figures involve using the equations for those figures to identify the specific coordinates of the points of intersection. But this question never asks us to identify the specific locations of the points of intersection! All it asks us to do is figure out how many of those points must exist, which is a much easier task and doesn't require any knowledge of the equations for the figures. Remember this kind of thing on test day—we always want to read every question carefully and consider it on its own terms, rather than leaping to a conclusion about what the question seems to be asking without actually reading it.

Test 1, Question 28 (Test 2 in the 2020-2021 Red Book—see page 23 for more)

- **What's the prompt asking for?** The number that produces the same result when multiplied by 0.6 that 250 produces when multiplied by 0.4.

- **Math concepts in the prompt:** percentages

- **Notable differences among choices:** (H) is the only choice that involves a fraction.

- **Concepts in the choices:** fractions

- **Things to look out for:** Don't accidentally find 40% of 60 or 40% of one of the answer choices! Don't accidentally find 60% of 250! Don't make any small mistakes in your reading or calculations!

Solution 1: Arithmetic/Backsolving: Find 40% of 250. Then find 60% of each answer choice, and pick the choice that produces the same result as 40% of 250.

$$250 \times 0.4 = 100 \qquad \text{(find 40\% of 250)}$$

Now let's find 60% of each answer choice and see which one gives a result of 100:

(F) $150 \times 0.6 = 90$

(G) $160 \times 0.6 = 96$

(H) $166\frac{2}{3} \times 0.6 = 100$

(J) $270 \times 0.6 = 162$

(K) $375 \times 0.6 = 225$

We found that 60% of (H) is 100, so (H) is right.

Solution 2: Algebra: Create an algebraic statement equating 40% of 250 to 60% of an unknown number, and solve for the unknown number.

$250 \times 0.4 = 0.6x$	(equation based on the prompt)
$100 = 0.6x$	(simplify)
$166.6666666 \approx x$	(divide both sides by 0.6)

So we can see that (H) is right.

Solution 3: Test-smart: Note that the right answer must involve a fraction, and pick the only choice that satisfies that requirement.

Once we realize that we need to figure out what number 100 is "60% of," we might notice that the result has to involve a fraction or decimal, since 100 won't divide by 0.6 evenly. Only (H) satisfies this requirement, so (H) is right.

ANSWER CHOICE ANALYSIS

(F): This is 60% of 250, which could be the result of misreading the prompt, or of an algebra mistake when trying Solution 2 above. **(G):** This is the result of finding 40% of 250, and then finding 160% of the result, which could reflect a misreading of the prompt or an algebra error when attempting Solution 2 above. **(J):** This could reflect the mistake of assuming that the right answer must be 20 more than 250 because the second percentage is 20 more than the first percentage. **(K):** This reflects the mistake of assuming that the right answer must be 50% greater than 250 because the second percentage is 50% more than the first percentage. It could also be the result of trying Solution 2 above but accidentally setting up the equation $250 \times 0.6 = 0.4x$, rather than the equation $250 \times 0.4 = 0.6x$.

How to check? Try an alternate approach above. Note that the right answer must be less than 250, because the prompt describes taking a larger percentage from the second number than the first, which means the second number must be smaller than the first number in order for the results to come out equal. Also note that the right answer must involve a fraction in order to allow us to multiply 60% by the number and arrive at 100.

Test 1, Question 29 (Test 2 in the 2020-2021 Red Book—see page 23 for more)

- **What's the prompt asking for?** The choice containing a statement that's equivalent to the one in the prompt.
- **Math concepts in the prompt:** algebra, inequalities, negative numbers, subtraction
- **Elements of the choices:** Each choice is an inequality statement that begins with x and ends with 2.
- **Notable differences among choices:** (A), (C), and (D) all involve a less-than sign, while (B) and (E) involve a greater-than sign. (A) and (B) both have -4 as the coefficient of y, while (D) and (E) have 4 as the coefficient of y, and (C) is the only choice with 2 as a coefficient of y.

- **Concepts in the choices:** addition, algebra, inequalities, negative numbers
- **Pre-solution patterns (see p. 149):** wrong answers try to imitate right answers; halves and doubles; opposites
- **Things to look out for:** Don't make a mistake with respect to the signs of numbers! Remember to reverse the direction of the inequality symbol if your algebra requires you to multiply or divide every term in the inequality by a negative number! Don't forget that there are y-terms on both sides of the inequality in the prompt! Don't make any small mistakes in your reading or algebra!

Solution 1: Algebra: Isolate x on the left-hand side of the given inequality, and pick the choice that matches your result.

$-2x - 6y > 2y - 4$	(given inequality)
$-2x > 8y - 4$	(add $6y$ to both sides)
$x < -4y + 2$	(divide both sides by -2 and reverse inequality sign)

This matches (A), so (A) is right.

ANSWER CHOICE ANALYSIS

(B): This choice reflects the mistake of not reversing the direction of the inequality symbol when dividing by -2 during Solution 1 above. **(C):** This reflects the mistake of subtracting $6y$ from $2y$ while trying Solution 1 above, which would result in the inequality $-2x > -4y - 4$, ultimately producing the inequality in this choice. **(D):** This choice is similar to (C), but reflects a different mistake when combining y-terms during Solution 1: writing $-8y$ on the right-hand side of the inequality as the result of adding $6y$ and $2y$. **(E):** This choice is a combination of the mistakes in (B) and (D).

How to check? Be especially careful when it comes to the direction of the inequality symbol, the sign of the y coefficient, and whether the *y* coefficient should involve 4 or 2, since the answer choices clearly indicate that the ACT expects test takers to make mistakes when considering those issues.

Test 1, Question 30 (Test 2 in the 2020-2021 Red Book—see page 23 for more)

- **What's the prompt asking for?** The cosine of α according to the prompt.

- **Math concepts in the prompt:** angles, cosine, fractions, right triangles, sine, tangent

- **Elements of the choices:** Each choice is a fraction with 9 either in the numerator or the denominator.

- **Notable differences among choices:** (F) and (G) are reciprocals of one another. (J) and (K) have radical expressions in their denominators, while the other choices only have integers in their numerators and denominators. (G) is the only choice with nine in the denominator instead of the numerator.

- **Concepts in the choices:** fractions, radical expressions, reciprocals

- **Pre-solution patterns (see p. 149):** wrong answers try to imitate right answers; opposites

- **Things to look out for:** Don't confuse the numerators and denominators of the fractions in the question, or the ratios in SOHCAHTOA! Don't confuse the trig functions in the prompt!

Solution 1: Trigonometry: Use SOHCAHTOA to determine the lengths of the sides of the triangle in the prompt, and then use the side lengths to construct the fraction that represents $\cos \alpha$.

We know from SOHCAHTOA that $Sine = \frac{Opposite}{Hypotenuse}$, $Cosine = \frac{Adjacent}{Hypotenuse}$, and $Tangent = \frac{Opposite}{Adjacent}$. If we want to find $\cos \alpha$, we need to know the proportion of the adjacent side to the hypotenuse. The adjacent side is the denominator in the tangent fraction, which the prompt tells us is 9, and the hypotenuse is the denominator in the sine fraction, which the prompt tells us is 41. So $\cos \alpha = \frac{9}{41}$, which means (F) is right.

Solution 2: Calculator: Use $\sin^{-1}$ or $\tan^{-1}$ to find α directly, and then find $\cos \alpha$. Finally, use your calculator to find numerical equivalents for each fraction in the answer choices, and then pick the choice whose value is equal to the value you found for $\cos \alpha$.

We can use our calculators to find that $\sin^{-1}\left(\frac{40}{41}\right) = 77.31961651$. Then we can find the cosine of that value, which gives us $\cos(77.31961651) = 0.2195121951$. Now let's find decimal equivalents of each choice to see which one is 0.2195121951:

(F) $\frac{9}{41} = 0.2195121951$

(G) $\frac{41}{9} = 4.\overline{5}$

(H) $\frac{9}{40} = 0.225$

(J) $\frac{9}{\sqrt{1,519}} = 0.2309211026$

(K) $\frac{9}{\sqrt{3,281}} = 0.1571228667$

We can see that (F) is equal to 0.2195121951, so (F) is right.

ANSWER CHOICE ANALYSIS

(G): This is the reciprocal of the correct answer, so it will attract test takers who try to use Solution 1 above but accidentally use the hypotenuse for the numerator and the adjacent side for the denominator. (Remember that, by definition, the cosine or sine of an angle must be less than 1, which means this choice can't possibly be the right answer.) **(H):** This is the reciprocal of the tangent of α (also known as the cotangent of α), which isn't what the prompt asked for. It could reflect a mistaken application of SOHCAHTOA in which the denominator of the fraction is the length of the opposite side, instead of the hypotenuse. **(J):** The number in the radical expression for this choice is the result of squaring 40 and then subtracting 9^2. There's no need to do this because the information in the prompt makes it clear that the hypotenuse of the right triangle is 41—and, even if that weren't the case, the idea of subtracting the square of the length of one side of a triangle from the square of the length of another side isn't relevant to anything in this question. **(K):** The number in the radical expression for this choice is the sum of the squares of 40 and 41, reflecting a mistake in recreating the right triangle in the prompt using SOHCAHTOA and the given values for α. The hypotenuse of the right triangle in the prompt is 41; there's no need to square 40 and 41 and add them together in an attempt to find that hypotenuse (and doing so won't give you the length of the hypotenuse anyway).

How to check? Try an alternate approach above. Be especially careful to make sure that you apply SOHCAHTOA correctly if you try an approach like Solution 1 above, because the similarities and differences among the answer choices make it clear that the ACT expects a lot of people to make that kind of mistake on this question.

▶ **Post-solution patterns (see p. 151):** most like the other choices; right answer to the wrong question

Note Solution 2 above may strike some people as unnecessarily complicated, but I mention it here for two reasons. First, it actually makes it easier to avoid falling for any of the wrong answer choices in the question, because those choices are all based on the expectation that an untrained test-taker will apply SOHCAHTOA incorrectly. Second, I want to keep making it clear that it's smart to look for novel approaches to questions, and those novel approaches will sometimes involve using a calculator in a way that wouldn't be rewarded in a classroom setting.

Test 1, Question 31 (Test 2 in the 2020-2021 Red Book—see page 23 for more)

- **What's the prompt asking for?** The length of $\overline{AB}$.
- **Math concepts in the prompt:** perimeter, ratios, rectangles
- **Elements of the choices:** Each choice is a multiple of 6.
- **Notable differences among choices:** (B) is half of (D), and (C) is half of (E). (B) is 3 times as much as (A) and (C) is 5 times as much as (A), which may be relevant because the question mentions a 3:5 ratio, suggesting that we may need to multiply or divide by 3 and by 5 at some point in order to find the answer. (A), (B), and (C) form a series in which each choice is

12 more than the choice before it.

- **Concepts in the choices:** Multiplying 6 by some combination of 3, 5, and/or 2.
- **Pre-solution patterns (see p. 149):** halves and doubles
- **Things to look out for:** Don't accidentally find the length of the wrong side! Don't confuse the two parts of the ratio! Don't forget that 96 is the perimeter of the entire rectangle, not the sum of $\overline{AB}$ and $\overline{BC}$! Don't make any small mistakes in your reading or calculations!

Solution 1: Algebra: Write an equation that compares $\overline{AB}$ to $\overline{BC}$ and to 96, and solve it to find $\overline{AB}$.

We'll use w (for "width") to represent $\overline{AB}$, and l (for "length") to represent $\overline{BC}$. (Note that it doesn't matter which we call the length and which we call the width, as long as we keep them straight, and remember that the question asks for the length of $\overline{AB}$.)

We know that the perimeter of a rectangle is the sum of the lengths of its sides, which is the same as twice the width of the rectangle added to twice the length of the rectangle, which is the same as $2w + 2l$. The prompt tells us that the perimeter of the rectangle is 96, so we know that $2w + 2l = 96$. The prompt also tells us that the ratio of $\overline{AB}$ to $\overline{BC}$ is 3:5, which means the ratio of w to l is 3:5. We can express this as $\frac{w}{l} = \frac{3}{5}$. Remember that the prompt wants us to find the length of $\overline{AB}$, and that w represents $\overline{AB}$. So let's solve for l in terms of w in one equation, then plug the result into the other equation and solve for w.

$$\frac{w}{l} = \frac{3}{5} \qquad \text{(second equation we found)}$$

$$5w = 3l \qquad \text{(cross-multiply)}$$

$$\frac{5w}{3} = l \qquad \text{(divide both sides by 3)}$$

We can now plug $l = \frac{5w}{3}$ into the first equation:

$$2w + 2l = 96 \qquad \text{(first equation we found)}$$

$$2w + 2\left(\frac{5w}{3}\right) = 96 \qquad \text{(plug in } l = \frac{5w}{3}\text{)}$$

$$2w + \frac{10w}{3} = 96 \qquad \text{(simplify)}$$

$$6w + 10w = 288 \qquad \text{(multiply both sides by 3)}$$

$$16w = 288 \qquad \text{(simplify)}$$

$$w = 18 \qquad \text{(divide both sides by } w\text{)}$$

So the length of $\overline{AB}$ is 18 centimeters, and (B) is the right answer.

Solution 2: Backsolve: Try each choice as the length of $\overline{AB}$, and see which choice results in a rectangle with a perimeter of 96, as the prompt requires.

The prompt tells us that the perimeter of the rectangle is 96 centimeters. We know that the perimeter of a rectangle is the sum of the lengths of its sides, which is the same as twice the width of the rectangle added to twice the length of the rectangle, which is the same as $2w + 2l$. So we know that $2w + 2l = 96$.

The prompt tells us that the ratio of $\overline{AB}$ to $\overline{BC}$ is 3:5, so we can multiply $\overline{AB}$ by $\frac{5}{3}$ to get $\overline{BC}$. That means we can multiply the length of $\overline{AB}$ in each answer choice by $\frac{5}{3}$ to get the corresponding $\overline{BC}$ value. If the answer is correct, we'll be able to add twice the $\overline{AB}$ value to twice the $\overline{BC}$ value to get 96, the perimeter of the rectangle.

(A) $6 \times \frac{5}{3} = 10$	$2(6) + 2(10) = 32$
(B) $18 \times \frac{5}{3} = 30$	$2(18) + 2(30) = 96$
(C) $30 \times \frac{5}{3} = 50$	$2(30) + 2(50) = 160$
(D) $36 \times \frac{5}{3} = 60$	$2(36) + 2(60) = 192$
(E) $60 \times \frac{5}{3} = 100$	$2(60) + 2(100) = 320$

Only (B) results in a $\overline{BC}$ value that would generate a perimeter of 96, so (B) is right.

Solution 3: Test-smart: Consider the lengths of the sides if the rectangle were a square, and use this information along with the information in the prompt to select the only possible choice.

If the rectangle described in the prompt were a square, then each side would be 24 centimeters long, because $\frac{96}{4} = 24$. The prompt tells us that the ratio of $\overline{AB}$ to $\overline{BC}$ is $3:5$, so $\overline{AB}$ must be a little smaller than $\overline{BC}$. That means $\overline{AB}$ must be a little less than 24. Only (B) meets this requirement, so (B) is right.

ANSWER CHOICE ANALYSIS

(A): This choice is the greatest common factor of the lengths of $\overline{AB}$ and $\overline{BC}$, so it's a number that you might run across in a more formal algebraic solution, but it isn't the answer to the question in the prompt. To find the length of $\overline{AB}$, we need to multiply this choice by 3, since $\overline{AB}$ is the shorter of the two sides in the $3:5$ ratio described in the prompt. **(C):** This is the length of $\overline{BC}$, but the question asked us to find the length of $\overline{AB}$. A lot of untrained test-takers will pick this choice because they forgot which side's length the prompt asked us to find, or because they accidentally reversed the ratio in the prompt. **(D):** This choice is twice as much as the right answer. It would be the answer to the question if the sum of the lengths of $\overline{AB}$ and $\overline{BC}$ themselves were 96, but we have to remember that 96 is the perimeter of the *entire* rectangle, which means that $\overline{AB}$ and $\overline{BC}$ only add up to 48. **(E):** This choice combines the mistakes from (C) and (D) above: it corresponds to the larger value in the ratio instead of the smaller one, and it forgets that the two sides in the prompt must add up to 48, not 96.

How to check? Try an alternate approach above. Be especially careful not to reverse the ratio in the prompt or forget that 96 is the perimeter of the entire rectangle, not the sum of $\overline{AB}$ and $\overline{BC}$.

▶ **Post-solution patterns (see p. 151):** right approach, wrong step; opposites; right answer to the wrong question

Test 1, Question 32 (Test 2 in the 2020-2021 Red Book—see page 23 for more)

- **What's the prompt asking for?** The side length of a square whose area is equal to the area of $\triangle ABC$.

- **Math concepts in the prompt:** altitude, area of a square, area of a triangle, base of a triangle, triangles

- **Math concepts in the diagram:** altitude, base of a triangle, isosceles triangles, right triangles

- **Elements of the choices:** Each choice is an even number.

- **Notable differences among choices:** (F) is half of (H). (G) is half of (J), which is half of (K).

- **Concepts in the choices:** Multiplying and dividing by 2.

- **Pre-solution patterns (see p. 149):** halves and doubles

- **Things to look out for:** Don't find the area of the wrong triangle! Don't confuse the dimensions in the diagram! Don't forgot that the question is asking for the side length of the square, not for the area of the square! Don't make any small mistakes in your calculations!

Solution 1: Geometry: Find the area of $\triangle ABC$. Then find the square root of that area.

$$\frac{1}{2}bh \qquad \text{(area of a triangle)}$$
$$\frac{1}{2}(16)(8) \qquad \text{(plug in 16 for the base and 8 for the height)}$$
$$64 \qquad \text{(simplify)}$$

The area of the triangle is 64 square inches, so the area of the square is 64 square inches. We find the area of a square by squaring the length of a side, so the length of one side of this square is the square root of 64, or 8 inches. That means (G) is right.

Solution 2: Geometry/Test-smart: Note that $\triangle ABD$ can be "rotated" about point B so that it forms a square with $\triangle BCD$, and that the resulting square has a side length of 8 inches.

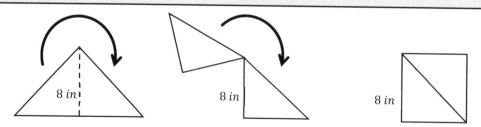

We can see that if we split this triangle into two triangles along the dashed line, we could make a square with a side length of 8 inches. So the right answer is (G).

ANSWER CHOICE ANALYSIS

(F): This choice could reflect a fundamental misunderstanding of the concepts in the question, because it would be the result of adding the two numbers in the diagram and dividing by four. The idea of dividing by four might seem to be related to the idea of a square, since a square has four sides, but finding the side length of a square from its area involves taking the square root of the area, not dividing the area into four equal parts. More importantly, there's no reason to think that the area of any figure in the question would be found by adding two given numbers together. Perimeters are found through addition, but areas are found through multiplication. **(H):** This choice could be the result of adding the two numbers in the diagram together and dividing by two, which might be a misguided attempt to find the area of $\triangle ABC$. The formula for the area of the triangle involves multiplying base by height, not adding the base to the height. More importantly, the question didn't ask us to find the area of $\triangle ABC$; it essentially asked us to find the square root of that area. **(J):** This choice could reflect the mistake of dividing the area of $\triangle ABC$ by four—rather than finding the square root of the area—which might happen if a test-taker confuses the area and perimeter of a square. **(K):** This choice could reflect a calculator mistake, because it's half of the area of $\triangle ABC$, rather than the square root of the area. It could also reflect a misreading of the question, because 32 is the perimeter of the square referred to in the prompt—not the side length of that square, which is what the prompt asked for.

> **How to check?** Try an alternate approach above. Be especially careful that you're not off by a factor of two, since the choices are clearly trying to set us up to make that kind of a mistake. Also make sure you're answering the specific question the prompt asked.

▶ **Post-solution patterns (see p. 151):** right answer to the wrong question

Test 1, Question 33 (Test 2 in the 2020-2021 Red Book—see page 23 for more)

- **What's the prompt asking for?** The percentage of $\overline{AD}$ that's represented by $\overline{EH}$.
- **Math concepts in the prompt:** diameter, dimension labels, midpoints, percentages, rectangles, semicircles, squares
- **Math concepts in the diagram:** diameter, dimension labels, midpoints, rectangles, semicircles, squares
- **Elements of the choices:** Each choice is a percentage between 0% and 50%.

- **Notable differences among choices:** (A) and (D) both involve decimal points, while the other choices don't.
- **Concepts in the choices:** decimal points, percentages
- **Things to look out for:** Don't accidentally find the percentage of $\overline{EH}$ represented by $\overline{AD}$! Don't misread the lengths indicated in the diagram, or the labels on any of the points. Don't make any small mistakes in your calculations! Don't forget that the right answer must fit with the scale of the diagram!

Solution 1: Geometry: Use the information in the prompt and the diagram to determine the lengths of $\overline{EH}$ and $\overline{AD}$, and then find the percentage of $\overline{AD}$ represented by $\overline{EH}$.

The prompt tells us $ABCD$ is a rectangle. We can see that $\overline{AD}$ is the side of the rectangle opposite $\overline{BC}$, and $\overline{BC}$ is 12 meters long, so $\overline{AD}$ must be 12 meters long also. The prompt tells us $EFGH$ is a square, so $\overline{EH} = \overline{HG} = 3.6$. We can divide the length of $\overline{EH}$ by the length of $\overline{AD}$ to find the answer to the question. The result is $\frac{3.6}{12} = 0.3$, which is the same as 30%. So (B) is right.

Solution 2: Test-smart/Estimation: Notice that $\overline{EH}$ must be more than 15.6% of $\overline{AD}$, but less than a third of $\overline{AD}$. Pick the only choice that satisfies that requirement.

If you look at the diagram, you can see that $\overline{EH}$ is less than a third the length of $\overline{AD}$ (it may help to imagine three segments the length of $\overline{EH}$ laid end to end; the result would be less than the length of $\overline{AD}$). $\overline{EH}$ is also clearly more than 15.6% of $\overline{AD}$, otherwise you could lay more than 6 line segments the length of $\overline{EH}$ and they would still be less than the length of $\overline{AD}$. Only (B) is less than 33% (approximately one third) and greater than 15.6%, so (B) must be the right answer.

(Notice that not every student will be comfortable concluding that $\overline{EH}$ must be less than one third the length of $\overline{AD}$, especially because choice (C) is relatively close to choice (B). If you aren't comfortable with this type of solution in a situation like this, you can always go with a solution more like Solution 1 above.)

ANSWER CHOICE ANALYSIS

(A): This choice is the result of accidentally adding $\overline{EH}$ and $\overline{AD}$ and then including a percent sign for some reason, rather than properly finding the percentage of $\overline{AD}$ represented by $\overline{EH}$. **(C):** This choice will catch test-takers who misread point D as point B, either in the prompt or in the diagram, because it's true that $\overline{EH}$ is 36% of $\overline{AB}$—but the question asked about $\overline{EH}$ relative to $\overline{AD}$. This choice will also catch test-takers who think that the length of $\overline{AD}$ is 10. **(D):** This choice is the result of multiplying the length of $\overline{EH}$ by the length of $\overline{AD}$ and then adding a percentage sign, but that isn't what the question asked us to do. **(E):** This choice is probably here to attract untrained test-takers who don't really understand the question, but notice that it frequently refers to midpoints, which are halfway between two other points by definition.

> **How to check?** Try an alternate approach above. Be especially careful that you didn't accidentally compare the wrong two lengths. Make sure your answer fits with the scale of the diagram.

▶ **Post-solution patterns (see p. 151):** right answer to the wrong question

Test 1, Question 34 (Test 2 in the 2020-2021 Red Book—see page 23 for more)

- **What's the prompt asking for?** The length of $\overline{JD}$.
- **Math concepts in the prompt:** diameter, dimension labels, midpoints, rectangles, semicircles, squares
- **Math concepts in the diagram:** diameter, dimension labels, midpoints, rectangles, semicircles, squares
- **Notable differences among choices:** (F) and (H) are integers. (G) involves a decimal. (J) and (K) are radical expressions.
- **Concepts in the choices:** decimal points, radical expressions, two-digit numbers
- **"Bridge" concepts:** $\overline{JD}$ is the hypotenuse of right triangle $\triangle AJD$.
- **Things to look out for:** Don't misread the lengths indicated in the diagram, or the labels on any of the points. Don't make any small mistakes in your calculations! Don't forget that the right answer must fit with the scale of the diagram!

Solution 1: Geometry: $\overline{JD}$ is the hypotenuse of $\triangle AJD$. Use the Pythagorean theorem to determine the length of $\overline{JD}$.

The prompt tells us J is the midpoint of $\overline{AB}$, so the length of $\overline{AJ}$ is half that of $\overline{AB}$, which means the length of $\overline{AJ}$ is 5. $ABCD$ is a rectangle, so the length of $\overline{AD}$ is equal to that of $\overline{BC}$, which means the length of $\overline{AD}$ is 12. We can plug these values into the Pythagorean Theorem to find the length of $\overline{JD}$.

$a^2 + b^2 = c^2$	(Pythagorean Theorem)
$5^2 + 12^2 = c^2$	(plug in $a = 5$ and $b = 12$)
$169 = c^2$	(simplify)
$13 = c$	(take square root of both sides)

So $\overline{JD}$ is 13 meters long, and (F) is right.

Solution 2: Geometry/Test-smart: Recognize that $\triangle AJD$ is a 5-12-13 right triangle and pick the appropriate choice.

Once we realize that $\triangle AJD$ is a right triangle with legs of 5 and 12 meters long, we can recognize that we're dealing with a 5-12-13 triangle, and the hypotenuse must be 13 meters long. So (F) is right.

ANSWER CHOICE ANALYSIS

(G): Like (A) in the previous question, this choice represents the mistake of adding $\overline{EH}$ and $\overline{AD}$. But $\overline{EH}$ is irrelevant to what the prompt is asking us to do. **(H):** This is the sum of $\overline{AJ}$ and $\overline{AD}$, but we know that $\overline{JD}$ must be shorter than that sum, not equal to it. **(J):** This choice reflects a combination of mistakes in trying to apply the Pythagorean theorem to this question. First, it involves squaring the lengths of $\overline{AB}$ and $\overline{AD}$ rather than $\overline{AJ}$ and $\overline{AD}$; second, it involves subtracting one of those squared numbers from the other, rather than adding them. **(K):** This choice is the length of $\overline{BD}$ rather than the length of $\overline{JD}$. It could attract untrained test-takers who misread either the prompt or the diagram.

How to check? Check your answer against the scale of the diagram. Make sure you read the prompt correctly and accurately identified points J and D in the diagram.

▶ Post-solution patterns (see p. 151): right answer to the wrong question

Test 1, Question 35 (Test 2 in the 2020-2021 Red Book—see page 23 for more)

- **What's the prompt asking for?** The length, in meters, of arc $\overset{\frown}{CD}$.
- **Math concepts in the prompt:** arc, diameter, dimension labels, midpoints, rectangles, semicircles, squares
- **Math concepts in the diagram:** diameter, dimension labels, midpoints, rectangles, semicircles, squares
- **Elements of the choices:** Each is a number ending in π.
- **Notable differences among choices:** (A) and (C) involve decimal points, while the other choices don't. (A), (B), and (D) form a series in which each choice is twice as much as the choice before it. The integer in (C) is the square of the integer in (A), and the integer in (E) is the square of the integer in (B).
- **Concepts in the choices:** multiplying by 2, π, squaring
- **Pre-solution patterns (see p. 149):** halves and doubles
- **Things to look out for:** Make sure you find the length of arc $\overset{\frown}{CD}$ and not line segment $\overline{CD}$! Make sure you don't misread the names of the points in the prompt or the diagram! Don't make any small mistakes in your calculations—especially with respect to the number 2, since the answer choices are clearly trying to get you to make a mistake related to squaring or dividing by 2! Don't forget that the right answer must fit with the scale of the diagram!

Solution 1: Geometry: Use the information in the prompt and the diagram to determine the length of line segment $\overline{CD}$, and use that information to find the length of arc $\overset{\frown}{CD}$.

$ABCD$ is a rectangle and $\overline{CD}$ and $\overline{AB}$ are opposite sides, so the length of $\overline{CD}$ is equal to that of $\overline{AB}$, which means the length of $\overline{CD}$ is 10. The prompt tells us that $\overline{CD}$ is the diameter of a semicircle. So arc $\overset{\frown}{CD}$ is half the circumference of a circle with a diameter of 10. The circumference of a circle equals πd, so half the circumference of a circle is $\frac{\pi d}{2}$. That means the length of arc $\overset{\frown}{CD}$ is $\frac{\pi 10}{2}$, or 5π. So (B) is right.

ANSWER CHOICE ANALYSIS

(A): This choice is half of the right answer. It might appeal to test-takers who confuse radius and diameter when finding the length of arc $\overset{\frown}{CD}$, or who misremember the formula for the circumference of a circle. **(C):** This choice involves the square of the integer from (A), which may be tempting for test-takers who mistakenly try to apply the formula for the area of a circle. **(D):** This would be the circumference of circle K (with radius DK) if that whole circle existed in the diagram, but the diagram asks us to find the length of arc $\overset{\frown}{CD}$, which is only half the circumference of circle K. **(E):** This is the square of the right answer; it would also be the area of circle K (with radius DK) if that entire circle were in the diagram.

How to check? Carefully reconsider your reading and your calculations. Make sure your answer fits the scale of the diagram. Make sure you're not accidentally off by a factor of 2, and make sure you haven't accidentally found the square or the square root of the right answer, since the relationships among the choices show that the ACT thinks an untrained test-taker would be likely to make one or both of those mistakes.

▶ **Post-solution patterns (see p. 151):** right approach, wrong step; right answer to the wrong question

Test 1, Question 36 (Test 2 in the 2020-2021 Red Book—see page 23 for more)

- **What's the prompt asking for?** The y-coordinate of H, given that K is $(0,0)$ and 1 meter in the diagram corresponds to 1 coordinate unit.

- **Math concepts in the prompt:** diameter, dimension labels, midpoints, origin, parallel lines, plotting points in the xy-coordinate plane, rectangles, semicircles, squares

- **Math concepts in the diagram:** diameter, dimension labels, midpoints, rectangles, semicircles, squares

- **Notable differences among choices:** (F), (G), and (H) all involve decimal points, while the other choices don't. (F) is half of (G). (K) is the sum of (G) and (H).

- **Concepts in the choices:** addition, multiplying by 2

- **Pre-solution patterns (see p. 149):** opposites; halves and doubles

- **Things to look out for:** Don't find the x-coordinate of H! Don't find the y-coordinate of some point besides H! Don't make any small mistakes in your calculations!

Solution 1: Geometry: Use the diagram and your understanding of the coordinate plane to determine the y-coordinate of H.

We know that the y-coordinate of H will be equal to the vertical separation between H and the origin (which the prompt says is at K). The length of $\overline{BC}$ is 12, so we know that the line $\overline{AB}$ is 12 units up from the origin. The information above the diagram tells us that $EFGH$ is a square, so we know that $\overline{EH} = \overline{HG} = 3.6$, which means point H is 3.6 units below the line $\overline{AB}$. So the vertical separation between K and H is equal to $12 - 3.6$, or 8.4, and (H) is right.

Solution 2: Test-smart: Note that the right answer must have a value slightly less than 10 and involve a decimal, and pick the only choice that satisfies those requirements.

Once we realize that we're subtracting the length of $\overline{EH}$ from 12, we know that the right answer must be a little less than 10 and involve a decimal. Only (H) satisfies these requirements, so (H) is right.

ANSWER CHOICE ANALYSIS

(F): This is the absolute value of the x-coordinate of H under the conditions in the prompt. It might appeal to untrained test-takers who misread which coordinate of H the prompt is asking for. **(G):** This is the amount that has to be subtracted from 12 in order to find the y-coordinate of H. **(J):** This choice is the length of $\overline{AB}$ or $\overline{DC}$, which may appeal to untrained test-takers who don't understand what the prompt is asking for and simply note that 10 is one of the numbers in the diagram. **(K):** This is a number we have to consider on the way to identifying the right answer, since finding the y-coordinate of H involves subtracting the length of $\overline{EH}$ from the length of $\overline{AD}$ or $\overline{BC}$.

How to check? Carefully reconsider the answer choices and your calculations. Make sure your answer fits in the scale of the diagram. Make sure you haven't identified the x-coordinate of H, since the question asks for the y-coordinate of H.

▶ **Post-solution patterns (see p. 151):** right approach, wrong step; right answer to the wrong question

Test 1, Question 37 (Test 2 in the 2020-2021 Red Book—see page 23 for more)

- **What's the prompt asking for?** The length of the altitude from C to $\overline{AB}$.

- **Math concepts in the prompt:** altitudes, length, plotting points in a coordinate plane, triangles

- **Math concepts in the diagram:** plotting points in a coordinate plane, triangles

- **Notable differences among choices:** (A), (B), and (C) are single-digit integers, while (D) and (E) are radical expressions

involving two-digit numbers. (A) is half of (C), and (B) is half of the integer in the radical expression in (D).

- **Concepts in the choices:** integers, radical expressions

- **"Bridge" concepts:** By definition, an altitude of a triangle is a line segment with one endpoint at a vertex of the triangle that meets the line containing the other two points of the triangle at a right angle. So, in this case, the altitude from C to $\overline{AB}$ will meet line segment $\overline{AB}$ at $(2, 1)$.

- **Pre-solution patterns (see p. 149):** halves and doubles
- **Things to look out for:** Don't find the wrong altitude! Don't

misread the labels of the points in the diagram, or the coordinates of those points! Don't make any small mistakes in your calculations!

Solution 1: Geometry: Realize that the altitude must be the vertical separation between C and $\overline{AB}$, and calculate that distance.

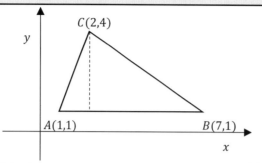

The length of the altitude will be the vertical separation between C and the line $\overline{AB}$. The y-coordinate of C is 4, and the y-coordinate of every point on $\overline{AB}$ is 1. $4 - 1 = 3$, so the answer is (A), 3.

ANSWER CHOICE ANALYSIS

(B): This choice is the difference between the x-coordinates of B and C, but the question requires us to find the difference between the y-coordinates of C and any point on $\overline{AB}$. **(C):** This is the length of $\overline{AB}$ itself, but the length of $\overline{AB}$ isn't relevant to the length of the altitude from C. **(D):** This choice will attract a lot of untrained test-takers because it's the length of $\overline{AC}$. But $\overline{AC}$ isn't an altitude of the triangle—it's just the length of one side of the triangle. **(E):** This choice is the distance from C to the midpoint of $\overline{AB}$, which is at $(4, 1)$. This will attract some untrained test-takers who think that an altitude of a triangle is determined using the midpoint of the side opposite a given vertex of the triangle, but the altitude of a triangle requires us to draw a line segment from a given vertex of the triangle so that it meets the line containing the opposite side of the triangle at a right angle, as we can see in the diagram in the solution above.

How to check? Carefully reconsider the definition of the term "altitude" and make sure you've correctly identified the points on the triangle and read their coordinates accurately.

▶ **Post-solution patterns (see p. 151):** right answer to the wrong question

Note It would have been easy for the ACT to make this question significantly more difficult in several ways. For one thing, the triangle in the question could have been arranged so that none of its sides were perfectly horizontal or vertical, which would have made it much harder for us to draw in the altitude with precision. The question would also have been more likely to mislead test-takers if the altitude had been a horizontal or diagonal line segment, rather than a vertical line segment. When we consider the ACT's choice to present this question the way it did, we see that the question is essentially testing whether we know the meaning of the word "altitude." We won't see a lot of questions on the ACT that test our knowledge of math vocabulary so directly, and you probably won't see a question on test day that specifically tests the meaning of "altitude." Still, if you were unfamiliar with the term before attempting this question, it would be a good idea to remember the meaning for the future—after reading this walkthrough, you'll probably be able to recall what an altitude of a triangle is if the situation ever arises.

Test 1, Question 38 (Test 2 in the 2020-2021 Red Book—see page 23 for more)

- **What's the prompt asking for?** The choice that's closest to the probability that exactly 2 customers are in line when the post office closes.
- **Math concepts in the prompt:** averages, e, exponents, factorials, fractions, function models, negative numbers, probability, variables
- **Elements of the choices:** Each choice is a decimal expression carried out to the hundredths place.
- **Notable differences among choices:** (F) is the only choice with a

zero in the tenths place. (F) and (H) add up to (J). (G) is approximately half of (J), and (J) is approximately half of (K).

- **Concepts in the choices:** addition, decimal points
- **Pre-solution patterns (see p. 149):** opposites; halves and doubles; be aware of series
- **Things to look out for:** Don't find the probability for some number of customers besides 2! Don't forgot that the prompt defines e^{-3} for you! Don't make any small mistakes in your reading, algebra, or calculator usage!

Solution 1: Calculator: Plug $n = 2$ and $e^{-3} \approx 0.05$ into the expression from the prompt. Use a calculator to simplify the expression on the right-hand side of the equation, and pick the choice that's closest to the P-value you find.

$$P = \frac{3^n e^{-3}}{n!}$$
(given equation)

$$P \approx \frac{3^2(0.05)}{2!} \qquad \text{(plug in } e^{-3} \approx 0.05 \text{ and } n = 2\text{)}$$

$$P \approx 0.225 \qquad \text{(simplify with a calculator)}$$

The answer choice that is closest to 0.225 is 0.23 from choice (J). The prompt asked us to find which value was "closest," so (J) is the right answer.

ANSWER CHOICE ANALYSIS

(F): This choice could reflect a misreading of the expression in the prompt in which we overlook the first exponent in the numerator, causing us to find $\frac{3(0.05)}{2!}$ instead of $\frac{3^2(0.05)}{2!}$. **(G):** This could reflect the mistake of assuming that 2! is equal to 2^2 instead of 2×1. **(H):** This choice could reflect the mistake of finding the probability that 1 person is standing in line, rather than the probability that 2 people are standing in line. **(K):** This reflects the mistake of overlooking the denominator in the equation in the prompt—in other words, this choice is the value of $3^2(0.05)$, not the value of $\frac{3^2(0.05)}{2!}$, which is what the prompt requires.

How to check? Note that (J) is the middle term in a series of choices including (G), (J), and (K), in which each choice is twice as much as the previous choice (remembering that the choices are approximate values according to the prompt). This reminds us that we especially need to make sure we're not off by a factor of two.

▶ **Post-solution patterns (see p. 151):** easy calculation mistake; right approach, wrong step

Note Notice that the provided equation involves the value e^{-3}, which might intimidate some test-takers who have never encountered the number e, or who have but don't completely remember what that number represents. Also notice that the prompt tells us e^{-3} is approximately equal to 0.05—so all we have to do is plug in 0.05 for e^{-3}, and we don't need to worry about what e represents or what it's equal to. This is one more example of the way the ACT tries to intimidate untrained test-takers with material that seems advanced or unfamiliar—but if we remain calm, remember our training, and look for efficient ways to answer each question, we'll almost always find a simple way to deal with any intimidating or unfamiliar idea that appears in a question.

Test 1, Question 39 (Test 2 in the 2020-2021 Red Book—see page 23 for more)

- **What's the prompt asking for?** The amplitude of the function in the prompt.
- **Math concepts in the prompt:** addition, amplitude, fractions, multiplication, π, radians, trig functions, variables
- **Notable differences among choices:** (A), (B), and (C) are all fractions involving the numbers 1, 2, and 3 in the numerators or denominators, while (D) and (E) are the integers 2 and 3, respectively. (A) is the reciprocal of (E), and (B) is the reciprocal of (D).
- **Concepts in the choices:** dividing by three, dividing by two, fractions, integers

- **"Bridge" concepts:** The amplitude of the cosine function is one-half of the vertical separation between the highest value the function can have and the lowest value the function can have—in other words, it's the distance from the function's highest (or lowest) possible value to its average value.
- **Pre-solution patterns (see p. 149):** wrong answers try to imitate right answers; opposites
- **Things to look out for:** Don't accidentally choose the reciprocal of the correct answer! Don't get confused about which part of the function affects the amplitude! Don't forget the definition of amplitude! Don't accidentally misread the prompt or the answer choices!

Solution 1: Graphing/Backsolve: Graph the given function on your calculator, and pick the choice that reflects the amplitude of your graphed function.

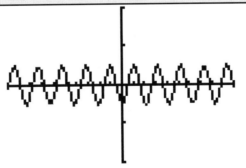

We can see that the amplitude is $\frac{1}{2}$, because the distance from the center line of the wave to either the highest or lowest point on the wave is $\frac{1}{2}$. So (B) is right.

Solution 2: Trigonometry/Abstract: Think about the properties of the cosine function and the way it would be affected by the elements of the equation in the prompt, and pick the choice that reflects the resulting cosine.

The amplitude of $y = \cos x$ is normally 1. The only part of the given expression that would impact the amplitude would be the $\frac{1}{2}$ coefficient being multiplied by $\cos(3x + 4)$. This results in the output of $\cos(3x + 4)$ being multiplied by $\frac{1}{2}$, which means the maximum and minimum values of the equation are half as big as they would otherwise be. So the amplitude must be half the normal amplitude of $y = \cos x$. Since the normal amplitude of $y = \cos x$ is 1, half of that amplitude is $\frac{1}{2}$, which means (B) is right.

ANSWER CHOICE ANALYSIS

(A): This choice might tempt an untrained test-taker who was confused about the difference between the amplitude of a graph and its period, because finding the period of a graph can involve dividing a number by the coefficient of the variable, as we see here. (Of course, when we find the period of a graph, we divide 2π by that coefficient, and not 1.) **(C):** This choice, like (A), could reflect confusion related to the period of a graph, since it involves dividing the coefficient of x by 2 (rather than dividing 2π by the coefficient of x, which is the correct way to find a graph's period—and, again, the prompt doesn't ask about the period anyway). **(D):** This is the inverse of the coefficient of the cosine function, which might appeal to an untrained test-taker who had incorrectly memorized a formulaic way to find amplitude, rather than actually understanding the concept of amplitude. **(E):** This is the coefficient of the x-term, but the right answer is the coefficient of the cosine function, because the coefficient of cosine is the part of the function that modifies the normal range of possible cosine values.

How to check? Try an alternate approach above. Be especially careful not to pick the reciprocal of the right answer, since the choices are clearly setting us up to make that mistake!

▶ **Post-solution patterns (see p. 151):** most like the other choices

Test 1, Question 40 (Test 2 in the 2020-2021 Red Book—see page 23 for more)

- **What's the prompt asking for?** The expression that reflects the number of distinct license plates that are possible under the conditions in the prompt.
- **Math concepts in the prompt:** combinations
- **Elements of the choices:** Each choice is an expression involving the numbers 3, 10, and 26.
- **Notable differences among choices:** Each choice uses 3 as an exponent except (J), which uses an expression with 3 as a base. Each choice uses parentheses except (F). (F) involves only multiplication and exponents; (G) and (J) involve addition and exponents; (H) involves multiplication, exponents, and factorials; (K) involves addition, factorials, multiplication, and exponents.
- **Concepts in the choices:** addition, exponents, factorials, multiplication
- **Pre-solution patterns (see p. 149):** wrong answers try to imitate right answers
- **Things to look out for:** Don't make any small mistakes in your reading! Don't confuse the number of possible letters with the number of possible digits! Don't confuse the roles of exponents, addition, and/or factorials when it comes to combinations!

Solution 1: Algebra: Use your knowledge of the properties of combinations to write an expression that reflects the prompt, and then pick the choice that matches your result.

We can find the answer to this question by figuring out how many possible options there are for each of the 6 spots on the license plates, and then multiplying those values together.

The prompt says each of the first 3 spots is any of the 26 letters of the alphabet, and that letters can be repeated. So the first spot can be any of 26 letters, and the second spot can also be any of 26 letters, and the third spot can also be any of 26 letters. We can find all the different possible combinations of these three spots with the expression $26 \times 26 \times 26$, which is the same as 26^3.

The prompt then says that the numbers are followed by 3 spots with digits, and that each of those 3 spots can be any of the 10 digits, and that digits can be repeated. So the first spot can be any of 10 digits, and the second spot can also be any of 10 digits, and the third spot can also be any of 10 digits. We can find all the different possible combinations of these three spots with the expression $10 \times 10 \times 10$, which is the same as 10^3.

We can multiply 26^3 by 10^3 to find the total number of combinations of the three letters followed by the three digits. The result is $26^3 \times 10^3$, which is equal to the expression in (F), so (F) is right.

Solution 2: Backsolve: Consider the elements of each choice in light of the situation in the prompt, and pick the appropriate choice.

(F): This choice incorporates the idea of multiplying 10 by itself 3 times—to reflect the process of picking one of 10 digits three times—and then incorporates the idea of multiplying that result by the result of multiplying 26 by itself 3 times—to reflect the process of picking one of 26 letters three times. In other words, this choice is equal to $10 \times 10 \times 10 \times 26 \times 26 \times 26$, which seems to reflect what the prompt asks for. (F) appears to be right, but let's check the other answer choices to make sure we haven't overlooked anything.

(Note that the prompt mentions the 26 letters first and then the 10 digits, while this answer choice includes the number 10 before the number 26. But since the order in which we multiply a string of numbers doesn't affect the result of the multiplication, this detail doesn't stop (F) from being right.)

(G): This choice would be equal to 36^3, which would tell us the number of possible permutations of 3 things chosen from a set of 36 possibilities. But that doesn't reflect what's in the prompt, so (G) is wrong.

(H): This choice includes several factorials, but factorials shouldn't play a role in the right answer because, for example, 10! is equal to $10 \times 9 \times 8 \times 7 \times 6 \times 5 \times 4 \times 3 \times 2 \times 1$, and nothing in the prompt describes a situation in which we choose first from 10 things, and then from 9 things, and so on, all the way down to 1 thing. This choice is probably intended to attract test-takers who have memorized formulas for permutations and combinations without understanding them.

(J): This choice is equivalent to 6^{36}, so it would reflect a situation in which we were choosing from six possible options 36 times in a row, but the prompt doesn't describe anything like that.

(K): This choice is similar to (H) in the sense that it was probably intended to attract people who vaguely remembered that factorials are sometimes involved in questions about permutations. As we discussed for (H), nothing in the prompt describes a situation in which we need to start with one number and then multiply it by a constantly diminishing series of other numbers. There's also no reason to think that we should be adding the results of any multiplication or exponent operations, since the combination described in the prompt only involves one string of possible options.

After considering each choice, we know that (F) is the only choice that reflects the concepts in the prompt.

ANSWER CHOICE ANALYSIS

See Solution 2 above.

How to check? Be especially careful about the differences between addition, multiplication, exponents, and factorials, since the choices are clearly setting you up to make a mistake with respect to those concepts.

Note A lot of untrained test takers will see this prompt and panic—but, as we've just seen, the key idea in this question is that we find the total number of possible outcomes for a series of events by multiplying together the number of possible outcomes for the individual events in the series. On test day, remember that the ACT often likes to trick us into thinking that its math questions are more sophisticated than they actually are. Don't be thrown off just because you see a particular word, diagram, or concept! Instead, remember your training, focus on figuring out what each question is really asking you to do, and then use your knowledge of mathematical principles and the ACT's design to find the answer. (Of course, you'll often find that the best way to answer an ACT Math question doesn't involve a formulaic approach at all.)

Test 1, Question 41 (Test 2 in the 2020-2021 Red Book—see page 23 for more)

- **What's the prompt asking for?** The interval that contains the median, according to the table.
- **Math concepts in the prompt:** median, ranges, reading data from a table
- **Math concepts in the diagram:** frequency, ranges
- **Elements of the choices:** Each choice is a range that covers 5 integers (inclusive) and appears in the provided table.
- **Concepts in the choices:** ranges
- **Pre-solution patterns (see p. 149):** be aware of series
- **Things to look out for:** Don't misread the data in the tables! Don't misread the answer choices!

Solution 1: Abstract: Note that the median must be the average of the 10th-highest and 11th-highest scores, and pick the choice that would contain both of those scores.

The prompt tells us that there are 20 quiz scores. We know that the median value in a set of data is the value that appears in the middle when the values are listed from least to greatest. When there is an even number of values (as there is in this case), the median is the average of the two values in the middle.

So the median will be the average of the 10th and 11th scores when the scores are ordered from greatest to least (or from least to greatest), because the 10th and 11th scores are the two scores in the middle of a set of 20 values.

When we look at the table and count from the highest scores in the range, we can see that the first 7 scores appear in the top 3 ranges in the table. Then the 8th, 9th, 10th and 11th scores all appear in the 81-85 point range. Since the 10th and 11th scores both fall in the 81-85 range, their average (and therefore the median) must also fall in that range. So (D) is the correct answer.

ANSWER CHOICE ANALYSIS

(E): This choice could reflect the mistake of assuming that the interval containing the most quiz scores was guaranteed to contain the median score. But, as we saw in our solution above, that doesn't have to be true.

How to check? Pay special attention to the meaning of the word "median," and make sure you correctly account for the specified numbers of scores in each range.

Test 1, Question 42 (Test 2 in the 2020-2021 Red Book—see page 23 for more)

- **What's the prompt asking for?** The choice that's equivalent to the product of the two fractions in the prompt.
- **Math concepts in the prompt:** addition, complex numbers, fractions, i, multiplication, subtraction
- **Elements of the choices:** Each choice is an expression that includes at least the numbers 1 and i.

- **Notable differences among choices:** (J) and (K) both involve fractions with a denominator of 2, while the other choices don't involve fractions. (F), (H), and (J) involve subtraction, while (G) and (K) involve addition. (F) is the opposite of (H). (J) is half of (H). (K) is half of (G).
- **Concepts in the choices:** 1, addition, dividing by two, i, subtraction

- **Pre-solution patterns (see p. 149):** wrong answers try to imitate right answers; halves and doubles; opposites
- **Things to look out for:** Don't forget that $i^2 = -1$! Don't make any small mistakes with respect to sign, because the choices clearly indicate that the test expects those mistakes to be easy to make!

Solution 1: Algebra: Multiply out the fractions in the prompt, and use your knowledge of algebra and the fact that $i^2 = -1$ to simplify the resulting expression. Pick the choice that's equivalent to your result.

$$\frac{1}{1+i} \cdot \frac{1-i}{1-i} \qquad \text{(given expression)}$$

$$\frac{1(1-i)}{(1+i)(1-i)} \qquad \text{(combine fractions)}$$

$$\frac{1-i}{1-i+i-i^2} \qquad \text{(distribute 1 in numerator, FOIL denominator)}$$

$$\frac{1-i}{1-(-1)} \qquad \text{(combine like terms and plug in } i^2 = -1\text{)}$$

$$\frac{1-i}{2} \qquad \text{(simplify)}$$

So (J) is the right answer.

Solution 2: Test-smart: Note that the right answer must have a numerator that involves subtracting i, and a denominator of 2. Pick the only choice that satisfies those requirements.

We can see that multiplying the numerators would involve multiplying 1 from the first numerator by $-i$ from the second numerator, which means the resulting numerator must include $-i$ (because $1 \times -i = -i$.) We can also see that multiplying the denominators would involve FOILing $1 + i$ and $1 - i$, which includes adding 1 (the result of multiplying the first terms) and $-i^2$, or 1 (the result of multiplying the last terms). We can also see that the inner and outer terms will cancel each other out. That means the resulting denominator must be 2. Only (J) involves a numerator with $-i$ and has a denominator of 2, so (J) must be right.

ANSWER CHOICE ANALYSIS

(H): This choice could reflect the mistake of thinking the $+i$ and $-i$ in the denominators of the two fractions would somehow cancel out completely, resulting in a denominator of 1. **(K):** This choice could reflect a misreading of the numerator in the second fraction as $1 + i$ rather than $1 - i$.

How to check? Be especially careful about correctly substituting -1 in for i^2, and about other issues related to sign, for the reasons noted above.

Test 1, Question 43 (Test 2 in the 2020-2021 Red Book—see page 23 for more)

- **What's the prompt asking for?** The temperature whose degree measurement is the same in both the Celsius and Fahrenheit systems.
- **Math concepts in the prompt:** equal values, functions
- **Elements of the choices:** Each is a multiple of 8.
- **Notable differences among choices:** (A), (B), and (C) are negative values, while (D) is 0 and (E) is positive. (C) is the opposite of (E).
- **Concepts in the choices:** multiples of eight, negative numbers, positive numbers, zero
- **Pre-solution patterns (see p. 149):** wrong answers try to imitate right answers; opposites
- **Things to look out for:** Don't make any small mistakes in your reading or calculations!

Solution 1: Concrete/Backsolve: For each answer choice, plug the given value in for F and C in the equation from the prompt. The right answer will be the one that results in a valid statement.

$$F = \frac{9}{5}C + 32 \qquad \text{(given equation)}$$

$$(-72) = \frac{9}{5}(-72) + 32 \qquad \text{(plug in } F = -72 \text{ and } C = -72 \text{ from (A))}$$

$$-72 = -97.6 \qquad \text{(simplify)}$$

The value from (A) results in an invalid statement, so (A) can't be correct. Let's try (B).

$$(-40) = \frac{9}{5}(-40) + 32 \qquad \text{(plug in } F = -40 \text{ and } C = -40 \text{ from (B))}$$

$$-40 = -40 \qquad \text{(simplify)}$$

The value from (B) results in a valid statement, so (B) appears to be correct. Let's take a look at the remaining choices to make sure we haven't made a mistake.

$$(-32) = \frac{9}{5}(-32) + 32 \qquad \text{(plug in } F = -32 \text{ and } C = -32 \text{ from (C))}$$
$$-32 = -25.6 \qquad \text{(simplify)}$$

The value from (C) results in an invalid statement, so (C) can't be right. Let's take a look at (D):

$$(0) = \frac{9}{5}(0) + 32 \qquad \text{(plug in } F = 0 \text{ and } C = 0 \text{ from (D))}$$
$$0 = 32 \qquad \text{(simplify)}$$

The value from (D) also results in an invalid statement, so (D) is wrong. Finally, let's try (E):

$$(32) = \frac{9}{5}(32) + 32 \qquad \text{(plug in } F = 32 \text{ and } C = 32 \text{ from (E))}$$
$$32 = 89.6 \qquad \text{(simplify)}$$

The value from (E) results in an invalid statement, so (E) can't be correct.

So, after checking each choice, we can be confident that (B) is right.

Solution 2: Algebra: Substitute both variables in the original equation with x. Solve for x. Pick the choice that matches your result.

$$F = \frac{9}{5}C + 32 \qquad \text{(given equation)}$$
$$x = \frac{9}{5}x + 32 \qquad \text{(plug in } F = x \text{ and } C = x)$$
$$5x = 9x + 160 \qquad \text{(multiply both sides by 5)}$$
$$-4x = 160 \qquad \text{(subtract } 9x \text{ from both sides)}$$
$$x = -40 \qquad \text{(divide both sides by } -4)$$

So (B) is right.

ANSWER CHOICE ANALYSIS

(A): This choice could result from trying Solution 2 above and accidentally multiplying 32 by $\frac{9}{5}$ during that solution. **(C):** This choice could result from trying Solution 2 above and plugging in $F = 0$ and $C = 0$, and then accidentally misreading the remaining 32 value in the equation as the number of degrees in both systems. **(D):** This choice could reflect the mistaken assumption that both temperature systems would establish the same temperature at 0 degrees. **(E):** This choice reflects a mistake similar to the one in (C).

How to check? Try an alternate approach above.

Note Many untrained test takers might try to use outside knowledge to answer this question, if they happen to have been taught in school that a particular temperature is the same in both systems. But, as trained test takers, we know that we should only rely on the equation provided in the prompt, and use it to determine our answer without paying attention to what we think we might remember from science class. Of course, it's unlikely that you'll see a question relating temperatures in degrees Celsius to temperatures in degrees Fahrenheit on test day, but it's still important to be aware of the larger point that the ACT isn't a test of obscure outside knowledge; instead, it's a test of how well you can take the information in front of you and use it to answer questions. Keep this idea in mind, because you'll find that it applies across the entire test!

Test 1, Question 44 (Test 2 in the 2020-2021 Red Book—see page 23 for more)

- **What's the prompt asking for?** The choice that's closest to the constant of variation in the given data.
- **Math concepts in the prompt:** constant of variation, direct variation, reading data from a figure
- **Math concepts in the diagram:** coordinate pairs, decimal points
- **Elements of the choices:** Each choice is a number with a decimal point, a tenths digit, and a hundredths digit.
- **Notable differences among choices:** (F) is the only negative number. (K) is the only integer.

- **Concepts in the choices:** decimal points, negative numbers, positive numbers
- **Things to look out for:** Don't confuse the x-values and y-values in the table! Don't forget that the prompt is discussing direct variation, not indirect variation! Don't misread any of the numbers in the figure or the answer choices! Don't make any small algebra mistakes when you work with the equation from the note in the prompt!

Solution 1: Algebra: Plug an x-value and its corresponding y-value into the equation from the note and use them to determine k. Then pick the choice whose value is approximately k.

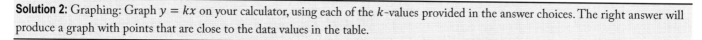

$$y = kx \qquad \text{(given equation)}$$
$$0.140 = k(2.75) \qquad \text{(plug in values from row 1)}$$
$$0.05\overline{09} = k \qquad \text{(divide both sides by 2.75)}$$

This value is very close to the value in (G). Let's plug in the values from row 2 to make sure we haven't made a mistake.

$$0.425 = k(8.50) \qquad \text{(plug in values from row 2)}$$
$$0.05 = k \qquad \text{(divide both sides by 8.5)}$$

This value is equal to the value in (G), so we can conclude that (G) is correct.

Solution 2: Graphing: Graph $y = kx$ on your calculator, using each of the k-values provided in the answer choices. The right answer will produce a graph with points that are close to the data values in the table.

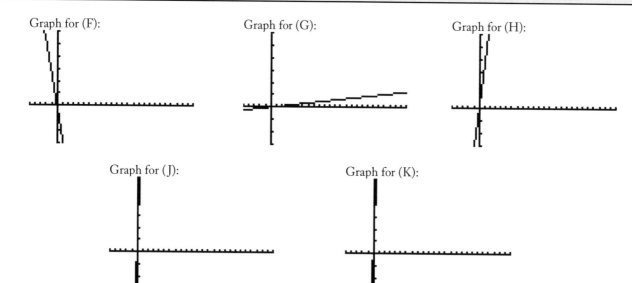

Graph for (F): Graph for (G): Graph for (H):

Graph for (J): Graph for (K):

We can see that the graph of (G) roughly follows the data points in the table, while the other graphs are quite far off from the values in the table—for example, (F) doesn't even have any points with positive x and y values, and (H), (J), and (K) all have y-values that are far higher than the corresponding values in the table. So (G) must be right.

Solution 3: Test-smart: Note that the right answer must be a positive number smaller than 1, and pick the only choice that satisfies that requirement.

The note in the prompt tells us that the "constant of variation" is some number that can be multiplied by an x-value to produce a corresponding y-value. The chart shows that y is always positive when x is positive, which means the "constant of variation" must be positive as well, since it would be impossible to multiply a negative number by a positive number and get a positive result. The chart also shows that every y-value is less than its corresponding x-value, which means the "constant of variation" must be smaller than 1. Only (G) satisfies both requirements, so we know it must be right.

ANSWER CHOICE ANALYSIS

(F): This is the difference between the terms in the first row, but k is the *ratio* of those two terms, not their difference. **(H):** This choice is the result of multiplying the two numbers from the second row of data, but the k in the prompt is a ratio of y to x, not the product of y and x. **(J):** Like (F), this choice represents the difference between two numbers in a row of data (specifically, the next-to-last row), but the question asked us for a ratio, not a difference. **(K):** This choice is the approximate difference between the last two numbers in the table. But the prompt asked us for k, which represents a ratio between two numbers in a row of the given data, not a difference between two numbers.

How to check? Try an alternate approach above. The fact that we can explain the various mistakes that lead to the wrong answers should help reassure us that we've probably thought of the question correctly.

▶ **Post-solution patterns (see p. 151):** easy calculation mistake

Note Even though many trained test takers will be familiar with the idea of direct variation, they may not have heard the phrase "constant of variation" before attempting this question. Notice that the ACT goes out of its way to define this term, which means it wasn't necessary for us to know that term beforehand—all we needed to do was remain calm and read carefully. Keep this in mind on test day, and don't let the test intimidate you by using unfamiliar phrases to refer to concepts that you already know and/or that are defined on the page.

Test 1, Question 45 (Test 2 in the 2020-2021 Red Book—see page 23 for more)

- **What's the prompt asking for?** The choice that accurately models the equation in the prompt.
- **Math concepts in the prompt:** function modeling, graphing functions in the xy-coordinate plane, positive numbers
- **Elements of the choices:** Each choice is the graph of a line segment in Quadrant I of the xy-coordinate plane.
- **Notable differences among choices:** (A) and (B) both have a y-intercept of 1, while (D) and (E) both have a y-intercept of 5, and (C) has a y-intercept of 0. (A) and (D) appear to have the same slope as each other.
- **Concepts in the choices:** graphing functions in the xy-coordinate plane, positive numbers
- **Pre-solution patterns (see p. 149):** wrong answers try to imitate right answers
- **Things to look out for:** Don't make any mistakes with respect to slope and y-intercept, since the choices are clearly trying to trick people who make those kinds of mistakes!

Solution 1: Graphing/Backsolve: Use a calculator to graph the equation in the prompt, and pick the choice that matches your graph.

We can put the provided equation into slope-intercept form:

$$2x - 5y = -5 \qquad \text{(given equation)}$$
$$-5y = -2x - 5 \qquad \text{(subtract } 2x \text{ from both sides)}$$
$$y = \frac{2}{5}x + 1 \qquad \text{(divide both sides by } -5)$$

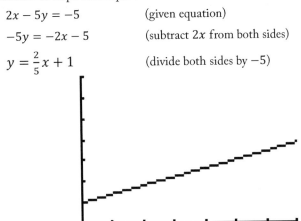

We can see that the graph matches (A), so (A) is correct. (Note that we can confirm that this matches (A) by checking a few points—for example, this graph has a point at $(0,1)$, which eliminates (C), (D), and (E), and it has a point roughly around $(3,2)$, which eliminates (B), leaving only (A).)

Solution 2: Algebra/Backsolve: Plug some x-values into the given equation to see what the corresponding y-values are, and pick the choice whose line goes through the correct coordinate points.

Let's see what we get when we plug in $x = 0$.

$$2x - 5y = -5 \qquad \text{(given equation)}$$
$$2(0) - 5y = -5 \qquad \text{(plug in } x = 0)$$
$$-5y = -5 \qquad \text{(simplify)}$$
$$y = 1 \qquad \text{(divide both sides by } -5)$$

The graph should contain the point $(0, 1)$. Only the graphs in choices (A) and (B) contain that point, so we can rule out the other three answer choices. We can see that (A) and (B) have different y values when $x = 1$, so we should be able to eliminate the wrong answer if we plug $x = 1$ into the given equation.

$$2x - 5y = -5 \qquad \text{(given equation)}$$
$$2(1) - 5y = -5 \qquad \text{(plug in } x = 1)$$
$$2 - 5y = -5 \qquad \text{(simplify)}$$
$$-5y = -7 \qquad \text{(subtract 2 from both sides)}$$
$$y = \frac{7}{5} \qquad \text{(divide both sides by } -5)$$

The graph should contain the point $\left(1, \frac{7}{5}\right)$. Only the graph in choice (A) appears to contain this point, while the graph in (B) appears to have a point near $(1, 3)$. That means (A) is correct.

Solution 3: Algebra: Determine the slope and y-intercept of the equation in the prompt, and pick the corresponding answer choice.

We can put the provided equation into slope-intercept form:

$$2x - 5y = -5 \qquad \text{(given equation)}$$
$$-5y = -2x - 5 \qquad \text{(subtract } 2x \text{ from both sides)}$$
$$y = \frac{2}{5}x + 1 \qquad \text{(divide both sides by } -5)$$

Based on our understanding of slope-intercept form (or "$y = mx + b$" form) the graph should have a y-intercept of 1 and a slope of $\frac{2}{5}$. Only choice (A) matches these requirements, so (A) must be right.

(B): This choice has the right y-intercept, but its slope is wrong. This could reflect an algebra mistake by a test-taker who tried Solution 3 above. **(D):** This choice has the reverse of the problem in (B): it has the correct slope, but its y-intercept is 5 instead of 1, which could reflect an algebra mistake made by a test-taker who was trying to use Solution 3 above.

How to check? Try an alternate approach above. Pay particular attention to slope and y-intercept, for the reasons we noted above.

Test 1, Question 46 (Test 2 in the 2020-2021 Red Book—see page 23 for more)

- **What's the prompt asking for?** The number of cups of flour that Diana will use.
- **Math concepts in the prompt:** mixed fractions, ratios
- **Notable differences among choices:** (F), (G), (H), and (J) are all mixed fractions, while (K) is the integer 4. (G), (H), and (J) all have 3 as their whole number, while (F) has 1. (F) is the only choice whose fraction is in eighths; the fractions in (G) and (J) are in fourths, and the fraction in (H) is in halves. (F) is half of (J). (G), (H), (J), and (K) form a series in which each choice is $\frac{1}{4}$ more than the previous choice.
- **Concepts in the choices:** integers, mixed fractions
- **Pre-solution patterns (see p. 149):** wrong answers try to imitate right answers; halves and doubles
- **Things to look out for:** Don't confuse the three different numbers that are in the prompt! Don't make any mistakes when converting among fractions with different denominators! Don't misread any of the small differences among the answer choices!

Solution 1: Algebra: Write an equation that compares the original ratio in the recipe to the ratio of yeast in the packet and the unknown quantity of flour. Solve your equation and pick the corresponding answer choice.

$$\frac{1.5}{2.5} = \frac{2.25}{x}$$ (ratio of yeast called for/flour called for set equal to ratio of yeast actually used/flour actually used)

$1.5x = 5.625$ (cross-multiply)

$x = 3.75$ (divide both sides by 1.5)

So the answer is (J).

Solution 2: Arithmetic: Note that the amount of yeast Diana has is 50% greater than the amount called for in the recipe, and pick the choice that's 50% greater than the amount of flour called for in the recipe.

$$\frac{2.25}{1.5} = 1.5$$ (ratio of yeast Diana used to yeast recipe calls for)

So Diana used 1.5 times as much yeast as the recipe called for; that means she'll need to use 1.5 times as much flour as well.

$$2.5 \times 1.5 = 3.75$$ (cups of flour recipe calls for multiplied by 1.5)

3.75 is equivalent to the value in (J), so (J) is correct.

(F): This is half of the right answer. It could reflect the mistake of multiplying the amount of flour in the recipe by the difference between the amounts of yeast in the prompt, rather than multiplying by the ratio of the larger amount of yeast to the smaller amount. **(G):** This choice reflects the mistake of thinking that the difference between the amounts of yeast should also be the difference between the amounts of flour, but, as we discussed in Solution 2 above, the *ratio* between the amounts of flour should be equal to the *ratio* between the corresponding amounts of yeast.

How to check? Try an alternate approach above.

▶ **Post-solution patterns (see p. 151):** easy calculation mistake

Test 1, Question 47 (Test 2 in the 2020-2021 Red Book—see page 23 for more)

- **What's the prompt asking for?** The choice that's equal to the fraction in the prompt.
- **Math concepts in the prompt:** algebra, exponents, fractions, multiplication, subtraction
- **Elements of the choices:** Each is a binomial expression that begins with $4x$ and involves subtracting the second term.
- **Notable differences among choices:** In (A) and (B), the exponent of the first term is 3, while in (C), (D), and (E) the exponent of the first term is 4. (A) and (D) have $3x$ as the second term, while (B) and (E) have only 3, and (C) has $9x^2$.
- **Concepts in the choices:** algebra, exponents, multiplication, subtraction
- **Pre-solution patterns (see p. 149):** wrong answers try to imitate right answers
- **Things to look out for:** Don't forget that when we divide one exponent expression by another with a common base, we subtract the exponents, rather than dividing the exponents! Don't misread the answer choices, or overlook any of the small differences among them!

Solution 1: Backsolve: Pick an arbitrary value, plug it in for x in the expressions in the prompt and the choices, and use your calculator to find the value of each expression. Then pick the choice whose value matches the value of the expression in the prompt.

Let's say that $x = 5$. First, we can plug $x = 5$ into the given expression on a calculator:

$$\frac{12(5)^6 - 9(5)^2}{3(5)^2} = 2497$$

Now we can plug $x = 5$ into each expression in the answer choices. The right answer will produce a result of 2497.

(A) $4(5)^3 - 3(5) = 485$

(B) $4(5)^3 - 3 = 497$

(C) $4(5)^4 - 9(5)^2 = 2275$

(D) $4(5)^4 - 3(5) = 2485$

(E) $4(5)^4 - 3 = 2497$

We can see that only the value from (E) matched the value we found for the given expression, so (E) is right.

Solution 2: Graphing/Backsolve: Graph all the expressions in the problem as functions, and then pick the choice that produces the same graph as the expression in the prompt.

First, let's graph the given expression:

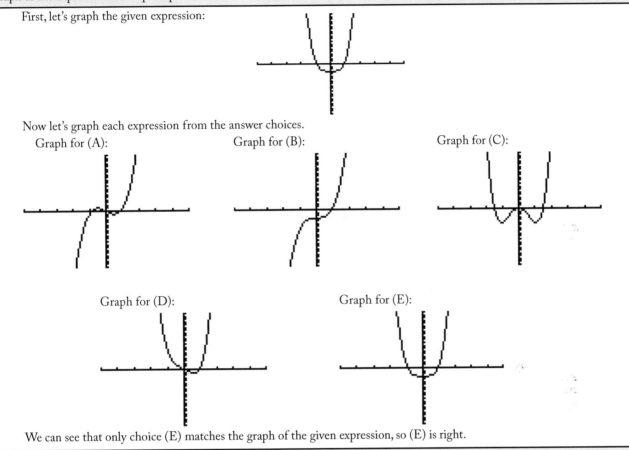

Now let's graph each expression from the answer choices.

Graph for (A):   Graph for (B):   Graph for (C):

Graph for (D):   Graph for (E):

We can see that only choice (E) matches the graph of the given expression, so (E) is right.

Solution 3: Algebra: Divide the numerator and denominator of the given expression by $3x^2$ to find the simplified version of the fraction, and pick the choice that matches your result.

$\dfrac{12x^6 - 9x^2}{3x^2}$ (given expression)

$4x^4 - 3$ (divide each term in the numerator by $3x^2$)

So (E) is right.

ANSWER CHOICE ANALYSIS

(A): This choice reflects the mistake of thinking that dividing one exponent expression by another expression with a common base involves dividing the exponents, rather than subtracting one exponent from the other. **(B):** This choice reflects the same mistake that we saw in (A), but only applies that mistake to the first term in the numerator. **(C):** The first term in this answer is the same first term that we find in the right answer, but the second term hasn't been changed from the original numerator. This could reflect the mistake of trying Solution 3 above, correctly determining what the first term should be, and then accidentally ignoring the second term. **(D):** This choice is essentially the opposite of (B): it represents the mistake of correctly finding the first term of the right answer, but then trying to use division instead of subtraction to determine the correct exponent on the second term.

How to check? Try an alternate approach above. Pay particular attention to the exponents in the choice you pick, since the test is clearly setting us up to make a mistake when it comes to exponents!

▶ **Post-solution patterns (see p. 151):** opposites

- **What's the prompt asking for?** The choice whose matrix product is undefined.
- **Math concepts in the prompt:** matrices, matrix products
- **Elements of the choices:** Each choice is a product of two of the matrices in the prompt.
- **Notable differences among choices:** W appears first in (F) and (G), and W appears second in (J). X appears first in (J) and (K), but X appears second in (F). Y appears first in (H) and second in (G). Z appears second in (H) and (K); Z never appears first. (F) is the opposite of (J).

- **Concepts in the choices:** matrix products
- **"Bridge" concepts:** In order for the product of a matrix to exist, the number of columns in the first matrix must equal the number of rows in the second matrix.
- **Pre-solution patterns (see p. 149):** wrong answers try to imitate right answers; opposites
- **Things to look out for:** Don't miscount the rows or columns in any of the matrices! Don't confuse the letters of the matrices with each other! Don't forget that the number of columns in the first matrix must equal the number of rows in the second matrix, not the other way around!

Solution 1: Calculator/Concrete: Try to use your calculator to multiply each pair of matrices in the answer choices. Pick the choice that has an undefined product according to the calculator.

When we try to use our calculators to multiply the matrices in each answer choice, we get an error message doing the multiplication from (K). So (K) is right. (If you don't know how to multiply matrices with your calculator, search online for your calculator model and a phrase like "multiply matrices" or "matrix multiplication.")

Solution 2: Matrices: Using your knowledge of matrices, pick the choice in which the number of columns in the first matrix is not equal to the number of rows in the second matrix.

We know that when we multiply one matrix by another matrix, the number of columns in the first matrix must be equal to the number of rows in the second matrix. For (F), (G), and (J), the first matrix has two columns and the second matrix has two rows. For (H), the first matrix has three columns and the second matrix has three rows. But for (K), the first matrix has two columns and the second matrix has three rows. So the product of X and Z is undefined, and (K) is the right answer.

ANSWER CHOICE ANALYSIS

(F) and (J): (F) could attract a test-taker who incorrectly believed that matrices couldn't be multiplied together if they had the same dimensions. But notice that, if this were a valid reason to pick (F), it would also mean that (J) had to be right, too—and, as trained test-takers, we know that each question has only one acceptable choice, which means both (F) and (J) must be wrong.

How to check? Try an alternate approach above. Be especially careful about the potential issues we identified above before coming up with possible approaches.

▶ **Post-solution patterns (see p. 151):** most like the other choices

- **What's the prompt asking for?** The equation that defines the family of parabolas described in the prompt.
- **Math concepts in the prompt:** graphing functions in the xy-coordinate plane, parabolas, variables
- **Math concepts in the diagram:** graphing functions in the xy-coordinate plane, parabolas, variables
- **Elements of the choices:** Each choice is a function with y on the left-hand side, and some combination of $x^2, n,$ and 1 on the right-hand side.
- **Notable differences among choices:** (A) involves multiplying x

by n, while (B) involves multiplying x by the reciprocal of n, (D) involves multiplying x by the opposite of n, and (E) involves multiplying x by the opposite of the reciprocal of n. (C) involves adding n.

- **Concepts in the choices:** addition, fractions, functions, multiplication, negative numbers, positive numbers, reciprocals, squaring
- **Pre-solution patterns (see p. 149):** wrong answers try to imitate right answers; opposites
- **Things to look out for:** Be careful not to make any mistakes with respect to the signs of numbers or their inverses, since the choices are clearly trying to set you up to do that!

Solution 1: Graphing: Test each choice with your calculator. Try using $n = 3$ first to graph the equations in each choice; the differences in the graphs may be more pronounced with a larger n-value. Pick the choice that matches the graph in the figure.

Graph for (A) when $n = 3$:

This seems to match the graph in the prompt when $n = 3$. Let's check the other choices to see if any others look similar.

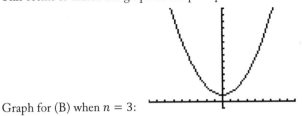

Graph for (B) when $n = 3$:

This graph shares a point at $(0,1)$ with the graph in the prompt, but the other points are much farther away from the y-axis. For example, when $x = 2$, the graph in the prompt has a y-value around 15, but the above graph has a y-value around 2.

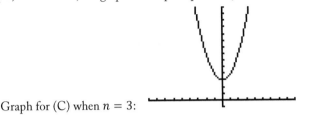

Graph for (C) when $n = 3$:

Each of the three graphs in the prompt has a point at $(0,1)$, but this graph has a point at $(0,3)$, so this choice must be wrong.

Graph for (D) when $n = 3$:

The parabola in this graph opens down, but the parabolas in the prompt all open up, so this choice must be wrong.

Graph for (E) when $n = 3$:

This choice has the same basic problem as (D).

After we consider each choice, we can see that only (A) matches the provided graph, so (A) is the right answer.

Solution 2: Algebra: Use your knowledge of graphing parabolas to see which choice reflects the features of the graphs in the figure.

We can choose a point on the curve with clearly identifiable values for x and y and then plug those values into each answer choice, and see which choice is a valid expression for those two values. The only point on the curves in the prompt that's easily identifiable is $(0,1)$. If we plug in $x = 0$ and $y = 1$ for each answer choice, the only one that doesn't work is (C), and we're still left with four possible answer choices.

Next, we could notice that (D) and (E) would both produce some negative y-values, since they involve multiplying x^2 by negative numbers. (This is another way to say that both (D) and (E) would produce graphs that "open down.") Since the parabolas in the graph from the prompt don't open down or include any negative y-values, we know (D) and (E) must be wrong.

From there, we need to see if we can figure out a way to tell whether (A) or (B) is correct. The only difference between them is that (A) multiplies the x^2 value by n, while (B) multiplies it by $\frac{1}{n}$. So now we need to decide which of those is an accurate description of what we see in the graph from the question. The graph shows that the curves become narrower when n is greater—in other words, when n is greater, the y-value is higher for a given x-value than it is when n is lower. This indicates (A) is the correct answer, because (A) will give us a bigger y-value for any single x-value as n gets bigger, since we'll be multiplying x^2 by a larger value when n is larger. On the other hand, (B) would have us multiplying x^2 by smaller and smaller fractions as n gets larger, because $\frac{1}{3}$ is less than $\frac{1}{2}$, and so on. So (A) must be right.

ANSWER CHOICE ANALYSIS

(B): This choice might attract untrained test-takers who forgot how the coefficient of x affects the graph of a parabola. This choice would create a family of parabolas that became wider as n increased, not narrower, as the diagram requires. **(C):** This choice might attract untrained test takers who tested the value $(0, 1)$ when $n = 1$, but it fails to reflect the figure when we consider the y-intercepts of this equation when $n = 2$ or $n = 3$. **(D):** This choice could attract untrained test takers who forget how a negative x-term will affect a parabola: all the parabolas described by this function will open downward, rather than upward. **(E):** This choice combines the mistakes from (B) and

(D).

How to check? Try an alternate approach above. Also consider testing individual points from the graph and making sure they satisfy the answer choice you're picking.

Note Many untrained test takers will be bothered by this question because they're not familiar with the term "family of parabolas." But, as trained test takers, we notice that the question essentially explains this term in the prompt and in the figure, which allows us to find the answer with total certainty even if we've never heard that term before. On test day, remember that you shouldn't be intimidated by concepts that seem new and different at first—you'll often find that you can easily work through them with the information provided on the page.

Test 1, Question 50 (Test 2 in the 2020-2021 Red Book—see page 23 for more)

- **What's the prompt asking for?** The minimum number of students who play both the guitar and piano.
- **Math concepts in the prompt:** minimums, surveys
- **Elements of the choices:** Each choice is an integer from 0 to 17 inclusive.
- **Notable differences among choices:** (G) and (H) add up to (J).

(H) and (J) add up to (K).

- **Concepts in the choices:** addition, subtraction
- **Things to look out for:** Make sure you find the minimum number of students who play both instruments, and not just any number of students who could possibly play both instruments!

Solution 1: Diagramming: Sketch out a diagram of the 20 students in the class, and then mark off the number of students who play the piano and the number of students who play the guitar, trying to create as little overlap in the two groups as possible. Pick the choice that reflects your conclusion.

For purposes of this demonstration, we'll make a grid with 20 squares, and each square will represent one student. (Of course, if you were sketching this out in your test booklet on test day, you wouldn't necessarily have to make a grid—there are a lot of other ways you could represent this visually that would allow you to answer the question with confidence.) Starting from the top-left square, we'll put a "G" in 8 of the squares to represent 8 students who play the guitar. Then, starting from the bottom-right square, we'll put a "P" for piano on 9 squares, to represent 9 students who play the piano. This should allow us to have the fewest possible number of squares contain both a "G" and a "P":

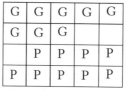

We can see that it's possible for 8 students to play guitar and 9 students to play piano and for there to be 0 students who play both instruments. So (F) is the right answer.

Solution 2: Abstract: Use your understanding of the information in the prompt to determine the minimum number of students who play both the guitar and the piano.

If there are 20 students in the class and 8 students play the guitar, then there are 12 students who don't play the guitar. If 9 students in the class play the piano, then it's possible that those 9 students could all come from the group of 12 students who don't play the guitar. So it's possible for none of the students in the class to play both guitar and piano. That means (F) is right.

ANSWER CHOICE ANALYSIS

(G): This choice could reflect a couple of different possible mistakes. It could be the result of accidentally subtracting 8 from 9, which isn't an appropriate way to handle the question because there's no reason to think that the difference between the numbers of students playing the two instruments is relevant to the question. It could also be the result of correctly noticing that there doesn't have to be any overlap between the group of students playing the piano and the group of students playing the guitar, but then incorrectly thinking that there must be at least one student who plays both in order to satisfy the prompt; the prompt only asks for the minimum number of students, and 0 is a number, which means 0 is a perfectly valid answer to the question and there's no need to assume 1 student must exist who plays both instruments. **(H):** This choice is kind of the opposite of what the prompt asks for, since it represents the maximum number of students who could possibly play both instruments. **(K):** This choice is the maximum possible number of students in the group who could play one of the instruments, but that isn't what the prompt asked us to find.

How to check? Try an alternate approach above. Make sure that you've read the prompt carefully, and remember that 0 is an acceptable answer, because the prompt never says otherwise.

▶ **Post-solution patterns (see p. 151):** opposites; right answer to the wrong question

Test 1, Question 51 (Test 2 in the 2020-2021 Red Book—see page 23 for more)

- **What's the prompt asking for?** The number of the student who   must be paired with a student whose number is 1.

- **Math concepts in the prompt:** integers, ranges, square numbers
- **Elements of the choices:** Each choice is an integer between 1 and 18.
- **Notable differences among choices:** (A) is twice as much as (D). (A) and (C) are the only square numbers. (B), (D), and (E) are the only numbers that are 1 less than a square number.

- **Concepts in the choices:** square numbers
- **Pre-solution patterns (see p. 149):** halves and doubles
- **Things to look out for:** Don't forget that the right answer must allow all of the other numbers to be paired according to the prompt! Don't forget which numbers are square numbers!

Solution 1: Arithmetic: Reason through the requirements in the prompt to determine how the pairings must go, and pick the choice that reflects your conclusion.

The first requirement is that the sum of 1 and the answer choice must be a perfect square. Let's test each choice with this in mind:

(A) $16 + 1 = 17$

(B) $15 + 1 = 16$

(C) $9 + 1 = 10$

(D) $8 + 1 = 9$

(E) $3 + 1 = 4$

As we can see, only (B), (D), and (E) can be added to 1 to make a perfect square. Remember that the prompt says all 9 pairs of students follow the rule from the prompt, and the prompt asks which number *must* be paired with the number 1. So it seems like out of 15, 8, and 3, two of those numbers, when paired with 1, will make it impossible for all 9 pairs of students to be paired off according to the rule in the prompt. Let's think this through.

The smallest sum of two integers from 1 to 18 is 3 (because $1 + 2 = 3$), and the largest sum of two integers from 1 to 18 is 35 (because $18 + 17 = 35$). So the perfect squares that each pair adds up to must be between 3 and 35. The only perfect squares in this range are 4, 9, 16, and 25, so each pair must add up to either 4, 9, 16, or 25.

Let's list out each number and see which numbers can be paired together to add up to perfect squares. The top row of the following grid contains each number from 1 to 18, and then the numbers below those numbers are the ones that can be added to the original number to make a perfect square:

1	2	3	4	5	6	7	8	9	10	11	12	13	14	15	16	17	18
3	7	1	5	4	3	2	1	7	6	5	4	3	2	1	9	8	7
8	14	6	12	11	10	9	17	16	15	14	13	12	11	10			
15		13				18											

We can see that 16, 17, and 18 can only match up with 9, 8, and 7.

Since 9, 8, and 7 have to be paired with 16, 17, and 18, we know that 9, 8, and 7 aren't available to pair with any other numbers. So now we can modify our table, and cross out the numbers that we've definitely accounted for so far—that is, the numbers that can't possibly pair with 1, since we know they have to pair with something else:

1	2	3	4	5	6	X	X	X	10	11	12	13	14	15	X	X	X
3	X	1	5	4	3	2	1	X	6	5	4	3	2	1	X	X	X
X	14	6	12	11	10	X	X	X	15	14	13	12	11	10			
15		13				X											

This lets us draw some further conclusions. For example, we can see that 2 must be paired with 14, because 7 is no longer available. If we cross out all the 2s and 14s on the table, we get this:

1	X	3	4	5	6	X	X	X	10	11	12	13	X	15	X	X	X
3	X	1	5	4	3	X	1	X	6	5	4	3	X	1	X	X	X
X	X	6	12	11	10	X	X	X	15	X	13	12	11	10			
15		13				X											

We can now see that 11 must be paired with 5, because no number is available underneath 11 besides 5. (I won't keep showing the new version of the table with the additional numbers crossed out, in order to keep this explanation as simple as possible. If you'd like, you can follow along as I describe the numbers we could cross out as we match them up, and you can cross them out yourself.)

Crossing out all the 11s and 5s shows us that 4 must be paired with 12; crossing out all the 4s and 12s shows us that 13 must be paired with 3. At that point, we can see on the table that 15 is the only possible number that can be paired with 1, so (B) must be right. (If this solution didn't make a lot of sense to you, try reading it another time or two, and refer back to the tables; consider crossing out each set of numbers as they're eliminated.)

ANSWER CHOICE ANALYSIS

(A): This choice can be thought of as a "right approach, wrong step" answer, since the 16 is the number that results when the number 1 is paired up with the number 15 as the prompt requires. But the prompt asked us for the number that should be paired with 1, not for the sum of the two paired numbers. **(D):** This number can be added to 1 to make a perfect square, but as we discussed above, 8 needs to pair with 17. **(E):** This number can be added to 1 to make a perfect square, but as we discussed above, 3 needs to pair with 13.

How to check? Consider listing out all of the pairings to make sure you've thought about the question in a way that satisfies the prompt.

▶ **Post-solution patterns (see p. 151):** right approach, wrong step

Note This is a great example of the kind of question that's based on extremely simple concepts but still requires more time and effort from most test-takers than most of the other questions on the ACT Math section. On test day, remember that we always have to be prepared to encounter unusual combinations of familiar math concepts, and we'll often find that relatively challenging ACT Math questions don't involve formulas, just as this one doesn't.

Test 1, Question 52 (Test 2 in the 2020-2021 Red Book—see page 23 for more)

- **What's the prompt asking for?** The number of quarters that Lucky found in the given week.
- **Math concepts in the prompt:** adding one, counting money, multiplying by two, subtracting one
- **Notable differences among choices:** (F), (G), and (J) are all multiples of 3, while the numbers in the other choices aren't. (H), (J), and (K) form a series in which each choice is 5 more than the one before it.
- **Concepts in the choices:** multiples of 3, series

- **"Bridge" concepts:** Quarters are worth $0.25. Dimes are worth $0.10. Nickels are worth $0.05. Pennies are worth $0.01.
- **Pre-solution patterns (see p. 149):** be aware of series
- **Things to look out for:** Don't misread the relationships in the prompt! Don't confuse the values of the different kinds of coins! Don't accidentally put down the number of some other kind of coin as your answer! Don't make any small mistakes in your calculations!

Solution 1: Concrete/Backsolve: Using the relationships described in the prompt, try each choice as the number of quarters that Lucky found. Pick the choice that results in Lucky finding $8.25 when the rest of the conditions in the prompt are met.

(F): According to the prompt, if Lucky found 3 quarters, she must have found 2 nickels, 1 dime, and 1 penny. That's $3(0.25) + 2(0.05) + 1(0.10) + 1(0.01)$, which is the same as $0.96. So (F) is wrong.

(G): According to the prompt, if Lucky found 9 quarters, she must have found 8 nickels, 7 dimes, and 4 pennies. That's $9(0.25) + 8(0.05) + 7(0.10) + 4(0.01)$, which is the same as $3.39. So (G) is wrong.

(H): According to the prompt, if Lucky found 16 quarters, she must have found 15 nickels, 14 dimes, and 7.5 pennies. That's $16(0.25) + 15(0.05) + 14(0.10) + 7.5(0.01)$, which is the same as $6.225. So (H) is wrong.

(J): According to the prompt, if Lucky found 21 quarters, she must have found 20 nickels, 19 dimes, and 10 pennies. That's $21(0.25) + 20(0.05) + 19(0.10) + 10(0.01)$, which is the same as $8.25. So (J) seems to be right; let's check the last choice to make sure we haven't made a mistake.

(K): According to the prompt, if Lucky found 26 quarters, she must have found 25 nickels, 24 dimes, and 12.5 pennies. That's $26(0.25) + 25(0.05) + 24(0.10) + 12.5(0.01)$, which is the same as $10.275. So (K) is wrong.

After considering each choice, we can see that only (J) results in a total of $8.25, so (J) must be right.

Notice that testing (H) and (K) was a little weird because each one involved half a penny. Instead of taking time to wonder about whether the ACT would let us pick a solution that involved half a penny, we can just multiply those choices out on our calculators, confirm that they don't produce a result of $8.25, eliminate them, and move on.

Solution 2: Algebra: Write an algebraic equation that captures the relationships among $8.25 and the numbers of quarters, dimes, nickels, and pennies described in the prompt. Solve your equation and use the result to determine how many quarters Lucky found.

We need to come up with algebraic expressions to represent the number of each type of coin Lucky found. We don't want to just use a different variable for each coin, because then we'll have an expression with four different variables (one for each coin), and that won't be very helpful. The prompt tells us how many coins there are relative to each other, though, so we can use that information to express each quantity of coins in terms of the same variable. The smallest denomination of coin is the penny, so we'll put everything in terms of pennies to avoid having too many fractions. We'll use the variable p to represent the number of pennies Lucky found, and we'll put everything else in terms of p.

So we know she found p pennies. The prompt says she found twice as many nickels as pennies, so she must have found $2p$ nickels. The prompt says she found one fewer dime than nickels, and we just said she found $2p$ nickels, so she must have found $2p - 1$ dimes. Finally, we're told she found 1 more quarter than nickels, so that's $2p + 1$ quarters. Now we can multiply the value of each coin by the number of that type of coin, set the whole thing equal to $8.25, and solve for p:

$$(\$0.01 \times p) + (\$0.05 \times 2p) + (\$0.10 \times (2p - 1)) + (\$0.25 \times (2p + 1)) = \$8.25 \quad \text{(initial equation)}$$

$$\$0.01p + \$0.10p + \$0.20p - \$0.10 + \$0.50p + \$0.25 = \$8.25 \qquad \text{(multiply expressions in parentheses)}$$

$0.81p + $0.15 = 8.25 $\quad$ (simplify)

$0.81p = 8.10 $\quad$ (subtract $0.15 from both sides)

$p = 10$ $\quad$ (divide both sides by $0.81)

So we found that $p = 10$. Remember that we determined that there are $2p + 1$ quarters, so that means there are $2(10) + 1$ quarters, or 21 quarters. So (J) is right.

Solution 3: Test-smart: Consider the requirements for the total amount of money to end with a 5, and pick the only choice that meets these requirements.

We are told that the total amount of money Lucky finds ends in a 5. Quarters, nickels, and dimes are all denominations that are already multiples of 5, so any combination of those coins would be a multiple of 5—but pennies are 1 cent each, so we know the correct number of pennies must be a multiple of 5, or the total can't possibly end in a 5. When we read the prompt, we can see that there are half as many pennies as nickels, and 1 more quarter than nickels. So when we subtract 1 from the number of quarters and divide that number in half—which gives us the number of pennies Lucky found—the result has to be a multiple of 5, or the number of quarters we started with can't be right. With this logic, we can eliminate (F), (G), (H), and (K), because when we subtract 1 from those numbers and then divide them by 2, we get 1, 4, 7.5, and 12.5 respectively, which aren't divisible by 5. That only leaves (J), which is the correct answer. (Note that when we subtract 1 from the value in (J) and divide by 2 we get 10, which is divisible by 5.)

ANSWER CHOICE ANALYSIS

(G): This choice is the difference between the number of dimes and the number of pennies in the situation required by the right answer. **(H):** This choice is 5 less than the right answer, which could tempt test-takers because the value of most of the coins is divisible by 5, and a number of different algebra mistakes could lead test-takers to be off by 5. **(K):** This choice is 5 more than the right answer, and is probably here for the same reasons (H) is here.

How to check? Try an alternate approach above.

Note $\quad$ The math in this question is relatively simple, but the question can still frustrate some test-takers because of the extreme importance of reading carefully through the details and relationships described in the prompt. Remember that reading comprehension is the most important aspect of any section of the ACT, including the Math section!

Test 1, Question 53 (Test 2 in the 2020-2021 Red Book—see page 23 for more)

- **What's the prompt asking for?** The value of x in the given equation.
- **Math concepts in the prompt:** exponents, fractions
- **Notable differences among choices:** (A) and (B) are negative, while the other choices are positive. (A) is the opposite of (C). (E) is 1, and all the other choices are fractions with absolute values less than 1.
- **Concepts in the choices:** fractions, negative numbers, one, positive numbers

- **"Bridge" concepts:** Raising any number to an exponent of 0 gives a result of 1.
- **Pre-solution patterns (see p. 149):** opposites
- **Things to look out for:** Don't forget that the value of the fraction in the equation needs to be zero in order for the equation to be valid, because any number raised to a zero exponent equals 1! Don't make any small mistakes in your algebra! Pay special attention to the sign of your answer, since the choices seem to be setting us up to make a mistake related to sign!

Solution 1: Calculator/Backsolve: Using a calculator, try each choice as the value of x in the given equation. Pick the choice that makes the equation true.

$$10^{\left(\frac{2\left(-\frac{1}{2}\right)-1}{\left(-\frac{1}{2}\right)}\right)} = 1 \quad \text{(plug } x = -\frac{1}{2} \text{ into the given expression to test (A))}$$

$$10^{\left(\frac{-2}{\left(-\frac{1}{2}\right)}\right)} = 1 \quad \text{(simplify)}$$

$$10^4 = 1 \quad \text{(simplify)}$$

$$10,000 = 1 \quad \text{(simplify)}$$

When we test (A) we get an invalid statement, so (A) is wrong. Let's try the next choice.

$$10^{\left(\frac{2\left(-\frac{1}{8}\right)-1}{\left(-\frac{1}{8}\right)}\right)} = 1 \quad \text{(plug } x = -\frac{1}{8} \text{ into the given expression to test (B))}$$

$$10^{\left(\frac{-\frac{5}{4}}{\left(-\frac{1}{8}\right)}\right)} = 1 \qquad \text{(simplify)}$$

$$10^{10} = 1 \qquad \text{(simplify)}$$

$$10{,}000{,}000{,}000 = 1 \qquad \text{(simplify)}$$

Testing (B) also gives us an invalid statement, so (B) is wrong. Let's try (C):

$$10^{\left(\frac{2\left(\frac{1}{2}\right)-1}{\left(\frac{1}{2}\right)}\right)} = 1 \qquad \left(\text{plug } x = \tfrac{1}{2} \text{ into the given expression to test (C)}\right)$$

$$10^{\left(\frac{0}{\left(\frac{1}{2}\right)}\right)} = 1 \qquad \text{(simplify)}$$

$$10^{0} = 1 \qquad \text{(simplify)}$$

$$1 = 1 \qquad \text{(simplify)}$$

When we test (C) we get a valid statement, so (C) appears to be right. Of course, we still have to try the remaining choices to make sure we haven't made any mistakes, so let's try (D):

$$10^{\left(\frac{2\left(\frac{10}{19}\right)-1}{\left(\frac{10}{19}\right)}\right)} = 1 \qquad \left(\text{plug } x = \tfrac{10}{19} \text{ into the given expression to test (D)}\right)$$

$$10^{\left(\frac{\frac{1}{19}}{\left(\frac{10}{19}\right)}\right)} = 1 \qquad \text{(simplify)}$$

$$10^{\left(\frac{1}{10}\right)} = 1 \qquad \text{(simplify)}$$

$$\sqrt[10]{10} = 1 \qquad \text{(simplify)}$$

When we test (D) we get an invalid statement, so (D) is wrong. Let's try the last choice.

$$10^{\left(\frac{2(1)-1}{(1)}\right)} = 1 \qquad \left(\text{plug } x = 1 \text{ into the given expression to test (E)}\right)$$

$$10^{1} = 1 \qquad \text{(simplify)}$$

$$10 = 1 \qquad \text{(simplify)}$$

When we test (E) we get an invalid statement, so (E) is wrong. After checking each answer choice, we can be sure that (C) is the right answer.

Solution 2: Algebra: Set the exponent equal to zero, and solve for x.

We know that when a number is raised to an exponent and the result is 1, that exponent must be 0. So we can set the expression in the exponent equal to 0 and solve for x.

$$\frac{2x-1}{x} = 0 \qquad \text{(exponent set equal to 0)}$$

$$2x - 1 = 0 \qquad \text{(multiply both sides by } x)$$

$$2x = 1 \qquad \text{(add 1 to both sides)}$$

$$x = \frac{1}{2} \qquad \text{(divide both sides by 2)}$$

So the answer is (C).

ANSWER CHOICE ANALYSIS

(A): This is the opposite of the right answer; this choice reflects the kind of mistake with the sign of a number that's common when untrained test-takers do algebra too carelessly on test day. (By the way, the fact that most of the choices are positive strongly suggests, but doesn't guarantee, that the right answer is also positive; noticing that might help a trained test-taker realize that she needed to re-check her work if she thought (A) was right.) **(D):** This choice reflects the mistake of thinking that we multiply a number by its exponent. If we multiplied 10 by $\frac{1}{10}$, we would get a result of 1, but that isn't how exponents work. **(E):** This choice could reflect a mistaken understanding of exponents. If an untrained test-taker accidentally thought that raising a number to an exponent of 1 led to a value of 1, then he might pick this choice, which results in the exponent of having a value of 1.

How to check? Try an alternate approach above. Pay special attention to the issues that we noted above.

▶ **Post-solution patterns (see p. 151):** most like the other choices

Test 1, Question 54 (Test 2 in the 2020-2021 Red Book—see page 23 for more)

- **What's the prompt asking for?** The chance that a randomly selected person who plays an instrument also likes to read.
- **Math concepts in the prompt:** probability, reading data from a table, surveys
- **Math concepts in the diagram:** addition, probability, surveys
- **Elements of the choices:** Each choice is a fraction.
- **Notable differences among choices:** (F) has 5 as its denominator, while (G) and (H) have it as their numerator. (G) has 9 as its denominator, while (J) has it as a numerator. (J) and (K) both have 25 as their denominators, which may be relevant since 25 is a multiple of 5, which appears in the other answer choices.
- **Concepts in the choices:** fractions, multiples of 5
- **"Bridge" concepts:** When we construct a probability fraction, the denominator represents the total number of possible outcomes, and the numerator represents the number of those outcomes whose probability we're trying to determine.
- **Pre-solution patterns (see p. 149):** wrong answers try to imitate right answers
- **Things to look out for:** Don't misread the data in the prompt! Don't focus on the wrong part of the table!

Solution 1: Data: Use the table to determine the number of people who play a musical instrument, and make that number the denominator of your probability fraction. Then use the table to find the number of people who both play a musical instrument and read, and make that number the numerator of your probability fraction. Finally, pick the choice that's equivalent to the fraction you've just constructed.

The denominator of the probability fraction is the number of possible outcomes. In this case, that's the total number of people who play a musical instrument, which the table tells us is 90 people. (Note that the phrase from the prompt "given that the person plays a musical instrument" tells us we're only selecting from people who play a musical instrument.)

The numerator of the probability fraction is the number of desired outcomes. In this case, that's the number of people who play a musical instrument and who also like to read, which the table tells us is 50 people.

So the probability fraction is $\frac{50}{90}$, or $\frac{5}{9}$, and (G) is right.

ANSWER CHOICE ANALYSIS

(F): This choice reflects the mistake of comparing the number of people who both like to read and play a musical instrument to the total number of people who answered the survey, resulting in a fraction of $\frac{50}{250}$. **(H):** This choice could reflect a misreading of the prompt, since it indicates the chance that a person who likes to read also plays a musical instrument, not the chance that a person who plays a musical instrument also likes to read. The chance that a person who likes to read also plays a musical instrument is $\frac{50}{110}$. **(J):** This reflects the chance that a person who answered the survey plays a musical instrument, but that isn't what the prompt asked us for. **(K):** This indicates a mistake similar to the one in (J). It's the chance that a person who answered the survey likes to read, but that isn't what the prompt asked us for.

How to check? Carefully reconsider your reading of the prompt and the data, to make sure that you have compared the right numbers in the right way. Being able to explain the mistakes that lead to the wrong answers, as described above, should give us extra confidence that we've thought about the question correctly.

▶ **Post-solution patterns (see p. 151):** most like the other choices; right answer to the wrong question

Test 1, Question 55 (Test 2 in the 2020-2021 Red Book—see page 23 for more)

- **What's the prompt asking for?** Mario's average speed, in feet per second, during the minute described in the prompt.
- **Math concepts in the prompt:** circles, diameters, minutes, ratios, speed, unit conversions
- **Elements of the choices:** Each choice involves multiplying π by an improper fraction.
- **Notable differences among choices:** (A) and (B) both include 65 in the numerator. (B) is half of (A), and (A) is half of (C). (A), (C), and (E) have 9 in the denominator, while (B) and (D) have 18 in the denominator.
- **Concepts in the choices:** fractions, multiplying by two, π
- **"Bridge" concepts:** There are 12 inches in a foot and 60 seconds in a minute. The formula for the circumference of a circle is πd. The distance that Mario travels during the minute described in the prompt will be equal to the product of 200 and the circumference of his wheels, since the wheels roll along the ground 200 times in the given minute.
- **Pre-solution patterns (see p. 149):** wrong answers try to imitate right answers; halves and doubles
- **Things to look out for:** Don't forget to convert from inches to feet! Don't forget to convert from minutes to seconds! Don't confuse diameter with radius! Don't make any small mistakes in your reading or calculations!

Solution 1: Geometry: Use πd to determine the circumference of Mario's wheel in inches, and multiply that by 200 to determine the number of inches he traveled during the given minute. Then divide that number by 12 to find the number of feet he traveled in the given minute, and divide this new number by 60 to find the number of feet traveled on average per second.

Before we get into this solution, we should notice that all of the answers choices are expressed as fractions, not decimals. So let's try to keep our expression as a fraction, and then reduce it if we need to at the end.

$$\pi d \qquad \text{(formula for circumference)}$$

$$\pi(26) \qquad \text{(plug in } d = 26)$$

So the circumference of Mario's wheel is 26π inches. We can multiply this value by 200 to find the distance in inches that Mario traveled during one minute, since we're told the wheel revolved 200 times in one minute.

$$\pi(26) \times 200 = 5200\pi \qquad \text{(circumference multiplied by number of revolutions)}$$

So Mario traveled 5200π inches during his one-minute ride. We can divide this number by 12 to find how many feet he traveled, since there are 12 inches in a foot.

$$5200\pi \times \frac{1}{12} = \frac{5200\pi}{12} \qquad \text{(divide by 12 to convert to feet)}$$

Finally, we can divide this number by 60 to find the number of feet he traveled in one second, because there are 60 seconds in a minute:

$$\frac{5200\pi}{12} \times \frac{1}{60} = \frac{5200\pi}{720} \qquad \text{(divide by 60 to convert to seconds)}$$

We've found our answer, but it doesn't look like the answers from the answer choices. Let's try to reduce it. We can divide the numerator and denominator by 10, which gives us $\frac{520\pi}{72}$. We need to reduce it even more, though, so let's think of a number that goes evenly into 520 and 72. We might realize that 8 goes into 72, and if we try dividing 520 by 8 on a calculator, we'll see that 8 goes into 520 evenly too. So let's divide the numerator and denominator by 8. The result is $\frac{65\pi}{9}$, which is equal to the expression in (A), so (A) is the right answer.

If we didn't want to bother with reducing the fractions, we could also just use a calculator to find a decimal approximation of the answer we found, and then find a decimal approximation of each answer choice. If we did that, we would find that our expression $\frac{5200\pi}{720}$ was approximately equal to 22.689, and the five answer choices were approximately equal to 22.689, 11.344, 45.379, 147.480, and 589.921, in order. Again, we would see that our expression was equal to (A), the right answer.

ANSWER CHOICE ANALYSIS

(B): This choice could reflect the mistake of thinking that the formula for the circumference of a circle was πr instead of πd. **(C):** This choice could reflect the mistake of thinking that the wheel's radius was 26 inches, rather than its diameter, resulting in a diameter of 52 inches. **(D):** This choice reflects the mistake of using the formula for the area of a circle in place of the formula for circumference of a circle. **(E):** This choice combines the mistakes from (C) and (D).

How to check? Carefully reconsider your reading and your calculations. Be especially careful about the correct denominator, since the choices are clearly setting you up to be off by a factor of two there.

▶ **Post-solution patterns (see p. 151):** easy calculation mistake; most like the other choices

▌ Test 1, Question 56 (Test 2 in the 2020-2021 Red Book—see page 23 for more)

- **What's the prompt asking for?** The value of $\frac{j}{k}$ as described in the prompt.

- **Math concepts in the prompt:** exponents, fractions, integers, positive numbers, radical expressions

- **Notable differences among choices:** (F) is the reciprocal of (K). (G) is half of (H), and (H) is half of (K). (F) and (G) are fractions, while the other numbers are integers.

- **Concepts in the choices:** dividing by 2, fractions

- **"Bridge" concepts:** $\sqrt{3}$ and 27 are both numbers that can be expressed as powers of 3; rewriting each number as an exponent expression with a base of 3 will make it easier to answer the question using the abstract/algebra approach.

- **Pre-solution patterns (see p. 149):** halves and doubles; opposites

- **Things to look out for:** Don't confuse the numerator and denominator in the fraction described by the prompt! Don't confuse j and k in the original equation! Don't make any small mistakes in your reading or calculations!

Solution 1: Concrete/Backsolve: Try each choice as the value of $\frac{j}{k}$, and pick the one that makes the original equation valid.

Remember that any integer is understood to have a denominator of 1, so when we check an answer choice that's just an integer, that integer will be the value of j, and k will be 1.

$$\left(\sqrt{3}\right)^{1} = 27^{6} \qquad \text{(plug in } j = 1 \text{ and } k = 6 \text{ to test (F))}$$

$$1.732 = 387{,}420{,}489 \qquad \text{(simplify)}$$

This doesn't result in a valid statement, so (F) is wrong. Let's check the next answer choice.

$$\left(\sqrt{3}\right)^3 = 27^2 \qquad \text{(plug in } j = 3 \text{ and } k = 2 \text{ to test (G))}$$
$$5.196 = 729 \qquad \text{(simplify)}$$

This doesn't result in a valid statement, so (G) is wrong. Let's check the next answer choice.

$$\left(\sqrt{3}\right)^3 = 27^1 \qquad \text{(plug in } j = 3 \text{ and } k = 1 \text{ to test (H))}$$
$$5.196 = 27 \qquad \text{(simplify)}$$

This doesn't result in a valid statement, so (H) is wrong. Let's check the next answer choice.

$$\left(\sqrt{3}\right)^4 = 27^1 \qquad \text{(plug in } j = 4 \text{ and } k = 1 \text{ to test (J))}$$
$$9 = 27 \qquad \text{(simplify)}$$

This doesn't result in a valid statement, so (J) is wrong. Let's check the last answer choice.

$$\left(\sqrt{3}\right)^6 = 27^1 \qquad \text{(plug in } j = 6 \text{ and } k = 1 \text{ to test (K))}$$
$$27 = 27 \qquad \text{(simplify)}$$

This results in a valid statement. We've checked every other answer choice, so we can be sure that (K) is right.

Solution 2: Abstract/Algebra: Re-write the original equation so that both sides involve an exponent term with base 3, and then find the ratio of j to k.

We know that taking the square root of a number is the same as raising that number to an exponent of $\frac{1}{2}$, so we can rewrite $\sqrt{3}$ as $3^{\left(\frac{1}{2}\right)}$. We also know that 27 is equal to $3 \times 3 \times 3$, which is the same as 3^3. So we can rewrite the expression from the prompt like this:

$$3^{\left(\frac{1}{2}\right)^j} = (3^3)^k \qquad \text{(expression from the prompt rewritten with base 3)}$$
$$3^{\left(\frac{j}{2}\right)} = 3^{3k} \qquad \text{(simplify exponents)}$$

Because the bases are equal and the expressions are equal, we know the exponents on each side must equal each other.

$$\frac{j}{2} = 3k \qquad \text{(exponents set equal to one another)}$$
$$j = 6k \qquad \text{(multiply both sides by 2)}$$
$$\frac{j}{k} = 6 \qquad \text{(divide both sides by } k)$$

So $\frac{j}{k} = 6$, and the right answer is (K).

ANSWER CHOICE ANALYSIS

(F): This choice is the inverse of the right answer, which might tempt untrained test takers who either confuse the variables in the original equation or in the fraction at the end of the prompt. **(G):** This could be the result of thinking that $\left(\sqrt{3}\right)^j$ was equal to 3^{2j} instead of $3^{\frac{j}{2}}$, and then solving $2j = 3k$ for $\frac{j}{k}$. **(H):** This choice represents the common base that we need to find if we try Solution 2 above, so it may attract untrained test takers who don't remember what the prompt was asking for. This could also be the result of thinking that $\left(\sqrt{3}\right)^j$ was equal to 3^j instead of $3^{\frac{j}{2}}$, and then solving $j = 3k$ for $\frac{j}{k}$.

How to check? Try an alternate approach above. Be especially careful about not switching j and k in your answer, since the choices are clearly setting you up to make that kind of mistake!

▶ **Post-solution patterns (see p. 151):** opposites

Test 1, Question 57 (Test 2 in the 2020-2021 Red Book—see page 23 for more)

- **What's the prompt asking for?** The difference between the mean and the median of the terms described in the prompt.
- **Math concepts in the prompt:** arithmetic sequences, fractions, mean (average), median, subtraction
- **Notable differences among choices:** (A), (D), and (E) are integers. (B) and (C) present both possible combinations of (D) and (E) as the components of a fraction. (A) is zero.
- **Concepts in the choices:** denominators, fractions, numerators, zero

- **"Bridge" concepts:** The mean of a series is the result when the terms in the series are added together, and the sum is divided by the number of terms. The median of a series is the number in the middle when the terms in the series are written in order from least to greatest.
- **Pre-solution patterns (see p. 149):** wrong answers try to imitate right answers
- **Things to look out for:** Don't make any small mistakes in your reading, reasoning, or calculations! Don't forget the difference between mean and median!

Solution 1: Concrete/Arithmetic: List out some possible terms in the sequence and use them to determine the mean and median of the sequence. Then subtract one number from the other and pick the corresponding answer choice.

Let's imagine that the sequence works by adding 1 to the previous term. The prompt tells us that the first term is $\frac{3}{4}$, so the second term would be $1\frac{3}{4}$, the third would be $2\frac{3}{4}$, then $3\frac{3}{4}$, $4\frac{3}{4}$, $5\frac{3}{4}$, and $6\frac{3}{4}$. We can find the mean by adding up these 7 terms and dividing by 7. The result is 3.75. We know that the median is the term in the middle when all the values are listed from least to greatest. In this case, that's the fourth term, which is $3\frac{3}{4}$. The mean, 3.75, and the median, $3\frac{3}{4}$, are equal, so the difference between them is 0, and the answer is (A).

Solution 2: Abstract: Given the properties of the sequence in the prompt, realize that the mean and median must be identical.

We know that the median in a set of values is the value in the middle when the set is ordered from least to greatest. In this case, that would have to be the fourth term in the series, because the series has seven terms, and the fourth one is the one in the middle. How would this relate to the mean?

Well, we know that the mean is the average of the 7 terms. We would expect this number to be relatively close to the median, because the 7 terms are evenly spaced out, and the median is the term right in the middle. In fact, because we know that each term is a constant amount greater than the previous term, we can reason that the median and the mean must be the same number. Think about it this way: the fourth term is $\frac{3}{4}$ more than the third term, and $\frac{3}{4}$ less than the fifth term. The fourth term is also $1\frac{1}{2}$ more than the second term, and $1\frac{1}{2}$ less than the sixth term. Finally, the fourth term is $2\frac{1}{4}$ more than the first term, and $2\frac{1}{4}$ less than the seventh term. In other words, the differences between the fourth term and each term before and after it sort of "cancel out." So the fourth term, which is the median, is also the mean. That means there's no difference between the mean and the median, since they're the same number, so (A) is right.

(If this solution didn't make a lot of sense to you, don't worry about it—it's perfectly fine to use an approach like the one we used in the previous solution.)

ANSWER CHOICE ANALYSIS

(E): This choice might appeal to some untrained test-takers who don't read the question carefully enough, because it is true that the fourth term in the sequence is both the mean and the median. But the prompt asked us for the difference between the mean and the median, not the number of the term in the center of the sequence.

How to check? Try an alternate approach above.

▶ **Post-solution patterns (see p. 151):** right answer to the wrong question

Test 1, Question 58 (Test 2 in the 2020-2021 Red Book—see page 23 for more)

- **What's the prompt asking for?** The choice whose expression represents the length in centimeters of arc $\overset{\frown}{AC}$.

- **Math concepts in the prompt:** angles, arcs, center of a circle, circles, degrees, dimension measurements, radii, right angles

- **Math concepts in the diagram:** angles, arcs, center of a circle, circles, dimension labels, radii, right angles

- **Elements of the choices:** Each choice is an expression that involves multiplying a fraction with a denominator of 45 by a parenthetical expression featuring the inverse of a trig function and the fraction $\frac{1}{4}$.

- **Notable differences among choices:** (F) and (G) both have π as

the numerator of the first fraction, while (H), (J), and (K) have 2π. (F) and (H) both involve sine, while (G) and (J) both involve cosine, and (K) involves tangent.

- **Concepts in the choices:** fractions, inverse trig functions, multiplication, π

- **"Bridge" concepts:** Arc length can be found by finding the central angle associated with the arc, dividing that angle by 360, and then multiplying the result by the circumference. In other words, we need to find what percentage of the 360 degrees of the circle is represented by the arc, and then multiply that percentage by the circumference of the whole circle.

Solution 1: Concrete/Algebra: Find the measure of the central angle, divide the result by 360, then multiply that result by the circumference of the circle.

We'll start by finding the measure of the central angle, $\angle ADC$, which is the same as $\angle BDC$ from $\triangle BDC$. We'll call the measure of that angle x. We can see that $\triangle BDC$ is a right triangle, and we know the length of the hypotenuse of that triangle is 4, and the length of the side opposite $\angle BDC$ is 1. We know from SOHCAHTOA that $sine = \frac{opposite}{hypotenuse}$, so it must be true that $\sin x = \frac{1}{4}$.

If $\sin x = \frac{1}{4}$, then we can find the arcsine of each side of that equation to find the value of x. That gives us $x = \sin^{-1}\left(\frac{1}{4}\right)$.

So the measure of $\angle ADC$ is $\sin^{-1}\left(\frac{1}{4}\right)$. We need to divide this value by 360 to find which proportion of the 360° of arc of the whole circle is represented by $\angle ADC$. That gives us $\dfrac{\sin^{-1}\left(\frac{1}{4}\right)}{360}$.

Finally, we need to multiply this amount by the circumference of the whole circle. We know that $C = 2\pi r$, where C is the circumference of the circle, and r is the radius of the circle. In this case, the prompt tells us that the radius of the circle is 4, so the circumference of the circle is $2\pi(4)$, or 8π. Now we can multiply $\dfrac{\sin^{-1}\left(\frac{1}{4}\right)}{360}$ by 8π to get $\dfrac{8\pi \sin^{-1}\left(\frac{1}{4}\right)}{360}$.

This expression doesn't look like any of the expressions from the answer choices, but we can see that our expression could be reduced and re-written a little bit. We can divide the numerator and denominator by 8 to get $\dfrac{\pi \sin^{-1}\left(\frac{1}{4}\right)}{45}$, which is equal to the expression in (F). So (F) is right.

Solution 2: Test-smart: We can see from the diagram that the length of the arc should be only a little more than 1. Calculate the actual decimal value of each expression in the answer choices and eliminate all the answer choices that are too large to be right.

(F) $\dfrac{\pi}{45}\left(\sin^{-1}\left(\frac{1}{4}\right)\right) \approx 1.0107$

(G) $\dfrac{\pi}{45}\left(\cos^{-1}\left(\frac{1}{4}\right)\right) \approx 5.2724$

(H) $\dfrac{2\pi}{45}\left(\sin^{-1}\left(\frac{1}{4}\right)\right) \approx 2.0214$

(J) $\dfrac{2\pi}{45}\left(\cos^{-1}\left(\frac{1}{4}\right)\right) \approx 10.5450$

(K) $\dfrac{2\pi}{45}\left(\tan^{-1}\left(\frac{1}{4}\right)\right) \approx 1.9598$

We can see that only (F) is just a little more than 1, so (F) must be right. (Notice that the prompt tells us the angle is measured in degrees, so we should make sure our calculator is in degree mode, not radian mode.)

ANSWER CHOICE ANALYSIS

(G): This choice reflects the mistake of confusing sine and cosine. **(H):** This choice reflects the mistake of mixing up radius and diameter, or thinking the radius of the circle was 8 instead of 4, or thinking that the formula for circumference was $C = 2\pi d$ instead of $C = 2\pi r$. **(J):** This choice reflects a combination of the error in (G) and the error in (H). **(K):** This choice reflects the error in (H) and also the mistake of confusing sine and tangent.

How to check? Try an alternate approach above.

Test 1, Question 59 (Test 2 in the 2020-2021 Red Book—see page 23 for more)

- **What's the prompt asking for?** The area of the triangle in the diagram.
- **Math concepts in the prompt:** triangles, trigonometric functions
- **Math concepts in the diagram:** angle measurements, dimension labels, triangles
- **Notable differences among choices:** (A) is half of (C) and (B) is half of (D).
- **Concepts in the choices:** dividing by 2

- **"Bridge" concepts:** The note in the prompt itself gives us the formula for determining the area of the triangle, so all we have to do is take the provided numbers, plug them into the provided formula, and simplify.
- **Pre-solution patterns (see p. 149):** halves and doubles
- **Things to look out for:** Don't confuse the different side lengths when you plug the information from the diagram into the given formula! Don't accidentally use cosine instead of sine! Don't forget the $\frac{1}{2}$ that appears in the beginning of the formula!

Solution 1: Trigonometry: Plug the values from the diagram into the provided formula, and use your calculator to find the result.

The only angle measure we know is that the bottom left angle is $30°$, so for the purposes of the formula we'll have to make that angle C, and make the side lengths opposite the other (unmarked) angles a and b. So $C = 30°$, $a = 4$, and $b = 8$.

$\dfrac{1}{2}ab \sin C$ (provided formula for area of the triangle)

$\dfrac{1}{2}(4)(8) \sin 30°$ (plug in $C = 30°$, $a = 4$, and $b = 8$)

$(16) \sin 30°$ (simplify)

8 (simplify)

So the answer is (C).

ANSWER CHOICE ANALYSIS

(A): This is half of the right answer, which could reflect the mistake of multiplying by $\sin 30°$ twice instead of once. **(B):** This choice could be the result of confusing the side lengths when applying the formula, using 4 and 5 for a and b instead of 4 and 8. **(D):** This choice could reflect the mistake similar to the one in (B), except that it would use the side lengths 5 and 8 for a and b instead of 4 and 8. **(E):** This choice could result from using cosine instead of sine in the given formula and rounding up.

How to check? Carefully recheck your work, especially with respect to plugging in the right values for the right side lengths, and using the right trig function.

▶ **Post-solution patterns (see p. 151):** easy calculation mistake

(see p. 151)

Test 1, Question 60 (Test 2 in the 2020-2021 Red Book—see page 23 for more)

see page 23 for more

- **What's the prompt asking for?** The expected value of x according to the table.
- **Math concepts in the prompt:** expected value, probability distribution
- **Math concepts in the diagram:** fractions, probability distribution, zero
- **Notable differences among choices:** (F) is half of (G). (H) is half of (J). (F) and (G) are fractions, while (H) and (J) are integers, and (K) is the only choice that's a mixed fraction.
- **Concepts in the choices:** 1, fractions
- **Pre-solution patterns (see p. 149):** halves and doubles
- **Things to look out for:** Don't make any small mistakes when multiplying out the probabilities of each discrete value and adding those products together on your calculator! Don't confuse which probability applies to which expected value!

(see p. 149)

Solution 1: Probability: Multiply each discrete value by its probability, and add together all the products as a result of doing that.

$$\left(0 \times \tfrac{1}{6}\right) + \left(1 \times \tfrac{1}{12}\right) + \left(2 \times \tfrac{1}{4}\right) + \left(3 \times \tfrac{1}{12}\right) + \left(4 \times \tfrac{1}{12}\right) + \left(5 \times 0\right) + \left(6 \times \tfrac{1}{3}\right)$$ (sum of the discrete values multiplied by their probabilities)

$$\tfrac{1}{12} + \tfrac{1}{2} + \tfrac{3}{12} + \tfrac{4}{12} + 2$$ (simplify)

$$\tfrac{8}{12} + \tfrac{1}{2} + 2$$ (simplify)

$$\tfrac{8}{12} + \tfrac{6}{12} + \tfrac{24}{12}$$ (put in terms of twelfths)

$$\tfrac{38}{12}$$ (simplify)

$\tfrac{38}{12}$ is the same $3\tfrac{2}{12}$, or $3\tfrac{1}{6}$. So (K) is right.

Notice that instead of dealing with the fractions, we could have just added all those products on a calculator, which would give us a result of 3.16666667. We could then see that only (K) had a value that was 3 plus some fraction, and we could find $3 + \tfrac{1}{6}$ on a calculator to confirm that $3\tfrac{1}{6} \approx 3.16666667$.

Solution 2: Test-smart: Note that the right answer must be greater than 2, and pick the only choice that fits that requirement.

Once we realize that we need to multiply each x value by its probability and add the results together, and we notice that the last value by itself will be $6 \times \tfrac{1}{3}$, which equals 2, we can be sure that the value must be more than 2. Only (K) is more than 2, so the answer must be (K).

ANSWER CHOICE ANALYSIS

(F): This choice is the average of the probability fractions in the right-hand column of the table (not counting 0), but the right answer is the weighted average of the possible outcomes in the left-hand column, not the average of the fractions in the right-hand column. **(H):** This is the sum of the probability fractions in the table, but that isn't what the prompt is asking for.

How to check? Try an alternate approach above. Especially note that the right answer must make sense in the context of the distribution in the table (which, again, means (K) must be right).

▶ **Post-solution patterns (see p. 151):** right answer to the wrong question

(see p. 151)

Note This question is one more great example of how the ACT often writes questions so that they seem like they will take much longer than they really need to take. Many untrained test-takers will go through the hassle of Solution 1 above, but, as trained test-takers, we know that we always need to consider the answer choices before we get started on an ACT Math question, which would allow us to see that a much faster approach, like Solution 2, is possible. Remember this kind of thing on test day!

TEST 2 (TEST 3 IN 2020-2021 RED BOOK)

Test 2, Question 1 (Test 3 in the 2020-2021 Red Book—see page 23 for more)

see page 23 for more

- **What's the prompt asking for?** The degrees turned after 1 hour.
- **Math concepts in the prompt:** degrees, ratio, time
- **Elements of the choices:** Each choice is a number of degrees.
- **Notable differences among choices:** Every choice except (A) is a

3-digit number, while (A) is 2 digits. (A), (B), and (D) are multiples of 90, while (C) and (E) aren't; (A), (B), and (D) also form a series in which each choice is 90 more than the choice before it. (A) and (D) add up to a full circle, or 360°. (B) is the only number that appears in the prompt.

- **Concepts in the choices:** degrees
- **"Bridge" concepts:** There are 60 minutes in one hour.
- **Pre-solution patterns (see p. 149):** opposites; halves and doubles
- **Things to look out for:** Don't forget how many minutes are in an hour! Don't misread the prompt!

Solution 1: Arithmetic: Determine the number of degrees that the restaurant turns in one minute; then, multiply that number by 60 to find the number of degrees it will turn in one hour.

If the restaurant turns 180° in 45 minutes, then it must turn $\frac{180°}{45}$ in one minute, or 4° in one minute. If the restaurant turns 4° in one minute, then it must turn $60 \times 4°$, or 240°, in an hour, because there are 60 minutes in an hour. That means (C) is correct.

Solution 2: Algebra: Let x be the number of degrees that the restaurant turns in one hour. Write an equation that sets the following ratios equal to one another: $\frac{180}{45}$, and $\frac{x}{60}$. Then cross-multiply and solve for x.

$$\frac{180}{45} = \frac{x}{60}$$ (degree rotation in 45 minutes set equal to degree rotation in 1 hour)

$$10,800 = 45x$$ (cross-multiply)

$$240 = x$$ (divide both sides by 45)

So (C) must be right.

Solution 3: Test-smart: Notice that the correct answer must be a number that's more than 180 but less than 270, and note that only (B) satisfies that requirement.

We know that restaurant turns 180° in 45 minutes, and we know that an hour is more than 45 minutes long, so the correct answer must be more than 180°. That eliminates (A) and (B). We also know that 270° is 50% more than 180° (in other words, it's $180° + 90°$), and that 60 minutes (or 1 hour) is *less than* 50% more than 45 minutes, so 270° must be too large. That eliminates (D) and (E), which means (C) must be right.

ANSWER CHOICE ANALYSIS

(A): This choice corresponds to one-quarter of a circle, and may attract untrained test-takers who notice that 45 minutes differs from 60 minutes by one-quarter of an hour, and accidentally think that's relevant to the prompt. **(B):** This represents the number of degrees turned after 45 minutes according to the prompt, so the number of degrees turned after one hour must be more than (B). **(D):** This choice is the complement of (A). It must be too large to be the right answer for the reason we noted in Solution 3 above.

How to check? Make sure that your answer choice fits with the scale and context of the ideas in the prompt, and/or consider an alternative approach above.

Test 2, Question 2 (Test 3 in the 2020-2021 Red Book—see page 23 for more)

- **What's the prompt asking for?** The number of months paid for by a $500 check, including the onetime fee.
- **Math concepts in the prompt:** arithmetic, monthly fees, onetime fees
- **Elements of the choices:** one- and two-digit numbers

- **Notable differences among choices:** (F), (G), and (H) are all single-digit numbers, while (J) and (K) are two-digit numbers.
- **Things to look out for:** Don't confuse the onetime fee with the monthly fee! Don't make any small mistakes in your arithmetic! Don't assume that the onetime fee also pays for a month!

Solution 1: Arithmetic: Subtract the one-time fee from $500 to figure out how much of the money will be spent on monthly fees. Then, the divide the remaining amount by $40 to figure out how many months Brendan can pay for.

$$500 - 140 = 40x$$ (one-time $140 fee subtracted from $500 and set equal to $40x$)

$$360 = 40x$$ (simplify)

$$9 = x$$ (divide both sides by 40)

So (H) is right.

Solution 2: Backsolve: Test each answer choice as the number of months that Brendan paid for. To do this, multiply the number in the choice by $40, and then add $140. The right answer will be the one that results in a sum of $500.

$$140 + 40(3) = 260$$ (plug in value from (F))

$$140 + 40(4) = 300$$ (plug in value from (G))

$$140 + 40(9) = 500$$ (plug in value from (H))

$$140 + 40(12) = 620 \qquad \text{(plug in value from (J))}$$
$$140 + 40(13) = 660 \qquad \text{(plug in value from (K))}$$

We can see that only (H) results in a value of $500, so (H) is correct.

ANSWER CHOICE ANALYSIS

(F): This choice could appeal to untrained test-takers who accidentally thought the prompt was asking them to divide 500 by 140 (or even divide 140 by 40), and who also accidentally thought it was okay for Brendan's check to be larger than the amount that he owed. **(G):** This could be the result of misreading the size of the check, and thinking it was a $300 check. **(J):** This could be the result of forgetting about the onetime fee and finding the number of months that $500 would pay for without that fee included. **(K):** This could be the result of making the mistake from (J) and then rounding up the number of months.

How to check? Try an alternate approach above.

Test 2, Question 3 (Test 3 in the 2020-2021 Red Book—see page 23 for more)

- **What's the prompt asking for?** The total amount of the refund owed to the tour group.
- **Math concepts in the prompt:** arithmetic, costs
- **Elements of the choices:** Each is an amount of money.
- **Notable differences among choices:** (A) is half of (E). (B) and (E) both end in .00, while (D), (A), and (C) end in .25, .50, and .75, respectively.
- **Pre-solution patterns (see p. 149):** halves and doubles
- **Things to look out for:** Don't forget that the number of people in the group is 27, not 25! Don't confuse the two given costs when you do your calculations!

Solution 1: Arithmetic: Multiply $9.25 by 27 people to find the amount paid by the group. Multiply $8.50 by 27 people to find the amount that the group should have paid according to the prompt. Subtract the smaller amount from the larger amount to find the amount of the refund.

$$(9.25 \times 27) - (8.50 \times 27) \qquad \text{(cost of tour at higher price minus cost of tour at lower price)}$$
$$249.75 - 229.50 \qquad \text{(simplify)}$$
$$20.25 \qquad \text{(simplify)}$$

We can see that (D) is correct.

Solution 2: Arithmetic: Figure out how much each individual person overpaid, and then multiply that amount by 27 to find the amount the entire group overpaid.

Each person in the group paid $9.25, and each person should have paid $8.50. So each person overpaid by $0.75, because $9.25 − $8.50 = $0.75. If 27 people overpaid by $0.75, then the museum owes the group $0.75 × 27, or $20.25. So (D) is right.

ANSWER CHOICE ANALYSIS

(A): This choice is half of (E). **(C):** This is the result of correctly figuring out that each individual person overpaid by $0.75, but then accidentally multiplying that number by 25 instead of 27. **(E):** This number appears several times in the prompt, and could be tempting for test-takers who misread one or more parts of the prompt.

How to check? Try an alternate approach above.

Test 2, Question 4 (Test 3 in the 2020-2021 Red Book—see page 23 for more)

- **What's the prompt asking for?** The probability that a person who is a member—but not an officer—will be chosen.
- **Math concepts in the prompt:** probability
- **Elements of the choices:** Most of the choices are fractions. ((F) could also be seen as the equivalent of a fraction with a numerator of 0.)
- **Notable differences among choices:** (G), (H), and (K) all have a numerator of 1, while (J) has a numerator of 3. (G) and (J) have a denominator of 13, while (H) has a denominator of 10 and (K) has a denominator of 3.
- **Concepts in the choices:** fractions, zero
- **Pre-solution patterns (see p. 149):** wrong answers try to imitate right answers
- **Things to look out for:** Don't forget that the probability fraction should not include the officers of the club! Make sure to notice that Samara isn't an officer!

Solution 1: Probability: Construct a probability fraction that reflects the scenario in the prompt (which is that there are 10 eligible members, and only one will be chosen).

The numerator of the probability fraction is the number of desired outcomes. In this case, that's 1, because the prompt asks us the about the probability of one particular person being chosen.

The denominator of the probability fraction is the number of possible outcomes. In this case, that's the total number of people in the group from which a representative is chosen, which the prompt tells us is the number of members who are NOT officers. The prompt says there are 13 members and 3 of them are officers, so there are 10 members who aren't officers.

So the probability fraction is $\frac{1}{10}$, and (H) is right.

Solution 2: Test-smart: Notice that the right answer cannot be zero, because Samara meets the requirements to be selected, and it must have a denominator that's a factor of 10, because 10 students are eligible to be chosen. So only (H) can be right.

ANSWER CHOICE ANALYSIS

(F): This reflects one of two mistakes: either thinking that Samara is an officer (which would mean she was ineligible to be the representative, and would therefore have a zero probability of being chosen), or that the representative was being chosen from the 3 officers (in which case Samara would have been ineligible, and would therefore have a zero probability of being chosen). **(G):** This choice reflects the mistake of thinking the three officers are also eligible to be chosen. **(J):** This choice is the probability that a randomly chosen member of the club would be an officer; this might tempt test-takers who didn't read the prompt carefully. **(K):** This choice would represent the probability that Samara would be chosen if Samara were an officer AND if the representative was being chosen from among the 3 officers; this choice would tempt test-takers who misread at least two aspects of the prompt.

How to check? Try an alternate approach above.

Test 2, Question 5 (Test 3 in the 2020-2021 Red Book—see page 23 for more)

- **What's the prompt asking for?** The equation that, when solved for s, accurately describes the score Mele needs on the sixth test.
- **Math concepts in the prompt:** algebra, averages, variables
- **Elements of the choices:** Each choice is an algebraic equation with at least one fraction in it.
- **Notable differences among choices:** (A) and (B) include fractions with only 429 in the numerator, while (C), (D), and (E) include fractions with $s + 429$ in the numerator. (E) also involves dividing 85 by 100, while all the other choices set the left hand side of the equation equal to 85.
- **Concepts in the choices:** algebra, fractions
- **Pre-solution patterns (see p. 149):** wrong answers try to imitate right answers
- **Things to look out for:** Don't forgot that we need to find the average for six test scores, not five! Don't make small mistakes in your reading or algebra!

Solution 1: Algebra: Using the definition of the term "average," construct an algebraic equation that captures the scenario in the prompt.

We know that the average of a group of numbers is the sum of those numbers divided by the number of numbers. The prompt tells us that the test scores are 75, 70, 92, 95, 97, and s, the score Mele needs to earn on the 6th test. The sum of those six values is $s + 429$. When we divide that value by the number of numbers, we get $\frac{s + 429}{6}$. That expression tells us the average of the 6 numbers, and the prompt tells us that the average needs to be 85. When we set that expression equal to 85, we get $\frac{s + 429}{6} = 85$, which is the same as (D). So (D) is right.

Solution 2: Test-smart: Keeping in mind the similarities and differences among the choices that we noted above, consider each answer choice individually and compare it to the scenario in the prompt.

Choice (A) involves adding the 5 provided test scores and then dividing the result by 5, which gives us the average of those numbers. Then choice (A) adds the average of the 5 provided test scores to the score s that Mele must get on the 6th test, and sets the result equal to 85. It doesn't make any sense to say that 85 should be equal to the average of Mele's first 5 scores added to his 6th score itself, so (A) can't be correct.

Choice (B) has basically the same problem as (A), except it involves dividing the sum of the five provided scores by 6, which doesn't solve any of the problems in (A).

Choice (C) involves adding all 6 test scores together and dividing the result by 5—but there are 6 test scores, so if we want to find the average of the 6 test scores, we need to divide by the number of scores, which is 6, not 5. So (C) can't be right.

(D) involves adding all 6 test scores together and dividing the result by 6, which makes sense, because finding the average of a group of number means adding the numbers together and then dividing by the number of numbers. Choice (D) also sets the result equal to 85, which makes sense because the prompt told us to find the value for s that allows Mele "to average exactly 85 points for all 6 tests." So (D) appears to satisfy the requirements of the prompt—let's look at (E) to make sure we haven't made a mistake.

Choice (E) starts out the same as (D), but then sets the expression on the left equal to $\frac{85}{100}$. There's no reason to think that we want the average of the test scores to be equal to $\frac{85}{100}$, because the prompt told us they need to average 85. So (E) must be wrong.

After considering each choice, we can see that (D) is correct.

ANSWER CHOICE ANALYSIS

(A): This choice reflects the mistake of forgetting to include s in the average, and then thinking we could just add s to the average of the other 5 scores. **(B):** This is similar to (A) but with the added mistake of thinking 429 points is the sum of the scores for 6 tests, not 5. **(C):**

This reflects the mistake of forgetting that we need to find the average of six test scores, not five. **(E):** This reflects the mistake of thinking that 85 points should be expressed as $\frac{85}{100}$, even though the prompt just uses the number 85.

How to check? Try an alternate approach above.

▶ **Post-solution patterns (see p. 151):** most like the other choices

Test 2, Question 6 (Test 3 in the 2020-2021 Red Book—see page 23 for more)

- **What's the prompt asking for?** The measure of angle C.
- **Math concepts in the prompt:** angles, quadrilaterals
- **Math concepts in the diagram:** angles, quadrilaterals
- **Elements of the choices:** Each choice is the measure of an angle in degrees.
- **Notable differences among choices:** (J) and (K) add up to 180. The difference between (F) and (G) is 5, and so is the difference between (H) and (J). (F), (J), and (K) form a series in which each choice is 20 less than the previous choice.
- **Concepts in the choices:** 180°
- **"Bridge" concepts:** The angles in a quadrilateral must add up to 360°.
- **Pre-solution patterns (see p. 149):** opposites
- **Things to look out for:** Don't make a small mistake in your addition or subtraction, because the answer choices are clearly set up to anticipate that kind of mistake!

Solution 1: Geometry: Subtract the measures of the given angles from 360°.

We know that the four angles in a quadrilateral always add up to 360°, so we can subtract the 3 provided angle measures from 360° to find the value of the missing angle measure: $360° - 100° - 75° - 65° = 120°$

So the answer is (F).

ANSWER CHOICE ANALYSIS

Each wrong answer reflects a small mistake in reading and/or arithmetic—see the note below.

How to check? Carefully re-check your reading and arithmetic.

▶ **Post-solution patterns (see p. 151):** easy calculation mistake

Note This is a great example of a math question that many untrained test takers will miss without realizing it. The question seems simple, and it is, but there are still a lot of opportunities to make small mistakes in your reading or calculations and arrive at a wrong answer. Remember that you can't take anything for granted on test day, and that the ACT is specifically trying to get you to make tiny errors you won't catch. Don't let them get away with that!

Test 2, Question 7 (Test 3 in the 2020-2021 Red Book—see page 23 for more)

- **What's the prompt asking for?** The perimeter of ΔDEF.
- **Math concepts in the prompt:** perimeter, similar triangles
- **Math concepts in the diagram:** triangles
- **Elements of the choices:** Each choice is a one-or two-digit number.
- **Notable differences among choices:** (A) and (B) add up to (C).
- (C), (D), and (E) form a series in which each choice is one more than the previous choice.
- **Pre-solution patterns (see p. 149):** be aware of series
- **Things to look out for:** Don't confuse which sides of the similar triangles correspond to one another! Don't make small mistakes in your addition!

Solution 1: Geometry: Determine the length of side $\overline{DE}$, and then add that to the lengths of the other sides of ΔDEF to find the perimeter of ΔDEF.

We can see that each side of ΔDEF is half the corresponding side of ΔABC—for example, the longest side of ΔABC is 10 meters long, and the longest side of ΔDEF is 5 meters long. $\overline{DE}$, the missing side length of ΔDEF, corresponds to $\overline{BC}$, which has a length of 6, so the missing side length must be half of 6, or 3. So the perimeter of ΔDEF is $3 + 3 + 5$, or 11. That means (C) is right.

Solution 2: Geometry: Find the perimeter of ΔABC, then divide the result by 2, since each side of ΔABC is twice the corresponding side of ΔDEF.

We can see that each side of ΔDEF is half the corresponding side of ΔABC—for example, the longest side of ΔABC is 10 meters long, and the longest side of ΔDEF is 5 meters long—so the perimeter of ΔDEF must be half the perimeter of ΔABC. We can find the perimeter of ΔABC and divide by 2 to get our answer.

$$\frac{6 + 6 + 10}{2} = 11$$

Again, we can see that (C) is right.

ANSWER CHOICE ANALYSIS

(A): This "right approach, wrong step" answer is the length of side $\overline{DE}$, which we have to find in order to answer the question—but it isn't what the prompt actually asked us for. **(B):** This is the sum of the two given sides of ΔDEF. **(E):** This is equal to $5 + 5 + 3$, which is the calculation you'd make if you accidentally thought $\overline{DE}$ was equal to 5 instead of 3.

How to check? Carefully reconsider your reading and arithmetic, especially in light of the issues to look out for that were noted above, and our analysis of the choices. Especially note that (A) and (B) add up to (C), which makes sense from the ACT's perspective, considering that 3 (the length of $\overline{DE}$) must be added to 8 (the sum of $\overline{DF}$ and $\overline{EF}$) to find the correct answer, and many untrained test-takers will forget what the question was asking for and mark one of those choices without completing the process of answering the question.

▶ **Post-solution patterns (see p. 151):** right approach, wrong step; right answer to the wrong question

Test 2, Question 8 (Test 3 in the 2020-2021 Red Book—see page 23 for more)

- **What's the prompt asking for?** The value of the expression in the prompt.
- **Math concepts in the prompt:** absolute value, arithmetic, PEMDAS
- **Elements of the choices:** The choices are one-and two-digit numbers.
- **Notable differences among choices:** (F) is the opposite of (G).
- **Pre-solution patterns (see p. 149):** opposites
- **Things to look out for:** Don't execute your calculations in the wrong order!

Solution 1: Arithmetic: Multiply 3 by -2, add 4, and then take the absolute value of the result.

$|3(-2) + 4|$	(given expression)
$|-6 + 4|$	(multiply)
$|-2|$	(simplify)
2	(take absolute value)

So (G) is right.

Solution 2: Calculator: Carefully enter the expression from the prompt into your calculator and evaluate it.

When we enter the expression from the prompt into a calculator and evaluate it, the calculator indicates that the expression is equal to 2. So, again, (G) is right.

ANSWER CHOICE ANALYSIS

(F): This is the opposite of the right answer; it's also the value of the expression in the prompt without the absolute value brackets. **(H):** This would be the result if an untrained test-taker thought $3(-2)$ was equal to $3 - 2$ and evaluated the rest of the expression correctly. **(J):** This would be the result if an untrained test-taker thought $3(-2)$ was equal to $3 - (-2)$, or $3 + 2$, and evaluated the rest of the expression correctly. **(K):** This would be the result if an untrained test-taker thought $3(-2)$ was equal to $3(2)$ and evaluated the rest of the expression correctly.

How to check? Carefully reread the prompt and rework your calculations or try an alternate approach above, especially keeping in mind the answer choice analysis above, which demonstrates how the ACT tries very hard to take advantage of small mistakes and misreadings by untrained test-takers who are nervous on test day.

▶ **Post-solution patterns (see p. 151):** easy calculation mistake; most like the other choices; opposites

Test 2, Question 9 (Test 3 in the 2020-2021 Red Book—see page 23 for more)

- **What's the prompt asking for?** The values for x that satisfy the given equation.
- **Math concepts in the prompt:** algebra, multiplication, zero
- **Elements of the choices:** The choices present different combinations of the variables a and b from the prompt.
- **Notable differences among choices:** (A), (B), (D), and (E) present every possible combination of positive or negative a and positive or negative b. (C) involves multiplying a, b, and -1.
- **Concepts in the choices:** multiplication, opposites, variables
- **"Bridge" concepts:** In order for the product of two numbers to be zero, at least one of the numbers being multiplied must be zero.
- **Pre-solution patterns (see p. 149):** wrong answers try to imitate right answers; opposites
- **Things to look out for:** Don't get confused between positive and negative numbers!

Solution 1: Concrete: Pick values for a and b, and then use those values to determine x in terms of a and b. Choose the answer that accurately describes your value for x in terms of a and b.

Let's say that $a = 3$ and $b = 4$. That would give us the following expression: $(x + 3)(x + 4) = 0$

We might notice that the only values that appear in the answer choices are a, b, $-a$, $-b$, and $-ab$. So we can just test these five values to see which ones make the expression above true, and then check them against the answer choices. We'll start by plugging in a.

$(3 + 3)(3 + 4) = 0$	(our expression with a plugged in)
$(6)(7) = 0$	(simplify)

$$42 = 0 \qquad \text{(simplify)}$$

We can see that a doesn't satisfy the given equation. Let's try b.

$$(4 + 3)(4 + 4) = 0 \qquad \text{(our expression with } b \text{ plugged in)}$$

$$(7)(8) = 0 \qquad \text{(simplify)}$$

$$56 = 0 \qquad \text{(simplify)}$$

We can see that b doesn't satisfy the given equation. Let's try $-a$.

$$(-3 + 3)(-3 + 4) = 0 \qquad \text{(our expression with } -a \text{ plugged in)}$$

$$(0)(1) = 0 \qquad \text{(simplify)}$$

$$0 = 0 \qquad \text{(simplify)}$$

We can see that $-a$ does satisfy the given equation. Let's try $-b$.

$$(-4 + 3)(-4 + 4) = 0 \qquad \text{(our expression with } -b \text{ plugged in)}$$

$$(-1)(0) = 0 \qquad \text{(simplify)}$$

$$0 = 0 \qquad \text{(simplify)}$$

We can see that $-b$ also satisfies the given equation. Finally, let's try $-ab$.

$$(-12 + 3)(-12 + 4) = 0 \qquad \text{(our expression with } -ab \text{ plugged in)}$$

$$(-9)(-8) = 0 \qquad \text{(simplify)}$$

$$72 = 0 \qquad \text{(simplify)}$$

We can see that $-ab$ doesn't satisfy the given equation. After testing $a, b, -a, -b,$ and $-ab$, we can see that only $-a$ and $-b$ satisfy the equation, which means that (A) must be right.

(Notice that after testing a and finding out that it didn't satisfy the equation, we could have saved some time by ruling out (D) and (E), then testing $-b$ or b, which would have let us rule out (B), and so on. But we can also just test each value as we did above, and we should still be able to find the answer and move on relatively quickly.)

Solution 2: Algebra: Use your knowledge of the properties of zero to find the correct answer.

The expression on the left is two expressions in parentheses multiplied together. We know that the expression on the left can only equal zero if at least one of the parenthetical expressions is equal to zero. Let's consider the first parenthetical expression, $(x + a)$. We can see that the only x value that will make this expression equal to 0 is $-a$, because $(-a + a) = 0$. Similarly, the only x value that will make the second parenthetical expression equal to 0 is $-b$, because $(-b + b) = 0$. So when $x = -a$ or $x = -b$, the equation in the prompt will be satisfied. That means choice (A) is right.

ANSWER CHOICE ANALYSIS

(C): This choice might be tempting for test-takers who make a mistake while attempting a solution that involves somehow FOILing and/or factoring the expression in the prompt. **(E):** This could be the result if an untrained test-taker mistakenly switched the signs in the right answer.

How to check? Try an alternate approach above. Make sure you haven't made a mistake with respect to the sign of the right answer, because the ACT is clearly trying to get you to do that!

▶ **Post-solution patterns (see p. 151):** most like the other choices

Test 2, Question 10 (Test 3 in the 2020-2021 Red Book—see page 23 for more)

- **What's the prompt asking for?** The answer choice with the largest degree measure.
- **Math concepts in the prompt:** angles, circles, line segments, lines, minor arcs, points, tangents
- **Math concepts in the diagram:** angles, circles, line segments, lines, minor arcs, points, tangents
- **Elements of the choices:** Each choice uses geometric notation to indicate a part of the diagram.
- **Notable differences among choices:** (F) and (G) indicate minor arcs, while (H), (J), and (K) indicate angles. Every choice except (J) includes point M. The other points each appear in one, two, or three answer choices.
- **Concepts in the choices:** angles, minor arcs
- **"Bridge" concepts:** A tangent to a circle is perpendicular to the radius of the circle that it shares a point with. All radii of a circle are the same length. The diameter of a circle is twice the length of the radius of that circle. The degree measure of a minor arc is measured from the center of the circle that contains the arc.
- **Pre-solution patterns (see p. 149):** opposites; wrong answers try to imitate right answers
- **Things to look out for:** Don't confuse minor arcs with major arcs! Don't confuse minor arcs and angles! Don't misread the orders of the points in the answer choices! Don't confuse the letters of the answer choices with the letters in the diagram! Don't forget that the prompt asked for the largest degree measure, not the smallest!

Solution 1: Geometry: Use your knowledge of geometry to compare the relative sizes of the items in the answer choices.

The first thing we probably notice about $\overset{\frown}{LM}$ is that it pretty clearly looks like it's greater than 90°. The prompt tells us that $\overline{LK}$ is a diameter and G is the center of the circle, and we can see that M is closer to K than to L, which further supports that idea that $\overset{\frown}{LM}$ is greater than 90°. (If $\overset{\frown}{LM}$ were equal to 90°, then M would be exactly between K and L.) Let's come back to this idea that $\overset{\frown}{LM}$ is greater than 90° after we consider the other answer choices: if no other choice is greater than 90°, then we know that (F) must be the choice with the largest degree measure.

We can see that $\overset{\frown}{MK}$ from choice (G) must be less than 90°: we know $\angle GMJ$ is a 90° angle (because it's the angle formed by a radius and a tangent line), so $\angle MGK$ must be less than 90°, since both angles are part of triangle GMJ. (This also confirms that $\overset{\frown}{LM}$ must be greater than 90, as we just discussed for (F), since $\angle MGK$ is the supplement of $\angle LGM$.)

For (H), we know that $\angle JMG$ is equal to 90° because the prompt tells us $\overleftrightarrow{JM}$ is tangent to the circle at M, and G is the center of the circle, which means $\overline{MG}$ is a radius of the circle and $\overleftrightarrow{JM}$ must be perpendicular to $\overline{MG}$, by definition.

$\angle LHK$ from (J) must be 90°, because it's an angle inscribed in a semicircle and, by definition, that kind of angle must be 90°.

$\angle MJL$ from (K) must be less than 90°, because $\angle MJL$ has the same measure as $\angle MJG$, and $\angle MJG$ is one of the angles of right triangle $\triangle MJG$. Since $\angle JMG$ is the right angle in that right triangle, the other two angles must be acute angles—so $\angle MJG$ is an acute angle, which means $\angle MJL$ is an acute angle, which means $\angle MJL$ must be less than 90°.

After considering all the answer choices, we can see that only $\overset{\frown}{LM}$ from choice (F) is greater than 90°, while every other choice is less than or equal to 90°. So (F) must be right.

Solution 2: Test-smart: Remember the diagram is drawn to scale. Visually compare the parts to determine which is largest.

As trained test-takers, we know that every diagram on the ACT is drawn to scale, unless otherwise noted. When we look at each answer choice, we can see that only $\overset{\frown}{LM}$ from choice (F) is clearly greater than 90° according to the scale of the diagram, while every other choice is less than or equal to 90°. So (F) must be right.

ANSWER CHOICE ANALYSIS

(G): This choice could appeal to untrained test-takers who confused the minor arc $\overset{\frown}{MK}$ with the major arc $\overset{\frown}{MK}$. **(H):** Some untrained test-takers will pick this choice because it's an angle measurement we can determine with certainty from the information in the prompt, without incorporating judgments based on the scale of the diagram—but we can still tell (F) must be larger, even if we don't know the exact size of (F). **(J):** Some untrained test takers will accidentally assume this choice refers to the *arc* passing from L to K through H, which would make it the largest choice. **(K):** Some untrained test takers will pick this because they forget that the prompt asks for the choice with the *largest* measurement, not the *smallest*.

How to check? Carefully reconsider your reading and assumptions, especially in light of the answer choice analysis and things to look out for noted above.

Note   This question will frustrate a lot of untrained test takers who don't realize that it can be answered with total certainty even though the specific measurements of most of the things in the answer choices can't be determined. But, as trained test takers, we notice that the prompt only asks us to compare the relative sizes of things, not to determine their sizes objectively. We also know that we can rely on the scale of the diagram, which makes answering this question an easy thing to do as long as we make sure not to misread the points on the diagram and in the answer choices. Keep this kind of thing in mind on test day!

Test 2, Question 11 (Test 3 in the 2020-2021 Red Book—see page 23 for more)

- **What's the prompt asking for?** The length of $\overline{BC}$ (assuming it can be determined).
- **Math concepts in the prompt:** length, lines, points
- **Math concepts in the diagram:** length, lines, points
- **Elements of the choices:** Four of the choices are one-and two-digit numbers.
- **Notable differences among choices:** (A) and (B) add

up to (C). (A) and (C) add up to (D). (E) indicates that the length of $\overline{BC}$ cannot be found from the provided information.

- **Concepts in the choices:** insufficient information
- **Things to look out for:** Don't confuse the points! Don't find any distance besides $\overline{BC}$! Don't make small mistakes in your arithmetic!

Solution 1: Backsolve: Try the first four answer choices as the distance between B and C. The right answer will be the choice that allows all of the statements in the prompt to be true. (If none of the first four choices is correct, then we know (E) must be right.)

Based on the given diagram, we can see that if we add the lengths of $\overline{AC}$ and $\overline{BD}$, we would get the length of $\overline{AD}$ *plus* $\overline{BC}$, because both $\overline{AC}$ and $\overline{BD}$ include the length of $\overline{BC}$—in other words, if we just added the lengths of $\overline{AC}$ and $\overline{BD}$, then the length of $\overline{BC}$ would get counted twice. So the length of $\overline{AD}$ must be equal to $\overline{AC} + \overline{BD} - \overline{BC}$.

With this in mind, we can plug the given length of $\overline{BC}$ from each choice into the expression we just found to see which option gives us a length of 30 for $\overline{AD}$. (Remember that the prompt told us that $\overline{AC} = 16$ units, $\overline{BD} = 20$ units, and $\overline{AD} = 30$ units.)

$$\overline{AC} + \overline{BD} - \overline{BC} = \overline{AD} \qquad \text{(formula for length of } \overline{AD} \text{ we came up with based on the diagram)}$$

(At this point, we might realize that we can just plug in the given values and solve for BC. That's basically what we'll see in our next solution, and it's absolutely a fast and easy way to solve the problem—but not every test-taker will notice it, so we'll finish this backsolving solution and then look at that quicker option in Solution 2.)

$$16 + 20 - 4 = 32 \qquad \text{(plug in the given values, plus } \overline{BC} = 4 \text{ from (A))}$$

We can see that the $\overline{BC}$ value from (A) gives us a length of 32 for $\overline{AD}$, so (A) must be wrong. Let's take a look at (B).

$$16 + 20 - 6 = 30 \qquad \text{(plug in the given values, plus } \overline{BC} = 6 \text{ from (B))}$$

We can see that the $\overline{BC}$ value from (B) gives us a length of 30 for $\overline{AD}$, which matches the information from the prompt. So (B) appears to be correct—but we'll take a look at the other answer choices to make sure we haven't made a mistake.

$$16 + 20 - 10 = 26 \qquad \text{(plug in the given values, plus } \overline{BC} = 10 \text{ from (C))}$$

We can see that the $\overline{BC}$ value from (C) gives us a length of 26 for $\overline{AD}$, so (C) must be wrong. Let's look at (D).

$$16 + 20 - 14 = 22 \qquad \text{(plug in the given values, plus } \overline{BC} = 14 \text{ from (D))}$$

We can see that the $\overline{BC}$ value from (D) gives us a length of 22 for $\overline{AD}$, so (D) must be wrong. Finally, let's consider (E).

Choice (E) says that the answer can't be determined—but we already determined that choice (B) satisfies the requirement in the prompt, so (E) can't be right either.

After looking at each choice, we can see that (B) must be right.

Solution 2: Geometry: Given that the points are on a line, either determine how far B is from A, or how far C is from D, and then use that distance to determine $\overline{BC}$.

The prompt tells us that the length of $\overline{AD}$ is 30 units. We also know that the length of $\overline{AC}$ is 16 units. When we subtract the length of $\overline{AC}$ from the length of $\overline{AD}$, we're left with the length of $\overline{CD}$. That means $\overline{CD}$ must be 14 units, because $30 - 16 = 14$.

Now we know that $\overline{CD}$ is 14 units long, and the prompt told us that $\overline{BD}$ was 20 units long. The length of $\overline{BC}$ is the difference between the length of $\overline{BD}$ and the length of $\overline{CD}$, so the length of $\overline{BC}$ must be 6 units, because $20 - 14 = 6$. So (B) is right.

ANSWER CHOICE ANALYSIS

(A): This is the difference between the length of $\overline{AC}$ and the length of $\overline{BD}$, which might be attractive to untrained test-takers who misread the prompt. **(C):** This is the length of $\overline{AB}$, which will be tempting to untrained test takers who correctly attempt a solution like Solution 2 above but forget what the question actually asks for. **(D):** This is the length of $\overline{CD}$, which will be tempting to untrained test takers who correctly attempt Solution 2 above but forget what the question actually asks for. **(E):** This choice will appeal to untrained test takers who can't figure out how to find what the prompt is asking for and assume incorrectly that it must be impossible to find.

How to check? Consider an alternate approach above. Remember that the diagram is drawn to scale, and make sure that your answer makes sense according to that scale.

▶ **Post-solution patterns (see p. 151):** right approach, wrong step; right answer to the wrong question

Note This is an excellent example of a question that's probably easier to answer correctly if we backsolve than if we use a formal mathematical approach: if we backsolve, all we need to do is read carefully and add one-and two-digit numbers, but if we try the kind of approach we might use in a geometry class on a non-multiple-choice question then we could easily make a variety of small mistakes and arrive at one of the wrong answer choices without realizing it. On test day, remember that the goal is to find the correct answer as quickly and easily as possible, and that will often mean using approaches that wouldn't be acceptable in a math class!

▌Test 2, Question 12 (Test 3 in the 2020-2021 Red Book—see page 23 for more)

- **What's the prompt asking for?** The value of x in the given equation.
- **Math concepts in the prompt:** algebra, negative numbers, PEMDAS
- **Notable differences among choices:** (F) and (K) are opposites of

each other. (H) and (J) each include a fraction.

- **Concepts in the choices:** fractions, negative numbers
- **Pre-solution patterns (see p. 149):** opposites
- **Things to look out for:** Don't make any small mistakes in your algebra!

Solution 1: Backsolve: Plug each answer choice in for x to determine the choice that makes the equation true. Remember that you can enter the expressions into your calculator (carefully!) if you don't want to deal with the improper fractions.

$$12(20) = -8\big(10 - (20)\big) \qquad \text{(plug in value from (F))}$$

$$240 = 80 \qquad \text{(simplify)}$$

The value from (F) creates an invalid statement, so (F) can't be right. Let's look at (G).

$$12(8) = -8\big(10 - (8)\big) \qquad \text{(plug in value from (G))}$$
$$96 = -16 \qquad \text{(simplify)}$$

The value from (G) creates an invalid statement, so (G) can't be right. Let's look at (H).

$$12\left(7\tfrac{3}{11}\right) = -8\left(10 - \left(7\tfrac{3}{11}\right)\right) \qquad \text{(plug in value from (H))}$$
$$87.\overline{27} = -21.\overline{81} \qquad \text{(simplify)}$$

The value from (H) creates an invalid statement, so (H) can't be right. Let's look at (J).

$$12\left(6\tfrac{2}{13}\right) = -8\left(10 - \left(6\tfrac{2}{13}\right)\right) \qquad \text{(plug in value from (J))}$$
$$\sim 73.846 = \sim -30.769 \qquad \text{(simplify)}$$

The value from (J) creates an invalid statement, so (J) can't be right. Let's look at (K).

$$12(-20) = -8\big(10 - (-20)\big) \qquad \text{(plug in value from (K))}$$
$$-240 = -240 \qquad \text{(simplify)}$$

The value from (K) creates a valid statement. After checking each choice, we know that (K) is right.

Solution 2: Algebra: Solve for x in the usual way, by performing identical operations on both sides of the equation until x is isolated.

$$12x = -8(10 - x) \qquad \text{(given equation)}$$
$$12x = -80 + 8x \qquad \text{(distribute } -8\text{)}$$
$$4x = -80 \qquad \text{(subtract } 8x \text{ from both sides)}$$
$$x = -20 \qquad \text{(divide both sides by 4)}$$

We can see that (K) is right.

Solution 3: Test-smart: Once we realize that isolating x will result in a negative number on the other side of the equation, we can quickly realize that (K) must be correct because it's the only choice with a negative number.

ANSWER CHOICE ANALYSIS

(F): This is the opposite of the correct answer choice. When we see it, we should be very careful to make sure that the correct answer really is negative, especially considering that four of the five choices are positive. **(H):** This is the result of making a mistake distributing the -8, ending up with $80 + x$. **(J):** This is the result of making a mistake distributing the -8, ending up with $80 - x$.

How to check? Try an alternate approach above.

▶ **Post-solution patterns (see p. 151):** opposites

Note This is a great example of a question that's actually not very different from a question you might see in a high school math class. It's very important not to get lazy on a question like this: as trained test takers, we should still try to answer it as quickly and efficiently as possible, while making sure that we avoid small mistakes.

Test 2, Question 13 (Test 3 in the 2020-2021 Red Book—see page 23 for more)

- **What's the prompt asking for?** The area of the aluminum foil that isn't covered by the cake.
- **Math concepts in the prompt:** area, dimensions, rectangles, units of distance
- **Math concepts in the diagram:** dimensions, rectangular prisms, units of distance
- **Elements of the choices:** The choices are all two- and three-digit even numbers.
- **Notable differences among choices:** (A), (B), (C), and (D) are all 2-digit numbers, while (E) is a 3-digit number. (B) is half of (E). (B), (D), and (E) form a series in which each number is 32 more than the one before it.
- **Pre-solution patterns (see p. 149):** halves and doubles
- **Things to look out for:** Don't confuse the dimensions in the diagram! Don't confuse the dimensions of the cardboard and the cake! Don't find the area of the cake instead of the area of the cardboard that's exposed! Don't forget that the cardboard extends beyond the cake by 2 inches on all sides of the cake!

Solution 1: Geometry: Find the surface area of the cardboard and the area of the top of the cake. Subtract the area of the top of the cake from the area of the cardboard.

If the cardboard extends beyond the cake by two inches on all sides, then each dimension of the cardboard must be 4 inches greater than the corresponding dimension of the cake (2 inches wider on each side makes the cardboard a total of 4 inches wider than the cake, and 2 inches longer on each side makes the cardboard a total of 4 inches longer than the cake). That means the cardboard is 16 inches wide by 20 inches long.

So the surface area of the cardboard is 20 × 16, or 320 inches. The surface area of the top of the cake is 16 × 12, or 192 inches. The difference between the two is 320 − 192, or 128 inches. So (E) is right.

ANSWER CHOICE ANALYSIS

(A): This is the exposed surface area when the cardboard only extends 1 inch beyond the cake on all sides—not two inches, as described in the prompt. **(B):** This is the exposed surface area when the cardboard extends 2 inches beyond the cake on both sides only in its width—not on all sides, as described in the prompt. This is also half of the right answer. **(C):** This is the exposed surface area when the cardboard extends 2 inches beyond the cake on both sides in its length, and 1 inch beyond the cake on both sides in its width—not 2 inches on all sides, as described in the prompt. **(D):** This is the exposed surface area when the cardboard extends 2 inches beyond the cake on both sides in its width, and 1 inch beyond the cake on both sides in its length—not 2 inches on all sides, as described in the prompt.

How to check? Carefully reread the prompt and rework the question, making sure to avoid any small mistakes.

Test 2, Question 14 (Test 3 in the 2020-2021 Red Book—see page 23 for more)

- **What's the prompt asking for?** The number of pieces after the principal finished cutting.
- **Math concepts in the prompt:** dimensions, division, units of length
- **Math concepts in the diagram:** dimensions, rectangular prisms, units of distance
- **Elements of the choices:** The choices are all two-digit even numbers.
- **Notable differences among choices:** (G) and (H) add up to (J). (J) is half of (K).
- **Pre-solution patterns (see p. 149):** halves and doubles
- **Things to look out for:** Don't confuse the dimensions! Don't make small mistakes in your reading or calculations!

Solution 1: Geometry: Figure out how many pieces would fit along each dimension of the cake in the diagram, and then multiply the numbers of pieces per dimension to find the answer.

The top of each slice is 2 inches by 2 inches. Since the cake is 12 inches wide, 6 slices can fit along the width of the cake (because 12 ÷ 2 = 6). Since the cake is 16 inches long, 8 slices can fit along the length of the cake (because 16 ÷ 2 = 8). So the cake is 6 slices wide by 8 slices long, which means the cake contains 6 × 8 slices, or 48 slices. So (J) is correct.

(The height of the pieces may confuse some test takers—but we can focus on the area of the top of each slice and the area of the top of the cake, since the height of each piece and the height of the cake is the same.)

Solution 2: Geometry: Find the volume of the whole cake, and then divide that volume by the volume of each piece to find the number of pieces contained in the whole cake.

We know that the dimensions of the slices described in the prompt will divide evenly into the cake, because the length and width of the cake are both divisible by 2, and the height of the cake is divisible by 3. So we can just find the volume of the entire cake and divide that by the volume of one slice of cake; the result will be the number of slices of the given dimensions that can be cut from the cake described in the test.

$$\frac{12 \times 16 \times 3}{2 \times 2 \times 3} = 48 \qquad \text{(volume of the cake divided by volume of 1 slice)}$$

Again, we can see that (J) is right.

Solution 3: Geometry/Test-smart: Find the area of the top of the whole cake, and then divide that area by the area of the top of each piece to find the number of pieces contained in the whole cake.

We know that the cake and the slices are both 3 inches high, so we can ignore the height and just focus on comparing the length and width of one slice to the length and width of the whole cake. When we divide the area of the top of the whole cake by the area of the top of one slice, we get this:

$$\frac{12 \times 16}{2 \times 2} = 48 \qquad \text{(area of the top of the whole cake divided by area of the top of 1 slice)}$$

Again, we can see that (J) is right.

ANSWER CHOICE ANALYSIS

(F): This is the result of dividing the *surface area* of the top of the whole cake by the *volume* of one slice. **(H):** This is the length and width of the whole cake added together. **(K):** This is twice the right answer, and could be the result of attempting Solution 3 above and accidentally dividing by 2 instead of dividing by 2 × 2.

How to check? Carefully review the prompt and reconsider your calculations to make sure you haven't made any small mistakes.

Test 2, Question 15 (Test 3 in the 2020-2021 Red Book—see page 23 for more)

- **What's the prompt asking for?** The amount that Ken will receive from the Math Club.
- **Math concepts in the prompt:** arithmetic, percentages, prices, sales tax

- **Elements of the choices:** Each choice is a price under $10.00.
- **Notable differences among choices:** (A) is significantly less than the other choices. (A) and (E) both end in 7. (B) is the only choice that ends in 0.
- **Things to look out for:** Don't misread the prices! Don't forget the sales tax! Don't accidentally apply the sales tax to the $5.00 Ken is receiving for making the cake!

Solution 1: Arithmetic: Add the cost of the cake mix and the frosting mix, and multiply that sum by 1.05 to find the total cost with sales tax added in. Then add that to the $5.00 Ken receives for making the cake.

$$1.05(\$1.73 + \$2.67) + \$5.00 = \$9.62$$

(cost of cake mix and frosting mix added and multiplied by 1.05, and the result added to $5.00)

So (D) is right.

ANSWER CHOICE ANALYSIS

(A): This is the cost of the cake mix and frosting mix, plus tax, added to 5 *cents*, instead of 5 *dollars*. We know this choice must be wrong because it's less than $5.00, and the prompt says Ken gets $5.00 just for making the cake. **(B):** This is the result if a test-taker finds the sum of the costs of the mixes and the money that Ken receives from the club for preparing the cake, but fails to apply the 5% sales tax to the mixes. **(C):** This choice reflects the mistake of finding the sum of the costs of the mixes and Ken's preparation fee, and then simply adding 5¢ to the total—rather than applying a 5% sales tax to the costs of the mixes. **(E):** This choice reflects the mistake of applying the 5% sales tax to the mixes *and* to the $5.00 that Ken receives from the Math Club. But the prompt makes it clear that the sales tax only applies to the two mixes.

How to check? Carefully reread the prompt and reconsider your work.

▶ **Post-solution patterns (see p. 151):** easy calculation mistake; right approach, wrong step

> **Note** Once again, we can clearly see that the ACT is deliberately trying to anticipate the various types of mistakes that untrained test-takers might make under the pressures of test day. Always keep this in mind, and make sure that you don't let small mistakes lower your score for no good reason!

Test 2, Question 16 (Test 3 in the 2020-2021 Red Book—see page 23 for more)

- **What's the prompt asking for?** The y-intercept of the line that passes through $(-3, 6)$ and $(3, 2)$.
- **Math concepts in the prompt:** graphing coordinate pairs, the xy-coordinate plane, y-intercept
- **Elements of the choices:** The five choices form a series from 0 to 8 in which each choice is 2 more than the one before it.
- **Pre-solution patterns (see p. 149):** halves and doubles
- **Things to look out for:** Don't graph the points incorrectly! Don't try to find the x-intercept instead of the y-intercept! Don't make any small mistakes in your algebra!

Solution 1: Graphing: Sketch the two points and use your sketch to determine the y-intercept.

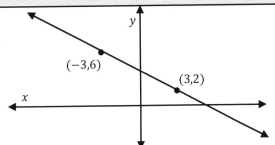

When we sketch the points and a line between them, we can see that the line crosses the y-axis somewhere between 6 and 2. The only answer choice that is less than 6 and more than 2 is (H), 4. So (H) is correct.

Solution 2: Formal Algebra: Use the given points to find the slope of the line, and then use the slope to write an equation for the line in point-slope form. Finally, convert the formula in point-slope form to the slope-intercept form, and use the slope-intercept form of the equation to find the y-intercept of the line.

$$\frac{y_2 - y_1}{x_2 - x_1}$$ (formula for slope)

$$\frac{2 - 6}{3 - (-3)}$$ (plug in the given values)

$$\frac{-4}{6}$$ (simplify)

$$-\frac{2}{3} \qquad \text{(reduce)}$$

So the slope is $-\frac{2}{3}$. We can use the slope with the coordinates of either point in point-slope form to create an equation for the line:

$$y - y_1 = m(x - x_1) \qquad \text{(generic point-slope form)}$$

$$y - 2 = -\frac{2}{3}(x - 3) \qquad \text{(plug in } m = -\frac{2}{3} \text{ and } (3, 2))$$

Now we can solve for y to put the equation for the line in slope-intercept or "$y = mx + b$" form:

$$y - 2 = -\frac{2}{3}(x - 3) \qquad \text{(point-slope form of the equation for the line in the prompt)}$$

$$y - 2 = -\frac{2}{3}x + 2 \qquad \text{(distribute } -\frac{2}{3})$$

$$y = -\frac{2}{3}x + 4 \qquad \text{(add 2 to both sides)}$$

Now we have the equation for the line in slope-intercept form, or "$y = mx + b$" form. We can see that the value for b, the y-intercept, is 4. So the right answer is (H), 4.

Solution 3: Test-smart: Note that the two points are on opposite sides of the y-axis, so the y-intercept must be between the y-values of the given points. That means the correct answer must be a number less than 6 and more than 2, and only one answer choice satisfies that requirement. That means (H) must be correct.

ANSWER CHOICE ANALYSIS

(F): This is the x-coordinate at the y-intercept of the line, but that isn't what the prompt asks for. **(J):** This is the x-intercept of the line, but the prompt asks for the y-intercept.

How to check? Try an alternate approach above.

▶ Post-solution patterns (see p. 151): be aware of series; easy calculation mistake

Test 2, Question 17 (Test 3 in the 2020-2021 Red Book—see page 23 for more)

- **What's the prompt asking for?** The distance in inches between the centers of the two holes in the diagram.
- **Math concepts in the prompt:** circles, distance, parallel lines, points on a line
- **Math concepts in the diagram:** circles, distance, points on a line
- **Elements of the choices:** The choices are all numbers between $4\frac{3}{16}$ and $5\frac{3}{16}$.
- **Notable differences among choices:** (A), (B), (D), and (E) all involve fractions with 16 in the denominator, while (C) does

not. (A) and (E) both have 3 in the numerator, while (B) has 1 and (D) has 13. (A), (C), and (D) form a series in which each choice is $\frac{3}{16}$ less than the choice before it.

- **Concepts in the choices:** fractions
- **Pre-solution patterns (see p. 149):** wrong answers try to imitate right answers
- **Things to look out for:** Don't make any small mistakes in your arithmetic, especially when dealing with the fractions in the question!

Solution 1: Algebra: Create an expression to equate the two shorter distances on the diagram, the missing distance, and the full length of the part, and then solve for the missing distance.

When we look at the diagram, we can see that the width of the entire part is $11\frac{5}{8}$ inches, and that we must be able to add $2\frac{1}{16}$, the missing distance, and $4\frac{3}{4}$ to get $11\frac{5}{8}$. With that in mind, we can write an expression to find the missing distance.

To make this easier, we'll convert each number to sixteenths of an inch. We can convert $\frac{3}{4}$ to sixteenths by multiplying the fraction by $\frac{4}{4}$ to get $\frac{12}{16}$, so $4\frac{3}{4}$ is the same as $4\frac{12}{16}$. We can convert $\frac{5}{8}$ to sixteenths by multiplying the fraction by $\frac{2}{2}$ to get $\frac{10}{16}$, so $11\frac{5}{8}$ is the same as $11\frac{10}{16}$. Now let's set up our equation, using d to represent the missing distance.

$$2\frac{1}{16} + 4\frac{12}{16} + d = 11\frac{10}{16} \qquad \text{(our expression to find } d)$$

$$6\frac{13}{16} + d = 11\frac{10}{16} \qquad \text{(simplify)}$$

$$d = 4\frac{13}{16} \qquad \text{(subtract } 6\frac{13}{16} \text{ from both sides)}$$

So the correct answer is (D).

Solution 2: Arithmetic: Subtract $2\frac{1}{16}$ and $4\frac{3}{4}$ from $11\frac{5}{8}$ to find the right answer.

$$11\frac{5}{8} - 2\frac{1}{16} - 4\frac{3}{4}$$ (the two shorter distances subtracted from the full width of the part)

$$11\frac{10}{16} - 2\frac{1}{16} - 4\frac{12}{16}$$ (convert each expression to sixteenths)

$$4\frac{13}{16}$$ (simplify)

Again, the correct answer is (D).

ANSWER CHOICE ANALYSIS

(A): This choice might tempt an untrained test-taker who attempts one of the solutions above and then loses track of the whole numbers while performing the arithmetic involving fractions. **(C):** This choice might tempt an untrained test-taker who notices that $2 + 4 + 5 = 11$, and then forgets to consider the fractions in the diagram, or incorrectly thinks that $\frac{5}{8}$ is the sum of $\frac{1}{16}$ and $\frac{3}{4}$.

How to check? Try an alternate approach above. Be especially careful to make sure that you correctly handle the fractions in the diagram, since the answer choices are clearly trying to set you up to make a mistake with them.

▶ **Post-solution patterns (see p. 151):** easy calculation mistake; right approach, wrong step

Test 2, Question 18 (Test 3 in the 2020-2021 Red Book—see page 23 for more)

- **What's the prompt asking for?** The approximate number of weeks until the ponds reach the same depth.
- **Math concepts in the prompt:** constant rates, measurements of depth
- **Elements of the choices:** The choices are all 2- or 3-digit multiples of 10.
- **Notable differences among choices:** (F), (G), (H), and (J) form a series in which each number is twice the number before it. (K) is the sum of (G), (H), and (J).
- **Concepts in the choices:** addition, doubling
- **Pre-solution patterns (see p. 149):** halves and doubles
- **Things to look out for:** Don't get confused about which pond is being reduced at which rate! Don't make small mistakes in your reading or arithmetic!

Solution 1: Backsolve: Try each answer choice as the number of weeks described in the prompt. The right answer is the one that causes both ponds to be equal in depth.

The prompt tells us that the first pond is 180 cm deep and is reduced by 1 cm per week. We can model that by saying that the first pond is $180 - x$ cm deep after x weeks. We're also told that the second pond is 160 cm deep and is reduced by $\frac{1}{2}$ cm per week. We can model that by saying that the second pond is $160 - 0.5x$ cm deep after x weeks. Now we can plug in the values from each answer choice to find out which one satisfies the requirement from the prompt. We'll start with (F):

$180 - x$	$160 - 0.5x$	(expressions for the depth of each pond after x weeks)
$180 - 10$	$160 - 0.5(10)$	(plug in the value from (F))
170	155	(simplify)

When we plug in the value from (F) the depths of the two ponds aren't equal, so (F) doesn't appear to be right. Let's look at (G):

$180 - 20$	$160 - 0.5(20)$	(plug in the value from (G))
160	150	(simplify)

When we plug in the value from (G), the depths aren't equal, so (G) doesn't appear to be right either. Let's try (H):

$180 - 40$	$160 - 0.5(40)$	(plug in the value from (H))
140	140	(simplify)

When we plug in the value from (H) the depths of the two ponds are equal, so this choice appears to be right. Let's look at the remaining answer choices to make sure we haven't made a mistake. Here's (J):

$180 - 80$	$160 - 0.5(80)$	(plug in the value from (J))
100	120	(simplify)

Plugging in the value from (J) doesn't cause the depths of the two ponds to be equal, so (J) doesn't appear to be right. Let's try (K):

$180 - 140$	$160 - 0.5(140)$	(plug in the value from (K))
40	90	(simplify)

The value from (K) also doesn't make the depths of the two ponds equal, so (K) is wrong.

Now that we've checked each answer, we can be confident that (H) is right.

Solution 2: Concrete/ Guess-and-check: Pick a number from the answer choices to test, then try a lower or higher number from the answer choices as needed until you find the choice that satisfies the requirement in the prompt.

Let's try 40 from (H), since that option is right in the middle—that will either allow us to find the correct answer, or eliminate three wrong answer choices (choice (H), plus the two options that are higher or lower, depending on our result).

$180 - x$	$160 - 0.5x$	(expressions for the depth of each pond after x weeks)
$180 - 40$	$160 - 0.5(40)$	(plug in $x = 40$ from (H))

When we plug in the value from (H), the depths of the two ponds are equal—so this choice appears to be right. Of course, when we try this guess-and-check method, we won't always pick the right answer on the first try, but this time we were able to do that. We should carefully check our algebra and our reading to confirm that (H) is correct.

Solution 3: Algebra: Create algebraic expressions to model the change in depth of each pond over time. Set these two expressions equal to each other in an equation, and solve for the number of weeks at which the two expressions are equal. Then pick the answer choice that matches the value that satisfies your equation.

$$180 - x = 160 - 0.5x \quad \text{(pond depths set equal to one another)}$$
$$180 = 160 + 0.5x \quad \text{(add } x \text{ to both sides)}$$
$$20 = 0.5x \quad \text{(subtract 160 from both sides)}$$
$$40 = x \quad \text{(divide both sides by 0.5)}$$

So the answer is (H).

Note that once we figure out expressions to represent the depth of each pond, we could also graph these two expressions on a calculator. The x-value of their point of intersection will tell us how many weeks pass before the depths of the ponds are equal. Here is the graph of $y = 180 - x$ and $y = 160 - 0.5x$:

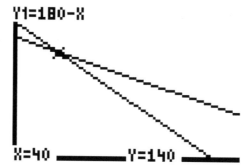

We can see that the ponds have the same depth after 40 weeks, so (H) is right.

Solution 4: Test-smart: Note that the first pond is 20 cm higher than the second pond, and its depth decreases at twice the rate. Also note that the answer choices indicate the concept of doubling is probably highly relevant to the question. With that in mind, test the number of weeks that's equal to 2 times as much as the difference in depth between the 2 ponds.

The difference in depth of the two ponds is 20 cm, and twice that difference is 40 cm. As we saw in the first two solutions, when we test $x = 40$ from (H) we find that both ponds have a depth of 140 cm, and we can confirm that (H) is correct.

ANSWER CHOICE ANALYSIS

(F): This choice is half the difference between the depths of the 2 ponds, rather than twice that difference. It may be present to attract test takers who tried Solution 4 above but divided by two instead of multiplying by two and then neglected to test the result. **(G):** This is the number of weeks it will take for the first pond to have a depth of 160 cm, which is the starting depth of the second pond—but the depth of the second pond will change over that period as well. In other words, this choice would be right if the depth of the second pond didn't change. This choice is also the difference between the depths of the two ponds. **(J):** This choice is twice the correct answer. Like (F), it could reflect mistakes related to misreading the prompt or performing algebra incorrectly in a way that caused a test-taker to be off by a factor of 2. **(K):** This is the depth that both ponds will have when their depths are equal. Many untrained test takers will attempt Solution 1, 2, or 3 above and correctly work out the depth at which the ponds will have equal depths, but forget that this value isn't what the prompt actually asked us to find.

How to check? Try an alternate approach above. Be especially careful to make sure that you're finding the value the prompt asked for, instead of a "right approach, wrong step" answer.

▶ **Post-solution patterns (see p. 151):** right approach, wrong step; right answer to the wrong question; most like the other choices

Note   The right answer is actually exactly 40, even though the prompt uses the phrase "about how many," indicating that approximation would be acceptable here.

Test 2, Question 19 (Test 3 in the 2020-2021 Red Book—see page 23 for more)

- **What's the prompt asking for?** The answer choice that does not represent a line when graphed.
- **Math concepts in the prompt:** equations, graphing in the xy-coordinate plane, lines
- **Elements of the choices:** Each choice is an equation.

- **Notable differences among choices:** (A) and (B) each include only one variable, while (C), (D), and (E) each include both x and y. (D) is the only choice that includes a fraction. (E) is the only choice with a variable raised to an exponent.
- **Concepts in the choices:** equations, exponents,

fractions, variables

- **"Bridge" concepts:** The equation for a straight line in the xy-coordinate plane can take a variety of formats, but any such equation with no variable raised to an exponent and no fraction with a variable in the denominator will be a straight line.

- **Pre-solution patterns (see p. 149):** wrong answers try to imitate right answers

- **Things to look out for:** Don't overlook the word "not" in the prompt! Don't make small mistakes with your graphing calculator!

Solution 1: Concrete/Graphing: Use your graphing calculator to graph each choice, and pick the choice that doesn't create a line.

Graph of (A):

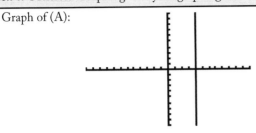

This is a line, so (A) isn't right.

Let's try (B). We can isolate the y-term in (B) as follows:

$$3y = 6 \qquad \text{(expression from (B))}$$
$$y = 2 \qquad \text{(divide both sides by 3)}$$

So here's the graph of $y = 2$, which is equivalent to (B):

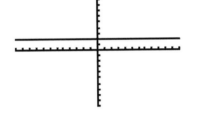

This is also a line, so (B) isn't right, either.

Now we'll try (C). We can isolate the y-term in (C) as follows:

$$x - y = 1 \qquad \text{(expression from (C))}$$
$$x = y + 1 \qquad \text{(add } y \text{ to both sides)}$$
$$x - 1 = y \qquad \text{(subtract 1 from both sides)}$$

Here's the graph of $y = x - 1$, which is equivalent to (C):

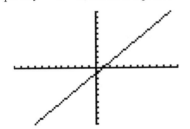

This is a line, too, so (C) is wrong.

Let's try (D):

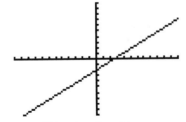

This is also a line, so (D) isn't right, either.

Finally, let's try (E). We can isolate the y-term in (E) as follows:

$$x^2 + y = 5 \qquad \text{(expression from (E))}$$

$$y = -x^2 + 5 \qquad \text{(subtract } x^2 \text{ from both sides)}$$

Here is the graph of $y = -x^2 + 5$, which is equivalent to (E):

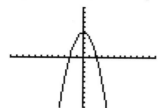

When we look at the graphs, it's clear that (E) is the only choice that isn't a straight line, so (E) is right.

Solution 2: Algebra: Use your knowledge of algebra to identify the only choice that involves raising a variable to an exponent.

When we consider the answer choices, we can see that only (E) involves raising one of the variables to an exponent, and no choice involves a fraction with a variable in the denominator—so we know that (E) must be the correct answer, and that the graph of every other choice will be a line.

ANSWER CHOICE ANALYSIS

(A): This choice produces a vertical line with an x-intercept of 4. Many untrained test takers will be drawn to (A), because they'll accidentally confuse the idea of an equation that doesn't create a line and an equation that's not a function, and (A) doesn't pass the vertical line test—but (A) still produces a line when it's graphed, which is what the prompt asks about. **(B):** This choice produces a horizontal line with a y-intercept of 2. **(C):** This choice produces a diagonal line. **(D):** Like (C), this produces a diagonal line.

How to check? Try an alternate approach above, and/or carefully reread the prompt to make sure you're answering the specific question it asks.

▶ **Post-solution patterns (see p. 151):** easy calculation mistake

Test 2, Question 20 (Test 3 in the 2020-2021 Red Book—see page 23 for more)

- **What's the prompt asking for?** The choice with a true statement about $\angle A$.
- **Math concepts in the prompt:** angles, right triangles, true statements
- **Math concepts in the diagram:** Pythagorean triples, right triangles
- **Elements of the choices:** Each choice equates a trig-function value of $\angle A$ with a fraction involving the numbers 12 and 13.
- **Notable differences among choices:** (F) and (J) involve cosine, while (G) and (K) involve sine and (H) is the only choice that mentions tangent. (F), (G), and (H) all have 12 in the numerator and 13 in the denominator, while (J) and (K) have 13 in the numerator and 12 in the denominator.
- **Concepts in the choices:** cosine, sine, tangent
- **"Bridge" concepts:** SOHCAHTOA
- **Pre-solution patterns (see p. 149):** wrong answers try to imitate right answers; opposites
- **Things to look out for:** Don't accidentally find values for angles besides $\angle A$! Don't confuse the side lengths in the triangle! Don't confuse which values go in the numerator or denominator according to SOHCAHTOA! Make sure you consider each answer choice, in order to give yourself every opportunity to catch any mistakes you might have made!

Solution 1: Backsolve: Compare each choice to the diagram, and pick the choice that accurately reflects it.

(F) We know that the cosine of an angle is equal to $\frac{adjacent}{hypotenuse}$, but in this case the adjacent side is 5 and the hypotenuse is 13, so this choice can't be correct.

(G) We know that the sine of an angle is equal to $\frac{opposite}{hypotenuse}$, and we can see that the opposite side is 12 and the hypotenuse is 13, so this choice seems to be right. Let's check the remaining choices to make sure we haven't made any mistakes.

(H) We know that the tangent of an angle is equal to $\frac{opposite}{adjacent}$, but in this case the opposite side is 12 and the adjacent side is 5, so this choice can't be correct.

(J) We know that the cosine of an angle is equal to $\frac{adjacent}{hypotenuse}$, but in this case the adjacent side is 5 and the hypotenuse is 13.

(K) We know that the sine of an angle is equal to $\frac{opposite}{hypotenuse}$, but in this case the opposite side is 12 and the hypotenuse is 13.

After looking at each choice, we can conclude that (G) must be right.

ANSWER CHOICE ANALYSIS

(F): This choice is wrong because the cosine of A is $\frac{5}{13}$ according to SOHCAHTOA. **(H):** This choice is wrong because the tangent of A is $\frac{12}{5}$ according to SOHCAHTOA. **(J):** This is wrong because the cosine of A is $\frac{5}{13}$, as we discussed for (F). **(K):** This is wrong because the sine of A is $\frac{12}{13}$, as we saw for the right answer.

How to check? Carefully reconsider the prompt, the answer choices, and the diagram. Note that the ACT is clearly trying to get you to make a small mistake in your application of SOHCAHTOA, so triple-check yourself to make sure you don't fall for that trick!

Note This is a great example of the type of question that many untrained test takers will miss because they aren't diligent enough on test day, even though the vast majority of them are familiar with SOHCAHTOA and understand it perfectly. Keep this in mind on test day: knowing the relevant concepts isn't enough. Instead, you have to take the time to make sure you apply them carefully and correctly, which is what the ACT actually rewards!

Test 2, Question 21 (Test 3 in the 2020-2021 Red Book—see page 23 for more)

- **What's the prompt asking for?** The answer choice that accurately describes how to move from point *A* to the water fountain's location as described in the prompt.
- **Math concepts in the prompt:** locating a point halfway between two other points
- **Math concepts in the diagram:** distance labels on a diagram, perpendicular lines
- **Elements of the choices:** Each choice describes moving a certain number of blocks east and north.
- **Notable differences among choices:** (A) involves a fraction in the number of blocks moved east, while (B) and (E) involve a fraction for the number of blocks moved north, and (D) is the only choice that involves a fraction for movement in both

directions. (A) and (C) both involve moving 6 blocks north, while (B) and (D) both involve moving $4\frac{1}{2}$ blocks north, and (B) and (C) both involve moving 5 blocks east. The eastward movements in (A) and (B) (or (C)) add up to the eastward movement in (D).

- **Concepts in the choices:** addition, plotting points in a coordinate plane
- **Pre-solution patterns (see p. 149):** wrong answers try to imitate right answers
- **Things to look out for:** Don't confuse east and north when you read the answer choices! Don't confuse the points on the diagram!

Solution 1: Backsolve: Plot the point from each choice, and pick the one that's halfway between *B* and *D* on the diagram.

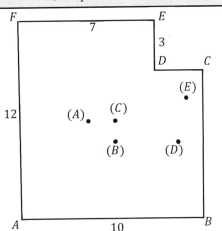

When we sketch in each point as in the diagram above, we can see that only choice (D) refers to a point that's halfway between points *B* and *D* in the diagram, so (D) is right.

Solution 2: Geometry: Note that a point halfway between *B* and *D* must have a horizontal separation from point *A* that's equal to the average of 7 and 10. Further, note that a point halfway between *B* and *D* must have a vertical separation from point *A* that's equal to the average of 0 and 9. Find the only choice that satisfies these requirements.

If the point we're looking for is halfway between *B* and *D*, then that point must be equally horizontally separated from both points, as well as equally vertically separated from both points. In order for the point to have equal horizontal separation between *B* and *D*, it must be halfway between 7 blocks and 10 blocks horizontally separated from *A*, which is the same as $8\frac{1}{2}$ blocks east of *A*. In order for the point to have equal vertical separation between *B* and *D*, it must be halfway between 0 blocks and 9 blocks vertically separated from *A*, which is the same as $4\frac{1}{2}$ blocks north from *A*. That means (D) must be correct.

Solution 3: Test-smart: Note that a point halfway between *B* and *D* must have a horizontal separation from point *A* that's greater than seven and a vertical separation that's less than six, and only one answer choice satisfies that requirement.

Using logic similar to what we discussed for the previous solution, we know that the horizontal/east component of the answer must be greater than 7, because point *D* is 7 units east of point *A*, and the water fountain must be further east than point *D*. The only two choices that satisfy that requirement are (D) and (E). But (E) includes a vertical/north component that would involve traveling closer to point F than point A, and we can see in the diagram that a point halfway between B and D must be lower than a point halfway between F and A. In fact, the water fountain must have a vertical separation from A that's less than 6, since it can't possibly be greater than half the distance of FA. So (D) must be right.

ANSWER CHOICE ANALYSIS

(A): This choice reflects the mistake of trying to find the point halfway between A and E. **(B):** This choice correctly reflects the idea of moving $4\frac{1}{2}$ blocks north, but incorrectly moves only half the distance between point A and point B horizontally, rather than moving halfway between points D and B horizontally. This choice would be right if the prompt has asked for the midpoint between A and C instead of between B and D. **(C):** This choice reflects the mistake of trying to find the point halfway between F and B.

How to check? Try an alternate approach above, making sure not to confuse the different points and labels on the diagram.

▶ **Post-solution patterns (see p. 151):** almost like the other choices

Test 2, Question 22 (Test 3 in the 2020-2021 Red Book—see page 23 for more)

- **What's the prompt asking for?** The maximum speed that Damon can drive so that his breaking distance is no more than 150 feet.
- **Math concepts in the prompt:** exponents, fractions, function modeling, inequalities, speed
- **Elements of the choices:** Each choice is a multiple of 10 between 10 and 60 inclusive.
- **Notable differences among choices:** (G), (H), (J),

and (K) form a series in which each number is 10 more than the number before it, and (F) is 10 itself. (K) is twice as much as (G).

- **Concepts in the choices:** adding 10
- **Pre-solution patterns (see p. 149):** halves and doubles
- **Things to look out for:** Don't misread the function model in the prompt! Don't make any small mistakes in your reading or algebra!

Solution 1: Backsolve: Try each answer choice as the value of x in the function in the prompt. Pick the choice that results in the largest value of y that's no more than 150 feet.

$$y = \frac{3((10)^2 + 10(10))}{40} \quad \text{(plug in } x = 10 \text{ from (F))}$$
$$y = 15 \quad \text{(simplify)}$$

When we plug in the value from this choice, the braking distance is 15 feet, so this choice probably isn't right. Let's try the next choice and see if it produces a higher braking distance that's still less than 150 feet.

$$y = \frac{3\left((30)^2 + 10(30)\right)}{40} \quad \text{(plug in } x = 30 \text{ from (G))}$$
$$y = 90 \quad \text{(simplify)}$$

When we plug in the value from this choice, the braking distance is 90 feet, so this choice probably isn't right. Let's try the next choice and see if it produces a higher braking distance that's still less than 150 feet.

$$y = \frac{3\left((40)^2 + 10(40)\right)}{40} \quad \text{(plug in } x = 40 \text{ from (H))}$$
$$y = 150 \quad \text{(simplify)}$$

When we plug in the value from this choice, the braking distance is 150 feet, so this choice seems to be right. Let's try the remaining choices to make sure we haven't made a mistake.

$$y = \frac{3\left((50)^2 + 10(50)\right)}{40} \quad \text{(plug in } x = 50 \text{ from (J))}$$
$$y = 225 \quad \text{(simplify)}$$

When we plug in the value from this choice, the braking distance is 225 feet, which is more than 150, so this choice can't be right. Let's try the last choice.

$$y = \frac{3\left((60)^2 + 10(60)\right)}{40} \quad \text{(plug in } x = 60 \text{ from (K))}$$
$$y = 315 \quad \text{(simplify)}$$

When we plug in the value from this choice, the braking distance is 315 feet, which is more than 150, so this choice can't be right either. Now that we've tested every answer choice, we can see that (H) is right.

Solution 2: Algebra: Re-write the model in the prompt, plug in $y = 150$, and then solve for x.

$$y = \frac{3(x^2+10x)}{40} \qquad \text{(given equation)}$$

$$150 = \frac{3(x^2+10x)}{40} \qquad \text{(plug in } y = 150)$$

$$6000 = 3(x^2 + 10x) \qquad \text{(multiply both sides by 40)}$$

$$2000 = x^2 + 10x \qquad \text{(divide both sides by 3)}$$

$$0 = x^2 + 10x - 2000 \qquad \text{(subtract 2000 from both sides)}$$

$$0 = (x + 50)(x - 40) \qquad \text{(reverse-FOIL)}$$

We can see that the equation will be equal to 0 when $x = -50$ or $x = 40$. Since it doesn't make sense in context for Damon's car to go at a negative speed (and even if it did, the "maximum speed" would still be the higher value, which is still $x = 40$), we can see that the correct answer is 40, and (H) is right.

Solution 3: Graphing: Use your graphing calculator to graph the function in the prompt. The right answer will be the highest answer choice that is no greater than the x-coordinate whose y-coordinate is 150 in the graph.

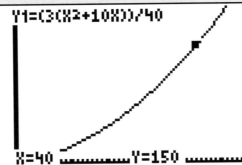

When we look at the graph, we can see that the greatest speed Damon can travel so that the braking distance is less than or equal to 150 feet is 40 miles per hour. (H) is 40, so (H) must be the right answer.

ANSWER CHOICE ANALYSIS

(F): This choice reflects the mistake of being off by a factor of 10 in your algebra: when $x = 10$, the value of y is 15, not 150.

How to check? Try an alternate approach above. Be especially careful about being off by a factor of 10 or by 10 miles per hour, since the question is clearly setting up some kind of mistake related to the number 10.

▶ **Post-solution patterns (see p. 151):** easy calculation mistake

---

Test 2, Question 23 (Test 3 in the 2020-2021 Red Book—see page 23 for more)

- **What's the prompt asking for?** The value of $\frac{g(4)}{f(1)}$.
- **Math concepts in the prompt:** exponents, functions, square roots
- **Notable differences among choices:** (A), (B), and (C) are fractions, while (D) and (E) are single-digit numbers. (A), (C), and (D) all involve the number 2. (A) and (B) both involve the number 7. (B) and (C) both involve 25.

- **Concepts in the choices:** fractions
- **Pre-solution patterns (see p. 149):** wrong answers try to imitate right answers
- **Things to look out for:** Don't confuse the numerator and denominator in the fraction in the prompt! Don't confuse the two functions in the prompt! Don't make any small mistakes in your algebra or arithmetic!

Solution 1: Algebra: Evaluate $g(4)$ and $f(1)$ using the functions in the prompt, and construct the fraction requested in the prompt.

$$g(x) = \sqrt{x} \qquad \text{(given } g(x) \text{ function)}$$

$$g(4) = \sqrt{4} \qquad \text{(plug in } x = 4)$$

$$g(4) = 2 \qquad \text{(simplify)}$$

Now we have a value for $g(4)$; let's find a value for $f(1)$.

$$f(x) = x^2 + x + 5 \qquad \text{(given } f(x) \text{ function)}$$

$$f(1) = (1)^2 + (1) + 5 \qquad \text{(plug in } x = 1)$$

$$f(1) = 7 \qquad \text{(simplify)}$$

We've now found both values, and we can construct the fraction from the prompt: $\frac{g(4)}{f(1)} = \frac{2}{7}$. So (A) is right.

ANSWER CHOICE ANALYSIS

(B): This choice is equal to $\frac{f(4)}{f(1)}$. **(C):** This choice is equal to $\frac{g(4)}{f(4)}$. **(D):** This choice represents $g(4)$ alone. It could tempt an untrained test-taker who forgot to evaluate the denominator of the fraction in the prompt, or who incorrectly thought that $f(1)$ was equal to 1, or who found $\frac{g(4)}{g(1)}$. **(E):** This choice could be tempting for a test-taker who thought $\frac{g(4)}{f(1)}$ could reduce to $\frac{(4)}{(1)}$, or 4.

How to check? Carefully reconsider the prompt, the answer choices, and your calculations.

▶ **Post-solution patterns (see p. 151):** most like the other choices; right approach, wrong step

Note This is another great example of a question that isn't really based on advanced math; instead, it tries to trick us with a complicated presentation of very basic ideas, which is very common on the ACT. Notice, for example, that the question presents function f before function g, but then asks about a fraction in which g appears above f. This small choice by the ACT will momentarily confuse most test takers, because they'll instinctively expect the function that was defined first to be the first one they encounter in the fraction. Things like this can slowly add up and frustrate an untrained test-taker who isn't expecting to deal with them, so be on the lookout for those kinds of issues and don't get nervous when you run into them!

Test 2, Question 24 (Test 3 in the 2020-2021 Red Book—see page 23 for more)

- **What's the prompt asking for?** The number of two-person combinations according to the prompt.
- **Math concepts in the prompt:** combinations
- **Elements of the choices:** Each is a multiple of 25.
- **Notable differences among choices:** (G) is the only choice that doesn't include the digits 2 and 5. (G) and (H) are the only two numbers in the answer choices that appear in the prompt. (F) is the difference between (G) and (H), while (J) is the sum of (G) and (H), and (K) is the product of (G) and (H). (F) is the only two-digit number and (K) is the only five-digit number; the other choices are all three-digit numbers.

- **Concepts in the choices:** addition, multiples of 25, multiplication, subtraction
- **"Bridge" concepts:** The number of combinations of two things can be found by multiplying the number of possible choices for each of the two things individually.
- **Pre-solution patterns (see p. 149):** wrong answers try to imitate right answers
- **Things to look out for:** Don't accidentally think there are 125 of each group of students, or 100 of each group of students! Don't make small mistakes in your calculation!

Solution 1: Arithmetic: Multiply 125 and 100 to find the number of possible two-person combinations.

Each of the 125 juniors could be paired with each of 100 different seniors, so there must be 125×100 possible 2-person combinations. $125 \times 100 = 12,500$

So the right answer is (K), 12,500.

ANSWER CHOICE ANALYSIS

(F): This choice is the difference between the sizes of the two groups of students; this might tempt a test-taker who thought the question asked for the number of juniors left over if each senior was paired with one junior. **(G):** This is the number of seniors, which might be tempting for test-takers who don't realize that each senior can be used more than one time in determining the number of possible pairs. In other words, even after the first senior is paired with the first junior, that first senior can make another pair with the second junior, and the third junior, and the fourth junior, and so on. **(H):** This is the number of juniors. This choice might be tempting for reasons similar to the reasons (G) might be tempting, and it's wrong for the same basic reasons. **(J):** As we noted above, this is the sum of the two choices. But when we find the number of combinations of one student from each group, we use *multiplication*, not addition, to reflect the idea that each student of the first group could conceivably be paired with any of the students in the other group.

How to check? Note the relationships among the answer choices as described above and consider how they relate to the idea of combining individual members of two groups.

Note As you know if you've ever studied combinations in school, there are much more difficult and complicated ideas related to combinations and permutations than what we see in this question. Questions like this make it clear that the ACT isn't actually evaluating whether we have a thorough understanding of advanced math concepts. Instead, it only evaluates whether we have a half-decent familiarity with relatively basic concepts, and we can recognize when and how to use them. For example, in this question, it was possible to find the right answer if you only remember that combinations involve multiplying the things being combined. Keep this kind of thing in mind on test day, and don't let the ACT intimidate you when it tries to throw around words that might scare a lot of untrained test takers!

Test 2, Question 25 (Test 3 in the 2020-2021 Red Book—see page 23 for more)

- **What's the prompt asking for?** The choice with an equation that describes the line in the diagram.
- **Math concepts in the prompt:** graphing lines in a coordinate plane, scatterplots

- **Math concepts in the diagram:** axis labels, graphing lines in a coordinate plane, scatterplots
- **Elements of the choices:** Each choice is an equation of a line in slope-intercept form (or $y = mx + b$ form).
- **Notable differences among choices:** (A), (B), and (C) all include negative slopes, while (D) and (E) include positive slopes. (A) and (B) each have a 3 in the x-term, while (C), (D), and (E) all have a 2 in the x-term. (A) and (E) feature a y-intercept of 8,

while the other choices all have a y-intercept of 10.
- **Concepts in the choices:** equations, lines, slope-intercept form
- **Pre-solution patterns (see p. 149):** wrong answers try to imitate right answers
- **Things to look out for:** Don't make a mistake on the sign of the slope in the answer you pick! Don't overlook the fact that the x-axis is divided into half-unit increments!

Solution 1: Backsolve: Compare the slope and y-intercept of each choice to the graph, and pick the choice that accurately describes the line.

(Note that each hash mark on the horizontal axis of the graph in the prompt represents 0.5 units, not 1 unit.)

(A) has a y-intercept of 8, but the line in the graph has a y-intercept of 10, so this choice can't be right.

(B) has a y-intercept of 10, which matches the y-intercept of the graph. Also, this choice has a slope of -3, and we can see that as the line in the graph moves down 3 units, it moves right 1 unit—in other words, the line in the graph has a slope of -3 as well. For example, the line passes through the point $(0,10)$, then travels down 3 units and right 1 unit to pass through the point $(1,7)$. Since the slope and y-intercept of the graph match the slope and y-intercept of the equation in (B), we know (B) must be right. Still, we'll check out all the other choices to make sure we haven't made a mistake.

(C) has a y-intercept of 10, which matches the y-intercept of the graph, but the slope of -2 doesn't match the graph's slope of -3 as we saw in our discussion of (B), so this choice must be wrong.

(D) has a positive slope, but the line in the graph has a negative slope, so (D) can't be right.

(E) combines the problems from (A) and (D).

After considering each choice, we can see that the correct answer is (B).

Solution 2: Graphing: Graph each answer choice on your calculator, and look to see which one has the same y-intercept and x-intercept as the graph in the diagram.

Let's look at the graph of each choice. (Note that to make the comparison easier, I've made the scale of the graphs below match the scale of the graph in the prompt—so every hash mark on the x-axis is 0.5 units, and every hash mark on the y-axis is 1 unit.)

Here is the graph of (A):

Here is the graph of (B):

Here is the graph of (C):

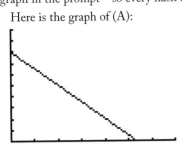 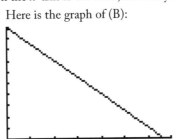 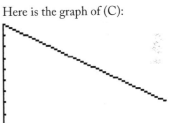

Here is the graph of (D):

Here is the graph of (E):

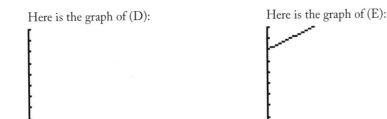

Notice that the graph in the prompt crosses the y-axis at $y = 10$, and the x-axis between $x = 3$ and $x = 3.5$. Only the graph of (B) shares these characteristics, so (B) must be right.

Solution 3: Algebra: Use your knowledge of algebra to observe the key aspects of the line in the figure, determining in advance what the correct slope and y-intercept should be, and then pick the choice that reflects your conclusions.

When we look at the graph of the line, we can see that it crosses the y-axis at $y = 10$, so we know the correct answer should also have a y-intercept of 10. We can also see that the line passes through the point $(0,10)$, then travels down 3 units and right 1 unit to pass through the point $(1,7)$, which means the line has a slope of $\frac{-3}{1}$, or -3. The only choice with a slope of -3 and a y-intercept of 10 is (B), the correct answer.

ANSWER CHOICE ANALYSIS

(A): This choice reflects the mistake of thinking that the y-intercept should be 8. **(C):** This choice reflects the mistake of thinking that the slope is -2, which might be tempting if an untrained test-taker overlooks the fact that the x-axis is marked off in half-units. If the gridlines indicated full units on both axes, then the slope of the line would almost be -2 (if you look carefully, you can see that the line nearly goes down two gridlines and over one, but not exactly). **(D):** This choice includes the mistake from (C) and adds the mistake of forgetting that a positive slope indicates a line rising from left to right, not falling from left to right. **(E):** This choice combines the mistakes in (D) and (A).

How to check? Try an alternate approach above. Pay special attention to the size and sign of the slope, and to the y-intercept, since the ACT is clearly trying to encourage you to make a mistake on those issues!

▶ **Post-solution patterns (see p. 151):** most like the other choices

Test 2, Question 26 (Test 3 in the 2020-2021 Red Book—see page 23 for more)

- **What's the prompt asking for?** The choice with a temperature that doesn't fall inside the range from the prompt.
- **Math concepts in the prompt:** absolute value, inequalities, subtraction
- **Notable differences among choices:** (F), (G), and (H) are all negative numbers, while (J) is 0 and (K) is positive. (K) is significantly larger than the other choices.
- **Concepts in the choices:** negative numbers, positive numbers, zero
- **Things to look out for:** Don't make any small mistakes in your reading or calculations, especially with respect to absolute value and inequalities!

Solution 1: Backsolve: Plug each choice into the inequality from the prompt, and pick the choice that makes the inequality invalid.

We'll start by plugging in the value from (F):

$\lvert t - 24 \rvert \le 30$	(given inequality)
$\lvert(-10) - 24\rvert \le 30$	(plug in $t = -10$ from (F))
$\lvert -34 \rvert \le 30$	(simplify)
$34 \le 30$	(take absolute value)

When we plug in the value from (F), we get a value that isn't in the range described in the prompt—which is exactly what the prompt asks for. So (F) seems to be right, but, of course, we'll check the other choices to make sure we haven't made a mistake. As trained test-takers, we know that it's always critical to consider every answer choice for a question. So let's plug in the values from (G):

$\lvert(-6) - 24\rvert \le 30$	(plug in $t = -6$ from (G))
$\lvert -30 \rvert \le 30$	(simplify)
$30 \le 30$	(take absolute value)

When we plug in the value from (G), we get a value that *is* in the range described in the prompt—but the question asks for a value that "is NOT in this range," so this choice can't be right.

Now, let's take a look at (H):

$\lvert(-5) - 24\rvert \le 30$	(plug in $t = -5$ from (H))
$\lvert -29 \rvert \le 30$	(simplify)
$29 \le 30$	(take absolute value)

When we plug in the value from (H), we get a value that *is* in the range described in the prompt—but the question asks for a value that "is NOT in this range," so this choice can't be right. So let's try (J):

$\lvert(0) - 24\rvert \le 30$	(plug in $t = 0$ from (J))
$\lvert -24 \rvert \le 30$	(simplify)
$24 \le 30$	(take absolute value)

When we plug in the value from (J), we get a value that *is* in the range described in the prompt—but the question asks for a value that "is NOT in this range," so this choice can't be right. Finally, let's consider (K):

$\lvert(54) - 24\rvert \le 30$	(plug in $t = 54$ from (K))
$\lvert 30 \rvert \le 30$	(simplify)
$30 \le 30$	(take absolute value)

When we plug in the value from (K), we get another value that *is* in the range described in the prompt—but again, the question asks for a value that "is NOT in this range," so this choice can't be right.

After testing each answer choice, we can be sure that (F) is right.

Solution 2: Algebra: Solve the inequality in the prompt for t. Pick the choice that's outside the valid range for t.

$$|t - 24| \le 30 \qquad \text{(given inequality)}$$
$$-30 \le t - 24 \le 30 \qquad \text{(account for absolute value)}$$
$$-6 \le t \le 54 \qquad \text{(add 24 to each expression)}$$

Only the value in (F) is not in this range, so (F) is correct.

Solution 3: Test-smart: Note that the correct answer must be either the largest number or the smallest number in the answer choices; test those two numbers to see which one makes the inequality statement false.

The correct answer must be the largest or the smallest number in the answer choices, because we know that there can only be one correct answer to the question, and if the correct answer is a number that's too large to fall in the given range, any larger number would also be too large for the range, and if the correct answer is a number that's too small to fall in the given range, any smaller number would also be too small for the range. We can save some time in applying the backsolving solution by only checking the smallest and largest options. If we do that, we'll find again that the correct answer is (F), -10.

ANSWER CHOICE ANALYSIS

(K): This choice may tempt some untrained test-takers because it's so much larger than the other numbers in the range, but, when we plug it into the original inequality, we see that it results in a true statement, since $30 \le 30$.

How to check? Try an alternate approach above. Carefully reconsider your reading and your calculations.

Test 2, Question 27 (Test 3 in the 2020-2021 Red Book—see page 23 for more)

- **What's the prompt asking for?** The possible values of n according to the prompt.
- **Math concepts in the prompt:** multiple valid solutions for a variable, multiplication, negative numbers, subtraction, translating text into algebra
- **Notable differences among choices:** (A), (B), and (C) all indicate only one number, while (D) and (E) indicate ranges of numbers. (B), (D), and (E) all involve 3. (D) and (E) present ranges on opposite sides of 3.

- **Concepts in the choices:** inequalities, solution sets, zero
- **"Bridge" concepts:** If a number is negative, then it's less than zero by definition.
- **Pre-solution patterns (see p. 149):** opposites
- **Things to look out for:** Don't make any mistakes translating the text into algebra! Don't make any small mistakes in your algebraic solving! Pay special attention to the direction of the inequality sign!

Solution 1: Backsolve: Plug a value from each answer choice into the situation described in the prompt. Pick the choice that accurately describes the results of your testing.

The prompt mentions "5 times a number n." We can represent this idea with the expression $5n$. The prompt then says that $5n$ "is subtracted from 15," which is the same as saying $15 - 5n$. Finally the prompt says that the result of $15 - 5n$ is negative, which we can represent with the inequality $15 - 5n < 0$. Now let's use that inequality to check each answer choice; the one that satisfies the inequality will be the correct answer.

$$15 - 5n < 0 \qquad \text{(inequality from prompt)}$$
$$15 - 5(0) < 0 \qquad \text{(plug in } n = 0 \text{ from (A))}$$
$$15 - 0 < 0 \qquad \text{(simplify)}$$
$$15 < 0 \qquad \text{(simplify)}$$

We got an invalid statement when we plugged in $n = 0$, so (A) can't be correct. Let's test (B).

$$15 - 5n < 0 \qquad \text{(inequality from prompt)}$$
$$15 - 5(3) < 0 \qquad \text{(plug in } n = 3 \text{ from (B))}$$
$$15 - 15 < 0 \qquad \text{(simplify)}$$
$$0 < 0 \qquad \text{(simplify)}$$

We got an invalid statement when we plugged in $n = 3$, so (B) can't be correct. Let's test (C).

$$15 - 5n < 0 \qquad \text{(inequality from prompt)}$$
$$15 - 5(10) < 0 \qquad \text{(plug in } n = 10 \text{ from (C))}$$
$$15 - 50 < 0 \qquad \text{(simplify)}$$
$$-35 < 0 \qquad \text{(simplify)}$$

We got a valid statement when we plugged in $n = 10$, so (C) *could* be correct—but we're not sure yet. Choice (D) says that the values for n include all numbers greater than 3. We need to try another number greater than 3 to see whether (C) or (D) is right. Let's test $n = 7$, since 7 is a number other than 10 that is greater than 3.

$$15 - 5n < 0 \qquad \text{(inequality from prompt)}$$
$$15 - 5(7) < 0 \qquad \text{(plug in } n = 7 \text{ to test (D))}$$
$$15 - 35 < 0 \qquad \text{(simplify)}$$
$$-20 < 0 \qquad \text{(simplify)}$$

We got a valid statement when we plugged in $n = 7$. That means (C) can't be correct, because (C) says that only 10 is a possible value for n, and we just saw that 7 is a possible value for n. (D) appears to be correct, because we know that 10 and 7 are both possible values for n, and (D) is the only choice that includes those two values. Let's take a look at (E) to make sure that we haven't overlooked anything.

We know that (E) can't be correct, because 0 is less than 3, and when we tested 0 we got an invalid statement. After considering each answer choice, we can be confident that (D) is correct.

Solution 2: Algebra: Translate the scenario from the prompt into an inequality statement. Solve the inequality statement for n, and pick the appropriate answer choice.

As we saw in the previous solution, we can translate the information from the prompt into the inequality $15 - 5n < 0$.

$$15 - 5n < 0 \qquad \text{(inequality from prompt)}$$
$$15 < 5n \qquad \text{(add } 5n \text{ to both sides)}$$
$$3 < n \qquad \text{(divide both sides by 5)}$$

We found that the inequality is true when $3 < n$, which is the same as when $n > 3$. So (D) is right.

Solution 3: Test-smart: Note that the situation in the prompt would be true for really large values of n, because subtracting a larger number from a smaller number always gives a negative result. Only one choice would allow for infinitely large values of n, and that choice is the correct answer, (D).

ANSWER CHOICE ANALYSIS

(B): Solving the problem algebraically does involve arriving at the number 3, but 3 isn't the answer to the question. (In fact, 3 isn't even an acceptable value for n, as we saw in our solutions above.) **(E):** This choice could appeal to test-takers who made a mistake in their algebra, and reversed the inequality sign. It could also attract test-takers who misread the prompt and thought that 15 was being subtracted from $5n$, not the other way around, or that the result of the given inequality should be positive, not negative.

How to check? Try an alternate approach above. Be especially sure to test your answer back in the scenario from the prompt.

▶ Post-solution patterns (see p. 151): right approach, wrong step; opposites

Test 2, Question 28 (Test 3 in the 2020-2021 Red Book—see page 23 for more)

- **What's the prompt asking for?** The choice that's equal to the fraction in the prompt when x is larger than 21.
- **Math concepts in the prompt:** addition, exponents, fractions, inequalities, multiplication, subtraction
- **Notable differences among choices:** (F) is the only choice that's not a fraction. (G) is the only fraction without a variable in it. (H), (J) and (K) all include $(x - 3)$ in the numerator. (J) and (K) both include $x + 1$ in the denominator. (H) is the only choice with $(x + 3)$ in the denominator. (K) is the only negative choice.
- **Concepts in the choices:** addition, fractions, multiplication, one, subtraction, variables
- **"Bridge" concepts:** Some of the numbers in the numerator of the fraction are factors of numbers in the denominator of the fraction, which suggests that it may be possible to factor out the expressions in the numerator and denominator and reduce them.
- **Pre-solution patterns (see p. 149):** wrong answers try to imitate right answers
- **Things to look out for:** Don't make small mistakes in your arithmetic or algebra! If you use a calculator, make sure you enter everything accurately! Don't confuse the signs on the numbers or the answer choices!

Solution 1: Algebra: Factor out the expressions in the numerator and denominator of the given fraction, and then reduce to find the right answer.

$$\frac{(x^2 + 8x + 7)(x - 3)}{(x^2 + 4x - 21)(x + 1)} \qquad \text{(given expression)}$$
$$\frac{(x + 7)(x + 1)(x - 3)}{(x + 7)(x - 3)(x + 1)} \qquad \text{(reverse-FOIL)}$$

So we can see that the correct answer is (F).

Solution 2: Calculator: Choose a value for x that's greater than 21 (such as 22), plug it in everywhere that x appears in the prompt or in the answer choices, and determine the numerical values for each expression. The right answer will be the one with the same numerical value as the fraction in the prompt.

$$\frac{(x^2+8x+7)(x-3)}{(x^2+4x-21)(x+1)} \quad \text{(given expression from the prompt)}$$

$$\frac{(22^2+8(22)+7)(22-3)}{(22^2+4(22)-21)(22+1)} \quad \text{(plug in the value } x=22, \text{ since 22 is more than 21)}$$

$$\frac{(484+176+7)(19)}{(484+88-21)(23)} \quad \text{(simplify)}$$

$$\frac{(667)(19)}{(551)(23)} \quad \text{(simplify)}$$

$$\frac{12673}{12673} \quad \text{(simplify)}$$

$$1 \quad \text{(simplify)}$$

Now let's consider the answer choices. We can see that our result matches the value in (F), and it doesn't match the value in (G). At this point, for all we know, it's possible that the expressions in (H), (J), and (K) might also match our result, if we happen to have picked a value for x that causes more than one of the expressions to come out to the same value. So we'll need to plug $x = 22$ into the other answer choices, to see if any of them are also equal to 1 when $x = 22$, in which case we would need to try a new x-value. We'll start with (H):

$$\frac{x-3}{x+3} \quad \text{(expression from (H))}$$

$$\frac{22-3}{22+3} \quad \text{(plug in } x = 22)$$

$$\frac{19}{25} \quad \text{(simplify)}$$

The expression in (H) doesn't match the value of the expression in the prompt. Let's try (J):

$$\frac{2(x-3)}{x+1} \quad \text{(expression from (J))}$$

$$\frac{2(22-3)}{22+1} \quad \text{(plug in } x = 22)$$

$$\frac{2(19)}{23} \quad \text{(simplify)}$$

$$\frac{38}{23} \quad \text{(simplify)}$$

The expression in (J) doesn't match the value of the expression in the prompt, either. Let's try the last choice, (K):

$$-\frac{4(x-3)}{x+1} \quad \text{(expression from (K))}$$

$$-\frac{4(22-3)}{22+1} \quad \text{(plug in } x = 22)$$

$$-\frac{4(19)}{23} \quad \text{(simplify)}$$

$$-\frac{76}{23} \quad \text{(simplify)}$$

The expression in (K) doesn't match the prompt either. So, after considering each choice, we can see that (F) must be right.

Solution 3: Graphing: Using a graphing calculator, graph a function that sets y equal to the expression in the prompt. Then, for each answer choice, graph a function that sets y equal to the expression in the choice. The right answer will be the choice whose graph matches the graph of the expression in the prompt for all values of x larger than 21.

Let's start out by graphing the given expression. (Note that for this graph and all following graphs in this solution, we've set the window on the calculator so the x-value starts at $x = 21$, because the prompt tells us that we're only concerned with what the given expression is equal to when $x > 21$. I've also set the scale on the y axis to 0.5 instead of 1—in other words, each hash mark on the vertical axis represents 0.5 units, not 1 unit—so it's easier to see small differences between graphs.) Here's the graph of the given expression from the prompt:

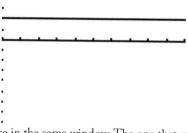

Now let's look at the graph of each answer choice in the same window. The one that matches our graph for the given expression will be the right answer. Here's the graph for (F):

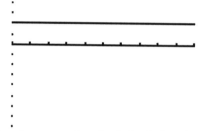

This appears to be identical to the graph for the given expression. Let's check the other options to make sure we haven't made a mistake or overlooked anything. Here's the graph for (G):

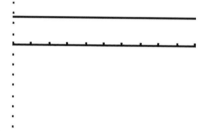

This is a horizontal line, like our graph for (F) and the graph of the expression from the prompt, but those lines are at $y = 1$, while this one is slightly above $y = 1$. So this choice doesn't match the graph of the expression from the prompt, which means it can't be right. Here's the graph of (H):

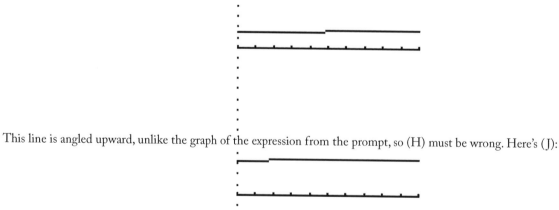

This line is angled upward, unlike the graph of the expression from the prompt, so (H) must be wrong. Here's (J):

This line has the same basic problem as (H), so it can't be right either. Finally, let's look at (K):

Facebook.com/TestingIsEasy Youtube.com/TestingIsEasy

This graph has negative values sloping downward, while the graph of the expression from the prompt has only positive values, so this choice can't be right. After considering each choice, we know that (F) must be the right answer.

ANSWER CHOICE ANALYSIS

(H), (J), and (K): These choices could each be the result of factoring incorrectly if you attempt Solution 1 above.

How to check? Try an alternate approach above.

Note   Many untrained test takers will try an approach similar to Solution 1 above—in fact, that's what the ACT's official solution in the Red Book recommends. But notice that the calculator-based solutions will be much faster and easier for test-takers who aren't comfortable with the algebra in Solution 1. Always remember that there's no reward on the ACT for doing questions the way a math teacher would want you to! You should always take a moment or two to figure out the fastest and easiest way for you to approach a question—and remember that it may also involve using a calculator in a way that a teacher wouldn't reward in class.

Test 2, Question 29 (Test 3 in the 2020-2021 Red Book—see page 23 for more)

- **What's the prompt asking for?** The statement that must be true about the median of the new set.

- **Math concepts in the prompt:** medians, sets

- **Elements of the choices:** Each choice is a sentence dealing with concepts related to different kinds of averages.

- **Notable differences among choices:** (A) and (C) both refer to the average of two values—(A) to the lower two values, and (C) to the higher. (B), (D), and (E) all refer to the original median, with one choice saying the new one is the same as the original

one, one choice saying it's greater than the original one, and one choice saying it's less than the original one.

- **Concepts in the choices:** averages, inequalities, medians

- **Pre-solution patterns (see p. 149):** wrong answers try to imitate right answers; opposites

- **Things to look out for:** Don't misread the prompt or the answer choices! Don't forget the difference between medians and averages!

Solution 1: Concrete: Write down nine numbers as described in the prompt and note which number is the median. Then insert two numbers that are greater than the median, and two numbers that are less than the median. See which answer choice accurately reflects that change in the dataset.

Let's use the numbers 11, 12, 13, 14, 15, 16, 17, 18, and 19. The median of this set is the value in the middle when they're listed from least to greatest, so the median is 15. We can add the values 20 and 21 to the set, because the prompt says to add two numbers greater than the original median, and we can also add the values 9 and 10 to the set, because the prompt says to add two numbers less than the original median.

The resulting set of data would be 9, 10, 11, 12, 13, 14, 15, 16, 17, 18, 19, 20, and 21. We can see that the value in the middle is still 15, which means the median didn't change. Only (B) describes this situation accurately, so (B) must be correct.

Solution 2: Abstract: Use your knowledge of the definition of median to identify what happens to a median if an equal number of items are added above and below it.

We know that the median of a set of values is the number in the middle when the values are ordered from least to greatest. The prompt tells us about a set of numbers with a median, then says that four items are added to the set—two items less than the median, and two items greater than the median. Well, if we're adding two items less than the median, and two items greater than the median, then that same median will still be in the middle of the set of values, just with two extra values before it and two extra values after it. So that means the median must remain unchanged, which means (B) is correct.

(If the reasoning in this solution was unclear, please check the previous solution to this problem.)

ANSWER CHOICE ANALYSIS

(A): This choice could be tempting for students who confuse median and average and/or misremember the properties of medians. **(C):** This choice could be tempting for reasons similar to those we saw in our discussion of (A). **(D):** This choice could be tempting for students who attempt Solution 1, but make some mistake either in adding the new data or finding the new median. **(E):** This choice could be tempting for reasons similar to those we saw in our discussion of (D).

How to check? Try an alternate approach above. Make sure to read and think very carefully, because the answer choices clearly indicate that the ACT hopes you'll make a small mistake in your reading.

Test 2, Question 30 (Test 3 in the 2020-2021 Red Book—see page 23 for more)

- **What's the prompt asking for?** The area of the shaded region.
- **Math concepts in the prompt:** area, circles, diameters, radii, tangents
- **Math concepts in the diagram:** area, circles, diameters, dimension labels, radii, tangents
- **Notable differences among choices:** (F) and (G) don't involve π, while (H), (J) and (K) do. (F) and (J) both involve 10, while (G) and (K) both involve 75.
- **Concepts in the choices:** π

- **"Bridge" concepts:** There's not really a set formula for determining the area of the shaded region in the figure directly, but we can determine it by subtracting the area of the smaller circle from the area of the larger circle.
- **Pre-solution patterns (see p. 149):** wrong answers try to imitate right answers
- **Things to look out for:** Don't confuse radius and diameter! Don't confuse the dimensions of the two different circles! Don't make any small mistakes in your calculations!

Solution 1: Geometry: Use the formula $A = \pi r^2$ to find the area of the smaller circle and the area of a larger circle. Then subtract the smaller number from the larger number to find the answer to the question.

We know that the area of a circle can be found using the formula $A = \pi r^2$, where A represents the area and r represents the radius. We can see from the diagram that the radius of the larger circle is 10, and the radius of the smaller circle is half of 10, or 5 (because the diameter of the smaller circle is 10, and half the diameter must be the radius). With that in mind, we can subtract the area of the smaller circle from the area of the larger circle:

$$\pi(10)^2 - \pi(5)^2 \qquad \text{(the area of the larger circle minus the area of the smaller circle)}$$
$$100\pi - 25\pi \qquad \text{(simplify)}$$
$$75\pi \qquad \text{(simplify)}$$

So we can see that (K) is correct.

Solution 2: Test-smart: When you realize that both circles must have areas that involve π, that the smaller circle must have an area of 25π, and that the shaded area is larger than the smaller circle, you can pick the only choice that involves π and is larger than 25π—the correct answer, (K).

ANSWER CHOICE ANALYSIS

(F): This is the radius of the larger circle, which is something that we need to find if we decide to use Solution 1 above. **(G):** This choice reflects the mistake of neglecting π in the expression of the circles' areas. **(J):** This is the difference between the *circumferences* of the two circles, not the *areas* of the two circles. Wrong answer choices like this one remind us of the fundamental importance of careful reading on the ACT Math section!

How to check? Try an alternate approach above.

▶ **Post-solution patterns (see p. 151):** most like the other choices; right answer to the wrong question

Test 2, Question 31 (Test 3 in the 2020-2021 Red Book—see page 23 for more)

- **What's the prompt asking for?** The sign of the average of a and b, if it can be determined.
- **Math concepts in the prompt:** averages, negative numbers, positive numbers
- **Notable differences among choices:** The choices contain every possible combination of positive and negative numbers, and (E) says the answer can't be found.
- **Concepts in the choices:** insufficient information, negative numbers, positive numbers, zero

- **"Bridge" concepts:** The mean of 2 numbers is the result when the numbers are added together and divided by 2—in other words, what we commonly think of as the average of the 2 numbers.
- **Pre-solution patterns (see p. 149):** wrong answers try to imitate right answers
- **Things to look out for:** Don't forgot that the prompt doesn't indicate the absolute value of a or b! Don't assume that a and b are opposites! Don't make small mistakes in your reading!

Solution 1: Concrete: Run a variety of tests in which you choose different numbers for a and b that satisfy the prompt. Pick the answer choice that describes the results of all of your tests.

Let's test the situation described in the prompt using $a = 3$ and $b = -3$. The mean of these two values can be found by adding the values together and dividing by 2.

$$\frac{3+(-3)}{2} \qquad \text{(mean when } a = 3 \text{ and } b = -3\text{)}$$
$$0 \qquad \text{(simplify)}$$

So we can see that with the values we picked, the mean of the two numbers would be neither positive nor negative. That eliminates (A), (B), and (C). But we can't be sure that (D) is right, because we only tested one set of numbers. So let's try $a = 5$ and $b = -10$:

$$\frac{5 + (-10)}{2} \quad \text{(mean when } a = 5 \text{ and } b = -10)$$

$$-\frac{5}{2} \quad \text{(simplify)}$$

With these values the mean was negative, which means (D) can't be right either. At this point we can be confident that the correct answer is (E), because we've found an example that contradicts each of the other choices.

Solution 2: Abstract: Think about the properties of a and b as described in the prompt, and pick the choice that reflects those properties. (Consider using a number line for this if you want.)

When we start to think about the situation described in the prompt, we might realize that the result could be a very low negative number if the absolute value of b was a lot larger than the absolute value of a. On the other hand, the result could be a very high positive number if the absolute value of a was a lot larger than the absolute value of b. But the result could also be 0 if a and b had equal absolute values—something like 5 and -5, or 328 and -328. So we can see that a positive or negative result is possible, as well as a result that is neither positive nor negative. Once again, we can confidently choose (E).

ANSWER CHOICE ANALYSIS

(C): This choice is impossible because the mean of a and b must be a single number, since the mean of any set of numbers must be a single number by definition, and a single number can only have one sign. So it's logically impossible for a single number to be both positive and negative. **(D):** This choice could reflect the mistake of assuming that a and b must be opposites of each other—in other words, assuming that a must be 5 if b is -5, for example. If the two numbers were opposites, then their mean would necessarily be zero. But the prompt doesn't say that a and b are opposites, only that one is positive and one is negative. So, for example, it would be possible for a to be 7 while b is -926, or for a to be 15 while b is -1, and so on.

How to check? Try an alternate approach above. Make sure that you don't assume anything that isn't stated in the prompt.

Test 2, Question 32 (Test 3 in the 2020-2021 Red Book—see page 23 for more)

- **What's the prompt asking for?** The y-coordinate for the point on the curve whose x-coordinate is 20.
- **Math concepts in the prompt:** exponents, graphing functions, plotting points in the xy plane, ranges
- **Math concepts in the diagram:** plotting functions in the xy-coordinate plane

- **Elements of the choices:** The choices are the series of even numbers from 160 to 168.
- **Concepts in the choices:** even numbers, series
- **Pre-solution patterns (see p. 149):** be aware of series
- **Things to look out for:** Don't misread the graph, the function, or the answer choices!

Solution 1: Algebra: Plug $x = 20$ into the function from the prompt, and find the corresponding y-value.

$$y = 0.005x^2 - 2x + 200 \quad \text{(given equation)}$$
$$y = 0.005(20)^2 - 2(20) + 200 \quad \text{(plug in } x = 20\text{)}$$
$$y = 0.005(400) - 40 + 200 \quad \text{(simplify)}$$
$$y = 2 + 160 \quad \text{(simplify)}$$
$$y = 162 \quad \text{(simplify)}$$

So the correct answer is (G), 162.

Solution 2: Graphing: Enter the given function in your calculator. Find the y-coordinate that corresponds to an x-coordinate of 20.

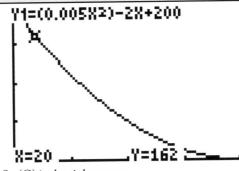

We can see that when $x = 20$, $y = 162$. So (G) is the right answer.

ANSWER CHOICE ANALYSIS

(F): See the note below. **(H):** This choice could the result of trying to read the value off the provided graph, or making a simple algebra mistake in attempting Solution 1. **(J):** This choice could be tempting for the same reasons we saw in our discussion of (H). **(K):** This choice could be tempting for the same reasons we saw in our discussions of (H) and (J).

How to check? Carefully rework the question, being sure not to make any small mistakes in your reading or calculations.

▶ **Post-solution patterns (see p. 151):** easy calculation mistake

Note The ACT's explanation for this question in the Red Book indicates that you might arrive at (F) if you make a small mistake of miscalculating $0.005(20^2)$ as .2 instead of 2. But you would still have to make another mistake on top of that miscalculation in order to arrive at (F): the mistake of thinking it was okay to round off 160.2 to 160 when choosing your answer, even though the prompt doesn't say anything about approximation or estimation.

Test 2, Question 33 (Test 3 in the 2020-2021 Red Book—see page 23 for more)

- **What's the prompt asking for?** The approximate length of $\overline{FG}$ in the graph.
- **Math concepts in the prompt:** graphing lines in a plane, length
- **Math concepts in the diagram:** plotting functions in the xy-coordinate plane

- **Notable differences among choices:** (A) is the square root of (E). (C) is half of (E).
- **Concepts in the choices:** squaring
- **Things to look out for:** Don't forget that the diagram is drawn to scale! Don't make small mistakes in your calculations!

Solution 1: Geometry: Use the Pythagorean Theorem to find the length of $\overline{FG}$, which is the hypotenuse of a right triangle.

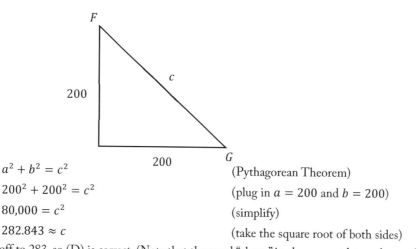

$$a^2 + b^2 = c^2 \quad \text{(Pythagorean Theorem)}$$
$$200^2 + 200^2 = c^2 \quad \text{(plug in } a = 200 \text{ and } b = 200\text{)}$$
$$80,000 = c^2 \quad \text{(simplify)}$$
$$282.843 \approx c \quad \text{(take the square root of both sides)}$$

Our answer rounds off to 283, so (D) is correct. (Note that the word "about" in the prompt lets us know that it's okay to choose an approximate answer.)

Solution 2: Geometry: Use your knowledge of isosceles right triangles to find the length of $\overline{FG}$, which is the hypotenuse of an isosceles right triangle.

We can see that the triangle in question is an isosceles right triangle, and therefore a 45°-45°-90° triangle, and that a 45°-45°-90° triangle has a side length ratio of $1:1:\sqrt{2}$. We can multiply the length of either side by $\sqrt{2}$ to find the length of the hypotenuse, which in this case is $200\sqrt{2}$, or approximately 282.843, which rounds off to 283. So (D) is correct.

Solution 3: Test-smart: Note that the length of $\overline{FG}$ must be larger than 200 but smaller than 400, and only one answer choice satisfies that requirement.

We know that the hypotenuse will be longer than either of the legs of the triangle—but not twice as long as either leg. That means the correct answer must be between 200 and 400, and only one choice satisfies that requirement—the correct answer, (D).

ANSWER CHOICE ANALYSIS

(A): This could be the result of trying to apply Solution 2 above but finding $\sqrt{2 \times 200}$ rather than $(\sqrt{2})200$ when trying to use the special right triangle ratio of $1:1:\sqrt{2}$, which applies to isosceles right triangles. This mistake would also require us not to check our work against the scale of the given diagram, because doing so would show us immediately that 20 is much too small to be the right answer. **(B):** This could be the result of trying to apply Solution 2 above but finding $\sqrt{2}\left(\frac{200}{2}\right)$ rather than $(\sqrt{2})200$ when trying to use the special right triangle ratio of $1:1:\sqrt{2}$, which applies to isosceles right triangles. Like (A), this mistake would also require us not to check our work against the scale of the given diagram, because doing so would show us immediately that 141 is smaller than either leg and therefore too small to be the right answer. **(C):** This could be the result of assuming incorrectly that if two sides of a right triangle are 200 units each, then the third side must also be 200 units. This choice could also tempt test-takers who thought 45°-45°-90° triangles were equilateral triangles. **(E):** This could be the result of assuming incorrectly that the hypotenuse of an isosceles right triangle is twice the length of either leg, rather than the result of multiplying the length of either leg by $\sqrt{2}$.

How to check? Try an alternate approach above. Be especially careful to compare the answer choices to the diagram.

▶ **Post-solution patterns (see p. 151):** easy calculation mistake

Note This is another good example of how simply relying on the design rules of the test (in this case, using the scale of a diagram) can let you avoid wrong answer choices that might be tempting for other test-takers who decide to apply formal math. The wrong answer choices are positioned here to trick people who make mistakes in their calculations related to $\sqrt{2}$, but no wrong answer is positioned to take advantage of people who try to eyeball the length of $\overline{FG}$ using the scale of the diagram!

Test 2, Question 34 (Test 3 in the 2020-2021 Red Book—see page 23 for more)

- **What's the prompt asking for?** The answer choice with the accurate statement about the shaded region.
- **Math concepts in the prompt:** area of a triangle, area under the curve of a function, evaluating a function, line segments
- **Math concepts in the diagram:** plotting functions in the xy-coordinate plane
- **Notable differences among choices:** Each choice relates the area under the curve to 20,000 square units, and each choice except (H) provides reasoning for the stated relationship.
- **Concepts in the choices:** equality, function curves, inequalities, straight lines
- **Pre-solution patterns (see p. 149):** wrong answers try to imitate right answers; opposites
- **Things to look out for:** Don't misread the prompt or the answer choices!

Solution 1: Geometry/Abstract: Read each answer choice and compare it to the diagram. Pick the choice that accurately describes the diagram.

(F) We can see that the curve *does* lie under $\overline{FG}$, and it makes sense that if the curve lies under $\overline{FG}$, then the area of the shaded region would be *less* than the area of the triangle created by the origin and points F and G. This choice appears to be correct, but we'll take a look at the other options to make sure we haven't misread something or made some other mistake.

(G) This choice follows the logic we discussed in (F) regarding the area of the shaded region—but this choice says that the curve lies *over* $\overline{FG}$. We can see that the curve lies *under* $\overline{FG}$, so this choice must be wrong.

(H) This choice doesn't make any sense because we can see that the shaded region has a smaller area than the triangle created by the origin and points F and G, so we would expect the area of that shaded region to be less than 20,000 units.

(J) This choice correctly indicates that the curve lies under $\overline{FG}$, but incorrectly says that we would expect the area of the shaded region to be *greater than* 20,000 units. The shaded region is smaller than the triangle created by the origin and points F and G, so we would expect the area of the shaded region to be *less than* 20,000 units.

(K) This choice combines the mistakes from (G) and (J).

After considering each choice, we can see that (F) is right.

ANSWER CHOICE ANALYSIS

(G): This choice may attract some untrained test-takers who recognize that (F) is right but accidentally mark (G) because the choices begin with the same nine words and the test-takers don't read carefully enough. This choice could also tempt test-takers who get confused about which is the curve and which is $\overline{FG}$. **(H):** This choice may attract untrained test takers who don't read the prompt carefully enough, and assume that the prompt says the area under the curve is 20,000 square units, not the area under $\overline{FG}$.

How to check? Carefully reread the answer choices to make sure you haven't accidentally picked the wrong choice, possibly by letting your eyes skip a line while you read.

Test 2, Question 35 (Test 3 in the 2020-2021 Red Book—see page 23 for more)

- **What's the prompt asking for?** The expression that gives the approximate distance in miles from cargo ship to fishing boat.
- **Math concepts in the prompt:** algebraic formulas, angles, distance, law of cosines
- **Math concepts in the diagram:** angles, distance, triangles
- **Elements of the choices:** Each choice is a radical expression.
- **Notable differences among choices:** (A) involves subtracting $(4.2)^2$ from $(5.0)^2$, but all the other choices add those two values. (A) is the only choice that doesn't include a cosine expression. (B), (C), (D), and (E) all include the expression $2 \times 4.2 \times 5.0\cos$; in (B) and (C), the cosine of 5° is taken, while in (D) and (E), the cosine of 85° is taken. (B) and (D) involve subtracting the expression that begins with 2×4.2, while (C) and (E) involve adding the expression that begins with 2×4.2.
- **Concepts in the choices:** addition, angle measurements, cosine, multiplication, square roots, squaring

- **"Bridge" concepts:** The question isn't actually asking us to use the law of cosines to find the distance from the cargo ship to the fishing boat on our own—instead, it's asking us to identify the correct expression that uses the law of cosines to find that distance.

- **Pre-solution patterns (see p. 149):** wrong answers try to imitate right answers; opposites
- **Things to look out for:** Don't confuse the variables in the law of cosines formula! Don't misread the answer choices!

Solution 1: Algebra: Apply the law of cosines from the prompt to the numbers in the prompt and pick the answer choice that matches your expression.

The prompt provides the following formula for the law of cosines:

$$c^2 = a^2 + b^2 - 2ab\cos C$$

Most test-takers won't know which values to substitute for the different variables, but we know from the note that the side lengths are given as the lowercase letters a, b, and c. We also know that the capital letters A, B, and C correspond to the angles of the vertices that are opposite the sides a, b, and c. Further, we know that we're looking for the distance from the ship to the boat, and that the angle opposite that side of the triangle is a 5° angle.

Since we're looking for that unlabeled distance from the ship to the boat, and since that distance is opposite a 5° angle, we'll make that unlabeled distance our lower-case c variable, and our upper-case C variable will be 5°. (Note that we know we have to use 5° for the C value because the formula involves the measure of an angle, and the 5° angle is the only angle whose measure we know.) The only other values we have in the question are the distances 4.2 and 5.0, and those will be our values for a and b. (For our purposes, it doesn't matter which one is a and which one is b, because the result will be the same either way.) Plugging those values into the equation from the note gives us the following:

$$^2 = a^2 + b^2 - 2ab\cos C \qquad \text{(provided formula for law of cosines)}$$
$$c^2 = 4.2^2 + 5.0^2 - 2(4.2)(5.0)\cos 5° \qquad \text{(plug in } a = 4.2, b = 5.0, \text{ and } C = 5°)$$
$$c = \sqrt{4.2^2 + 5.0^2 - 2(4.2)(5.0)\cos 5°} \qquad \text{(take the square root of both sides to solve for } c)$$

This expression matches (B), so we can see that (B) is right.

Solution 2: Backsolve: Compare the elements of each answer choice to the concepts in the prompt and the diagram to determine the following: whether the correct answer should involve cosine, whether the cosine expression should be added or subtracted, and whether the cosine should be taken of 5° or 85°. Then pick the appropriate answer choice.

We can see that 4 of the 5 answer choices involve cosine, and one doesn't. The provided formula involves cosine, and we don't have any reason to think that the cosine expression will be canceled out or left out for any reason, so it makes sense to say that the correct expression should involve cosine.

Of the 4 remaining choices, each one involves adding 4.2^2 and 5.0^2, so we know that will be part of the right answer. 2 of those 4 include a minus sign in front of the 2 in the middle of the expression, while 2 of them include a plus sign. If we look back at the note in the question, we can see that the sign before the 2 should be a minus sign, and there's no reason to think we're subtracting negative values (which would effectively turn the minus sign into a plus sign).

Finally, we need to determine whether the correct expression should involve the cosine of a 5° angle or an 85° angle. If we look carefully, we see that the only angle measurement anywhere in the question is a 5° measurement. (Some test-takers might incorrectly assume that an 85° angle measurement is still relevant to the question, since $5° + 85° = 90°$, and the idea of a 90° angle is often relevant to trig questions on the ACT. But there's no mention of a 90° angle in this question, so we have no reason to believe that an 85° angle would be relevant to the question.)

With all of that in mind, we can be confident that the right answer should involve a cosine expression, should include a minus sign before the 2 in the middle of the expression, and should involve the cosine of a 5° angle, not an 85° angle. Only choice (B) matches all of these requirements, so (B) is right.

ANSWER CHOICE ANALYSIS

(A): This choice reflects a fundamental misreading of the prompt and/or the diagram.

How to check? Carefully reconsider the prompt and reread the answer choices to make sure you haven't made a small mistake with respect to sign or the question of which angle's cosine should be considered.

▶ **Post-solution patterns (see p. 151):** most like the other choices

Note This question is one that very often frustrates untrained test takers, and gets them to think that the trigonometry tested on the ACT is much more advanced and sophisticated than it actually is. As we can see, all the question actually requires us to do is to use relatively basic algebra to manipulate a given equation and then pick an answer choice that correctly plugs values into that equation. As trained test-takers, we know that the ACT can't actually require us to know trig formulas like the law of sines or law of cosines; we also know that roughly one question per ACT Math section will require us to plug provided values into a provided trig formula like this question does. Keep this in mind on test day, and don't be surprised or distracted when you encounter it.

- **What's the prompt asking for?** The choice that accurately relates a and c according to the prompt.
- **Math concepts in the prompt:** equations, exponents, real numbers, variables
- **Elements of the choices:** Each choice is an equation relating c to an expression with a.
- **Notable differences among choices:** (F), (G), and (H) all involve exponents, while (J) and (K) don't. (H) and (J) involve coefficients that include the number 2, while (F), (G), and (K) have no coefficients.
- **Concepts in the choices:** equations, exponents, multiplying or dividing by 2, real numbers, variables
- **"Bridge" concepts:** When we take an expression with an exponent and raise that expression itself to an exponent, we multiply the two exponents together to find the final expression.
- **Pre-solution patterns (see p. 149):** wrong answers try to imitate right answers
- **Things to look out for:** Don't confuse the variables in the prompt! Don't misread the exponents in the answer choices! Don't make small mistakes in your algebra!

Solution 1: Concrete/Backsolve: Assign arbitrary values to a, b, and c that satisfy the conditions in the prompt, and then plug those values for a and c into the expressions from the answer choices. The right answer will be the choice that contains a true statement.

Let's say that $a = 2$. Since the prompt tells us that $a^3 = b$ and $b^2 = c$, that means b would have to be 2^3, or 8, and c would have to 8^2, or 64. Let's test these values in the answer choices to see which one makes a valid statement.

$$c = a^6 \quad \text{(expression from (F))}$$
$$64 = 2^6 \quad \text{(plug in } a = 2 \text{ and } c = 64)$$
$$64 = 64 \quad \text{(simplify)}$$

This is a valid statement, so it looks like (F) is the right answer. Let's check the remaining choices to make sure we haven't made a mistake or gotten a false positive.

$$c = a^5 \quad \text{(expression from (G))}$$
$$64 = 2^5 \quad \text{(plug in } a = 2 \text{ and } c = 64)$$
$$64 = 32 \quad \text{(simplify)}$$

This isn't a valid statement, so it looks like (G) is wrong. Let's try (H).

$$c = 2a^3 \quad \text{(expression from (H))}$$
$$64 = 2(2^3) \quad \text{(plug in } a = 2 \text{ and } c = 64)$$
$$64 = 16 \quad \text{(simplify)}$$

This isn't a valid statement, so it looks like (H) is wrong. Let's try (J).

$$c = \tfrac{1}{2}a \quad \text{(expression from (J))}$$
$$64 = \tfrac{1}{2}(2) \quad \text{(plug in } a = 2 \text{ and } c = 64)$$
$$64 = 1 \quad \text{(simplify)}$$

This isn't a valid statement, so it looks like (J) is wrong. Finally, let's try (K).

$$c = a \quad \text{(expression from (K))}$$
$$64 = 2 \quad \text{(plug in } a = 2 \text{ and } c = 64)$$

This isn't a valid statement, so it looks like (K) is wrong. After checking each choice, we can be confident that (F) is right.

Solution 2: Abstract: Use your knowledge of exponents to determine an expression with a that's equivalent to c.

Since all the choices are equations in terms of c and a only, we know that we need to find a way to combine the equations in the prompt in a way that gets rid of the b term. We can do that by plugging $b = a^3$ into the other equation:

$$b^2 = c \quad \text{(provided information)}$$
$$(a^3)^2 = c \quad \text{(plug } b = a^3 \text{ in for } b)$$
$$a^6 = c \quad \text{(simplify)}$$

So we can see that (F) is right.

ANSWER CHOICE ANALYSIS

(G): This choice will appeal to untrained test takers who incorrectly think that raising one exponent expression to another exponent involves adding the exponents, rather than multiplying them. **(H):** This choice will appeal to untrained test takers who incorrectly think that raising one exponent expression to another exponent involves multiplying the first expression by the second exponent, rather than multiplying the exponents together and leaving the base unchanged. **(K):** This choice probably reflects multiple mistakes in reading and/or algebra.

How to check? Try an alternate approach above. Make sure you read the prompt and the answer choices carefully, especially with respect to exponents.

▶ **Post-solution patterns (see p. 151):** most like the other choices

Test 2, Question 37 (Test 3 in the 2020-2021 Red Book—see page 23 for more)

- **What's the prompt asking for?** The name of the company that allows Francisco to travel more miles for $255—if one does—and the number of miles extra he can travel with that company.
- **Math concepts in the prompt:** rental costs
- **Notable differences among choices:** (A) and (D) both say Sea Horse allows more miles for $255, while (B) and (C) both say Ocean Blue allows more miles for $255. (A), (B), (C), and (D) all mention different numbers of miles by which one company's allowance exceeds the other's. (E) says the two companies' allowances would be equal for $255.
- **Concepts in the choices:** equality
- **Things to look out for:** Don't confuse the names of the two companies, or the rates charged by each company! Don't make small mistakes in your algebra or arithmetic! Don't forget to consider the daily rental rates in addition to the mileage rates!

Solution 1: Concrete: Use algebra and/or arithmetic to determine the number of miles that Francisco can travel with each company, and then pick the choice that reflects your conclusions.

First, let's calculate the number of miles Francisco can travel with each car company, and then we can subtract one from the other to find out which company allows him to travel more miles, and by how much.

We'll start out by looking at the information for Sea Horse Car Rental. The prompt says that Sea Horse Car Rental charges $50 per day, and we know that Francisco will be renting a car for 2 days—so that's the same as $2 \times \$50$, or $100. It also says that Sea Horse Car Rental charges $0.25 per mile, which is the same as $0.25m$, if we use m to represent the number of miles Francisco travels. So the total cost of Francisco's trip with Sea Horse Car Rental will be $100 + 0.25m$. We can set that expression equal to 255 to find the maximum number of miles m that Francisco can travel for $255.

$$100 + 0.25m = 255 \qquad \text{(equation we just figured out for Sea Horse Car Rental)}$$
$$0.25m = 155 \qquad \text{(subtract 100 from both sides)}$$
$$m = 620 \qquad \text{(divide both sides by 0.25)}$$

So Francisco can travel 620 miles for $255 with Sea Horse Car Rental. Let's figure out how far he can travel for that much money with Ocean Blue Car Rental. The prompt says that Ocean Blue Car Rental charges $60 per day, and we know that Francisco will be renting a car for 2 days—so that's the same as $2 \times \$60$, or $120. It also says that Ocean Blue Car Rental charges $0.20 per mile, which is the same as $0.20m$, if we use m to represent the number of miles Francisco travels. So the total cost of Francisco's trip with Ocean Blue Car Rental will be $120 + 0.20m$. We can again set that expression equal to 255 to find the maximum number of miles m that Francisco can travel for $255.

$$120 + 0.20m = 255 \qquad \text{(equation we just figured out for Ocean Blue Car Rental)}$$
$$0.20m = 135 \qquad \text{(subtract 120 from both sides)}$$
$$m = 675 \qquad \text{(divide both sides by 0.20)}$$

So Francisco can travel 675 miles for $255 with Ocean Blue Car Rental. We can see that Francisco can travel $675 - 620$ miles, or 55 miles more with Ocean Blue Car Rental, which means (B) is correct.

ANSWER CHOICE ANALYSIS

(A): This is how much cheaper Sea Horse Car Rental is compared to Ocean Blue Car Rental when you consider just the daily rate after two days, without taking into account the rate per mile. **(C):** This choice is the difference between the base cost per day of each company divided by the per mile rate of that company, or $\frac{\$60}{\$0.20} - \frac{\$50}{\$0.25}$. **(D):** This is the amount of money spent on mileage if Francisco uses Ocean Blue Car Rental. **(E):** This will tempt test-takers who think that the differences in the per day rate and the per mile rate for each company will cancel each other out for some reason.

How to check? Carefully reconsider your reading and calculations.

▶ **Post-solution patterns (see p. 151):** easy calculation mistake

Test 2, Question 38 (Test 3 in the 2020-2021 Red Book—see page 23 for more)

- **What's the prompt asking for?** The area of the given parallelogram in square units.
- **Math concepts in the prompt:** area, parallelograms, plotting points in the xy-coordinate plane, square units

- **Math concepts in the diagram:** area, parallelograms, plotting points in the xy-coordinate plane
- **Notable differences among choices:** (F) and (G) are the only choices without a radical expression. (F), (H), and (J) all involve the number 30, while (G) and (K) involve the number 60. (J) and (K) involve $\sqrt{5}$, while (H) involves $\sqrt{3}$.
- **Concepts in the choices:** multiplying or dividing by two, radical expressions
- **"Bridge" concepts:** The formula for the area of a parallelogram is $area = (base)(height)$.
- **Pre-solution patterns (see p. 149):** wrong answers try to imitate right answers; halves and doubles
- **Things to look out for:** Don't misread the coordinates of the corners of the parallelogram! Don't forget or misapply the formula for the area of a parallelogram!

Solution 1: Geometry: Apply the formula for the area of a parallelogram to the question, and pick the appropriate answer choice.

If we know the formula for the area of a parallelogram, we can apply it here. That formula is $A = bh$, where A is the area of the parallelogram, b is the length of the base of the parallelogram, and h is the height of the parallelogram.

When we look at the diagram, we can see that the base of the parallelogram is 10 units, because it stretches from the point $(0, 0)$ 10 units over to the point $(10, 0)$. We can also see that the height of the parallelogram must be 6, because the base runs along the x-axis, and the vertical distance from the x-axis to point $(3, 6)$ must be 6 units. Let's plug the values we found in to the equation for the area of a parallelogram.

$$A = bh \qquad \text{(formula for area of a parallelogram)}$$
$$A = (10)(6) \qquad \text{(plug in } b = 10 \text{ and } h = 6\text{)}$$
$$A = 60 \qquad \text{(simplify)}$$

So we can see that the area of the parallelogram is 60, and the right answer is (G).

Solution 2: Concrete: If we don't know the formula for the area of a parallelogram, we can still break up the shape into two triangles and a rectangle, then find the sum of their areas.

We can figure out the area of the figure by breaking it up into three shapes: two triangles and a rectangle.

Now we need to figure out the dimensions of the rectangle, and the bases and heights of the two triangles.

We know that the bottom of the figure is 10 units long, because it stretches from the point $(0, 0)$ 10 units over to the point $(10, 0)$. We can tell that the bottom of the rectangle must be 7 units long, because the vertical line separating the triangle on the left from the rectangle is 3 units to the right of the origin, and $10 - 3 = 7$. The top of the rectangle must be the same length, because opposite sides of a rectangle have the same length, and also because the same relationship exists between the rectangle and the triangle on the right as between the rectangle and the triangle on the left. We can also see that the height of the rectangle (and the heights of the triangles) must be 6, because the bottom of the figure runs along the x-axis, and the vertical distance from the x-axis to point $(3, 6)$ must be 6 units. With all of this information in mind, we can label the distances on the figure:

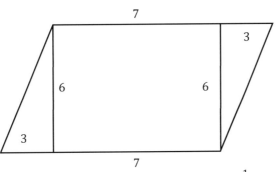

Now we can apply the formula for the area of a triangle, which is $A = \frac{1}{2}bh$, where A is the area of the triangle, b is the length of the base of the triangle, and h is the height of the triangle.

$$A = \frac{1}{2}bh \qquad \text{(formula for area of a triangle)}$$

$$A = \frac{1}{2}(3)(6) \qquad \text{(plug in } b = 3 \text{ and } h = 6)$$
$$A = 9 \qquad \text{(simplify)}$$

So the area of the triangle is 9, and both triangles have the same dimensions, which means the area of both triangles combined is 18. Now let's find the area of the rectangle. The formula for the area of a rectangle is $A = lw$, where A is the area of the rectangle, l is the length of the rectangle, and w is the width of the rectangle.

$$A = lw \qquad \text{(formula for area of a rectangle)}$$
$$A = (7)(6) \qquad \text{(plug in } l = 7 \text{ and } w = 6)$$
$$A = 42 \qquad \text{(simplify)}$$

So the area of the rectangle is 42. When we add that to the combined area of the two triangles, we get $42 + 18 = 60$, and we can see that (G) is correct.

Solution 3: Test-smart/Backsolve: Consider the answer choices and compare them to the prompt and the diagram to identify the choice with the appropriate elements.

If we realize that finding the area of a parallelogram (or the area of a rectangle and two triangles, as we saw in Solution 2) doesn't involve taking the square root of anything, and that none of the relevant dimensions of the shapes in the figure involve radical expressions, we can eliminate (H), (J), and (K). If we realize that just the rectangle in the middle of the figure must have an area greater than 30 (as we saw in Solution 2), we can eliminate (F). That leaves only the right answer, (G).

ANSWER CHOICE ANALYSIS

(F): This choice would result from incorrectly applying the formula for the area of a *triangle*—which is $\frac{1}{2}bh$—rather than the area of a parallelogram. **(H):** This choice reflects the same mistake as (J), with the added mistake of finding the wrong length for the short side of the parallelogram. **(J):** This choice reflects the mistake of trying to find the length of one of the short sides of the parallelogram and then multiplying that by the length of the long side. The problem with this approach is that the area of a parallelogram must be calculated using the *base* and the *height* of the parallelogram, not the base and the length of an adjacent side. **(K):** This choice results from the same mistake as (J), with the added mistake of multiplying by 2 at some point.

How to check? Try an alternate approach above.

Test 2, Question 39 (Test 3 in the 2020-2021 Red Book—see page 23 for more)

- **What's the prompt asking for?** The choice with all the Roman numerals that include sets that the result of $n + m$ must belong to, according to the prompt.
- **Math concepts in the prompt:** addition, complex numbers, integers, natural numbers, rational numbers, real numbers, sets
- **Elements of the choices:** Roman numerals
- **Notable differences among choices:** Every choice includes III. Only (A) and (E) include I. Every choice except (C) includes II. Every choice except (A) includes IV. Only (C), (D), and (E) include V.
- **Concepts in the choices:** addition, complex numbers, integers, natural numbers, rational numbers, real numbers, sets
- **"Bridge" concepts:** The natural numbers are the numbers that can be counted as discrete, whole objects in nature: 1, 2, 3, 4, 5, etc. The integers are all whole numbers (negative or positive)

and zero: ...$-5, -4, -3, -2, -1, 0, 1, 2, 3, 4, 5,...$. The rational numbers are the numbers that can be expressed as a ratio of integers, so all integers are examples of rational numbers. The real numbers are the numbers that don't involve taking the square root of -1, so all rational numbers are also real. The complex numbers are numbers that can include an imaginary component, but don't have to include an imaginary component, so all real numbers are also complex numbers—but see the note below.

- **Pre-solution patterns (see p. 149):** wrong answers try to imitate right answers
- **Things to look out for:** Don't misread the phrases that accompany the Roman numerals! Don't confuse the attributes of the different sets described in the question!

Solution 1: Theoretical: Use your knowledge of the attributes of the different sets in the Roman numerals to identify the answer.

Since natural numbers are basically positive integers, any two natural numbers together must equal another positive integer, which means that result must be another natural number. So Roman numeral I must be part of the right answer.

As we just discussed, any number $n + m$ as described in the prompt must be an integer, so II must be part of the right answer as well.

Every integer is a rational number, because every integer can be expressed as a ratio, so for the reasons we've discussed so far, III must be part of the right answer too.

Every integer must be a real number, because integers aren't expressed using the square root of -1, which means IV must also be part of the right answer.

Complex numbers can include an imaginary component, but they don't have to—so every real number is also a complex number. For that reason we know that the right answer must include V.

The only choice that includes Roman numerals I, II, III, IV, and V is the right answer, choice (E). (Note that once we were sure I, II, III, and IV had to be in the right answer, we could be sure that (E) was correct, even if we weren't sure about V—see the note below for more on that.)

Solution 2: Test-smart: Note that the sum must be a natural number and a real number, and only one choice includes Roman numerals I and IV. That choice is (E), the correct answer.

ANSWER CHOICE ANALYSIS

(A): Many untrained test-takers pick this answer choice because they incorrectly feel certain that the right answer should not include V, because they assume that complex numbers must include an imaginary component. But, even if we make that mistake, we should still know that (A) can't be right because it doesn't include IV, and the defining attribute of real numbers is that they don't include an imaginary component. **(B):** Some untrained test-takers pick this choice because they like that it doesn't include V, for the reasons we discussed for (A), and they don't read carefully enough to see that it also doesn't include I.

How to check? Carefully reconsider the prompt, the Roman numerals, and the answer choices. Make sure that the choice you pick definitely includes all of the sets that it should according to your understanding of math.

Note Many untrained test takers will see this question during their practice sessions and incorrectly assume that they need to be well versed in number theory for the ACT. But there are three reasons why we know that isn't true. First, as we just demonstrated in Solution 2, we actually didn't need to know the key details of the definitions for most of the sets named in the Roman numerals: we only needed to know for sure that adding natural numbers would result in a natural number, and that the set of real numbers includes the set of natural numbers. Knowing those two facts would allow us to see that (E) must be right without needing to know that complex numbers can appear not to have imaginary components (because $+0i$ could always be implied in any real number). Second, and perhaps more importantly, the exact subject matter needed to answer this question is very unlikely to appear on test day, since it doesn't come up often on the ACT. Third, in theory, we could miss this question and still answer every other question right and score a 36 on the test overall. This demonstrates once again why it's so important to understand how the ACT actually functions, and not just assume that the subject-matter you think you're encountering in a given practice question will be important for you to know on test day. We must remember to practice the concepts that appear repeatedly on the ACT Math section—like careful reading and simple math—and not get distracted or intimidated by the few questions that appear to be more advanced before we really understand what they're asking.

▌ Test 2, Question 40 (Test 3 in the 2020-2021 Red Book—see page 23 for more)

- **What's the prompt asking for?** The number of digits in the square root of the perfect square described in the prompt.
- **Math concepts in the prompt:** digits, integers, positive numbers, ranges, square numbers
- **Notable differences among choices:** (F), (G), (H), and (J) include every possible integer from 1 to 4, inclusive. (K)

indicates that the answer is unknowable from the given information.

- **Concepts in the choices:** insufficient information, integers
- **Pre-solution patterns (see p. 149):** halves and doubles
- **Things to look out for:** Don't miscount the digits! Don't make any small mistakes in your reading or calculations!

Solution 1: Concrete/Backsolve: As a test, square the smallest and largest numbers consisting of one digit, two digits, three digits, and four digits, to establish the possible ranges of the resulting square numbers. Then pick the choice that reflects your results.

We can test (F) by squaring 1 and 9, since 1 is the smallest one-digit number and 9 is the largest. 1^2 is 1, and 9^2 is 81. That range doesn't overlap with the range from 1,000 to 9,999 that appears in the question. So (F) must be wrong.

We can test (G) by squaring 10 and 99, since 10 is the smallest two-digit number and 99 is the largest. 10^2 is 100, and 99^2 is 9,801. That range of numbers does overlap with the range from 1,000 to 9,999, so this looks like a promising answer choice. But it's always important to check every answer choice when we're trying to test out numbers like this, just to make sure we haven't made a mistake. So let's try the others.

We can test (H) by squaring 100 and 999, because they're the smallest and largest 3-digit numbers. 100^2 is 10,000, and 999^2 is 998,001. Those numbers are outside of our target range of 1,000 to 9,999.

Finally, we can test (J) by squaring 1,000 and 9,999—the smallest and largest 4-digit numbers. $1,000^2$ is 1,000,000, and $9,999^2$ is 99,980,001. Those squares also fall well outside our target range of 1,000 to 9,999.

What about (K)? We know that (K) must be wrong, because we tested the largest 1-digit number, the smallest 2-digit number, the largest 2-digit number, and the smallest 3-digit number, and we found that all the perfect squares between 1,000 and 9,999 had to have 2-digit roots—we know this because squaring the largest 1-digit number (which is 9) gives us a result of 81, which is too low to be part of the target range of 1,000 to 9,999, and squaring the smallest 3-digit number (which is 100) gives us a result of 10,000, which is too high to be part of the target range of 1,000 to 9,999. So it wouldn't be true to say that the answer can't be determined, because we've determined that 2 must be the answer.

So we know that (G) is correct.

Solution 2: Abstract/Backsolve: As a test, take the square root of 1,000 and 9,999 and see what you can conclude about the choices.

We can use our calculators to find that the square root of 1,000 is about 31.62, and the square root of 9,999 is about 99.99. So the square root of any perfect square between 1,000 and 9,999 must be an integer greater than approximately 31.6 and less than approximately 99.99. All integers in that range have 2 digits, so the right answer must be (G).

ANSWER CHOICE ANALYSIS

(K): Many untrained test takers will choose (K) because they'll assume that we can't know any attributes of the square root described in the prompt if we don't know exactly what the square itself is. But as we demonstrated above, it's possible to establish with certainty that the square root of any square with four digits must be a number with two digits, which means that (G) is the right answer no matter which specific number the prompt is describing.

How to check? Try an alternate approach above.

Test 2, Question 41 (Test 3 in the 2020-2021 Red Book—see page 23 for more)

- **What's the prompt asking for?** The number of rooms that we should expect to be occupied on any given day during the summer season, according to the table (rounded to the nearest whole number).
- **Math concepts in the prompt:** decimals, probability, rates, reading data from a table
- **Math concepts in the diagram:** probability, rates
- **Elements of the choices:** Each choice is a two-digit number.
- **Notable differences among choices:** (B) and (E) are complements of one another with respect to the ideas of probability, since they add up to 100. (A) and (D) are complements of one another with respect to the prompt, because they add up to 80, the number of rooms in the hotel. (D) is the result when (C) is rounded to the nearest tens digit.
- **Concepts in the choices:** complements
- **"Bridge" concepts:** To find the expected occupancy rate on any given day, multiply the total number of rooms by each occupancy rate and the corresponding probability of that occupancy rate, and add up those four products. This is the same thing as multiplying the total number of rooms by the weighted average of the occupancy rates.
- **Pre-solution patterns (see p. 149):** opposites
- **Things to look out for:** Don't confuse the probabilities of the individual occupancy rates! Don't forget to round to the nearest whole number! Don't make any small mistakes in your multiplication! Don't forget that there are 80 rooms in the hotel, not 100!

Solution 1: Probability: Multiply the total number of rooms by each occupancy rate and the corresponding probability of that occupancy rate, and add up those four products.

We can find the expected number of occupied rooms for each occupancy rate and probability like so:

$$0.60 \times 0.20 \times 80 = 9.6$$
$$0.70 \times 0.40 \times 80 = 22.4$$
$$0.80 \times 0.30 \times 80 = 19.2$$
$$0.90 \times 0.10 \times 80 = 7.2$$

Now we can add the four results we just found:

$$9.6 + 22.4 + 19.2 + 7.2 = 58.4$$

The choice that's the nearest whole number to 58.4 is the right answer, (C), 58.

ANSWER CHOICE ANALYSIS

(A): This choice could be the result of averaging the probabilities, which results in a 0.25 average probability, and multiplying that number by 80. This approach doesn't take into account the issue of which occupancy rate has any particular probability, among other problems. **(B):** This choice combines the mistakes from (A) and (E). **(D):** This choice could represent the mistake of rounding the result of Solution 1 to the tens digit instead of the nearest whole number. **(E):** This is close to the result if a test-taker attempts Solution 1, but incorrectly thinks there are 100 rooms instead of 80 rooms.

How to check? Pay special attention to your reading and calculations, as always.

▶ **Post-solution patterns (see p. 151):** right approach, wrong step

Test 2, Question 42 (Test 3 in the 2020-2021 Red Book—see page 23 for more)

- **What's the prompt asking for?** The product of the two matrices in the prompt.
- **Math concepts in the prompt:** matrices, multiplication
- **Elements of the choices:** Each choice is a matrix.
- **Notable differences among choices:** (F) and (G) each have three columns and three rows, while (H) and (J) each have three columns and one row. (K) has only one column and one row.

(F) and (G) both include the same elements, but (F) has a central column of zeros and (G) has a central row of zeros. (J) is the only choice that includes $6a$ and $-6a$, which are the possible products of either $2a$ or $-2a$ and $3a$ or $-3a$.

- **Concepts in the choices:** matrices, multiplication, zero
- **"Bridge" concepts:** When we multiply these particular matrices, the result will be a 3×3 matrix in which the top row is the

result of multiplying a by each of the numbers in the second matrix, the middle row is the result of multiplying $2a$ by each of the numbers in the second matrix, and the bottom row is the result of multiplying $3a$ by each of the numbers in the second matrix.

- **Pre-solution patterns (see p. 149):** wrong answers try to imitate right answers; opposites
- **Things to look out for:** Don't confuse the steps for multiplying matrices! Don't make any small mistakes in your multiplication! Don't mis-key anything into your calculator!

Solution 1: Algebra: Use your knowledge of multiplying matrices to multiply the two matrices together.

$$\begin{bmatrix} a \\ 2a \\ 3a \end{bmatrix} \times \begin{bmatrix} 1 & 0 & -1 \end{bmatrix} = \begin{bmatrix} a & 0 & -a \\ 2a & 0 & -2a \\ 3a & 0 & -3a \end{bmatrix}$$

When we multiply the two matrices, we can see that (F) must be right.

Solution 2: Concrete/Calculator: Assign an arbitrary value to a, and then use that a-value to enter the two matrices from the prompt into your calculator and multiply them. Pick the answer choice that corresponds to your result.

Let's decide that $a = 5$. That gives us the following expression:

$$\begin{bmatrix} 5 \\ 10 \\ 15 \end{bmatrix} \times \begin{bmatrix} 1 & 0 & -1 \end{bmatrix}$$

If we enter the above expression into our calculator, we get the following result:

$$\begin{bmatrix} 5 & 0 & -5 \\ 10 & 0 & -10 \\ 15 & 0 & -15 \end{bmatrix}$$

When we check the answer choices, we can see that only (F) and (G) are even in the same format as our result, so we don't need to consider the other answer choices. Let's plug $a = 5$ into (F) and (G) to see which one matches our result.

$$\begin{bmatrix} 5 & 0 & -5 \\ 10 & 0 & -10 \\ 15 & 0 & -15 \end{bmatrix} \qquad \text{(choice (F) when } a = 5\text{)}$$

$$\begin{bmatrix} 5 & 10 & 15 \\ 0 & 0 & 0 \\ -5 & -10 & -15 \end{bmatrix} \qquad \text{(choice (G) when } a = 5\text{)}$$

We can see that only (F) matches the result when $a = 5$, so (F) must be the right answer.

Solution 3: Abstract: Use your knowledge of the properties of matrix multiplication to determine the attributes of the correct product matrix. Pick the answer choice that reflects your conclusions.

We know from our training that when we multiply a 3×1 matrix by a 1×3 matrix, the result will be a 3×3 matrix. Based on that, we can eliminate (H), (J), and (K). Between (F) and (G), we can focus on the zeros—should the right answer include a vertical column of zeros, or a horizontal row of zeros? We can see that the second matrix is a 1×3 matrix, and it includes a 0 as the middle term. We know that the middle term in this matrix will be multiplied to produce each of the terms in the middle column of the product matrix—in other words, each term in the middle column of the product matrix will be multiplied by 0, which means each of those terms will be 0. So the middle column of the right answer should contain three zeros, which means (F) must be right.

ANSWER CHOICE ANALYSIS

(G): This choice reflects the mistake of taking the individual terms from the correct matrix in (F) but arranging them in the wrong orientation, so that, among other things, the middle *row* consists of zeros, rather than the middle *column*. **(H):** This choice could reflect the mistake of simply multiplying across the central row of the entire expression in the prompt, ignoring a and $3a$ in the first matrix because there appear to be no corresponding rows for them in the second matrix. **(K):** This choice could reflect the mistake of assuming that the product of any matrix including zero must ultimately be zero.

How to check? Try an alternate approach above.

Note   The ACT made this question much easier than it had to. First of all, only two of the answer choices involve a 3×3 matrix, so just knowing the dimensions of the matrix product allows you to eliminate three choices immediately. Second, the terms in the second matrix in the prompt produce a kind of visual symmetry that can be easily observed when we scan through the answer choices. It would have been much harder to answer this question quickly if the numbers in the two matrices had been less similar to one another and had avoided zero, because then it might have been necessary to keep careful track of the value and location of each term in all seven matrices in the prompt and the answer choices. Instead, the choices are arranged so that we can easily identify the answer if we just realize the product should be a 3×3 matrix with a central column of zeros. It's also important to point out that we can use a graphing calculator to answer this question, so you don't need to learn the intricacies of matrix multiplication for the purposes of the ACT if you're comfortable doing those calculations on your calculator.

- **What's the prompt asking for?** The size of the smaller angle in the diagram, in degrees.
- **Math concepts in the prompt:** angles, degrees, lines, rays, reading diagrams
- **Math concepts in the diagram:** addition, algebra, angles, degrees, lines, rays
- **Notable differences among choices:** (A), (B), (C), and (D) are all degree measurements, while (E) says the question can't be answered. (A) is half of (B) and (C) is half of (D).
- **Concepts in the choices:** insufficient information, degrees, multiplying or dividing by 2
- **"Bridge" concepts:** Since there are 180° in a straight line, we can write an equation that compares the angle measurements in the diagram to 180°.
- **Pre-solution patterns (see p. 149):** halves and doubles
- **Things to look out for:** Don't forget that the smaller angle in the diagram has a size of $2x$, not x! Don't make any small mistakes in your algebra! Don't forget that the prompt is asking about the smaller angle, not the larger!

Solution 1: Concrete/Backsolve: Try the value from each answer choice as $2x$ in the diagram. The right answer will be the one that causes the measurements of the two angles in the diagram to add up to 180°.

The question asks for the measure of the smaller angle, which is $2x$—so we have to remember that if we're going to attempt a backsolving solution, we have to plug in the value in each answer choice for $2x$ in our equation, because that's what the value represents: the measure of the smaller angle, which is $2x$—not just x!

Now let's plug in the values from each answer choice for $2x$ to see which one causes the angles in the diagram to add up to 180°. We'll start with the value from (A). If the smaller angle had a measurement of 14°, then x would have a value of 7°. This would mean the value of the larger angle was 34°, because $4(7) + 6 = 34$. Since 34° and 14° don't add up to 180°, we know (A) can't be right.

Now, let's look at (B). If $2x$ were 28°, then x would be 14°. That would make the larger angle 62°, because $4(14) + 6 = 62$. But 62° and 28° don't add up to 180° either, so (B) isn't right.

Let's try (C) next. If $2x$ were 29°, then x would be 14.5°, and the larger angle would have a measurement of 64°, because $4(14.5) + 6 = 64$. But 64° and 29° don't add up to 180°, so (C) must also be wrong.

Now let's try (D). If $2x$ were 58°, then x would be 29°. That would cause the larger angle in the diagram to be 122°, because $4(29) + 6 = 122$. As it turns out, 122° and 58° do add up to 180°, just as the diagram requires. So we can see that (D) appears to be right.

Of course, as trained test-takers, we know that we need to check the remaining answer choice to help make sure we haven't made a mistake in our approach. (E) says that we can't determine the answer with the given information. Well, when we tested (D), we found that the measure of the smaller angle must be 58°, so it doesn't make sense to say we can't determine the answer from the given information. So (E) must be wrong.

After considering each choice, we can conclude that (D) is right.

Solution 2: Algebra: Write an equation that sets the sum of the two angles from the diagram equal to 180°, and solve that equation for x. Finally, use this value to find the size of the smaller angle.

First, we will need to solve for x. Then, in order to answer the question, we will need to find the measure of the smaller of the two angles, which is given in the diagram as $2x$.

$(4x + 6) + (2x) = 180$	(relationship between given angles in the diagram)
$6x + 6 = 180$	(simplify)
$6x = 174$	(subtract 6 from both sides)
$x = 29$	(divide both sides by 6)

Now we know that $x = 29$. But remember that the prompt didn't ask us to find x! It asked us to find the measure of the smaller angle, which is $2x$. So now we need to multiply x by 2, which gives us 58° as the size of the smaller angle. So (D) is right.

Solution 3: Test-smart: Note that the question must have an answer, and remember that the diagram is drawn to scale, and then pick the answer choice that reflects the diagram.

The diagram clearly shows that the angles have definite sizes relative to each other, which means there must be some value of x that makes the diagram valid—which means (E) must be wrong. Once we realize this, and we remember that the diagram is drawn to scale (because that's the ACT's unwritten rule), we can confidently choose the right answer, because the angle in the diagram is clearly greater than 45°, which means only one answer choice is possible: the correct answer, (D), 58°.

ANSWER CHOICE ANALYSIS

(A): This choice would be the value of x if there were 90° in a straight line, rather than 180°. **(B):** This choice would be the value of $2x$ if there were 90° in a straight line, rather than 180°. **(C)**: This is the value of x by itself, but the question asks for the size of the smaller angle, which is listed as $2x$ in the diagram.

How to check? Try an alternate approach above. Triple-check to make sure you correctly remembered that there are 180° in a straight line, and that the question is ultimately asking for the value of $2x$, not x.

▶ **Post-solution patterns (see p. 151):** opposites; right approach, wrong step

Test 2, Question 44 (Test 3 in the 2020-2021 Red Book—see page 23 for more)

- **What's the prompt asking for?** The effect on a after the changes to the other variables described in the prompt.
- **Math concepts in the prompt:** addition, algebra, functions, subtraction
- **Elements of the choices:** Each choice is a statement describing a possible change in a.
- **Notable differences among choices:** (F), (G), and (H) all indicate that a would increase, while (J) indicates it wouldn't change at all and (K) indicates it would decrease. The amounts

of the increases mentioned in (F), (G), and (H) are 4, 2, and 1 respectively, and the amount of the decrease in (K) is 2.

- **Concepts in the choices:** decreasing, increasing, multiplying or dividing by 2
- **Pre-solution patterns (see p. 149):** be aware of series; halves and doubles; opposites
- **Things to look out for:** Don't confuse the variables in the prompt, or the changes that occur to them! Don't misread the answer choices!

Solution 1: Concrete: Assign arbitrary values for a, b, and c that satisfy the initial conditions in the prompt. Then change the values of b and c as described later in the prompt, and note the resulting change in a. Pick the answer choice that reflects this change.

Let $b = 4$ and $c = 7$:

$$a = 2b + 3c - 5 \quad \text{(given equation)}$$
$$a = 2(4) + 3(7) - 5 \quad \text{(plug in } b = 4 \text{ and } c = 7)$$
$$a = 24 \quad \text{(simplify)}$$

So we know that when $b = 4$ and $c = 7$, $a = 24$.

Now let's decrease b by 1 and increase c by 2 as described in the prompt, so that $b = 3$ and $c = 9$:

$$a = 2(3) + 3(9) - 5 \quad \text{(plug in } b = 3 \text{ and } c = 9)$$
$$a = 28 \quad \text{(simplify)}$$

So a increased by 4, which means (F) is correct.

Solution 2: Abstract: Use your understanding of algebra to determine the net effect on a as a result of the changes in the prompt.

The prompt says the value of b *decreases* by 1. In the given expression, b is multiplied by 2, so the effect of decreasing b by 1 must be that a decreases by 2, because $-1 \times 2 = -2$. The prompt also says that the value of c *increases* by 2. In the given expression, c is multiplied by 3, so the effect of increasing c by 2 must be that a increases by 6, because $2 \times 3 = 6$. So the changes described in the prompt cause a to decrease by 2 and then increase by 6, which is the same as increasing by 4, because $-2 + 6 = 4$. So (F) is right.

ANSWER CHOICE ANALYSIS

(G): This could result from misreading the coefficient of c as 2, rather than 3. **(H)**: This could result from misreading the increase in c as 1 instead of 2, or thinking that b increases by 2 and c decreases by 1, instead of the other way around as the prompt describes.

How to check? Try an alternate approach above. Pay special attention to whether the increase should be one, two, or four.

▶ **Post-solution patterns (see p. 151):** almost like the other choices

Test 2, Question 45 (Test 3 in the 2020-2021 Red Book—see page 23 for more)

- **What's the prompt asking for?** The expression that accurately describes the number of gallons of fertilizer that Shima will mix according to the prompt.
- **Math concepts in the prompt:** algebraic expressions, ratios, unit conversion
- **Elements of the choices:** Each choice is a fraction that includes the numbers 0.5, 40, 128, and 43,560. No other numbers are included in any of the choices.
- **Notable differences among choices:** (A) has 43,560 in the denominator, and the other three numbers in the numerator, while (D) is the reciprocal of (A). (B) has 40 and 128 in the

numerator, with the other two numbers in the denominator; (C) is the reciprocal of (B). (E) has 128 in the denominator and the other three numbers in the numerator; (E) is the only choice without a reciprocal in the answer choices.

- **Concepts in the choices:** division, multiplication, reciprocals
- **Pre-solution patterns (see p. 149):** wrong answers try to imitate right answers; opposites
- **Things to look out for:** Don't confuse the numerator and denominator of the correct expression! Don't confuse the numbers involved in the unit conversions! Don't misread the answer choices!

Solution 1: Concrete/Arithmetic: First, convert one fluid ounce to gallons as a decimal expression, and divide the number of square feet in an acre by 40. Multiply the decimal expression in gallons that represents 1 fluid ounce by the number of times that 40 square feet can fit into an acre. Finally, multiply by 0.5 to find the amount of fertilizer required for half an acre. The result will be a decimal expression of the actual number of gallons of fertilizer that Shima will need, according to the prompt. Finally, use your calculator to determine the numerical values of the expressions in each answer choice: the choice that matches the number of gallons you just found will be the right answer.

The prompt tells us that one fluid ounce is $\frac{1}{128}$ of a gallon, or 0.0078125 gallons, and the number of 40-square-foot sections in an acre is $\frac{43,560}{40}$, or 1089. We can multiply these numbers together to find the number of gallons of fertilizer required for an acre of soil, and we can multiply the result by 0.5 to find the amount required for half an acre, as required by the prompt. The result is approximately 4.2540. Now let's find the value of each expression from the answer choices to find which one matches our value.

The value from (A) is approximately 0.0588, which doesn't match our value—so (A) appears to be wrong.

The value from (B) is approximately 0.2351, which doesn't match our value—so (B) appears to be wrong.

The value from (C) is approximately 4.2540, which matches our value. This choice appears to be right, but let's check the remaining choices to help make sure we didn't misread something or make some other mistake.

The value from (D) is approximately 17.0156, which doesn't match our value—so (D) appears to be wrong.

Finally, the value from (E) is 6806.25, which doesn't match our value—so (E) appears to be wrong.

After considering each choice, we can see the only (C) matches the value we found, which means (C) must be right.

Solution 2: Abstract/Algebraic: Perform a standard unit conversion to convert the ratio from the prompt into a ratio that compares gallons to half-acres. Pick the answer choice that reflects your result.

The prompt tells us that Shima uses 1 fluid ounce of fertilizer per 40 square feet of soil, and we need to find this measurement in gallons per acre. The prompt tells us that 1 gallon = 128 fluid ounces, so we know that one fluid ounce is $\frac{1}{128}$ of a gallon. The prompt also tells us that 1 acre = 43,560 square feet, so there must be $\frac{43,560}{40}$ sections in an acre that measure 40 square feet. So we can say that Shima uses $\frac{1}{128}$ of a gallon of fertilizer on each of $\frac{43,560}{40}$ sections, which means she must use $\frac{1}{128} \times \frac{43,560}{40}$ gallons of fertilizer on an acre, or $\frac{43,560}{(128)(40)}$ gallons.

The amount we just found was for one acre, but the prompt asks how much she would use on 0.5 acres, so we need to multiply that expression by 0.5. That gives us $\frac{(0.5)(43,560)}{(128)(40)}$, which equals the expression in the correct answer, (C).

Solution 3: Test-smart/Backsolve: Consider the differences among the answer choices and compare them to the concepts in the prompt. Reason that the right answer must involve multiplying by half and dividing by 40, and note that only one choice satisfies these requirements.

When we read the prompt, we can see that we have a conversion for square feet to acres, and we can also see that Shima will need to fertilize 0.5 acres. So the right answer should involve multiplying by 0.5, to reflect the idea of applying the ratio to 0.5 acres. We also know that our original situation involves Shima fertilizing an area of 40 square feet, and that we need to compare this number of square feet to the number of square feet in an acre. It makes sense, then, that the right answer will have to involve dividing the number of square feet in an acre by 40, to figure out how many of these 40 square-foot sections are in an acre. So the right answer must involve multiplying by 0.5 as well as dividing by 40, and only one choice does that—the right answer, (C).

ANSWER CHOICE ANALYSIS

(A): This choice reflects the mistake of multiplying by $\frac{40}{43,560}$, instead of $\frac{43,560}{40}$, and multiplying by 128 instead of $\frac{1}{128}$. **(B):** This choice is the reciprocal of the right answer, probably reflecting the mistake of trying Solution 2 above but being confused as to which numbers should be on which side of the fraction bar. **(D):** This choice is the reciprocal of (A), possibly reflecting a combination of the mistakes described for (A) and (B).

How to check? Try an alternate approach above. Pay special attention to which numbers should be multiplied and which should be divided, because the answer choices are clearly trying to set us up to make a mistake on that!

Note As we can see in Solution 3 above, this question can actually be answered very quickly and efficiently if we pause for a moment to take stock of the similarities and differences among the answer choices, and consider them in light of the prompt. Remember this on test day!

Test 2, Question 46 (Test 3 in the 2020-2021 Red Book—see page 23 for more)

- **What's the prompt asking for?** The largest number of booths that could be filled with 4 people, according to the prompt.
- **Math concepts in the prompt:** largest possible number
- **Notable differences among choices:** (F), (G), (H), and (J) form a sequence of integers from 0 to 3. (K) is 5; the number 4 doesn't appear in the choices.
- **Concepts in the choices:** series, zero

- **Pre-solution patterns (see p. 149):** be aware of series
- **Things to look out for:** Don't confuse the number of booths and the number of people! Don't get confused about the largest number of people that can fit in a booth! Don't accidentally find the smallest possible number of booths that could have four people! Don't forget that each booth must have at least one person in it!

Solution 1: Concrete/Backsolve: Try each answer choice to see if it could possibly be a number of booths that has four people according to the prompt. The largest answer choice that makes this possible will be the correct answer.

(F) can't be right, because if one booth has four people in it, that still leaves 16 people (because $20 - 4 = 16$), which is more than enough to satisfy the requirement that none of the 10 booths can be empty (or, put another way, that each of the 10 booths must have at least one person sitting there). So at least one booth can be filled without violating the rules in the prompt, and (F) can't be right; let's check the next answer.

(G) can't be right either, because when we follow our logic from the last choice, 2 booths filled with 4 people each still leaves 12 people, which is more than enough to place at least one person at each of the 8 remaining booths. So at least two booths can be filled without violating the rules in the prompt, and (G) must be wrong.

(H) also can't be right, because 3 booths filled with 4 people each leaves 8 people, which is still enough to seat one person at each of the 7 remaining booths. So at least three booths can be filled without violating the rules in the prompt, and (G) must be wrong. Let's check (J)

(J) looks like a right answer, because we just saw that filling up 3 booths is possible without breaking the rules in the prompt, but when we fill up four booths with 4 people each, we only have 4 people left, and that's not enough to seat at least one person in each of the 6 remaining booths. So it seems like 3 *is* the greatest number of booths that could be filled with four people while making sure that no booths are empty. Let's take a look at (K) to make sure we haven't made a mistake.

(K) is wrong because if 5 booths are filled with 4 people each, then all 20 people are sitting at those booths, and there's no one left to sit at the other booths, which is required by the prompt.

After considering each choice, we can be confident that (J) is right, because we can seat 4 people at each of 3 booths and still have 8 people left over, which is more than enough to seat at least one person in each of the 7 remaining booths—but when we try to fill up 4 booths with 4 people each, only 4 people remain, which isn't enough to seat at least one person in each of the 6 remaining booths.

Solution 2: Abstract: In order to save as many people as possible for four-person booths, presume that each of the 10 booths begins with one person in it, since the prompt specifies that no booth can be empty. Then imagine that three-person groups come join some of the individual people already sitting in the booths, until a total of 20 people are sitting in the booths. The right answer is the number of booths with four people in this scenario.

If each of the 10 booths has one person in it, then 10 people have sat down and we've already satisfied the rule that says no booth can be empty. If 3 people show up and sit down at one booth, then 13 people are seated in booths, and one booth is full. If 3 more people show up and sit down at another booth, then 16 people are seated in booths, and two booths are full. If 3 more people show up and sit down at another booth, then 19 people are seated in booths, and three booths are full. At this point there's only one person left to seat, because the question said that only 20 people are seated in booths—and that person isn't enough to fill up another booth. So the maximum number of booths that can be filled is 3, if no booths can be empty. That means (J) is right.

ANSWER CHOICE ANALYSIS

(F): This could be the result of misreading the prompt, and finding the smallest possible number of booths that could have four people, instead of the largest possible number. It could also be the result of thinking that the prompt asked for the number of booths that MUST be filled with four people, rather than the largest number of booths that COULD be filled with four people. **(H):** This choice probably reflects the mistake of miscounting the number of booths that could be full. It could also represent the mistake of assuming that the prompt is asking how many people would sit in each booth if the people were evenly distributed. **(K):** This choice reflects the mistake of figuring out how many booths could be filled with 4 people if 20 total people are sitting at the booths, while ignoring the requirement that none of the 10 booths can be empty.

How to check? Try an alternate approach above. Be sure not to be off by one table in either direction.

Note This question is a great example of how ACT Math questions can still be "difficult" even though they don't involve advanced math. Most people who miss this question will do so because they don't read carefully enough, or because they don't pay attention to their table-counting. Don't make that kind of mistake on test day—don't assume you'll automatically answer a question correctly just because it's about something simple like counting tables!

▌Test 2, Question 47 (Test 3 in the 2020-2021 Red Book—see page 23 for more)

- **What's the prompt asking for?** The answer choice that must be true under the conditions in the prompt.
- **Math concepts in the prompt:** notation, probability
- **Elements of the choices:** Each choice equates two different probability expressions.
- **Notable differences among choices:** (A) and (B) are the only choices without $P(A \cap B)$. (B) is the only choice that contains a number. (B) and (C) involve subtraction and addition, respectively. (D) involves multiplication. (E) involves addition, subtraction, and multiplication.
- **Concepts in the choices:** addition, multiplication, notation, one, probability, subtraction
- **"Bridge" concepts:** By definition, the probability that two individual events will both occur is equal to the product of the individual probabilities of each event.
- **Pre-solution patterns (see p. 149):** opposites; wrong answers try to imitate right answers
- **Things to look out for:** Don't misread the notation in the prompt or the choices! Don't confuse the mathematical operations described in each choice! Don't forget that the prompt asks what *must* be true, not just what *might* be true!

Solution 1: Abstract: Using your knowledge of the rules of probability, consider each answer choice in turn and identify the choice that must be true.

(A) If A and B are independent events, we have no reason to believe that the probability of one event happening is the same as the probability of the other event happening. This equation *could* be true, but the prompt asks which equation *must* be true, so (A) can't be right.

(B) This choice has the same basic problem as (A)—if A and B are independent events, we also have no reason to believe that the probability of one event happening is the same as the probability of the other event *not* happening, which is what $1 - P(B)$ would represent. Again, this equation *could* be true, but the prompt asks which equation *must* be true, so (B) also can't be right.

(C) This choice is wrong because the probability of both events happening isn't the same as the sum of the probabilities of the two separate events happening. One reason we know that this is true is that if both events are guaranteed to happen, then the probability of each event would be 1—but it wouldn't make any sense to say that the probability of both events happening would be $1 + 1$, or 2.

(D) In order to calculate the probability of both events happening, we multiply the probability of one event happening by the probability of the other event happening, which is exactly what this choice says. This choice looks right, but we'll take a look at (E) to make sure we haven't made a mistake.

(E) This choice might be tempting, because it includes the idea of multiplying the probabilities of the two events happening together, but this choice still involves the mistake from (C), among other issues, so it's wrong.

After considering each choice, we can see that (D) must be right.

ANSWER CHOICE ANALYSIS

(A): This choice says the probabilities of the two events must be equal. While it's possible that they might be equal, the prompt doesn't provide enough information for us to know what the probability of B actually is, or how it compares to the probability of A. **(C):** This choice will appeal to a lot of untrained test-takers who misremember the proper method for determining compound probability, and incorrectly think that it involves adding the probabilities of two events, rather than multiplying them. This choice could also attract an untrained test-taker who meant to mark (D) but didn't pay enough attention to the choices and picked this one by accident, since they look similar. **(E):** The right hand side of this equation is actually the formula for determining the probability that either A or B occurs, rather than the probability that both A and B occur—although you don't need to know that to recognize that (D) is the right answer, and (E) is wrong. (Most test-takers who know enough about probability to be familiar with this formula will probably also know that (D) is right.)

How to check? Carefully reread the prompt and the answer choices.

▶ **Post-solution patterns (see p. 151):** most like the other choices

> **Note** This is another example of the kind of question that will cause people who don't understand the ACT to waste a lot of time in their preparation. Many people will assume from this question that the ACT requires them to know a lot about mathematical probability and the various ideas related to it, but, as trained test-takers, we realize that this question is only asking us about one of the most basic concepts in probability: the idea that we multiply the probabilities of two independent events in order to find the probability of the two independent events both happening. This is about as complicated as an ACT Math question about probability will get. Further, it's important to remember that this question is only one out of 60 on the math section, which means it's possible to miss this question and still score very high—in fact, you could theoretically miss this one question, never see another question about probability formulas, answer everything else right, and still score a "perfect" 36. Don't let the ACT trick you into believing that it's a more advanced and complicated test than it is!

Test 2, Question 48 (Test 3 in the 2020-2021 Red Book—see page 23 for more)

- **What's the prompt asking for?** The cosine of the given angle under the conditions in the prompt and the diagram.
- **Math concepts in the prompt:** angles, cosine, origin, plotting points in the xy-coordinate plane, positive numbers, vertices,

x-axis, xy-coordinate plane

- **Math concepts in the diagram:** angles, origin, plotting points in the xy-coordinate plane, positive numbers, vertices, x-axis, xy-coordinate plane

- **Elements of the choices:** Every choice is a fraction.

- **Notable differences among choices:** (F) and (G) involve the numbers 3 and 4, while (J) and (K) involve the numbers 4 and 5. (F) and (G) are reciprocals of each other, and (J) and (K) are reciprocals of each other. (H) has no reciprocal and is the only choice that includes both 3 and 5. (F), (G), and (H) are all

negative, while (J) and (K) are positive.

- **Concepts in the choices:** fractions, negative numbers, positive numbers, reciprocals

- **Pre-solution patterns (see p. 149):** wrong answers try to imitate right answers; halves and doubles

- **Things to look out for:** Don't confuse the numerator and denominator of the fraction! Don't confuse the sign of the right answer! Don't forget which trig function you've been asked to find! Don't confuse the order of the coordinates of the given point!

Solution 1: Trigonometry: Determine the distance of the given point from the origin, then use SOHCAHTOA to construct the appropriate cosine fraction.

In order to execute this solution, we'll need to know the distance from the point to the origin. In order to find that distance, we'll have to treat it like the hypotenuse of a triangle, and use the Pythagorean theorem to find that hypotenuse. (Note that this technique is the same as applying the distance formula, but thinking about it in terms of the Pythagorean theorem usually makes it much easier to remember.)

We know the horizontal leg must be 4 units long, because the given point has an x-coordinate of 4, which represents a horizontal separation of 4 units from the origin. We also know the vertical leg must be 3 units long, because the given point has a y-coordinate of -3, which represents a vertical separation of 3 units from the origin. We can add those values to our diagram:

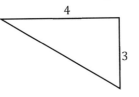

(At this point we might realize that this is a 3-4-5 Pythagorean triple, in which we case we know that the hypotenuse is 5 units long, and we don't need to apply the Pythagorean theorem, but if we don't recognize that, we can still go ahead and apply the Pythagorean theorem anyway.)

$$a^2 + b^2 = c^2 \qquad \text{(Pythagorean theorem)}$$
$$3^2 + 4^2 = c^2 \qquad \text{(plug in } a = 3 \text{ and } b = 4)$$
$$25 = c^2 \qquad \text{(simplify)}$$
$$5 = c \qquad \text{(take the square root of both sides)}$$

Again, we can see that the length of the hypotenuse is 5. Let's add that measurement to the diagram:

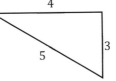

The angle we need to know about involves the longer leg and the hypotenuse of the triangle. The prompt asks for the cosine of that angle; we know from SOHCAHTOA that $cosine = \frac{adjacent}{hypotenuse}$, so the cosine of the angle in question must be $\frac{4}{5}$. So the correct answer is (J).

(You may notice in the diagram that the angle opens from the positive portion of the x-axis and then goes counter-clockwise "the long way" around the origin; this might throw off some test-takers, but in this case it doesn't change the sign of the cosine value—and anyway, the ACT doesn't include $-\frac{4}{5}$ as an answer choice to trip you up, so as long you figured out that the adjacent side was 4 units long and the hypotenuse was 5 units long, you didn't need to worry about this detail.)

Solution 2: Test-smart: Remember that cosine is equal to the adjacent side over the hypotenuse, and that the adjacent side has a length of 4, so the numerator of the right answer should be 4. At this point you've already narrowed it down to (F) or (J), because those are the only two choices with 4 in the numerator. You can eliminate (F) for any of the following reasons: you can realize that cosine in this quadrant should be positive, and (F) is negative. You can also realize that the denominator can't be 3, because the opposite side is 3 units long (and cosine doesn't involve the opposite side, and the hypotenuse can't be 3 because the hypotenuse must be longer than either side length). Finally, you can realize that cosine must be a fraction with an absolute value less than 1, because the numerator is the length of the adjacent side, and the denominator is the length of the hypotenuse, and the length of the adjacent side must be less than the length of the hypotenuse—the absolute value of (F) is greater than 1, so (F) can't be right. Based on this logic, you can confidently choose (J) without even finding the length of the hypotenuse.

ANSWER CHOICE ANALYSIS

(F): This is the cotangent of the given angle, not its cosine. **(G):** This is the tangent of the given angle, not its cosine. **(H):** This is the sine of the given angle, not its cosine. **(K):** This is the reciprocal of the correct answer, probably included to attract untrained test-takers who forgot how to apply SOHCAHTOA.

How to check? Try an alternate approach above. Carefully reread the prompt and the answer choices, because the question is clearly setting you up to make a small mistake with respect to trig functions, reciprocals, and signs.

▶   **Post-solution patterns (see p. 151):** opposites; right answer to the wrong question

▌ Test 2, Question 49 (Test 3 in the 2020-2021 Red Book—see page 23 for more)

- **What's the prompt asking for?** Which of the given expressions are equal for all real numbers x.
- **Math concepts in the prompt:** radical expressions, real numbers, Roman numerals, squaring, variables
- **Elements of the choices:** Each choice except (E) is either 2 or 3 Roman numerals.

- **Notable differences among choices:** (A), (B), (C), and (D) include Roman numerals. (E) says that none of the expressions are equivalent.
- **Things to look out for:** Be very careful with the signs of the numbers in the expressions from the prompt, especially when dealing with negative signs and absolute values!

Solution 1: Concrete: Pick a few different values for x, and see what happens in each expression. Use what you learn to determine which expressions must be equal for all real numbers x.

Let's see what happens when $x = 5$.

$$\sqrt{(-5)^2} = \sqrt{25} = 5 \qquad \text{(plug } x = 5 \text{ into the expression from I)}$$
$$|-5| = 5 \qquad \text{(plug } x = 5 \text{ into the expression from II)}$$
$$-|5| = -5 \qquad \text{(plug } x = 5 \text{ into the expression from III)}$$

We can see that when $x = 5$, the expressions from I and II are equal to each other, but not to the expression from III. But this doesn't tell us that I and II are necessarily equivalent for all real numbers x. Let's try a negative number next to see what we can figure out. We'll use $x = -3$.

$$\sqrt{\left(-(-3)\right)^2} = \sqrt{(3)^2} = \sqrt{9} = 3 \qquad \text{(plug } x = -3 \text{ into the expression from I)}$$
$$|-(-3)| = 3 \qquad \text{(plug } x = -3 \text{ into the expression from II)}$$
$$-|(-3)| = -3 \qquad \text{(plug } x = -3 \text{ into the expression from III)}$$

We got the same result as last time—the first two expressions were equivalent, but not the third one. Let's think about why this happens. In the first expression, you start out by squaring the opposite of the x value. Whether the x-value was positive or negative to start with, this will result in a positive number, because multiplying two negative numbers or multiplying two positive numbers will both result in a positive number. Then that positive number, which is equivalent to x^2 (whether x was positive or negative to start with), goes under the radical sign, so we end up with the positive square root of x^2, which is the same as $|x|$. The second expression is just the absolute value of the opposite of x, which will always the be the same as $|x|$, by definition. So we can be sure that the first two expressions will always be equal to $|x|$, which means I and II should be included in the right answer. We've already seen that III produces values that aren't equivalent to the values from I and II, so we know that III won't be part of the right answer—that means (A) must be right.

Solution 2: Abstract: Using your understanding of exponents, radical expressions, and absolute value, consider the characteristics of each of the Roman numerals and then select the answer choice that fits your analysis.

Roman numeral I starts with a $-x$ value, and then squares it. The result will be the same as x^2, because whether we multiply x by x or $-x$ by $-x$, we get x^2. The result of squaring $-x$ is under a radical sign, and we know that a radical sign represents the positive square root of whatever is under the radical sign—in this case, the positive square root of $(-x)^2$, which is the same as the positive square root of x^2. In other words, Roman numeral I is equal to the positive square root of x^2, which is $|x|$.

Roman numeral II is the absolute value of $-x$, which by definition is equal to $|x|$.

Roman numeral III is the opposite of the absolute value of x. We know that the absolute value of x is positive x by definition, so the opposite of that must always be negative x.

After considering each Roman numeral, we know that only I and II must be equal for all real numbers x, so (A) must be right.

(D): This choice would be tempting for test-takers who thought that an expression involving absolute value was positive no matter what, even with a negative sign outside of the absolute value brackets. **(E):** This choice would be tempting for test-takers who thought that a radical expression represented the positive and negative square root of the quantity under the radical.

How to check? Try an alternate approach above. Carefully reread the prompt and the Roman numeral expressions, because the question is clearly setting you up to make a small mistake with respect to signs.

Test 2, Question 50 (Test 3 in the 2020-2021 Red Book—see page 23 for more)

- **What's the prompt asking for?** The choice with a statement that does not have to be true according to the provided information.
- **Math concepts in the prompt:** angles, geometric points, labels on a diagram, lines, right angles
- **Math concepts in the diagram:** angles, geometric points, labels on a diagram, lines, opposite angles, right triangles, right angles
- **Elements of the choices:** Each choice is a statement that incorporates geometric notation and terminology, and asserts a relationship between two different elements of the diagram.
- **Notable differences among choices:** (H) and (K) both refer to things being congruent, while the other choices mention things being parallel, perpendicular, or similar. (G) and (K) both refer to line segments, while other choices refer to lines, angles, and triangles.
- **Concepts in the choices:** angles, congruence, geometric points, parallel lines, perpendicular lines, similarity, triangles
- **Pre-solution patterns (see p. 149):** wrong answers try to imitate right answers
- **Things to look out for:** Don't confuse any of the points or lines in the diagram or the answer choices! Don't confuse terms like "parallel" and "perpendicular!" Don't forget that the prompt asked you to find the statement that does not have to be true!

Solution 1: Geometry/Backsolve: Compare each answer choice to the concepts in the prompt and the diagram. Pick the choice that does not have to be true.

(F) We can see that $\overleftrightarrow{AB}$ and $\overleftrightarrow{EF}$ are both perpendicular to $\overleftrightarrow{AD}$, because they both meet $\overleftrightarrow{AD}$ at right angles. If $\overleftrightarrow{AB}$ and $\overleftrightarrow{EF}$ are both perpendicular to the same line, they must be parallel to each other—so (F) must be true. Remember that we're looking for the choice that is "NOT justifiable" based on the diagram, so (F) doesn't look like the right answer. Let's check the other choices.

(G) $\overline{DE}$ and $\overline{BE}$ meet at a right angle, so $\overline{DE}$ must be perpendicular to $\overline{BE}$, and we know (G) must be true as well, which means (G) isn't the right answer.

(H) $\angle ACB$ and $\angle FCE$ are vertical angles, so they must be congruent, and (H) must be true, and can't be the right answer.

(J) $\triangle BAC$ and $\triangle EFC$ each have a right angle, and as we saw in our discussion of (H), $\angle ACB$ and $\angle FCE$ are congruent, because they're vertical angles. So each triangle has two angles which are congruent with two angles on the other triangle. Since the sum of the angles of any triangle must equal 180°, the third angles of the two triangles must be congruent as well, which means all the angles of the triangles are congruent, and the two triangles must be similar. So (J) must be true.

(K) At first glance we might think (K) is true, but we can't actually justify the statement in (K) based on the diagram or the information in the prompt. In order for (K) to be true, $\angle ECF$ would have to be congruent to $\angle EDF$, and there isn't anything in the prompt or the diagram to tell us that this is the case. The statement in (K) isn't justifiable based on the given information, so (K) is the right answer.

(F): Many untrained test takers will pick this choice because they'll misread the prompt and think they need to pick the answer choice that *does* have to be true. Someone who made this mistake and bothered to look at the other choices would realize that four of the choices must be true, and they must have made a mistake somewhere. **(G), (H), and (J):** See Solution 1 above.

How to check? Carefully reconsider the prompt, the diagram, and the answer choices.

Test 2, Question 51 (Test 3 in the 2020-2021 Red Book—see page 23 for more)

- **What's the prompt asking for?** The perimeter of the figure.
- **Math concepts in the prompt:** dimensions, horizontal lines, perimeter, vertical lines
- **Math concepts in the diagram:** dimensions, horizontal lines, perimeter, vertical lines
- **Elements of the choices:** Each choice is a two-digit number.
- **Notable differences among choices:** (A), (C), and (E) form a series in which each number is three more than the one before it; (A), (B), (D), and (E) form a series in which each number is two more than the one before it. (C) is the only odd number.
- **Concepts in the choices:** series
- **"Bridge" concepts:** In order to find the perimeter, we'll need to figure out the lengths of the unlabeled sides.
- **Pre-solution patterns (see p. 149):** be aware of series
- **Things to look out for:** Don't forget to find the perimeter, not some other attribute of the figure (like the area)! Don't make a mistake when you determine the length of the unlabeled sides! Don't make any small mistakes when you add up all the side lengths together!

We know the length of the unlabeled side on the left must be 3, because the two vertical sides on the right add up to 3. We also know that the length of the shorter, unlabeled horizontal side near the bottom right must be 1, because the bottom horizontal side is 4 units long, which means the two opposite horizontal pieces must add up to 4, and the other horizontal component is 3 units long, and $4 - 3 = 1$. We can add this information to the diagram:

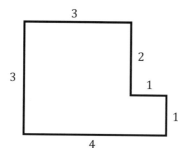

After we've added that information, we can add up the different side lengths to find the perimeter:

$$3 + 2 + 1 + 1 + 4 + 3 = 14 \qquad \text{(sum of all the side lengths)}$$

So the right answer is (D), 14.

ANSWER CHOICE ANALYSIS

(A): This choice indicates the *area* of the figure in square units, not the perimeter. It also reflects the mistake of simply adding the numbers that are already given in the figure, without finding the lengths of the unlabeled sides. **(B):** This choice could reflect the mistake of thinking that the vertical unlabeled side has a length of two, instead of three, and also forgetting to count the unlabeled horizontal side of the figure. **(C):** This choice could reflect the mistake of forgetting the unlabeled horizontal side of the figure, which has a length of one unit.

How to check? Carefully reconsider the prompt, the diagram, and the answer choices. The question is obviously trying to set you up to be off by a unit or two, so make sure you don't fall for that!

▶ **Post-solution patterns (see p. 151):** easy calculation mistake; right answer to the wrong question

> **Note** This question is another great example of the kinds of tricks that the test can play on untrained test-takers. Most test-takers could easily determine the lengths of the unlabeled sides in this diagram if they were asked to do that directly, and most could easily find the sum of six single-digit numbers. But the ACT used a diagram that distracts many test-takers from noticing the unlabeled horizontal side, and positioned the answer choices to take advantage of a variety of likely small mistakes, so lots of people will miss this question even though they have all the necessary skills to answer it correctly. Look out for this kind of thing on test day, because you'll see it over and over again!

Test 2, Question 52 (Test 3 in the 2020-2021 Red Book—see page 23 for more)

- **What's the prompt asking for?** The slope of the line along which point C could be moved without changing the area of the triangle in the diagram.

- **Math concepts in the prompt:** area of a triangle, lines, plotting points in the xy-coordinate plane, slope, vertices

- **Math concepts in the diagram:** lines, plotting points in the xy-coordinate plane, triangles, vertices

- **Notable differences among choices:** (F) and (G) are negative, while (J) and (K) are positive and (H) is neither negative nor positive. (F) is the negative reciprocal of (K) and (G) is the negative reciprocal of (J).

- **Concepts in the choices:** negative numbers, negative reciprocals, perpendicular slopes, positive numbers, zero

- **"Bridge" concepts:** The area of a triangle is given by the formula $\frac{1}{2}bh$. The base of the triangle can be any of its sides, and the height of the third point is determined by drawing a line through that point that meets the line along the base at a 90° angle. So, in order to move C in a way that doesn't change the area of the triangle, we have to move it on a line parallel to $\overline{AB}$, so that the perpendicular height measurement from C will always be the same distance from the line that contains A and B.

- **Pre-solution patterns (see p. 149):** wrong answers try to imitate right answers; opposites

- **Things to look out for:** Don't confuse the points in the question! Don't find a perpendicular slope instead of a parallel slope! Don't forget the diagram is drawn to scale!

The slope of $\overline{AB}$ is equal to the difference in the y-coordinates of A and B divided by the difference in their x-coordinates:

$$\frac{2-6}{8-0} \qquad \text{(y-coordinate of A minus y-coordinate of B over x-coordinate of A minus x-coordinate of B)}$$

$$-\frac{1}{2} \qquad \text{(simplify)}$$

So the slope of the line described in the prompt is $-\frac{1}{2}$, and (F) is the right answer.

ANSWER CHOICE ANALYSIS

(G): This would be the slope of a line perpendicular to $\overline{BC}$, which isn't what the prompt asked for. **(H):** This would be the correct answer if the prompt had asked us about moving B, but it asked about moving C. **(J):** This would be the right answer if the prompt had asked about moving A, but it asked about moving C. **(K):** This choice could reflect the mistake of thinking that the slopes of parallel lines were negative reciprocals of one another, or that we needed to find a slope perpendicular to the slope of $\overline{AB}$, instead of a slope parallel to $\overline{AB}$.

How to check? Carefully reconsider the prompt, the diagram, and the answer choices, as we can see that the question is clearly setting you up to confuse the points that define the triangle.

▶ **Post-solution patterns (see p. 151):** right answer to the wrong question

Note A lot of test-takers might have difficulty understanding what the prompt is talking about when it mentions moving C without changing the area of the triangle. That's very understandable, and one way to try to work around that might be to imagine moving C along lines with slopes that reflect each answer choice. The important lesson to learn from this question isn't something about moving the points on a triangle without changing the triangle's area, because that idea probably won't come up on test day. The much deeper lesson here is that the ACT can find a lot of ways to confuse test-takers without using advanced concepts, but we can still find ways to work around whatever confuses us if we keep our training in mind!

▮ Test 2, Question 53 (Test 3 in the 2020-2021 Red Book—see page 23 for more)

- **What's the prompt asking for?** The total number of calls that Marshall made after 20 days as a telemarketer, according to the conditions in the prompt.
- **Math concepts in the prompt:** addition, series, word problems
- **Elements of the choices:** Each is a three- or four-digit integer.
- **Notable differences among choices:** (A), (B), and (C) are three-digit numbers, while (D) and (E) are four-digit numbers. Every choice but (C) ends in a zero.
- **Things to look out for:** Don't think that Marshall starts making 5 extra calls on the first day—the 5 extra calls start on the second day!

Solution 1: Concrete: List out the number of calls for each day, and then add all the numbers in the list.

The prompt says that Marshall made 24 calls on his first day, and then increased his call total every day by 5 calls compared to the day before. If we wanted to list out the number of calls on each day, we'd get this:

Day 1: 24	44	64	84	104
29	49	69	89	109
34	54	74	94	114
39	59	79	99	Day 20: 119

When we add the number of calls from each day, we get 1430, which is (D), the right answer. This approach requires you not to make a mistake in listing out or adding the number of calls, but it's actually relatively quick and (for many people) can be a faster, more reliable approach than trying to reason through the question in a more abstract way. Still, it may be time-consuming for some test-takers.

Solution 2: Test-smart: Realize that Marshall must have made at least 24 calls each day, and then come up with a simple way to model the additional calls over the course of the 20 day period.

We can think of the calls that Marshall makes as belonging to 2 groups: the 24 calls he makes each day that match his first day's calls, and then the additional calls he makes to satisfy the requirements of the question.

The 24 calls per day are equal to 24×20 calls, or 480 calls. Now we need to figure out how many additional calls Marshall makes. We know that he doesn't make any additional calls the first day, and then he makes 5 additional calls the second day, 10 additional calls the third day, 15 additional calls the fourth day, and so on. Following that patterns, he must make 95 additional calls on his twentieth and final day. If he makes 0 additional calls on his first day, and 95 additional calls on the 20th day, and the number of calls per day increases at a steady rate, then the average number of additional call per day over the 20 day period must be equal to the average of the first day's additional calls and the last day's additional calls, or $\frac{0+95}{2}$, which is the same as 47.5. When we multiply the average number of additional calls per day by the number of days, we get $47.5 \times 20 = 950$, and when we add 480 and 950 we get 1430, which is (D), the right answer.

If this logic didn't feel totally comfortable to you, don't worry—the other solution is equally valid, and you don't need to feel comfortable approaching questions in this way on test day, as long as you're comfortable with one of the approaches we discuss.

ANSWER CHOICE ANALYSIS

(A): This choice reflects the mistake of thinking that Marshall makes only one extra call per day starting on the second day, instead of 5 extra calls per day. **(B):** This choice reflects the mistake from (A) and the additional mistake of thinking that the extra calls start on the first day, rather than the second day. **(C):** This choice is the result of correctly calculating the 950 extra calls that Marshall makes on top of this 24 calls each day—but then mistakenly adding 950 to 24, instead of adding 950 to *24 calls per day for 20 days*, or 480. **(E):** This is the result if we think that Marshall's 5 additional calls started on his first day, rather than his second day.

How to check? Try an alternate approach above. Reread the prompt to make sure you understand the details describing the calls Marshall makes.

Test 2, Question 54 (Test 3 in the 2020-2021 Red Book—see page 23 for more)

- **What's the prompt asking for?** The choice whose graph reflects the function defined in the prompt.
- **Math concepts in the prompt:** exponents, function definitions, piecewise functions, ranges
- **Elements of the choices:** Each choice is a diagram showing the graphs of three curves; for each graph, the left-most curve is part of a parabola.
- **Notable differences among choices:** (F) and (G) have parabolas that open "down," while the other choices have parabolas that open "up." The slope of the middle line segment in each choice is the same, and the slope of the right-most line segment in

each choice is the same. (F) and (K) are the only choices that pass the vertical line test. The lengths and intercepts of the three components of each graph generally vary from choice to choice.

- **Concepts in the choices:** line segments, parabolas, piecewise functions, slope, vertical line test
- **Pre-solution patterns (see p. 149):** wrong answers try to imitate right answers; opposites
- **Things to look out for:** Don't misread the function definition in the prompt! Don't forget to make sure that the ranges in your answer match the ranges in the function definition!

Solution 1: Calculator: Graph the function in the prompt and pick the answer choice that reflects the result.

Most students won't know how to graph a piecewise function on their graphing calculators. But let's just graph the three provided expressions anyway—because of the way ACT Math questions are written, there's a very good chance we'll still be able to find the answer from the resulting graph. Here's the graph of the three expressions from the prompt:

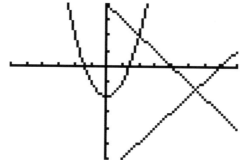

Based on this graph, we can eliminate (F) and (G) right away, because they include parabolas that open down. We can also eliminate (H), because the parabola in (H) isn't centered on the vertical axis, but the parabola in our graph is centered on the vertical axis. That leaves only (J) and (K). There are a few different reasons that we can eliminate (J). One way is to notice that the parabola in (J) has a point at $(1,0)$, and the parabola in our graph doesn't. Another would be to notice that the line with the negative slope in (J) touches the x-axis at $x = 5$, but the line with the negative slope in our graph touches the x-axis at $x = 4$. Either way, we can eliminate (J) as well, which leaves only (K), the right answer.

Solution 2: Test-smart: Note that the right answer must pass the vertical line test and include a parabola that opens "up." Pick the only choice that fits those requirements.

The prompt says we're talking about the graph of a "function," and a function must pass the vertical line test. Choices (G), (H), and (J) all fail the vertical line test, so they can be ruled out. (Remember that the "vertical line test" is when we check to see if drawing a vertical line anywhere on the graph of an equation causes that vertical line to intersect the graph more than once. If any vertical line can intersect the graph of the equation more than once, that equation isn't a function.) That leaves only (F) and (K).

There are a couple of ways we could choose between (F) and (K). The easiest way is probably to realize that (F) involves a parabola that opens down, while (K) involves a parabola that opens up. The parabola in the function is defined by $x^2 - 2$, which is a parabola that opens up—so (K) must be right.

ANSWER CHOICE ANALYSIS

(F): This choice is very similar to the right answer except that it features a parabola that opens "down," to trap untrained test-takers who forget the graphing rules of parabolas and don't take the time to consult their calculators.

How to check? Try an alternate approach above.

▶ **Post-solution patterns (see p. 151):** most like the other choices

- **What's the prompt asking for?** The choice that expresses the number of permutations of 15 objects taken 5 at a time.
- **Math concepts in the prompt:** permutations
- **Elements of the choices:** Each choice is an expression involving the numbers 15 and 5.
- **Notable differences among choices:** (A) is the only choice without a factorial expression. (A) and (B) are the only choices without fractions. (C), (D), and (E) all have 15! in the numerator. (D) has $(15 - 5)!$ in the denominator, and (E) has a similar expression—but with the exclamation point inside the parentheses: $(15 - 5!)$.
- **Concepts in the choices:** factorials, fractions, multiplication, PEMDAS
- **"Bridge" concepts:** Factorial notation uses an exclamation point to indicate the idea of multiplying an integer by every natural number lower than that integer; for example, $5! = 5 \times 4 \times 3 \times 2 \times 1$. To find the number of permutations of a given selection, we multiply together the number of possible options for each slot in the selection. Thus, the number of permutations of 15 objects taken 5 at a time is equal to $15 \times 14 \times 13 \times 12 \times 11$, because there will be 15 possibilities for the first object, 14 possibilities for the second object, 13 possibilities for the third object, 12 possibilities for the fourth object, and 11 possibilities for the fifth object.
- **Pre-solution patterns (see p. 149):** wrong answers try to imitate right answers
- **Things to look out for:** Don't misread the answer choices! Remember that the prompt asks for the number of permutations, not combinations!

Solution 1: Permutations: Use your knowledge of the rules of permutations to identify the correct answer choice.

In order to find the number of permutations of 15 objects taken 5 at a time, we would need to multiply together the number of possibilities for each object. So the first of the 5 objects would have 15 possibilities, the second would have 14 possibilities (because one has already been taken), the third would have 13 possibilities (because two have already been taken), the fourth would have 12 possibilities (because three have already been taken), and the fifth would have 11 possibilities (because four have already been taken). Multiplying each of those numbers of possibilities together gives us $15 \times 14 \times 13 \times 12 \times 11$, which equals 360,360.

This number doesn't appear in any of the answer choices, though. We have two ways to find the right answer choice. We can realize that $15 \times 14 \times 13 \times 12 \times 11$ is equal to $\frac{15!}{(15-5)!}$, because $\frac{15!}{(15-5)!}$ is the same as $\frac{15!}{10!}$, which is the same as $\frac{15 \times 14 \times 13 \times 12 \times 11 \times 10 \times 9 \times 8 \times 7 \times 6 \times 5 \times 4 \times 3 \times 2 \times 1}{10 \times 9 \times 8 \times 7 \times 6 \times 5 \times 4 \times 3 \times 2 \times 1}$, and the $10 \times 9 \times 8 \times 7 \times 6 \times 5 \times 4 \times 3 \times 2 \times 1$ part cancels out of that expression, leaving only $15 \times 14 \times 13 \times 12 \times 11$. This analysis tells us that (D) must be right. We can also just enter each of the values in the answer choices in our calculator, and we'll find that only (D) is equal to 360,360, and therefore equal to $15 \times 14 \times 13 \times 12 \times 11$, which makes (D) right.

Solution 2: Calculator: Use your graphing calculator to find the number of permutations of 15 objects taken 5 at a time, and then use the calculator to find the numerical value of each answer choice. Pick the choice whose value matches the value you found when you calculated the permutation.

If your calculator can calculate permutations, you can use that functionality to find the right answer here. Not all calculators are the same, so you may need to find out how your calculator does permutations, but on a TI-84 Plus you can enter 15, then the nPr command (which tells us the number of permutations when we choose r objects from a group of n objects), then 5. That will look more or less like this on the screen: $15 \ nPr \ 5$

When you hit enter, the result will be 360,360. Using the same process we saw in the previous solution, we can determine that this is equal to (D), the right answer.

ANSWER CHOICE ANALYSIS

(A): This isn't really relevant to the concepts in the prompt. This choice would indicate the number of possible combinations from one group of 15 items and another group of 5 items. **(B):** This choice represents the denominator in the expression of the right answer, not the entire expression. **(E):** This is intended to be an expression that would tell us the number of *combinations* of 15 objects taken five at a time—while the prompt asked for the number of *permutations* of 15 objects taken five at a time—but the ACT actually made a mistake, and left the final exclamation point inside the parentheses, when it should be outside the parentheses. So the denominator was supposed to be $(5!)(15 - 5)!$ instead of $(5!)(15 - 5!)$. Either way it's a wrong answer, but it's not as tricky as the ACT meant it to be, and we thought you'd like to know about the mistake the ACT made here.

How to check? Try an alternate approach above.

▶ **Post-solution patterns (see p. 151):** easy calculation mistake; right answer to the wrong question

- **What's the prompt asking for?** The expression that's equivalent to the expression in the prompt.
- **Math concepts in the prompt:** fractions, i, positive numbers, radicals
- **Notable differences among choices:** (F), (J), and (K) involve i. Every choice except (F) is a fraction with $\sqrt{x}$ in the numerator. (H) and (K) have $x + 1$ as a denominator, while (G) has x and

(J) has $x - 1$.
- **Concepts in the choices:** fractions, i, radicals
- **"Bridge" concepts:** We can get rid of a binomial with a square root in the denominator of a fraction by multiplying that fraction by its complex conjugate.
- **Things to look out for:** Don't make any small mistakes in your calculations, especially with respect to i, plus signs, and minus signs!

Solution 1: Algebra: Multiply the numerator and denominator by the complex conjugate of the denominator in the prompt.

$$\frac{i}{\sqrt{x}-i}$$ (original expression from the prompt)

$$\frac{i}{\sqrt{x}-i} \times \frac{\sqrt{x}+i}{\sqrt{x}+i}$$ (multiply top and bottom by complex conjugate of the denominator)

$$\frac{i\sqrt{x}+i^2}{x-i^2}$$ (simplify)

$$\frac{i\sqrt{x}-1}{x+1}$$ (substitute $i^2 = -1$)

So we can see that $\dfrac{i}{\sqrt{x}-i}$ is equal to $\dfrac{i\sqrt{x}-1}{x+1}$, and (K) is right.

ANSWER CHOICE ANALYSIS

(F): This choice would be right if $\sqrt{x} - 1$ were equal to 1, but it isn't. **(H):** This choice is the same as the right answer, except the numerator is missing the i next to $\sqrt{x}$. This choice could tempt a test-taker who almost executed the solution correctly but made a small mistake related to i. **(J):** This choice is the same as the right answer, except the plus sign and minus sign are switched. This choice could tempt a test-taker who almost executed the solution correctly but made a small mistake related to sign.

How to check? Carefully reread the prompt and the answer choice you selected to make sure you didn't make a mistake related to whether a value was positive or negative.

Test 2, Question 57 (Test 3 in the 2020-2021 Red Book—see page 23 for more)

- **What's the prompt asking for?** The unit vector notation of $\overrightarrow{AB} + \overrightarrow{CD}$.
- **Math concepts in the prompt:** vectors, xy-coordinate plane
- **Elements of the choices:** Each choice is an expression in unit vector notation.
- **Notable differences among choices:** (B) and (C) both have a coefficient of 3 for i, while (D) and (E) have a coefficient of 9.
- **Concepts in the choices:** coefficients, unit vectors
- **"Bridge" concepts:** We add vectors by breaking them down into

horizontal components and vertical components, and adding the corresponding components together. In unit vector notation, $\mathbf{i}$ represents a horizontal vector 1 unit long, and $\mathbf{j}$ represents a vertical vector 1 unit long.
- **Things to look out for:** Don't switch the horizontal components of the vectors with the vertical components of the vectors! Don't confuse unit vector notation and (x, y) coordinate pairs! Don't make an error related to sign!

Solution 1: Concrete: Use your knowledge of unit vector notation to find $\overrightarrow{AB} + \overrightarrow{CD}$.

We can use the grid in the diagram to see that $\overrightarrow{AB}$ represents 9 units moving from left to right and 6 units moving up, so this corresponds to a unit vector notation of $9\mathbf{i} + 6\mathbf{j}$. We can also see that $\overrightarrow{CD}$ represents 0 units moving from left to right and 5 units moving up, so this corresponds to a unit vector notation of $0\mathbf{i} + 5\mathbf{j}$. When we add the components of these two vectors we get $9\mathbf{i} + 11\mathbf{j}$, which corresponds to (E), the right answer.

Solution 2: Test-smart: Once you realize that the vertical component of the resulting vector is $5 + 6$, or 11, you can eliminate every choice but (E), the right answer.

ANSWER CHOICE ANALYSIS

(A): Neither vector moves left, so there's no reason to have a negative value in the $\mathbf{i}$ position. This choice could be tempting for test-takers who thought the unit vector notation of $\overrightarrow{AB}$ was $-6\mathbf{i} - 2\mathbf{j}$ based on the fact that the coordinates of A are $(-6, -2)$. **(B):** Neither vector moves down, so there's no reason to have a negative value in the $\mathbf{j}$ position. This could trick test-takers who thought the unit vector notation of $\overrightarrow{AB}$ was $3\mathbf{i} + 4\mathbf{j}$ (based on the fact that the coordinates of B are $(3, 4)$), and who also thought that $\overrightarrow{CD}$ was pointed down instead of up. **(C):** This choice could be tempting for test-takers who thought the unit vector notation of $\vec{AB}$ was $3\mathbf{i} + 4\mathbf{j}$, based on the fact that the coordinates of B are $(3, 4)$. **(D):** This is $\vec{AB} - \vec{CD}$, but the prompt asks for $\vec{AB} + \vec{CD}$.

How to check? Try an alternate approach above. Make sure your conclusions make sense when considered along with the diagram.

Test 2, Question 58 (Test 3 in the 2020-2021 Red Book—see page 23 for more)

- **What's the prompt asking for?** The number of times larger the first pendulum's string is than the second pendulum's string according to the prompt—in other words, the result we would get if we divided the length of the first string by the length of the second string.
- **Math concepts in the prompt:** function models, mass, π, square roots, time
- **Notable differences among choices:** (F) is equal to 3^{-1}, (G) is equal to 3^1, (J) is equal to 3^2, and (K) is equal to 3^3. (H) is equal to 3×2.

- **Concepts in the choices:** exponents, fractions, multiples, three
- **"Bridge" concepts:** Since the model involves taking the square root of the L-term, any change in t must be accompanied by a change in L that is the square of the change in t.
- **Pre-solution patterns (see p. 149):** wrong answers try to imitate right answers; halves and doubles; opposites
- **Things to look out for:** Don't misread the prompt! Don't make any small mistakes in your calculations, especially with respect to the number 3! Don't confuse the variables in the model! Don't compare the pendulum strings in the wrong order!

Solution 1: Concrete: Pick an arbitrary starting value for L, and calculate the corresponding t-value. Then, return to the function and plug in a t-value that's one-third as much as your first t-value, and calculate the corresponding L-value. Pick the choice that reflects how many times larger the first L is than the second L; that is, pick the result when you divide the first L by the second L.

Let's say that $L = 128$ (you'll notice soon that I'm picking this particular number because it will make the math a little cleaner, but you don't have to pick this specific t-value when you try this approach if you don't want to). That gives us this:

$$t = 2\pi\sqrt{\frac{L}{32}} \qquad \text{(given equation)}$$

$$t = 2\pi\sqrt{\frac{128}{32}} \qquad \text{(plug in } L = 128\text{)}$$

$$t = 2\pi\sqrt{4} \qquad \text{(simplify)}$$

$$t = 4\pi \qquad \text{(simplify)}$$

Now we need a t-value that's one third this size; we can plug in that t-value and solve for the resulting L-value to see how much bigger the first L is than the second L.

$$t = 2\pi\sqrt{\frac{L}{32}} \qquad \text{(given equation)}$$

$$\frac{4}{3}\pi = 2\pi\sqrt{\frac{L}{32}} \qquad \text{(plug in } t = \frac{4}{3}\pi\text{)}$$

$$\frac{2}{3} = \sqrt{\frac{L}{32}} \qquad \text{(divide both sides by } 2\pi\text{)}$$

$$\frac{4}{9} = \frac{L}{32} \qquad \text{(square both sides)}$$

$$\frac{128}{9} = L \qquad \text{(multiply both sides by 32)}$$

So the length of Pendulum 1's string was 128 feet, and the length of Pendulum 2's string was $\frac{128}{9}$ feet, which means Pendulum 1's string was 9 times longer than Pendulum 2's string, and (J) is right.

Solution 2: Abstract: Think about the square-root relationship between t and L that appears in the model, and figure out the kind of change in L that would cause t to triple.

In order to increase the t value by 3 times, we have to increase the L value by the square of 3 times, or 9 times, because L is under a radical, which means its square root will be taken in the process of calculating t. So if the t-value for Pendulum 1 is 3 times as much as the t-value for Pendulum 2, then the L-value for Pendulum 1 must be 9 times as much as the L-value for Pendulum 2. Again, we can see that (J) is right.

ANSWER CHOICE ANALYSIS

(F): This choice could reflect the mistake in (G), along with the mistake of finding how many times the length of Pendulum 2's string is of Pendulum 1's string, instead of the other way around. **(G):** This choice reflects the mistake of assuming that every variable in the model must change by a factor of three if one of them does. **(H):** This choice reflects the mistake of multiplying 3 by 2, rather than raising 3 to the power of 2. **(K):** This choice reflects the mistake of raising 3 to the power of 3, but nothing in the prompt indicates a relationship involving the power of 3, or a cube-root.

Test 2, Question 59 (Test 3 in the 2020-2021 Red Book—see page 23 for more)

- **What's the prompt asking for?** The expression that is equal to $\log_a(xy)^2$.

- **Math concepts in the prompt:** logarithms, squaring, variables

- **Elements of the choices:** Each choice is an expression involving s and t.

- **Notable differences among choices:** (A) and (B)

involve adding s and t, while (C), (D), and (E) involve multiplying s and t.

- **Concepts in the choices:** addition, coefficients, multiplication, variables

- **Things to look out for:** Don't mix up the variables in the prompt or the answer choices!

Solution 1: Backsolving: Find values for $a, x, s, y,$ and t that satisfy the requirements of the prompt, then use those values to find which answer choice is equal to $\log_a xy^2$.

Let's say that $a = 5$ and $x = 125$. That means s would equal 3, because $\log_5 125 = 3$. Let's also say that $y = 625$; that means t would equal 4, because $\log_5 625 = 4$. Now we have values for $a, x, s, y,$ and t. We can plug these values into $\log_a(xy)^2$ and then use our calculators to find that $\log_5((125 \times 625)^2) = 14$. Now let's plug our values into each choice to see which is equal to 14. (Remember that when we started our solution we came up with the values $a = 5, x = 125, s = 3, y = 625,$ and $t = 4$.)

$2(s + t)$	(expression from (A))
$2(3 + 4)$	(plug in $s = 3$ and $t = 4$)
14	(simplify)

This value matches the one we found for $\log_a(xy)^2$, so this looks like the right answer. Let's check the others to make sure we haven't overlooked anything or made any mistakes.

$s + t$	(expression from (B))
$3 + 4$	(plug in $s = 3$ and $t = 4$)
7	(simplify)

This value doesn't match the one we found for $\log_a(xy)^2$, so this seems to be wrong. Let's check the next answer choice.

$4st$	(expression from (C))
$4(3)(4)$	(plug in $s = 3$ and $t = 4$)
48	(simplify)

This value doesn't match the one we found for $\log_a(xy)^2$, so this seems to be wrong. Let's check the next answer choice.

$2st$	(expression from (D))
$2(3)(4)$	(plug in $s = 3$ and $t = 4$)
24	(simplify)

This value doesn't match the one we found for $\log_a(xy)^2$, so this seems to be wrong. Let's check the last answer choice.

st	(expression from (E))
$(3)(4)$	(plug in $s = 3$ and $t = 4$)
12	(simplify)

This value doesn't match the one we found for $\log_a(xy)^2$ either, so this seems to be wrong. After considering each answer choice, we can see that (A) must be right.

Solution 2: Algebra: Use your knowledge of the properties of logarithms to find the right answer.

Based on the properties of logarithms, we should know that $\log_a(xy)^2 = 2\log_a(xy)$, and that $2\log_a(xy) = 2(\log_a x + \log_a y)$. Since the prompt tells us that $\log_a x = s$ and $\log_a y = t$, we know that $2(\log_a x + \log_a y) = 2(s + t)$. So (A) is right.

ANSWER CHOICE ANALYSIS

(B): This is the value of $\log_a(xy)$ according to the conditions in the prompt, but the prompt asked for the value of $\log_a(xy)^2$. **(C):** This is the result of making the mistake from (D) and also thinking of each variable in $\log_a(xy)^2$ as being squared separately, and making the exponent of 2 a coefficient of the expression twice, effectively multiplying the expression by 4 instead of 2. **(D):** This is the result of thinking that $2\log_a(xy) = 2(\log_a x \times \log_a y)$, instead of $2\log_a(xy) = 2(\log_a x + \log_a y)$. **(E):** This choice combines the mistakes from (B) and (D).

How to check? Try an alternate approach above.

- **What's the prompt asking for?** The percent increase in Jennifer's best long jump distance from 1990 to 1992.
- **Math concepts in the prompt:** percentage increase
- **Elements of the choices:** Each answer choice is a percentage.
- **Notable differences among choices:** Every answer choice but (K) is a two-digit percentage, while (K) is a one-digit percentage. (G) and (K) add up to (F).
- **Concepts in the choices:** addition, percentages
- **Things to look out for:** Remember that the 20% increase is based on the distance from the previous year, which already increased by 10% compared to the first year. The 20% increase doesn't just represent a 20% increase over her original distance!

Solution 1: Concrete: Calculate the 10% increase from 1990 to 1991, and then calculate the 20% increase from 1991 to 1992. Subtract the original percentage from the 1992 percentage to find the percent increase from 1990 to 1992.

We know that Jennifer's best long jump distance increased by 10% from 1990 to 1991. We can calculate that like this:

$$100\% \times 1.1 = 110\% \qquad \text{(increase from 1990 to 1991)}$$

(Notice that we find 10% more than a number by multiplying the number by 110%, which is the same as multiplying by 1.1.)

Then her best long jump distance increased by a further 20% from 1991 to 1992. Starting with the 110% we calculated for 1991, we can calculate that increase like this:

$$110\% \times 1.2 = 132\% \qquad \text{(increase from 1991 to 1992)}$$

(As before, we find a 20% increase by multiplying by 1.2.)

Now we can subtract the initial percentage from the final percentage to find the percent increase:

$$132\% - 100\% = 32\% \qquad \text{(initial percentage subtracted from the final percentage)}$$

So the total percent increase was 32%, and (F) is right.

Solution 2: Abstract/backsolving: Consider the answer choices and rule out any that can't be right.

We know that Jennifer's best long jump distance increased by 20% from 1991 to 1992 alone, and that increase was on top of an existing 10% increase from 1990 to 1991, so the total percent increase since 1990 must be greater than 20%, which means (H), (J), and (K) must be wrong. That only leaves (F) and (G). If we understand that there was a 10% increase first, and then a 20% increase *on top of the already increased number*, then we know that that the total percent increase since 1990 must be more than simply 10% + 20%, or 30%. That only leaves one choice: the right answer, (F).

ANSWER CHOICE ANALYSIS

(G): This choice reflects the common mistake of assuming that you can just add 10% and 20% to get 30%, without realizing that the 20% increase is on top of an existing 10% increase; in other words, the additional 20% is 20% of 110% of the original number, not of 100%. **(H):** This choice is the percent increase from 1991 to 1992, but the prompt asks for the increase from *1990* to 1992. **(J):** This choice is the average of the two percentages that appear in the prompt, which may tempt test-takers who misunderstand the question. **(K):** This choice is the difference between the right answer, (F), and the most likely wrong answer, (G).

How to check? Try an alternate approach above.

TEST 3 (FORM 16MC3—SEE PAGE 23)

- **What's the prompt asking for?** The height of the flagpole.
- **Math concepts in the prompt:** dimension measurements, right angles
- **Elements of the choices:** Each choice is a multiple of 4.
- **Notable differences among choices:** (A), (B), and (C) form a series in which each choice is 4 more than the one before it. (B) is twice as much as (A). (A), (C), and (E) form a series in which each choice is 3 times as much as the choice before it.
- **Concepts in the choices:** adding four, multiplying by three
- **Pre-solution patterns (see p. 149):** halves and doubles
- **Things to look out for:** Don't confuse the various measurements in the prompt! Don't make any small mistakes in your reading or calculations!

Solution 1: Geometry: Sketch the situation described in the prompt, and use your understanding of similar triangles to find the height of the flagpole.

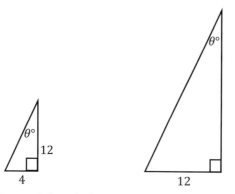

When we sketch the two objects and their shadows, we can see that these are similar triangles, because corresponding angles have the same measurements. We know that the corresponding sides of similar triangles are in constant ratios to each other. We can see that the base of the triangle on the right (which corresponds to the shadow cast by the flagpole) is three times greater than the base of the triangle on the left (which corresponds to the shadow cast by the rod), so we know that the vertical section of the triangle on the right (which corresponds to the height of the flagpole) must be three times greater than the vertical section of the triangle on the left (which corresponds to the height of the rod). So the height of the flagpole must be three times greater than 12, which means the height is 36. So (E) is right.

Solution 2: Algebra: Set up a ratio of the height of the rod to the shadow of the rod and set it equal to the ratio of the height of the flagpole to the shadow of the flagpole, then solve for the height of the flagpole.

Let f equal the height of the flagpole.

$$\frac{12}{4} = \frac{f}{12} \qquad \left(\frac{\text{rod height}}{\text{rod shadow}} = \frac{\text{flagpole height}}{\text{flagpole shadow}}\right)$$

$$144 = 4f \qquad \text{(cross-multiply)}$$

$$36 = f \qquad \text{(divide both sides by 4)}$$

We can see that the height of the flagpole is 36 feet, and (E) is right.

Solution 3: Test-smart: Note that the shadow of the rod is one-third the height of the rod, which means the shadow of the pole is one-third the height of the pole. So the right answer is 12 times 3, or 36, which is choice (E).

ANSWER CHOICE ANALYSIS

(A): This choice could be the result of trying Solution 3 above and accidentally *dividing* 12 by 3 rather than *multiplying* 12 by 3. It could also be the result of reasoning incorrectly that if a 12-foot-tall rod goes with a 4-foot shadow, then a 12-foot shadow must go with a 4-foot-tall pole. **(B):** This is the difference between the shadows of the two objects, which isn't what the question asks for. **(D):** This choice reflects the mistake of assuming that the height of the flagpole must be 8 feet more than its shadow, just because the height of the rod is 8 feet more than the shadow of the rod. But, as trained test takers, we know that we need to focus on the *ratio* of the height to the length of the shadow, not the on the *difference* between the height and the length of the shadow.

How to check? Try an alternate approach above. Be especially careful not to confuse the heights of the two objects, or the lengths of their shadows.

▶ **Post-solution patterns (see p. 151):** easy calculation mistake

Test 3, Question 2 (Form 16MC3 if you have the 2020-2021 Red Book—see page 23 for more)

- **What's the prompt asking for?** The number of points Kalino must earn in order to average 90 points for the five tests.
- **Math concepts in the prompt:** addition, averages
- **Elements of the choices:** The choices are all two-digit numbers from 87 to 97.
- **Notable differences among choices:** (G), (H), and (J) form a sequence in which each choice is 2 more than the choice before it.
- **Pre-solution patterns (see p. 149):** wrong answers try to imitate right answers
- **Things to look out for:** Don't misread the numbers of points that Kalino has already earned! Don't forget that you need to average five scores instead of four! Don't make any small mistakes in your reading or calculations!

Solution 1: Concrete/Backsolve: Try each answer choice as the number of points scored on the fifth test, and pick the choice that results in an average of 90 points for the five tests.

We can find the average of the scores that would result from each answer choice by adding them up and dividing the sum by the number of scores, which is 5:

$$\frac{85 + 95 + 93 + 80 + (87)}{5} = 88 \qquad \text{(average using the value from (F))}$$

$$\frac{85 + 95 + 93 + 80 + (88)}{5} = 88.2 \qquad \text{(average using the value from (G))}$$

$$\frac{85 + 95 + 93 + 80 + (90)}{5} = 88.6 \qquad \text{(average using the value from (H))}$$

$$\frac{85 + 95 + 93 + 80 + (92)}{5} = 89 \qquad \text{(average using the value from (J))}$$

$$\frac{85 + 95 + 93 + 80 + (97)}{5} = 90 \qquad \text{(average using the value from (K))}$$

When we try each value from the answer choices as the score for the fifth test, we can see that only (K) produces an average of 90 points as the prompt requires, so (K) is right.

Solution 2: Arithmetic: Determine the total number of points necessary in order to have an average of 90, and then subtract the existing scores from that total to find the number of points that Kalino still needs.

If there are 5 test scores and together they average 90 points, the total number of points from all 5 tests must be 450, because $5 \times 90 = 450$. We can subtract the provided test scores from 450 to find the missing test score.

$$450 - 85 - 95 - 93 - 80 = 97$$

So the missing test score is 97, and (K) is right.

Solution 3: Algebra: Write an equation that sets the average of the five test scores equal to 90. Solve the equation you've written.

$$\frac{85 + 95 + 93 + 80 + x}{5} = 90 \qquad \text{(set the average of the 5 test scores equal to 90)}$$

$$353 + x = 450 \qquad \text{(combine like terms and multiply both sides by 5)}$$

$$x = 97 \qquad \text{(subtract 353 from both sides)}$$

So Kalino's average will be 90 points if he gets a 97 on his fifth test, which means (K) is right.

Solution 4: Test-smart: Note that the answer must end in 7 and be greater than 90. Pick the choice that satisfies these requirements.

When we add up the four test scores given in the prompt, the total is 353. If the average of all 5 scores is 90, then we'll have to add a number to 353 and divide the result by 5 to get 90. In other words, after the missing score is added to 353, the result has to be a number that can be divided by 5 to get 90. So the sum of all the scores must end in zero, because every multiple of 90 ends in a zero.

In order for the result of adding the missing test score to 353 to end in a 0, the missing score must end in a 7—because any number ending in a 7, when added to 353, will produce a sum that ends in a zero. So the right answer must end in a 7.

Further, the average of the provided scores is 88.25, because $\frac{85 + 95 + 93 + 80}{4} = 88.25$. We're told that the additional score needs to raise this average to 90, which means that additional score must be greater than 90, since the starting average is below 90. The only choice that ends in a 7 and is greater than 90 is (K), so we know (K) is right.

ANSWER CHOICE ANALYSIS

(F): This choice could attract untrained test-takers who make a small mistake in their arithmetic and end up with a value in the tens place that's off by one, giving them a result of 87 instead of 97. **(G):** This is the average of the 4 scores in the prompt, rounded off to the nearest whole number. **(H):** This choice could result from an untrained test-taker making an algebraic mistake and accidentally finding 90 as the value of x, rather than setting up 90 as the average of the five tests. This could also be the result if an untrained test-taker assumes that Kalino will need a score of 90 to make 90 the average of the 5 tests. **(J):** This choice could be the result if an untrained test-taker found that the average of the provided scores was around 88, and then reasoned that a score of 92 would raise that average to 90, because $\frac{88+92}{2} = 90$. This solution is wrong because it gives the one remaining test the same weight as the four previous tests combined, instead of giving equal weight to each of the five tests.

How to check? Try an alternate approach above. Make sure to consider your reading and calculations very carefully.

▶ **Post-solution patterns (see p. 151):** easy calculation mistake; most like the other choices

Test 3, Question 3 (Form 16MC3 if you have the 2020-2021 Red Book—see page 23 for more)

- **What's the prompt asking for?** The value of the fraction in the prompt when $x = -5$.
- **Math concepts in the prompt:** addition, algebra, exponents, fractions, negative numbers, PEMDAS, subtraction
- **Notable differences among choices:** (A) and (B) are the only

negative numbers. (B) is the opposite of (C). (D) is the only mixed fraction. (E) is the only two-digit number.

- **Concepts in the choices:** mixed fractions, negative numbers, positive numbers
- **Pre-solution patterns (see p. 149):** opposites

- **Things to look out for:** Don't forget that the value of x is -5, not 5! Don't make any small mistakes in your reading or calculations!

Solution 1: Algebra: Plug in $x = -5$ to the given fraction, simplify the resulting expression, and pick the choice matching the result.

$$\frac{x^2-1}{x+1} \qquad \text{(given expression)}$$

$$\frac{(-5)^2-1}{(-5)+1} \qquad \text{(plug in } x = -5\text{)}$$

$$\frac{24}{-4} \qquad \text{(simplify)}$$

$$-6 \qquad \text{(reduce)}$$

So the answer is (A), -6.

Solution 2: Graphing: Graph the equation $y = \frac{x^2-1}{x+1}$ on your calculator, and note the value of the function at $x = -5$.

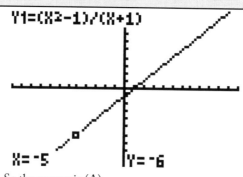

We can see that when $x = -5$, $y = -6$. So the answer is (A).

ANSWER CHOICE ANALYSIS

(B): This could be the result if an untrained test-taker accidentally read $x + 1$ as $x - 1$. **(C):** This is the result of plugging in $x = 5$ instead of $x = -5$. **(D):** This choice potentially combines two mistakes. The first mistake is thinking that the square of -5 is 30 instead of 25, and the second mistake would be thinking that the denominator of the fraction would be equal to 5 instead of -4. **(E):** This could be the result of finding the value of the numerator and then subtracting 5 for some reason.

How to check? Try an alternate approach above, and/or carefully reconsider your calculations to make sure you haven't made a mistake like the ones described above.

Note Solution 2 above would probably strike most test takers as unnecessary, because most people would probably find it easy enough to plug the given value of x into the given fraction and simplify. But I wanted to point out that Solution 2 is possible in this case because I want you to be able to use this kind of approach on questions that might be more challenging. Seeing the technique in action against a question that's relatively straightforward can often help students start to realize how it could be applied in other situations.

Test 3, Question 4 (Form 16MC3 if you have the 2020-2021 Red Book—see page 23 for more)

- **What's the prompt asking for?** The total number of miles that Kaya ran.
- **Math concepts in the prompt:** mixed fractions, units of measurement
- **Elements of the choices:** Each choice is a mixed fraction that includes the integer 3.
- **Notable differences among choices:** (F), (J), and (K) all include 15 in their denominators, while (G) has 8 and (H) has 5. (F) and (H) both include 2 in their numerators, while (G) has 3, (J) has 7, and (K) has 11.
- **Concepts in the choices:** mixed fractions
- **Pre-solution patterns (see p. 149):** wrong answers try to imitate right answers
- **Things to look out for:** Don't make any mistakes when you convert the given fractions to similar denominators! Don't make any mistakes when you simplify a fraction! Don't confuse the numerators and denominators of the fractions in the prompt!

Solution 1: Concrete/Arithmetic: Convert the given fractions into fractions with the same denominator, add them, simplify the sum, and pick the choice that matches your result.

$1\frac{2}{5}$ miles is the same as $1\frac{6}{15}$ miles, because $\frac{2}{5} \times \frac{3}{3} = \frac{6}{15}$. $2\frac{1}{3}$ miles is the same as $2\frac{5}{15}$ miles, because $\frac{1}{3} \times \frac{5}{5} = \frac{5}{15}$. When we add $1\frac{6}{15}$ to $2\frac{5}{15}$ we get $3\frac{11}{15}$, so (K) is the right answer.

Solution 2: Concrete/Backsolving: Add the decimal equivalents of the fractions from the prompt, then find the decimal equivalents of the numbers in the choices. The answer choice that matches the value you found from the prompt will be the right answer.

$$1\frac{2}{5} + 2\frac{1}{3} = 1.4 + 2.\overline{3} = 3.7\overline{3}$$

(F) $3\frac{2}{15} = 3.1\overline{3}$

(G) $3\frac{3}{8} = 3.375$

(H) $3\frac{2}{5} = 3.4$

(J) $3\frac{7}{15} = 3.4\overline{6}$

(K) $3\frac{11}{15} = 3.7\overline{3}$

The value from (K) matches the value we found from the prompt, so (K) is the right answer.

Notice that after we added the numbers from the prompt, if we noticed that our value was closer to 4 than to 3 we could have picked the only answer choice that was closer to 4 than 3, without having to find the decimal approximation of each choice.

Solution 3: Test-smart: Note that the right answer must involve a fraction that's more than one half, because each of the distances in the prompt involves a fraction that is more than one quarter. The only choice that satisfies this requirement is (K), the right answer.

ANSWER CHOICE ANALYSIS

(F): The fraction in this choice would be the result of multiplying $\frac{2}{5}$ and $\frac{1}{3}$, rather than adding them. **(G):** The fraction in this choice would be the result of incorrectly "adding across" the numerators and denominators of the two fractions in the prompt—in other words, adding 2 and 1 to get a new numerator of 3, and adding 5 and 3 to get a new numerator of 8—rather than converting those fractions so they have the same denominators, and adding the converted fractions. **(H):** This choice could be the result of misreading the second number in the prompt as just 2, rather than $2\frac{1}{3}$. **(J):** This could be the result of reading $1\frac{2}{5}$ from the prompt as $1\frac{2}{15}$.

How to check? Try an alternate approach above. Carefully reconsider your reading and your calculations. Remember that trying to figure out the kinds of mistakes that could lead to some of the wrong answers can help reassure you that you're on the right track.

Test 3, Question 5 (Form 16MC3 if you have the 2020-2021 Red Book—see page 23 for more)

- **What's the prompt asking for?** The choice with the statement that must be true.
- **Elements of the choices:** Each choice is a sentence.
- **Notable differences among choices:** (A), (B), and (C) make statements about Insect I, while (D) and (E) make statements about Insect J. (A) and (D) mention an insect not being attracted to honey, while (B) and (C) mention an insect being attracted to honey. (A), (B), and (E) all mention an insect being an ant.
- **Pre-solution patterns (see p. 149):** wrong answers try to imitate right answers; opposites
- **Things to look out for:** Don't confuse the two insects! Don't accidentally pick a choice that *can* be true—remember that you need to find a choice that *must* be true! Don't use outside knowledge—only answer based on the 3 provided statements!

Solution 1: Reading Comprehension: Carefully read the statements in the prompt and pick the only choice that must be true.

(A) The second statement in the prompt says that Insect I is not an ant, and this choice says that Insect I *is* an ant. This statement directly contradicts the second statement, so it must not be true.

(B) This choice has the same basic problem as (A).

(C) The first statement says that all insects that are attracted to honey are ants, but the second statement says that Insect I is not an ant. If Insect I isn't an ant, then Insect I can't be attracted to honey, so (C) is wrong. (According to the first statement, if Insect I *were* attracted to honey, Insect I would be an ant, but that would violate the second statement.)

(D) This statement directly contradicts the third statement, so (D) is wrong.

(E) The third statement says that Insect J is attracted to honey, and the first statement says that all insects that are attracted to honey are ants. So Insect J must be an ant, and this statement must be true. That means (E) is the right answer.

ANSWER CHOICE ANALYSIS

(A): The first part of this choice directly contradicts the sentence about Insect I in the prompt, which says Insect I is not an ant. Notice that this is exactly the kind of wrong answer we'd often find on a reading comprehension question in the Reading or Science sections of the ACT. **(B):** This choice could tempt an untrained test-taker who misreads it and thinks it refers to Insect J, not Insect I. **(C):** This choice could attract test-takers who misread the third statement of the prompt as though it were talking about Insect I, because then this choice would exactly restate the misread version of the third statement. **(D):** Like (A), this choice directly contradicts a statement from the prompt—just as we might expect to see on the Reading or Science sections of the ACT.

How to check? Carefully re-read the prompt and the answer choices, paying particular attention to the issues we identified above to help

Test 3, Question 6 (Form 16MC3 if you have the 2020-2021 Red Book—see page 23 for more)

- **What's the prompt asking for?** The value of the expression in the prompt under the conditions in the prompt.
- **Math concepts in the prompt:** fractions, PEMDAS, square roots, variables
- **Elements of the choices:** Each involves the number 2.
- **Notable differences among choices:** (F) is the only negative choice. (H) and (K) both involve $\sqrt{2}$. (J) and (K) both involve i.

- **Concepts in the choices:** 2, i, negative numbers, positive numbers, radical expressions
- **Pre-solution patterns (see p. 149):** wrong answers try to imitate right answers; opposites
- **Things to look out for:** Don't make any small mistakes in your reading or calculations, especially with respect to PEMDAS or sign! Don't confuse the values of x and m!

Solution 1: Algebra: Insert the given values for x and m into the expression from the prompt and simplify. Pick the answer choice that matches your result.

$$\sqrt{\frac{m}{x-3}}$$ (given expression)

$$\sqrt{\frac{-16}{-1-3}}$$ (plug in $x = -1$ and $m = -16$)

$$\sqrt{\frac{-16}{-4}}$$ (simplify)

$$\sqrt{4}$$ (simplify)

$$2$$ (take square root)

So the correct answer is (G), 2.

ANSWER CHOICE ANALYSIS

(F): This could confuse test-takers who forget that a radical expression only refers to the positive square root of the expression under the radical, or test-takers who make a mistake with the sign of the numerator or denominator and think the square root of -4 must be -2. **(H):** This would be the result of misreading the value of x as 1, rather than -1. **(J):** This would be the result of mistakenly assuming that the expression under the radical sign is negative, rather than positive. This could happen if an untrained test-taker only noticed the negative sign in the numerator or the denominator, rather than noticing both of them, or if an untrained test-taker forgot that dividing a negative number by a negative number results in a positive number. **(K):** This choice reflects the mistake of thinking that the value of x was 1 instead of -1, and thinking that the expression under the radical was negative (which could be the result of a variety of mistakes related to sign).

How to check? Be especially careful with issues related to sign, since the answer choices clearly show that the ACT expects people to make some kind of mistake when it comes to signs!

▶ **Post-solution patterns (see p. 151):** most like the other choices

Test 3, Question 7 (Form 16MC3 if you have the 2020-2021 Red Book—see page 23 for more)

- **What's the prompt asking for?** The smallest number of tickets that must be sold at the door in order for the group to meet its goal of $2,000 in sales.
- **Math concepts in the prompt:** addition, inequalities, multiplication, prices
- **Elements of the choices:** Each choice is a three-digit number.
- **Notable differences among choices:** (E) is significantly larger than the other choices.
- **Things to look out for:** Don't confuse the prices for tickets bought in advance and tickets bought at the door! Don't make any small mistakes in your calculations!

Solution 1: Concrete/Backsolve: Try each choice as the number of tickets sold at the door. The right answer will be the smallest choice that still results in total sales of at least $2,000.

The prompt says that 142 tickets were sold in advance, and that advance tickets cost $6 each. So the advance ticket sales were $142 \times \$6$, or $852. The prompt says that tickets sold at the door were $8. We can multiply the value from each answer choice by $8 to get the sales at the door, and we can add that amount to $852 to find the total sales. The answer choice that produces the smallest value over $2,000 will be the minimum number of tickets they need to sell to make their goal, as required by the prompt.

(A) $\$852 + (143 \times \$8) = \$1996$

(B) $\$852 + (144 \times \$8) = \$2004$

(C) $\$852 + (192 \times \$8) = \$2388$

(D) $\$852 + (250 \times \$8) = \$2852$

(E) $\$852 + (357 \times \$8) = \$3708$

We got the smallest number that was greater than $2,000 with (B), so we know that (B) is right.

Solution 2: Abstract/Algebra: Write an inequality that relates the amount of money earned so far, the price of tickets at the door, and the goal of $2,000. Solve the inequality to find the lowest possible number of tickets that will still allow the goal to be met.

The prompt says that 142 tickets were sold in advance, and that advance tickets cost $6 each, so we can multiply 6 by 142 to find the sales from advance tickets. The prompt also tells us that tickets at the door are $8 each, so if we make x the number of tickets sold at the door, then sales from tickets sold at the door are equal to $8x$. We can add these values together and set the result greater than 2000, since we're trying to find the smallest x-value that makes total sales greater than $2,000.

$$6(142) + 8x > 2000 \quad \text{(expression based on prompt)}$$
$$852 + 8x > 2000 \quad \text{(simplify)}$$
$$8x > 1148 \quad \text{(subtract 852 from both sides)}$$
$$x > 143.5 \quad \text{(divide both sides by 8)}$$

So x has to be greater than 143.5 in order for the inequality above to be true. Since x represents a number of tickets sold, and can't be a decimal, the smallest x-value greater than 143.5 is 144. So they would have to sell 144 tickets to meet the goal, which means (B) is correct.

ANSWER CHOICE ANALYSIS

(A): This choice could reflect the mistake of trying Solution 2 above but rounding 143.5 down to 143 for some reason, or accidentally finding the largest possible number of tickets sold that still *fails* to meet the goal, rather than the smallest number of tickets that *does* meet the goal. **(C):** This would be the correct answer if the tickets sold at the door were the same price as the tickets sold in advance ($6, instead of $8). **(D):** This is the total number of $8 tickets they would have to sell to hit the goal of $2,000 if they didn't sell any $6 tickets at all. **(E):** This is the result of attempting Solution 2 above but accidentally *adding* 852 to the right side of the inequality, instead of subtracting it—in other words, this is the minimum number of tickets that needs to be sold to make $2,852 in ticket sales at the door.

How to check? Try an alternate approach above.

▶ **Post-solution patterns (see p. 151):** easy calculation mistake

Note   Each of the wrong answers above is more likely to tempt an untrained test-taker who uses a formal approach to the question like Solution 2 above; if you try Solution 1 above, it's much less likely that you'll fall for any of the wrong answers unless you use your calculator incorrectly. In a sense, this means that it might be "smarter" to approach this question in a less formal, less algebra-dependent way, because doing so would decrease the likelihood of making a mistake and getting the question wrong. We'll see this kind of thing over and over again on the ACT: responding to ACT questions in the same way you'd respond to a similar question in school will often increase the chances that you fall for a wrong answer choice, while attacking the question in the most basic, straightforward, test-aware way will make it easier to answer.

Test 3, Question 8 (Form 16MC3 if you have the 2020-2021 Red Book—see page 23 for more)

- **What's the prompt asking for?** The number of types of sandwich that can be made at the shop.
- **Math concepts in the prompt:** combinations
- **Notable differences among choices:** (K) is the only three-digit number. (G), (H), and (J) form a series in which each choice is 15 more than the choice before it.
- **"Bridge" concepts:** We can find the total number of possible sandwich combinations if we identify the number of possible outcomes for each part of a sandwich, and multiply those numbers of possible outcomes together.
- **Pre-solution patterns (see p. 149):** be aware of series
- **Things to look out for:** Don't misread the numbers of available breads, meats, and cheeses! Don't make any small mistakes in your calculation!

Solution 1: Concrete: Create a diagram of the possible combinations, and use it to answer the question.

Let's call the breads B1, B2, and B3, the meats M1, M2, M3, M4, and M5, and the cheeses C1, C2, and C3. We can write out the different possible combinations below:

Starting with B1 first:	B1-M3-C3	B2-M1-C2
B1-M1-C1	B1-M4-C1	B2-M1-C3
B1-M1-C2	B1-M4-C2	B2-M2-C1
B1-M1-C3	B1-M4-C3	B2-M2-C2
B1-M2-C1	B1-M5-C1	B2-M2-C3
B1-M2-C2	B1-M5-C2	B2-M3-C1
B1-M2-C3	B1-M5-C3	B2-M3-C2
B1-M3-C1	Starting with B2 first:	B2-M3-C3
B1-M3-C2	B2-M1-C1	B2-M4-C1

B2-M4-C2	B3-M1-C2	B3-M3-C3
B2-M4-C3	B3-M1-C3	B3-M4-C1
B2-M5-C1	B3-M2-C1	B3-M4-C2
B2-M5-C2	B3-M2-C2	B3-M4-C3
B2-M5-C3	B3-M2-C3	B3-M5-C1
Starting with B3 first:	B3-M3-C1	B3-M5-C2
B3-M1-C1	B3-M3-C2	B3-M5-C3

So there are 45 combinations, which means (J) is right. (Notice that we can tell there must be 45 combinations once we figure out there are 15 possibilities starting with B1, because we know the number of possibilities that begin with B1 must be equal to the number of possibilities that begin with B2 or with B3. Since there are 15 possibilities starting with B1, and $15(3) = 45$, there must be 45 possibilities in total. So we wouldn't have to write out the second and third columns if we didn't want to.)

Solution 2: Abstract/Combinations: Using your knowledge of the properties of combinations, multiply together the numbers of available breads, meats, and cheeses.

To find the total number of possible combinations of the three ingredients, we can multiply the number of different types of each ingredient in a way that reflects the possible combinations described in the prompt. The prompt tells us that any one each of 3 kinds of bread, 5 kinds of meat, and 3 kinds of cheese are combined to make a sandwich. When we multiply these possibilities together, we get $3 \times 5 \times 3 = 45$, so we know there are 45 different combinations, and (J) is right.

ANSWER CHOICE ANALYSIS

(F): This choice is the sum of the numbers in the prompt, but finding the right answer involves multiplying those numbers, not adding them. **(G):** This choice could reflect a misreading of the text that caused an untrained test-taker to overlook either the bread or the cheese in the sandwich, causing him to think that only 5 meats and either 3 breads or 3 cheeses were available for the sandwich, which would lead to the calculation 5×3. **(H):** This choice could reflect misreading the number of available breads or cheeses as 2, resulting in the calculation $5 \times 3 \times 2$. **(K):** This choice is equal to 5!, or $5 \times 4 \times 3 \times 2 \times 1$. But 5! would tell us the number of possible permutations of 5 objects, which isn't what the question is asking for.

How to check? Try an alternate approach above. Carefully re-check your reading to make sure you haven't used the wrong numbers in your calculations!

Test 3, Question 9 (Form 16MC3 if you have the 2020-2021 Red Book—see page 23 for more)

- **What's the prompt asking for?** The value of x in the given equation.
- **Math concepts in the prompt:** equations, multiplication, negative numbers, positive numbers, subtraction
- **Elements of the choices:** Each choice is a fraction.
- **Notable differences among choices:** Every choice

except (E) is negative. (A), (C), and (E) have 4 as the denominator. (D) is the only choice whose absolute value is less than 1.

- **Concepts in the choices:** fractions, negative numbers, positive numbers
- **Things to look out for:** Don't make any mistakes in your reading or calculations, especially with respect to sign!

Solution 1: Concrete/Backsolve: Try each answer choice as the value of x in the original equation. Pick the choice that makes the original equation valid.

$$12(x - 11) = -15 \qquad \text{(given equation)}$$

$$12\left(-\frac{49}{4} - 11\right) = -15 \qquad \text{(plug in } (x = -\frac{49}{4} \text{ from (A))}$$

$$12\left(-\frac{49}{4} - \frac{44}{4}\right) = -15 \qquad \text{(create a common denominator in the parenthetical expression)}$$

$$12\left(-\frac{93}{4}\right) = -15 \qquad \text{(simplify)}$$

$$-279 = -15 \qquad \text{(simplify)}$$

This value doesn't create a valid statement, so (A) must be wrong. Let's take a look at the next choice:

$$12(x - 11) = -15 \qquad \text{(given equation)}$$

$$12\left(-\frac{13}{6} - 11\right) = -15 \qquad \text{(plug in } (x = -\frac{13}{6} \text{ from (B))}$$

$$12\left(-\frac{13}{6} - \frac{66}{6}\right) = -15 \qquad \text{(create a common denominator in the parenthetical expression)}$$

$$12\left(-\frac{79}{6}\right) = -15 \qquad \text{(simplify)}$$

$$-158 = -15 \qquad \text{(simplify)}$$

This value doesn't create a valid statement, so (B) must also be wrong. Now let's take a look at (C):

$$12(x - 11) = -15 \quad \text{(given equation)}$$
$$12\left(-\frac{5}{4} - 11\right) = -15 \quad \left(\text{plug in } \left(x = -\frac{5}{4} \text{ from (C)}\right)\right)$$
$$12\left(-\frac{5}{4} - \frac{44}{4}\right) = -15 \quad \text{(create a common denominator in the parenthetical expression)}$$
$$12\left(-\frac{49}{4}\right) = -15 \quad \text{(simplify)}$$
$$-147 = -15 \quad \text{(simplify)}$$

This isn't a valid statement either, so (C) must be wrong too. Let's try (D):

$$12(x - 11) = -15 \quad \text{(given equation)}$$
$$12\left(-\frac{1}{3} - 11\right) = -15 \quad \left(\text{plug in } \left(x = -\frac{1}{3} \text{ from (D)}\right)\right)$$
$$12\left(-\frac{1}{3} - \frac{33}{3}\right) = -15 \quad \text{(create a common denominator in the parenthetical expression)}$$
$$12\left(-\frac{34}{3}\right) = -15 \quad \text{(simplify)}$$
$$-136 = -15 \quad \text{(simplify)}$$

(D) is wrong too, since this value doesn't create a valid statement. Let's try (E):

$$12(x - 11) = -15 \quad \text{(given equation)}$$
$$12\left(\frac{39}{4} - 11\right) = -15 \quad \left(\text{plug in } \left(x = \frac{39}{4} \text{ from (E)}\right)\right)$$
$$12\left(\frac{39}{4} - \frac{44}{4}\right) = -15 \quad \text{(create a common denominator in the parenthetical expression)}$$
$$12\left(-\frac{5}{4}\right) = -15 \quad \text{(simplify)}$$
$$-15 = -15 \quad \text{(simplify)}$$

This value creates a valid statement. After checking each choice, we can be confident that (E) is right.

Solution 2: Algebra: Solve for x by applying the same changes to both sides of the given equation until x is isolated.

$$12(x - 11) = -15 \quad \text{(given equation)}$$
$$12x - 132 = -15 \quad \text{(distribute the 12)}$$
$$12x = 117 \quad \text{(add 132 to both sides)}$$
$$x = 9.75 \quad \text{(divide both sides by 12)}$$

The value we found for x was positive, and only (E) has a positive value. Also, when we divide 39 by 4, we see that (E) is equal to 9.75, so (E) must be right.

Solution 3: Test-smart: Notice that the answer must be a positive number, and pick the only choice that satisfies that requirement.

We can see that we need to multiply 12 by the expression in parentheses to get a result of -15. If x is 0, or any number less than 0, then the expression in parentheses will be a negative number at least as low as -11. We'd be multiplying 12 by that negative number, which would give us a result of -132 or lower, because $12 \times (-11) = -132$. But we can see the result needs to be -15, which is much higher than -132. So the expression in parentheses must be greater than -11, which means the x-value must be positive. Only (E) has a positive value, so (E) must be right.

ANSWER CHOICE ANALYSIS

(A): This choice reflects the mistake of trying Solution 2 above and adding 132 to the left-hand side of the equation while subtracting 132 from the right-hand side. That would result in the equation $12x = -147$, instead of $12x = 117$. **(B):** This choice reflects the combination of the mistakes in (A) and (D), because it requires a test-taker to distribute 12 incorrectly, resulting in the equation $12x - 11 = -15$, and then add 11 to the left-hand side of the equation while subtracting 11 from the right-hand side, resulting in the equation $12x = -26$. **(C):** This choice reflects the mistake of ignoring the -11 in the original equation, resulting in the equation $12(x) = -15$. **(D):** This choice could be the result of distributing the 12 incorrectly or thinking the original equation was equal to $12x - 11 = -15$, rather than $12(x - 11) = -15$.

How to check? Try an alternate approach above. Be especially careful not to make any mistakes with respect to sign, since the question is clearly trying to encourage us to do that!

Test 3, Question 10 (Form 16MC3 if you have the 2020-2021 Red Book—see page 23 for more)

- **What's the prompt asking for?** The measurement of $\angle BCE$.
- **Math concepts in the prompt:** angles, congruent line segments, points on a line
- **Math concepts in the diagram:** angles, supplementary angles, congruent line segments, isosceles triangles, points on a line
- **Elements of the choices:** The choices are all degree

measurements.

- **Notable differences among choices:** (H) ends in 5, while the other choices all end in 0.
- **Concepts in the choices:** angle measurements
- **"Bridge" concepts:** The measures of the angles of a triangle must add up to 180°. In an isosceles triangle, the angles that are opposite the sides of the same length have the same degree measurements as each other. If two angles combine to form a straight line, then the measures of those angles add up to 180°.
- **Pre-solution patterns (see p. 149):** halves and doubles
- **Things to look out for:** Don't find the measure of the wrong angle! Don't make any mistakes in your calculations!

Solution 1: Geometry: Use your knowledge of isosceles triangles to allow you to determine the measures of $\angle BAD$ and $\angle ADB$. Use the measure of $\angle ADB$ to find $\angle BDC$. Use the measure of $\angle BDC$ to find $\angle BCD$. Finally, use the measure of $\angle BCD$ to find $\angle BCE$.

The prompt tells us that $\overline{AD}$ and $\overline{BD}$ are the same length, so ΔABD must be an isosceles triangle. That means $\angle ABD$ must be equal to $\angle BAD$. The diagram shows us that $\angle ABD = 25°$, so $\angle BAD$ must be 25° as well. We can now find the measure of $\angle BDA$, because the sum of the measures of the interior angles of any triangle is 180°. $180° - 25° - 25° = 130°$, so $\angle BDA = 130°$.

Now that we know $\angle BDA = 130°$, we can find the measure of $\angle BDC$. We can see that $\angle BDA$ and $\angle BDC$ are supplementary angles, because together they create a 180° angle (or straight line). So $\angle BDC$ must be $180° - 130°$, or 50°. The prompt tells us that $\overline{BD}$ and $\overline{BC}$ are the same length, so ΔBDC must be an isosceles triangle. That means $\angle BCD$ must be equal to $\angle BDC$, so $\angle BCD = 50°$. Finally, $\angle BCD$ and $\angle BCE$ are also supplementary angles, which means $\angle BCD$ and $\angle BCE$ must add up to 180°. Since $\angle BCD = 50°$, $\angle BCE$ must equal 130°. That means (J) is right.

Solution 2: Test-smart: Note that $\angle ADB$ must be equal to $\angle BCE$, and use your knowledge of isosceles triangles to find $\angle ADB$.

Once we realize that $\angle BDA = 130°$, we can recognize that $\angle BDA$ must have the same measure as $\angle BCE$ if we notice the following:

- $\overline{BD}$ and $\overline{BC}$ are the same length, so ΔBDC must be an isosceles triangle.
- $\angle BDA$ and $\angle BDC$ are supplementary angles, because added together they create a 180° angle (or straight line)
- $\angle BDC$ must be equal to $\angle BCD$
- $\angle BCD$ and $\angle BCE$ are also supplementary angles

If $\angle BDA$ and $\angle BCE$ are supplementary with two angles that have the same measure, than $\angle BDA$ and $\angle BCE$ must have the same measure. So $\angle BDA = \angle BCE = 130°$, and (J) is right.

Solution 3: Test-smart: Use the scale of the diagram and pick the only answer choice that makes sense in that context.

When we consider the scale of the diagram, we can see that the angle in question has a degree measure that is roughly similar to a 90° plus a 45° angle, which would be around 135°. The only answer choice fairly close to this is the right answer, (J).

(Note that you should only attempt this solution in a situation like this if you feel comfortable recognizing that the angle in the diagram is large enough to be 130°, but not large enough to be 160°. If you ever feel unsure of this kind of an approach, then look for a solution more like Solution 1 or 2 above.)

ANSWER CHOICE ANALYSIS

(F): This is the sum of angles $\angle ABD$ and $\angle BAD$, which is something we need to calculate on the way to finding the right answer for Solutions 1 and 2 above—but it's not what the prompt actually asks for, so it's wrong. This is also the value of $\angle BDC$ and $\angle BCD$ —but, again, those angles aren't the ones we were asked to measure. This choice is also the supplement of the right answer.

How to check? Try an alternate approach above. Be especially careful about solving for the correct angle!

▶ Post-solution patterns (see p. 151): right approach, wrong step

---

Test 3, Question 11 (Form 16MC3 if you have the 2020-2021 Red Book—see page 23 for more)

- **What's the prompt asking for?** The result when -2 is plugged into the function from the prompt.
- **Math concepts in the diagram:** functions, negative numbers, trinomials
- **Notable differences among choices:** (A) is 3 times as much as (B). (B) is the opposite of (C). (C) is half of (D).
- **Concepts in the choices:** multiplying by 2, multiplying by 3, negative numbers, positive numbers
- **Pre-solution patterns (see p. 149):** halves and doubles; opposites
- **Things to look out for:** Don't make any mistakes in your calculations, especially as they could relate to PEMDAS and negative numbers!

Solution 1: Algebra: Plug -2 into the function as x, and calculate the resulting value.

$$f(x) = 9x^2 + 5x - 8 \qquad \text{(given function)}$$
$$f(-2) = 9(-2)^2 + 5(-2) - 8 \qquad \text{(plug } x = -2 \text{ into given function)}$$
$$f(-2) = 9(4) + (-10) - 8 \qquad \text{(simplify)}$$

$$f(-2) = 18 \qquad \text{(simplify)}$$

So (C) is right.

Solution 2: Graphing: Graph the function in the prompt, and pick the choice that reflects the y-value when $x = -2$.

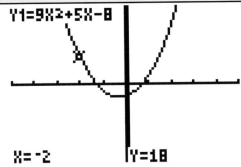

We can see that when $x = -2$, $y = 18$. So the answer is (C).

(Notice that I changed the graphing window of the calculator so the shape of the graph would be a little easier to see; you don't need to do this as long as you enter the function correctly and find the value when $x = -2$.)

ANSWER CHOICE ANALYSIS

(A): This choice could reflect the mistake of thinking that $(-2)^2$ was equal to -4, instead of 4. **(B):** This is the opposite of the right answer, which could reflect an algebra mistake related to sign. **(D):** This is twice the right answer, and also the value of $9(-2)^2$, which we have to find as part of Solution 1. **(E):** This choice reflects the mistake of thinking that $5(-2)$ is 10, instead of -10.

How to check? Try an alternate approach above. Be especially careful with PEMDAS and the signs of numbers, since the answer choices are clearly trying to set you up to make a mistake with relation to those ideas.

▶ **Post-solution patterns (see p. 151):** easy calculation mistake

Test 3, Question 12 (Form 16MC3 if you have the 2020-2021 Red Book—see page 23 for more)

- **What's the prompt asking for?** The least common multiple of 30, 20, and 70.
- **Math concepts in the prompt:** least common multiple
- **Notable differences among choices:** (G) is the only choice that doesn't end in 0. (F) and (G) are two-digit numbers, while (H) and (J) are three-digit numbers and (K) is a five-digit number. The non-zero digits in (G), (J), and (K) are 42, while the non-

zero digit in (F) is 4 and the non-zero digits in (H) are 1 and 2.
- **Concepts in the choices:** multiplying by 10
- **Pre-solution patterns (see p. 149):** wrong answers try to imitate right answers
- **Things to look out for:** Don't misread the numbers in the prompt or the answer choices! Don't make small mistakes in your calculations!

Solution 1: Concrete/Backsolve: Divide each answer choice by the numbers 30, 20, and 70. The right answer is the smallest answer choice that's evenly divisible by all three numbers.

(F) $40 \div 30 = 1.\overline{3}$

This choice can't be divided evenly by 30, so (F) must be wrong. Now we'll try (G):

(G) $42 \div 30 = 1.4$

This choice can't be divided evenly by 30, so (G) must be wrong too. Now we'll try (H):

(H) $120 \div 30 = 4$ $120 \div 20 = 6$ $120 \div 70 \approx 1.714$

This choice can't be divided evenly by 70, so (H) must be wrong. Let's take a look at (J):

(J) $420 \div 30 = 14$ $420 \div 20 = 21$ $420 \div 70 = 6$

This choice can be divided evenly by all the numbers, and every smaller answer choice was wrong, so this choice looks correct. Let's check the last choice just to be sure:

(K) $42,000 \div 30 = 1400$ $42,000 \div 20 = 2100$ $42,000 \div 70 = 600$

This choice can also be divided evenly by all the numbers, but it's larger than the value in (J). The prompt asked for the <u>least</u> common multiple, so (J) must be the right answer.

Solution 2: Abstract/Backsolving: Consider each answer choice and rule out any that can't be the least common multiple that the prompt asks for.

(F) and (G) don't work right off the bat, because they're both less than 70, so they can't possibly be multiples of 70.

(H) doesn't work because it isn't a multiple of 70 either; $70 \times 1 = 70$ and $70 \times 2 = 140$.

(J) is the correct answer. 30 goes into 420 exactly 14 times, 20 goes into it 21 times, and 70 goes into it 6 times. Since it's a multiple of all the numbers, and since all the answer choices with smaller numbers are wrong, this must be the least common multiple. We'll look at (K) just to be safe.

(K) is the product of the 3 numbers multiplied together—so it's definitely a common multiple of all three numbers, but it's not the least common multiple, so it's not the right answer.

After considering each choice, we can be confident that (J) is right.

Solution 3: Abstract/Algebra: Find the prime factorizations of 30, 20, and 70, and use them to determine the least common multiple.

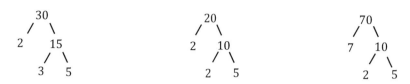

After doing the prime factorizations, we can multiply each prime number from the factorizations together, with each prime number getting multiplied the maximum number of times it appears in any *one* of the factorizations.

2 appears twice in the factorization for 20, 3 appears once in the factorization for 30, 5 appears once in each factorization, and 7 appears once in the factorization for 70. So we multiply $2 \times 2 \times 3 \times 5 \times 7$ and get 420. That means the least common multiple is 420, and (J) is right.

ANSWER CHOICE ANALYSIS

(F): This choice could reflect a fundamental misunderstanding of the phrase "least common multiple." 40 is the smallest result when we multiply one of the numbers in the prompt by an integer larger than 1, but that's not what "least common multiple" means—the least common multiple is the smallest number that's a multiple of *all* of the numbers in the list, not the smallest number that's a multiple of *any one* of the numbers in the list. **(G):** This is one-tenth of the right answer, probably put here in an attempt to trick test-takers who don't read carefully enough, or who make a mistake attempting Solution 3. **(H):** This choice might be here to trick test-takers who accidentally think 120 is twice as much as 70, when, in reality, 140 is twice as much as 70. If 120 were a multiple of 70, then this choice would be correct, because it's a multiple of 30 and 20. **(K):** This choice is the result of multiplying all the numbers in the list together, so it's definitely a multiple of those numbers—it's just not the smallest one, as the prompt requires. This might attract test-takers who try Solution 3 above but don't know the right way to find the least common multiple from a set of prime factors, and ultimately just multiply all the prime factors together no matter how many times they occur.

How to check? Try an alternate approach above.

▶ **Post-solution patterns (see p. 151):** right answer to the wrong question

▌Test 3, Question 13 (Form 16MC3 if you have the 2020-2021 Red Book—see page 23 for more)

- **What's the prompt asking for?** The calculation that Tom could do to produce the result he originally wanted.
- **Math concepts in the prompt:** division, multiplication
- **Elements of the choices:** division, multiplication, subtraction
- **Notable differences among choices:** (B), (C), (D), and (E) present every possible combination of multiplication or division and 2 or 4. (A) involves subtracting the original number.

- **Concepts in the choices:** division, doubling, multiplication
- **Pre-solution patterns (see p. 149):** wrong answers try to imitate right answers; halves and doubles
- **Things to look out for:** Don't forget that the prompt is asking us to figure out how Tom can reach the result he originally wanted in one step, not how Tom can get his calculator back to the original number that he entered!

Solution 1: Arithmetic/Concrete: With your own calculator, pick an arbitrary number to be the number Tom starts with, and divide that number by two to show the target number that Tom is trying to reach. Then, go back to Tom's original number and multiply it by 2, to recreate Tom's mistake. Finally, go through each answer choice and apply what it describes to the number that reflects Tom's mistake. The right answer will be the one that produces the result you found as Tom's target number.

Let's imagine that Tom had a 10 on his screen before he made his mistake. $10 \div 2 = 5$, so in this example, 5 would be the target number that Tom wanted to find. If he multiplied 10 by 2, then he would have 20 on his screen. Let's imagine following the step in each answer choice using the number 20, and we can see which one gives us a result of 5.

(A) $20 - 10 = 10$

(B) $20 \times 2 = 40$

(C) $20 \times 4 = 80$

(D) $20 \div 2 = 10$

(E) $20 \div 4 = 5$

Only (E) gives us the value we're looking for, so (E) must be right.

Solution 2: Algebra/Abstract: Think about the properties of multiplication and division, and determine what step would need to be taken to find half of a starting number when your calculator's screen shows twice the starting number.

If Tom had a certain number on his screen, and he wanted to divide that number by 2, but he accidentally multiplied the number by 2, his screen would now show a number that was twice as much as the original number. That original number must be twice as much as the number Tom wanted, because he was going to divide that original number by 2 in the first place.

So the number on Tom' screen is twice as much as a number that's twice as much as the number he wants to find. That means it must be 4 times as much as the number he wants, so he should divide the number by 4 to get the number he wanted in the first place. That means (E) is correct.

ANSWER CHOICE ANALYSIS

(A): This choice will trick a lot of untrained test takers who don't read the prompt carefully enough, because it will cause the calculator to display the number Tom started with. But the prompt asks us how Tom can find the number that he wanted, not the number that he started with; the number that he wants to find is half of the starting number, not the starting number itself. **(C):** This choice would be the way Tom would get from his target number to the number on his screen after he made his mistake, which is the opposite of what the prompt asks for. **(D):** Like (A), this choice would cause Tom's calculator to display the number he originally entered, not the number that the prompt asked for.

How to check? Try an alternate approach above.

▶ **Post-solution patterns (see p. 151):** opposites; right answer to the wrong question

Note Many untrained test takers might try an approach like Solution 1 above and stop after testing (A), because they misread the prompt and think they need to find the number that Tom started with. But, as trained test takers, we know that we always need to consider every answer choice before moving on to the next question. In this case, considering every answer choice would also cause us to try (D), which is another choice that leads back to the number that Tom originally entered in the calculator. Seeing that two choices lead to the same result, and knowing that every question has exactly one correct answer, we would be forced to reconsider our reading and our calculations, which would allow us to see that we had misunderstood the prompt, and give us the chance to get the question right. Keep questions like this in mind when you attempt a backsolving solution and you're tempted not to consider all the answer choices—one of the best ways to turn potential wrong answers into right answers is to get in the habit of looking for ways that you might have made a mistake.

Test 3, Question 14 (Form 16MC3 if you have the 2020-2021 Red Book—see page 23 for more)

- **What's the prompt asking for?** The perimeter of the figure, in inches.
- **Math concepts in the prompt:** area, congruent shapes, division, perimeter, squares
- **Math concepts in the diagram:** squares
- **Notable differences among choices:** (G), (H), and (J) form a series in which each choice is 20 more than the choice before it. (K) is the sum of (F) and (J).

- **"Bridge" concepts:** By definition, the side length of a square is the square root of its area.
- **Pre-solution patterns (see p. 149):** be aware of series
- **Things to look out for:** Don't confuse perimeter with area! Don't forget that the perimeter of the figure isn't the same as the sum of the perimeters of each square! Don't make any small mistakes in your reading and calculations!

Solution 1: Geometry: Determine the side length of each square, and then multiply that length by the number of side lengths on the border of the figure.

In order to find the perimeter of the figure, we need to know the side length of each square. We can find the side length of each square by finding the area of each square, and then taking the square root, because the area of a square is the length of one of its sides squared.

We are given the area of all 5 squares; we can find the area of one square by dividing that value by 5.

$$\frac{125}{5} = 25 \qquad \text{(total area divided by 5 to find area of each square)}$$

So each square has an area of 25. We can now find the square root of 25 to get the length of one side of each square.

$$\sqrt{25} = 5 \qquad \text{(square root of area of each square to find side length)}$$

So each square has side lengths of 5. We can count the side lengths that make up the perimeter of the figure; that number is 12. So we'll multiply 5 by 12 to get the perimeter of the figure.

$$5 \times 12 = 60 \qquad \text{(side length multiplied by number of side lengths in perimeter)}$$

So the perimeter is 60 inches, and (G) is the right answer.

ANSWER CHOICE ANALYSIS

(F): This choice is the area of any individual square in the diagram, which is something we need to figure out on the way to figuring out the side length of each square. But it isn't the thing that the prompt asked us to find, so it's wrong. **(H):** This choice reflects the mistake of counting the dashed lines in the diagram as part of the perimeter of the figure, but those dashed lines aren't on the perimeter of the figure, and they shouldn't be counted. **(J):** This choice takes the perimeter of a single square with side length of 5, which would be 20, and multiplies that number by 5, but that isn't the same as the perimeter of the figure in the prompt. **(K):** This could reflect the mistake of assuming that the perimeter and area of the figure should be the same for some reason.

How to check? Carefully reconsider your reading, calculations, and assumptions. Make sure that you haven't miscounted the number of sides that are on the perimeter, since the question is clearly setting us up to do that!

▶   **Post-solution patterns (see p. 151):** right approach, wrong step; right answer to the wrong question

Test 3, Question 15 (Form 16MC3 if you have the 2020-2021 Red Book—see page 23 for more)

- **What's the prompt asking for?** The maximum number of drives that Hai can buy under the conditions in the prompt.
- **Math concepts in the prompt:** largest possible number, prices, sales tax
- **Elements of the choices:** The choices form a series of integers from 11 to 15.

- **Concepts in the choices:** series
- **Pre-solution patterns (see p. 149):** be aware of series
- **Things to look out for:** Don't forget to calculate the sales tax! Don't make any small mistakes with your reading or calculations!

Solution 1: Concrete/Backsolve: For each answer choice, calculate the result of buying that many USB drives and paying sales tax. The largest choice that doesn't require spending more than $100 is the right answer.

Each USB drive is $8 plus 7% tax, which is the same as $8 × 1.07. If Hai buys 11 USB drives, as choice (A) says, his cost will be 11 × $8 × 1.07, or $94.16. This looks like it might be the right answer, but let's check the other choices—the right answer will be the highest number that is still less than or equal to $100:

(B) 12 × $8 × 1.07 = $102.72   (D) 14 × $8 × 1.07 = $119.84

(C) 13 × $8 × 1.07 = $111.28   (E) 15 × $8 × 1.07 = $128.40

The highest value that is still less than or equal to $100 is actually the only value that is less than or equal to $100—$94.16, the value we found using (A). So (A) is right.

Solution 2: Arithmetic: Determine the price of a single USB drive including sales tax. Divide $100 by that price, and round down to the nearest whole number (since every answer choice is a whole number, and the money spent can't be more than $100). Pick the choice that reflects your result.

One USB drive will be $8 plus 7% tax, or 1.07 × $8, or $8.56. Now we can divide the amount of money Hai has by the total cost of one USB drive plus tax to find out how many USB drives Hai can buy.

$$\frac{\$100}{\$8.56} \approx 11.682$$ (Hai's money for USB drives divided by the cost of one USB drive, including tax)

So he can buy between 11 and 12 USB drives. Since he can't buy a partial USB drive, and he can't go over $100, we have to round down to 11. That means the right answer is (A).

Solution 3: Algebra/Abstract: Write an algebraic expression for the total cost of a number of USB drives, and then create an inequality showing that expression to be less than or equal to $100. Solve the inequality and pick the highest answer choice in the range of the inequality.

Each USB drive is $8 plus 7% tax, which is the same as $8 × 1.07. If Hai buys x USB drives, we can represent the cost of those drives with the expression $8x × 1.07$. We can then set that value less than or equal to $100, and solve for x to find the number of USB drives Hai can buy with $100.

$8x \times 1.07 \leq 100$ (inequality based on prompt)

$8x \leq 93.458$ (divide both sides by 1.07)

$x \leq 11.682$ (divide both sides by 8)

Again, we know that Hai can't buy a partial USB drive, so the largest number of whole USB drives he can buy with $100 is 11, and (A) is right.

Solution 4: Test-smart: Note that Hai would be able to buy 12 drives if there were no sales tax, and that adding sales tax would put the total over $100 for 12 drives. Pick the only choice that's less than 12.

If we realize that 12 USB drives without tax would be $96 (which would only leave $4 extra out of the $100), and that adding in the 7% tax would be more than $4 extra, then we can be sure that Hai doesn't have enough money for 12 USB drives, including tax. Once we're sure that 12 is too many, we can be confident that (A) is right, because every other option is 12 or more.

ANSWER CHOICE ANALYSIS

(B): This choice could reflect the mistake of trying Solution 2 or 3 above and accidentally rounding up instead of down. It could also reflect the mistake of neglecting to consider sales tax.

How to check? Try an alternate approach above.

Test 3, Question 16 (Form 16MC3 if you have the 2020-2021 Red Book—see page 23 for more)

- **What's the prompt asking for?** The number of seconds that would be necessary to perform 6.0×10^{16} calculations according to the prompt.
- **Math concepts in the prompt:** rates, scientific notation
- **Elements of the choices:** Each choice is a quantity expressed in scientific notation.
- **Notable differences among choices:** (F) is the only choice with a negative exponent. (G) is the only choice with a zero exponent. (G) and (K) both involve 9.0, while (H) and (J) involve 4.0.
- **Concepts in the choices:** exponent of zero, negative exponents, scientific notation
- **"Bridge" concepts:** When we have two exponential expressions with the same base and we need to divide one by the other, we subtract exponent values.
- **Pre-solution patterns (see p. 149):** wrong answers try to imitate right answers
- **Things to look out for:** Don't make any small mistakes in your calculations, especially with respect to exponents!

Solution 1: Scientific notation: Divide the larger number in the prompt by the smaller number to determine how many seconds will be necessary to perform the calculations.

$$\frac{6.0 \times 10^{16}}{1.5 \times 10^{8}} = 4 \times 10^{8}$$

So (J) is right. Note that it may help to think of the above expression this way:

$$\frac{6.0 \times 10 \times 10 \times 10 \times 10 \times 10 \times 10 \times 10 \times 10 \times 10 \times 10 \times 10 \times 10 \times 10 \times 10 \times 10 \times 10}{1.5 \times 10 \times 10 \times 10 \times 10 \times 10 \times 10 \times 10 \times 10}$$

When we cancel out the eight 10s on the bottom and eight 10s on the top, we're left with this:

$$\frac{6.0 \times 10 \times 10 \times 10 \times 10 \times 10 \times 10 \times 10 \times 10}{1.5}$$

$\frac{6}{1.5}$ is equal to 4, so when we simplify the expression above and put it back in scientific notation, we get:

$$4 \times 10^{8}$$

So again, we can be sure that (J) is right.

Solution 2: Test-smart: Recognize that the answer must have an exponent of 8, and pick the only choice satisfying this requirement.

Since the numerator involves 10^{16} and the denominator involves 10^{8}, we know that the result will involve canceling out 8 of those 10s on the top and bottom of the fraction, and the result will involve 10^{8}. Only choice (J) includes a 10^{8} term, so (J) is right.

ANSWER CHOICE ANALYSIS

(F): This choice performs the division in the wrong direction. One way that we could know this choice must be wrong, if we reached it by accident, is that it would require all of the calculations to be done in under one second, since the exponent is negative. But the second number in the prompt is larger than the number of calculations that can be done in one second, which means that doing them in only a fraction of a second would contradict the prompt. **(G):** This choice is 6.0 multiplied by 1.5, which would tempt test-takers who decided to ignore the exponent expressions and multiply the remaining numbers. **(H):** This choice reflects the mistake of dividing the larger exponent by the smaller exponent, rather than subtracting the smaller exponent from the larger exponent. **(K):** This choice is the result of multiplying the two numbers in the prompt, rather than dividing one by the other, as the prompt requires us to do.

How to check? Try an alternate approach above. Be especially careful about the exponent in the answer you pick.

▶ **Post-solution patterns (see p. 151):** easy calculation mistake

Test 3, Question 17 (Form 16MC3 if you have the 2020-2021 Red Book—see page 23 for more)

- **What's the prompt asking for?** The answer choice with an equation for the line in the diagram.
- **Math concepts in the prompt:** equations for lines, the xy-coordinate plane
- **Math concepts in the diagram:** graphing lines in the xy-coordinate plane
- **Elements of the choices:** Each choice is an equation with y isolated on one side and an expression involving an x-term on the other.
- **Notable differences among choices:** (A) and (C) use 5 as the coefficient of x, while (B), (D), and (E) use 2. (C) has 2 as the y-intercept, while (D) has -5, (E) has 5, and the other choices have zero.
- **Concepts in the choices:** slope-intercept form
- **Pre-solution patterns (see p. 149):** wrong answers try to imitate right answers; opposites

- **Things to look out for:** Don't confuse the coefficient of x with the constant (in other words, don't confuse the slope with the y-intercept)! Don't make any small mistakes related to the sign of a number!

Solution 1: Concrete/Graphing: Use your calculator to graph each choice, and pick the choice whose graph looks like the diagram.

We can graph the expression from each answer choice; the right answer will be the one that matches the graph in the prompt. Note that the following graphs are on the same scale as the graph in the prompt, so each hash mark represents 2 units, not 1 unit. With that in mind, let's look at (A):

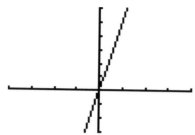

This one clearly doesn't match the graph from the prompt, because the graph from the prompt doesn't go through the origin.
Here's the graph of (B):

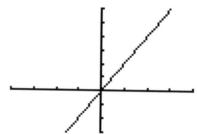

This one has basically the same problem as (A), because it also goes through the origin.
Here's the graph of (C):

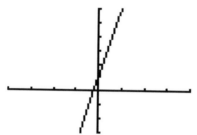

This one crosses the vertical axis at $y = 2$, but the graph from the prompt crosses that axis at $y = 5$.
Now let's look at the graph of (D):

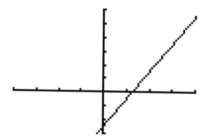

This one definitely doesn't match the graph from the prompt because it has a negative y-intercept.
Finally, here's the graph of (E):

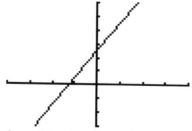

We can see that this graph crosses the y-axis at around $y = 5$, just like the graph in the prompt, and crosses the x-axis between $x = -2$ and $x = -4$, just like the graph in the prompt (each hash mark at the scale in the graph represents 2 units, not 1 unit). This graph matches the graph in the prompt, so (E) is right.

Solution 2: Concrete/Backsolving: Notice that $(0, 5)$ lies on the line. Plug $x = 5$ into each equation in the answer choices, and find the one that produces a y-value of 0.

When we plug in $x = 0$, the result should be $y = 5$.

$$y = 5(0) = 0 \qquad (x = 0 \text{ plugged into the equation from (A)})$$
$$y = 2(0) = 0 \qquad (x = 0 \text{ plugged into the equation from (B)})$$
$$y = 5(0) + 2 = 2 \qquad (x = 0 \text{ plugged into the equation from (C)})$$
$$y = 2(0) - 5 = -5 \qquad (x = 0 \text{ plugged into the equation from (D)})$$
$$y = 2(0) + 5 = 5 \qquad (x = 0 \text{ plugged into the equation from (E)})$$

Only the equation in (E) produces a result of $y = 5$ when $x = 0$, so (E) must be right.

(Note that we couldn't know for sure that this approach would work, because a wrong answer may have also had a point at $(0, 5)$ as well—but it was relatively quick to plug $x = 0$ into each equation, and the way ACT Math questions are written, this approach was likely to eliminate at least some of the wrong answer choices, and ended up eliminating all the wrong answer choices.)

Solution 3: Abstract/Algebra: Using your knowledge of the slope-intercept form, look at the line in the diagram and determine its equation. Then pick the choice that matches your conclusion.

The equations in the answer choices all appear to be in slope-intercept form (or "$y = mx + b$" form). We know m is the slope of the line. The only m values that appear in the answer choices are 2 and 5. When we consider the graph, we can see that the line moves roughly 2 units up for every 1 unit to the right, so the slope must be 2. We can also see the graph crosses the y-axis halfway between 4 and 6, so the b-value (which represents the y-intercept) appears to be 5. That means the equation of the line must be $y = 2x + 5$, and (E) must be right.

Solution 4: Test-smart: Notice the y-intercept of the line in the diagram must be 5. Only (E) has that y-intercept, so (E) must be right.

ANSWER CHOICE ANALYSIS

(A): This choice might attract test-takers who realize the line should have a y-intercept of 5, but incorrectly think that the coefficient of x corresponds to the y-intercept. **(B):** This choice shows the correct slope, but would have a y-intercept of zero. It might attract untrained test takers who simply forgot to consider the intercept of the right answer, and stopped working on the question when they figured out the slope. **(C):** This choice reverses the positions of 2 and 5 in the right answer, possibly to trick test-takers who confuse the rules of the various parts of a slope-intercept equation. **(D):** This choice uses a minus sign in place of the plus sign that should appear in the right answer. As with most of the other choices, it might appeal to a test-taker who has forgotten how a slope-intercept equation relates to a graph. In this case, the test-taker might have thought that the constant in the equation was the opposite of the y-intercept.

How to check? Try an alternate approach above. Make sure you've read the answer choices and the graph very carefully, because the choices are clearly setting you up to make some small mistake in your reading.

▶ **Post-solution patterns (see p. 151):** most like the other choices

Test 3, Question 18 (Form 16MC3 if you have the 2020-2021 Red Book—see page 23 for more)

- **What's the prompt asking for?** The area of the square in the diagram.
- **Math concepts in the prompt:** area, circles, radii, squares
- **Math concepts in the diagram:** circles, radii, squares
- **Notable differences among choices:** (J) is the only choice that involves π. The only difference between (F) and (J) is that the value in (J) is multiplied by π. (F), (H), and (K) form a sequence in which each choice is twice as much as the choice before it. (F), (J), and (K) are the only choices that include a square number.
- **Concepts in the choices:** multiplying by two, π, square numbers
- **Pre-solution patterns (see p. 149):** be aware of series; wrong answers try to imitate right answers; halves and doubles
- **Things to look out for:** Don't confuse the radius of the circle with the side length of the square! Don't make any small mistakes in your calculations!

Solution 1: Geometry: Determine the side length of the square, and square it to find the area of the square.

This question becomes a lot more straightforward if we redraw the diagram with a slight tweak:

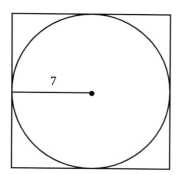

This makes it more obvious that the radius is half as long as a side length of the square, which makes sense—the side length of the square extends all the way from one side of the square to the opposite side, and the diameter of the circle (which is twice the radius) must extend all the way from one side of the square to the opposite side as well, since the circle is drawn inside the square so its edges touch the edges of the square. The radius of this circle is 7, so the diameter must be twice that, or 14, which means the side length of the square is 14 as well. We know that the area of a square is equal to one of the side lengths squared, so the area of this square is 14^2, or 196. That means (K) is right.

Solution 2: Test-smart: Notice that the right answer must be more than 100, and must not include π. Pick the only choice that satisfies those requirements.

Once we realize that the side length must be twice as much as 7, and that 14 squared is well over 100, and that calculating the area of this square won't involve π, we can be sure that the right answer is (K), 196.

ANSWER CHOICE ANALYSIS

(F): This choice reflects the common mistake of simply squaring 7 on the assumption that the length of one of the sides of the square should be equal to the radius of the circle. **(G):** This is the perimeter of the square, but the prompt asked for the area. **(H):** This is half the area of the square. It's probably here just to fit with the halves and doubles pattern. **(J):** This is the area of the circle, which will tempt a lot of untrained test-takers who forgot which figure the prompt was talking about when it asked for the area.

How to check? Try an alternate approach above. The fact that we can identify simple mistakes that could lead untrained test takers to the wrong answers strongly suggests, but doesn't guarantee, that we thought about the question correctly.

▶ **Post-solution patterns (see p. 151):** right answer to the wrong question

█ **Test 3, Question 19 (Form 16MC3 if you have the 2020-2021 Red Book—see page 23 for more)**

- **What's the prompt asking for?** The equation that would indicate the number of years after which B's salary will match A's.
- **Math concepts in the prompt:** algebra, rates
- **Elements of the choices:** Each choice is an algebraic equation expressing different relationships among five quantities: 20,000; 800; 15,200; 2,000; and x.
- **Notable differences among choices:** (A), (B), and (C) all have x-terms on both sides of the equation, while (D) and (E) have x-terms on only the left-hand side of the equation. (A), (B), (C), and (D) involve addition on the left-hand side of the equation, while (E) involves subtraction on that side; (A), (B),

(C), and (E) all involve addition on the right-hand side of the equation, while (D) has subtraction there.

- **Concepts in the choices:** addition, equations, multiplication
- **Pre-solution patterns (see p. 149):** wrong answers try to imitate right answers
- **Things to look out for:** Don't accidentally confuse the dollar values associated with the workers! Make sure you think carefully about whether addition or subtraction is appropriate! Don't misread the prompt or the answer choices, which will be especially important on this question since the answer choices are so long and so similar!

Solution 1: Concrete/Backsolve: Using arithmetic, determine the number of years after which the two salaries become equivalent. Then, use that number of years as the value of x in each answer choice, and pick the answer choice whose equation is a true statement with the x-value that you found.

Let's write out the salaries of these two workers after the first several years and see what we come up with.

Full years of employment	Worker A	Worker B
0	$20,000	$15,200
1	$20,800	$17,200
2	$21,600	$19,200
3	$22,400	$21,200
4	$23,200	$23,200

We can see that the two workers had equivalent salaries after 4 years, and that salary was \$23,200. That means if we plug $x = 4$ into the equation in the right answer, we should end up with \$23,200 on each side. Let's plug $x = 4$ into the equation from each answer choice and see which one satisfies this requirement.

$$20,000 + 800x = 15,200 + 2,000x \quad \text{(equation from (A))}$$
$$20,000 + 800(4) = 15,200 + 2,000(4) \quad \text{(plug in } x = 4\text{)}$$
$$\$23,200 = \$23,200 \quad \text{(simplify)}$$

This equation shows both salaries at \$23,200 after 4 years, just as we found in our table, so this choice looks right. Let's check the other choices to make sure we haven't misread anything or made a careless error.

$$20,000 + 2,000x = 15,200 + 800x \quad \text{(equation from (B))}$$
$$20,000 + 2,000(4) = 15,200 + 800(4) \quad \text{(plug in } x = 4\text{)}$$
$$\$28,000 = \$18,400 \quad \text{(simplify)}$$

This equation doesn't show both salaries at \$23,200 after 4 years, so it must not be right. Let's take a look at the next choice.

$$(20,000 + 800)x = (15,200 + 2,000)x \quad \text{(equation from (C))}$$
$$(20,000 + 800)(4) = (15,200 + 2,000)(4) \quad \text{(plug in } x = 4\text{)}$$
$$\$83,200 = \$68,800 \quad \text{(simplify)}$$

This equation doesn't show both salaries at \$23,200 after 4 years, so it must not be right. Let's take a look at the next choice.

$$(2,000 + 800)x = 20,000 - 15,200 \quad \text{(equation from (D))}$$
$$(2,000 + 800)(4) = 20,000 - 15,200 \quad \text{(plug in } x = 4\text{)}$$
$$\$11,200 = \$4,800 \quad \text{(simplify)}$$

This equation doesn't show both salaries at \$23,200 after 4 years, so it must not be right. Let's take a look at the last choice.

$$(2,000 - 800)x = 20,000 + 15,200 \quad \text{(equation from (E))}$$
$$(2,000 - 800)(4) = 20,000 + 15,200 \quad \text{(plug in } x = 4\text{)}$$
$$\$4,800 = \$35,200 \quad \text{(simplify)}$$

This equation doesn't show both salaries at \$23,200 after 4 years, so it must not be right. After we consider each choice, we can be confident that (A) is right.

Solution 2: Abstract/Algebra: Translate the prompt's description of each salary into an algebraic expression, and then pick the answer choice that sets these expressions equal to each other.

The prompt says that Worker A has a starting salary of \$20,000, with an increase of \$800 per year. We can model this with the expression $20,000 + 800x$, where x equals the number of years that Worker A has worked. As x increases by 1 with each passing year, Worker A's salary will increase by an additional \$800. The prompt also says that Worker B has a starting salary of \$15,200, with an increase of \$2,000 per year. We can model this with the expression $15,200 + 2,000x$, where x equals the number of years that Worker B has worked. As x increases by 1 with each passing year, Worker B's salary will increase by an additional \$2,000.

To find when the salaries are equal, we can set these expressions equal to one another. When we do that, we get the following expression: $20,000 + 800x = 15,200 + 2,000x$

This matches (A), so (A) must be right.

ANSWER CHOICE ANALYSIS

(B): This choice makes the mistake of mixing Worker A's annual increase with Worker B's starting amount, and Worker B's annual increase with Worker A's starting amount. This will trap a lot of untrained test-takers who don't read the prompt very carefully. **(C):** This choice makes the mistake of multiplying both the yearly increase and the starting amount by the number of years worked, since the x-values would be distributed to both terms in the two parenthetical expressions. **(D):** This choice would set the total amount of annual increases for both people equal to the difference between their starting salaries, which doesn't really make sense in the context of the prompt. **(E):** This is similar to (D), and reflects a similar fundamental misunderstanding of the prompt.

How to check? Try an alternate approach above. Make sure you're very careful with all the details in this question, since they will be especially easy to confuse.

Test 3, Question 20 (Form 16MC3 if you have the 2020-2021 Red Book—see page 23 for more)
- **What's the prompt asking for?** The height of the highest point on the ramp.
- **Math concepts in the prompt:** distances
- **Math concepts in the diagram:** labeled dimensions, right

triangles
- **Notable differences among choices:** (F), (G), and (H) form a series in which each choice is twice as much as the one before it. (J) is the sum of (F) and (H).
- **"Bridge" concepts:** We can use the Pythagorean theorem to

find the height of the highest point on the ramp.
- **Pre-solution patterns (see p. 149):** halves and doubles
- **Things to look out for:** Don't make any small mistakes in your reading or calculations!

Solution 1: Pythagorean theorem: Apply the Pythagorean theorem to determine the unknown side of the given right triangle.

We can see that the triangle is a right triangle, and we know the length of the hypotenuse and one of the sides, so we can apply the Pythagorean theorem to find the missing side length.

$a^2 + b^2 = c^2$	(Pythagorean theorem)
$12^2 + b^2 = 13^2$	(plug in $a = 12$ and $c = 13$)
$144 + b^2 = 169$	(simplify)
$b^2 = 25$	(subtract 144 from both sides)
$b = 5$	(take square root of both sides)

So (J) is right.

Solution 2: Pythagorean triples: If you recognize the 5-12-13 right triangle right away, then you know the missing side length is 5, and you can pick (J).

ANSWER CHOICE ANALYSIS

(F): This choice is the difference between 13 and 12, so some people will pick it accidentally because they see that the unlabeled side is joining line segments of 12 and 13 feet. This choice could also reflect the mistake of applying the Pythagorean theorem but not squaring any of the terms. **(G):** This choice is twice the difference between the lengths of the two given sides, which could reflect the mistake of doubling the terms in the Pythagorean theorem instead of squaring them. **(H):** This is the square of (G), which might possibly reflect a misunderstanding or miscalculation with respect to the Pythagorean theorem. **(K):** This is the difference of the squares of the lengths in the diagram divided by 4, which could reflect a mistake in applying the Pythagorean theorem.

How to check? Carefully re-check your reading and analysis.

Test 3, Question 21 (Form 16MC3 if you have the 2020-2021 Red Book—see page 23 for more)

- **What's the prompt asking for?** The expression that's equivalent to the expression in the prompt.
- **Math concepts in the prompt:** addition, multiplication, PEMDAS, subtraction, variables
- **Elements of the choices:** Each choice is an algebraic expression with a different positive constant added to x.
- **Notable differences among choices:** (B), (C), (D), and (E) form

a series in which the constant of each expression is 4 more than the constant of the previous expression.
- **Concepts in the choices:** addition, constants, variables
- **Pre-solution patterns (see p. 149):** be aware of series
- **Things to look out for:** Don't make any mistakes in your calculations, especially with respect to the order of basic operations or the signs of numbers!

Solution 1: Concrete/Backsolve: Assign an arbitrary value to x, and determine the value of the expression in the prompt that results from your x-value. Then plug the same x-value into each answer choice and pick the one that has the same value as the expression in the prompt.

Let's say that $x = 5$. When we plug this value into the given expression, we get the following:

$7(5 + 3) - 3(2(5) - 2)$	(plug $x = 5$ into given expression)
$7(8) - 3(10 - 2)$	(simplify)
$56 - 24$	(simplify)
32	(simplify)

So when $x = 5$, the expression is equal to 32. Now let's plug $x = 5$ into each answer choice to see which one is also equivalent to 32.

(A) $(5) + 1 = 6$ (D) $(5) + 23 = 28$

(B) $(5) + 15 = 20$ (E) $(5) + 27 = 32$

(C) $(5) + 19 = 24$

Only the expression in (E) is equal to 32 when $x = 5$, so (E) must be right.

Solution 2: Abstract/Algebra: Using your knowledge of PEMDAS, carefully simplify the expression in the prompt and pick the choice that matches it.

$7(x + 3) - 3(2x - 2)$	(given expression)

$$7x + 21 - 6x + 6 \qquad \text{(distribute 7 and } -3)$$
$$x + 27 \qquad \text{(simplify)}$$

So we can see that (E) is right.

ANSWER CHOICE ANALYSIS

(A): This choice could reflect a mistake in distributing the 7 and the -3 in the expression in the prompt—if we only multiple those numbers by the x-terms and not by the other numbers inside the parenthetical expressions, we end up with $7x + 3 - 6x - 2$, which can be simplified to give the expression in (A). **(B):** This choice could reflect the mistake of not "distributing the minus sign" in the $-3(2x - 2)$, which could cause you to try to simplify $7x + 21 - 6x - 6$, resulting in the expression in (B). **(C):** This could be the result of making the mistake described in (A), but only making it on the second parenthetical expression, which would give you $7x + 21 - 6x - 2$. **(D):** This is sort of the opposite of (B), in that it could reflect the mistake of accidentally distributing only the minus sign (and not the 3) in the second half of the expression in the prompt, causing you to try to simplify $7x + 21 - 6x + 2$.

How to check? Try an alternate approach above. Be especially careful about issues related to things like the sign of a number, because the answer choices clearly indicate that the test thinks you could easily make a small mistake and be off by just a little bit.

Test 3, Question 22 (Form 16MC3 if you have the 2020-2021 Red Book—see page 23 for more)

- **What's the prompt asking for?** 75% of the number referred to in the prompt.
- **Math concepts in the prompt:** percentages
- **Elements of the choices:** Each choice is a three-digit number from 280 to 400.
- **Notable differences among choices:** (F), (G), and (H) form a series in which each choice is 20 more than the choice before it. (G) is 75% of (K). (J) is the only choice that doesn't end in 0.
- **Pre-solution patterns (see p. 149):** be aware of series
- **Things to look out for:** Don't confuse the relationships among the percentages in the prompt, the "number" mentioned in the prompt, and 460! Don't make any small mistakes with your calculations!

Solution 1: Abstract/Algebra: Create an algebraic equation relating the number 460 to 115% and then to 75%, and then solve your equation and pick the resulting answer.

Let x equal the number referred to in the prompt.

$$1.15x = 460 \qquad \text{(equation based on prompt)}$$
$$x = 400 \qquad \text{(divide both sides by 1.15)}$$

So the original number that the prompt refers to is 400. Now let's find 75% of 400:

$$0.75(400) = 300 \qquad \text{(find 75\% of 400)}$$

We can see that the right answer is (G), 300.

ANSWER CHOICE ANALYSIS

(J): This choice is 115% of the right answer; it's also 75% of 460. This choice may tempt test-takers who get confused about which percentage to find of which number. **(K):** Many untrained test takers will pick this choice because it's the value of the "number" referred to in the prompt. But the prompt asked us for 75% of this number, not for this number itself. Once more, we see the extreme importance of critical reading on the ACT Math section!

How to check? Carefully reconsider your reading and calculations. The fact that (G) is 75% of (K) should give us a lot of confidence that we've probably thought about the question correctly.

▶ **Post-solution patterns (see p. 151):** right approach, wrong step; right answer to the wrong question

Note Again, we see that the ACT could have made this question harder if the "number" referred to in the prompt hadn't been a multiple of 100, which made it much easier to notice right away that 300 is 75% of 400 than it would have been if the number had been, say, 317.524. Remember that the ACT generally doesn't require us to deal with calculations that are as tedious and awkward as they can often be in a school math class. On test day, if you find yourself doing a lot of calculations with unwieldy numbers, there's a good chance you're not approaching the question in the most efficient way possible!

Test 3, Question 23 (Form 16MC3 if you have the 2020-2021 Red Book—see page 23 for more)

- **What's the prompt asking for?** The sum of $a, b,$ and c under the conditions in the prompt.
- **Math concepts in the prompt:** squaring binomials, trinomials
- **Notable differences among choices:** (A) and (B) are negative, while the other choices are positive. (E) is the square of (B).
- **Concepts in the choices:** negative numbers, positive numbers, squaring
- **Things to look out for:** Don't make any small mistakes when you square the expression in the prompt, or when you add the resulting terms, especially when it comes to the signs of the numbers you're dealing with!

Solution 1: Algebra/FOIL: Square the binomial expression and add the resulting terms to find the right answer.

Solution 1: Algebra/FOIL: Square the binomial expression and add the resulting terms to find the right answer.

$(2x - 3)(2x - 3)$ (expression from prompt)

$4x^2 - 6x - 6x + 9$ (FOIL)

$4x^2 - 12x + 9$ (simplify)

Now we can plug $a = 4$, $b = -12$, and $c = 9$ into $a + b + c$, which gives us this: $4 + (-12) + 9 = 1$

So the right answer is (C), 1.

ANSWER CHOICE ANALYSIS

(A): This choice could reflect the mistake of thinking that -3 multiplied by -3 results in -9, because $4 - 12 - 9 = -17$. **(D):** This choice would tempt test-takers who thought the result of squaring the given binomial would be $4x^2 + 9$, instead of $4x^2 - 12x + 9$. **(E):** This choice is the sum of the absolute values of all of the coefficients in the resulting trinomial, which would reflect the mistake of thinking the coefficient of x in that trinomial should be 12 instead of -12.

How to check? Carefully reconsider your reading and calculations. Since we can see clearly that the answer choices are set up to catch a variety of mistakes that untrained test-takers might make with respect to the signs of numbers, we should pay careful attention to how we handled those signs in our calculations.

▶ **Post-solution patterns (see p. 151):** right approach, wrong step

Test 3, Question 24 (Form 16MC3 if you have the 2020-2021 Red Book—see page 23 for more)

- **What's the prompt asking for?** The area, in square feet, of the figure in the diagram.
- **Math concepts in the prompt:** area
- **Math concepts in the diagram:** dimension labels, right angles
- **Notable differences among choices:** (F) and (G) are two-digit numbers, while the other choices are three-digit numbers. (F), (G), and (K) all end in 0, while the other choices end in 5.

- **"Bridge" concepts:** We can find the area of a figure like the one in the diagram by subdividing it into rectangles, finding the areas of the rectangles, and adding them together.
- **Things to look out for:** Don't confuse the lengths of the different sides of the figure! Don't make any small mistakes with your calculations!

Solution 1: Geometry: Subdivide the given figure into one 15×15 rectangle and one 10×5 rectangle. Calculate the area of each rectangle and add them together.

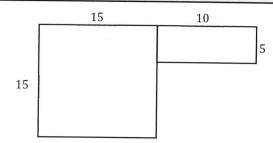

When we add the areas of these two figures, we get $(15 \times 15) + (5 \times 10) = 275$. So the right answer is (H).

Solution 2: Geometry: Find the area of a 15×25 rectangle and then subtract the area of a 10×10 rectangle, since the figure could be described as a 15×25 rectangle with a 10×10 "chunk" taken out of the bottom right-hand corner.

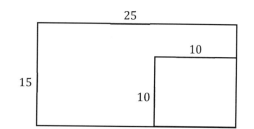

When we subtract the area of the smaller figure from the area of the larger figure, we get $(25 \times 15) - (10 \times 10) = 275$. Again, the right answer is (H).

ANSWER CHOICE ANALYSIS

(F): This is the sum of the numbers that are present in the diagram, but that sum isn't relevant to what the prompt is asking. **(G):** This is the perimeter of the figure in the diagram, not its area. **(J):** This would be the area of a 15×25 rectangle, but, as we noted in Solution 2 above, the figure isn't a 15 × 25 rectangle.

How to check? Try an alternate approach above.

▶ **Post-solution patterns (see p. 151):** right approach, wrong step; right answer to the wrong question

Test 3, Question 25 (Form 16MC3 if you have the 2020-2021 Red Book—see page 23 for more)

- **What's the prompt asking for?** The smallest number of paving blocks that Barb will need.

- **Math concepts in the prompt:** area, dimensions, minimums, unit conversions

- **Notable differences among choices:** (A) is a two-digit number, while (E) is a four-digit number and the other choices are all three-digit numbers. (C) and (E) are the only two choices that end in non-zero digits.

- **"Bridge" concepts:** The prompt specifies that all of the blocks must be turned in the same direction, which can only mean that the face that's pointing up must have the same dimensions for each block—in other words, it's either the case that all of the blocks have the 4 × 8 side facing up, or they all have the 4 × 2 side facing up, or they all have the 8 × 2 side facing up. The prompt says it's not possible for some of the blocks to have the 4 × 2 side facing up while others have the 4 × 8 side facing up, for example.

- **Things to look out for:** Don't forget that all of the blocks have to be in the same orientation! Don't make any mistakes during the unit conversion between feet and inches! Don't make any small mistakes in your calculations!

Solution 1: Geometry/Concrete: Sketch out a diagram of the rectangular area, and then determine how many blocks would fit along each dimension of the area, with the blocks oriented so that they take up the most area possible. Once you find the smallest possible number of blocks that can fit along each dimension, multiply the number of blocks in the two dimensions to find the answer.

The prompt tells us that the blocks are 4 inches by 8 inches by 2 inches, and asks for the minimum number of blocks that will be needed to cover the given area. If we want to find the minimum number of blocks to do this job, then we need each block to cover the maximum area; that means we want the block oriented so that an 8 inch by 4 inch side faces up, because 8 inches and 4 inches are the two largest dimensions.

Let's assume the blocks will have the following orientation:

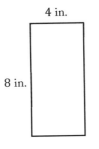

4 in.

8 in.

And let's assume that the area to be covered looks like this:

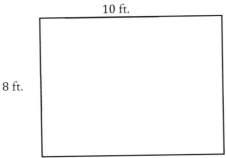

10 ft.

8 ft.

So the vertical dimension is 8 feet, which is the same 8 × 12 inches, or 96 inches. In the vertical dimension, we can fit 12 blocks, because $\frac{96\ inches}{8\ inches} = 12$. The horizontal dimension is 10 feet, which is the same 10 × 12 inches, or 120 inches. In the horizontal dimension, we can fit 30 blocks, because $\frac{120\ inches}{4\ inches} = 30$. So the area can be covered by an arrangement 30 blocks wide and 12 blocks long, for a total of 30 × 12 blocks, or 360 blocks. That means (B) is right.

Solution 2: Geometry/Abstract: Determine the total area that Barb wants to cover in square inches, and then determine the largest number of square inches that can be covered by a paving block. Divide the larger number by the smaller number to find the number of paving blocks that will cover Barb's area when the paving blocks are taking up as much space as possible.

As discussed in the previous solution, we want the blocks to be oriented so that an 8 inch by 4 inch side faces up. That means the area covered by each block will be 8×4 square inches, or 32 square inches. We can find the total area to be covered by converting the side lengths to inches as well—the 8 foot side will be 8×12 inches, or 96 inches, and the 10 foot side will be 10×12 inches, or 120 inches. So the total area to be covered by blocks is 96×120 square inches, or 11,520 square inches. We can divide 11,520 square inches by 32 square inches to find the number of blocks required to cover the given area:

$$\frac{11,520}{32} = 360$$

So the right answer is (B).

Solution 3: Test-smart: Notice that the answer choices are relatively far apart from one another on a number line, suggesting that it will be possible to estimate the correct answer. If we realize that the area is 80 square feet, and that each square foot can be covered by a little more than 4 blocks, then we know that the area can be covered by a little more than 320 blocks, because 80 times 4 blocks is 320 blocks. The only answer choice that's a little more than 320 is the correct answer, (B).

ANSWER CHOICE ANALYSIS

(A): This is the number of square feet of the rectangular area Barb wants to cover. It can't be the right answer because each rectangular block clearly takes up less than 1 square foot of area according to the prompt. **(D):** This choice could be the result of incorrectly converting the number of square feet in the rectangular area Barb wants to cover to square inches; in this case, rather than multiply 80 by 12×12 to reflect the fact that the conversion needs to take place in two dimensions, an untrained test-taker might just multiply 80 by 12.

How to check? Try an alternate approach above. Be especially careful to look out for the issues that we noted earlier.

▶ **Post-solution patterns (see p. 151):** right approach, wrong step; right answer to the wrong question

Test 3, Question 26 (Form 16MC3 if you have the 2020-2021 Red Book—see page 23 for more)

- **What's the prompt asking for?** The slope of the line in the prompt.
- **Math concepts in the prompt:** lines, slope, the equation of a line
- **Notable differences among choices:** (F) is the opposite of (K). (G) and (H) are the only fractions, and (G) is the only choice whose absolute value is less than 1. (H) is the only choice that doesn't include numbers from the original equation in the prompt (but each number in (H) is half of a number in the prompt).
- **Concepts in the choices:** fractions, negative numbers, opposites
- **Pre-solution patterns (see p. 149):** opposites
- **Things to look out for:** Don't confuse x and y! Don't make any mistakes with respect to sign!

Solution 1: Algebra: Convert the line into slope-intercept form by isolating y, then determine the slope.

$6y - 14x = 5$	(given equation)
$6y = 14x + 5$	(add $14x$ to both sides)
$y = \frac{14}{6}x + \frac{5}{6}$	(divide both sides by 6)

We can see that the slope is $\frac{14}{6}$, which reduces to $\frac{7}{3}$. So (H) is correct.

ANSWER CHOICE ANALYSIS

(F): This choice could reflect the mistake of assuming that the coefficient of x is equal to the slope of the line in the format that we see in the prompt, but, as trained test-takers, we know the coefficient of x is only the slope of the line when the equation is in slope-intercept form, which involves isolating y on one side of the equation. **(G):** This choice might be tempting for test-takers who put the equation into slope-intercept form and mistakenly think that the constant $\frac{5}{6}$ represents the slope (it's actually the y-intercept). **(J):** This choice is the coefficient of y in the given equation, but slope is equal to the coefficient of x when the equation is in slope-intercept form, not the coefficient of y in the form in the prompt. **(K):** This choice could be tempting to test-takers who attempt Solution 1 above and add $14x$ to both sides of the equation, but then forget to divide both sides by 6 to isolate y on one side of the equation.

How to check? Our ability to explain each of the wrong answers in ways that remind us why (H) is still correct is a good sign, but not a guarantee, that we've thought about the question correctly.

▶ **Post-solution patterns (see p. 151):** right approach, wrong step

Test 3, Question 27 (Form 16MC3 if you have the 2020-2021 Red Book—see page 23 for more)

- **What's the prompt asking for?** The choice that must be true when m and n are positive integers and $m < n$.
- **Math concepts in the prompt:** inequalities, integers, positive numbers
- **Elements of the choices:** Each choice is an inequality with at least one square root expression.
- **Notable differences among choices:** (A) involves zero and (B) involves one, but the other choices only involve expressions

with m and n.

- **Concepts in the choices:** addition, compound inequalities, multiplication, one, square roots, subtraction, zero
- **Pre-solution patterns (see p. 149):** wrong answers try to imitate right answers

- **Things to look out for:** Don't confuse m and n! Don't forget that both numbers are positive integers, and m is smaller than n! Don't misread the prompt or the answer choices! Don't forget that an expression with a radical sign indicates the positive square root!

Solution 1: Concrete/Backsolve: Pick arbitrary values for m and n that satisfy the requirements in the prompt. Plug your values into each answer choice to determine which one must be true.

Let's use $m = 3$ and $n = 6$.

$$0 < \sqrt{mn} < m \qquad \text{(inequality from (A))}$$
$$0 < \sqrt{(3)(6)} < 3 \qquad \text{(plug in } m = 3 \text{ and } n = 6\text{)}$$
$$0 < 4.24 < 3 \qquad \text{(simplify)}$$

This statement isn't true, so (A) must be wrong. Let's take a look at the next choice.

$$1 < \sqrt{mn} < m \qquad \text{(inequality from (B))}$$
$$1 < \sqrt{(3)(6)} < 3 \qquad \text{(plug in } m = 3 \text{ and } n = 6\text{)}$$
$$1 < 4.24 < 3 \qquad \text{(simplify)}$$

This statement isn't true, so (B) must be wrong. Let's take a look at the next choice.

$$m < \sqrt{mn} < n \qquad \text{(inequality from (C))}$$
$$3 < \sqrt{(3)(6)} < 6 \qquad \text{(plug in } m = 3 \text{ and } n = 6\text{)}$$
$$3 < 4.24 < 6 \qquad \text{(simplify)}$$

This statement is true, so (C) could be right. Let's take a look at the remaining choices to see if we've overlooked anything or made some other mistake.

$$\sqrt{m} < \sqrt{mn} < \sqrt{n} \qquad \text{(inequality from (D))}$$
$$\sqrt{3} < \sqrt{(3)(6)} < \sqrt{6} \qquad \text{(plug in } m = 3 \text{ and } n = 6\text{)}$$
$$1.73 < 4.24 < 2.45 \qquad \text{(simplify)}$$

This statement isn't true, so (D) must be wrong. Let's take a look at the final choice.

$$\sqrt{m - n} < \sqrt{mn} < \sqrt{m + n} \qquad \text{(inequality from (E))}$$
$$\sqrt{3 - 6} < \sqrt{(3)(6)} < \sqrt{3 + 6} \qquad \text{(plug in } m = 3 \text{ and } n = 6\text{)}$$
$$1.73i < 4.24 < 3 \qquad \text{(simplify)}$$

This statement isn't true, so (E) must be wrong. After checking each choice, we can see that (C) must be right.

Solution 2: Abstract: Think about the properties that each expression in the answer choices must have, given the properties of m and n as described in the prompt. Use these properties to determine which choice must always be true, and pick it.

We know that the statement in (A) can't be right, because the square root of m multiplied by a larger number than n must be larger than m, since it involves multiplying m by n (which is larger than m), and then dividing the result by a number that's less than n. In other words, the square root of m multiplied by m is m, so the square root of m multiplied by a number larger than m must also be larger than m. (B) has the same problem as (A), and must also be wrong. (C) makes sense, though—m must be smaller than a number that's the square root of m multiplied by a number larger than m. Following similar logic, n must be greater than a number that's the square root of n multiplied by a number smaller than n. Let's check the remaining two choices to make sure we haven't made a mistake. (D) doesn't make sense, because the square root of n multiplied by a positive integer couldn't be less than the square root of n by itself. (E) must also be wrong, because the square root of two positive integers multiplied together would almost always be larger than the square root of two positive integers added together—we can see an example of this in Solution 1 above.

After considering each choice, we can be confident that (C) must be right.

ANSWER CHOICE ANALYSIS

(A): As we saw in the solutions above, $\sqrt{mn}$ must be larger than m, because it involves multiplying m by n (which is larger than m), and then dividing the result by a number that's less than n. This choice could trick test-takers who didn't read carefully enough, or who forgot which variable was larger. **(B):** This choice has the same basic problem as (A). **(E):** Among other things, this choice will cause the first term in the compound inequality to be imaginary, and it's not really possible to say that an imaginary number is necessarily less than a real number under the conditions in this question. This introduces a variety of mathematical concerns that are outside the scope of the ACT Math section, so, as trained test-takers, we would already know from the first term that this choice must be wrong. Further, we can see that the product mn will nearly always be larger than the sum of m and n, as long as m is an integer larger than 1. This means the square root of *mn* will also be larger than the square root of the sum of *m* and *n*.

How to check? Try an alternate approach above.

▶ **Post-solution patterns (see p. 151):** most like the other choices

Test 3, Question 28 (Form 16MC3 if you have the 2020-2021 Red Book—see page 23 for more)

- **What's the prompt asking for?** The perimeter, in centimeters, of the larger triangle described in the prompt.
- **Math concepts in the prompt:** perimeter, ratios, similar triangles
- **Elements of the choices:** The choices are all two-digit numbers.
- **Notable differences among choices:** (F), (H), and (J) form a series in which each choice is five more than the

previous choice. (G) is half of (K).
- **Concepts in the choices:** difference of 5, doubling
- **Pre-solution patterns (see p. 149):** halves and doubles
- **Things to look out for:** Don't confuse the two triangles in the prompt, or which triangle corresponds to which part of the ratio! Don't get confused by the fact that two of the measurements for the smaller triangle involve the same numbers as the two numbers in the ratio!

Solution 1: Geometry/Sides-first: Sketch the smaller triangle described in the prompt, and assign the proper dimensions. Then sketch the larger triangle, and assign dimensions to its sides that make them $\frac{5}{3}$ as large as the corresponding sides in the smaller triangle. Finally, add up the sides of the larger triangle to find the answer.

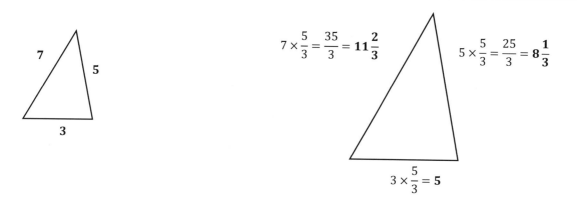

As we can see above, when we multiply each side by $\frac{5}{3}$, we find that the perimeter of the larger triangle is 25, because $5 + 8\frac{1}{3} + 11\frac{2}{3} = 25$. So (J) is right.

Solution 2: Geometry/Perimeter-first: Determine the perimeter of the smaller triangle first. Then multiply that perimeter by $\frac{5}{3}$ to find the perimeter of the larger triangle, and pick the appropriate answer choice.

The perimeter of the first triangle must be 15, because $3 + 5 + 7 = 15$. The prompt says the ratio of the perimeter of the smaller triangle to the perimeter of the larger triangle is $3:5$, so we can multiply 15 by $\frac{5}{3}$ to find the perimeter of the larger triangle: $15 \times \frac{5}{3} = 25$. So (J) is right.

ANSWER CHOICE ANALYSIS

(F): This choice is the perimeter of the *smaller* triangle, to attract untrained test-takers who forgot what the prompt was asking for.

How to check? Try an alternate approach above. Pay special attention to the issues we noted in "things to look out for" above. As trained test-takers, if someone provided us with the prompt for this question and then asked us to predict some of the answer choices, we'd predict that one of the wrong answers was likely to be the perimeter of the smaller triangle, just as we see in (F). When we see that there are only two choices in the prompt that are in the ratio $3:5$, we can be even more confident that we've probably thought about the question correctly (although we still want to double-check and make sure that the prompt is, indeed, asking for the perimeter of the larger triangle!).

▶ **Post-solution patterns (see p. 151):** right approach, wrong step; right answer to the wrong question

Test 3, Question 29 (Form 16MC3 if you have the 2020-2021 Red Book—see page 23 for more)

- **What's the prompt asking for?** The percentage chance that Thomas will win the game.
- **Math concepts in the prompt:** centers, circles, geometric probability, inequalities, points, probability percentages, radii,

series
- **Math concepts in the diagram:** circles, labels
- **Elements of the choices:** Each chance is a percentage.
- **Notable differences among choices:** (E) is the only choice that

involves a fraction.

- **Concepts in the choices:** fractions, percentages
- **"Bridge" concepts:** The percentage chance that Thomas will win the game is equal to the chance that he will score at least 30 points on his throw, since the prompt tells us that he needs at least 30 points to win. The prompt also tells us his dart will hit a random point on the board, so the percentage probability will be equal to the probability fraction in which the numerator

is the area of the target that would result in Thomas winning, and the denominator is the area of the entire target.

- **Things to look out for:** Don't confuse the point values of the different circles in the diagram! Don't confuse the ratio of the different circles in the diagram! Don't accidentally treat the radius like a diameter! Don't make any small mistakes in your calculations!

Solution 1: Geometry/Probability: Create a probability fraction that compares the area that scores at least 30 points to the entire area of the circle, and then pick the choice whose percentage is equal to that fraction.

The prompt tells us that the outside circle has a radius of 10 inches, and that each smaller circle has a radius 2 inches smaller than the next largest circle. So the circle worth 30 points must have a radius of 6 inches. We can divide the area of the smaller circle by the area of the larger circle to find out what percentage of the larger circle is covered by the smaller circle, which will also be the probability that a random dart thrown at the larger circle hits the smaller circle. Remember that the area of a circle can be found using $A = \pi r^2$, where A is the area and r is the radius.

$$\frac{\pi 6^2}{\pi 10^2} \qquad \left(\frac{area\ of\ smaller\ circle}{area\ of\ larger\ circle}\right)$$

$$\frac{36\pi}{100\pi} \qquad \text{(simplify)}$$

$$\frac{36}{100} \qquad \text{(simplify)}$$

$\frac{36}{100}$ is equal to 36%, so (A) is correct.

ANSWER CHOICE ANALYSIS

(B): This is the number of points Thomas needs to score, but the question asked for the probability he would hit the 30-point region of the board. **(C):** This is the percent chance that Thomas will score 40 points, but the prompt said he only needs 30 points to win the game. This choice would also attract test-takers who miscounted and thought that the radius of the 30-point circle was 4 instead of 6. **(D):** This choice would attract test-takers who thought that the *diameter* of the 30-point region was 6—rather than the *radius*—and that it was necessary to divide 6 by 2 to find the radius of that circle.

How to check? Carefully reconsider your reading and your calculations, especially with respect to the issues we noted above that need to be looked out for.

Note The ACT could have made this question much more challenging by using different dimensions for the diagram. For example, if the radius of the largest circle had been something besides 10, then it would have been more challenging for us to determine the percentage of the larger circle that was covered by the point-regions that would allow Thomas to win; similarly, if the circles' radii were different from each other by irregular amounts, instead of always differing by two inches, then it would have been easier to make a mistake in calculating the radius of the region that would allow Thomas to win.

Test 3, Question 30 (Form 16MC3 if you have the 2020-2021 Red Book—see page 23 for more)

- **What's the prompt asking for?** The algebra teacher's age.
- **Math concepts in the prompt:** multiplication, squaring, subtraction
- **Elements of the choices:** Each choice is a two-digit integer.
- **Notable differences among choices:** (F), (G), and (H) form a series in which each choice is 2 more than the previous choice.

(F) is half of (J), and (G) is half of (K). (F) and (K) are both mentioned in the prompt.

- **Pre-solution patterns (see p. 149):** halves and doubles
- **Things to look out for:** Don't confuse the steps in the prompt! Don't confuse the operations in the prompt! Don't make any mistakes in your calculations!

Solution 1: Backsolving: Take each answer choice and run it through the process described by the teacher in the prompt. The one that produces a result of 50 will be the right answer.

We can use x to represent the teacher's age. The teacher says "if you square my age," so we can represent his age squared with x^2. Then he says "and subtract 23 times my age," which we can represent with "$-23x$." Finally, he says the result is 50, so we can set our expression equal to 50. That gives us $x^2 - 23x = 50$:

(F) $23^2 - 23(23) = 0$

(G) $25^2 - 23(25) = 50$

(H) $27^2 - 23(27) = 108$

(J) $46^2 - 23(46) = 1,058$

(K) $50^2 - 23(50) = 1,350$

For free sample video demonstrations, go to www.ACTprepVideos.com

Only (G) produces a result of 50, so (G) is correct.

Solution 2: Algebra: Translate the teacher's statement into algebra, and then solve the equation you've come up with and pick the appropriate answer choice.

As we saw in the previous solution, we can translate the teacher's statement into the equation $x^2 - 23x = 50$. Once we have that equation, we can solve for x.

$$x^2 - 23x = 50 \qquad \text{(algebraic equivalent of the teacher's statement)}$$
$$x^2 - 23x - 50 = 0 \qquad \text{(subtract 50 from both sides)}$$
$$(x - 25)(x + 2) \qquad \text{(reverse-FOIL)}$$

So the statement is true when $x = 25$ and when $x = -2$. Since it doesn't make sense to say the teacher is -2 years old, and (more importantly) since only 25 appears in the answer choices, we know that the right answer is (G), 25.

ANSWER CHOICE ANALYSIS

(F): This choice is the result of using Solution 2 above and then adding the x-values of 25 and -2. It's also the value we get for x if we set the expression equal to 0 instead of 50. **(H):** This choice could reflect the same basic mistake that we saw in (F), but with the added mistake of adding 2 to 25 instead of -2. **(K):** This choice could reflect the mistake of assuming that the number 50 at the end of the teacher's sentence must have been the square root of the square of the teachers age, which would mean that the age itself would be 50.

How to check? Try an alternate approach above. Use the value you found in the statement made by the teacher to make sure the result is 50.

Note   Once again, we see that an approach that would be unacceptable in a classroom setting is arguably the best possible approach on an ACT Math question: many test-takers will have an easier time using the backsolving approach above than the formal algebraic approach. (On top of that, they'll be less likely to make mistakes with the backsolving approach.) On test day, remember that the important thing is to find the right answer efficiently and confidently, not to force yourself to use a certain approach just because you think your teacher would prefer it.

Test 3, Question 31 (Form 16MC3 if you have the 2020-2021 Red Book—see page 23 for more)

- **What's the prompt asking for?** The approximate number of seconds the car traveled under the conditions in the prompt.
- **Math concepts in the prompt:** acceleration, distance, exponents, fractions, function models, rate
- **Notable differences among choices:** (A), (B), and (C) are all ranges of numbers with whole numbers as their boundaries, starting at 1 and ending up at 4. (D) and (E) are whole numbers, not ranges. (D) is the upper boundary of choice (C), and (D) is also half of (E).
- **Concepts in the choices:** ranges, whole numbers
- **Pre-solution patterns (see p. 149):** wrong answers try to imitate right answers; halves and doubles
- **Things to look out for:** Don't misread the prompt! Don't make any small mistakes in your calculation! Don't confuse the variables in the function model!

Solution 1: Algebra: Substitute the values in the prompt for their corresponding variables in the function model, and then solve for the number of seconds, t. Pick the answer choice that reflects your result.

$$d = \frac{1}{2}at^2 \qquad \text{(given equation)}$$
$$80 = \frac{1}{2}(20)t^2 \qquad \text{(plug in } d = 80 \text{ and } a = 20)$$
$$80 = 10t^2 \qquad \text{(simplify)}$$
$$8 = t^2 \qquad \text{(divide both sides by 10)}$$
$$2.828 \approx t \qquad \text{(take square root of both sides)}$$

So the car travels between 2 and 3 seconds, which means (B) is right.

Solution 2: Backsolve: Go through the choices and plug in the numbers 2, 3, 4, and 8 as t in the equation from the prompt. Use the resulting d-values to figure out which choice is correct. (Notice that we don't need to test $t = 1$. If $t = 2$ is too large, we'll know that (A) is right without needing to test $t = 1$.)

$$d = \frac{1}{2}at^2 \qquad \text{(given equation)}$$
$$d = \frac{1}{2}20(2)^2 = 40 \qquad \text{(plug in } a = 20 \text{ and } t = 2)$$
$$d = \frac{1}{2}20(3)^2 = 90 \qquad \text{(plug in } a = 20 \text{ and } t = 3)$$
$$d = \frac{1}{2}20(4)^2 = 160 \qquad \text{(plug in } a = 20 \text{ and } t = 4)$$

$$d = \frac{1}{2}20(8)^2 = 640 \qquad \text{(plug in } a = 20 \text{ and } t = 8)$$

We can see that a distance of 80 meters should occur in between 2 and 3 seconds, because 2 seconds resulted in a distance of 40 meters and 3 seconds resulted in a distance of 90 meters. So (B) is right.

ANSWER CHOICE ANALYSIS

(D): This choice could reflect the mistake of dividing the 80 meters value from the prompt by the 20 meters per second per second value from the prompt. **(E):** This is the value of t^2, which we found as part of Solution 1—but the prompt asks for the number of seconds that the car traveled, which is equal to t, not t^2.

How to check? Try an alternate approach above.

Note Many untrained test-takers will be concerned when they read this question because they're not familiar with the formula in the prompt. But as trained test-takers, we realize that all we need to do is plug the given values into the function model and solve for the unknown variable; no previous knowledge of any formula is necessary. On test day, you almost certainly won't need this particular formula (and if by some coincidence you do, it will be provided for you), but you will need to remain flexible and use basic algebra to handle some other formula.

Test 3, Question 32 (Form 16MC3 if you have the 2020-2021 Red Book—see page 23 for more)

- **What's the prompt asking for?** The choice with the set that satisfies the prompt.
- **Math concepts in the prompt:** inequalities, real numbers, sets, variables
- **Elements of the choices:** Each describes a set of numbers.
- **Notable differences among choices:** (H) and (J) are opposites or complements of one another. The set in (G) contains the sets from every other choice except (F). (J) contains (K).

- **Concepts in the choices:** negative numbers, real numbers, sets, zero
- **Pre-solution patterns (see p. 149):** opposites; wrong answers try to imitate right answers
- **Things to look out for:** Don't make any small mistakes in your reading or algebra! Don't forgot that the prompt says that the right answer must *only* contain numbers that satisfy the inequality in the prompt!

Solution 1: Algebra/Abstract: Simplify the inequality in the prompt and pick the answer choice that reflects what you find.

$$x + 3 > x + 5 \qquad \text{(given inequality)}$$
$$x > x + 2 \qquad \text{(subtract 3 from both sides)}$$

x can't ever be greater than $x + 2$, by definition. So no value of x makes this inequality true, and the right answer is (F).

Solution 2: Number line/Abstract: Note that the inequality in the prompt would mean that starting at some point on a number line and moving 3 units to the right would have to cause you to be further to the right then if you had started at the same point and moved 5 units to the right. In other words, 3 more than a number would have to be greater than 5 more than that same number. Since this idea isn't possible, choose the only answer that reflects this impossibility: (F).

Solution 3: Test-smart: Realize that 3 more than a number can never be greater than 5 more than that number, so no x-value makes this inequality true, and (F) must be right.

ANSWER CHOICE ANALYSIS

(G): This choice could reflect the mistake of misreading the direction of the inequality in the prompt. **(H):** This choice could reflect the mistake of assuming that x must be valid when it's negative since the inequality in the prompt is wrong, and the numbers in the prompt are positive. But, as we saw in Solution 2 above, the statement in the prompt is impossible no matter what kinds of numbers we try to use for x, because the idea of adding 3 or adding 5 necessarily involves moving 3 or 5 units to the right on a number line, no matter where we began on that number line. **(K):** This choice could reflect confusion between the idea that there are zero solutions to the inequality, and the idea of zero itself being a solution to the inequality. It's true that there are zero solutions to the inequality, but that's why the correct answer is (F), the empty set: since the set of solutions has zero things inside of it, it is empty. On the other hand, if we try to say that $x = 0$ is a solution to the inequality, we still end up with the untrue statement $3 > 5$ when we plug in $x = 0$.

How to check? Try an alternate approach above. Make sure you carefully read and consider the differences among the choices.

Test 3, Question 33 (Form 16MC3 if you have the 2020-2021 Red Book—see page 23 for more)

- **What's the prompt asking for?** The fraction of the students who said they had spent less than 3 hours studying.
- **Math concepts in the prompt:** reading data from a graph, rounding, surveys

- **Math concepts in the diagram:** axis labels, bar graphs
- **Elements of the choices:** Each choice is a fraction between zero and one.
- **Notable differences among choices:** (A) and (D) both have 13

for their numerators. (D) and (E) both have 20 for their denominators. The denominators in (B), (C), (D), and (E) are factors of the denominator in (A).

- **Concepts in the choices:** fractions, simplifying fractions
- **Pre-solution patterns (see p. 149):** wrong answers try to imitate right answers

- **Things to look out for:** Don't accidentally include the number of students who spent exactly 3 hours! Don't misread the prompt, the graph, or the answer choices!

Solution 1: Fractions: Create a fraction whose numerator is the number of students who spent 0, 1, or 2 hours studying, and whose denominator is the total number of students surveyed. Pick the answer choice with the equivalent fraction.

We can see that 2 students spent 0 hours studying, 5 students spent 1 hour studying, and 6 students spent 2 hours studying, so 2 + 5 + 6 or 13 students spent less than 3 hours studying. That means 13 should be the numerator in our fraction, and the total number of students, 20, should be the denominator in the fraction. So the right answer is $\frac{13}{20}$, and (D) is right.

ANSWER CHOICE ANALYSIS

(A): This choice could reflect the mistake of correctly realizing that the numerator in the fraction should be 13, but accidentally thinking in terms of percentages when determining the denominator. **(B):** This choice could reflect the mistake of thinking that the prompt asked for the number of students who studied exactly 3 hours, instead of the ones who studied less than 3 hours. **(C):** This choice could reflect the mistake of focusing only on the students who studied exactly 2 hours, forgetting that the phrase "less than three" would include the people who studied zero hours or 1 hour as well. **(E):** This choice reflects the mistake of counting the people who studied *3 hours or less*—that is, 0, 1, 2, or 3 hours—rather than just the people who studied *less than 3 hours*—that is, 0, 1, or 2 hours.

How to check? Carefully reconsider what the prompt asks and what each of the answer choices reflects, and make sure that you picked the choice that accurately answers the prompt.

▶ **Post-solution patterns (see p. 151):** most like the other choices; right answer to the wrong question

Test 3, Question 34 (Form 16MC3 if you have the 2020-2021 Red Book—see page 23 for more)

- **What's the prompt asking for?** The measure of the central angle for the part of the pie chart that would reflect the number of students who studied for 3 hours, according to the graph and the prompt.
- **Math concepts in the prompt:** reading data from a graph, rounding, surveys, circles
- **Math concepts in the diagram:** axis labels, bar graphs
- **Elements of the choices:** The choices are all degree measures less than or equal to 90°.
- **Notable differences among choices:** (F), (H), and (J) form a series in which each choice is twice the one before it. The difference between (F) and (H) is the same as the difference between (J) and (K). (F) and (J) are complements, and add up to (K).

- **Concepts in the choices:** complements, degree measurements, right angles
- **"Bridge" concepts:** The central angle should take up a proportion of the circle equal to the proportion of the students who studied for 3 hours.
- **Pre-solution patterns (see p. 149):** opposites; halves and doubles
- **Things to look out for:** Don't accidentally find the measure of the central angle for the number of students who studied for some other amount of time besides 3 hours! Don't forget that there are 360° in a circle! Don't make any small mistakes in your reading or arithmetic!

Solution 1: Pie charts/Percentages: Determine the percentage of the students who studied for 3 hours, and pick the answer choice that reflects the same percentage of 360°.

When we look at the histogram, we can see that 4 students studied for 3 hours. We can divide 4 by 20 to find that 4 is 20% of 20, so the sector of the pie chart representing those students should be 20% of the pie chart as well, which means the central angle should be 20% × 360°, or 72°. So the right answer is (J).

Solution 2: Pie charts/Ratios: Set up a ratio comparing the fraction of students who studied for exactly 3 hours to a fraction with an unknown numerator and a denominator of 360°. Solve for the unknown numerator and pick the appropriate choice.

$$\frac{4}{20} = \frac{x}{360°} \quad \left(\frac{students\ who\ studied\ for\ 3\ hours}{total\ number\ of\ students} = \frac{central\ angle\ representing\ students\ who\ studied\ for\ 3\ hours}{total\ number\ of\ degrees\ in\ a\ circle}\right)$$

$$1440° = 20x \quad \text{(cross-multiply)}$$

$$72° = x \quad \text{(divide both sides by 20)}$$

So the right answer is (J).

ANSWER CHOICE ANALYSIS

(F): This choice might attract untrained test-takers who accidentally found 20% of 90°, instead of 20% of 360°. **(G):** This choice could reflect the mistake of trying Solution 1 above, and confusing percentages with degree measurements, because the correct answer should be 20% of the 360° of a circle, rather than a 20° angle. **(H):** This choice is half of the right answer, and could reflect the mistake of finding 20% of 180°, instead of 20% of 360°. **(K):** This choice is one-quarter of a circle when measured from the center, so it might reflect the mistake of thinking that the number of students who studied for 3 hours was $\frac{1}{4}$ of the total number of students simply because it was 4 actual students, or of thinking that $\frac{4}{20}$ reduced to $\frac{1}{4}$.

How to check? Try an alternate approach above. Also, the fact that (G) and (K) both reflect mistakes related to reading the number of students who studied for 3 hours and then trying to convert that into an angle measurement is a strong suggestion, but not a guarantee, that we've thought about the question correctly.

▶ **Post-solution patterns (see p. 151):** right approach, wrong step

▌ **Test 3, Question 35 (Form 16MC3 if you have the 2020-2021 Red Book—see page 23 for more)**

- **What's the prompt asking for?** The average number of hours for the 20 survey responses, rounded to the nearest 10th of an hour.
- **Math concepts in the prompt:** averages, decimals, reading data from a graph, rounding, surveys
- **Math concepts in the diagram:** axis labels, bar graphs
- **Elements of the choices:** The choices are each numbers from 2.0 to 3.0, with one digit after the decimal point.
- **Notable differences among choices:** (A) and (E) are both exact integers ending in .0. (D) is the average of (A) and (E). (C) is the average of (B) and (D).
- **Concepts in the choices:** averages, decimal points
- **Things to look out for:** Make sure you don't overlook any of the data in the graph! Make sure you don't misread the answer choices! Make sure you divide by the right number when calculating the average! Make sure you round off your answer correctly!

Solution 1: Arithmetic: Add up the number of hours studied by the students in the graph, and divide by 20 to find the average. Then round your answer choice to one decimal point and pick the appropriate answer.

$$\frac{2(0) + 5(1) + 6(2) + 4(3) + 2(4) + 1(5)}{20} = 2.1$$

So the right answer is (B), 2.1.

ANSWER CHOICE ANALYSIS

(A): This choice is the median of the values in the graph, not the average of those values, which is what the prompt asked for. **(C):** This choice could represent the result an untrained test-taker would reach if he didn't include the two students who studied for 0 hours in the calculation, and incorrectly divided 42 by 18 instead of by 20.

How to check? Since we see that most of the answer choices are clustered around values between 2.0 and 2.5, we know that we need to be very precise in our data-reading and calculations, because we see that the test is clearly trying to set us up to make a mistake and be off by a small fraction. So carefully re-check your reading and your calculations to make sure you haven't fallen for this trap!

▶ **Post-solution patterns (see p. 151):** easy calculation mistake

▌ **Test 3, Question 36 (Form 16MC3 if you have the 2020-2021 Red Book—see page 23 for more)**

- **What's the prompt asking for?** The number of diagonals in the octagon.
- **Math concepts in the prompt:** diagonals, octagons, pentagons
- **Math concepts in the diagram:** diagonals, octagons, pentagons
- **Notable differences among choices:** (F) is half of (G) and (H) is half of (K). (H), (J), and (K) form a series in which each number is 10 more than the number before it.
- **Pre-solution patterns (see p. 149):** halves and doubles
- **Things to look out for:** Don't assume that octagons have eight diagonals just because pentagons have five diagonals! If you draw the diagonals into the octagon, make sure that your result accurately connects all the points appropriately! Don't miscount the number of diagonals!

Solution 1: Geometry/Concrete: Connect the diagonals in the octagon, count them accurately, and pick the corresponding answer choice.

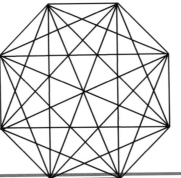

Once we count up all the diagonals, we can see that there are 20, and that (H) is the right answer. Notice that if you have trouble keeping track of which diagonals you've counted already as you move around the shape, you can realize that there are 8 vertices, and that every vertex has 5 diagonals coming out of it, and that every diagonal must connect two vertices. If we count all the diagonals coming out of each vertex, we'll count both ends of each diagonal. So the number of diagonals must be half of 5 × 8, which is half of 40, or 20. So (H) is right.

ANSWER CHOICE ANALYSIS

(F): This choice reflects the mistake of assuming that the number of diagonals is equal to the number of sides for all shapes, just because this was true with the pentagon in the example. **(G):** This is the result if a test-taker reasoning through the solution incorrectly decided to multiply the 8 vertices by the number of endpoints for each diagonal, which would produce 8 × 2, or 16. **(K):** This choice reflects the mistake of forgetting that we'll count every diagonal twice if we look at every vertex of the shape and count each diagonal leaving that vertex. As we saw above, if part of our process to calculate the number includes doing this, we need to divide our count by two because otherwise we'll double-count each diagonal, since we're considering each diagonal from both vertices that are its endpoints.

How to check? Make sure you didn't accidentally count each diagonal twice!

▶ **Post-solution patterns (see p. 151):** right approach, wrong step

Note There is a formula for determining the number of diagonals in a given polygon, but, as trained test-takers, we know it would be a mistake to learn that formula for the purposes of the ACT Math section, even though we just answered a question about diagonals. We can tell that this question doesn't require us to know that formula, or even to know the definition of the word "diagonal," for two reasons: first, the question gives us an example of what a diagonal is, which it wouldn't do if it were trying to test us on the meaning; second, the shape whose diagonals we're asked to count has a relatively small number of vertices, which allows us to count them individually instead of requiring us to apply a formula. Remember on test day that the ACT is often trying to trick us into thinking that the test is harder than it is!

▌ Test 3, Question 37 (Form 16MC3 if you have the 2020-2021 Red Book—see page 23 for more)

- **What's the prompt asking for?** The expression that gives the distance in feet from the bottom of the basket to the ground.
- **Math concepts in the prompt:** angles, height, parallel lines
- **Math concepts in the diagram:** angles, height, right angles, right triangles
- **Elements of the choices:** Every choice includes a trig function and the numbers 72 and 144.
- **Notable differences among choices:** (A) and (B) involve fractions, while (C), (D), and (E) don't. (A) and (D) both involve cosine, while (B) and (E) involve sine and

(C) involves tangent.

- **Concepts in the choices:** angles, coefficients, cosine, fractions, sine, tangent
- **"Bridge" concepts:** SOHCAHTOA
- **Pre-solution patterns (see p. 149):** wrong answers try to imitate right answers; opposites
- **Things to look out for:** Don't confuse the numbers 144 and 72! Don't confuse the appropriate values for SOHCAHTOA! Don't make any small mistakes in your reading or calculations!

Solution 1: SOHCAHTOA: Since we know the hypotenuse of the right triangle and we need to find the length of the side opposite the given angle, use the SOH part of SOHCAHTOA to determine the length of the opposite side.

$$\sin x° = \frac{opposite}{hypotenuse}$$ (definition of sine)

$$\sin 72° = \frac{d}{144}$$ (plug in $x = 72°$, d for the unknown distance, and 144 for the hypotenuse)

$$144 × \sin 72° = d$$ (multiply both sides by 144 to isolate d)

This matches the expression in (E), so (E) must be right.

ANSWER CHOICE ANALYSIS

(A): This choice combines the mistakes from (B) and (D). **(B):** This choice reflects a mistake in algebra, resulting in a fraction with 144 being divided by the trig expression, rather than that expression being multiplied by 144. **(C):** This choice would make sense if the length of the side adjacent to the given angle was 144, because then we could use the TOA part of SOHCAHTOA to determine the length of the side opposite to the angle. But the diagram tells us the *hypotenuse* of the triangle is 144, so we can't draw a conclusion relative to tangent from the given information. **(D):** This accidentally refers to cosine instead of sine; we know that sine is appropriate because the question involves the ratio of the length of the opposite side to the length of the hypotenuse.

How to check? Carefully verify that sine is the appropriate function here, and that sine is equal to $\frac{opposite}{hypotenuse}$. Also make sure it's correct for 144 to be multiplied by the trig expression rather than divided by that expression, since the question is clearly trying to set us up to make a mistake in connection with this issue.

▶ **Post-solution patterns (see p. 151):** opposites

Test 3, Question 38 (Form 16MC3 if you have the 2020-2021 Red Book—see page 23 for more)

- **What's the prompt asking for?** The x-coordinate of the midpoint of $\overline{GH}$.

- **Math concepts in the prompt:** line segments, midpoints, plotting points in the xy-coordinate plane

- **Notable differences among choices:** (G) is the opposite of (J). (F) and (G) are both negative, while (J) and (K) are both positive, and (H) is neither negative nor positive. (F), (G), (H), and (J) form a series in which each number is three more than the number before it.

- **Concepts in the choices:** negative numbers, opposites, positive numbers, zero

- **Pre-solution patterns (see p. 149):** be aware of series

- **Things to look out for:** Don't accidentally find the y coordinate of the midpoint! Don't confuse the x and y coordinates of the given points! Don't make any small mistakes in your arithmetic!

Solution 1: Graphing/Concrete: Graph the line segment described in the prompt and pick the answer choice that corresponds to the x-coordinate of the midpoint of the line you graphed.

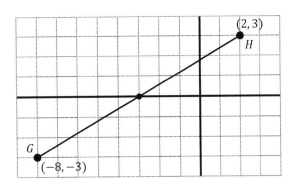

After we graph the given points, we can see that the x-coordinate of the midpoint of $\overline{GH}$ is -3, and (G) is right.

Solution 2: Geometry/Abstract: Average the x-coordinates of the two points in the prompt, and pick the corresponding choice.

$$x = \frac{-8 + 2}{2} = -3$$

Once again, we see that (G) is right.

ANSWER CHOICE ANALYSIS

(F): This is the sum of the two x-coordinates, but we need to find their average. **(H):** This is the average of the two y-coordinates, not the average of the two x-coordinates. **(J):** This is the opposite of the right answer, which could reflect a mistake related to the signs of the numbers in the prompt. **(K):** This choice will tempt a lot of untrained test takers, because it reflects the horizontal distance between either endpoint and the midpoint—but the prompt asked us for the x-coordinate of the midpoint itself, not the horizontal distance from either endpoint to the midpoint.

How to check? Try an alternate approach above. Note that our ability to explain all the mistakes that could lead to the wrong answers strongly suggests, but doesn't guarantee, that we have dealt with the question correctly.

▶ **Post-solution patterns (see p. 151):** right approach, wrong step; right answer to the wrong question

Test 3, Question 39 (Form 16MC3 if you have the 2020-2021 Red Book—see page 23 for more)

- **What's the prompt asking for?** The value of $8x + 9y$ under the conditions in the prompt.

- **Math concepts in the prompt:** addition, systems of equations

- **Notable differences among choices:** (A) is the opposite of (E). (A) and (B) are both negative, while the other choices are positive.

- **Concepts in the choices:** negative numbers, opposites, positive numbers

- **"Bridge" concepts:** A single x-value and a single y-value can be combined to make the first two equations in the prompt valid. Once we know those values, we can find the value of the equation that the prompt is asking about.

- **Pre-solution patterns (see p. 149):** opposites

- **Things to look out for:** Don't accidentally find x or y by itself! Don't accidentally find the value of $9x$ plus $8y$! Don't misread the equations in the prompt! Don't pick the opposite of the right answer, or make any other mistake related to the sign of a number!

Solution 1: Algebra: Add the two equations together to isolate one of the variables, and then use the value of that variable to find the other variable. Finally, find the value of $8x + 9y$.

When we add two equations, our goal is to eliminate one of the variables so we can find the value of the other variable. In this case, the easiest way to eliminate one variable is probably to multiply the first equation by -2. That way, the coefficient of the y-value in the first equation will be -6, and the coefficient of the y-value in the second equation will be 6, so that when we add the equations together, the two y-terms will cancel out, and we can solve for the x-term.

$$\begin{array}{r} -4x - 6y = -8 \\ +\quad 5x + 6y = \ 7 \\ \hline x \qquad\ = -1 \end{array}$$ (the first equation multiplied by -2 and added to the second equation)

Now we know that $x = -1$. We can plug this value into either of the original equations and then solve for y.

$5x + 6y = 7$ (second equation)

$5(-1) + 6y = 7$ (plug in $x = -1$)

$6y = 12$ (add 5 to both sides)

$y = 2$ (divide both sides by 6)

Now we know that $x = -1$ and $y = 2$. We can use these values to find $8x + 9y$.

$8x + 9y$ (given expression)

$8(-1) + 9(2)$ (plug in $x = -1$ and $y = 2$)

$-8 + 18$ (simplify)

10 (simplify)

So (E) is right.

Solution 2: Graphing: Graph both of the given equations on your calculator in order to find the values of x and y. Then use those values to find $8x + 9y$.

We can put each of the provided equations into slope-intercept form by isolating y. We'll start with the first one:

$2x + 3y = 4$ (first equation)

$3y = -2x + 4$ (subtract $2x$ from both sides)

$y = -\frac{2}{3}x + \frac{4}{3}$ (divide both sides by 3)

Now let's put the other equation into slope-intercept form:

$5x + 6y = 7$ (second equation)

$6y = -5x + 7$ (subtract $5x$ from both sides)

$y = -\frac{5}{6}x + \frac{7}{6}$ (divide both sides by 6)

We can graph those equations to find their point of intersection:

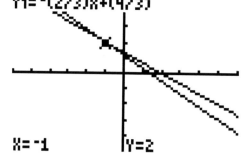

So the point of intersection for these two graphs is $(-1, 2)$, or the point where $x = -1$ and $y = 2$. As we did in the previous solution, we can use these values to find $8x + 9y$.

$8x + 9y$ (given expression)

$8(-1) + 9(2)$ (plug in $x = -1$ and $y = 2$)

$-8 + 18$ (simplify)

10 (simplify)

So (E) is right.

Solution 3: Test-smart: Notice that the difference between the first equation and the second equation is $3x + 3y$ on the left side, and 3 on the right side. (In other words, when we add $3x + 3y$ to the left side of the first equation, we get the left side of the second equation, and when we add 3 to the right side of the first equation, we get the right side of the second equation). So adding $3x + 3y$ must be the same as adding 3. Then notice that the question asks about $8x + 9y$, which is $3x + 3y$ greater than the expression $5x + 6y$ in the second equation. Since adding $3x + 3y$ is the same as adding 3, we can just add 3 to 7 (which the prompt tells us is equal to $5x + 6y$) to find the value of $8x + 9y$. That gives us 10, which means (E) is right.

ANSWER CHOICE ANALYSIS

(A): This choice is the opposite of the right answer, which could reflect a mistake in handling the signs of the equations in the prompt. **(B):** This is the value of x, which will attract untrained test-takers who forget that the prompt was asking for the value of $8x + 9y$, not just x by itself. **(C):** This is the value of y, which will attract untrained test-takers who forget that the prompt was asking for the value of $8x + 9y$, not just y by itself. **(D):** This is the value of $8y + 9x$, but the prompt asked for $8x + 9y$.

How to check? Try an alternate approach above. We should also feel especially confident in our answer when we realize that (B) and (C) reflect the values we found for x and y, strongly suggesting that our reasoning and calculations were probably on the right track. Of course, we still have to make sure that we're actually answering the question that the prompt is asking!

▶ **Post-solution patterns (see p. 151):** right approach, wrong step; opposites; right answer to the wrong question

Test 3, Question 40 (Form 16MC3 if you have the 2020-2021 Red Book—see page 23 for more)

- **What's the prompt asking for?** The choice with the values of θ that allow $\tan \theta$ to be equal to -1.

- **Math concepts in the prompt:** π, radians, range, tangent, θ

- **Elements of the choices:** Each choice contains two or more values that involve $\frac{\pi}{4}$.

- **Notable differences among choices:** The choices combine the numbers 3, 5, and 7 in addition to $\frac{\pi}{4}$. 3 appears in four choices, 5 appears in three choices, 7 appears in three choices, and $\frac{\pi}{4}$

- appears by itself in two choices.

- **Concepts in the choices:** fractions, π, radians

- **Pre-solution patterns (see p. 149):** wrong answers try to imitate right answers

- **Things to look out for:** Don't confuse the trig function that's mentioned in the prompt! Don't misread the answer choices! Don't forget to put your calculator in radians mode, since we're dealing with trigonometry and π!

Solution 1: Concrete: Use your calculator to evaluate $\tan \frac{\pi}{4}$, $\tan \frac{3\pi}{4}$, $\tan \frac{5\pi}{4}$, and $\tan \frac{7\pi}{4}$ to determine which of those values are equal to -1. Pick the choice that reflects your results.

A calculator reveals the following equivalent values:

$$\tan \frac{\pi}{4} = 1 \qquad \tan \frac{3\pi}{4} = -1 \qquad \tan \frac{5\pi}{4} = 1 \qquad \tan \frac{7\pi}{4} = -1$$

After we find the values of tangent from the answer choices, we can see that only $\tan \frac{3\pi}{4}$ and $\tan \frac{7\pi}{4}$ equal -1, so (H) is right.

Solution 2: Graphing: Use a graphing calculator to graph $\tan \theta$ over the interval 0 to 2π, and then see which x-coordinates on the graph correspond to a y-coordinate of -1, and pick the appropriate answer choice.

Let's graph $y = \tan x$ and see when $y = -1$ between $x = 0$ and $x = 2\pi$. The answer choices include expressions with a π term over 4, so I made each hash mark on the x-axis in the graph below equal to $\frac{\pi}{4}$.

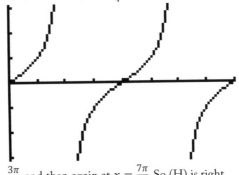

We can see that $y = -1$ right around $x = \frac{3\pi}{4}$, and then again at $x = \frac{7\pi}{4}$. So (H) is right.

ANSWER CHOICE ANALYSIS

(K): $\frac{\pi}{4}$ and $\frac{5\pi}{4}$ are values of θ where $\tan \theta$ is 1, not -1. This choice might have appealed to test-takers who misread the prompt and thought that 1 was also an acceptable value for $\tan \theta$ under the conditions in the prompt.

How to check? Try an alternate approach above.

Note In this case, misreading the prompt might have led you to look for the values of $\tan \theta$ that were equal to 1 instead of -1.

But notice that none of the answer choices reflects this specific mistake: $\tan \theta = 1$ when $\theta = \frac{\pi}{4}$ or when $\theta = \frac{5\pi}{4}$, and no choice combines only $\frac{\pi}{4}$ and $\frac{5\pi}{4}$. A lot of untrained test-takers who initially thought the right answer should be $\frac{\pi}{4}$ and $\frac{5\pi}{4}$ would notice that and then decide to pick one of the wrong answers as a sort of compromise, hoping that somehow they'd get lucky. But, as trained test-takers, if we thought we were looking for an answer choice with only $\frac{\pi}{4}$ and $\frac{5\pi}{4}$, then seeing there wasn't a choice with our answer should cause us to realize that we must have made a fundamental mistake in our approach to the question. Rather than compromise with ourselves and pick a choice that didn't reflect our exact conclusions about the question, we should go back and try to discover and fix our mistake (or decide to skip the question and come back to it later). We always keep in mind that the right answer to an ACT question must answer that question exactly (unless the prompt uses a word like "approximately," of course); if no choice seems to meet that requirement, then we've done something wrong. Keep that in mind on test day, and don't let yourself be tricked into marking an answer choice that isn't right!

Test 3, Question 41 (Form 16MC3 if you have the 2020-2021 Red Book—see page 23 for more)

- **What's the prompt asking for?** The answer choice that could be the result when i is raised to an exponent that's an integer.
- **Math concepts in the prompt:** complex numbers, exponents, i, integers
- **Elements of the choices:** Choices form a series from 0 to 4.
- **Concepts in the choices:** one, zero
- **"Bridge" concepts:** $i^2 = -1$, by definition.
- **Pre-solution patterns (see p. 149):** halves and doubles
- **Things to look out for:** Don't forget that i has unique properties when it's raised to an exponent!

Solution 1: Concrete: Test a variety of integer values for x and pick the choice that corresponds to a possible value of i^x.

- $i^0 = 1$
- $i^1 = i$
- $i^2 = -1$
- $i^3 = -i$
- $i^4 = 1$
- $i^5 = i$

We can see that the only possible value of i^x (as described in the prompt) that appears in the answer choices is 1. So (B) is right.

Solution 2: Abstract: Think about the properties of i and pick the only answer choice that can be the result when i is multiplied by itself a number of times.

We know that i is the square root of -1, so that means i^2 must be -1, and $(i^2)^2$, or i^4, must be 1. We can see that no matter how many times i is multiplied by itself, the result will never involve 0, 2, 3, 4, or any number other than positive or negative i, or positive or negative 1. Again, we can see that (B) is right.

ANSWER CHOICE ANALYSIS

(A): This choice might tempt some untrained test-takers who don't read the question carefully enough, because zero is one of the values of x that causes i^x to have a value of 1. Some test-takers may also think that i^0 is equal to 0, instead of 1. But zero itself isn't one of the values that i^x can have under the conditions in the prompt. **(C):** Like (A), this choice might attract test-takers who incorrectly think the question is asking for a value of x that causes i^x to be an integer, because i^2 is -1. **(E):** This choice has the same problem as (A) and (C): it's a value of x that causes i^x to be an integer, but it's not a possible value of i^x itself.

How to check? Try an alternate approach above. Make sure you have correctly assessed what the prompt is asking you for.

▶ **Post-solution patterns (see p. 151):** right answer to the wrong question

Test 3, Question 42 (Form 16MC3 if you have the 2020-2021 Red Book—see page 23 for more)

- **What's the prompt asking for?** The height of the soda in the glass, in inches.
- **Math concepts in the prompt:** cylinders, height, radius, volume
- **Notable differences among choices:** (J) is the sum of (F) and (G). (F) and (J) are the only choices that involve a fraction, and they both involve $\frac{2}{3}$. (G) is half of (K).
- **Concepts in the choices:** adding 4, fractions
- **"Bridge" concepts:** Since the volume of the soda will be the same in both containers, the question is asking us for the height of a "cylinder" of the same volume of soda when the radius is 3 inches instead of 2.
- **Pre-solution patterns (see p. 149):** halves and doubles
- **Things to look out for:** Don't confuse the dimensions of the two

containers! Don't confuse radius and diameter! Don't make any small mistakes when you calculate volume from radius and height, or when you use volume and radius to find height!

Solution 1: Geometry: Use the provided formula to calculate the volume of the soda in the can, and then use the volume of the soda and the diameter of the glass to find the height of the soda when it's poured into the glass. (Be sure not to confuse radius and diameter—the prompt tells us the *diameter* of the two objects, but the provided formula for volume uses the *radius* of those objects, which is half of the diameter.)

$$\pi r^2 h = V \qquad \text{(given formula for the volume of a right circular cylinder)}$$

$$\pi(1)^2 6 = 6\pi \qquad \text{(volume of soda can where } r = 1 \text{ and } h = 6; \text{ notice that } r = \tfrac{d}{2})$$

Now we know that the can holds 6π cubic inches of soda. We can set this equal to the volume of the glass and then solve for h to find the height in inches of the soda poured into the glass. (Notice that we use $r = \frac{3}{2}$ for the radius of the glass, because the prompt says the diameter of the glass is 3, and we know that radius is half of diameter.)

$$6\pi = \pi \left(\frac{3}{2}\right)^2 h \qquad \text{(volume of soda can set equal to volume of glass)}$$

$$6\pi = \pi \frac{9}{4} h \qquad \text{(simplify)}$$

$$6 = \frac{9}{4} h \qquad \text{(divide both sides by } \pi)$$

$$24 = 9h \qquad \text{(multiply both sides by 4)}$$

$$\frac{24}{9} = h \qquad \text{(divide both sides by 9)}$$

$\frac{24}{9}$ reduces to $\frac{8}{3}$, which is the same as $2\frac{2}{3}$. So (F) is correct.

Solution 2: Test-smart: Note that the answer must be less than half of six, and pick the only choice that satisfies that requirement.

The prompt tells us that when the soda is in the can with a diameter of 2 inches, the height of the soda in the can is 6 inches. When that same volume of soda is poured into a glass with a diameter of 3 inches—which is larger than the diameter of the can—the height must drop to less than 6 inches. That eliminates choices (J) and (K)—but let's follow this line of reasoning a little farther and see what we can figure out.

The provided formula for the volume of the cylinder is $\pi r^2 h = V$. We know that πr^2 is equal to the area of a circle—in this case, it's the area of the circle that we would see on top of the cylinder if we looked down at it from above. The other part of the volume is h, which represents the height of the cylinder. So the two things that determine the volume of the cylinder are the area of the circle on either end of the cylinder, which is given by πr^2, and the height of the cylinder, h.

In this question, the diameter of the can is 2, and the diameter of the glass is 3, which means their radii are 1 and 1.5, respectively. So the πr^2 part of the volume of those cylinders goes from 1π to 2.25π. In other words, the area of the circle on either end of the glass is more than twice the area of the circle on either end of the can. Since that area—the πr^2 part of the volume formula—more than doubles moving from the can to the glass, the other part of the volume—h—must decrease by more than half for the volume to remain unchanged. So the height of the soda in the glass must be less than half of 6, which means only (F) can be right.

ANSWER CHOICE ANALYSIS

(G): This choice could reflect the mistake of assuming that the height of the new container must be $\frac{2}{3}$ the height of the old container, since the diameter of the new container is $\frac{3}{2}$ the diameter of the old container. But this logic doesn't work here because the formula for volume involves squaring the radius, but not squaring the height. **(H):** This could reflect the mistake of assuming that the height must decrease by 1 inch in order to offset an increase of 1 inch in the diameter. **(K):** This could reflect an algebra mistake in attempting Solution 1 that results in $\frac{6\pi}{\frac{3}{4}\pi}$, which reduces to 8.

How to check? Try an alternate approach above. Pay particular attention to the things we noted that we should look out for above.

Test 3, Question 43 (Form 16MC3 if you have the 2020-2021 Red Book—see page 23 for more)

- **What's the prompt asking for?** The volume of the given cylinder in cubic meters.
- **Math concepts in the prompt:** cylinders, height, radius, volume
- **Math concepts in the diagram:** cylinders, dimension labels, height, radius
- **Elements of the choices:** Each choice is a two- or three-digit number involving π.
- **Notable differences among choices:** (C) is 5 times more than (A). (D) is 6 times more than (A), just as (E) is 6 times more than (C). The integer in (E) is the square of the integer in (A). (B) contains the only prime number.
- **Concepts in the choices:** multiples, multiplying by 5,

multiplying by 6, π, squaring

- **"Bridge" concepts:** The formula for the volume of a right circular cylinder is $V = \pi r^2 h$. In other words, we find the volume of a cylinder by finding the area of one of the circular bases, and then multiplying that area by the height of the cylinder.

- **Things to look out for:** Don't confuse the height and the radius of the cylinder, because they are similar numbers! Don't make any small mistakes in your calculations!

Solution 1: Geometry: Apply the formula for the volume of a right circular cylinder. Pick the choice that corresponds to the result.

$\pi r^2 h$	(volume of a cylinder)
$\pi(5)^2(6)$	(plug in $r = 5$ and $h = 6$)
150π	(simplify)

So the right answer is (C).

ANSWER CHOICE ANALYSIS

(A): This is the product of the two numbers in the diagram and π. Untrained test-takers might accidentally reach this result if they forgot the formula for calculating the volume of a cylinder and tried to make one up. **(B):** This choice could be the result of squaring the radius correctly, then adding the height rather than multiplying by the height, and then multiplying by π. **(D):** This is the result of accidentally switching the values for r and h. **(E):** This is the result of squaring both the radius and the height, and then multiplying by π—but the formula only calls for squaring the radius, not the height.

How to check? Carefully reconsider your reading and calculations, especially in light of the relationships among the answer choices noted above. Satisfy yourself that you've read the question accurately and multiplied correctly.

Test 3, Question 44 (Form 16MC3 if you have the 2020-2021 Red Book—see page 23 for more)

- **What's the prompt asking for?** The ratio of AC to CE in the given diagram.

- **Math concepts in the prompt:** line segments, parallel lines, perimeters, ratios, reading diagrams, triangles

- **Math concepts in the diagram:** line segments, parallel lines, perimeters, ratios, similar triangles, triangles

- **Elements of the choices:** The answer choices are all ratios involving the numbers 1, 2, or 3.

- **Notable differences among choices:** (G) is the opposite of (J), and (H) is the opposite of (K). ((F) can't really have an opposite present, since reversing 1:1 results in the same ratio of 1:1.)

- **Concepts in the choices:** opposites, ratios

- **"Bridge" concepts:** Triangles ABC, ADE, and AFG must be similar to one another, because we know from the prompt that they all have the same angle measurements at corresponding angles.

- **Pre-solution patterns (see p. 149):** opposites

- **Things to look out for:** Don't confuse the points in the diagram! Don't pick an answer choice that reverses the correct ratio! Don't forget that you can compare your answer to the diagram, since the diagram is drawn to scale! Don't overlook any of the given information in the prompt!

Solution 1: Geometry: Use your knowledge of similar triangles and the given information to determine the ratio of AC to CE.

We know that $\triangle ABC$ and $\triangle AFG$ are similar triangles, because their angle measures are the same: they share the same angle with vertex A, and the prompt tells us that their bottom sides ($\overline{BC}$ and $\overline{FG}$, which run along l_3 and l_5 respectively) are parallel, and intersect the same lines (l_1 and l_2) to create equal angles in the bottom left and right vertices of each triangle. If $\triangle ABC$ and $\triangle AFG$ are similar triangles, and if the ratio of the perimeter of $\triangle ABC$ to the perimeter of $\triangle AFG$ is 1:3, then every side length of $\triangle AFG$ must be three times the corresponding side length of $\triangle ABC$.

We also know that $\triangle ABC$ and $\triangle ADE$ are similar triangles, using the same logic we applied to $\triangle ABC$ and $\triangle AFG$. Now we know that all three triangles are similar, since we proved that $\triangle ABC$ was similar to both $\triangle ADE$ and $\triangle AFG$. The prompt tells us that the ratio of $\overline{DE}$ to $\overline{FG}$ is 2:3. Since $\overline{DE}$ and $\overline{FG}$ are corresponding sides of similar triangles $\triangle ADE$ and $\triangle AFG$, we know that the ratio of the perimeter of $\triangle ADE$ to the perimeter of $\triangle AFG$ is 2:3.

If the ratio of the perimeter of $\triangle ABC$ to the perimeter of $\triangle AFG$ is 1:3, and the ratio of the perimeter of $\triangle ADE$ to the perimeter of $\triangle AFG$ is 2:3, then the ratio of the perimeter of $\triangle ABC$ to the perimeter of $\triangle ADE$ must be 1:2. Since $\overline{AC}$ and $\overline{AE}$ are corresponding sides of similar triangles $\triangle ABC$ and $\triangle ADE$, and the ratio of the perimeter of $\triangle ABC$ to the perimeter of $\triangle ADE$ is 1:2, the ratio of $\overline{AC}$ to $\overline{AE}$ must be 1:2.

So we know that $\overline{AE}$ is twice as long as $\overline{AC}$, and we can see from the diagram that the length of $\overline{AE}$ is the length of $\overline{AC}$ plus the length of $\overline{CE}$. So the length of $\overline{CE}$ must be equal to the length of $\overline{AC}$, which means the ratio of $\overline{AC}$ to $\overline{CE}$ must be 1:1, and (F) is right.

Solution 2: Test-smart: Remember that the diagram is drawn to scale, and pick the only answer choice that seems plausible according to

When we look at $\overline{AC}$ and $\overline{CE}$, it's clear that neither is two or three times the size of the other. The only ratio that could possibly make sense in the context of the diagram is $1:1$, the ratio in (F), so (F) is right.

ANSWER CHOICE ANALYSIS

(G): This could reflect incorrectly thinking that the prompt asked us to compare AC to E. **(H):** This could reflect incorrectly thinking that the prompt asked us to compare AC to AG. **(J):** This could involve a mistake similar to the one we described in (G), but in the opposite direction. **(K):** This could involve a mistake similar to the one we described in (H), but in the opposite direction.

How to check? Try an alternate approach above. Especially remember that you can consider the scale, since diagrams on the ACT Math section are drawn to scale and the answer choices in this question are different enough from each other to allow us to eyeball which one is appropriate.

▶   **Post-solution patterns (see p. 151):** right answer to the wrong question

Test 3, Question 45 (Form 16MC3 if you have the 2020-2021 Red Book—see page 23 for more)

- **What's the prompt asking for?** The height of the rocket above the launch pad.
- **Math concepts in the prompt:** angles, distance, height
- **Math concepts in the diagram:** angles, distance, height, right angles, triangles
- **Elements of the choices:** The answer choices all involve integers and/or radical expressions.
- **Notable differences among choices:** (A), (B), and (C) are integers, while (D) is the sum of two radical expressions and

(E) is the sum of an integer and two radical expressions.
- **Concepts in the choices:** addition, integers, radical expressions
- **"Bridge" concepts:** We can use our knowledge of triangles to calculate the height of each separate portion of the rocket's trip.
- **Things to look out for:** Don't confuse the angle measures in the diagram! Don't confuse the distances in the diagram! Don't forget the vertical distance of 30 km! Don't forget that you can compare your answer to the diagram, since the diagram is drawn to scale!

Solution 1: Geometry: Consider each section of the rocket's trip separately, and use your knowledge of special triangles to figure out the vertical portion of each section.

We can see that the first portion of the trip is 30 km straight up, so we know that 30 km will be one of the numbers we add to find the answer to the question.

The diagram shows us that the next portion of the trip is 30° off from vertical, which we know is the same as being 60° off from horizontal (see the diagram below if that doesn't make sense to you).

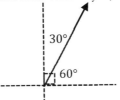

So if we drew in a vertical line at the end of the second portion of the rocket's trip, we could make a triangle, and fill in some more information:

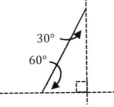

So this is a 30°-60°-90° triangle, and we know that the ratio of the hypotenuse of a 30°-60°-90° triangle to the length of the longer leg of a 30°-60°-90° triangle is $2:\sqrt{3}$. We know the length of the hypotenuse of this triangle from the given diagram, so we can set up an equation with the ratio of the hypotenuse of a 30°-60°-90° triangle to its longest side length and the ratio of the distance traveled by the rocket to the height traveled by the rocket over this section of the trip:

$$\frac{2}{\sqrt{3}} = \frac{40}{x} \qquad \text{(equation we just described above)}$$
$$2x = 40\sqrt{3} \qquad \text{(cross-multiply)}$$
$$x = 20\sqrt{3} \qquad \text{(divide both sides by 2)}$$

So the height that the rocket climbed during the second portion of the rocket's trip was $20\sqrt{3}$ km. Now let's find the third portion.

Using the same analysis from the last triangle, we can see that this portion of the trip can be seen as the hypotenuse of a 45°-45°-90° triangle. We know that the ratio of the hypotenuse of a 45°-45°-90° triangle to the length of either of its legs is $\sqrt{2}:1$. With this information, we can set up an equation with the ratio of the hypotenuse of a 45°-45°-90° triangle to the length of one of its legs and the ratio of the distance traveled by the rocket to the height traveled by the rocket over this section of the trip:

$$\frac{\sqrt{2}}{1} = \frac{100}{x}$$ (equation we just described above)

$$x\sqrt{2} = 100$$ (cross-multiply)

$$x = \frac{100}{\sqrt{2}}$$ (divide both sides by $\sqrt{2}$)

We can remove the radical expression from the denominator by multiplying our expression by $\frac{\sqrt{2}}{\sqrt{2}}$, like this:

$$\frac{100}{\sqrt{2}} \times \frac{\sqrt{2}}{\sqrt{2}} = \frac{100\sqrt{2}}{2} = 50\sqrt{2}$$

So the height that the rocket climbed during the third portion of the rocket's trip was $50\sqrt{2}$ km. We can now add these three numbers together to get the full height of the rocket in the diagram. That gives us $30 + 20\sqrt{3} + 50\sqrt{2}$, which is the same as the expression in (E). So (E) is right.

Solution 2: Test-smart: Reason that the answer must include multiple values added together, since the choices involve radical expressions and not decimals. Note that one of those values must be 30. Pick the only choice that meets this requirement.

We can see that we'll probably need to calculate the height by adding up three different numbers: the 30 km height from the first part of the launch, and whatever the vertical portions of the other two parts of the launch will be. We can see that finding the height of those vertical portions will probably involve radicals, because this looks like a question that's going to involve the Pythagorean theorem, or special triangles, or something like that. So we would expect the right answer to involve adding 30 km and 2 radical expressions, and only choice (E) has those characteristics—and even if the math in this question involved two expressions using the same radical that could be combined, (E) is still the only choice that involves any radical expression <u>and</u> 30 km. So we can be confident that (E) is right.

ANSWER CHOICE ANALYSIS

(A): This is the length of the last leg of the rocket's trip. **(B):** This is the total distance the rocket travels, but it isn't the height of the rocket at the end of the trip, because the rocket doesn't travel straight up for its whole trip. **(D):** This is the height the rocket travels in the second and third portions of its trip, but this ignores the 30 km that the rocket traveled straight up initially.

How to check? Try an alternate approach above. Make sure your answer makes sense in the scale of the diagram.

Test 3, Question 46 (Form 16MC3 if you have the 2020-2021 Red Book—see page 23 for more)

- **What's the prompt asking for?** The expected number of defective springs produced by Machine A in a given day.
- **Math concepts in the prompt:** constant rate, probability distribution, reading data from a table
- **Math concepts in the diagram:** probability distribution
- **Elements of the choices:** Each choice is a number from 0 to 2, with two digits after the decimal point.
- **Concepts in the choices:** 1, decimal points, zero
- **"Bridge" concepts:** To find the expected number of defective springs produced on any given day, multiply each possible total number of defective springs produced in any single day (in the first column) by the corresponding probability of that number of defective springs being produced in any single day (in the second column), and add up those four products. This is the same thing as finding the weighted average of the possible total numbers of defective springs produced in any single day.
- **Pre-solution patterns (see p. 149):** opposites
- **Things to look out for:** Don't make any mistakes in your reading or calculation! Don't confuse the rows of data in the chart!

Solution 1: Probability: Multiply the numbers of defective springs by their corresponding probabilities, and add up the four resulting products to find the answer.

$$0 \times 0.70 = 0$$
$$1 \times 0.20 = 0.2$$ (the products of the numbers of defective springs and their corresponding probabilities)
$$2 \times 0.05 = 0.10$$
$$3 \times 0.05 = 0.15$$

$$0 + 0.20 + 0.10 + 0.15 = 0.45$$ (add the four products from the previous step)

So the answer is (G), 0.45.

ANSWER CHOICE ANALYSIS

(F): This choice might appeal to test-takers who aren't familiar with this kind of analysis, and assume that zero must be the answer because, according to the table, the most commonly occurring outcome is a day in which zero defective springs are produced. But the prompt asked for the expected value of the number of defective springs per day, which isn't the same thing as asking for the natural number of actual defective springs that is most likely to be produced on a single day. **(J):** This is the sum of the probabilities in the table, but we need to find the result when these probabilities are multiplied by their respective outcomes, and those products are added together. **(K):** This is the average of the numbers in the left-hand column of the table, but we needed to find the weighted average of these numbers to answer the question (as discussed above), not just the normal, unweighted average.

How to check? Double-check that you used the right numbers from the figure.

▶   **Post-solution patterns (see p. 151):** easy calculation mistake; right answer to the wrong question

Test 3, Question 47 (Form 16MC3 if you have the 2020-2021 Red Book—see page 23 for more)

- **What's the prompt asking for?** The statement from the answer choices that is shown by the factored form of the given equation.
- **Math concepts in the prompt:** equations, height, time
- **Elements of the choices:** Each choice is a statement about the object.
- **Notable differences among choices:** (B) and (C) mention the maximum height of the object, while (D) and (E) mention the time when the object reaches the ground, and only (A) mentions the starting height of the object. (B) and (D) involve the number 3, while (C) and (E) involve the number 8, and only (A) involves the number 2.
- **Concepts in the choices:** maximum height, starting height
- **Things to look out for:** Don't forget to check any statement in the answer choice against the provided equation!

Solution 1: Graphing: Graph the given equation, and eliminate any answer choice that makes an untrue statement. Pick the only remaining choice. (Note that x corresponds to t and y corresponds to h for this solution.)

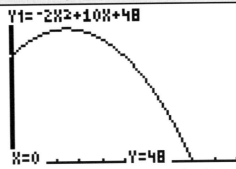

First, let's consider (A). We can see that when $x = 0$, $y = 48$. In other words, the object starts 48 units off the ground, not 2 units. So (A) is wrong. We can see that (B) and (C) are also wrong, because the graph shows that the object starts at 48 units off the ground, which is already higher than 3 units or 8 units. Now let's consider (D).

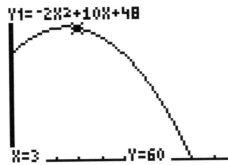

We can see that when $x = 3$, $y = 60$. So at 3 seconds, the object is still 60 feet in the air, not on the ground, as (D) says. That means (D) is wrong. Finally, let's consider (E).

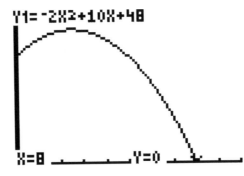

When we look at the graph, we can see that when $x = 8$, $y = 0$. That means the object is at a height of 0—in other words, it's on the ground—at 8 seconds. This matches up exactly with the statement in (E), so (E) is right.

Notice that we didn't need to worry about any "equivalent factored form" of the equation as mentioned in the prompt; we were able to eliminate every wrong answer just by figuring out which choices made untrue statements about the given equation.

Solution 2: Test-smart: Consider each answer choice, and eliminate any choice that makes an untrue statement. Pick the only remaining choice.

The point where the object "starts" must be when $t = 0$, because that's when no time has passed yet. We can see that when $t = 0$, h will be 48, because $-2(0^2) + 10(0) + 48 = 48$. So we can rule out (A). We can also rule out (B), because we just established that the object starts out with a height of 48 units, so the maximum height must be at least 48. For the same reason, we can also rule out (C).

We can test (D) by plugging in $t = 3$. If (D) is right, our h-value will be 0 (because the ground must be at a height of 0). When we plug in $t = 3$, we get $-2(3^2) + 10(3) + 48$, which is the same as $-18 + 30 + 48$, which is the same as 60. So (D) isn't true either. That leaves (E). We can test (E), as we just tested (D), by plugging in $t = 8$. That gives us $-2(8^2) + 10(8) + 48$, which is the same as $-128 + 80 + 48$, which is the same as 0. So the object has a height of 0 at 8 seconds, which means the object reaches the ground at 8 seconds. Only (E) makes a true statement about the given equation, so (E) is the right answer.

ANSWER CHOICE ANALYSIS

(A): This choice might be tempting for students who notice the 2 that appears in the given equation. **(B):** This choice might be tempting for students who try to answer this question by factoring, and misinterpret the results. **(C):** This choice might be tempting for reasons similar to those that make (B) tempting. **(D):** This choice might be tempting for reasons similar to those that make (B) and (C) tempting.

How to check? Try an alternate approach above. Make sure that your answer choice doesn't contradict the equation in the prompt.

Note Notice that we couldn't know for sure when we started eliminating untrue statements whether there would only be one choice left, or we would have to figure out some other way to pick the right answer—but we ended up being able to find the right answer using only this approach. Sometimes when you're not sure what else to do, just looking for reasons to eliminate certain answer choices can be a good start.

Test 3, Question 48 (Form 16MC3 if you have the 2020-2021 Red Book—see page 23 for more)

- **What's the prompt asking for?** The expression that is equivalent to the given expression.
- **Math concepts in the prompt:** exponents, radical expressions, variables
- **Elements of the choices:** Each choice is an exponential expression involving g and h.
- **Notable differences among choices:** (F) involves a fifth root expression, (G) and (H) involve fourth root expressions, (J) involves a square root expression, and (K) doesn't involve any radical expression.
- **Concepts in the choices:** exponents, radical expressions, variables
- **Things to look out for:** Don't forget the rules related to exponents, especially fractional exponents! Don't mistake a fifth-root expression or a fourth-root expression for a square root expression! Don't mix up g and h!

Solution 1: Backsolving: Pick arbitrary values for g and h, plug those values into the given expression, and then plug the values into each answer choice. The answer choice that matches the value of the given expression will be the right answer.

Let $g = 9$ and $h = 11$.

$$9^2\sqrt{9^5} \cdot 11^2\sqrt[4]{11^5} \approx 47{,}710{,}890.14 \qquad \text{(given expression)}$$

Now we can plug $g = 9$ and $h = 11$ into the expressions from the prompt to see which one is equal to 47,710,890.14.

$9^2 11^2 \sqrt[5]{9^2 11^2} \approx 61{,}592.023$ (plug $g = 9$ and $h = 11$ into expression from (F))

$9^3 11 \sqrt[4]{9^2 11^3} \approx 145{,}306.815$ (plug $g = 9$ and $h = 11$ into expression from (G))

$9^4 11^3 \sqrt[4]{9^2 11} \approx 47{,}710{,}890.14$ (plug $g = 9$ and $h = 11$ into expression from (H))

$9^4 11^4 \sqrt{9 \cdot 11} \approx 955{,}780{,}962.1$ (plug $g = 9$ and $h = 11$ into expression from (J))

$9^7 11^7 \approx 9.321 \times 10^{13}$ (plug $g = 9$ and $h = 11$ into expression from (K))

We can see that only (H) matched the value of the original expression, so we know that (H) is right.

Solution 2: Algebra/Abstract: Use your knowledge of exponents to determine which choice is equivalent to the given expression.

$$g^2\sqrt{g^5} \cdot h^2 \sqrt[4]{h^5} \qquad \text{(given expression)}$$

$$g^2 g^{\frac{5}{2}} \cdot h^2 h^{\frac{5}{4}}$$ (simplify)

$$g^{2+\frac{5}{2}} \cdot h^{2+\frac{5}{4}}$$ (simplify)

$$g^{\frac{9}{2}} \cdot h^{\frac{13}{4}}$$ (simplify)

A lot of test-takers won't know how to get from this step to matching this value with a value from the answer choices. One way to do that is by simplifying each answer choice into one g term raised to an exponent multiplied by one h term raised to an exponent.

When we do this, we'll find that we can actually eliminate (F), (J), and (K) right away because each of those expressions has the same exponent for each variable, while we found that each variable should have a different exponent. In other words, (F) shows each variable squared, and then the fifth root of each variable squared, (J) shows each variable raised to the fourth power, and then the square root of each variable, and (K) shows each variable raised to the seventh power. Now let's focus on the two remaining choices, (G) and (H).

$$\text{(G) } g^3 h^4 \sqrt[4]{g^2 h^3} = g^3 g^{\frac{2}{4}} \cdot (h) h^{\frac{3}{4}} = g^{\frac{7}{2}} \cdot h^{\frac{7}{4}}$$

This choice isn't equivalent to the expression we found above. Now let's check (H):

$$\text{(H) } g^4 h^3 \sqrt[4]{g^2 h} = g^4 g^{\frac{2}{4}} \cdot h^3 h^{\frac{1}{4}} = g^{\frac{9}{2}} \cdot h^{\frac{13}{4}}$$

This choice *is* equivalent to the expression we found above. After considering each choice, we know that (H) is right.

ANSWER CHOICE ANALYSIS

(K): This reflects the mistake of ignoring the fractional exponents associated with the radical expressions in the original expression.

How to check? Try an alternate approach above. Double-check to make sure your conclusions follow the rules of exponents, especially fractional exponents.

Test 3, Question 49 (Form 16MC3 if you have the 2020-2021 Red Book—see page 23 for more)

- **What's the prompt asking for?** The pair of numbers between which the value of the given logarithmic expression falls.
- **Math concepts in the prompt:** consecutive integers, logarithms
- **Elements of the choices:** Each choice is a range between two consecutive integers.
- **Notable differences among choices:** (B), (C), and (D) form a series in which the numbers on either end of the range are one more than the corresponding numbers from the previous choice.

- **Concepts in the choices:** integers, ranges
- **Pre-solution patterns (see p. 149):** be aware of series
- **Things to look out for:** Don't forget the basic definition of a logarithm! Don't make a simple calculator mistake if you choose to use a calculator in your solution!

Solution 1: Calculator: Enter the given expression in your calculator and pick the answer choice that matches the result.

When we enter this expression into a calculator, we'll get a result of 6.5, which is between 6 and 7, so the right answer is (D).

Solution 2: Abstract/Algebra: Use your understanding of logarithms to find the value of the given expression.

We know that we can read the expression $\log_5\left(5^{\frac{13}{2}}\right)$ as "to what exponent can we raise 5 to make it equal to $5^{\frac{13}{2}}$?" Of course, we would have to raise 5 to an exponent of $\frac{13}{2}$ to make it equal to $5^{\frac{13}{2}}$. So the right answer is $\frac{13}{2}$, which is equivalent to 6.5. 6.5 is between 6 and 7, so again the right answer is (D).

ANSWER CHOICE ANALYSIS

(C): This choice might attract someone who understands the logarithm involved but accidentally think that $\frac{13}{2}$ is between 5 and 6.

How to check? Try an alternate approach above.

Test 3, Question 50 (Form 16MC3 if you have the 2020-2021 Red Book—see page 23 for more)

- **What's the prompt asking for?** The percentage decrease from the regular 12-month rate that Daria will pay.
- **Math concepts in the prompt:** percentages, prices, reading data from a table, sales
- **Math concepts in the diagram:** dimensions, prices
- **Elements of the choices:** Each is a percentage between 8% and 10%, with two digits to the right of the decimal point.
- **Notable differences among choices:** (H) is 0.09 larger than (G), and (K) is 0.09 larger than (J).

- **Concepts in the choices:** percentages
- **Pre-solution patterns (see p. 149):** be aware of series
- **Things to look out for:** Don't accidentally find the percentage increase that the regular rate represents over the sale rate! Don't misread the table and calculate the discount for the wrong room! Don't forget that Daria's 12-month rate will mean she pays the $1 discounted price for 1 month, and the full price for the other 11 months, rather than paying full price for all 12 months!

Solution 1: Formal Algebra: If you remember the classic formula for percentage decrease, use it to calculate the answer. (You can translate the text in the prompt and in the diagram into mathematical expressions as part of this solution.)

First we'll find what percentage the special rate is of the normal rate, by dividing 12 months of the special rate by 12 months of the normal rate. Remember that 12 months of the special rate is equal to one month with rent of $1 and 11 months with rent at the normal rate, which the table tells us is $100 for a Size 3 unit.

$$\frac{1+11(100)}{12(100)} = 0.9175 \qquad \left(\frac{12 \; months \; at \; special \; rate}{12 \; months \; at \; regular \; rate}\right)$$
$$0.9175 \times 100\% = 91.75\% \qquad \text{(convert to percentage)}$$

The cost of renting a Size 3 unit for 12 months at the special rate is 91.75% of the cost of renting the same unit at the regular rate, so the special rate represents a 100% − 91.75% decrease, or 8.25% decrease in cost. That means (F) is right.

Solution 2: Arithmetic: Figure out how much the 12-month rental would cost at the regular rate, and then figure out how much Daria will pay for her 12-month rental with her one-month discount. Then find the decrease from the larger number to the smaller number, and divide that by the larger number to calculate the percentage decrease.

We can see from the chart that the 12-month rental at the regular rate for a Size 3 unit would be $100 × 12, or $1200. The discounted rate would be $1 + $100 × 11, or $1101. The difference between the two rentals is $1200 − $1101, or $99. We can find out what percentage $99 is of $1200 by dividing $99 by $1200 and multiplying the result by 100%:

$$\frac{\$99}{\$1200} \times 100\% = 8.25\%$$

Again, we see that the right answer is (F).

ANSWER CHOICE ANALYSIS

(G): This would be the right answer if the special rate made the first month's rent free, but the prompt says that under the special rate, the first month's rent is $1. **(H):** This is the result of dividing $101 by $1200, which could come from accidentally subtracting the first month's rent of $1 from the $1100 for the rest of the year, instead of adding that $1. **(J):** This choice could reflect accidentally comparing the difference between Daria's discounted 12-month rate and the normal 12-month rate to $1100, rather than to the normal 12-month rate of $1200—in other words, dividing 99 by 1100 and multiplying the result by 100%. **(K):** This could be the result of combining the mistakes in (G) and (J): incorrectly thinking that the first month's rent was free under the special rate, and then comparing the difference between Daria's discounted 12-month rate and the normal 12-month rate to $1100, rather than the normal 12-month rate of $1200—in other words, dividing 100 by 1100 and multiplying the result by 100%.

How to check? Since there are a lot of ways to miscount things in this question, and the answer choices only have small differences between them, it's pretty clear that the ACT is trying to get us to make a small mistake we won't catch. So make sure you triple-check your reading and your calculations.

▶ Post-solution patterns (see p. 151): easy calculation mistake

Test 3, Question 51 (Form 16MC3 if you have the 2020-2021 Red Book—see page 23 for more)

- **What's the prompt asking for?** The largest number of Size 1 units that can be formed from a Size 5 unit.
- **Math concepts in the prompt:** division
- **Math concepts in the diagram:** dimensions
- **Notable differences among choices:** (A), (B), (C), and (E) form a series in which each number is twice as much as the one before it. (D) is the only choice that's not a power of two. (A) and (C) add up to (D), while (A), (B), and (D) add up to (E).
- **Concepts in the choices:** addition, doubling, series
- **Pre-solution patterns (see p. 149):** halves and doubles
- **Things to look out for:** Don't compare units of the wrong size! Don't make any small mistakes in your reading or calculations! Be especially careful about being off by a factor of two, since the answer choices are clearly trying to set you up to do that!

Solution 1: Area: Calculate the area of a Size 1 unit and the area of a Size 5 unit. Divide the larger area by the smaller area, and pick the corresponding answer choice.

The area of a Size 5 unit is 8 × 16, and the area of a Size 1 unit is 2 × 4.

$$\frac{8 \times 16}{2 \times 4} = 16$$

So one Size 5 unit can be divided into 16 Size 1 units, which means (E) is right.

Solution 2: Diagramming: Quickly sketch a diagram of an 8 × 16 unit space, and then draw lines to subdivide it into 2 × 4 unit spaces. Count the resulting subdivisions and pick the corresponding answer.

16

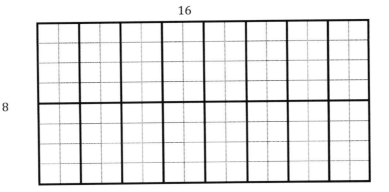

8

We can conclude from the sketch above that one Size 5 unit can be divided into 16 Size 1 units, which means (E) is right.

Solution 3: Abstract/Dimensions: Note how many times each dimension of a Size 1 unit could fit into the corresponding dimension of a Size 5 unit. Multiply these numbers together to figure out how many times a Size 1 unit could fit in a Size 5 unit.

Let's assume the Size 1 unit will have the following orientation:

2

4

And let's assume that the Size 5 unit will have the following orientation:

8

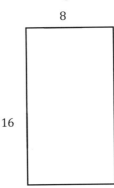

16

We can see that the 2 meter side of the Size 1 unit will fit 4 times along the 8 meter side of the Size 5 unit, and the 4 meter side of the Size 1 unit will fit 4 times along the 16 meter side of the Size 2 unit. So that's 4 Size 1 units wide by 4 Size 1 units tall, which is the same as 16 Size 1 units in a Size 5 unit. So (E) is right.

(Notice that the orientation of the units was different in this solution from the orientation of the units in the solution with the sketch, but we found the same answer anyway.)

ANSWER CHOICE ANALYSIS

(A): This could be the result of misreading the prompt and seeing how many times the Size 1 unit could fit into a Size 2 unit, rather than a Size 5 unit. **(B):** Similar to what we saw in (A), this could be the result of comparing a Size 1 unit to a Size 3 unit, instead of a Size 5 unit. **(C):** As with (A) and (B), this could be the result of comparing a Size 1 unit to a Size 4 unit, instead of a Size 5 unit.

How to check? Try an alternate approach above. Carefully consider your reading and your calculations, to make sure you haven't made a small mistake like accidentally comparing the wrong units.

▶   **Post-solution patterns (see p. 151):** easy calculation mistake; right answer to the wrong question

▌ Test 3, Question 52 (Form 16MC3 if you have the 2020-2021 Red Book—see page 23 for more)

- **What's the prompt asking for?** The choice with the algebraic expression that accurately relates the area of a unit to its size number.

- **Math concepts in the prompt:** dimensions, ratios, reading data from a table

- **Math concepts in the diagram:** dimensions

- **Elements of the choices:** Each choice is an algebraic expression involving 2, an exponent, and x.

- **Notable differences among choices:** (F), (G), and (H) all involve raising the number 2 to an exponent. (J) and (K) involve exponential expressions with x in the base rather than in the exponent. (F) and (G) both include an exponent that involves

3. (H) and (K) both involve adding 2 and x, while (J) involves adding x and 1, and the other two choices don't involve addition at all.

- **Concepts in the choices:** addition, exponents, function modeling, multiplication, variables
- **Pre-solution patterns (see p. 149):** wrong answers try to imitate right answers
- **Things to look out for:** Don't make any mistakes with respect to PEMDAS! Don't accidentally associate the wrong dimensions with the wrong size numbers! Don't make any small mistakes in your reading or calculations!

Solution 1: Concrete: Test each answer choice against the unit sizes in the table; the only choice that accurately describes the relationship between dimension and unit size will be the right answer.

Let's find the areas of the different units, so we can compare them to the values we find when we check the answer choices.

Size	Dimensions	Area
1	2×4	8
2	4×4	16
3	4×8	32
4	8×8	64
5	8×16	128

First, let's test the expression from (F).

$$2^3 \times (1) = 8 \qquad \text{(area of Size 1 unit using expression from (F))}$$
$$2^3 \times (2) = 16 \qquad \text{(area of Size 2 unit using expression from (F))}$$
$$2^3 \times (3) = 24 \qquad \text{(area of Size 3 unit using expression from (F))}$$

The expression from (F) fails for the Size 3 unit. Let's try the expression from (G).

$$2^{3(1)} = 8 \qquad \text{(area of Size 1 unit using expression from (G))}$$
$$2^{3(2)} = 64 \qquad \text{(area of Size 2 unit using expression from (G))}$$

The expression from (G) fails for the Size 2 unit. Let's try the expression from (H).

$$2^{(2+(1))} = 8 \qquad \text{(area of Size 1 unit using expression from (H))}$$
$$2^{(2+(2))} = 16 \qquad \text{(area of Size 2 unit using expression from (H))}$$
$$2^{(2+(3))} = 32 \qquad \text{(area of Size 3 unit using expression from (H))}$$
$$2^{(2+(4))} = 64 \qquad \text{(area of Size 4 unit using expression from (H))}$$
$$2^{(2+(5))} = 128 \qquad \text{(area of Size 5 unit using expression from (H))}$$

The expression from (H) gives the floor area for all 5 unit sizes, so (H) appears to be correct. Let's check the remaining expressions to make sure we haven't made a mistake.

$$2\big((1) + 1\big)^2 = 8 \qquad \text{(area of Size 1 unit using expression from (J))}$$
$$2\big((2) + 1\big)^2 = 18 \qquad \text{(area of Size 2 unit using expression from (J))}$$

The expression from (J) fails for the Size 2 unit. Finally, let's check the expression from (K).

$$\big((1) + 2\big)^2 = 9 \qquad \text{(area of Size 1 unit using expression from (K))}$$

The expression from (K) fails for the Size 1 unit. After considering each answer choice, we can be confident that (H) is right.

Solution 2: Abstract: Notice that each unit size in the table after the first one involves doubling one of the dimensions of the previous unit size, which must mean that each unit size has twice the area of the size before it. Pick the only choice that involves a doubling in area every time x increases by 1. Choice (H) involves raising 2 to an exponent that increases by 1 as the unit size increases by 1, which is the same as doubling the area as the unit size increases by 1. No other choice will result in each unit doubling the area of the next smallest unit, so (H) must be right.

ANSWER CHOICE ANALYSIS

(F): This could reflect the mistake of thinking that each unit size was an increase of 8 m² over the previous unit size, instead of being double the previous unit size. **(G):** This choice accurately reflects the area of the Size 1 unit, but not the areas of the other unit sizes. **(J):** This choice reflects the areas of unit sizes 1 and 3, but not the areas of the other unit sizes. **(K):** This choice only accurately reflects the area of the

Size 2 unit.

How to check? Try an alternate approach above. Recheck your answer choice to make sure it accurately generates the correct area for each unit size.

Test 3, Question 53 (Form 16MC3 if you have the 2020-2021 Red Book—see page 23 for more)

- **What's the prompt asking for?** The period of the function in the diagram.
- **Math concepts in the prompt:** graphing functions in the xy-coordinate plane, positive numbers, real numbers, sine, the period of a function, trig functions
- **Math concepts in the diagram:** graphing functions in the xy plane, π, sine, the period of a function, trig functions
- **Notable differences among choices:** Every choice except (E) involves π. (A), (B), (C), and (D) form a series in which each number is twice as large as the one before it.

- **Concepts in the choices:** 2, doubling, π
- **"Bridge" concepts:** We can determine the period of a trig function just by looking at its graph, without knowing or considering the underlying equation of the function.
- **Pre-solution patterns (see p. 149):** wrong answers try to imitate right answers; halves and doubles
- **Things to look out for:** Don't miscount the number of π-intervals on the x-axis! Don't forget that the period of a graph covers a single repetition of the graph! Don't misread the prompt, the diagram, or the answer choices!

Solution 1: Concrete: Remembering the definition of the term "period," look carefully at the given diagram and determine the shortest horizontal span over which the graph repeats itself. Pick the corresponding answer choice.

When we look at the graph, we can see that the graph repeats itself every π units, so the period must be π, and (B) is right.

ANSWER CHOICE ANALYSIS

(A): This may tempt test-takers who don't fully understand the concept of the period of a graph. An interval of $\frac{\pi}{2}$ on the x-axis of this graph is enough space for the graph to go from its highest point to its lowest point . . . but the period must contain the other half of this cycle. (See the note below.) **(C):** This is the period of $y = \sin x$, but that's not the graph the prompt asks about. **(D):** This choice reflects the span of the domain labeled in the diagram, from -2π to 2π, but the amount of the domain shown in the diagram isn't relevant to the function's period. **(E):** This is the function's amplitude, but the amplitude isn't relevant to the period.

How to check? Carefully reconsider the prompt and the graph, to make sure that you've correctly identified the smallest repeatable horizontal span of the graph as the period.

▶ **Post-solution patterns (see p. 151):** right answer to the wrong question

Note   Many untrained test-takers will waste time trying to figure out what the ACT is talking about when it spends a whole paragraph providing a technical, abstract definition of the term "period," since that term is one that a lot of test-takers would already know from math class. But as trained test-takers, we know that our first instinct when we encounter a strange question—on any part of the ACT—should be to stay calm and read carefully, and see what the text says. When we do that, we see two things: first, that the technical definition is really just describing the idea of a period that we've already learned in school, which is the minimum amount of horizontal separation between any two corresponding points on the repeating curve of a trig function, and, second, that the diagram itself already gives us enough information to find the period of the graph, whether we understand the technical definition of the term "period" that appears in the question or not. You probably won't see a question that specifically asks about the period of a trig function on test day, but you'll definitely see other questions that present relatively basic ideas in ways that are designed to intimidate you for no reason. When that happens, remember to stay calm and read carefully, and keep the design limitations of the test in mind!

Test 3, Question 54 (Form 16MC3 if you have the 2020-2021 Red Book—see page 23 for more)

- **What's the prompt asking for?** The component form of the vector **w**.
- **Math concepts in the prompt:** equations, vectors
- **Notable differences among choices:** (F) is the opposite of (K). (G) is the opposite of (J).

- **Elements of the choices:** Each choice is the component form of a vector.
- **Pre-solution patterns (see p. 149):** opposites
- **Things to look out for:** Don't confuse **u** and **v**! Don't make a mistake involving sign when manipulating the given equation!

Solution 1: Concrete: Use your knowledge of the component forms of vectors to find the component form of **w**.

Let's plug the component forms of **u** and **v** into the equation in the prompt and solve for **w**.

$2\mathbf{u} + (-3\mathbf{v}) + \mathbf{w} = 0$	(given equation)
$2\langle 5, 3 \rangle + (-3\langle 2, -7 \rangle) + \mathbf{w} = 0$	(plug $\mathbf{u} = \langle 5, 3 \rangle$ and $\mathbf{v} = \langle 2, -7 \rangle$ into given equation)
$\langle 10, 6 \rangle + \langle -6, 21 \rangle + \mathbf{w} = 0$	(distribute the 2 and the -3)

$$\langle 4, 27 \rangle + \boldsymbol{w} = 0 \qquad \text{(simplify)}$$
$$\boldsymbol{w} = \langle -4, -27 \rangle \qquad \text{(subtract } \langle 4, 27 \rangle \text{ from both sides)}$$

So (G) is right.

ANSWER CHOICE ANALYSIS

(F): This is equal to $-2\boldsymbol{u} - 3\boldsymbol{v}$, and could be the result of mixing up one or more negative signs when executing the solution. **(H):** This is equal to $\boldsymbol{u} - \boldsymbol{v}$. **(J):** This is the right answer multiplied by -1; this choice might be tempting for a test-taker who mixed up a negative sign at some point in the solution. **(K):** This is equal to $2\boldsymbol{u} + 3\boldsymbol{v}$, and could be the result of mixing up one or more negative signs when executing the solution.

How to check? Make sure you don't make a mistake related to sign, because the answer choices are clearly setting you up to do that!

Test 3, Question 55 (Form 16MC3 if you have the 2020-2021 Red Book—see page 23 for more)

- **What's the prompt asking for?** The number of integer values for x that would make the equation in the prompt true.
- **Math concepts in the prompt:** equations, exponents, variables
- **Notable differences among choices:** (A), (B), (C), and (D) form a series of integers from 0 to 3. (E) says there would be an infinite number of solutions.
- **Concepts in the choices:** infinity, zero
- **"Bridge" concepts:** In order to solve equations that involve exponents, it's usually preferable to express the exponent terms with a common base.
- **Pre-solution patterns (see p. 149):** be aware of series
- **Things to look out for:** Don't forget that the original equation features exponent expressions with different bases! Don't confuse the two different exponent expressions! Don't forget that the question is asking you for the number of valid solutions, not the valid solutions themselves!

Solution 1: Concrete: Note that the numbers involved in the question are relatively small, which suggests that it might be possible to test individual integer values of x in the original equation to see if you can observe trends in the values of the two sides of the equation as different values of x are tested.

$3^{0+1} = 3^1 = 3$	$9^{0-2} = 9^{-2} = \frac{1}{81}$	(value when $x = 0$)
$3^{1+1} = 3^2 = 9$	$9^{1-2} = 9^{-1} = \frac{1}{9}$	(value when $x = 1$)
$3^{2+1} = 3^3 = 27$	$9^{2-2} = 9^0 = 1$	(value when $x = 2$)
$3^{3+1} = 3^4 = 81$	$9^{3-2} = 9^1 = 9$	(value when $x = 3$)
$3^{4+1} = 3^5 = 243$	$9^{4-2} = 9^2 = 81$	(value when $x = 4$)
$3^{5+1} = 3^6 = 729$	$9^{5-2} = 9^3 = 729$	(value when $x = 5$)
$3^{6+1} = 3^7 = 2187$	$9^{6-2} = 9^4 = 6561$	(value when $x = 6$)
$3^{7+1} = 3^8 = 6561$	$9^{7-2} = 9^5 = 59049$	(value when $x = 7$)

When we test these values, we can see that the two expressions are only equivalent one time (when $x = 5$). We can also see that, as x decreases from $x = 5$, the value of the first expression gets proportionally greater and greater compared to the value of the second expression: at $x = 4$ the first expression is 3 times the second expression, at $x = 3$ the first expression is 9 times the second expression, at $x = 2$ the first expression is 27 times the second expression, at $x = 1$ the first expression is 81 times the second expression, and so on. As x increases from $x = 5$, the second expression starts to get extremely large in proportion to the first expression: at $x = 6$ the second expression is 3 times the first expression, at $x = 7$ the second expression is 9 times the first expression, and we can see that this trend will continue. So the two expressions are only equivalent for one x-value, which means (B) is right.

Solution 2: Algebra: Try to solve the original equation for x. If you find solutions, count them and pick the corresponding choice.

$$3^{x+1} = 9^{x-2} \qquad \text{(given equation)}$$
$$3^{x+1} = (3^2)^{x-2} \qquad \text{(rewrite 9 as } 3^2)$$
$$3^{x+1} = 3^{2x-4} \qquad \text{(simplify)}$$
$$x + 1 = 2x - 4 \qquad \text{(set exponents equal to one another)}$$
$$1 = x - 4 \qquad \text{(subtract } x \text{ from both sides)}$$
$$5 = x \qquad \text{(add 4 to both sides)}$$

The equation is only true when $x = 5$, so (B) is correct.

ANSWER CHOICE ANALYSIS

(A): This could reflect the mistake of attempting Solution 2 above and forgetting to rewrite the expressions in the equation with a common base, and simply trying to solve the equation $x + 1 = x - 2$, which has no solution. **(E):** This choice could reflect the mistaken conclusion that there must be an infinite number of solutions to the equation simply because there are an infinite number of possible values for the individual expressions 3^{x+1} and 9^{x-2}. But the fact that there are an infinite number of possible values for 3^{x+1} doesn't guarantee that there are an infinite number of values of x that make 3^{x+1} and 9^{x-2} equal to each other, which is what the equation in the prompt requires. As we saw in the solutions above, only one value of x makes the equation true.

How to check? Reconfirm that $x = 5$ makes the equation true, and satisfy yourself that it's the only possible value by considering the points raised above.

▶ **Post-solution patterns (see p. 151):** right approach, wrong step

Test 3, Question 56 (Form 16MC3 if you have the 2020-2021 Red Book—see page 23 for more)

- **What's the prompt asking for?** The time, t, when the triangle in the prompt will have $\frac{1}{2}$ of its original area.
- **Math concepts in the prompt:** area, functions, length, line segments, sine, time, triangles
- **Math concepts in the diagram:** length, triangles
- **Notable differences among choices:** Every choice except (F) is a fraction. (G) and (J) have a denominator of 8, while (H) and

(K) have a denominator of 4. (G) and (H) have a numerator of 15, while (J) and (K) have a numerator of 45.

- **Concepts in the choices:** doubling, fractions, tripling
- **Pre-solution patterns (see p. 149):** wrong answers try to imitate right answers; halves and doubles
- **Things to look out for:** Don't divide by 2 any more or less than is appropriate!

Solution 1: Concrete: Pick a value for θ, and use the provided formula to find the area of the triangle. Then find the length of $\overline{BC}$ when the area of the triangle is half the initial area. Finally, find out how many seconds must pass for the length of $\overline{BC}$ to shrink to the length you found.

Let $\theta = 100°$. (Note that we can just pick a value for θ here because the prompt doesn't provide a value, and we're picking our own value as we would in any other solution where we can choose our own values to test a concrete version of an abstract idea from a prompt.)

$$\frac{1}{2} ab \cdot \sin x = area \qquad \text{(provided formula for area of the triangle)}$$

$$\frac{1}{2}(15)(20) \cdot \sin(100°) \approx 147.721 \qquad \text{(area of original triangle when } a = 15, b = 20, \text{ and } \theta = 100°)$$

Note that a corresponds to the length of $\overline{BC}$. Now we can solve for the length of $\overline{BC}$ when the area of the triangle is $\frac{147.721}{2}$:

$$\frac{1}{2}(a)(20) \cdot \sin(100°) \approx \frac{147.721}{2} \qquad \text{(set area formula equal to } \frac{147.721}{2} \text{ and remove length of } \overline{BC})$$

$$(a)(20) \cdot \sin(100°) \approx 147.721 \qquad \text{(multiply both sides by 2)}$$

$$a \approx \frac{147.721}{(20)\cdot\sin(100°)} \qquad \text{(divide both sides by } (20) \cdot \sin(100°))$$

$$a = 7.5 \qquad \text{(solve)}$$

So the area of the triangle will be half its original area when the length of $\overline{BC}$ is 7.5. But that isn't what the prompt asks for! We need to find the *time* that must pass before the triangle's area will be half the area of the original triangle. Now that we know $\overline{BC}$ has to be 7.5 inches long for that to be the case, we can find the number of seconds required for the length of $\overline{BC}$ to be 7.5.

$$7.5 = 15 - 2t \qquad \text{(set the equation for the length of } \overline{BC} \text{ equal to 7.5)}$$

$$-7.5 = -2t \qquad \text{(subtract 15 from both sides)}$$

$$3.75 = t \qquad \text{(divide both sides by } -2)$$

3.75 is equal to $\frac{15}{4}$, so (H) is correct.

Solution 2: Test-smart: Realize that the area of the triangle will decrease by half when one of the side lengths decreases by half, then find the amount of time necessary for $\overline{BC}$ to shrink to 7.5 inches.

The provided formula for the area of this triangle is $\frac{1}{2} ab \cdot \sin x$, and we are told that a and b are the lengths of the sides of the triangle that form the angle with measure x. When we look at this formula, we can see that the value for the area will decrease by half if the length of either leg decreases by half. For example, if b were replaced with $\frac{b}{2}$, the area of the triangle would be cut in half. So the area of the triangle in question will be half the original area when $\overline{BC}$ is half of its original length, or $\frac{15}{2}$, or 7.5. We can find the number of seconds it will take for the length of $\overline{BC}$ to be 7.5 by setting the equation for the length of $\overline{BC}$ equal to 7.5, as we did in the earlier solution, or we can look at that equation and realize that the length decreases by 2 inches every second, and it will decrease by 7.5 inches in $\frac{7.5}{2}$ seconds, which is the same as $\frac{15}{4}$ seconds. So (H) is right.

ANSWER CHOICE ANALYSIS

(F): This choice could be the result of trying a more formal solution and accidentally finding the amount of time it takes for the triangle to have the same area as the original triangle—which would be zero seconds, because the original triangle already has the same area as the original triangle. **(G):** This is half of the right answer, and could be the result of an error when solving for t in the function $f(t) = 15 - 2t$, or of accidentally multiplying by $\frac{1}{2}$ one too many times when plugging values into the given equation for the area of a triangle. Choices (J) or (K) could be the result of an algebra mistake in a more formal solution.

How to check? Try an alternate approach above.

Test 3, Question 57 (Form 16MC3 if you have the 2020-2021 Red Book—see page 23 for more)

- **What's the prompt asking for?** The number of permutations of the letters in PEOPLE.
- **Math concepts in the prompt:** permutations
- **Elements of the choices:** Each choice is an expression involving a factorial.
- **Notable differences among choices:** (C), (D), and (E) all involve fractions. (B) is the only choice that doesn't involve 6. (D) is half of (A), and (E) is half of (D).
- **Concepts in the choices:** factorials, fractions
- **Pre-solution patterns (see p. 149):** halves and doubles
- **Things to look out for:** Don't forget to account for the two Ps and the two Es in PEOPLE!

Solution 1: Abstract: Use your understanding of permutations to reason through the solution to this problem.

We know that the answer to a question like this would normally be 6!, which is the same as $6 \times 5 \times 4 \times 3 \times 2 \times 1$, because we would multiply together the number of possibilities at each position: 6 possible letters in the first position times 5 possible letters in the second position times 4 possible letters in the third position, and so on. But in this case, the word includes two sets of two letters that are the same: there are two Ps and two Es. How do we account for that?

Let's think about the Ps first. Not accounting for the Ps when we did the normal permutation multiplication above means that there is basically a whole extra set of possibilities that are redundant. In other words, for every permutation of letters—like PPEOLE, for example—there is a duplicate permutation where the Ps are switched that looks identical—a second PPEOLE. In these two examples the Ps are switched, but since the Ps are identical, the actual permutation is the same. We don't want to count any permutation more than once, so we need to get rid of this set of duplicates in our calculation. To get rid of this set of duplicates, we can divide the result of our multiplication by 2. That way we're accounting for the fact that in our original calculation, every permutation that contains two Ps got counted twice—and since every permutation contains two Ps, that means all the permutations got counted twice.

So we divided by 2 to account for the two Ps. The number of permutations we're left with after correcting for the two Ps still contains duplicates for every possible position of the two Es: for example, in our current calculation, LEEPOP and LEEPOP would be counted as two different permutations because the Es are switched—but again, since the Es are identical, this is really the same permutation, and should only be counted once. So, to account for this set of duplicate permutations, we divide by 2 a second time.

Those were the only two letters that appeared twice, so we've now accounted for everything we need to account for in this solution. Now we just need to find the answer choice that is equal to the calculation we just figured out. Choice (E) is $\frac{6!}{(2!)(2!)}$, which is the same as $\frac{6 \times 5 \times 4 \times 3 \times 2 \times 1}{(2 \times 1)(2 \times 1)}$, which is the same as $\frac{6 \times 5 \times 4 \times 3 \times 2 \times 1}{(2)(2)}$. So (E) is the right answer.

ANSWER CHOICE ANALYSIS

(A): This reflects the mistake of failing to account for the fact that there are two Ps and two Es, which means there aren't 6 unique letters, as this answer would require. **(B):** This choice is the number of unique letters in PEOPLE multiplied by the factorial of the number of unique letters in PEOPLE, but it isn't the answer to the question in the prompt. **(C):** This choice is the factorial of the number of *total* letters in PEOPLE divided by the factorial of the number of *unique* letters in PEOPLE, but it isn't the answer to the question in the prompt. **(D):** This choice reflects the mistake of accounting for either the two Ps or the two Es, but not both.

How to check? Make sure you didn't divide by 2 too many or too few times; the answer choices are clearly setting you up to do that.

Test 3, Question 58 (Form 16MC3 if you have the 2020-2021 Red Book—see page 23 for more)

- **What's the prompt asking for?** The choice that's equivalent to the binomial in the prompt.
- **Math concepts in the prompt:** addition, binomials, equivalent expressions, square numbers
- **Notable differences among choices:** (G), (H), and (K) all involve i. (F), (G), and (H) all involve squaring a binomial, while (J) and (K) involve the factoring for a difference of squares.
- **Concepts in the choices:** addition, binomials, difference of squares, FOIL, i, square roots, squaring, subtraction
- **Pre-solution patterns (see p. 149):** wrong answers try to imitate right answers; opposites

- **Things to look out for:** Don't misread the prompt or the answer choices, especially when it comes to negative numbers, positive numbers, and i!

Solution 1: Algebra/Backsolve: Use your knowledge of the rules for multiplying binomials to multiply out the expressions in each answer choice. Then pick the choice that results in a product that matches the expression in the prompt.

$$(7x + 9)(7x + 9) \qquad \text{(expression from (F))}$$
$$49x^2 + 63x + 63x + 81 \qquad \text{(FOIL)}$$
$$49x^2 + 126x + 81 \qquad \text{(simplify)}$$

The expression in (F) isn't equal to the expression from the prompt. Let's take a look at the next choice.

$$(7x + 9i)(7x + 9i) \qquad \text{(expression from (G))}$$
$$49x^2 + 63ix + 63ix + 81i^2 \qquad \text{(FOIL)}$$
$$49x^2 + 126ix + 81i^2 \qquad \text{(simplify)}$$
$$49x^2 + 126ix - 81 \qquad \text{(substitute } i^2 = -1)$$

The expression in (G) isn't equal to the expression from the prompt. Let's take a look at the next choice.

$$(7x - 9i)(7x - 9i) \qquad \text{(expression from (H))}$$
$$49x^2 - 63ix - 63ix + 81i^2 \qquad \text{(FOIL)}$$
$$49x^2 - 126ix + 81i^2 \qquad \text{(simplify)}$$
$$49x^2 - 126ix - 81 \qquad \text{(substitute } i^2 = -1)$$

The expression in (H) isn't equal to the expression from the prompt. Let's take a look at the next choice.

$$(7x - 9)(7x + 9) \qquad \text{(expression from (J))}$$
$$49x^2 + 63x - 63x - 81 \qquad \text{(FOIL)}$$
$$49x^2 - 81 \qquad \text{(simplify)}$$

The expression in (J) isn't equal to the expression from the prompt. Let's take a look at the last choice.

$$(7x - 9i)(7x + 9i) \qquad \text{(expression from (K))}$$
$$49x^2 + 63ix - 63ix - 81i^2 \qquad \text{(FOIL)}$$
$$49x^2 - 81i^2 \qquad \text{(simplify)}$$
$$49x^2 + 81 \qquad \text{(substitute } i^2 = -1)$$

The expression in (K) is equal to the expression from the prompt. After considering each choice, we see that (K) is right.

Solution 2: Algebra/Abstract: Consider the attributes of each answer choice and pick the only choice that could possibly generate the expression in the prompt.

The prompt asks which expression is equivalent to the binomial $49x^2 + 81$. We know that when we square a binomial, we'll end up with a trinomial, so (F), (G), and (H) must all be wrong, because each of those involves squaring a binomial.

When we consider (J), we can see that this expression will be a binomial, like the expression in the prompt, because the outer and inner calculations ($63x$ and $-63x$) will cancel out. But the final term in the resulting binomial will be the result of multiplying -9 and 9, which is -81. The final term in the binomial from the prompt is positive 81, so (J) looks like a wrong answer choice.

We can see that (K) will be a binomial, like (J). Also, the final term in the binomial resulting from (K) will be the result of multiplying $-9i$ and $9i$, which will be $-81i^2$, or $-81(-1)$, or 81. (K) is the only choice that will produce a binomial that ends with a positive 81, so (K) must be right.

ANSWER CHOICE ANALYSIS

(F): This choice could reflect the mistake of forgetting the middle term that results from squaring a binomial—in other words, it reflects the mistake of assuming we can just square $7x$ and square 9 and then add the results to get $49x^2 + 81$, without having to do the normal FOIL process. **(G):** This choice reflects the mistake from (F), and adds the mistake of forgetting that the square of i is -1, so squaring $9i$ will result in -81, not 81, as the prompt requires. **(H):** This choice also includes the mistake from (F) of forgetting FOIL and just trying to square each term individually, but mistakenly tries to correct for the mistake involving i that we saw in (G) by switching the sign of $9i$. **(J):** This choice could reflect a misreading of the prompt or a mistake in FOILing the provided expression: it would result in the expression $49x^2 - 81$, not $49x^2 + 81$, as the prompt requires.

How to check? Try an alternate approach above. Be especially careful about issues related to sign and i, because the question is clearly trying to get you to make mistakes with respect to those ideas.

▶ **Post-solution patterns (see p. 151):** most like the other choices

---

- **What's the prompt asking for?** The absolute value of the largest residual, as defined in the prompt.
- **Math concepts in the prompt:** data, lines of best fit, xy-coordinate plane
- **Math concepts in the diagram:** data, graphs of equations, lines of best fit, xy-coordinate plane
- **Elements of the choices:** Each choice is a number below 50 with a single digit after the decimal.
- **Notable differences among choices:** Every choice but (A) and (B) has a zero in the tenths place.
- **Concepts in the choices:** decimal numbers, integers
- **Things to look out for:** Don't be intimidated by the academic-sounding text in the prompt!

Solution 1: Algebra/Concrete: Carefully read the information in the prompt, and then calculate the absolute value of the residual for each of the 4 points in the diagram. Pick the answer choice that corresponds to the largest absolute value you find.

This prompt is intentionally written in a way that makes the question sound more complicated and intimidating than it really is. As always, if we read carefully, we can figure out what's going on in the question, and how to find the right answer.

The second sentence tells us that the "residual" can be found by subtracting two different y-values. The first value, y_i, "is the observed y-value corresponding to the input x_i." In the context of data and lines of best fit, we know that an observed value is just an actual data point, as opposed to a line of best fit. (Remember that a line of best fit represents a *trend* in data, and not actual data.) So the "observed value" y_i is just the y value for the actual data points on the graph, whose coordinates are (x_i, y_i). Also, the subscript i for $i = 1, 2, 3, 4$ just refers to the 4 different coordinate pairs on the graph $((x_1, y_1), (x_2, y_2)$, and so on).

The second y-value in the calculation for the residual is given as $y(x_i)$. Toward the end of the prompt, we see that $(x_i, y(x_i))$ is a point on the line of best fit. So $y(x_i)$ just refers to the y-value on the line of best fit that corresponds to x_i.

So the information in this unnecessarily complicated prompt basically boils down to the idea that there are 4 data points on a graph, and there's also a line of best fit on the graph, and that for each x-value in the 4 data points, there is the corresponding y-value in that data point, and also a corresponding y-value on the line of best fit. When we subtract the y-value on the line of best fit from the y-value in the actual data point for a given x-value, we get something the prompts calls a "residual," and we need to find the residual that has the largest absolute value—in other words, the biggest difference between the actual y-value and the y-value on the line of best fit for any given x value.

So let's find the absolute values of the residuals for each labeled point, working from left to right. Notice that the graph contains the equation for the line of best fit, $y = 1.1x + 93$.

The first point on the left is $(27, 120)$. We can plug $x = 27$ into the given equation for the line of best fit to find the $y(x_i)$ value for this data point.

$y = 1.1x + 93$ (provided equation for line of best fit)

$y = 1.1(27) + 93$ (plug in $x = 27$ from the first point)

$y = 122.7$ (simplify)

Now we can subtract this value from the actual y-value in the data point to find the residual:

$120 - 122.7 = -2.7$ (actual y-value from the data minus the y-value on the line of best fit)

Finally, we can take the absolute value of the result:

$|-2.7| = 2.7$ (absolute value of the residual we just found)

So the absolute value of the residual for the first point from the left is 2.7. Let's repeat this process using the remaining points:

$|135 - (1.1(32) + 93)| = 6.8$ (absolute value of the residual of the second point)

$|130 - (1.1(37) + 93)| = 3.7$ (absolute value of the residual of the third point)

$|140 - (1.1(42) + 93)| = 0.8$ (absolute value of the residual of the fourth point)

After we find the absolute value of the residual of all four points, we can see that the largest value is 6.8, so (B) is right.

Solution 2: Test-smart: Realize that the residual described in the prompt must be the vertical distance from the labeled points on the graph to the line of best fit. Notice that the second data point from the left has the largest vertical separation from the line of best fit, so it must have the largest residual as defined in the prompt. Calculate the absolute value of that residual as described in the previous solution, and then pick the right answer, (B).

ANSWER CHOICE ANALYSIS

(A): If an untrained test-taker correctly used the coordinates $(32, 135)$ to calculate the largest residual, but used $y = 1.1(32 + 93)$ instead of $y = 1.1(32) + 93$ in that calculation, this choice would be the resulting residual. **(C):** This is the difference between the largest and smallest x-values in the 4 provided data points. **(D):** This is the difference between the largest and smallest y-values in the 4 provided data points. **(E):** This is the largest x-value in the provided data points.

How to check? Re-read the prompt to make sure you understand the meaning of "residual" in context, and take a second look at the graph to make sure your conclusion makes sense, given the points and line on the graph.

Test 3, Question 60 (Form 16MC3 if you have the 2020-2021 Red Book—see page 23 for more)

- **What's the prompt asking for?** The approximate probability that the machine will make at least one error in a given day, according to the table.
- **Math concepts in the prompt:** inequalities, probability
- **Math concepts in the diagram:** probability, reading a table
- **Elements of the choices:** Each choice is a four-digit decimal expression between 0 and 1.
- **Notable differences among choices:** (F) is the only choice with a number that appears in the table. (F) and (J) are nearly complements of one another, but not exactly. (F) is the only number that's below 0.5.
- **Concepts in the choices:** decimal numbers, probability
- **Pre-solution patterns (see p. 149):** opposites
- **Things to look out for:** Don't accidentally find the probability that the machine will make exactly one error! Don't accidentally find the probability that the machine will make at most one error! Don't accidentally find the complement of the right answer! Don't overlook the fact that the probability values in the table don't add up to 1!

Solution 1: Probability: Remember that the probability of making at least 1 error is the complement of the probability of making zero errors, by definition. Pick the answer choice that reflects the complement of the probability of making zero errors—or, to put it another way, the probability that the machine will NOT make zero errors.

The table tells us that the probability that the machine will make 0 errors is 0.0823. The probability that the machine will make at least 1 error is the same as the probability that it won't make 0 errors, so that probability must be $1 - 0.0823$, or 0.9177. That means (K) is right.

ANSWER CHOICE ANALYSIS

(F): This is the probability of making exactly 1 error, so it will attract a lot of untrained test-takers who don't read the question carefully enough. **(G):** This choice combines the mistake in (J) with the mistake of forgetting that you would still need to add the likelihood of making exactly 1 error, even if the approach in (J) were valid, which it isn't. In other words, (G) reflects the decision to try to answer the question by adding the probabilities of 2, 3, or 4 errors. **(H):** This is the probability of making at least 2 errors, but the prompt asked for the probability of making at least 1 error. **(J):** This is the result of adding the probabilities of making 1, 2, 3, or 4 errors, which reflects the incorrect assumption that every possible number of errors is shown on the chart. But, as we can see, the probability values in the chart don't add up to 1, which means that some possible numbers of errors have been left out of the chart (such as the probability of making 5, 6, 7, or more errors), so we can't just add the probabilities that are in the chart to answer the question in the prompt.

How to check? Carefully reread the question and reconsider your assumptions and your calculations.

▶ **Post-solution patterns (see p. 151):** right answer to the wrong question

Part 8: Science Test Training and Walkthroughs

In Part 8, we'll talk about how to apply the careful reading we already used against the Reading and Math sections to the ACT Science section—along with a little bit of math and even less actual science. You'll learn that for the most part, ACT Science is a lot like ACT Reading with charts and graphs thrown in.

Among other things, you'll learn the following:

- the main reason that people struggle with ACT Science
- what to do when you encounter unfamiliar scientific terms on test day
- the limited role that actual scientific knowledge plays on the ACT Science section
- the simple math ideas that can appear in the ACT Science section
- what you need to know about chemical equations
- three options for reading passages on the ACT Science section, and how to pick the best one for you
- the 5 different ACT Science question types, and how to deal with each one
- why you shouldn't be intimidated by exotic scientific vocabulary
- how to approach the "Yes yes no no" answer-choice pattern
- how to apply these concepts to every Science question from three official ACT practice tests
- and more . . .

ACT Science

Science is the belief in the ignorance of experts.
Richard Feynman

Overview and Important Reminders for ACT Science

A lot of people worry about the ACT Science section. They think it makes the ACT more like an advanced high school test than like a regular standardized test, because they think it requires a wide range of subject-matter knowledge.

The reality, of course, is very different. Just as you need relatively basic reading and math skills to beat the ACT Reading and ACT Math sections, you only need basic scientific knowledge for the ACT Science section—and even that basic level of knowledge only comes into play on a minority of questions on any given ACT. All of the other questions on the section require only careful reading of text, charts, graphs, and diagrams, with a little bit of simple math occasionally thrown in.

In other words, the majority of ACT Science questions require no scientific knowledge at all, even though they sometimes talk about obscure areas of science; they're just reading comprehension questions that involve charts, graphs, and diagrams.

If you think about it, it would be difficult to make a meaningful standardized science test that used any challenging scientific subject matter, because students all across the country take different science classes. So ACT Science can only test very basic scientific skills or knowledge—stuff that any high school student could reasonably be expected to know, regardless of which specific types of science classes that student had taken. That's the only way the ACT can ensure that most test-takers have the potential to score extremely well on the section. (This is the same issue we identified when we discussed the design of the ACT Math section.)

The Big Secret of ACT Science

For the majority of the questions, all the information you need to answer correctly and confidently will be right there on the page, just like on the Reading section. You'll see that the ACT tries to mix in as much scientific terminology as it can, often from sciences most students would never study in high school, in order to make you panic because you're unfamiliar with the material. But you never actually have to know any of those terms; you only need to be able to match them up with phrases in a related paragraph, chart, or diagram.

There's even more to it than that, though—being scientifically knowledgeable can actually be harmful to your score on the ACT Science section in some instances, if you don't know what the ACT Science section actually rewards.

Why is that?

People who get ready for ACT Science by studying actual science might try to apply some scientific knowledge or bias on questions where it seems relevant, instead of just realizing that the information they need to answer the question is nearly always right there on the page, staring them in the face. Then they run the risk of misremembering or misapplying what they think they know, instead of simply reading the right answer off the page.

So please, by all means, avoid studying actual science in preparation for the ACT Science section! Instead, you should learn the rules for the section and the test-taking techniques in this Black Book, see those ideas in action in the question walkthroughs, and then practice them against real ACT Science questions from the Red Book, just as you would with any other section of the test.

Why Some People Struggle with ACT Science

At this point, you might be wondering why so many people struggle with the ACT Science section, if it just requires us to read carefully and find information in charts and diagrams.

Here's the answer: people struggle because they're not used to seeing unfamiliar material on tests.

In school, a test covers the material you've already been studying for weeks. On the ACT, you'll be asked questions about all kinds of scientific areas you've never studied before, and maybe never even heard of—astronomy, nuclear chemistry, ecology, meteorology, geology, and who-knows-how-many-other ologies.

The goal of all of this is to make you think, "Oh no! I've never studied this stuff before. I bet every other kid in this room has done this experiment, or built this model, and I'm the only one who's sitting here, totally lost, feeling like an idiot. I'll never get into college or find a meaningful relationship . . .," at which point you break into tears and forget all about filling in bubbles. Or at least I imagine that's the ACT's dream scenario. The test's designers wants you to panic, and not realize that no high school student on Earth has previous experience with all the concepts (or even most of the concepts) in an ACT Science section.

For a quick example of this, just look at the beginning of the very first paragraph of the first Science passage of practice test 1 in the Red Book, which is test 2 in the 2020-2021 Red Book (remember that the first practice test in the Red Book is usually found about 50 pages into the Red Book, separate from the other practice tests near the end of the book!):

> In a study of fur pigmentation in deer mice, *Peromyscus polionotus*, scientists compared the brightness of the fur of mice from populations located different distances directly inland from a coastal site.

How many high school students (or college students, for that matter) have ever heard of *Peromyscus polionotus,* or studied how bright its fur is near the coast? Almost none. But it doesn't matter, because the questions in this passage don't require you to know anything about *Peromyscus polionotus* ahead of time; the questions simply reward you for reading information right out of the passage. (My walkthroughs of the questions on that passage start on page 348 of this Black Book and end on page 351.)

On test day, you'll see much stranger things than the phrase *Peromyscus polionotus*, so let's talk about how to deal with those kinds of things.

Dealing with strange terms and units

You must remember that any exotic term or unit that you see on the ACT Science section will fall into one of three groups:

1. It will be explained in the text.

2. It won't be explained, and it won't be relevant to answering any of the questions—in other words, you won't have to understand the concept in order to answer a question correctly.

3. It won't be explained, but you'll be able to match a concept in a question or answer choice with the same concept somewhere in the passage, like on a chart or a graph.

The first two situations are probably clear enough, but let's elaborate on the third one for a moment—the idea that a concept might not really be explained, but that you can still work around it by matching up a concept in a question with the same concept in a chart or something.

Imagine we see this question on the ACT:

"According to Table 1, which experimental group had the most phosportence?"

(Of course, that's not a real ACT question. The people who write the ACT wouldn't know phosportence if it kicked them in the shins.)

We don't know what phosportence is. But then we notice that Figure 1 has this information:

Figure 1: Observed Phosportence by Group

Group A	14pkl
Group B	7pkl
Group C	23pkl
Group D	29pkl

The answer to the made-up question would be Group D, because the table shows that Group D has a phosportence value of 29pkl, which is more than any other group.

So the question is actually very straightforward if we just ignore the fact that we don't know what phosportence is, or what the pkl unit is. Even though you've never heard "phosportence" before in your life, and even though you'll probably never hear it again, the answer is completely clear, based on the information in front of you.

On the Science section of the ACT, you'll definitely have to deal with concepts you've never heard of before. Expect it. Welcome it. The important thing isn't to know a lot of science in advance; the important thing is just to get used to reading carefully and finding the relevant parts of texts, charts, graphs, and figures. In the next pages, we'll learn more about how to do that, and then we'll see examples of it in action when we do our walkthroughs starting on page 345 of this Black Book.

"Science" on the ACT Science Section: What You Need to Know, and What You Don't

As we've mentioned, the majority of ACT Science questions will be based completely on information that the test provides to you, and you won't need to have any outside knowledge in order to answer these questions with total certainty. At the same time, you will need a little bit of outside knowledge if your goal is to answer every ACT Science question with total certainty. But we don't want you to waste your ACT prep time on learning more science than you actually need for the test, which is a common mistake among untrained test-takers. In this section, we'll explain how to identify questions that require a little outside knowledge, and how to react to those questions when you find them.

(It's very important to note that we're NOT saying you shouldn't learn actual, "real-world" science in general, just for the pure love of science and the natural universe! We're only saying that our goal is to get you ready for the ACT Science section as efficiently as possible, and you just don't need to know much about real-world science in order to do well on this part of the test.)

Basic Science Facts

A few times per Science section, you'll see a question that requires you to use real scientific knowledge.

You'll typically (but not always) be able to spot these questions because they'll involve terms that don't appear anywhere else in the passage.

When you do see a question like this, it will depend on very basic science—the kind of thing that almost any high school student would have a good chance of knowing after years of basic science education. (Remember that a standardized test like the ACT is only useful if it tests skills that almost all test-takers could be expected to have. That means any outside scientific knowledge required by the test can't be too exotic.)

As with most other stuff on the ACT Science section, the ACT will often try to make these questions appear more advanced and challenging than they actually are, so you'll need to be prepared for that.

This is another situation that might be best explained with an example from a real test question, so let's look at question 35 from the Science section of practice test 3 in your copy of *The Official ACT Prep Guide* (form 16MC3 online if you have the 2020-2021 Red Book). The prompt states that, in osmosis, water moves through a semi-permeable barrier. It then asks which answer choice contains the name of the structure involved in osmosis.

When we look back at the passage, we see that the only mention of osmosis comes in the first bullet-point, which describes

> a net movement of H_2O between the cytoplasm of the plants' cells and the environment via osmosis

The answer choices, as we might expect, are scientific-sounding and intimidating, just as we know the ACT wants them to be: "Chromosomes," "Nuclear envelope," "Cell membrane," and "Rough endoplasmic reticulum."

At this point, most untrained test-takers would be wondering what a rough endoplasmic reticulum is, or wondering if everyone else in the testing room already knew what osmosis was when they read the question. That's exactly what the ACT wants us to do, so we won't notice how simple the question actually is.

Let's look at it again.

What does the passage describe? As we just saw, it describes water moving "between the . . . plants' cells and the environment via osmosis."

So we're told that osmosis involves moving water between the cells and the environment.

If we think about it, that means the water must be moving between the *inside* of the cells and the *outside* of the cells, because "the environment" of the cells must, by definition, be an area outside of the cells, surrounding the cells.

If you remember anything about cells, you probably remember that a cell, by definition, is enclosed in some sort of membrane, which is a structure that selectively lets some stuff through and keeps other stuff out.

There's no way that water can pass between the inside of a cell and the cell's environment without going through that membrane, so the answer must be (C).

Even though that question might have seemed intimidating, it actually came down to some relatively basic science. We had to know that the phrase "the environment" described something outside of a cell, and we had to know that a cell membrane is the barrier between the inside of a cell and the outside of a cell. That's all.

We never needed to know what the term "osmosis" meant, because it was described in the passage for us. We never needed to know what a rough endoplasmic reticulum was, because another answer choice ended up being right.

It was just a matter of cutting through the unnecessary information in the question to see the relatively simple concept the test was actually asking about.

". . . but what if I didn't know that?!"

Don't worry if you didn't know what a cell membrane was, and you don't think you could have answered that example question correctly. From an ACT standpoint, there's no point in memorizing that osmosis involves fluid passing through a cell membrane, because you almost certainly won't see that fact tested again on test day. Instead, you'll see some other relatively basic fact tested in some other strange way on test day. There's no way to know in advance which basic facts will be tested, so there's no efficient way to memorize scientific facts in advance. Instead, you should focus your energies on the following goals, all of which will be discussed throughout our ACT Science training:

- Correctly answering every ACT Science question that involves the following kinds of concepts:
    - information stated directly on the page (this will account for the large majority of questions on test day)
    - trends in provided data (this will account for a few questions on test day—see page 333 of this Black Book for more)
    - provided chemical equations (one or two questions on test day, usually—see page 334 of this Black Book for more)
    - basic experimental design (one or two questions on test day, usually—see page 336 of this Black Book for more)
- Learning to identify questions that require basic scientific knowledge and answer them to the best of your ability as quickly as you can, so you can invest as much time as possible in the rest of the section

How you'll need to think about this on test day

If you see a question on test day that uses terms you can't find in the provided passage, then you should consider the possibility that the question relies on basic scientific knowledge. You should expect to see a handful of these questions on any given test.

An ACT Science question that really depends on outside knowledge will involve the kind of thing you might expect the average high school student to know. For example, the question we discussed above was ultimately about the idea that a cell membrane is the structure that separates the cell from its environment, which is something that most people who've had a biology class would know on some level. It's important to distinguish between questions like this, which really do require basic outside knowledge, and questions about more advanced topics whose answers must be spelled out on the page somewhere. If a question really does focus on something very exotic and uncommon, like the number of weeks of average gestation for a particular kind of squirrel or the wavelength of a particular kind of radiation in a particular kind of quasar, then you should realize that the answer must be spelled out on the page somewhere, because the ACT won't ask questions about such obscure concepts without providing the answer somewhere in the passage!

If you run into a question that definitely tests basic outside knowledge, and you still aren't sure which choice to go with, then all you can really do is pick the one that seems most closely related to the subject matter in the question. You'll probably be right, and, even if you aren't, staring at a question whose answer you don't know means you're wasting time that could be spent on questions whose answers are right there in the passage. Since there's no penalty for wrong answers on the ACT, you may as well pick the one that looks best to you, and then move on.

Only Fall Back on Outside Knowledge after Trying to Find the Answer in the Passage!

Just to make sure we're perfectly clear on this important concept, we'll restate it yet again: We only ever consider using outside knowledge on the ACT Science section if we're confident that the answer to the relevant question doesn't appear in the passage. We should check the passage—including all diagrams and figures—for information we can use to answer the relevant question, and only consider what kind of basic scientific information we could use to answer a question when we're certain that the passage doesn't contain the answer.

Math on the ACT Science Section

You'll be able to answer most ACT Science questions by reading the relevant question, answer choices, and passage carefully. But sometimes you'll need to use a little math as well. That math could involve something like basic addition or subtraction—which we don't need to review here—or it could involve any of the relatively simple, slightly science-y math ideas we'll cover now:

- Using Simple Trends in Data
- The Metric System
- Chemical Equations

Using Simple Trends in Data

On the ACT Science section, you'll occasionally need to make simple predictions based on clear trends in data from the passage. That data might be found in a chart, graph, table, or diagram—basically, anything with numbers.

The predictions will essentially require you to determine whether a number that hasn't been provided by the passage should be

- greater than a number in the provided data,
- less than a number in the provided data, or
- between two numbers in the provided data

The best way to discuss this is probably just to use a real ACT practice question as an example, so let's use question 7 from the Science section of practice test 1 in the Red Book, which is test 2 in the 2020-2021 Red Book (remember the first practice test in the Red Book is usually found about 50 pages in, separate from the other practice tests near the end of the book!).

The prompt mentions the phrases "reaction time," "Experiment 1," and "CNF." We can see all of those phrases in Table 1, so Table 1 seems like a good place to start as we figure out the answer to this question.

When we take a closer look at Table 1, we see that it shows data for Experiment 1, and that this data involves different amounts of time in a column called "Reaction time," and then corresponding numbers in a separate column called "CNF."

(As a side note, notice that we don't know at this point what "CNF" is, or what was involved in the reaction, or really anything about the experiment at all! But we do know that Table 1 contains information related to the question we're answering, which is all we need to know for question 7. This is a great demonstration of how the ACT Science section is almost completely a test of careful reading, and outside scientific knowledge plays only a small role.)

Anyway, we can see that the CNF values are listed for Experiment 1 with reaction times of 10 minutes, 3 days, and 7 days . . .

. . . but the question asks about a reaction time of 2 days, and Table 1 doesn't have information for a reaction time of 2 days! So how are we supposed to answer the question?

Well, first of all, we should notice that the prompt includes the phrase "would most likely have been," which signals to us that the experiment didn't actually include a trial with a reaction time of 2 days—so we're not wrong to think that the passage doesn't provide explicit data for a reaction time of 2 days. And, as trained test-takers, we know that the ACT can't ask us a question unless the answer to that question is absolutely certain, with no possibility of argument or disagreement. So that means it must be possible to answer this question with total certainty, even though the data doesn't directly provide any information about a reaction time of 2 days.

At this point, we should notice there's a clear trend in the data: in Table 1, as reaction time increases, CNF also increases.

Now we can use this simple trend in the provided data to answer the prompt. We were asked to find the CNF value for a reaction time of 2 days. Table 1 shows us that the following is true for Experiment 1:

- CNF for 10 minutes was 6 mg/kg
- CNF for 3 days was 39 mg/kg

Since the CNF increases as reaction time increases, we know that a reaction time 2 days will have a CNF somewhere between 6 mg/kg and 39 mg/kg, since a reaction time of 2 days is between 10 minutes and 3 days. Sure enough, that's exactly what (B) says, and (B) is the right answer.

Notice that the question doesn't include more than one choice with a value between 6 and 39—in fact, the rules of the ACT wouldn't allow more than one choice like that! This is because we only have enough information to say for certain that the right answer must be somewhere between 6 and 39; we can't get any more specific than that, because the provided information doesn't get any more specific than that. Whenever you see a question like this, there will be only one clearly correct answer choice supported by the data—just like there is on any other real ACT Science question that relies on data.

In this question, we were asked about a reaction time that was in between two values that appeared in Table 1. On another question, we might be asked about a value that's greater or less than any value in a given table or graph. The same principle would apply, and we would just answer based on a clear trend in the data.

For example, what if this prompt had asked us about the CNF value for a reaction time of 15 days in Experiment 1?

Well, Table 1 doesn't have data for a reaction time of 15 days, but we can see that the greatest reaction time in the table is 7 days, and the CNF value at 7 days is 42 mg/kg. Since we know that Table 1 shows CNF increasing as reaction time increases, we know that the answer to our made-up question would be something like "greater than 42 mg/kg," because 15 days is longer than 7 days, so the CNF for 15 days must be greater than the CNF for 7 days, according to the clear trend in the table. (For our full discussion of this question, see its walkthrough on page 351 in this Black Book.)

How you'll need to think about this on test day

Most questions on the ACT Science section will ask about data or concepts that actually appear directly on the page, but you'll have to use simple trends like this a few times on most test days. Still, you'll only need to think in these terms when you see that a prompt is asking you about "missing" data in a table or graph that shows a clear trend in the data, as we saw in the example question above.

As we also noted above, another major indication that you'll need to use a trend in the provided data is a phrase like "would most likely have been" in the prompt, which indicates clearly that the ACT hasn't included the relevant data in the passage.

The Metric System

The ACT Science section may ask you a question that involves converting between different metric prefixes. For example, you may be asked to pick the answer choice that correctly expresses 2500 grams in terms of kilograms (the right answer would be 2.5 kilograms in this case).

To make these conversions, you'll need to know the following:

- "Deci-" means that a unit is divided by 10, so a decigram is 0.1 grams.
- "Centi-" means that a unit is divided by 100, so a centigram is 0.01 grams.
- "Milli-" means that a unit is divided by 1000, so a milligram is 0.001 grams.
- "Kilo-" means that a unit is multiplied by 1000, so a kilogram is 1000 grams.

How you'll need to think about this on test day

You'll see a lot of scientific units mentioned in ACT Science passages on test day, but you generally won't need to think about converting any of those units (in fact, for the most part, you won't have to understand the names or purposes of any of the units you see on test day, beyond making sure that units mentioned in a prompt or an answer choice match with units mentioned in the passage). But if a question specifically asks you to convert between different sizes of the same units, then you can use your knowledge of the prefixes above. (This situation doesn't arise very often—it usually accounts for something like zero or one question per test.)

Chemical Equations

As part of the ACT's strategy of making the Science section seem more challenging than it really is, the passages on this section will occasionally include a chemical equation, even though most or all of the questions in the passage won't rely on that equation.

But, roughly once or twice per test, you may need a very basic understanding of chemical equations to answer a question. (Please note that you will NOT need to know any advanced chemistry for the ACT, even when a question involves a chemical equation!)

On the ACT Science section, our required understanding of chemical equations is actually very similar to the idea of basic algebraic equations, in the sense that the elements on both sides of an equation need to be balanced. Before we discuss this further, let's define a few key terms and conventions.

Basic terms and an example equation

A "chemical reaction" is a process in which two or more molecules interact with each other and produce something new. (For our purposes on the ACT, an "atom" is the smallest possible unit of a chemical element, and a "molecule" is a group of atoms that are stuck together.)

A "chemical equation" is a written expression of what happens in a chemical reaction. A chemical equation on the ACT will look something like this:

$$CH_4 + 2O_2 \rightarrow CO_2 + 2H_2O$$

So a chemical equation will include the following elements:

- some letters and numbers representing molecules or atoms on the left-hand side. These are called the "reactants" or the "reagents." They're the chemicals that exist before the reaction happens.
- an arrow. This indicates that the reaction is starting with the things on the left of the arrow, and producing the things on the right of the arrow.
- some letters and numbers representing molecules or atoms on the right-hand side. These are the "products." They're the chemicals that result from the chemical reaction.

In the sample equation above, the letters C, H, and O represent elements. (Note that you may know that these symbols stand for carbon, hydrogen, and oxygen, respectively, but you won't actually need to know that when you answer a question on the ACT! If that information is relevant to the question, it will be provided in the text.)

Determining the numbers of atoms in an equation

The elements in the above example equation are grouped into molecules.

If a small number (a "subscript") appears *after* an element, it indicates the number of atoms of that element present in each molecule of that kind. Based on the equation above, we know the following:

- CH_4 is a molecule with one C atom and four H atoms.

- O_2 is a molecule with two O atoms.
- CO_2 is a molecule with one C atom and two O atoms.
- H_2O is a molecule with two H atoms and one O atom.

If a number appears *before* a molecule, it indicates how many of those molecules are involved in the equation.

In the equation above, the "2" that appears before "O_2" in "$2O_2$" tells us that there are two O_2 molecules. Also, because we already know there are two O atoms in an O_2 molecule, and there are two O_2 molecules in the equation, we know that there must be a total of four O atoms on the left side of the equation.

If no number appears before a molecule, then there is only one of that molecule. For example, no number appears before CH_4 in the above equation, so we know there is only one CH_4 molecule in that equation.

So with all of this in mind, we know that the chemical equation above basically says this:

> One CH_4 molecule and two O_2 molecules react to form one CO_2 molecule and two H_2O molecules.

Balancing chemical equations

This brings us to our next important idea: chemical equations must be balanced. In other words, the number of each type of atom on one side must match the number of that type of atom on the other side.

Let's look again at our example above. The first atom we encounter on the left side is C:

- There's no small subscript after C, so we know this molecule only contains one C atom.
- There's no number at the front of this molecule, so we know there's only one CH_4 molecule in this equation.
- No other molecule on the left side of the equation involves C.

So we can tell there's only one C atom on the left side of the equation. When we check the right side of the equation, we can see that there's only one C atom on that side as well—the one in the CO_2 molecule. So there's one C atom on the left side of the equation, and one C atom on the right side of the equation.

The next atom we encounter on the left side is H:

- There's a small subscript after H that says "4," so we know this molecule contains four H atoms.
- There's no number at the front of this molecule, so we know there's only one CH_4 molecule in this equation.
- No other molecule on the left side of the equation involves H.

So that means there are four H atoms on the left side of the equation. When we check the right side of the equation, we can see that H only appears in the H_2O molecule. The subscript after the H in that molecule tells us there are two H atoms in one H_2O molecule, and the "2" that appears before H_2O tells us there are two H_2O molecules. Since each H_2O molecule has two H atoms, and there are two H_2O molecules, we know there are a total of four H atoms in those two molecules. So there are four H atoms on the left side of the equation, and four H atoms on the right side of the equation.

Repeating this analysis, we can see that are four O atoms on each side of the equation: all four on the left side are in the two molecules of O_2, and the four on the right side are evenly split between the one CO_2 molecule and the two H_2O molecules.

So each side of the equation has one C atom, four H atoms, and four O atoms. This means every atom in the equation appears the same number of times on the left-hand side of the equation as it does on the right-hand side of the equation.

That means the equation is balanced.

Chemical equations as ratios

The equation we've been discussing so far is basically a ratio. It tells us that for every one molecule of CH_4 and two molecules of O_2, the reaction will produce one molecule of CO_2 and two molecules of H_2O.

But what if the reaction uses three CH_4 molecules? Well, the equation would have to stay balanced, so every other part of the equation would have to be multiplied by three as well, and the result would look like this:

$$3CH_4 + 6O_2 \rightarrow 3CO_2 + 6H_2O$$

An example from the Red Book

Question 13 from the Science section of practice test 1 in the Red Book (test 2 in the 2020-2021 Red Book) covers these concepts. You can read our walkthrough for that question on page 353 of this Black Book.

(Conversely, question 12 on the same page of the Red Book is a good example of a question that will fool many untrained test-takers into thinking they can't answer it without knowing some chemistry, when, in fact, no knowledge of chemistry is necessary for that question. See our walkthrough of that question on page 353 of this Black Book for more.)

How you'll need to think about this on test day

If you see a chemical equation on test day, don't assume that you'll need to understand much about it. You won't have to understand or explain anything about why the equation works the way it does, or do any of the other kinds of analysis that you might expect to do in a chemistry class. Instead, you'll only have to answer one or two questions that cover the kinds of general concepts we talked about above.

Special Article: Basics of Experimental Design

Roughly once per test, you may see questions on the ACT Science section that require a basic understanding of experimental design. These questions may require you to know terms and concepts like the following:

- Hypothesis
- Experiment
- Control Group
- Experimental Group
- Independent Variable
- Dependent Variable
- Constant

On the other hand, you won't have to know anything advanced about experimental design, such as the history of experimentation itself, or the application of statistics and computer modeling to scientific experimentation.

To help you understand the basic terms in the bulleted list above, we'll talk about them in the context of a made-up experiment.

Let's say that you have some tomato plants, and you hear a rumor that they'll grow faster if you add sugar to their water. You decide that you want to do a test to find out if this idea is true.

Before you can run a good test, you'll need to come up with a specific statement of what you'll be testing. This statement is called a "hypothesis." The hypothesis is a statement—not a question!

In our scenario with the tomato plants and the sugar water, a good hypothesis might be the following:

> Tomato seeds and plants that are watered with sugar water will grow taller after 30 days than tomato seeds and plants that are watered with pure water during that time.

This statement works okay as a hypothesis because you can test it pretty directly. You'll do this test by designing an "experiment," which is a systematic test of a hypothesis.

In this case, one way to test the hypothesis would be to create an area in your garden with two groups of tomato seeds:

1. Group 1 will get 100mL of pure water every day
2. Group 2 will get 100mL of water with 10mg of table sugar dissolved into it every day

At the end of 30 days, you measure the heights of all the plants in each group, and compare the average height of the plants in Group 1 to the average height of the plants in Group 2:

- If the average height of plants in Group 1 is greater than the average height of plants in Group 2, or if the two averages are equal, then you have disproved the hypothesis, and you know the hypothesis is a false statement.
- If the average height of plants in Group 2 is greater than the average height of plants in Group 1, then the hypothesis hasn't been disproved, and your experiment provides support that the hypothesis might be true.

In this experiment,

- the "control group" is Group 1, because we're deliberately setting up Group 1 and trying to make it be as normal as we can, so we can use it as a reference for how different the results are from Group 2.
- the "experimental group" is Group 2, because Group 2 is the one that we're deliberately treating differently from normal tomato seeds, so we can observe the impact of that difference while we're trying to disprove our hypothesis.

Note that experiments need a control group, or else there would be nothing to compare the results of the experimental group to—in this case, if we only had the experimental group and not the control group, then we couldn't compare the average height of the tomato plants watered with sugar water *to* anything, and we wouldn't know if the sugar water made the plants grow taller or shorter than watering the plants without sugar.

Experiments also involve things called "independent variables," "dependent variables," and "constants:"

- An independent variable is an attribute of the experiment that you change directly, and on purpose, so you can find out the effects of these deliberate changes. In our scenario, the independent variable is the presence of sugar in the water, because we're deliberately controlling whether the sugar has water in it, so we can see what the effect of sugar water is on the average height of tomato plants after 30 days.
- A dependent variable is an attribute of an experiment that changes unpredictably in response to the changes that we create in the independent variable—in other words, a dependent variable is one that *depends* on a different variable. In this scenario, the dependent variable is the average height of the two groups of plants after the 30-day period.
- Constants are attributes of an experiment that we keep the same for all the groups in the experiment, so we can make sure that what happens to the dependent variable is really the result of the changes we made to the independent variable. In our experiment, we would need to keep the following things constant, among others:
  - the soil used for the two groups
  - the specific kind of tomato seed used for the two groups
  - the amount of sunlight received by the two groups

For example, imagine if you tried to run the experiment we're describing, but you used heirloom tomato seeds for Group 1 and cherry tomato seeds for Group 2, and then you planted the seeds for Group 2 in sand at the beach, and the seeds for Group 1 in potting soil in your backyard. In this scenario, you would have no idea if the difference in average height after

30 days was due to the effect of the soil, or the amount of sun, or the seeds, or any combination of those factors. This is why a good experiment requires us to hold everything constant between the different groups, except for the independent variable that we're using to test the hypothesis.

Slightly more advanced experimental design

There's one more concept we need to address in order to make this hypothetical situation fully relevant to the kinds of experiments you might see in the passages of an ACT Science section on test day.

What if we wanted to modify our experiment so that we could compare the effects of different amounts of sugar in the water, instead of just comparing one group with some sugar to another group without sugar?

We might decide to set up multiple experimental groups, each with a different amount of sugar dissolved in the water:

1. Group 1 would still receive 100mL of pure water.
2. Group 2 would receive 100mL of water with 10mg of table sugar dissolved in it.
3. Group 3 would receive 100mL of water with 20mg of table sugar dissolved in it.
4. Group 4 would receive 100mL of water with 30mg of table sugar dissolved in it.

In this experiment,

- The control group is still Group 1, because we're deliberately setting up Group 1 and trying to make it be as normal as we can, so we can use it as a reference for how different the results are from Groups 2, 3, and 4.
- The experimental groups are Groups 2, 3, and 4, because those are the groups that we're deliberately treating differently from normal tomato seeds, so we can observe the impact of differing amounts of dissolved sugar
- The independent variable is the amount of sugar dissolved in the water, because we're deliberately controlling how much sugar is in the water, so we can see the effect of the amount of sugar on the average height of tomato plants after 30 days.
- The dependent variable is the average height of each group after the 30-day period.
- All of the other attributes of the experiment should still be held constant, like the following:
  - the soil used for the four groups
  - the specific kind of tomato seed used for the four groups
  - the amount of sunlight received by the four groups

How you'll need to think about this on test day

You won't need to think about any aspect of experimental design unless a question specifically requires you to do so, and the vast majority of questions won't do that!

So you can ignore all aspects of experimental design unless a prompt or an answer choice uses terms like "hypothesis" or "control group." If that happens, you'll need to remember the relatively basic principles we described above so you can answer the relevant question with certainty.

An example of a question that requires knowledge of basic experimental design is question 40 from the Science section of practice test 3 in the Red Book (form 16MC3 online if you have the 2020-2021 Red Book). Our walkthrough for that question is on page 407 of this Black Book.

How to Read Passages on the ACT Science Section

Just as a lot of people ask about the best way to read ACT Reading passages, a lot of people ask about the best way to read ACT Science passages—and the answer is basically the same. There's no single "best" way to do this. There are three basic ways to approach it, and you should try each one in practice to see what works best for you.

Option 1: Read the whole passage first.

This is probably the most popular approach with untrained test-takers. In this method, you just read the entire passage before looking at the questions. When you get to any tables or figures, you don't need to read all of the values, but you should take note of any labels on axes, headings on columns, and so on. This way, you'll know which parts of the passage to refer back to when a question asks about a specific type of data.

Don't bother trying to grasp everything you read if you take this approach. The point isn't to understand everything that's going on in the passage—the point is just to see generally which parts of the passage talk about particular concepts, so you'll know where to look in more detail when a question asks about those concepts.

Option 2: Skip the passage and go right to the questions.

In this method, you don't even look at the passage first; you just start in with the first question. This method is a little easier with ACT Science passages than it is with ACT Reading passages, because ACT Science passages are shorter, and the questions tend to refer to specific parts of the passage more clearly.

For example, imagine that a question says something like, "In Figure 1, what was the regromination index of slappentonium?" (I know that "regromination" and "slappentonium" aren't actually words. I'm using them in my imaginary question to demonstrate once more how we can often work around unknown words on the ACT Science section.) To answer this imaginary question without reading the passage first, we'd just find Figure 1, find a column with a label like "Regromination Index," and then locate the value for slappentonium. At no point in that process would we need to know anything about the rest of the passage. Then we could just repeat the process with the next question—we'd identify the key terms and values in the question, and then locate those terms and/or values in the passage and find the answer.

You'll see several examples of this idea in the walkthroughs.

Some people find this approach helpful because they can just focus on the relevant part of each passage with a given question in mind; other people just find this technique confusing, because it means skipping around in the passage and they're not comfortable with that. Try it out and see how it works for you.

(By the way, you'll find that our ACT Science walkthroughs—which start on page 345 of this Black Book—include a section that tells you which parts of the passage were actually critical to finding the right answer for each question, so you can develop your instincts for identifying and focusing on important information.)

Option 3: Skim the passage, then read the questions.

This method combines the previous two methods, and it's the one I generally prefer (though, again, you should give each one a shot and use the one you personally like best). In this method, we're going to start out by *quickly* skimming the passage. Take note of any unusual technical terms, formulas, or italicized phrases. Glance at any figures, read the labels on charts and graphs, and so on. In just a minute or so, you can have a reasonable idea of where different pieces of information are in the passage.

Then, you'll be in a good position to find the relevant information in the passage after you've read an individual question, even though you only invested a minimal amount of time skimming beforehand.

Conclusion

As I said, these are basically the same options we have for reading passages on the ACT Reading section (which we discussed on page 55 of this Black Book), except that ACT Science passages are shorter and can include charts, graphs, and so on, and the Science questions will tend to direct you more specifically to the relevant areas of the passage. Just try out the different methods and see what you prefer.

ACT Science Question Types

I like to think of the ACT Science section in terms of five main question types. I'm not advising you to take the time to classify each question before you do it, since the basic approach to each type will still be the same. I'm just breaking them into groups like this so we can discuss what kinds of questions you should expect to see on this section of the test.

Let's take a look.

"Pure Data"

Many of the questions you'll see will be what I call "Pure Data" questions. These questions are exactly what they sound like—they ask you a relatively simple, straightforward question about the provided data, and you'll need to read the data accurately and choose the appropriate answer.

This process is essentially the same one you use for ACT Reading. The only difference is that you'll usually be reading tables, graphs, and diagrams instead of sentences or paragraphs. If you're comfortable with ACT Reading, and if you can get comfortable applying the same basic technique to charts, graphs, and diagrams, you'll be fine. Like everything else on the ACT, it just takes some careful thought and some careful practice, and then you'll get the hang of it and find it very repetitive. (Remember that it's good for the ACT to be repetitive, because that means we can predict its behavior and use that predictability to answer questions correctly and score high.)

Question 2 from the Science section of practice test 1 in the Red Book (test 2 in the 2020-2021 Red Book) is a good example of a "pure data" question. Our walkthrough for that question is on page 348 of this Black Book.)

"Pure Paragraph"

The next type of question we'll talk about is what I call the "Pure Paragraph" question. As you might guess, this type of question is based purely on what you read in a paragraph in the passage. These are just reading comprehension questions, and we'll approach them in basically the same way we approach questions on the ACT Reading section. These questions can appear in any passage on the Science section, but they'll usually appear in the heaviest concentration on the "Scientist 1 vs. Scientist 2" or "Student 1 vs. Student 2" type of passage.

Just like we do on the ACT Reading section, we'll pick the answer choice that's restated or demonstrated by the relevant part of the text, without contradicting it. We'll read carefully, and we won't be thrown off by scientific terms we're not familiar with, as we discussed in "Dealing with strange terms and units" on page 330.

Question 10 from the Science section of practice test 1 in the Red Book (test 2 in the 2020-2021 Red Book) is a good example of this kind of question. You can see its walkthrough on page 352 of this Black Book.

"Data Plus Paragraph"

As you might imagine from the name, answering a "Data Plus Paragraph" question will require us to combine information from a paragraph in the passage with data found in a chart, graph, diagram, etc.

Again, we'll just look carefully at the information that's relevant to the question, and then we'll apply what we find to answer the question.

Question 8 from the Science section of practice test 1 in the Red Book (test 2 in the 2020-2021 Red Book) is an example of this kind of question. Our walkthrough for that question is on page 351 of this Black Book.

"Data Plus Data"

Finally, there are the "Data Plus Data" questions. These will require us to use two different data sources from the passage—for instance, we might have to answer based on a data point from a line graph and a separate data point from a table in the same passage.

These types of questions are often a little harder than other questions on the Science section, just because they involve processing a little more information than other questions do. But, as with every other major question type on the ACT Science section, all we really have to do is read carefully and use the available information to answer the question.

An example of this kind of question is number 31 from the Science section of practice test 1 in the Red Book (test 2 in the 2020-2021 Red Book). The walkthrough for that question is on page 362 of this Black Book.

"Outside Info"

Some questions will require you to understand the basics of experimental design or chemical equations, and some will even require you to know basic scientific facts like the idea that the moon revolves around the Earth. We've already discussed the kinds of questions that require outside information in ""Science" on the ACT Science Section: What You Need to Know, and What You Don't" on page 331 of this Black Book. Refer to that section for more details on these kinds of questions.

Unwritten Test Design Rules of ACT Science

By now it should be clear that the ACT Science section has little in common with the kind of science tests you might take in a normal high school class. The majority of this section of the test comes down to being able to read questions carefully, and then being able to find the information you need to answer those questions in the text, charts, graphs, and diagrams in the relevant passage.

These are the rules you need to remember as you train for the ACT Science section.

ACT Science Rule 1: Every Part of the Answer is Almost Always on the Page in Front of You

Each ACT Science section will have roughly a handful of questions (or fewer) that test actual scientific knowledge. (This knowledge is always relatively basic, by the way, which we'll talk about in Rule 5 below.) For the rest of the 40 questions, everything you need to answer a question with total certainty will be on the page in front of you—whether in the text, in a figure, or even in the prompt itself (or in some combination of those things), as we saw in "ACT Science Question Types" on page 339 of this Black Book.

The ACT never requires you to know about obscure branches of science; the necessary information related to those branches of science will always be somewhere on the page.

ACT Science Rule 2: Labels are Important

You'll often need to find information on a chart, graph, or table. Get used to identifying the labels on these kinds of figures and matching them up to the words and phrases in the prompt and answer choices to find the information you need. Look for labels on the top, bottom, left, and right sides of graphs and diagrams, as well as within the graphs and diagrams themselves.

(This might sound like a very obvious piece of advice, but you'd be surprised how often test-takers mistakenly think they can't answer a question just because they failed to locate a label on an axis of a graph or something. A good example of a question that shows the importance of noting all labels on a figure is question 2 from the Science section of practice test 1 in the Red Book—test 2 in the 2020-2021 Red Book—which requires us to note two axis-labels and one label for an entire graph in a single figure that includes four separate graphs. The walkthrough for that question is on page 348 of this Black Book.)

ACT Science Rule 3: Be Sure to Use the Right Data

Most questions will require you to look somewhere in the passage for some kind of information. *Make sure you're looking in the right place.* There may be more than one experiment, or table, or chart, or graph in a given passage, and they often use similar (or even identical) labels for their data.

So when you refer back to a figure or table in the passage, make sure the one you check is actually the one the prompt is asking about!

Again, I know this might sound kind of obvious, but we have to remember that one of the ACT's most effective tactics, on any section, is to give untrained test-takers the opportunity to make small, simple mistakes. As trained test-takers, we have to make ourselves look out for those small mistakes at all times. On the Science section, accidentally looking at the wrong piece of data is one of the easiest ways to fall for a wrong answer.

(Question 19 from the Science section of practice test 2 in the Red Book, which is test 3 in the 2020-2021 Red Book, provides an example of how easy it can be for an untrained test-taker to fall for this kind of thing. Our walkthrough of that question is on page 376 of this Black Book.)

ACT Science Rule 4: Don't Get Intimidated by Vocabulary, Especially with Italicized Words

The ACT loves to try to intimidate untrained test-takers with scientific vocabulary that sounds advanced.

Think about it. In school, any time we see a strange word in a science class, we have a teacher there to tell us what it means. We aren't used to reading a strange scientific term and having to figure it out on our own, or just work around it. The ACT knows this, and it will intentionally make very straightforward questions seem intimidating simply by sticking in scary, unfamiliar words and phrases (such as "rostrum" from Passage I of the Science section of practice test 1 in the Red Book, which is test 2 in the 2020-2021 Red Book, and "accrete" from Passage III of that same test, to pick two examples out of many).

Don't let this throw you. Remember our hypothetical discussion of phosportence from page 330 of this Black Book. In the walkthroughs, you'll see several examples of effective solutions to ACT Science questions that involve working around unknown terms and concepts.

(By the way, you'll frequently find that new or exotic terms are italicized when they first appear in a passage on the ACT Science section, and these italicized first mentions of a term are often followed by a definition or explanation of the italicized term. For an example of this, see Passage VI from the Science section of practice test 1 in the Red Book (test 2 in the 2020-2021 Red Book), which italicizes the phrase "mean free path" and then defines it as

> the average distance a gas atom will travel between collisions with other gas atoms

Also note that you never actually have to use the term "mean free path" to answer any of the questions in the passage. See their walkthroughs on pages 365-367 of this Black Book.)

ACT Science Rule 5: You'll Need to Know BASIC Science a Few Times per Test

There will be a few times per test when actual scientific knowledge will come into play. This scientific knowledge will be very basic—something like knowing that the sun is at the center of the solar system, or that animals that blend into their surroundings are less likely to get eaten by predators, or that a cell membrane is located on the outside of the cell, or that a molecule of water contains two hydrogen atoms and one oxygen atom.

But these questions often won't seem so basic on the surface! The ACT will try to use complicated phrasing to make them sound more advanced and specialized than they really are. We've already seen an example of this kind of question in "Basic Science Facts" on page 331 of this Black Book, which discussed question 35 from the Science section of practice test 3 in the Red Book (form 16MC3 online if you have the 2020-2021 Red Book)—a question that required us to identify the phrase "cell membrane" as the name of the structure that separates a cell from its environment. A slightly less challenging example of this kind of question can be found in question 9 from the Science section of practice test 1 in the Red Book (test 2 in the 2020-2021 Red Book), which requires us to know that a vacuum pump exerts some amount of force; our walkthrough for that question is on page 352 of this Black Book.

ACT Science Answer-Choice Patterns

Let's take a look at some common answer choice patterns on the ACT Science section.

ACT Science Answer-Choice Pattern 1: All the ACT Reading Patterns Apply

As we explained earlier, the ACT Science section is very similar to the ACT Reading section, in the sense that most ACT Science questions require you to find an answer that's stated directly on the page, without requiring outside knowledge.

With this in mind, it should be no surprise that the wrong answers on this section will often incorporate many of the same wrong answer patterns that we saw in the ACT Reading section:

- Some wrong answers will confuse relationships among the concepts in the passage. For example, the passage might describe a sequence of steps in an experiment, and a wrong answer choice might mention those steps in a different order.
- Some wrong answers will be barely relevant to what appears in the passage.
- Some wrong answers will directly contradict the right answer.
- Some wrong answers will be only one or two words away from accurately restating what the passage says.
- Some wrong answers will reflect data or concepts from the wrong part of the passage. For example, a question might refer to data from Figure 1 in the passage, while a wrong answer following this pattern will refer to data from Figure 2 instead.

You'll see these wrong-answer patterns throughout the ACT Science walkthroughs in a few pages. You can also refresh yourself on these patterns by referring to "ACT Reading Wrong Answer Patterns" on page 53 of this Black Book.

ACT Science Answer-Choice Pattern 2: All of One Type

On ACT Science questions, you'll often see a set of answer choices that includes the full range of possible values from a table or chart. In other words, the question might refer to groups 1, 2, 3, and 4, and the answer choices for a given question might be:

(A) Group 1
(B) Group 2
(C) Group 3
(D) Group 4

Similarly, a passage might talk about four periods of time, and your answer choices might just be those four time periods. In a situation like this, it might seem like you're not going to get much use out of analyzing the answer choices—but this kind of answer choice set is still helpful, because it can point you to a certain part of the data being presented to you.

For example, if the set of answer choices only includes four time periods, and there's a graph in the passage that gives information about those time periods, then that graph is likely to contain information relevant to the answer. The answer choices can help make that extra clear.

Similarly, if all the choices are different types of metal, and those metal names match up to labels on one of the charts in the passage, then that's a good indicator that you'll probably find that chart to be useful in answering the question.

If the answer choices are all names of gases, there's probably a chart or a graph somewhere that talks about those different gases.

You get the idea. As in ACT Math, ACT Science answer choices can give you an idea of the sorts of thing you might need to consider when finding the answer for a question. Basically, one of the biggest possible challenges on any ACT Science question is to find the relevant information in the given passage, and the answer choices can provide a set of relevant keywords or values that can help you find what you're looking for.

(Question 40 from the Science section of practice test 3 in the Red Book, which is form 16MC3 online if you have the 2020-2021 Red Book, is one clear example of this type of question. You can read its walkthrough on page 407 of this Black Book.)

ACT Science Answer-Choice Pattern 3: Numbers in a Series

It's not uncommon to find that the answer choices for an ACT Science question form a mathematical series in which each choice differs from the previous choice by a constant amount. This pattern probably exists because many ACT Science questions will require us to read data from a table or graph, and those tables and graphs will include axes with number labeling at regular intervals, which makes it easy to misread the data in a way that causes you to be off by an interval that's reflected in the answer choices. For example, if a graph has an x-axis that's labelled in 10-unit increments, and a prompt requires you to read a value from that axis, it's not uncommon for the answer choices to form a series in which each choice is 10 more than the choice before it. This makes it easy for an undisciplined test-taker to misread the relevant figure without realizing it.

You'll also see this answer choice pattern even when questions don't refer to a chart or graph with data marked at consistent intervals.

When you encounter this pattern, make sure to read the relevant data carefully, and be especially careful about making any mistake that might cause you to be off by an amount that reflects the common difference in the series. (You can find an example of this pattern in question 2 from the Science section of practice test 1 in the Red Book, which is test 2 in the 2020-2021 Red Book. Its walkthrough is on page 348 of this Black Book.)

ACT Science Answer-Choice Pattern 4: Yes Yes No No

This is an answer-choice pattern that shows up on other sections as well, but it's probably most prevalent on the ACT Science and ACT

English sections.

This pattern takes two major forms. The first form appears on the ACT Science and ACT English sections; the second form is very common on the ACT Science section but not on the ACT English section.

Yes Yes No No with four different reasons

You'll see a question that asks which of two possibilities might happen. The answer choices will feature two choices that support one possibility and two choices that support another possibility, and every choice will offer a different reason to support that possibility.

That might sound confusing, so let's make up an example. Imagine a portion of the text says this:

It was very cloudy Tuesday night. When there is a very cloudy night, it always rains the next day.

Now imagine a question that says,

Based on the text, will it rain on Wednesday?

You might see answer choices like this:

(A) Yes, because it always rains on Wednesdays.

(B) Yes, because it was very cloudy on Tuesday night.

(C) No, because Tuesday night wasn't cloudy.

(D) No, because it didn't rain Tuesday.

Notice that there are two answer choices to support each possibility (two "yes" answers and two "no" answers), but just knowing whether the answer is "yes" or "no" isn't enough, because each question offers its own support that must be taken into consideration.

Here's the thing: in most cases, you can rule out three answers by ignoring the yes/no part of the answer and just checking whether the rest of the answer choice is supported by the text.

In this case, (A) must be wrong because the text doesn't say that it always rains on Wednesdays. (C) must be wrong because the text says Tuesday night was cloudy. (D) must be wrong because the text doesn't say whether it rained Tuesday, and it doesn't say that rain on Tuesday has anything to do with rain on Wednesday.

(B) is right because it's directly restated in the text.

You can often handle these questions on test day just by checking to see whether the passage restates or demonstrates the *reason* given for each answer, without considering whether "yes" or "no" makes sense to you. If you eliminate all the choices whose reasons aren't reflected in the text and you're still left with more than one choice whose reason is restated or demonstrated in the passage, then you'll find that the "yes" or "no" answer will follow logically from one of the remaining choices, and that choice must be right. (If this doesn't make any sense in the abstract, don't worry—you can see an example of this pattern in question 4 from the Science section of practice test 3 in the Red Book, which is form 16MC3 online if you have the 2020-2021 Red Book. Its walkthrough is on page 388 of this Black Book.)

Yes Yes No No with two reasons

In this version of the pattern, each of the "yes" and "no" options is paired with one of two reasons, so that the choices provide every possible combination of "yes" or "no" and one of the two reasons. This pattern is very common on the ACT Science section, but rarely (if ever) appears on the ACT English section.

Let's imagine that a question asks whether total rainfall increased over a given period of time, and then refers us to a graph of total rainfall that points up over that period. In this version of the answer choice pattern, the two reasons might be "because the graph points up" and "because the graph points down." The result would be four choices like this:

(A) Yes, because the graph points up.

(B) Yes, because the graph points down.

(C) No, because the graph points up.

(D) No, because the graph points down.

In this case, we can only eliminate two of the choices based on the given reasons, because one reason won't be demonstrated in the text, and that reason appears in two answer choices: in this hypothetical example, if we could see that the graph pointed up, then we'd know that (B) and (D) must be wrong based on that alone. Then we'd be left with (A) and (C), and we'd have to decide whether "yes" or "no" logically goes with the given reason that accurately describes the text. In this case, a graph of total rainfall that points up over a given period supports the idea that rainfall *did* increase over that period, which would make (A) right.

One more thing about this pattern

I call this the "Yes Yes No No" pattern, but the two choices aren't always "yes" and "no." You might see a question that asks whether something was hot or cold, in which case there will be two choices that say "hot" and two that say "cold," each with its own supporting reason. There might also be a question that asks whether Group 1 or Group 2 from a passage will do something, and there will be two choices that say "Group 1" does it and two choices that say "Group 2" does it, each for different reasons. You'll get used to recognizing the pattern as you work with practice ACT Science questions.

The General Process for Answering (Most) ACT Science Questions

Now that we've discussed all the important aspects of ACT Science questions, we can take a look at the recommended step-by-step process for answering most of them—that is, all of the questions that involve material presented in the passage, which will account for the majority of questions on any given Science section. (The "Outside Info" questions, as I call them, don't really call for a methodical approach. We simply recognize that we're dealing with one of those questions when we see that we can't answer based only on information from the passage, and then we do our best to answer them based on our outside scientific knowledge and our awareness of the concepts in the answer choices, as we demonstrated on page 331 of this Black Book, in ""Science" on the ACT Science Section: What You Need to Know, and What You Don't," and also in the training on page 339 of this Black Book.)

So the following approach is intended for use on the majority of ACT Science questions—the ones that don't require any outside knowledge because all the relevant information is present in the passage. As always, you can see examples of this process in the walkthroughs starting on page 345 of this Black Book.

1. Read, skim, or skip the passage.

As we discussed in "How to Read Passages on the ACT Science Section" on page 338 of this Black Book, you'll want to either read, skim, or skip the passage, according to your preference.

2. Read the prompt carefully, noting key terms and units.

We've covered this over and over again, and it never stops being important: you must take the time to read carefully on the ACT Science section, just as you would for any other part of the test. Notice any key scientific terms—in other words, any technical-sounding terms that aren't part of most people's everyday conversation. Don't worry if you don't know what an exotic scientific term means: either the passage will explain it, or none of the questions will require you to understand it. (Refer to "ACT Science Rule 4: Don't Get Intimidated by Vocabulary, Especially with Italicized Words" on page 340 for a refresher on this.)

3. Read the answer choices carefully.

This step is very important as well, because reading the answer choices will tell you where to look in the passages and/or which options to consider while you look for the answer to the question. See "ACT Science Question Types" on page 339 of this Black Book and "ACT Science Answer-Choice Patterns" on page 342 of this Black Book for more on this.

4. Find the relevant part of the passage.

Once you've read the whole question carefully, you know what information you need to find. If the text mentions a specific area of the passage, like "Study 2" or "Table 1," then look there. If there are no specific indications of tables or figures to look at in the passage, you can still match up technical terms from the question and answer choices with key phrases in the text, or in labels on a chart, graph, or table. (Again, we'll see plenty of examples of this in the walkthroughs starting on page 345 of this Black Book.)

5. Find the right answer, or eliminate three wrong answers.

Some questions will lend themselves to eliminating wrong answers, and in some cases it'll be easier just to find the right answer. Either way, use the information in the passage to select the correct answer. In most cases, you'll either be matching a specific value from the data to a specific value in an answer choice, or you'll be treating "Pure Paragraph" questions from the passage the same way you would treat ACT Reading questions. Either way, actually finding the answer is a relatively minor step (in terms of difficulty) once you've taken the time to understand the question and locate the relevant part of the text. Remember to read carefully!

6. Double-check your answer. Anticipate likely mistakes.

Once you've done everything and found your answer, take another look at the question. Did you refer to the right study? Did you find the right figure? Did you look at the right date range or temperature or depth (or whatever) on the right chart or graph? Did you overlook a word? Can you look at the choices you think are wrong and figure out which mistakes the ACT wants untrained test-takers to make to arrive at those answers? (Remember that high-scoring test-takers still make mistakes—they're just better at catching them afterwards! Get in the habit of double-checking yourself.) Once you're satisfied, mark your choice and move on.

Closing Thoughts

Doing well on the ACT Science section comes down to a few things:

- Read carefully. Don't make any assumptions about what isn't explicitly mentioned.
- Don't be intimidated. You WILL see unfamiliar scientific terms; you'll probably see a lot of them. Don't let them scare you. Either they don't matter, or their meaning will be made clear enough in the passage for you to answer the questions. (Refer back to "Dealing with strange terms and units" on page 330 of this Black Book for more.)
- Rely on the passages. The information you need to answer almost every question is on the page in front of you. Match up key terms and units from the question and the answer choices to figure out where to find the answer in the passage.

ACT Science Quick Summary

This is a one-page summary of the major concepts for the ACT Science section. Use it to evaluate your comprehension or jog your memory. For a more in-depth treatment of these ideas, see the rest of the section.

The Big Secret: Almost all ACT Science questions reward you for reading the passage and finding the correct answer spelled out on the page. ACT Science is a lot like ACT Reading, except that it involves charts and graphs and scientific terminology.

Don't get nervous when you see scientific terms you don't know. They'll either be explained in the passage somewhere, or you won't need to know them to answer the question.

Use the right data. Many passages involve multiple tables, graphs, etc., with similar information. Check to make sure you're using the right data to answer a given question.

Pay close attention to the labels on graphs, charts, and diagrams. These will tell you whether the data you're looking at is relevant to the question you're trying to answer.

There will be a few questions that require you to know a little basic science on your own—plan on roughly 5 per test. These questions are often designed to seem like they're advanced to an untrained test-taker, but they really hinge on basic ideas. You'll often know you're dealing with one of these questions when it involves terms that aren't in the passage.

You will need a basic understanding of the following around once per test each:

- trends in data
- the metric system
- chemical equations
- experimental design

Answer choices are important because they can tell you what you'll need to think about to answer the question. They're as important as any other part of the question, so always read them carefully.

Here are some of the common answer choice patterns you'll see:

- Because most ACT Science questions function like ACT Reading questions, you'll see all of the ACT Reading answer choice patterns.
- Answer choices may contain all the answers of a certain type that are relevant to the question—this could mean every date range on a chart, every type of metal used in an experiment, each temperature on a graph, and so on. This will tell you to focus on the part of the passage that deals with this concept.
- Wrong-answer choices are often numbers in a series.
- Wrong-answer choices often follow the "Yes yes no no" pattern, with either two different reasons or four different reasons appearing in the answer choices—see the relevant training earlier in this section for more on this pattern. Eliminate supporting statements that aren't restated or demonstrated in the text, or are irrelevant.

Here's the general ACT Science process:

1. Read, skim, or skip the passage depending on your preference.
2. Read the question carefully, noting key scientific terms.
3. Read the answer choices carefully.
4. Look at the relevant part of the passage.
5. Find the correct answer, or eliminate three wrong answers.
6. Double-check your answer, mark it, and move on.

Science Question Walkthroughs

In this section, we'll go through every official ACT Science question from three practice tests in the Red Book, so you can see the ideal process in action against real questions. (As always, I recommend that you only prepare with official practice questions, because those are the only questions that are guaranteed to play by the rules of the actual ACT. For more on that, see "Using the Official ACT Prep Guide (the "Red Book")" on page 21 of this Black Book.)

> **IMPORTANT NOTE:** If you have the 2020-2021 edition of the Red Book (ISBN: 978-1119685760), then "Test 1" in this Black Book refers to Practice Test 2 in your edition of the Red Book, and "Test 2" in this Black Book refers to Practice Test 3 in your Red Book. What we refer to as "Test 3" in this Black Book has been removed from the 2020-2021 edition of the Red Book, but it can be found online as ACT test form 16MC3. (See "**The 2020-2021 Red Book**" on page 23 of this Black Book for more.)

Before we get started, I'll explain how the ACT Science walkthroughs are set up. (If you'd like to see some video demonstrations of these ideas, go to www.ACTprepVideos.com for a selection of demonstration videos that are free to readers of this Black Book.)

Sample Science Walkthrough

The ACT Science walkthroughs in this book are laid out in a way that allows us to do the following:

- capture the ideal thought process for attacking individual questions, from initial assessment of the question through consideration of each answer choice
- make it easier for you to pick and choose specific parts of the walkthrough to focus on, while also allowing you to read the entire solution easily
- present the walkthroughs so they can stand on their own, while still making it easy to refer back to the relevant parts of the training for more details on key ideas if you want a refresher
- demonstrate how mechanical and repetitive real ACT questions are

Here's a diagram of an example walkthrough, with the elements of the walkthrough explained on the next page:

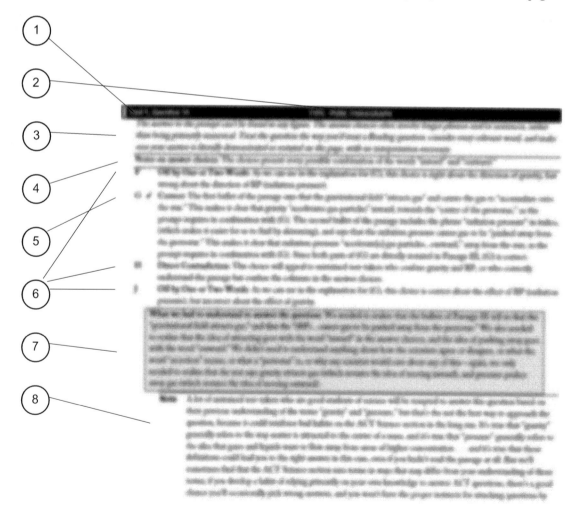

Explanation of Walkthrough Elements

The elements of the walkthrough are presented in a way that reflects the ideal mental process for approaching an ACT Science question:

1. This shows the test number and question number of the question being analyzed in the walkthrough, so you can find it in the Red Book.

2. This indicates the question's type, as discussed in "ACT Science Question Types" on page 339 of this Black Book. Having an idea of a question's type isn't critical on test day, and there's no need to spend a lot of time consciously deciding what type of question you're dealing with, but question types are included in walkthroughs so you can start to get a sense of the different ways that evidence from the passage can be used to answer ACT Science questions with total certainty. The classification isn't what really matters—all that really matters is that you stay in the habit of answering every question based on a literal reading of the words and figures on the page. Item 3 will give you an idea of how to use the information from Item 2.

3. This reminds you of the general characteristics of the question type from Item 2, and gives you an idea of how to approach the question based on its type. But, again, it's important not to get too hung up on this information—it's just here to help remind you of key ideas that will become second nature as you keep reading these walkthroughs and practicing on your own.

4. This Item points out the differences and similarities among the answer choices, just as you might identify them through a vertical scan like the kind we talked about on page 46 of this Black Book. Identifying the similarities and differences among the choices can help you figure out which part of the passage to consult when answering the question, and help make you aware of small mistakes that the ACT is trying to trick you into making.

5. The right answer will be noted with a checkmark, and the explanation that follows will explain how the right answer follows the rules and patterns of the ACT Science section.

6. The wrong answers will also be analyzed. Each explanation starts with a brief description of the general type of wrong answer, followed by a longer description showing how the answer choice fits that general pattern of wrong answer. Again, remember that it isn't critical for you to agree with me on the specific classification of each wrong answer! Ultimately, all that matters on the ACT Science section is that wrong answers fail to reflect exactly what's on the page.

7. After discussing all of the answer choices, we'll clarify exactly which parts of the passage were relevant to finding the right answer. This will help you develop your instincts for finding the key parts of the passage on test day, without getting bogged down in concepts that don't help you answer questions correctly.

8. If I feel that something is noteworthy about the question but I can't fit it in the rest of the walkthrough, then I'll note that at the end of the walkthrough. Be sure to pay attention to these notes when they appear, as they'll often contain useful information about what a particular question can teach us generally about future ACT questions.

Note that some walkthroughs are missing some of the Items in this list! If one of the Items above isn't relevant to a particular question, then it's omitted.

Remember that the ultimate goal of these walkthroughs is to help you see how I attack each question, and how I recommend you do the same. But, in the end, what matters most is that you develop an approach for ACT Science questions that allows you to find one right answer and three wrong answers with certainty. Feel free to modify my approach as you see fit, as long as your modifications still bring you the results you want.

TEST 1 (TEST 2 IN 2020-2021 RED BOOK)

Test 1, Question 1 (Test 2 in the 2020-2021 Red Book—see page 23 for more)   **TYPE: DATA PLUS PARAGRAPH**

Finding the answer requires information from the text as well as information from a figure. Read carefully, and be very particular about matching up exact values in the figure and the answer choices, unless the prompt calls for estimation. See p. 339.

Notes on answer choices: The choices form a series in which each choice is 50 km inland more than the choice before it. (Note that "at the coastal site" is technically 0 km inland according to the passage and the figures.)

A ✓ **Correct:** Untrained test-takers may struggle with this question because Figure 2 doesn't include the word "brightness" or the phrase "surface soil," even though the prompt tells us to consider Figure 2. But when we read the paragraph above Figure 2, we see that "the average brightness of surface soil" (which restates the phrase "on average...the brightest surface soil" from the prompt) is depicted on the Figure as "the average percent relative reflectance." So the vertical axis of Figure 2, which is labeled "average percent relative reflectance," literally indicates the brightness of the soil, according to the paragraph. With that in mind, we can see that the highest level of "relative reflectance," or brightness, occurred at 0 km inland. In other words, the highest level of soil brightness was measured at no distance at all from the coast, which means the brightest surface soil was found directly on the coast itself—so (A) is right.

B **Wrong Part of the Passage:** This choice might tempt an untrained test-taker who incorrectly looked at the "cheek" graph in Figure 1, instead of looking at Figure 2, as the prompt required.

C **Direct Contradiction:** This choice might attract an untrained test-taker who thought that a lower value in Figure 2 corresponded to higher brightness; it might also attract someone who misread the prompt and thought it was asking where the least bright surface soil was found. This choice may also simply be present because the ACT wanted to provide answer choices that created a series in which each choice was 50 km more than the choice before it.

D **Confused Relationships:** This choice might have been tempting for a test-taker who thought that the greatest distance from the coast would correspond to the brightest soil, for some reason. Like (C), it may also simply be present to complete a series in which each choice is 50 more than the choice before it.

What we had to understand to answer the question: We had to realize that the "bright[ness]" of "surface soil" referred to in the prompt was measured on the vertical axis of Figure 2, labeled "average percent relative reflectance." We also had to realize that "at the coastal site" in (A) corresponded to an inland distance of 0 in Figure 2. (For more on that, see the explanation for (A) above.) None of this required previous knowledge of anything in the passage, nor of anything outside of Figure 2 and the text immediately surrounding it. We didn't need to know what the word "reflectance" meant—we only needed to realize that it corresponded to "brightness" in the prompt, which is explained in the text above Figure 2.

Test 1, Question 2 (Test 2 in the 2020-2021 Red Book—see page 23 for more)   **TYPE: PURE DATA**

Finding the answer requires information from a figure. Read carefully, and be very particular about matching up exact values in the figure and the answer choices, unless the question calls for estimation. See p. 339.

Notes on answer choices: The choices form a series in which each choice is 20 km more than the choice before it.

F **Barely Relevant:** (F) is probably here because it completes a series in which each choice is 20km more than the one before it.

G **Barely Relevant:** (G) might attract an untrained test-taker who noticed that the *x*-value on the graph that corresponds to a *y*-value of 0.25 is one tick-mark more than 50, and then got confused and picked a value that was one tick-mark less than 50. But it's probably here because it helps complete a series in which each choice is 20 km more than the choice before it.

H ✓ **Correct:** We can see that Figure 1 involves 4 different graphs. The question asks about the "average relative brightness of the dorsal stripe;" the vertical axis of each graph in Figure 1 is labeled "average relative brightness," and the top right graph is labeled "dorsal stripe," so we know the top-right graph in Figure 1 is the relevant graph for this question. On that graph, we can see that an average relative brightness value of 0.25 corresponds to an inland distance about one tick-mark more than 50, and definitely less than 75. The only answer choice in this range is the right answer, 60 km.

J **Barely Relevant:** Like (F) and (G), this choice is probably here because it helps complete a series.

What we had to understand to answer the question: We needed to realize that the "dorsal stripe" graph in Figure 1 had all of the information relevant to this question. We didn't need to read or understand any other part of the passage for this question. We didn't need to know what the phrase "dorsal stripe" means.

Test 1, Question 3 (Test 2 in the 2020-2021 Red Book—see page 23 for more)   **TYPE: PURE DATA**

Finding the answer requires information from a figure. Read carefully, and be very particular about matching up exact values in the figure and the answer choices, unless the question calls for estimation. See p. 339.

Notes on answer choices: The first three choices form a series in which the boundaries for each range are 25 more than the corresponding boundary for the previous choice.

A   **Barely Relevant:** There is some change in the brightness in this range—from 1.00 to about 0.80. But that change isn't as large as the change between 50 km and 75 km, so (A) is wrong. This choice might also be tempting for test-takers who try to answer this question based on the graph in Figure 2.

B   **Barely Relevant:** This choice has the same basic problem as (A): it reflects *some* change, but the prompt asked us to find the interval with the greatest amount of change.

C ✓ **Correct:** We can see that Figure 1 involves 4 different graphs. The question asks about the "average relative brightness of the fur on the rostrum;" the vertical axis of each graph in Figure 1 is labeled "average relative brightness," and the top left graph is labeled "rostrum," so we know that we need to focus on the top left graph in Figure 1. When we do that, we see that the greatest change in brightness of the fur on the rostrum occurs between 50 km inland and 75 km inland on the horizontal axis. We can tell this in either of the following ways: we can note that the line changes from a value of about 0.7 at $x = 50$ to about 0.2 at $x = 75$, or we can simply note that the line is steepest for the longest interval between $x = 50$ and $x = 75$.

D   **Barely Relevant:** We can see from the graph of the rostrum that there's relatively little change over this range.

What we had to understand to answer the question: We needed to understand that the "rostrum" graph in Figure 1 had all the relevant information for this question. It would help to understand that the slope or steepness of a line indicates a rate of change, but it's not necessary to understand that in order to answer this question. (See the explanation for (C) for more.) We didn't need to know what the word "rostrum" meant at any time while answering this question.

Test 1, Question 4 (Test 2 in the 2020-2021 Red Book—see page 23 for more)   **TYPE: DATA PLUS PARAGRAPH**

Finding the answer requires information from the text as well as information from a figure. Read carefully, and be very particular about matching up exact values in the figure and the answer choices, unless the prompt calls for estimation. See p. 339.

Notes on answer choices: The wording of each choice is identical except for two words: the first word in (F) and (G) is "lighter" and the first word in (H) and (J) is "darker;" the last word in (F) and (H) is "greater" and the last word in (G) and (J) is "less."

F   **Direct Contradiction:** (F) might attract a test-taker who misread either axis on the graph and thought that lower values corresponded to lighter fur pigmentation for some reason. It could also appeal to someone who misread the prompt or the answer choice, and got the direction of the comparison backwards (that is, someone who thought the phrase in (F) described the coastal measurement in relation to the inland measurement, not the inland measurement in relation to the coastal one).

G   **Direct Contradiction:** This choice might attract an untrained test-taker who correctly identified that the brightness inland was less, but mistakenly assumed that lower "brightness" would correspond to lighter pigmentation.

H   **Off by One or Two Words:** (H) is probably here to round out the "yes-yes-no-no" pattern present in these answer choices, combining the correct word "darker" with the incorrect word "greater." Arriving at (H) might involve misreading the second half of the choice, or possibly thinking (J) was right but marking (H) instead because the text in these choices is very similar.

J ✓ **Correct:** This question about "fur pigmentation" might confuse an untrained test-taker, because Figure 1 doesn't mention "fur pigmentation" anywhere. But the first sentence in Passage 1 describes "a study of fur pigmentation" in which "scientists compared the brightness of the fur of mice." So we can see that "fur pigmentation" refers to the "brightness of the fur," according to the paragraph. With that in mind, we can notice that the vertical axis of each graph in Figure 1 is labeled "average relative brightness," with an asterisk leading to a footnote indicating that the brightness is related to a measurement of "fur pigmentation." We see that the bottom right graph in Figure 1 is labeled "ventrum," just as the prompt requires. The prompt asks whether fur pigmentation is "lighter" or "darker" 150 km inland, compared to the coastal region. (According to the footnote in Figure 1, "lighter" describes something with greater relative brightness, and "darker" describes something with less relative brightness.) When we compare the relative brightness of the ventrum fur 150 km inland to the relative brightness of the ventrum fur at the coastal site, we can see that the ventrum fur was *darker* at 150 km inland, because the relative brightness was *less* than it was at the coastal site, so (J) is right.

What we had to understand to answer the question: We needed to realize that the ventrum graph in Figure 1 demonstrates the relative lightness or darkness referred to in the right answer. We didn't need to understand the diagram of facial regions and body regions, nor the scientific name that appears in the prompt.

Test 1, Question 5 (Test 2 in the 2020-2021 Red Book—see page 23 for more)   **TYPE: OUTSIDE INFO**

Answering requires some information that can't be found in the passage. Any required outside knowledge must be relatively basic. Don't try to use outside knowledge on a question unless you're sure you can't answer based on the passage. See p. 339.

Notes on answer choices: The wording of each choice is identical except for two words: the first word in (A) and (B) is "less" and the first word in (C) and (D) is "more;" the fourth word in the second line of (A) and (C) is "less" and the corresponding word in (B) and (D) is "more."

A   **Off by One or Two Words:** The first "less" in this choice makes sense, because it should be harder to detect a mouse when its coloring is a close match to the soil, which means that it should be "less likely the mouse will be found," as (A) and (B) require. But being harder to find makes it *more* likely the mouse will pass its traits to its offspring, because a mouse that doesn't get caught by a predator is more likely to live long enough to reproduce, which we'll talk more about in our discussion of (B). This choice could appeal to untrained test-takers who aren't careful about distinguishing (A) from (B), since this choice is identical to (B) except for one word.

B ✓ **Correct:** This is a great example of the kind of fundamental scientific knowledge that we occasionally need on the ACT Science section. Each choice involves two basic ideas: whether fur pigmentation on a mouse matching the surrounding soil makes it more likely that the mouse will be found by a predator, and whether being found by a predator makes it more likely that the mouse will pass its traits to its offspring. As we noted for (A), if a mouse's fur matches the mouse's surroundings, then predators should be less likely to find the mouse, because the mouse will be harder to distinguish from its surroundings. And it also makes sense that a mouse who's less likely to be found by a predator will also be more likely to pass its traits along to any offspring—because animals that get found by predators are more likely to be killed, and animals that don't get found by predators are more likely to live long enough to reproduce, which means they're "more likely" to "pass fur pigmentation traits" to those offspring. So (B) is right.

C **Direct Contradiction:** As we saw in our discussion of (B), this is essentially the opposite of the right answer. Interestingly, the internal logic of this choice is actually consistent: if a mouse were more likely to be found by a predator, then it would be less likely to pass on its traits, which is what the text of (C) says. But when we combine (C) with the prompt, we see that the idea of being *more* likely to be found doesn't go with the idea in the prompt, which talks about mouse pigmentation matching the color of the soil, not contrasting with the color of the soil. So (C) could appeal to people who misread the prompt and think it's asking for what would happen when the mouse's coloring differed more from the coloring of the soil, or people who forgot exactly what the prompt said and just thought (C) sounded like it made sense on its own.

D **Off by One or Two Words:** This choice has the reverse of the same basic problem as (A). It may attract some untrained test-takers because it only differs from the right answer by one word.

> **What we had to understand to answer the question:** We needed to realize that having coloring similar to the soil would make it harder for a mouse to be seen, which would also make it harder for a predator to find the mouse. We also needed to know that an animal that's less likely to get killed by a predator is more likely to have offspring, and therefore more likely to pass long traits to those offspring. We didn't need to know what the "geographic variation in the fur pigmentation of *P. polionotus*," as mentioned in the prompt, even is. This question could have been answered just as easily without any of the text or diagrams in the passage.

Note Many test-takers who read this question will be reminded of Darwin and the theory of evolution, because this question involves the ability to survive and pass genetic material on to offspring. But we didn't actually need to know anything about Darwin or evolution specifically to answer this question, as long as we were able to work through the reasoning in the answer choice explanations above. Keep in mind that the ACT Science section requires much less outside scientific knowledge than most people believe!

Test 1, Question 6 (Test 2 in the 2020-2021 Red Book—see page 23 for more)   **TYPE: DATA PLUS PARAGRAPH**

Finding the answer requires information from the text as well as information from a figure. Read carefully, and be very particular about matching up exact values in the figure and the answer choices, unless the prompt calls for estimation. See p. 339.

Notes on answer choices: The wording of each choice is identical except for two words: the first word in (F) and (G) is "lighter" and the first word in (H) and (J) is "darker;" the last two words of (F) and (H) are "was 100%" and the corresponding words in (G) and (J) are "was less than 100%."

F **Off by One or Two Words:** The word "lighter" might appeal to some untrained test-takers because Figure 2 does show that the soil at the coast was lighter *than the other soil that was tested.* But the prompt asks whether the coastal soil was lighter than the "standard that was used for comparison," and the footnote for Figure 2 makes it clear that the standard of comparison was "assigned 100% reflectance," which means that it corresponds to a value of 100 on the vertical axis of Figure 2. So it's clear that none of the soil tested for Figure 2 was lighter than the standard, because being lighter than the standard would involve having a y-value on the graph that was greater than 100%.

G **Off by One or Two Words:** (G) is similar to (F), except that it correctly observes that the y-value of the coastal site at Figure 2 (and all sites for Figure 2) was less than 100%. Still, "lighter" is the wrong way to begin this phrase, as noted for (F).

H **Barely Relevant:** The word "darker" is correct, as we'll see for (J), but none of the soil in Figure 2 had a relative reflectance of 100%, as we just saw in our discussions of (F) and (G).

J ✓ **Correct:** The description above Figure 2 says that "the average brightness of surface soil" is "given as the average percent relative reflectance." So the vertical axis of Figure 2, which is labeled "average percent relative reflectance," is a measure of "brightness," which means it tells us whether one thing is "lighter" or "darker" than another thing, as the prompt requires. There's an asterisk (*) on the label of the vertical axis, and the corresponding note at the bottom of Figure 2 says that the "average percent reflectance" is "compared to a standard that was assigned 100% reflectance." So the prompt asks about "the standard that was used for the comparison," and the footnote on Figure 2 tells us that the standard has "100% reflectance." We can see in Figure 2 that the surface soil at the coastal site—that is, where the inland distance is 0 km—is around 75%. So the surface soil at the coastal sight is less

---

bright than the standard used for comparison, which means it's darker than the standard—again, because the *y*-value for the coastal readings is less than 100%. This is exactly what (J) says, so (J) is correct.

> **What we had to understand to answer the question:** We needed to refer to Figure 2 and realize that "lighter" soil corresponded to higher "reflectance," and we needed to notice the footnote that said the "standard...was assigned 100% reflectance." We never needed to know how the standard referred to in the asterisk for Figure 2 was selected.

Test 1, Question 7 (Test 2 in the 2020-2021 Red Book—see page 23 for more) **TYPE: PURE DATA**

Finding the answer requires information from a figure. Read carefully, and be very particular about matching up exact values in the figure and the answer choices, unless the question calls for estimation. See p. 339.

Notes on answer choices: Each of the numbers in the answer choices is a value in the CNF column of Table 1.

A   **Barely Relevant:** According to the logic discussed in the explanation for (B), this is what we'd expect in Experiment 1 from a reaction time of less than 10 minutes—not a reaction time of 2 days, as the prompt requires.

B ✓ **Correct:** Table 1 gives us the results from Experiment 1, which is mentioned in the prompt. When we read that table, we can see that the CNF value always increases as the reaction time gets longer. This indicates that there's a predictable relationship between how long the reaction takes and the CNF. Since 2 days is a length of time between 10 minutes and 3 days, we expect a CNF between the CNF measurements for 10 minutes and 3 days—in other words, we expect the CNF for 2 days to be between 6 mg/kg and 39 mg/kg. So (B) is right.

C   **Barely Relevant:** According to the logic discussed in the explanation for (B), this is what we would expect in Experiment 1 from a reaction time of between 3 days and 7 days—not a reaction time of 2 days, as the prompt requires.

D   **Barely Relevant:** According to the logic discussed in the explanation for (B), this is what we would expect in Experiment 1 from a reaction time of more than 7 days—not a reaction time of 2 days, as the prompt requires.

> **What we had to understand to answer the question:** This question didn't require us to understand any of the terms in the passage—all it required us to do was to refer to the table that included information about Experiment 1, and then figure out which range of CNF values corresponded to the range of reaction times that included a reaction time of 2 days.

Test 1, Question 8 (Test 2 in the 2020-2021 Red Book—see page 23 for more) **TYPE: DATA PLUS PARAGRAPH**

Finding the answer requires information from the text as well as information from a figure. Read carefully, and be very particular about matching up exact values in the figure and the answer choices, unless the prompt calls for estimation. See p. 339.

Notes on answer choices: (F) and (H) both have "10 min" as their reaction times, while (G) and (J) both have "7 days." (F) and (G) both have "standard" as their filtration method, while (H) and (J) both have "vacuum." So the choices offer every possible combination of two reaction times and two filtration methods.

F ✓ **Correct:** An untrained test-taker might be confused by the phrase "concentration of dissolved nickel" in the prompt, because that exact phrase doesn't appear in Passage II. But when we read carefully, we can see that the first sentence of the passage tells us that dissolved nickel is Ni^{2+}, and the 4th step of Experiment 1 tells us that CNF represents the concentration of Ni^{2+}—dissolved nickel—in the filtrate. So when the prompt asks us about the "concentration of dissolved nickel in the filtrate," it's asking us about the CNF. Further, we can see that the answer choices all mention either a "standard" or "vacuum" filtration method—but Table 1 doesn't mention a filtration method when reporting the results of Experiments 1 and 2. We can see that the phrase "standard filtration" appears in two places: it's italicized in Step 3 of Experiment 1, and it's the caption for Figure 1. This tells us that Experiment 1 used "standard filtration." We see that the phrase "vacuum filtration" also appears in two places: it's italicized in the description of Experiment 2, and it's the caption for Figure 2. This tells us that Experiment 2 used vacuum filtration. With all of that in mind, we can see that the lowest CNF in Table 1 (the lowest "concentration of dissolved nickel" as described in the prompt) was 6 mg/kg, which corresponds to a reaction time of 10 minutes in Experiment 1. And we now know the passage indicates Experiment 1 used standard filtration, so (F) is right.

G   **Off by One or Two Words:** Table 1 shows us that this combination of reaction time and filtration method resulted in a concentration of dissolved nickel in the filtrate (CNF) of 42 mg/kg, but the lowest CNF is the one described in choice (F), as we can see in the explanation for that choice.

H   **Off by One or Two Words:** Table 1 shows us that this combination of reaction time and filtration method resulted in a concentration of dissolved nickel in the filtrate (CNF) of 58 mg/kg, but the lowest CNF is the one described in choice (F), as we can see in the explanation for that choice.

J   **Direct Contradiction:** Table 1 shows us that this combination of reaction time and filtration method resulted in the *highest* concentration of dissolved nickel in the filtrate, but the question asks for the *lowest*.

> **What we had to understand to answer the question:** We needed to use the information in the first sentence of the passage and also in Step 4 of Experiment 1 to figure out that the phrase "concentration of dissolved nickel" corresponded to the "CNF" column in Table 1, as we discussed for (F) above. We also needed to realize that Experiment 1 used standard filtration, while Experiment 2 used vacuum filtration; we could figure this out as described in the explanation for (F) above. But we never needed

to know why nickel is being concentrated or dissolved, or what the words "nickel" and "filtrate" mean, or how filtration works in general and why somebody would want to use a vacuum for it. We also never needed to understand the experimental diagrams in Figure 1 or Figure 2.

Test 1, Question 9 (Test 2 in the 2020-2021 Red Book—see page 23 for more)   TYPE: OUTSIDE INFO

Answering requires some information that can't be found in the passage. Any required outside knowledge must be relatively basic. Don't try to use outside knowledge on a question unless you're sure you can't answer based on the passage. See p. 339.

Notes on answer choices: The choices are identical except for two differences. (A) and (B) begin with "Trial 3," while (C) and (D) begin with "Trial 6." (A) and (C) have the phrase "was connected" at the end of the first line, while (B) and (D) have the phrase "was not connected" at the end of the first line. Since those are the only differences, we know that the issue of being "connected to a vacuum pump" is relevant to the question.

A   **Off by One or Two Words:** We can see that Trial 3 was part of Experiment 1. When we look at Figure 1, which relates to Experiment 1, we see that the trials in Experiment 1 *did NOT* involve a vacuum pump, so (A) contradicts the passage.

B   **Direct Contradiction:** As we just saw for (A), it's true that Trial 3 didn't involve a vacuum pump, because it was part of Experiment 1. But as we can see in the explanation for (C), we can use our basic scientific knowledge to conclude that more net force would be exerted when a vacuum pump was used, so this choice must be wrong.

C ✓   **Correct:** This is another great example of the kind of fundamental scientific knowledge we occasionally need on the ACT Science section. When we read the choices, we can see that we need to decide whether the force exerted on the mixture in the funnel was greater in Trial 3 or in Trial 6, and whether the filtration apparatus was connected to a vacuum pump. We can conclude that the use of a vacuum pump would exert *more* force, as opposed to using no pump at all. The most obvious and straightforward way to realize this is to remember that a vacuum is a machine that's designed to generate some kind of force, so it makes sense that the trial with a force-generating machine would involve more force than the trial without a force-generating machine. This leads us to conclude that the trial with more force would have involved a vacuum pump, which means the right answer must accurately indicate which trial involved a vacuum pump. We see that the vacuum pump is mentioned in Figure 2 as part of Experiment 2, and we see in the table that Experiment 2 covered Trials 4, 5, and 6. This means that Trials 4, 5, and 6 were the ones that involved a vacuum pump. So the right answer should refer to one of those three trials, and mention that it included a vacuum pump. (C) is the only choice that does that, so (C) must be right.

D   **Off by One or Two Words:** When we look at the description for Experiment 2 in the passage, we can see that Trial 6 was part of that experiment. When we look at Figure 2, we can see that the trials in this experiment *did* involve a vacuum pump—so this choice contradicts the passage, and must be wrong.

Test 1, Question 10 (Test 2 in the 2020-2021 Red Book—see page 23 for more)   TYPE: PURE PARAGRAPH

Answering requires information from the text. Choices often primarily involve phrases rather than numbers. Consider every relevant word. Be sure your answer is literally demonstrated or restated on the page, with no interpretation necessary. See p. 339.

Notes on answer choices: Each choice includes the same three steps separated by semicolons, but in a different order.

F   **Confused Relationships:** We can see in the steps for Experiment 1 that measuring the CNF happens last, in step 4. But it's the first step listed in (F), so (F) must be wrong.

G ✓   **Correct:** We can see in the steps for Experiment 1 that Step 1 involved pouring an amount of OH^- solution and Ni^{2+} solution into the same flask, which restates "mixing the Ni^{2+} and the OH^- solutions" from (G). This is actually all we need to know in order to realize that (G) is right, since no other choice starts with mixing the chemicals together. Further, Step 3 in Experiment 1 says the "solid monohydrate was recovered by standard filtration," and the description for Experiment 2 says that in Step 3, "the solid monohydrate was recovered by vacuum filtration." So both versions of Step 3 restate the idea of "recovering the solid by filtration," as (G) requires after the step of mixing the solutions. Finally, Step 4 says the CNF "was determined," which restates "measuring the CNF" from (G). Since the order of the steps in (G) matches the order described in the passage, (G) must be right.

H   **Confused Relationships:** This choice has the recovery step first, but the text for Experiment 1 in Passage II says the mixing step happened first, as we saw above for (G).

J   **Confused Relationships:** This choice has the same problem we just saw in our discussion of (H).

What we had to understand to answer the question: We needed to realize that the steps listed out for Experiment 1 in Passage II must be restated in the right answer. We didn't need to know the meanings of the words "aqueous," "mole," "flask," or "monohydrate" from those steps; it was enough to realize "mixing the...solutions" from the choices restated the idea that a "...solution and...[another] solution were poured into the same..." from Step 1. Above all, we didn't need to understand anything about the purpose behind the design of the experiments in order to find the answer with certainty.

Test 1, Question 11 (Test 2 in the 2020-2021 Red Book—see page 23 for more)   TYPE: DATA PLUS PARAGRAPH

Finding the answer requires information from the text as well as information from a figure. Read carefully, and be very particular about matching up exact values in the figure and the answer choices, unless the prompt calls for estimation. See p. 339.

A   **Barely Relevant:** Trials 1 and 2 aren't relevant to this question, since they don't involve "vacuum filtration" as required by the prompt, so (A) can't be right (see the explanation for (D)).

B   **Off by One or Two Words:** This choice makes an accurate statement about the relevant trials, but the fact that Trial 5 had a reaction time of 3 days and Trial 4 had a reaction time of 10 minutes—and Trial 5 had a greater CNF than Trial 4—means that these trials *do* support the prediction in the prompt, as we can see in the discussion of (D).

C   **Barely Relevant:** This choice has the same basic problem as (A): neither of the trials it mentions involved vacuum filtration.

D ✓   **Correct:** We can see in the description of Experiment 2 that Experiment 2 involved recovering solid monohydrate with "*vacuum filtration*" (italics in original). So we need to figure out whether there was a greater CNF when Experiment 2 was performed with a reaction time of 3 days, or when the same experiment was performed with a reaction time of 10 minutes. Table 1 tells us that Trial 5 used a reaction time of 3 days and was part of Experiment 2. The same table tells us that Trial 4 used a reaction time of 10 minutes and was also part of Experiment 2. We can see that the CNF for Trial 5 is 69, which is greater than the CNF for Trial 4, at 58. So Trial 5 had a greater CNF than did Trial 4, which supports the student's prediction. That means (D) is right.

> **What we had to understand to answer the question:** We didn't need to understand what solid monohydrate actually was, or how vacuum filtration actually recovers it. We also didn't need to understand anything about the diagrams or chemical reactions in Passage II. All we had to realize was that the phrase "vacuum filtration" in the prompt meant that we had to pay attention to Experiment 2—which we could know because the description of Experiment 2 and the caption of Figure 2 tells us that Experiment 2 involved "vacuum filtration"—and that Table 1 provided the data for the trials involving vacuum filtration with reaction times of 3 days and 10 minutes.

Test 1, Question 12 (Test 2 in the 2020-2021 Red Book—see page 23 for more)   **TYPE: DATA PLUS PARAGRAPH**

Finding the answer requires information from the text as well as information from a figure. Read carefully, and be very particular about matching up exact values in the figure and the answer choices, unless the prompt calls for estimation. See p. 339.

F   **Off by One or Two Words:** This choice may tempt some untrained test-takers because there's a single trial where standard filtration was used and the reaction went on for *exactly* 3 days. But the prompt uses the phrase "*for at least 3 days*" (emphasis added), and Experiment 1 has two trials that went for *at least* 3 days: Trial 2, and Trial 3. So (F) is wrong. (Note that step 3 of Experiment 1 tells us that "*standard filtration*" was used for that experiment, while the description for Experiment 2 tells us that "*vacuum filtration*" was used for that experiment.)

G ✓   **Correct:** As we discussed for (F), only Experiment 1 used "standard filtration," as the prompt calls for, and Table 1 tells us that only 2 trials in Experiment 1 (Trials 2 and 3) involved a reaction time of at least 3 days, as the prompt also calls for. So (G) is correct.

H   **Off by One or Two Words:** This choice will tempt untrained test-takers who misread the prompt and think it's just asking how many trials involved a reaction that went on for 3 days or more, no matter what type of filtration was involved. It's true that a total of 4 trials were allowed to react for at least 3 days, but 2 of those trials were in Experiment 2, so they involved vacuum filtration, not the "standard filtration" required by the prompt, as we saw in our discussion of (F).

J   **Barely Relevant:** Some untrained test-takers who didn't understand the question and/or passage might pick this choice because Table 1 shows a total of 6 trials. But, as trained test-takers, we know that 4 of those trials aren't relevant to the prompt, as discussed above for (F).

> **What we had to understand to answer the question:** We didn't really need to understand what "nickel hydroxide monohydrate," OH^-, and Ni^{2+} are, since none of the answer choices is zero and Passage II only mentions one reaction, and one substance to be filtered out after that reaction (it does mention using two different methods to filter stuff out, but it never says that the stuff being filtered with either method is different from the stuff being filtered with the other method). All we needed to understand was that we needed to locate the parts of Table 1 that dealt with "standard filtration" for "at least 3 days," as we discussed above for (F.

Test 1, Question 13 (Test 2 in the 2020-2021 Red Book—see page 23 for more)   **TYPE: PURE PARAGRAPH**

Answering requires information from the text. Choices often primarily involve phrases rather than numbers. Consider every relevant word. Be sure your answer is literally demonstrated or restated on the page, with no interpretation necessary. See p. 339.

A ✓   **Correct:** When we look at the "balanced chemical equation in the passage," we can see that 2 OH^- on the left side of the equation corresponds to a single $Ni(OH)_2 \cdot H_2O$ on the right side of the equation. This means that 6 OH^- would be 3 times as many as the 2 OH^- that are in the given equation, so we'll see 3 times as many of the $Ni(OH)_2 \cdot H_2O$ produced on the right side. 3 times 1 is 3, so this choice is correct. (Note that realizing we need to multiply by 3 helps us to understand why all the choices in this question are multiples of 3.)

B   **Confused Relationships:** This choice would tempt an untrained test-taker who simply assumed that each OH^- would correspond to a $Ni(OH)_2 \cdot H_2O$, without considering the equation in Passage II (as we saw in our discussion of (A)).

C   **Direct Contradiction:** This choice would attract someone who correctly noticed that the equation calls for twice as much OH^- as $Ni(OH)_2 \cdot H_2O$, but then mentally reversed that relationship and thought that $6\ OH^-$ should correspond to $12\ Ni(OH)_2 \cdot H_2O$ instead of 3.

D   **Barely Relevant:** This choice might attract an untrained test-taker who thought that each OH^- would correspond to $3\ Ni(OH)_2 \cdot H_2O$, perhaps due to a mistake similar to the one we discussed above for (C).

> **What we had to understand to answer the question:** We definitely didn't need to understand or remember anything about Passage II apart from the equation mentioned in the prompt, which appears after the second paragraph in the passage. The prompts specifically mentions that the string of symbols is a "balanced chemical equation," and the same phrase is used to refer to it at the end of the second paragraph. Once we're told that the given string of symbols is a "balanced...equation," we can probably figure out that this automatically means that any change applied to one side of the equation requires the same change to be applied to the other side. Since $6\ OH^-$ involves multiplying the original $2\ OH^-$ on the left-hand side by 3, we know we need to multiply $Ni(OH)_2 \cdot H_2O$ on the right-hand side by 3 as well. (See "Chemical equations as ratios" on page 335 of this Black Book for more.)

Test 1, Question 14 (Test 2 in the 2020-2021 Red Book—see page 23 for more)   **TYPE: PURE PARAGRAPH**

Answering requires information from the text. Choices often primarily involve phrases rather than numbers. Consider every relevant word. Be sure your answer is literally demonstrated or restated on the page, with no interpretation necessary. See p. 339.

Notes on answer choices: The choices present every possible combination of the words "inward" and "outward."

F   **Off by One or Two Words:** As we can see in the explanation for (G), this choice is right about the direction of gravity, but wrong about the direction of RP (radiation pressure).

G ✓   **Correct:** The first bullet of the passage says that the gravitational field "attracts gas" and causes the gas to "accumulate onto the star." This makes it clear that gravity "accelerates gas particles" inward, towards the "center of the protostar," as the prompt requires in combination with (G). The second bullet of the passage includes the phrase *radiation pressure* (RP)" in italics, (which makes it easier for us to find by skimming), and says that the radiation pressure causes gas to be "pushed away from the protostar." This makes it clear that radiation pressure "accelerate[s] gas particles...outward," away from the star, as the prompt requires in combination with (G). Since both parts of (G) are directly restated in Passage III, (G) is correct.

H   **Direct Contradiction:** This choice will appeal to untrained test-takers who confuse gravity and RP, or who correctly understand the passage but confuse the columns in the answer choices.

J   **Off by One or Two Words:** As we can see in the explanation for (G), this choice is correct about the effect of RP (radiation pressure), but incorrect about the effect of gravity.

> **What we had to understand to answer the question:** We needed to realize that the bullet points in Passage III tell us that the "gravitational field attracts gas," and that the "(RP)…causes gas to be pushed away from the protostar." We also needed to realize that the idea of attracting goes with the word "inward" in the answer choices, and the idea of pushing away goes with the word "outward." We didn't need to understand anything about how the scientists agree or disagree, or what the word "accretion" means, or what a "protostar" is, or why any scientist would care about any of this—again, we only needed to realize that the text says gravity attracts gas (which restates the idea of moving inward), and pressure pushes away gas (which restates the idea of moving outward).

Note   A lot of untrained test-takers who are good students of science will be tempted to answer this question based on their previous understanding of the terms "gravity" and "pressure," but that's the not the best way to approach the question, because it could reinforce bad habits on the ACT Science section in the long run. It's true that "gravity" generally refers to the way matter is attracted to the center of a mass, and it's true that "pressure" can generally refer to the idea that gases and liquids want to disperse from areas of higher concentration … *and* it's true that those definitions could lead you to the right answer in this case, even if you hadn't read the passage at all. But we'll sometimes find that the ACT Science section uses terms in ways that may differ from your understanding of those terms; if you develop a habit of relying primarily on your own knowledge to answer ACT questions, there's a good chance you'll occasionally pick wrong answers, and you won't have the proper instincts for attacking questions by depending on the information on the page in front of you. Of course, there are a few questions per test that require some outside knowledge—but remember that you should always try to find the answer to any ACT Science question by looking in the provided passage first, and only fall back on basic outside scientific knowledge when you can't find the answer in the passage. (For more on this, see "Basic Science Facts" on page 331 of this Black Book.)

Answering requires information from the text. Choices often primarily involve phrases rather than numbers. Consider every relevant word. Be sure your answer is literally demonstrated or restated on the page, with no interpretation necessary. See p. 339.

Notes on answer choices: Choices are identical except for two differences. (A) and (B) start with "near the equator," while (C) and (D) start with "near the poles." (A) and (C) end with "is increased there," while (B) and (D) end with "is reduced there."

A   **Off by One or Two Words:** As we can see in the explanation for (B), this choice is correct about the location where the gas particles accrete, but not about what happens to the effect of RP near the equator, so it's wrong. This will attract untrained test-takers who misread the last part of the choice.

B ✓ **Correct:** Scientist 2 says that "a disk of gas" in the "protostar's equator…reduces the effect of RP…in that plane, allowing gas from the disk to readily accrete." The phrase "disk of gas" in that sentence tells us we've found the part of Scientist 2's argument that's relevant to the prompt, since the prompt mentions a "protostar with a disk." The phrase "in the plane of the protostar's equator" in Scientist 2's argument restates the phrase "near the equator" in (B). Finally, the phrase "reduces the effect of RP" in Scientist 2's argument restates the phrase "the effect of RP is reduced" from (B). Since every part of (B) is directly restated by the relevant text mentioned in the prompt, (B) is right.

C   **Confused Relationships:** In one sense, this choice is exactly the opposite of Scientist 2's argument, as we saw for (B), because it uses the wrong phrases for both parts of the answer choice. But in another sense, this choice may seem like it's logically true to some test-takers who don't base their response exactly on the text and don't refer back to the prompt before picking an answer. They might think it could make sense to assume that RP is *relatively* stronger at the poles (since we know it's weaker at the equator, as we saw in our discussion of (B))…but, even if it were true that RP was stronger at the poles, the text still doesn't say that gas particles would accrete there, which is what the prompt requires. (It also doesn't have to be true that the effect of RP is increased at the poles just because it's decreased at the equator—it's entirely possible that RP is just unchanged at the poles and only weakened at the equator, according to Scientist 2's statements.) If you picked (C), you probably need to focus more on working directly from the wording on the page, just as we do for an ACT Reading question. See the explanation of (B) for a detailed description of how the right answer to this question is literally restated on the page.

D   **Off by One or Two Words:** This choice has the same basic problem as (A), and is wrong for the same reason—in this case, the word "poles" should be "equator" in order for this choice to match what Scientist 2 says.

What we had to understand to answer the question: We needed to realize that the second sentence of Scientist 2's statement specifically mentions a "disk of gas," which is relevant to the phrase "with a disk" in the prompt. Then we needed to read that sentence and the following sentence, matching up words like "accrete" in both the prompt and in Scientist 2's statement to verify that we were considering the right part of the text. We never actually needed to understand the meanings of the words "protostar," "accrete," or "RP," nor the actual physical mechanics of the model that Scientist 2 is proposing. We also never needed to read or understand any part of Passage III apart from the two sentences we just mentioned above. All we needed to do was to match up the phrases mentioned in the explanation for (B) above.

Answering requires information from the text. Choices often primarily involve phrases rather than numbers. Consider every relevant word. Be sure your answer is literally demonstrated or restated on the page, with no interpretation necessary. See p. 339.

Notes on answer choices: Scientist 2 is the only scientist that doesn't appear alone in her own answer choice. No choice combines all of the scientists, and no choice includes Scientist 2 and Scientist 3.

F   **Confused Relationships:** As we can see in the explanation for (H), the results discussed in the prompt *are* inconsistent with Scientist 1's argument. But Scientist 2 agrees with Scientist 1 about the likelihood of stellar mergers, so those results are also inconsistent with Scientist 2's argument, which means this choice is incorrect.

G   **Direct Contradiction:** (G) will attract a lot of untrained test-takers who misread the prompt and think that we need to figure out whose argument is *consistent* with the results in the prompt—if that were what the prompt was really asking for, then (G) would be right. But the prompt asks whose argument is *inconsistent* with those results, so (G) is precisely wrong.

H ✓ **Correct:** Scientist 1 finishes his argument with the words "stellar mergers are likely," and Scientist 2 begins by saying that "Scientist 1 is correct that stellar mergers are likely." But Scientist 3 says, "stellar mergers are *very unlikely*" (emphasis added). So if a survey found no evidence of stellar mergers, as the prompt describes, then that lack of evidence would be inconsistent with Scientists 1 and 2, because they both said that stellar mergers were likely. So (H) is right.

J   **Confused Relationships:** This choice might tempt untrained test-takers who got confused between Scientists 2 and 3.

What we had to understand to answer the question: We needed to locate each scientist's direct statements about "stellar mergers" and whether they were likely. We also needed to realize that the idea of something never happening during the history of the whole galaxy is consistent with the idea of that thing being unlikely, not with the idea that it's likely to happen. We didn't need to understand what a stellar merger actually is, or why it might be likely, or how someone would survey star clusters to see if one ever happened, or any part of Passage III besides the sentence in each scientist's argument that specifically mentioned the likelihood of stellar mergers.

Answering requires information from the text. Choices often primarily involve phrases rather than numbers. Consider every relevant word. Be sure your answer is literally demonstrated or restated on the page, with no interpretation necessary. See p. 339.

Notes on answer choices: The choices present every possible combination of two options. The first option is whether Scientist 1 will say 5 or 6; the second option is whether the other scientists will say 3 and 1, or 4 and 2.

A   **Off by One or Two Words:** This choice is right about what Scientists 2 and 3 would say, but it's wrong about what Scientist 1 would say, as we'll see in our discussion of (C). This choice might attract untrained test-takers who made small mistakes in their reading or math, and didn't catch those mistakes.

B   **Barely Relevant:** This choice is wrong about each of the 3 scientists, for reasons we'll see when we talk about (C).

C ✓ **Correct:** Scientist 1 says that stars can reach a size of 20 M_s by accretion, and any further increase in size requires a stellar merger. According to this theory, a star with a mass of 120 M_s would have to involve the merging of at least 6 stars, each being the maximum size of 20 M_s, since $6 \times 20 = 120$. Scientist 2 says that stars can reach a size of 40 M_s by accretion; according to this theory, a star with a mass of 120 M_s would have to involve the merging of at least 3 stars that were each as big as possible, since $3 \times 40 = 120$. Scientist 3 says that a star can grow to an unlimited size by accretion, limited only by the amount of available gas; according to this theory, a star with a mass of 120 M_s wouldn't have to involve the merging of any stars, and could be achieved with only 1 star formed by accretion. (C) is the only choice that accurately reflects all of these values, so it must be right.

D   **Off by One or Two Words:** This choice is correct about what Scientist 1 would say, but it's wrong about what the other 2 scientists would say, as we saw for (C) above.

What we had to understand to answer the question: We needed to find and read the portion of each scientist's argument that stated the maximum size a star could reach through accretion, since those statements are relevant to the prompt's statements about a star with a mass of 120 M_s. We needed to be able to divide 120 by 20 and by 40. We never needed to know anything about Eta Carinae (other than its mass), nor how its size was determined, nor what the word "accretion" actually means, nor any part of Passage III apart from each scientist's statement about the maximum possible size a star can reach without a stellar merger.

Answering requires information from the text. Choices often primarily involve phrases rather than numbers. Consider every relevant word. Be sure your answer is literally demonstrated or restated on the page, with no interpretation necessary. See p. 339.

Notes on answer choices: The difference between any choice and the next choice is twice as much as the difference between that choice and the previous two choices—so the difference between (H) and (J) is 20 M_s, while the difference between (G) and (H) is 10 M_s, and the difference between (F) and (G) is 5 M_s.

F   **Barely Relevant:** Both scientists say that a star can reach this size by accretion: Scientist 1 says a star can grow to a size of up to 20 M_s by accretion, and Scientist 2 says a star can grow to a size of up to 40 M_s by accretion. Since both scientists allow for the possibility of a start growing through accretion to the size in (F), it's impossible for a star this size to support the claims of one scientist while weakening the claims of the other. (See our discussion of (H) for more on the connection between the prompt and the idea of a star reaching a certain size by accretion.)

G   **Barely Relevant:** This choice has the same problem as (F), and is wrong for the same reason: both scientist's arguments allow for stars to reach the size in (G) through accretion, so the idea of a star doing that can't have different implications for the theories of the two scientists. (See our discussion of (H) for more on the connection between the prompt and the idea of a star reaching a certain size by accretion.)

H ✓ **Correct:** The first paragraph after the bullet points in the passage says that "Star formation ends when the effect of RP overcomes that of gravity. At that point, the protostar can no longer gain mass by accretion." This sentence uses a technical phrase that appears word-for-word in the prompt: "when the effect of RP overcomes that of gravity." The prompt calls this the moment when a star has "'emerged from its envelope.'" So, according to the information we're given, the moment of "emerging from its envelope" is also the moment of no longer growing by accretion, and these are both different ways to describe the moment "when the effect of RP overcomes that of gravity." Scientist 1 says that stars can only grow by accretion until they reach a size of 20 M_s, but Scientist 2 says that stars can grow by accretion until they reach a size of 40 M_s. If a star reached a size of 30 M_s by accretion, that would contradict Scientist 1's argument, which says it's impossible for a star to grow above 20 M_s that way. But a star that grew to 30 M_s through accretion would be consistent with Scientist 2's argument, since 30 M_s is still less than 40 M_s, which is the limit that Scientist 2 proposes. So (H) is correct.

J   **Barely Relevant:** Both scientists say that a star can't reach this size by accretion, so a star "emerging from its envelope" at this size would undermine both scientists' arguments. See our discussion of (H) above for more.

> **What we had to understand to answer the question:** One way to approach this question involves comparing the prompt to the passage and realizing that the phrase "emerged from its envelope" in the prompt is just another way to say that a star has reached the point at which it no longer grows through accretion, as we discussed for (H). Using this approach, we need to realize that Scientist 1 says this point is reached when a star grows to 20 M_s, and Scientist 2 says the point is reached when a star grows to 40 M_s. We can tell those parts of the arguments are relevant because we can see that the answer choices are numbers followed by the M_s unit, just as we see in the part of each scientist's argument that addresses the maximum size a star can reach through accretion. And that leads us to the second way to approach the question, which is just to realize that two of the choices are below both scientist's stated maximum sizes for a star to reach through accretion, and one of the choices is above both scientist's stated maximum size for a star to reach through accretion; all of those choices must be wrong, since the prompt asks for a choice that would have different implications for the two theories, which means the right answer must be above one scientist's maximum number and below the other scientist's maximum number. Neither of these approaches requires us to understand the metaphor behind the phrase "emerged from its envelope," or any other part of Passage III besides the paragraph immediately after the bullet points and the statements made by Scientist 1 and Scientist 2 about numbers in M_s units.

Test 1, Question 19 (Test 2 in the 2020-2021 Red Book—see page 23 for more)   **TYPE: PURE PARAGRAPH**

Answering requires information from the text. Choices often primarily involve phrases rather than numbers. Consider every relevant word. Be sure your answer is literally demonstrated or restated on the page, with no interpretation necessary. See p. 339.

Notes on answer choices: The choices appear to be unrelated phrases with no obvious similarities.

A ✓ **Correct:** Scientist 2 says that "a disk of gas forms in the plane of the protostar's equator," which restates the idea from the prompt that "a disk forms around a protostar." Scientist 2 explains that the disk forms "because a protostar rotates about its axis," which restates the idea from (A) that "motion" is what causes the disk to form, since rotation is a kind of motion. Scientist 3 says that "Scientist 2 is correct about the formation…of the disk." So we can see that both Scientist 2 and Scientist 3 agree on how the disk is formed, and their opinion is that motion causes the disk to form around the protostar, just as (A) requires.

B **Confused Relationships:** This choice might tempt some test-takers who don't read carefully, because Scientist 3 does mention "regions of radiation that increase the effect of RP…, promoting the flow of gas into the disk." But Scientist 2 doesn't say anything connecting the protostar's "emission of radiation" to the formation of the disk, so this choice can't be correct, because the prompt asked for a subject that both scientists agree on.

C **Barely Relevant:** Neither Scientist 2 nor 3 makes any connection between the star's presence in a star cluster and the formation of the disk—in fact, Scientist 2 never mentions star clusters at all.

D **Barely Relevant:** Neither Scientist 2 nor 3 makes any connection between the merging of stars and the formation of the disk—in fact, Scientist 3 calls stellar mergers "very unlikely."

> **What we had to understand to answer the question:** We needed to recognize which parts of Scientist 2's argument were about how a disk forms, and we needed to recognize that Scientist 3 claims to agree with Scientist 2 about disk formation, as discussed for (A) above. We didn't need to know or understand anything about radiation, star clusters, mergers, or anything else in Passage III.

Test 1, Question 20 (Test 2 in the 2020-2021 Red Book—see page 23 for more)   **TYPE: PURE PARAGRAPH**

Answering requires information from the text. Choices often primarily involve phrases rather than numbers. Consider every relevant word. Be sure your answer is literally demonstrated or restated on the page, with no interpretation necessary. See p. 339.

Notes on answer choices: Scientist 2 is the only one who doesn't appear alone in an answer choice.

F **Off by One or Two Words:** Scientist 1 would agree with the statement from the prompt—but so would scientists 2 and 3, as we can see in the discussion of (H) below.

G **Off by One or Two Words:** This choice has the same basic problem as (F): it says that only one of the scientists would agree with something that all of the scientists would actually agree with, as we'll see for (H) below. This choice might also tempt a test-taker who didn't realize that the mass of the sun was equal to 1 M_s, and might have assumed that the mass of the sun would be 100 M_s, so that other stars could be expressed in terms of a "percentage" of the sun—so that a 20 M_s star would be 20% of the size of the sun, etc. But the first parenthetical statement in the argument made by Scientist 1 makes it clear that 1 M_s is the size of the sun, so all of the size limits discussed by the scientists are larger than the size of the Sun.

H ✓ **Correct:** The paragraph under "Scientist 1" tells us that "1 M_s = mass of the Sun." Scientist 1 says that "the maximum mass that a protostar can reach by accretion is 20 M_s." Scientist 2 says that "the maximum mass that a protostar can reach by accretion is 40 M_s." Scientist 3 says that "the maximum mass that a protostar can reach by accretion is limited only by the amount of available gas"—in other words, a protostar can reach any size by accretion as long as there's enough gas available. So all three scientists agree that a protostar can grow through accretion to a mass that's many times larger than the mass of the Sun, which means that all three scientists agree that the Sun itself could have formed entirely by accretion, since size limitation is the only factor in any of the

For free sample video demonstrations, go to www.ACTprepVideos.com   Page 357

scientist's discussions.

J   **Direct Contradiction:** As we can see in the discussion of (H), all 3 scientists would agree with the statement from the prompt. This choice could tempt a test-taker who misread the word "agree" from the prompt as "disagree."

> **What we had to understand to answer the question:** We needed to realize that each scientist allowed for the possibility that stars forming by accretion could be larger than the Sun. We could figure this out by focusing on the statements that included units of solar mass and/or mentions of how large a star can get through accretion, which we had to think about for questions 17 and 18. We didn't need to understand any other part of Passage III to answer this question.

Test 1, Question 21 (Test 2 in the 2020-2021 Red Book—see page 23 for more)   **TYPE: DATA PLUS DATA**

Finding the right answer requires information from more than one figure. Read carefully, and be very particular about matching up exact values in the figure and the answer choices, unless estimation is called for. See page 339.

Notes on answer choices: Choices offer every possible one- or two-option combination of the words "increased" and "decreased."

A   **Confused Relationships:** This choice might have attracted an untrained test-taker who only focused on the second portion of Figures 1 and 2, or who simply reacted to her general impression of the graphs in each study, and didn't notice that two of the answer choices combine the idea of increasing and decreasing.

B   **Confused Relationships:** This choice might have tricked an untrained test-taker who only focused on the first two bars of Figures 1 and 2, and disregarded the rest of the data.

C   **Direct Contradiction:** This choice is probably here to fill out the pattern of offering every possible combination of increasing and decreasing. If you picked it, you probably need to make sure you read more carefully in the future.

D ✓   **Correct:** In the prompt, we see the phrase "percent by volume of vermicompost," and the numbers 0% and 100%, so we'll need to figure out what that's referring to in order to identify the relevant part of Passage IV. When we look at Table 1, we see a label that reads "Percent by volume of," and beneath that label we see "vermicompost." In the "vermicompost" column, we can see that Mixture 1 starts at 0 percent vermicompost, Mixture 2 is at 20 percent vermicompost, and the mixtures increase by 20 percent up to Mixture 6 at 100 percent vermicompost. So these numbers and their labeling definitely reflect the ideas in the prompt, but now we need to figure out how they're relevant to the idea of "average yield" in the prompt, and the ideas of decreasing and increasing in the answer choices. The phrase "average yield" is the label for the vertical axes of both graphs in Passage IV, and we can see that both graphs demonstrate trends related to increasing and decreasing. So we still need to figure out how those graphs are relevant to the idea of the percentage of vermicompost. When we look at Table 1 and at both figures, we can see that what they have in common is a references to Mixtures 1-6. From Table 1, we see that each mixture corresponds to a percentage of vermicompost, and in the figures we can see how average yield was affected by the different percentages of vermicompost. With all of that figured out, we can turn our attention to "both studies," as required in the prompt, to figure out the answer to the question. We see that Figure 1 displays data from Study 1, and Figure 2 displays data from Study 2, and both studies involved plants growing in the Mixtures 1-6 that appeared in Table 1; both figures show that average yield initially increases and then decreases from left to right on the graph, as the percentage of vermicompost increases. So the right answer is (D).

> **What we had to understand to answer the question:** We needed to locate the technical phrase "percent by volume of vermicompost" in Table 1, and the data it referred to, after reading that phrase in the prompt. We also needed to locate the phrase "average yield" in Figure 1 and Figure 2 after reading it in the prompt. Finally, we needed to recognize that the 6 mixtures in Table 1 vary by percentage, and are the same mixtures referred to in the label on the horizontal axes of both figures. We never actually needed to read any of the paragraphs in Passage IV, nor to understand what the word "vermicompost" means or why anyone would care about testing percentages of it.

Test 1, Question 22 (Test 2 in the 2020-2021 Red Book—see page 23 for more)   **TYPE: PURE PARAGRAPH**

Answering requires information from the text. Choices often primarily involve phrases rather than numbers. Consider every relevant word. Be sure your answer is literally demonstrated or restated on the page, with no interpretation necessary. See p. 339.

Notes on answer choices: The choices include every mixture except 3 and 6.

F ✓   **Correct:** This is another example of the kind of relatively fundamental scientific knowledge that's occasionally required on the ACT Science section. Speaking very simply, the "control" is the part of an experiment that doesn't include the thing being tested, so that when we include the thing being tested, we have something to compare the results to. (The "control" allows the researchers to make a meaningful comparison to the thing that is being tested.) We can see that the first sentence of Passage IV tells us that studies were done "to examine how the proportion of vermicompost...affects the yield...;" since the researchers are studying the effects of vermicompost on yield, the control would logically be the sample without vermicompost. That way, the mixtures with vermicompost can be compared to the control—the sample without vermicompost—and the researchers can use that comparison to figure out the impact of using the different percentages of vermicompost. Table 1 shows us that Mixture 1 is 0% vermicompost, so Mixture 1 must be the control and (F) is correct.

G   **Barely Relevant:** See the explanation for choice (F). The prompt doesn't restate or demonstrate any reason why the control should be a mixture including vermicompost, and there's no reason to think a mixture would make a good control in this situation. (See "Special Article: Basics of Experimental Design" on page 336 of this Black Book for more.)

H   Barely Relevant: Again, see the explanation for (F).

J   Barely Relevant: See (F) above.

> **What we had to understand to answer the question:** We needed to have the outside knowledge mentioned in (F), and we needed to be able to read the first row of data in Table 1 to know that Mixture 1 was the only mixture that contained no vermicompost.

Test 1, Question 23 (Test 2 in the 2020-2021 Red Book—see page 23 for more)   **TYPE: PURE DATA**

Finding the answer requires information from a figure. Read carefully, and be very particular about matching up exact values in the figure and the answer choices, unless the question calls for estimation. See p. 339.

Notes on answer choices: (A) and (C) assume that the yield for Mixture 5 in Study 1 will involve the numbers 1, 4, and 5; (B) and (D) assume it will include the numbers 3, 5, and 0. (A) and (B) assume that two digits will be to the right of the decimal point, while (C) and (D) assume that one digit will be to the right of the decimal point.

A   Confused Relationships: This choice would be correct if the question asked about Mixture 5 from *Study 2*, but the prompt asks about Mixture 5 from *Study 1*, so this is incorrect.

B ✓ Correct: Figure 1 gives the results for Study 1, and Figure 1 shows us that the average yield for Mixture 5 was 3,500 g/plant. 1 kilogram is equal to 1,000 grams, so 3,500 grams is equal to 3.5 kilograms. That means the average yield for Mixture 5 in kilograms/plant is 3.5 kg/plant, and (B) is correct.

C   Confused Relationships: This choice combines the mistake from (A) with the mistake of thinking that a kilogram is equal to 100 grams, instead of 1,000 grams.

D   Same Ballpark: This would attract test-takers who mistakenly thought that a kilogram was equal to 100 grams, instead of 1,000 grams (or who simply made a mental mistake when dividing by 1,000).

> **What we had to understand to answer the question:** We needed to realize that we should consider the column of data for Mixture 5 in Figure 1, and we needed to realize that we should divide 3,500 grams by 1,000 in order to find the number of kilograms in 3,500 grams. No other part of Passage IV was relevant to this question at all.

Test 1, Question 24 (Test 2 in the 2020-2021 Red Book—see page 23 for more)   **TYPE: PURE PARAGRAPH**

Answering requires information from the text. Choices often primarily involve phrases rather than numbers. Consider every relevant word. Be sure your answer is literally demonstrated or restated on the page, with no interpretation necessary. See p. 339.

Notes on answer choices: The choices offer every possible combination of two of the Roman numerals, as well as the possibility of picking all three Roman numerals.

F   Confused Relationships: See the explanation for (G).

G ✓ Correct: The description of Study 2 says that "*the procedures of Study 1 were repeated*, except that...the pots received water and light for 149 days instead of 158 days" (emphasis added). So the description mentions that the length of time for Study 2 was different from the length of time for Study 1. (It also mentions a few other differences, but the Roman numerals don't mention those differences.) The description of the differences doesn't say anything about changing the number of pots, or changing the volume of each pot. That means (G) is right.

H   Confused Relationships: See the explanation for (G).

J   Off by One or Two Words: This choice would attract untrained test-takers who correctly read the phrase "the procedures of Study 1 were repeated," but then didn't see the rest of that sentence, which mentions the different length of time for the second study, as described in (G).

> **What we had to understand to answer the question:** We needed to find the part of Study 2 that explains how it differed from Study 1. As it turns out, the sentence explaining that Study 2 involved different timing from Study 1 takes up nearly all of the paragraph that describes how Study 2 was run. We didn't need to consider either of the Figures, or the Table. We didn't need to read any part of the text other than the first sentence in the paragraph about Study 2.

Test 1, Question 25 (Test 2 in the 2020-2021 Red Book—see page 23 for more)   **TYPE: DATA PLUS PARAGRAPH**

Finding the answer requires information from the text as well as information from a figure. Read carefully, and be very particular about matching up exact values in the figure and the answer choices, unless the prompt calls for estimation. See p. 339.

Notes on answer choices: Each choice is identical except for two differences. (A) and (B) both begin with "yes," while (C) and (D) both begin with "no." (A) and (C) both say that Mixture 2 had the greatest yield in the first study and Mixture 3 had the greatest yield in the second study, while (B) and (D) both say that Mixture 3 had the greatest yield in the first study and Mixture 2 had the greatest yield in the second study.

A ✓ **Correct:** The description of Study 1 says it involved *S. lycopersicum* seeds. The first paragraph of Passage IV says that *Solanum lycopersicum* is a tomato plant, so we know that Study 1 involved tomato plants. On the other hand, the description of Study 2 says it involved *C. annuum* seeds, and the first paragraph of Passage IV says that *Capsicum annuum* is a pepper plant, so we know that Study 2 used pepper plants. When we look at Figure 1, which gives the results for the tomato plants from Study 1, we can see that the highest average yield came from Mixture 2; Table 1 shows us that Mixture 2 was 20% vermicompost. So the highest yield for the tomato plants came from 20% vermicompost. When we look at Figure 2, we see that the highest average yield for Study 2 came from Mixture 3. Table 1 says Mixture 3 was 40% vermicompost. So the pepper plants had the highest yield with 40% vermicompost. This means the statement in the prompt *is* consistent with the results of the studies: the tomato plants in Study 1 produced their maximum yield with a lower percentage (20%) of vermicompost, while the pepper plants produced their maximum yield with a higher percentage (40%) of vermicompost. That takes care of the "yes" part of the answer choices, so we know that either (A) or (B) is right—but now we have to make sure we confirm the specific numbers of the mixtures, so we don't pick a wrong answer accidentally. We can see that Figure 1, which is about Study 1, clearly shows that Mixture 2 had the highest yield. And we see that Figure 2, which is about Study 2, clearly shows Mixture 3 had the highest yield. So (A) is right. See the note below.

B **Off by One or Two Words:** This choice would attract untrained test-takers who correctly determined that the right answer should begin with "yes" as we saw above for (A), but then didn't read carefully enough to confirm that Mixture 2 did best in Study 1, and Mixture 3 did best in Study 2. In particular, a lot of people will have a hard time reading this choice without confusing the idea of Study 2 and Mixture 2, which could confuse them into picking (B). See the note below.

C **Off by One or Two Words:** This choice could attract test-takers who thought the prompt asked whether the statement in the prompt was *inconsistent* with the results. See the note below.

D **Direct Contradiction:** (D) might attract a test-taker who made some combination of the errors anticipated by choices (B) and (C), and/or who misread the question, passage, answer choice, or data in some other way. See the note below.

What we had to understand to answer the question: We needed to understand that tomato plants were used in Study 1, and pepper plants were used in Study 2, for the reasons that we noted in (A). We also needed to be able to read the figures and realize that the tallest bars indicated the highest average yields, and then refer to Table 1 to determine the percentages of the mixtures in the figures. We didn't need to understand what "vermicompost" is, or why the results were different for the two different plants.

Note More than perhaps any other question on this ACT Science section, this question demonstrates that the ACT is often interested in trying to confuse and trick test-takers, rather than evaluating how well a student understands science. Understanding what's going on in this question fundamentally involves the ability to read a bar graph, and to match up specific phrases when they appear in multiple places on the page (such as "tomato plant[s]," "pepper plant[s]," "proportion of vermicompost," "yield," "mixture," and so on). Then the ACT deliberately created a 32-word prompt that included a 20-word quoted statement, and came up with four answer choices that are each 26 words long, with each phrase in the choices repeated exactly in at least one other answer choice. Clearly, the ACT's goal in constructing this question is to frustrate test-takers and lead them to make some small mistake that has almost nothing to do with actual science, such as confusing pepper plants with tomato plants, or Study 1 with Study 2, or Mixture 2 with Mixture 3, or the idea of being consistent with the idea of being inconsistent, etc. Throughout your preparation, remember that keeping track of small details like these is one of the most important skills when it comes to the ACT! When you're confronted with these kinds of questions on test day—which happens often, as we've seen—remember to focus on the specific differences among the choices and resolve them with certainty. For example, in this question, we can take each phrase in each choice one at a time, and focus completely on confirming that Mixture 2 really did give the highest yield in Study 1, for example, on the way to picking (A). Don't forget that the ACT is always trying to get you to feel frustrated—and don't give in!

Test 1, Question 26 (Test 2 in the 2020-2021 Red Book—see page 23 for more) **TYPE: PURE PARAGRAPH**

Answering requires information from the text. Choices often primarily involve phrases rather than numbers. Consider every relevant word. Be sure your answer is literally demonstrated or restated on the page, with no interpretation necessary. See p. 339.

Notes on answer choices: (F) and (G) talk about how many things were planted, while (H) and (J) talk about how many things were removed. (F) and (H) talk about seeds, but (G) and (J) talk about seedlings.

F **Direct Contradiction:** The description of Study 1 says that "3 *S. lycopersicum* seeds were added to each pot," and the description of Study 2 says that "5 *C. annuum* seeds...were added to each pot." This choice directly contradicts those sentences, so it's wrong.

G **Direct Contradiction:** We can see in the explanation for (F) that multiple *seeds* were added to each pot—not a single *seedling*, as (G) would require.

H **Off by One or Two Words:** As we can see in the explanation for (J), the text tells us that the plants removed from the pot were seedlings—not seeds, as (H) would require. A lot of test-takers will misread the word "seedling" in the description of Study 1, or the word "seed" in this choice, and pick (H) by accident.

J ✓ **Correct:** The description of Study 1 says that "all the seedlings...were removed from the pots with the exception of a single seedling in each pot." Study 2 says that "the procedures of Study 1 were repeated" and also mentions "seedling removal." All of this restates (J), so (J) is right.

> **What we had to understand to answer the question:** We needed to find the part of Study 1 that talked about the numbers of seeds in each pot and the number of seedlings in each pot, and the part of Study 2 that said the procedures of Study 1 were repeated in Study 2, and we needed to realize the difference between the words "seed" and "seedling." We didn't need to understand any of the text in the first sentence of the prompt, because the right answer is the only choice that's restated in the text anyway. We didn't need to read or understand any part of Passage IV beyond the part of the description of Study 1 that mentioned seeds and seedlings, and the part of the description of Study 2 that mentioned repeating the procedures of Study 1.

Test 1, Question 27 (Test 2 in the 2020-2021 Red Book—see page 23 for more)   **TYPE: OUTSIDE INFO**

Answering requires some information that can't be found in the passage. Any required outside knowledge must be relatively basic. Don't try to use outside knowledge on a question unless you're sure you can't answer based on the passage. See p. 339.

Notes on answer choices: Each choice includes the following elements in a unique order: water, light, glucose, oxygen, and carbon dioxide. Carbon dioxide appears last in each choice except (D), where it appears first. Water and light always appear in the first two or three positions.

A   **Confused Relationships:** This choice could attract an untrained test-taker who forgot that plants *consume* carbon dioxide, instead of *producing* carbon dioxide, as (A) would require. See the discussion of (D) below for more.

B   **Confused Relationships:** This choice has basically the same problem as (A): it says the plants produce carbon dioxide, but carbon dioxide is one of the things plants use, not one of the things they produce.

C   **Confused Relationships:** This choice has the same problem as (A) and (B).

D ✓ **Correct:** This is another example of the kind of relatively basic scientific knowledge that's occasionally required on the ACT Science section. We should know that plants require water and light to grow. Similarly, we should also know that plants use up carbon dioxide. (There are two main ways you might have learned this. One is the standard elementary school explanation that animals use oxygen and produce carbon dioxide, while plants use carbon dioxide and produce oxygen. Another is the fact that environmentalists and ecologists often point to forests and other plant life as potential consumers of carbon dioxide, which is a greenhouse gas.) Only (D) shows carbon dioxide on the left side of the expression, being consumed. So (D) must be right.

> **What we had to understand to answer the question:** We needed to understand that the italicized names in the prompt refer to plants (this is spelled out in the first sentence of Passage IV). We also needed to remember that plants use carbon dioxide to produce energy, or that plants don't produce carbon dioxide—either idea would have shown us that (D) must be right. We didn't need to read or understand anything else beyond the first sentence of Passage IV.

Test 1, Question 28 (Test 2 in the 2020-2021 Red Book—see page 23 for more)   **TYPE: PURE PARAGRAPH**

Answering requires information from the text. Choices often primarily involve phrases rather than numbers. Consider every relevant word. Be sure your answer is literally demonstrated or restated on the page, with no interpretation necessary. See p. 339.

Notes on answer choices: The choices present different combinations of the following things being changed in the two studies: electric potential, plate length, and the magnitude and direction of the electric field. "Plate length" appears as the first phrase in (G) and (J), while the other phrases appear as the first phrase in one other choice each. "The magnitude and direction of the electric field" appears as the last phrase in (F) and (J), while "electric potential" appears as the last phrase in (G) and (H).

F   **Direct Contradiction:** (F) would attract test-takers who mixed up Study 1 and Study 2, as we'll see when we discuss (H).

G   **Off by One or Two Words:** (G) makes a correct statement about Study 2, but Study 1 involved determining how the spot's location varied with the magnitude and direction of the electric field—not plate length—as we'll see for (H).

H ✓ **Correct:** The description of Study 1 says, "the students…varied both the direction and the magnitude…of *E*," while the description of Study 2 says, "the students…varied *V*." An untrained test-taker might get confused here, because none of the choices mentions *E* or *V* directly—but, as trained test-takers, we know that the right answer to this question must be spelled out somewhere on the page, since the specifics of this experiment aren't the kind of generalized, basic scientific knowledge that the ACT Science section occasionally requires us to know. We see that the paragraph under Figure 1 tells us that the "electric field" is "*E*," and the "electrical potential" is "*V*," so we can see that Study 1 involved varying the direction and magnitude of the electric field, and Study 2 involved varying electrical potential. Only (H) reflects both of these elements correctly, so (H) is right. (In fact, even if we couldn't figure out what *E* and *V* referred to, we could still tell that that (H) was right because the description of Study 1 says it involved "var[ying] both the direction and the magnitude" of something, and (H) is the only choice that says Study 1 involved varying the magnitude and direction of anything.)

J   **Barely Relevant:** (J) joins the wrong statement about Study 1 from (G) with the wrong statement about Study 2 from (F).

> **What we had to understand to answer the question:** As described in (H), this question really only requires us to realize that the phrase "varied both the direction and the magnitude" appears in the description of Study 1, and also in the first part of (H).

For free sample video demonstrations, go to www.ACTprepVideos.com   Page 361

We never needed to know anything about CRT systems, or about electric fields, or kilovolts, or newtons, or any other technical detail that appears anywhere in Passage V.

Test 1, Question 29 (Test 2 in the 2020-2021 Red Book—see page 23 for more) TYPE: PURE DATA

Finding the answer requires information from a figure. Read carefully, and be very particular about matching up exact values in the figure and the answer choices, unless the question calls for estimation. See p. 339.

Notes on answer choices: All of the numbers in the answer choices appear as values in the V(kV) column of Table 2.

A **Confused Relationships:** According to the logic discussed in the explanation for (B), a V-value less than 1.0 kV would correspond to a y-value greater than 3.2 cm—but the prompt mentions a y-value of 2.6 cm, so (A) is wrong. This choice might attract a test-taker whose eyes accidentally skipped up a line when trying to read Table 2.

B ✓ **Correct:** Table 2 shows us the results from Study 2, which is mentioned in the prompt. The question asks about "the value of V," and the middle column of Table 2 is labeled "V(kV)" and includes the same numbers that appear in the answer choices for 29, so we know that Table 2 is relevant to this question. A y-value of 2.6 would be between the y-values in Trials 8 and 9, so we expect the corresponding V-value to be between the V-values from Trials 8 and 9. That means the V-value should be between 1.0 and 1.5 kV, so (B) is correct.

C **Confused Relationships:** According to the logic discussed in the explanation for (B), a V-value between 1.5 kV and 2.0 kV would correspond to a y-value between 1.6 cm and 2.1 cm—but the prompt mentions a y-value of 2.6 cm, so this choice is wrong. It might attract a test-taker whose eyes accidentally skipped down a line when trying to read Table 2.

D **Barely Relevant:** According to the logic discussed in the explanation for (B), a V-value greater than 2.0 kV would correspond to a y-value of less than 1.6 cm—but the prompt mentions a y-value of 2.6 cm, so this choice is incorrect.

What we had to understand to answer the question: We needed to realize that Table 2 was relevant to the prompt, for the reasons discussed above for (B). We also needed to know how to use basic trends in the provided data to figure out that the right answer was between 1.0kV and 1.5kV. (See "Using Simple Trends in Data" on page 333 of this Black Book for a refresher on that.) We didn't need to read or understand anything else in the passage, including anything about why Study 2 was done, or what V(kV) means in the table.

Test 1, Question 30 (Test 2 in the 2020-2021 Red Book—see page 23 for more) TYPE: DATA PLUS DATA

Finding the right answer requires information from more than one figure. Read carefully, and be very particular about matching up exact values in the figure and the answer choices, unless estimation is called for. See page 339.

Notes on answer choices: The choices offer different combinations of Trials 1, 4, and 8. 1 and 8 each appear alone in one choice, while 4 only appears in combination with one other trial.

F **Direct Contradiction:** This choice might attract an untrained test-taker who forgets about the negative sign in the y-value from Trial 1, because Trial 1 has a y-value of -3.2, but Figure 2 shows a y-measurement around *positive* 3, not negative 3.

G **Off by One or Two Words:** It's true that Trial 8 resulted in a y-value of around 3 cm, as Figure 2 reflects. But Trial 4 also resulted in a y-value of around 3 cm, so the word "only" makes this choice wrong.

H **Confused Relationships:** This choice might attract a test-taker who made the mistake from (F), and also didn't notice that Trial 8 resulted in a y-value of around 3 cm.

J ✓ **Correct:** In Figure 2, we see that the vertical ruler shows the y-value in cm. The bright spot corresponds to a y-value of around positive 3 cm. Tables 1 and 2 show us that Trials 4 and 8 each produced a y-value around 3 cm while Trial 1 didn't, so (J) is correct.

What we had to understand to answer the question: We needed to realize that Figure 2 shows a y-value of about 3 cm. (We could figure this out by noting that the ruler in the figure is labeled "y (cm)," and the spot appears around 3 tick-marks up from the spot labeled zero.) We also needed to realize that the results of the trials referred to by number in the answer choices are recorded in Tables 1 and 2, and that these tables have values in a column labeled "y (cm)." Then we needed to find the trials from the answer choices whose y-values were roughly 3, matching Figure 2. We never needed to understand anything at all about how the experiments in Passage V were carried out, or why anybody bothered to do them. We never needed to read a word of text outside of Figure 2 and the y-values for Trials 1, 4, and 8 in the tables.

Test 1, Question 31 (Test 2 in the 2020-2021 Red Book—see page 23 for more) TYPE: DATA PLUS DATA

Finding the right answer requires information from more than one figure. Read carefully, and be very particular about matching up exact values in the figure and the answer choices, unless estimation is called for. See page 339.

Notes on answer choices: Choices offer every possible combination of an up arrow and a down arrow for each of the two studies.

A **Off by One or Two Words:** This choice might attract an untrained test-taker who realized which direction E was pointing in Study 3, but who made a mistake figuring it out for Study 2. (See our discussion of (C) for more information.)

B **Direct Contradiction:** This choice might attract an untrained test-taker who mixed up Study 2 and Study 3. But it will also attract a lot of people who just assume that a positive *y*-value should be associated with an upward arrow, without bothering to pay attention to the arrows in Table 1, as we'll discuss for (C).

C ✓ **Correct:** We can see in Table 1 that when the direction of ***E*** is *upward*, the resulting *y*-value is *negative*, as with Trials 1, 2, and 3. We also see in the same table that when the direction of ***E*** is *downward*, the resulting *y*-value is *positive*, as with Trials 4, 5, and 6. The *y*-values in Study 2 are positive, so the direction of ***E*** in Study 2 must be downward. And the *y*-values in Study 3 are negative, so the direction of ***E*** in Study 3 must be upward. That means (C) is correct.

D **Off by One or Two Words:** This choice is basically the inverse of (A). It might attract an untrained test-taker who realized which direction ***E*** was pointing in Study 2, but who made a mistake figuring that out for Study 3.

> **What we had to understand to answer the question:** As noted for (C), we needed to use Table 1 to compare the direction of the arrow with the sign of the number in the *y*(cm) column, and then we needed to consider that information with respect to the signs of the *y*(cm) numbers in Table 2 and Table 3. We didn't need to read or understand any of the text or either of the diagrams in the passage apart from the relevant columns in each table (that is, the "direction" column in Table 1 and the "*y*(cm)" column in each of the three tables). We didn't need to understand what ***E*** means or why it has a direction.

Test 1, Question 32 (Test 2 in the 2020-2021 Red Book—see page 23 for more) **TYPE: DATA PLUS PARAGRAPH**

Finding the answer requires information from the text as well as information from a figure. Read carefully, and be very particular about matching up exact values in the figure and the answer choices, unless the prompt calls for estimation. See p. 339.

Notes on answer choices: The choices are all numbers that appear in the "Trial" column of one of the tables in Passage V.

F **Reasonable Statement Not in the Text:** This choice might attract an untrained test-taker who assumed that one CRT could be used for all 3 studies without reading carefully enough to note that the plate length (*L*) of a CRT can't be changed, and that the text for Study 3 specifically refers to "various CRTs," meaning that the same CRT couldn't be used for every trial in Study 3. See the explanation of (G) for more.

G ✓ **Correct:** This question might confuse an untrained test-taker, because Passage V never specifically explains which characteristics of a CRT can't be changed. But, as trained test-takers, we know that the ACT Science section must provide us with any information that's necessary to answer a question with total certainty (apart from fundamental scientific knowledge, but the details of constructing a CRT definitely don't fall into that category). So let's start by looking at the text and the tables for each study, and see if any of them mention using multiple CRTs. The text for Study 1 mentions "a CRT having *L* = 2.5 cm." The description from Study 1 doesn't mention any other CRTs, so it looks like the students would have needed 1 CRT to complete Study 1. Now let's move on to Study 2, whose description begins with "using the CRT from Study 1...." No other CRT is mentioned anywhere for Study 2, so we can see that only 1 CRT—in total—was used for both Study 1 and Study 2. Now let's check out Study 3. The description for Study 3 tells us that "the students obtained various CRTs, each having a different *L*." Table 3 then shows us 5 different *L*-measurements. Since each different *L*-value indicates a different CRT, there must have been 5 CRTs used in Study 3. At this point, it looks like 1 CRT was used in Studies 1 and 2, and 5 CRTs were used in Study 3, so the number of different CRTs must be 6...but 6 isn't one of the answer choices, so we must have made a mistake. The choices are 1, 5, 11, and 16, so our mistake is one of the following: we either misunderstood that the same CRT could be used for every trial, in which case (A) is right; or we double-counted one of the CRTs, in which case (G) is right; or we under-counted by 5, in which case (H) is right; or we under-counted by 10, in which case (J) is right. We know that we must not have made the first of those mistakes, because Study 3 clearly refers to "various CRTs." And we know that the number must be lower than 11 or 16, because the first line of text for Study 2 says that all of Study 2 was done with the same CRT as the one used for Study 1, so all 11 trials in Study 1 and Study 2 together were done with only one CRT. So now we have to figure out if it's possible that we could have double-counted a CRT when we originally thought the answer was 6. As it turns out, the description of Study 1 mentions "a CRT having *L* = 2.5 cm." In Table 3, we can see that one of the CRTs from Study 3 has *L* = 2.5 cm. So it's possible that the CRT from Study 1 and the CRT from Study 3 that both have *L* = 2.5 are the same CRT! That means it would be possible that only 5 CRTs were required to complete the 3 studies, so (G) is correct.

H **Direct Contradiction:** This choice might attract an untrained test-taker who thought that the *first 11 trials* had to be done with different CRTs, but that the last 5 trials could be done with one of the CRTs used in the first 11 trials—but this is the exact opposite of the situation described in the studies, as we saw in our explanation of (G).

J **Reasonable Statement Not in the Text:** This choice might attract an untrained test-taker who simply assumed that a different CRT had to be used for each of the 16 trials, without bothering to read any part of the text to see if that was true.

> **What we had to understand to answer the question:** We needed to notice the first sentence in the description of Study 2, which specifically says that Study 2 and Study 1 used the same CRT for all 11 trials. We also needed to read the first sentence in the description of Study 3, which says that each *L*-value in Table 3 requires a unique CRT. Finally, as we discussed for (G) above, we needed to realize that the *L*-value of Trial 14 was the same as the *L*-value of the one CRT used for Study 1 and Study 2. None of this required us to understand why the *L*-value of a CRT is important, or what experiments were actually done with the CRTs, or any other aspect of Passage V.

Finding the right answer requires information from more than one figure. Read carefully, and be very particular about matching up exact values in the figure and the answer choices, unless estimation is called for. See page 339.

Notes on answer choices: The choices present every possible combination of both V and E being either zero or nonzero.

A   **Direct Contradiction:** As we can see in the explanation for (B), this is the exact opposite of the correct answer. (A) would attract untrained test-takers who mixed up V and E, which could be easy to do because V isn't mentioned until the second study, but it's mentioned first in the answer choices, while E is mentioned first in the studies but second in the choices.

B ✓   **Correct:** As we mentioned in our brief notes on the answer choices above, we need to decide whether V was zero or nonzero, and whether E was zero or nonzero. Let's look at V first. V appears in Table 2, where we can see that y becomes a smaller and smaller number as V increases. In other words, V is an increasing positive number as y approaches zero in Table 2. From this pattern, we can see that V will be a positive number when y reaches zero, so V will be nonzero when y equals zero. Now we need to figure out what's going on with E. We see that E appears in Table 1. In Trial 3, at a magnitude of 3.0×10^4, the y-value is -9.5. In Trial 2, at a magnitude of 2.0×10^4, the y-value is -6.3. In Trial 1, at a magnitude of 1.0×10^4, the y-value is -3.2. So every time the magnitude decreases by 1.0×10^4, the y-value increases by about 3.1 or 3.2. That means when the magnitude in Trial 1 decreases from 1.0×10^4 to 0, we would expect the y-value to increase from -3.2 to right around 0. Similarly, when we look at Trials 4-6, we can see the same trend coming from the other side of 0—the y-values start out at 9.5, and decrease by around 3.1 or 3.2 every time the magnitude decreases by 1.0×10^4. Based on that same trend, we can see that when the magnitude in Trial 4 decreases from 1.0×10^4 to 0, we would expect the y-value to decrease from 3.2 to right around 0. All of this shows us that E will be zero when $y = 0$. So (B) is right.

C   **Confused Relationships:** (C) might attract an untrained test-taker who correctly concluded that E should be zero, but made a mistake about V, or who assumed (without reading Table 2) that when $y = 0$, both V and E should equal zero as well.

D   **Confused Relationships:** This choice might attract an untrained test-taker who correctly concluded that V should be nonzero, but then simply assumed that E must also be nonzero since V would have to be nonzero.

> **What we had to understand to answer the question:** We needed to find the parts of Table 1 and Table 2 that showed y trending towards zero, and figure out the corresponding trend in E and V. We didn't need to know what y, E, or V were measuring, or why anybody would be interested in that. We didn't need to understand any of the technical terms in the prompt, like "cathode rays" and "filament." We didn't need to read or understand any part of Passage V besides the two columns in Table 1 and the two columns in Table 2 that are referred to in our explanation for (B).

Answering requires some information that can't be found in the passage. Any required outside knowledge must be relatively basic. Don't try to use outside knowledge on a question unless you're sure you can't answer based on the passage. See p. 339.

Notes on answer choices: The choices are identical except for two differences. (F) and (G) start with the phrase "the top plate," while (H) and (J) start with the "bottom plate." The second line in (F) and (H) begins with the word "attracted," while the second line in (G) and (J) begins with the word "repelled."

F   **Direct Contradiction:** See our explanation of (J) for more on why this is wrong. This choice might attract an untrained test-taker who got everything exactly backwards in trying to reason through the question, and who forgot that like charges repel.

G   **Off by One or Two Words:** (G) might attract a test-taker who remembered that charges of like sign are repelled from each other, but who overlooked the fact that Figure 1 shows us that the ray travels *up* when E is directed *down*.

H   **Off by One or Two Words:** This choice might attract an untrained test-taker who realized that the bottom plate was negatively charged, but who got confused when reading the second half of the choice.

J ✓   **Correct:** This is another example of the kind of fundamental scientific knowledge that's occasionally required on the ACT Science section. We should know that positive and negative charges attract each other, while two positive charges repel each other, and two negative charges repel each other. (There are a few ways we might know this. One would be from playing with magnets, and seeing that similar poles repel each other while opposite poles attract. Another way might be from a basic physics or chemistry class.) The prompt tells us that cathode rays are negatively charged, and that "E is directed downward as shown in Figure 1." When we look at Figure 1, we can see that the cathode ray is pushed *upward* as it travels between the two conducting plates in the middle of the figure. So we know from the prompt that the cathode ray is negatively charged, and we know from Figure 1 that the cathode ray travels up when E is directed downward, and we know from outside knowledge that a negatively charged thing will travel away from things that are also negatively charged. Since the negatively charged cathode ray travels away from the bottom plate, we know the bottom plate is negatively charged, because two negative charges repel each other. So (J) is correct.

> **What we had to understand to answer the question:** We needed to have the outside knowledge that like charges repel one another. We needed to realize from the prompt that we had to look at Figure 1 to see which direction the ray traveled when E was pointed down. We needed to read the statement in the prompt about charged electric plates. Other than that, we didn't need

to read or understand a single other part of Passage V.

Finding the answer requires information from a figure. Read carefully, and be very particular about matching up exact values in the figure and the answer choices, unless the question calls for estimation. See p. 339.

Notes on answer choices: The four choices provide different options for ordering Ar, Kr, Ne, and Xe. (A) and (B) begin with Ne and end with Xe, while (C) and (D) begin with Xe and end with Ne. (A) and (C) have Ar second and Kr third, while (B) and (D) have Kr second and Ar third.

A   **Direct Contradiction:** This choice lists the gas samples from *longest* λ to *shortest* λ, but the question asks for a list of gas samples from *shortest* λ to *longest* λ. So this choice is the exact reverse of the right answer.

B   **Confused Relationships:** This choice combines the mistake from (A) with the mistake from (C).

C   **Confused Relationships:** This choice correctly begins with the gas sample whose λ is shortest, and it correctly ends with the gas sample whose λ is longest, but it mixes up Ar and Kr in the middle. It might attract an untrained test-taker who didn't read carefully enough to notice the difference between the A and the K in the two middle terms.

D ✓ **Correct:** When we look at Figure 2, we can see that λ is measured along the vertical axis, and N is measured along the horizontal axis. When $N = 15 \times 10^{23}$ atoms, the order of gas samples from shortest λ to longest λ is Xe, Kr, Ar, Ne, so (D) is correct. (In fact, the same shortest-to-longest order applies for every single N-value in Figure 2, since the lines for the different gases for Figure 2 never cross each other at any N-value.)

> **What we had to understand to answer the question:** We needed to identify Figure 2 and realize that the λ-value on the *y*-axis of Figure 2 goes from shortest to longest as we read up from bottom to top, so we needed to order the elements in the right answer as we encounter them moving up from the bottom of Figure 2 to the top of Figure 2. We didn't need to understand what λ refers to, or why it's being measured, or how the measurement was obtained, or anything else that appears in Passage VI.

Finding the answer requires information from a figure. Read carefully, and be very particular about matching up exact values in the figure and the answer choices, unless the question calls for estimation. See p. 339.

Notes on answer choices: (F) is the inverse of (J) and (G) is the inverse of (H). (F) is half of (G) and (H) is half of (J).

F   **Confused Relationships:** (F) might attract someone who misread Figure 2, or who made a mental math mistake and thought 1600 was four times as much as 800, or who accidentally thought the prompt was asking him to compare the λ-value of Ne to the λ-value of Ar or Kr at $N = 6$.

G ✓ **Correct:** The prompt refers to "a sample size of 6×10^{23} atoms" being represented in Figure 2. When we look at Figure 2, we can see "a sample size of 6×10^{23}" corresponds to an N-value of 6 on the horizontal axis. Similarly, a sample size of 12×10^{23} corresponds to an N-value of 12 on the horizontal axis. For Ne, the λ-value at $N = 6$ is 1,600 nm, and the λ-value at $N = 12$ is 800 nm. We have to multiply 1,600 by $\frac{1}{2}$ to get 800, which means (G) is correct.

H   **Direct Contradiction:** A lot of untrained test-takers will pick this choice, because they misread "multiplied" in the prompt as "divided," or because they mixed up the λ-value at 6×10^{23} atoms with the λ-value at 12×10^{23} atoms, or because they just didn't expect to multiply by a fraction.

J   **Confused Relationships:** This choice combines the error from (F) with the error from (H).

> **What we had to understand to answer the question:** We needed to realize that $N = 6$ and $N = 12$ on Figure 2 correspond to samples of 6×10^{23} atoms and 12×10^{23} atoms respectively, as described in the prompt. We needed to read the correct λ-values for Ne off of Figure 2, and we needed to realize that $1,600 \times \frac{1}{2} = 800$. We didn't need to read or understand any other part of Passage VI.

Finding the right answer requires information from more than one figure. Read carefully, and be very particular about matching up exact values in the figure and the answer choices, unless estimation is called for. See page 339.

Notes on answer choices: (A) is the inverse of (D) and (B) is the inverse of (C). (A) is half of (B) and (C) is half of (D).

A   **Barely Relevant:** This choice combines the errors we'll discuss from (B) and (D). It's probably here to fill out the pattern in the answer choices that was also used for question 36.

B   **Direct Contradiction:** This choice might attract an untrained test-taker who accidentally finds λ for the 25 L sample relative to λ for the 50 L sample, instead of the other way around, which is what the prompt asked for.

C ✓ **Correct:** We need to compare two samples of Kr that are similar except that one has a V-value of 25 L, and the other has a V-value of 50 L. The prompt mentions Figure 1, so we should consider that graph as we try to answer the question. The horizontal axis of Figure 1 doesn't go out to $V = 50$, so we have to use the data that does appear for Kr and see if we can observe a trend for the λ-value of Kr relative to V, and then determine the λ-value of Kr at $V = 50$. We can see that its λ-value doubles from around 120 nm to around 240 nm when the V-value for Kr doubles from 10 L to 20 L. In fact, for all V-values of Kr that we see in Figure 1, doubling the V-value of Kr results in doubling the corresponding λ-value. So, at $V = 50$, the λ-value of Kr should be twice as much as the λ-value at $V = 25$, which means (C) is correct.

D   **Confused Relationships:** This choice combines the error from (A) with the error from (B) It might attract an untrained test-taker who misread Figure 1 or made a simple mistake in calculation.

> **What we had to understand to answer the question:** We needed to realize that the prompt was referring us to Figure 1, and then use the information in Figure 1 to observe the trend in λ-values for Kr. We never needed to know what Kr stands for, or what a λ-value corresponds to in real life, or what a V-value corresponds to in real life. We never needed to understand anything else in Passage VI apart from the data mentioned above in Figure 1.

Test 1, Question 38 (Test 2 in the 2020-2021 Red Book—see page 23 for more)   TYPE: PURE DATA

Finding the answer requires information from a figure. Read carefully, and be very particular about matching up exact values in the figure and the answer choices, unless the question calls for estimation. See p. 339.

Notes on answer choices: The choices form a series in which each choice is 50 nm more than the choice before it.

F   **Confused Relationships:** This choice might attract an untrained test-taker who mistakenly compares two other values from Figure 1 with an approximate difference in λ of 50 nm, such as Kr and Xe at $V = 10$.

G   **Confused Relationships:** This is similar to (F) in the sense that it might trap someone who mistakenly compared two other values from Figure 1 with a difference in λ of 100 nm, such as the values for Ar and Kr at $V = 15$.

H   **Confused Relationships:** This is similar to (F) and (G). It might result from accidentally comparing the λ-values of Ar and Kr at $V = 25$.

J   ✓   **Correct:** In Figure 1, when $V = 20$ L, λ for Xe is a little less than 200 nm, while λ for Ar is a little less than 400 nm. So λ for Ar is around 200 nm longer than λ for Xe at 20 L, and (J) is right.

> **What we had to understand to answer the question:** We needed to identify the data for Xe and Ar when $V = 20$ in Figure 1, just as the prompt directed us to do. Apart from that, we didn't need to read or understand any other part of Passage VI.

Test 1, Question 39 (Test 2 in the 2020-2021 Red Book—see page 23 for more)   TYPE: DATA PLUS PARAGRAPH

Finding the answer requires information from the text as well as information from a figure. Read carefully, and be very particular about matching up exact values in the figure and the answer choices, unless the prompt calls for estimation. See p. 339.

Notes on answer choices: The choices have identical wording except for two differences. (A) and (B) use the number 5 in two places, while (C) and (D) use the number 25 in those places. (A) and (C) include the word "shorter" in the middle of each choice, while (B) and (D) have the word "longer" in that position.

A   ✓   **Correct:** As we noted above, reading the choices makes it clear that we need to decide whether the collision frequency would be higher in the 5 L sample or the 25 L sample, and whether atoms traveling shorter distances to each other or longer distances to each other would correlate with the atoms colliding more often, as the end of each choice mentions. We can see in Figure 1 that λ is smaller for the Xe sample at 5 L than at 25 L. We know from the first sentence of Passage VI that λ is "the average distance a gas atom will travel between collisions with other gas atoms," so having a lower λ means that gas atoms travel shorter distances between collisions. The prompt tells us that the atoms "have the same average speed in both samples." Thus, if the atoms are traveling a shorter distance at the same speed before colliding, then they must be colliding more frequently. (For example, imagine that some atoms travel for 5 seconds at a given speed before colliding, and other atoms travel for 30 seconds at the same speed before colliding. The first atoms will collide 12 times in a minute, while the second atoms will collide only twice a minute. So our hypothetical example shows that atoms with lower λ must collide more frequently than atoms with higher λ at the same speed.) Since (A) is the only choice that correctly says the 5 L sample would have a higher collision frequency, and (A) correctly states that a shorter λ distance corresponds to more collisions in a given period of time, we know (A) is right.

B   **Off by One or Two Words:** This choice might attract an untrained test-taker who was confused about the meaning of mean free path (λ) as discussed in the passage, or who misread Figure 1.

C   **Confused Relationships:** This choice might attract an untrained test-taker who misread it and thought it used the number 5 instead of the number 25, or who misread Figure 1, or who thought the data for N in Figure 2 was the data for V.

D   **Off by One or Two Words:** This choice might attract an untrained test-taker who was confused about the meaning of mean free path (λ) as discussed in the passage, or who misread Figure 1 or this answer choice. It's wrong for two reasons: first, it uses the wrong number; second, it makes a mistake in the logic we discussed for (A), and concludes that longer distances between collisions would lead to higher collision frequency, instead of lower.

> **What we had to understand to answer the question:** We needed to find the two data points for Xe in Figure 1 that are mentioned in the prompt, we needed to understand what λ represented as described in the first sentence of the passage, and we needed to understand how traveling a longer distance at a constant speed between collisions would automatically result in fewer

collisions per second, as we saw in our discussion of (A). Apart from that, we didn't need to read or understand anything in Passage VI.

Test 1, Question 40 (Test 2 in the 2020-2021 Red Book—see page 23 for more)   **TYPE: DATA PLUS DATA**

Finding the right answer requires information from more than one figure. Read carefully, and be very particular about matching up exact values in the figure and the answer choices, unless estimation is called for. See page 339.

Notes on answer choices: All of the numbers in the answer choices are marked values on the horizontal axis of Figure 2.

F ✓ **Correct:** We can see in Table 1 that d for Rn is greater than d for Xe. When we compare the d-values in Table 1 to the λ-values in Figure 2, we can see that λ decreases as d increases. So a gas with a higher d-value will have a lower λ-value at any given value of N. This means that if the data for Rn were added to Figure 2, then the resulting curve would be entirely underneath the curve for Xe. We can see in Figure 2 that in order for a sample of Rn to have a λ-value of 320 nm and be underneath the curve for Xe, that sample would definitely have to have an N-value *less than* 6×10^{23} atoms. So (F) is right.

G **Barely Relevant:** See the explanation for (F).

H **Barely Relevant:** See the explanation for (F).

J **Barely Relevant:** See the explanation for (F).

> **What we had to understand to answer the question:** We needed to realize that a larger d-value correlates to a lower N-value at a given λ-value, as described in our explanation for (F). But we never needed to know what N-values, λ-values, or d-values correlate to in real life, and we never needed to read or understand any of the other text or information for Passage VI.

TEST 2 (TEST 3 IN 2020-2021 RED BOOK)

Test 2, Question 1 (Test 3 in the 2020-2021 Red Book—see page 23 for more)   **TYPE: OUTSIDE INFO**

Answering requires some information that can't be found in the passage. Any required outside knowledge must be relatively basic. Don't try to use outside knowledge on a question unless you're sure you can't answer based on the passage. See p. 339.

Notes on answer choices: (C) and (D) are significantly larger numbers than (A) and (B).

A **Off by One or Two Words:** This choice might attract an untrained test-taker who isn't careful enough when counting the generations as described for (B) below, and accidentally misses one, or who doesn't realize that the two individuals at the top of the diagram count as a generation.

B ✓ **Correct:** This is an example of the kind of relatively basic scientific knowledge that's occasionally required on the ACT Science section. The passage doesn't define the term "generation," but we should know that when two individuals reproduce, those two individuals are part of one generation, and their offspring are part of the next generation. When those offspring find mates and reproduce, their offspring are part of *another* generation, and so on. When we look at the figure, we can see that individuals 1 and 2 are one generation, individuals 3 - 8 are part of a second generation, individuals 9 - 17 are part of a third generation, and individuals 18 - 24 are part of a fourth generation—basically, every horizontal level in the diagram is a separate generation. So (B) is correct.

C **Confused Relationships:** (C) might attract an untrained test-taker who makes the mistake mentioned in the explanation for (D), and also forgets to count 2 of the individuals—probably the two at the top of the diagram, possibly as a result of not realizing that the first two individuals are also part of a generation even though their parents aren't present in the diagram.

D **Confused Relationships:** This choice might attract an untrained test-taker who mistakenly thinks that the question is asking for the total number of *individuals* in the figure, rather than the number of generations, as the prompt requires—or who thinks that every individual represents a generation.

> **What we had to understand to answer the question:** As discussed for (B) above, we needed to realize that the number of generations referred to in the prompt is reflected in the horizontal levels of the diagram. Otherwise, we didn't need to understand anything in Passage I, including anything about Trait G, the idea of dominant and recessive alleles, etc.

Test 2, Question 2 (Test 3 in the 2020-2021 Red Book—see page 23 for more)   **TYPE: PURE DATA**

Finding the answer requires information from a figure. Read carefully, and be very particular about matching up exact values in the figure and the answer choices, unless the question calls for estimation. See p. 339.

Notes on answer choices: The choices all present different numbers.

F **Direct Contradiction:** These individuals have neither the same shape nor the same color, so we wouldn't expect them to be genetically similar according to the diagram.

G ✓ **Correct:** This question will intimidate some untrained test-takers, because they won't feel like they have enough information to measure the "genetic similarity" referred to in the prompt—especially since only one gene is explicitly discussed in Passage I. But when we compare (G) to the other choices, we can see that Individuals 12 and 13 are the only pair of individuals in the choices that are represented with the exact same symbol—a white circle. According to the key in the diagram, this means that 12 and 13 are both females without trait G. These are the only individuals in the answer choices that are represented by the exact same symbol, which means they must have the "greatest…similarity," as the prompt requires. So (G) is right.

H **Confused Relationships:** These individuals are somewhat similar in that they're both represented by black symbols, but those symbols have different shapes, which means one individual is a male with Trait G, and the other is a female with Trait G. So these individuals aren't as similar as the individuals from (G).

J **Confused Relationships:** These individuals are somewhat similar in that they're both represented by circles, but those circles have different colors, meaning one individual is a female with Trait G, and the other is a female without Trait G, according to the key—so they aren't as similar as the individuals from (G).

> **What we had to understand to answer the question:** We needed to realize that the diagram provides enough information to assess the relative genetic similarity of the pairs in the answer choices, and then we needed to read the diagram and the answer choices carefully while considering those pairs, as described for (G) and the other choices above. We needed to recognize that the only pair with two individuals represented by identical symbols must be the individuals with "greatest…similarity." We didn't need to read any of the text for Passage I outside of the diagram and its key.

Test 2, Question 3 (Test 3 in the 2020-2021 Red Book—see page 23 for more) **TYPE: PURE DATA**

Finding the answer requires information from a figure. Read carefully, and be very particular about matching up exact values in the figure and the answer choices, unless the question calls for estimation. See p. 339.

Notes on answer choices: The choices present every whole number from 0 to 4 inclusive, except 2.

A **Confused Relationships:** This choice might attract an untrained test-taker who mistakenly thought that neither 23 nor 24 had Trait G, possibly as a result of misreading the key and thinking that black symbols indicated a lack of Trait G.

B **Confused Relationships:** This choice might attract an untrained test-taker who mistakenly tried to apply some outside knowledge about genetics, and didn't notice individuals 9, 10, 18, 19, and 20, as discussed in the explanation for (D).

C **Confused Relationships:** This choice might attract an untrained test-taker who noticed the offspring of Individuals 9 and 10 from the diagram, but mistakenly concluded that those results indicated that any pair of individuals with Trait G would automatically have exactly 3 offspring with Trait G, instead of concluding that 100% of their offspring would have Trait G.

D ✓ **Correct:** When we compare Individuals 23 and 24 to the key, we can see that those individuals both have Trait G. The only other reproductive pair in the figure that both have Trait G is found in Individuals 9 and 10. All of the offspring of 9 and 10 have Trait G, so we can conclude that all of the offspring of 23 and 24 will have Trait G as well. That means (D) is right.

> **What we had to understand to answer the question:** We needed to recognize that Individuals 9 and 10 presented the same kind of mating pair as Individuals 23 and 24 according to the diagram, and we needed to realize that all of the offspring of Individuals 9 and 10 had Trait G, as described for (D). Beyond that, we didn't need to read or understand any part of Passage I.

Test 2, Question 4 (Test 3 in the 2020-2021 Red Book—see page 23 for more) **TYPE: PURE DATA**

Finding the answer requires information from a figure. Read carefully, and be very particular about matching up exact values in the figure and the answer choices, unless the question calls for estimation. See p. 339.

Notes on answer choices: The choices provide different single-digit integers.

F **Confused Relationships:** This choice might attract an untrained test-taker who got confused about which symbol represents an individual with Trait G, or who wasn't sure which individuals were the grandchildren of Individuals 1 and 2, or who thought that only 12 and 13 were grandchildren of 1 and 2.

G **Confused Relationships:** This choice might attract an untrained test-taker who didn't notice either Individual 10 or Individual 16 for some reason.

H ✓ **Correct:** We know that someone's grandchildren are the children of that person's children—in the given diagram, the grandchildren of 1 and 2 appear two levels down from the level of 1 and 2. So the grandchildren of 1 and 2 are Individuals 10, 11, 12, 13, 15, 16, and 17. The key tells us that Individuals with Trait G are represented by a black circle or square. So two of the grandchildren of 1 and 2 have Trait G, because two of them are represented by black symbols: Individual 10 and Individual 16. So (H) is correct.

J **Confused Relationships:** This choice might attract an untrained test-taker who thought the prompt was only asking how many total grandchildren Individuals 1 and 2 had, rather than the number of those grandchildren with Trait G.

> **What we had to understand to answer the question:** As we discussed for (H) above, we needed to realize that 10, 11, 12, 13, 15, 16, and 17 were the grandchildren of 1 and 2, and we needed to read from the key that the individuals represented by black symbols were the ones with Trait G. Beyond that, we didn't need to read or understand anything about Trait G, or anything else in Passage I.

Test 2, Question 5 (Test 3 in the 2020-2021 Red Book—see page 23 for more) **TYPE: PURE DATA**

Finding the answer requires information from a figure. Read carefully, and be very particular about matching up exact values in the

Notes on answer choices: The choices are identical except for two differences. (A) and (B) both begin with the word "yes," while (C) and (D) begin with the word "no." (A) and (C) include the phrase "always passed," while (B) and (D) include the phrase "did not always pass."

A   **Direct Contradiction:** This choice incorrectly states that "mothers with Trait G always passed Trait G to their sons," which isn't true in the case of Individuals 4 and 11. (See the explanation for (D) for more info.)

B   **Off by One or Two Words:** This choice is almost identical to (D), which is the right answer. It might attract an untrained test-taker who simply misread the first word in (B), or misread the word "likely" in the prompt as "unlikely."

C   **Direct Contradiction:** This choice has the same basic problem as (A).

D ✓ **Correct:** When we look at the figure, we see that there are two situations in which mothers with Trait G had sons: Individual 4 had a son who was Individual 11, and Individual 10 had a son who was Individual 20. In one case (with 4 and 11), we can see that the mother didn't pass Trait G to the son, while in the other case (with 10 and 20) the mother did pass Trait G to her son. So we can see that mothers with Trait G didn't always pass Trait G on to their sons, as the part of (D) after "no" requires. It may be a little less obvious whether we can call the trait "sex-linked," but we can think about the ideas in the prompt and the answer choices, and reason through it. If the trait is "sex-linked," then we'd expect it to be connected to an individual's sex in some way. If such a connection existed, then we'd expect to see some kind of pattern in the figure—like that every female had the trait, or that every father with the trait passed it on to any sons he had, or something like that. The only possible pattern like this that appears in the answer choices is the idea of mothers passing on the trait to their sons. But we just established that mothers don't always pass the trait on to their sons: one mother in the diagram did, and one mother in the diagram didn't. Since the only possible sex-related pattern in the answer choices doesn't appear in the figure, and since the answer choices require us to answer this question with either a "yes" or a "no," we can conclude that the trait likely isn't "sex-linked," which means the beginning of this choice should say "no," and which also confirms that (D) is right.

What we had to understand to answer the question: We needed to read the key carefully to know that black circles in the diagram represented females with Trait G, and that black squares represented males with Trait G, while white squares represented males without Trait G. We also needed to read the answer choices carefully in order to determine that, for this question, being "sex-linked" is related to the idea of demonstrating a consistent pattern of mother-son inheritance, as we described for (D). Beyond that, we never needed to read or understand anything in Passage I.

Test 2, Question 6 (Test 3 in the 2020-2021 Red Book—see page 23 for more)   **TYPE: DATA PLUS PARAGRAPH**

Finding the answer requires information from the text as well as information from a figure. Read carefully, and be very particular about matching up exact values in the figure and the answer choices, unless the prompt calls for estimation. See p. 339.

Notes on answer choices: The choices are identical except for two differences. (F) and (G) both begin with "yes," while (H) and (J) both begin with "no." (F) and (H) both include the word "dominant," while (G) and (J) both include the word "recessive."

F   **Direct Contradiction:** We know this choice is incorrect because the last sentence of Passage I tells us that "scientists concluded that Trait G is a recessive trait." This choice might attract untrained test-takers who misread that last sentence as though it said "dominant trait."

G   **Direct Contradiction:** This choice is wrong because the passage tells us that "the Gene G genotype of Individual 21 is *Gg*," and we can see in the diagram that Individual 21 is represented by a white symbol, which means she doesn't have Trait G—so the correct answer should start with "no," not "yes."

H   **Direct Contradiction:** This choice has the same basic problem as (F), and is wrong for the same reason.

J ✓ **Correct:** The second sentence of the second paragraph in Passage I tells us that "the Gene G genotype of Individual 21 is *Gg*," and we can see in the diagram that Individual 21 is represented by a white symbol, which means she doesn't have Trait G. Also, the last sentence of the passage tells us that "scientists concluded that Trait G is a recessive trait." So (J) is the correct answer, since it's the only choice that's directly restated and demonstrated in Passage I.

What we had to understand to answer the question: We needed to read the second and third sentences of the second paragraph of Passage I, and we needed to locate the symbol for Individual 21 in the diagram. We didn't need to read or understand any other part of Passage I in order to answer this question correctly.

Test 2, Question 7 (Test 3 in the 2020-2021 Red Book—see page 23 for more)   **TYPE: OUTSIDE INFO**

Answering requires some information that can't be found in the passage. Any required outside knowledge must be relatively basic. Don't try to use outside knowledge on a question unless you're sure you can't answer based on the passage. See p. 339.

Notes on answer choices: The choices are each names of scientific equipment.

A ✓ **Correct:** This is another example of the kind of fundamental scientific knowledge that's occasionally required on the ACT Science section. The prompt refers us to Figure 2; when we look at that figure, we can see that the label on the vertical axis mentions "mass," and the results are reported in milligrams, which are a measure of mass. Of the four answer choices, only a balance can measure mass, so (A) is correct.

B   **Barely Relevant:** As we saw in the explanation for (A), the results in Figure 2 were measured in mg, a measure of mass, and a pH meter doesn't measure mass.

C   **Barely Relevant:** This choice is wrong for the same basic reason that (B) is wrong: a telescope doesn't measure mass.

D   **Barely Relevant:** This choice is wrong for the same basic reason that (B) and (C) are wrong.

> **What we had to understand to answer the question:** We needed to look at Figure 2 and realize that it involved milligrams, and we needed to know milligrams are units of mass (or just notice the word "mass" in the label), and we needed to know mass can be measured with a balance. We didn't need to read or understand any other part of Passage II.

Test 2, Question 8 (Test 3 in the 2020-2021 Red Book—see page 23 for more)   TYPE: PURE PARAGRAPH

Answering requires information from the text. Choices often primarily involve phrases rather than numbers. Consider every relevant word. Be sure your answer is literally demonstrated or restated on the page, with no interpretation necessary. See p. 339.

Notes on answer choices: The choices are fairly dissimilar for an ACT Science question.

F   **Barely Relevant:** The study couldn't answer this question because the study doesn't involve testing flowers in different locations.

G ✓   **Correct:** The first paragraph of Passage II says that the "study was conducted to investigate the effects of different pollination treatments on fruit production and seed mass in a population of *H. metallica*." The phrase "percent of flowers that produce fruit" from the answer choice restates the phrase "fruit production" from the passage. The phrase "average mass per seed" in the answer choice restates the phrase "seed mass" from the passage. The phrases "when flowers are self-pollinated" and "when flowers are cross-pollinated" from the answer choice demonstrate the "different pollination treatments" mentioned in the passage. Since every part of this choice literally restates or demonstrates an element from the passage, (G) is right.

H   **Barely Relevant:** The study couldn't answer this question because the passage doesn't mention fruit ripening at all.

J   **Confused Relationships:** Some untrained test-takers will pick (J) because the first paragraph of Passage II plainly states that "*H. metallica* flowers are normally pollinated by hummingbirds." But the prompt asks us which choice has a question that's answered by the study, and Passage II doesn't say anything about the study testing anything related to hummingbirds.

> **What we had to understand to answer the question:** We needed to read both paragraphs of Passage II and the labels on the Figures in order to tell that (G) was the only choice literally demonstrated by the passage. Apart from that, we didn't need to read or understand any part of Passage II. (See "Special Article: Basics of Experimental Design" on page 336 of this Black Book for more.)

Test 2, Question 9 (Test 3 in the 2020-2021 Red Book—see page 23 for more)   TYPE: DATA PLUS PARAGRAPH

Finding the answer requires information from the text as well as information from a figure. Read carefully, and be very particular about matching up exact values in the figure and the answer choices, unless the prompt calls for estimation. See p. 339.

Notes on answer choices: (A) and (B) both say that one group of flowers received pollen from the same plant, while the other group received pollination from one other plant. (C) and (D) both say that one group was pollinated with pollen from one plant, while the other was pollinated by pollen from 6 plants.

A ✓   **Correct:** The prompt refers to "the pollination treatments," so we'll need to find the part of Passage II that refers to those treatments. We can find the phrase "pollination treatment" as the heading of the second column in Table 1, and Table 1 also refers to groups, just like the prompt does. So we can tell that Table 1 is the relevant part of Passage II. Table 1 tells us the plants in Group 1 were pollinated by "self-pollination." Paragraph 1 explains that self-pollination is when "egg and pollen are from the same *H. metallica* plant," which restates the idea in (A) that the pollen is "from the same plant as the flower." Table 1 also tells us that the plants in Group 2 were pollinated by "cross-pollination;" paragraph 1 explains that cross-pollination is when "egg and pollen are from different *H. metallica* plants," which restates the idea in (A) that "the pollen received by each Group 2 flower was from a different plant than the flower." Since every part of (A) is literally restated in the relevant parts of Passage II, we know it's right.

B   **Direct Contradiction:** This choice might attract untrained test-takers who misread Table 1 or choice (B) and mixed up Group 1 and Group 2.

C   **Off by One or Two Words:** This choice might attract untrained test-takers who misread Table 1 and thought Group 1 was Group 2, and who also thought that Group 2 was Group 3.

D   **Confused Relationships:** This choice might attract untrained test-takers who thought Group 1 was Group 3.

> **What we had to understand to answer the question:** We needed to realize that the phrase "pollination treatments" in the prompt corresponded to the phrase in Table 1, as we discussed for (A). We also needed to read Table 1 and the answer choices carefully, and we needed to read the explanations related to self-pollination and cross-pollination from the first paragraph of Passage II. We didn't need to read or understand any other part of Passage II.

Finding the answer requires information from a figure. Read carefully, and be very particular about matching up exact values in the figure and the answer choices, unless the question calls for estimation. See p. 339.

Notes on answer choices: The fractions in (F) and (G) are reciprocals of each other, as are the fractions in (H) and (J). (F) and (G) compare the number of seeds to the mass of seeds, while (H) and (J) compare the number of flowers producing fruit to the number of flowers.

F   **Confused Relationships:** This choice is the reciprocal of the mistake from (G).

G   **Confused Relationships:** This expression would almost give us the values from *Figure 2* if it didn't involve multiplying by 100. But it doesn't actually give us the values from Figure 2, and the prompt actually asked for the expression that would give us the values from *Figure 1* anyway.

H ✓   **Correct:** The prompt refers us to Figure 1, and the label on the vertical axis of Figure 1 says, "percent of flowers that produced fruit." If we want to find the percent of flowers that produced fruit, then we need to divide the number of flowers that produced fruit by the total number of flowers, and then multiply the result by 100. Only (H) describes this process correctly, so (H) is right. (Another way to tell that (H) is right is to notice that only (H) and (J) refer to the idea of producing fruit, and, of those two choices, only (H) would produce a result not more than 100%, because the number of flowers that produce fruit can't be more than the total number of flowers, since the flowers that produce fruit are a subset of the total number of flowers, and the numerator of the fraction in the right answer must be less than the denominator in order for the percentage to be less than 100.)

J   **Confused Relationships:** This choice would give us the reciprocal of the right answer, which would result in percentages greater than 100%, as we can see in the explanation for (H). This choice would attract an untrained test-taker who forgot how to construct a percentage fraction, or who misread the answer choices and meant to pick (H).

> **What we had to understand to answer the question:** We needed to realize that the prompt was referring us to Figure 1, and that the label on Figure 1 refers to fruit, as we discussed in our analysis of (H). We also needed to realize the proper way to construct a percentage fraction. We didn't need to read or understand any other part of Passage II.

Answering requires information from the text. Choices often primarily involve phrases rather than numbers. Consider every relevant word. Be sure your answer is literally demonstrated or restated on the page, with no interpretation necessary. See p. 339.

Notes on answer choices: (A) and (C) both begin with the word "would," while (B) and (D) begin with the phrase "would not." (A) and (B) both refer to self-pollination, while (C) and (D) both refer to hummingbirds.

A   **Direct Contradiction:** As we can see in the explanation for (B), the anthers produce pollen, so removing the things that produce pollen would contradict the idea of "ensur[ing]" that the flowers "spontaneously self-pollinate."

B ✓   **Correct:** The prompt refers to the idea of removing the anthers, so we'll need to read some part of Passage II to find out why anthers are relevant to the study and why they were removed. The first sentence of the second paragraph says the anthers are "pollen-producing structures," and they were removed "before pollination could occur." The rest of the paragraph, and Table 1, provide descriptions of the different ways the *H. metallica* plants were pollinated during the experiment. So we can see from Passage II that the anthers were cut off, and that they contained pollen. (B) mentions the idea of "self-pollinat[ing]," which is referred to in the fourth sentence of the first paragraph of Passage II: "the flowers can be self-pollinated (egg and pollen are from the same *H. metallica* plant)." We can see that removing the flowers' pollen-producing structures would prevent them from self-pollinating, just as (B) requires. (B) is the only choice that can logically be demonstrated by the text in Passage II, so we know it's right.

C   **Confused Relationships:** It's true that Passage II says the flowers are normally pollinated by hummingbirds, as we'll see below for (D). But nothing in the passage connects the idea of being pollinated by hummingbirds with the idea of removing the anthers. (In fact, since the anthers had to be specially removed for the study, we know that the anthers aren't normally removed as part of the normal life-cycle of the flowers, so the behavior of the hummingbirds (which are the "normal pollinators" of the flowers according to Passage II) can't be dependent on the removal of the anthers. Of course, you don't have to realize all of this to know that (C) isn't literally restated or demonstrated in the passage, and must be wrong.)

D   **Confused Relationships:** The third sentence of the first paragraph of Passage II says that "*H. metallica* flowers are normally pollinated by hummingbirds," and the second sentence of the second paragraph says that "the flowers were covered with nylon bags to prevent the normal pollinators from pollinating the flowers." So we can see that a step *was* taken to prevent hummingbirds from pollinating the flowers—but that step was to cover the flowers with nylon bags, not to remove the anthers. Further, since Passage II makes it clear that the flowers can be pollinated with pollen from other flowers, we know that simply removing the anthers from a set of flowers wouldn't prevent those flowers from being pollinated by hummingbirds who brought pollen from other flowers. So (D) can't be right.

> **What we had to understand to answer the question:** We needed to understand from the text that the anthers were required for

the process of self-pollination, but they weren't directly relevant to the process of being pollinated by hummingbirds. We didn't need to read or understand either figure in Passage II.

Test 2, Question 12 (Test 3 in the 2020-2021 Red Book—see page 23 for more)   **TYPE: DATA PLUS PARAGRAPH**

Finding the answer requires information from the text as well as information from a figure. Read carefully, and be very particular about matching up exact values in the figure and the answer choices, unless the prompt calls for estimation. See p. 339.

Notes on answer choices: The choices are identical except for two differences. (F) and (G) begin with the word "yes," while (H) and (J) begin with the word "no." (F) and (H) use the number 20% and refer to self-pollination, while (G) and (J) use the word "none" and refer to the "no pollination treatment."

F   **Confused Relationships:** (F) contains the statement "only 20% of the flowers receiving the self-pollination treatment produced fruit," which is consistent with Figure 1—but no part of Passage II connects the idea of a 20% pollination rate in the self-pollination group to success in preventing the normal pollinators from pollinating the flowers, as (F) would require.

G ✓ **Correct:** The second sentence of the second paragraph tells us that "the flowers were covered with nylon bags to prevent the normal pollinators from pollinating the flowers." Table 1 tells us that flowers in Group 4 received no pollination treatment, and Figure 1 shows us that none of the flowers in Group 4 produced fruit. If none of the flowers in Group 4 produced any fruit, then it must be true that the flowers in Group 4 weren't pollinated—by the "normal pollinators," or by anything else. So the nylon bags successfully prevented pollination by the normal pollinators, which means (G) is correct.

H   **Confused Relationships:** To some untrained test-takers who didn't read carefully enough, it might seem possible that a 20% rate of fruit production in the self-pollination group could mean that the bags didn't keep out all of the normal pollinators, which would seem to explain how some of the pollination was able to take place. But Passage II makes it clear that the controlled pollination treatments in the study must have been carried out by researchers, not by the "normal pollinators" referred to in the prompt, because otherwise there would be no way to control the types of pollination applied to each group (remember that the third sentence in the first paragraph told us that the "normal pollinators" were hummingbirds). And, as we saw for (G) above, the data in Figure 1 for Group 4 make it clear that Group 4 was never exposed to any kind of pollination, which means the first part of the right answer should be "yes."

J   **Off by One or Two Words:** This choice cites the relevant evidence, as discussed in the explanation for (G) above, but it makes the wrong conclusion—the correct answer should start with "yes," not "no," because the evidence from Group 4 indicates that pollination by normal pollinators *was* totally prevented for that group. So this choice might attract an untrained test-taker who misread its first word.

What we had to understand to answer the question: We needed to understand that all the groups were covered with nylon bags, and that Group 4 specifically never got any pollination treatment. As discussed above for (G), we also needed to understand that the result for the "no pollination" group referred to in (G) and (J) was a clear indication that pollination had been totally prevented in that group, which meant that the "normal pollinators" referred to in the prompt had been prevented from pollinating the flowers.

Test 2, Question 13 (Test 3 in the 2020-2021 Red Book—see page 23 for more)   **TYPE: PURE DATA**

Finding the answer requires information from a figure. Read carefully, and be very particular about matching up exact values in the figure and the answer choices, unless the question calls for estimation. See p. 339.

Notes on answer choices: (A), (B), and (C) provide numerical values, while (D) says it's impossible to know the numerical value.

A   **Confused Relationships:** This choice might attract untrained test-takers who accidentally looked at the information in Figure 2 for *Group 4*, not Group 3, as the prompt requires.

B   **Confused Relationships:** This choice is the "percent of flowers that produced fruit" in Group 3 according to Figure 1, but that number isn't relevant to the "total mass of seeds" mentioned in the prompt, so (B) is wrong.

C   **Confused Relationships:** As discussed in (D), this is the *average mass per seed* in Group 3 according to Figure 2, but it's not the "total mass of the seeds," as the prompt requires. This choice will attract a lot of untrained test-takers who don't read the label on the vertical axis of Figure 2 carefully enough, or who don't understand the difference between the average mass and the total mass of a group of objects.

D ✓ **Correct:** The only data we have on the mass of the seeds produced by Group 3 flowers is in Figure 2, and the vertical axis label tells us that Figure 2 provides information about *average mass per seed*, not the "total mass of seeds," as the prompt requires. In order to find that total mass, we'd have to multiply the average mass by the number of seeds (because, by definition, the average is the result when we divide the total mass by the number of seeds). Passage II never provides any information about the total number of seeds in Group 3, so it's impossible for us to know what the total mass of those seeds was. That means (D) is right. (Strictly speaking, we can also know (D) must be right even if we don't know the definition of the word "average," just because no piece of information anywhere in Passage II tells us about all the seeds as a group.)

What we had to understand to answer the question: As noted for (D) above, we needed to realize that no part of Passage II provides information about the seeds as a group. We didn't need to understand anything else about Passage II.

Test 2, Question 14 (Test 3 in the 2020-2021 Red Book—see page 23 for more)   **TYPE: OUTSIDE INFO**

Answering requires some information that can't be found in the passage. Any required outside knowledge must be relatively basic. Don't try to use outside knowledge on a question unless you're sure you can't answer based on the passage. See p. 339.

Notes on answer choices: (F) and (G) each say that only one kind of bacteria breaks down organic matter in the summer, and the other kind does it in the winter. (H) and (J) each say that both kinds of bacteria are more active in either summer or winter.

F   **Barely Relevant:** The results from Figure 1 and Figure 2 show that CH_4 was produced during the summer, and the first paragraph of Passage III says CH_4 is produced by anaerobic bacteria, which contradicts the idea that anaerobic bacteria don't break anything down in the summer, as this choice would require.

G   **Barely Relevant:** This choice has basically the same problem as (F). Figure 1 and Figure 2 both show that CO_2 was produced during the summer, and the first paragraph of Passage III says that CO_2 is produced by aerobic bacteria, so there's no reason to think that aerobic bacteria would only be active in the summer, as (G) would require.

H ✓   **Correct:** This is another example of the kind of basic scientific information we need to know on the ACT Science section. This choice might sound very intimidating and technical, but it's basically just saying that "organic matter" will break down faster in the heat than it will in the cold. In other words, organic stuff rots and breaks down more quickly when it's warm out than when it's cold out—this is why food lasts longer in refrigerators or freezers, so we can see that (H) is right.

J   **Direct Contradiction:** In order for this choice to be correct, it would have to be true that things break down more quickly when it's cold than they do when it's hot, which would mean refrigerators and freezers would cause food to go bad faster, among other things. As we saw in the explanation for (H), this isn't the case—so this choice must be wrong.

> **What we had to understand to answer the question:** In order to tell that (F) and (G) were wrong, it helped to notice that both kinds of gases were produced in both figures, and the first paragraph of Passage III says that means both kinds of bacteria were active during the experiment. Apart from that, we didn't need to read or understand anything else in Passage III—we just needed to be aware of the relatively basic fact that bacteria breaks stuff down more quickly in the heat than in the cold.

Test 2, Question 15 (Test 3 in the 2020-2021 Red Book—see page 23 for more)   **TYPE: DATA PLUS DATA**

Finding the right answer requires information from more than one figure. Read carefully, and be very particular about matching up exact values in the figure and the answer choices, unless estimation is called for. See page 339.

Notes on answer choices: The choices offer every possible combination of the words "increased" and "decreased."

A ✓   **Correct:** The prompt refers to "the results of the study," which are tabulated in Figure 1 and Figure 2 (note that Passage III only includes one study, so there's no danger that we're looking at the results of the wrong study, as there might be on other passages with multiple studies). The prompt also mentions the idea of the "water table" getting "progressively lower," which is reflected in the way the values on the horizontal WT-axis get lower as we read from left to right on all four graphs (Note that the first sentence of the third paragraph tells us WT stands for water table). Since the first column in the answer choices refers to "total CO_2 emission," we'll start by considering the CO_2 graphs for both figures, which we know are the left-most graphs, because those graphs have vertical axis labels that refer to CO_2 emissions. We can see that the bars for CO_2 in both graphs get bigger as we read from left to right, which means that they get bigger as the water table gets lower. So the first word in the right answer should be "increased." When we consider the CH_4 values for the second column in the answer choices, we see that the values for CH_4 are in the right-most graphs for both figures, because those graphs have vertical axes labeled "total CH_4 emission." In those graphs, we can see that the bars representing CH_4 emission get smaller as we read from left to right, which means they get smaller as the water table gets lower. So the second word in the right answer should be "decreased." This means (A) is right.

B   **Direct Contradiction:** This choice might attract untrained test-takers who mixed up CO_2 and CH_4, either in the figures themselves or in the columns in the answer choices. It would also attract untrained test-takers who misread the horizontal axes on the graphs and thought the water table was getting higher as we moved from left to right across each graph.

C   **Confused Relationships:** (C) might attract test-takers who mistakenly thought that one of the graphs on the left-hand side of one of the figures represented CH_4 emissions, and who ignored the two graphs on the right-hand side of each figure.

D   **Confused Relationships:** This choice has a similar problem to the one in (C). It would attract an untrained test-taker who accidentally thought one of the graphs on the right-hand side of the figures was a graph for CO_2, and who accidentally ignored the two graphs to the left.

> **What we had to understand to answer the question:** We needed to understand that the prompt was referring us to the four graphs in Figure 1 and Figure 2, and we needed to read those graphs accurately to understand which ones were related to CO_2 and which ones were related to CH_4, and how they showed values changing in connection with changes in the water table, as described above for (A). We also needed to read the answer choices carefully to make sure we weren't confused by them. None of this required us to understand the purpose of the experiment, or anything about CO_2, CH_4, or water tables in general. We also didn't need to read any part of Passage III apart from the two figures, and the sentence in the third paragraph that tells us "WT"

Test 2, Question 16 (Test 3 in the 2020-2021 Red Book—see page 23 for more)   **TYPE: PURE PARAGRAPH**

Answering requires information from the text. Choices often primarily involve phrases rather than numbers. Consider every relevant word. Be sure your answer is literally demonstrated or restated on the page, with no interpretation necessary. *See p. 339.*

Notes on answer choices: The choices are largely dissimilar, compared to the choices for other ACT Science questions. (F) and (H) talk about preventing things from getting out of the tank, while (G) and (J) talk about things getting into the tank. (F) and (G) both talk about gases, while (H) and (J) talk about other things mentioned in Passage III.

F ✓ **Correct:** The prompt refers to the idea of the lid being closed, so, in order to answer the question, it will be a good idea to find the parts of Passage III that refer to the lid, and how it's used. The second paragraph says each sample was "placed in a separate 100 L tank having sides and a lid made entirely of glass." It then says that "an instrument to measure gas emissions was mounted on the underside of the lid." Then the last sentence of the third paragraph says all the lids were closed during the experiment, and the first sentence of the last paragraph says, "gas emissions from each soil section were measured." So we can see that the lids are essential for measuring the gas, since the instrument for the measurement is placed on the underside of the lids. We can also see that the lids are closed the whole time (rather than, for example, being left half on and half off, or being slightly misaligned with the tank so that the tanks aren't fully sealed). All of this literally demonstrates the idea of "minimiz[ing] the amount of emitted gas that exited the tank," as (F) requires: the gas is the stuff that needs to be measured in the experiment, and the lids make that measurement possible and keep the gases from escaping.

G   **Direct Contradiction:** As we saw for (F), the experiment involves an instrument on the underside of the lid that measures the gas emitted from the sealed tank. Placing a lid on a tank wouldn't "maximize...the gas that entered the tank," as (G) would require; instead, it would keep gas from entering or exiting the tank, allowing accurate measurements of the gases produced in the tank during the experiment. So this choice must be wrong. This choice might attract an untrained test-taker who fundamentally misunderstood or misread Passage III or this answer choice.

H   **Reasonable Statement Not in the Text:** It might seem to make sense that a closed lid would "prevent bacteria from leaving the tank," since the lid seems to create a barrier. But there are a few problems with this choice. The biggest one is that the passage doesn't mention the idea of bacteria entering or leaving the tank, nor the idea of needing to measure bacteria or keep tabs on how much bacteria was in a certain place at a certain time, or anything like that—instead, the passage repeatedly refers to the idea of measuring the gas emissions, as we see in the first sentence of the last paragraph of text, and in all four graphs in the figures. Since the idea of using the lid to keep all the bacteria in the tank isn't literally demonstrated or restated in the passage, (H) is wrong. This choice might attract untrained test-takers who didn't read the passage carefully and just assumed that the bacteria would need to be sealed into the tanks, and/or who assumed the bacteria themselves were being measured, rather than the gases produced by the bacteria.

J   **Direct Contradiction:** The second sentence of the second paragraph says the lid was "made...of glass," and the end of that paragraph says all the tanks were "placed at an outdoor site." Since the lid is made of glass and the whole tank is outside, the description of the experiment contradicts the idea of "prevent[ing] sunlight from entering the tank," as (J) would require. This choice might attract untrained test-takers who didn't read the study carefully and simply assumed that a lid would be opaque, and would keep out sunlight.

What we had to understand to answer the question: We needed to find the references to the lids in the study, and we needed to read the answer choices carefully. We didn't need to understand anything about either figure.

Test 2, Question 17 (Test 3 in the 2020-2021 Red Book—see page 23 for more)   **TYPE: DATA PLUS PARAGRAPH**

Finding the answer requires information from the text as well as information from a figure. Read carefully, and be very particular about matching up exact values in the figure and the answer choices, unless the prompt calls for estimation. *See p. 339.*

Notes on answer choices: The choices present every possible combination of the words "bogs" and "fens."

A   **Off by One or Two Words:** This choice might attract untrained test-takers who mixed up the data for bogs with the data for fens. See the explanation of (D) for more.

B   **Off by One or Two Words:** This choice could attract an untrained test-taker who somehow misread the two left-most graphs and thought the bars for bogs were larger than the bars for fens, or who misread the labels on those two graphs, or misread the answer choice.

C   **Off by One or Two Words:** This choice has basically the same problem as (B), but for the two right-most graphs rather than the two left-most graphs.

D ✓ **Correct:** The prompt refers to the idea of different levels of nutrients being present in bogs and fens, but no part of Passage III specifically mentions nutrients, or food. At first, this might seem to suggest that we're supposed to know whether bogs or fens have more nutrients for different kinds of bacteria...but, as trained test-takers, we know that the ACT Science section can only occasionally require us to know some basic scientific facts in order to answer a question, and we can tell that this doesn't seem to be one of those facts. For one thing, the italics on the words "*bog*" and "*fen*" in the first paragraph of the study indicate that the ACT thinks these are specialized terms we haven't encountered before, as we discussed in "ACT Science Rule 4: Don't Get Intimidated by Vocabulary, Especially with Italicized Words" on page 340 of this Black Book. So it seems like we should use the provided information to answer this question, which means we need to figure out how we can possibly know anything from the study about the relative amounts of nutrients for different kinds of bacteria. Well, we can see pretty clearly that the only measured results presented as part of the study are found in the two graphs in Figure 1 and the two graphs in Figure 2. In each figure, the left-most graph shows "total CO_2 emissions," and the right-most graph shows "total CH_4 emissions." Since the only data in the study refers to CO_2 and CH_4, we'll need to see if we can draw any connection between those two chemical compounds and different types of bacteria. We see that the first paragraph in Passage III says that "gases are generated" when certain kinds of bacteria "break down organic matter." The idea of "break[ing] down organic matter" actually restates the idea of feeding on "nutrients" from the prompt—the "organic matter" is the "nutrient." Further, the first paragraph says, "aerobic bacteria…generate CO_2," while "anaerobic bacteria…generate CH_4." So we know that the left-most graphs in both figures show quantities related to *aerobic* bacteria processing nutrients, and the right-most graphs in both figures show quantities related to *anaerobic* bacteria processing nutrients. When we look at Figure 1 and Figure 2, we can see that all the bars in Figure 2 are taller than the corresponding bars in Figure 1, and the unit measurements and scales on all the vertical axes are the same. This means that more CO_2 and more CH_4 are emitted by the fens in Figure 2 than by the bogs in Figure 1, for any given water table level. Since both aerobic and anaerobic bacteria emit more gas in fens than in bogs, and those gases are generated when the bacteria break down nutrients in organic matter, we know the bacteria must be breaking down more organic matter in fens than in bogs…which means fens have higher levels of nutrients for both aerobic bacteria and anaerobic bacteria. So (D) is correct.

What we had to understand to answer the question: See the explanation for (D) above.

Test 2, Question 18 (Test 3 in the 2020-2021 Red Book—see page 23 for more)   **TYPE: DATA PLUS PARAGRAPH**

Finding the answer requires information from the text as well as information from a figure. Read carefully, and be very particular about matching up exact values in the figure and the answer choices, unless the prompt calls for estimation. See p. 339.

Notes on answer choices: The choices are identical except for two differences. (F) and (G) both begin with "yes," while (H) and (J) both begin with "no; only." (F) and (H) both mention CO_2, while (G) and (J) both mention CH_4.

F ✓ **Correct:** The prompt asks about aerobic bacteria, so we know that we need to pay attention to CO_2, because the first paragraph in Passage III says that "aerobic bacteria…generate CO_2." When we look at the first graph in Figure 1 and the first graph in Figure 2, we can see CO_2 *was* emitted in the bog soil and in the fen soil when WT was at +1 cm—so aerobic bacteria were present in those sections, and (F) is correct. ("Submerged" in the prompt means "underwater," and the third paragraph says that the "+1 cm" soil section had a water table 1 cm above its surface. If the water table is above the surface of the soil section, then that soil section must be "submerged" by definition, as the prompt requires. But note that, strictly speaking, we don't have to realize which parts of the graphs indicate a "soil section[]…completely submerged in water," as the prompt describes, because CO_2 is present in all three tanks, so the answer to this question would be the same no matter which water table the prompt referred to.)

G **Off by One or Two Words:** The first word in this choice is accurate, as we saw in the explanation for (F). But, as we saw for (F), Passage III tells us that aerobic bacteria produce CO_2, not CH_4, so the statement in (G) about CH_4 isn't relevant to the question. The presence of CH_4 only indicates that *anaerobic* bacteria are present, according to Passage III; it doesn't provide any indication of whether *aerobic* bacteria are present, as the prompt requires. This choice would attract an untrained test-taker who misread Passage III and thought that CH_4 was produced by aerobic bacteria, or who misread the prompt and thought it was asking about anaerobic bacteria.

H **Off by One or Two Words:** As we saw in the explanation for (F), the correct answer should start with "yes," not "no." Also, this choice says that "*only* CO_2 was emitted" (emphasis added), but Figure 1 and Figure 2 show us that submerged soil sections produced both CO_2 *and* CH_4. Either issue is enough to make this choice wrong. This choice is probably here to fill out a common wrong answer pattern on the ACT of offering every possible combination of two different options.

J **Confused Relationships:** This choice could be said to combine the mistakes from (G) and (H). But it may attract an untrained test-taker who misreads the figures, ignoring the left-most graphs in both figures and focusing only on the right-most graphs. That could lead to the mistaken conclusion that no CO_2 was measured, which, if true, would make (J) right. (See our explanation of (F) above to understand the proper approach to this question.)

What we had to understand to answer the question: As described for (F), we needed to realize (based on the first paragraph) that CO_2 emissions came from aerobic bacteria, and we needed to look at the graphs in Figure 1 and Figure 2, and we needed to read the prompt and the answer choices carefully. Beyond that, we didn't need to read or understand any other part of Passage III.

Note Some untrained test-takers will get this question wrong because they'll incorrectly assume that aerobic bacteria must be unable to live underwater, since they require oxygen to metabolize nutrients, and it may seem like it would be hard or impossible to get oxygen underwater. That would lead to the incorrect conclusion that only CH_4 was produced in the tanks where the soil was underwater, which would make (J) right. Of course, there are scientific issues with that line of thought, but the bigger concern for us, as trained test-takers, is that we should never base our answers on some obscure scientific concept that we think we recall accurately when we can simply base our answers on information provided in the passage. In this case, Passage III clearly tells us that CO_2 is produced by aerobic bacteria, and that CO_2 was measured in each tank, and that's all we need to know in order to answer the question. Keep this in mind on test day—always base your conclusions on the provided information, and only fall back on your basic scientific knowledge when the provided information isn't enough to answer the question, as we discussed in "Basic Science Facts" on page 331 of this Black Book.

Test 2, Question 19 (Test 3 in the 2020-2021 Red Book—see page 23 for more)   TYPE: PURE DATA

Finding the answer requires information from a figure. Read carefully, and be very particular about matching up exact values in the figure and the answer choices, unless the question calls for estimation. See p. 339.

Notes on answer choices: The choices are all 2-digit numbers of mol C/m^2.

A   **Wrong Part of the Passage:** (A) might attract test-takers who accidentally used the CO_2 data for *bog soil* at -10 cm, instead of fen soil, as the prompt requires, because a little more than 30 mol C/m^2 divided by 3 would be around 10 mol C/m^2.

B   **Confused Relationships:** This choice might attract untrained test-takers who misread the value of the CO_2 bar for -10 cm in fen soil as being just barely below 40, rather than just barely below 50. That would lead to the conclusion that the average would be around 13, because $13 \times 3 = 39$.

C ✓   **Correct:** The prompt refers to the total CO_2 emission from the fen soil section with a WT of -10 cm, which we can find by looking at the middle bar in the left-most graph in Figure 2. When we look there, we can see that the total CO_2 emission at a WT of -10 cm was a little less than 50 mol C/m^2. The prompt asks for the average emission per month for that soil section over the 3 months of the study, so we'll need to divide the total emission for the 3 months by 3. 50 divided by 3 is a little less than 17, so the result when a little less than 50 mol C/m^2 is divided by 3 would be around 16 mol C/m^2. That means (C) is correct.

D   **Wrong Part of the Passage:** This choice might attract untrained test-takers who accidentally used the CO_2 data for fen soil at *-20* cm, instead of -10 cm, as the prompt requires.

> **What we had to understand to answer the question:** We needed to use the information in the prompt to focus our attention on the middle bar of the left-most graph in Figure 2, and we needed to divide that amount by 3, as we saw in (C). We didn't need to read or understand any other part of Passage III. We also didn't need to understand the unit "mol C/m^2," even though it appeared in every answer choice and in Figure 2 itself.

Test 2, Question 20 (Test 3 in the 2020-2021 Red Book—see page 23 for more)   TYPE: PURE PARAGRAPH

Answering requires information from the text. Choices often primarily involve phrases rather than numbers. Consider every relevant word. Be sure your answer is literally demonstrated or restated on the page, with no interpretation necessary. See p. 339.

Notes on answer choices: The choices are fairly dissimilar for an ACT Science question.

F   **Barely Relevant:** Precipitation is rain, but the last sentence of the third paragraph tells us that all the tanks were closed up with lids, which means no rain would have gotten into the samples. This choice might have attracted an untrained test-taker who assumed that rainfall would be important to wetland environments like the ones described in the passage, without reading the passage carefully enough.

G   **Direct Contradiction:** The second paragraph tells us that the sections of soil were removed "after all live plants had been removed." That means these soil sections must have had plants before they were put in the tanks, which means the wetlands had plants, while the samples in the tanks didn't—so the wetlands and the tanks weren't identical in terms of the "types of plants present," as (G) would require. This choice might attract an untrained test-taker who assumed that soil would contain plants and didn't read the passage closely enough to note that the plants had been removed.

H   **Confused Relationships:** This choice will attract a lot of untrained test-takers who misread the prompt and think it's asking about the similarities among the samples themselves, because it's true that each sample is the same size according to the second paragraph, and is put in a tank of the same size. But the prompt asks us to find a similarity between the tanks *and the wetlands themselves!* Nothing in the passage restates or demonstrates the idea that the volume of the soil in the samples was "nearly identical" to the volume of soil of the wetlands, as the prompt requires, so (H) is wrong.

J ✓   **Correct:** If the tanks were kept outside near the wetlands, as the prompt describes, then they'd receive "nearly identical" hours of daylight compared to the wetlands, as (J) requires. We know this must be the case because the second sentence in the second paragraph says that the tanks that held the samples had "sides and a lid made entirely of glass," which would allow light through—so (J) is right.

> **What we had to understand to answer the question:** We needed to read the parts of Passage III referred to in the analyses for the answer choices above, and we needed to read the prompt carefully, as we described for (H) above. We didn't need to pay any attention to the data from the experiment, or the figures containing that data.

Finding the answer requires information from the text as well as information from a figure. Read carefully, and be very particular about matching up exact values in the figure and the answer choices, unless the prompt calls for estimation. See p. 339.

Notes on answer choices: The choices offer the possibility of picking any individual study, or of not picking any study.

A   **Off by One or Two Words:** As we'll see in the discussion of (B), Study 1 used a 61 lb door, which has less mass than the 76 lb door in Study 2. This choice might attract an untrained test-taker who correctly noted that the study at the top of the second column includes the heaviest door, but who incorrectly thinks that study is Study 1, possibly because he overlooks the study at the bottom of the first column and doesn't read the name of the study at the top of the second column.

B ✓ **Correct:** The prompt refers to "the door with the greatest mass," but Passage IV doesn't specifically refer to mass; instead, it refers to weight. Part of our general science knowledge is the fact that increased mass correlates to increased weight (since weight is just the result of the Earth's gravity acting on the mass of an object). So we'll need to see if any study uses a door that weighs more than the doors in the other studies. The first sentence in the description for Study 1 says that study was done with a door that weighed 61 lb. The description for Study 2 says that study was done with multiple doors with "a different W." When we look at Figure 2 to learn more about the weights of the doors in Study 2, we can see that the highest W-value is 76 lb. Finally, the first sentence of the description for Study 3 says that study was done with 3 doors that each weighed 61 lb. So we can see that the heaviest door was the 76 lb door from Study 2, which means (B) is correct.

C   **Off by One or Two Words:** As we discussed for (B), the door in Study 3 isn't as heavy as the 76 lb door in Study 2. This choice might attract untrained test-takers who misread the title of Study 2 as Study 3.

D   **Direct Contradiction:** This choice might attract untrained test-takers who didn't notice that Study 2 involved doors with different weights, which might happen if a test-taker didn't look at Figure 2 in Study 2, since the other studies state the weights of their doors in text above the figures.

What we had to understand to answer the question: We needed to realize that "mass" in the prompt is correlated to "weight" in Passage IV, as we discussed for (B). We also needed to read the first sentence in the description of Study 1 and the first sentence in the description of Study 3, and we needed to note that Figure 2 indicates the weights of the different doors used in Study 2. Beyond that, we didn't need to read or understand any part of Passage IV, including the diagram of a door and the subscripted notation.

Note   Answering this question *does* require a little bit of outside basic scientific knowledge, because we have to know that we can answer this question about "mass" based on the information in the passage about "weight." (Some test-takers might not even notice this distinction, because they think of mass and weight as basically interchangeable, which they often are.) For that reason, you could make an argument that this should be classified as an "Outside Info" question, instead of a "Data Plus Paragraph" question—in reality, this question incorporates a little bit of both types. The important thing to remember here is that these question types are guidelines to prepare you for the kinds of things you'll see on test day. Most questions will fit neatly into one classification, and a few will blur the boundaries little bit. But on test day, you don't need to classify each question before you answer it; you only need to read carefully and apply your training to find the right answer. Don't get distracted trying to figure out exactly how to classify the questions you see on test day!

Answering requires information from the text. Choices often primarily involve phrases rather than numbers. Consider every relevant word. Be sure your answer is literally demonstrated or restated on the page, with no interpretation necessary. See p. 339.

Notes on answer choices: The choices combine statements about whether W and/or D was held constant or varied in Study 2 and Study 3. (F) and (G) both say that one variable was held constant and the other was varied in each study. (H) and (J) both say that both of the variables were held constant in one of the studies, and both were varied in the other study.

F ✓ **Correct:** The first sentence of Study 2 says it includes "3 doors, each with $D = 30$ in but a different W." This specifically indicates that "W was varied" in Study 2, "while D was held constant," just as the first part of (F) requires. The first sentence of the description for Study 3 says it includes "3 doors, each with $W = 61$ lb but a different D." This restates the idea in (F) that "W was held constant while D was varied" in Study 3, just as the second half of (F) requires. So (F) is right.

G   **Direct Contradiction:** This choice confuses the details of Study 2 and Study 3, as we saw in our discussion of (F) above. It could attract untrained test-takers who have a hard time keeping the details of the individual studies straight in their heads.

H   **Confused Relationships:** As we saw for our discussion of (F), each study varied one of the things in the answer choices and held the other one constant; neither study varied both values. This choice could confuse untrained test-takers who accidentally misread Study 1 as Study 3, because Study 1 does involve every door having a constant weight of 61 lb and a constant width of 30 in.

J   **Confused Relationships:** As we saw for our discussion of (F), each study varied one of the things in the answer choices and held the other one constant; neither study varied both values. This choice could confuse untrained test-takers who accidentally misread

Study 1 as Study 2, because Study 1 does involve every door having a constant weight of 61 lb and a constant width of 30 in.

What we had to understand to answer the question: We needed to focus in on the specific differences among the answer choices, and we needed to read the sentences at the beginning of Study 2 and Study 3 that indicate which values were changed for those studies. Beyond that, we didn't need to read or understand any part of Passage IV, including the diagrams, graphs, and subscripts.

Test 2, Question 23 (Test 3 in the 2020-2021 Red Book—see page 23 for more)   **TYPE: PURE DATA**

Finding the answer requires information from a figure. Read carefully, and be very particular about matching up exact values in the figure and the answer choices, unless the question calls for estimation. See p. 339.

Notes on answer choices: The choices include numbers between 20 and 45.

A   **Direct Contradiction:** As we can see in the explanation for (D), the right answer reflects the idea that a 90 lb door would have a curve in Figure 2 that's *above* the curves for the lighter doors that are already present on the graph. But this choice reflects the idea that the data points for the 90 lb door would be *below* the points for the other doors that already appear in Figure 2. This choice might attract an untrained test-taker who correctly realized that the trend in the data indicates the value for the 90 lb door should be outside of the provided values for the other doors (instead of being between the values provided for other doors), but who then accidentally chose a value that was *less than* all of the provided data points, instead of a value that was *greater than* the provided data points, as we see in (D). (A) could also attract a test-taker who misread the number 90 in the prompt as the number 9, or who thought the 30 that appeared in the prompt was the weight of the door.

B   **Barely Relevant:** There's no reason to think that any data point in Figure 2 related to a 90 lb door would be in the range between 20 and 30 on the vertical axis, as (B) would require. See the explanation of (D) for more.

C   **Barely Relevant:** This choice has the same basic problem as (B), and is wrong for the same reason.

D ✓   **Correct:** The prompt refers to Study 2, so we should start by consulting that part of Passage IV. The results of Study 2 are given in Figure 2, which includes one axis labeled $F_{n,av}$ and another labeled S; since these are terms that appear in the prompt, we can be sure that Figure 2 is relevant to this question. Neither the description for Study 2 nor the axes for Figure 2 mention a door with a weight of 90, as we see in the prompt, but we do see in the description of Study 2 that all the doors in Figure 2 have $D = 30$ in, as the prompt describes. Further, we can see that one of the possible S-values in Figure 2 is $S = 50$, since 50 is one of the labels on the horizontal S-axis. So it looks like the only concept in the prompt that isn't already depicted in Figure 2 is the idea of a door weighing 90 pounds. In Figure 2, we can see that $F_{n,av}$ increases as weight increases—in other words, at $S = 50$, $F_{n,av}$ is about 28 for a 51 lb door, about 37 for a 61 lb door, and about 46 for a 76 lb door. Following this trend, we know that a door that weighs even more than 76 lb must have an even higher $F_{n,av}$ than 46. So (D) is right.

What we had to understand to answer the question: We needed to realize that the prompt was telling us to look at Study 2 and Figure 2, and that a 90 lb door would have a curve above the curves of the existing doors in Figure 2, as we saw for (D). We didn't need to read or understand any other text, diagram, or figure in Passage IV outside of Study 2. We didn't have to understand the meanings of $W, D, S,$ or $F_{n,av}$; we only needed to find the places in Figure 2 where those expressions were used.

Test 2, Question 24 (Test 3 in the 2020-2021 Red Book—see page 23 for more)   **TYPE: PURE DATA**

Finding the answer requires information from a figure. Read carefully, and be very particular about matching up exact values in the figure and the answer choices, unless the question calls for estimation. See p. 339.

Notes on answer choices: The choices present every possible combination of the words "less" and "greater."

F   **Off by One or Two Words:** See the explanation for (H) to understand why (F) is wrong. (F) might attract an untrained test-taker who assumed that $F_{h,av}$ was always less than $F_{v,av}$ because Figure 1 shows the label $F_{h,av}$ positioned below $F_{v,av}$.

G   **Direct Contradiction:** This choices reverses the relationship between $F_{h,av}$ and $F_{v,av}$. It might trap an untrained test-taker who didn't read carefully enough to note the difference between $F_{h,av}$ and $F_{v,av}$; it might also trap an untrained test-taker who got confused by the grammatical structure of the prompt or the similarity of the subscripts.

H ✓   **Correct:** The prompt refers us to Study 1, and mentions values related to $F_{h,av}$ and $F_{v,av}$ when S is greater than or less than 30. The only part of Study 1 that shows actual values for $F_{h,av}$ and $F_{v,av}$ is Figure 1, so we know we should consider that figure as we try to answer the question. In Figure 1, we see that $F_{h,av}$ is represented by the curve with white circles, and $F_{v,av}$ is represented by the line with black squares. As it turns out, the two lines cross each other where $S = 30$. To the left of the point where they cross, S is less than 30 inches. For those values, $F_{h,av}$ is greater than $F_{v,av}$. To the right of the point where the lines cross, which is where S is greater than 30 inches, we see that $F_{h,av}$ is less than $F_{v,av}$. So (H) is correct.

J   **Off by One or Two Words:** This choice is probably here to fill out the pattern presented in the answer choices.

What we had to understand to answer the question: We needed to realize that the question was directing us to consider the data in Figure 1, and we needed to be able to determine which curve was higher to the left of $S = 30$, and which was higher to the right of $S = 30$, as we discussed for (H). We also needed to read the prompt and the answer choices carefully to make sure we were correctly comparing $F_{h,av}$ to $F_{v,av}$, and not the other way around.

Finding the right answer requires information from more than one figure. Read carefully, and be very particular about matching up exact values in the figure and the answer choices, unless estimation is called for. See page 339.

Notes on answer choices: The choices present different combinations of values for W, D, and S. (A) and (B) share one set of W- and D-values, while (C) and (D) share a different set of W- and D-values. (A) and (C) both have S-values of 20, while (B) and (D) both have S-values of 70.

A   **Confused Relationships:** This choice includes the W and D values of the door with the lowest $F_{n,av}$, but this S-value actually corresponds to the *highest* $F_{n,av}$ for the 51 lb door, which isn't what the prompt asked for. This choice might attract an untrained test-taker who simply assumed that a lower S-value would automatically correspond to a lower $F_{n,av}$-value, without actually checking Passage IV to see if that was true.

B ✓ **Correct:** The prompt refers to Studies 2 and 3, and also refers to values for W, D, S, and $F_{n,av}$. When we look at those studies, we see that $F_{n,av}$ is the label of the vertical axis in both figures—this fits with the prompt's idea of finding the lowest $F_{n,av}$ value. We see that the lowest $F_{n,av}$ value in both figures is the $F_{n,av}$ value of approximately 26, which is in the bottom-right corner of Figure 2. We see that the $F_{n,av}$ value of 26 was created by the 51 lb door, and it's right over the spot where $S = 70$ on the horizontal S-axis. So we can see that the lowest $F_{n,av}$ value of any door in the two studies is associated with 51 lbs and $S = 70$. That's actually enough information to determine that (B) is right, since (B) is the only choice with $W = 51$ and $S = 70$. Still, as trained test-takers, we know that it's a good idea to verify every part of this choice, so we need to make sure that $D = 30$ from (B) is still accurate for the 51 lb door in Figure 2. We see that the description for Study 2 says $D = 30$ for all the doors in Study 2 and Figure 2. So (B) is correct.

C   **Confused Relationships:** This choice includes the W- and D-values of the door with the lowest $F_{n,av}$ in Study 3, as we can see in our discussion of (D), but the question asks about Studies 2 *and* 3...and this S-value actually corresponds to the *highest* $F_{n,av}$ for this particular door—not the *lowest*, as the prompt would require. So this choice might attract an untrained test-taker who combined the mistakes from choices (A) and (D).

D   **Wrong Part of the Passage:** This choice might attract an untrained test-taker who overlooked the part of the prompt that mentions Study 2, because this choice corresponds to the lowest $F_{n,av}$-value *in Study 3*, but the prompt asks about the lowest $F_{n,av}$-value out of both Studies 2 *and* 3, so (D) is wrong.

What we had to understand to answer the question: We needed to realize that the prompt was referring us to the data in Figure 2 and Figure 3, and then we needed to find the door with the lowest $F_{n,av}$-value among both of those figures, and observe the data points relevant to that door, as described for (B) above. We didn't need to read or understand any other part of Passage IV, including any part of the diagram. We didn't need to understand how W, D, and S might affect $F_{n,av}$, or even what $F_{n,av}$ actually stands for or means. We just needed to find the lowest data point on either figure (literally the lowest dot), and determine which numbers from the figure were relevant for that data point.

Finding the answer requires information from a figure. Read carefully, and be very particular about matching up exact values in the figure and the answer choices, unless the question calls for estimation. See p. 339.

Notes on answer choices: The choices are identical except for two changes. (F) and (G) refer to $F_{h,av}$, while (H) and (J) refer to $F_{v,av}$. (F) and (H) end with the word "decreased," while (G) and (J) end with the phrase "remained constant."

F   **Confused Relationships:** (F) correctly describes what happened to $F_{h,av}$ as S increased, but incorrectly says that $F_{h,av}$ was independent of S. By definition, $F_{h,av}$ can't be "independent of S" as the prompt requires if S and $F_{h,av}$ change together in the data. This choice might attract an untrained test-taker who though that being "independent" of a variable meant changing in the opposite direction of the variable; it actually means that one variable doesn't change in response to the other.

G   **Confused Relationships:** This choice combines the problems from (F) and (H): it misidentifies the independent variable, and it contradicts Figure 1, which shows that $F_{h,av}$ decreased as S increased. This choice could attract an untrained test-taker who understood the question perfectly but misread $F_{h,av}$ as $F_{v,av}$.

H   **Confused Relationships:** This choice is wrong because its statement that "as S increased, $F_{v,av}$ decreased" contradicts Figure 1, which shows that $F_{v,av}$ was unchanged as S increased. (It's true that $F_{v,av}$ is independent of S, but, as trained test-takers, we know that the reason provided in the answer choice must be demonstrated in the passage, so this choice is still wrong.) This choice could attract an untrained test-taker who thought (J) was right but marked (H) because the choices look similar.

J ✓ **Correct:** As trained test-takers, we should know that the idea of a variable being "independent of S" (as required by the prompt) means that the variable is unaffected by changes in S (see "Special Article: Basics of Experimental Design" on page 336 of this Black Book for more). We might start by looking in the text description of Study 1 to see if we can find a written explanation of the independent variable, since the prompt refers to Study 1, but there isn't any such description there. That means we'll need to look at Figure 1. Figure 1 makes it clear that $F_{v,av}$ isn't affected by changes in S, because $F_{v,av}$ never changes for any different value of S;

$F_{v,av}$ always stays at 30 lbs, no matter what S is. So (J) is the correct answer.

> **What we had to understand to answer the question:** We needed to know that an independent variable is one that doesn't change in response to changes in another variable. We also needed to realize that the prompt was telling us to look at Figure 1, and we needed to realize that Figure 1 shows that $F_{v,av}$ remains unchanged no matter what the value of S is, as the prompt requires. Finally, we needed to read the choices closely, to make sure we picked the appropriate one, since they're all highly similar to each other. We didn't need to understand what $F_{h,av}$ and $F_{v,av}$ actually are in real life, or how they might affect S in real life. We didn't need to look at any part of Passage IV except for Figure 1.

Test 2, Question 27 (Test 3 in the 2020-2021 Red Book—see page 23 for more)   TYPE: PURE DATA

Finding the answer requires information from a figure. Read carefully, and be very particular about matching up exact values in the figure and the answer choices, unless the question calls for estimation. See p. 339.

Notes on answer choices: Choices offer every combination of either 30 or 36 in the first column, and either 20 or 70 in the second.

A   **Off by One or Two Words:** The results of Study 3 appear in Figure 3, which shows the $F_{n,av}$-values for different kinds of doors (see the explanation for (C) if you want to know how we know $F_{n,av}$-values are relevant to this question). Based on that figure, when $D = 30$ and $S = 20$, $F_{n,av}$ will be around 55 lb. The prompt tells us that the hinges will break when a net force of greater than 57 lb is applied, so this combination of D and S won't cause the hinge to break. This choice might be here to attract untrained test-takers who think the right answer needs to be *as close to 57 as possible*, instead of being *greater than 57*, which is what the prompt actually calls for.

B   **Confused Relationships:** This choice is probably here to fill out the pattern of offering every combination of two different options, which is common on the ACT Science section. It combines the mistakes from (A) and (D).

C ✓   **Correct:** The prompt refers us to the results of Study 3, which appear in Figure 3. The prompt talks about a "net force greater than 57 lb," which may seem odd at first because Figure 3 doesn't include the words "net force." But we see that Figure 3 does mention $F_{n,av}$, and we know that the ACT has to define obscure technical terms like that if they're relevant to a question. When we skim through the provided information to see where $F_{n,av}$ is defined, we see that the last sentence of the paragraph under the diagram of the door says $F_{n,av}$ is "the average net force per hinge." So we know that the $F_{n,av}$ being measured in Figure 3 corresponds to the "net force" referred to in the prompt, which confirms that Figure 3 is the right place for us to look as we answer this question. In Figure 3, we see that when $D = 36$ and $S = 20$, $F_{n,av}$ will be a little less than 65 lb. The prompt tells us that the hinges will break "when a net force greater than 57 lb is exerted," so this combination of D and S will cause the hinge to break, which means (C) is right.

D   **Off by One or Two Words:** As we saw in our discussion of (C), an $F_{n,av}$-value greater than 57 lb does include a D of 36 in, just as this choice does. After noticing that, some untrained test-takers will just assume that the highest S-value must correlate to the highest net force, without bothering to check the figure, where they could realize that lower S-values actually correlate to higher $F_{n,av}$-values for a given D-value.

> **What we had to understand to answer the question:** We needed to realize that the prompt is referring us to Figure 3, and that the $F_{n,av}$-values in Figure 3 are the "net force" referred to in the prompt, as we discussed for (C) (which we found out from the last sentence in the paragraph below the diagram). From there, we needed to make sure we were careful and precise in picking the answer choice whose D-value and S-value corresponded to an $F_{n,av}$-value in Figure 3 that was greater than 57 lb. We didn't need to read or understand any other part of Passage IV, including the diagram of the door and the material in the other studies.

Test 2, Question 28 (Test 3 in the 2020-2021 Red Book—see page 23 for more)   TYPE: PURE PARAGRAPH

Answering requires information from the text. Choices often primarily involve phrases rather than numbers. Consider every relevant word. Be sure your answer is literally demonstrated or restated on the page, with no interpretation necessary. See p. 339.

Notes on answer choices: Choices allow us to pick different selections of 2 of the 4 students, or all the students, or none of them.

F   **Barely Relevant:** See the explanation for (J).

G   **Barely Relevant:** See the explanation for (J).

H   **Direct Contradiction:** See the explanation for (J).

J ✓   **Correct:** None of the students' explanations mentions Argon in any way. Further, the small amount of Argon mentioned in the prompt (less than 1% by volume) isn't enough to contradict any of the explanations presented by any of the students, since those explanations all refer to rough estimates in the neighborhood of 20% or 80% of the air volume.

> **What we had to understand to answer the question:** We needed to be generally aware that the students' explanations all deal with inexact estimates (which we know from the word "about" in phrases like "about 75% O_2") of substances that make up at least roughly 20% of a sample, and we needed to know that a small amount of another substance wouldn't affect the general validity of any of the student's statements. We didn't need to understand the details of any of the students' arguments, nor what Argon actually is, or what it does in the air.

Answering requires information from the text. Choices often primarily involve phrases rather than numbers. Consider every relevant word. Be sure your answer is literally demonstrated or restated on the page, with no interpretation necessary. See p. 339.

Notes on answer choices: The choices offer every possible combination of two Roman numerals, as well as the option to pick all 3 Roman numerals.

A ✓ **Correct:** The prompt asks which of "the properties listed below" was a reason that "silicone was…used" in the experiment described in the passage. When we read those properties, we see that III is "high solubility in water." Water isn't mentioned a single time in the passage, so we know the passage doesn't say that any property related to water was a reason that silicone hoses were used in the experiment. That means III can't be part of the right answer, and the only choice without III is (A), which mentions Roman numerals I and II. We can feel confident in our decision that (A) is right and Roman numerals I and II are part of the right answer because the passage mentions the quartz tube is "heat-resistant," and that the contents of the quartz tube were heated, and the diagram shows that the quartz tube is directly connected to the silicone hoses. If the silicone hoses are attached to something that's heat resistant and gets exposed to heat, then it makes sense that the silicone hoses need to be heat-resistant too, as property I describes. Further, each of the students in the passage talks about how chemical reactions take place in the apparatus, but none of those chemical reactions involves anything reacting with silicone—so we know it's likely that silicone must have low chemical reactivity, which means Roman numeral II is probably a property of silicone hoses as well. With all of this in mind, we can be confident that (A) is correct.

B **Confused Relationships:** See the explanation for (A). This choice might attract untrained test-takers who misread the Roman numerals in the choice, and think they're picking Roman numerals I and II instead of I and III.

C **Confused Relationships:** See the explanation for (A). This choice is probably here to round out the pattern of offering every possible combination of two out of three Roman numerals.

D **Off by One or Two Words:** See the explanation for (A). This choice is probably here for people who tried to use outside knowledge to answer this question instead of relying on the information in the passage.

> **What we had to understand to answer the question:** As described in (A), we arguably didn't need to know any properties of silicone hoses in order to answer this question. All we had to do was notice which options the answer choices were giving us, and then look in the passage for information about the experiment and use that information to eliminate the Roman numeral that wasn't relevant to the experiment. We never needed to understand what actually happened during the experiment, or anything in all of Passage V, apart from the idea that the experiment involved heat and some kind of chemical reaction, and the idea that water was never mentioned.

Answering requires information from the text. Choices often primarily involve phrases rather than numbers. Consider every relevant word. Be sure your answer is literally demonstrated or restated on the page, with no interpretation necessary. See p. 339.

Notes on answer choices: The choices offer every possible combination of the words "increase" and "decrease."

F **Off by One or Two Words:** See the explanation for (J). This choice might attract untrained test-takers who just assumed that all types of gas would increase since O_2 increases, without confirming that idea in Passage V.

G **Direct Contradiction:** See the explanation for (J). This choice might attract untrained test-takers who confuse the labels on the columns in the answer choices, and think the first column corresponds to O_2 and the second one corresponds to CO_2.

H **Off by One or Two Words:** See the explanation for (J). This is probably here to round out the pattern in the set of choices.

J ✓ **Correct:** The prompt tells us to consider Student 4's statement, which says that the Fe "reacted with all the CO_2 in the air to form solid iron carbonate." If all the CO_2 in the air reacted to form a solid, then we know that there *was* some CO_2 in the air *before* the reaction, but there was no longer any CO_2 in the air *after* the reaction. So the percentage of CO_2 in the air must have decreased to 0%. Student 4 also says that "air contains about 20% CO_2 by volume," but that "almost all the gas remaining in the apparatus was O_2" after the reaction. The phrase "almost all" indicates that the percentage of O_2 must have increased to practically 100%, even though it had to start out being around 80% or less (since CO_2 made up 20%, according to Student 4). So the CO_2 decreased in percentage, and the O_2 increased in percentage, which means (J) is correct.

> **What we had to understand to answer the question:** We needed to notice that the prompt referred to Student 4, and then focus on Student 4's statement, and see that it described CO_2 decreasing to basically 0% and O_2 increasing to basically 100%. We also needed to read the choices carefully to make sure we picked the one that accurately reflected our conclusions. We never needed to understand why Student 4 thinks CO_2 would decrease, or O_2 would increase, or how any of the proposed chemical reactions would work, or how the teacher decided on the construction of the apparatus in the diagram, or anything else in Passage V apart from what's mentioned in the explanation of (J) above.

Answering requires information from the text. Choices often primarily involve phrases rather than numbers. Consider every relevant word. Be sure your answer is literally demonstrated or restated on the page, with no interpretation necessary. See p. 339.

Notes on answer choices: Each choice contains Student 1. It's impossible to choose Student 4 without also choosing Student 2 or Student 3. It's impossible to choose both Student 2 and Student 3 together.

A   **Off by One or Two Words:** It's true that Students 1 and 2 believe the air has more O_2 than N_2, as (A) requires, but the word "only" makes this choice wrong, because Student 4 also thinks the air has more O_2 than N_2. This choice will attract untrained test-takers who misread or ignore Student 4's statement. See the explanation of (C) for more.

B   **Confused Relationships:** It's true that Student 1 agrees the air has more O_2 than N_2, as we'll discuss in (C) below. But Student 3 says, "air contains about 20% O_2 by volume," and that the Fe reacted with "all the O_2 in the air." Then Student 3 says that, after the reaction, "almost all the gas remaining in the apparatus was N_2." If air is "about 20% O_2 by volume," and then almost all the remaining gas is N_2 when the O_2 is removed from the air, then the air must have originally been around 80% N_2. Since 80% is greater than 20%, we can see that Student 3 thinks air contains more N_2 than O_2. This choice might appeal to untrained test-takers who confuse Student 2 and Student 3, or who confuse the statements of Student 3 with respect to the percentages of the different compounds—and who also ignore or misunderstand Student 4. See the explanation of (C) for more on the other students' opinions.

C   ✓   **Correct:** Student 1 says, "air contains about 20% N_2 by volume," and that the Fe reacted with "all the N_2 in the air." Then Student 1 says that after the reaction, "almost all the gas remaining in the apparatus was O_2." If air is "about 20% N_2 by volume," and then all the N_2 is removed from the air, and almost all the remaining gas is O_2, then the air must have originally been around 80% O_2—so we can see that Student 1 thinks air contains more O_2 than N_2 by volume, as the prompt and (C) both require. Student 2 says, "air contains about 80% O_2 by volume." If air contains about 80% O_2 by volume, then the absolute maximum possible percentage of N_2 in air would be about 20%—so we can see that Student 2 must also think air contains more O_2 than N_2, as the prompt and (C) require. Finally, Student 4 says after the reaction, the "gas...decreased by about 20%," and "almost all the gas remaining...was O_2." If the volume of the gas decreased by 20%, and almost all the remaining gas was O_2, then the air must have originally been around 80% O_2. By the same logic we applied with Student 2, who also thought the air must have originally been around 80% O_2, we can see that Student 4 must agree there's more O_2 than N_2 in the air. So we can see that Students 1, 2, and 4 think air contains more O_2 than N_2, which means (C) is right.

D   **Off by One or Two Words:** This choice could attract untrained test-takers who confuse Student 2 and Student 3. See the explanations of (B) and (C) for more on the different students' opinions.

> **What we had to understand to answer the question:** We needed to find, read, and understand the students' statements about the percentages of different compounds in the air, as we discussed for (B) and (C) above. We didn't need to understand any of the chemical reactions proposed by any of the students—beyond the proportions of the relevant gases—or understand why the apparatus was built the way it was, or anything else in Passage V.

Test 2, Question 32 (Test 3 in the 2020-2021 Red Book—see page 23 for more)   **TYPE: PURE PARAGRAPH**

Answering requires information from the text. Choices often primarily involve phrases rather than numbers. Consider every relevant word. Be sure your answer is literally demonstrated or restated on the page, with no interpretation necessary. See p. 339.

Notes on answer choices: (F) and (H) both include the compounds Fe_2O_3, Fe, and O_2, in different orders. (G) and (J) both include the compounds FeN, Fe, and N_2 in different orders. (F) is the reverse of (H), and (G) is the reverse of (J).

F   **Direct Contradiction:** This is the reverse of the chemical reaction in the correct answer, choice (H). It could attract an untrained test-taker who got confused about which things were reacting in Student 3's analysis, and which things were produced by that reaction.

G   **Barely Relevant:** This describes the reverse of the chemical reaction in (J). See the explanation for (J) to understand why (G) and (J) are both irrelevant to the prompt.

H   ✓   **Correct:** The prompt tells us to consider Student 3's statement. We can see that Student 3 says, "the Fe...reacted with all the O_2." As trained test-takers, we know that the compounds on the left-hand side of the arrow in a chemical equation are the ones that react together, and the compounds to the right-hand side of the arrow are the products of that reaction. So we need to find the answer choice that shows Fe and O_2 on the left-hand side of the arrow, since Student 2 says those two things "reacted." (H) is the only choice that has Fe and O_2 on the left, so (H) must be right. (Notice that we didn't need to worry about whether the equation was balanced, or what was on the right side of the arrow, because only one choice had Fe and O_2 as the things reacting together to the left of the arrow.)

J   **Wrong Part of the Passage:** This is the reaction described in Student 1's explanation, but the prompt asked for the reaction described by Student 3. This choice will attract a lot of untrained test-takers who misread the prompt and think it's asking about Student 1, or misread Passage V and think that Student 1's statement is being made by Student 3.

> **What we had to understand to answer the question:** We needed to find Student 3's statement and note which substances Student 3 said were reacting, as discussed in our explanation of (H) above. We also needed to know that the chemicals on the left-hand side of a chemical equation are the ones that react together. We didn't need to read or understand any part of Passage V.

apart from the phrase "the Fe...reacted with all the O_2" in Student 3's statement.

Note This choice requires a very basic understanding of conventions related to chemical equations, as we discussed in "Chemical Equations" on page 334 of this Black Book.

Answering requires information from the text. Choices often primarily involve phrases rather than numbers. Consider every relevant word. Be sure your answer is literally demonstrated or restated on the page, with no interpretation necessary. See p. 339.

Notes on answer choices: Student 2 is included in every choice that says any student agrees with the given statement.

A   **Off by One or Two Words:** This choice correctly notes that Student 2 would agree with the statement from the prompt, as we can see in the explanation for (B). But the word "only" in this choice ignores the fact that Student 3 would also agree with the prompt, so (A) is wrong.

B ✓ **Correct:** Students 1 and 4 both say that, after the reaction, "almost all the gas remaining in the apparatus was O_2," so they wouldn't agree that the remaining gas was at least 20% N_2 by volume, as the statement in the prompt requires. Student 2 says the remaining gas was "25% N_2 by volume." Since 25% is more than 20%, we can see that Student 2 agrees with the statement in the prompt. Student 3 says, "almost all the gas remaining in the apparatus was N_2;" since "almost all" means "almost 100%," and 100% is more than 20%, we can see that Student 3 also agrees with the statement in the prompt. So Students 2 and 3 both clearly say that they agree with the statement in the prompt, just as (B) requires.

C   **Confused Relationships:** It's true that Student 1 says, "air contains about 20% N_2 by volume," but that statement is about "air" in general, not specifically about "the gas remaining in the apparatus," as the prompt requires. Further, we saw in our discussion of (B) that Student 4 doesn't agree with the statement made in the prompt. Either of these issues by itself is enough to make (C) wrong. (C) might attract a test-taker who misread Student 1's statement and thought Student 1 believed air was 20% N_2 even after the experiment, if that test-taker also ignored or misread the statement by Student 4.

D   **Confused Relationships:** As we can see in the explanation for (B), Students 2 and 3 would agree with the statement in the prompt. This choice might attract an untrained test-taker who misread or ignored the statements of Students 2 and 3.

What we had to understand to answer the question: We needed to find and understand the statements about N_2 and O_2 that came up in our discussions of (B) and (C). We didn't need to read or understand any other part of Passage V.

Answering requires information from the text. Choices often primarily involve phrases rather than numbers. Consider every relevant word. Be sure your answer is literally demonstrated or restated on the page, with no interpretation necessary. See p. 339.

Notes on answer choices: Each student can be selected individually.

F   **Confused Relationships:** Student 1 thinks the limiting reactant was N_2, because Student 1 says, "the Fe...reacted with the all the N_2." If all the N_2 was used up, then we know that N_2 was "in the shortest supply," as the prompt describes. This choice might attract an untrained test-taker who misread the statement of Student 1 and thought it referred to "all the Fe," or who thought the symbol for "iron" as described in the prompt was N_2 instead of Fe.

G ✓ **Correct:** The prompt tell us that the limiting reactant "limits the amount of product that can be produced." Student 2 says that "Fe...reacted with some of the O_2," and also that "the gas remaining...was...about 75% O_2." Student 2 clearly believes there was O_2 left in the apparatus after the Fe was done reacting with the O_2, which means that Fe was "in the shortest supply" as described by the prompt, which means that Fe must have been the limiting reactant according to Student 2. (Note that the first sentence of the passage tells us that "Fe" is iron.)

H   **Confused Relationships:** Student 3 refers to the reaction using up "all the O_2," which means Student 3 thought that O_2 was "in the shortest supply" as the prompt describes. As with (F), this choice could attract an untrained test-taker who misread Student 3's statement and thought it referred to "all the Fe," or who incorrectly thought the chemical symbol for the "iron" in the prompt was O_2.

J   **Confused Relationships:** Student 4 says the action used up "all the CO_2," which means the CO_2 must have been the compound "in the shortest supply," as described by the prompt. As with (F) and (H), this choice could attract an untrained test-taker who misread Student 4's statement and thought it mentioned "all the Fe," or who incorrectly thought the symbol for the "iron" referred to in the prompt was CO_2, rather than Fe.

What we had to understand to answer the question: We needed to note that the "iron" referred to in the prompt had a chemical symbol of Fe, which is spelled out in the first sentence of Passage V. We needed to realize that the substance that was completely used up in the reaction must have been "in the shortest supply." We also needed to find the specific phrases in each student's statement that indicated which element was "in the shortest supply," as required by the prompt. Beyond that, we didn't need to read or understand any part of Passage V.

Finding the answer requires information from a figure. Read carefully, and be very particular about matching up exact values in the figure and the answer choices, unless the question calls for estimation. See p. 339.

Notes on answer choices: The choices are different combinations of plus signs, minus signs, and the fractions $\frac{1}{2}$ and $\frac{3}{2}$.

A   **Direct Contradiction:** This choice is the opposite of the right answer, so it might attract an untrained test-taker who didn't notice the negative signs at the beginning of each fraction, or who got confused by the prompt and through spin-up was associated with a negative spin, and spin-down was associated with a positive spin.

B   **Confused Relationships:** This choice might attract an untrained test-taker who accidentally thought the value in the first column should be negative, and who didn't notice the difference between the two Greek letters in the answer choices, and thought both columns should have the same value.

C ✓   **Correct:** The prompt refers us to Table 2, and we see that Table 2 includes terms like "baryon" and "spins" that are directly reflected in the prompt, so we know that Table 2 is relevant to this question. The right-hand column of Table 2 shows us that the quark spins for Λ^0 are up, down, and up. The prompt tells us that spin-up quarks have $\frac{1}{2}\hbar$ spin, and spin-down quarks have $-\frac{1}{2}\hbar$ spin, and that the spin of the baryon is equal to the sum of its quark spins. With that in mind, the spin of Λ^0 must be equal to $\frac{1}{2}\hbar - \frac{1}{2}\hbar + \frac{1}{2}\hbar$, which adds up to $\frac{1}{2}\hbar$. By similar logic, we see that Table 2 tells us that the quark spin for Δ^0 is up, up, and up, so the spin for that baryon must be equal to $\frac{1}{2}\hbar + \frac{1}{2}\hbar + \frac{1}{2}\hbar$, or $\frac{3}{2}\hbar$. So (C) is right.

D   **Confused Relationships:** (D) might attract an untrained test-taker who correctly figured out the spin for Δ^0, but then misread the table and thought the same spin applied to Λ^0. It could also attract an untrained test-taker who didn't notice a difference between the symbols for Λ^0 and Δ^0, and thought both columns in the right answer should have the same value.

> **What we had to understand to answer the question:** We needed to know how to use Table 2 to find the spins for the two particles with the symbols used in the prompt. We needed to be able to add and subtract $\frac{1}{2}$. We never needed to know where the term baryon comes from, or what the word "spin" actually means, or why Greek letters are used as symbols for baryons, or why the quarks have the names they have, or how anybody figured out that quarks exist, or why any scientist cares about them. We only needed to match the symbols from the prompt to a row of information in Table 2, and then add together $+\frac{1}{2}$ for every up arrow in that row, and $-\frac{1}{2}$ for every down arrow in that row, because the prompt told us to do that.

Finding the answer requires information from a figure. Read carefully, and be very particular about matching up exact values in the figure and the answer choices, unless the question calls for estimation. See p. 339.

Notes on answer choices: Each choice is a diagram with lower-case italicized letters like the ones in Table 1 and Table 2, and arrows like the ones in Table 2.

F   **Off by One or Two Words:** This choice does satisfy the prompt's requirement of having "only 2 quark spins oriented in the same direction." But, according to Table 1, all 3 quarks in the diagram—"up," "charm," and "top"—have charges of $+\frac{2}{3}$, which add up to a charge of $+2$. The prompt says the right answer must be "electrically neutral," and a charge of $+2$ isn't electrically neutral, so this choice is wrong.

G ✓   **Correct:** Choice (G) shows 2 "spin-down" quarks and 1 "spin-up" quark, which satisfies the requirement from the prompt of "having only 2 quark spins oriented in the same direction." The prompt also mentions the idea of being "electrically neutral." We may not know what that phrase means at first, but we can tell that the only mention of anything having to do with electricity appears in Table 1, which mentions the "electric charge" of each quark. Table 1 tells us that the electric charges of u, d, and s are $\frac{2}{3}$, $-\frac{1}{3}$, and $-\frac{1}{3}$, respectively. These charges add up to a total electric charge of 0, which means that the baryon in (G) is electrically neutral. Since (G) has all the attributes required in the prompt, we know (G) is correct.

H   **Barely Relevant:** We know this choice must be wrong because all 3 quark spins are down, and the prompt says the right answer must have "only 2 quark spins oriented in the same direction." This choice must also be wrong because it has 3 "top" quarks, and Table 1 tells us that each "top" quark has an electric charge of $+\frac{2}{3}$. That means the charge of this baryon must be $3 \times \frac{2}{3}$, or $+2$, which isn't "electrically neutral," as the prompt requires. Either issue is enough by itself to make (H) wrong.

J   **Confused Relationships:** This choice does satisfy the prompt's requirement that the baryon be "electrically neutral," because Table 1 tells us that the quarks "strange," "charm," and "down" have electric charges of $-\frac{1}{3}$, $\frac{2}{3}$, and $-\frac{1}{3}$, respectively, and those charges add up to 0. But we know this choice is still wrong because all 3 quark spins are up, and the prompt says the right answer must have "only 2 quark spins oriented in the same direction."

What we had to understand to answer the question: We needed to be able to refer to Table 1 to find the electrical charges that corresponded to the lower-case letters in the answer choices, and we needed to be able to add those charges together to see which diagram had a net charge of zero. We also needed to read the last sentence of the first paragraph so we could tell that the arrows in the answer choices indicated the spin of the quarks, allowing us to eliminate any choices with three arrows pointing in the same direction. We didn't need to read or understand anything in Table 2, or in any part of Passage VI outside of Table 1.

Test 2, Question 37 (Test 3 in the 2020-2021 Red Book—see page 23 for more)   **TYPE: OUTSIDE INFO**

Answering requires some information that can't be found in the passage. Any required outside knowledge must be relatively basic. *Don't try to use outside knowledge on a question unless you're sure you can't answer based on the passage. See p. 339.*

Notes on answer choices: The choices are identical except for two differences. (A) and (B) begin with the word "no," while (C) and (D) begin with the word "yes." (A) and (C) end with 0, while (B) and (D) end with +1.

A   **Direct Contradiction:** This choice is the total opposite of the right answer, in the sense that it uses the "no" and "0" options instead of the "yes" and "+1" options. It would attract an untrained test-taker who remembered that a proton has a positive charge, but who misread the tables and ended up thinking that they showed a net charge of 0 for a proton.

B   **Off by One or Two Words:** This choice might have attracted untrained test-takers who confused protons with neutrons, and thought that a proton should have neutral charge. It could also attract an untrained test-taker who misread or overlooked the first word in (B), because (B) would be correct if that word were "yes."

C   **Off by One or Two Words:** This choice combines the mistake of thinking that a proton has a neutral charge and the mistake of misreading the tables so that they seem to say a proton has a neutral charge.

D ✓ **Correct:** From our basic outside scientific knowledge, we should know that the "known electric charge for the proton" is +1. Table 1 lists the charges of different quarks, but it doesn't tell us which quarks make up a proton. So we need to look at Table 2 to find the makeup of a proton. We see from the first row of data that a proton is made up of two u-quarks and a d-quark. When we go back to Table 1 and find the charges for u-quarks and d-quarks, we see that those electric charges are $+\frac{2}{3}$ and $-\frac{1}{3}$, respectively. So the combined charges of a u-quark, another u-quark, and a d-quark would add up to $+\frac{2}{3} + \frac{2}{3} - \frac{1}{3}$, or +1. This reflects the idea of a proton having a positive charge. So the first word in the right answer should be "yes," and the last number in the right answer should be +1, which means (D) is right.

What we had to understand to answer the question: We needed to know that a proton has a charge of +1. We also needed to find the word "proton" in Table 2 and read that its makeup was uud; then, we needed to find the charges for u-quarks and d-quarks in Table 1, and add them up to see if they added up to 0 or 1. Finally, we needed to notice the differences among the answer choices and make sure we picked the one that accurately reflected our findings.

Note   Some untrained test-takers might have answered this question correctly just by knowing that a proton has a positive charge, and assuming that the data in Passage VI would correctly reflect that information, which would allow someone to pick (D) without bothering to consult the data provided in the passage. But, as we discussed in the training, we strongly advise you not to make assumptions about what the data on the ACT Science section will say—instead, you should always verify your answers with the provided data when the provided data make that possible. Test-takers often misremember details from their science classes, and passages on the ACT may cover material that differs from what your teachers have told you in school. In any case, the ACT will only give credit for the answer that directly reflects the data provided in the passage, so there's no reason not to refer to the provided data when you answer a question.

Test 2, Question 38 (Test 3 in the 2020-2021 Red Book—see page 23 for more)   **TYPE: DATA PLUS DATA**

Finding the right answer requires information from more than one figure. Read carefully, and be very particular about matching up exact values in the figure and the answer choices, unless estimation is called for. See page 339.

Notes on answer choices: The choices combine three lower-case letters each. (G) and (H) differ only in their last letter, while (G) and (J) differ only in the first letter. Every choice has at least one s.

F ✓ **Correct:** The prompt refers to an "electric charge," which is the name of the third column in Table 1. So Table 1 provides the charges of the quarks associated with the lower-case letters in the answer choices, but Table 1 doesn't say anything about Greek letters like the one in the prompt. But we can see that the second column of Table 2 contains the specific symbol referred to in the prompt, and tells us that the baryon associated with the symbol is made up of 3 s-quarks. Since "electric charge" only appears in Table 1, we'll have to consult Table 1 to find the total charge the Ω^- baryon has. Table 1 tells us that each s-quark has a charge of $-\frac{1}{3}$, so the Ω^- baryon must have a charge of -1, because $-\frac{1}{3} - \frac{1}{3} - \frac{1}{3} = -1$. Table 1 also tells us that d, s, and b each have a charge of $-\frac{1}{3}$, which means the total charge of the quarks in (F) is also -1. So (F) is correct.

G   **Confused Relationships:** As we saw in our discussion of (F), the Ω^- baryon must have a charge of -1. Table 1 tells us that s and c

have charges of $-\frac{1}{3}$ and $\frac{2}{3}$, so 2 s-quarks and a c-quark would add up to 0, because $-\frac{1}{3} - \frac{1}{3} + \frac{2}{3} = 0$. So (G) is wrong. This choice might attract an untrained test-taker whose eye skipped up a line when trying to read the charge for a c-quark, since the charge of the s-quark is listed directly above the charge of a c-quark in Table 1.

H   **Confused Relationships:** As we saw in our discussion of (F), the Ω^- baryon must have a charge of -1. Table 1 tells us that s and t have charges of $-\frac{1}{3}$ and $\frac{2}{3}$, so 2 s-quarks and a t-quark would add up to 0, since $-\frac{1}{3} - \frac{1}{3} + \frac{2}{3} = 0$, which makes (H) wrong. As we saw with (G), this choice could attract an untrained test-taker whose eye skipped up a line while reading the charge for a t-quark.

J   **Direct Contradiction:** As we saw in our discussion of (F), the Ω^- baryon must have a charge of -1. Table 1 tells us that u, s, and c have charges of $\frac{2}{3}$, $-\frac{1}{3}$, and $\frac{2}{3}$, respectively, which would add up to 1, so (J) is wrong. This choice may attract untrained test-takers who made a careless error when adding up the charge for Ω^- baryon, causing them to believe the charge for the Ω^- baryon was 1, instead of -1.

> **What we had to understand to answer the question:** As we discussed for (F) above, we needed to be able to use Table 2 and Table 1 to determine the overall charge on the Ω^- baryon, and then we needed to use Table 1 to find the charges on the sets of 3 quarks in the answer choices. We also needed to be able to add combinations of $\frac{1}{3}$, $-\frac{1}{3}$, $\frac{2}{3}$, and $-\frac{2}{3}$ correctly. We didn't need to understand anything about what a quark or a baryon actually does or why any scientist would care about that—we only needed to be able to read the charges for the relevant lower-case letters off of Table 1, and to find the quarks in the Ω^- baryon on Table 2.

Test 2, Question 39 (Test 3 in the 2020-2021 Red Book—see page 23 for more)   **TYPE: OUTSIDE INFO**

Answering requires some information that can't be found in the passage. Any required outside knowledge must be relatively basic. Don't try to use outside knowledge on a question unless you're sure you can't answer based on the passage. See p. 339.

Notes on answer choices: The choices offer different combinations of the letters u, d, and s.

A ✓   **Correct:** As part of our basic scientific knowledge that the ACT Science section can choose to test, we need to know that an atomic nucleus is made up of protons and neutrons, which means that the only baryons in Table 2 that can be part of a nucleus are protons and neutrons. In all of Passage VI, the words "proton" and "neutron" only appear in Table 2, which means we'll need to consult Table 2 to answer this question. When we do that, we see that protons and neutrons are only made up of u-quarks and d-quarks, so (A) is right.

B   **Barely Relevant:** According to Table 2, the only baryons made up of just d-quarks and s-quarks are delta-minuses and omega-minuses. We should know that an atomic nucleus is made up of protons and neutrons, not delta-minuses and omega-minuses (in fact, most test-takers will never have heard of the phrase "delta-minus" or "omega-minus" at all), so (B) can't be right.

C   **Barely Relevant:** According to Table 2, only the omega-minus is made from just s-quarks, and none of the baryons is made from only u-quarks, or only from u-quarks and s-quarks. So this choice basically combines the issue from (B) with the mistake of mentioning u-quarks for no apparent reason, which means it must be wrong.

D   **Confused Relationships:** As we saw in the explanation for (A), atomic nuclei do contain u-quarks and d-quarks, but they don't contain any s-quarks, so (D) can't be right. But (D) will trap untrained test-takers whose eyes skip down one line while trying to use Table 2 to read the makeup of protons and neutrons, because those people might accidentally read the makeup of neutrons and lambda-zeros instead.

> **What we had to understand to answer the question:** We needed to know that "proton" and "neutron" were the only terms in Table 2 that were related to the "atomic nuclei" mentioned in the prompt, and we needed to be able to read the "quark content" values for protons and neutrons. We didn't need to read or understand any other part of Passage VI.

Test 2, Question 40 (Test 3 in the 2020-2021 Red Book—see page 23 for more)   **TYPE: PURE DATA**

Finding the answer requires information from a figure. Read carefully, and be very particular about matching up exact values in the figure and the answer choices, unless the question calls for estimation. See p. 339.

Notes on answer choices: The choices offer us the option of choosing any generation by itself, or none of the generations.

F ✓   **Correct:** The prompt mentions "charged quarks" being "more massive." The only part of Passage VI that mentions quarks having charge and mass is Table 1, so we'll need to look at Table 1 to answer this question. When we look at Table 1, we can see that the d-quark from Generation 1 has a charge of $-\frac{1}{3}$, while the u-quark has a charge of $+\frac{2}{3}$. We also see that the d-quark has a mass of 5 MeV, while the u-quark has a mass of 3 MeV. So, for Generation 1, the statement in the prompt is NOT true, just as the prompt requires, and (F) must be right. (Of course, we'll check the other answer choices to make sure we understand why the statement IS true for those choices, so we can verify our work and make sure we haven't misread or misunderstood something.)

G   **Off by One or Two Words:** According to the table in the prompt, the Generation 2 quarks are the s-quark and the c-quark. Table

1 shows us that the *s*-quark is negatively charged and has a mass of 104 MeV, while the *c*-quark is positively charged and has a mass of 1,270 MeV, which is larger than the mass of the negatively charged *s*-quark. So the statement in the prompt IS true for this generation, which means (G) is wrong. This choice could attract an untrained test-taker who correctly understood that the statement in the prompt is accurate with respect to this generation, but who overlooked or forgot about the word "NOT" in the prompt.

H   **Off by One or Two Words:** According to the table in the prompt, the Generation 3 quarks are *b*-quarks and *t*-quarks. Table 1 shows us that *b*-quarks are negatively charged and have a mass of 4,200 MeV, while *t*-quarks are positively charged and have a mass of 171,200 MeV, which is larger than the mass of the negatively charged *b*-quark. So, as with (G), the statement in the prompt IS true for this generation, which means (H) is wrong. And like we also saw in (G), some untrained test-takers will pick this choice because they understand everything going on in the prompt and in Table 1 but accidentally overlook or forget the word "NOT" in the prompt.

J   **Confused Relationships:** As we saw in the explanation for (F), the statement from the prompt isn't true for Generation 1. This choice could attract someone who misread the data for *d*-quarks and *u*-quarks in Table 1 while evaluating (F).

> **What we had to understand to answer the question:** We needed to use Table 1 to identify the masses and the charges of the quarks in the prompt, and we needed to compare the masses of the negatively charged quarks to the masses of the positively charged quarks within each generation. We didn't need to understand the meaning of the MeV unit, nor why some of the quarks are so much larger than the others. We didn't need to read or understand the paragraph at the beginning of Passage VI, or any part of Table 2.

TEST 3 (FORM 16MC3—SEE PAGE 23)

Test 3, Question 1 (Form 16MC3 if you have the 2020-2021 Red Book—see page 23 for more)   **TYPE: PURE DATA**

Finding the answer requires information from a figure. Read carefully, and be very particular about matching up exact values in the figure and the answer choices, unless the question calls for estimation. See p. 339.

Notes on answer choices: The choices are identical except for two differences. (A) and (C) refer to Day 1, while (B) and (D) refer to Day 30. (A) and (B) refer to Site 1, while (C) and (D) refer to Site 2.

A   **Barely Relevant:** The choices refer to days and sites, which indicates we'll need to consider the data either from Figure 1 or from Figure 2, since those figures mention specific days and sites. The prompt refers to the number of "colonies formed per 100 mL of water," which is reflected in the vertical axis of Figure 1. So we know that Figure 1 is where we need to look when we answer this question. When we look at that figure, we can see that there were 101 colonies per 100 mL of water on Day 1 at Site 1. That's less than the 400 colonies mentioned in the prompt, so (A) is wrong. This choice might attract an untrained test-taker who misread the word "unsafe" in the prompt as "safe," and who forgot to check the other choices, which would have shown him that more than one choice would be a safe day to swim according to the prompt.

B ✓ **Correct:** As discussed for (A), we can see that Figure 1 contains the data relevant to this question. The only value in Figure 1 that's over 400 colonies per 100 mL of water, as required by the prompt, was recorded at Site 1 on Day 30, so (B) is right.

C   **Direct Contradiction:** This choice might attract an untrained test-taker who thought the prompt was asking for the day from the answer choices with the lowest number of recorded colonies, possibly as a result of misreading the word "unsafe" in the prompt as "safe."

D   **Barely Relevant:** This choice has basically the same problem we saw in (A) and (C): it's lower than the 400 colonies mentioned in the prompt.

> **What we had to understand to answer the question:** As noted above for (A) and (B), we needed to realize that Figure 1 had the data that was relevant to the prompt, and then we needed to read that figure (including the key) and the answer choices carefully. Otherwise, we never needed to read or understand any part of Passage I. We never needed to know why *E. Coli* is harmful above a certain concentration.

Test 3, Question 2 (Form 16MC3 if you have the 2020-2021 Red Book—see page 23 for more)   **TYPE: DATA PLUS DATA**

Finding the right answer requires information from more than one figure. Read carefully, and be very particular about matching up exact values in the figure and the answer choices, unless estimation is called for. See page 339.

Notes on answer choices: The choices offer every possible combination of Site 1 and Site 2.

F ✓ **Correct:** The prompt tells us to answer "based on Figures 1 and 2," so we'll start by looking at those figures. Since the prompt asks which sites had the higher averages—and since this is the ACT Science section, which never requires us to do much math—we know that we can probably figure out which values have the highest averages by glancing at the data. Sure enough, both graphs show significantly more black than grey. Since black is associated with Site 1, we know that Site 1 has the higher average values in both figures, so (F) is right.

G   **Off by One or Two Words:** This choice is probably here to fill out the ACT's pattern of providing every possible combination of Site 1 and Site 2 as an answer choice.

H   **Off by One or Two Words:** This choice has basically the same issue as (G).

J   **Direct Contradiction:** This choice might attract an untrained test-taker who thought the Site 1 data was represented by the grey bars and the Site 2 data was represented by the black bars, or who misread the words "higher" in the prompt as "lower."

> **What we had to understand to answer the question:** As noted in our discussion of (F) above, we needed to realize that the prompt was directing us to look at the values in Figure 1 and Figure 2. We never needed to read or understand any other part of Passage I. We never needed to understand whether a connection exists between the number of colonies and the water flow, either.

Test 3, Question 3 (Form 16MC3 if you have the 2020-2021 Red Book—see page 23 for more)   **TYPE: DATA PLUS PARAGRAPH**

Finding the answer requires information from the text as well as information from a figure. Read carefully, and be very particular about matching up exact values in the figure and the answer choices, unless the prompt calls for estimation. See p. 339.

Notes on answer choices: Choices are identical except for two differences. (A) and (B) include the word "improves," while (C) and (D) include the word "degrades." (A) and (C) include the word "increases," while (B) and (D) include "remains the same."

A ✓   **Correct:** The prompt refers to Table 1, and uses the phrases "water quality" and "biotic index." When we look at Table 1, we can see that it includes column headings called "BI" and "Water quality rating." The phrase "Water quality rating" clearly restates the idea of "water quality" from the prompt, and the abbreviation "BI" definitely looks like it could refer to the "biotic index" in the prompt. Sure enough, when we skim the rest of Passage I for "BI," we see that the first sentence of Passage I tells us BI is an abbreviation for "biotic index." So we know that Table 1 contains the relevant data for this question. When we look at that table, we can see that a higher biotic index is associated with a better water quality rating: the highest BI in the table, greater than or equal to 3.6, corresponds to an "excellent" water quality rating, and the next highest BI in the table, 2.6 to 3.5, corresponds to a "good" water quality rating, and so on. So (A) is right.

B   **Barely Relevant:** (B) might attract an untrained test-taker who fundamentally misunderstands Table 1, because there are multiple values for BI in Table 1; there's no way to say that the BI in Table 1 "stays the same," as (B) would require.

C   **Direct Contradiction:** This choice expresses the reverse of the relationship we saw in the correct answer. This choice might attract someone who misread the word "increases" as "decreases."

D   **Barely Relevant:** This choice has basically the same problem as (B), and is wrong for the same reasons.

> **What we had to understand to answer the question:** We needed to realize that the prompt was telling us to look at Table 1, and we needed to verify that "BI" in Table 1 was referring to the "biotic index" mentioned in the prompt, as we described for (A) above. Then we needed to see what happened to water quality in relation to BI, according to Table 1. Apart from that, we didn't need to read or understand any other part of Passage I, including the reason for the correlation between higher BI and higher water quality.

Test 3, Question 4 (Form 16MC3 if you have the 2020-2021 Red Book—see page 23 for more)   **TYPE: DATA PLUS DATA**

Finding the right answer requires information from more than one figure. Read carefully, and be very particular about matching up exact values in the figure and the answer choices, unless estimation is called for. See page 339.

Notes on answer choices: The choices are identical except for two differences. (F) and (G) begin with "yes," while (H) and (J) begin with "no." The ratings for Site 1 are "good," "excellent," "poor," and "fair" in (F), (G), (H), and (J) respectively, while the ratings for Site 2 are "poor," "fair," "good," and "excellent" in those choices.

F   **Off by One or Two Words:** As we can see in the explanation for (G), the part of this choice that says "yes" is correct. But the statement afterward isn't true. As we can also see in the explanation for (G), Site 1 had a water quality rating of "excellent"—not "good," as (F) would require—and Site 2 had a water quality rating of "fair"—not "poor," as (F) would require. This choice might have attracted an untrained test-taker who misread Table 1 in a way that caused her to be off by one line in each rating, so that the "excellent" rating for Site 1 seemed to be a "good" rating, and the "fair" rating for Site 2 seemed to be a "poor" rating.

G ✓   **Correct:** The prompt tells us that "as water quality improves, the number of stone fly larvae…increases." So when the prompt asks whether Table 2 supports the idea that there are more stone fly larvae at Site 1 than at Site 2, it's really asking whether Table 2 supports the idea that the water quality is better at Site 1 than at Site 2, because the prompt says that an increased number of larvae is an indicator of increased water quality. When we look at Table 2, we can see that Site 1 has an "Average BI" of 6.3, and Site 2 has an "Average BI" of 2.5. But the answer choices don't specifically refer to any numbers as part of the water quality description, so we'll need to figure out the meanings of the numbers in Table 2. As trained test-takers, we know that the ACT Science section must provide us with all the information we need to answer ACT Science questions—outside of some occasional basic scientific knowledge—so there must be something in the passage to tell us how "Average BI" relates to water quality. When we look elsewhere for information about BI, we see that Table 1 equates BI-values with water quality ratings like the ones in the answer choices. Table

1 says a BI of 6.3 corresponds to a water quality rating of "excellent," and a BI of 2.5 corresponds to a water quality rating of "fair." So the water quality at Site 1 *is* "excellent," as (G) requires, and the water quality at Site 2 *is* "fair," as (G) also requires. And, since the water quality at Site 1 is better than the quality at Site 2, we know there should be more larvae present at Site 1, which means the student's hypothesis is consistent with Table 2, so the first word in the right answer should be "yes." This means (G) is right.

H **Barely Relevant:** Every part of this choice is wrong; see the explanation for (G) for more information. This choice might attract an untrained test-taker who fundamentally misread and misunderstood the prompt and the data in Table 2.

J **Direct Contradiction:** This choice gets the water quality ratings of the two sites reversed. It might trap someone who confused the values in Table 2 for Site 1 and Site 2.

What we had to understand to answer the question: We needed to realize that the prompt was asking us whether Site 1 or Site 2 had a higher quality rating, and we needed to realize that Table 1 and Table 2 were both critical in the process of answering the question, as we discussed for (G). Apart from those two tables, we didn't need to read or understand any part of Passage I.

Note The ACT only mentions the stone fly larvae and the phrase "aquatic invertebrate" to make the prompt sound more scientific to an untrained test-taker; as we saw in our discussion of (G), the key issue is just whether the water quality is better at Site 1 or at Site 2, and what the specific quality ratings are at those two sites. Keep this kind of thing in mind on test day, and don't get intimidated just because the ACT occasionally throws in terms like "aquatic invertebrate!"

Test 3, Question 5 (Form 16MC3 if you have the 2020-2021 Red Book—see page 23 for more)   TYPE: DATA PLUS PARAGRAPH

Finding the answer requires information from the text as well as information from a figure. Read carefully, and be very particular about matching up exact values in the figure and the answer choices, unless the prompt calls for estimation. See p. 339.

Notes on answer choices: The choices include every figure and table in Passage I.

A ✓ **Correct:** Figure 1 compares the amount of *E. coli* at each site, and it clearly shows that Site 1 has more E. coli than Site 2. But Figure 1, itself, doesn't include the phrase "water quality" anywhere. When we skim the text for information related to *E. coli*, we see that the first paragraph tells us that one measure of water quality is "the number of *Escherichia coli* bacteria present," and the second paragraph says that "*E. coli* levels that are above 100 colonies formed per 100 mL of water indicate reduced water quality." So having more *E. coli* indicates lower water quality, which means that Site 1 has lower water quality than Site 2, according to Figure 1. That means (A) is correct.

B **Barely Relevant:** The description above Figure 2 tells us that this figure "shows the water flow at each site on the 5 collection days." But when we skim the rest of Passage I to find more information about "water flow," we see that nothing in the passage specifically connects water flow to water quality. So Figure 2 doesn't tell us anything about water quality, which means it can't tell us that "Site 1 has lower water quality than Site 2," as the prompt requires.

C **Barely Relevant:** Table 1 just tells us how different BI numbers correspond to different water quality ratings. This table provides no information whatsoever about Site 1 or Site 2 specifically, which means it can't possibly indicate that "Site 1 has lower water quality than Site 2," as the prompt requires.

D **Direct Contradiction:** Table 2 tells us that Site 1 has a higher average BI than Site 2, but it doesn't specifically mention the words "water quality." When we skim the rest of Passage I to find some indication of what "BI" refers to, we see that Table 1 tells us that a higher BI corresponds to higher water quality, so Table 2 indicates that Site 1 has higher water quality than Site 2. But the prompt asked us for data to support the claim that "Site 1 has *lower* water quality than Site 2." So the data in Figure 2 does the opposite of what the prompt requires, which means (D) is wrong.

What we had to understand to answer the question: We needed to consider each of the figures and tables in the answer choices, and we needed to skim various parts of Passage I to figure out how *E. coli*, water flow, and BI were correlated to water quality.

Test 3, Question 6 (Form 16MC3 if you have the 2020-2021 Red Book—see page 23 for more)   TYPE: OUTSIDE INFO

Answering requires some information that can't be found in the passage. Any required outside knowledge must be relatively basic. Don't try to use outside knowledge on a question unless you're sure you can't answer based on the passage. See p. 339.

Notes on answer choices: Choices are identical except for two differences. (F) and (G) begin with the word "increase," while (H) and (J) begin with "decrease." (F) and (H) end with the word "increase," while (G) and (J) end with "decrease."

F **Direct Contradiction:** (F) would attract someone who thought adding fertilizer to a water supply would increase the water quality. See our discussion of (J) for a couple of ways we might have known that adding fertilizer would lower water quality.

G **Off by One or Two Words:** This choice might attract an untrained test-taker who understands that adding fertilizer to a water supply decreases the quality of that water supply, but who then accidentally thinks that decreased water quality results in a higher BI, rather than a lower BI, which would contradict Table 1. It could also attract someone who misread the first word in the choice as "decrease" instead of "increase."

H **Off by One or Two Words:** This choice combines the errors from (F) and (G). It could also attract someone who misread the last word in the choice as "decrease" instead of "increase."

J ✓ **Correct:** This is another example of the kind of fundamental scientific knowledge that's occasionally required on the ACT Science section; in this case, we're expected to know that adding large amounts of fertilizer to a water supply will reduce the quality of that water. (Think of it this way: would you rather drink water that contains fertilizer, or water that doesn't contain fertilizer? Do bottled water brands advertise their purity, or do they advertise that they contain a lot of fertilizer?) The prompt refers to BI, which is mentioned in Table 1 and Table 2. Table 1 shows us that lower BI ratings indicate lower water quality. So if fertilizer were added to the water supply, then the water quality would decrease, and the BI of the water would also go down. This is what (J) says, so (J) is right.

> **What we had to understand to answer the question:** As we discussed for (J), we needed to know that BI decreases as water quality decreases (which is reflected in Table 1). We also needed to know that adding fertilizer would decrease water quality. Otherwise, we didn't need to read or understand any part of Passage I. We also didn't need to understand exactly how fertilizer in a water supply would be expected to influence the biotic index—we just needed to know that Table 1 from the passage says lower BI means lower water quality.

Test 3, Question 7 (Form 16MC3 if you have the 2020-2021 Red Book—see page 23 for more) **TYPE: PURE DATA**

Finding the answer requires information from a figure. Read carefully, and be very particular about matching up exact values in the figure and the answer choices, unless the question calls for estimation. See p. 339.

Notes on answer choices: The choices present every combination of the ideas of the volume of H_2 increasing and decreasing and the idea of the graph inflecting up or inflecting down.

A **Confused Relationships:** See the discussion of (B) for an explanation of why this is wrong. This choice would appeal to untrained test-takers who accidentally refer to the solid line in the graph in Figure 1, and then try to pick an answer choice that reflects the shape of that curve.

B ✓ **Correct:** The prompt tells us to answer "based on Table 1," so we should start by looking at that table. The prompt also mentions "volume of H_2," which is a label on Table 1 for the values under Days 2, 4, 6, and 8 in Table 1. Finally, the prompt mentions AWP 2, which corresponds to the second row of data in Table 1, because the left-most column in Table 1 is called "AWP," and the second number under AWP is 2. So we can see that we need to find the graph that reflects the numbers from that second row of data in Table 1. According to that data, on Day 2, the AWP 2 number is 21 mL of H_2. So we can tell that (C) and (D) are wrong, because they both show a value close to 800 on Day 2. On Day 4, Table 1 says the value for AWP 2 is 187, so we can tell (A) is wrong, because the value on Day 4 in (A) is about 400. Only (B) is consistent with the data for every day in the row of data for AWP 2 in Table 1, so (B) is right.

C **Confused Relationships:** See the discussion of (B) for an explanation of why (C) is wrong. (C) joins the issues from (A) and (D): it uses the same general shape from (A) and Figure 1, and then reverses the trend from increasing to decreasing.

D **Direct Contradiction:** See the discussion of (B) for an explanation of why this is wrong. (D) might attract a test-taker who accidentally read the numbers on the x-axis backwards, or read the data for Days 2, 4, and 8 backwards in Table 1.

> **What we had to understand to answer the question:** We needed to realize that the prompt was telling us to consider the second row of data in Table 1, as we discussed for (B) above. Apart from that, we never needed to read or understand anything in Passage II, including what AWP stands for or why the volume of H_2 is relevant to anything.

Test 3, Question 8 (Form 16MC3 if you have the 2020-2021 Red Book—see page 23 for more) **TYPE: PURE DATA**

Finding the answer requires information from a figure. Read carefully, and be very particular about matching up exact values in the figure and the answer choices, unless the question calls for estimation. See p. 339.

Notes on answer choices: The choices present ranges of numbers whose boundaries are all numbers from Table 1.

F **Off by One or Two Words:** (F) might attract a test-taker in a hurry who knew the answer should involve a number greater than the value for AWP 1 on Day 8, saw the number 133 in (F), and then overlooked or misread the phrase "less than."

G ✓ **Correct:** The prompt tells us to answer "based on Table 1," and it uses the words "if the volume...had been measured" and "would most likely have been," which tell us that the right answer isn't specifically included in Table 1, but it must follow a clear trend in Table 1. So we'll need to find the trend in the volume of H_2 produced by AWP 1. On Day 2, the number for AWP 1 is 4 mL. On Day 4, the number for AWP 1 is 33 mL—that's roughly 8 times the amount of H_2 produced on Day 2. On Day 6, the number for AWP 1 is 81 mL, which is between 2 times and 3 times as much as the 33 mL for Day 4. On Day 8, the AWP 1 number is 133 mL, which is less than twice the amount on Day 6—in fact, it's about 50% more than the number from Day 6. So we can see that the AWP number is always increasing as the number of days increases, but the rate of its increase is slowing down: first it went up by around 8 times, then it roughly doubled or tripled, then it increased by about 50%. So this trend indicates that the value will increase from Day 8 to Day 10, but not double in that time. That means the number on Day 10 should be between 133 mL and 266 mL, which falls into the range in (G). So (G) is right. (See "Using Simple Trends in Data" on page 333 of this Black Book for more on this thought process.)

H   **Wrong Part of the Passage:** This choice mentions the values for H_2 produced from the AWP 2 sample on days 6 and 8, but there's no reason to think that the volume produced from AWP 1 on Day 10 would depend on that data from AWP 2. This choice might attract an untrained test-taker who somehow got confused and tried to find the volume of AWP 2 on Day 7, which isn't what the prompt asks for.

J   **Wrong Part of the Passage:** This choice might attract untrained test-takers who accidentally considered the data from AWP 2 instead of AWP 1, or who misread AWP 1 in the prompt as AWP 2, because it's true that the Day 10 number for AWP 2 would be greater than 760.

> **What we had to understand to answer the question:** We needed to look at the row of data for AWP 1 in Table 1, as described for (G) above. Otherwise, we didn't need to look at any other part of Passage II. We also didn't need to understand why H_2 is produced, why the rate of increase in its production slows down, or what AWP 1 means.

■ **Test 3, Question 9 (Form 16MC3 if you have the 2020-2021 Red Book—see page 23 for more)**   **TYPE: PURE DATA**

Finding the answer requires information from a figure. Read carefully, and be very particular about matching up exact values in the figure and the answer choices, unless the question calls for estimation. See p. 339.

Notes on answer choices: (B) and (C) are numbers from Table 1. (A) is the difference between those numbers, and (D) is the sum of those two numbers.

A ✓   **Correct:** The prompt tells us to answer "according to Table 1," and that table shows that AWP 1 had produced 81 mL of H_2 by Day 6. By Day 8, that amount had increased to 133 mL of H_2. So AWP 1 must have produced 52 mL of H_2 between Day 6 and Day 8, because 133 mL − 81 mL = 52 mL. So (A) is right.

B   **Confused Relationships:** This is the amount of H_2 produced by AWP 1 by Day 6 according to Table 1. But the prompt asked for the amount of H_2 produced by AWP 1 *from* Day 6 *to* Day 8, so (B) is wrong. (B) would appeal to untrained test-takers who got distracted in the middle of answering the question and thought that the value for Day 6 was the right answer, instead of being a piece of information that we needed to find on the way to the right answer, as we saw for (A).

C   **Confused Relationships:** This choice reflects a mistake similar to the one for (B): it's the amount of H_2 produced by AWP 1 by Day 8, but the prompt asked for the amount of H_2 produced by AWP 1 *from Day 6 to Day 8*, so this choice is wrong.

D   **Direct Contradiction:** This would be the result of *adding* the AWP 1 value for Day 6 to the AWP 1 value for Day 8, instead of subtracting the Day 6 value from the Day 8 value, as we discussed for (A) above.

> **What we had to understand to answer the question:** We needed to use Table 1 to identify the two values for AWP 1 that are mentioned in the prompt, and then subtract the smaller value from the larger value, as we discussed above for (A). Otherwise, we didn't need to read or understand any part of Passage II, including the chemical reaction or Figure 1, or even what "AWP" means or what H_2 is.

■ **Test 3, Question 10 (Form 16MC3 if you have the 2020-2021 Red Book—see page 23 for more)**   **TYPE: PURE PARAGRAPH**

Answering requires information from the text. Choices often primarily involve phrases rather than numbers. Consider every relevant word. Be sure your answer is literally demonstrated or restated on the page, with no interpretation necessary. See p. 339.

Notes on answer choices: (F) and (G) are the reverse of each other, and (H) and (J) are the reverse of each other. (F) and (G) mention H_2O, while (H) and (J) mention $AL(OH)_3$.

F   **Confused Relationships:** The prompt mentions Table 1 and Figure 1, but the data from Table 1 and Figure 1 don't specifically mention any of the chemicals in the answer choices, so we know we'll need to look elsewhere in order to answer this question. As it turns out, the chemical reaction at the beginning of Passage II includes all of the chemicals in the answer choices, so we'll start by considering that reaction. (F) mentions H_2O turning into Al, but the reaction shows Al and H_2O both on the left side of the arrow, which means they're being converted into other things, not being converted into each other. So this choice can't be right.

G   **Confused Relationships:** This choice has the same basic problem as (F): the reaction from the passage shows Al and H_2O on the same side of the reaction, both being converted into other things. So this choice is also wrong.

H ✓   **Correct:** This question sounds like it requires some outside scientific knowledge. But as trained test-takers we know that we should always try to answer a question based on information in the passage before we fall back on any outside knowledge. If we look in the passage, we can see that the chemical reaction that appears after the first paragraph of Passage II includes all of the chemicals in the answer choices. We know that the arrow in the middle of that reaction indicates the process of reaction, which means that this reaction produces $AL(OH)_3$ and H_2. (H) is the only choice that talks about something from the left side of the reaction being converted into something that appears on the right side of the reaction. So (H) must be right, because only (H) is literally demonstrated in Passage II.

J   **Direct Contradiction:** This is the reverse of (H), because it describes $AL(OH)_3$ being converted to Al. But the reaction in Passage II clearly shows Al on the left side of the equation and $AL(OH)_3$ on the right side of the equation, so we know that Al is being converted into $AL(OH)_3$, and not the other way around, as (J) would require. So (J) must be wrong as well.

What we had to understand to answer the question: We needed to realize that all of the chemicals in the answer choices are in the reaction in Passage II, and we needed to pick the only choice that reflects what's going on in that reaction. We didn't need to read or understand any other part of Passage II, including any explanatory text or data; we definitely didn't need to try to read the minds of "the experimenters" mentioned in the prompt. We didn't really have to understand any chemistry, beyond knowing that a chemical equation shows the chemicals being produced on the right-hand side of the arrow (see "Chemical Equations" on page 334 for more). We didn't need to know what the different chemical symbols in the question refer to.

Note Always remember to keep the answer choices in mind from the very beginning, because they often offer strong clues about the best way to approach a question. And remember not to get intimidated when the ACT tries to make a question look more technical than it is!

Test 3, Question 11 (Form 16MC3 if you have the 2020-2021 Red Book—see page 23 for more) **TYPE: OUTSIDE INFO**

Answering requires some information that can't be found in the passage. Any required outside knowledge must be relatively basic. Don't try to use outside knowledge on a question unless you're sure you can't answer based on the passage. See p. 339.

Notes on answer choices: The choices are identical except for two differences. (A) and (B) include the word "acid," while (C) and (D) include the word "base." (A) and (C) include the word "decreases," while (B) and (D) include the word "increases."

A   **Off by One or Two Words:** This choice might attract an untrained test-taker who realized that acids have lower pH than bases, but who misread the last sentence before Table 1 as though it said "decreases" instead of "increases." See the discussion of (D) for more.

B   **Confused Relationships:** This choice might attract an untrained test-taker who thought that acids had a higher pH than bases. See the discussion of (D) for more.

C   **Barely Relevant:** This choice combines the mistakes from (A) and (B). See the discussion of (D) for more.

D ✓ **Correct:** The prompt doesn't refer to any particular part of Passage II, but it does use the name DMEA, which we can skim for relatively easily because it consists of 4 capital letters. When we find DMEA in the passage, we see it appears in the last sentence before Table 1, which says that DMEA "increases pH." The only two choices that accurately restate the words "increases pH" from the text are (B) and (D). Of those two choices, only (D) makes the logical statement that a substance that increases pH is likely a base, so (D) is right. (Note that it's technically possible for (D) to be a weaker acid than some other acid, instead of being a base. But no answer choice mentions a weak acid; the only choice that restates the idea of increasing pH and offers a plausible reason for DMEA to do that is (D).)

What we had to understand to answer the question: We needed to find the one sentence in Passage II that included the word "DMEA," and read that sentence carefully. We also needed to be aware of the relatively fundamental scientific fact that bases have higher pH than acids, by definition. Otherwise, we didn't need to look at or understand any other part of Passage II, or any other idea related to chemistry.

Test 3, Question 12 (Form 16MC3 if you have the 2020-2021 Red Book—see page 23 for more) **TYPE: DATA PLUS PARAGRAPH**

Finding the answer requires information from the text as well as information from a figure. Read carefully, and be very particular about matching up exact values in the figure and the answer choices, unless the prompt calls for estimation. See p. 339.

Notes on answer choices: The choices form a series in which each choice is 3 days later than the previous choice.

F   **Wrong Part of the Passage:** This choice might attract an untrained test-taker who accidentally considered the data for AWP 1 or AWP 2 in Table 1, instead of for AWP 3, as we discuss below for (J). That would lead to the mistaken conclusion that we needed to find the day in Figure 1 where the EDTA curve had a value of 4 or 21 mL.

G   **Wrong Part of the Passage:** This choice might attract an untrained test-taker who accidentally compared the line for gluconic acid or citric acid to the Day 4 data from AWP 2 in Table 1.

H   **Confused Relationships:** This choice represents the day when the EDTA curve has a value a value of roughly 100 in Figure 1, so it might attract an untrained test-taker who rounded off the value for AWP 3 in Day 2 of Table 1 to 100, instead of remembering that the relevant value from Table 1 is 121.

J ✓ **Correct:** The prompt refers to "EDTA" and "the AWP 3 sample that contained no corrosion inhibitor," and tells us to answer "based on Table 1 and Figure 1." When we look at Table 1 and Figure 1, we can see that the only specific mention of data for AWP 3 within the table or the graph is in the bottom row of Table 1, and the only mention of EDTA is in the dot-dash line for Figure 1 (the third line down on the graph). But what does the prompt mean by the phrase "that contained no corrosion inhibitor?" We'll need to find out, in case we're somehow looking at the wrong AWP 3 data. One way to try to find out what the prompt means is to skim Passage II for any other mentions of AWP 3. When we do that, we see that the text between Table 1 and Figure 1 tells us that Figure 1 shows the data from the repetitions of the AWP 3 trial with "corrosion inhibitors." This means that the AWP 3 data in Table 1 was obtained without the corrosion inhibitors in Figure 1, which means that the phrase "the AWP 3 sample that contained no corrosion inhibitor" in the prompt is referring to the AWP 3 data in Table 1. Table 1 shows us that AWP 3 had produced 121 mL by Day 2. Figure 1 shows us that the sample of AWP containing EDTA had produced 121 mL around Day 10, so (J) is correct.

Test 3, Question 13 (Form 16MC3 if you have the 2020-2021 Red Book—see page 23 for more)   **TYPE: DATA PLUS PARAGRAPH**

Finding the answer requires information from the text as well as information from a figure. Read carefully, and be very particular about matching up exact values in the figure and the answer choices, unless the prompt calls for estimation. See p. 339.

Notes on answer choices: The choices offer us the chance to pick any trial from Study 2 individually, or to pick none of the trials.

A   **Barely Relevant:** The prompt refers us to Study 2, and the choices mention Trials 4, 5, and 6 within that study. Trials 4, 5, and 6 are represented in Figure 4. When we look at the diagram for Trial 4, which is at the top of Figure 4, we can see that the hands on each scale are rotated away from the zero on the scale, which tells us that each scale is bearing some non-zero amount of weight—but those hands are in two different positions: the hand on the scale to the left is pointing up and right, while the hand on the scale to the right is pointing down and right. This means each scale is bearing a different weight. (One way to know that the scales are bearing different amounts of force is to note that the first sentence in Passage III says the scales are "identical platform scales," which means that they must be holding different amounts of weight if their hands aren't in the same positions. Another way is to read the last sentence before Study 1, which says, "the amount of rotation [of the hand on the scale] was directly proportional to the strength of the force." If the hands on the two scales in Trial 4 have rotated different amounts, then those two scales must be experiencing different forces.) So we can tell that (A) can't be right. This choice might attract someone who thought that the "Trial 4" label in Figure 4 referred to the trial *below* the label, rather than the trial *above* the label. We can see that the label for each trial must refer to the diagram above that label, or else the topmost trial in Figure 4 would have no name, and the label "Trial 6" wouldn't refer to anything. (By the way, another way to tell that (A) can't be right is to note that the diagram for Trial 6 shows two scales with arrows in orientations similar to those in Trial 4, except that the scale on the left is pointing down and the scale on the right is pointing up—since (C) refers to Trial 6, and Trial 6 presents two scales in the same orientations as the scales in Trial 4 for (A), we know that both (A) and (C) must be wrong, since they can't both be right.)

B ✓   **Correct:** As we noted for (A), the prompt indicates that we should be considering Study 2 when answering this question, and (B) refers to Trial 5 in that study, which is depicted in the second diagram in Figure 4. When we look at the diagram for Trial 5, we can see that the hands on both scales are in the same position: each one is pointing horizontally to the right, which indicates that the forces on them are equal, for reasons we discussed in our analysis of (A). So (B) is correct.

C   **Barely Relevant:** This choice has the same basic problem as (A); see the discussion of (A) for more.

D   **Wrong Part of the Passage:** As we can see in the explanation for (B), the force was equally distributed in Trial 5, which means (D) can't be right. But (D) might attract some untrained test-takers who thought that the phrase "Study 2" in the prompt meant they should look at *Figure 2* in Passage III; in that figure, it's true that none of the three trials depict equal forces being distributed between the two scales. But, as we saw when discussing (A) and (B) above, Figure 4—not Figure 2!—is the one that's relevant to this question, because it's the one that shows the trials in Study 2.

Test 3, Question 14 (Form 16MC3 if you have the 2020-2021 Red Book—see page 23 for more)   **TYPE: PURE DATA**

Finding the answer requires information from a figure. Read carefully, and be very particular about matching up exact values in the figure and the answer choices, unless the question calls for estimation. See p. 339.

Notes on answer choices: The choices present a series in which each choice is 2.5 N more than the choice before it.

F   **Confused Relationships:** This choice can't be correct for the reasons discussed in the explanation for (G). It might have attracted untrained test-takers who thought they should divide the weight of each scale by 2, possibly as a result of finding the weight of one scale and then getting confused by the fact there are two identical scales in the diagram.

G ✓   **Correct:** The prompt refers us to Trials 1 and 2, which are diagrammed in Figure 2. The only concrete information we receive about the weight of an object in Trial 1 or Trial 2 is the fact that the triangular weight on the top scale in Trial 2 weighs 5.0 N, so we'll need to see how we can use that fact to determine the weights of the scales themselves. We can see that when the triangular 5.0 N weight is placed on the top scale, the hand on that scale points directly to the right, which means that a 5.0 N weight causes the hand on a scale to point directly to the right. And in Trial 1, the hand on the bottom scale (Scale B) is pointing directly to the right under the weight of the top scale (Scale A). This means the top scale—Scale A—must weigh 5.0 N, just like the triangular weight in Trial 2. From here, there are at least two ways to know that each scale must weigh 5.0 N. One is to note that the first sentence in Passage III says the scales are "identical," which means they're the same, which means they must have the same weight. Another way is to note that the prompt says, "Scale A and Scale B each weighed," which also directly indicates that each scale has the same weight as the other. Since we now know that Scale A weighs 5.0 N, and that each scale has the same weight, we know that the answer to the question is 5.0 N.

H   Confused Relationships: This choice might have attracted untrained test-takers who looked at Trial 2 and noted that the top scale is registering a weight of 5.0 N and the bottom scale is registering a weight of 10.0 N, and then added those two weights and divided by the two scales. Among other things, this approach would be wrong because it would add the weight of the triangle in Trial 2 to the weights of the scales.

J   Confused Relationships: This choice might have attracted untrained test-takers who misread the prompt and thought it was asking for the combined weight of both scales, rather than the individual weight of each scale.

> **What we had to understand to answer the question:** We needed to refer to Trials 1 and 2 as described above for (G), and we needed to know that the scales had the same weight as each other, either from reading the first paragraph of Passage III or by noticing that the wording of the prompt tells us the scales' weights are equal, as we also noted in our analysis of (G). Otherwise, we didn't need to read or look at any other part of Passage III. We also didn't need to know what kind of unit is indicated by the capital letter N in the answer choices and in Figure 2.

Test 3, Question 15 (Form 16MC3 if you have the 2020-2021 Red Book—see page 23 for more)   **TYPE: OUTSIDE INFO**

Answering requires some information that can't be found in the passage. Any required outside knowledge must be relatively basic. Don't try to use outside knowledge on a question unless you're sure you can't answer based on the passage. See p. 339.

Notes on answer choices: The choices are identical except for two differences. (A) and (B) mention Trial 1, while (C) and (D) mention Trial 3. (A) and (C) include the word "greater," while (B) and (D) include the word "less."

A   Confused Relationships: (A) might attract an untrained test-taker who understands the connection between springs and potential energy as discussed in the explanation for (C), but who misreads Figure 2 and thinks that Scale A is bearing more weight in Trial 1 than in Trial 3, possibly as a result of ignoring the square weight in Trial 3 and thinking that the scales are registering their lowest possible weight when they're pointing straight down. Note that we could eliminate this answer choice based solely on the fact that the second half of the statement in this choice contradicts Figure 2 from the passage.

B   Direct Contradiction: This choice might attract an untrained test-taker who understood Figure 2 and realized that Scale A held more weight in Trial 3 than in Trial 1, but who doesn't understand that a compressed spring holds potential energy, and an uncompressed spring doesn't.

C ✓ Correct: As trained test-takers, our relatively basic outside scientific knowledge should include the fact that the phrase "potential energy" in the prompt refers (very roughly) to energy that's stored in a system. A compressed spring stores potential energy that will be released when the compression is released. The more compressed a spring is, the more potential energy is stored inside of the spring. In Trial 1, there's no weight on Scale A, so the "spring inside the scale" that's mentioned in the prompt would be totally uncompressed in Trial 1. But in Trial 3, there's a 10.0 N weight on Scale A, so the spring inside the scale would be compressed. Since a compressed spring has more potential energy than an uncompressed spring, we know that the spring in Scale A has more potential energy when it's compressed under a weight in Trial 3 than when it's uncompressed in Trial 1, with no weight on it. (C) directly reflects this, so (C) is right.

D   Off by One or Two Words: This choice would be right if the word "less" were the word "greater." It might attract some untrained test-takers who confuse choices (C) and (D) because they're so similar to each other, and end up picking (D) by accident. Note that we could eliminate this answer choice based solely on the fact that the second half of the statement in this choice contradicts Figure 2 from the passage.

> **What we had to understand to answer the question:** We needed to consider the diagrams of Trials 1 and 3 in Figure 2, with the concept of potential energy in mind, as we discussed for (C) above. Apart from that, we didn't need to look at or understand any other part of Passage III.

Test 3, Question 16 (Form 16MC3 if you have the 2020-2021 Red Book—see page 23 for more)   **TYPE: DATA PLUS PARAGRAPH**

Finding the answer requires information from the text as well as information from a figure. Read carefully, and be very particular about matching up exact values in the figure and the answer choices, unless the prompt calls for estimation. See p. 339.

Notes on answer choices: Choices are identical except for two differences. (F) and (G) show the upper scale pointing left, while (H) and (J) show it pointing up. (F) and (H) show the lower scale pointing right, while (G) and (J) show it pointing down.

F ✓ Correct: The prompt doesn't refer us to any specific part of Passage III, but the choices do show scales stacked on each other, which is very similar to what we see in the diagrams for Figure 2, so we'll probably need to consult Figure 2 at some point. In order to answer this question, we need to figure out where the hand would point on each scale—and to figure that out, we need to know how much force is being applied to the platform on each scale, since the direction of the hand is determined by the force on the platform, according to the second sentence under Figure 1. It's probably easier to start by considering the scale on the bottom, since it's right-side up, like all the scales in Passage III. The only force being applied to the bottom scale is the weight of the scale on top. (Note that the scale being upside-down doesn't have any impact on how much of the scale's weight is pushing down on the bottom scale.) In Trial 1 from Figure 2, we can see that the hand on the bottom scale points directly to the right when a scale is placed on top of it, so we know that the bottom scale in the right answer should point to the right as well. Now we need to consider the scale on top. If we think about it, the force pushing on the platform of the top scale is just the weight of the top scale itself. (Remember that the first sentence after Figure 1 says, "the weight of the platform of each scale was insignificant," so subtracting the weight of the platform doesn't change the weight of the scale overall.) That means the force acting on the top scale is the same as the force acting on the bottom scale—both scales are really just registering the weight of the top scale. Remember that the scale is upside down, so when the hand rotates 90 degrees away from 0, it ends up pointing straight to the left, just like the top scale in this answer choice. (Actually, all we have to notice is that the hand on the top scale should be pointing to the side, rather than pointing up or down, because our only options in the answer choice are to have the hand pointing to the left, or to have it pointing straight "up" in the diagram.) Each scale in (F) shows the hand pointing to the right side of the scale (if we imagine looking at the scales when they're right-side up), so (F) is right.

G Confused Relationships: As we can see in our discussion of (F), the top scale in this choice shows the correct amount of force, but the bottom scale doesn't. This choice would attract untrained test-takers who think the bottom scale should be registering the weight of 2 scales—but, as we discussed for (F), the bottom scale can only be weighing the top scale, no matter how the top scale is oriented.

H Confused Relationships: As we can see in our discussion of (F), the bottom scale in this choice shows the correct amount of force. But the top scale is registering the weight of two scales. This choice might attract someone who thinks the top scale should somehow be weighing itself twice, or should weigh both scales.

J Confused Relationships: As we can see in our discussion of (F), neither scale in this answer choice shows the correct amount of force. This choice would attract a test-taker who thought that both scales should register the weight of 2 scales, instead of each registering the weight of the top scale. It would also attract someone who thought that each scale's weight was twice its actual weight, which would cause each scale's hand to point straight down, away from its platform (when right-side up)—possibly as a result of misreading the diagram for Trial 2 and ignoring the triangular weight in that diagram.

What we had to understand to answer the question: We needed to notice that Figure 2 included stacked scales, and that Trial 1 in Figure 2 shows the way the bottom scale in the stack should look, as we noted in our discussion of (F) above. We also needed to know that the scales were "identical," as we can see in the first sentence of Passage III, and that the weight of each platform was "insignificant," as the first sentence after Figure 1 states. Apart from that, we didn't need to read or understand any other part of Passage III.

Test 3, Question 17 (Form 16MC3 if you have the 2020-2021 Red Book—see page 23 for more)   TYPE: PURE DATA

Finding the answer requires information from a figure. Read carefully, and be very particular about matching up exact values in the figure and the answer choices, unless the question calls for estimation. See p. 339.

Notes on answer choices: The choices provide a set of possible explanations that are all pretty different from each other.

A ✓ Correct: The passage refers us to Study 2, which includes Figures 3 and 4. The diagrams in those figures all show that the placement of the pencil on each scale is the reference point for the distance measurements in those diagrams. Since (A) is the only choice that's literally demonstrated in the relevant diagrams, we know (A) is right.

B Barely Relevant: No part of Passage III mentions the board rolling from side to side at any point during the experiment, so (B) isn't literally restated or demonstrated by the text, which means it's wrong.

C Direct Contradiction: The prompt refers us to Study 2, and the first paragraph under Study 2 says the students "set the dial readings...to zero" after putting the pencils and boards on the scales. This would remove the weight of the pencils and board from the future readings of the scales, and nothing else in Study 2 indicates that the students needed or wanted extra weight from the pencils in conducting the experiment. Since (C) isn't restated or demonstrated in the relevant text, it's wrong.

D Barely Relevant: Passage III never mentions air pressure as part of the experiment—further, there's no reason to think that using a pencil would cause the air pressure above and below the platform to be equal, as (D) describes.

What we had to understand to answer the question: We needed to realize that the prompt was referring us to Study 2, and that the diagrams in Study 2 demonstrated the idea in (A), as we saw above when discussing (A).

Test 3, Question 18 (Form 16MC3 if you have the 2020-2021 Red Book—see page 23 for more)   TYPE: PURE DATA

Finding the answer requires information from a figure. Read carefully, and be very particular about matching up exact values in the figure and the answer choices, unless the question calls for estimation. See p. 339.

Notes on answer choices: The choices offer every possible correlation between the distance and the force mentioned in the prompt.

F Confused Relationships: As we can see in the discussion of (H), the answer should be "decreased only." This choice might attract an untrained test-taker who thought the prompt asked about the total weight on both scales.

G Direct Contradiction: As we can see in the discussion of (H), the answer should be "decreased only." This choice might attract an untrained test-taker who thought the question asked about the amount of force on the surface of Scale A as the weight moved farther from Scale B.

H ✓ **Correct:** The prompt refers us to Study 2, and mentions the idea of the "distance between the...weight and the pencil on Scale B." Both the text description of Study 2 and the diagrams in Figure 4 reflect a change in the distance between the weight and the pencil on Scale B, so we know that we've found the relevant part of Passage III to answer this question. In Trials 4, 5, and 6, the 10.0 N weight moves farther and farther from the pencil on Scale B. As the weight moves farther away, the hand on Scale B points closer and closer to the "0" marker at the top of the scale. So we can see that the force exerted on Scale B gets closer to zero as the weight moves farther away, which means it decreases. So (H) is right.

J **Confused Relationships:** As we can see in the discussion of (H), the answer should be "decreased only." This choice might attract an untrained test-taker who had trouble reading the scales in the different trials in Figure 4.

> **What we had to understand to answer the question:** We needed to realize that the prompt was referring us to Study 2, and then consider the changes in Scale B as the weight was moved further from it, just as we discussed in (H). We also needed to understand the way the hands on the scales moved clockwise when force was applied to them, as described in the first two paragraphs of the passage. Otherwise, we didn't need to read or understand a single word in Passage III.

Test 3, Question 19 (Form 16MC3 if you have the 2020-2021 Red Book—see page 23 for more)   TYPE: PURE PARAGRAPH

Answering requires information from the text. Choices often primarily involve phrases rather than numbers. Consider every relevant word. Be sure your answer is literally demonstrated or restated on the page, with no interpretation necessary. See p. 339.

Notes on answer choices: Choices are identical except for two differences. (A) and (B) begin with "to add," while (C) and (D) begin with "to subtract." (A) and (C) include the phrase "the scales," while (B) and (D) include "the board and pencils."

A **Barely Relevant:** (A) might attract an untrained test-taker who thinks that the stacked scales from Figure 2 are somehow relevant to this question, and who doesn't realize that setting the dials back to zero is a way to remove weight, not add it.

B **Direct Contradiction:** As we can see in the explanation for (D), this is the opposite of the right answer—setting the scales to zero after adding the board and pencils will have the effect of subtracting their weight from the readings. This choice might appeal to an untrained test-taker who gets confused by the idea of setting the scales to zero.

C **Off by One or Two Words:** This choice might attract an untrained test-taker who has some understanding of the purpose of setting the dial to zero, but also thinks that the stacked scales from Figure 2 are somehow related to the question, or thinks that the scales are somehow registering their own weights in some other way.

D ✓ **Correct:** The prompt refers us to Trials 4-6, which appear in Study 2. When we read the text description of Study 2, we see that the students put a pencil on each scale, and then laid a board on top of the pencils so that it spanned the distance from one scale to the other. After that, they set the dials to zero. So what was the impact of setting the dials to zero? Well, before the dials were set to zero, they must have showed some kind of reading, because the two pencils and the board were on the scales. (On top of that, if they weren't showing any reading, there would be no need to reset them to zero—they'd already be at zero if there were no reading.) If the students hadn't set the dials to zero at this point, then the scales would show the weight of the pencils and the board that were already on there, plus the weight of any additional object. By setting the scale to zero, the students removed the weight of the pencils and board from the reading, so that when other objects were added to the scales, the scales would only show the weight of the new objects. That means any measurement they took after setting the dial to zero would be made without the weight of the pencils and board. This means (D) is literally demonstrated in the relevant part of the text, so (D) is right.

> **What we had to understand to answer the question:** We needed to realize that the prompt was referring us to Study 2, and then read Study 2 and think carefully about the effect of setting the scales to zero, as we discussed for (D). We didn't need to read or understand any part of Passage III outside of the text description of Study 2.

Test 3, Question 20 (Form 16MC3 if you have the 2020-2021 Red Book—see page 23 for more)   TYPE: PURE DATA

Finding the answer requires information from a figure. Read carefully, and be very particular about matching up exact values in the figure and the answer choices, unless the question calls for estimation. See p. 339.

Notes on answer choices: The choices offer every possible combination of the idea of increasing and the idea of decreasing.

F **Direct Contradiction:** This choice is the exact opposite of the right answer. It might attract an untrained test-taker who misread the phrase "as engine speed increases" in the prompt as though it had said "as engine speed *decreases*," or someone who accidentally read the "Engine speed" column in Table 2 from top to bottom, but then accidentally read the "EOR" column from bottom to top without realizing it.

G ✓ **Correct:** The prompt refers to Experiment 3, and also mentions the phrase "minimum octane number of fuel required for an engine to operate without becoming damaged," which exactly restates the definition of "EOR" from the description of Experiment 3. This makes it clear that we need to consider Experiment 3 when answering this question. When we look at Table 2 in Experiment 3, we can see that values in the "EOR" column consistently decrease as values in the "engine speed" column increase. (For example, an engine speed of 1,500 has an EOR of 97.4, while an engine speed of 2,000 has an EOR of 95.3.) So (G) is correct.

H **Barely Relevant:** As it turns out, no data series (such as the values in a column on a table or the y-values of data in a graph) in all of Passage IV shows a trend of increasing and then decreasing, as (H) would require. This choice is probably here because it allows the ACT to use a common answer-choice pattern in this question.

J **Barely Relevant:** This choice has basically the same issue as (H), and is probably also here just because it fits a common answer-choice pattern on the ACT Science section.

> **What we had to understand to answer the question:** As we discussed for (G) above, we needed to realize that the prompt was referring us to the information for Experiment 3, and that the "EOR" column in Table 2 corresponds to the phrase "minimum octane number...for an engine to operate" in the prompt. Apart from that, we didn't need to read or understand any part of Passage IV, including the names, structures, or attributes of the various chemical compounds referred to in the passage.

Test 3, Question 21 (Form 16MC3 if you have the 2020-2021 Red Book—see page 23 for more)   **TYPE: PURE DATA**

Finding the answer requires information from a figure. Read carefully, and be very particular about matching up exact values in the figure and the answer choices, unless the question calls for estimation. See p. 339.

Notes on answer choices: The choices include numbers within the general ranges of the values for Fuel A and Fuel B in Table 2.

A **Confused Relationships:** These are the octane numbers for Fuel A and Fuel B from Table 2 for an engine speed of 2,500 rpm...but the question asked for the octane numbers at 2,200 rpm. This choice will attract a lot of untrained test-takers who misread "2,200 rpm" in the prompt as "2,500 rpm," or who misread the number 2,500 in Table 2 as 2,200. As trained test-takers, we should notice that this question requires us to answer based on a trend in data—rather than reading it directly off of Table 2 somewhere—because of the phrases "suppose a trial had been performed" and "would most likely have been determined." If the prompt were asking us to read data directly off of Table 2, it would have simply asked what the octane numbers were for Fuel A and Fuel B at an engine speed of 2,200 rpm, without telling us to "suppose a trial had been performed" and asking us what the result "would most likely have been."

B ✓ **Correct:** The prompt refers us to Experiment 3, and we see that Experiment 3 includes Table 2. That table provides data related to rpm, Fuel A, and Fuel B, which are all terms appearing in the prompt, so we know that Table 2 is relevant to the prompt. When we look at Table 2, we can see that it shows a clear trend in which octane number decreases as engine speed increases. Table 2 provides a row of data for an engine speed of 2,000 rpm, and another row of data for an engine speed of 2,500 rpm, but the prompt asks about the data that would correspond to an engine speed of 2,200 rpm, which is between 2,000 rpm and 2,500 rpm. We would expect the corresponding data for Fuel A and Fuel B to be between the values for those fuels at 2,000 rpm and 2,500 rpm (see "Using Simple Trends in Data" on page 333 of this Black Book for more on this logic). Fuel A has a value of 96.6 at 2,000 rpm and a value of 95.0 at 2,500 rpm. Fuel B has a value of 96.1 at 2,000 rpm and a value of 95.4 at 2,500 rpm. (B) offers a value for Fuel A of 96.1, which is between the values of 96.6 and 95.0; (B) also offers a value for Fuel B of 95.8, which is between the values of 96.1 and 95.4. Since the values for Fuel A and Fuel B in (B) are between the values for Fuel A and Fuel B at 2,000 rpm and 2,500 rpm, (B) is right.

C **Confused Relationships:** The issue with (C) is similar to the issue we discussed above for (A): these are the octane numbers for an engine speed of 2,000 rpm, which are already reflected in Table 2. But the question asked for the likely octane numbers at 2,200 rpm, as we discussed for (B). Like (A), this choice might appeal to untrained test-takers who misread the number 2,200 in the prompt as 2,000, or who misread the number 2,000 in Table 2 as 2,200.

D **Confused Relationships:** According to the logic used in our discussion of (B), these octane numbers would correspond to an engine speed between 1,500 rpm and 2,000 rpm—but the question asked for the octane numbers at 2,200 rpm, which is between 2,000 rpm and 2,500 rpm. (D) might attract untrained test-takers who correctly realized that they needed to find a choice between existing values in the columns for Fuel A and Fuel B, but who then read the wrong lines of data in Table 2.

> **What we had to understand to answer the question:** We needed to realize that the prompt was asking us to pick a choice whose values fell inside a range of values from Table 2, as we discussed for (B) above. We never needed to read or understand any other part of Passage IV, including anything about what octane is, or why it's relevant to engine speed.

Test 3, Question 22 (Form 16MC3 if you have the 2020-2021 Red Book—see page 23 for more)   **TYPE: PURE DATA**

Finding the answer requires information from a figure. Read carefully, and be very particular about matching up exact values in the figure and the answer choices, unless the question calls for estimation. See p. 339.

Notes on answer choices: (F) and (G) are the reciprocals of one another. (F) and (H) both have isooctane alone in the numerator, while (G) and (J) both have heptane alone in the numerator. (H) and (J) both involve adding the volumes of heptane and isooctane, while (F) and (G) don't.

F **Confused Relationships:** The first row of data from Table 1 shows that when the volume of heptane is 0 mL, the volume of isooctane is 100 mL, and the octane number is 100. If we plug those values into choice (F), we'll end up dividing by zero, since the value for "volume of heptane" is zero, and that's the only thing in the denominator for (F). Since it's mathematically impossible to divide a number by zero, we know that (F) must be wrong. (F) might appeal to untrained test-takers who try to come up with the appropriate calculation on their own, rather than plugging in numbers from the provided data, and don't realize that the formula needs to involve comparing the amount of isooctane to the amount of the entire mixture, rather than the amount of heptane. (See the note below for more.)

G   **Confused Relationships:** As we did in our discussion of (F), we can plug the first row of data from Table 1 into the formula in (G) and see if it's valid. When we do that, we'll find that the expression in (G) has the volume of heptane by itself in the numerator, so it would have us divide zero by whatever is in the denominator, and then multiply by 100, which would produce a result of zero...but the octane number in the first row of data from Table 1 is 100, not zero, so we know (G) is also wrong. This choice combines the mistakes from (F) and (J): it only uses one chemical in the denominator, rather than a combination of both chemicals, and it places the amount of *heptane* in the numerator, rather than the amount of *isooctane*. (See the note below for more.)

H ✓   **Correct:** If we take the values from the first row of data in Table 1 and plug them into the formula in (H), as we did for choices (F) and (G) above, we'll get an expression that won't be undefined or equal to zero, even when we plug in zero for the volume of heptane. Instead, we get this:

$$\frac{100}{0+100} \times 100$$ (plug in the data from the first row of Table 1)

$$\frac{100}{100} \times 100$$ (simplify the denominator)

$$1 \times 100$$ (simplify the fraction)

$$100$$ (multiply)

In other words, when we take the values for the first row of data in Table 1 and plug them into choice (H), we get a result of 100, which matches the octane number from the first row of Table 1. That means this equation works, at least for the first row of values. As we can see in the discussion of the other answer choices, none of them works for the first row of values in Table 1, so (H) must be right.

J   **Confused Relationships:** The formula in choice (J) leaves heptane alone in the numerator again, like choice (G) did, so plugging in the values from the first row of data in Table 1 will cause the product to be zero again, and not 100, which is the correct octane number for the first row of data in that table. So we can see that (J) is wrong—but (J) might appeal to an untrained test-taker who accidentally confused isooctane with heptane in the numerator.

> **What we had to understand to answer the question:** We needed to notice that the prompt was telling us to refer to Table 1, and we needed to make sure we didn't confuse the words "isooctane" and "heptane." We also needed to know the properties of the number zero when it comes to multiplication, addition, and division, as we saw in our discussion of the answer choices above. Apart from that, we didn't need to read or understand any part of Passage IV. We definitely didn't need to know the formula for an octane number beforehand!

Note   If we just look at the table and glance through the choices, and if we realize that plugging in 0 for heptane has to be able to produce a result of 100, as we saw above for (H), then we can rule out (F), (G), and (J) immediately, since a heptane value of zero in those expressions results in either zero or an undefined result no matter what the value for isooctane is. Since we know that the ACT Science section doesn't like to make us do much actual math, we can understand why the test included data points with a value of zero: they're much easier to plug into this set of answer choices. Of course, if more than one expression in the answer choices had worked for the first row of data in Table 1, then we would have had to try the next row of values until we found that only one expression worked for all the values that we tested in the table. But in this case we were able to rule out three of the four choices just by testing the first row of values in Table 1.

Test 3, Question 23 (Form 16MC3 if you have the 2020-2021 Red Book—see page 23 for more)   **TYPE: DATA PLUS DATA**

Finding the right answer requires information from more than one figure. Read carefully, and be very particular about matching up exact values in the figure and the answer choices, unless estimation is called for. See page 339.

Notes on answer choices: The choices involve ranges defined by the numbers 55, 90, and 125; of those numbers, 90 is the only one that appears in one of the tables from Passage IV, and 125 is the only one that appears in the graph from Passage IV.

A   **Confused Relationships:** This choice might attract untrained test-takers who thought the prompt described a mixture of 900 mL of heptane and 100 mL of isooctane, not the other way around, and who thought that the added TEL would have no effect. That mixture would have resulted in an octane of 10, according to the fifth row of data from Table 1.

B   **Confused Relationships:** This choice might attract untrained test-takers who got confused and thought that adding 3 mL of TEL would *decrease* the octane number by 25, rather than increasing it by 25, as Figure 1 shows.

C ✓   **Correct:** The prompt refers us to "Table 1 and Experiment 2," so we know that we'll need to use those data sources to answer the question. The prompt then describes a mixture of "100 mL of heptane and 900 mL of isooctane." Table 1 contains information about mixtures of different volumes of heptane and isooctane, so we'll start our approach with Table 1. When we look at that table, we see that it doesn't have any information about mixtures that include 900 mL of anything, so we may think that we're looking at the wrong table—but, when we look through the rest of Passage IV, we don't see any other mentions of anything being 900 mL either. Since Passage IV talks about mixtures repeatedly, we need to realize that the *ratio* of the mixture in the prompt is what matters. Once we understand that, we see that Table 1 says a mixture of 10 mL of heptane and 90 mL of isooctane has an octane number of 90. Since that's the same ratio as the mixture of 100 mL of heptane to 900 mL of isooctane from the prompt, we know that the mixture in the prompt also has an octane number of 90. At this point, we might think that we're done, but there are two problems with that: the first one is that we haven't accounted for the 3 mL of TEL mentioned in the prompt, and the second one is that no answer choice accounts for the possibility of an octane number being exactly 90. So let's figure out what effect the TEL will have on the octane number. Figure 1 shows us that adding 3 mL of TEL to a 100-octane fuel caused the octane number to increase by 25 points, to 125. So if 3 mL of TEL were added to a 90-octane fuel, we'd expect the resulting octane number to be roughly 25 points higher than 90—but we wouldn't expect the new octane number to be higher than the octane number achieved by adding 3 mL of TEL to a 100-octane fuel, as shown in Figure 1. So we'd expect the mixture in the prompt to have an octane number higher than 90 (which is the octane number before the TEL is added), and lower than 125 (which is the result of adding the TEL to a 100-octane mixture, not a 90-octane mixture). So (C) is right. (Note that the description for Experiment 2 describes the TEL being "added to 1,000 mL samples of isooctane," and that the sample described in the prompt would also be 1,000 mL, because 100 mL + 900 mL = 1,000 mL.)

D   **Barely Relevant:** This choice might attract untrained test-takers who thought that adding 3 mL of TEL would somehow raise the octane number beyond anything depicted in Figure 1—or anything else in Passage IV.

> **What we had to understand to answer the question:** As we saw for (C), we needed to use Table 1 to realize that the ratio of 10:90 (or 100:900, or even 1:9 if you prefer) was the key piece of information for finding the octane of the mixture described in the prompt before the TEL was added, and then we used the information in Experiment 2 and Figure 1 to figure out the effect of adding the TEL.

Test 3, Question 24 (Form 16MC3 if you have the 2020-2021 Red Book—see page 23 for more)   **TYPE: PURE DATA**

Finding the answer requires information from a figure. Read carefully, and be very particular about matching up exact values in the figure and the answer choices, unless the question calls for estimation. See p. 339.

Notes on answer choices: Identical except for two differences. (F) and (G) begin with "Fuel A," while (H) and (J) begin with "Fuel B." (F) and (H) say the octane number was *lower* than the EOR, while (G) and (J) say the octane number was *higher*.

F   **Confused Relationships:** This choice might attract an untrained test-taker who accidentally mixed up the values for the EOR column and the Fuel A column in Table 2, and who also misunderstood the explanation of EOR in the passage.

G ✓ **Correct:** The prompt refers to Experiment 3, which contains Table 2. Table 2 includes columns with headings for "Engine speed," "EOR," "Fuel A," and "Fuel B," which all appear in the prompt and in the answer choices, so we know that Table 2 is relevant to the question. When we look at Table 2, we can see that the octane number of Fuel A is higher than the corresponding EOR at all engine speeds. As we'll see after checking the remaining choices, (G) is the only choice that accurately reflects the data in Table 2, so it must be right.

H   **Direct Contradiction:** This choice might attract an untrained test-taker who misread the data for Fuel B in Table 2, and overlooked the fact that the Fuel B octane number was only lower than the EOR at an engine speed of 1,500 rpm, without considering the data for the other engine speeds.

J   **Direct Contradiction:** As we saw in our discussion of (H), the octane numbers for Fuel B in Table 2 are higher than the EOR numbers for all the engine speeds *except* 1,500 rpm, so the phrase "at each of the engine speeds tested" in (J) isn't literally demonstrated by the data, which means (J) is wrong. This choice might have attracted an untrained test-taker who accidentally overlooked the first row of data in Table 2.

> **What we had to understand to answer the question:** We needed to realize that the prompt was referring us to Table 2, and then we needed to find the only choice that was literally demonstrated by the data in Table 2. Otherwise, we didn't need to read or understand any part of Passage IV, including the paragraph above Table 2 explaining what EOR means.

Test 3, Question 25 (Form 16MC3 if you have the 2020-2021 Red Book—see page 23 for more)   **TYPE: DATA PLUS PARAGRAPH**

Finding the answer requires information from the text as well as information from a figure. Read carefully, and be very particular about matching up exact values in the figure and the answer choices, unless the prompt calls for estimation. See p. 339.

Notes on answer choices: (C) is ten times as much as (A), and (D) is ten times as much as (B).

A   **Barely Relevant:** This choice combines the errors described in the discussions of (B) and (C).

B   **Confused Relationships:** This choice might attract an untrained test-taker who thought the octane number would be divided by 10 because the amounts in the prompt are 1/10 the size of the amounts in Table 1. But the text before Table 1 indicates that the *proportion* of heptane to isooctane determines octane number, not the specific *amounts* of either chemical.

C   **Confused Relationships:** This would be the octane number of a mixture of 8 mL heptane and 2 mL isooctane, not the other way around. (See the explanation of (D) below for more.) This choice will attract a lot of untrained test-takers who try to answer this question quickly and don't bother to verify which amount in the prompt corresponds to which chemical, or who confuse the

"Volume of heptane" and "Volume of isooctane" columns in Table 1.

D ✓ **Correct:** As we saw in our discussion of (B) above, the octane numbers mentioned in Table 1 are related to the ratios of the heptane-isooctane mixtures in Table 1. So we can see that a mixture of 2 mL heptane and 8 mL isooctane would have the same proportion of heptane to isooctane as a mixture of 20 mL heptane and 80 mL isooctane...but Table 1 doesn't include any specific information about a mixture of 20 mL heptane and 80 mL isooctane! We can see that the prompt clearly tells us to answer the question "based on Table 1," so we'll need to figure out how Table 1 can be used to determine the octane number of a mixture of 2 mL heptane and 8 mL isooctane (or of 20 mL heptane and 80 mL isooctane, which we know would come out to the same thing). We can start by looking to see if there's any noticeable correlation between octane numbers and the other numbers in Table 1. As it turns out, there is: we see that the octane number is always equal to the volume of isooctane, as long as the volume of isooctane and the volume of heptane add up to 100 mL. (This is the same thing as saying that the octane number is the percentage of the mixture of heptane and isooctane that's made up of isooctane.) By that logic, the octane number of the mixture in the prompt is 80, because the mixture in the prompt would have the same ratio as a mixture of 20 mL heptane and 80 mL isooctane. S (D) is right.

What we had to understand to answer the question: We needed to refer to Table 1, as instructed by the prompt, and we needed to realize that the octane numbers in Table 1 are related to the *ratio* of isooctane to heptane—which we saw in the second paragraph of Passage IV (as we discussed for (B) above). And as we saw in our discussion of (D), we also needed to realize that the octane number is equal to the volume of isooctane in mL, as long as the volume of heptane can be added to the volume of isooctane to produce a volume of 100 mL (in other words, the octane number is the percentage of isooctane in the mixture). So we didn't need to read or understand anything at all about the descriptions of the experiments in Passage IV.

Test 3, Question 26 (Form 16MC3 if you have the 2020-2021 Red Book—see page 23 for more) TYPE: DATA PLUS PARAGRAPH

Finding the answer requires information from the text as well as information from a figure. Read carefully, and be very particular about matching up exact values in the figure and the answer choices, unless the prompt calls for estimation. See p. 339.

Notes on answer choices: The choices are essentially identical except for two differences. (F) and (G) both begin with the word "higher," while (H) and (J) begin with the word "lower." (F) and (J) end with the phrase "lower than 115," while (G) and (H) end with the phrase "higher than 115."

F ✓ **Correct:** The prompt tells us to answer "based on Experiment 2," which describes the addition of TEL to "1,000 mL samples of isooctane." But the prompt talks about adding TEL to "1,000 ml of *heptane*" (emphasis added), not isooctane, as in Experiment 2. So we'll need to look elsewhere in Passage IV to help figure out what the impact of TEL would be on 1,000 mL of heptane—we can probably start doing this by skimming Passage IV for the word "heptane." When we do that, we see that the third sentence of the first paragraph says, "heptane...is given an octane number of 0," and the next sentence says, "isooctane...is given an octane number of 100." So we can see from these sentences that the octane number of heptane is 0, and that it's lower than the octane number of isooctane. But we still need to figure out how 1 mL of TEL will affect this initial octane of 0 for heptane, since that's what the prompt is asking us about. The only mention of 1 mL of TEL in all of Passage IV occurs in Figure 1, which shows that adding 1 mL of TEL to 1,000 mL of *isooctane* raises its octane number from 100 to 115. So we know that adding 1 mL or TEL to 1,000 mL of *heptane* will also raise its octane number—we don't know how high the octane number will go, but we know from the first paragraph of Passage IV that pure heptane has an octane number of 0, which is much lower than the octane number of pure isooctane. So we can see that adding 1 mL of TEL to 1,000 mL of heptane will result in an octane number higher than 0 (the octane number of pure heptane) but less than 115 (the result of adding 1 mL of TEL to 1,000 mL of *isooctane*). So we can see that (F) is right.

G **Off by One or Two Words:** (G) might attract a test-taker who thought the prompt was asking about adding 1 mL of TEL to 1,000 mL of isooctane, rather than heptane, and who didn't notice that Figure 1 indicates the result of adding 1 mL of TEL to 1,000 mL of isooctane was an octane number right around 115, not "higher than 115," as (G) would require.

H **Barely Relevant:** We know this choice must be wrong because the first paragraph of Passage IV tells us that the octane number of pure heptane is 0—so the octane number of the mixture described in the prompt can't be both lower than 0 and higher than 115, since no number could possibly satisfy that description. This choice is probably here because it completes a common pattern on the ACT Science section by combining the mistakes from (G) and (J).

J **Off by One or Two Words:** As we saw in our discussion of (F), this choice is right to say the number should be lower than 115—but we also saw in our discussion of (F) that the octane number of pure heptane was 0, and nothing in the passage demonstrates that it's possible to have an octane number that's less than 0, or that adding TEL to any mixture would result in a lower octane number—so (J) is wrong.

What we had to understand to answer the question: We needed to refer to Experiment 2, as the prompt indicated. We also needed to realize that Experiment 2 involves pure isooctane, which is different from the heptane mentioned in the prompt—so we needed to find the information in the first paragraph of Passage IV that would allow us to make some kind of determination about the result of adding TEL to heptane, as we discussed for (F) above. We didn't need to read or understand anything in Table 1, Experiment 1, or Experiment 3. We also didn't need to know anything about the chemical structures of heptane or isooctane, of course.

Answering requires information from the text. Choices often primarily involve phrases rather than numbers. Consider every relevant word. Be sure your answer is literally demonstrated or restated on the page, with no interpretation necessary. See p. 339.

Notes on answer choices: (A) and (C) make statements about long-period comets becoming short-period comets. (B) makes a statement about short-period comets becoming long-period comets. (D) makes a statement about both types of comets' orbits.

A　Direct Contradiction: This directly contradicts a statement made by Scientist B, as we'll see in the explanation for (C). It might attract an untrained test-taker who misread or misunderstood Scientist B's position, or an untrained test-taker who misread the word "cannot" in (A) as "can."

B　Barely Relevant: Neither scientist makes any statement about whether short-period comets can become long-period comets. This choice might attract some untrained test-takers who understand that Scientist B believes long-period comets can become short-period comets (as we'll see in our discussion of (C)) and just assume that Scientist B believes the reverse isn't possible, even though Scientist B doesn't say that. As trained test-takers, we know that the answer to this question must be literally restated or demonstrated in the text; since (B) doesn't meet that standard, (B) must be wrong.

C　✓　Correct: The second sentence of Scientist B's statement says "short-period comets were once long-period comets," which restates the idea from (C) that "long-period comets can become short-period comets." This directly restates a statement by Scientist B as the prompt requires, so (C) is the right answer.

D　Barely Relevant: Scientist B mentions "short-period comets" with "orbital planes," and the diagram shows these "orbital plane[s]" going around the Sun. So Scientist B seems to allude to the idea of short-period comets going around the Sun—but certainly never says that no long-period or short-period comets orbit the Sun, as (D) would require, so (D) is wrong.

What we had to understand to answer the question: We needed to read Figure 1 and the statement by Scientist B and compare them to the answer choices. We didn't need to read or understand any other part of Passage V.

Answering requires information from the text. Choices often primarily involve phrases rather than numbers. Consider every relevant word. Be sure your answer is literally demonstrated or restated on the page, with no interpretation necessary. See p. 339.

Notes on answer choices: (G) and (H) are identical except that one refers to a 90° inclination and one refers to a 0°-30°-degree inclination. (F) and (J) mention areas that are pretty different from the ones in (G) and (H).

F　Barely Relevant: The prompt tells us to consider the opinion of Scientist A, and Scientist A never says anything about a region 100,000 A.U. beyond our solar system. So this choice is neither demonstrated nor restated by the relevant portion of the text, which means it's wrong. It might appeal to an untrained test-taker who simply assumes that a "more powerful" telescope like the one mentioned in the prompt would automatically be used to look at things that are really far away, even though nothing in Passage V mentions a need to do that.

G　Off by One or Two Words: As we'll see in the explanation for (H), (G) *almost* describes the location of the Kuiper Belt according to Scientist A, but Scientist A says the Kuiper Belt "has a small inclination with respect to the ecliptic plane," while (G) mentions "an angle of 90° with respect to the ecliptic plane." An angle of 90° can't be "small" in this context, as (G) would require, because 90° is the largest possible inclination that one plane can have with respect to another: it makes the two planes perpendicular. This means (G) isn't demonstrated or restated in Scientist A's statement, so (G) is wrong.

H　✓　Correct: The prompt mentions Scientist A and "objects in the KB," so we know that we'll need to locate Scientist A's statement and see what he means by "the KB." When we do that, we see that the first sentence in Scientist A's statement says that "comets in our solar system" come from "the *Kuiper Belt* (KB)" (emphasis in original). He goes on to say that the Kuiper Belt (KB) "has a small inclination with respect to the ecliptic plane" and that it's "between 30 A.U. and 50 A.U. from the Sun." The phrase "at angles of 0° to 30° with respect to the ecliptic plane" from (H) demonstrates the idea of having "small inclination with respect to the ecliptic plane" as described by Scientist A, so we know that the region in (H) is the same region where the KB is, according to Scientist A. Since (H) is the only choice that literally demonstrates a region that fits with Scientist A's statements about the KB, we know (H) is right. (Note that the label on the left of the diagram shows us that "inclination" refers to the angle created by the ecliptic plane and an orbit that intersects that plane.)

J　Confused Relationships: It's true that Scientist B briefly mentions Jupiter as a planet that might exert some gravitational influence on comets, but the prompt refers to Scientist A, not Scientist B, and we see that Scientist A never says anything about Jupiter. This choice is probably here to attract untrained test-takers who get the elements of the two Scientists' statements confused, and don't go back to verify their ideas about those statements before picking an answer.

What we had to understand to answer the question: We needed to realize that the prompt was referring us to Scientist A's statement, and that an inclination of 0° to 30° (as mentioned in (H)) is smaller than an inclination of 90° (as mentioned in (G)). We didn't need to read or understand the introduction or any part of Scientist B's statement.

Answering requires information from the text. Choices often primarily involve phrases rather than numbers. Consider every relevant word. Be sure your answer is literally demonstrated or restated on the page, with no interpretation necessary. See p. 339.

Notes on answer choices: The choices present a range of angle measurements from 5° to 45°. (B), (C), and (D) form a series in which each measurement is 15° more than the previous measurement.

A   **Direct Contradiction:** The first sentence of the third paragraph of the introduction says that short-period comets have inclinations of "30° or less"—but the question asked which inclination "would most likely NOT be observed" for a short-period comet. Since (A) mentions an inclination of 5°, and 5° is less than 30°, this choice WOULD most likely be observed for the orbital plane of a short-period comet, so (A) is wrong. (A) might still attract untrained test-takers who answered this question in a hurry and didn't notice the word "NOT" in the prompt, and also didn't notice that (B) and (C) are also measurements of 30° or less.

B   **Direct Contradiction:** (B) has the same basic problem as (A): it's a measurement that's less than or equal to 30°, so it's not a measurement that would likely "NOT be observed for the orbital planes of short-period comets," as the prompt requires.

C   **Direct Contradiction:** This choice has the same basic problem as (A) and (B).

D ✓ **Correct:** The first sentence of the third paragraph of the introduction says that short-period comets have inclinations of "30° or less." Only choice (D) falls outside of that range, so it must be correct.

> **What we had to understand to answer the question:** We needed to notice that the prompt referred us to the introduction, and then we needed to read the sentence in the introduction that mentions the inclinations of short-period comets (which is the first sentence of the third paragraph, as we noted for (A) and (D) above). Apart from that, we didn't need to read or understand any part of Passage V. We also didn't need to understand *why* short-period comets would have smaller inclinations—we only needed to understand that the introduction says they do.

Answering requires some information that can't be found in the passage. Any required outside knowledge must be relatively basic. Don't try to use outside knowledge on a question unless you're sure you can't answer based on the passage. See p. 339.

Notes on answer choices: Each choice is the name of a planet.

F   **Confused Relationships:** As we see in the explanation for (J), we need to find the choice that mentions a "giant planet[] (for example, Jupiter)." Mercury isn't a giant planet, so (F) is wrong.

G   **Confused Relationships:** This choice has the same basic problem as (F): it's not a giant planet. Some people may be drawn to this choice because Passage V does refer to Earth a few times, but Scientist B never mentions Earth as a planet that can change the period of a comet, as the prompt requires.

H   **Confused Relationships:** This choice has the same basic problem as (F) and (G).

J ✓ **Correct:** The prompt refers us to Scientist B, who says that long-period comets can be "influenced by the gravitational fields of the giant planets;" Scientist B also mentions Jupiter as an example of a giant planet. We need to know that Saturn is the only giant planet in the answer choices, so (J) is correct. This is another example of the kind of fundamental scientific knowledge that's occasionally required on the ACT Science section.

> **What we had to understand to answer the question:** We needed to realize that the prompt was referring us to Scientist B's statement, which told us that giant planets can affect the periods of comets. We needed to know the relatively basic scientific fact that, of the planets in the answer choices, only Saturn was a giant planet. Apart from that, we didn't need to read or understand any other part of Passage V.

Answering requires information from the text. Choices often primarily involve phrases rather than numbers. Consider every relevant word. Be sure your answer is literally demonstrated or restated on the page, with no interpretation necessary. See p. 339.

Notes on answer choices: Choices are identical except for two differences. (A) and (B) start with the word "short," while (C) and (D) start with the word "long." (A) and (C) end with the phrase "Oort Cloud," while (B) and (D) end with the letters "KB."

A ✓ **Correct:** The prompt mentions Scientist B, so we know that we'll need to consult Scientist B's statement in order to answer the question. When we consider the differences among the answer choices, we see that the question comes down to whether the comet in the prompt is a short-period comet or a long-period comet, and whether it originated in the Oort Cloud or the KB. When we read Scientist B's statement, we see that the second and third sentences of that statement describe a process by which long-period comets pass close to giant planets and then become short-period comets, which Scientist B refers to as "comets with orbital periods less than 200 yr." Since the prompt says Comet Halley has a "76 yr" orbital period, and 76 is less than 200, we know that Scientist B will say Comet Halley is a short-period comet. Further, the first sentence of Scientist B's statement says, "The KB does not exist," so we can see clearly that Scientist B doesn't believe any comets can come from the KB, since he doesn't think there's any such thing as the KB in the first place. Still, as trained test-takers, we want to confirm that Scientist B believes the Oort Cloud is the source of short-period comets, instead of just assuming that (A) must be right without confirming every part of it. Well, as we just saw, Scientist B believes that "short-period comets were once long-period comets," but Scientist B doesn't explain where he thinks long-period comets come from. Knowing that (A) and (C) mention the Oort Cloud as the only alternative choices to the KB, we might decide to skim Passage V for mention of the Oort Cloud, which we can find italicized in the first sentence of the second paragraph of the introduction. That sentence says, "Long-period comets...originate...in the *Oort Cloud*" (emphasis in original). Since we know that Scientist B believes all short-period comets used to be long-period comets, and we see in the introduction that long-period comets originate in the Oort Cloud, and we see that Scientist B doesn't make any other statements about the origins of long-period comets, we know for sure that the relevant text states that Scientist B believes short-period comets (and all other comets) originated in the Oort Cloud. So (A) is right.

B   **Confused Relationships:** Scientist A says that short-period comets originated in the KB—but the prompt asks about the perspective of *Scientist B*, not Scientist A, so (B) is wrong. This choice will attract a lot of untrained test-takers who confuse the positions of the two scientists, or who misread "Scientist B" in the prompt as "Scientist A."

C   **Off by One or Two Words:** The prompt says that Comet Halley "currently has an orbital period of 76 yr," so Comet Halley isn't a long-period comet according to Scientist B, as we saw for (A) above. It's true that Scientist B says, "short-period comets *were once* long-period comets" (emphasis added), but the question asks how Scientist B would "currently" classify Comet Halley—and, again, we saw in our discussion of (A) that Comet Halley is currently a short-period comet according to Scientist B. This choice could attract some untrained test-takers who misread the word "short" in (B) as part of (C), or who overlook the word "currently" in the prompt.

D   **Confused Relationships:** This choice combines the errors from (B) and (C).

> **What we had to understand to answer the question:** We needed to realize the prompt was referring us to Scientist B's statement. We needed to read that statement, the introduction, and the choices carefully, as we saw for (A), (B), and (C).

Test 3, Question 32 (Form 16MC3 if you have the 2020-2021 Red Book—see page 23 for more)   **TYPE: PURE PARAGRAPH**

Answering requires information from the text. Choices often primarily involve phrases rather than numbers. Consider every relevant word. Be sure your answer is literally demonstrated or restated on the page, with no interpretation necessary. See p. 339.

Notes on answer choices: The choices indicate ranges in intervals of 10 km.

F   **Barely Relevant:** In light of our discussion of (J) below, we can tell that icy bodies with diameters under 10 km must not be the "much larger icy bodies" that Scientist A mentions. This choice might attract an untrained test-taker who noticed "10 km" in the passage, or someone who just assumes that an icy body up to 10 km in diameter must be pretty big, without checking Scientist A's statement.

G   **Barely Relevant:** As with (F), this choice is wrong for reasons we'll explore in more detail when we discuss (J) in a moment. (We also know (G) must be wrong because Scientist A never mentions the number 20 in particular.)

H   **Barely Relevant:** This choice has basically the same problem as (G), and is wrong for the same reason.

J ✓ **Correct:** Scientist A mentions "icy bodies with diameters between 10 km and 30 km," and then goes on to mention "much larger icy bodies" than those. So the "much larger icy bodies" must be larger than the ones with diameters between 10 km and 30 km, which means (J) is right.

> **What we had to understand to answer the question:** We needed to realize the prompt was referring us to Scientist A's statement, and then we needed to read that statement carefully as described for (J) above. Otherwise, we never needed to read or understand any portion of Passage V.

Test 3, Question 33 (Form 16MC3 if you have the 2020-2021 Red Book—see page 23 for more)   **TYPE: PURE PARAGRAPH**

Answering requires information from the text. Choices often primarily involve phrases rather than numbers. Consider every relevant word. Be sure your answer is literally demonstrated or restated on the page, with no interpretation necessary. See p. 339.

Notes on answer choices: The choices offer different combinations of the ideas of weakening or strengthening the scientists' arguments, or leaving those arguments unaffected.

A   **Barely Relevant:** See the explanation for (D). An untrained test-taker might be attracted to this choice if he thought that the missing "spherical shell" in the prompt had any implications for the likely existence of the KB in our own solar system, as mentioned by Scientist A. But Scientist A describes the KB as "a thin ring-shaped region," not as a "shell" like the one in the prompt. Further, when Scientist A concludes that "nearby stars have similar regions of icy bodies," Scientist A is, again, referring to thin rings of icy bodies, not to spherical shells of icy bodies. So this choice could appeal to untrained test-takers who didn't notice the difference between the "thin ring-shaped region" discussed by Scientist A and the "spherical shell" mentioned in the prompt.

B   **Barely Relevant:** Scientist B never makes any claim about nearby stars having spherical shells, so the lack of a shell around a nearby star as mentioned in the prompt wouldn't have any impact on Scientist B's viewpoint. (Note that Scientist B *does* mention long-period comets, which the second paragraph of the passage tells us "originate...in the *Oort Cloud*, a spherical shell of many icy bodies." But no part of Scientist B's discussion mentions the idea of the presence or absence of such a spherical shell around any other star, so the idea in the prompt still doesn't impact Scientist B's viewpoint.) This choice might be tempting for test-takers who think that such a spherical shell around another star would have some impact on the presence or absence of the Oort Cloud in the solar system, but that idea isn't restated by Scientist B.

C   Direct Contradiction: See the explanation for (D). This choice might attract an untrained test-taker who somehow assumed that the absence of a shell around a nearby star would support both scientists' differing views on the formation of short-period comets, possibly because neither scientist makes a claim that specifically contradicts the idea in the prompt.

D ✓ Correct: The scientists disagree on the existence of the KB, which is a "thin, ring-shaped region" according to Scientist A, and which "does not exist" according to Scientist B. Scientist A never mentions anything related to a "spherical shell of material" like the one in the prompt, and, as we saw in our discussion of (B), Scientist B only indirectly discusses the Oort Cloud, a spherical shell of material around the Sun. So neither scientist's viewpoint relies on the presence or absence of a spherical shell around some nearby star, and (D) is right.

> **What we had to understand to answer the question:** We needed to realize that the prompt required us to read through both scientists' statements and identify any phrase relating to a "spherical shell of material" like the one mentioned in the prompt. This included referring back to the second paragraph of the passage, which provides information about long-period comets and the Oort Cloud.

Test 3, Question 34 (Form 16MC3 if you have the 2020-2021 Red Book—see page 23 for more)   **TYPE: PURE DATA**

Finding the answer requires information from a figure. Read carefully, and be very particular about matching up exact values in the figure and the answer choices, unless the question calls for estimation. See p. 339.

Notes on answer choices: The choices are identical except for two differences. (F) and (G) mention L2, while (H) and (J) mention L4. (F) and (H) include the number 60, while (G) and (J) include the number 120.

F   Barely Relevant: Table 2 shows the data for plants that were given a 10 L nutrient solution containing 60 g of NaCl, as (F) describes. We can see that L2 plants given this solution produced fruit (since the value for those plants in the "fruit mass" column isn't zero), and had an average height over 100 cm. So there's no reason to think that the plant described in the prompt was an L2 plant given a 10 L nutrient solution containing 60 g of NaCl, which means (F) is wrong.

G   Off by One or Two Words: Table 3 shows the data for plants that were given a 10 L nutrient solution containing 120 g of NaCl, as (G) describes. We can see that L2 plants given this solution produced fruit (since the value in the "fruit mass" column for these plants isn't zero), and had an average height over 100 cm. So we can't conclude that the plant described in the prompt was an L2 plant given a 10 L nutrient solution containing 120 g of NaCl. This choice might attract untrained test-takers who noticed the line of data for L3 plants in Table 3, but then misread that data as though it related to the L2 plants that appear one line up in that table.

H   Off by One or Two Words: Table 2 shows the data for plants that were given a 10 L nutrient solution containing 60 g of NaCl, as (H) describes. We can see that the L4 plants in the table produced fruit (since they have a value in the "fruit mass" column that isn't zero) and had an average height over 60 cm. So there's no reason to conclude that the plant described in the prompt was an L4 plant given a 10 L nutrient solution containing 60 g of NaCl.

J ✓ Correct: Table 3 shows data for plants that were given a 10 L nutrient solution containing 120 g of NaCl, as (J) describes. We can see that L4 plants given this solution didn't produce any fruit (since the value in the "fruit mass" column for these plants is zero), and had an average height of 36 cm. The plant described in the prompt produced no fruit, like this plant, and was much closer in height to this plant than to any of the other plants described in the choices—so we can conclude that the plant in the prompt was an L4 plant given a 10 L nutrient solution containing 120 g of NaCl, which means (J) is correct.

> **What we had to understand to answer the question:** We needed to note the small differences among the four choices, which allowed us to zero in on the L2 and L4 plants in Table 2 (which was the table where plants got the solution with 60 g of NaCl) and in Table 3 (which was the table where plants got the solution with 120 g of NaCl). After we did that, we needed to pick the choice that allowed for a plant not to produce any fruit, and to be 21 cm tall. Apart from reading the information for L2 and L4 plants on Table 2 and Table 3, we didn't need to read or understand any other part of Passage VI.

Test 3, Question 35 (Form 16MC3 if you have the 2020-2021 Red Book—see page 23 for more)   **TYPE: OUTSIDE INFO**

Answering requires some information that can't be found in the passage. Any required outside knowledge must be relatively basic. Don't try to use outside knowledge on a question unless you're sure you can't answer based on the passage. See p. 339.

Notes on answer choices: Each choice is the name of a different cellular component.

A   Barely Relevant: If we know what chromosomes are, then we know they're not directly involved in osmosis. If we don't know what they are, there's still no real reason to guess (A)—nothing in the word "chromosomes" or in Passage VI suggests that chromosomes are relevant to this prompt, which is unlike what we'll see for (C) below.

B   Confused Relationships: As we saw for (A), if a test-taker knows what the nuclear envelope is, then there's no reason to think that (B) is right. If a test-taker isn't familiar with the term in this choice, then he should consider all the other choices, and will probably realize that "cell membrane" is likely to be the right answer. See the explanation of (C) for more.

C ✓ **Correct:** This is one more example of the kind of fundamental scientific knowledge that's occasionally required on the ACT Science section. But the question doesn't really require the kind of in-depth knowledge of cell structure that an untrained test-taker might expect! The first bullet point in Passage VI describes a "movement...between the cytoplasm of the plants' cells and the environment via osmosis." That bullet point says that osmosis involves something moving from inside a cell to the cell's environment—in other words, osmosis must involve something moving from the inside cell to the outside of the cell. If something does that, then it must pass through the cell membrane, which is the barrier between the inside of the cell and the environment. That means the correct answer is choice (C). Note that the cell membrane is a part of the cell that most test-takers will probably be familiar with, since it's the structure that defines the boundary of the cell—even if we've somehow never heard the phrase before, we can probably still work out that it's some kind of membrane that surrounds the cell, which is exactly what it is—and which is basically enough information for us to choose (C) as the right answer.

D **Barely Relevant:** As we saw for (A), if a test-taker knows what the rough endoplasmic reticulum is, then there's no reason to think that (D) is right. If a test-taker isn't familiar with the term in this choice, there's no reason to guess that it's likely to be right based on the term itself or the wording in Passage VI. See the explanation of (C) above for more.

> **What we had to understand to answer the question:** We could answer this question either by already knowing that osmosis involves movement through the cell membrane, or by reasoning through to the correct answer as described above for (C). Apart from reading this question and the first bullet in Passage VI, we didn't need to read or understand any other part of Passage VI in order to arrive at the answer.

Test 3, Question 36 (Form 16MC3 if you have the 2020-2021 Red Book—see page 23 for more)   **TYPE: PURE DATA**

Finding the answer requires information from a figure. Read carefully, and be very particular about matching up exact values in the figure and the answer choices, unless the question calls for estimation. See p. 339.

Notes on answer choices: Every combination of increasing or decreasing all the time, or doing first one and then the other.

F **Direct Contradiction:** (F) might attract test-takers who thought the prompt said "decreased" instead of "increased."

G ✓ **Correct:** Tables 1, 2, and 3, in that order, show an increasing concentration of salt in the nutrient solution, from 3g / 10 L in Table 1, up to 120 g / 10L in Table 3. The average plant mass for any line of plants decreases consistently as the concentration of salt increases. For example, the mass of L1 was 1.2 kg in Table 1, then 1.1 kg in Table 2, and finally 1.0 kg in Table 3. So (G) is right.

H **Barely Relevant:** (H) just fills out the pattern of offering every combination of increasing and decreasing, as noted above.

J **Wrong Part of the Passage:** (J) might attract test-takers who made the mistake of reading down the "Mass" column on each table, instead of comparing the masses for the same lines across multiple tables. For example, reading down the mass column of Table 2 would lead us to think about the numbers 1.1, 1.1, 0.4, and 0.5, instead of considering numbers for the same line on different tables as we described for (G). There are many ways we might realize this is the wrong approach; one would be to notice that the numbers in the "Mass" column for Table 1 don't decrease or increase as we read down the column.

> **What we had to understand to answer the question:** We needed to read the prompt and the answer choices carefully, and then observe the trend in plant masses for each individual line across Tables 1, 2, and 3, as we saw for (G) above. Apart from that, we didn't need to read or understand any part of Passage VI. (But see the note below.)

Note Some test-takers may feel that this question requires us to know that NaCl is the formula for table salt, but a strong argument can be made that this information is basically provided in Passage VI. The text repeatedly mentions salt, such as when the first sentence refers to "high-salt environments," and then we see that the only chemical mentioned is NaCl, which makes it pretty clear that NaCl is salt. Similarly, we see that the prompt refers to an increase in salt concentration, and we see in Passage VI that the only thing being increased in the solution in each table is NaCl—this also makes it clear more salt is being added. Otherwise, the prompt would be meaningless and impossible to answer.

Test 3, Question 37 (Form 16MC3 if you have the 2020-2021 Red Book—see page 23 for more)   **TYPE: PURE PARAGRAPH**

Answering requires information from the text. Choices often primarily involve phrases rather than numbers. Consider every relevant word. Be sure your answer is literally demonstrated or restated on the page, with no interpretation necessary. See p. 339.

Notes on answer choices: The choices all mention different aspects of the experiment. Two of them begin with the word "whether," and two of them correspond to the names of columns in the tables provided in Passage VI.

A ✓ **Correct:** As trained test-takers, we should know that an "independent variable" is something directly manipulated by the researchers so they can observe the results of that manipulation. The second paragraph in Passage VI after the bullet points describes how the "researcher created" 4 lines of tomato plants that were "genetically identical" (L1-L4). Then, 2 copies of "an *AtNHX1* gene" were incorporated into L1, while L2 and L3 each had "a different *AtNHX1* allele," and L4 didn't get any version of the *AtNHX1* gene. Since the manipulated variable is "whether a line received *AtNHX1*," as (A) describes, we know that (A) must represent the independent variable, as the prompt requires.

B **Barely Relevant:** Tomato plants were the only plants used in the experiment: as we saw for (A), the last paragraph before the description of the experiment specifically mentions that L1-L4 are "4 genetically identical lines of tomato plants." Since every plant in the experiment was a tomato plant, the use of a tomato plant can't be any kind of variable, so (B) is wrong. This choice might appeal to an untrained test-taker who incorrectly though that an independent variable was an aspect of the experiment that was unchanged throughout the experiment—but, as trained test-takers, we know that those unchanging aspects of an experiment are called constants, not variables.

C   **Confused Relationships:** This is a *dependent* variable, not an independent variable, as the prompt requires. Dependent variables are the things that change (and get measured or recorded) as a result of the researcher's deliberate modifications to the independent variables. In the last paragraph of text before Table 1, we can see that the "average mass (without fruit)" is one of the things that was measured by the scientist and recorded in each table. In this experiment, one independent variable was the *AtNHX1* gene, and one of the dependent variables was the average mass of the lines of plants—without fruit—which was affected by the different versions of that gene. This choice might have attracted an untrained test-taker who misread the word "independent" in the prompt as "dependent" (and who also forgot to consider (D), which is another dependent variable), or who got confused about the attributes of these two kinds of variables.

D   **Confused Relationships:** This choice has the same basic problem as (C): plant height is an attribute of the plants that changes as a result of the researcher's deliberate modifications of the plant's genetic makeup, as we discussed in (A). Like (C), this choice could appeal to an untrained test-taker who confused the two kinds of variables, or who misread the word "independent" as the word "dependent" in the prompt.

> **What we had to understand to answer the question:** We needed to know the meaning of the term "independent variable" from the prompt, and we needed to read the last paragraph before the explanation of the experiment, as we saw for our explanation of (A) above. We also needed to realize that the concepts in (B), (C), and (D) weren't independent variables, which we could determine by looking at the last paragraph of text before Table 1, and/or by looking at Tables 1, 2, and 3, as we discussed for (C) and (D) above. See "Special Article: Basics of Experimental Design" on page 336.

Test 3, Question 38 (Form 16MC3 if you have the 2020-2021 Red Book—see page 23 for more)   **TYPE: PURE PARAGRAPH**

Answering requires information from the text. Choices often primarily involve phrases rather than numbers. Consider every relevant word. Be sure your answer is literally demonstrated or restated on the page, with no interpretation necessary. See p. 339.

Notes on answer choices: Choices are identical except for two differences. (F) and (G) include "heterozygous," while (H) and (J) include "homozygous." (F) and (H) end with the word "different," while (G) and (J) end with the word "identical."

F   **Confused Relationships:** The last paragraph before the description of the experiment says that "2 *identical* copies of [*AtNHX1*] were incorporated into L1's genome," so the relevant text doesn't restate or demonstrate the idea that they were "different," as (F) would require. (See the note below for more on the meaning of the word "allele".) This choice might attract untrained test-takers who didn't read the text carefully enough, and incorrectly thought that the "different *AtNHX1* allele[s]" mentioned for L2 and L3 in Passage VI were relevant to L1, as the prompt requires.

G   **Off by One or Two Words:** (G) would be right if "heterozygous" were changed to "homozygous." (G) might attract people who accidentally thought that the word "heterozygous" referred to two things being the same, rather than different.

H   **Off by One or Two Words:** (H) has basically the same problem as (F): the text says the two *AtNHX1* genes in L1 were "identical," so the word "different" in (H) contradicts the text. (See the note below for more on the meaning of "allele".)

J ✓   **Correct:** The prompt refers to the "genotype of L1 for *AtNHX1*," so we'll need to skim through Passage VI to find the part of the text that's relevant to that. When we do that, we see that "2 identical copies of [*AtNHX1*] were incorporated into L1's genome," which appears in the last paragraph before the description of the experiment. That idea is restated in the part of (J) that says the "2 *AtNHX1* alleles were identical." This choice also says the genotype of L1 for *AtNHX1* was "homozygous;" if we know the term "homozygous," then we can just select (J) and move on to the next question, because "homozygous" describes an individual with two of the same allele. But, even if we don't know the term "homozygous," we still have a good shot at answering this question correctly. We know from looking at the choices that we have to decide between the terms "heterozygous" and "homozygous." We probably know that "hetero-" means "different," and "homo-" means "same." Since the alleles are "identical"—the same as one another—we should pick the choice that includes "homo-" instead of the one that includes "hetero-." (See the note below for more on the meaning of the word "allele".)

> **What we had to understand to answer the question:** We needed to locate the relevant paragraph of Passage VI, which mentioned that L1 had two identical copies of the gene, as we described above for (J). We also needed to know, or figure out, the difference between the words "homozygous" and "heterozygous." Apart from that, we didn't need to read or understand any other part of Passage VI—including what the *AtNHX1* gene actually does, or why anybody cares.

Note   This question may seem to require us to know the word "alleles," since it appears in each choice. But in order to answer this question, we have to determine that 2 (somethings) related to the genotype of L1 for *AtNHX1* were either "different" or "identical," because each choice includes one of those options. When we see that the text refers to "2 identical copies of this gene" for L1, and doesn't refer to L1 having 2 "different" things of any type, we can conclude that the "2 identical copies" mentioned in Passage VI must be 2 identical alleles, even if we don't know what alleles are.

Test 3, Question 39 (Form 16MC3 if you have the 2020-2021 Red Book—see page 23 for more) **TYPE: PURE DATA**

Finding the answer requires information from a figure. Read carefully, and be very particular about matching up exact values in the figure and the answer choices, unless the question calls for estimation. See p. 339.

Notes on answer choices: The choices describe every possible slope of a line.

A **Barely Relevant:** In order for the best-fit line to be vertical, there would have to be a lot of points with similar x-values and a variety of y-values, which would create a vertical trend in the data. The prompt tells us that the height of the plants is plotted on the x-axis. When we look at Tables 1, 2, and 3, we can see that there are lots of different values for the heights of the plants, not just one value, so (A) must be wrong. This choice is probably here because the ACT wanted to present every possible type of slope as an answer choice. It might attract an untrained test-taker who only considered Table 1, instead of considering all three tables, because the values in the "Height" column of Table 1 are all clustered around 124.

B **Wrong Part of the Passage:** If the slope were zero, then the line would be horizontal, by definition. In order for the best-fit line to be horizontal, there would have to be a lot of points with similar y-values and a variety of x-values, which would create a horizontal trend in the data. The prompt tells us that the mass of the plants (without fruit) is plotted on the y-axis. When we look at Tables 1, 2, and 3, we can see that there are lots of different values for the masses of the plants, not just one value, so (B) can't be correct. This choice might attract an untrained test-taker who only considered Table 1, instead of considering all three tables, because every value in the "Mass" column of Table 1 is identical.

C **Direct Contradiction:** If the slope were negative, that would mean that the masses of the plants got *smaller* as the height of the plants increased. But the opposite is true, as we can see in the explanation for (D): taller plants generally had larger masses, which means the slope would be positive, and (C) is wrong. This choice could trick an untrained test-taker who incorrectly thought that a negative slope was one that went up as it moved from left to right.

D ✓ **Correct:** There are two main ways to approach this question. One way would be to sketch out the graph described in the prompt and observe the slope of the line. If we do that, we get something like this:

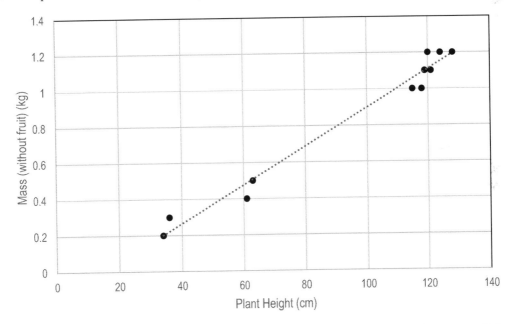

Another much quicker and simpler approach is to observe that, across all three tables, the taller plants generally have more mass than the much shorter plants. For example, all the plants in Table 1 have heights between 120 and 128 cm and masses of 1.2 kg, while, in Table 3, L3 and L4 have heights around 35 cm and masses of 0.2 and 0.3 kg, respectively. If increased height typically corresponds to increased weight, then the graph described in the prompt must have a positive slope.

> **What we had to understand to answer the question:** We needed to read the prompt carefully, then look at the tables in Passage VI and observe the relationships described in (D) (or simply create the graph ourselves, also as described in (D)). We also needed to know the attributes of the four different kinds of slopes in the answer choices. We didn't need to read or understand anything else in Passage VI, including any discussion of the genes of the different types of tomato plants.

Test 3, Question 40 (Form 16MC3 if you have the 2020-2021 Red Book—see page 23 for more) **TYPE: OUTSIDE INFO**

Answering requires some information that can't be found in the passage. Any required outside knowledge must be relatively basic. Don't try to use outside knowledge on a question unless you're sure you can't answer based on the passage. See p. 339.

Notes on answer choices: Each choice is one of the lines of tomato plants described in Passage VI.

F   **Confused Relationships:** (F) might attract some test-takers who just assume that the first line would be the control group without bothering to read Passage VI, but that's not the case for this experiment. See the explanation of (J) for more details.

G   **Confused Relationships:** L2 can't be the control because the last paragraph before the description of the experiment shows that the researcher modified L2 in much the same way that L1 and L3 were modified. See the explanation for (J). This choice is probably here because the ACT wanted to have each line present in the answer choices.

H   **Confused Relationships:** This choice has essentially the same issue as (G): Passage VI describes modifications being made to L3 that are very similar to the modifications that were made to L1 and L2. See the explanation for (J).

J   √   **Correct:** As trained test-takers with an understanding of the basics of experimental design (as discussed in "Special Article: Basics of Experimental Design" on page 336 of this Black Book), we should know that the "control" in an experiment is (basically) the group that isn't manipulated by the researchers, so that the changes observed in the other groups can be compared to a baseline result. The second paragraph below the bullet points says that "L1, L2, and L3 had different genotypes for *AtNHX1*," and no part of Passage VI mentions any changes made to L4. Since L4 is the only line without an *AtNHX1* gene, L4 is the control.

What we had to understand to answer the question: The question required us to know the meaning of the term "control," and to identify the part of Passage VI that mentioned how each line of tomato plants was created, as described for (J) above. Apart from that, we didn't need to read or understand any part of Passage VI.

Part 9: English Test Training and Walkthroughs

By now, we've addressed the Reading, Math, and Science sections of the ACT. We've seen how those sections reward careful reading and attention to detail above all. Now we'll turn our attention to the English section, which requires us to know some basic principles of grammar, style, and punctuation. But, just as with the other sections, we'll find that the best way to attack this section is to stay focused on careful reading, attention to detail, and ACT-specific strategies that let us exploit the weaknesses inherent in the test's design.

In this part of the ACT Prep Black Book, Second Edition, you'll learn the following:

- the most important secret of the ACT English section
- the two major groups of questions on this section
- how demonstration and restatement, which we discussed for the ACT Reading section, apply here as well
- all about the specific types of questions within each group, and how to approach them
- the specific grammatical rules that appear on the ACT—some of which might differ from what your teacher would accept in an essay
- the unwritten rules that shape this section
- the hidden patterns that often appear among answer choices, and how to use them on test day
- how to recognize intervening phrases and work around them
- how to use "parallelism" to determine which choice is correct when the rules of grammar alone aren't enough
- the recommended process for answering questions on this section
- how to apply these ideas to every English question from three ACT practice tests
- and more . . .

ACT English

Thus I got into my bones the essential structure of the ordinary British sentence, which is a noble thing.
Winston Churchill

Overview and Important Reminders for ACT English

At this point, we've definitely seen that the ACT is highly standardized and repetitive. This is just as true on the English section as it is everywhere else on the test. Of course, before you can learn to take advantage of the repetition and the standardization that make the ACT so beatable, you have to take the time to familiarize yourself with the specific ideas and patterns that keep appearing on each section of the test. The English section is no exception.

The ACT English section repeatedly tests a specific set of concepts related to the grammar and style conventions of written American English. Unfortunately for our purposes, most test-takers don't really know very much about the grammar and style of American English, because those things are almost never taught in American high schools—and even when teachers do try to cover those topics, they almost never teach them in a way that agrees with the ACT, because the ACT English section is based on the rules of written grammar that were popular in the middle of the 20th century.

So here's the bottom line: most test-takers who want to score very high on the ACT English section will need to learn some grammar concepts, even if their English teachers have praised their writing ability in class.

But don't panic!

There aren't very many grammar concepts on the ACT, and the few concepts that do appear on the test aren't very advanced. Also, the ACT English section itself often gives you clues to help you identify the right answer to a question, if you know where to look for them.

On top of that, there are three general ways to learn the grammar you need for the ACT:

1. You can read through the test-taking advice in this Black Book, take a look at the walkthroughs in this Black Book, and just sort of "get the hang of it" without obsessing over rules.
2. You can study all the strategies, rules, and principles in this section until you have complete and total mastery of them, and the entire English section of the ACT cowers before you.
3. You can take a sort of middle path, which involves making a conscious effort to learn a few of the major concepts that the ACT tests, and then relying on practical experience with walkthroughs and sample tests to fill in the rest.

Any of those three approaches can work great, depending on your personality and the type of score you need.

In general, most of the students I've worked with prefer the more informal approach of reading through some question walkthroughs from this Black Book and trying some practice questions from the Red Book to develop an intuitive understanding of how the ACT English section works. Some prefer the middle approach of deliberately learning a few concepts in detail and then soaking up the rest through a relatively short period of trial and error.

One important note, though: if you're shooting for a 34 or higher on the ACT English section, you'll have very little room for error, which means you'll probably need to make a conscious decision to master the ACT's rules for grammar, style, and punctuation. If you want to score in that range, you basically have to go through all 75 questions on the entire English section and only miss about 3 or 4 questions at most, and it's hard to reach that level of accuracy without being consciously aware of the ACT's idea of grammar rules. (And even if you think you already have a perfect understanding of modern English grammar, I want to caution you gently that the ACT will probably disagree with you on at least a few issues.)

By the way, the ACT will never test you on the specific names of grammatical terms like "participle," "gerund," "nominative," and so on, so don't worry if you can't keep those terms straight (or if you've never even heard of them). Instead, the ACT tests your awareness of its principles of grammar and style by having you choose the form of a phrase that it considers acceptable within the context of a passage. So even if you choose to learn all the rules and principles in this Black Book, you'll never have to answer direct questions about grammatical terminology on the ACT.

Now that we've addressed some of the important preliminary issues with the ACT English section, let's talk about the section's big secret.

The Big Secret of ACT English

The big secret of the ACT English section is that it doesn't follow the same rules and conventions that many educated people follow when they write or speak in American English today. Instead, it follows a set of rules that might loosely be described as the rules that governed standard written American English in the early-to-mid 20th century.

Most test-takers don't realize this. Whenever they come across a new ACT English question, they just think,

Which choice would make this phrase sound best *to me?*

This is a huge mistake. By now we should realize that the ACT doesn't care what sounds good to you, or to me, or to anybody else who doesn't write the ACT. So instead of looking at an ACT question and answering based on what sounds good to us, we should be answering based on what the ACT consistently rewards. That's all. What you and I think sounds good or bad isn't important if it disagrees with the

ACT's rules and patterns.

Let me say it again: when you're faced with an ACT English question, you should immediately ask yourself,

> Which answer satisfies the ACT's standards and patterns for this type of question?

When we talked about the ACT Reading section earlier in this Black Book, we talked about how one of the biggest reasons people struggle with those questions is that they're used to classroom discussions in which almost any interpretation of a text has some value, while the ACT Reading section only rewards a literal reading of each text. Well, a lot of test-takers have a similar issue when it comes to ACT English, because most English teachers have very loose standards for grammar and writing style. This means that most test-takers find the ACT penalizes them for things that their English teachers would accept.

For example, many people are taught in school that a comma can be placed almost anywhere in a sentence, whether to indicate that a reader would take a breath at that point in the sentence if it were being read out loud, or just to break up a lot of text, or for any number of other reasons. But the ACT English section doesn't reward us for using commas like that—instead, it has its own rigid rules about comma usage (you can find these rules on page 431 of this Black Book, by the way).

Just as we learned to attack the questions on the Reading, Math, and Science sections in a systematic and dependable way—even though they mostly ask us to do things we don't normally do in school—we can learn to beat ACT English questions in a reliable way. As we did with the other sections, we'll use an approach that's tailored to the repetitive patterns and issues that come up in this part of the test. We'll see that most of the questions in the ACT English section test only a handful of concepts over and over again.

ACT English Question Groups

I generally encourage test-takers to think of the questions on the ACT English section as falling into three rough groups. These groups are my own personal classifications, not official classifications from the ACT, so you won't see them listed or described this way on the actual test, or in the Red Book.

The names of these groups are pretty self-explanatory:

1. "Reading Comprehension" questions
2. Grammar/Style/Punctuation questions
3. Questions that combine grammar/style/punctuation elements with reading comprehension elements

Training yourself to recognize these broad question groups will make it easier for you to focus on the concepts that might be tested in a particular question. This, in turn, will make the ACT English section easier to approach.

Don't get stressed out at the thought of learning to recognize these different question types! It'll become second nature pretty quickly, and it's not really something that can lead you to a wrong answer if you do it wrong; it'll usually just save you some time if you do it right. As I said, it's more about helping you focus your mind on the specific tricks the ACT is trying to play on you with any particular question.

Now let's talk about each question group in more detail, and about some of the major issues that the ACT will test with them.

Reading Comprehension Questions

The first major group of question is what I call a "Reading Comprehension" question. These questions are relatively easy to spot because ACT English questions with prompts generally focus on some aspect of reading comprehension (as opposed to questions that simply offer a set of answer choices, which usually focus on grammar, style, and/or punctuation).

The correct answers to these questions generally reward the same kind of literal approach to the text that we've already seen in the Reading and Science sections of the ACT: they're directly restated or demonstrated in the relevant part of the passage.

As you might imagine, we'll also find that the wrong-answer choices on these kinds of questions are frequently similar to the types of wrong answers we'll encounter on the ACT Reading section: some wrong answers will directly contradict the text, some will confuse the relationships among concepts from the text, and so on. (For a refresher on these types of wrong answers, see "ACT Reading Wrong Answer Patterns" on page 53 of this Black Book.)

There are a few different specific forms that these questions can take. We'll look at them now.

"Best accomplishes X"

Some questions will ask which answer choice best accomplishes some goal, such as providing relevant information, or illustrating a certain idea. We'll find that the right answer is always the only one that plainly and directly demonstrates the idea required by the prompt, with no interpretation or judgment calls involved.

We can see a real-life example of this question type in question 44 from the English section of practice test 1 in the Red Book (test 2 in the 2020-2021 Red Book). The prompt of the question asks which answer choice "most effectively suggests the shape of blue holes as described earlier in the essay." (As trained test-takers, of course, we know that phrases like "most effectively suggests" are designed to make other people think that subjectivity or interpretation might be necessary to find the answer. Since this is a real ACT question, it must be the case that only one answer choice is restated or demonstrated by the text, with no interpretation necessary.)

The right answer ends up being (G), which includes the word "dot." Dots are circles, and this word refers back to the word "circular" in the first line of the previous paragraph. In fact, the word "dot" is the only mention of any kind of shape in any of the answer choices.

Notice that there was no interpretation involved here. One choice clearly accomplished what the prompt asked for, and the other choices clearly didn't. (For a full analysis of this question, see its walkthrough on page 468 of this Black Book.)

We just discussed one instance of the "best accomplishes X" question type. A lot of questions on the ACT English section fall into this category. Some of them will have prompts that are pretty specific to the relevant passage, and won't really be directly repeated in another prompt—in other words, you probably won't see another question about "suggest[ing] the shape" of something on test day.

On the other hand, some prompts for questions of this type *do* get repeated across multiple questions. But this doesn't really change your approach to the question. No matter what the prompt specifically asks about, it will still be your job to pick the choice that plainly accomplishes whatever the prompt requires. Still, since the following "sub-types" of this question type do appear relatively frequently on the ACT, I thought we'd go ahead and take a look at each one to make sure you're fully comfortable with them.

"Most relevant information"

Some questions ask which of the answer choices provides the "most relevant information" regarding something. The right answer to this type of question will be the only one that talks about what the question asks about without adding extra information that doesn't appear in the passage.

For a real life example of this type of question, let's look at question 25 from the English section of practice test 3 in the Red Book (form 16MC3 online if you have the 2020-2021 Red Book). The prompt asks which version of the sentence provides "the most relevant information at this point in the essay." When we look at what's being discussed "at this point in the essay," we can see that the text is listing women and their accomplishments regarding social movements.

All four answer choices provide information about Ida B. Wells. Three of them don't say anything about what she did in connection to any movement or cause:

- (B) mentions the man she married, along with information about the man's occupation.
- (C) mentions that she wrote for papers in three cities.
- (D) tells us some basic information about her birth and family.

These three answers are wrong because they introduce information that's unrelated to what's being discussed "at this point in the essay."

Only the right answer, (A), focuses exclusively on Ida's accomplishments in fighting for a cause. The fact that she "courageously spoke out for social and racial justice" is relevant "at this point in the essay," because the text immediately before the underlined portion describes other women who fought for similar causes, and the text immediately after does the same. (For a full analysis of this question, see its walkthrough on page 529 of this Black Book.)

"Best conclusion"

Some questions will offer different sentences and ask which one is the "best conclusion" for the passage. According to the unwritten rules of the ACT, the best conclusion will be the one that focuses on the main topic of the passage, often on something that's mentioned in the title of the passage itself.

A prompt of this type might even ask something like, "Which sentence would best conclude this essay while tying the end of the essay back to the beginning?" In this case, you just want to find the choice that talks about the main topic of the passage, and also mentions something related to the beginning of the essay.

For a real-life example of a "best conclusion" question, look at question 59 from the English section of practice test 2 in the Red Book (test 3 in the 2020-2021 Red Book). The prompt asks us which sentence, if true, "would best conclude the paragraph and the essay by referring back to the opening paragraph."

We know the right answer will be the one that mentions ideas from this paragraph and also from the opening paragraph, because that's what the prompt mentioned. In this case, choice (A) is right because it mentions concepts from this paragraph and a concept from the first paragraph, as the prompt requires:

1. "these features" (the "star cluster" mentioned earlier in the same paragraph)
2. "my winter trek" (the narrator's experience using his telescope in the cold, as described in the first paragraph)
3. "a change in focus…help[ing] to see more clearly" (the "principle of averted vision," as mentioned at the end of the previous paragraph and described in this paragraph)

Meanwhile, choices (B), (C), and (D) are wrong, because none of those choices mentions concepts from both this paragraph and the first paragraph. (For a more detailed examination of this question, see its walkthrough on page 510 of this Black Book.)

"Most effective introduction"

Along similar lines, the ACT might also ask which sentence is the "most effective" introduction, usually to a paragraph. The answer will be the sentence that discusses the same topics that are discussed in the other sentences in that paragraph. Again, if more than one choice mentions a topic that's already in the paragraph, then the right answer will be the one that mentions the largest number of concepts from the paragraph, as we saw in "What about Main Purpose, Main Idea, Best Description Questions?" on page 58 of this Black Book.

You might see wrong-answer choices related to the previous paragraph, or wrong-answer choices that make some broad statement related to the passage as a whole, but that don't restate any ideas from the paragraph being introduced.

Let's look at an example. Question 32 on the English section of practice test 1 from the Red Book (test 2 in the 2020-2021 Red Book) asks us which choice "would most effectively introduce" the paragraph it would appear in. The paragraph is about how the Bahamas formed from calcium carbonate in seawater. The right answer, (F), mentions the idea of the Bahamas forming, and also mentions that calcium carbonate is part of seawater; both of these concepts are restated directly in the paragraph, in the phrases "the formation process" and "calcium carbonate separated from the seawater." (For a more detailed discussion of this question, see its walkthrough on page 463 in this Black Book.)

"Most specific information"

A prompt that asks for the "most specific information" wants you to find the choice that provides the type of information required by the question. That might sound pretty subjective, but the ACT always make sure that there's a concrete, objective reason why the information in one choice is more "specific" than the information in the other choices. Let's look at an example and you'll see what I mean.

Question 54 on the English section of practice test 1 in the Red Book (test 2 in the 2020-2021 Red Book) asks for the choice that "provides the most specific information about how posterns and towers served as defensive positions." The right answer is (G), which says, "by providing cover for armed guards during the attack." This is the only choice that specifies *how* the "posterns and towers served as defensive positions," as the prompt requires; in other words, the other choices only say *that* the posterns and towers kept Rome safe or protected Rome, but they don't say *how* the posterns and towers actually did that. (For a more detailed discussion of this question, see its walkthrough on page 472 in this Black Book.)

(Notice, also, that we didn't need to know what the word "postern" meant. All we needed to do was find the choice that told us how posterns and towers served as defensive positions—we never needed to know what a "postern" actually was.)

"Most effective transition"

When you see a prompt that asks for the "most effective transition" from one sentence or paragraph to another, you just need to find the choice that refers to something from the passage before the transition and something from the passage after the transition, without adding extra information that doesn't get discussed in either paragraph.

So, for example, if the first paragraph is about wooden roller coasters, and the second paragraph is about carousels, then you should pick the choice that refers to both wooden roller coasters and carousels.

We can see a real-life example of a "most effective transition" question in question 55 from the English section of practice test 1 in the Red Book (test 2 in the 2020-2021 Red Book). This question asks which choice "provides the most effective transition to Paragraph 5." We know the right answer will be the one that mentions something from paragraph 4, and something from paragraph 5.

The only choice that does this is (B). It starts with the word "today," the timeframe discussed in Paragraph 5, and also mentions "the Aurelian wall," which was discussed in the previous paragraph. That means (B) is correct.

(See the full walkthrough of this question on page 473 of this Black Book for a more detailed discussion of this question.)

Sentence or paragraph placement

You'll sometimes encounter questions that ask where a sentence or paragraph should best be placed. In a question like this, the ACT wants sentences and paragraphs to appear in a sequence that makes them refer to each other in a logical order.

For example, if one sentence says, "My brother had a dog named Snowflake," then that sentence needs to come *before* a sentence that says, "That dog would follow him everywhere." It wouldn't make sense to use the word "that" to refer to the dog unless there's already a previous sentence that introduces the dog.

Also, if one sentence refers to something in another sentence, then the ACT will want those sentences as close together as possible.

Let's look at a real-life example: question 13 from the English section of practice test 1 in *The Official ACT Prep Guide* (test 2 in the 2020-2021 Red Book). The prompt asks about the placement of Sentence 7.

If you read the paragraph, you'll see that Sentence 7 mentions Ely's "deformed feet." But Sentences 5 and 6 already discussed how Echo and Enid helped Ely out, and how Ely "overcame his early limitations." In other words, the original version of the paragraph has Sentences 5 and 6 discuss problems related to Ely's deformed feet before Sentence 7 even mentions that he has deformed feet. And as we keep inspecting the paragraph, we see that Ely isn't even introduced until Sentence 4. So, according to the ACT's rules of sentence ordering, Sentence 7 must be moved so that it comes after Sentence 4, which introduces Ely, and before Sentence 5, so that Sentence 7's information about Ely's deformed feet will appear before the sentences that explain what happened as a result of his deformed feet.

With all of this in mind, we know that (D) is right, because it's the only choice that causes the information about Ely's deformed feet to appear *after* Ely has been introduced, but *before* the discussion of the problems related to Ely's deformed feet. (For a more detailed discussion of this question, see its walkthrough on page 453 in this Black Book.)

Precision Vocabulary

A few times per test, you might see a question with an underlined word and three alternatives for that word. There won't be any punctuation involved, or different forms of the same word—just four different words with somewhat similar meanings.

Even though these questions don't have any prompts, they're basically reading comprehension questions. The words in the answer choices will often be words you could use interchangeably in a classroom discussion, but their specific meanings won't be quite the same, and one will clearly be a better choice than the others when you think carefully about the meaning of each word and the sentence it would be inserted into.

Typically, these words aren't exotic—they tend to be words that most test-takers are familiar with, but whose specific meanings might not be something the average test-taker normally pays any attention to.

The key to answering these questions correctly is to think in a precise way about what each relevant word actually means, and what it can be used to describe. For a real-life example, look at question 66 from the English section of practice test 2 in your copy of *The Official ACT Prep Guide* (test 3 in the 2020-2021 Red Book). That question asks us whether "voluminous," "immeasurable," "mountainous," or "large" is the right word to use in a sentence that describes paintings that are "about six feet by eight feet" according to the passage, which also describes them as "expansive."

All of these answer choices might seem to be vaguely appropriate, and each one would probably be acceptable in an English class discussion of this passage. But we know by now that the ACT isn't satisfied if we just pick an answer choice that feels vaguely appropriate. Instead, we need to think about what each word actually means, and how it fits into the sentence.

The first choice, (F), says the paintings are "voluminous." Does that really make sense? We might say that a suitcase is "voluminous," or even that a big coat is "voluminous," but does it make sense to call a painting "voluminous?" The word "voluminous" could describe something that's bulky, taking up and/or containing a lot of space in three dimensions. It can't really be used to describe a flat object like a painting—at least, not with the specificity that the ACT demands.

What about the word "immeasurable," from (G)? This choice might be pretty tempting for a lot of untrained test-takers because the paintings are apparently pretty big, and this word can be used to describe something pretty big. But remember—we have to think very carefully about what words actually mean on the ACT, and this word literally describes something that *can't be measured*. That can't be appropriate here, because the sentence where this word appears gives the paintings' measurements as "about six feet by eight feet." We can't logically say that something is "immeasurable" and then provide its measurements. So (G) is definitely wrong.

How about the word "mountainous?" This means something like "enormous" or "huge," with the added idea of something that projects upward, like a mountain. A huge pile of something could be "mountainous," or a wave on the ocean could even be "mountainous," but it doesn't really work to call flat paintings "mountainous," no matter how big they are, because paintings aren't shaped like mountains. So this won't be right, either, even though most teachers wouldn't stop to correct you if you referred to large paintings as mountainous in a classroom discussion.

Finally, let's consider the word "large." This one's pretty straightforward. Something that's "large" is big. We know the paintings are big, because they're described as "expansive" later in the paragraph. Only (J) expresses the idea of being large without also including a connotation that isn't literally restated or demonstrated in the passage, so (J) is right.

Again, if you just skimmed these words, or if you heard any of them used in this context in a classroom discussion, you'd probably think any of them could be adequate. But if you take the time to think carefully about each one, you'll find that only one can actually describe a painting in a way that makes sense and fits the context of the passage.

So when you see a precision vocabulary question, be sure to check the surrounding text in the passage, including the sentences before and after the one in question, for key phrases that might help you pick the right answer choice.

One more thing—there's no point in memorizing hundreds of vocabulary words to get ready for a question like this, in case you were thinking of doing that! Most of the words in the choices are ones that test-takers are already familiar with, and the real issue is being very particular about the meanings of those words. We'll see more examples of this in the walkthroughs, which start on page 446 of this Black Book.

(You might also see a question of this type where the *sounds* of the answer choices are similar, rather than the meanings. For example, question 57 from the English section of practice test 2 in the Red Book (test 3 in the 2020-2021 Red Book) includes the choices "illuminated," "emanated," "emulated," and "eliminated." We'll still attack this sort of question the same way—just think carefully about what each word means, and choose the only one that makes sense in context. For a complete walkthrough of that question, see page 509 of this Black Book.)

Transitions

There are a lot of instances where the ACT English section will ask us to identify the word or phrase that indicates some type of relationship between things or ideas in a sentence. Here are some examples of the kinds of words I'm talking about:

unless	during	while
because	except	but

There's an example of a real ACT question involving transition words in question 29 from the English section of practice test 2 in the Red Book (test 3 in the 2020-2021 Red Book), which rewards us for choosing the phrase "for example" as the phrase to begin a sentence that provides an example of an idea from a previous sentence. (See the question's walkthrough on page 496 of this Black Book for more.)

Effect of deleting a phrase or sentence

Sometimes the prompt will tell you that the author is considering deleting something from the passage, and you'll be asked what the impact of that change would be.

The answers to these types of questions depend on all the same principles of reading comprehension that we've been discussing for other ACT questions. You won't have to interpret anything; you'll just need to pick the answer that plainly describes the relationship between the deleted phrase and the rest of the text.

Let's look at an example from the Red Book. Question 65 from the English section of practice test 1 in that book (test 2 in the 2020-2021 Red Book) asks what the essay would lose if the previous sentence were deleted.

Choice (B) is right because it's the only choice that's demonstrated by the relationship of the previous sentence to the rest of the passage. (B) says the previous sentence is "a transition," which is an accurate description of the sentence according to the ACT's unwritten rules. (On the ACT, we know that a sentence is a "transition" between two ideas if that sentence appears between the two ideas and refers to both of them—see "Most effective transition" on page 414 of this Black Book for a refresher on that idea).

For a more detailed discussion of this question, see its walkthrough on page 477 of this Black Book.

Including or excluding a phrase or sentence

The key identifying element of these questions is that their answer choices will demonstrate the "yes yes no no" pattern we saw in the ACT Science training: two choices will include a word like "yes," the other two choices will include a word like "no," and each of the four choices will include a different reason to support the "yes" or "no." (Sometimes the answer choices will say "kept" or "deleted," or something similar, instead of "yes" or "no," but the pattern is the same, and the approach to the question is the same. See "ACT Science Answer-Choice Pattern 4: Yes Yes No No" on page 342 of this Black Book for a refresher on this pattern.)

Some questions of this type tell you that the author is considering adding a sentence provided in the question, and then ask you whether that sentence should be included. Other questions of this type ask whether the author should keep or delete a sentence that's already in the passage. We answer either version of this question type with the same process.

As we've seen on other reading comprehension questions in the ACT English section, the correct answer will (usually) be the only choice that plainly describes the relationships demonstrated in the relevant text. In other words, for most questions of this type, you can ignore the "yes" or "no" (or "kept" or "deleted") portion of each answer choice, and just check to see whether the reasoning after the "yes" or "no" is demonstrated by the sentence and/or passage. (We'll discuss how to handle a question with more than one answer choice that's demonstrated by the text in just a moment.)

We can see a real-life example of this in question 4 from the English section of practice test 1 in the Red Book (test 2 in the 2020-2021 Red Book). That question asks whether the following sentence should be added to the passage:

> Humans are among the threats to the animal's survival.

The right answer is (J), which is the only choice that's literally demonstrated by the relevant text. (J) tells us that "the information is already provided in the paragraph." Since the passage says that elephants face an "array of threats to their survival," and that one of those threats is "human encroachment," we can see that the idea of humans being "among the threats to the animal's survival" *is* already literally in the text, just as (J) says.

Note that, as trained test-takers, we never actually had to look at the "yes" or "no" part of any of the answer choices for this question; we simply picked the only choice that described the text accurately. (Also note that we don't need to know what the word "encroachment" means to answer this question correctly. As long as we understand that "human [something]" in the text is a threat to the elephant's survival, we know that (J) is right, and we don't have to know the meaning of the word that comes after "human." For a more detailed discussion of this question, see its walkthrough on page 449 of this Black Book.)

The approach we just discussed will be sufficient for most questions of this type. But there will be some questions with more than one answer choice that accurately describes the text. In this situation, we should pick the choice that follows the broader standards of ideal sentences and paragraphs on the ACT English section, which are basically the following:

- DO include details and examples that are relevant to the main topic of the text (see "What about Main Purpose, Main Idea, Best Description Questions?" on page 58 for more on how to determine the main topic of a text).
- DO include introductions for ideas that appear in the next sentence.
- DO include a transition between ideas that are different (see "Most effective transition" on page 414 for more on the ACT's rules for transitions).
- DO include phrases that reflect relationships present in the text.
- DON'T include irrelevant ideas that aren't obviously connected to the text or don't get explained or discussed elsewhere.

So if there's more than one answer choice left after we eliminate all the choices that don't accurately describe the text, then the right answer will be the one that correctly says to include or exclude the sentence based on the standards we just listed. Let's take a look at these ideas in action in question 40 from the English section of practice test 1 in the Red Book (test 2 in the 2020-2021 Red Book).

That prompt asks about the following sentence:

> At 663 feet deep, Dean's Blue Hole in Long Island, Bahamas, is a popular cave-diving destination.

Choices (G), (H), and (J) could all arguably describe the sentence in the prompt and its relationship to the text. But (H) is right because it's the only choice with reasoning that follows the standards we just listed: specifically, it says the sentence shouldn't be included because it's "unrelated to the paragraph's focus." For a more detailed explanation of this question, see its walkthrough on page 467 of this Black Book.

"Would this essay fulfill the writer's goal?"

Sometimes, at the end of a passage, you'll see a question that states a possible goal of the essay's writer, and then asks if that goal was fulfilled. The answer choices for this type of question will typically demonstrate the "yes yes no no" pattern we saw in our discussion of the ACT Science section on page 342 of this Black Book; in this case, two answer choices will say the writer's goal was fulfilled, and the other two will say it wasn't fulfilled; each choice will offer a different reason for saying yes or no.

The right answer will be the only one that meets both of the following criteria:

1. It's literally restated or demonstrated by the passage, and
2. It's logically connected to the goal mentioned in the prompt.

For a real-life example of this idea, see question 15 from the English section of practice test 2 in the Red Book (test 3 in the 2020-2021 Red Book). This question asks us whether the passage would fulfill the writer's goal "to . . . outline[] the steps . . . to restore the Kam Wah Chung & Co. building."

The right answer is (C), which says the essay has not accomplished that goal, because it "instead focuses on describing the history" of the building and its "uses." The accuracy of this statement is literally demonstrated by the passage, and the "no" part of the answer shows the logical relationship between the rest of the choice and the question in the prompt. (C) is the only choice that satisfies the two requirements above, so we know it's right.

On the other hand, choices (A) and (B) both include statements that accurately reflect the passage, but they're both wrong because they say the essay successfully fulfills the goal in the prompt, which isn't logically reflected in the statements made about the passage. (A) says the essay fulfills its goal because it says the "building was renovated in the 1970s," but that simple statement doesn't "outline[] the steps" involved in the renovation, as the prompt required, so the "yes" part of (A) is illogical. (B) accurately says that the essay "explains why the artifacts…were preserved," but, like (A), it illogically says that this statement is a reason that the goal in the prompt was fulfilled. (For a more detailed analysis of this question, see its walkthrough on page 489 of this Black Book.)

Now that we've addressed the various kinds of Reading Comprehension questions you're likely to encounter on the ACT English section on test day, it's time to take a look at the other major group of questions.

Grammar/Style/Punctuation Questions

These questions test your ability to identify the form of a phrase or sentence that follows the ACT's rules for grammar, style, and punctuation.

These questions can often test rule-based concepts like proper verb conjugations, the proper use of punctuation, the formation of possessives, and so on. They also sometimes offer us more than one answer choice that's grammatically acceptable, and ask us to indicate which one sounds the most appropriate according to the ACT. (I know that may sound like a pretty subjective exercise, and like exactly the kind of thing the ACT would never ask. But we'll find that the right answers to these questions are just as predictable as the right answer to any other ACT question, because the test consistently rewards the same attributes in the right answers to ACT English questions, and I'll teach you what those are.)

You'll typically be able to identify these questions because of the following attributes:

- The question won't have a separate prompt—it's usually just a list of answer choices.
- The first answer choice will usually say, "NO CHANGE."

These grammar/style/punctuation questions can cover a lot of different areas of grammar, style, and punctuation, but don't be intimidated by that. You may already know some or most of the subject matter that they'll test. We'll just need to highlight the important things that will come up in ACT English questions. Furthermore, most individual questions will only cover one or two topics each.

Also, because of the ways that different parts of a sentence interact with each other, there will be some overlap among the concepts we talk about, so don't worry if some of these ideas run together a little bit in your mind. As long as you can understand the right answer when you're practicing, you're in good shape.

One more thing—if you're feeling confused as you're reading through any one of these topics, just finish reading all the way through it. I'll always follow up with examples when necessary, and the examples will tend to clear things up. Then you can re-read the difficult topic one more time and it will probably feel easier to understand. So just keep at it, even if things don't seem clear right away.

This is also a good time for me to remind you of the importance of the question walkthroughs you'll see after this training. We'll cover a lot of stuff in the ACT English Toolbox, but you'll really get the best sense of how to beat ACT English questions by following along in your copy of *The Official ACT Prep Guide* with the walkthroughs in this Black Book. That way, you can see all of this material in action, which will really help you recognize these concepts when you see them on test day.

And after that, of course, the most important thing is always for you to do some real practice ACT English questions on your own after you've learned the material in this Black Book. So let's get started!

ACT English Toolbox

Important note:

In this section, I'll show you a lot of different sample sentences—some with errors, some without. To keep things clear, the examples with errors will have an asterisk (*) at the beginning of the example.

So if you see an example that begins with an asterisk, you'll know that it shows something you should *avoid* on the ACT English section.

Nouns

Nouns are words that describe objects or ideas, essentially. Some nouns describe objects, like these:

apple	bicycle	toy	umbrella
watch	computer	shoe	train
mall	sign	book	car

The name for any object you can touch or point to is a noun.

But nouns can also refer to abstract concepts or ideas, like these:

happiness	anger	weather	peace
hope	idealism	love	election
talent	operation	biology	speed

These aren't things you can touch or point to, but they're still nouns. Often, you can recognize nouns like these because they have suffixes like "-ness", "-ism," "-ion," "-ology," "-hood," and so on.

Nouns can be singular or plural. We typically form a plural of a noun by adding "-s" or "-es" to the singular version of the noun, but some nouns have irregular plurals that are formed differently. Here are some examples of regular and irregular nouns in their singular and plural forms:

Nouns with regular plural forms:

houses	clouds	foxes

Nouns with irregular plural forms:

| geese | children | mice |

Pronouns

Pronouns are a particular type of noun that we use to refer to a noun we've already mentioned. These are pronouns:

| I | you | he | she | it | we | they | which |
| me | him | her | us | them | one | that | |

(**NOTE:** the words "that" and "which" are special types of pronouns called "relative pronouns." Both words can also be used in other ways that aren't related to pronouns, depending on the context. Don't worry about those other usages right now—just know that the words "that" and "which" are often, but not always, pronouns.)

Pronouns are useful because they save us from having to say the same noun over and over again. Consider this sentence:

Ashley says she has to leave by Monday.

In the above sentence, we use the pronoun "she" to refer back to the word "Ashley." That way, we don't have to say this:

Ashley says Ashley has to leave by Monday.

Pronoun number and ambiguity on the ACT

When a pronoun appears on the ACT, it must agree in number with the noun it refers to:

Last week I saw an antique car. <u>It</u> was over 100 years old.

In the above example, the singular pronoun "it" is correctly used to refer to the singular noun "car."

Let's look at a sentence that breaks this rule:

*Last week I saw an antique car. At over 100 years old, <u>they</u> were in great shape.

The above sentence incorrectly uses the plural pronoun "they" to refer to the singular noun "car."

If a question on the ACT English section tests us on the use of a pronoun, then that pronoun has to follow two rules:

1. There must be a noun phrase in the surrounding text that the pronoun can possibly refer to.
2. The pronoun must have the same grammatical number as the noun it's referring to (that is, a plural pronoun has to refer to a plural noun, and a singular pronoun must refer to a singular noun).

For an example of a question that involves this pronoun issue, see question 42 from the English section of practice test 1 in the Red Book (test 2 in the 2020-2021 Red Book). Our walkthrough for that question is on page 468 of this Black Book.

Subjects and objects

Every sentence that you're asked about on the ACT English section must have a main verb. The main verb is the word (or phrase) that describes an action being performed in the sentence.

The thing that performs the action is called the "subject" of the sentence (or the subject of the verb). If there's a noun that receives the action in the sentence, then that noun is called the "object" in the sentence (or the object of the verb). Sentences don't have to have objects.

Consider the following sentence:

John grabbed the pencil.

In the above sentence,

- the word "John" is the subject, because "John" is the thing doing the action—in this case, the action is described by the word "grabbed"
- the word "pencil" is the object of the verb, because "pencil" is the thing receiving the action of being grabbed

Some pronouns are subject pronouns, and some are object pronouns.

The following pronouns are subject pronouns, because they can be used to replace words that serve as subjects of verbs:

| I | you | he | she | it |
| we | they | who | what | |

The following pronouns are object pronouns, because they can be used to replace words that serve as objects of verbs:

| me | you | him | her | it |
| us | them | whom | what | |

Notice that the words "you," "it," and "what" each have identical subject and object forms.

Subject pronouns can only be used as subjects; they must be the thing in the sentence that does an action.

Object pronouns can only be used as objects; they must be the thing in a sentence that receives an action.

So the following sentences would be acceptable on the ACT English section:

He gave her a present.

They sent a letter to us.

In the above sentences,

- "He" and "they" are subject pronouns that are doing the actions in the sentences.
- "Her" and "us" are object pronouns that are receiving the actions in the sentences.

The following sentences would be unacceptable on the ACT English section:

*He gave she a present.

*Them sent a letter to us.

In the above sentences,

- "She" is a subject pronoun that can't properly receive the action of the verb "gave."
- "Them" is an object pronoun that can't properly do the action of the verb "sent."

Personal pronouns

Personal pronouns are pronouns that can be used to replace a noun that describes a person. When a pronoun is used in place of a noun that describes a person, that pronoun must be a personal pronoun.

The following would be an acceptable sentence on the ACT English section:

This is my uncle, who got me interested in physics.

In the above sentence, the word "who" is a personal pronoun that takes the place of the personal noun "uncle."

The following would be an unacceptable sentence on the ACT English section:

*This is my uncle that got me interested in physics.

In this sentence, the word "that" isn't a personal pronoun, so it can't be used to refer to the word "uncle" on the ACT English section.

Verbs

Generally speaking, a verb is a word that refers to an action.

One way to test whether a word is a verb is to try to think of a sentence that places that word immediately after the word "cannot." If you can do that with the word, then that word is a verb, like the following words:

| run | do | make | swim |
| cook | imagine | follow | think |

You can see that any of these words can be placed into a logical sentence after the word "cannot:"

I cannot run far.

He cannot do that for very long.

They cannot make a sports car.

We cannot swim here.

Verbs can be "conjugated," which means they change their forms according to how they're used in a sentence. On the ACT, we need to pay attention to two different things when it comes to conjugating verbs:

1. We sometimes need to know whether the verb should be singular or plural (to match its subject).
2. We sometimes need to know the verb's tense (whether it describes an action in the past, present, or future).

Singular verbs and plural verbs

When a present-tense verb goes with a third-person, singular noun, that verb needs to end in "-s" or "-es." (A third-person, singular noun is any noun that can be replaced by the pronouns "he," "she," or "it.")

Other forms of verbs don't require "-s" or "-es."

Consider these sentences:

Rhonda drives to the dentist.

My friends drive downtown.

In these sentences,

- The singular noun "Rhonda" requires the singular verb form "drives." (Again, note that the present-tense, third-person singular form of a regular verb ends in "-s" or "-es.")
- The plural noun "friends" requires the plural verb form "drive."

A verb must always agree in number with the noun or nouns it modifies. This would be an acceptable sentence on the ACT English section:

Charles and Adam speak German.

In this sentence,

- The phrase "Charles and Adam" requires a plural verb form, because it describes more than one person.
- The word "speak" is a plural verb form to match the plural subject.

This would be an unacceptable sentence on the ACT English section:

> ¯*Charles and Adam speaks German.

In this sentence,

- the singular verb form "speaks" is incorrect, because it's being used with the plural subject "Charles and Adam."
- the phrase "Adam speaks" may sound correct on its own, but when we read the whole sentence we can see that the subject is actually the noun phrase "Charles and Adam," not just the word "Adam"

Here is the verb "to speak" conjugated in the present tense. Note that the third-person singular form ends in -*s*:

> I speak   we speak
>
> you speak   you speak
>
> he/she/it speaks   they speak

The ACT English section has a lot of questions that mix up singular nouns with plural verbs, or plural nouns with singular verbs. When a verb form is being tested in a question, always figure out which noun phrase is its subject, then see whether the verb is in the correct form.

Singular and plural verbs on test day

There are two primary ways the ACT will try to trick you into not noticing that a verb is conjugated incorrectly.

Sometimes, the ACT uses a question's answer choices to try to confuse us about the focus of a question about the proper form of a verb, so that we think we're being asked about the proper tense of a verb. For example, you might see something like this:

> The man has swept the kitchen floor.
>
> (A) NO CHANGE
>
> (B) have been sweeping
>
> (C) sweep
>
> (D) are sweeping

If you scan through the answer choices, it might look like the question is asking which tense the verb should be in, since the answer choices all present different tenses and aspects of the verb "to sweep." That can be confusing, especially when the sentence doesn't give us any clues about a particular time-frame.

When you look more closely, you'll notice that choices (B), (C), and (D) are all *plural* verb-forms, but the word "person" is *singular*, so the right answer should actually be a singular verb-form. The original phrase is the only singular one, so (A) would be the correct answer if this were an ACT question.

A real-life example of this issue (in question 31 from the English section of practice test 3 in the Red Book, which is form 16MC3 online if you have the 2020-2021 Red Book) involves this phrase:

> *our technologically advanced times has allowed filmmakers to create....

The answer choices include three singular verb forms: two are different past-tense forms, and one is in the present tense. To the untrained test-taker, it might seem like we need to figure out which tense of the verb is appropriate. But, in reality, the verb needs to agree with the plural noun "times," which means it needs to be a plural verb form, and the only choice with a plural verb form is the correct answer, choice (B). In other words, the tense of the verb ends up being irrelevant to the question because only one verb is plural. (See this question's walkthrough on page 532 of this Black Book for more.)

The other trick that the ACT likes to play relies on the "intervening phrase," which we'll cover in more detail on page 439 of this Black Book.

For now, we can see a real-life example of the intervening phrase at work in question 42 from the English section of practice test 2 in the Red Book (test 3 in the 2020-2021 Red Book). The question includes this phrase:

> *a channel that is composed of granite—and previously unexposed rhyolite rock—and contain rocks from at least three other geological eras

In this example, the phrase "—and previously unexposed rhyolite rock—" makes it more difficult to see what the verb "contain" should agree with. Once we mentally remove that intervening phrase, we're left with this:

> *a channel that is composed of granite and contain rocks from at least three other geological eras.

This version of the sentence makes it easier to see that "contain" must agree with the singular noun "channel." So we know that we need the verb form "contains," which is choice (J), the right answer. (See this question's walkthrough on page 502 of this Black Book for more.)

Verb tenses

Verbs are actions that take place at a certain time. The action described by a verb can take place in the past, present, or future, and the form of a verb phrase changes according to the time frame when the verb's action takes place. We call these different forms of the verb "tenses."

In the following sentence, the verb "enjoyed" is in the past tense, which shows that the act of enjoying elementary school happened in the past. We can tell this because of the "*-ed*" suffix on the verb:

> I enjoyed elementary school.

In the following sentence, the verb "enjoy" is in the present tense, showing that the act of enjoying high school is happening now:

> I enjoy high school.

In the following sentence, the verb form "will enjoy" is in the future tense, which shows that the act of enjoying college will happen in the future:

> I will enjoy college.

You'll see some other verb forms on the test as well. These verb forms often involve forms of the verbs "to have" and "to be," which are often called "helping verbs" in this context. We don't need to know the names of these forms for ACT purposes, but we do need to be able to tell whether they describe actions in the past, present, or future.

On the ACT English section, any verb-form that uses the helping verb "to have" describes a completed action:

> We have gone there.

> Brian had considered studying Spanish before he went to Madrid.

In the above sentences, the verb forms "have gone" and "had considered" both involve the helping verb "to have," so we know they both describe completed actions:

- The phrase "we have gone" emphasizes that the action of going is completed at the time the sentence is being spoken.
- The phrase "had considered" shows that the action of considering was completed before Brian went to Madrid.

Verb forms that use a past-tense form of the helping verb "to be" describe an action in the past.

> She was looking for a computer.

In this sentence, the verb form "was looking" involves the word "was," which is a past-tense form of the helping verb "to be," so we know it describes an action taking place in the past.

On the ACT English section, any verb-form that uses a present-tense form of the helping verb *to be* describes an action in the present:

> She is thinking about buying a computer.

In the above sentence, the verb form "is thinking" involves the word "is," which is the present-tense form of the helping verb "to be," so we know it describes an action taking place in the present.

On the ACT English section, verbs in a sentence should generally describe actions in the same time frame whenever possible—that is, unless the passage involves words like "before" or "after," which specifically indicate that verb phrases are taking place in different time frames.

This would be an acceptable sentence on the ACT English section:

> I was making dinner when my parents arrived.

In the above sentence, all the verb forms ("was making" and "arrived") take place in the same time frame (the past).

This would be an unacceptable sentence on the ACT English section:

> *I was making dinner when my parents will arrive.

In the above sentence, the word "when" tells us that the two events happen simultaneously, but the verb forms "was making" and "will arrive" are in different tenses (past and future, respectively). This makes the above sentence logically impossible.

On the ACT English Section, verb tenses must be used in a way that's logically possible: we can't pick a choice that would cause the verb phrases in a sentence to describe events happening in an impossible order. For an example of a question that tests this issue, see question 33 from the English section of practice test 1 in the Red Book (test 2 in the 2020-2021 Red Book). The walkthrough for that question is on page 463 of this Black Book.

It can also sometimes be helpful to consider parallel structures in the surrounding text when determining which tense is appropriate for a verb. For more on that, see "Special Technique: Considering Parallelism when Answering ACT English Questions" on page 440.

Conjugating irregular verbs

English verbs are conjugated in ways that show their tenses. The ACT will sometimes test your familiarity with irregular verbs (in this case, verbs whose past-tense forms end in something other than "*-ed*").

> The manager has left for the day.

"Has left" is the past participle conjugation of the irregular verb "to leave."

Sometimes you'll see a verb-form on the ACT English section that isn't conjugated correctly. For example, this would be an unacceptable sentence on the ACT English section:

> *When he left to take a call, he <u>had gave</u> up his seat.

This sentence is wrong because "had gave" isn't the correct form of the verb "to give" in this situation. For some irregular verbs like "to give," a helping verb like "had" requires a special participle form of the verb—in this case, the proper form would be "he had given." (You don't have to know what the phrase "past participle" means to answer an ACT English question correctly—you just have to be able to recognize that some verb forms are inappropriate when a helping verb is present.)

There are at least two ways to fix a phrase like this: we can either switch in the proper participle form of the irregular verb "to give," or we can change "had gave" to a form that doesn't need a helping verb. So here are two corrected versions of this sentence:

When he left to take a call, he <u>had given</u> up his seat.

When he left to take a call, he <u>gave</u> up his seat.

Either of those two versions of the sentence could be grammatically acceptable on the ACT.

We can see a real-life example of this issue in question 42 from the English section of practice test 3 in the Red Book (form 16MC3 online if you have the 2020-2021 Red Book). The original sentence refers to a time "*long before interplanetary explorations <u>had began</u>." In this example, "*had began" is an inappropriate conjugation of the verb "to begin;" the correct past-participle form of this irregular verb in this phrase would be "had begun," which is what (J) says, so (J) is right. See this question's walkthrough on page 537 of this Black Book for more.

Verb-forms used as nouns
There are two verb forms that can be used as nouns: the "-ing" form of a verb, and the "to" form of a verb.

I love to dance.

Running is her hobby.

In these sentences, the verb phrase "to dance" is the object of the verb "love," and the verb form "running" is the subject of the verb "is."

It's also possible to make a verb phrase function like a noun within a sentence by placing the word "that" before the verb phrase. For example, the following phrase is a verb phrase:

you sing

If we place the word "that" in front of the verb phrase, then the phrase with "that" can function as a noun phrase in the following sentence:

I love that you sing.

In the above sentence, "that you sing" is essentially the object of the verb "love."

This issue comes up rarely on the ACT English section, but it's worth pointing out because it sometimes confuses people. We can see a question with a sentence that involves this issue in question 34 from the English section of practice test 3 in the Red Book (form 16MC3 online if you have the 2020-2021 Red Book). The walkthrough for that question is on page 534 of this Black Book.

Singular vs plural
One of the broadest and most common issues that comes up on the ACT English section is the distinction between the singular and plural forms of different kinds of words (whether nouns, verbs, or pronouns). This can come up in a lot of ways, and you should learn to keep a sharp eye out for all of them. For example, you might see the singular word "it" used incorrectly to refer to a plural noun. You might even see an incorrect sentence that says something like

*My brother and my sister both want to be an astronaut.

when the correct version would be

My brother and my sister both want to be astronauts.

since two people can't become a single astronaut.

This idea of the difference between singular and plural forms has already come up in this section in other situations, and we'll see plenty more of it in the walkthroughs starting on page 446 in this Black Book—it's just such a common issue that I wanted to call it to your attention here. Always remember to be on the lookout for issues related to the difference between singular and plural forms of words, especially in the context of verbs and pronouns.

Adjectives and adverbs
Adjectives are single words that describe nouns. You'll usually find an adjective right before the noun it describes, or as part of a list of other adjectives describing that noun.

Bowser is a tiny dog.

In this sentence, the word "tiny" is an adjective that describes the noun "dog."

If you want to modify something that isn't a noun—like a verb, adjective, or adverb—then you'll need to use the adverb form of the adjective. The adverb form of an adjective almost always ends in " -ly."

I quickly ran across the street to see what was happening.

In this sentence, the adverb "quickly" is used to modify the verb "ran." Notice that "ran" isn't a noun, so we must use an adverb to modify it.

On the ACT English Section, you'll sometimes see wrong answers that involve adjectives modifying words that aren't nouns, or adverbs modifying words that are nouns. Watch out for this!

This would be an unacceptable sentence on the ACT English section:

> *I walked slow through the halls so no one would hear me.

In the above sentence, the adjective "slow" is being incorrectly used to modify the verb "walked," which is not a noun. That means we should use the adverb form "slowly."

This would be an acceptable sentence on the ACT English section:

> I walked slowly through the halls so no one would hear me.

In the above sentence, the adverb "slowly" is correctly being used to modify the verb "walked."

Question 41 from the English section of practice test 1 in the Red Book (test 2 in the 2020-2021 Red Book) is an example of an ACT English question that focuses on this issue. You can find its walkthrough on page 467 of this Black Book.

Possessives

Luckily, the ACT's rules for possessives are actually pretty simple, even if they differ from today's common usage.

There are three things you need to know if you want to form possessives on the ACT.

First, you need to know how possessive pronouns are formed. Most people are comfortable with these possessive pronouns:

- my
- his
- her

The ones that sometimes cause trouble tend to be these:

- your
- its
- whose
- their

People often mix up those possessive pronouns with these contractions:

- The possessive pronoun "your" is confused with the contraction "you're," which is short for "you are."
- The possessive pronoun "its" is confused with the contraction "it's," which is short for "it is."
- The possessive pronoun "whose" is confused with the contraction "who's," which is short for "who is."
- The possessive pronoun "their" is confused with the contraction "they're," which is short for "they are."

So here's the rule to remember for these three troubling possessive pronouns: these possessive pronouns contain no apostrophes. If you're in a position where you have to choose between "its" and "it's," or "whose" and "who's," or "their" and "they're," remember that the choice with the apostrophe is a contraction, and the other is a possessive form. Whenever you see these contractions in a sentence or an answer choice, imagine them in their "un-contracted" state, and you should be able to tell if they're appropriate.

- "You're" with an apostrophe can always be read as "you are."
- "It's" with an apostrophe can always be read as "it is."
- "Who's" with an apostrophe can always be read as "who is."
- "They're" with an apostrophe can always be read as "they are."

Many people are unsure about sentences like these:

> *She sat in the car and honked <u>it's</u> horn.

> *<u>Who's</u> house is this?

But if we imagine the contractions in their "un-contracted" forms, the grammatical errors become a lot more obvious:

> *She sat in the car and honked <u>it is</u> horn.

> *<u>Who is</u> house is this?

When you get used to reading "it's" as "it is," "who's" as "who is," and "they're" as "they are," you won't be tricked by that kind of sentence.[1]

---

[1] One more bonus mistake: People sometimes confuse the word "there," which indicates a place, with the possessive pronoun "their," which indicates that something belongs to a group of people. In this case, the easiest thing to remember is probably that the word "there" has a spelling very similar to the spellings of the words "here" and "where," and all of those words are related to physical positions.

So, one more time, just to be clear:

The word "their" is a possessive pronoun and shows that a group of people own something: "They invited me to <u>their</u> house."

The word "they're" is always interchangeable with the phrase "they are:" "They said <u>they're</u> going to decide tomorrow."

The word "there" has a similar spelling to the word "where," and always shows position: "The car isn't here; it's over <u>there</u>."

The second thing to remember about possessives is that a PLURAL noun ending in "-s" will always form its possessive with a single apostrophe, and nothing more. Here are some examples:

> This toy belongs to the cats. It is the <u>cats'</u> toy.
>
> Those are the <u>girls'</u> bikes. Those bikes belong to the girls.
>
> That lawn mower belongs to the neighbors. It is the <u>neighbors'</u> lawn mower.

In each of these three situations, there's a plural noun that ends in "-s:"

- cats
- girls
- neighbors

To form a plural for each of those words, you just add an apostrophe, and don't change anything else:

- cats'
- girls'
- neighbors'

So that's the second rule: to form the possessive of a plural noun ending in "-s," just add an apostrophe to the end.

The third rule is that EVERY OTHER KIND OF NOUN forms its possessive by adding an apostrophe AND an "s." That's right: with the exception of pronouns, and plural nouns ending in "-s," every noun on the ACT forms its possessive with an apostrophe and an "s."

Here are a few examples of words that get an apostrophe and an "s" on the ACT. Note that many of these possessive forms differ from modern usage (and that includes the things your teachers might write):

> This ball belongs to my dog. It is my <u>dog's</u> ball.
>
> The game belongs to the children. It is the <u>children's</u> game.
>
> Jess has a car. It is <u>Jess's</u> car.
>
> The abacus has wooden beads. They are the <u>abacus's</u> wooden beads.
>
> The geese live on a pond. It is the <u>geese's</u> pond.

So let's do a quick review of the three possessive rules you need to know for the ACT:

1. The possessive pronouns "their," "whose," and "its" don't include apostrophes.
2. The possessive form of a plural noun ending in "-s" is formed by adding an apostrophe and nothing else.
3. The possessive form of EVERY OTHER KIND OF NOUN is formed by adding an apostrophe and an "-s," no matter what letter or sound the base noun ends in.

Once you learn these rules and see them in action on some real ACT practice questions, they'll become second nature.

For a real-life example of a question involving possessives, take a look at question 19 on page 481. The text says,

> *One panel is sewn into the piece's top border, the other into <u>it's</u> bottom border.

and we're given the opportunity to change "it's" to "its." Let's think about what's being said here. Are we trying to say "*into <u>it is</u> bottom border?" No, we're saying that the bottom border belongs to "it," which refers to the "piece." That means we need the possessive form of "it," which is choice (C), "its." (For more on this question, see its walkthrough on page 527 of this Black Book.)

Conjunctions

Conjunctions are words that we use to link ideas to each other, like the following:

> and   but   yet   either
> or   nor   because neither

On the ACT English section, two or more ideas that are linked by a conjunction must appear in the same form if possible. (This is one example of parallelism on the test, which we'll discuss in more detail on page 440 in this Black Book.) So this would be an acceptable sentence on the ACT English section:

> We like reading, learning, and thinking.

In the above sentence, the words "reading," "learning," and "thinking" are connected by the conjunction "and," and they're all in the same form (the "-ing" form), so this would be a good sentence on the ACT English section.

But the following would be an unacceptable sentence on the ACT English section:

> *We like to read, learning, and thinking.

In the above sentence, the phrases "to read," "learning," and "thinking" are all connected with the conjunction "and," but they're not all in the same form (one is in the "to" form, and two are in the "-ing" form), so this wouldn't be a good ACT English sentence. For an example of this issue, see question 5 from the English section of practice test 2 in the Red Book (test 3 in the 2020-2021 Red Book). Our walkthrough is on

Correlative conjunctions

Correlative conjunctions are sets of words that typically appear in the same sentence together, like the common expressions "either . . . or" and "neither . . . nor."

The following are some common examples of correlative conjunction pairs:

- both . . . and
- either . . . or
- just as . . . so
- neither . . . nor
- no sooner . . . than
- not only . . . but (also)
- whether . . . or

The following would be ACCEPTABLE uses of correlative conjunctions on the ACT English section:

> <u>Not only</u> is that my favorite chair, <u>but</u> it's <u>also</u> a family heirloom.

> Still, you have <u>neither</u> the right <u>nor</u> the power to make me call it a "chairloom."

(Note that in the case of the correlative conjunction "not only . . . but (also)," the word "also" doesn't *always* appear; when it does appear, it doesn't have to follow the word "but" immediately.)

The following would be UNACCEPTABLE uses of correlative conjunctions on the ACT English Section:

> *<u>Not only</u> is that my favorite chair, <u>or</u> it's a family heirloom.

> *Still, you have <u>neither</u> the right <u>and</u> the power to make me call it a "chairloom."

You can see an example of an ACT English question that involves this issue in question 35 from the English section of practice test 1 in the Red Book (test 2 in the 2020-2021 Red Book). Our walkthrough is on page 464 of this Black Book. (Remember you don't have to know the term "correlative conjunction" when you take the ACT; you just have to spot this issue when it comes up, and pick the choice that uses constructions like "either . . . or" correctly.)

Phrases and clauses

A phrase is a group of words that serves a particular function in a sentence. A phrase can include one word, or multiple words.

We refer to types phrases based on what they do in a given sentence—such as "noun phrases," "verb phrases," "prepositional phrases," etc. Consider this example sentence:

> My new neighbor really likes to build wooden furniture in his spare time.

In the above sentence,

- "My new neighbor" is a noun phrase.
- "Likes to build" is a verb phrase.
- "Wooden furniture" is a noun phrase.
- "In his spare time" is a prepositional phrase.

It's possible to pick out other phrases from this sentence, but I think you get the idea.

The ACT won't directly ask about names or roles of phrases, so don't worry if you're not totally comfortable with this concept. I'm just talking about it because it will make this section easier to understand.

Independent and dependent clauses

A clause is a group of words that includes a subject noun phrase, a verb phrase, and an object noun phrase (if necessary). The following is a clause:

> That gorilla doesn't like you.

In the above clause,

- "that gorilla" is a subject noun phrase
- "doesn't like" is a verb phrase
- "you" is an object noun phrase

Clauses are either "dependent" or "independent." An independent clause can stand on its own as a sentence, but a dependent clause can't.

A dependent clause generally begins with one of the following words or phrases:

- after
- although
- and
- as
- because
- before
- but
- even if
- even though
- if
- in order that
- once
- provided that
- rather than
- since
- so
- so that
- than
- that
- though
- unless
- until
- where/ wherever
- whether
- which/whichever
- while
- who/whom/whose
- whoever/ whomever/ whosever
- why

Most of the words and phrases in this list are conjunctions or relative pronouns, but you won't need to know those terms on test day, because the ACT English section doesn't require us to know the names of grammatical concepts. Just be aware that we might refer to a "conjunction" or a "relative pronoun" in the walkthroughs later in this book when we discuss dependent clauses that appear in official ACT practice questions, and that all you need to know is that those kinds of words often introduce dependent clauses.

(You may have heard of the acronym FANBOYS as a way to remember the set of words in the list above that are thought to appear most commonly in written American English: "for," "and," "nor," "but," "or," "yet," and "so." But you don't really need to memorize the above list, nor the acronym FANBOYS. Instead, you can just read through the above list a couple of times. After you start to work with real practice ACT English questions and read through the walkthroughs in this Black Book, you'll get comfortable with spotting dependent clauses.)

A dependent clause CANNOT stand on its own as a complete sentence, as we see in the following example:

> *so I barely move that toe

In the dependent clause above, which CANNOT stand alone as a sentence,

- "so" is a conjunction
- "I" is a subject pronoun
- "barely move" is a verb phrase
- "that toe" is a noun phrase

Every complete sentence in the ACT English section must include at least one independent clause. That clause can be as simple as a subject and a verb. (It may include an object, but it doesn't have to.)

Sentence fragments

On the ACT, a proper sentence isn't just any group of words with a period after it. Some groups of words are acceptable sentences, and some are missing key elements. These are all sentences:

> My sister loves to play basketball.
>
> The dog is barking in the front yard.
>
> If I don't hurry, I'm going to be late for work.

All of these groups of words describe someone or something doing something. They express a complete thought.
These are NOT sentences:

> *The man driving in the car next to me.
>
> *While I was waiting in line at the bank.
>
> *Because I was too tired to stand up anymore.

These groups of words are called "sentence fragments" because they aren't complete sentences by ACT standards. They might describe things, but they aren't complete in the way that a correct sentence is complete. These fragments leave questions unanswered, like the following:

- What *about* the man driving in the car next to you—what did he do, apart from just driving next to you?
- What happened *while* you were waiting in line at the bank?
- What happened *because* you were too tired to stand up anymore?

Notice that the problem with these fragments isn't just that it's possible to ask questions about them. The problem is that the fragment itself invites a question without offering an answer. Take another look at this fragment:

> *While I was waiting in line at the bank.

The word "while" specifically indicates the idea of some other thing that also happened during the period when "I was waiting in line at the bank." Without the word "while," we'd have a complete sentence, which would look like this:

> I was waiting in line at the bank.

Anything that prevents a sentence from containing an independent clause (as discussed on pages 426-427) turns that sentence into a fragment, and it's not really necessary or possible to go over all of those potential issues in this space. As a speaker of English, you already have an innate understanding of what makes something a sentence, and any major gaps in your understanding should be filled in by this training section, the question walkthroughs, and your own practice.

It's very important for you to be able to tell the difference between a complete sentence (which is acceptable on the ACT) and a fragment (which isn't). You might see a question about some text that looks like this:

> *I had the radio playing so I could listen to some <u>music. As</u> I was gardening.

The problem with this example is that "as I was gardening" is just a fragment, not a sentence, because the word "as" indicates a connection with something else that needs to be in the same sentence. In this case, the phrase about the gardening needs to be joined with the sentence "I had the radio playing so I could listen to some music."

So, for example, the following sentence would be one way to fix the above issue:

> I had the radio playing so I could listen to some <u>music as</u> I was gardening.

There's a real-life example of a sentence fragment issue in question 23 from the English section of practice test 2 in the Red Book (test 3 in the 2020-2021 Red Book). The original version of the underlined text in this question creates the following "sentence:"

> *Substituting *good morrow* for "good morning" and *gramercy* for "thank you."

The only choice that fixes this issue without creating other problems is (C), the right answer, which uses a comma to connect the original sentence fragment to the previous sentence:

> We also incorporated sixteenth-century English vocabulary into our speech, substituting *good morrow* for "good morning" and *gramercy* for "thank you."

(For a more detailed discussion of this question, see its walkthrough on page 492 later in this Black Book.)

Run-on sentences and comma splices

You may also see something like this:

> *I grabbed my umbrella on my way out the <u>door it was</u> raining outside and I didn't want to get wet.

In this case, you need to recognize that you're actually looking at two groups of words that could each be independent sentences on their own—only there's no punctuation separating them. This situation is called a "run-on sentence," and it's not acceptable on the ACT.

A similar problem with the same "sentence" could look like this:

> *I grabbed my umbrella on my way <u>out the door, it was</u> raining outside and I didn't want to get wet.

In this case, the two groups of words that could each be sentences are separated by a comma. We call this situation a "comma splice," and it's also not acceptable on the ACT. So the difference between a run-on sentence and a comma splice is that a run-on sentence is two sentences with no punctuation in between them, and a comma splice is two sentences with only a comma between them. You don't actually have to remember which one is which when you take the ACT; you just have to be able to recognize that both of them are unacceptable.

On the ACT, there are two equally acceptable types of punctuation for separating two groups of words that could be complete sentences on their own:

- the period
- the semicolon

That means that either of the two following versions would be equally acceptable on the ACT English section:

> I grabbed my umbrella on my way out the <u>door. It was</u> raining outside and I didn't want to get wet.

> I grabbed my umbrella on my way out the <u>door; it was</u> raining outside and I didn't want to get wet.

The first version adds a period and capitalizes the letter "I" in the word "it." The second version just adds a semicolon between "door" and "it."

Again, these are both equally acceptable ways to divide the two sentences. Neither version is better or worse than the other on the ACT. If you see a situation like this on the ACT, you won't have to choose between a period or a semicolon to separate the two sentences, since both are acceptable. Either you'll see only one of the two in the answer choices, or—if you *do* see both—there will be some other difference between the options that makes one or both of them wrong.

The issue of run-on sentences and comma splices comes up in Question 41 from the English section of practice test 3 in the Red Book (form 16MC3 online if you have the 2020-2021 Red Book). Choice (A), the original version of the underlined portion, creates a comma splice because it uses a comma to join two sets of words that could each be a sentence by themselves. Choice (B) removes the comma and changes the wording slightly, which results in a run-on sentence. Choice (C) appropriately puts a period where the comma appeared in the original version of the sentence, creating two acceptable sentences. (Choice (D) combines the problems in (A) and (B), resulting in a slightly different comma splice from the one in the original version.) The right answer is (C), the only choice that doesn't create a run-on sentence or a comma splice. (For a more detailed discussion of this question, see its walkthrough on page 537 of this Black Book.)

Who versus whom

You'll occasionally see ACT English questions that require you to choose between "who" and "whom." For example, you may see a sentence like this:

> This is the man <u>who</u> taught me how to ride a bike.

Then, you may have to decide whether "who" or "whom" (or something else) is appropriate in this space. In the case above, "who" is the correct choice. You use the word "who" to describe something or someone doing an action. Here, the word "who" refers to "the man," and "the man" does the action indicated by the word "taught."

You use "whom" to describe someone who's being acted upon, like in this sentence:

> He is also the man <u>whom</u> I accidentally hit with my bike before I knew how to ride it.

In this sentence, the word "whom" is correct because it refers to someone receiving the action of getting hit. "Whom" refers to "the man," and in this sentence "the man" receives the action of being "hit with my bike."

Here's another way to think about it that's simpler for most people. It involves turning a sentence into a question, and then figuring out how that question would be answered. Let's take a look.

Imagine you need to evaluate a sentence like this:

This is the man <u>who</u> taught me how to ride a bike.

Turn it into a question:

*(Who/whom) taught me how to ride a bike?

Then answer it:

<u>He</u> taught me how to ride a bike.

If you'd use "he" to answer the question, then "who" is the proper form.

If you'd use "him" to answer the question, then "whom" is the proper form (you can remember this because they both end in "m").

Let's do it with the other sentence:

He is also the man <u>whom</u> I accidentally hit with my bike before I knew how to ride it.

Turn it into a question:

*(Who/whom) did I accidentally hit with my bike?

Then answer it:

I hit <u>him</u> with my bike.

Since we'd answer the question with "him," we know the proper form in the original sentence would be "whom."

So remember that "who" corresponds with "he," and "whom" corresponds with "him" (again, you can remember that because both "whom" and "him" end with the letter "m").

Of course, if the sentence has to do with a girl or a woman, you can just mentally switch out "she" for "he," and "her" for "him," or you can always think of it in terms of female pronouns if you want to. I just prefer to teach it in terms of "he" and "him" because "he" and "who" sound kind of similar, and so do "him" and "whom," which usually makes it easier for people to remember the correct usages of the words.

Let's look at this in one more example. Imagine we had to choose the correct version of this sentence:

*That's the boy to (who/whom) I gave all my toys.

When we read that, we might ask ourselves, "To (who/whom) did you give all your toys?" The answer to this question would be "I gave all my toys to him." Because I'd answer with "him" (or "her" if it were a girl), I know that the correct form in the original sentence is "whom:"

That's the boy to <u>whom</u> I gave all my toys.

There's a real-life example of this in question 25 from the English section of practice test 2 in the Red Book (test 3 in the 2020-2021 Red Book). The original sentence mentions the idea of

*pretending to be a person <u>whom had lived</u> in a different country and century.

When we look at the original sentence, we can see that "whom" is wrong and "who" would be correct, because the sentence describes "a person" doing the action of the verb "had lived." Since the person being described by who/whom is *doing* the action of living in this case, not receiving the action, we know that we need the "who" form, as in choice (D).

If we wanted to turn the sentence into a question, we would say "(Who/whom) had lived in a different country and century?" The answer would be "He had lived in a different country and century." Since we know that "he" corresponds to "who," we can again see that the "who" form is needed, which we find in the right answer, choice (D). (For a more detailed discussion of this question, see the walkthrough on page 494 in this Black Book.)

We can still use this approach when a question involves a plural noun; we just use "they" or "them" to answer the question:

- "they" functions like "he" or "who." It refers to nouns that perform actions (note that each word ends in a vowel sound).
- "them" functions like "him" or "whom." It refers to nouns that receive actions (note that all three words end in "m").

Let's look at an example with a plural noun this time. Imagine we had to choose the correct version of this sentence:

*Those are the kids to (who/whom) I gave all my toys.

When we read that, we might ask ourselves,

To (who/whom) did you give all your toys?

The answer to this question would be

I gave all my toys to <u>them</u>.

Because I'd answer with "them," I know that the correct form in the original sentence is "whom:"

> Those are the kids to <u>whom</u> I gave all my toys.

Comparisons

On the ACT English section, we can only make comparisons between things of the same kind. For example, we're not allowed to choose a sentence like this on the ACT:

> *The population of Tokyo is larger than Idaho.

The ACT wouldn't accept that sentence because it technically compares a *population* to a *place*, instead of comparing a population to a population, or a place to a place.

Acceptable versions of the above sentence could look like this:

> The population of Tokyo is larger than the population of Idaho.

> The population of Tokyo is larger than that of Idaho.

In these sentences, it's clear that we're comparing the populations of the two places, instead of comparing the population of one place to the other place itself, which is illogical.

This idea doesn't appear frequently, but if an underlined phrase on the ACT English section involves a comparison, then you should check whether that comparison is between two things of the same type. One example of an ACT question that involves this concept is number 73 from the English section of practice test 2 in the Red Book (test 3 in the 2020-2021 Red Book); our walkthrough for that question is on page 517 of this Black Book.

Comparatives and superlatives

Comparatives and superlatives are types of words that are used to describe how some things relate to other things. The comparative version of an adjective or adverb either ends in "-er" or begins with the word "more" or "less." Here are some examples of comparatives:

> smarter   bigger   happier
>
> more intelligent   less disgusting   more quickly

The superlative version of an adjective or adverb either ends in "-est" or begins with the word "most" or "least." Here are some examples of superlatives:

> smartest   biggest   happiest
>
> most intelligent   least disgusting   most quickly

Some words have irregularly-formed comparatives and superlatives, but luckily they're very common, well-known forms. Here are a couple of examples:

> better, best
>
> more, most

There's one more important note on this topic. Comparative forms are created using EITHER "-er" OR "more/less," and superlative forms are created using EITHER "-est" OR "most/least." You NEVER form a comparative using both "-er" AND "more/less," or a superlative using both "-est," AND "most/least." That means phrases like these are wrong on the ACT:

> *more happier
>
> *most biggest

Like a lot of concepts that come up on the English section, this is something you're probably already familiar with on an unconscious level, but you might not be sure which version is correct when someone asks you about it—so make sure you're comfortable with this idea.

There's an example involving a comparative phrase in question 50 from the English section of practice test 1 in the Red Book (test 2 in the 2020-2021 Red Book). The underlined portion of the sentence is "*more sturdier than." As we just discussed, we know that we can't form a comparative with both "-er" AND "more/less," so we know that the original version of the underlined phrase must be wrong. Choice (G) is right, because it gets rid of the word "more" and substitutes the word "much," which doesn't cause any problems in this context. Note that (J) incorrectly uses the word "then" instead of "than" in the comparison, and (H) combines the errors in (F) and (J). (For more on this question, see its walkthrough on page 471 in this Black Book.)

Finally, as we just saw in our brief discussion of (J) for question 50 from the English section of practice test 1 in the Red Book (test 2 in the 2020-2021 Red Book), remember that we use the word "than" to compare two things—not the word "then."

Colons

Colons can be used on the ACT to introduce a phrase that demonstrates a previously mentioned concept.

> Marian brought three things with her to the beach: a towel, some sunscreen, and a hat.

In this sentence, the phrase "a towel, some sunscreen, and a hat" demonstrates the previously mentioned concept of Marian bringing "three things with her to the beach."

On the ACT English section, a colon can only be placed after a group of words that could stand on its own as a sentence, as we saw in the above two examples: both "there's one thing I love about going to the movies" and "Marian brought three things with her to the beach" could be sentences on their own.

On the ACT, a single sentence can't have more than one colon.

Semicolons

Semicolons are acceptable in two situations on the ACT English section, and the first one is far more common than the second:

    1. Semicolons can separate two sets of words that could each stand on their own as sentences

    2. Semicolons can separate listed items in a "super series."

Two sets of words that could each stand on their own as sentences on the ACT can be separated by a semicolon. So this would be an acceptable sentence on the ACT English section:

> I wonder what time it is; I'll go check the clock.

In the above sentence, the phrases "I wonder what time it is" and "I'll go check the clock" are both acceptable sentences, so they can be correctly separated by a semicolon.

This would be an unacceptable sentence on the ACT English section:

> *They decided to stay home; because it was raining.

In the above sentence, the phrase "they decided to stay home" is an acceptable sentence, and the phrase "because it was raining" is a sentence fragment. Since these aren't both acceptable sentences, we can't separate them with a semicolon on the ACT English section.

We can see an example of an ACT English question that tests this concept directly if we look at question 39 from the English section of practice test 1 in the Red Book (test 2 in the 2020-2021 Red Book). The right answer to that question is (C), which would result in the following sentence:

> Some of these blue holes open to small contained <u>caves;</u> others open to miles-long interconnected tunnels.

Note, once more, that all the words before the semicolon could stand on their own as a sentence, and all the words after the semicolon could also stand on their own as a sentence. (For a full analysis of this question, see its walkthrough on page 466 of this Black Book.)

The second usage of semicolons on the ACT English section comes up much less frequently, and you almost certainly won't see it on test day. Still, the ACT has tested it in the past, so I'll cover it here.

This second issue is that the ACT also allows semicolons to be used to separate items in a "super series." A super series is a series of things that includes another series of things. The items in the sub-series are separated by commas, and the items in the super series are separated by semicolons. That might sound confusing, so let's look at an example.

> I like indoor sports; water sports, including water skiing, kneeboarding, and surfing; and outdoor sports.

In the above sentence, the sub-series is "water skiing, kneeboarding, and surfing." The super series is "indoor sports; water sports . . . ; and outdoor sports."

Commas on the ACT English Section

Commas can appear in a variety of ways on test day, so it's important that you read the walkthroughs starting on page 446 of this Black Book, so you can get a strong idea of what ACT comma placement questions are actually like.

Before we get started, it's important to note that we should approach comma placement with the attitude that it's better to *avoid* commas unless we have an actual, concrete reason to use one! In other words, if a phrase would be grammatically acceptable without commas, then the ACT wants us to leave out commas.

The acceptable comma usages that we might see tested on the ACT English section fall into the following main categories:

    1. commas used to divide items in a list of three or more things (including the so-called "Oxford comma," which we'll discuss in a moment)

    2. commas between dependent clauses and independent clauses

    3. "comma sandwiches," which show that the sandwiched phrase could be removed from a sentence without creating any grammatical issues or changing the meaning of the rest of the sentence

We'll discuss each of these uses in more detail now.

Commas in a list of three or more things

On the ACT, if we have a list of three or more items, then a comma is placed after each item except the last item, and the word "and" appears before the last item in the list. For example, the following sentence would be acceptable on the ACT English section:

> Thomasina had always liked falcons, ravens, eagles, and cardinals.

But the following sentence wouldn't be okay on this section, because it omits the comma before the word "and:"

> *Thomasina had always liked falcons, ravens, eagles and cardinals.

(You may have heard someone call the comma that appears before the word "and" in these kinds of lists the "Oxford comma." If you've never heard that term, don't worry about it—you don't need to know it on the ACT. I only mention it because it has become fashionable in the last few years to omit the Oxford comma in some types of writing. It's important to remember that the ACT English section REQUIRES the Oxford comma, even if your teachers might prefer you to avoid it in school.)

Also note that the ACT doesn't want us to use both a comma and the word "and" if we're only dealing with a list of two items. In other words, if a list only includes two things, then we should join those two things with the word "and;" there should NOT be a comma before or after the "and" in that case.

Finally, note that this issue isn't always the entire focus of a question on the ACT, but it may play a role in helping you identify the right answer to a question that touches on other grammatical issues as well. For an example of this, see question 43 from the English section of practice test 1 in the Red Book (test 2 in the 2020-2021 Red Book), which involves creating a comma-separated list of three groups of things that divers have found in an area. The walkthrough for that question is on page 468 of this Black Book.

Lists of two things

Sometimes you'll encounter an underlined phrase on the ACT that involves a list of two things—in other words, just any two nouns joined by the word "and." It's important to remember there should NOT be a comma immediately before or after the word "and" in a list of two things on the ACT English section.

Let's look at an example of this in the Red Book.

Question 20 from the English section of practice test 1 (test 2 in the 2020-2021 Red Book) involves the underlined phrase "products and businesses." Choice (H) gives us the option to add a comma before "and" to create the phrase ""*products, and businesses." We know (H) can't be correct, because no comma should appear before the word "and" in a list of two things. (See the walkthrough for this question on page 457 in this Black Book for more.)

Commas between dependent clauses and independent clauses

When a dependent clause appears immediately before an independent clause in a sentence, a comma is placed after the dependent clause.

No comma is necessary between an independent clause and a dependent clause when the independent clause comes immediately before the dependent clause—unless the dependent clause begins with a form of "which" or "who." Consider the following examples:

> Before I fell asleep, I was watching the movie.
>
> I was watching the movie until I fell asleep.
>
> The movie was directed by my great-aunt, who studied under Kubrick.

In the first example sentence above, the dependent clause "before I fell asleep" appears before the independent clause "I was watching the movie," so the clauses are separated by a comma. In the second example sentence, the order of the clauses is reversed, so no comma is necessary. In the third example sentence, the dependent clause begins with "who," so we separate that clause from the independent clause with a comma.

"Comma sandwiches"

"Comma sandwich" isn't a technical grammatical term, of course. It's something I made up to help test-takers remember a useful concept. As the name implies, a "comma sandwich" is a phrase "sandwiched" between two commas (or between a comma and a period, if the end of the comma sandwich is also the end of the sentence). This type of phrase isn't a complete sentence or a part of a list. Instead, it's a descriptive phrase that provides additional information about something in a sentence.

When a comma sandwich is used properly according to the rules of the ACT English section, the entire sandwiched phrase can be removed, leaving behind a complete sentence, without changing the meaning of the rest of the sentence.

Let's look at a couple of examples of this so you can actually see what I'm talking about. In these examples, I'll underline the "comma sandwich:"

> The man next door, <u>who told us we could borrow his lawn mower</u>, was always very helpful.

In the above sentence, removing the comma sandwich gives us this:

> The man next door was always very helpful.

Here's another example. Imagine we start with this sentence:

> The orange shirt, <u>which is the one I wanted to wear</u>, isn't clean right now.

Removing the comma sandwich gives us this:

> The orange shirt isn't clean right now.

In each case, we see that a complete sentence with the same original meaning is still left behind when the commas and the phrase between them are removed.

Let's look at our two examples again, this time with comma placement that wouldn't be okay on the ACT English section:

> *The man next door, <u>who told us we</u>, could borrow his lawn mower was always very helpful.

Removing the phrase between the commas in the above sentence would leave us with the following, which would be unacceptable on the ACT:

> *The man next door could borrow his lawn mower was always very helpful.

Here's another example of an unacceptable use of commas on the ACT:

> *The orange shirt, which is the one I wanted to wear isn't clean, right now.

Removing the phrase between the commas would give us this unacceptable fragment:

> *The orange shirt right now.

(Note that in cases where three commas are potentially involved in comma sandwiches, all the normal rules apply, and we must be able to remove either comma sandwich—or both comma sandwiches—and leave behind an acceptable sentence with the same core meaning.)

There are a few different ways that the ACT might test us on comma sandwiches. We might see something like the previous examples where the whole sandwich is underlined, or there might be an underlined segment that only overlaps with a portion of the comma sandwich.

For a real-life example of the comma sandwich, take a look at question 28 from the English section of practice test 1 in the Red Book (test 2 in the 2020-2021 Red Book). The walkthrough for that question appears on page 461 of this Black Book.

No comma sandwich when a profession is indicated immediately before a name

We'll sometimes find that a passage mentions a person's occupation immediately before the person's name, instead of after the person's name with the help of a phrase like "who is a." When the profession is mentioned immediately before the name, the ACT doesn't allow us to use a comma sandwich. So, for example, these phrases would be acceptable on the ACT English section:

> We read about famous astronaut Buzz Aldrin in class.

> My favorite song is *Hungarian Rhapsody #2* by composer Ferenc Liszt.

When the profession is mentioned immediately after the name, a comma sandwich is needed:

> Buzz Aldrin, a famous astronaut, was the subject of an article we read.

> Ferenc Liszt, a composer, created some of my favorite music.

Comma sandwiches at the beginning or end of a sentence

Of course, if a sandwiched phrase appears at the very beginning of a sentence, then the initial comma is omitted, because we can't start a sentence with a comma.

Similarly, if a sandwiched phrase appears at the very end of a sentence, then the final comma is omitted, because we can't include a comma immediately next to a period, exclamation point, or question mark.

Other "punctuation sandwiches"

You may see the "comma sandwich" concept on the test with dashes or parentheses around the sandwiched phrase, instead of commas. These other "punctuation sandwiches" function just like "comma sandwiches" on the ACT.

One last note: any punctuation sandwich must have the same punctuation on either side of the sandwich. For example, on the ACT English section, you could have a comma sandwich with commas on either end, or you could have a dash sandwich with dashes on either end, but you can't have a sandwich with a dash on one end and a comma on the other end. (The only exception to this would be the situation we described earlier where the sandwich appears at the beginning of the sentence—in which case there is no punctuation at the beginning of the sandwich—or the sandwich appears at the end of the sentence, in which case the sandwich ends with a period.)

No commas after conjunction expressions (unless a comma sandwich is involved)

Some people will be tempted to use commas by default after conjunction phrases, especially "and," "unless," and "such as." But we're not allowed to use commas after these expressions on the ACT (unless the comma is part of a comma sandwich), so the following sentences would be unacceptable on the ACT English section, for example:

> *The Senator picked up the phone and, ordered a pizza.

> *Unless, this time will be different, I don't think playing canasta is a good idea.

> *Jerry has always had a problem with dogs, such as, Pomeranians and Malamutes.

Instead, these versions would be acceptable on the ACT:

> The Senator picked up the phone and ordered a pizza.

> Unless this time will be different, I don't think playing canasta is a good idea.

> Jerry has always had a problem with dogs, such as Pomeranians and Malamutes.

Of course, it's possible to insert a comma sandwich immediately after a conjunction expression:

> The Senator picked up the phone and, with tears in his eyes, ordered a pizza.

Commas between two adjectives

Sometimes you'll encounter ACT English questions that give you the option to place a comma between two adjectives that describe a noun:

- When both adjectives describe the noun interchangeably, and could appear in either order, a comma should be placed between them.
- When the adjectives aren't interchangeable, and must appear in a set order, no comma should be placed between them.

That may sound a little a confusing, but it will make more sense after we look at a couple of examples.

Question 71 from the English section of practice test 1 in the Red Book (test 2 in the 2020-2021 Red Book) gives us the option to put a comma between the adjectives "smaller" and "quicker." Both of these adjectives describe the noun "vessels." The relevant phrase appears in the passage as "smaller, quicker vessels." We could also switch those two adjectives without changing the meaning of the sentence or creating any issues, so the phrase would say "quicker, smaller vessels". Because we can switch the adjectives in this way, we know the comma should appear between the two adjectives. (See this question's walkthrough on page 480 of this Black Book for more.)

On the other hand, question 48 from the English section of practice test 3 in the Red Book (form 16MC3 online if you have the 2020-2021 Red Book) gives us the option to put a comma between the adjectives "dusty" and "back," which both describe the noun "rooms." The relevant phrase appears in the passage as "*dusty, back rooms." In this case, we can't switch the adjectives without causing an issue, because "*dusty, back rooms" refers to back rooms that are dusty, while "*back, dusty rooms" describes rooms that are both "back" and "dusty," which doesn't really make any sense. Since we can't switch the two adjectives without causing problems, the comma shouldn't appear, and the right version of the phrase is "dusty back rooms." (See this question's walkthrough on page 540 of this Black Book for more.)

Dashes

A dash is a punctuation mark that looks like an elongated hyphen (—). On the ACT English section, dashes can only be used in two scenarios:

1. to create a punctuation sandwich as described on page 433 of this Black Book
2. to function as a colon would, by providing an example or explanation of a concept from a preceding group of words that could be a sentence on their own (see page 430 for a description of the proper usage of colons on the ACT)

Dangling participles

A participle is a special verb-form; on the ACT English section, a question that focuses on a participle will most likely use a verb that ends in "-ing," but it might also use a verb that ends in "-ed" or "-en." A phrase that begins with a participle can be called a "participial phrase." A participle will often appear in a phrase at the beginning of a sentence, joined to an independent clause with a comma. (But participial phrases can also appear at the end of a sentence, joined to an independent clause with a comma.)

On the ACT English section, participial phrases are always understood to refer to the first noun phrase in the independent clause in the sentence. Consider this example, which would be acceptable on the ACT:

Sitting on the park bench, Alma watched the sun set.

In the sentence above,

- "sitting" is a participle
- "sitting on the park bench" is the participial phrase (beginning with the participle "sitting," an "-ing" word)
- "Alma watched the sun set" is the independent clause (see "Independent and dependent clauses" on page 426)

This sentence specifically says that the action of the word "sitting" is performed by Alma, because "Alma" is the first noun phrase in the independent clause.

The following sentence, on the other hand, would be unacceptable on the ACT:

*Sitting on the park bench, the sun set while Alma watched.

In the sentence above,

- "sitting" is a participle
- "sitting on the park bench" is the participial phrase (beginning with the participle "sitting," an "-ing" word)
- "the sun set while Alma watched" is the independent clause (see "Independent and dependent clauses" on page 426)

What's wrong with the above sentence? We still have a participial phrase ("sitting on the park bench") and an independent clause ("the sun set while Alma watched"), but the problem is that the participle in this sentence can't be an action performed by the first noun phrase in the independent clause, which is "the sun." This sentence literally says that the sun is the thing that's sitting on the bench as it sets.

Let's look at one more example, this time with the participial phrase appearing at the end of the sentence:

Moira began to forget what hope felt like, waiting at the DMV.

We can see that "Moira" is the first noun in the independent clause, so this sentence says that Moira was the one doing the waiting, according to the rules of ACT English.

An unacceptable version of a similar sentence might look like this:

*Hopelessness overwhelmed Moira, waiting at the DMV.

This sentence would be unacceptable on the ACT English section because it technically says that the *hopelessness* was the thing waiting at the DMV.

You can see an example of this issue in question 27 from the English section of practice test 3 in your copy of *The Official ACT Prep Guide* (form 16MC3 online if you have the 2020-2021 Red Book). This question asks about an underlined phrase that appears right after a phrase that begins "establishing her own hair products business…" The only noun in each version of the underlined phrase that could possibly be described by the phrase "establishing her own hair products business" is "Madam C. J. Walker."

Every answer choice features the noun phrase "Madam C. J. Walker," but only the right answer places this phrase at the beginning of the underlined portion of the text, so that the phrase "Madam C. J. Walker" would come immediately after the phrase that begins "establishing her own hair products business…" The resulting sentence reads,

> Establishing her own hair products business in the first decade of the twentieth century, Madam C. J. Walker later bequeathed…

(For a more detailed discussion of this question and the other answer choices, see its walkthrough on page 530 in this Black Book.)

Proximity

When a phrase on the ACT English section describes or refers to another phrase, the ACT wants those two phrases to be as close to each other as possible, to keep the meaning clear. Let's look at a couple of examples.

This is an example of poor phrase placement on the ACT:

> *Tomorrow I'll get that report done, which is when it's due.

This is an example of good phrase placement on the ACT:

> I'll get that report done tomorrow, which is when it's due.

The phrase "which is when it's due" refers to "tomorrow," so we want the word "tomorrow" to be moved so that the two phrases are next to each other if possible.

Here's another example of poor phrase placement on the ACT:

> *The station won't dispense gasoline for anyone in plastic containers.

This is an example of good phrase placement on the ACT:

> The station won't dispense gasoline in plastic containers for anyone.

The first version of the sentence says that the station won't dispense gas for you if you show up in a plastic container. The second version says that nobody who comes to the station can get gas dispensed into a plastic container, no matter who they are. For an example of an ACT question that tests this idea, see question 68 from the English section of practice test 2 in the Red Book (test 3 in the 2020-2021 Red Book). Our walkthrough for that question is on page 514 of this Black Book.

Prepositional idioms

We need to take a minute to talk about prepositional idioms for two main reasons: they occasionally come up on the ACT, and they involve a concept that many test preparation resources explain poorly.

The word "idiom" has two different meanings. In a loose sense, the "idiom of a language" is the natural way that native speakers of that language communicate. In a stricter sense, an idiom is an individual phrase that's considered to be grammatically correct for reasons that can't be predicted or explained by a grammatical rule. In other words, this second type of idiom is an expression that's simply right because it's right, even though it has no detectable similarity to any other correct phrase.

This second type of idiom is the type I'm referring to when I talk about idioms on the ACT. Let's consider a quick example. You're probably familiar with the phrase "to fall in love." Why isn't it "*to fall *with* love" or "*to fall *to* love?" There's no logical reason for one of those phrases to be acceptable while the other two aren't—love isn't a physical substance or location, so people can't literally fall "in" love any more than they can literally fall "to" love or "with" love. This phrase just uses the preposition "in" because that's how English-speakers have spoken for a long time.

In other words, if you weren't already familiar with this phrase and you had to pick which preposition to use with it, there would be no rule you could follow that would predict the right answer. You'd just have to guess and hope you were right. And that's what makes this phrase's use of "in" truly idiomatic in the strict sense of that word: it's a one-of-a-kind expression that it doesn't follow any rule that applies to any other use of the word "in."

Luckily, on the ACT we only need to think about things being strictly "idiomatic" in a limited number of questions.

These questions will often involve prepositional phrases you've probably heard before, like "to fall in love." Prepositions are short words like "in," "at," "to," "by," "with," "for," and so on. (Not all short words are prepositions, and not all prepositions are short words, but prepositions are usually short words.) Many languages use prepositions idiomatically, and English is one of them. Here are a few more phrases that depend on idiomatic usage of prepositions, with those prepositions underlined:

> to be <u>on</u> time
>
> to depend <u>on</u> something
>
> to jump <u>to</u> a conclusion

to be all <u>for</u> something

In these phrases, the only way to know which preposition is correct is to be familiar with each phrase beforehand. If you've never heard the phrase before, there's no way to predict the correct preposition to go with it.

Some students have asked me if they should try to memorize a list of idioms in the hope that something from the list might show up on test day, but the odds are very much against that, and the energy you'd spend on that would definitely be better spent somewhere else. For one thing, there are tons of these kinds of idioms in English, and there doesn't seem to be any restriction on the ones the ACT occasionally tests; for another thing, you probably already know a lot of idioms if you're halfway decent at speaking English; for a third thing, there aren't very many ACT English questions that rely on idioms anyway.

So if you see a question that seems to be asking about a prepositional idiom, you should go with your gut instinct about which version of the phrase sounds right to you. There's no point in wasting time trying to figure something out that literally can't be figured out, because it doesn't follow any rules by definition.

As an example, Question 63 from the English section of practice test 1 in the Red Book (test 2 in the 2020-2021 Red Book) asks about the prepositional idiom in the phrase "chance of surviving," as opposed to the phrase "*chance to survive." In the context of the sentence, "of" is the correct preposition—but, again, this is impossible to predict from any broad rules about the word "of" and "to." It's just something you have to know already to answer with total certainty. (For more on this question, see the walkthrough on page 476 in this Black Book.)

Since there's no real rule governing this type of question, and since it appears rarely, I suggest you spend your energies working on other issues. When you do see a question like this on test day, go with your gut instinct and move on.

Remember that most ACT English questions *do* follow rules and patterns, so you should be able to answer almost every ACT English question you see with certainty and confidence if you know the test's rules. If you feel like you're encountering lots of idiomatic phrases (in the strict sense) when you practice with the Red Book, then you're misunderstanding or misreading the passages and/or the questions—because they just aren't that common.

(By the way, a lot of test-prep resources like to describe almost any acceptable word usage as "idiomatic," using the loose sense of the term. This is basically like saying that something is correct because it's correct—which isn't very helpful if you're trying to learn *why* a phrase is acceptable or unacceptable. Look out for that. On the ACT, the only strictly idiomatic phrases you'll encounter are similar to the ones we just talked about. When talking about ACT English questions, this Black Book will only use the word "idiomatic" in its strict sense, to describe the few phrases on the ACT that can't be predicted by rules.)

Confused homophones

A homophone group is a group of words or phrases that have the same pronunciation, but different meanings and spellings. The ACT occasionally likes to test your awareness of these groups by requiring you to choose which homophone is appropriate in a given context.

Some frequently confused homophones are listed below.

"then" and "than"

- "Then" is an adverb used to indicate a time when something occurred, as in this sentence:

> Then it happened.

The word "then" can also be used to signal the second half of a conditional statement with the word "if," as in this sentence:

> If it keeps raining then we'll need to wear boots when we go outside.

We can remember that "then" is related to time expressions because it has a spelling that's very similar to the word "when."

- "Than" is used when we're comparing two things, as in the sentence:

> This dog is nicer than that one.

"*Would of"

This doesn't come up too often on the ACT, but you still need to be aware of it.

When people speak, they often pronounce the phrase "would have" so it sounds just like the nonsense phrase "*would of." This is such a widespread error that some test-takers will read a sentence like this one and never notice a mistake:

> *I <u>would of</u> done that sooner if I were you.

The sentence should read:

> I <u>would have</u> done that sooner if I were you.

You can see a real-life example of this issue in question 47 on the English section of test 3 in the Red Book. The underlined portion of the text is "would of been," which needs to be changed to "would have been," so choice (B) is correct. (For a more detailed discussion of this question, see its walkthrough on page 540 in this Black Book.)

"there," "their," and "they're"

We discussed this homophone group earlier, when we talked about possessive pronouns on page 424. As a refresher, we should remember that "there" indicates location (and has a spelling very similar to "where"), while "their" is a possessive pronoun and "they're" is always short for "they are."

"its" and "it's"

We also discussed this homophone group on page 424. To review, we should remember that "its" is a possessive pronoun and "it's" is always short for "it is."

"your" and "you're"

This is another homophone group we discussed earlier, when we talked about possessive pronouns on page 424. We should remember that "your" is a possessive pronoun and "you're" is always short for "you are."

"whose" and "who's"

This is another homophone group we mentioned on page 424. "Whose" is the possessive form of "who," while "who's" is always short for "who is."

Less commonly confused homophones

Homophones that are confused relatively rarely could include groups like "past" and "passed," or "principle" and "principal." It's unlikely that you'll see these particular homophones on test day, but the ACT could decide to test you on some other group of rarely confused homophones.

"Which would be least acceptable?"

This is a special type of style question that has a prompt. The prompt will ask which answer choice is the LEAST acceptable alternative to the underlined portion of the sentence. Three of the choices will be acceptable according to the ACT, and one will not.

It may sound silly to point this out, but I want to stress the importance of noticing the word LEAST in all capital letters in the prompt. You'd be surprised how often test-takers ignore this word and pick one of the three acceptable options instead of the one unacceptable option. Always read each prompt carefully, and make sure you consider every answer choice before moving on to the next question as we discussed on page 42 of this Black Book!

(Question 57 from the English section of practice test 3 in the Red Book, which is form 16MC3 online if you have the 2020-2021 Red Book, is a good example of this kind of situation. You can read its walkthrough on page 545 of this Black Book.)

Redundancy

Redundancy is an important concept in ACT English questions that deal with grammar, style, and punctuation. In these questions, we basically want to avoid answer choices with a word or phrase that restates something that's already clearly stated somewhere else in the surrounding text. (You may notice that this is different from how we treat the concept of restatement when dealing with ACT English questions based on reading comprehension! More on that in a minute.)

For example, imagine we have a choice between these two sentences:

> *My house is in the space next to the library.
>
> My house is next to the library.

The ACT would reward the second sentence, because the first sentence contains the unnecessary phrase "in the space." When we say that something is "next to" something else, it's already understood that we're talking about physical spaces, so the phrase "in the space" would need to be avoided if this were a sentence on the ACT English section.

Here's another example:

> *John always chose the aisle seat every time he flew.
>
> John chose the aisle seat every time he flew.

In this example, the second sentence would be preferred on the ACT. The original sentence already contains the phrase "every time he flew," so the word "always" isn't necessary, and the ACT would reward you for avoiding it in this situation.

Notice that the example about the seat requires us to notice more of the sentence than the example about the house did, because the sentence about the seat included some other words between the redundant phrases.

The ACT likes to look for opportunities to separate important phrases from one another on the English section, to decrease the likelihood that test-takers will notice the key elements in a question. This is why it's always important for us to pay attention!

Still, our job won't be to read through every single sentence in every single ACT English passage and look out for redundant phrases, so please don't try to do that—it would be far too time-consuming. Instead, when we see an answer choice that allows us to get rid of a phrase (or part of a phrase), we just need to remember to take a look at the whole sentence and see whether that phrase is redundant and should be removed.

There's a real-life example of this kind of redundancy in question 46 from the English section of practice test 1 in the Red Book (test 2 in the 2020-2021 Red Book). The underlined portion describes "walls intended to defend the city protectively." The word "defend" already expresses the idea of doing something "protectively;" there's no reason to use both words to express that idea, according to the rules of ACT English. Only choice (J), the correct answer, solves the problem by simply using the phrase "defensive walls." (For a more detailed discussion of this question, see its walkthrough on page 469 later in this Black Book.)

Remember that if two nearby words or phrases on the ACT English section express the same idea, one of them needs to go (assuming we're given the option).

Questions that combine grammar/style/punctuation elements with reading comprehension elements

We'll occasionally see questions that mix elements from both grammar/style/punctuation questions and reading comprehension questions. They'll typically look like grammar/style/punctuation questions, with one key difference: more than one answer choice will be grammatically and stylistically acceptable to the ACT, but one of those choices will change the intended meaning of the sentence in a way that doesn't fit with the surrounding text. Let's take a look at an example so you can see what I mean.

Question 59 from the English section of practice test 3 in the Red Book (form 16MC3 online if you have the 2020-2021 Red Book) refers to a sentence from the passage that should look like this:

> They don't need to be reminded that girls can be <u>successful; they know</u> that.

This sentence uses a parallel structure and a semicolon to make three things clear:

1. The word "they" is referring to the same group of people in both cases (that group is identified in the previous sentence in the passage).

2. The word "they" refers to a group that's different from the general word "girls" in this sentence.

3. The word "that" refers back to the idea in the previous independent clause that "girls can be successful," which the sentence says "they don't need to be reminded" of.

Further, there's a logical connection between the idea that they "know" something and "don't need to be reminded" of that thing, because the relevant verbs are in the same form and are describing actions in the same time frame.

Two of the wrong answers for the question, (A) and (B), would create run-on sentences, because they would each join two sets of words that could be sentences on their own without placing any punctuation between them. This means (A) and (B) are wrong for grammatical reasons.

(D), on the other hand, would create a sentence that was arguably grammatically acceptable, but with multiple possible meanings, at least one of which would have a different meaning from the original sentence:

> *They don't need to be reminded that girls can be successful, knowing that.

In this version, the verb form "knowing" is no longer in the same tense as the verb phrase "don't need," which fails to create the parallelism we saw in the correct version above, and which also makes it unclear what the word "that" refers to: it could refer to the idea that a group of people doesn't need to be reminded of something, or it could refer to the idea that "that girls can be successful," or it could refer to an idea from the previous sentence in the passage.

In short, the right version of the sentence clearly says that "they" know "girls can be successful," which fits logically with the meaning of the surrounding text in the passage. The only way we can tell that (C) is right and (D) is wrong is to consider the actual meanings of two grammatically acceptable sentences and pick the one that clearly maintains the literal meaning of the surrounding text, which is a skill we'd normally associate with reading comprehension questions on the ACT English section. (For our full walkthrough of this question, see page 545 of this Black Book.)

So if you look carefully at a grammar/style/punctuation question and end up concluding that more than one choice is acceptable according to the normal rules of that question type, then you should use the rules of reading comprehension to identify the choice that's right by eliminating any choice that changes the original meaning of the sentence. But there are two important caveats to this:

1. If considering the reading comprehension aspect of the answer choices still doesn't make it clear which one is right, then you should consider the possibility that you've misread the question or the answer choices.

2. This kind of hybrid question only comes up a handful of times per ACT English section, at most. So if you find yourself considering both grammar and reading comprehension to answer a large number of ACT English questions, then you need to reconsider your approach to the section, because you're mis-diagnosing some questions.

The Intervening Phrase

The ACT will use something I call the "intervening phrase" to try to trick you into overlooking a situation in which two phrases don't agree with each other as they should.

Just as the name suggests, the intervening phrase is a phrase that the ACT sticks between a noun and its verb, or a noun and the pronoun it refers to. The test does this because it's hoping you'll get confused and think that the grammatical agreement should be with a word in the intervening phrase, instead of with the noun that's actually related grammatically to the verb or pronoun.

We can see a real-life example of this issue in question 56 from the English section of practice test 1 in the Red Book (test 2 in the 2020-2021 Red Book), which refers to this sentence:

> *However, only small portions of the Servian Wall <u>remains,</u> some of which can be seen inside a chain restaurant located beneath Rome's central train station.

The choices for this question make it clear we need to choose the correct form of the verb "remains."

When we identify and mentally remove the intervening phrase "of the Servian Wall," we're left with this:

> *However, only small portions <u>remains,</u> some of which can be seen inside a chain restaurant located beneath Rome's central train station.

This makes it more obvious that the verb form in the underlined portion of the sentence needs to agree with the plural noun "portions," so it needs to be a plural verb form like "remain," which appears in (J), the right answer. (For more on this question, see its walkthrough on page 473 of this Black Book.)

Intervening phrases can also cause problems for untrained test-takers even when verb conjugations aren't directly involved. For example, consider question 64 from the English section of practice test 1 in the Red Book (test 2 in the 2020-2021 Red Book). That question refers to a phrase from the following long, complicated sentence:

> Forten also knew that if released at the war's end or as part of an exchange, he, a free black man, might be captured and sold into slavery as he journeyed home to Philadelphia.

That sentence includes the following intervening phrases, among others:

- "if released at the war's end or as part of an exchange"
- "a free black man"
- "and sold into slavery"
- "to Philadelphia"

When we mentally remove those intervening phrases, we end up with this much less complicated sentence:

> Forten also knew that he might be captured as he journeyed home.

This version of the sentence makes it much easier to see that the original version of the sentence is grammatically acceptable on the ACT. (For a full discussion of this question, see its walkthrough on page 477 in this Black Book.)

So when you read a sentence on the ACT English section, it can be very helpful to ignore these intervening phrases and focus on the core relationships in the sentence to make sure the appropriate words agree with one another, and that punctuation is used in ways that the ACT accepts. We'll see several examples of this when we look at walkthroughs of real ACT questions, starting on page 446 of this Black Book.

(Note, by the way, that many intervening phrases will appear in comma sandwiches, as we discussed on page 432 of this Black Book.)

Special Technique: Considering Parallelism when Answering ACT English Questions

The term "parallelism" is used much too loosely by most people when it comes to standardized test prep, in my opinion, but it's actually useful on ACT English questions if you understand what it really means, and you use it in the proper context.

Ultimately, in order to use parallelism as a tool to beat the ACT, we should think of it as the idea of looking at the text surrounding an underlined portion of a passage when we're trying to find clues about what to do with that underlined portion. This often helps on the ACT English section because the test sometimes does us a favor by demonstrating its idea of proper style and punctuation in a part of the passage that's near the part we're being asked to consider.

That may sound confusing, so let's look at an example.

Question 24 from the English section of practice test 2 in your copy of *The Official ACT Prep Guide* (test 3 in the 2020-2021 Red Book) asks us to pick the appropriate form of the verb "to introduce" in the following phrase:

> while I served the queen's meals or <u>introduced</u> her to guests

In addition to (F), which is the original version above, (G) and (H) could arguably also be grammatically acceptable in a classroom setting: (G) would change the underlined phrase to "to introduce," and (H) would change it to "introducing."

As trained test-takers, we know that the ACT often allows us to resolve these issues by consulting parallel phrases in the surrounding text, and picking the choice with the same structure as those phrases.

In this case, the phrase "while I served" is in the past tense, which tells us that the ACT will reward the choice that uses the past tense form "introduced," since the word "or" tells us that both "served" and "introduced" are done by the same person and in the same context relative to the rest of the sentence. (For a more detailed discussion of this question, see its walkthrough on page 493 in this Black Book.)

Unfortunately, it's not possible to use this technique on every single question, simply because the ACT doesn't structure its texts in a way that makes this possible on every question. Depending on the context, though, we might use this technique to determine something like the right form of a verb (as in this example), the right pronoun, or even the right punctuation for a phrase. We'll see examples of this in the walkthroughs starting on page 446 of this Black Book.

Of course, you shouldn't double-check every sentence in every passage for these kinds of parallel structures—that would take up a lot of time, for one thing, and the test doesn't include parallelism on every question, as we just discussed. Instead, keep this parallelism idea in mind for situations where more than one choice seems equally grammatically acceptable. It may be that the right answer becomes clear when you compare the underlined phrase to other phrases in the surrounding lines, as we just did in the example above.

How to Read Passages on the ACT English Section

Earlier in this Black Book, we talked about the best ways to read passages on the ACT Reading and ACT Science sections. I said there were three main ways to approach those passages—reading, skimming, or skipping—and that you should experiment with them and pick the approach you're most successful with.

But my advice for the passages on the ACT English section is different. This section is structured differently from the way those other two sections are structured.

For the ACT English section, my recommendation is that you just start reading the passage from the very beginning (including the title). Every time you see an underlined, numbered portion of text, or a number with a square around it in the text, finish the sentence you're reading in the passage, and then look to the right of the page to find the question that corresponds to the text you've just read. In most cases, you'll be able to answer that question based on the text you've read so far; you may sometimes need to read a little further, especially if a question involves one of the following elements (which were all discussed in the preceding "ACT English Question" section, starting on page 413):

- introducing a paragraph (see page 414 of this Black Book)
- placing a set of sentences in the right order (see page 415 of this Black Book)
- providing a transition between paragraphs or sentences (see page 416 of this Black Book)
- the option to eliminate a phrase or sentence (see page 416 of this Black Book)
- redundancy (see page 437 of this Black Book)
- parallelism (see page 440 of this Black Book)

You may also see questions at the end of a passage that ask about the passage as a whole; these will usually involve some kind of reading comprehension, which means the right answer will be restated or demonstrated directly in the text. You'll probably be able to answer these questions after answering the other questions about the passage, without needing to re-read the entire passage for each question. Still, make sure you check back over the relevant portions of the passage before deciding on your answer.

You'll get used to this general approach as you do some practice of your own and look through the walkthroughs in this Black Book, which start on page 446.

ACT English Answer-Choice Patterns

The ACT deliberately positions wrong-answer choices to take advantage of the mistakes that it believes test-takers are likely to make, as we've repeatedly seen in our discussion of wrong-answer choices for the Reading, Math, and Science sections of the test. We'll find many of the same general patterns at work in the English section that we've already seen in the other sections.

We already discussed a variety of answer-choice patterns when we talked about the question types you'll encounter on the ACT English section. For example, we saw that some reading comprehension questions on the ACT demonstrate a "yes yes no no" pattern in their answer choices, just like some ACT Science questions do.

But there are some other answer-choice patterns that apply more generally on this section, and we'll take a look at them now.

ACT English Pattern 1: On Grammar/Style/Punctuation questions, shorter is better if possible

This is an idea that overlaps with some of what we've already talked about on page 437, but it's worth mentioning on its own: for ACT English questions based on grammar, style, and punctuation, shorter is better, all else being equal. In other words, if two answer choices on a grammar/style/punctuation question are both grammatically acceptable according to the ACT, and neither one changes the meaning from the original passage, then the right answer will be the shorter of the two choices.

This would be an example of an unnecessarily long sentence on the ACT:

> *If I were the one who had the choice about going, I would choose to stay home.

This would be an improved version of the sentence, according to the ACT:

> If it were up to me, I would stay home.

Technically speaking, there isn't anything grammatically *wrong* with the first choice: all the words in the sentence agree grammatically with the words they should agree with. But the ACT English section would prefer the second version, because it's the shorter version and also has no grammatical issues of its own.

I want to make it clear that shortness has nothing to do with grammar in real life! It's just something the ACT English section has arbitrarily decided to reward.

We can see a real-life example of this "shorter is better" principle in question 34 from the English section of practice test 1 in the Red Book (test 2 in the 2020-2021 Red Book). Many test-takers might be unsure how to choose from (F), (G), and (H), because they don't seem to have any concrete grammatical or stylistic problems (at least as far as ACT grammar and style are concerned). In cases like this, the right answer will be the shortest choice with no grammar or style problems, so (F) is the right answer to this question. (For a more detailed discussion of this question, see its walkthrough on page 464 this Black Book.)

Two important notes

As a corollary to this pattern, it's worth noting that the shortest answer choice on a grammar/style/punctuation question must be the right answer if it's grammatically acceptable on the ACT English, and if it doesn't change the meaning of the original sentence. This is because any other grammatically acceptable answer choice would "lose" to the shortest choice, because of the pattern we just noted above.

It's also important to remember that this pattern only applies on questions that test grammar, style, and/or punctuation! The answer choices for Reading Comprehension questions on the ACT English section will nearly always be grammatically acceptable on the ACT English section, and the relative lengths of those answer choices won't be important for determining the right answers to those questions. (For more on the distinction between these two groups of ACT English questions, see "ACT English Question Groups" on page 413 of this Black Book.)

ACT English Pattern 2: Wrong answers try to imitate right answers

This answer-choice pattern works more or less the same way as the pattern with the same name that we discussed for the ACT Math section, on page 150 of this Black Book.

The ACT often likes to incorporate elements of the correct answer in the incorrect answers, so that test-takers who figure out part of a question will still have to work to figure out the rest of it, instead of being able to choose the only answer choice that includes the part of the question they've worked out.

When the ACT does this on the English section, it often generates a set of answer choices that are highly similar to one another, such as choices that include identical wording with slightly different punctuation, or the same base words with slightly different conjugations, or sentences composed of mostly the same phrases but in slightly different orders. Noticing these slight differences among a set of answer choices can help us key in on the specific concepts that the ACT wants to test with a given question. (Of course a vertical scan like the kind discussed on page 44 of this Black Book can help us identify those issues quickly.)

For an example of this pattern in action, take a look at question 43 from the English section of practice test 1 in the Red Book (test 2 in the 2020-2021 Red Book). All of the answer choices for the question contain the same four words: "alligators now extinct on." The only differences among the answer choices are the locations of periods in the phrase.

This situation tells us right away that the ACT is focusing on concepts related to complete sentences with this question, and that it hopes some untrained test-takers will make mistakes that lead them to put a period in the wrong place.

(Note, by the way, that this question would follow the "Most Like the Others" pattern that we discussed in the Math training on page

- 3 of the 4 choices have no punctuation after the word "alligators."
- 3 of the 4 choices have no punctuation after the word "now."
- 3 of the 4 choices have no punctuation after the word "extinct."

So the most common characteristic after the word "alligators" is to have no punctuation. The most common characteristic after "now" is also not to have punctuation. And, similarly, most of the choices have no punctuation after "extinct," either. So, in light of the "most like the others" pattern, we'd expect the right answer to be the choice that has no punctuation after any of the words—and it is, because (C) is correct. Unfortunately, this "Most Like the Others" pattern doesn't apply 100% of the time on the ACT English section, so it should *never* be the only factor in determining your answer (unless you've completely given up on a question and decided to guess—see "Guessing on the ACT" on page 38 of this Black Book for more on that). Instead, we should use this pattern to help us identify which concepts are being tested in a question, and to help us re-check our answer to a question before finally deciding on it. For a more detailed discussion of this question, see its walkthrough on page 468 in this Black Book.)

ACT English Pattern 3: Functionally equivalent answer choices

As you go through the ACT English section, you'll find some questions in which 2 or 3 of the choices are phrases that would serve the same purpose in the context of the question. Because there can only be one valid right answer for every ACT question, if you find two or three choices that are effectively the same as each other, then you know they must all be wrong, since they can't all be right.

You can see an example of this concept in *The Official ACT Prep Guide*, in question 35 from the English section of practice test 1 (test 2 in the 2020-2021 Red Book).

In this example, the underlined phrase from the passage is the following:

▌ *faster than either <u>rainwater—or seawater—</u>could alone

As we can see, the ACT has placed the phrase "or seawater" in a punctuation sandwich, with dashes used as the punctuation in the sandwich. (See "Other "punctuation sandwiches" on page 433 of this Black Book for a reminder on that.) Choice (B) uses commas instead of dashes to create the same punctuation sandwich around the phrase "or seawater."

As trained test-takers, we know that the ACT doesn't care which punctuation is used to surround a phrase: whether it's surrounded by dashes, commas, or parentheses, a "sandwiched" phrase like this is only grammatically acceptable if the phrase could be removed from the sentence without causing any grammatical issues in the remaining sentence, and without changing the meaning of the remaining sentence. So if one of these choices with a sandwiched phrase were grammatically acceptable on the ACT, that would mean that both choices were equally grammatically acceptable—and that would mean both choices were right. We know that the ACT never creates a question with two right answers that are equally valid, so we know that both of these choices must be wrong, since they would serve equivalent functions in the sentence and they can't both be right. (For a more detailed discussion of this question, including an explanation of the right answer, see the walkthrough on page 464 of this Black Book.)

ACT English Pattern 4: No special consideration for "NO CHANGE"

Don't be afraid to select "NO CHANGE" on a grammar/style/punctuation question if you think the original version of the phrase is correct according to the rules and patterns of the ACT English section.

A lot of people start to worry if they think they've chosen "NO CHANGE" too many times (or too few times). But those answer choices aren't any more or less likely to be correct than any other answer choices are.

On school tests, teachers often use trick answer choices like "none of the above" that are rarely correct to make multiple-choice questions seem harder. But the ACT doesn't do that with the "no change" answer choice. On some days the "no change" choice is correct a little more often than other answer choices are, and on other days it's correct a little less often. So there's no magical number of times that this kind of answer choice has to be correct.

The General Process For Answering ACT English Questions

Now that we've learned all the basics, let's take a look at the general process I recommend for answering this type of question.

1. Read the passage until you come to a question.

The questions will appear to the right of the passage, and they'll either correspond to a certain portion of the passage (which will be underlined or marked with a number in a box), or they'll appear at the end of the passage and ask about that passage as a whole. When you come to a question, finish the sentence you're on, then stop reading the passage and shift your attention to the question.

2. Carefully read the prompt (if there is one) and the answer choices, and determine which type of question it is.

Not all questions will have a prompt; some will only offer four answer choices as possible versions of an underlined portion of the text. Either way, read the prompt if there is one, and carefully read the answer choices. Determine whether you're dealing with a grammar/style/punctuation question, or a reading comprehension question (see "ACT English Question Groups" on page 413 of this Black Book).

3a. For a reading comprehension question, look for any of the relevant issues we discussed in "Reading Comprehension Questions" on page 413 of this Black Book.

There are several different issues we talked about regarding reading comprehension questions in ACT English, but they generally have to do with finding an answer choice that's directly restated or demonstrated by the concepts and relationships in the text.

3b. For grammar/style/punctuation questions, look for any of the relevant issues we discussed in "Grammar/Style/Punctuation Questions" on page 418 of this Black book.

Look at the words in the underlined portion, and see how they relate to the other words in the sentence. Are verbs in the right number and tense? Are possessives formed correctly? Are periods, commas, and semicolons in the right place according to the ACT's grammar rules?

Consider all the answer choices. Are any choices unnecessarily long? Are there any transition words that don't make sense? And so on.

4. Find the right answer, or eliminate three wrong answers.

Sometimes you can immediately see which concept the question is testing, and you can tell that a particular choice is correct. If not, you should still be able to start eliminating wrong-answer choices based on the issues we discussed for that question type. For example, on a grammar/style/punctuation question, you might be able to tell that an answer choice has a verb in the wrong tense, or a comma in the wrong place; on a reading comprehension question, you might be able to see that an answer choice differs from the passage. Keep considering answer choices until you've identified the one correct choice that follows the rules and patterns of the ACT English section, and the three wrong-answer choices that break those rules and patterns.

5. Take a second look to reconsider the question, the answer choices, and the passage.

Now that you've chosen a correct answer, take another look at the question, answer choices, and passage to make sure you haven't overlooked or misread anything. Did you miss an intervening phrase between a subject and its verb? Did you overlook a word like "NOT," "EXCEPT," or "LEAST?" Did you overlook a parallel structure in the surrounding text? Always remember that the ACT is trying to trick you into making a small mistake on every single question. Stay on your toes.

6. Mark your answer choice and move on.

Once you've gone through the process and double-checked your answer, mark your choice and move on. Keep going through the passage until you reach the next question.

ACT English Quick Summary

This is a one-page summary of the major concepts you'll need to know for the ACT English section. Use it to evaluate your comprehension or jog your memory. For a more in-depth treatment of these ideas, see the rest of this section in this Black Book.

The Big Secret: ACT English is all about learning the ACT's standards and then applying them, rather than relying on your own sense of what sounds good to you personally.

There are 2 main groups of ACT English questions: reading comprehension questions and grammar/style/punctuation questions. (A very few questions on this section will combine elements of both.)

<u>Reading comprehension questions will tend to include a prompt.</u> Generally speaking, the correct answers to reading comprehension questions on the English section will be directly restated or demonstrated in the relevant passage, or will demonstrate an idea that appears in the prompt.

Depending on the context, the correct answer might also be the one that keeps related ideas together, or that places sentences or paragraphs in a logical order, or that uses a particular word in a precise way.

<u>Grammar/style/punctuation questions won't include a prompt. They'll usually require you to pick which version of an underlined phrase fits with the ACT's rules.</u>

- Common grammatical issues for these kinds of questions include agreement in tense and number between/among verbs and nouns, agreement in number between pronouns and their nouns, idiomatic usage of prepositions, parallel structures of phrases, and similar topics.
- Common style issues will include the idea of avoiding redundancy and unnecessary length.
- Common punctuation issues will include comma placement, the formation of possessives, and the proper use of semicolons and colons.

<u>Questions that include elements of both reading comprehension and grammar/style/punctuation will tend to look like pure grammar/style/punctuation questions at first.</u> But you'll find that more than one answer is grammatically acceptable according to the ACT, and then you'll have to choose the answer that doesn't contradict other concepts in the surrounding text. These kinds of questions are relatively rare.

Here's the general ACT English process:

1. Read the passage until you come to a question.
2. Carefully read the prompt (if there is one) and the answer choices and determine whether the question is primarily based on reading comprehension or on grammar/style/punctuation.
3. Look for any of the issues we discussed in the training according to the question type.
4. Find the right answer, or eliminate three wrong answers.
5. Take another look at the question and answer choices.
6. Mark your answer choice and move on.

Go through the ACT English walkthroughs in this Black Book, and follow along in your copy of *The Official ACT Prep Guide* to see demonstrations of these ideas.

English Question Walkthroughs

Now that we've discussed everything you need to know in order to tackle the ACT English section, we'll show this approach in action against all the English questions from three practice tests in the Red Book (which, of course, is the *The Official ACT Prep Guide*—see "Using the Official ACT Prep Guide (the "Red Book")" on page 21 of this Black Book for details on why official questions are so important.)

IMPORTANT NOTE: If you have the 2020-2021 edition of the Red Book (ISBN: 978-1119685760), then "Test 1" in this Black Book refers to Practice Test 2 in your edition of the Red Book, and "Test 2" in this Black Book refers to Practice Test 3 in your Red Book. What we refer to as "Test 3" in this Black Book has been removed from the 2020-2021 edition of the Red Book, but it can be found online as ACT test form 16MC3. (See "**The 2020-2021 Red Book**" on page 23 of this Black Book for more.)

Sample English Walkthroughs

There are actually two types of ACT English walkthroughs, reflecting the two general groups of ACT English questions we identified on page 413: one type of walkthrough for Reading Comprehension questions, and one for Grammar/Style/Punctuation questions. The walkthroughs for Reading Comprehension questions look more or less similar to the walkthroughs for ACT Reading questions on page 62 of this Black Book, and should be self-explanatory for that reason. The walkthroughs for Grammar/Style/Punctuation questions look like this:

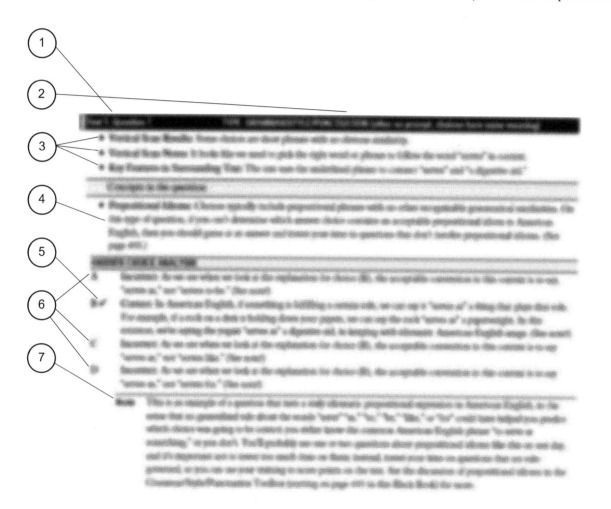

Explanation of Walkthrough Elements

The elements of the walkthrough are presented in an order that reflects "The General Process For Answering ACT English Questions" on page 444 of this Black Book, as we can see when referring to the diagram above:

1. This shows the test number and question number of the question being analyzed in the walkthrough, so you can find the question in the Red Book.

2. This Item indicates whether the question is a Reading Comprehension question, or a Grammar/Style/Punctuation question, and how we know that. See page 413 for more on that distinction.

3. For Grammar/Style/Punctuation questions, this Item reflects the attributes of the question that a trained test-taker would notice when he first reads it:
   - the results of a vertical scan of the choices (see page 42 of this Black Book for more on that)
   - the relevant features of the surrounding text, which might reveal phrases that should be paralleled in the correct answer, or phrases that must agree grammatically with the underlined phrase in the question

4. This Item reflects the Grammar/Style/Punctuation concepts that might be relevant to this question, based on the observations we made in Item 3, and provides page numbers where you can read up on those concepts in this Black Book if you've forgotten them.

5. The correct answer will be indicated with a check-mark icon, and the explanatory text will show how the correct answer follows the ACT's rules as discussed in our training for the English section.

6. For each of the three wrong answers, the walkthrough will explain how they fail to satisfy the ACT's requirements.

7. If I feel that something is noteworthy about the question but I can't fit it in the rest of the walkthrough, then I'll note that at the end of the walkthrough. Be sure to pay attention to these notes when they appear, as they'll often contain useful information about what a particular question can teach us generally about future ACT questions.

Note that some walkthroughs are missing some of the items in this list! If one of the Items above isn't relevant to a particular question, then it's omitted.

Remember that the ultimate goal of these walkthroughs is to show you how I recommend you diagnose a question and evaluate the answer choices to find the correct answer. As always, you should feel free to modify this approach if you want, as long as your modifications still bring you the results you're looking for.

TEST 1 (TEST 2 IN 2020-2021 RED BOOK)

- **Vertical Scan Results:** Some choices have the same words with different punctuation.
- **Vertical Scan Notes:** We need to decide whether there should be a comma, an apostrophe, or nothing after "elephants," and whether there should be a comma after "1972."
- **Key Features in Surrounding Text:** The underlined phrase is followed by the phrase "when she started the now-famous Amboseli Elephant Research Project in Amboseli National Park in Kenya," which is a dependent clause that follows "Cynthia Moss…1972." The current version of the sentence is unacceptable on the ACT because a dependent clause can't appear immediately after an independent clause with no comma between the two clauses.

Concepts in the question:

- **Commas:** Choices include commas. Commas can separate a list of 3 or more items, form sandwiches, separate interchangeable adjectives, or introduce an independent clause after a dependent clause. They can't appear for no reason. (p. 431)
- **Dependent and Independent Clauses:** Choices would create or join clauses. An independent clause has a main verb and can be a sentence by itself. A dependent clause can't, and starts with a conjunction or relative pronoun. (p. 426)
- **Parallelism:** Choices include options that would ignore a parallel structure in the surrounding text. The right answer should match the phrasing and grammatical structures in the surrounding text when possible. (See p. 440)
- **Punctuation Sandwich:** Choices involve phrases "sandwiched" between similar punctuation marks. When removed from the sentence, a proper sandwich leaves behind a grammatical sentence with the same original meaning. (See p. 432 and 433)
- **Verb Tense/Conjugation:** Choices include different forms of the same verb. Look at the surrounding text to find the verb's subject. Also look for other verbs that could indicate the proper tense or form for the verbs in the choices. (See p. 420-423)

ANSWER CHOICE ANALYSIS

A   **Incorrect:** This version is unacceptable for reasons mentioned in the "Key Features in Surrounding Text" section above.

B   **Incorrect:** This choice resolves the problem in (A), but we can't make a punctuation sandwich around "since 1972" because removing the phrase "since 1972" would cause the remaining sentence to have an unacceptable shift in the tenses of two verbs ("has been" and "started") linked by the word "when." (See page 421 in this Black Book for more.)

C ✓   **Correct:** As we saw in the "Key Features in Surrounding Text" above, we need to have a comma after "1972" to join the dependent clause "when she…Kenya" to the rest of the sentence. This choice avoids the problem in the original version of the sentence without creating any other problems, so it's the right answer.

D   **Incorrect:** We can't use the plural possessive form "elephants'" (notice the apostrophe after the "s") because it doesn't make sense to say that "elephants" possess "since 1972." Also, a comma should appear after "1972," as we saw for (C).

- **Vertical Scan Results:** Some choices have different forms of the same base word.
- **Vertical Scan Notes:** Two options involve the adjective "famous." Two involve the adverb "famously." Two involve hyphens.
- **Key Features in Surrounding Text:** The underlined phrase describes the noun "Amboseli Elephant Research Project," so we know the correct answer must be something that can describe a noun.

Concepts in the question:

- **Adjective/Adverb:** Choices involve a word in its adjective or adverb form. Remember that adverb forms often end in "-ly," but not always. Adjectives can modify nouns; adverbs can modify anything else (verbs, adjectives, other adverbs). (p. 423)
- **Confused Homophones:** Choices include different homophone pairs (such as "their"/"they're" or "too"/"to"). Remember the correct formation of possessives. Remember to read contractions as their uncontracted forms (e.g. "it's" = "it is"). (p. 436)

ANSWER CHOICE ANALYSIS

F ✓   **Correct:** The ACT allows us to use an adjective ("famous") to describe a noun phrase ("Amboseli Elephant Research Project"). We can also use the word "now" to indicate that the project is famous at the current time. (Some test-takers may be put off by the hyphen in this answer choice, but see the note below.)

G   **Incorrect:** This choice incorrectly uses the word "then," which sounds like the word "than," but has a different meaning: "then" is used to indicate a specific point in time. (Note that "then" can be an answer to the question "when?", just as "there" can be an answer to the question "where?")

H   **Incorrect:** The ACT doesn't allow us to use an adverb (such as "famously") to describe a noun phrase (such as "Amboseli Elephant Research Project"), so this choice can't be correct.

J   Incorrect: This choice has the same problem as (H).

Note   Some test-takers will be confused by the hyphens in (F) and (G). From a test-taking standpoint, it's still possible for a trained test-taker to know that (F) must be correct because all the other choices clearly violate the rules of ACT grammar, as we discussed above, while (F) follows the rules related to adjectives and adverbs. If you want to make a perfect score on the English section on test day, that's all you need to know. If you'd like a more detailed grammatical explanation (and who wouldn't, really?), then you may be interested to know that hyphens can be used to show that a cluster of words is operating as a single phrase with a single grammatical function in a sentence: in this case, the phrase "now-famous" is an adjective phrase modifying the noun phrase "Amboseli Elephant Research Project," and "now-famous" is composed of the adverb "now" and the adjective "famous" joined by a hyphen, as we noted for (F). If the hyphen had been omitted in this case, leaving us with the words "the now famous Amboseli Elephant Research Project," then the word "now" would just be an isolated adverb modifying the isolated adjective "famous," and the adjective "famous" would still be modifying the noun phrase with the word "Project." So the difference created by the hyphen in this case is very minimal and, again, has no impact on the reasoning that we need to apply in order to know that (F) will be right on the ACT—I just wanted to provide a little more of an explanation for students who might be interested.

T1, Q3 (Test 2 in the 2020-2021 Red Book—see page 23)   **TYPE: G/S/P (often no prompt; choices w/similar meanings—see page 418)**

- **Vertical Scan Results:** Some choices have the same words with different punctuation.
- **Vertical Scan Notes:** We must decide whether there should be a dash, colon, comma, or no punctuation after "encroachment."
- **Key Features in Surrounding Text:** There's a dash earlier in the sentence at the beginning of a phrase that can be removed from the sentence without creating any grammatical problems.

Concepts in the question:

- **Colons:** Choices include colons. A colon can only be placed after a set of words that could be a sentence on their own, and only before a demonstration or example of the idea before the colon. No more than one colon per sentence. (p. 430)
- **Commas:** Choices include commas. Commas can separate a list of 3 or more items, form sandwiches, separate interchangeable adjectives, or introduce an independent clause after a dependent clause. They can't appear for no reason. (p. 431)
- **Dependent and Independent Clauses:** Choices would create or join clauses. An independent clause has a main verb and can be a sentence by itself. A dependent clause can't, and starts with a conjunction or relative pronoun. (p. 426)
- **Punctuation Sandwich:** Choices involve phrases "sandwiched" between similar punctuation marks. When removed from the sentence, a proper sandwich leaves behind a grammatical sentence with the same original meaning. (See p. 432 and 433)

ANSWER CHOICE ANALYSIS

A   Incorrect: This option causes the phrase describing elephants not to be separate from the information about "Moss," and also makes it unclear that the phrase "an author, lecturer, filmmaker, and a fierce advocate for elephants" is a description of "Moss." On top of that, it causes the whole "sentence" to lack a main verb and an independent clause, since everything in the sentence starting with the word "which" would be part of a dependent clause.

B ✓   Correct: This option completes the punctuation sandwich around "which face…encroachment," turning the sandwiched phrase into a description of the word "elephants," and showing that the phrase "an author, lecturer, filmmaker, and a fierce advocate for elephants" is a phrase describing the noun "Moss." We know this sandwiched phrase is acceptable on the ACT because we can remove it without creating any grammatical errors or changing the meaning of the rest of the sentence.

C   Incorrect: The ACT won't let us use a colon after "encroachment" because the words before the colon can't stand on their own as a complete sentence, and because we would fail to create the punctuation sandwich as shown in (B).

D   Incorrect: We can't put a comma after "encroachment" because we need to complete the punctuation sandwich around "which face…encroachment." That punctuation sandwich has a dash on the other end, and punctuation sandwiches must have the same punctuation on both ends (unless they start at the beginning of a sentence or end at the end of a sentence).

T1, Q4 (Test 2 in the 2020-2021 Red Book—see page 23)   **TYPE: RC (usually has a prompt; choices w/different meanings—see page 413)**

- **RC Question sub-type:** Including/excluding a phrase/sentence. (The question asks whether a given sentence or phrase should be included in the passage. The correct choice will include a comment that plainly describes the role of the phrase or sentence in the passage. Sentences that should be included will follow broad ACT standards for ideal sentences and paragraphs, while sentences that shouldn't be included will not follow those standards. See p. 416)

ANSWER CHOICE ANALYSIS

F   Reasonable statement not in the text: An untrained test-taker might imagine that Moss wants to work with elephants specifically to keep them safe from humans and that this was a "crucial factor" in her choice of a career, but that idea isn't actually stated in the passage. The passage only says that elephants face threats that include "human encroachment," and that Moss is an "advocate for elephants." Since the reasoning for this choice isn't literally restated or demonstrated in the text, it can't be right.

G   Direct contradiction: The idea of humans threatening elephants doesn't come up again after this point in the passage, so the ACT

---

won't let us say that this idea "becomes the focus of the rest of the essay," as (G) would require. Since the reasoning for this choice isn't demonstrated in the rest of the text, we know it's wrong.

H   **Direct contradiction:** The text mentions "human encroachment" in the portion underlined for question 3, which is an example of "a human presence in [elephants'] lives," so the statement in (H) directly contradicts the evidence in the passage.

J ✓   **Correct:** The sentence before this question in the passage mentions an "array of threats," and says one of those threats is "human encroachment," which literally demonstrates that the information in the prompt is "already provided in the paragraph," just as (J) requires. (Note that we didn't need to know the meaning of "encroachment" in order to answer this question. We only needed to realize that the word "human" in the passage was describing something that the passage describes as a "threat to [elephants'] survival," which means that the idea of humans threatening elephants' survival is already in the paragraph, just as (J) requires.)

T1, Q5 (Test 2 in the 2020-2021 Red Book—see page 23)   **TYPE: G/S/P (often no prompt; choices w/similar meanings—see page 418)**

- **Vertical Scan Results:** Some choices have the same words with different punctuation.
- **Vertical Scan Notes:** Should there be a comma after "intensive," "field," and/or "studies?"
- **Key Features in Surrounding Text:** The original version of the phrase uses commas to separate "intensive," "field," and "studies," which isn't okay on the ACT because those things aren't items in a series, nor are they separate, interchangeable adjectives all describing some other noun.

> ### Concepts in the question:

- **Commas:** Choices include commas. Commas can separate a list of 3 or more items, form sandwiches, separate interchangeable adjectives, or introduce an independent clause after a dependent clause. They can't appear for no reason. (p. 431)
- **Punctuation Sandwich:** Choices involve phrases "sandwiched" between similar punctuation marks. When removed from the sentence, a proper sandwich leaves behind a grammatical sentence with the same original meaning. (See p. 432 and 433)

ANSWER CHOICE ANALYSIS

A   **Incorrect:** As trained test-takers, we know that the ACT English section allows us to use commas in specific types of situations, and none of those situations appears in the underlined phrase for this question, as we noted above. So (A) is wrong. See the explanation of (B) for more.

B ✓   **Correct:** This choice would allow the word "field" to modify "studies," and then the word "intensive" would modify the phrase "field studies." (In other words, we can't switch the order of "intensive" and "field," because the resulting phrase "*field intensive studies" doesn't make any sense. Since we can't switch those two adjectives, we know that no comma should appear between them, according to the rules of ACT English.) Further, we know that there's no reason to put a comma between the word "field" and the word it modifies, "studies." Since there's no reason for a comma in the underlined phrase, (B) is right.

C   **Incorrect:** This comma doesn't fit any of the acceptable examples of comma usage on the ACT, so we can't put a comma after this phrase on the ACT English section.

D   **Incorrect:** As we saw in the explanation for (B), there's no reason for a comma in the underlined phrase.

T1, Q6 (Test 2 in the 2020-2021 Red Book—see page 23)   **TYPE: RC (usually has a prompt; choices w/different meanings—see page 413)**

- **RC Question sub-type:** Transition Phrase. (The choices reflect different kinds of transitions between two concepts, with words or phrases like "however," "instead of," or "for example." The right answer must reflect the relationship between the previous concept in the passage and the following concept in the passage. See p. 416)

ANSWER CHOICE ANALYSIS

F   **Confused relationships:** "However" would be appropriate if this sentence were somehow in contrast with the previous sentence, but that's not the case, as we'll discuss for (G).

G ✓   **Correct:** The previous sentence mentions that "elephant survival depends on learned behavior," and this sentence provides an example about an elephant learning a behavior. "For instance" shows that this sentence provides an example of the idea from the previous sentence, so (G) is right.

H   **Confused relationships:** "As always" could be appropriate if some other part of this sentence or paragraph were indicating that something was always true, but the text doesn't say anything about that, so (H) is wrong.

J   **Confused relationships:** "By now" could be appropriate if this sentence involved the idea of something being the case as of the start of the sentence or the current moment, but it doesn't do that.

T1, Q7 (Test 2 in the 2020-2021 Red Book—see page 23)   **TYPE: G/S/P (often no prompt; choices w/similar meanings—see page 418)**

- **Vertical Scan Results:** Similar phrases with different short words and/or punctuation.
- **Vertical Scan Notes:** We need to choose between "sipped," "sips," and "sipping," and also to consider the other short words in the answer choices.
- **Key Features in Surrounding Text:** The underlined phrase describes one of the steps done by the "young elephant" so it can drink. The other step is the parallel phrase "kneeling down by the water's edge." According to the ACT, the verb in the underlined phrase should be in the same form as the verb in the parallel phrase from the context.

Concepts in the question:

- **Parallelism:** Choices include options that would ignore a parallel structure in the surrounding text. The right answer should match the phrasing and grammatical structures in the surrounding text when possible. (See p. 440)
- **Verb Tense/Conjugation:** Choices include different forms of the same verb. Look at the surrounding text to find the verb's subject. Also look for other verbs that could indicate the proper tense or form for the verbs in the choices. (See p. 420-423)

ANSWER CHOICE ANALYSIS

A   **Incorrect:** As we discussed above, the verb needs to be in the "-ing" form, so the verb form "sipped" can't be correct.

B   **Incorrect:** Again, as we said above, the verb needs to be in the "-ing" form, so the verb form "sips" is wrong. (Many untrained test-takers will be drawn to this choice because they won't read carefully enough, and they'll think that the word "it" refers to the water in the sentence. But the structure of the sentence in the text means that "it" could only refer to the "water's edge," and it makes no sense to say the elephant learns to drink by sipping the edge of something. As trained test-takers, we know that we don't need to worry about this issue with the edge of the water, though—the right answer has to be the choice whose structure is parallel with the appropriate phrase in the surrounding text, which in this case involves the "-ing" form of a verb.)

C ✓   **Correct:** As we saw above, the verb needs to be in the "-ing" form so it can parallel the verb "kneeling," which means the form "sipping" is acceptable.

D   **Incorrect:** This choice has an issue similar to the one in (B), except in this case the sentence would say that the "water's edge," and not the elephant, is the thing "that sips."

T1, Q8 (Test 2 in the 2020-2021 Red Book—see page 23)   **TYPE: G/S/P (often no prompt; choices w/similar meanings—see page 418)**

- **Vertical Scan Results:** Similar phrases with different short words and/or punctuation.
- **Vertical Scan Notes:** Should the word "then" be included? If so, should it be preceded by "and," or followed by "by"?
- **Key Features in Surrounding Text:** In the original version of the phrase, the text leading up to the underlined period is a sentence fragment, and so is the text that comes after the underlined period. The paragraph is talking about how baby elephants learn to drink with their trunks, and the previous sentence makes it clear the water has to end up in the elephant's mouth.

Concepts in the question:

- **Dependent and Independent Clauses:** Choices would create or join clauses. An independent clause has a main verb and can be a sentence by itself. A dependent clause can't, and starts with a conjunction or relative pronoun. (p. 426)
- **Intervening Phrase:** A phrase appears between two words that need to agree with each other grammatically. Remember to identify pairs of words that need to agree with each other, and ignore phrases that appear between those words. (See page 439)

ANSWER CHOICE ANALYSIS

F   **Incorrect:** As we noted above, (F) creates the fragment "the habit of pulling water into its trunk." We know that the right answer to an ACT English question can't create a sentence fragment, so (F) must be wrong.

G ✓   **Correct:** This choice is the only one that results in a grammatically acceptable sentence on the ACT English section: it causes the intervening phrase "of pulling water into its trunk and then releasing that water into its mouth" to modify the noun "habit," and uses "habit" as the subject of the verb "develops." Since it fixes the issue in the original version and doesn't create any other issues, we know it's right.

H   **Incorrect:** (H) causes the sentence to be grammatically unacceptable on the ACT. The phrase "by releasing that water into its mouth" can't logically modify anything in the sentence, because the action of releasing water into the elephant's mouth doesn't cause anything else to happen in the sentence. In other words, if "releasing that water into its mouth" caused the elephant to stop being thirsty, the sentence could say "by releasing that water into its mouth, the elephant quenches its thirst." But no idea like this appears in the sentence, so the word "by" can't be appropriate here. (Note that some test-takers might assume this action would quench the elephant's thirst, but, without a phrase that actually says that, the word "by" still can't work in this sentence.)

J   **Incorrect:** The phrase "pulling water into its trunk releasing that water into its mouth" doesn't include any word or phrase to connect the actions of "pulling" and "releasing." These two verb phrases need a conjunction like "and" to join them.

Note   As is often the case with sentences on the ACT English section, there are a variety of ways that the underlined words could have been changed to create an acceptable sentence on the ACT...but only one of those ways was reflected in the answer choices. Many test-takers would want to fix the error in these two sentences in other ways, such as by removing the period and changing "then" to "and," or by creating a comma sandwich around the phrase "then releasing that water into its mouth." But, as trained test-takers, we know that it doesn't help to come up with our own solutions to the problems that appear in an ACT English section, because there's no guarantee that our proposed solution will be among the answer choices. Instead, we should read the answer choices without any expectations, looking only for the choice that conforms to the ACT's unwritten rules.

- **Vertical Scan Results:** Similar phrases with different short words and/or punctuation.
- **Vertical Scan Notes:** Three choices involve the "-ing" form of the word "witness," while one doesn't. The words "as if," "when," "of," and "then" appear before the form of "witness" in each choice.
- **Key Features in Surrounding Text:** The phrase before the underlined phrase is "only after months," so the underlined phrase needs to modify "months."

Concepts in the question:

- **Intervening Phrase:** A phrase appears between two words that need to agree with each other grammatically. Remember to identify pairs of words that need to agree with each other, and ignore phrases that appear between those words. (See page 439)
- **Parallelism:** Choices include options that would ignore a parallel structure in the surrounding text. The right answer should match the phrasing and grammatical structures in the surrounding text when possible. (See p. 440)
- **Verb Tense/Conjugation:** Choices include different forms of the same verb. Look at the surrounding text to find the verb's subject. Also look for other verbs that could indicate the proper tense or form for the verbs in the choices. (See p. 420-423)

ANSWER CHOICE ANALYSIS

A   **Incorrect:** There are multiple problems with this choice. The biggest one is that, grammatically, the phrase "as if witnessing" would be modifying the grammatical subject of the sentence, which is the word "habit"—in other words, this choice would be saying that the habit "develops" as if the habit itself were "witnessing other elephants." Since habits aren't people or animals, they can't witness things, and this version of the sentence wouldn't make any sense.

B   **Incorrect:** This choice shares an issue with (A): the word "when" would refer back to the development of the habit, which means that (B) would also be saying the habit itself was doing the "witnessing" while it was "develop[ing]." As we noted for (A), habits can't witness things, so this choice must be wrong. It might attract untrained test-takers who never read back over the entire sentence, and are vaguely aware that the elephants must be witnessing other elephants, but don't realize that the grammatical subject of the sentence isn't the word "elephants."

C ✓ **Correct:** Unlike (A) and (B), this choice provides a prepositional phrase that would modify the word "months," showing that the months were "months of witnessing other elephants." In other words, this is the only choice that shows the witnessing was happening during the months, and the only choice that makes any sense in the sentence.

D   **Incorrect:** (D) is grammatically unacceptable to the ACT. One reason for this is that the word "witness" would have to be meant as a verb here, since verbs indicate actions and the word "then" indicates a time when an action occurs…but there's no noun in the sentence that could be performing the action of the verb "witness" as it's conjugated here.

- **Vertical Scan Results:** Similar phrases with different short words and/or punctuation.
- **Vertical Scan Notes:** (F) and (G) differ only by the word "which." (H) is the only choice that doesn't share a word with any other choice.
- **Key Features in Surrounding Text:** The correct answer will come after the word "observations" without any punctuation after it, so it will probably have to modify the word "observations."

Concepts in the question:

- **Dependent and Independent Clauses:** Choices would create or join clauses. An independent clause has a main verb and can be a sentence by itself. A dependent clause can't, and starts with a conjunction or relative pronoun. (p. 426)
- **Intervening Phrase:** A phrase appears between two words that need to agree with each other grammatically. Remember to identify pairs of words that need to agree with each other, and ignore phrases that appear between those words. (See page 439)
- **Pronoun Ambiguity:** Choices include pronouns that could refer to more than one phrase in the surrounding text. We can't use a pronoun on the ACT when it isn't clear what that pronoun refers to. (See page 419)

ANSWER CHOICE ANALYSIS

F   **Incorrect:** There are several issues here. The easiest way to describe the problem with this choice is that it simply inserts the word "which" into the middle of the phrase "in this regard;" as we'll see when we talk about (G), "in this regard" would have been fine by itself. The word "which" isn't okay here because it isn't introducing a dependent clause or referring back to some other noun.

G ✓ **Correct:** This choice appropriately uses the pronoun phrase "in this regard" to modify the word "observations," showing us that the observations are related to a particular topic indicated by the phrase "this regard"—specifically, the topic of senior female elephants teaching other female elephants, which was mentioned in the previous sentence. Further, because this choice is the only one without a relative pronoun like "which" or "that," it's the only choice that doesn't create a sentence fragment in this scenario, which means it must be right.

H   **Incorrect:** One issue with this choice is that the word "that" would cause the main verb in the original version of the sentence ("involved") not to be a main verb anymore, causing problems similar to those caused by "which" in (F) and (J).

J   **Incorrect:** This choice has problems similar to those we discussed in (F). This use of "which" would cause the original sentence not to have a main verb anymore, since "involved" would come immediately after "which." It might attract untrained test-takers who didn't consider each choice in light of the entire surrounding sentence before picking it.

T1, Q11 (Test 2 in the 2020-2021 Red Book—see page 23)   TYPE: G/S/P (often no prompt; choices w/similar meanings—see page 418)

- **Vertical Scan Results:** Some choices are short phrases with no obvious similarity.
- **Vertical Scan Notes:** The choices are all different details that describe "Ely."
- **Key Features in Surrounding Text:** The sentence describes two elephants in a row in two parallel phrases: "Enid, a ten-year-old female" and "Ely, (blank)." The description of the first elephant involves the word "a," then a phrase telling the elephant's age ("ten-year-old") and sex ("female"), so the underlined phrase should parallel this structure.

Concepts in the question:

- **Parallelism:** Choices include options that would ignore a parallel structure in the surrounding text. The right answer should match the phrasing and grammatical structures in the surrounding text when possible. (See p. 440)
- **Redundancy:** Choices and/or surrounding text could combine to repeat the same concept unnecessarily. On grammar/style/punctuation questions, we should avoid words that directly repeat ideas in the immediate surrounding text. (See p. 437)

ANSWER CHOICE ANALYSIS

A   **Incorrect:** This detail tells us who named the elephant; it doesn't create a phrase that is parallel to the phrase "a ten-year-old female" as discussed in the "Key Features in Surrounding Text" section above.

B ✓   **Correct:** This detail provides the age ("a baby") and sex ("male") of the elephant, which makes the underlined phrase parallel to the phrase "a ten-year-old female" from earlier in the sentence.

C   **Incorrect:** This detail only repeats that the other elephant is an elephant, which we know from the previous sentence in the passage. This kind of redundancy isn't allowed on grammar/style/punctuation questions on the ACT English section. This choice also fails to create the parallel structure we saw in (B).

D   **Incorrect:** This just repeats the fact that the other elephant is the third one being described, so it has basically the same problem as (A) and (C). We already know the passage is talking about three elephants because of the previous sentence, and we can see that the other two have already been named, so the phrase "the third" is redundant according to the ACT. Like (C), this choice also fails to create the parallel structure we saw in (B).

T1, Q12 (Test 2 in the 2020-2021 Red Book—see page 23)   TYPE: G/S/P (often no prompt; choices w/similar meanings—see page 418)

- **Vertical Scan Results:** Some choices have different forms of the same base word.
- **Vertical Scan Notes:** The only differences among the choices relate to the form of the verb "to grow," and whether the word "he" should be in the underlined phrase.
- **Key Features in Surrounding Text:** The underlined phrase appears after the phrase "Ely not only overcame..." The right answer needs to be a verb in the same past-tense form as "overcame."

Concepts in the question:

- **Parallelism:** Choices include options that would ignore a parallel structure in the surrounding text. The right answer should match the phrasing and grammatical structures in the surrounding text when possible. (See p. 440)
- **Verb Tense/Conjugation:** Choices include different forms of the same verb. Look at the surrounding text to find the verb's subject. Also look for other verbs that could indicate the proper tense or form for the verbs in the choices. (See p. 420-423)

ANSWER CHOICE ANALYSIS

F ✓   **Correct:** This choice uses the past-tense form "grew," which is in the same form as the parallel verb "overcame" from earlier in the sentence.

G   **Incorrect:** As we saw above, the right answer needs to have the same form as the past tense verb "overcame" in the first half of the sentence. But this choice is in a different form, so it's wrong.

H   **Incorrect:** This choice has the same basic problem as (G). It does reflect an event in the past, but it doesn't use the same simple past-tense form as the verb "overcame" earlier in the sentence. Instead, it uses a form with the helping verb "had," which doesn't appear with the verb "overcame." This choice might attract untrained test-takers who didn't realize that the right answer needs to be in exact same form as "overcame," not just in a similar time frame.

J   **Incorrect:** This choice has the same basic problem as (G) and (H).

T1, Q13 (Test 2 in the 2020-2021 Red Book—see page 23)   TYPE: RC (usually has a prompt; choices w/different meanings—see page 413)

- **RC Question sub-type:** Sentence or paragraph placement. (The prompt asks us where a sentence should go in a paragraph, or where a paragraph should go in the passage. The correct order will reflect a logical chronology, and/or will allow for pronouns to refer to nouns in a logical way, and/or will place related concepts near one another. See page 415)

ANSWER CHOICE ANALYSIS

A   **Causes text to introduce an idea that has already been discussed:** In its current placement, the sentence mentions Ely's "deformed feet" *after* the text already discusses how "Echo" and "Enid" worked to take care of Ely, and how Ely "overcame his early limitations." The ACT English section will want us to place the sentence that explains what Ely's limitations are (his "initial[]" problems with "walking") before any sentence that refers back to those limitations as though the reader were already familiar with them. So (A) must be wrong.

B   **Causes text to refer to an idea that hasn't been mentioned yet:** In this placement, the sentence would refer to "Ely" as though the reader already knew who Ely was, even though Ely isn't introduced until Sentence 4. This choice might appeal to untrained test-takers who realize that the sentence needs to appear earlier than its original placement in the passage, and simply respond by moving the sentence to the very beginning of the paragraph without considering anything else.

C   **Causes text to refer to an idea that hasn't been mentioned yet:** This choice has the same problem as (B): it refers to Ely as though the reader should already be familiar with that name, even though the name isn't explained until Sentence 4.

D ✓   **Correct:** This placement is the only one that provides the information about Ely's deformed feet *after* Ely has been described to the reader as a young elephant, and *before* the text mentions Ely being helped through his problems.

▌T1, Q14 (Test 2 in the 2020-2021 Red Book—see page 23)   TYPE: G/S/P (often no prompt; choices w/similar meanings—see page 418)

- **Vertical Scan Results:** Some choices are short phrases with no obvious similarity.
- **Vertical Scan Notes:** Three of the choices begin with "is," and the other choice doesn't involve "is." Three of the choices involve verbs with different endings. Three of the choices involve the word "to."
- **Key Features in Surrounding Text:** The first three words of the sentence are the main subject "Moss" and the main verb "has brought." The original version of the sentence uses "and" to join two groups of words that could each be sentences on their own—but the first group of words ("Moss has brought compelling stories") doesn't specify who Moss brought the stories to.

Concepts in the question:

- **Dependent and Independent Clauses:** Choices would create or join clauses. An independent clause has a main verb and can be a sentence by itself. A dependent clause can't, and starts with a conjunction or relative pronoun. (p. 426)
- **Intervening Phrase:** A phrase appears between two words that need to agree with each other grammatically. Remember to identify pairs of words that need to agree with each other, and ignore phrases that appear between those words. (See page 439)
- **Verb Tense/Conjugation:** Choices include different forms of the same verb. Look at the surrounding text to find the verb's subject. Also look for other verbs that could indicate the proper tense or form for the verbs in the choices. (See p. 420-423)

ANSWER CHOICE ANALYSIS

F   **Incorrect:** As we discussed above, this would basically join two sentences with the word "and:" "Moss has brought compelling stories," and "information about elephants is provided to an ever-expanding audience." This isn't grammatically wrong in itself, but (J) has the advantage of being shorter and also being grammatically acceptable, which means it's right according to the ACT.

G   **Incorrect:** (G) has the same basic problem as (F): it would use "and" to join two independent clauses, but (J) is shorter.

H   **Incorrect:** This choice has the same problem as (F) and (G).

J ✓   **Correct:** This choice causes the sentence to have only one subject ("Moss") and one main verb ("has brought"), and uses the preposition "to" so that "stories and information about elephants" becomes the direct object of "has brought," and "to an ever-expanding audience" becomes the indirect object, telling us who received the "stories and information about elephants." This choice is also the shortest one and results in a grammatically acceptable sentence, so it's right.

Answer choice patterns (page 442): shortest grammatically acceptable choice is correct

▌T1, Q15 (Test 2 in the 2020-2021 Red Book—see page 23)   TYPE: RC (usually has a prompt; choices w/different meanings—see page 413)

- **RC Question sub-type:** Would essay fulfill goal? (The question describes a goal that the author had in writing the passage, and asks whether the author achieved that goal. The right answer choice will be directly restated or demonstrated by the passage, and logically answer the question in the prompt. See page 417)

ANSWER CHOICE ANALYSIS

A   **Barely relevant:** The text doesn't demonstrate the idea from the second part of (A), which is that the essay focuses on how elephants learn to identify family members: the idea of elephants identifying family members is never mentioned in the essay.

B ✓   **Correct:** The part of this choice after the comma is literally demonstrated by the passage, because the passage mentions elephant behaviors observed by Moss, such as the way "a calf [will] stick its trunk into the mouth of its mother" or the way "Echo showed Enid how to care for Ely." As we'll see after we consider all the other choices, (B) is the only one that's literally restated or demonstrated by the text, so (B) must be right.)

C   **Barely relevant:** The essay does describe elephants in Kenya, but it doesn't say how those elephants "have evolved," as (C) would

---

require, and it doesn't compare them to elephants in other parts of Africa, as (C) would also require. Either of these issues is enough to make (C) a wrong answer to an "author's purpose" question on the ACT English section, regardless of whether (C) begins with the word "yes" or "no."

D   **Pattern:** Off by one or two words. **Incorrect:** The essay does describe elephants that Moss studies, as (D) would require, but it never says those elephants are in zoos, and it doesn't describe Moss researching elephants "around the world." Either of those issues would be enough to keep (D) from being a literal restatement or demonstration of the passage, which means (D) can't be right.

T1, Q16 (Test 2 in the 2020-2021 Red Book—see page 23)   **TYPE: G/S/P (often no prompt; choices w/similar meanings—see page 418)**

- **Vertical Scan Results:** Similar phrases with different short words and/or punctuation.
- **Vertical Scan Notes:** All choices include the word "remnants." Two choices include a form of the verb "see" before "remnants." (G) is the only choice that includes "sight."
- **Key Features in Surrounding Text:** The underlined phrase appears immediately before the phrase "of outdoor advertisements," and is part of a longer phrase that ends with a comma and is followed by the word "they." The word "they" must logically refer to some part of the underlined phrase.

Concepts in the question:

- **Changed Meaning:** Choices would change the meaning of the original text, or cause the relevant phrase/sentence not to make sense. The right answer must be grammatically acceptable and still preserve the original meaning. (See p. 438)
- **Dangling Participle:** When a phrase is joined to the main sentence by a comma and the phrase starts with an -ing/-ed/-en word, the first noun phrase in the independent clause is performing the action of the -ing/-ed/-en word. (See page 434.)
- **Dependent and Independent Clauses:** Choices would create or join clauses. An independent clause has a main verb and can be a sentence by itself. A dependent clause can't, and starts with a conjunction or relative pronoun. (p. 426)
- **Intervening Phrase:** A phrase appears between two words that need to agree with each other grammatically. Remember to identify pairs of words that need to agree with each other, and ignore phrases that appear between those words. (See page 439)
- **Pronoun Ambiguity:** Choices include pronouns that could refer to more than one phrase in the surrounding text. We can't use a pronoun on the ACT when it isn't clear what that pronoun refers to. (See page 419)

ANSWER CHOICE ANALYSIS

F   **Incorrect:** Since "seeing" is a participle and "they" is the first noun (or pronoun) in the independent clause, this choice would cause "they" to be the things doing the "seeing." But the sentence tells us "they" refers to "ghost signs," and signs can't see things, because they don't have functioning eyes. Since "seeing" isn't a verb that can be performed by "they" in this sentence, (F) can't be right.

G   **Incorrect:** This choice has a problem similar to what we saw in (F), though (G) doesn't involve a participle. The rules of ACT English would require (G) to say that "the sight" was referred to by "they," but "sight" isn't a plural noun, and the plural pronoun "they" must refer to a plural noun.

H   **Incorrect:** (H) uses the verb form "to see" in a way that doesn't make it clear who's seeing, or why "see" isn't conjugated. As we noted for (F), there's no noun in the sentence that can be performing the action of seeing, so (H) must be wrong.

J ✓ **Correct:** This choice solves the problem from the other choices by causing the sentence to begin with the phrase "remnants…from a bygone era," which provides the noun phrase that "they" is referring to.

T1, Q17 (Test 2 in the 2020-2021 Red Book—see page 23)   **TYPE: G/S/P (often no prompt; choices w/similar meanings—see page 418)**

- **Vertical Scan Results:** Similar phrases with different short words and/or punctuation.
- **Vertical Scan Notes:** All the choices include "era." Three choices include a phrase after "era."
- **Key Features in Surrounding Text:** The surrounding text includes ideas that are repeated in some of the answer choices.

Concepts in the question:

- **Redundancy:** Choices and/or surrounding text could combine to repeat the same concept unnecessarily. On grammar/style/punctuation questions, we should avoid words that directly repeat ideas in the immediate surrounding text. (See p. 437)
- **Shorter is Better:** Choices include words or phrases that can be removed without impacting meaning or creating grammatical problems. The shortest grammatically acceptable choice that doesn't change the meaning is right. (p. 442)

ANSWER CHOICE ANALYSIS

A ✓ **Correct:** This choice avoids the redundancy from the other choices without creating any other issues. Also, this is the shortest choice and it's grammatically acceptable on the ACT, so it's right. See the note below.

B   **Incorrect:** The phrase "that is no more" expresses exactly the same idea as the word "bygone" already expresses in the sentence, so (B) is redundant, which makes it the wrong answer to a style/grammar/punctuation question on the ACT English section. See the note below.

C   **Incorrect:** This choice has essentially the same issue as (B): "of another time" expresses an idea that "bygone" already expressed, making (C) redundant. See the note below.

D   **Incorrect:** Like (B) and (C), this choice expresses an idea that "bygone" already expresses, so this choice is redundant. See the note below.

T1, Q18 (Test 2 in the 2020-2021 Red Book—see page 23)   **TYPE: G/S/P (often no prompt; choices w/similar meanings—see page 418)**

- **Vertical Scan Results:** Some choices have the same words with different punctuation.
- **Vertical Scan Notes:** We have to decide whether no punctuation, a dash, a comma, or a colon should appear after "remain."
- **Key Features in Surrounding Text:** The original sentence includes a dash that isn't acceptable according to the rules of the ACT English section, because it isn't part of a "punctuation sandwich." In other words, no phrase that's set off by the dash could be removed from the sentence and leave behind a set of words that could stand on their own as a sentence, with the same essential meaning as the original sentence.

Concepts in the question:

- **Colons:** Choices include colons. A colon can only be placed after a set of words that could be a sentence on their own, and only before a demonstration or example of the idea before the colon. No more than one colon per sentence. (p. 430)
- **Commas:** Choices include commas. Commas can separate a list of 3 or more items, form sandwiches, separate interchangeable adjectives, or introduce an independent clause after a dependent clause. They can't appear for no reason. (p. 431)
- **Punctuation Sandwich:** Choices involve phrases "sandwiched" between similar punctuation marks. When removed from the sentence, a proper sandwich leaves behind a grammatical sentence with the same original meaning. (See p. 432 and 433)

ANSWER CHOICE ANALYSIS

F   **Incorrect:** As we discussed above, the sentence currently uses a dash in a way that doesn't follow the ACT's standards.

G ✓   **Correct:** This choice creates a punctuation sandwich (in this case, a dash sandwich) around the phrase "Fruiterer...Apothecary...Gramophones...Pan-Handle Coffee." This punctuation sandwich is acceptable on the ACT English section because it surrounds a phrase that can be removed from the original sentence, leaving behind a grammatically acceptable sentence with the same essential meaning as the original sentence.

H   **Incorrect:** This choice fails to solve the dash problem described in the explanation for (F), so it's wrong. It might attract some untrained test-takers who glance through the rest of the sentence, notice that it seems to list a certain kind of word, and assume incorrectly that commas are relevant to the kind of list in the sentence.

J   **Incorrect:** This choice fails to solve the dash problem described in the explanation for (F). Further, as trained test-takers, we know that a colon can only appear on the ACT English section after a group of words that could stand on their own as a sentence, which isn't the case here. This choice might attract an untrained test-taker who knows that lists are often introduced by colons, but who doesn't read the rest of the sentence, and/or doesn't know the rules for colons and dashes on the ACT English section.

T1, Q19 (Test 2 in the 2020-2021 Red Book—see page 23)   **TYPE: G/S/P (often no prompt; choices w/similar meanings—see page 418)**

- **Vertical Scan Results:** Similar phrases with different short words and/or punctuation.
- **Vertical Scan Notes:** All four choices include "should." Two choices also include "they," and one choice includes "that." The word "should" comes first in one of the choices, last in two of the choices, and stands alone in the other choice.
- **Key Features in Surrounding Text:** The underlined phrase is part of a group of words that could stand on their own as a grammatically acceptable sentence on the ACT English section: "Pale fragments...should strike me as silly or sad." But that group of words is joined to the first half of the sentence by a comma, and the first half of the sentence *could also stand on its own as a sentence:* "Whatever words remain...are often barely legible." The ACT English section doesn't allow us to use a comma to join two groups of words together if each group could stand on its own as a sentence, so the original version of the sentence is unacceptable according to the ACT.

Concepts in the question:

- **Comma Splice:** Choices and/or surrounding text use commas to join two groups of words that could each be sentences on their own. A comma can't be used in this way on the ACT English section. (See page 428)
- **Commas:** Choices include commas. Commas can separate a list of 3 or more items, form sandwiches, separate interchangeable adjectives, or introduce an independent clause after a dependent clause. They can't appear for no reason. (p. 431)
- **Dependent and Independent Clauses:** Choices would create or join clauses. An independent clause has a main verb and can be a sentence by itself. A dependent clause can't, and starts with a conjunction or relative pronoun. (p. 426)

ANSWER CHOICE ANALYSIS

A   **Incorrect:** As we noted above, this choice would create a comma splice, because "whatever words...are often barely legible" and "pale fragments...should strike me as silly or sad" could each stand on their own as sentences.

B ✓   **Correct:** (B) uses the relative pronoun "that" before the verb "should," which turns the second half of the sentence into the dependent phrase "pale fragments...that should strike me as silly or sad." This causes the original sentence to begin with an independent clause and end with a dependent clause joined by a comma, which is acceptable on the ACT English section.

C   Incorrect: This choice is flawed for multiple reasons. One of the most obvious reasons is that it creates the following independent clause: "they should strike me as silly or sad." That clause would then be stuck on to the phrase "pale fragments of yesterday's consumer culture" with no punctuation, and then all of those words together would still be joined to the independent clause in the first half of the sentence with a comma, which is an unacceptable use of a comma on the ACT English section, as we saw in our discussion of (A).

D   Incorrect: This choice has essentially the same issue as (C). Everything in the sentence up to the comma after "legible" can stand on its own as sentence, and this choice makes the rest of the sentence either an awkward independent clause, which would make the sentence a comma splice (as we saw with (A) and (C)), or a nonsensical clause with two main nouns ("fragments" and "they") that aren't joined by any conjunction. Either way, this choice doesn't create an acceptable sentence on the ACT.

T1, Q20 (Test 2 in the 2020-2021 Red Book—see page 23)   TYPE: G/S/P (often no prompt; choices w/similar meanings—see page 418)

- **Vertical Scan Results:** Some choices have the same words with different punctuation.
- **Vertical Scan Notes:** The choices give us the options of including a comma, a colon, or nothing after "products," and a comma or nothing after "businesses." Once choice also omits "and."
- **Key Features in Surrounding Text:** The underlined words are part of a phrase telling us what kinds of things the signs are "advertising."

ANSWER CHOICE ANALYSIS

- **Changed Meaning:** Choices would change the meaning of the original text, or cause the relevant phrase/sentence not to make sense. The right answer must be grammatically acceptable and still preserve the original meaning. (See p. 438)
- **Colons:** Choices include colons. A colon can only be placed after a set of words that could be a sentence on their own, and only before a demonstration or example of the idea before the colon. No more than one colon per sentence. (p. 430)
- **Commas:** Choices include commas. Commas can separate a list of 3 or more items, form sandwiches, separate interchangeable adjectives, or introduce an independent clause after a dependent clause. They can't appear for no reason. (p. 431)
- **Dependent and Independent Clauses:** Choices would create or join clauses. An independent clause has a main verb and can be a sentence by itself. A dependent clause can't, and starts with a conjunction or relative pronoun. (p. 426)
- **Intervening Phrase:** A phrase appears between two words that need to agree with each other grammatically. Remember to identify pairs of words that need to agree with each other, and ignore phrases that appear between those words. (See page 439)

ANSWER CHOICE ANALYSIS

F ✓   Correct: This choice avoids the problems from the other choices without creating any additional problems. (As trained test-takers, we know that we should omit commas and other punctuation unless they're specifically required by the rules of the ACT English section. In this case, there's no need for punctuation: "products and businesses" are the things that no longer exist, and we don't need punctuation before the word "that," which refers back to the products and businesses.)

G   Incorrect: According to the rules of ACT English, there's no need for a comma to separate the phrase "that no longer exist" from the phrase "products and businesses" that it's modifying. See the explanation of (F) for more.

H   Incorrect: The easiest way to know this choice is wrong is to recognize that it would use a comma to separate two things in a list ("advertising products" and "businesses"), which the ACT English section doesn't allow. Even if we miss that issue, this choice would also fundamentally change the meaning of the sentence, which isn't allowed on the ACT English section. The original sentence says that "they" (the ghost signs) advertise things that don't exist anymore, and the nonexistent things being advertised were "products and businesses." But (H) would make the sentence say that there were two types of things present: (1) some "advertising products," which could be things like branded t-shirts, etc., and (2) "businesses that no longer exist." In other words, this placement of a comma would cause the sentence to mention "advertising products," and would make it so that the "advertising products" are no longer described as being things that don't exist—only the businesses would be things that don't exist, according to this version of the sentence. So this choice would create a sentence that doesn't make any sense in the passage, because the paragraph doesn't mention the idea that "advertising products" and "businesses that no longer exist" are "there;" the only things described as being anywhere are the "ghost signs," which is clear in the correct version of this sentence as well. See the explanation of (F) above for more.

J   Incorrect: There are multiple ways to describe the issues with (J). One of them would be to note that we can't have two colons in one sentence. Another would be to note that this colon would turn the phrase "businesses that no longer exist" into an explanation of what "advertising products" are, and the "advertising products" would be an explanation of what "there they are" means—none of which makes any sense. See the explanation of (F) for more.

Answer choice patterns (page 442): wrong answers try to imitate right answers

T1, Q21 (Test 2 in the 2020-2021 Red Book—see page 23)   TYPE: G/S/P (often no prompt; choices w/similar meanings—see page 418)

- **Vertical Scan Results:** Some choices have the same words with different punctuation.
- **Vertical Scan Notes:** The choices offer us a combination of comma placements after "apology," "with," and/or "instead"

- **Key Features in Surrounding Text:** The original version of the underlined phrase creates a comma sandwich around the phrase "with instead," which is unacceptable on the ACT English section, because the sandwiched phrase wouldn't leave behind a grammatically acceptable sentence if it were removed.

Concepts in the question:

- **Comma Splice:** Choices and/or surrounding text use commas to join two groups of words that could each be sentences on their own. A comma can't be used in this way on the ACT English section. (See page 428)
- **Commas:** Choices include commas. Commas can separate a list of 3 or more items, form sandwiches, separate interchangeable adjectives, or introduce an independent clause after a dependent clause. They can't appear for no reason. (p. 431)
- **Intervening Phrase:** A phrase appears between two words that need to agree with each other grammatically. Remember to identify pairs of words that need to agree with each other, and ignore phrases that appear between those words. (See page 439)
- **Punctuation Sandwich:** Choices involve phrases "sandwiched" between similar punctuation marks. When removed from the sentence, a proper sandwich leaves behind a grammatical sentence with the same original meaning. (See p. 432 and 433)

ANSWER CHOICE ANALYSIS

A Incorrect: As we noted above, the original version of the underlined phrase creates a comma sandwich around the phrase "with instead" that's unacceptable on the ACT English section.

B ✓ Correct: The series of commas that appears in this question makes it difficult for some test-takers to think about. The easiest way to realize what should be going on in this sentence is probably to imagine the sentence without the word "instead." The sentence that remains would be "Yet, they themselves survive without apology, with their simple claims and complex colors." This makes it easier to see that there needs to be a comma after "apology," because otherwise there would be two consecutive phrases describing the word "survive" ("without apology" and "with their simple claims and complex colors") with no punctuation between them. Now we need to think about how "instead" fits back in, since each choice includes "instead." We've already determined that the sentence is acceptable without the word "instead," so it must be okay to add "instead" back in, sandwiched between two commas—because any phrase sandwiched between two commas on the ACT English section can be removed and leave behind an acceptable sentence. So there should be a comma after "apology," "with," and "instead," which means (B) must be right.

C Incorrect: This choice would create a comma sandwich around "they…instead," which would leave behind a sentence fragment if removed.

D Incorrect: See the explanation for (B) to understand why commas must appear in the underlined phrase.

T1, Q22 (Test 2 in the 2020-2021 Red Book—see page 23)　　　**TYPE: G/S/P (often no prompt; choices w/similar meanings—see page 418)**

- **Vertical Scan Results:** Choices are long phrases/sentences.
- **Vertical Scan Notes:** The choices offer a variety of ways to arrange similar phrases relating to the ideas of driving home from school, a chilly evening, and the beginning of the collection.
- **Key Features in Surrounding Text:** The entire sentence is underlined in this case. The previous sentence tells us the "collection" in the question is a collection of photographs. As trained test-takers, we know that the original version of the sentence actually says that the collection itself was the thing driving home, because we know that the rules of ACT English say that if a phrase beginning with an "-ing" verb is attached to an independent clause with a comma, then the first noun in the independent clause is the thing performing the action of the "-ing" verb.

Concepts in the question:

- **Changed Meaning:** Choices would change the meaning of the original text, or cause the relevant phrase/sentence not to make sense. The right answer must be grammatically acceptable and still preserve the original meaning. (See p. 438)
- **Commas:** Choices include commas. Commas can separate a list of 3 or more items, form sandwiches, separate interchangeable adjectives, or introduce an independent clause after a dependent clause. They can't appear for no reason. (p. 431)
- **Dangling Participle:** When a phrase is joined to the main sentence by a comma and the phrase starts with an -ing/-ed/-en word, the first noun phrase in the independent clause is performing the action of the -ing/-ed/-en word. (See page 434.)
- **Dependent and Independent Clauses:** Choices would create or join clauses. An independent clause has a main verb and can be a sentence by itself. A dependent clause can't, and starts with a conjunction or relative pronoun. (p. 426)
- **Intervening Phrase:** A phrase appears between two words that need to agree with each other grammatically. Remember to identify pairs of words that need to agree with each other, and ignore phrases that appear between those words. (See page 439)

ANSWER CHOICE ANALYSIS

F Incorrect: As we noted above, this version of the sentence says that "my collection" was the thing "driving home" according to the rules of ACT English. Since a collection can't drive, this choice can't be right.

G Incorrect: This version of the sentence says that "the beginning of my collection" was "driving home," which could mean one of two things: either the beginning itself was driving, which is logically impossible, or the act of driving home was the first thing in the collection, which is impossible since the text tells us that the collection involves photographs.

H ✓   **Correct:** This version fixes the problem that we noted above. According to the ACT's rules for participles, (H) says that "I" was the thing "driving home," because the independent clause "I started…one…evening" is followed by a comma and then the "-ing" word "driving." (H) is the only choice that provides a logically possible statement about who was driving.

J   **Incorrect:** This version of the sentence says that "the start of my collection" was the thing "driving home," which is logically impossible. Some untrained test-takers will misread this sentence or think that it says something like "The start…came to me…*while* I was driving home." But, when we read carefully, we see that the word "me" is used, not the word "I;" grammatically speaking, the word "me" always indicates receiving an object or an action, not performing it. So this version of the sentence makes it impossible for the speaker to have been doing the driving.

T1, Q23 (Test 2 in the 2020-2021 Red Book—see page 23)   **TYPE: RC (usually has a prompt; choices w/different meanings—see page 413)**

- **RC Question sub-type:** Best accomplishes X. (The prompt describes a goal of the author, and asks which choice achieves that goal. The right answer will be plainly demonstrated in the passage. See page 413)

ANSWER CHOICE ANALYSIS

A   **Barely relevant:** As trained test-takers, we know that the idea of "echo[ing] a central point…about ghost signs" as described in the prompt will require us to find an answer choice that literally restates or demonstrates some concept about ghost signs from the passage. This means that (A) can't be right, because the idea of a sign being "upright," "vertical," or any other kind of similar word or phrase doesn't appear anywhere in the passage.

B   **Direct contradiction:** The idea of an old ad not being interesting to the author isn't a "central point the writer makes," as the prompt would require. In fact, it's the opposite of what the author says: she mentions "search[ing] for them on city streets" and "collect[ing]…photos of them," and says they "draw [her] in every time," and that she's "happily haunted" by them.

C   **Barely relevant:** This choice has a flaw similar to the one we discussed for (A): it mentions an idea that doesn't appear anywhere in the passage. Some untrained test-takers will be drawn to this choice because they will simply assume that old signs would be made of wood, without realizing that the ACT English section is asking us to pick a choice that "echoes" something from the passage—that's literally restated or demonstrated elsewhere in the text—which this choice doesn't do.

D ✓   **Correct:** As we noted in our discussion of (A) and (C) above, the right answer must be literally restated or demonstrated in the passage. Throughout the passage, the author describes ghost signs as "faded," "barely legible," and "pale." The word "disappearing" in this choice causes the sign in the sentence to demonstrate those ideas.

T1, Q24 (Test 2 in the 2020-2021 Red Book—see page 23)   **TYPE: G/S/P (often no prompt; choices w/similar meanings—see page 418)**

- **Vertical Scan Results:** Similar phrases with different short words and/or punctuation.
- **Vertical Scan Notes:** The choices provide different orders for words related to sunset and illumination. "Illuminated" appears in two choices, while "illumination" and "illuminating" appear in one choice each. "Setting" appears in three choices, while "set" appears in one.
- **Key Features in Surrounding Text:** The phrase "the way the…" in the original sentence requires a verb after it, but the original version of the underlined phrase doesn't provide one. (In this sentence, the words "setting" and "yellowing" are adjectives, and "illumination" is a noun.)

Concepts in the question:

- **Dependent and Independent Clauses:** Choices would create or join clauses. An independent clause has a main verb and can be a sentence by itself. A dependent clause can't, and starts with a conjunction or relative pronoun. (p. 426)
- **Shorter is Better:** Choices include words or phrases that can be removed without impacting meaning or creating grammatical problems. The shortest grammatically acceptable choice that doesn't change the meaning is right. (p. 442)
- **Verb Tense/Conjugation:** Choices include different forms of the same verb. Look at the surrounding text to find the verb's subject. Also look for other verbs that could indicate the proper tense or form for the verbs in the choices. (See p. 420-423)

ANSWER CHOICE ANALYSIS

F   **Incorrect:** As we noted above, the original version of the sentence is lacking a verb to complete the idea that begins with the phrase "the way the…."

G   **Incorrect:** This choice has the same problem as (F): it lacks a verb to tell us what was done in the "way" mentioned earlier in the sentence.

H   **Incorrect:** Strictly speaking, this choice creates a sentence that could be grammatically acceptable on the ACT English section: the main verb would be "illuminated," and the word "set" would have to be a noun (like in "tea set" or "movie set"), and the set would have to be located on some kind of "yellowing plastic." Of course, this choice is still wrong, for two reasons. First, it changes the meaning of the sentence by introducing the idea of a "set," which isn't mentioned anywhere else (in addition to the fact that a "set" being on some "yellowing plastic" and getting "illuminated" by the sun doesn't make any sense in the context of the passage). Second, as trained test-takers, we should note that (J) is both grammatically acceptable and shorter than (H), which means (J) must be right.

J ✓ **Correct:** This is the shortest grammatically acceptable answer choice, so we know it must be right, since this question is a grammar/style/punctuation question. The word "illuminated" is the verb that was done in the particular "way" referred to in the sentence.

Note Many untrained test-takers will incorrectly assume that they can rely on the concept of parallelism to attack this question successfully, which may cause them to pick (G) because it includes two "-ing" words, which look like they might be parallel to the word "yellowing" in the sentence. But, as trained test-takers, we know that we should only think about parallelism when the proper form of a word can't be determined by using grammar alone, as we discussed in the training on parallelism on page 440 of this Black Book. In this case, it's clear that the original version of the sentence requires us to provide a verb to complete the phrase "the way the...." (Further, as we noted above, "yellowing" is actually an adjective describing "plastic" in this sentence—not a verb being performed by the sun, which is what "illuminated" is in the right answer.)

T1, Q25 (Test 2 in the 2020-2021 Red Book—see page 23)   **TYPE: G/S/P (often no prompt; choices w/similar meanings—see page 418)**

- **Vertical Scan Results:** Some choices have different forms of the same base word.
- **Vertical Scan Notes:** Two choices include a version of the word "evidence," one choice mentions a "clue," and one choice is to delete the underlined phrase.
- **Key Features in Surrounding Text:** The word "or" connects the ideas of both "vandalism" and "a hailstorm" to the "small hole" mentioned earlier in the sentence.

Concepts in the question:

- **Intervening Phrase:** A phrase appears between two words that need to agree with each other grammatically. Remember to identify pairs of words that need to agree with each other, and ignore phrases that appear between those words. (See page 439)
- **Prepositional Idioms:** Choices typically include prepositional phrases with no other recognizable similarities. If you can't tell which choice contains an acceptable prepositional idiom in American English, guess and invest your time elsewhere. (p. 435)

ANSWER CHOICE ANALYSIS

A **Incorrect:** This choice would create two incorrect versions of a prepositional idiom: "clue to vandalism" and "clue...of a hailstorm." We'll actually consider the second incorrect idiom first, because it probably sounds more obviously unacceptable than the first one. The phrase "clue of a hailstorm" (or "clue of" anything else, for that matter) isn't acceptable in English, which is enough to make this choice wrong. Even though this phrase is more obviously wrong to most people than the first one (which we'll discuss in a minute), many test-takers won't notice that "clue" needs to create a prepositional idiom with "of a hailstorm," because the use of "or" in the original sentence creates distance between "clue" and "of a hailstorm." Now let's consider the first incorrect prepositional idiom. The phrase "clue to" does exist in English, but its use is slightly different from what we see here. We could call something a "clue to a mystery," or a "clue to a puzzle," where what comes after "to" is an article like "a," and then something that needs to be solved or figured out—like a puzzle, or a mystery, or a riddle, or something along those lines. But the phrase that would appear in the passage if we picked this choice lacks any kind of article after "to," and "vandalism" isn't something that needs to be solved or figured out. (The question of who committed vandalism could be something that needs to be solved or figured out, but "vandalism" doesn't mean the same thing as "the question of who committed vandalism.") So (A) must be wrong. (Notice that in order to realize that this choice was wrong, we only had to be able to recognize the problem with one of the two prepositional idioms—as soon as we did that, we could eliminate this choice and move on.)

B ✓ **Correct:** "Evidence of vandalism" is an acceptable prepositional idiom in American English, and so is "evidence of a hailstorm." In this sense, the word "evidence" means "an indication" or "a trace." See the explanations of the other choices, and the note below, for more.

C **Incorrect:** It's grammatically acceptable (though maybe a little strange in this sentence) to say that something is "evidently vandalism," but the underlined phrase also has to work with the phrase "of a hailstorm," and "evidently of a hailstorm" isn't a prepositional idiom in American English and doesn't make sense in context, so (C) is wrong.

D **Incorrect:** This choice would cause the sentence to say the small hole itself was "vandalism or of a hailstorm." This is ungrammatical for multiple reasons; one of the easier ones to see is probably that we can't say something was a "hole of a hailstorm." Another issue with this choice is that the phrase "the small hole, vandalism or of a hailstorm" is just meaningless as it appears in this sentence.

Note It's true that the right answer to this question creates two parallel structures ("evidence of vandalism" and "evidence...of a hailstorm"), but that parallelism isn't the *reason* for the right answer to be right! The right answer is right because "evidence of X" is an acceptable idiomatic expression in American English; the fact that it appears twice in this sentence isn't what makes it right. It's also arguably true to say that the wrong answers are wrong because they don't use the word "of"—but, again, this isn't related to the fact that "of" appears elsewhere in the sentence. It's just that "evidence of X" is an acceptable prepositional idiom in American English, while "a clue to X" and "evidently...of X" and "vandalism or of a hailstorm" aren't prepositional idioms. To a lot of people, it may seem like we're splitting hairs by pointing this out, but the distinction is important if your goal is to score very high. This isn't a parallelism question, but a prepositional idiom question. Remember that you should only consider parallelism when you can't use grammar alone to find the answer because more than one choice would be grammatically acceptable. In this case, only one choice is grammatically acceptable because only one choice creates a prepositional idiom that's acceptable in American English. (And, as always, remember that you shouldn't spend a lot of time trying to figure out the right answer to a prepositional idiom question, because they don't follow generalized rules for using particular prepositions. Instead, you should read carefully and then pick the choice that feels right to you as quickly as you can, so you'll be able to invest more of your time in all the non-idiom questions, since those questions are far more common and you can analyze them in terms of general rules and principles.)

T1, Q26 (Test 2 in the 2020-2021 Red Book—see page 23)   TYPE: RC (usually has a prompt; choices w/different meanings—see page 413)

- **RC Question sub-type:** Transition Phrase. (The choices reflect different kinds of transitions between two concepts, with words or phrases like "however," "instead of," or "for example." The right answer must reflect the relationship between the previous concept in the passage and the following concept in the passage. See p. 416)

ANSWER CHOICE ANALYSIS

F   **Confused relationships:** The word "instead" indicates a contradiction between two ideas, but the idea that "something about the sign touched [the author]" doesn't contradict the idea of a "small hole" from the previous sentence.

G   **Confused relationships:** This choice would be acceptable if this sentence expressed an idea that was an alternative to the idea from the preceding sentence, but that's not the case here.

H   **Confused relationships:** This choice would be acceptable if this sentence and the previous sentence described two things that were happening in different places at the same time, but that's not the case here.

J ✓ **Correct:** None of the transition phrases from the other choices are acceptable on the ACT, for the reasons we discussed above. That means this choice, with no transition, must be right.

T1, Q27 (Test 2 in the 2020-2021 Red Book—see page 23)   TYPE: G/S/P (often no prompt; choices w/similar meanings—see page 418)

- **Vertical Scan Results:** Some choices have different forms of the same base word.
- **Vertical Scan Notes:** The choices are all similar to the word "solo." Two are nouns, one is an adverb, and one is an adjective.
- **Key Features in Surrounding Text:** The underlined word comes after the verb phrase "have been" and before the noun "trips."

    Concepts in the question:

- **Adjective/Adverb:** Choices involve a word in its adjective or adverb form. Remember that adverb forms often end in "-ly," but not always. Adjectives can modify nouns; adverbs can modify anything else (verbs, adjectives, other adverbs). (p. 423)

ANSWER CHOICE ANALYSIS

A   **Incorrect:** This choice would use the noun "solitude" to modify the noun "trips." There are at least two reasons this choice is wrong on the ACT English section. The first reason is that a word that comes immediately before a noun and modifies that noun as we see it being done here should be an adjective, not another noun. (There are situations in American English when it would be acceptable to use a noun to modify another noun, like in the phrase "cheese pizza," but "solitude trips" isn't a situation like this.)

B   **Incorrect:** This choice basically has the same issue we noted for (A): it's an unacceptable part of speech in this context on the ACT English section. The slight technical difference between these two choices is that "solitarily" is an adverb, not a noun like "solitude," and it's basically never acceptable in American English to use an adverb to modify a noun in the way that (B) would require.

C   **Incorrect:** This choice would also use a noun to modify a noun, as we discussed for (A) above. It might appeal to untrained test-takers who misread it as the adjective "solitary."

D ✓ **Correct:** This choice provides the only adjective we can use to modify the noun "trips."

T1, Q28 (Test 2 in the 2020-2021 Red Book—see page 23)   TYPE: G/S/P (often no prompt; choices w/similar meanings—see page 418)

- **Vertical Scan Results:** Some choices have the same words with different punctuation.
- **Vertical Scan Notes:** We need to decide whether commas should appear after "I," "like," and/or "signs."
- **Key Features in Surrounding Text:** The text following the underlined phrase includes the verb "am," which can only be acceptable with the subject "I." So we need to make sure that the underlined word "I" can agree with "am."

    Concepts in the question:

- **Changed Meaning:** Choices would change the meaning of the original text, or cause the relevant phrase/sentence not to make sense. The right answer must be grammatically acceptable and still preserve the original meaning. (See p. 438)

- **Commas:** Choices include commas. Commas can separate a list of 3 or more items, form sandwiches, separate interchangeable adjectives, or introduce an independent clause after a dependent clause. They can't appear for no reason. (p. 431)

- **Intervening Phrase:** A phrase appears between two words that need to agree with each other grammatically. Remember to identify pairs of words that need to agree with each other, and ignore phrases that appear between those words. (See page 439)

- **Punctuation Sandwich:** Choices involve phrases "sandwiched" between similar punctuation marks. When removed from the sentence, a proper sandwich leaves behind a grammatical sentence with the same original meaning. (See p. 432 and 433)

- **Verb Tense/Conjugation:** Choices include different forms of the same verb. Look at the surrounding text to find the verb's subject. Also look for other verbs that could indicate the proper tense or form for the verbs in the choices. (See p. 420-423)

ANSWER CHOICE ANALYSIS

F **Incorrect:** This choice could attract an untrained test-taker who thought the sentence ended at the word "signs," because that would leave us with the grammatically acceptable sentence "I appreciate…when I like the signs." But this would ignore the words "am alone" at the end of the original sentence, which wouldn't be able to refer back to "I" because the verb "like" would already be associated with "I," and there's no word like "and" to allow a second verb to be associated with "I." So "am alone" would just be floating at the end of the sentence, not relating back to anything else.

G **Incorrect:** This choice would form a punctuation sandwich around "like," indicating that "like" could be removed from the sentence without creating an ungrammatical sentence. But removing "like" would leave us with the verb phrase "*when I the signs am alone." In this phrase, "the signs" would have no grammatical relationship to any other words in the sentence, which would mean that the comma sandwich around "like" would be unacceptable on the ACT English section.

H ✓ **Correct:** (H) creates a punctuation sandwich around "like the signs." When we remove that phrase, we're left with the phrase "when I am alone," which is grammatically acceptable on the ACT, and preserves the clear meaning of the sentence.

J **Incorrect:** This choice creates a comma sandwich around "the signs," but removing "the signs" from the original sentence results in this phrase: "*when I like am alone." In that version of the sentence, "like" would have no grammatical relationship to any other word in the sentence, which would mean that the sentence was grammatically unacceptable on the ACT English section.

T1, Q29 (Test 2 in the 2020-2021 Red Book—see page 23)   TYPE: RC (usually has a prompt; choices w/different meanings—see page 413)

- **RC Question sub-type:** Sentence or paragraph placement. (The prompt asks us where a sentence should go in a paragraph, or where a paragraph should go in the passage. The correct order will reflect a logical chronology, and/or will allow for pronouns to refer to nouns in a logical way, and/or will place related concepts near one another. See page 415)

ANSWER CHOICE ANALYSIS

A ✓ **Correct:** The first paragraph tells us what ghost signs are. The second paragraph tells us the narrator collects pictures of ghost signs and mentions the start of the narrator's collection. The third paragraph tells us about the first time the narrator took a picture of a ghost sign. Nothing in the original sequence of events is logically impossible. None of these paragraphs refers to a concept as though the reader should already know what it is without properly introducing it. For these reasons, the ACT won't let us move this paragraph to any other position in the passage.

B **Causes text to refer to an idea that hasn't been mentioned yet:** This would cause the narrator to discuss ghost signs as though the reader already knows what they are, even though the author hasn't explained the term yet.

C **Causes text to introduce an idea that has already been discussed:** This would cause the narrator to explain her collection of pictures of ghost signs *after* she has already told the story of how she took her first picture in that collection.

D **Causes text to introduce an idea that has already been discussed:** This choice has the same problem as (C).

T1, Q30 (Test 2 in the 2020-2021 Red Book—see page 23)   TYPE: RC (usually has a prompt; choices w/different meanings—see page 413)

- **RC Question sub-type:** Would essay fulfill goal? (The question describes a goal that the author had in writing the passage, and asks whether the author achieved that goal. The right answer choice will be directly restated or demonstrated by the passage, and logically answer the question in the prompt. See page 417)

ANSWER CHOICE ANALYSIS

F ✓ **Correct:** This choice is the only one whose description of the passage is literally demonstrated by the passage. The third paragraph describes how the narrator first noticed a ghost sign, then stopped and took a picture of the sign. It then says that "since that dusky evening, [the narrator has] been happily haunted by ghost signs." So we can see that noticing the first ghost sign was "the event that led to the narrator becoming interested in finding ghost signs and taking photographs of them," just as (F) requires. (Remember that we don't have to worry about whether "yes" or "no" is an ideal answer to the question if only one of the answer choices is literally restated or demonstrated by the passage, which is the case here.)

G **Confused relationships:** In the fourth paragraph, the narrator mentions the idea of taking a friend out to hunt for ghost signs, but she never says that a friend *taught her* "how much fun the search itself can be," as (G) would require. Since (G) doesn't describe the passage accurately, it can't be right.

H **Confused relationships:** The narrator does use the word "forlorn"—but she uses it to describe the "beauty of [a] discovery," not her "experience" searching for ghost signs, as (H) would require. Furthermore the narrator never uses the word "lonely" to describe anything, even though (H) says she does. Any of these differences would be enough to make this choice wrong. (Remember that we don't have to concern ourselves with whether "yes" or "no" is an appropriate answer if the description of the relevant text is inaccurate, as it is here.)

J **Confused relationships:** The text never describes two separate hobbies—the only hobby described in the passage is taking photographs of ghost signs, which the narrator calls "collect[in]g ghost signs." So the photography described in the passage is photography of ghost signs, and "collecting ghost signs" *is* taking pictures of ghost signs. Again, the passage only describes one hobby. Since the description in (J) differs from the relevant text, we know (J) must be wrong.

T1, Q31 (Test 2 in the 2020-2021 Red Book—see page 23)　　TYPE: G/S/P (often no prompt; choices w/similar meanings—see page 418)

- **Vertical Scan Results:** Similar phrases with different short words and/or punctuation.
- **Vertical Scan Notes:** We need to decide whether the phrase should include "which," whether it should include "are," and whether it should include a comma after "States."
- **Key Features in Surrounding Text:** The original version of the sentence doesn't include a main verb, because the word "which" makes the verb "are" part of a description of either the islands or the United States, and not the main verb corresponding to the subject "the Bahamas."

Concepts in the question:

- **Commas:** Choices include commas. Commas can separate a list of 3 or more items, form sandwiches, separate interchangeable adjectives, or introduce an independent clause after a dependent clause. They can't appear for no reason. (p. 431)
- **Dependent and Independent Clauses:** Choices would create or join clauses. An independent clause has a main verb and can be a sentence by itself. A dependent clause can't, and starts with a conjunction or relative pronoun. (p. 426)
- **Intervening Phrase:** A phrase appears between two words that need to agree with each other grammatically. Remember to identify pairs of words that need to agree with each other, and ignore phrases that appear between those words. (See page 439)
- **Punctuation Sandwich:** Choices involve phrases "sandwiched" between similar punctuation marks. When removed from the sentence, a proper sandwich leaves behind a grammatical sentence with the same original meaning. (See p. 432 and 433)

ANSWER CHOICE ANALYSIS

A　　Incorrect: As we noted above, the word "which" makes the original "sentence" a fragment with no independent clause.

B　✓　Correct: This choice deletes the word "which" and creates a comma sandwich around the phrase "a series of semitropical islands…States," which is acceptable on the ACT English section because removing the phrase leaves behind a complete sentence with the same essential meaning as the original sentence.

C　　Incorrect: This choice omits the necessary comma that was included in (B). This causes the "sentence" not to have a main verb, since there's no main subject and "are" doesn't clearly apply to any particular plural noun.

D　　Incorrect: This choice is missing the word "are," which makes this a sentence fragment that doesn't include a main verb for the subject "Bahamas." Instead, this fragment would include the phrases "a series of semitropical islands off the…States" and "home to some of the…blue holes" as two separate comma sandwiches possibly describing the Bahamas.

T1, Q32 (Test 2 in the 2020-2021 Red Book—see page 23)　　TYPE: RC (usually has a prompt; choices w/different meanings—see page 413)

- **RC Question sub-type:** Best accomplishes X. (The prompt describes a goal of the author, and asks which choice achieves that goal. The right answer will be plainly demonstrated in the passage. See page 413)

Subjective Phrases to Ignore: "most effectively"

ANSWER CHOICE ANALYSIS

F　✓　Correct: There are a couple of ways we know that this choice must be right. First, the next sentence after the sentence we'll need to insert mentions "the formation process," and this choice is the only one that mentions anything forming ("the Bahamas were formed…"). Second, this paragraph is about how the Bahamas formed from calcium carbonate, and this choice is the only one that mentions both the Bahamas and calcium carbonate.

G　　Barely relevant: This choice can't be an acceptable introduction because this paragraph is about how the Bahamas formed from calcium carbonate, and this choice doesn't even mention the Bahamas. Also, the next sentence after the sentence we'll need to insert mentions "the formation process," and this choice doesn't mention anything forming.

H　　Barely relevant: This choice can't be an acceptable introduction because this paragraph is about how the Bahamas formed from calcium carbonate, and this choice doesn't even mention calcium carbonate. Also, the next sentence after the sentence we'll need to insert mentions "the formation process," and this choice doesn't mention anything forming.

J　　Barely relevant: This choice has basically the same problem as (G).

T1, Q33 (Test 2 in the 2020-2021 Red Book—see page 23)　　TYPE: G/S/P (often no prompt; choices w/similar meanings—see page 418)

- **Vertical Scan Results:** Some choices have different forms of the same base word.
- **Vertical Scan Notes:** The choices include different tenses of the verb "build."
- **Key Features in Surrounding Text:** The underlined text is followed by the phrase "then compacted." So the action in the underlined text is something that happened *before* the action of the verb "compacted." That means the right answer must be a verb in the past tense, because it describes an action that happened before the past-tense verb "compacted."

Concepts in the question:

- **Parallelism:** Choices include options that would ignore a parallel structure in the surrounding text. The right answer should match the phrasing and grammatical structures in the surrounding text when possible. (See p. 440)

- **Verb Tense/Conjugation:** Choices include different forms of the same verb. Look at the surrounding text to find the verb's subject. Also look for other verbs that could indicate the proper tense or form for the verbs in the choices. (See p. 420-423)

ANSWER CHOICE ANALYSIS

A ✓ **Correct:** "Built" is the only past tense verb form in the answer choices, so it's the only choice that describes something that can happen before the past-tense verb "compacted" in the sentence, as we noted above.

B **Incorrect:** "Are building" is a present-tense verb form, so it can't happen before the past-tense verb "compacted," as the word "then" would require.

C **Incorrect:** "Will build" is a future-tense verb form, so it has basically the same issue as (B): it can't describe an action that occurs before the action in the past-tense verb "compacted."

D **Incorrect:** "Build" is a present-tense verb form, so this choice has the same basic flaw as the other wrong answer choices, because it can't be used to describe an action that happens before a past-tense verb.

T1, Q34 (Test 2 in the 2020-2021 Red Book—see page 23)   TYPE: G/S/P (often no prompt; choices w/similar meanings—see page 418)

- **Vertical Scan Results:** Similar phrases with different short words and/or punctuation.

- **Vertical Scan Notes:** All the choices include some form of "buoy" along with some combination of the words "being," "by," "because of," "it," and "was."

- **Key Features in Surrounding Text:** All the choices include some form of the verb "buoy," so it will probably be useful to realize that the noun that's connected to that verb is the word "seawater." The other verbs in the sentence are "permeated" and "was trapped."

Concepts in the question:

- **Changed Meaning:** Choices would change the meaning of the original text, or cause the relevant phrase/sentence not to make sense. The right answer must be grammatically acceptable and still preserve the original meaning. (See p. 438)

- **Comma Splice:** Choices and/or surrounding text use commas to join two groups of words that could each be sentences on their own. A comma can't be used in this way on the ACT English section. (See page 428)

- **Intervening Phrase:** A phrase appears between two words that need to agree with each other grammatically. Remember to identify pairs of words that need to agree with each other, and ignore phrases that appear between those words. (See page 439)

- **Parallelism:** Choices include options that would ignore a parallel structure in the surrounding text. The right answer should match the phrasing and grammatical structures in the surrounding text when possible. (See p. 440)

- **Pronoun Ambiguity:** Choices include pronouns that could refer to more than one phrase in the surrounding text. We can't use a pronoun on the ACT when it isn't clear what that pronoun refers to. (See page 419)

- **Shorter is Better:** Choices include words or phrases that can be removed without impacting meaning or creating grammatical problems. The shortest grammatically acceptable choice that doesn't change the meaning is right. (p. 442)

- **Verb Tense/Conjugation:** Choices include different forms of the same verb. Look at the surrounding text to find the verb's subject. Also look for other verbs that could indicate the proper tense or form for the verbs in the choices. (See p. 420-423)

ANSWER CHOICE ANALYSIS

F ✓ **Correct:** This is the shortest choice and it's grammatically acceptable on the ACT, so, as trained test-takers, we know it's right. The phrase "buoyed by" describes an action being performed on the rainwater in the past, just like the phrase "was trapped" earlier in the sentence.

G **Incorrect:** The quickest way to tell that this answer choice is wrong is that (F) is shorter and grammatically correct, so (F) must be right. This choice would arguably be an acceptable sentence outside of the ACT English section, because each word and phrase in the choice agrees grammatically and logically with the other words and concepts in the sentence—but, again, this choice is longer than (F), and (F) is also grammatically acceptable, so (F) is right.

H **Incorrect:** As with (G), the quickest way to tell that this answer choice is wrong is that (F) is shorter and grammatically correct, so (F) must be right.

J **Incorrect:** This choice has multiple issues. One is the same problem as (G) and (H): it's longer than a choice that's grammatically acceptable. Another issue is that it turns the sentence into a comma splice, because "over time, rainwater…was trapped just above sea level," and "buoying it was the denser seawater below" could both be complete sentences by themselves—although the second one is pretty weird—and the ACT English section doesn't allow us to use a comma to join two groups of words that could each be sentences by themselves.

Answer choice patterns (page 442): shortest grammatically acceptable choice is correct; wrong answers try to imitate right answers

T1, Q35 (Test 2 in the 2020-2021 Red Book—see page 23)   TYPE: G/S/P (often no prompt; choices w/similar meanings—see page 418)

- **Vertical Scan Results:** Some choices have the same words with different punctuation.

- **Vertical Scan Notes:** Should there be a dash, comma, or no punctuation after "rainwater" and/or "seawater?"
- **Key Features in Surrounding Text:** As it's used here, the word "either" requires the word "or" to be present in the same sentence.

Concepts in the question:

- **Commas:** Choices include commas. Commas can separate a list of 3 or more items, form sandwiches, separate interchangeable adjectives, or introduce an independent clause after a dependent clause. They can't appear for no reason. (p. 431)
- **Correlative Conjunction:** Choices typically include variations on phrases that occur in common correlative conjunctions, such as "not only…but also," or "both…and." Pick the choice that creates a standard correlative conjunction. (See p. 426)
- **Punctuation Sandwich:** Choices involve phrases "sandwiched" between similar punctuation marks. When removed from the sentence, a proper sandwich leaves behind a grammatical sentence with the same original meaning. (See p. 432 and 433)

ANSWER CHOICE ANALYSIS

A   Incorrect: This creates an unacceptable punctuation sandwich around "or seawater," because removing it would leave behind the ungrammatical phrase "faster than either rainwater could alone." As it's used here, "either" must be accompanied by the word "or" in the same sentence, so we can't create a punctuation sandwich that includes "or," because such a sandwich would indicate that the phrase with "or" could be removed. Further, as trained test-takers, we should notice that this choice is functionally equivalent to (B), because both choices create punctuation sandwiches around the same words, and we know that the ACT English section doesn't prefer dashes or commas when it comes to punctuation sandwiches. Since it's not possible for both of these functionally identical choices to be right, they must both be wrong.

B   Incorrect: This choice has the same problem as (A).

C   Incorrect: As trained test-takers, we know that the ACT will only allow us to insert commas under certain conditions: in a list of more than two things, as part of a comma sandwich, between interchangeable adjectives, etc. Since this choice isn't an example of any of those situations, it's wrong.

D ✓ Correct: This is the shortest choice and it's grammatically acceptable on the ACT, so it's right. This choice also avoids the problems from the other choices without creating any other problems.

Answer choice patterns (page 442): functionally equivalent answer choices; shortest grammatically acceptable choice is correct

T1, Q36 (Test 2 in the 2020-2021 Red Book—see page 23)   TYPE: G/S/P (often no prompt; choices w/similar meanings—see page 418)

- **Vertical Scan Results:** Some choices have the same words with different punctuation.
- **Vertical Scan Notes:** Should there be a comma after "limestone," "eroded," or "caves"—or no comma at all?
- **Key Features in Surrounding Text:** At best, the original version of the "sentence" is actually a fragment made up of the dependent clause "as the…caves formed," with the caves being described as "limestone eroded"—that is, eroded by limestone.

Concepts in the question:

- **Commas:** Choices include commas. Commas can separate a list of 3 or more items, form sandwiches, separate interchangeable adjectives, or introduce an independent clause after a dependent clause. They can't appear for no reason. (p. 431)
- **Dependent and Independent Clauses:** Choices would create or join clauses. An independent clause has a main verb and can be a sentence by itself. A dependent clause can't, and starts with a conjunction or relative pronoun. (p. 426)

ANSWER CHOICE ANALYSIS

F   Incorrect: This choice is a sentence fragment, as we described above when we considered the surrounding text.

G   Incorrect: This choice would create the independent clause "eroded caves formed" (in this sense, the word "eroded" would be an adjective describing "caves"). But it would also create the ungrammatical phrase "as the limestone," which would be attached to the independent clause, so (G) is wrong.

H ✓ Correct: This choice creates the grammatically acceptable independent clause "caves formed," and uses a comma to attach the dependent clause "as the limestone eroded."

J   Incorrect: This choice has the same underlying problem as the original version of the "sentence," which is that it has no independent clause or main verb. (A verb in the past tense, like "formed," can't exist on its own as an independent clause without a subject, but the comma after "caves" in this choice would prevent "caves" from being the subject of "formed." Also, the word "as" makes the first part of the sentence a dependent clause, and prevents "the limestone eroded caves" from being an independent clause.)

T1, Q37 (Test 2 in the 2020-2021 Red Book—see page 23)   TYPE: RC (usually has a prompt; choices w/different meanings—see page 413)

- **RC Question sub-type:** Best accomplishes X. (The prompt describes a goal of the author, and asks which choice achieves that goal. The right answer will be plainly demonstrated in the passage. See page 413)

ANSWER CHOICE ANALYSIS

A   Pattern: Same ballpark. Incorrect: The information in (A) is less specific than the information in (B), because (A) doesn't tell us how long the "time periods" are. "Time periods" that see drastic shifts in weather could be less than a day; on the other hand, they could describe decades, centuries, millennia, or really any length of time at all. This is far more vague than what we see in (B), so (A) is wrong.

B ✓ **Correct:** This choice specifically mentions "ice ages" and "more temperate eras." Since "ice ages" are specific periods of time in Earth's history, as are "the more temperate eras that followed them," this choice tells us about a span of time on the scale of an age or an era. As we saw above, (A) only mentions the idea of weather changing in an undefined period of time, so (B) is more specific than (A). And as we'll see, (C) and (D) just mention the passage of time without providing any further details. Since (B) is the most specific choice, which is what the prompt asked for, (B) is right.

C **Pattern:** Same ballpark. **Incorrect:** This choice mentions an "extended time," but that phrase is pretty vague: an extended time for a movie could be 5 hours, an extended time for a vacation could be a month, and so on. So this choice is no more specific than (A) was, and much less specific than (B) was.

D **Pattern:** Same ballpark. **Incorrect:** This choice has the same problem as (A) and (C)—it doesn't say anything about *how much* time passed, which makes it less specific than (B).

T1, Q38 (Test 2 in the 2020-2021 Red Book—see page 23)   TYPE: G/S/P (often no prompt; choices w/similar meanings—see page 418)

- **Vertical Scan Results:** Similar phrases with different short words and/or punctuation.
- **Vertical Scan Notes:** Each choice includes the word "at" and the phrase "different depths," and some form of the word "repeat." Two choices include a form of the word "vary." Some choices are significantly shorter or longer than others.
- **Key Features in Surrounding Text:** All of the choices would end up creating a grammatically acceptable sentence on the ACT English section—in other words, they use punctuation properly, they conjugate verbs correctly, etc.

Concepts in the question:

- **Redundancy:** Choices and/or surrounding text could combine to repeat the same concept unnecessarily. On grammar/style/punctuation questions, we should avoid words that directly repeat ideas in the immediate surrounding text. (See p. 437)
- **Shorter is Better:** Choices include words or phrases that can be removed without impacting meaning or creating grammatical problems. The shortest grammatically acceptable choice that doesn't change the meaning is right. (p. 442)

ANSWER CHOICE ANALYSIS

F **Incorrect:** This choice is redundant. It re-uses the word "process" from earlier in this sentence, and repeats the idea of sea levels rising and falling hundreds of feet from the previous sentence.

G **Incorrect:** This choice is also redundant. The phrase "again and again" expresses the same idea as "repeat," and "various" and "different" both express the same idea as each other.

H **Incorrect:** It's redundant to describe the depths as "varied" after saying they were "different," since both of those words express the same idea in this sentence.

J ✓ **Correct:** This is the only choice that isn't redundant. Also, it's the shortest choice and it's grammatically acceptable on the ACT English section, so, as trained test-takers, we know it's right.

Answer choice patterns (page 442): shortest grammatically acceptable choice is correct

---

T1, Q39 (Test 2 in the 2020-2021 Red Book—see page 23)   TYPE: G/S/P (often no prompt; choices w/similar meanings—see page 418)

- **Vertical Scan Results:** Similar phrases with different short words and/or punctuation.
- **Vertical Scan Notes:** Should "caves" be followed by nothing, the word "that," a semicolon, or a comma?
- **Key Features in Surrounding Text:** The text leading up to the underlined word, and including the underlined word, can stand on its own as a sentence; the text following the underlined word can also stand alone as its own sentence.

Concepts in the question:

- **Changed Meaning:** Choices would change the meaning of the original text, or cause the relevant phrase/sentence not to make sense. The right answer must be grammatically acceptable and still preserve the original meaning. (See p. 438)
- **Comma Splice:** Choices and/or surrounding text use commas to join two groups of words that could each be sentences on their own. A comma can't be used in this way on the ACT English section. (See page 428)
- **Dependent and Independent Clauses:** Choices would create or join clauses. An independent clause has a main verb and can be a sentence by itself. A dependent clause can't, and starts with a conjunction or relative pronoun. (p. 426)
- **Pronoun Ambiguity:** Choices include pronouns that could refer to more than one phrase in the surrounding text. We can't use a pronoun on the ACT when it isn't clear what that pronoun refers to. (See page 419)
- **Run-on Sentence:** Choices and/or surrounding text include consecutive sentences not separated by any punctuation. If two consecutive sets of words can stand on their own as sentences, they need to be separated by a period or a semicolon. (p. 428)
- **Semicolons:** Choices include one or more semicolons. Semicolons can be used to separate two sets of words that could each stand on their own as complete sentences. (See page 431.)

ANSWER CHOICE ANALYSIS

A   Incorrect: As we noted above when discussing the surrounding text, this choice would result in a sentence consisting of two consecutive groups of words that could each be a sentence by themselves, with no punctuation between them, so it's not grammatically acceptable on the ACT English section. (This error is technically called a "run-on sentence," but you don't need to know that term on test day.)

B   Incorrect: This choice will attract some untrained test-takers who overlook the word "others" in the original sentence. Accidentally leaving out that word would cause this choice to make the sentence say "Some of these blue holes open to small contained caves that open to...tunnels," which would be a grammatically acceptable sentence. But, of course, the word "others" *does* appear in the sentence, so this choice would actually cause the sentence to say, "Some of these...caves that others open to...tunnels." This is a confusing, odd-sounding sentence, and the quickest and easiest way to tell this choice is wrong is to note that (C) is grammatically correct and shorter, so (C) must be right on the ACT English section. This choice also fundamentally changes the meaning of the sentence, so that an unidentified group of "others" is somehow "open[ing]" caves, whatever that would mean.

C ✓   Correct: This choice uses a semicolon to connect two consecutive independent clauses, which is grammatically acceptable on the ACT, so it's right.

D   Incorrect: This choice creates a comma splice by putting a comma between two independent clauses. Comma splices aren't acceptable on the ACT, so this choice is wrong.

T1, Q40 (Test 2 in the 2020-2021 Red Book—see page 23)   **TYPE: RC (usually has a prompt; choices w/different meanings—see page 413)**

- RC Question sub-type: Including/excluding a phrase/sentence. (The question asks whether a given sentence or phrase should be included in the passage. The correct choice will include a comment that plainly describes the role of the phrase or sentence in the passage. Sentences that should be included will follow broad ACT standards for ideal sentences and paragraphs, while sentences that shouldn't be included will not follow those standards. See p. 416)

ANSWER CHOICE ANALYSIS

F   Barely relevant: The previous sentence mentions *long* tunnels, but doesn't say anything about blue holes that are "deep," so the sentence in the prompt isn't "support[ing]" anything in the previous sentence, as (F) would require.

G   Barely relevant: The sentence doesn't describe a blue hole with any more detail or imagery than the other descriptions of blue holes throughout the passage, so there's no demonstration of the idea of "allow[ing] the reader to visualize a specific blue hole," as (G) would require. Further, even if we did think that the sentence in the prompt "allow[ed] the reader to visualize" something, (G) would still be wrong because its reasoning doesn't follow the ACT's standards for including a sentence in a paragraph, which are discussed in the training on page 416 of this Black Book.

H ✓   Correct: This choice contains a description that's literally demonstrated in the relevant text. It's true that this paragraph talks about "the cave-creating process," as (H) describes, and it's true that the sentence in the prompt doesn't mention anything about that process. Further, this choice is the only one whose reasoning reflects the standards listed in the training that starts on page 416 of this Black Book, which say that the ACT will want us to avoid adding irrelevant ideas into a paragraph on the ACT English section.

J   Barely relevant: This choice doesn't explain what would count as an "adequate description," so we can't say that the text literally demonstrates the idea in this choice, since we don't actually know what that idea is. Further, even if it were true that the description wasn't "adequate," the reasoning in (J) doesn't match the standards in the training on page 416 of this Black Book.

T1, Q41 (Test 2 in the 2020-2021 Red Book—see page 23)   **TYPE: G/S/P (often no prompt; choices w/similar meanings—see page 418)**

- Vertical Scan Results: Some choices have different forms of the same base word.
- Vertical Scan Notes: We have to choose between "striking" and "strikingly," and between "darker" and "darkly."
- Key Features in Surrounding Text: The underlined phrase makes a comparison between a "circular patch of water" and "the water surrounding."

Concepts in the question:

- Adjective/Adverb: Choices involve a word in its adjective or adverb form. Remember that adverb forms often end in "-ly," but not always. Adjectives can modify nouns; adverbs can modify anything else (verbs, adjectives, other adverbs). (p. 423)

ANSWER CHOICE ANALYSIS

A   Incorrect: On the ACT English section, an adjective (like "striking") can't describe another adjective, such as "darker." See the discussion of (B) for more.

B ✓   Correct: An adverb can be used to describe an adjective on the ACT English section, so the word "strikingly" can be used to describe the word "darker." And the adjective "darker" can be used to describe the noun "patch," so this choice is grammatically acceptable.

C   Incorrect: The adverb "strikingly" can be used to modify the adverb "darkly," since adverbs can be used to modify other adverbs. But the adverb "darkly" can't describe the noun "patch," because nouns can't be modified by adverbs; nouns can only be modified by adjectives.

D   Incorrect: This choice combines the problems from (A) and (C), because it starts with the adjective "striking," like (A) does, and finishes with the adverb "darkly," like (C) does. It might appeal to untrained test-takers who correctly observe that the right answer should include one adjective and one adverb, but then accidentally pick the choice with the adverb form of the wrong word.

Answer choice patterns (page 442): wrong answers try to imitate right answers

T1, Q42 (Test 2 in the 2020-2021 Red Book—see page 23)   TYPE: G/S/P (often no prompt; choices w/similar meanings—see page 418)

- **Vertical Scan Results:** Some choices are short phrases with no obvious similarity.
- **Vertical Scan Notes:** The choices are all different types of pronouns. (F) and (G) are plural, while (H) and (J) are singular.
- **Key Features in Surrounding Text:** The underlined phrase refers to the singular noun phrase "circular patch of water."

Concepts in the question:

- **Changed Meaning:** Choices would change the meaning of the original text, or cause the relevant phrase/sentence not to make sense. The right answer must be grammatically acceptable and still preserve the original meaning. (See p. 438)
- **Pronoun Ambiguity:** Choices include pronouns that could refer to more than one phrase in the surrounding text. We can't use a pronoun on the ACT when it isn't clear what that pronoun refers to. (See page 419)
- **Singular versus Plural:** Choices include singular and plural versions of the same base words that don't agree with other words in the surrounding text. Nouns, pronouns, and verbs must agree in number with the words they refer to or modify. (p. 423)

ANSWER CHOICE ANALYSIS

F   **Incorrect:** This choice is plural, but the underlined phrase needs to be singular in order to refer to the singular phrase "circular patch of water."

G   **Incorrect:** This choice has the same problem as (F).

H   **Incorrect:** The word "one" makes the meaning of this sentence unclear, and potentially changes that meaning, because we don't know what the number or pronoun "one" is referring to. This choice could make "the telltale sign of a blue hole" be a patch of water that's darker than the water around any one blue hole—as opposed to the water around the specific "blue hole" already mentioned earlier in the sentence. This choice could also make the "telltale sign" a patch of water around any person, if "one" is meant as a generic pronoun, similar to "anybody" or "you." Since the ACT doesn't allow ambiguous pronoun usage or choices that change the original meaning of the sentence, (H) must be wrong.

J ✓ **Correct:** The singular pronoun "it" is the only choice that clearly refers back to the singular noun phrase "circular patch of water" mentioned earlier in the sentence, so (J) is right.

T1, Q43 (Test 2 in the 2020-2021 Red Book—see page 23)   TYPE: G/S/P (often no prompt; choices w/similar meanings—see page 418)

- **Vertical Scan Results:** Some choices have the same words with different punctuation.
- **Vertical Scan Notes:** Should there be a period after "alligators," "now," "extinct," or nowhere in the underlined phrase?

Concepts in the question:

- **Commas:** Choices include commas. Commas can separate a list of 3 or more items, form sandwiches, separate interchangeable adjectives, or introduce an independent clause after a dependent clause. They can't appear for no reason. (p. 431)
- **Dependent and Independent Clauses:** Choices would create or join clauses. An independent clause has a main verb and can be a sentence by itself. A dependent clause can't, and starts with a conjunction or relative pronoun. (p. 426)

ANSWER CHOICE ANALYSIS

A   **Incorrect:** This choice would create a "sentence" ("Now extinct…human inhabitants") without a main verb.

B   **Incorrect:** This choice has the same basic problem as (A): it creates a sentence fragment that lacks a main verb ("extinct on the islands…inhabitants").

C ✓ **Correct:** This choice clearly indicates that "now extinct on the islands" describes "turtles and alligators," and creates one sentence with a main verb ("have found") and its subject ("divers"). It also creates a grammatically acceptable comma-separated list with these three elements: "turtles and alligators now extinct on the islands," "stalactites and stalagmites from a time when the caves were above sea level," and "artifacts of early human inhabitants."

D   **Incorrect:** This choice has the same basic problem as (A) and (B), which is that it creates a sentence fragment with no main verb ("on the islands…inhabitants").

T1, Q44 (Test 2 in the 2020-2021 Red Book—see page 23)   TYPE: RC (usually has a prompt; choices w/different meanings—see page 413)

- **RC Question sub-type:** Best accomplishes X. (The prompt describes a goal of the author, and asks which choice achieves that goal. The right answer will be plainly demonstrated in the passage. See page 413)

Subjective Phrases to Ignore: "most effectively suggests"

ANSWER CHOICE ANALYSIS

F   **Barely relevant:** This choice doesn't specifically say anything about the shape of the holes, which is what the prompt requires.

G ✓ **Correct:** The blue holes were described as "circular" in the passage and "dots" are also circular, so we know (G) is right. (As it turns out, (G) is the only choice that indicates any shape at all, as the prompt requires.)

H   **Barely relevant:** This choice has the same basic problem as (F): the idea of "dark[ness]" doesn't specifically indicate any particular shape, which is what the prompt asked us for.

J   **Barely relevant:** This choice has the same problem as (F) and (H).

T1, Q45 (Test 2 in the 2020-2021 Red Book—see page 23)   TYPE: RC (usually has a prompt; choices w/different meanings—see page 413)

- **RC Question sub-type:** Sentence or paragraph placement. (The prompt asks us where a sentence should go in a paragraph, or where a paragraph should go in the passage. The correct order will reflect a logical chronology, and/or will allow for pronouns to refer to nouns in a logical way, and/or will place related concepts near one another. See page 415)

    Subjective Phrases to Ignore: "most"

ANSWER CHOICE ANALYSIS

A   **Causes text to refer to an idea that hasn't been mentioned yet:** The sentence from the prompt mentions "these depths," but this placement comes *before* the mention of any "depths" for the word "these" to refer back to.

B   **Barely relevant:** This choice would insert a sentence about depths and preservation into a paragraph that doesn't talk specifically about either of those things, so this choice must be wrong on the ACT English section.

C ✓   **Correct:** The sentence from the prompt mentions "these depths," and the preceding sentence in this placement mentions "greater depth." Also, the next sentence mentions "the remains of turtles and alligators" (which restates the idea of "fossils" from the prompt sentence), and "stalactites and stalagmites" (which restates the idea of "rock formations" from the prompt sentence). Since this choice would add the sentence into a paragraph that already mentions the specific concepts from the sentence—and the other choices wouldn't—this choice is the right answer.

D   **Barely relevant:** This choice has the same problem as (B): it would involve inserting a sentence into a paragraph that doesn't specifically mention the concepts in that sentence. It would also fail to provide anything for the phrase "these depths" from the prompt sentence to refer to. This is unacceptable on the ACT English section, so (D) is wrong.

T1, Q46 (Test 2 in the 2020-2021 Red Book—see page 23)   TYPE: G/S/P (often no prompt; choices w/similar meanings—see page 418)

- **Vertical Scan Results:** Similar phrases with different short words and/or punctuation.
- **Vertical Scan Notes:** All of the choices include the word "walls" and some version of the word "defend." Some choices have a version of the word "protect" as well.
- **Key Features in Surrounding Text:** The underlined phrase tells us what "both were built as" according to the sentence.

    Concepts in the question:

- **Adjective/Adverb:** Choices involve a word in its adjective or adverb form. Remember that adverb forms often end in "-ly," but not always. Adjectives can modify nouns; adverbs can modify anything else (verbs, adjectives, other adverbs). (p. 423)
- **Redundancy:** Choices and/or surrounding text could combine to repeat the same concept unnecessarily. On grammar/style/punctuation questions, we should avoid words that directly repeat ideas in the immediate surrounding text. (See p. 437)
- **Shorter is Better:** Choices include words or phrases that can be removed without impacting meaning or creating grammatical problems. The shortest grammatically acceptable choice that doesn't change the meaning is right. (p. 442)

ANSWER CHOICE ANALYSIS

F   **Incorrect:** The adverb "protectively" is redundant because defending something already expresses the idea of protection.

G   **Incorrect:** It's redundant to describe walls as "defensive" and then say the walls are for "defending," so (G) is wrong.

H   **Incorrect:** This choice has a problem similar to the one in (F) and (G): the noun "protection" is redundant because "defensive" already expresses the idea of protection.

J ✓   **Correct:** This is the only choice that isn't redundant; it's also the shortest choice and it's grammatically correct, so it's right.

Answer choice patterns (page 442): shortest grammatically acceptable choice is correct

T1, Q47 (Test 2 in the 2020-2021 Red Book—see page 23)   TYPE: G/S/P (often no prompt; choices w/similar meanings—see page 418)

- **Vertical Scan Results:** Some choices have the same words with different punctuation.
- **Vertical Scan Notes:** Should there be a period, comma, semicolon, or no punctuation after "tall?"
- **Key Features in Surrounding Text:** "Although...tall" is a dependent clause, because a clause that starts with a conjunction like "although" is dependent by definition; "they...circumstances" is an independent clause, because it includes the main verb phrase "they were erected" and doesn't start with a conjunction.

    Concepts in the question:

- **Comma Splice:** Choices and/or surrounding text use commas to join two groups of words that could each be sentences on their own. A comma can't be used in this way on the ACT English section. (See page 428)
- **Dependent and Independent Clauses:** Choices would create or join clauses. An independent clause has a main verb and can be a

sentence by itself. A dependent clause can't, and starts with a conjunction or relative pronoun. (p. 426)

- **Intervening Phrase:** A phrase appears between two words that need to agree with each other grammatically. Remember to identify pairs of words that need to agree with each other, and ignore phrases that appear between those words. (See page 439)

- **Semicolons:** Choices include one or more semicolons. Semicolons can be used to separate two sets of words that could each stand on their own as complete sentences. (See page 431.)

ANSWER CHOICE ANALYSIS

A   **Incorrect:** This choice doesn't include any punctuation to separate the clauses we noted above in the surrounding text, so it's unacceptable on the ACT English section.

B   **Incorrect:** This choice would place a colon after a group of words that can't stand on its own as a sentence ("Although…tall"), which is unacceptable on the ACT English section. As trained test-takers, we also know (B) must be wrong because it's functionally equivalent to (D): periods and semicolons can both be placed between two groups of words that can be sentences on their own. Since both choices would play the same role in the text, and they can't both be right, they must both be wrong.

C ✓   **Correct:** This choice uses a comma to join a dependent clause ("Although…tall") to the independent clause that follows it ("they were erected…circumstances"), which is acceptable on the ACT English section.

D   **Incorrect:** This choice uses a semicolon to separate a dependent clause and an independent clause, but a semicolon can only separate two groups of words that can each stand on their own as sentences. It would also serve the same function as (B)—see the discussion of (B) above for more on that.

Answer choice patterns (page 442): functionally equivalent answer choices

T1, Q48 (Test 2 in the 2020-2021 Red Book—see page 23)   TYPE: G/S/P (often no prompt; choices w/similar meanings—see page 418)

- **Vertical Scan Results:** Similar phrases with different short words and/or punctuation.

- **Vertical Scan Notes:** We have to decide whether "its," "its'," or "it's" is appropriate, and whether or not to include "among historians."

- **Key Features in Surrounding Text:** The word "that" makes it clear the sentence is describing an idea that "[i]s thought."

Concepts in the question:

- **Dependent and Independent Clauses:** Choices would create or join clauses. An independent clause has a main verb and can be a sentence by itself. A dependent clause can't, and starts with a conjunction or relative pronoun. (p. 426)

- **Intervening Phrase:** A phrase appears between two words that need to agree with each other grammatically. Remember to identify pairs of words that need to agree with each other, and ignore phrases that appear between those words. (See page 439)

- **Plural/Possessive/Contraction:** Choices include nouns ending in "-s," with/without an apostrophe before or after the "-s." Recall the 3 rules for possessive forms (p. 424). Think of contractions in uncontracted forms ("you're" = "you are"). (p. 436)

- **Pronoun Ambiguity:** Choices include pronouns that could refer to more than one phrase in the surrounding text. We can't use a pronoun on the ACT when it isn't clear what that pronoun refers to. (See page 419)

ANSWER CHOICE ANALYSIS

F ✓   **Correct:** This choice uses the contraction "it's," which is the same as the phrase "it is," giving us the acceptable statement "it is thought that the Servian Wall was constructed."

G   **Incorrect:** This choice includes the possessive form "its," which isn't supported by the text for two reasons. One reason is that there's no singular noun that "it" could be referring to as the owner of the "thought." The other reason is that using the possessive pronoun "its" would turn the word "thought" into a noun, turning everything after "among historians" into a noun phrase with no main verb. Either of these issues by itself would make (G) wrong. We don't have to worry about the phrase "among historians," because we know the word "its" is unacceptable for the reasons we just mentioned.

H   **Incorrect:** For ACT English purposes, this form doesn't exist in American English and can never be correct.

J   **Incorrect:** This choice has the same problem as (G): it uses the possessive form "its." See our explanation of (G) for more.

Note   Notice that we didn't need to think about whether the phrase "among historians" was appropriate, because the form "its" from (G) wasn't acceptable in context.

T1, Q49 (Test 2 in the 2020-2021 Red Book—see page 23)   TYPE: G/S/P (often no prompt; choices w/similar meanings—see page 418)

- **Vertical Scan Results:** Similar phrases with different short words and/or punctuation.

- **Vertical Scan Notes:** Should there be a comma after "wall?" Should one of the short phrases from the answer choices come after "wall?"

- **Key Features in Surrounding Text:** The phrase following the underlined text describes the Aurelian Wall.

Concepts in the question:

- **Comma Splice:** Choices and/or surrounding text use commas to join two groups of words that could each be sentences on their own. A comma can't be used in this way on the ACT English section. (See page 428)

- **Dependent and Independent Clauses:** Choices would create or join clauses. An independent clause has a main verb and can be a sentence by itself. A dependent clause can't, and starts with a conjunction or relative pronoun. (p. 426)
- **Punctuation Sandwich:** Choices involve phrases "sandwiched" between similar punctuation marks. When removed from the sentence, a proper sandwich leaves behind a grammatical sentence with the same original meaning. (See p. 432 and 433)

ANSWER CHOICE ANALYSIS

A ✓   **Correct:** This choice creates an acceptable comma sandwich on the ACT English section, because the phrase "built in the late third century CE by the Roman Emperor Aurelian" can be removed from the rest of the sentence, leaving behind the following sentence: "The Aurelian Wall was [sturdier than] the older wall."

B   **Incorrect:** This choice creates two main verbs for the subject "Aurelian Wall" (the verb phrase "had been built" and the verb "was") with only a comma to join the two verb phrases. This might be acceptable (though a little poetic) in everyday English, but it's not an acceptable use of a comma on the ACT English section, so it's wrong.

C   **Incorrect:** This choice would create a punctuation sandwich that would leave behind a sentence fragment with no main verb, because everything after "which" would become a dependent clause containing another dependent clause. (One of the dependent clauses would be "which was more sturdier [sic] than the older wall," and the other dependent clause would be "built in the late third century CE by the Roman Emperor Aurelian.")

D   **Incorrect:** This choice has a problem similar to the one in (B).

Answer choice patterns (page 442): shortest grammatically acceptable choice is correct

T1, Q50 (Test 2 in the 2020-2021 Red Book—see page 23)   **TYPE: G/S/P (often no prompt; choices w/similar meanings—see page 418)**

- **Vertical Scan Results:** Similar phrases with different short words and/or punctuation.
- **Vertical Scan Notes:** We need to decide whether the right answer should include "much" or "more," and whether it should include "then" or "than."
- **Key Features in Surrounding Text:** The underlined phrase compares the "Aurelian Wall" to "the older wall."

     Concepts in the question:

- **Comparatives and Superlatives:** Choices and/or surrounding text include a comparison. A comparison can involve either the "-er" form of an adjective, or a word like "more" or "less." Comparisons often include the word "than," but not "then." (p. 430)
- **Confused Homophones:** Choices include different homophone pairs (such as "their"/"they're" or "too"/"to"). Remember the correct formation of possessives. Remember to read contractions as their uncontracted forms (e.g. "it's" = "it is"). (p. 436)

ANSWER CHOICE ANALYSIS

F   **Incorrect:** The phrase "more sturdier" is grammatically unacceptable on the ACT English section. "More sturdy" is acceptable in American English, and so is "sturdier," but we can't create the comparative form of and adjective by adding *both* "more" *and* "-er."

G ✓   **Correct:** This choice avoids the grammatical problems from the other answer choices, and doesn't create any other issues.

H   **Incorrect:** The phrase "more sturdier" is grammatically unacceptable, as we discussed for (F) above. Further, the word "then" can only be used in one of two situations, and neither applies here: as the second part of an if-then statement, or as an indication of the sequence in which something happens. The word "than," with an "a," is appropriate when making comparisons, as we can see in choice (G).

J   **Incorrect:** As we noted in our discussion of (H), "than," not "then," is used for making comparisons.

Answer choice patterns (page 442): wrong answers try to imitate right answers

T1, Q51 (Test 2 in the 2020-2021 Red Book—see page 23)   **TYPE: RC (usually has a prompt; choices w/different meanings—see page 413)**

- **RC Question sub-type:** Best accomplishes X. (The prompt describes a goal of the author, and asks which choice achieves that goal. The right answer will be plainly demonstrated in the passage. See page 413)

     Subjective Phrases to Ignore: "most"

ANSWER CHOICE ANALYSIS

A   **Confused relationships:** This original placement makes it seem like the thing that was "greatly expanded" was the word "it" from earlier in the sentence, and the word "it" refers to the Aurelian Wall from the previous sentence. Since the Aurelian Wall isn't Rome itself, which is what the prompt talks about, we know that (A) is wrong.

B ✓   **Correct:** This placement creates the phrase "the greatly expanded city of Rome," which makes it clear that Rome is the thing that has expanded, since we normally place adjectives and adverbs in front of the words they're modifying.

C   **Confused relationships:** This placement makes it unclear whether the thing being "greatly expanded" is Rome or the wall, because it puts the phrase "greatly expanded" in a position that wouldn't normally make it apply to either noun, which means we can't know which of the two nouns the writer wanted it to modify.

D   **Confused relationships:** This placement makes it seem like the "Tiber" is the thing that was "greatly expanded," because, as we noted for (B), the most common position for an adjective or adverb in English is directly in front of the noun that it's modifying.

- **RC Question sub-type:** Transition Phrase. (The choices reflect different kinds of transitions between two concepts, with words or phrases like "however," "instead of," or "for example." The right answer must reflect the relationship between the previous concept in the passage and the following concept in the passage. See p. 416)

ANSWER CHOICE ANALYSIS

F   **Confused relationships:** This choice would be acceptable on the ACT English section if this sentence restated the same information from the previous sentence, but that's not the case here. It's true that both sentences talk about ways to cross the boundary of the wall, but the first sentence talks about "eighteen large gateways," while the second sentence talks about "381 towers and eleven smaller side gates." The differences in the numbers in the two sentences—among other things—make it clear that they're discussing different entry points, so the phrase "in other words" isn't acceptable here.

G   **Confused relationships:** This choice would be acceptable if the previous sentence provided the reasoning or causation for the idea in this sentence, but that's not the case. The idea of "eighteen large gateways" doesn't cause or logically result in the idea of "a series of 381 towers and eleven smaller side gates."

H   **Confused relationships:** This would be acceptable if this sentence expressed the idea of some kind of substitution or replacement for something in the previous sentence, but it doesn't do that. The "381 towers and eleven smaller side gates" weren't a replacement for the "eighteen large gateways" in the previous sentence; they were just other types of openings in the wall, according to the text.

J ✓   **Correct:** None of the transition phrases from the other choices is acceptable on the ACT English section, as we discussed above. So (J), the only choice with no transition phrase, must be right.

- **Vertical Scan Results:** Some choices have the same words with different punctuation.
- **Vertical Scan Notes:** Should there be a comma after "both," "posterns," or "towers," or no comma in the underlined phrase?
- **Key Features in Surrounding Text:** The rest of the sentence describes an action performed by the nouns in the underlined phrase.

Concepts in the question:

- **Commas:** Choices include commas. Commas can separate a list of 3 or more items, form sandwiches, separate interchangeable adjectives, or introduce an independent clause after a dependent clause. They can't appear for no reason. (p. 431)
- **Pronoun Ambiguity:** Choices include pronouns that could refer to more than one phrase in the surrounding text. We can't use a pronoun on the ACT when it isn't clear what that pronoun refers to. (See page 419)
- **Punctuation Sandwich:** Choices involve phrases "sandwiched" between similar punctuation marks. When removed from the sentence, a proper sandwich leaves behind a grammatical sentence with the same original meaning. (See p. 432 and 433)

ANSWER CHOICE ANALYSIS

A ✓   **Correct:** As trained test-takers, we know that commas are only acceptable on the ACT English section in specific situations, as noted above. We can see that none of those situations applies here, so (A) is right: we don't need to add any commas to the original sentence.

B   **Incorrect:** Some untrained test-takers will be drawn to this answer choice because it might seem, at first, like a comma sandwich around "the posterns and the towers" is acceptable: if we remove that phrase, the remaining sentence seems like it would be grammatically acceptable in real life. But the problem is the word "both," which, by itself, would indicate that two things from a set of two things were involved in the rest of the sentence. As it turns out, the earlier part of the paragraph mentions *three* kinds of openings in the wall, not *two:* "large gateways," "towers," and "smaller side gates called posterns." Without the phrase "the posterns and the towers" in the sentence, the word "both" would be unacceptable on the ACT English section, because it would refer to two things from a set of three things, without specifying which two were meant.

C   **Incorrect:** As trained test-takers, we know that the ACT English section doesn't let us use a comma to separate items in a list of two things, so it won't let us place a comma between "posterns" and "towers" here.

D   **Incorrect:** Like the comma in (C), the comma after "towers" wouldn't perform any acceptable comma function on the ACT English section, so we can't insert it there.

- **RC Question sub-type:** Best accomplishes X. (The prompt describes a goal of the author, and asks which choice achieves that goal. The right answer will be plainly demonstrated in the passage. See page 413)

Subjective Phrases to Ignore: "most"

ANSWER CHOICE ANALYSIS

F   **Confused relationships:** This choice does mention the idea of "protecting Rome," but it doesn't say *how* they actually protected Rome, which is what the prompt asks about. This choice will attract untrained test-takers who read too quickly and don't notice that the prompt includes the word "how."

G ✓ **Correct:** This choice specifically describes *how* the posterns and towers provided defense: when an enemy was attacking, "armed guards" could have "cover" in the posterns and towers. This explains what the posterns and towers actually did to "serve[] as defensive positions," as the prompt requires.

H **Pattern:** Same ballpark. **Incorrect:** This choice is similar to (F): it says that the towers and posterns were designed to repel attacks, but it still doesn't say *how* they actually did this, as the prompt requires.

J **Pattern:** Same ballpark. **Incorrect:** Like (F) and (H), this choice says the towers and posterns "[kept] Rome safe," but it doesn't say *how* they did that, as the prompt requires.

T1, Q55 (Test 2 in the 2020-2021 Red Book—see page 23)   TYPE: RC (usually has a prompt; choices w/different meanings—see page 413)

- **RC Question sub-type:** Best accomplishes X. (The prompt describes a goal of the author, and asks which choice achieves that goal. The right answer will be plainly demonstrated in the passage. See page 413)

> **Subjective Phrases to Ignore:** "most effective"

ANSWER CHOICE ANALYSIS

A **Reasonable statement not in the text:** The idea of being built with bricks isn't mentioned in Paragraph 4 or Paragraph 5 at all, so it can't be part of a transition between the two paragraphs, according to the unwritten rules of the ACT English section. (A) would also cause the word "however" in the following sentence not to make any sense, because the content of that sentence isn't opposed to the content in this sentence. Either issue by itself would be enough to make (A) wrong.

B ✓ **Correct:** The previous paragraph discusses the Aurelian Wall as it appeared in the past, and Paragraph 5 discusses the Servian Wall as it stands today. Thus, an acceptable transition on the ACT English section could mention the condition of the Aurelian Wall today, because that description would combine elements of both paragraphs. Also note that this choice causes the word "however" in the next sentence to be logical, since the sentence about "only small portions of the Servian wall remain[ing]" is distinctly opposite to the idea of the Aurelian wall dominating the landscape "today."

C **Reasonable statement not in the text:** This choice has basically the same problem we saw in (A): it mentions something that doesn't appear in either paragraph (how long Emperor Aurelian survived), and it doesn't provide a reason for the word "however" to exist in the next sentence in the passage.

D **Reasonable statement not in the text:** This choice has the same issues as (A) and (C): it discusses something that isn't mentioned in either Paragraph 4 or Paragraph 5, so it's not an acceptable transition between those paragraphs according to the ACT. It also causes the word "however" in the next sentence to be illogical.

T1, Q56 (Test 2 in the 2020-2021 Red Book—see page 23)   TYPE: G/S/P (often no prompt; choices w/similar meanings—see page 418)

- **Vertical Scan Results:** Some choices have different forms of the same base word.
- **Vertical Scan Notes:** We need to choose the appropriate version of the verb "to remain."
- **Key Features in Surrounding Text:** The word doing the action in the underlined phrase is the plural noun "portions" (notice the intervening phrase "of the Servian Wall" that appears between "portions" and the version of the word "remain"), and the other verb phrase in this sentence is in the present tense ("can be seen"). (Note that "located" in this sentence isn't technically a verb like "remains" and "can be seen." Instead, it's a passive-voice conjugation of "to locate" that's functioning more like an adjective in this sentence, because it describes "restaurant." Not that you need to know that term for the ACT—we just didn't want you to wonder why we're not paying attention to the word "located" in our solution.)

> **Concepts in the question:**

- **Intervening Phrase:** A phrase appears between two words that need to agree with each other grammatically. Remember to identify pairs of words that need to agree with each other, and ignore phrases that appear between those words. (See page 439)
- **Parallelism:** Choices include options that would ignore a parallel structure in the surrounding text. The right answer should match the phrasing and grammatical structures in the surrounding text when possible. (See p. 440)
- **Verb Tense/Conjugation:** Choices include different forms of the same verb. Look at the surrounding text to find the verb's subject. Also look for other verbs that could indicate the proper tense or form for the verbs in the choices. (See p. 420-423)

ANSWER CHOICE ANALYSIS

F **Incorrect:** This is a singular verb form that would seem to agree with the singular noun "Wall" right in front of it...but we need a *plural* verb form to go with the plural noun "portions," because, grammatically speaking, the "portions" are the things doing the remaining. So (F) is wrong, even though it will trap a lot of untrained test-takers who don't read carefully.

G **Incorrect:** This choice includes the past-tense form "were remaining," which isn't parallel with the present-tense form "can be seen" elsewhere in the sentence (as trained test-takers, we know the ACT English section prefers us to create parallel grammatical structures when possible). Another issue is that "were remaining" makes no logical sense with the next part of the sentence, which says the portions "can be seen." Since they "can be seen" in the present tense, they must still be remaining in the present tense: you can't see something that doesn't remain anymore. Finally, we can see that (J) is grammatically acceptable and shorter than (G), so, thanks to our training, we know (G) is wrong.

H   Incorrect: This choice has the same problem as (F): it uses the singular verb "has," which would seem to agree with "Wall," but which needs to agree with "portions" instead. (Again, notice the intervening phrase "of the Servian Wall" that we mentioned above.)

J ✓   Correct: This choice appropriately uses the plural, present-tense verb form "remain" to agree with the plural noun "portions" and to match the idea that the portions "can be seen" in the present tense according to the rest of the sentence.

Answer choice patterns (page 442): shortest grammatically acceptable choice is correct

---

T1, Q57 (Test 2 in the 2020-2021 Red Book—see page 23)   **TYPE: RC (usually has a prompt; choices w/different meanings—see page 413)**

- **RC Question sub-type:** Including/excluding a phrase/sentence. (The question asks whether a given sentence or phrase should be included in the passage. The correct choice will include a comment that plainly describes the role of the phrase or sentence in the passage. Sentences that should be included will follow broad ACT standards for ideal sentences and paragraphs, while sentences that shouldn't be included will not follow those standards. See p. 416)

ANSWER CHOICE ANALYSIS

A   Direct contradiction: This paragraph talks about how the Servian Wall is mostly gone, so details about the construction of the Aurelian Wall don't "support[] the main idea of the paragraph," as (A) would require. Since the description of the text in this choice isn't literally restated or demonstrated by the text, this choice is wrong.

B   Barely relevant: The decision to use "existing architectural features" could be called practical, but the given sentence doesn't restate or demonstrate the idea that "incorporat[ing]" "existing architectural features" was "innovative"—for example, the text doesn't say that no one had ever thought of doing this before, or anything along those lines. This statement doesn't describe the given text accurately, so it must be wrong.

C ✓   Correct: The sentence from the prompt demonstrates the idea in this choice because it would "interrupt the passage's discussion of the Servian Wall in the present day," exactly as (C) requires—the paragraph talks about what remains of the Servian Wall, and the given sentence doesn't provide any information on that topic. Since (C) is the only choice whose description is literally restated or demonstrated by the passage and/or the sentence in the prompt, we know (C) is right.

D   Direct contradiction: The description in this choice isn't restated or demonstrated by the text, so this choice must be wrong. The level of detail in this sentence is basically consistent with the level of detail in Paragraph 4, which mentions other architectural features of the wall—so the text directly contradicts the statement in (D). (Note that if a choice like this were ever going to be right, the difference between the "level of detail" in the essay and the provided sentence would have to be very obvious, and not rely on a judgment call by the test-taker.)

T1, Q58 (Test 2 in the 2020-2021 Red Book—see page 23)   **TYPE: G/S/P (often no prompt; choices w/similar meanings—see page 418)**

- **Vertical Scan Results:** Similar phrases with different short words and/or punctuation.
- **Vertical Scan Notes:** All of the choices except (F) are a little unnatural-sounding to a native speaker, especially (G) and (J).
- **Key Features in Surrounding Text:** The clause with the underlined word uses the phrase "once protected" and "ancient world," showing that it's talking about the capital from the perspective of the past.

> **Concepts in the question:**

- **Redundancy:** Choices and/or surrounding text could combine to repeat the same concept unnecessarily. On grammar/ style/punctuation questions, we should avoid words that directly repeat ideas in the immediate surrounding text. (See p. 437)
- **Shorter is Better:** Choices include words or phrases that can be removed without impacting meaning or creating grammatical problems. The shortest grammatically acceptable choice that doesn't change the meaning is right. (p. 442)

ANSWER CHOICE ANALYSIS

F ✓   Correct: This is the shortest choice and it's grammatically acceptable on the ACT English section, so it's right. Within the sentence, it points out that, when the wall was built, the city of Rome was not yet a "capital of one of the ancient world's most famous empires," but would be at a later time.

G   Incorrect: This choice has multiple problems. The most important one, from a test-taking standpoint, is that this choice is longer than (F) and (F) is grammatically acceptable on the ACT, which means (G) can't be right. From a grammatical standpoint, we could also point out that (G) is redundant, since an "appoint[ment]" and a "designation" are basically the same thing in this context.

H   Incorrect: As we saw in (G), the biggest problem with (H) is that (F) is the shortest choice and (F) is grammatically correct; as trained test-takers, we know that means all other choices must be wrong.

J   Incorrect: Like (G), this choice has at least one issue apart from the fact that it's longer than (F) and (F) is grammatically correct. The phrases "would be" and "not yet" are redundant, because anything that "would be" is "not yet," by definition—since the word "would" is used to describe a state that doesn't currently exist.

Answer choice patterns (page 442): shortest grammatically acceptable choice is correct

---

T1, Q59 (Test 2 in the 2020-2021 Red Book—see page 23)   **TYPE: RC (usually has a prompt; choices w/different meanings—see page 413)**

- **RC Question sub-type:** Best accomplishes X. (The prompt describes a goal of the author, and asks which choice achieves that goal.

The right answer will be plainly demonstrated in the passage. See page 413)

Subjective Phrases to Ignore: "best"

ANSWER CHOICE ANALYSIS

A **Direct contradiction:** As trained test-takers, we know that "irony" on the ACT, by definition, involves some kind of contradiction, usually between what's expected and what actually happens; since (A) describes what would be expected of an ancient wall around an important city, (A) is basically the opposite of an "ironic" statement according to the ACT, which means (A) is wrong.

B **Direct contradiction:** This choice has the same problem as (A): rather than describe something contradictory or unexpected, it describes something that would be expected.

C ✓ **Correct:** As we noted for (A), the ACT uses the word "irony" to refer to a situation that involves a contrast, or something unexpected (see "What about "Irony?"" on page 59 of this Black Book for more). You may be able to sense the irony of a historically important wall being inside a modern fast food place without any further elaboration. On a more technical level, the idea of the wall "protect[ing]" a city contrasts with the idea of it being located "within" another structure, and the idea of an ancient wall contrasts with the idea of a modern fast food restaurant. So (C) demonstrates the ACT's idea of irony, which means it's right.

D **Barely relevant:** The text only mentions one kind of location for this wall: "inside a chain restaurant located beneath Rome's central train station." Since only one location is mentioned in the passage, (D) would contradict the text. Beyond that, the "remnants" being in "varied locations" wouldn't create any sort of unexpected contrast, which means it can't be called ironic, as we saw in our discussion of the other answer choices. Either problem is enough to make (D) wrong.

Note It's unusual for the ACT to include a more academic, literary term like "irony" in an ACT English question, but it can happen around once per test. You can often find the answer to such a question either by eliminating the wrong answer choices for relatively obvious reasons not connected to the term in question, or by having the most basic understanding of the relevant term. In this case, if we knew that something "ironic" involved the idea of something being unexpected, then we'd quickly realize that (C) was right, and we could also eliminate (D) for contradicting the passage. Remember that the vast majority of ACT English questions—possibly every one you see on test day—doesn't include literary terms like "irony," and the few that do will rely on very basic knowledge of such terms.

T1, Q60 (Test 2 in the 2020-2021 Red Book—see page 23)   TYPE: RC (usually has a prompt; choices w/different meanings—see page 413)

- **RC Question sub-type:** Sentence or paragraph placement. (The prompt asks us where a sentence should go in a paragraph, or where a paragraph should go in the passage. The correct order will reflect a logical chronology, and/or will allow for pronouns to refer to nouns in a logical way, and/or will place related concepts near one another. See page 415)

ANSWER CHOICE ANALYSIS

F ✓ **Correct:** In this placement, the previous sentence mentions "two ancient walls," and the sentence from the prompt refers back to "the two walls," providing information about the positions of those two walls relative to one another, and how they both "surrounded the city," as the previous sentence says. Since the ACT English section rewards us for adding a sentence to a paragraph if the sentence and the paragraph mention the same ideas, we know that (F) is right.

G **Confused relationships:** In this placement, the previous sentence describes a single wall, but the sentence from the prompt refers back to "the two walls," which would make no sense and be unacceptable on the ACT English section.

H **Confused relationships:** This choice has the same basic problem as (G): it would involve putting a sentence that mentions "the two walls" into a paragraph that's only talking about one wall.

J **Confused relationships:** This placement would make the sentence from the prompt the first sentence of Paragraph 4. But both Paragraph 3 and Paragraph 4 only discuss one wall, so the reference to "the two walls" wouldn't make any sense here, just as we saw with (G) and (H).

T1, Q61 (Test 2 in the 2020-2021 Red Book—see page 23)   TYPE: G/S/P (often no prompt; choices w/similar meanings—see page 418)

- **Vertical Scan Results:** Some choices have the same words with different punctuation.
- **Vertical Scan Notes:** Should a comma appear after "revolution," "war," and/or "Forten?"
- **Key Features in Surrounding Text:** The person doing the action of the verb "said" is James Forten.

Concepts in the question:

- **Commas:** Choices include commas. Commas can separate a list of 3 or more items, form sandwiches, separate interchangeable adjectives, or introduce an independent clause after a dependent clause. They can't appear for no reason. (p. 431)
- **Punctuation Sandwich:** Choices involve phrases "sandwiched" between similar punctuation marks. When removed from the sentence, a proper sandwich leaves behind a grammatical sentence with the same original meaning. (See p. 432 and 433)

ANSWER CHOICE ANALYSIS

A **Incorrect:** This choice would create a comma sandwich around "James Forten," which is unacceptable here according to the ACT English section, because removing the phrase would cause the remaining sentence to read, "Before entering a British-run prison during the American Revolution, prisoner of war said these words...." In other words, the "sentence" wouldn't have an article like "a" or "the" before the word "prisoner," so it would be ungrammatical.

B   **Incorrect:** This choice will fool a lot of test-takers who overlook the last comma and end up thinking that (B) says what (C) says. But (B) creates a comma sandwich around "prisoner of war James Forten," which can only be acceptable on the ACT if we can remove the sandwiched phrase and leave behind a grammatically acceptable sentence with the same basic meaning. In this case, removing that phrase would leave us with "Before...the American Revolution, said these words...." In other words, it would leave the sentence with no subject, because "prisoner of war James Forten" is the person who said the words in the previous sentence. Since it's ungrammatical on the ACT English section to use a verb without indicating who did the action of that verb, we can't put the subject of the sentence in a comma sandwich, so (B) is wrong.

C ✓   **Correct:** As trained test-takers, we know that the ACT only allows us to use commas in particular situations, and we can see that (C) follows those rules of comma use. The comma here creates a sandwich around the phrase "Before…the American Revolution," which is acceptable because we can remove that entire phrase and leave behind a grammatically acceptable sentence with the same basic meaning unchanged ("Prisoner of war James Forten said these words..."). We also know that it's not okay to put a comma between a title and a name when the title comes *before* the name, which means we don't need to put a comma between "prisoner of war" and "James Forten" (see "No comma sandwich when a profession is indicated immediately before a name" on page 433 of this Black Book for a refresher on this).

D   **Incorrect:** (D) would place a comma between a person's title and his name, which isn't acceptable on the ACT English section when the title comes before the name. So "prisoner of war James Forten" is correct, as we saw in (C), and "*prisoner of war, James Forten" is wrong on the ACT. (Note that we'd have to use a comma if the order were reversed, as in the following: "James Forten, prisoner of war." (See "No comma sandwich when a profession is indicated immediately before a name" on page 433 of this Black Book.) (D) is also missing the necessary comma after "Revolution," as we saw in (C).

T1, Q62 (Test 2 in the 2020-2021 Red Book—see page 23)   **TYPE: RC** (usually has a prompt; choices w/different meanings—see page 413)

- **RC Question sub-type:** Best accomplishes X. (The prompt describes a goal of the author, and asks which choice achieves that goal. The right answer will be plainly demonstrated in the passage. See page 413)

    Subjective Phrases to Ignore: "most logical"

ANSWER CHOICE ANALYSIS

F   **Barely relevant:** Neither Paragraph 1 nor Paragraph 2 discusses others who served in the American Revolution, and the ACT English section won't accept a transition between two paragraphs that doesn't mention an idea from either paragraph.

G ✓   **Correct:** Paragraph 1 mentions Forten's "patriotic rejection of his British captor's offer," and Paragraph 2 discusses the risks of Forten's decision, such as the fact that he had little "chance of surviving." On the ACT English section, an acceptable transition restates concepts from the previous paragraph and the following paragraph, just as we see with (G), so (G) is right.

H   **Reasonable statement not in the text:** Paragraph 1 mentions the "offer," but neither paragraph talks about whether the offer was "unusual." Many untrained test-takers will fall for this choice because they'll naturally assume that the offer really was unusual, without realizing that the right answer needs to restate concepts from the previous paragraph *and* the current paragraph.

J   **Barely relevant:** Paragraph 2 mentions Forten's success as a businessman, but neither Paragraph 1 nor Paragraph 2 calls Forten an innovator, or talks about whether people admired him later on, as (J) would require. (J) doesn't include ideas from both Paragraph 1 and Paragraph 2, so it can't be an acceptable transition between them on the ACT English section.

T1, Q63 (Test 2 in the 2020-2021 Red Book—see page 23)   **TYPE: G/S/P** (often no prompt; choices w/similar meanings—see page 418)

- **Vertical Scan Results:** Similar phrases with different short words and/or punctuation.
- **Vertical Scan Notes:** We need to choose between "chance" and "chances," "to" and "of," and "survive" and "surviving."
- **Key Features in Surrounding Text:** The plural verb "were" appears after the underlined text, so we know the noun in the underlined text must be plural.

    Concepts in the question:

- **Intervening Phrase:** A phrase appears between two words that need to agree with each other grammatically. Remember to identify pairs of words that need to agree with each other, and ignore phrases that appear between those words. (See page 439)
- **Prepositional Idioms:** Choices typically include prepositional phrases with no other recognizable similarities. If you can't tell which choice contains an acceptable prepositional idiom in American English, guess and invest your time elsewhere. (p. 435)
- **Singular versus Plural:** Choices include singular and plural versions of the same base words that don't agree with other words in the surrounding text. Nouns, pronouns, and verbs must agree in number with the words they refer to or modify. (p. 423)
- **Verb Tense/Conjugation:** Choices include different forms of the same verb. Look at the surrounding text to find the verb's subject. Also look for other verbs that could indicate the proper tense or form for the verbs in the choices. (See p. 420-423)

ANSWER CHOICE ANALYSIS

A   **Incorrect:** The plural verb form "were" requires a plural subject, but "chance" is singular.

B   Incorrect: This choice correctly pluralizes "chances," but it uses "to" to connect "chances" and "surviving;" the correct idiomatic phrase is "chances *of* surviving."

C ✓ Correct: This choice includes the plural subject "chances" to go with the plural verb form "were," and includes the acceptable idiomatic phrase "chances of surviving."

D   Incorrect: This choice has the same problem as (A): it uses a singular form of "chance" instead of the plural "chances." (Remember that this noun needs to be plural to agree with the plural verb form "were" later in this sentence.)

Answer choice patterns (page 442): wrong answers try to imitate right answers

Note   In another context, "chance to" could be an acceptable phrase to describe the opportunity to do something, as in the sentence "I had a chance to play professional foosball." But the given sentence for this question had to do with the *likelihood of something happening*, not with the *opportunity to do something*.

T1, Q64 (Test 2 in the 2020-2021 Red Book—see page 23)   **TYPE: G/S/P (often no prompt; choices w/similar meanings—see page 418)**

- **Vertical Scan Results:** Some choices have the same words with different punctuation.
- **Vertical Scan Notes:** Should there be a comma, semicolon, dash, or period after "exchange?" Should "as" appear after "he?"
- **Key Features in Surrounding Text:** The words in the sentence up to the word "exchange" can't stand on their own as a sentence. The text in the sentence starting at "he" can stand on its own as a sentence.

Concepts in the question:

- **Commas:** Choices include commas. Commas can separate a list of 3 or more items, form sandwiches, separate interchangeable adjectives, or introduce an independent clause after a dependent clause. They can't appear for no reason. (p. 431)
- **Dependent and Independent Clauses:** Choices would create or join clauses. An independent clause has a main verb and can be a sentence by itself. A dependent clause can't, and starts with a conjunction or relative pronoun. (p. 426)
- **Intervening Phrase:** A phrase appears between two words that need to agree with each other grammatically. Remember to identify pairs of words that need to agree with each other, and ignore phrases that appear between those words. (See page 439)
- **Punctuation Sandwich:** Choices involve phrases "sandwiched" between similar punctuation marks. When removed from the sentence, a proper sandwich leaves behind a grammatical sentence with the same original meaning. (See p. 432 and 433)
- **Semicolons:** Choices include one or more semicolons. Semicolons can be used to separate two sets of words that could each stand on their own as complete sentences. (See page 431.)

ANSWER CHOICE ANALYSIS

F ✓ Correct: The quickest and simplest way to know that this is the right answer is that the other three choices have specific grammatical problems that make them wrong. Another way we know that this choice is right is that the phrase "if released at the war's end or as part of an exchange" requires some phrase in the same sentence to explain the result of that "if" phrase—in other words, the sentence needs to tell us what will happen "if released…[etc.]." (F) is the only choice that satisfies this requirement ((G) and (J) both basically make that information part of another sentence, while (H) makes it part of an unacceptable descriptive phrase, as we will see in the explanation for that choice).

G   Incorrect: There shouldn't be a semicolon after "exchange" because the part of the sentence before the semicolon wouldn't stand on its own as a complete sentence, as the ACT English section would require. As trained test-takers, we also know this choice must be wrong because it would serve the same function as (J), and the ACT only allows one correct answer per question; since these two functionally equivalent choices can't both be right, they must both be wrong.

H   Incorrect: There shouldn't be a dash after "exchange" because the dash isn't part of an acceptable punctuation sandwich, so the ACT won't let us use it here.

J   Incorrect: This choice has the same basic problem as (G): there shouldn't be a period after "exchange" because the words leading up to the period couldn't stand on their own as a complete sentence.

Answer choice patterns (page 442): functionally equivalent answer choices

T1, Q65 (Test 2 in the 2020-2021 Red Book—see page 23)   **TYPE: RC (usually has a prompt; choices w/different meanings—see page 413)**

- **RC Question sub-type:** Effect of deletion. (The prompt asks what the effect would be if the author deleted a phrase or sentence. The right answer will be plainly and directly demonstrated by the text. See page 416)

Subjective Phrases to Ignore: "primarily"

ANSWER CHOICE ANALYSIS

A   Confused relationships: The preceding sentence *does* tell us that Forten survived imprisonment and became a businessman and abolitionist—but it doesn't say anything about the specific "tactics" he used to do these things, as (A) would require.

B ✓ Correct: The text before the sentence mentions the implications of Forten's decision, because it says he "might be captured and sold into slavery" as a result of his choice, which demonstrates the idea of a "discussion of the ramifications" as (B) requires. And the text after the sentence discusses how Forten became a successful sailmaker and abolitionist when it mentions that his "rise to prosperity began...when a sailmaker hired him," etc., as (B) also requires. As trained test-takers, we know that a "transition" on the ACT English section must restate some ideas that precede it and some that follow it. The sentence in question mentions how he "survived" the dilemma discussed earlier and went on to be successful, as discussed later—so this sentence demonstrates the idea of a "transition" as mentioned in (B). Since every part of (B) is literally restated or demonstrated on the page, (B) must be right.

C   **Confused relationships:** The preceding sentence tells us that Forten survived imprisonment and became a businessman and abolitionist, but that sentence doesn't compare those activities to each other, as (C) requires.

D   **Off by one or two words:** In this sentence, there's no "analysis" of the change "from a prisoner to a businessman and abolitionist," as (D) would require; there's only a mention of the fact that the change happened.

▌ T1, Q66 (Test 2 in the 2020-2021 Red Book—see page 23)   TYPE: G/S/P (often no prompt; choices w/similar meanings—see page 418)

- **Vertical Scan Results:** Similar phrases with different short words and/or punctuation; some choices have different forms of the same base word.

- **Vertical Scan Notes:** Should the phrase start with "had?" Should the verb be "rose," "arose," or "raised?"

- **Key Features in Surrounding Text:** The other actions in the paragraph are described with past-tense verbs like "began" and "gained," and nothing indicates that the action in the underlined phrase took place in a different time frame from the one in which the other verbs took place. Also, the action in the underlined phrase is followed by the phrase "to the position."

Concepts in the question:

- **Parallelism:** Choices include options that would ignore a parallel structure in the surrounding text. The right answer should match the phrasing and grammatical structures in the surrounding text when possible. (See p. 440)

- **Prepositional Idioms:** Choices typically include prepositional phrases with no other recognizable similarities. If you can't tell which choice contains an acceptable prepositional idiom in American English, guess and invest your time elsewhere. (p. 435)

- **Verb Tense/Conjugation:** Choices include different forms of the same verb. Look at the surrounding text to find the verb's subject. Also look for other verbs that could indicate the proper tense or form for the verbs in the choices. (See p. 420-423)

ANSWER CHOICE ANALYSIS

F ✓   **Correct:** This verb form matches the tense of the other verbs in the paragraph, and is conjugated correctly. Further, it makes sense in American English to say someone "rose to" a position or a particular job.

G   **Incorrect:** The form "had arose" doesn't exist in the kind of American English used on the ACT. An acceptable version of this form might be "arose" or "had arisen"—but even those would be wrong, because, as noted for (F), the appropriate prepositional idiom is "rose to the position," while "arose to the position" isn't acceptable. The verb "arise" basically describes someone or something standing up or emerging, and doesn't take an object. We can say that someone "arose," but we can't say someone "arose to" a position.

H   **Incorrect:** Like (G), this form is an incorrect conjugation. Acceptable forms of this verb would be "rose" or "had risen," not "*had rose."

J   **Incorrect:** "To raise" means to lift something else, or to cause something else to move up—not to move up yourself, which is what "rise" means. The phrase "*he raised to the position" isn't an acceptable prepositional idiom, so (J) is wrong. (A lot of untrained test-takers and non-native speakers may fall for this choice, because the word "raise" commonly appears in connection with business and professions—but a person receives a raise from a superior, instead of "*rais[ing] to the position" as (J) would require in connection with the passage. Also note that it's possible to say one person raises another person *to a position*, but this still isn't what appears in this answer choice, because no other person or object is being "raised.")

▌ T1, Q67 (Test 2 in the 2020-2021 Red Book—see page 23)   TYPE: G/S/P (often no prompt; choices w/similar meanings—see page 418)

- **Vertical Scan Results:** Similar phrases with different short words and/or punctuation.

- **Vertical Scan Notes:** Should there be a comma, colon, or no punctuation after "workers?" Should the phrase "whom were" appear after "workers?"

- **Key Features in Surrounding Text:** The words in the sentence up through "workers" create a phrase that describes "Forten."

Concepts in the question:

- **Colons:** Choices include colons. A colon can only be placed after a set of words that could be a sentence on their own, and only before a demonstration or example of the idea before the colon. No more than one colon per sentence. (p. 430)

- **Commas:** Choices include commas. Commas can separate a list of 3 or more items, form sandwiches, separate interchangeable adjectives, or introduce an independent clause after a dependent clause. They can't appear for no reason. (p. 431)

- **Punctuation Sandwich:** Choices involve phrases "sandwiched" between similar punctuation marks. When removed from the sentence, a proper sandwich leaves behind a grammatical sentence with the same original meaning. (See p. 432 and 433)

- **Who/Whom:** Choices involve "who" and "whom." "Who" is a subject pronoun (which does an action, like "he"). "Whom" is an object pronoun (which receives an action, like "him"). (See page 428)

ANSWER CHOICE ANALYSIS

A ✓ Correct: This choice creates a comma sandwich around "white and black," which is acceptable here because that phrase can be removed and leave behind a grammatically acceptable sentence with the same basic meaning as the original.

B Incorrect: The phrase "whom were" is ungrammatical, because "whom" is an object pronoun and can't be the subject of the verb "were" on the ACT. (We can use the he/who him/whom test here if we pluralize "he" and "him" to match the plural verb "were." We can see that "they were" would be acceptable, and "*them were" wouldn't be acceptable. Since "they" corresponds to "he" and to "who," we know that "who," not "whom," would be appropriate here.)

C Incorrect: The ACT English section won't let us use a colon after "workers" because the part of the sentence before the colon couldn't stand on its own as a complete sentence, as the ACT requires.

D Incorrect: Without a comma after "workers," the phrase "white and black" can't grammatically modify "workers," since it appears after that word—in fact, without the comma sandwich mentioned in (A), the phrase "white and black" has no definitive grammatical connection to the other words in the sentence at all.

❙ T1, Q68 (Test 2 in the 2020-2021 Red Book—see page 23)   TYPE: RC (usually has a prompt; choices w/different meanings—see page 413)

- RC Question sub-type: Including/excluding a phrase/sentence. (The question asks whether a given sentence or phrase should be included in the passage. The correct choice will include a comment that plainly describes the role of the phrase or sentence in the passage. Sentences that should be included will follow broad ACT standards for ideal sentences and paragraphs, while sentences that shouldn't be included will not follow those standards. See p. 416)

ANSWER CHOICE ANALYSIS

F Confused relationships: The sentence in question doesn't even mention the success of Forten's business, as the description part of (F) would require. Since the description in (F) isn't literally demonstrated or restated by the sentence, (F) is wrong.

G Confused relationships: The sentence does mention business records, but it doesn't specifically say anything to prove the idea that Forten employed 38 people, as (G) would require. (It's true that an earlier sentence in the paragraph says there were 38 employees, but the sentence mentioned in the prompt doesn't provide any evidence of that, which means this choice must be wrong.)

H ✓ Correct: The description in this choice is literally demonstrated by the text, because the business records aren't mentioned anywhere else in the paragraph outside of this question. This is an example of what the ACT means when it refers to "blur[ring] the focus," as we know from our training.

J Barely relevant: The fate of Forten's business records isn't related to Forten's expectations for his business, which means that the description in (J) isn't literally restated or demonstrated by the text.

Note This question specifically asks about a transition "into the next sentence of the essay." Normally when we talk about transitions on the ACT, we worry about the previous sentence *and* the next sentence, as we saw in "Most effective transition" on page 414 of this Black Book. But since this prompt specifically asks about a transition into the next sentence, that's what we needed to focus on.

❙ T1, Q69 (Test 2 in the 2020-2021 Red Book—see page 23)   TYPE: G/S/P (often no prompt; choices w/similar meanings—see page 418)

- Vertical Scan Results: Similar phrases with different short words and/or punctuation.
- Vertical Scan Notes: Every choice mentions that Forten was one of the best sailmakers.
- Key Features in Surrounding Text: Philadelphia is the place referred to by the word "city's" in the earlier part of the sentence.

Concepts in the question:

- Redundancy: Choices and/or surrounding text could combine to repeat the same concept unnecessarily. On grammar/style/punctuation questions, we should avoid words that directly repeat ideas in the immediate surrounding text. (See p. 437)
- Shorter is Better: Choices include words or phrases that can be removed without impacting meaning or creating grammatical problems. The shortest grammatically acceptable choice that doesn't change the meaning is right. (p. 442)

ANSWER CHOICE ANALYSIS

A Incorrect: The phrase "in Philadelphia" is redundant because the word "city's" already establishes the idea that the underlined statement is made in relation to the city where Forten lives.

B Incorrect: This choice has the same problem as (A). Also, "foremost" and "leading" mean the same thing in this context, so one of them is redundant.

C Incorrect: This choice has the same problem as (A), since it mentions Philadelphia even though the sentence already refers to "the city[]."

D ✓ Correct: This choice avoids the redundancy from the other choices. It's also the shortest choice and it's grammatically correct, so we know it must be right.

Answer choice patterns (page 442): shortest grammatically acceptable choice is correct

---

- RC Question sub-type: Best accomplishes X. (The prompt describes a goal of the author, and asks which choice achieves that goal. The right answer will be plainly demonstrated in the passage. See page 413)

Subjective Phrases to Ignore: "most effectively"

ANSWER CHOICE ANALYSIS

F   Barely relevant: This question asks for a transition into the next sentence—but that sentence doesn't say anything about abolitionist causes, so (F) can't be a good transition on the ACT English section. (This choice might tempt some test-takers who remember that the idea of Forten being an abolitionist is mentioned elsewhere in the passage, but the prompt asks about a transition "into the next sentence of the essay," and, again, that sentence doesn't say anything about abolition.)

G   Barely relevant: The next sentence doesn't say anything about Forten fighting in the Revolutionary War, as the ACT would require in order for (G) to be an acceptable transition in combination with the prompt. (It's true that the text mentions Forten being a prisoner of war during the Revolutionary War in an earlier paragraph, but this question asks about a transition for a sentence in Paragraph 5. It's also true that the next sentence refers to the War of 1812, but this choice refers to the Revolutionary War, not the War of 1812.)

H   Barely relevant: As we discussed for (F) and (G), we know that the prompt asked for a transition that mentions concepts in the following text. In this case, the next sentence doesn't say anything about schools or hospitals, or about Forten donating money to anyone, as (H) would require.

J ✓   Correct: The next sentence in the passage talks about a war shutting down the port, and how Forten managed to support his sailmaking enterprise anyway. This is a literal demonstration of the ideas in (J): the "difficult times" in (J) were when war "closed the port," and Forten "maintained his business" as (J) requires by "us[ing] his profits...to support his sailmaking enterprise." Since every part of (J) is literally demonstrated by the following sentence, (J) satisfies the prompt.

- Vertical Scan Results: Similar phrases with different short words and/or punctuation.

- Vertical Scan Notes: Should there be a comma after "smaller?" Should "more" or "and more" come after "smaller?"

- Key Features in Surrounding Text: The word "quicker" appears after the underlined phrase.

Concepts in the question:

- Commas: Choices include commas. Commas can separate a list of 3 or more items, form sandwiches, separate interchangeable adjectives, or introduce an independent clause after a dependent clause. They can't appear for no reason. (p. 431)

- Comparatives and Superlatives: Choices and/or surrounding text include a comparison. A comparison can involve either the "-er" form of an adjective, or a word like "more" or "less." Comparisons often include the word "than," but not "then." (p. 430)

ANSWER CHOICE ANALYSIS

A ✓   Correct: This choice uses a comma to separate the two adjectives "smaller" and "quicker." As trained test-takers, we know that we can switch these two adjectives to create the phrase "quicker, smaller vessels" without changing the meaning of the phrase, so a comma is appropriate between these two adjectives on the ACT English section. So (A) is right.

B   Incorrect: The phrase "more quicker" is ungrammatical on the ACT, which doesn't allow us to combine the word "more" with the "-er" form of a comparative adjective.

C   Incorrect: This choice has the same problem as (B): we can't use "more" with "quicker" on the ACT English section.

D   Incorrect: We need a comma to separate the adjectives "smaller" and "quicker," as we saw in our discussion of (A). Without the comma, "smaller" would be an adjective describing the noun phrase "quicker vessels," instead of the adjectives "smaller" and "quicker" both describing the noun "vessels."

- Vertical Scan Results: Similar phrases with different short words and/or punctuation.

- Vertical Scan Notes: All the answer choices express the idea of something being more than half.

- Key Features in Surrounding Text: The underlined phrase modifies the word "fortune," and includes the redundant phrase "over greater than."

Concepts in the question:

- Redundancy: Choices and/or surrounding text could combine to repeat the same concept unnecessarily. On grammar/style/punctuation questions, we should avoid words that directly repeat ideas in the immediate surrounding text. (See p. 437)

- Shorter is Better: Choices include words or phrases that can be removed without impacting meaning or creating grammatical problems. The shortest grammatically acceptable choice that doesn't change the meaning is right. (p. 442)

ANSWER CHOICE ANALYSIS

F   **Incorrect:** "Over" and "greater than" express the same idea, so one of them is redundant, which is unacceptable on the ACT English section.

G   **Incorrect:** This choice has a problem similar to what we saw in (F): "over" and "more than" express the same idea, so one of them is redundant.

H   **Incorrect:** This choice has the same problem as (G).

J ✓ **Correct:** This choice avoids the redundancy from the other choices. It's also the shortest choice and it's grammatically correct, so, as trained test-takers, we know it's right.

Answer choice patterns (page 442): shortest grammatically acceptable choice is correct

T1, Q73 (Test 2 in the 2020-2021 Red Book—see page 23)   **TYPE: G/S/P (often no prompt; choices w/similar meanings—see page 418)**

- **Vertical Scan Results:** Choices are long phrases/sentences.
- **Vertical Scan Notes:** All the choices start with "veteran," and three choices add another phrase.
- **Key Features in Surrounding Text:** The first part of the sentence mentions the Revolutionary War, and the end of the sentence mentions freedom.

Concepts in the question:

- **Redundancy:** Choices and/or surrounding text could combine to repeat the same concept unnecessarily. On grammar/style/punctuation questions, we should avoid words that directly repeat ideas in the immediate surrounding text. (See p. 437)
- **Shorter is Better:** Choices include words or phrases that can be removed without impacting meaning or creating grammatical problems. The shortest grammatically acceptable choice that doesn't change the meaning is right. (p. 442)

ANSWER CHOICE ANALYSIS

A   **Incorrect:** The word "veteran" already describes someone who fought in a war, so "veteran, who served in this war" is a redundant phrase, which means the ACT English section won't accept it.

B   **Incorrect:** "Cultivating" means "helping to grow," so it doesn't make sense to say that someone was "cultivating the sails," as (B) would require. Beyond that, there isn't anything in context to support the idea that the sails were like freedom, or vice-versa. Also, the idea of freedom is already mentioned at the end of this sentence, so discussing freedom here makes one of those mentions redundant. Most importantly, for test-taking purposes, we can see that (D) is grammatically acceptable and it's the shortest answer choice, which means (D) must be right according to our training. So (B) must be wrong.

C   **Incorrect:** This choice has problems similar to the ones we just discussed for (B). "Nurturing" means "feeding or taking care of," so it doesn't make sense to say that someone was "nurturing" a "road"—and, again, (D) is shorter and grammatically acceptable, so it's right.

D ✓ **Correct:** This choice avoids the issues from the other choices, creating the sentence "The Revolutionary War veteran believed...." Since this is the shortest choice and it's grammatically acceptable, we know it's right.

Answer choice patterns (page 442): shortest grammatically acceptable choice is correct

T1, Q74 (Test 2 in the 2020-2021 Red Book—see page 23)   **TYPE: RC (usually has a prompt; choices w/different meanings—see page 413)**

- **RC Question sub-type:** Sentence or paragraph placement. (The prompt asks us where a sentence should go in a paragraph, or where a paragraph should go in the passage. The correct order will reflect a logical chronology, and/or will allow for pronouns to refer to nouns in a logical way, and/or will place related concepts near one another. See page 415)

Subjective Phrases to Ignore: "most"

ANSWER CHOICE ANALYSIS

F   **Barely relevant:** This placement would cause the sentence to insert several ideas into Paragraph 1 that aren't already in there, such as the ideas of submitting articles, writing under a pen name, and calling for the end of slavery. Since the ACT doesn't allow us to add a sentence to a paragraph if ideas from that sentence aren't discussed or developed elsewhere in that paragraph, we know that (F) isn't the right place to insert the sentence in the prompt.

G   **Barely relevant:** This choice has the same basic problem as (F), because it would insert the sentence into a paragraph that doesn't discuss or develop ideas from that sentence.

H   **Causes text to refer to an idea that hasn't been mentioned yet:** The idea of Forten submitting articles and letters doesn't make sense here because the text hasn't mentioned yet that Forten was involved with a newspaper. (This choice will attract a lot of untrained test-takers because Paragraph 6 is the best paragraph to insert this sentence, but another choice presents a better spot in Paragraph 6, as we'll see when we discuss (J).)

J ✓ **Correct:** This placement would insert the sentence into a paragraph that already mentions a "newspaper" and "freedom," which means that the phrases "articles and letters" and "end of slavery" from the sentence aren't new ideas in this paragraph. Further, this spot provides a logical context for the idea of Forten submitting articles and letters, because it causes the text to mention Forten submitting those articles and letters immediately after the text mentions his involvement with a newspaper. Since this choice is the only one that observes the ACT's principles for an ideal paragraph and ideal sentence ordering, it must be right.

Note Some test-takers will try to approach this like a question that asks us whether we should include or exclude a given phrase or sentence in the passage—but this question doesn't give us the option to exclude the sentence, and the answer choices don't involve any description of the sentence or phrase in question. Instead, this is a sentence-ordering question that gives us the option to place the sentence in different paragraphs. As long as we remember the rules for sentence-ordering questions, along with the broader rules for ideal sentences and paragraphs on the ACT, we can find the right answer for this question.

T1, Q75 (Test 2 in the 2020-2021 Red Book—see page 23)   TYPE: RC (usually has a prompt; choices w/different meanings—see page 413)

- **RC Question sub-type:** Would essay fulfill goal? (The question describes a goal that the author had in writing the passage, and asks whether the author achieved that goal. The right answer choice will be directly restated or demonstrated by the passage, and logically answer the question in the prompt. See page 417)

ANSWER CHOICE ANALYSIS

A   **Barely relevant:** The description in this choice accurately describes the passage, because Paragraph 3 demonstrates the idea of Forten becoming a "successful businessman," and Paragraph 5 talks about two challenges that his business survived. At this point, we'd have to see if any other choices also have descriptions that are literally restated or demonstrated by the passage; if none of them do, then this choice must be right, but if some other description is also accurate, then we'll need to consider the "yes" or "no" aspect of this choice and any other such choice. When we get to our discussion of (C) below, we'll find that (C) is demonstrated by the text, and we'll see why (A) must be wrong: the concepts in the description of this choice have nothing to do with the goal of "describ[ing]" the "daily operations of a successful business," as the prompt requires. The essay doesn't "describe…the daily operations" of any business, so the "yes" part of this choice makes it wrong.

B   **Barely relevant:** The phrase "how the business evolved" is demonstrated in the passage, which describes how Forten started as the employee of a sailmaker and then eventually became the owner of multiple businesses. But the phrase "historical significance" isn't specifically reflected in the passage; it's true that the passage mentions "historians," and it's true that we're told Forten donated a lot of money to the cause of abolition, but the text never specifically says anything about the impact of Forten's business on history, as the phrase "historical significance" would require. (For example, the text doesn't say that Forten's business changed the results of some election, or caused the end of slavery, or started or ended a war, or caused any other specific historical event to happen. We might imagine that his businesses had "historical significance"—and they may have had historical significance in real life—but the essay doesn't say that.) Since the description part of this choice doesn't reflect the passage, we know the choice is wrong.

C ✓   **Correct:** The description part of this choice is exactly demonstrated by the text, because the passage says Forten is a patriot in Paragraph 1, a businessman in Paragraphs 3-5, and an abolitionist in Paragraph 6. It never discusses the day-to-day operations of his business. So we can see that the description part of this choice is accurate—and, in seeing that, we can also see that the passage never mentions the daily operations of a business as the prompt discusses, so the right answer needs to begin with "no." Since (C) begins with "no" and has an accurate description of the passage, we know (C) must be right.

D   **Confused relationships:** The article doesn't make any sort of contrast between Forten's work as an abolitionist and his work as a sailmaker, as (D) would require, so the statement in (D) is wrong, which makes (D) wrong.

TEST 2 (TEST 3 IN 2020-2021 RED BOOK)

T2, Q1 (Test 3 in the 2020-2021 Red Book—see page 23)   TYPE: G/S/P (often no prompt; choices w/similar meanings—see page 418)

- **Vertical Scan Results:** Similar phrases with different short words and/or punctuation.
- **Vertical Scan Notes:** Should the word "is" appear by itself, or with the word "that" or "it" in front of it? (Or should the whole phrase be deleted?)
- **Key Features in Surrounding Text:** The original "sentence" is just a sequence of comma-sandwiched phrases describing the building, without a main verb. It's also not clear which specific noun phrase is being referred to by the singular pronoun "that"—it could be "building" or "community" or "John Day," for example.

Concepts in the question:

- **Comma Splice:** Choices and/or surrounding text use commas to join two groups of words that could each be sentences on their own. A comma can't be used in this way on the ACT English section. (See page 428)
- **Commas:** Choices include commas. Commas can separate a list of 3 or more items, form sandwiches, separate interchangeable adjectives, or introduce an independent clause after a dependent clause. They can't appear for no reason. (p. 431)
- **Dependent and Independent Clauses:** Choices would create or join clauses. An independent clause has a main verb and can be a sentence by itself. A dependent clause can't, and starts with a conjunction or relative pronoun. (p. 426)

- **Intervening Phrase:** A phrase appears between two words that need to agree with each other grammatically. Remember to identify pairs of words that need to agree with each other, and ignore phrases that appear between those words. (See page 439)
- **Pronoun Ambiguity:** Choices include pronouns that could refer to more than one phrase in the surrounding text. We can't use a pronoun on the ACT when it isn't clear what that pronoun refers to. (See page 419)
- **Punctuation Sandwich:** Choices involve phrases "sandwiched" between similar punctuation marks. When removed from the sentence, a proper sandwich leaves behind a grammatical sentence with the same original meaning. (See p. 432 and 433)

ANSWER CHOICE ANALYSIS

A   **Incorrect:** The word "that" in this choice leaves the sentence without a main verb, and doesn't seem to be referring to any particular singular noun, as we discussed above.

B ✓   **Correct:** This choice is the only one that results in a complete, grammatically acceptable sentence according to the ACT. The subject of the sentence is "the Kam Wah Chung & Co. building," the verb is "is," and the thing that the building is being equated to is the noun phrase "a small, unassuming structure made of rock and wood." The comma-sandwiched phrase "to the casual observer" gives us a context for the rest of the sentence, and the comma-sandwiched phrase "located in the eastern Oregon community of John Day" tells us where the "building" is. The comma between "small" and "unassuming" shows that those adjectives are interchangeable for ACT purposes.

C   **Incorrect:** There are several issues with this choice. One of them is that the ACT English section only allows us to use the singular pronoun "it" in a situation where there's only one singular noun phrase that it can be referring to, but there are multiple singular nouns in this sentence that "it" might refer to, as we noted above. Another issue is that this choice would turn the phrase "the...building" into a misplaced modifier appearing after the word "observer," which isn't okay on the ACT because the building isn't "the casual observer."

D   **Incorrect:** This choice leaves the sentence without a main verb. See our explanation of (B) for more.

Answer choice patterns (page 442): wrong answers try to imitate right answers

T2, Q2 (Test 3 in the 2020-2021 Red Book—see page 23)   **TYPE: RC (usually has a prompt; choices w/different meanings—see page 413)**

- **RC Question sub-type:** Best accomplishes X. (The prompt describes a goal of the author, and asks which choice achieves that goal. The right answer will be plainly demonstrated in the passage. See page 413)

Subjective Phrases to Ignore: "most effectively"

ANSWER CHOICE ANALYSIS

F ✓   **Correct:** The phrase "preserves a part of the legacy of the Chinese community" literally demonstrates the idea of "the...cultural significance of the...building," as the prompt requires. The phrase "in the nineteenth-century American West" literally demonstrates the idea of "the historical...significance of the...building," as the prompt requires. Every part of the prompt is demonstrated in this answer choice, so (F) must be right.

G   **Reasonable statement not in the text:** This information about the rooms in the building doesn't specifically demonstrate that the building is historically or culturally significant in the literal, direct way the ACT requires, as we saw in (F). This choice might attract some untrained test-takers who assume that the layout of the house would be understood by an expert to be noteworthy from a historical and cultural standpoint, even though this choice doesn't literally say that.

H   **Barely relevant:** Information about the groups who preserve and operate the building doesn't literally demonstrate the idea of the building's "historical and cultural significance," as the prompt requires.

J   **Reasonable statement not in the text:** This choice could be tempting for test-takers because it mentions things that could be called both "historical" ("antique tables") and "cultural" ("a variety of Chinese teas and cooking utensils")—but the prompt asks for the choice that introduces "the historical and cultural significance of the...building," and these objects aren't the "building." Instead, they are things *inside* the building. Also, like (G), this choice might appeal to some untrained test-takers who simply assume that the design of a kitchen says a lot about the culture and time period of the people who built and used the kitchen. While this may seem like a thoughtful interpretation of the text in real life, we know that it must be a wrong answer on the ACT, because the description of the contents of the kitchen isn't a literal demonstration of the idea that the building itself is "historical[ly] and cultural[ly] significan[t]," as the prompt requires.

T2, Q3 (Test 3 in the 2020-2021 Red Book—see page 23)   **TYPE: G/S/P (often no prompt; choices w/similar meanings—see page 418)**

- **Vertical Scan Results:** Some choices have different forms of the same base word.
- **Vertical Scan Notes:** We need to choose between "attract" or some form of "are attracted" in the present, past, or future tense.
- **Key Features in Surrounding Text:** The other verb in the sentence is the past-tense form "served," and nothing in the sentence indicates that the action in the underlined phrase takes place in a different time frame from that verb.

Concepts in the question:

- **Parallelism:** Choices include options that would ignore a parallel structure in the surrounding text. The right answer should match the phrasing and grammatical structures in the surrounding text when possible. (See p. 440)

- **Verb Tense/Conjugation:** Choices include different forms of the same verb. Look at the surrounding text to find the verb's subject. Also look for other verbs that could indicate the proper tense or form for the verbs in the choices. (See p. 420-423)

ANSWER CHOICE ANALYSIS

A   **Incorrect:** One major, and more obvious, issue with this choice is that it changes the timeframe of the sentence for no reason, which the ACT won't allow: it makes no sense to use the past-tense verb "served" and then jump to the present-tense verb "attract" without any reason in the text for such a jump. A less obvious issue is that this version of the sentence would make the travelers the ones doing the attracting, and would tell us that the travelers were doing the attracting by means of "news of gold strikes," which makes no sense; this version of the sentence also wouldn't tell us what or who was being attracted by the news used by the attracting travelers. Any of these issues would be enough by itself to make (A) wrong. This choice might tempt test-takers who incorrectly assume that passive voice constructions must be wrong on the ACT English section (see the note below).

B   **Incorrect:** "Will be attracted" is a future-tense verb form, but the rules of the ACT require us to use a past-tense verb form to parallel "served," since nothing in the sentence indicates that the attraction of the travelers happened in a different time frame from when the "building first served as a trading post."

C ✓   **Correct:** The word "were" marks this as a past-tense verb form, which is what the rules of the ACT require, since the verb "served" is also in the past, and no word or phrase in the sentence indicates that the travelers were being attracted at a different time from when the "building first served as a trading post."

D   **Incorrect:** We know from the verb "are" that the phrase "are attracted" is a present-tense verb form, but the rules of the ACT require a past-tense verb form, as we saw in our discussion of (C) above.

Answer choice patterns (page 442): wrong answers try to imitate right answers

Note   Many untrained test-takers (and, unfortunately, many test-prep companies and tutors) believe that the ACT English test will punish the use of the passive voice, because many high school teachers punish the use of the passive voice. But there's nothing grammatically unacceptable about the passive voice in real life, and—more importantly for our purposes!—the ACT English section doesn't punish the use of the passive voice. This question is clear proof that the ACT will allow us to use passive-voice constructions when they're formed correctly (in other words, when they're in the right tense, they agree with the number of the subject, and they follow all the other normal style, grammar, and punctuation rules discussed in the training in this Black Book). Let this question remind you how important it is to know and follow the unwritten rules of the test, instead of incorrectly assuming that the test will reward and punish the arbitrary rules of some teachers!

T2, Q4 (Test 3 in the 2020-2021 Red Book—see page 23)   TYPE: RC (usually has a prompt; choices w/different meanings—see page 413)

- **RC Question sub-type:** Including/excluding a phrase/sentence. (The question asks whether a given sentence or phrase should be included in the passage. The correct choice will include a comment that plainly describes the role of the phrase or sentence in the passage. Sentences that should be included will follow broad ACT standards for ideal sentences and paragraphs, while sentences that shouldn't be included will not follow those standards. See p. 416)

ANSWER CHOICE ANALYSIS

F   **Barely relevant:** The preceding sentence doesn't mention Hay or On, as (F) would require.

G ✓   **Correct:** The next sentence in the passage describes something that "the men" did. The phrase from the prompt mentions "two...immigrants, Ing 'Doc' Hay and Lung On." Without this phrase, there is nothing in this sentence that the phrase "the men" at the beginning of the next sentence could logically refer to. So, as (G) indicates, the phrase "the men" can only have a "logical link" to the sentence in question if the phrase from the prompt is included in that sentence. Since the description in (G) is literally demonstrated by the ideas in the prompt and the passage, and since including a sentence or phrase that is logically connected to the passage would follow the broader rules for ideal sentences and paragraphs on the ACT, we know (G) is right.

H   **Direct contradiction:** The information in the phrase from the prompt isn't "implied" elsewhere in the passage, as the description in (H) would require: the other parts of the passage don't say things that would lead us to assume that Hay and On were "young Chinese immigrants" when they bought the building. Further, the statement in the prompt is necessary here because, otherwise, the phrase "the men" in the following sentence of the passage makes no sense, as we noted for (G).

J   **Barely relevant:** It's true that the description in (J) is literally demonstrated by the statement in the prompt, which does "provide[] little information about Hay and On's partnership," since it provides no information at all about their partnership. But, as we saw in our discussion for (G), including the phrase from the prompt would follow the broader rules of ideal sentences and paragraphs on the ACT, so it should be added—because it's the only thing that identifies "the men" mentioned in the next sentence. So the "no" part of this choice makes it wrong. Remember that when more than one answer choice in a question about including or excluding a phrase or sentence accurately describes the relevant text, the right answer will be the choice that follows the broader rules for ideal sentences and paragraphs on the ACT. See the relevant training for more on this idea.

- **Vertical Scan Results:** Some choices have different forms of the same base word.
- **Vertical Scan Notes:** We need to choose between different forms of the verb "to remain."
- **Key Features in Surrounding Text:** The sentence includes the verbs "combined" and "organized," and nothing in the sentence indicates that the action in the underlined phrase takes place in a different timeframe from that of those verbs. Also, the subject of the verb in the underlined phrase is the plural noun "men."

Concepts in the question:

- **Parallelism:** Choices include options that would ignore a parallel structure in the surrounding text. The right answer should match the phrasing and grammatical structures in the surrounding text when possible. (See p. 440)
- **Singular versus Plural:** Choices include singular and plural versions of the same base words that don't agree with other words in the surrounding text. Nouns, pronouns, and verbs must agree in number with the words they refer to or modify. (p. 423)
- **Verb Tense/Conjugation:** Choices include different forms of the same verb. Look at the surrounding text to find the verb's subject. Also look for other verbs that could indicate the proper tense or form for the verbs in the choices. (See p. 420-423)

ANSWER CHOICE ANALYSIS

A   **Incorrect:** "Remains" is a present-tense verb form, but the rest of the sentence makes it clear that the underlined phrase must be in the past tense, as we'll see in our discussion of (D) below.

B   **Incorrect:** As we saw above, the subject of the verb in the underlined phrase is the plural noun "men," so the right verb can't involve the singular verb form "has."

C   **Incorrect:** "Have remain" isn't a valid conjugation of the verb "to remain," so (C) can't be right. (Further, "have remained" would be valid in some situations, and "remain" would be valid in others, but neither would be appropriate here anyway, as we'll see when we discuss (D).)

D ✓   **Correct:** We can see that the right form of "remain" needs to fit in the comma-separated series with the verbs "combined" and "organized." We can see that those two verbs end in "-ed," and there's nothing in the sentence that indicates the underlined verb is happening in a different timeframe from that of those verbs—so the appropriate verb form is "remained," and (D) is right.

Answer choice patterns (page 442): wrong answers try to imitate right answers

- **Vertical Scan Results:** Some choices have different forms of the same base word.
- **Vertical Scan Notes:** Should the phrase include the word "make," "making," or "made?" Which pronouns and conjunctions should be present?
- **Key Features in Surrounding Text:** The text describes two actions that Hay did. The action that isn't part of the underlined phrase is "curing," so we need to make sure that the underlined phrase is in a form that works grammatically with "curing" according to the ACT's rules.

Concepts in the question:

- **Parallelism:** Choices include options that would ignore a parallel structure in the surrounding text. The right answer should match the phrasing and grammatical structures in the surrounding text when possible. (See p. 440)
- **Prepositional Idioms:** Choices typically include prepositional phrases with no other recognizable similarities. If you can't tell which choice contains an acceptable prepositional idiom in American English, guess and invest your time elsewhere. (p. 435)
- **Verb Tense/Conjugation:** Choices include different forms of the same verb. Look at the surrounding text to find the verb's subject. Also look for other verbs that could indicate the proper tense or form for the verbs in the choices. (See p. 420-423)

ANSWER CHOICE ANALYSIS

F   **Incorrect:** This choice creates a situation in which the phrase "and curing patients…failed" has no grammatical connection to the first half of the sentence, so it's wrong. It might attract untrained test-takers who accidentally stop reading the passage at the word "diagnoses" and think the resulting sentence sounds acceptable.

G ✓   **Correct:** The phrase "for making" allows the phrase "and curing…failed" to function grammatically in the sentence as another thing that made Hay famous: He was famous "for making…diagnoses," and he was famous "for…curing patients." This choice also allows the "-ing" form "making" to parallel "curing" from later in the sentence.

H   **Incorrect:** This choice has the same problem as (F): it causes the part of the sentence after the word "diagnoses" to have no grammatical connection to the first half of the sentence.

J   **Incorrect:** This choice has the same problem as (F) and (H).

- **Vertical Scan Results:** Similar phrases with different short words and/or punctuation.

- **Vertical Scan Notes:** The answer choices all describe people having previous treatments.
- **Key Features in Surrounding Text:** The underlined phrase modifies the word "patients," which appears right before the underlined phrase.

Concepts in the question:

- **Shorter is Better:** Choices include words or phrases that can be removed without impacting meaning or creating grammatical problems. The shortest grammatically acceptable choice that doesn't change the meaning is right. (p. 442)

ANSWER CHOICE ANALYSIS

A ✓ **Correct:** This is the shortest choice and it's grammatically acceptable to the ACT, so, as trained test-takers, we know it must be right.

B **Incorrect:** Strictly speaking, there wouldn't be anything grammatically wrong with this choice in real life. But this is the ACT English section, not real life; on the ACT English section, if (A) is shorter and grammatically acceptable to the ACT, then (B) can't be right.

C **Incorrect:** This choice has the same basic problem as (B) and (D), with the added issue that this choice makes it sound like the patients or Hay *were* the previous treatments, instead of saying that the patients *received* the treatments.

D **Incorrect:** As trained test-takers, we know that the unwritten rules of the ACT English section say that the shortest grammatically acceptable answer to a grammar/style/punctuation question must be the right answer as long as it doesn't change the meaning of the passage. For this question, we can see that (A) is grammatically acceptable on the ACT, and it's also shorter than (D), so (D) can't be right.

Answer choice patterns (page 442): shortest grammatically acceptable choice is correct

T2, Q8 (Test 3 in the 2020-2021 Red Book—see page 23)   TYPE: RC (usually has a prompt; choices w/different meanings—see page 413)

- **RC Question sub-type:** Including/excluding a phrase/sentence. (The question asks whether a given sentence or phrase should be included in the passage. The correct choice will include a comment that plainly describes the role of the phrase or sentence in the passage. Sentences that should be included will follow broad ACT standards for ideal sentences and paragraphs, while sentences that shouldn't be included will not follow those standards. See p. 416)

ANSWER CHOICE ANALYSIS

F ✓ **Correct:** The description in this choice is literally demonstrated in the text because the sentence in question describes how Hay "became famous," which tells us why "Hay's work was particularly noteworthy," as (F) requires. When we consider the other choices, we'll see that (H) also includes an accurate description of the passage. Between the two, we know that (F) is right, because the unwritten rules of the ACT require us to include a sentence that provides additional, relevant information about ideas that appear in context.

G **Confused relationships:** This choice might attract untrained test-takers, because the sentence in question *does* mention the idea of Hay diagnosing and curing "patients whose previous treatments had failed." But the sentence in question doesn't give any "examples" of "challenging and successful diagnoses," as (G) would require, which means the description in this choice isn't literally demonstrated by the text. So (G) must be wrong.

H **Confused relationships:** The description in this choice does accurately reflect the test: the sentence "doesn't make clear whether On was involved with Hay's...clinic." But, as we saw in our discussion of (F), the unwritten rules of the ACT say this sentence should remain in the paragraph, because it provides additional, relevant information about concepts that appear elsewhere in the paragraph, even if it doesn't discuss On's possible involvement with Hay's clinic. So, as trained test-takers, we know that the word "deleted" makes this choice wrong.

J **Confused relationships:** There are several things wrong with this choice. One of the more obvious issues is that the paragraph isn't only "about On's accomplishments," as (J) would require. Another issue is that the paragraph provides background information about On *and* Hay, so the sentence *does* "fit logically in this paragraph." This choice incorrectly describes the text, so it must be wrong.

T2, Q9 (Test 3 in the 2020-2021 Red Book—see page 23)   TYPE: RC (usually has a prompt; choices w/different meanings—see page 413)

- **RC Question sub-type:** Effect of deletion. (The prompt asks what the effect would be if the author deleted a phrase or sentence. The right answer will be plainly and directly demonstrated by the text. See page 416)

Subjective Phrases to Ignore: "primarily"

ANSWER CHOICE ANALYSIS

A ✓ **Correct:** The sentence in question mentions "a social, medical, and supply center" and "a post office, library, and herb shop" as things in "the partners' building," and we know from the previous paragraph that "the partners' building" is "the Kam Wah Chung & Co. building." So the sentence in the question literally demonstrates "the scope of services...in the Kam Wah Chung & Co. building," as (A) requires. The relevant sentence also says that this scope "evolved" "over time," which demonstrates the idea that these services were "eventually provided," as (A) also requires. Since every part of (A) is literally demonstrated by the relevant sentence, we know (A) is right.

B **Barely relevant:** The previous sentence includes the word "social," but it never mentions visitors, nor indicates that the social aspect of the company was more important than any other aspect, as (B) would require.

C **Barely relevant:** The sentence doesn't mention any specific person visiting the company, as (C) requires.

D **Pattern:** Wrong part of the passage. **Incorrect:** The *next* sentence in the text after the boxed number 9 *does* talk about the period of time during which the businesses prospered...but the prompt asks about the "preceding sentence," not the following sentence. The preceding sentence doesn't mention any particular length of time that the "businesses prospered," as (D) would require, so (D) is wrong—even though it will trick a lot of untrained test-takers who don't notice that the prompt refers to the "preceding sentence," not the following one.

T2, Q10 (Test 3 in the 2020-2021 Red Book—see page 23)   **TYPE: G/S/P** (often no prompt; choices w/similar meanings—see page 418)

- **Vertical Scan Results:** Some choices are short phrases with no obvious similarity.
- **Vertical Scan Notes:** The choices are all different ways to describe the idea of starting a period of time.
- **Key Features in Surrounding Text:** The underlined part of the sentence is the third item in a comma-separated list of times when the businesses did well, which includes "through the turn of the century" and "during the Great Depression." These phrases begin with the prepositions "through" and "during," so the underlined phrase should create a structure that's parallel to the structure of these phrases by also beginning with a preposition.

Concepts in the question:

- **Commas:** Choices include commas. Commas can separate a list of 3 or more items, form sandwiches, separate interchangeable adjectives, or introduce an independent clause after a dependent clause. They can't appear for no reason. (p. 431)
- **Parallelism:** Choices include options that would ignore a parallel structure in the surrounding text. The right answer should match the phrasing and grammatical structures in the surrounding text when possible. (See p. 440)
- **Pronoun Ambiguity:** Choices include pronouns that could refer to more than one phrase in the surrounding text. We can't use a pronoun on the ACT when it isn't clear what that pronoun refers to. (See page 419)

ANSWER CHOICE ANALYSIS

F **Incorrect:** "Beginning" isn't a preposition. As we discussed above, the underlined phrase must begin with a preposition in order to be parallel to the preceding phrases.

G **Incorrect:** This choice will attract a lot of untrained test-takers who read quickly and assume that the word "it" is referring to the company owned by Hay and On. But the word "businesses" earlier in the sentence is plural, and the ACT English section won't let us use a singular pronoun (such as "it") to refer to the plural noun "businesses." Grammatically speaking, we can't know whether "it" could refer to "turn," "century," or "Depression," which are the singular nouns in the sentence. Since the ACT English section won't let us use pronouns in ambiguous ways, (G) must be wrong. Another problem with (G) is that the parallel phrases "through the turn of the century" and "during the Great Depression" don't include a verb, so "as it entered the 1940s" can't be parallel to those phrases, since it includes the verb "entered."

H **Incorrect:** This choice has the same basic problem as (F).

J ✓ **Correct:** This choice would insert the preposition "into," creating the phrase "into the 1940s," which parallels the structure of the phrases in the first two parts of the three-part comma-separated list in the original sentence, as discussed above.

T2, Q11 (Test 3 in the 2020-2021 Red Book—see page 23)   **TYPE: G/S/P** (often no prompt; choices w/similar meanings—see page 418)

- **Vertical Scan Results:** Some choices have different forms of the same base word.
- **Vertical Scan Notes:** We need to pick the acceptable version of the verb "to become."
- **Key Features in Surrounding Text:** The earlier part of the sentence uses the verb phrase "was restored," and nothing in the sentence indicates that the action in the underlined phrase takes place in a different timeframe from the restoration. Further, the subject of the verb in the underlined phrase is the same as the subject of "was restored:" the singular noun "building."

Concepts in the question:

- **Parallelism:** Choices include options that would ignore a parallel structure in the surrounding text. The right answer should match the phrasing and grammatical structures in the surrounding text when possible. (See p. 440)
- **Verb Tense/Conjugation:** Choices include different forms of the same verb. Look at the surrounding text to find the verb's subject. Also look for other verbs that could indicate the proper tense or form for the verbs in the choices. (See p. 420-423)

ANSWER CHOICE ANALYSIS

A **Incorrect:** "*Has became" is never grammatically acceptable in American English. ("Has become" is one acceptable form, and "became" is another; in fact, the latter form happens to be the right answer to this question, as we'll see shortly.)

B **Incorrect:** The plural verb "have" doesn't agree with its singular subject, "building," so this choice is wrong no matter what tense the verb is in.

C ✓ **Correct:** The verb form "became" is in the past tense, like the verb phrase "was restored." "Became" also agrees in number with its singular subject, "building." Since this choice is the only one in the right tense and number, we know it's right.

D **Incorrect:** Both the tense and number of this verb are wrong: "become" is the present tense, and would require a plural subject in the third person. As we saw above, the right answer must be a third-person singular verb form (to match its singular subject, "building"), and it must also be in the past tense (to match the past-tense verb phrase "was restored").

Answer choice patterns (page 442): wrong answers try to imitate right answers

T2, Q12 (Test 3 in the 2020-2021 Red Book—see page 23)   TYPE: G/S/P (often no prompt; choices w/similar meanings—see page 418)

- **Vertical Scan Results:** Choices are long phrases/sentences.
- **Vertical Scan Notes:** Except for (J), the choices all include multiple short words.
- **Key Features in Surrounding Text:** The word before the underlined phrase is "designated," and the phrase after the underlined phrase is the title of the designation received by the building.

Concepts in the question:

- **Redundancy:** Choices and/or surrounding text could combine to repeat the same concept unnecessarily. On grammar/style/punctuation questions, we should avoid words that directly repeat ideas in the immediate surrounding text. (See p. 437)
- **Shorter is Better:** Choices include words or phrases that can be removed without impacting meaning or creating grammatical problems. The shortest grammatically acceptable choice that doesn't change the meaning is right. (p. 442)

ANSWER CHOICE ANALYSIS

F **Incorrect:** The word "called" is redundant because it means the same thing as "designated" in this context. As trained test-takers, we also know (F) must be wrong because it's longer than (J), and (J) is grammatically acceptable on the ACT.

G **Incorrect:** As with (F), we know this choice must be wrong because (J) is shorter and grammatically correct.

H **Incorrect:** The word "identified" is redundant because it means the same thing as "designated" in this context—and, again, (J) is shorter and grammatically acceptable, so (H) can't be right.

J ✓ **Correct:** This is the shortest choice and it's grammatically acceptable on the ACT, so, as trained test-takers, we know it must be right. This choice also avoids the redundancy from other choices.

Answer choice patterns (page 442): shortest grammatically acceptable choice is correct

T2, Q13 (Test 3 in the 2020-2021 Red Book—see page 23)   TYPE: RC (usually has a prompt; choices w/different meanings—see page 413)

- **RC Question sub-type:** Transition Phrase. (The choices reflect different kinds of transitions between two concepts, with words or phrases like "however," "instead of," or "for example." The right answer must reflect the relationship between the previous concept in the passage and the following concept in the passage. See p. 416)

ANSWER CHOICE ANALYSIS

A **Confused relationships:** This choice would be acceptable on the English section if the sentence in the question were providing additional, alternative support for an idea that was mentioned earlier, but that's not the case here.

B **Confused relationships:** The phrase "in conclusion" introduces a logical conclusion based on the preceding ideas in the text. But in this case, the idea of anything "encapsulating an era" isn't a logical conclusion that is supported by ideas in the preceding text—the text doesn't say anything about "the Kam Wah Chung & Co. Museum" (which was just mentioned for the first time in the previous sentence) doing anything at all, let alone anything to support the idea of the museum "encapsulat[ing] an era." So the phrase "in conclusion" isn't acceptable here, and (B) is wrong. (A lot of untrained test-takers will pick this choice because they think that any sentence that comes at the end of a passage can be called its conclusion, even if it doesn't serve to conclude an argument in the passage.)

C **Confused relationships:** This choice has at least two issues, either of which is enough to make it wrong on the ACT. One issue is that nothing in this sentence restates or demonstrates the idea that "encapsulat[ing] an era" is something that will happen in the future or after some period of time, as the phrase "in time" would require. Another issue is that something that happens "in time" is necessarily an action in the future, because "in time" basically means "after some amount of time has passed from this moment." But the only verb after the underlined phrase is the present-tense verb "encapsulates." We can't say that something "encapsulates" something else "in time," because if the present-tense verb form is used, then the action is happening now—not "in time." So (C) must be wrong.

D ✓ **Correct:** None of the transition phrases from the other choices is acceptable on the ACT English section for the reasons noted above, and this choice doesn't create any problems in the sentence.

T2, Q14 (Test 3 in the 2020-2021 Red Book—see page 23)   TYPE: RC (usually has a prompt; choices w/different meanings—see page 413)

- **RC Question sub-type:** Sentence or paragraph placement. (The prompt asks us where a sentence should go in a paragraph, or where a paragraph should go in the passage. The correct order will reflect a logical chronology, and/or will allow for pronouns to refer to nouns in a logical way, and/or will place related concepts near one another. See page 415)

F   **Causes text to refer to an idea that hasn't been mentioned yet:** Placing the sentence here makes it unclear what the word "inside" refers to, because the previous sentence doesn't mention a building or any other kind of structure where something could be "left inside."

G   **Causes text to refer to an idea that hasn't been mentioned yet:** The sentence includes phrases like "artifacts left inside" and "were preserved," which make it clear that this sentence refers to a time when the building was no longer being used for business—but this placement would make the preceding and following sentences refer to the building as though it were still in use. The idea of the businesses no longer being operated in the building doesn't appear until later in the passage, so this placement isn't acceptable on the ACT.

H   **Causes text to refer to an idea that hasn't been mentioned yet:** This choice has the same problem as (F).

J ✓ **Correct:** This placement makes it clear that "the building" in Sentence 4 (referred to by the word "it" in Sentence 5) is what the items were "left inside" according to the relevant sentence. It also addresses the chronological issue we saw in our discussion of (G). This choice avoids the problems we saw in the other choices without creating any other problems, so it must be right.

T2, Q15 (Test 3 in the 2020-2021 Red Book—see page 23)   TYPE: RC (usually has a prompt; choices w/different meanings—see page 413)

- **RC Question sub-type:** Would essay fulfill goal? (The question describes a goal that the author had in writing the passage, and asks whether the author achieved that goal. The right answer choice will be directly restated or demonstrated by the passage, and logically answer the question in the prompt. See page 417)

A   **Confused relationships:** The text does "make it clear that the...building was renovated in the 1970s," as the description in (A) requires. But that's not the same thing as specifically describing the "steps" that were taken to restore the building, as the prompt requires. This choice isn't logically connected to the prompt, so it must be wrong.

B   **Confused relationships:** As with (A), the description in (B) is literally demonstrated by the passage, which says the items in the building were preserved because of the "semi-arid" climate of "eastern Oregon." But these artifacts being preserved has nothing to do with "outlin[ing] the steps" that were taken "to restore the...building," which is what the prompt calls for.

C ✓ **Correct:** The essay literally demonstrates the description in this choice because it tells us the building was "built in the 1860s," sold in 1887, and "restored by the state of Oregon in the 1970s," which is a "history of the building," as (C) requires. It also describes the various "uses" of the building over the years, as (C) also requires: as "a trading post for travelers," "a social, medical, and supply center," a "post office, library, and herb shop," and as the Kam Wah Chung & Co. Museum. (C) also accurately says that this history of the building and its uses is not the same thing as an "essay that outlined the steps...to restore the...building." This choice accurately describes the text and is logically connected to the prompt, so it's right.

D   **Barely relevant:** The essay doesn't mentions On's business philosophies and doesn't critique Hay's diagnoses or treatments, so the description in this choice doesn't accurately describe the passage.

T2, Q16 (Test 3 in the 2020-2021 Red Book—see page 23)   TYPE: G/S/P (often no prompt; choices w/similar meanings—see page 418)

- **Vertical Scan Results:** Some choices have the same words with different punctuation.
- **Vertical Scan Notes:** Should there be a comma after "glance?" Should there be a comma or semicolon—or no punctuation—after "fair?"
- **Key Features in Surrounding Text:** The phrase "at first glance" indicates a time. The noun "fair" in the underlined phrase is the subject of the verb "looks."

Concepts in the question:

- **Commas:** Choices include commas. Commas can separate a list of 3 or more items, form sandwiches, separate interchangeable adjectives, or introduce an independent clause after a dependent clause. They can't appear for no reason. (p. 431)
- **Dependent and Independent Clauses:** Choices would create or join clauses. An independent clause has a main verb and can be a sentence by itself. A dependent clause can't, and starts with a conjunction or relative pronoun. (p. 426)
- **Semicolons:** Choices include one or more semicolons. Semicolons can be used to separate two sets of words that could each stand on their own as complete sentences. (See page 431.)

F   **Incorrect:** This choice would create one of two unacceptable comma sandwiches—either "at first glance a Renaissance fair" or "looks a lot like a theme park." Removing either comma sandwich leaves the other phrase, and neither phrase can stand on its own as a sentence. This comma usage also doesn't follow any other acceptable comma usage on the ACT, so this choice must be wrong.

G   **Incorrect:** This choice creates a comma sandwich around the phrase "a Renaissance fair." But that comma sandwich isn't acceptable on the ACT English section, because removing the sandwiched phrase would cause the main verb "looks" not to have a subject. This choice might attract untrained test-takers who only notice that a comma has been correctly inserted after "glance," and accidentally overlook the comma after "fair."

H ✓   **Correct:** This choice creates a comma sandwich around the phrase "at first glance" (remember that a sandwich at the very beginning or end of a sentence will only have one comma between it and the main sentence, since you can't put a comma as the first or last punctuation in a sentence). This sandwich is okay on the ACT because removing the sandwiched phrase would leave behind a grammatically acceptable sentence with the same essential meaning.

J   **Incorrect:** The ACT English section won't let us use a semicolon after "fair" because the part of the sentence before the semicolon and the part of the sentence after the semicolon wouldn't each be able to stand on their own as complete sentences.

▌T2, Q17 (Test 3 in the 2020-2021 Red Book—see page 23)   **TYPE: G/S/P (often no prompt; choices w/similar meanings—see page 418)**

- **Vertical Scan Results:** Some choices have different forms of the same base word.
- **Vertical Scan Notes:** We have to choose between "they're" and "their," and between "passed" and "past."
- **Key Features in Surrounding Text:** The words in the underlined phrase needs to refer back to the word "crowds" in the earlier part of the sentence, and to indicate a position relative to the "characters" and "booths" in the later part of the sentence.

Concepts in the question:

- **Confused Homophones:** Choices include different homophone pairs (such as "their"/"they're" or "too"/"to"). Remember the correct formation of possessives. Remember to read contractions as their uncontracted forms (e.g. "it's" = "it is"). (p. 436)
- **Dependent and Independent Clauses:** Choices would create or join clauses. An independent clause has a main verb and can be a sentence by itself. A dependent clause can't, and starts with a conjunction or relative pronoun. (p. 426)
- **Parallelism:** Choices include options that would ignore a parallel structure in the surrounding text. The right answer should match the phrasing and grammatical structures in the surrounding text when possible. (See p. 440)
- **Plural/Possessive/Contraction:** Choices include nouns ending in "-s," with/without an apostrophe before or after the "-s." Recall the 3 rules for possessive forms (p. 424). Think of contractions in uncontracted forms ("you're" = "you are"). (p. 436)

ANSWER CHOICE ANALYSIS

A   **Incorrect:** This choice uses the contraction "they're," which is equivalent to the phrase "they are." This is grammatically unacceptable on the ACT English section for multiple reasons. One reason is that it would make it unclear that the "way" belongs to the "crowds." This choice might tempt test-takers who mixed up "their" and "they're."

B   **Incorrect:** This choice uses the contraction "they're" instead of the possessive plural pronoun "their," which is wrong for the reason we discussed in (A). It also uses the verb form "passed" instead of the preposition "past," which is wrong for the reasons we'll discuss for (C).

C   **Incorrect:** This choice uses the past-tense verb form "passed" instead of the preposition "past." Among other issues, this would have to be wrong on the ACT English section because the earlier part of the sentence uses the main verb "mill" in the present tense, and there's nothing in the sentence that would allow us to change to the past tense when describing how the crowds' way is passing "characters" and "booths." This choice might appeal to test-takers who focus on the idea that "their" should appear in the right answer, and don't bother reading choice (D) or notice the issue with past/passed.

D ✓   **Correct:** This choice appropriately uses the plural possessive pronoun "their" and the preposition "past." Even if we're not familiar with the word "moseying" (which is a kind of slang way to refer to moving at a leisurely pace) we could still know that this choice must be right because of the issues with the verb phrases "they're" and "passed," as we discussed for choices (A) and (C) above.

▌T2, Q18 (Test 3 in the 2020-2021 Red Book—see page 23)   **TYPE: RC (usually has a prompt; choices w/different meanings—see page 413)**

- **RC Question sub-type:** Transition Phrase. (The choices reflect different kinds of transitions between two concepts, with words or phrases like "however," "instead of," or "for example." The right answer must reflect the relationship between the previous concept in the passage and the following concept in the passage. See p. 416)

ANSWER CHOICE ANALYSIS

F   **Confused relationships:** The phrase "being that" is somewhat commonly used, but it's grammatically questionable at best. Even if we put aside the grammatical problems of "being that," this choice must still be wrong, because it would make the sentence say that "roller coasters and Ferris wheels" are the "fair's attractions," which contradicts the passage—the next part of the passage makes it clear that "the fair's attractions are the "sights, sounds, and tastes inspired by sixteenth-century England," like "musicians, magicians, and archers" and "horses carrying knights to a jousting match," etc. So there are no actual "roller coasters" or "Ferris wheels," which means this choice must be wrong. (See the explanation for (G) for clarification about what the underlined phrase should say.)

G ✓   **Correct:** The word "instead" shows that the "sights, sounds, and tastes" are present at the fair *in place of* the "roller coasters and Ferris wheels" that one would expect at a "theme park." The word "yet" reinforces the contradiction between what would normally be found at a theme park (as mentioned in the first sentence of the essay), and what appears at the fair instead.

H   **Confused relationships:** This choice would be correct if the "roller coasters and Ferris wheels" were somehow the reason for the "sights, sounds, and tastes" at the fair, but the passage doesn't indicate that a causal relationship exists between those two phrases— in fact, the passage makes it clear that "roller coasters and Ferris wheels" aren't present at the fair the author is describing, so they

---

can't be causing anything to happen at that fair. So (H) can't be right.

J   Confused relationships: This choice has the same basic problems as (F), except for the grammatical issue associated with the phrase "being that."

- **Vertical Scan Results:** Some choices have the same words with different punctuation.
- **Vertical Scan Notes:** Should there be a comma after "horses" and/or after "knights?"
- **Key Features in Surrounding Text:** "Carrying knights to a jousting match" is a phrase in the sentence that describes horses.

Concepts in the question:

- **Commas:** Choices include commas. Commas can separate a list of 3 or more items, form sandwiches, separate interchangeable adjectives, or introduce an independent clause after a dependent clause. They can't appear for no reason. (p. 431)
- **Intervening Phrase:** A phrase appears between two words that need to agree with each other grammatically. Remember to identify pairs of words that need to agree with each other, and ignore phrases that appear between those words. (See page 439)
- **Punctuation Sandwich:** Choices involve phrases "sandwiched" between similar punctuation marks. When removed from the sentence, a proper sandwich leaves behind a grammatical sentence with the same original meaning. (See p. 432 and 433)

ANSWER CHOICE ANALYSIS

A ✓   **Correct:** This choice is correct because no commas are needed in the sentence: "carrying knights to a jousting match" is a phrase that describes what the horses are doing, and "walk" is the main verb in the sentence, being performed by the horses. See the note below for more.

B   **Incorrect:** This choice would create a comma sandwich around "carrying knights." But when this phrase is removed, we're left with the ungrammatical phrase "horses to a jousting match" as the subject of the verb "walk."

C   **Incorrect:** This choice would create one of two unacceptable comma sandwiches—either "horses carrying knights" or "to a jousting match walk along the streets." Removing either comma sandwich leaves the other phrase, and neither phrase can stand on its own as a sentence. This comma usage also doesn't follow any other acceptable comma usage on the ACT, so this choice must be wrong.

D   **Incorrect:** This choice would make everything after "horses" into a nonsensical phrase describing horses, and leave the sentence without a main verb. This choice might attract untrained test-takers who accidentally think there's also a comma after the word "match"—see the note below for more.

Answer choice patterns (page 442): wrong answers try to imitate right answers

Note   Many untrained test-takers will read the original version of this sentence and assume that the entire phrase "carrying knights to a jousting match" needs to be in a punctuation sandwich, because untrained test-takers often assume that the best way to approach the ACT English section is to "pre-form" the ideal answer before looking at the answer choices. But, as trained test-takers, we know that it's much more effective to read the text on the ACT passively but precisely, never assuming that we know what the text is going to say or how a particular problem is going to be resolved in the answer choices. As we discussed for (A), it's perfectly fine not to place "carrying...match" in a punctuation sandwich, which is what we find in the right answer to the question. But some people will pick (D) because their desire to put the phrase in a comma sandwich will cause them to misread the passage and think there's a comma between "match" and "walk," which would make (D) acceptable. This kind of issue is a great example of why it's so important to make sure you read carefully on test day!

- **RC Question sub-type:** Best accomplishes X. (The prompt describes a goal of the author, and asks which choice achieves that goal. The right answer will be plainly demonstrated in the passage. See page 413)

Subjective Phrases to Ignore: "best"

ANSWER CHOICE ANALYSIS

F   **Barely relevant:** The word "walk" doesn't involve any particular "sensory detail," as the prompt requires.

G ✓   **Correct:** "Clip-clop" is the sound the horses make as they walk down the street, so this choice includes a detail related to the sense of hearing, which satisfies the prompt.

H   **Barely relevant:** This choice has the same problem as (F).

J   **Barely relevant:** This choice has the same problem as (F) and (H).

- **Vertical Scan Results:** Choices are long phrases/sentences.
- **Vertical Scan Notes:** (A) includes two commas, while (B) and (C) include one comma and (D) has no commas. Each choice includes the "-ing" verb "ranging." (B) is the only choice with the "-ing" verb "peddling."

- **Key Features in Surrounding Text:** The underlined words for this question make up an entire sentence. The sentence appears in a paragraph about things that can be seen at a Renaissance fair.

Concepts in the question:

- **Changed Meaning:** Choices would change the meaning of the original text, or cause the relevant phrase/sentence not to make sense. The right answer must be grammatically acceptable and still preserve the original meaning. (See p. 438)
- **Dangling Participle:** When a phrase is joined to the main sentence by a comma and the phrase starts with an -ing/-ed/-en word, the first noun phrase in the independent clause is performing the action of the -ing/-ed/-en word. (See page 434.)
- **Intervening Phrase:** A phrase appears between two words that need to agree with each other grammatically. Remember to identify pairs of words that need to agree with each other, and ignore phrases that appear between those words. (See page 439)
- **Proximity:** Answer choice(s) would place descriptive phrases next to ideas they don't describe. (See page 434)
- **Punctuation Sandwich:** Choices involve phrases "sandwiched" between similar punctuation marks. When removed from the sentence, a proper sandwich leaves behind a grammatical sentence with the same original meaning. (See p. 432 and 433)
- **Verb Tense/Conjugation:** Choices include different forms of the same verb. Look at the surrounding text to find the verb's subject. Also look for other verbs that could indicate the proper tense or form for the verbs in the choices. (See p. 420-423)

ANSWER CHOICE ANALYSIS

A   **Incorrect:** The ACT's rules for participles would say that the phrase "ranging…of armor" must be performed by the noun "vendors." In other words, (A) literally says that *the vendors themselves* are the things that range from king-sized turkey legs to suits of armor. Since turkey legs and suits of armor clearly can't be vendors in this context, (A) must be wrong.

B   **Incorrect:** This choice would also say that vendors are "ranging from king-sized turkey legs to suits of armor." As we saw in our discussion of (A), turkey legs and suits of armor clearly can't be vendors in this context, so (B) must be wrong.

C   **Incorrect:** (C) has an issue similar to the one in (A): the "-ing" word "ranging" is performed by the noun "vendors," because "vendors" is the first noun after the comma that was used to join the phrase with "ranging" to the front of the sentence.

D ✓   **Correct:** (D) makes it clear that the wares are what "rang[e] from king-sized turkey legs to suits of armor," because the modifier "ranging from…armor" comes right after the noun "wares." This is the only choice that makes sense in context, so it's right.

T2, Q22 (Test 3 in the 2020-2021 Red Book—see page 23)   **TYPE: RC (usually has a prompt; choices w/different meanings—see page 413)**

- **RC Question sub-type:** Best accomplishes X. (The prompt describes a goal of the author, and asks which choice achieves that goal. The right answer will be plainly demonstrated in the passage. See page 413)

Subjective Phrases to Ignore: "best"

ANSWER CHOICE ANALYSIS

F   **Barely relevant:** By ACT standards, this isn't a good introduction to the subject of the paragraph and the rest of the essay, as the prompt requires, because we can see that the rest of the paragraph and essay discusses working at a Renaissance fair, which isn't mentioned in this version of the sentence.

G ✓   **Correct:** As trained test-takers, we know this is an acceptable introduction to the subject of the paragraph and the rest of the essay, as the prompt requires, because this paragraph and the rest of the essay literally demonstrate "working at [a Renaissance fair]" and "how much effort went into re-creating the past," as (G) requires. These literal demonstrations occur in phrases like "[we] spent weeks perfecting…accents and mannerisms," "it was exhausting…pretending," "the physical demands were…strenuous," and "three tiring months."

H   **Direct contradiction:** This isn't a good introduction by ACT standards because it mentions concepts that contradict the text being introduced. As we discussed for (G), the essay talks about the challenges of working at a Renaissance fair, not about working there being the "easiest way to…have fun at the same time," as (H) would require.

J   **Barely relevant:** As we saw in our discussion of (G), the rest of the essay describes the challenges of working as a performer at a Renaissance Fair, not about how the author and some friends "decided to attend a nearby fair."

T2, Q23 (Test 3 in the 2020-2021 Red Book—see page 23)   **TYPE: G/S/P (often no prompt; choices w/similar meanings—see page 418)**

- **Vertical Scan Results:** Some choices have the same words with different punctuation.
- **Vertical Scan Notes:** Should there be a period, comma, or semicolon after "speech?" Should the phrase be "substituting" or "we substituted?"
- **Key Features in Surrounding Text:** The words leading up to the underlined period in the original version of the underlined phrase form a complete sentence, but the words after the period in the underlined phrase create the sentence fragment "*Substituting…for 'thank you.'"

Concepts in the question:

- **Comma Splice:** Choices and/or surrounding text use commas to join two groups of words that could each be sentences on their own.

A comma can't be used in this way on the ACT English section. (See page 428)

- **Commas:** Choices include commas. Commas can separate a list of 3 or more items, form sandwiches, separate interchangeable adjectives, or introduce an independent clause after a dependent clause. They can't appear for no reason. (p. 431)
- **Dangling Participle:** When a phrase is joined to the main sentence by a comma and the phrase starts with an -ing/-ed/-en word, the first noun phrase in the independent clause is performing the action of the -ing/-ed/-en word. (See page 434.)
- **Dependent and Independent Clauses:** Choices would create or join clauses. An independent clause has a main verb and can be a sentence by itself. A dependent clause can't, and starts with a conjunction or relative pronoun. (p. 426)
- **Semicolons:** Choices include one or more semicolons. Semicolons can be used to separate two sets of words that could each stand on their own as complete sentences. (See page 431.)
- **Verb Tense/Conjugation:** Choices include different forms of the same verb. Look at the surrounding text to find the verb's subject. Also look for other verbs that could indicate the proper tense or form for the verbs in the choices. (See p. 420-423)

ANSWER CHOICE ANALYSIS

A   **Incorrect:** As we noted above, the original version of the underlined phrase creates a sentence fragment beginning with the word "substituting."

B   **Incorrect:** This choice creates a comma splice, which is unacceptable on the ACT English section, because each set of words on either side of the comma could stand on its own as a sentence, with a subject and a main verb. This choice will attract a lot of untrained test-takers who correctly note that the original version of the underlined phrase would be okay on the ACT if the period were changed into a comma, as we see in (C)...but who don't notice that (B) also introduces the word "we" and changes "substituting" to "substituted," creating the comma splice.

C ✓   **Correct:** This choice appropriately uses a comma to join the participial phrase "substituting...for 'thank you'" to the independent clause "we also incorporated...into our speech," so that the "substituting" is done by "we."

D   **Incorrect:** On the ACT English section, semicolons and periods are functionally equivalent in the sense that both are appropriate for separating two groups of words that could each stand on their own as a sentence. As we saw in our discussion of (A), the ACT won't allow us to use a period *or* semicolon here because the words after that punctuation mark couldn't stand on their own as a sentence. (Further, as trained test-takers, we recognize that (A) and (D) are identical except that one uses a period and one uses a semicolon—but if one of those types of punctuation were appropriate here, then the other one would be too. Since they can't both be right, we know they must both be wrong.)

Answer choice patterns (page 442): functionally equivalent answer choices

T2, Q24 (Test 3 in the 2020-2021 Red Book—see page 23)   **TYPE: G/S/P (often no prompt; choices w/similar meanings—see page 418)**

- **Vertical Scan Results:** Some choices have different forms of the same base word.
- **Vertical Scan Notes:** We need to pick the appropriate form of the verb "to introduce."
- **Key Features in Surrounding Text:** The sentence containing the underlined phrase describes two actions performed by the speaker, joined by the word "or:" "served the queen's meals," and the action involving the underlined phrase. Further, this sentence's use of the past-tense verbs "used" and "served," along with the word "while," indicates that all of the action in the sentence is in the past tense. For these reasons, the underlined phrase needs to parallel the verbs "used" and "introduced."

Concepts in the question:

- **Parallelism:** Choices include options that would ignore a parallel structure in the surrounding text. The right answer should match the phrasing and grammatical structures in the surrounding text when possible. (See p. 440)
- **Verb Tense/Conjugation:** Choices include different forms of the same verb. Look at the surrounding text to find the verb's subject. Also look for other verbs that could indicate the proper tense or form for the verbs in the choices. (See p. 420-423)

ANSWER CHOICE ANALYSIS

F ✓   **Correct:** "Introduced" is in the same form as "used" and "served," which is necessary for the reasons we discussed above.

G   **Incorrect:** This choice isn't in the same form as "served," so it would fail to create the parallel structure in (F)—and we know as trained test-takers that the ACT English section won't reward it. But note that the sentence created by (G) would be grammatically acceptable outside of the ACT! This choice would slightly alter the logical structure of the original sentence, because it would make "while I served..." and "or to introduce..." two phrases relating back to how the expressions were "used," instead of making "served..." and "introduced..." two phrases relating back to the word "while," as we see in (F). (Don't worry if that explanation doesn't make sense to you—it's more technical than anything you'll need to understand on test day. The important thing is that "to introduce" creates a subtle change in the relationships among the phrases in the sentence, but still allows for a sentence that would be grammatically acceptable outside of the ACT.) Many untrained test-takers will pick (G) because it would be grammatically acceptable in real life, and because they prefer the way it sounds, since they don't know the ACT's unwritten rules about parallel structures. Let this be one more reminder of why it's so important to know what the test actually rewards and punishes!

H   Incorrect: This choice doesn't use the same verb form as "used" and "served," so we know it's wrong on the ACT. (This choice also has the same issue as (G), in that it would be acceptable outside of the ACT for a similar reason.)

J   Incorrect: This choice doesn't use the same form as "used" and "served," so we know it's wrong.

T2, Q25 (Test 3 in the 2020-2021 Red Book—see page 23)   TYPE: G/S/P (often no prompt; choices w/similar meanings—see page 418)

- **Vertical Scan Results:** Similar phrases with different short words and/or punctuation.
- **Vertical Scan Notes:** We need to choose between "who" and "whom," and also among "had lived," "were to live," and "lived."
- **Key Features in Surrounding Text:** The underlined phrase and following text describe someone living in a previous century.

Concepts in the question:

- **Singular versus Plural:** Choices include singular and plural versions of the same base words that don't agree with other words in the surrounding text. Nouns, pronouns, and verbs must agree in number with the words they refer to or modify. (p. 423)
- **Verb Tense/Conjugation:** Choices include different forms of the same verb. Look at the surrounding text to find the verb's subject. Also look for other verbs that could indicate the proper tense or form for the verbs in the choices. (See p. 420-423)
- **Who/Whom:** Choices involve "who" and "whom." "Who" is a subject pronoun (which does an action, like "he"). "Whom" is an object pronoun (which receives an action, like "him"). (See page 428)

ANSWER CHOICE ANALYSIS

A   Incorrect: The underlined phrase involves performing the action "lived," so the object pronoun "whom" is unacceptable on the ACT. (Remember that we can use the "he/him" test: since it's not grammatical to say "*him had lived," it's also not grammatical to say "*whom had lived.")

B   Incorrect: The most obvious issue with this choice is probably that "who" refers back to the singular noun "person," so the plural verb form "were" isn't acceptable.

C   Incorrect: This choice also uses "whom," so it has the same problem as (A).

D ✓   Correct: The underlined phrase involves performing an action ("lived,") so the subject pronoun "who" is appropriate, as the "he/him" test makes clear: since we would say "he lived" and not "*him lived," we should say "who lived" and not "*whom lived." Further, the verb form "lived" agrees with the singular noun "person," unlike the plural phrase "were to live" in (B).

Answer choice patterns (page 442): wrong answers try to imitate right answers

T2, Q26 (Test 3 in the 2020-2021 Red Book—see page 23)   TYPE: G/S/P (often no prompt; choices w/similar meanings—see page 418)

- **Vertical Scan Results:** Similar phrases with different short words and/or punctuation.
- **Vertical Scan Notes:** Should the phrase begin with "of?" Should there be a comma after "costumes?" Should the phrase end with "they?"
- **Key Features in Surrounding Text:** The original version of the sentence uses the ungrammatical phrase "because our costumes," instead of using the phrase "because of our costumes," or stating directly what the costumes do without using a comma.

Concepts in the question:

- **Comma Splice:** Choices and/or surrounding text use commas to join two groups of words that could each be sentences on their own. A comma can't be used in this way on the ACT English section. (See page 428)
- **Commas:** Choices include commas. Commas can separate a list of 3 or more items, form sandwiches, separate interchangeable adjectives, or introduce an independent clause after a dependent clause. They can't appear for no reason. (p. 431)
- **Prepositional Idioms:** Choices typically include prepositional phrases with no other recognizable similarities. If you can't tell which choice contains an acceptable prepositional idiom in American English, guess and invest your time elsewhere. (p. 435)

ANSWER CHOICE ANALYSIS

F   Incorrect: This choice has multiple issues, as we noted above. One of the easiest ways to tell that this choice is wrong is to note that (J) is the shortest choice and that it's grammatically acceptable on the ACT, which means (J) must be right according to the test's unwritten rules.

G   Incorrect: This choice would create a comma splice, which is unacceptable on the ACT English section, because "The physical demands...of our costumes" and "they consisted...gowns" could each stand alone as separate sentences.

H   Incorrect: This choice would be correct without the word "of," because it would create the acceptable phrase "...because our costumes consisted..." But the word "of" creates an ungrammatical phrase, since the phrase "because of" must be followed by a noun phrase, not a complete clause with a subject and verb like "our costumes consisted of...gowns."

J ✓   Correct: This choice solves the issues noted above by removing the comma and the word "they" from the original version of the sentence. This makes it so that the dependent clause "because they consisted of...gowns" explains the reason behind the independent clause "The physical demands...ladies-in-waiting." Further, as trained test-takers, we should recognize that this is the shortest choice and it's grammatically acceptable to the ACT, so we know it must be right.

T2, Q27 (Test 3 in the 2020-2021 Red Book—see page 23)   TYPE: RC (usually has a prompt; choices w/different meanings—see page 413)

- **RC Question sub-type:** Including/excluding a phrase/sentence. (The question asks whether a given sentence or phrase should be included in the passage. The correct choice will include a comment that plainly describes the role of the phrase or sentence in the passage. Sentences that should be included will follow broad ACT standards for ideal sentences and paragraphs, while sentences that shouldn't be included will not follow those standards. See p. 416)

ANSWER CHOICE ANALYSIS

A   **Barely relevant:** The description in this choice is literally demonstrated by the prompt and the passage, since the sentence in the prompt does "develop[] the…comparison…[to] theme parks," as (A) requires. But, as trained test-takers, we know that the ACT won't allow us to add this sentence here because the broader rules of ideal sentences and paragraphs on the ACT say we can't add a sentence to a paragraph if that sentence mentions something that isn't discussed or developed in the rest of that paragraph. So the "yes" part of this choice makes it wrong.

B   **Barely relevant:** The given sentence doesn't "elaborate[] on the preceding sentence's point about costumes," because the preceding sentence's point was that uncomfortable costumes made it physically demanding to be a queen or lady-in-waiting at a Renaissance fair. This sentence that says theme park characters wear uncomfortable costumes doesn't "elaborate" on that point, as (B) would require, because it doesn't provide any more information about wearing uncomfortable costumes at a Renaissance fair. (B) doesn't accurately describe the sentence in question, so it's wrong.

C ✓   **Correct:** The description in this choice is literally demonstrated by the prompt and the passage, because the prompt's remark about costumes in theme parks is "only loosely related" to this paragraph, as (C) requires, since this paragraph doesn't mention theme parks—which is the reason that the ACT won't allow us to add the sentence to this paragraph, as we noted in our discussion of (A) above.

D   **Pattern:** Confused concepts. **Incorrect:** The reason in this choice isn't restated or demonstrated by the passage, because the passage doesn't say the costumes of *theme park characters* are uncomfortable; instead, it says the costumers of the speaker and the other "ladies-in-waiting" at the Renaissance fair are "confining" and "scratchy." This choice will attract a lot of test-takers who don't notice that the passage draws a clear distinction between theme park characters and people who work at a Renaissance fair. Since the reason in this choice doesn't accurately describe the passage, (D) can't be right.

T2, Q28 (Test 3 in the 2020-2021 Red Book—see page 23)   TYPE: G/S/P (often no prompt; choices w/similar meanings—see page 418)

- **Vertical Scan Results:** Choices are long phrases/sentences.
- **Vertical Scan Notes:** Some of the choices are much longer than the others. The specific words and phrases in the choices don't have much similarity to one another.
- **Key Features in Surrounding Text:** The underlined phrase must combine with the phrase "after the sixteenth century" to refer to objects being "explained in Renaissance terms."

Concepts in the question:

- **Changed Meaning:** Choices would change the meaning of the original text, or cause the relevant phrase/sentence not to make sense. The right answer must be grammatically acceptable and still preserve the original meaning. (See p. 438)
- **Comparatives and Superlatives:** Choices and/or surrounding text include a comparison. A comparison can involve either the "-er" form of an adjective, or a word like "more" or "less." Comparisons often include the word "than," but not "then." (p. 430)
- **Redundancy:** Choices and/or surrounding text could combine to repeat the same concept unnecessarily. On grammar/style/punctuation questions, we should avoid words that directly repeat ideas in the immediate surrounding text. (See p. 437)

ANSWER CHOICE ANALYSIS

F   **Incorrect:** As we noted above, the next phrase after the underlined portion of the sentence is "after the sixteenth century." The phrase "*more recently after the sixteenth century" would be a badly formed comparative phrase on the ACT English section; one way to fix it would be to write "more recently *than* the sixteenth century" (emphasis added). (Another way to fix this version of the sentence might be to sandwich "after the sixteenth century" in commas, dashes, or parentheses, so that "after the sixteenth century" would become a phrase clarifying the cutoff for things that needed "explain[ing] in Renaissance terms.")

G   **Incorrect:** The phrases "kind of object" and "type of item" from this choice mean the same thing, so one of them is redundant. Similarly, in this context, "created" and "introduced for use" mean the same thing, so one of those phrases is redundant as well. Either problem would be enough to make this choice wrong.

H ✓   **Correct:** This choice avoids the redundancy from (F) and (G), and doesn't change the meaning of the original text, like (J) does. Instead, it uses the phrase "anything invented," which refers to the kinds of things mentioned in the next sentence of the passage, like cameras.

J   **Incorrect:** As trained test-takers, we know that the ACT won't let us pick an answer to a grammar/style/punctuation question that changes the meaning of the original text. The phrase "stuff from" is more general than what the passage is talking about, because "stuff" could include any object at all that started existing after the sixteenth century, even if that general type of thing had been around for much longer—like a tree, or a mouse, or whatever. (In other words, the author isn't saying that she had to make a conscious effort to use "Renaissance terms" to describe the concept of a dress, because dresses in general existed during the Renaissance.) On the other hand, the passage makes it clear that the author was only concerned with using "Renaissance terms" for *inventions* that came after the sixteenth century, like the "camera" mentioned in the following sentence. So (J) changes the meaning of the passage, which makes it wrong. This is one more good example of the importance of reading carefully on test day, even on questions the might not seem to rely heavily on reading comprehension at first! (Review the training on page 438 of this Black Book if necessary.)

▌ T2, Q29 (Test 3 in the 2020-2021 Red Book—see page 23)   TYPE: RC (usually has a prompt; choices w/different meanings—see page 413)

- **RC Question sub-type:** Transition Phrase. (The choices reflect different kinds of transitions between two concepts, with words or phrases like "however," "instead of," or "for example." The right answer must reflect the relationship between the previous concept in the passage and the following concept in the passage. See p. 416)

ANSWER CHOICE ANALYSIS

A   **Confused relationships:** This choice would be acceptable on the ACT English section if "marvel[ing] at the camera" and asking about "lifelike paintings...inside the tiny box" were somehow in opposition to the idea of "explain[ing]" things "in Renaissance terms," which is mentioned in the previous sentence. Since there's no inherent opposition between those ideas, "however" is wrong.

B ✓ **Correct:** This choice is acceptable on the ACT English section because this sentence demonstrates an example of the kind of situation mentioned in the previous sentence.

C   **Confused relationships:** This choice would be appropriate if this sentence described an event that took place on one specific occasion, but that's not the case: the words "when," "a," and "would" all indicate that this is a general description of a type of event that happened more than once.

D   **Confused relationships:** This choice has an issue somewhat similar to what we saw in (A). Since there's no inherent contradiction between the ideas in this sentence and in the previous sentence—and since what appears in this sentence isn't something that takes the place of what appears in the previous sentence—we know the word "instead" is inappropriate on the ACT English section.

▌ T2, Q30 (Test 3 in the 2020-2021 Red Book—see page 23)   TYPE: G/S/P (often no prompt; choices w/similar meanings—see page 418)

- **Vertical Scan Results:** Choices are long phrases/sentences.
- **Vertical Scan Notes:** The choices are all long phrases describing the idea of something ending, except for (J), which would allow us to delete the underlined phrase completely.
- **Key Features in Surrounding Text:** The sentence with the underlined phrase already includes multiple indications of the time when the events in the sentence occurred.

    Concepts in the question:

- **Redundancy:** Choices and/or surrounding text could combine to repeat the same concept unnecessarily. On grammar/style/punctuation questions, we should avoid words that directly repeat ideas in the immediate surrounding text. (See p. 437)
- **Shorter is Better:** Choices include words or phrases that can be removed without impacting meaning or creating grammatical problems. The shortest grammatically acceptable choice that doesn't change the meaning is right. (p. 442)

ANSWER CHOICE ANALYSIS

F   **Incorrect:** This phrase is redundant, so it's unacceptable on the ACT English section: the sentence already uses the phrases "after three tiring months" and "the fair closed for the season," and we know from earlier in the passage that the author worked at the fair "in the hot summer temperatures."

G   **Incorrect:** The text already said "the fair closed for the season," so this phrase is redundant, like (F) was.

H   **Incorrect:** This choice has the same problem as (F) and (G)—it repeats an idea that already appears in the text.

J ✓ **Correct:** This choice avoids the redundant text from the other choices, and deleting the underlined portion doesn't create any grammatical problems in the text, so (J) is the only choice that follows the ACT's unwritten rules.

Answer choice patterns (page 442): shortest grammatically acceptable choice is correct

▌ T2, Q31 (Test 3 in the 2020-2021 Red Book—see page 23)   TYPE: G/S/P (often no prompt; choices w/similar meanings—see page 418)

- **Vertical Scan Results:** Some choices have the same words with different punctuation.
- **Vertical Scan Notes:** Should there be a comma after "water," "caused," or "by?"
- **Key Features in Surrounding Text:** The subject of the sentence is "blast," and the main verb is "roared."

    Concepts in the question:

- **Commas:** Choices include commas. Commas can separate a list of 3 or more items, form sandwiches, separate interchangeable adjectives, or introduce an independent clause after a dependent clause. They can't appear for no reason. (p. 431)
- **Dependent and Independent Clauses:** Choices would create or join clauses. An independent clause has a main verb and can be a

sentence by itself. A dependent clause can't, and starts with a conjunction or relative pronoun. (p. 426)

- **Intervening Phrase:** A phrase appears between two words that need to agree with each other grammatically. Remember to identify pairs of words that need to agree with each other, and ignore phrases that appear between those words. (See page 439)
- **Punctuation Sandwich:** Choices involve phrases "sandwiched" between similar punctuation marks. When removed from the sentence, a proper sandwich leaves behind a grammatical sentence with the same original meaning. (See p. 432 and 433)

ANSWER CHOICE ANALYSIS

A ✓ **Correct:** As trained test-takers, we can see that there's no need for any commas in the underlined portion of the sentence, and we know that the default preference of the ACT English section is to avoid commas unless they're necessary, so (A) is right. See the discussions of the other answer choices for more.

B **Incorrect:** The comma in this choice would create the comma sandwich "a one-billion-gallon blast...caused by." If this phrase were removed, the sentence left behind would read: "In Reynolds, Missouri, a breach of the Taum Sauk reservoir roared down Proffit Mountain…" But this sentence wouldn't make any sense, because a "breach" is a spot where something breaks through a barrier, and a spot where something breaks through a barrier can't "roar[] down" a mountain. This choice doesn't create an acceptable comma sandwich because removing that comma sandwich creates the problem we just discussed; it also doesn't involve any other acceptable use of a comma on the ACT, so it's wrong.

C **Incorrect:** This choice has an issue similar to the one in (B): it would create the unacceptable comma sandwich "a one-billion-gallon blast...caused," which would leave behind "In Reynolds, Missouri, by a breach of the Taum Sauk reservoir roared down Proffit Mountain…." This would cause a problem similar to the one in (B).

D **Incorrect:** This choice has a problem similar to the issue in (B) and (C), but it might attract more untrained test-takers than (B) and (C). This is because (D) could seem to be correct if an untrained test-taker were assuming there would also be a comma after "reservoir;" if a comma did appear in that position, then (D) would create an acceptable comma sandwich around the phrase "caused by a breach of the Taum Sauk reservoir," which would provide further information about the "blast." But, as we see when we read carefully, there is no comma after "reservoir," which means that adding a comma after "water" wouldn't satisfy any of the ACT's rules for comma usage. Always remember the importance of reading carefully on test day, so you can avoid these kinds of mistakes!

T2, Q32 (Test 3 in the 2020-2021 Red Book—see page 23)　　　**TYPE: G/S/P (often no prompt; choices w/similar meanings—see page 418)**

- **Vertical Scan Results:** Some choices are short phrases with no obvious similarity.
- **Vertical Scan Notes:** The choices are all different combinations of pronouns.
- **Key Features in Surrounding Text:** The underlined phrase must refer back to the singular noun "blast" from the previous sentence, because the blast is the thing that "ripped a channel."

Concepts in the question:

- **Dependent and Independent Clauses:** Choices would create or join clauses. An independent clause has a main verb and can be a sentence by itself. A dependent clause can't, and starts with a conjunction or relative pronoun. (p. 426)
- **Pronoun Ambiguity:** Choices include pronouns that could refer to more than one phrase in the surrounding text. We can't use a pronoun on the ACT when it isn't clear what that pronoun refers to. (See page 419)
- **Singular versus Plural:** Choices include singular and plural versions of the same base words that don't agree with other words in the surrounding text. Nouns, pronouns, and verbs must agree in number with the words they refer to or modify. (p. 423)
- **Who/Whom:** Choices involve "who" and "whom." "Who" is a subject pronoun (which does an action, like "he"). "Whom" is an object pronoun (which receives an action, like "him"). (See page 428)

ANSWER CHOICE ANALYSIS

F **Incorrect:** The plural pronoun "they" can't refer to the singular noun "blast."

G **Incorrect:** This choice has the same basic problem as (F), because it uses "they" to refer to the singular noun "blast." Some untrained test-takers will be drawn to this choice because they'll overlook the word "they," and think the word "that" is just referring back to the singular noun "blast" (as in "that ripped a channel...").

H **Incorrect:** In this position, the word "which" would turn this entire sentence into a dependent clause. A dependent clause that isn't attached to an independent clause is a sentence fragment, which is never acceptable on the ACT English section.

J ✓ **Correct:** The singular pronoun "it" matches the grammatical number of the singular noun "blast." This choice avoids the problems from the other choices without creating any other issues, so (J) is the only acceptable choice according to the rules of grammar on the ACT English test.

Note Choice (G) also uses "that" inappropriately, because placing the word "that" in front of a verb phrase like "they ripped a channel" actually causes the entire phrase to function as a noun phrase, like in the sentence "That you called means a lot." We don't have to pick up on this incorrect usage of "that" in order to know that (G) is wrong, because of the issue with "they," but this is an issue that shows up from time to time on the ACT English section.

- **Vertical Scan Results:** Some choices have the same words with different punctuation.
- **Vertical Scan Notes:** We have to choose among "parks," "park's," and "parks'," and decide whether a comma should appear after "time."
- **Key Features in Surrounding Text:** The choices give us the option of pluralizing "park," but the previous sentence mentions "Johnson's Shut-Ins, *one* of Missouri's most popular state parks" (emphasis added), so we need to make sure the underlined phrase refers to a single park, not multiple parks. Since the park must be singular, the "beauty" must belong to the single "park." Also, the phrase beginning with "though" is a dependent clause, so we need to make sure it's separated from the independent clause with a comma.

Concepts in the question:

- **Commas:** Choices include commas. Commas can separate a list of 3 or more items, form sandwiches, separate interchangeable adjectives, or introduce an independent clause after a dependent clause. They can't appear for no reason. (p. 431)
- **Dependent and Independent Clauses:** Choices would create or join clauses. An independent clause has a main verb and can be a sentence by itself. A dependent clause can't, and starts with a conjunction or relative pronoun. (p. 426)
- **Intervening Phrase:** A phrase appears between two words that need to agree with each other grammatically. Remember to identify pairs of words that need to agree with each other, and ignore phrases that appear between those words. (See page 439)
- **Plural/Possessive/Contraction:** Choices include nouns ending in "-s," with/without an apostrophe before or after the "-s." Recall the 3 rules for possessive forms (p. 424). Think of contractions in uncontracted forms ("you're" = "you are"). (p. 436)

ANSWER CHOICE ANALYSIS

A   **Incorrect:** The previous sentence refers to only one park, so the plural form "parks" makes no sense here. On top of that, the phrase "parks beauty," without an apostrophe to show possession, doesn't make sense in this context, because there's no grammatical connection between "parks" and "beauty" if there's no possessive relationship between them.

B ✓   **Correct:** This choice uses the possessive singular form "park's," which makes it clear that the "beauty" belongs to the "park." Also, "park's" matches in grammatical number with the singular noun "one" in the previous sentence—in other words, this choice makes it clear that the beauty belongs to one "park," not multiple parks, as the context requires. This choice also uses a comma after "time" to join the dependent clause ("though...for a time") to the independent clause ("the scar...history"). Since this choice is the only one that follows all the ACT's relevant grammatical rules, it's the right answer.

C   **Incorrect:** This choice uses the possessive plural form "parks'," but we know from the previous sentence in the passage that only a single park is being referred to: "Johnson's Shut-Ins," which is "one of Missouri's most popular state parks." A lot of untrained test-takers will incorrectly assume that "parks'" is the proper form because they'll think it's referring back to the plural word "Shut-Ins" or the plural word "parks" in the previous sentence, but, as we discussed above, the word "one" in the previous sentence tells us that this sentence is only referring to the beauty in a single park.

D   **Incorrect:** This choice includes no comma between the dependent clause and the independent clause in the sentence, but, as we discussed for (B), that comma is necessary.

- **RC Question sub-type:** Transition Phrase. (The choices reflect different kinds of transitions between two concepts, with words or phrases like "however," "instead of," or "for example." The right answer must reflect the relationship between the previous concept in the passage and the following concept in the passage. See p. 416)

ANSWER CHOICE ANALYSIS

F   **Barely relevant:** The word "specifically" would emphasize that one exact thing is happening. But nothing in the surrounding text indicates that the idea of an exact, specific event needs to be emphasized here.

G ✓   **Correct:** The dependent clause at the beginning of the sentence starts with the word "though," which indicates a contradiction of some kind. The sentence then describes how the short-term result of the flood "marred the park's beauty *for a time*" (emphasis added). The word "ultimately" (which means something like "finally" or "when all was said and done") indicates the long-term effect of the flood—"reveal[ing]...a billion years' worth of...history." The word "though" appropriately reflects the contrasting relationship between the short-term negative effect of "marr[ing]...beauty" and the long-term positive effect of "reveal[ing]...history," and that contrast is supported by "ultimately" as we just discussed, so (G) is right.

H   **Confused relationships:** The sentence describes two results of the flood: damage that "marred the park's beauty for a time," and the revealing of "over a billion years' worth of Earth's geologic history." The sentence doesn't demonstrate the idea that one thing happened *in place of* the other thing, which is what "instead" would require.

J   **Confused relationships:** As we saw in our discussion of (G), the right answer to this question needs to cause the text to demonstrate some kind of contrast or contradiction so that the word "though" will be justified. But (J) would reflect a kind of causation, rather than a contrast—in other words, (J) would say that the second result happened *because of* the first result. Many untrained test-takers will be drawn to this choice because they'll prefer the way it sounds, but our awareness of the unwritten rules of demonstration and restatement on the ACT will allow us to see that (J) must be wrong and (G) must be right, since (J) doesn't justify the presence of the word "though" in this sentence.

Note   Questions about transition phrases on the ACT English section usually offer four transition phrases in the answer choices, or three transition phrases and the option to delete the underlined phrase. This question offered three transition phrases and the word "specifically," which wouldn't normally be considered a transition phrase. The ACT will occasionally blur the lines between different question types by blending two or more types together. Remember on test day that if you just read carefully and apply your training for any relevant question type, you'll always be able to find one clear, right answer with certainty—it will never be the case that the standards for one question type point to one right answer, and the standards for another type point to another right answer, and you have to choose between them.

T2, Q35 (Test 3 in the 2020-2021 Red Book—see page 23)   **TYPE: G/S/P (often no prompt; choices w/similar meanings—see page 418)**

- **Vertical Scan Results:** Some choices have different forms of the same base word.
- **Vertical Scan Notes:** We need to choose from "had began," "begun," and "began," and we need to choose between "to develop" and "developing."
- **Key Features in Surrounding Text:** The action in the underlined phrase took place "when the volcanoes that created the St. Francois Mountains exploded." Since the action in the underlined phrase took place in the same timeframe as the past-tense verbs "created" and "exploded," the underlined verb should also be in the past tense, according to the ACT's unwritten rules.

Concepts in the question:

- **Parallelism:** Choices include options that would ignore a parallel structure in the surrounding text. The right answer should match the phrasing and grammatical structures in the surrounding text when possible. (See p. 440)
- **Verb Tense/Conjugation:** Choices include different forms of the same verb. Look at the surrounding text to find the verb's subject. Also look for other verbs that could indicate the proper tense or form for the verbs in the choices. (See p. 420-423)

ANSWER CHOICE ANALYSIS

A   Incorrect: This verb isn't in the same tense as "exploded"—and, on top of that, the verb form "*had began" isn't grammatically acceptable on the ACT in any context, anyway (acceptable forms of this verb include "began" or "had begun"). But, again, the right answer needs to be in the simple past tense, just like "created" and "exploded," so (A) is wrong either way.

B   Incorrect: This choice has an issue similar to the one in (A): it's not an acceptable conjugation of the irregular verb "begin." The simple past tense of that verb is "began," not "begun."

C ✓   Correct: "Began" is the simple past tense of the irregular verb "begin," which means that this choice would cause the underlined verb to be in the same tense as the verbs "created" and "exploded," just as the ACT requires in this situation.

D   Incorrect: This choice has the same basic problem as (B), because both use the incorrect form "begun" as the simple past tense of "begin."

Note   "Begin" is an irregular verb in English. This question is ultimately testing whether you know that "began" is the form of "begin" that corresponds to "created" and "exploded." The form of "develop" doesn't matter in this question, because only one choice has an acceptable version of "begin." If you weren't familiar with the forms of "begin," then you'd have to guess on this question. So remember that answering a question on the English section of the ACT will occasionally require you to know the conjugation of an irregular verb, but, if you don't know that conjugation, you'll be better off marking your best guess, and then investing your time and energy elsewhere.

T2, Q36 (Test 3 in the 2020-2021 Red Book—see page 23)   **TYPE: G/S/P (often no prompt; choices w/similar meanings—see page 418)**

- **Vertical Scan Results:** Similar phrases with different short words and/or punctuation.
- **Vertical Scan Notes:** Period, semicolon, or no punctuation after "ago?" Should "when" appear after "ago?"
- **Key Features in Surrounding Text:** In the current version of the underlined phrase, the words before the period could stand on their own as a sentence, but the "sentence" beginning with "when" is actually a sentence fragment, because it's just a dependent clause beginning with the word "when."

Concepts in the question:

- **Commas:** Choices include commas. Commas can separate a list of 3 or more items, form sandwiches, separate interchangeable adjectives, or introduce an independent clause after a dependent clause. They can't appear for no reason. (p. 431)
- **Dependent and Independent Clauses:** Choices would create or join clauses. An independent clause has a main verb and can be a sentence by itself. A dependent clause can't, and starts with a conjunction or relative pronoun. (p. 426)
- **Intervening Phrase:** A phrase appears between two words that need to agree with each other grammatically. Remember to identify pairs of words that need to agree with each other, and ignore phrases that appear between those words. (See page 439)
- **Semicolons:** Choices include one or more semicolons. Semicolons can be used to separate two sets of words that could each stand on their own as complete sentences. (See page 431.)

F — Incorrect: As we noted above, there shouldn't be a period after "ago," because the phrase "when…exploded" is a dependent clause, and can't stand on its own as a sentence.

G — Incorrect: This choice has basically the same issue as (F): a semicolon, like a period, would only be appropriate here if it separated two groups of words that could each stand on their own as sentences, but "when…exploded" is a dependent clause. (Further, as trained test-takers, we know that (F) and (G) are functionally equivalent, since they both involve punctuation that would have to separate two groups of words that could each stand on their own as sentences; both choices can't be right, so they must both be wrong.) This choice will attract some untrained test-takers who misread the semicolon as a comma, because it would be acceptable in real life to use a comma before the dependent clause introduced by "when."

H ✓ — Correct: This choice avoids the problems from the other choices, and doesn't create any new problems: it places the dependent clause "when…exploded" as a modifier after the phrase "1.5 billion years ago."

J — Incorrect: Without the word "when," there's no grammatical relationship between the phrase "the volcanoes…exploded" and the independent clause that precedes it.

Answer choice patterns (page 442): functionally equivalent answer choices

T2, Q37 (Test 3 in the 2020-2021 Red Book—see page 23)   TYPE: G/S/P (often no prompt; choices w/similar meanings—see page 418)

- Vertical Scan Results: Similar phrases with different short words and/or punctuation.
- Vertical Scan Notes: All the choices talk about something cooling.
- Key Features in Surrounding Text: The underlined phrase is an action performed by the "magma" in the sentence.

Concepts in the question:

- Redundancy: Choices and/or surrounding text could combine to repeat the same concept unnecessarily. On grammar/style/punctuation questions, we should avoid words that directly repeat ideas in the immediate surrounding text. (See p. 437)
- Shorter is Better: Choices include words or phrases that can be removed without impacting meaning or creating grammatical problems. The shortest grammatically acceptable choice that doesn't change the meaning is right. (p. 442)

ANSWER CHOICE ANALYSIS

A — Incorrect: By definition, when something "cool[s] down," we already know that the temperature is what's cooling down—so the phrase "its temperature" is redundant, and (A) is wrong.

B — Incorrect: This choice has an issue similar to the one in (A): when something "cool[s] down," we already know the temperature is getting lower—so "to a lower temperature" is redundant.

C — Incorrect: This choice has the same basic problem as (A) and (B).

D ✓ — Correct: This is the shortest choice and it's grammatically acceptable to the ACT, so, as trained test-takers, we know it must be right. Also, this choice avoids the redundancy from the other choices.

Answer choice patterns (page 442): shortest grammatically acceptable choice is correct

T2, Q38 (Test 3 in the 2020-2021 Red Book—see page 23)   TYPE: G/S/P (often no prompt; choices w/similar meanings—see page 418)

- Vertical Scan Results: Some choices have the same words with different punctuation.
- Vertical Scan Notes: Should there be a comma after "form," "silica-rich," and/or "rhyolite?"
- Key Features in Surrounding Text: All of the words in the underlined phrase relate to the word "rock" after the underline: "form" is a verb whose object is "rock," while "silica-rich" is an adjective describing the noun phrase "rhyolite rock."

Concepts in the question:

- Commas: Choices include commas. Commas can separate a list of 3 or more items, form sandwiches, separate interchangeable adjectives, or introduce an independent clause after a dependent clause. They can't appear for no reason. (p. 431)

ANSWER CHOICE ANALYSIS

F ✓ — Correct: As trained test-takers, we know the situations in which the ACT English section will require us to use commas, and we can see that the underlined phrase doesn't call for any commas, so (F) is right. As we noted above, the word "form" is a verb with "rock" as its object, so no comma needs to appear after "form." The phrase "silica-rich" is an adjective describing the noun phrase "rhyolite rock," so no comma needs to appear after "silica-rich." And the noun phrase "rhyolite rock" doesn't need a comma between the two nouns.

G — Incorrect: The simplest way to realize that this choice is wrong is to remember that the unwritten rules of the ACT require us to omit any punctuation unless there is a specific reason to include it, and that the shortest grammatically acceptable answer choice on a style/grammar/punctuation question is correct. Choice (F) omits punctuation without causing any problems, and it's also shorter than this choice and grammatically correct—so this choice must be wrong.

H — Incorrect: As we discussed for (F), there's no reason to place a comma in the middle of the noun phrase "rhyolite rock."

J — Incorrect: As we saw in our analysis of (F), there's no reason to insert a comma between the verb "form" and its object, the noun phrase "silica-rich rhyolite rock."

T2, Q39 (Test 3 in the 2020-2021 Red Book—see page 23) TYPE: RC (usually has a prompt; choices w/different meanings—see page 413)

- **RC Question sub-type:** Including/excluding a phrase/sentence. (The question asks whether a given sentence or phrase should be included in the passage. The correct choice will include a comment that plainly describes the role of the phrase or sentence in the passage. Sentences that should be included will follow broad ACT standards for ideal sentences and paragraphs, while sentences that shouldn't be included will not follow those standards. See p. 416)

ANSWER CHOICE ANALYSIS

A **Barely relevant:** The underlined phrase doesn't say anything about "how people feel." This choice makes an inaccurate statement about the text, so it's wrong.

B ✓ **Correct:** We know from earlier in the passage that the park is called "Johnson's Shut-Ins," and the underlined portion of the text explains what "shut-in" means in the context of the park, demonstrating the "inspiration for the park's name," as (B) requires. Since this is the only choice whose description is literally demonstrated by the passage, we know it must be correct.

C **Barely relevant:** The underlined phrase doesn't demonstrate informality or a lack of consistency with the essay's tone—in fact, as we saw for (B), the phrase "shut-ins" appears in other parts of the passage, so it makes no sense to say that this use of the same phrase would somehow not fit with the tone of the rest of the passage.

D **Confused relationships:** The underlined phrase does come in the middle of the description of the Black River, but it's part of that description, rather than an interruption of the description—the phrase "shut in" explains the word "confined," which is used to describe the relationship between "the Black River" and "the rhyolite." Logically speaking, if "shut-in" were an interruption, then "confined" would be an interruption too, because they're synonyms here, which means that removing "shut-in" (and leaving in "confined") wouldn't remove the interruption, as (D) would require. (Of course, "shut-in" isn't an interruption—as we've already said—which is the reason (D) is wrong.) Since (D) doesn't accurately describe the passage, we know (D) can't be right.

T2, Q40 (Test 3 in the 2020-2021 Red Book—see page 23) TYPE: G/S/P (often no prompt; choices w/similar meanings—see page 418)

- **Vertical Scan Results:** Some choices have the same words with different punctuation.
- **Vertical Scan Notes:** Should "rhyolite" be followed by "and," a comma, or a semicolon? Should the last word in the phrase be "creating," or "created?"

Concepts in the question:

- **Commas:** Choices include commas. Commas can separate a list of 3 or more items, form sandwiches, separate interchangeable adjectives, or introduce an independent clause after a dependent clause. They can't appear for no reason. (p. 431)
- **Dependent and Independent Clauses:** Choices would create or join clauses. An independent clause has a main verb and can be a sentence by itself. A dependent clause can't, and starts with a conjunction or relative pronoun. (p. 426)
- **Parallelism:** Choices include options that would ignore a parallel structure in the surrounding text. The right answer should match the phrasing and grammatical structures in the surrounding text when possible. (See p. 440)
- **Semicolons:** Choices include one or more semicolons. Semicolons can be used to separate two sets of words that could each stand on their own as complete sentences. (See page 431.)
- **Verb Tense/Conjugation:** Choices include different forms of the same verb. Look at the surrounding text to find the verb's subject. Also look for other verbs that could indicate the proper tense or form for the verbs in the choices. (See p. 420-423)

ANSWER CHOICE ANALYSIS

F **Incorrect:** If the word "and" appeared after "rhyolite" with no punctuation in the underlined phrase, then "was confined" and "creating" would be two verb phrases with "the Black River" as their subject. Those verbs would need to be parallel, but "was confined" and "creating" are different verb forms—one is an "-ed" form and the other is an "-ing" form—so this choice can't be right.

G **Incorrect:** There shouldn't be a semicolon after "rhyolite" because the part of the sentence after the semicolon wouldn't stand on its own as a complete sentence.

H ✓ **Correct:** This choice is right because it avoids the problems from the other choices, and it creates the acceptable punctuation sandwich "creating…visitors," which, when removed, leaves behind the grammatical sentence "In low places…rhyolite."

J **Incorrect:** This choice would create a list of two actions done by "the Black River:" "was confined…by the rhyolite" and "created the natural waterslides…." (This is technically called a compound predicate, but you don't need to know that term to get this question right.) These two different actions would need to be joined with a word like "and" or "but," but no such word appears in this choice, so it's wrong.

T2, Q41 (Test 3 in the 2020-2021 Red Book—see page 23) TYPE: G/S/P (often no prompt; choices w/similar meanings—see page 418)

- **Vertical Scan Results:** Similar phrases with different short words and/or punctuation.
- **Vertical Scan Notes:** Should the phrase include "in" or "on?" Should the phrase include "their" or "its?"

- **Key Features in Surrounding Text:** The pronoun in the underlined phrase refers to the singular noun "surge," and the preposition in the underlined phrase describes how "trees, soil, and sedimentary rock" relate to the "path" of the water surge.

Concepts in the question:

- **Intervening Phrase:** A phrase appears between two words that need to agree with each other grammatically. Remember to identify pairs of words that need to agree with each other, and ignore phrases that appear between those words. (See page 439)
- **Prepositional Idioms:** Choices typically include prepositional phrases with no other recognizable similarities. If you can't tell which choice contains an acceptable prepositional idiom in American English, guess and invest your time elsewhere. (p. 435)
- **Pronoun Ambiguity:** Choices include pronouns that could refer to more than one phrase in the surrounding text. We can't use a pronoun on the ACT when it isn't clear what that pronoun refers to. (See page 419)
- **Singular versus Plural:** Choices include singular and plural versions of the same base words that don't agree with other words in the surrounding text. Nouns, pronouns, and verbs must agree in number with the words they refer to or modify. (p. 423)

ANSWER CHOICE ANALYSIS

A ✓ **Correct:** This choice includes the preposition "in," which creates the idiomatically correct phrase "in its path" to describe how the position of the "trees, soil, and sedimentary rock" relates to the "path" of the "surge." This choice also includes the singular pronoun "its" to refer to the singular noun "surge."

B **Incorrect:** This choice uses "on" to express the relationship of the "trees, soil, and sedimentary rock" to the path, but the correct idiomatic preposition is "in," as we mentioned for (A). Also, this choice uses the plural pronoun "their" to refer to the singular noun "surge." Either issue is enough to make this choice wrong. See the note below for more.

C **Incorrect:** Like (B), this choice uses the plural pronoun "their" to refer to the singular noun "surge." This will appeal to a lot of untrained test-takers who think the underlined pronoun should refer to the plural noun "trees" or the plural noun "shut-ins." But we can see that the underlined pronoun is the thing that has a "path," which means it must be the singular noun "surge," since the text says the surge "tore through the park," and doesn't describe any other noun following any sort of "path."

D **Incorrect:** This choice uses "on" to describe what is in the path of the "surge," but the correct idiomatic preposition is "in," as we saw in our discussion of (A). See the note below for more.

Answer choice patterns (page 442): wrong answers try to imitate right answers

Note For this question, we were able to eliminate (B) and (C) because each one used a plural pronoun where a singular pronoun was required—but then we had to choose between "in its" from (A) and "on its" from (D). As trained test-takers, we know that the ACT English section occasionally asks questions that require us to know a prepositional idiom in English, such as the idiom "everything in its path" (as opposed to "*everything *on* its path*"). As we discussed in the training, there's usually no way that you can figure out the idiomatically correct preposition unless you happen to know it beforehand. So if you find yourself confronted with a prepositional idiom that you're not sure about on test day, the best thing you can do is mark down your best guess as quickly as possible, which allows you to invest your time in other questions that are based on the test's rules, rather than wondering about arbitrary prepositional phrases.

❚ T2, Q42 (Test 3 in the 2020-2021 Red Book—see page 23)   TYPE: G/S/P (often no prompt; choices w/similar meanings—see page 418)

- **Vertical Scan Results:** Some choices have different forms of the same base word.
- **Vertical Scan Notes:** Three choices involve a plural form of "to contain," and only (J) has a singular form of "to contain."
- **Key Features in Surrounding Text:** The verb in the underlined phrase is being done by the singular noun "channel."

Concepts in the question:

- **Singular versus Plural:** Choices include singular and plural versions of the same base words that don't agree with other words in the surrounding text. Nouns, pronouns, and verbs must agree in number with the words they refer to or modify. (p. 423)
- **Verb Tense/Conjugation:** Choices include different forms of the same verb. Look at the surrounding text to find the verb's subject. Also look for other verbs that could indicate the proper tense or form for the verbs in the choices. (See p. 420-423)

ANSWER CHOICE ANALYSIS

F **Incorrect:** This verb form is plural, but it needs to be singular to agree with the noun "channel," as we discussed above.

G **Incorrect:** This choice has the same basic problem as (F): it's plural, but it needs to be singular.

H **Incorrect:** Like (F) and (G), this choice is plural.

J ✓ **Correct:** This is the only singular verb form in the choices, which means it's the only choice that agrees with the singular noun "channel," as the sentence requires.

Note Many untrained test-takers will waste a lot of time on this question trying to figure out whether the right answer should contain an "-ed" verb, an "-ing" verb, or a verb form without a helping verb. But, as trained test-takers, we should notice that (F), (G), and (H) are all *plural* verb forms, while (J) is the only choice that contains a *singular* verb form. We can see

---

that the subject of the verb is the singular noun "channel," so the only choice with a singular verb form must be the right answer. Keep this kind of thing in mind on test day—if you can't see a meaningful difference between two or three choices that all seem acceptable, then you've probably overlooked the real issue in the question!

T2, Q43 (Test 3 in the 2020-2021 Red Book—see page 23)   TYPE: G/S/P (often no prompt; choices w/similar meanings—see page 418)

- **Vertical Scan Results:** Choices are long phrases/sentences.
- **Vertical Scan Notes:** The choices are different phrases that describe people who like the outdoors.
- **Key Features in Surrounding Text:** The original version of the underlined phrase says that "some have returned" to the park. As it's used here, the word "some" is a pronoun, and it's not clear what that pronoun is referring to. Have some of the "shut-ins" (which is the nearest plural noun to "some") returned somehow? Have the "years of work" returned somehow? Or does "some" refer to people, or animals, or what? The ACT won't allow this kind of ambiguity for an underlined pronoun. (The word "geologists" in the next sentence does describe a specific kind of person, which may be relevant here.)

Concepts in the question:

- **Commas:** Choices include commas. Commas can separate a list of 3 or more items, form sandwiches, separate interchangeable adjectives, or introduce an independent clause after a dependent clause. They can't appear for no reason. (p. 431)
- **Parallelism:** Choices include options that would ignore a parallel structure in the surrounding text. The right answer should match the phrasing and grammatical structures in the surrounding text when possible. (See p. 440)
- **Pronoun Ambiguity:** Choices include pronouns that could refer to more than one phrase in the surrounding text. We can't use a pronoun on the ACT when it isn't clear what that pronoun refers to. (See page 419)

ANSWER CHOICE ANALYSIS

A   **Incorrect:** As we noted above, "some" is a pronoun that doesn't clearly refer to anything in the surrounding text. The ACT won't allow this kind of ambiguous use of a pronoun, so (A) is wrong.

B   **Incorrect:** See the explanation for (C).

C ✓   **Correct:** When we consider (B), (C), and (D), we might think that they're pretty similar—all three seem to describe people who like being outdoors. But, as trained test-takers, we know there must be a reason why one choice is right and the other choices are wrong. When we think very carefully about the information expressed in each choice, and the text surrounding the underlined phrase in the question, we realize that (C) uses the parallel phrase "swimmers, hikers, and campers" to indicate specific kinds of people, echoing the use of the word "geologists" in the next sentence.

D   **Incorrect:** See the explanation for (C).

T2, Q44 (Test 3 in the 2020-2021 Red Book—see page 23)   TYPE: G/S/P (often no prompt; choices w/similar meanings—see page 418)

- **Vertical Scan Results:** Similar phrases with different short words and/or punctuation.
- **Vertical Scan Notes:** Three options have to do with coming back to the park, and one option is to delete the phrase entirely.
- **Key Features in Surrounding Text:** The word "returned" appears before the underlined phrase.

Concepts in the question:

- **Redundancy:** Choices and/or surrounding text could combine to repeat the same concept unnecessarily. On grammar/style/punctuation questions, we should avoid words that directly repeat ideas in the immediate surrounding text. (See p. 437)
- **Shorter is Better:** Choices include words or phrases that can be removed without impacting meaning or creating grammatical problems. The shortest grammatically acceptable choice that doesn't change the meaning is right. (p. 442)

ANSWER CHOICE ANALYSIS

F   **Incorrect:** The word "returned" already expresses the idea of people coming "back," so this choice is redundant, which means it's wrong on the ACT English section.

G   **Incorrect:** This choice has the same problem as (F).

H   **Incorrect:** The word "returned" already expresses the idea of people "revisit[ing] the park," so this choice is redundant, like (F) and (G).

J ✓   **Correct:** All the other choices are redundant, and removing the underlined portion doesn't create any grammatical issues in the sentence, so we know (J) is the right answer.

Answer choice patterns (page 442): shortest grammatically acceptable choice is correct

T2, Q45 (Test 3 in the 2020-2021 Red Book—see page 23)   TYPE: G/S/P (often no prompt; choices w/similar meanings—see page 418)

- **Vertical Scan Results:** Some choices have the same words with different punctuation.
- **Vertical Scan Notes:** We have to decide whether a comma, colon, or no punctuation should appear after "astronomer," and whether a comma or no punctuation should appear after "through."
- **Key Features in Surrounding Text:** "I was an inexperienced astronomer" is an independent clause, while "peering through light-

polluted skies" is a phrase describing what the speaker was doing while being an inexperienced astronomer.

Concepts in the question:

- **Colons:** Choices include colons. A colon can only be placed after a set of words that could be a sentence on their own, and only before a demonstration or example of the idea before the colon. No more than one colon per sentence. (p. 430)
- **Commas:** Choices include commas. Commas can separate a list of 3 or more items, form sandwiches, separate interchangeable adjectives, or introduce an independent clause after a dependent clause. They can't appear for no reason. (p. 431)
- **Dependent and Independent Clauses:** Choices would create or join clauses. An independent clause has a main verb and can be a sentence by itself. A dependent clause can't, and starts with a conjunction or relative pronoun. (p. 426)
- **Punctuation Sandwich:** Choices involve phrases "sandwiched" between similar punctuation marks. When removed from the sentence, a proper sandwich leaves behind a grammatical sentence with the same original meaning. (See p. 432 and 433)

ANSWER CHOICE ANALYSIS

A ✓ **Correct:** As trained test-takers, we can tell that none of the ACT's rules of punctuation require the presence of a comma or colon in this underlined phrase. Remember that the ACT always wants us to avoid using punctuation unless there is a specific reason to include punctuation. See the discussions of the other choices for more.

B **Incorrect:** This choice creates a punctuation sandwich around "peering though," which is unacceptable according to the ACT's rules, because removing the sandwiched phrase would leave behind the ungrammatical statement "*I was an inexperienced astronomer light-polluted skies," in which the phrase "light-polluted skies" has no grammatical relationship to the rest of the "sentence."

C **Incorrect:** The ACT English section won't allow a colon after "astronomer" because the part of the sentence after the colon isn't an example or explanation of what's stated before the colon, as the ACT English section requires: "peering through light-polluted skies" doesn't necessarily demonstrate or exemplify the idea of an "inexperienced astronomer."

D **Incorrect:** The rules of the ACT English section won't let us insert a comma in the middle of the prepositional phrase "through light-polluted skies"—this comma isn't part of a series, nor is it part of a comma sandwich, nor does it perform any other function that the ACT English section allows commas to perform in answer choices.

T2, Q46 (Test 3 in the 2020-2021 Red Book—see page 23) **TYPE: G/S/P (often no prompt; choices w/similar meanings—see page 418)**

- **Vertical Scan Results:** Similar phrases with different short words and/or punctuation.
- **Vertical Scan Notes:** All four choices involve a form of the verb "be," while two of the choices involve a form of the verb "say."
- **Key Features in Surrounding Text:** "But I...capabilities" could stand on its own as a sentence. The original version of the underlined phrase leaves the second half of the sentence without a main verb.

Concepts in the question:

- **Dependent and Independent Clauses:** Choices would create or join clauses. An independent clause has a main verb and can be a sentence by itself. A dependent clause can't, and starts with a conjunction or relative pronoun. (p. 426)
- **Pronoun Ambiguity:** Choices include pronouns that could refer to more than one phrase in the surrounding text. We can't use a pronoun on the ACT when it isn't clear what that pronoun refers to. (See page 419)
- **Shorter is Better:** Choices include words or phrases that can be removed without impacting meaning or creating grammatical problems. The shortest grammatically acceptable choice that doesn't change the meaning is right. (p. 442)
- **Verb Tense/Conjugation:** Choices include different forms of the same verb. Look at the surrounding text to find the verb's subject. Also look for other verbs that could indicate the proper tense or form for the verbs in the choices. (See p. 420-423)

ANSWER CHOICE ANALYSIS

F **Incorrect:** This choice would leave the second clause in the sentence—the one after the comma—without a main verb, which is unacceptable on the ACT English section.

G **Incorrect:** There's no obvious plural noun for the word "them" to refer to, which means we can't use "them," according to the ACT's unwritten rules. We'll also see that (H) is shorter and grammatically acceptable, which means (G) can't be right.

H ✓ **Correct:** This choice provides the clause with a main verb without creating any other problems. Since it's the only grammatically acceptable choice according to the ACT's rules, it must be right.

J **Incorrect:** This choice has the same problem as (F): its "-ing" verb causes the second clause not to have a main verb.

T2, Q47 (Test 3 in the 2020-2021 Red Book—see page 23)   **TYPE: G/S/P (often no prompt; choices w/similar meanings—see page 418)**

- **Vertical Scan Results:** Some choices have the same words with different punctuation.
- **Vertical Scan Notes:** Should there be a comma after "hunter," "who," "in," and/or "mythologies?"
- **Key Features in Surrounding Text:** The original version of the sentence creates a comma sandwich around "in some mythologies," which is acceptable on the ACT English section because we're left with a grammatically acceptable sentence with the same essential meaning if we remove the sandwiched phrase.

- **Commas:** Choices include commas. Commas can separate a list of 3 or more items, form sandwiches, separate interchangeable adjectives, or introduce an independent clause after a dependent clause. They can't appear for no reason. (p. 431)
- **Punctuation Sandwich:** Choices involve phrases "sandwiched" between similar punctuation marks. When removed from the sentence, a proper sandwich leaves behind a grammatical sentence with the same original meaning. (See p. 432 and 433)

ANSWER CHOICE ANALYSIS

A ✓ **Correct:** As we noted above, this choice creates an acceptable punctuation sandwich around the phrase "in some mythologies."

B **Incorrect:** This choice creates a punctuation sandwich around the phrase "who in some mythologies," which is unacceptable on the ACT English section because removing the sandwiched phrase would leave us with the sentence "Orion appears as a hunter is fighting Taurus...." Depending on how you read the sentence, this does one of two things: either it creates a sentence with two verb phrases ("appears as a hunter" and "is fighting Taurus") that aren't joined by a conjunction like "and," which is unacceptable on the ACT English section, or it changes the meaning of the original sentence. The new sentence would describe Orion appearing at the same moment some other hunter is fighting Taurus, instead of saying that Orion looks like a hunter fighting. Since removing this comma sandwich either results in an ungrammatical sentence or a change in the essential meaning of the original sentence, we know the sandwiched phrase is unacceptable on the ACT English section.

C **Incorrect:** This choice creates a punctuation sandwich around the phrase "in some mythologies...the Bull," which is unacceptable on the ACT, because removing the sandwiched phrase would leave us with the non-sentence "*Orion appears as a hunter who another constellation."

D **Incorrect:** This choice creates a punctuation sandwich around the phrase "some mythologies," which is unacceptable on the ACT English section because removing it would leave us with "*Orion appears as a hunter who in is fighting Taurus...." This choice might appeal to some untrained test-takers who overlook the word "in."

T2, Q48 (Test 3 in the 2020-2021 Red Book—see page 23)   **TYPE: G/S/P (often no prompt; choices w/similar meanings—see page 418)**

- **Vertical Scan Results:** Some choices have different forms of the same base word.
- **Vertical Scan Notes:** Two choices involve plural verb forms, while the other two choices involve singular verb forms. Also, two choices involve things happening in the past, while the other two involve things happening in the present.
- **Key Features in Surrounding Text:** The underlined verb needs to agree with the plural noun "stars." It also needs to be in the same tense as "appears" and "is fighting," since those verbs relate to the appearance of Orion, and the underlined verb also relates to the appearance of Orion.

Concepts in the question:

- **Intervening Phrase:** A phrase appears between two words that need to agree with each other grammatically. Remember to identify pairs of words that need to agree with each other, and ignore phrases that appear between those words. (See page 439)
- **Parallelism:** Choices include options that would ignore a parallel structure in the surrounding text. The right answer should match the phrasing and grammatical structures in the surrounding text when possible. (See p. 440)
- **Shorter is Better:** Choices include words or phrases that can be removed without impacting meaning or creating grammatical problems. The shortest grammatically acceptable choice that doesn't change the meaning is right. (p. 442)
- **Singular versus Plural:** Choices include singular and plural versions of the same base words that don't agree with other words in the surrounding text. Nouns, pronouns, and verbs must agree in number with the words they refer to or modify. (p. 423)
- **Verb Tense/Conjugation:** Choices include different forms of the same verb. Look at the surrounding text to find the verb's subject. Also look for other verbs that could indicate the proper tense or form for the verbs in the choices. (See p. 420-423)

ANSWER CHOICE ANALYSIS

F **Incorrect:** This choice uses the singular verb form "has been," which doesn't agree with the plural noun "stars."

G **Incorrect:** This choice uses the past-tense verb form "were being," which doesn't parallel the present-tense forms of "appears" and "is fighting."

H ✓ **Correct:** This choice uses the plural present-tense verb form "are," which agrees with the plural noun "stars," and matches the tense of "appears" and "is fighting," as we saw in our discussion above of key features in the surrounding text.

J **Incorrect:** This choice uses the singular verb form "is," which doesn't agree with the plural noun "stars," the subject of the verb.

Answer choice patterns (page 442): shortest grammatically acceptable choice is correct

T2, Q49 (Test 3 in the 2020-2021 Red Book—see page 23)   **TYPE: G/S/P (often no prompt; choices w/similar meanings—see page 418)**

- **Vertical Scan Results:** Similar phrases with different short words and/or punctuation.
- **Vertical Scan Notes:** All choices include with the word "collapse" followed by some way to say that stars form.
- **Key Features in Surrounding Text:** The original version of the underlined phrase has no independent clause, which results in a

sentence fragment; "when…collapse" is a dependent clause because of the word "when," and "forming stars" isn't a clause, because it lacks a subject and a main verb.

Concepts in the question:

- **Commas:** Choices include commas. Commas can separate a list of 3 or more items, form sandwiches, separate interchangeable adjectives, or introduce an independent clause after a dependent clause. They can't appear for no reason. (p. 431)
- **Dependent and Independent Clauses:** Choices would create or join clauses. An independent clause has a main verb and can be a sentence by itself. A dependent clause can't, and starts with a conjunction or relative pronoun. (p. 426)

ANSWER CHOICE ANALYSIS

A   **Incorrect:** As we noted above, this choice is a sentence fragment because it has no independent clause, and sentence fragments are unacceptable on the ACT English section.

B   **Incorrect:** This choice ultimately has the same problem as (A): it creates a sentence fragment without an independent clause. In this case, the entire fragment would be a dependent clause because of the word "when."

C ✓   **Correct:** This choice provides the sentence with the independent clause "stars form." The dependent clause "when…collapse" is joined to the independent clause with a comma, and tells us the conditions for the star formation described in the independent clause. This choice resolves the problems in the other choices without creating any other problems, so we know it's right.

D   **Incorrect:** This choice has the same basic problem as (B), because it makes all of the words a sentence fragment that's just one long dependent clause.

T2, Q50 (Test 3 in the 2020-2021 Red Book—see page 23)   TYPE: G/S/P (often no prompt; choices w/similar meanings—see page 418)

- **Vertical Scan Results:** Similar phrases with different short words and/or punctuation.
- **Vertical Scan Notes:** Two options include "is," and two options include "and." Only one option avoids both "is" and "and."
- **Key Features in Surrounding Text:** The current version of this sentence includes two verb phrases ("is home to…" and "is often called…") that aren't joined by a conjunction, which is unacceptable on the ACT English section.

Concepts in the question:

- **Commas:** Choices include commas. Commas can separate a list of 3 or more items, form sandwiches, separate interchangeable adjectives, or introduce an independent clause after a dependent clause. They can't appear for no reason. (p. 431)
- **Dependent and Independent Clauses:** Choices would create or join clauses. An independent clause has a main verb and can be a sentence by itself. A dependent clause can't, and starts with a conjunction or relative pronoun. (p. 426)
- **Intervening Phrase:** A phrase appears between two words that need to agree with each other grammatically. Remember to identify pairs of words that need to agree with each other, and ignore phrases that appear between those words. (See page 439)
- **Punctuation Sandwich:** Choices involve phrases "sandwiched" between similar punctuation marks. When removed from the sentence, a proper sandwich leaves behind a grammatical sentence with the same original meaning. (See p. 432 and 433)
- **Shorter is Better:** Choices include words or phrases that can be removed without impacting meaning or creating grammatical problems. The shortest grammatically acceptable choice that doesn't change the meaning is right. (p. 442)

ANSWER CHOICE ANALYSIS

F   **Incorrect:** As we noted above, the ACT English section doesn't allow two verb phrases in one sentence without a conjunction to join them, so (F) is wrong.

G   **Incorrect:** This choice would be grammatically acceptable in real life, but it's wrong on the ACT English section. In this case, the choice uses a comma and the word "and" to join a second main verb to the sentence (this is called a "compound predicate" in formal grammar, not that you need to know that term for the ACT). But, as trained test-takers, we know this choice is wrong because (J) is shorter and grammatically acceptable. See our discussion of (J) for more.

H   **Incorrect:** Like the correct answer, (J), this choice creates a punctuation sandwich around the phrase "home to thousands of young stars." But this choice includes the word "and," which creates an ungrammatical sentence when the punctuation sandwich is removed: "*The nebula and is often called a galactic 'nursery'."

J ✓   **Correct:** This choice creates an acceptable punctuation sandwich around the phrase "home to thousands of young stars," because when that phrase is removed, an acceptable sentence is left behind. As trained test-takers, we should also notice that (J) is the shortest answer choice, and it's grammatically acceptable on the ACT English section, which means it must be the right answer according to the ACT's unwritten rules.

Answer choice patterns (page 442): shortest grammatically acceptable choice is correct

Note   This choice is one more clear example of the importance of understanding the unwritten rules of the ACT. (G) and (J) would both be grammatically acceptable sentences if they appeared in a publication, but, on the ACT, one of them is wrong and one of them is right. As trained test-takers, we know that (J) must be right because it's grammatically acceptable and shorter, but most untrained test-takers won't be aware of that unwritten rule, which will cause them to waste time and energy on this question instead of confidently recognizing that (J) is right.

- **RC Question sub-type:** Sentence or paragraph placement. (The prompt asks us where a sentence should go in a paragraph, or where a paragraph should go in the passage. The correct order will reflect a logical chronology, and/or will allow for pronouns to refer to nouns in a logical way, and/or will place related concepts near one another. See page 415)

> Subjective Phrases to Ignore: "most"

ANSWER CHOICE ANALYSIS

A   **Causes text to refer to an idea that hasn't been mentioned yet:** The sentence in the prompt refers to "the nebula," but the nebula hasn't been mentioned in this paragraph by Point A.

B   **Causes text to refer to an idea that hasn't been mentioned yet:** This choice has the same problem as (A).

C   **Causes text to refer to an idea that hasn't been mentioned yet:** This choice has the same problem as (A) and (B).

D ✓   **Correct:** This is the only placement that causes the sentence to refer to "the nebula" *after* the phrase "the Great Orion Nebula" has already been mentioned in the paragraph, which lets the reader know which nebula the phrase "the nebula" refers back to.

- **RC Question sub-type:** Transition Phrase. (The choices reflect different kinds of transitions between two concepts, with words or phrases like "however," "instead of," or "for example." The right answer must reflect the relationship between the previous concept in the passage and the following concept in the passage. See p. 416)

ANSWER CHOICE ANALYSIS

F   **Confused relationships:** (F) would be acceptable if the switch of the eyepiece wasn't caused by the situation in the preceding sentences, and just happened for unrelated reasons. But, as we'll see when we discuss (J), the switch is clearly a deliberate decision by the author because she "just made out a dull smudge" with the other eyepiece.

G   **Confused relationships:** (G) would be right if "switch[ing] to a higher-powered eyepiece" were fundamentally like "[not] get[ting] much improvement" and/or "adjust[ing] the focuser," but that isn't the case.

H   **Confused relationships:** (H) would be acceptable on the ACT English section if the previous sentence provided support for an idea and then this sentence offered additional, unrelated support for the same idea, but that's not the case here.

J ✓   **Correct:** The preceding text mentions that the narrator wasn't able to see the nebula with the lowest-powered eyepiece. The word "so" makes it clear that the narrator "switched to a higher-powered eyepiece" and tried a different viewing technique *because* the lowest-powered eyepiece wasn't working.

- **Vertical Scan Results:** Some choices have different forms of the same base word.
- **Vertical Scan Notes:** Should "tried" or "try" appear in the phrase? Should "I'd," "I'd have," or "I" appear in the phrase?
- **Key Features in Surrounding Text:** The phrase "I switched…and" precedes the underlined phrase, so we know from the word "and" that the action in the underlined phrase takes place in the same time frame as "switched." We know the narrator must have read about the trick *before* the action in the sentence, because otherwise she wouldn't have known what the trick was. So the phrase describing the reading should indicate a time frame that takes place before the verb "switched."

> Concepts in the question:

- **Parallelism:** Choices include options that would ignore a parallel structure in the surrounding text. The right answer should match the phrasing and grammatical structures in the surrounding text when possible. (See p. 440)
- **Verb Tense/Conjugation:** Choices include different forms of the same verb. Look at the surrounding text to find the verb's subject. Also look for other verbs that could indicate the proper tense or form for the verbs in the choices. (See p. 420-423)

ANSWER CHOICE ANALYSIS

A ✓   **Correct:** "Tried" is in the same time frame as "switched," which is necessary because of the word "and," as we noted above. The phrase "I'd read," which is the contracted form of "I had read," indicates that the narrator read about the trick *before* switching the eyepiece and trying the trick. Since this is the only grammatically acceptable choice, we know it's right.

B   **Incorrect:** The phrase "I'd have read," which is the contracted form of "I would have read," would indicate that the author hasn't actually read about the trick, but would have read about it under some other condition that isn't specified in the sentence. This makes no logical sense in the context of the sentence, because it's impossible to try a trick you don't know about yet, so (B) must be wrong. (B) might attract some untrained test-takers who accidentally misread it as "tried a trick I have," because that phrase would be grammatically acceptable.

C   **Incorrect:** "Try" is a present tense verb form, but the word "and" indicates that the correct verb form must be in the same tense as "switched," so (C) must be wrong.

D   **Incorrect:** This choice has the same problem as (C). It might attract an untrained test-taker who misread it as "tried a trick I," because that phrase would have been grammatically acceptable.

- **Vertical Scan Results:** Similar phrases with different short words and/or punctuation.
- **Vertical Scan Notes:** Should "one" appear before "side," and, if so, should it be possessive? Should "of them," "their," or "they're" be used?
- **Key Features in Surrounding Text:** This phrase tells us where the "eye" can "look[]" to "see distant objects better."

Concepts in the question:

- **Confused Homophones:** Choices include different homophone pairs (such as "their"/"they're" or "too"/"to"). Remember the correct formation of possessives. Remember to read contractions as their uncontracted forms (e.g. "it's" = "it is"). (p. 436)
- **Plural/Possessive/Contraction:** Choices include nouns ending in "-s," with/without an apostrophe before or after the "-s." Recall the 3 rules for possessive forms (p. 424). Think of contractions in uncontracted forms ("you're" = "you are"). (p. 436)
- **Prepositional Idioms:** Choices typically include prepositional phrases with no other recognizable similarities. If you can't tell which choice contains an acceptable prepositional idiom in American English, guess and invest your time elsewhere. (p. 435)
- **Pronoun Ambiguity:** Choices include pronouns that could refer to more than one phrase in the surrounding text. We can't use a pronoun on the ACT when it isn't clear what that pronoun refers to. (See page 419)
- **Singular versus Plural:** Choices include singular and plural versions of the same base words that don't agree with other words in the surrounding text. Nouns, pronouns, and verbs must agree in number with the words they refer to or modify. (p. 423)

ANSWER CHOICE ANALYSIS

F   **Incorrect:** The phrase "their one side" may attract a lot of non-native speakers of English, because it might seem like "their one side" is grammatically equivalent to "one side of them." But "their one side" specifically indicates that the objects have only one side, which isn't logically possible—everything that has one side must have another side, which means nothing has only one side. This choice can't make any sense, so it must be wrong.

G ✓   **Correct:** This choice uses the prepositional idiom "to one side" as a way to indicate that "averted vision" just requires you to focus on any area next to an object, and it doesn't matter which side you pick. If we aren't familiar with the prepositional idiom "to one side," we can still probably answer this question with confidence, because we'll see that the other choices involve unrelated problems. See the note below for more.

H   **Incorrect:** This choice uses "they're," which is the contracted form of "they are." Since it makes no grammatical sense to say, "the eye can often see distant objects better by looking to they are one side," we know "they're" can't be right, even if we're not familiar with the prepositional idiom discussed in (G).

J   **Incorrect:** This choice uses the singular pronoun "one" to refer to the plural noun "objects," so we know it can't be right. (This is different from the use of "one" in (G), because (G) is using "one" in the sense of "a single thing out of multiple possibilities," rather than as a possessive pronoun that refers back to a noun in the text.) This choice may still attract a lot of people who've heard the prepositional idiom "to one side," but thought that it should be spelled "*to one's side," which would have a similar pronunciation to the correct version of the phrase.

Note   Questions involving prepositional idioms can be frustrating for some test-takers, because prepositional idioms—by definition—don't follow any kind of generalized rule that we can depend on. Instead, we just have to be familiar with the way a given preposition is used in a given situation. But the ACT often does something that works in our favor: the test will sometimes include wrong answer choices that are wrong for reasons unrelated to prepositional idioms. This allows us to eliminate some or all of the wrong answer choices for other reasons, which makes it easier for us to pick out the acceptable choice. In this case, we were able to eliminate all three wrong answer choices, and we didn't even actually have to know the relevant prepositional idiom if we were able to recognize the problems with the other choices. So when you encounter a question on test day that involves prepositional idioms, check and see if any of the answer choices can be eliminated for other reasons.

- **RC Question sub-type:** Including/excluding a phrase/sentence. (The question asks whether a given sentence or phrase should be included in the passage. The correct choice will include a comment that plainly describes the role of the phrase or sentence in the passage. Sentences that should be included will follow broad ACT standards for ideal sentences and paragraphs, while sentences that shouldn't be included will not follow those standards. See p. 416)

ANSWER CHOICE ANALYSIS

A   **Barely relevant:** The description in this choice isn't literally demonstrated by the given sentence, because the sentence doesn't say why the narrator can use averted vision, as (A) would require; in fact, it doesn't even refer to the narrator at all. The sentence just explains what the principle of averted vision is.

B ✓   **Correct:** The description is literally demonstrated by the given sentence, since it explains what averted vision is, and the text before and after this sentence shows how the narrator uses averted vision "to see the nebula more clearly," just as (B) requires. Since (B) is the only choice whose description is literally demonstrated in the text, we know it must be right.

C   **Barely relevant:** The description in this choice isn't literally demonstrated by the text, because the level of technical detail in the sentence isn't different from the level of technical detail in other parts of the passage, which mention terms like "scope," "nebula," "eyepiece," and so on. Since the description in this choice isn't literally demonstrated by the text, we know it's wrong.

D   **Direct contradiction:** The sentence doesn't "digress[] from the main point of the paragraph," as (D) would require: this paragraph only talks about the narrator using averted vision to see objects through the telescope, and the sentence in question explains what averted vision is.

▮ T2, Q56 (Test 3 in the 2020-2021 Red Book—see page 23)   TYPE: G/S/P (often no prompt; choices w/similar meanings—see page 418)

- **Vertical Scan Results:** Similar phrases with different short words and/or punctuation.
- **Vertical Scan Notes:** Should the phrase include "far" or "farther?" Should the phrase end with "more of a," or a comma, or no punctuation?
- **Key Features in Surrounding Text:** The underlined phrase describes the adjective "better" in the phrase "better view."

Concepts in the question:

- **Adjective/Adverb:** Choices involve a word in its adjective or adverb form. Remember that adverb forms often end in "-ly," but not always. Adjectives can modify nouns; adverbs can modify anything else (verbs, adjectives, other adverbs). (p. 423)
- **Changed Meaning:** Choices would change the meaning of the original text, or cause the relevant phrase/sentence not to make sense. The right answer must be grammatically acceptable and still preserve the original meaning. (See p. 438)
- **Commas:** Choices include commas. Commas can separate a list of 3 or more items, form sandwiches, separate interchangeable adjectives, or introduce an independent clause after a dependent clause. They can't appear for no reason. (p. 431)
- **Shorter is Better:** Choices include words or phrases that can be removed without impacting meaning or creating grammatical problems. The shortest grammatically acceptable choice that doesn't change the meaning is right. (p. 442)

ANSWER CHOICE ANALYSIS

F   **Incorrect:** The phrase "far more of a" means that this choice would indicate that peripheral vision offered a larger quantity of a "better view," instead of saying that peripheral vision simply offered a better view than direct vision did, as the context requires. (Further, as trained test-takers, we should notice that (H) is shorter and grammatically acceptable, so we know that (F) can't be right.)

G   **Incorrect:** The comma in this choice would make it sound like "farther" modifies "view," just like "better" does. In other words, it would make the sentence say that the view was "farther" and also "better." But there are two problems with this choice. One is that the surrounding text never says that averted vision lets the author see *farther* into space, in addition to seeing a *better* image of the nebula, so this choice would change the original meaning of the sentence and contradict the passage. The other issue, which is a little easier for a trained test-taker to spot, is that (H) is shorter than (G) and grammatically acceptable without changing the meaning of the passage, so (G) can't be right.

H ✓   **Correct:** The key issue in this choice is that "far" can be an adverb with a meaning like "much" or "greatly," so that "a far better view" is synonymous with "a much better view." This choice is the only one that preserves the meaning of the passage, because it avoids the introduction of "more" and the issue of comma-separated interchangeable adjectives.

J   **Incorrect:** The comma makes it sound like "far" modifies "view" just like "better" does. In other words, this choice makes it sound like the view is "far" and also "better," instead of "far better." So this choice has the same basic issues we saw in (G).

Answer choice patterns (page 442): shortest grammatically acceptable choice is correct

Note   Once more, we see a question that's much easier to answer if we're trained to understand the unwritten rules of the ACT. Most untrained test-takers would be confused by the fact that all of the answer choices in this question could arguably be grammatically acceptable (if a little strange) outside of the ACT. But, as trained test-takers, we know that (H) must be right, since it's the shortest of the grammatically acceptable choices. Keep this in mind on test day, and don't waste your time puzzling over questions just because more than one choice seems like it might be okay in real life!

▮ T2, Q57 (Test 3 in the 2020-2021 Red Book—see page 23)   TYPE: RC (usually has a prompt; choices w/different meanings—see page 413)

- **RC Question sub-type:** Precision Vocabulary. (Choices include words or short phrases that either sound similar, or have vaguely similar but not identical meanings. Most or all of the choices will seem vaguely appropriate, but only one choice will be correct when we think very carefully and specifically about the word means and how it can be used. See page 415)

ANSWER CHOICE ANALYSIS

A ✓   **Correct:** To "illuminate" means "to light up." We know that (A) must be correct because the "four...stars" doing the action in the underlined phrase are called "bright," and something that is "bright" gives off light.

B   **Barely relevant:** To "emanate" means "to come out from." The passage doesn't literally demonstrate or restate the idea of "the Trapezium star cluster" coming out of the "four bright young stars," so (B) must be wrong.

C   **Barely relevant:** To "emulate" means "to act like" or "to pretend to be like." Nothing in the passage literally restates or demonstrates the idea of the "four bright young stars" acting like the "star cluster," as (C) would require.

D   **Pattern:** Same ballpark. **Incorrect:** To "eliminate" means "to get rid of." The passage doesn't literally restate or demonstrate the idea of the "four bright young stars" getting rid of the "star cluster," as (D) would require.

<hr>

▌T2, Q58 (Test 3 in the 2020-2021 Red Book—see page 23)   **TYPE: G/S/P (often no prompt; choices w/similar meanings—see page 418)**

- **Vertical Scan Results:** Some choices have different forms of the same base word.
- **Vertical Scan Notes:** We need to choose from "birds'," "bird's," "birds," and "bird," and we also need to choose between "eggs" and "eggs'."
- **Key Features in Surrounding Text:** There's no article like "a" or "the" before the underlined phrase, so the underlined noun phrase must be plural, since "bird" and "egg" aren't abstract concepts or uncountable nouns, which can appear in the singular without an article. The first noun must also be possessive, because there's no preposition or other word between the two nouns to demonstrate a grammatical relationship. In other words, the context makes it clear that whichever version of "egg" is appropriate must belong to whichever version of "bird" is appropriate.

> **Concepts in the question:**

- **Plural/Possessive/Contraction:** Choices include nouns ending in "-s," with/without an apostrophe before or after the "-s." Recall the 3 rules for possessive forms (p. 424). Think of contractions in uncontracted forms ("you're" = "you are"). (p. 436)

ANSWER CHOICE ANALYSIS

F ✓   **Correct:** This is the only choice that begins with a plural possessive form, which is necessary for the reasons we noted above, so we know it's right.

G   **Incorrect:** The singular form "bird's" isn't acceptable here because a singular, countable noun like "bird" would need to be preceded by an article like "a" or "the," as we discussed above.

H   **Incorrect:** The plural noun "birds" isn't possessive, and doesn't show that the "eggs" belong to the birds, which is necessary for the reasons we discussed above.

J   **Incorrect:** There isn't anything in the text that could belong to the "eggs," so the possessive form of "eggs" isn't acceptable here.

<hr>

▌T2, Q59 (Test 3 in the 2020-2021 Red Book—see page 23)   **TYPE: RC (usually has a prompt; choices w/different meanings—see page 413)**

- **RC Question sub-type:** Best accomplishes X. (The prompt describes a goal of the author, and asks which choice achieves that goal. The right answer will be plainly demonstrated in the passage. See page 413)

> **Subjective Phrases to Ignore:** "best"

ANSWER CHOICE ANALYSIS

A ✓   **Correct:** The prompt asks for a sentence that will "conclude the paragraph" and "refer[] back to the opening paragraph," so we know that the right answer will mention ideas from the first paragraph and from this final paragraph. The opening paragraph mentions a "winter night" and how the narrator "bundled up" to use the telescope, so the phrase "winter trek outdoors" in this choice clearly refers back to that paragraph. This choice also mentions a "change in focus," which is demonstrated by the "principle of averted vision" elsewhere in this paragraph; it also mentions "see[ing] more clearly," which is restated in the paragraph when the author mentions "a better view." Since this choice refers back to the opening paragraph (as the prompt requires) and mentions ideas from this paragraph, we know it must be the right answer.

B   **Confused relationships:** This choice mentions "eliminat[ing] stray light," which is relevant to the term "light-polluted" in the opening paragraph, as the prompt requires—but this sentence doesn't mention any ideas from the last paragraph, as the prompt specifically requires. (The idea of different levels of magnification only appears in the *next-to-last* paragraph, which talks about different eyepieces—not the last paragraph.)

C   **Confused relationships:** The initial paragraph does mention looking for Orion, and the second paragraph mentions Taurus, but the prompt clearly requires an answer choice that mentions idea from the first and *last* paragraphs, and this sentence doesn't mention any ideas from the last paragraph.

D   **Barely relevant:** Nothing in this choice "refer[s] back to the opening paragraph," as the prompt requires.

<hr>

▌T2, Q60 (Test 3 in the 2020-2021 Red Book—see page 23)   **TYPE: RC (usually has a prompt; choices w/different meanings—see page 413)**

- **RC Question sub-type:** Would essay fulfill goal? (The question describes a goal that the author had in writing the passage, and asks whether the author achieved that goal. The right answer choice will be directly restated or demonstrated by the passage, and logically answer the question in the prompt. See page 417)

ANSWER CHOICE ANALYSIS

F   **Off by one or two words:** The description in (F) isn't literally demonstrated by the passage, because the narrator only describes one

<hr>

particular evening using the telescope, not "several past adventures," as (F) would require.

G ✓   **Correct:** This choice describes the text accurately. The passage describes one evening of stargazing, from setting out the telescope to cool down in the first paragraph, to looking for a constellation in the second paragraph, and then looking at a nebula within that constellation in the third and fourth paragraphs. This evening of stargazing demonstrates the idea of "a personal experience with astronomy," from the prompt, so we know that the word "yes" at the beginning of the answer choice is appropriate, and (F) must be right.

H   **Confused relationships:** The reasoning in this choice *does* accurately describe the passage, since every paragraph mentions the Orion Nebula at least once, and the second paragraph talks about "star formation" in that nebula. But as we saw in our discussion of (G), the passage's discussion of the nebula doesn't mean that the essay can't also be "about a personal experience with astronomy." So the "no" part of this choice makes it wrong.

J   **Confused relationships:** The description in (J) isn't literally demonstrated in the passage. While the text does describe a technique called "averted vision," it never says the technique is "universally used," as (J) would require.

T2, Q61 (Test 3 in the 2020-2021 Red Book—see page 23)   TYPE: G/S/P (often no prompt; choices w/similar meanings—see page 418)

- **Vertical Scan Results:** Similar phrases with different short words and/or punctuation.
- **Vertical Scan Notes:** Three options include additional words after "emotion," and one doesn't.
- **Key Features in Surrounding Text:** The original version of the sentence includes a comma splice, because all the words leading up to the first comma could stand on their own as a sentence, and all the words after the first comma could stand on their own as a separate sentence. Since comma splices aren't acceptable on the ACT English section, we know the original version of the sentence must be wrong.

Concepts in the question:

- **Comma Splice:** Choices and/or surrounding text use commas to join two groups of words that could each be sentences on their own. A comma can't be used in this way on the ACT English section. (See page 428)
- **Dependent and Independent Clauses:** Choices would create or join clauses. An independent clause has a main verb and can be a sentence by itself. A dependent clause can't, and starts with a conjunction or relative pronoun. (p. 426)
- **Punctuation Sandwich:** Choices involve phrases "sandwiched" between similar punctuation marks. When removed from the sentence, a proper sandwich leaves behind a grammatical sentence with the same original meaning. (See p. 432 and 433)
- **Run-on Sentence:** Choices and/or surrounding text include consecutive sentences not separated by any punctuation. If two consecutive sets of words can stand on their own as sentences, they need to be separated by a period or a semicolon. (p. 428)
- **Shorter is Better:** Choices include words or phrases that can be removed without impacting meaning or creating grammatical problems. The shortest grammatically acceptable choice that doesn't change the meaning is right. (p. 442)

ANSWER CHOICE ANALYSIS

A   **Incorrect:** As noted above, the original version of the sentence includes a comma splice, which isn't acceptable on the ACT English section. (A) might trick some untrained test-takers who thought the comma after "emotion" was a semicolon.

B   **Incorrect:** This choice has the same problem as (A): it creates a comma splice, which is something the ACT doesn't allow. It might attract an untrained test-taker who misread the comma after "emotion" as a semicolon.

C   **Incorrect:** This choice has an issue somewhat similar to the issue in (A) and (B)—but, instead of a comma splice, (C) would create a run-on sentence, which consists of two groups of words that could each be sentences on their own, presented one after the other in the same sentence, with no punctuation between them. In this case, "Others see them...emotion" could be one sentence by itself, and "the works offer...events" could also be a sentence by itself. Like (A) and (B), this choice might attract someone who misreads it and thinks there's a semicolon after "emotion."

D ✓   **Correct:** This choice removes the verb after the comma, which turns the phrase "metaphors for...events" into a modifier for the phrase "distillations of emotion," and resolves the problems from the other choices. Further, since this is the shortest choice and it's grammatically acceptable to the ACT, we know it must be right.

Answer choice patterns (page 442): shortest grammatically acceptable choice is correct

T2, Q62 (Test 3 in the 2020-2021 Red Book—see page 23)   TYPE: G/S/P (often no prompt; choices w/similar meanings—see page 418)

- **Vertical Scan Results:** Some choices have the same words with different punctuation.
- **Vertical Scan Notes:** Should there be a dash or a comma after "shapes?" Should there be a dash after "triangles?" Should there be a dash after "rectangles?"
- **Key Features in Surrounding Text:** The original version of the sentence places the phrase "in vibrant contrasting hues" immediately after the phrase "narrow rectangles," which makes it sound as though only the rectangles are in vibrant and contrasting hues—or, at most, like the triangles and rectangles are in vibrant and contrasting hues (remember that the prompt asks for the choice that "makes [it] clear that all the shapes...are painted in vibrant and contrasting hues"). Further, the phrase "vibrant contrasting hues," without a comma between "vibrant" and "contrasting," indicates that the hues are "contrasting," and that the "contrasting hues" are "vibrant,"

rather than indicating that the hues are equally "contrasting" and "vibrant," as the prompt requires. (See "Commas between two adjectives" on page 433 of this Black Book for more on this distinction.)

(See "Commas between two adjectives" on page 433 of this Black Book for more on this distinction.)

Concepts in the question:

- **Commas:** Choices include commas. Commas can separate a list of 3 or more items, form sandwiches, separate interchangeable adjectives, or introduce an independent clause after a dependent clause. They can't appear for no reason. (p. 431)
- **Punctuation Sandwich:** Choices involve phrases "sandwiched" between similar punctuation marks. When removed from the sentence, a proper sandwich leaves behind a grammatical sentence with the same original meaning. (See p. 432 and 433)

ANSWER CHOICE ANALYSIS

F   **Incorrect:** As we noted above, the original version of the sentence makes it seem like the phrase "in vibrant contrasting hues" refers specifically to "narrow rectangles," and possibly to "triangles," rather than referring to all the "shapes" that Little paints, as the prompt requires. This choice also omits a comma after "vibrant," which doesn't satisfy the prompt for the reasons we noted above.

G ✓   **Correct:** This choice creates a dash sandwich around "mostly triangles and narrow rectangles" to show that the sandwiched phrase gives us further information about the "shapes." Since properly sandwiched phrases can be removed from a sentence without fundamentally altering the meaning of the sentence, this sandwich also makes it clear that the underlying structure of the sentence would include the phrase "large-scale patterns of shapes in vibrant, contrasting hues." This shows clearly that "in vibrant, contrasting hues" is modifying the word "shapes," and not the words "rectangles" and "triangles," as the prompt requires.

H   **Incorrect:** This choice makes it seem like "in vibrant contrasting hues" refers specifically to "narrow rectangles," instead of referring to all the "shapes" that Little paints, as the prompt requires. (This choice also makes it sound like "narrow rectangles" aren't included in the word "shapes," which sounds odd but isn't directly related to the issue in the prompt.)

J   **Incorrect:** This choice has the same problems as (F): it doesn't allow the modifier "in vibrant contrasting hues" to apply to the word "shapes." It also doesn't have a comma between the adjectives "vibrant" and "contrasting," which is a problem for the reasons we discussed above in the key features in the surrounding text.

T2, Q63 (Test 3 in the 2020-2021 Red Book—see page 23)   **TYPE: G/S/P (often no prompt; choices w/similar meanings—see page 418)**

- **Vertical Scan Results:** Some choices have the same words with different punctuation.
- **Vertical Scan Notes:** Should there be commas after "but," "subject," and/or "says?"
- **Key Features in Surrounding Text:** The subject of this sentence is the word "subject," and the main verb is the word "is." The original version of the sentence puts the clause "he says" right in the middle of the main part of the sentence, with no punctuation to demonstrate the relationship between "but his subject is color" and "he says."

Concepts in the question:

- **Commas:** Choices include commas. Commas can separate a list of 3 or more items, form sandwiches, separate interchangeable adjectives, or introduce an independent clause after a dependent clause. They can't appear for no reason. (p. 431)
- **Dependent and Independent Clauses:** Choices would create or join clauses. An independent clause has a main verb and can be a sentence by itself. A dependent clause can't, and starts with a conjunction or relative pronoun. (p. 426)
- **Punctuation Sandwich:** Choices involve phrases "sandwiched" between similar punctuation marks. When removed from the sentence, a proper sandwich leaves behind a grammatical sentence with the same original meaning. (See p. 432 and 433)

ANSWER CHOICE ANALYSIS

A   **Incorrect:** As we noted above, the original version of the sentence inserts the clause "he says" right in the middle of the clause "but his subject is color," with no punctuation to demonstrate the relationship between the two clauses. Since one clause can't just interrupt another without any kind of punctuation, (A) is wrong.

B ✓   **Correct:** This choice creates a punctuation sandwich around the clause "he says," which shows that "he says" could be removed from the sentence without fundamentally altering the meaning of the rest of the sentence. Since this is the only grammatically acceptable choice, we know it must be right.

C   **Incorrect:** This choice would create a punctuation sandwich around "his subject," which is unacceptable on the ACT English section because we wouldn't be left with a grammatically complete sentence if we removed "his subject" from the surrounding text. Instead, we'd be left with this: "*But he says is color."

D   **Incorrect:** This choice would create one of two unacceptable comma sandwiches—either "but his subject" or "he says is color." Removing either comma sandwich leaves the other phrase, and neither phrase can stand on its own as a sentence. This comma usage also doesn't follow any other acceptable comma usage on the ACT, so this choice must be wrong.

T2, Q64 (Test 3 in the 2020-2021 Red Book—see page 23)   **TYPE: RC (usually has a prompt; choices w/different meanings—see page 413)**

- **RC Question sub-type:** Including/excluding a phrase/sentence. (The question asks whether a given sentence or phrase should be included in the passage. The correct choice will include a comment that plainly describes the role of the phrase or sentence in the passage. Sentences that should be included will follow broad ACT standards for ideal sentences and paragraphs, while sentences that shouldn't be included will not follow those standards. See p. 416)

ANSWER CHOICE ANALYSIS

F Barely relevant: The description in this choice isn't literally restated or demonstrated by the text, because the next paragraph doesn't have a "biographical focus," as (F) would require—instead, it talks about aspects of Little's painting style.

G Barely relevant: The description in this choice isn't literally demonstrated by the text, because the sentence in the prompt doesn't say anything about Little "first [becoming] focused on working with color," as (G) would require. In fact, the sentence doesn't say anything about a newly developing interest, or about color.

H ✓ Correct: This choice accurately describes the relationship between the prompt sentence and the paragraph. The information in this prompt sentence is "tangentially related to the essay," because the essay is about Little's painting, and the sentence is about Little. But the first paragraph doesn't say anything about MFAs, or Syracuse University, or going to college, or anything along those lines, so the prompt sentence doesn't address the focus of the paragraph. Since this choice is the only one that accurately describes the text, we know it must be right.

J Barely relevant: The sentence in the prompt doesn't cause any kind of confusion about Little's work with geometric figures, since nothing in the sentence calls into question the idea of Little working with geometric figures. So this choice doesn't accurately describe the text, which means (J) can't be the right answer to the question.

T2, Q65 (Test 3 in the 2020-2021 Red Book—see page 23)　　TYPE: G/S/P (often no prompt; choices w/similar meanings—see page 418)

- **Vertical Scan Results:** Similar phrases with different short words and/or punctuation.
- **Vertical Scan Notes:** Three of the four choices mention blends. Some choices are much longer than others. Some choices mention the idea that Little blended the paint himself.
- **Key Features in Surrounding Text:** The previous sentence says that Little is using "his own blends of beeswax and oil paint."

Concepts in the question:

- **Commas:** Choices include commas. Commas can separate a list of 3 or more items, form sandwiches, separate interchangeable adjectives, or introduce an independent clause after a dependent clause. They can't appear for no reason. (p. 431)
- **Intervening Phrase:** A phrase appears between two words that need to agree with each other grammatically. Remember to identify pairs of words that need to agree with each other, and ignore phrases that appear between those words. (See page 439)
- **Punctuation Sandwich:** Choices involve phrases "sandwiched" between similar punctuation marks. When removed from the sentence, a proper sandwich leaves behind a grammatical sentence with the same original meaning. (See p. 432 and 433)
- **Redundancy:** Choices and/or surrounding text could combine to repeat the same concept unnecessarily. On grammar/style/punctuation questions, we should avoid words that directly repeat ideas in the immediate surrounding text. (See p. 437)
- **Shorter is Better:** Choices include words or phrases that can be removed without impacting meaning or creating grammatical problems. The shortest grammatically acceptable choice that doesn't change the meaning is right. (p. 442)

ANSWER CHOICE ANALYSIS

A Incorrect: As we noted above, the previous sentence already says that Little uses "his own blends of beeswax and oil paint," so the phrase "that he blended himself" is redundant, and unacceptable on the ACT English section.

B Incorrect: This choice has the same basic issue as (A): the previous sentence already says that Little used "his own blends of beeswax and oil paint," so the phrase "which is of his own making" is redundant.

C Incorrect: This choice has the same basic issue as (A) and (B).

D ✓ Correct: This choice avoids the redundancy from the other choices. Also, this is the shortest choice and it's grammatically acceptable to the ACT, so, as trained test-takers, we know it must be right.

Answer choice patterns (page 442): shortest grammatically acceptable choice is correct

T2, Q66 (Test 3 in the 2020-2021 Red Book—see page 23)　　TYPE: RC (usually has a prompt; choices w/different meanings—see page 413)

- **RC Question sub-type:** Precision Vocabulary. (Choices include words or short phrases that either sound similar, or have vaguely similar but not identical meanings. Most or all of the choices will seem vaguely appropriate, but only one choice will be correct when we think very carefully and specifically about the word means and how it can be used. See page 415)

ANSWER CHOICE ANALYSIS

F Pattern: Same ballpark. Incorrect: "Voluminous" means something like "bulky" or "roomy," or something along those lines. But the text's description of the paintings as "about six feet by eight feet" doesn't specifically restate or demonstrate the idea of being "voluminous," so we can't say (F) is right.

G Direct contradiction: The paintings can't be "immeasurable," because the sentence provides two of their measurements: "about six feet by eight feet."

H Pattern: Same ballpark. Incorrect: In order for "mountainous" to be correct on the ACT, the text would need to describe the paintings with some kind of phrase that could be applied specifically to mountains (like "they projected upward out of the earth," or something along those lines), or it would need to say they were as large as really big hills, or something like that—in other words, there would need to be some specific, literal phrase or description in the text already that justified comparing the painting to mountains. Since no such phrase is in the text, (H) can't be right.

J ✓ Correct: The last sentence in this paragraph says Little's works are "expansive," which literally restates the idea of his paintings being large. This choice is right because it's the only one that describes the size of the paintings without adding an idea that contradicts the text or isn't literally supported by the text, as we saw in our discussions of the other choices.

T2, Q67 (Test 3 in the 2020-2021 Red Book—see page 23)   TYPE: RC (usually has a prompt; choices w/different meanings—see page 413)

- RC Question sub-type: Transition Phrase. (The choices reflect different kinds of transitions between two concepts, with words or phrases like "however," "instead of," or "for example." The right answer must reflect the relationship between the previous concept in the passage and the following concept in the passage. See p. 416)

ANSWER CHOICE ANALYSIS

A   Confused relationships: This choice would be acceptable on the ACT English section if the fact that the canvas is bisected were somehow something that should be done no matter the cost or difficulty, but nothing in the text literally restates or demonstrates this idea—and that idea doesn't really make any sense anyway.

B ✓ Correct: (B) is acceptable on the ACT English section because this sentence does provides an example of something discussed in the previous sentence: the previous sentence says Little "paints slashing diagonal lines and rays," and this paragraph describes a painting with triangles and "slanting" "bands," which, by definition, include diagonal lines and rays.

C   Direct contradiction: (C) would be right if this sentence offered some kind of information or viewpoint that was the opposite of what was discussed in the previous sentence, but, as we saw in the discussion of (B), this paragraph actually provides an *example* of what's discussed in the previous sentence, rather than a *contradiction* of it.

D   Confused relationships: The word "thereafter" includes the relative pronoun "there," so that "thereafter" means "starting after the thing that was just mentioned, and then continuing." In this case, the most recent noun before "thereafter" is "the 2005 painting," which would mean that (D) would cause the action of the "canvas" being "bisected" to happen *after* "the 2005 painting"—but it's clear that the 2005 painting *is* the painting that involves bisecting the canvas, not some painting that starts *after* the bisected canvas, as (D) would require.

T2, Q68 (Test 3 in the 2020-2021 Red Book—see page 23)   TYPE: G/S/P (often no prompt; choices w/similar meanings—see page 418)

- Vertical Scan Results: Similar phrases with different short words and/or punctuation.
- Vertical Scan Notes: The choices combine forms of the words "vertical," "bisect," "by," "a," and "beige" in different orders. One choice includes a comma, while the others don't. Three choices include the adverb "vertically," while one has the adjective "vertical."
- Key Features in Surrounding Text: In the original version of the sentence, the words "vertical" and "beige" are two adjectives that each describe the noun "line." We know this because the two adjectives are separated by a comma, which indicates that they each one applies to the noun equally. (See "Commas between two adjectives" on page 433 for more on this.)

Concepts in the question:

- Adjective/Adverb: Choices involve a word in its adjective or adverb form. Remember that adverb forms often end in "-ly," but not always. Adjectives can modify nouns; adverbs can modify anything else (verbs, adjectives, other adverbs). (p. 423)
- Commas: Choices include commas. Commas can separate a list of 3 or more items, form sandwiches, separate interchangeable adjectives, or introduce an independent clause after a dependent clause. They can't appear for no reason. (p. 431)
- Proximity: Answer choice(s) would place descriptive phrases next to ideas they don't describe. (See page 434)

ANSWER CHOICE ANALYSIS

F   Incorrect: Saying that something is "bisected by a vertical, beige line" is the same as saying it's "vertically bisected by a beige line," so (F) is an acceptable alternative to the original version of the sentence…which is the opposite of what the prompt asked for.

G ✓ Correct: In the passage, the adjective "vertical" describes the line, as we discussed above. But in (G), the adverb "vertically" describes the adjective "beige," because "vertically" appears directly in front of "beige." This fundamentally changes the meaning of the sentence, so (G) is not an acceptable version of the original sentence, which means (G) is right. (Notice that the phrase "vertically beige" makes no sense—but the fact that (G) is right isn't directly related to the absurdity of the phrase "vertically beige." (G) is right because it applies the idea of being vertical to something different from what's described as vertical in the original sentence, which changes the meaning of that sentence. This change in meaning is what causes (G) not to be an acceptable alternative, which in this case satisfies the prompt. In other words, we didn't have to decide whether the phrase "vertically beige" made any sense, or what that phrase would mean—we only had to recognize that "vertically beige" changes the meaning of the original version of the underlined phrase.)

H   Incorrect: Saying that something is "bisected by a vertical, beige line" is the same as saying it's "bisected vertically by a beige line," since the thing doing the bisecting in both cases is a line that's vertical and beige.

J   Incorrect: The phrase "vertical, beige" is equivalent to the phrase "beige, vertical," since both phrases involve the same two

---

adjectives with a comma between them. That means (J) has the same meaning as the original sentence, so it's not a valid answer according to the prompt.

T2, Q69 (Test 3 in the 2020-2021 Red Book—see page 23)   **TYPE: G/S/P (often no prompt; choices w/similar meanings—see page 418)**

- **Vertical Scan Results:** Some choices have different forms of the same base word.
- **Vertical Scan Notes:** We have to decide whether "which," "which by," or neither phrase should appear in the underlined phrase. We also have to decide whether "stretched," "stretching," or "stretches" should appear in the phrase.
- **Key Features in Surrounding Text:** The original version of the underlined phrase appears in the middle of the comma-sandwiched phrase "each one which stretched from the bottom to the top of the canvas's left half." The subject of the sentence is "triangles," and the verb is the present-tense verb "angle," so that a basic version of the sentence (with most intervening phrases removed) would be "Three triangles angle slightly to the right." The sandwiched phrase must describe the word "triangles."

Concepts in the question:

- **Comma Splice:** Choices and/or surrounding text use commas to join two groups of words that could each be sentences on their own. A comma can't be used in this way on the ACT English section. (See page 428)
- **Commas:** Choices include commas. Commas can separate a list of 3 or more items, form sandwiches, separate interchangeable adjectives, or introduce an independent clause after a dependent clause. They can't appear for no reason. (p. 431)
- **Dependent and Independent Clauses:** Choices would create or join clauses. An independent clause has a main verb and can be a sentence by itself. A dependent clause can't, and starts with a conjunction or relative pronoun. (p. 426)
- **Intervening Phrase:** A phrase appears between two words that need to agree with each other grammatically. Remember to identify pairs of words that need to agree with each other, and ignore phrases that appear between those words. (See page 439)
- **Parallelism:** Choices include options that would ignore a parallel structure in the surrounding text. The right answer should match the phrasing and grammatical structures in the surrounding text when possible. (See p. 440)
- **Verb Tense/Conjugation:** Choices include different forms of the same verb. Look at the surrounding text to find the verb's subject. Also look for other verbs that could indicate the proper tense or form for the verbs in the choices. (See p. 420-423)

ANSWER CHOICE ANALYSIS

A   **Incorrect:** There are multiple issues with this choice. One of the easiest issues to note is probably that the word "of" is missing, so that (A) says "*each one which" instead of "each one of which." Another issue is that "stretched" can't be used as a verb here (that is, it can't be an action the triangles have done) because the verb "angle" is in the present tense, and the ACT won't let us switch tenses from the past-tense "stretched" to the present-tense "angle" without a word or phrase that explains the difference in tense. Either of these issues would be enough to make (A) wrong by itself. See the note below.

B   **Incorrect:** This choice shares an issue with (A), because it's also missing the word "of." Without getting too technical in this explanation, another issue is that "by" doesn't make any sense here: the sentence never says what's accomplished "by stretching." See the note below.

C ✓   **Correct:** This choice gets rid of the word "which," and creates the sandwiched phrase "each one stretching from the bottom to the top...," which describes each of the "triangles." Since this is the only choice that's grammatically acceptable according to the ACT, we know it's right. See the note below.

D   **Incorrect:** This choice creates a comma sandwich around an independent clause, because it changes "stretched" in the original to the conjugated main verb form "stretches:" "each one stretches from the bottom to the top of the canvas's left half" could stand on its own as a sentence. Since the ACT doesn't let us to sandwich a set of words that could stand on their own as a sentence, we know (D) is wrong. See the note below.

Note   It may help to explain the ideal underlying structure of the entire sentence for this question, because it's a bit longer and more awkward than the average ACT English sentence. A basic version of the sentence, with the correct phrases supplied in questions 69 and 70, would be "Three orange triangles angle slightly to the right." This can be tricky for some people to realize, because the word "angle" is usually a noun, but this sentence uses it in the present tense, as the main verb in the whole sentence. The phrases "on the left half," "in a row," "each one stretching from the bottom to the top of the canvas," and "on a purple background" can all be thought of as intervening phrases (see page 439 in this Black Book) that have been added into that basic sentence. This is why "stretching" is correct here: it's part of a comma-sandwiched phrase that modifies the triangles. On test day, you'll probably see a few sentences that are as weird as this one. When you do, remember to stay focused, stick to your training, and always refer back to specific words, phrases, and punctuation marks as you decide on your answer—for example, in this case, we could tell that (A), (B), and (D) all violate grammatical rules without necessarily understanding the grammatical structure of the whole sentence, as we described above.

T2, Q70 (Test 3 in the 2020-2021 Red Book—see page 23)   **TYPE: G/S/P (often no prompt; choices w/similar meanings—see page 418)**

- **Vertical Scan Results:** Similar phrases with different short words and/or punctuation.

- **Vertical Scan Notes:** Three choices mention the left half of the canvas, and one choice doesn't.
- **Key Features in Surrounding Text:** The sentence begins with the phrase "on the left half," referring to "the canvas" from the previous sentence.

Concepts in the question:

- **Redundancy:** Choices and/or surrounding text could combine to repeat the same concept unnecessarily. On grammar/style/punctuation questions, we should avoid words that directly repeat ideas in the immediate surrounding text. (See p. 437)

ANSWER CHOICE ANALYSIS

F   **Incorrect:** As we discussed above, the sentence already tells us that this feature is on the left half of the canvas, so "left half" is redundant, which makes (F) wrong.

G   **Incorrect:** This choice has the same basic problem as (F): it repeats the phrase "left half."

H   **Incorrect:** This choice has the same problem as (F) and (G).

J ✓ **Correct:** This choice avoids the redundancy from the other choices. Also, it's the shortest choice and it's grammatically acceptable on the ACT, so we know it must be right.

Answer choice patterns (page 442): shortest grammatically acceptable choice is correct

---

T2, Q71 (Test 3 in the 2020-2021 Red Book—see page 23)   **TYPE: G/S/P (often no prompt; choices w/similar meanings—see page 418)**

- **Vertical Scan Results:** Some choices have different forms of the same base word.
- **Vertical Scan Notes:** We have to choose between "cuts" or "cut," and between "crossed" and "through."
- **Key Features in Surrounding Text:** The underlined phrase includes the main verb of the sentence. The subject of the sentence is the plural noun "bands," so the underlined phrase must be plural in order to agree with "bands."

Concepts in the question:

- **Confused Homophones:** Choices include different homophone pairs (such as "their"/"they're" or "too"/"to"). Remember the correct formation of possessives. Remember to read contractions as their uncontracted forms (e.g. "it's" = "it is"). (p. 436)
- **Prepositional Idioms:** Choices typically include prepositional phrases with no other recognizable similarities. If you can't tell which choice contains an acceptable prepositional idiom in American English, guess and invest your time elsewhere. (p. 435)
- **Singular versus Plural:** Choices include singular and plural versions of the same base words that don't agree with other words in the surrounding text. Nouns, pronouns, and verbs must agree in number with the words they refer to or modify. (p. 423)
- **Verb Tense/Conjugation:** Choices include different forms of the same verb. Look at the surrounding text to find the verb's subject. Also look for other verbs that could indicate the proper tense or form for the verbs in the choices. (See p. 420-423)

ANSWER CHOICE ANALYSIS

A   **Incorrect:** This choice involves the singular verb form "cuts," so it doesn't agree with "bands," for reasons discussed above.

B   **Incorrect:** This choice involves the singular verb form "cuts," like (A); it also inappropriately uses the verb form "crossed" instead of the preposition "across." Either issue by itself would be enough to make (B) wrong.

C ✓ **Correct:** This choice uses the plural verb form "cut," which is appropriate for the reasons discussed above. It also uses the preposition "through," which appropriately reflects the idea of cutting from one side of something to the other.

D   **Incorrect:** This choice has the same problem involving "crossed" that we saw in our discussion of (B); it might attract untrained test-takers who mistake the verb "crossed" for the preposition "across."

T2, Q72 (Test 3 in the 2020-2021 Red Book—see page 23)   **TYPE: G/S/P (often no prompt; choices w/similar meanings—see page 418)**

- **Vertical Scan Results:** Similar phrases with different short words and/or punctuation.
- **Vertical Scan Notes:** Each choice uses a different preposition: "to," "on," "into," and "with."
- **Key Features in Surrounding Text:** The preposition in the underlined phrase is used in conjunction with the verb "lends." Two of the choices use some version of the word "entire," and two choices use the word "whole."

Concepts in the question:

- **Prepositional Idioms:** Choices typically include prepositional phrases with no other recognizable similarities. If you can't tell which choice contains an acceptable prepositional idiom in American English, guess and invest your time elsewhere. (p. 435)

ANSWER CHOICE ANALYSIS

F ✓ **Correct:** In American English, it's idiomatically appropriate to use the preposition "to" after the verb "lends." This is the only choice that creates an acceptable prepositional idiom involving "lends," so it's right. See the note below for more.

G   **Incorrect:** As we saw in our discussion of (F), the idiomatically acceptable preposition to use after "lends" would be "to," not "on," so this choice is wrong. Note that we don't need to worry about whether the phrase "the entirety of the" is appropriate here, since the preposition "on" makes this choice wrong. See the note below for more.

H   Incorrect: This choice uses the preposition "into" instead of "to," and has the same basic problem as (G). See the note below for more.

J   Incorrect: This choice uses the preposition "with" instead of "to," and has the same basic problem as (G) and (H). See the note below for more.

Note   As trained test-takers, we know that the ACT will sometimes ask questions involving prepositional idioms, and that our best bet on these questions is to pick the choice that sounds right, and then move on. Sometimes these questions will involve other issues related to style, grammar, or punctuation, which will make it possible for us to eliminate wrong answer choices for reasons other than their use of prepositions, but that wasn't the case on this question. Also, notice that we didn't need to spend any time thinking about the phrases "the whole," "the entirety of the," or "the entire" that appeared in the answer choices, because only one choice had an acceptable preposition, and the others didn't.

T2, Q73 (Test 3 in the 2020-2021 Red Book—see page 23)   TYPE: G/S/P (often no prompt; choices w/similar meanings—see page 418)

- **Vertical Scan Results:** Choices are long phrases/sentences.
- **Vertical Scan Notes:** All the answer choices express the idea of one thing being like another thing.
- **Key Features in Surrounding Text:** The two things being compared are "effect" and "perfect jazz collaboration."

Concepts in the question:

- **Comparison:** The ACT English section only allows us to compare two things if those things are of the same type (for example, a person to a person, or a voice to a voice, but not a person's voice to a person herself). (See page 430)
- **Shorter is Better:** Choices include words or phrases that can be removed without impacting meaning or creating grammatical problems. The shortest grammatically acceptable choice that doesn't change the meaning is right. (p. 442)

ANSWER CHOICE ANALYSIS

A   Incorrect: The easiest way to tell that this choice is wrong is to notice that (C) is shorter and grammatically correct.

B   Incorrect: The easiest way to tell that this choice is wrong is to notice that (C) is shorter and grammatically correct.

C ✓ Correct: This choice is grammatically correct and shorter than (A) or (B), and it resolves the issue we'll see in our discussion of (D) by including the phrase "that of." The word "that" acts as a pronoun referring to "effect," which makes it clear that the sentence is making a comparison between the "effect" of the painting and the "effect" of a "perfect jazz collaboration." This choice avoids the problems in the other choices and makes a comparison between two things of the same kind, which is acceptable on the ACT English section, so it must be correct.

D   Incorrect: This choice would say that the "effect" is "like" a "collaboration." This would create a comparison between two different kinds of things, which isn't acceptable on the ACT English section. Instead, the underlined phrase must make it clear that the author is comparing the "effect" of the painting to the "effect" of a jazz collaboration. See the discussion of (C) for more on this.

Answer choice patterns (page 442): shortest grammatically acceptable choice is correct

T2, Q74 (Test 3 in the 2020-2021 Red Book—see page 23)   TYPE: RC (usually has a prompt; choices w/different meanings—see page 413)

- **RC Question sub-type:** Effect of deletion. (The prompt asks what the effect would be if the author deleted a phrase or sentence. The right answer will be plainly and directly demonstrated by the text. See page 416)

ANSWER CHOICE ANALYSIS

F ✓ Correct: This choice is literally demonstrated by the text, so it's right. The sentence before the one in the question refers to "rhythm" and the idea of "play[ing]," which are two "subtle musical references" that are "elsewhere in the paragraph," as (F) requires. And deleting the sentence in the question would cause the paragraph to lose the phrase "the effect is like that of a perfect jazz collaboration" (see the explanation for question 73), which is literally "a comparison between Little's paintings and jazz," as (F) also requires.

G   Reasonable statement not in the text: The sentence *does* compare Little's work to jazz, as we discussed for (F), but it doesn't say anything about the popularity of his paintings. (Some untrained test-takers might pick this choice because they assume that a "perfect...collaboration" would have to be "popular[]," as (G) requires, but the idea of perfection doesn't literally restate or demonstrate the idea of popularity: some popular things aren't perfect, and some perfect things aren't popular.) The sentence in question doesn't mention the idea of popularity at all, so this choice must be wrong.

H   Barely relevant: The following paragraph only talks about one assessment of Little's work, and the text never indicates that the person who assessed his work was an art critic, so (H) doesn't accurately describe the text. Further, the sentence doesn't provide any transition, as (H) would also require, because it doesn't mention anything about the following text.

J   Barely relevant: The sentence doesn't say anything about Little's goals for *Bittersweet Victory*, nor that those goals were unique, as (J) would require.

T2, Q75 (Test 3 in the 2020-2021 Red Book—see page 23)   TYPE: RC (usually has a prompt; choices w/different meanings—see page 413)

- **RC Question sub-type:** Would essay fulfill goal? (The question describes a goal that the author had in writing the passage, and asks whether the author achieved that goal. The right answer choice will be directly restated or demonstrated by the passage, and logically answer the question in the prompt. See page 417)

ANSWER CHOICE ANALYSIS

A **Confused relationships:** It's true that the passage says one woman told Little that his paintings in general were optimistic, but the passage doesn't say that the lines in *Bittersweet Victory*, specifically, were optimistic, as (A) would require. Further, the idea of optimism is only mentioned once in the final paragraph, so we can't call it the focus of the essay. Since this choice isn't literally restated or demonstrated by the passage, (A) can't be right.

B ✓ **Correct:** The passage routinely refers to Little's "shapes," "triangles," "rectangles," "lines," "rays," and "bands," which demonstrate the idea of "shapes" as (B) requires. The passage also uses words like "color," "color-soaked," "beige," "orange," "purple," "dark green," "lime-green," and "blocks of color," which demonstrate the idea of Little using "color" as (B) requires. The first two paragraphs discuss how Little "explore[s]...the energy of movement," and the last two paragraphs focus on how those shapes and colors express "rhythm" and "shifts," demonstrating the idea of "captur[ing]...movement," as (B) also requires. Finally, the last paragraph says Little thinks "his paintings reflect...our experiences as human beings," which restates the notion of the "human experience" from (B). Since the description in this choice is the only one that's literally demonstrated and restated by the passage, (B) is right.

C **Direct contradiction:** The third paragraph mentions *Bittersweet Victory*, but doesn't discuss any "metaphor that Little hoped to create" with that specific painting, as (C) would require. Further, the passage does describe the painting (we're told it's "bisected by a vertical, beige line," that it has "three orange triangles," and so on). Since every part of the description in this choice is contradicted by the text, (C) is wrong.

D **Direct contradiction:** The first paragraph describes the effect of Little's work when it says that "some viewers see the paintings...as impersonal..." and "others see them as minimalistic...." The fourth paragraph also describes the effect of Little's work on one observer, who tells Little his paintings are "optimistic." Since the description in this choice contradicts what's literally demonstrated in the text, (D) must be wrong.

TEST 3 (FORM 16MC3—SEE PAGE 23)

T3, Q1 (Form 16MC3 if you have 2020-2021 Red Book—see p. 23) TYPE: G/S/P (often no prompt; choices w/similar meanings—see p. 418)

- **Vertical Scan Results:** Some choices have the same words with different punctuation.
- **Vertical Scan Notes:** Should a comma, semicolon, or no punctuation appear after "tribe?" Should a comma appear after "American?" Should a comma appear after "people?"
- **Key Features in Surrounding Text:** The subject of the sentence is "family," and the main verb is "is." The original version of the underlined portion of the sentence doesn't show how the phrase "a Native American people..." is connected to the independent clause "my family is...tribe."

Concepts in the question:

- **Changed Meaning:** Choices would change the meaning of the original text, or cause the relevant phrase/sentence not to make sense. The right answer must be grammatically acceptable and still preserve the original meaning. (See p. 438)
- **Commas:** Choices include commas. Commas can separate a list of 3 or more items, form sandwiches, separate interchangeable adjectives, or introduce an independent clause after a dependent clause. They can't appear for no reason. (p. 431)
- **Dependent and Independent Clauses:** Choices would create or join clauses. An independent clause has a main verb and can be a sentence by itself. A dependent clause can't, and starts with a conjunction or relative pronoun. (p. 426)
- **Punctuation Sandwich:** Choices involve phrases "sandwiched" between similar punctuation marks. When removed from the sentence, a proper sandwich leaves behind a grammatical sentence with the same original meaning. (See p. 432 and 433)
- **Semicolons:** Choices include one or more semicolons. Semicolons can be used to separate two sets of words that could each stand on their own as complete sentences. (See page 431.)

ANSWER CHOICE ANALYSIS

A **Incorrect:** As trained test-takers who know the situations in which commas are acceptable on the ACT English section, we know that a single comma after "people" doesn't satisfy the ACT's rules. It would create a comma sandwich around the phrase "with strong ties...Illinois," which isn't okay because removing the sandwiched phrase would leave us with this non-grammatical "sentence:" "My family is part of the Miami tribe a Native American people." In that ungrammatical sentence, the phrase "a Native American people" has no connection to the rest of the sentence. So (A) is wrong.

B **Incorrect:** This choice creates an unacceptable comma sandwich around the phrase "a Native American." The sandwich is unacceptable because removing it would fundamentally alter the meaning of the sentence, which is something the ACT doesn't allow us to do. In this case, removing the phrase would leave us with this: "My family is part of the Miami tribe, people with strong ties..." This would change the use of the word "people" so that it goes from being a singular noun in the original sentence (as in "a people") to a plural noun meaning "more than one person" in the modified sentence.

C ✓ **Correct:** The comma after "tribe" joins the independent clause before the comma to the comma-sandwiched phrase "a Native American...and Illinois," demonstrating that the sandwiched phrase describes the "Miami tribe," and that the phrase can be removed from the sentence without fundamentally altering the meaning of the sentence. Since this is the only grammatically acceptable choice, we know it must be right.

D **Incorrect:** There shouldn't be a semicolon after "tribe" because the part of the sentence after the semicolon can't stand on its own as a complete sentence. This choice might attract untrained test-takers who misread the semicolon as a comma.

Answer choice patterns (page 442): wrong answers try to imitate right answers

---

T3, Q2 (Form 16MC3 if you have 2020-2021 Red Book—see p. 23) TYPE: RC (usually has prompt; choices w/different meanings—see p. 413)

- **RC Question sub-type:** Best accomplishes X. (The prompt describes a goal of the author, and asks which choice achieves that goal. The right answer will be plainly demonstrated in the passage. See page 413)

ANSWER CHOICE ANALYSIS

F ✓ **Correct:** This choice mentions two specific activities that the writer's grandmother loved: "making freezer jam" and "researching tribal history." This literally demonstrates the idea of the "grandmother's interests," as the prompt requires. (Further, this is the only choice that allows the phrase "whether it was..." in the passage to make sense, since it's the only choice that includes the word "or." (See the note below for more.))

G **Pattern: Same ballpark. Incorrect:** This choice mentions "pursuits," but doesn't describe or define those pursuits, so it doesn't demonstrate what "the grandmother's interests" actually are, as the prompt would require. ((G) also doesn't mention multiple alternatives, so it can't work logically with the phrase "whether it was" in the text. (See the note below for more.))

H **Barely relevant:** This choice doesn't literally demonstrate anything about what the "grandmother's interests" are at all, so it can't satisfy the prompt. (It also doesn't make any grammatical sense with the phrase "whether it was," because it doesn't include the word "or." (See the note below for more.))

J **Off by one or two words:** This choice broadly mentions "historical research" and "domestic projects" as examples of "something [the grandmother] loved," but it doesn't specify which "domestic projects" or what kind of "historical research" the grandmother likes with the same level of detail as the phrases "making freezer jam" and "researching tribal history" in (F). (Further, (J) uses the phrase "as well as" to join two ideas, and that phrase doesn't work grammatically with the word "whether." As we noted for (F), "whether" requires multiple options joined by the word "or." (See the note below for more.))

Note This question can be viewed as a hybrid of a reading comprehension question and a grammar/style/punctuation question. The question includes a prompt, and the right answer clearly demonstrates a "glimpse into the grandmother's interests," as the prompt requires; all of these are common features of reading-based questions on the ACT English section. But it's also true that the right answer is the only one that contains the word "or," which is necessary to complete the correlative conjunction (see page 426) that begins with phrase "whether it was;" this is the kind of issue we would expect to see in a grammar/style/punctuation question. On test day, remember that the major question types we discuss in the training are useful tools for helping you understand how to attack individual questions, but the ACT will occasionally present you with questions like this one, which seem to incorporate elements of both reading comprehension *and* style, grammar, and/or punctuation. The important thing to note here, and for all ACT questions, is that the right answer is always totally predictable if you remember your training and read carefully. On this question, (F) is right whether you lean more heavily on literal demonstration or on grammar in your analysis, and it will never happen that the ACT will ask you a question that might seem to have one right answer if you consider it from one valid perspective, and another right answer if you consider it from another valid perspective. Once you know the rules of the test, each official ACT question has only one right answer, no matter how you look at it!

T3, Q3 (Form 16MC3 if you have 2020-2021 Red Book—see p. 23)   TYPE: G/S/P (often no prompt; choices w/similar meanings—see p. 418)

- **Vertical Scan Results:** Similar phrases with different short words and/or punctuation.
- **Vertical Scan Notes:** All four choices mention the idea of rushing; three choices also mention another word that's synonymous with rushing.
- **Key Features in Surrounding Text:** The original phrase involves two phrases that both refer to the idea of someone moving quickly, which is redundant according to the rules of the ACT English section.

Concepts in the question:

- **Redundancy:** Choices and/or surrounding text could combine to repeat the same concept unnecessarily. On grammar/style/punctuation questions, we should avoid words that directly repeat ideas in the immediate surrounding text. (See p. 437)
- **Shorter is Better:** Choices include words or phrases that can be removed without impacting meaning or creating grammatical problems. The shortest grammatically acceptable choice that doesn't change the meaning is right. (p. 442)

ANSWER CHOICE ANALYSIS

A   **Incorrect:** Being "rushed" and being "in a hurry" are synonyms in this context, so one of these phrases is redundant, which makes this choice wrong on the ACT.

B   **Incorrect:** This choice has the same basic issue as (A): being "hurried" and being "rushed" are the same thing in this context, so one of these phrases is redundant.

C   **Incorrect:** This choice has the same issue as (A) and (B).

D ✓   **Correct:** This is the only choice that avoids redundancy. Also, it's the shortest choice and it's grammatically correct, so, as trained test-takers, we know it's right.

Answer choice patterns (page 442): shortest grammatically acceptable choice is correct

T3, Q4 (Form 16MC3 if you have 2020-2021 Red Book—see p. 23)   TYPE: G/S/P (often no prompt; choices w/similar meanings—see p. 418)

- **Vertical Scan Results:** Some choices have the same words with different punctuation.

- **Vertical Scan Notes:** Should "appointment" be followed by a period, a semicolon, a comma, or the word "and?"

- **Key Features in Surrounding Text:** The original version of the phrase places a period after "appointment," which isn't acceptable on the ACT English section because the words leading up to "appointment" contain the word "if" in a way that causes them to be a dependent clause, and a sentence can't consist of only a dependent clause on the ACT English section. (In other words, the following can't stand on its own as a sentence: "*Conversely, if we were running late for an appointment.")

     Concepts in the question:

- **Commas:** Choices include commas. Commas can separate a list of 3 or more items, form sandwiches, separate interchangeable adjectives, or introduce an independent clause after a dependent clause. They can't appear for no reason. (p. 431)

- **Dependent and Independent Clauses:** Choices would create or join clauses. An independent clause has a main verb and can be a sentence by itself. A dependent clause can't, and starts with a conjunction or relative pronoun. (p. 426)

- **Semicolons:** Choices include one or more semicolons. Semicolons can be used to separate two sets of words that could each stand on their own as complete sentences. (See page 431.)

ANSWER CHOICE ANALYSIS

F   **Incorrect:** As we noted above, there can't be a period after "appointment" because "Conversely, if…appointment" is a dependent clause, and the ACT won't allow us to create a sentence that consists entirely of a dependent clause. Another way to know that a period can't be placed here is to note that (G) involves placing a semicolon in the same position, and semicolons (like periods) are used to separate two sets of words that could each be sentences on their own. If (F) were acceptable according to the rules of the ACT English section, then (G) would also be acceptable—but, as trained test-takers, we know it's not possible for an ACT question to have two choices that are both acceptable. Since the two choices can't both be right, they must both be wrong.

G   **Incorrect:** See our discussion of (F).

H   **Incorrect:** The word "and" makes it sound like "if" refers to both "running late" and "she would chide us," so that the sentence still never says what would happen "if we were running late…and she would chide us." This means that this choice still results in one long dependent clause making up an entire sentence, which isn't allowed on the ACT English section.

J ✓   **Correct:** This choice appropriately uses a comma to join the dependent clause "Conversely, if we…appointment" to the independent clause "she would chide us…." This is the only grammatically acceptable choice, so we know it's right.

T3, Q5 (Form 16MC3 if you have 2020-2021 Red Book—see p. 23) TYPE: RC (usually has prompt; choices w/different meanings—see p. 413)

- **RC Question sub-type:** Best accomplishes X. (The prompt describes a goal of the author, and asks which choice achieves that goal. The right answer will be plainly demonstrated in the passage. See page 413)

ANSWER CHOICE ANALYSIS

A ✓   **Correct:** This choice allows the word "it" to refer to "Miami time" in the next sentence. Further, we can see that the idea of being "difficult…to grasp" in this choice is literally demonstrated by the fact that the grandmother "tried to explain" Miami time to the writer, and the fact that the "meaning" had only "recently" "started to sink in." Since this choice is the only one connected to the ideas in the rest of the paragraph, we know it's the one the test will reward.

B   **Confused relationships:** The *previous* paragraph is the one that mentions the idea of sometimes "running late for an appointment," which means this choice is relevant to the previous paragraph. But the prompt asks us for a sentence that's relevant to "this paragraph," so this choice relates to the wrong part of the text, which makes it wrong.

C   **Reasonable statement not in the text:** As trained test-takers, we know that the right answer must mention concepts that are already present in the paragraph. The rest of this paragraph doesn't actually restate or demonstrate that the narrator lived with the grandmother, nor that they became close. Some untrained test-takers will assume on their own that it's okay to say the narrator and the grandmother share a home and are close, but we know that we can't assume anything is true unless it's stated or demonstrated in the text!

D   **Barely relevant:** The paragraph doesn't say anything about the son asking about the grandmother, or about his never meeting her, so the ACT English section won't reward us for adding a sentence to this paragraph that mentions those ideas.

- **Vertical Scan Results:** Some choices have the same words with different punctuation.
- **Vertical Scan Notes:** Should "moments" have a comma after it? Should the phrases "when," "as if," or "because" come after "moments?"
- **Key Features in Surrounding Text:** On the ACT English section, the original version of this sentence is unacceptable because the comma after "moments" makes it unclear what the word "those" refers to. (The original version of the sentence would probably be grammatically acceptable *outside* of the ACT English section, but, strictly speaking, it would refer to "those moments" without specifying exactly what the word "those" meant: with a comma after "moments," the sentence is saying that the grandmother tried to explain something, and, when she did that explaining, time slowed down. This is because the comma in the original version of the sentence would create a "punctuation sandwich" around the second half of the sentence—remember that a punctuation sandwich involves only one comma when the "sandwiched" phrase occurs at the beginning or the end of the sentence. This problem is probably a little clearer if we move the sandwiched phrase to the beginning of the sentence: "When time seemed to slow down or stand still, my grandmother tried to explain that "Miami time" referred to those moments." This makes it unclear what "those moments" refers to, and is also different from saying that the phrase "Miami time" by itself refers to a type of slowed-down moment.)

Concepts in the question:

- **Changed Meaning:** Choices would change the meaning of the original text, or cause the relevant phrase/sentence not to make sense. The right answer must be grammatically acceptable and still preserve the original meaning. (See p. 438)
- **Commas:** Choices include commas. Commas can separate a list of 3 or more items, form sandwiches, separate interchangeable adjectives, or introduce an independent clause after a dependent clause. They can't appear for no reason. (p. 431)
- **Dependent and Independent Clauses:** Choices would create or join clauses. An independent clause has a main verb and can be a sentence by itself. A dependent clause can't, and starts with a conjunction or relative pronoun. (p. 426)
- **Pronoun Ambiguity:** Choices include pronouns that could refer to more than one phrase in the surrounding text. We can't use a pronoun on the ACT when it isn't clear what that pronoun refers to. (See page 419)
- **Punctuation Sandwich:** Choices involve phrases "sandwiched" between similar punctuation marks. When removed from the sentence, a proper sandwich leaves behind a grammatical sentence with the same original meaning. (See p. 432 and 433)

ANSWER CHOICE ANALYSIS

F   **Incorrect:** As we discussed above, placing a comma after "moments" technically causes the word "those" to be ambiguous, which isn't acceptable on the ACT English section. Instead of making it clear that "those moments" are the moments "when time seemed to slow down or stand still," this placement makes it seem like "those moments" refers to some other moments that would need to have been mentioned elsewhere in the text, but weren't.

G ✓ **Correct:** No punctuation is necessary in the underlined phrase, because placing the word "when" immediately after the word "moments," with no comma, shows that the word "those" is referring to the kinds of moments "when time seemed to slow down...."

H   **Incorrect:** This choice has the same basic issue as (F): its comma causes "those" to be ambiguous, which isn't okay on the ACT English section.

J   **Incorrect:** This choice has a comma after "moments," just like (F) and (G).

Note   This is one more excellent example of a time when the right answer is clear to someone who knows the rules of the test and reads carefully, even though an untrained test-taker might be drawn to a wrong answer (in this case, (F)) because she incorrectly assumes that the ACT will reward exactly the same kind of decision-making that's rewarded in school. On test day, remember to read everything carefully and consider each choice in light of your training, and remember that pronouns can't be used ambiguously on the ACT English section!

- **Vertical Scan Results:** Choices are long phrases/sentences.
- **Vertical Scan Notes:** Each choice except for (A) includes a longer phrase that makes the same point as (A).
- **Key Features in Surrounding Text:** The underlined word is referred to as something with a "meaning" that "started to sink in."

Concepts in the question:

- **Redundancy:** Choices and/or surrounding text could combine to repeat the same concept unnecessarily. On grammar/style/punctuation questions, we should avoid words that directly repeat ideas in the immediate surrounding text. (See p. 437)
- **Shorter is Better:** Choices include words or phrases that can be removed without impacting meaning or creating grammatical problems. The shortest grammatically acceptable choice that doesn't change the meaning is right. (p. 442)

ANSWER CHOICE ANALYSIS

A ✓ **Correct:** This choice avoids the redundancy of the other options. It's also the shortest choice and it's grammatically acceptable, so, as trained test-takers, we know it's right.

B   **Incorrect:** A "statement" can only reach someone's "ears" if it's "spoken," so everything but "statements" is redundant in this choice. Further, we see that (A) is shorter and grammatically acceptable, so we know that (B) can't be right.

C   **Incorrect:** This choice has the same basic problem as (B): the phrase "on the matter" is redundant, because the paragraph makes it clear that the "expressed opinions" are about "Miami time." Also, the "opinions" couldn't "sink in" if they weren't "expressed," which means "expressed is redundant as well.

D   **Incorrect:** This choice has the same basic problem as (B) and (C): everything but "remarks" is redundant, and (A) is shorter and grammatically acceptable.

Answer choice patterns (page 442): shortest grammatically acceptable choice is correct

T3, Q8 (Form 16MC3 if you have 2020-2021 Red Book—see p. 23)   TYPE: G/S/P (often no prompt; choices w/similar meanings—see p. 418)

- **Vertical Scan Results:** Some choices have different forms of the same base word.

- **Vertical Scan Notes:** One choice involves a future-tense verb form, two involve present-tense verb forms, and one involves a past-tense verb form. All include the word "inadvertently."

- **Key Features in Surrounding Text:** The previous sentence begins with "recently" and uses the verb "started," both of which indicate that the action in this sentence takes place in the past. This sentence begins with the phrase "one morning, my son and I," and then the next two paragraphs (which start with the next sentence) mention the narrator and her son doing something on a morning in the past. All of this indicates that the underlined verb needs to indicate some kind of action in the past.

     Concepts in the question:

- **Parallelism:** Choices include options that would ignore a parallel structure in the surrounding text. The right answer should match the phrasing and grammatical structures in the surrounding text when possible. (See p. 440)

- **Verb Tense/Conjugation:** Choices include different forms of the same verb. Look at the surrounding text to find the verb's subject. Also look for other verbs that could indicate the proper tense or form for the verbs in the choices. (See p. 420-423)

ANSWER CHOICE ANALYSIS

F   **Incorrect:** The word "will" in this choice marks it as a future-tense verb, which is unacceptable here for the reasons noted above.

G   **Incorrect:** This choice uses a present-tense verb, which is wrong here for the reasons we discussed above.

H   **Incorrect:** This choice uses a present-tense verb, so it has the same basic problem as (G).

J   ✓   **Correct:** This choice uses a past-tense verb, so it's appropriate for the reasons we noted above.

T3, Q9 (Form 16MC3 if you have 2020-2021 Red Book—see p. 23)   TYPE: G/S/P (often no prompt; choices w/similar meanings—see p. 418)

- **Vertical Scan Results:** Similar phrases with different short words and/or punctuation.

- **Vertical Scan Notes:** Each choice except (D) includes an -ing verb. (A) and (B) include the plural helping verb "were," while (C) doesn't. (D) provides the option of deleting the underlined phrase.

- **Key Features in Surrounding Text:** The subject of the underlined verb is the singular pronoun "I;" the earlier part of the sentence makes it clear that the underlined phrase should be parallel to "pushing," which also has the singular subject "I."

     Concepts in the question:

- **Parallelism:** Choices include options that would ignore a parallel structure in the surrounding text. The right answer should match the phrasing and grammatical structures in the surrounding text when possible. (See p. 440)

- **Prepositional Idioms:** Choices typically include prepositional phrases with no other recognizable similarities. If you can't tell which choice contains an acceptable prepositional idiom in American English, guess and invest your time elsewhere. (p. 435)

- **Singular versus Plural:** Choices include singular and plural versions of the same base words that don't agree with other words in the surrounding text. Nouns, pronouns, and verbs must agree in number with the words they refer to or modify. (p. 423)

- **Verb Tense/Conjugation:** Choices include different forms of the same verb. Look at the surrounding text to find the verb's subject. Also look for other verbs that could indicate the proper tense or form for the verbs in the choices. (See p. 420-423)

ANSWER CHOICE ANALYSIS

A   **Incorrect:** As we noted above, the subject of the verb in the phrase is the singular noun "I," so the plural verb form "were" is unacceptable here.

B   **Incorrect:** This choice also includes the plural verb "were," so it has the same problem as (A).

C   ✓   **Correct:** "Thinking" is in the same form as the parallel verb "pushing," and doesn't include any plural helping verbs like "were," so it's the only grammatically acceptable choice.

D   **Incorrect:** Without the underlined phrase, the sentence would read "*...I was pushing Jeremy in his stroller and of the day ahead...," so the phrase "of the day ahead and the tasks I had to complete" wouldn't have any grammatical or logical relationship to the rest of the sentence, since there would be no verb to form an acceptable prepositional idiom with the preposition "of."

- **Vertical Scan Results:** Some choices have the same words with different punctuation.
- **Vertical Scan Notes:** Should commas appear after "does," "and," or "fawns?"
- **Key Features in Surrounding Text:** The underlined phrase describes the things that "stood watching" the author—in other words, they provide the subject for the verb "stood."

Concepts in the question:

- **Changed Meaning:** Choices would change the meaning of the original text, or cause the relevant phrase/sentence not to make sense. The right answer must be grammatically acceptable and still preserve the original meaning. (See p. 438)
- **Commas:** Choices include commas. Commas can separate a list of 3 or more items, form sandwiches, separate interchangeable adjectives, or introduce an independent clause after a dependent clause. They can't appear for no reason. (p. 431)
- **Dependent and Independent Clauses:** Choices would create or join clauses. An independent clause has a main verb and can be a sentence by itself. A dependent clause can't, and starts with a conjunction or relative pronoun. (p. 426)
- **Punctuation Sandwich:** Choices involve phrases "sandwiched" between similar punctuation marks. When removed from the sentence, a proper sandwich leaves behind a grammatical sentence with the same original meaning. (See p. 432 and 433)

ANSWER CHOICE ANALYSIS

F ✓ **Correct:** There's no reason for any punctuation in the underlined phrase: as we saw above, the subject "two does and three fawns" is performing the action in the phrase "stood watching," and no punctuation is necessary to make that grammatical relationship clear.

G **Incorrect:** This choice can't be right because the ACT doesn't allow us to use a comma in a list of two items (in this case, the two grammatical items are "two does" and "three fawns.") This choice also creates an unacceptable comma sandwich around "two does." Since it doesn't follow the ACT's rules for comma usage, we know it's wrong. (This choice might attract some untrained test-takers who misread it and think it's forming a comma sandwich around the phrase "and three fawns"—but there's no comma after "fawns," so no such sandwich is formed. And, even if it were formed, removing the phrase "and three fawns" from the sandwich would fundamentally change its meaning, and cause the phrase "five pairs of ears" in the next sentence to make no sense.)

H **Incorrect:** This choice would create a comma sandwich around the phrase "two does and three fawns," which would be unacceptable because removing that phrase doesn't leave behind a full sentence.

J **Incorrect:** This choice is wrong because it would create the unacceptable comma sandwich "two does and." If that sandwiched phrase were removed, it would change the meaning of the sentence by failing to mention the two does, which would cause the phrase "five pairs of ears" in the next sentence to make no sense. This choice is also wrong because we can't use a comma to join the items in a two-item list on the ACT English section.

Note The singular noun "doe" refers to an adult female deer, and its plural form is "does." Some test-takers will be confused by the reference to "does" in this question because it looks like the third-person singular form of the verb "to do." But, when we read carefully, we see that there's no way the underlined word "does" can be a verb form, because it's preceded by the number "two," and because the first phrase in the next sentence refers to "five pairs of ears," which only makes sense if "does" and "fawns" are things that each have a pair of ears. On test-day, you almost certainly won't see another question that involves more than one doe, but you'll probably see some other phrase that looks strange at first—when that happens, remember to stay calm, read carefully, and work out what's going on with the question in a way that allows you to apply your training effectively.

- **RC Question sub-type:** Sentence or paragraph placement. (The prompt asks us where a sentence should go in a paragraph, or where a paragraph should go in the passage. The correct order will reflect a logical chronology, and/or will allow for pronouns to refer to nouns in a logical way, and/or will place related concepts near one another. See page 415)

ANSWER CHOICE ANALYSIS

A ✓ **Correct:** The previous sentence mentions a clearing, which provides a reference for the word "there" in Sentence 3. The following sentence also begins with the phrase "five pairs of ears," which makes sense with the current placement of Sentence 3 because does and fawns each have a pair of ears, and this placement allows the phrase "two does and three fawns" to explain why "five pairs of ears" are mentioned in the next sentence. Since the current placement is the only one that allows both "there" and "five pairs of ears" to make logical sense, (A) must be right.

B **Pattern:** Causes events to be discussed out of chronological order. **Incorrect:** In this placement the word "there" in Sentence 3 could only refer to "one [world] measured by curiosity and sensation," instead of the "clearing" where the deer "stood." Also, it would be unclear what caused the "squeal[ing]" and "point[ing]" in Sentence 2, and what the "five pairs of ears" refers to in Sentence 4.

C **Pattern:** Causes events to be discussed out of chronological order. **Incorrect:** This choice has some issues in common with (B); among other things, it makes it unclear what the "five pairs of ears" refers to in Sentence 4.

D   Causes text to introduce an idea that has already been discussed: In this placement, the "two does and three fawns" would be introduced after the text already mentioned their "five pairs of ears." This placement would also cause the word "there" not to refer to anything in the previous sentence.

T3, Q12 (Form 16MC3 if you have 2020-2021 Red Book—see p. 23) TYPE: G/S/P (often no prompt; choices w/similar meanings—see p. 418)

- **Vertical Scan Results:** Some choices have different forms of the same base word.
- **Vertical Scan Notes:** We need to pick the appropriate form of "rustle," or decide to delete the underlined phrase.
- **Key Features in Surrounding Text:** If we read carefully, the sentence makes it clear that the underlined word should be in the same form as the parallel word "lazing." (The main verb in the sentence is "surprised," and the subject phrase includes the nouns "lizards" and "quail," so that the lizards and the quail are the things that surprised the author. One way we can know that the underlined verb shouldn't parallel "surprised" is that this would give the sentence two mains verbs—"rustled" and "surprised"—with no conjunction like "and" to join them.)

Concepts in the question:

- **Parallelism:** Choices include options that would ignore a parallel structure in the surrounding text. The right answer should match the phrasing and grammatical structures in the surrounding text when possible. (See p. 440)
- **Verb Tense/Conjugation:** Choices include different forms of the same verb. Look at the surrounding text to find the verb's subject. Also look for other verbs that could indicate the proper tense or form for the verbs in the choices. (See p. 420-423)

ANSWER CHOICE ANALYSIS

F   **Incorrect:** As we discussed above, the underlined word has to have the same form as the word "lazing," not the word "surprised."

G ✓   **Correct:** "Rustling" is parallel to "lazing," so this choice is right, for the reasons mentioned above—it makes clear that "lizards lazing" and "quail rustling" are the things that "surprised us."

H   **Incorrect:** This choice does include the word "rustling," like (G), but it also includes the word "were," which would turn "were rustling" into a main verb like "surprised." One problem with this, as we discussed above, is that it would require the word "and" to appear right before "surprised" so that the two main verbs could both be associated with the subject of the sentence. Since "and" doesn't appear right before "surprised," (H) can't be right.

J   **Incorrect:** Deleting the underlined phrase would create the phrase "and quail through grasses," which doesn't provide any grammatical connection between "quail" and "through grasses"—in other words, it doesn't explain what the "quail" were doing "through grasses."

T3, Q13 (Form 16MC3 if you have 2020-2021 Red Book—see p. 23) TYPE:RC (usually has prompt; choices w/different meanings—see p. 413)

- **RC Question sub-type:** Transition Phrase. (The choices reflect different kinds of transitions between two concepts, with words or phrases like "however," "instead of," or "for example." The right answer must reflect the relationship between the previous concept in the passage and the following concept in the passage. See p. 416)

ANSWER CHOICE ANALYSIS

A   **Confused relationships:** This choice would be appropriate if "the aroma of crushed eucalyptus tingl[ing] in our noses" were some kind of specific example of "blackberries melt[ing] on our tongues." But that isn't the case, so (A) must be wrong.

B   **Confused relationships:** This would be appropriate if "blackberries melt[ing] on our tongues" were some sort of alternative that was separate from "the aroma of crushed eucalyptus," but both of those phrases describe some kind of pleasant sensation that "we" experienced, so there's no reason to think these are two separate, distinct options.

C   **Confused relationships:** This would be right if "the aroma of crushed eucalyptus leaves tingl[ing] in our noses" were something done to guard against a potential problem caused by "blackberries melt[ing] on our tongues," but the text gives us no reason to think that's the case.

D ✓   **Correct:** The phrases from the other choices didn't make sense, as we saw above. Omitting the phrase before "the" doesn't create any grammatical or logical problems with the sentence, so we know (D) is right.

T3, Q14 (Form 16MC3 if you have 2020-2021 Red Book—see p. 23) TYPE: G/S/P (often no prompt; choices w/similar meanings—see p. 418)

- **Vertical Scan Results:** Some choices have different forms of the same base word.
- **Vertical Scan Notes:** We have to decide whether "shorter," "more shorter," or "the shortest" should appear in the underlined phrase, and whether "then" or "than" should appear in the underlined phrase.
- **Key Features in Surrounding Text:** The underlined phrase is part of a comparison to the word "ever." It appropriately uses the "-er" form to compare the hike to one other thing, but it inappropriately uses the word "then" instead of "than" in the comparison. "Then," with an "e," is used to indicate a particular point in time, or the consequence of a statement that starts with "if." But "than," with an "a," is used for comparisons.

Concepts in the question:

- **Comparatives and Superlatives:** Choices and/or surrounding text include a comparison. A comparison can involve either the "-er" form of an adjective, or a word like "more" or "less." Comparisons often include the word "than," but not "then." (p. 430)

- **Confused Homophones:** Choices include different homophone pairs (such as "their"/"they're" or "too"/"to"). Remember the correct formation of possessives. Remember to read contractions as their uncontracted forms (e.g. "it's" = "it is"). (p. 436)

ANSWER CHOICE ANALYSIS

F   Incorrect: When we make a comparison, we need to use "than," not "then," as we discussed above. This choice might attract an untrained test-taker who misread it and thought the second word was "than," with an "a."

G   Incorrect: "*More shorter" is wrong, because we can use either the word "more" or the "-er" form to create a comparative, but not both. This choice also has the "then" issue we saw in (F). Either problem would be enough by itself to make (G) wrong.

H   Incorrect: "Shortest" is inappropriate here because, strictly speaking, the word "hike" is being compared to the word "ever." When we compare two things, we have to use the comparative form of an adjective, which is the "more" form or the "-er" form, not the "-est" form. "Shortest" would only be appropriate if we were comparing three or more things. Further, we can never use the "-est" form with the word "than." This choice will attract a lot of untrained test-takers who read it too quickly, because the phrase "the shortest ever" might sound acceptable to some test-takers, and they'll accidentally overlook the word "than" in the choice.

J ✓ Correct: This choice appropriately uses the comparative form "shorter" and the word "than" to make a comparison between two things (the "hike" and "ever").

Answer choice patterns (page 442): wrong answers try to imitate right answers

T3, Q15 (Form 16MC3 if you have 2020-2021 Red Book—see p. 23) TYPE:RC (usually has prompt; choices w/different meanings—see p. 413)

- **RC Question sub-type:** Would essay fulfill goal? (The question describes a goal that the author had in writing the passage, and asks whether the author achieved that goal. The right answer choice will be directly restated or demonstrated by the passage, and logically answer the question in the prompt. See page 417)

ANSWER CHOICE ANALYSIS

A ✓ Correct: The second, third, fourth, and fifth paragraphs are a detailed description of a "morning spent in Miami time," as the description for this choice requires. Since this is the only choice that accurately describes the passage, we know it must be right.

B   Direct contradiction: The second paragraph mentions how the narrator's grandmother explained to him what Miami time was, and then the essay tells about a morning spent "in Miami time." But the text never says that the narrator *decided* to live in Miami time at any point, as the description in this choice would require. In fact, the text says the narrator slipped "inadvertently" into Miami time, which means the narrator did it without meaning to. Since the text directly contradicts this choice, we know it's wrong.

C   Direct contradiction: The passage only gives the grandmother's view on "the meaning of Miami time," so the description in this choice differs from the passage, which makes (C) wrong. (It's true that the passage does discuss one time when the narrator *experienced* Miami time with her son, but the passage never tells us the author's views on "the *meaning* of Miami time," as (C) would require.)

D   Confused relationships: The grandmother provides information about Miami time, but the text never says that the term "belonged" to her or anyone else, as (D) would require. Since (D) doesn't accurately describe the text, (D) must be wrong.

T3, Q16 (Form 16MC3 if you have 2020-2021 Red Book—see p. 23) TYPE: G/S/P (often no prompt; choices w/similar meanings—see p. 418)

- **Vertical Scan Results:** Some choices have the same words with different punctuation.
- **Vertical Scan Notes:** We have to decide whether "that," "and," a period, or a comma should appear between "flowers" and "eight."
- **Key Features in Surrounding Text:** The original version of the underlined phrase creates a couple of issues—among other things, the sentence describes a "field of towering yellow flowers" where women are working on a quilt, but the word "that" in the underlined phrase would make the "field of towering yellow flowers" itself something "that eight African American women sit around," while that same phrase "eight African American women" describes the people who "sit around" the quilt . . . trying to understand what this "sentence" might possibly mean is like being stuck in some kind of recursive quilted dreamworld.)

Concepts in the question:

- **Comma Splice:** Choices and/or surrounding text use commas to join two groups of words that could each be sentences on their own. A comma can't be used in this way on the ACT English section. (See page 428)
- **Dependent and Independent Clauses:** Choices would create or join clauses. An independent clause has a main verb and can be a sentence by itself. A dependent clause can't, and starts with a conjunction or relative pronoun. (p. 426)
- **Shorter is Better:** Choices include words or phrases that can be removed without impacting meaning or creating grammatical problems. The shortest grammatically acceptable choice that doesn't change the meaning is right. (p. 442)

ANSWER CHOICE ANALYSIS

F   Incorrect: As we noted above, this choice uses "that" twice in a way that makes no sense. This choice may attract some untrained test-takers who misread the original sentence and think it stops with the word "around," because that version of the sentence would seem like an acceptable thing to say in everyday English to most test-takers. (The ACT doesn't test us on whether a preposition like "around" can be the last word in a sentence).

G   **Incorrect:** This choice is arguably grammatically acceptable, even if the word "and" might not be obviously appropriate as a conjunction. But, as trained test-takers, we know that we have to consider every choice before we commit to one...and, as we'll see in a moment, (H) is also grammatically acceptable, and it's shorter than (G), which means (G) can't be right according to the unwritten rules of the ACT English section.

H ✓   **Correct:** This choice deletes the word "that," which is an unacceptable word here for the reasons we noted above, and places a period between the two resulting independent clauses. This is perfectly acceptable, since an independent clause can always stand on its own as a separate sentence, by definition. And since this is the shortest grammatically acceptable answer choice, we know it must be the right answer.

J   **Incorrect:** This choice would use a comma to join two independent clauses, creating a comma splice—which isn't acceptable on the ACT English section.

Answer choice patterns (page 442): shortest grammatically acceptable choice is correct

---

T3, Q17 (Form 16MC3 if you have 2020-2021 Red Book—see p. 23)TYPE:RC (usually has prompt; choices w/different meanings—see p. 413)

- **RC Question sub-type:** Transition Phrase. (The choices reflect different kinds of transitions between two concepts, with words or phrases like "however," "instead of," or "for example." The right answer must reflect the relationship between the previous concept in the passage and the following concept in the passage. See p. 416)

ANSWER CHOICE ANALYSIS

A   **Barely relevant:** This choice would be right if the idea of the answers "be[ing] found in the artwork itself" were somehow the logical conclusion of the questions being asked in the previous sentence. But the questions in the preceding sentences don't logically lead to the idea of the answers appearing in the artwork, so there's no reason to think that "thus" is appropriate here.

B   **Barely relevant:** This choice would be appropriate if the idea of the "answers...be[ing] found in the artwork itself" were some kind of substitution for the questions asked in the previous sentences, but that isn't the case.

C   **Barely relevant:** This would be right if the idea of the "answers...be[ing] found in the artwork itself" were some kind of continuation from the questions themselves being posed in the previous sentences, but including an answer in an artwork isn't a continuation of asking questions about that artwork.

D ✓   **Correct:** The phrases from the other choices don't make any sense in context, for the reasons we just described. Omitting the phrase before "the" doesn't create any problems with the sentence, and the word "these" in the sentence already refers back to the previous questions. This choice avoids the problems from the other choices without creating any problems of its own, so it must be right.

T3, Q18 (Form 16MC3 if you have 2020-2021 Red Book—see p. 23) TYPE: G/S/P (often no prompt; choices w/similar meanings—see p. 418)

- **Vertical Scan Results:** Choices are long phrases/sentences.
- **Vertical Scan Notes:** Each choice includes a different ordering of exactly the same words, in exactly the same forms.
- **Key Features in Surrounding Text:** The beginning of the sentence makes it clear that the first words in the underlined phrase must be something that can be "told." The next sentence after the underlined phrase begins by talking about "one panel."

     Concepts in the question:

- **Intervening Phrase:** A phrase appears between two words that need to agree with each other grammatically. Remember to identify pairs of words that need to agree with each other, and ignore phrases that appear between those words. (See page 439)
- **Proximity:** Answer choice(s) would place descriptive phrases next to ideas they don't describe. (See page 434)

ANSWER CHOICE ANALYSIS

F ✓   **Correct:** The ordering of the ideas in this choice expresses relationships among the concepts that are logically and grammatically sound, because this order allows all the phrases to follow as soon as possible after the phrases they modify: "the story" is the thing being told, and "of this gathering" explains what kind of story it is, and "on two horizontal panels" tells where the story was told, and "of text" tells us what kind of panels they are.

G   **Incorrect:** This choice places the modifier "of this gathering" *before* the word that it modifies, which is "story." This also makes it sound like the story is the thing that was gathered.

H   **Incorrect:** Among other things, this choice makes it sound like the text is the thing that was gathered ("this gathering of text"), instead of "this gathering" referring to the group of women described in the previous paragraph, because of the unacceptable placement of modifying phrases.

J   **Incorrect:** Among other things, this choice makes it sound like the text is "of" the gathering, which doesn't make any sense.

Answer choice patterns (page 442): wrong answers try to imitate right answers

---

- **Vertical Scan Results:** Some choices have different forms of the same base word.
- **Vertical Scan Notes:** We need to decide whether the word "their" or a form of "it" should appear in the underlined phrase.
- **Key Features in Surrounding Text:** The underlined phrase refers to the singular noun "piece," and shows that the "piece" possesses the "bottom border," just as the word "piece's" earlier in the sentence shows that the piece possesses the "top border."

Concepts in the question:

- **Confused Homophones:** Choices include different homophone pairs (such as "their"/"they're" or "too"/"to"). Remember the correct formation of possessives. Remember to read contractions as their uncontracted forms (e.g. "it's" = "it is"). (p. 436)
- **Parallelism:** Choices include options that would ignore a parallel structure in the surrounding text. The right answer should match the phrasing and grammatical structures in the surrounding text when possible. (See p. 440)
- **Plural/Possessive/Contraction:** Choices include nouns ending in "-s," with/without an apostrophe before or after the "-s." Recall the 3 rules for possessive forms (p. 424). Think of contractions in uncontracted forms ("you're" = "you are"). (p. 436)
- **Singular versus Plural:** Choices include singular and plural versions of the same base words that don't agree with other words in the surrounding text. Nouns, pronouns, and verbs must agree in number with the words they refer to or modify. (p. 423)

ANSWER CHOICE ANALYSIS

A   Incorrect: This is the contracted form of "it is," not a possessive form of "it;" picking this choice would create the nonsense phrase "the other into it is bottom border."

B   Incorrect: This is an ungrammatical form of "it" that might look possessive, but actually doesn't mean anything and is never acceptable on the ACT; as we'll see in our discussion of (C), "its," without an apostrophe, is the proper possessive form for the singular noun "it."

C ✓ Correct: This is the singular possessive pronoun "its," which correctly reflects that the pronoun is referring back to the singular noun "piece" and possesses the noun phrase "bottom border."

D   Incorrect: This is a plural possessive pronoun, which would only be appropriate if we needed to refer back to a plural noun. This choice might attract some untrained test-takers who misread the possessive singular noun "piece's" as though it were the plural noun "pieces."

- **Vertical Scan Results:** Some choices have the same words with different punctuation.
- **Vertical Scan Notes:** Should there be a comma after "women?" Should there be a dash or a comma after "explains?"
- **Key Features in Surrounding Text:** The subject of the sentence is the phrase "these eight women," and the main verb performed by the women is "strove."

Concepts in the question:

- **Commas:** Choices include commas. Commas can separate a list of 3 or more items, form sandwiches, separate interchangeable adjectives, or introduce an independent clause after a dependent clause. They can't appear for no reason. (p. 431)
- **Punctuation Sandwich:** Choices involve phrases "sandwiched" between similar punctuation marks. When removed from the sentence, a proper sandwich leaves behind a grammatical sentence with the same original meaning. (See p. 432 and 433)

ANSWER CHOICE ANALYSIS

F   Incorrect: This choice would create one of two unacceptable comma sandwiches—either "these eight…explains" or "strove in…world." Removing either comma sandwich leaves the other phrase, and neither phrase can stand on its own as a sentence. This comma usage also doesn't follow any other acceptable comma usage on the ACT, so (F) must be wrong.

G   Incorrect: This choice might seem similar to (J) in the eyes of an untrained test-taker, but, as trained test-takers, we know that punctuation sandwiches must use identical punctuation marks on both sides of the sandwich unless the sandwich appears at the very beginning or very end of a sentence. Since this sandwich is in the middle of the sentence, it needs to be surrounded either by two commas, or by two dashes, but not by a comma and a dash.

H   Incorrect: This choice has basically the same problem as (F), except that it would use a dash instead of a comma to create the unacceptable sandwiched phrases.

J ✓ Correct: This choice creates a punctuation sandwich around "the story explains." This sandwich is acceptable on the ACT English section because removing it from the sentence would leave behind a grammatically acceptable sentence with the same basic meaning: "These eight women strove in their various ways to support the cause of justice in the world."

- **Vertical Scan Notes:** Each choice would place the underlined phrase in a different position in the sentence.
- **Key Features in Surrounding Text:** The underlined phrase includes the word "their," which refers back to the plural noun "women"

earlier in the sentence.

Concepts in the question:

- **Intervening Phrase:** A phrase appears between two words that need to agree with each other grammatically. Remember to identify pairs of words that need to agree with each other, and ignore phrases that appear between those words. (See page 439)
- **Proximity:** Answer choice(s) would place descriptive phrases next to ideas they don't describe. (See page 434)

ANSWER CHOICE ANALYSIS

A   **Incorrect:** This choice is grammatically acceptable because it puts the phrase "in their various ways" right after a verb that phrase can logically modify, which tells us more about how the women "strove." This choice doesn't create any other issues in the sentence, so it can't be the right answer here.

B   **Incorrect:** This choice is somewhat similar to (A): it places "in their various ways" immediately after a noun that could logically be modified by that phrase, without causing any other problems in the sentence. (It's true that this placement causes "in their various ways" to come between the verb "support" and its object, "the cause of justice." But there's nothing automatically wrong with putting a phrase between a verb and its object when the phrase is behaving like an adverb and telling us more information about how the verb happened, which is the case here.)

C ✓   **Correct:** (C) would create the phrase "to support the cause in their various ways of justice in the world," which would make it sound like the women had "various ways of justice," and like the cause was somehow contained in those various ways. This makes no logical sense, so (C) is right, because the prompt asked us to find the single choice that isn't acceptable.

D   **Incorrect:** This choice would cause "in their various ways" to modify the way the women "support the cause of justice in the world," which is logically and grammatically acceptable, so (D) is wrong.

T3, Q22 (Form 16MC3 if you have 2020-2021 Red Book—see p. 23) TYPE:RC (usually has prompt; choices w/different meanings—see p. 413)

- **RC Question sub-type:** Transition Phrase. (The choices reflect different kinds of transitions between two concepts, with words or phrases like "however," "instead of," or "for example." The right answer must reflect the relationship between the previous concept in the passage and the following concept in the passage. See p. 416)

ANSWER CHOICE ANALYSIS

F ✓   **Correct:** (F) indicates that the scene in the painting never actually happened. This is literally restated in the next sentence, which says that the scene is from "the artist's imagination," meaning it didn't happen in real life. Since (F) is the only one that accurately reflects relationships in the text, we know it must be right according to the hidden rules of ACT English.

G   **Confused relationships:** (G) would be appropriate if the idea that the "women never met" were a shortened version of the previous sentences, which describe two panels of text and say the women "strove...to support the cause of justice." But since "never [meeting]" isn't a shortened form of "support[ing]...justice," (G) is wrong. This choice will attract a lot of untrained test-takers who assume that "in summary" is always a valid phrase to use when transitioning into a related paragraph.

H   **Confused relationships:** This choice would be okay if the idea of "never [meeting]" was a continuation of the ideas from the previous sentence that mentioned "support[ing]...justice," but this isn't the case; these ideas just happen to be mentioned sequentially in different paragraphs.

J   **Confused relationships:** This choice would be right if "never [meeting]" were a direct contradiction of "support[ing] justice" from the previous sentence, but that isn't the case. A lot of untrained test-takers will be drawn to this choice because they think the idea that the women never met seems to contrast the idea that they're in a painting together. But there are two problems with this line of thinking. One is that those two ideas don't actually contradict each other: it's probably true to say that most paintings depict scenes that never actually happened as they appear in the painting. The other problem is that the idea of the women appearing in the same painting is only explicitly mentioned in the first paragraph, and the underlined phrase for this question occurs in the third paragraph; the ACT won't allow us to use "in contrast" to introduce an idea unless the contrast is between two consecutive ideas— and, again, the idea in this sentence isn't a direct contradiction of the idea in the first paragraph anyway.

T3, Q23 (Form 16MC3 if you have 2020-2021 Red Book—see p. 23) TYPE: G/S/P (often no prompt; choices w/similar meanings—see p. 418)

- **Vertical Scan Results:** Some choices have the same words with different punctuation.
- **Vertical Scan Notes:** We have to decide whether "artists'," "artist's," or "artists" is appropriate, and whether a comma should appear after "imagination."
- **Key Features in Surrounding Text:** We know that the correct version of "artist" must be singular, because the previous paragraphs tell us that only one artist (Faith Ringgold) made the painting.

Concepts in the question:

- **Commas:** Choices include commas. Commas can separate a list of 3 or more items, form sandwiches, separate interchangeable adjectives, or introduce an independent clause after a dependent clause. They can't appear for no reason. (p. 431)
- **Plural/Possessive/Contraction:** Choices include nouns ending in "-s," with/without an apostrophe before or after the "-s." Recall the

3 rules for possessive forms (p. 424). Think of contractions in uncontracted forms ("you're" = "you are"). (p. 436)

- **Singular versus Plural:** Choices include singular and plural versions of the same base words that don't agree with other words in the surrounding text. Nouns, pronouns, and verbs must agree in number with the words they refer to or modify. (p. 423)

ANSWER CHOICE ANALYSIS

A		Incorrect: This is the plural form of "artist," not the singular possessive form. This choice will attract a lot of untrained test-takers because it sounds like the singular possessive form when read out loud.
B	✓	Correct: (B) uses a singular possessive form of "artist"—in fact, it's the only choice that uses a singular form of "artist," which is necessary because we know that only one artist, Faith Ringgold, created the painting, as we discussed above.
C		Incorrect: This is the plural possessive form of "artist," which would only be okay if the imagination in the sentence belonged to more than one artist. But, for reasons we discussed above, we know that's not the case.
D		Incorrect: This choice has the same basic issue as (A). It might attract untrained test-takers who think that a comma should appear at the end of the phrase, and overlook the incorrect form of "artist."

▌ T3, Q24 (Form 16MC3 if you have 2020-2021 Red Book—see p. 23) TYPE: G/S/P (often no prompt; choices w/similar meanings—see p. 418)

- **Vertical Scan Results:** Some choices have different forms of the same base word.
- **Vertical Scan Notes:** Three choices have singular verb forms, because they include the singular helping verb "was;" only (J) has a plural verb form.
- **Key Features in Surrounding Text:** The subject in this sentence is "Sojourner Truth and Harriet Tubman," so we need a plural verb form to agree with the subject.

Concepts in the question:

- **Singular versus Plural:** Choices include singular and plural versions of the same base words that don't agree with other words in the surrounding text. Nouns, pronouns, and verbs must agree in number with the words they refer to or modify. (p. 423)
- **Verb Tense/Conjugation:** Choices include different forms of the same verb. Look at the surrounding text to find the verb's subject. Also look for other verbs that could indicate the proper tense or form for the verbs in the choices. (See p. 420-423)

ANSWER CHOICE ANALYSIS

F		Incorrect: This is a singular verb form, so it can't agree grammatically with the compound subject "Sojourner Truth and Harriet Tubman," as we discussed above.
G		Incorrect: This choice has the same basic problem as (F): it uses a singular verb instead of a plural verb.
H		Incorrect: This choice has the same issue as (F) and (G).
J	✓	Correct: This is the only plural verb form in the set of answer choices, so we know it must be right, since the sentence requires a plural verb to agree with the compound subject "Sojourner Truth and Harriet Tubman," as we discussed above.

Note	Many untrained test-takers will assume that this question focuses on whether "active," "engaged," or "actively engaged" is the best phrase to describe Truth and Tubman, without noticing that the underlined phrase must be plural. This will be very frustrating for them, because there's no solid reason to like one of those three phrases more than the other two—they all basically indicate that someone was involved in something. Of course, as trained test-takers, we would note that the answer choices also involve singular and plural verbs, which lets us know that we need to figure out which noun phrase in the sentence is the subject of the verb in the underlined phrase. On test day, look out for questions that might seem to offer identical choices at first—remember that you might have overlooked some detail of the answer choices, which could cause you to focus on something unimportant while overlooking the key issue in the question.

▌ T3, Q25 (Form 16MC3 if you have 2020-2021 Red Book—see p. 23)TYPE:RC (usually has prompt; choices w/different meanings—see p. 413)

- **RC Question sub-type:** Best accomplishes X. (The prompt describes a goal of the author, and asks which choice achieves that goal. The right answer will be plainly demonstrated in the passage. See page 413)

ANSWER CHOICE ANALYSIS

A	✓	Correct: The prompt asks us for the choice that provides "the most relevant information at this point in the essay." When we consider what is being discussed "at this point in the essay," we can see that the previous sentence and the following sentence mention the social and political accomplishments of the women who were depicted on the quilt. This sentence describes a social and political accomplishment of Ida B. Wells, so we know that it must be "relevant information at this point in the essay," as the prompt requires.
B		Barely relevant: As we saw in our discussion of (A), the right answer must provide "relevant information at this point in the essay," according to the prompt. This part of the essay doesn't discuss who these women married or what their husbands did, so (B) can't be right.
C		Reasonable statement not in the text: This choice has the same basic problem as (B): it doesn't talk about the political or social accomplishments of Ida B. Wells, which makes it unlike the other statements "at this point in the essay." Instead, (C) tells us the

locations of the newspapers Wells wrote for. This choice might attract some test-takers who assume that Wells's social and political accomplishments were related to her job writing for a newspaper—and that might indeed be the case in real life for all we know—but (C) doesn't actually say that. It only says she wrote for papers in a few different cities.

D   **Barely relevant:** This choice has the same basic problem as (B) and (C), because it mentions information that isn't similar to other information at this point in the essay, which makes it irrelevant according to the ACT's rules. The details of Wells's birth and her siblings aren't similar to the discussion of political and social accomplishments of the women that are mentioned at this point in the essay.

T3, Q26 (Form 16MC3 if you have 2020-2021 Red Book—see p. 23) TYPE: G/S/P (often no prompt; choices w/similar meanings—see p. 418)

- **Vertical Scan Results:** Similar phrases with different short words and/or punctuation.
- **Vertical Scan Notes:** All four choices mention a business, and three of the four choices refer to "her" or "herself."
- **Key Features in Surrounding Text:** The part of the sentence that's not underlined already includes the phrase "her own."

Concepts in the question:

- **Commas:** Choices include commas. Commas can separate a list of 3 or more items, form sandwiches, separate interchangeable adjectives, or introduce an independent clause after a dependent clause. They can't appear for no reason. (p. 431)
- **Punctuation Sandwich:** Choices involve phrases "sandwiched" between similar punctuation marks. When removed from the sentence, a proper sandwich leaves behind a grammatical sentence with the same original meaning. (See p. 432 and 433)
- **Redundancy:** Choices and/or surrounding text could combine to repeat the same concept unnecessarily. On grammar/style/punctuation questions, we should avoid words that directly repeat ideas in the immediate surrounding text. (See p. 437)

ANSWER CHOICE ANALYSIS

F   **Incorrect:** "Herself" is redundant because the sentence already says that Walker was the one who "establish[ed] her own...business."

G   **Incorrect:** "Belonging to her" is redundant because the sentence already says Walker's business was "her own."

H   **Incorrect:** This choice has the same basic problem as (F). Some untrained test-takers will be drawn to this choice because it includes a comma sandwich around "herself," and the comma sandwich follows the test's rules for comma sandwiches—but the sandwich is around a phrase that violates the ACT's rules against redundancy, so (H) is still wrong. Also, we can see that (J) is shorter and grammatically acceptable, so, as trained test-takers, we know that (H) can't be right.

J ✓ **Correct:** This choice avoids the redundancy from the other choices without creating any other issues: it uses "business" as the object of the verb "establishing," and the prepositional phrase "in the first decade..." tells us when the business was established. Also, since this is the shortest choice and it's grammatically correct, we know it must be right according to the ACT's unwritten rules.

T3, Q27 (Form 16MC3 if you have 2020-2021 Red Book—see p. 23) TYPE: G/S/P (often no prompt; choices w/similar meanings—see p. 418)

- **Vertical Scan Results:** Choices are long phrases/sentences.
- **Vertical Scan Notes:** Only choice (B) begins by mentioning a person.
- **Key Features in Surrounding Text:** The sentence begins with the participial phrase "establishing her own hair products business," so the underlined phrase must start with a noun that could perform the action of establishing.

Concepts in the question:

- **Commas:** Choices include commas. Commas can separate a list of 3 or more items, form sandwiches, separate interchangeable adjectives, or introduce an independent clause after a dependent clause. They can't appear for no reason. (p. 431)
- **Dangling Participle:** When a phrase is joined to the main sentence by a comma and the phrase starts with an -ing/-ed/-en word, the first noun phrase in the independent clause is performing the action of the -ing/-ed/-en word. (See page 434.)
- **Pronoun Ambiguity:** Choices include pronouns that could refer to more than one phrase in the surrounding text. We can't use a pronoun on the ACT when it isn't clear what that pronoun refers to. (See page 419)
- **Proximity:** Answer choice(s) would place descriptive phrases next to ideas they don't describe. (See page 434)

ANSWER CHOICE ANALYSIS

A   **Incorrect:** The first noun phrase in this choice is "millions of dollars," but millions of dollars can't "establish[] her own hair products business," as the participial phrase at the beginning of the sentence would require under the ACT's rules.

B ✓ **Correct:** The first noun phrase in this choice is "Madame C. J. Walker," which is the name of a particular woman; it's grammatically and logically possible that she could "establish her own hair products business," as the participle at the beginning of the sentence would require. Since this is the only choice that begins by describing a single person, it's the only grammatically acceptable choice, which means it must be right.

C   **Incorrect:** The first noun phrase in this choice is the plural noun phrase "charities and educational institutions." This plural noun phrase can't be referred to with the singular pronoun "her," as the modifier at the beginning of the sentence would require under the grammar rules of the ACT English section.

D   **Incorrect:** This choice has the same basic problem as (A), because it also begins with the noun phrase "millions of dollars."

- **Vertical Scan Results:** Some choices have the same words with different punctuation.
- **Vertical Scan Notes:** Should "generosity" be followed by a comma, a semicolon, or no punctuation at all? Should "were" have a colon after it?
- **Key Features in Surrounding Text:** The original version of the sentence would create a "comma sandwich" around the phrase "among…generosity." This is unacceptable on the ACT English section because removing the sandwiched phrase would leave us with the non-sentence "*were those…for Black students."

Concepts in the question:

- **Colons:** Choices include colons. A colon can only be placed after a set of words that could be a sentence on their own, and only before a demonstration or example of the idea before the colon. No more than one colon per sentence. (p. 430)
- **Commas:** Choices include commas. Commas can separate a list of 3 or more items, form sandwiches, separate interchangeable adjectives, or introduce an independent clause after a dependent clause. They can't appear for no reason. (p. 431)
- **Intervening Phrase:** A phrase appears between two words that need to agree with each other grammatically. Remember to identify pairs of words that need to agree with each other, and ignore phrases that appear between those words. (See page 439)
- **Pronoun Ambiguity:** Choices include pronouns that could refer to more than one phrase in the surrounding text. We can't use a pronoun on the ACT when it isn't clear what that pronoun refers to. (See page 419)
- **Punctuation Sandwich:** Choices involve phrases "sandwiched" between similar punctuation marks. When removed from the sentence, a proper sandwich leaves behind a grammatical sentence with the same original meaning. (See p. 432 and 433)
- **Semicolons:** Choices include one or more semicolons. Semicolons can be used to separate two sets of words that could each stand on their own as complete sentences. (See page 431.)

ANSWER CHOICE ANALYSIS

F   Incorrect: As we noted above, this choice would create an unacceptable comma sandwich, so it's wrong.

G   Incorrect: There shouldn't be a semicolon after "generosity" because the groups of words before and after the semicolon can't stand on their own as complete sentences.

H ✓   Correct: The underlined phrase doesn't need any punctuation according to the rules of the ACT English section. The easiest way to see this is probably to note that all of the other answer choices clearly violate rules of ACT English punctuation. (We could try to explain that the sentence doesn't need any punctuation because it's an inverted construction of the base sentence "The schools that Mary McLeod Bethune opened and ran in order to provide a better education for Black students were among those that benefited from this generosity," but, on test day, the much smarter and more efficient way to approach a question like this would be to notice that all of the other choices clearly violate the ACT's rules, and then to work backwards and realize that this choice doesn't break any rules. This would take a lot less effort for most people than seeing the original sentence right away, mentally unraveling it to realize that the right answer shouldn't include any punctuation, double-checking all the other choices, and so on.) Remember that the unwritten rules of the ACT say that we should avoid punctuation unless there is a specific reason to include it.

J   Incorrect: According to the rules of the ACT English section, there shouldn't be a colon after "were" because the part of the sentence before the colon can't stand on its own as a complete sentence. (J) might attract a lot of untrained test-takers who would feel comfortable using a colon this way in school, and who didn't know the test's rules for colon usage.

- **Vertical Scan Results:** Similar phrases with different short words and/or punctuation.
- **Vertical Scan Notes:** Three choices include a pronoun ("it" or "that") and a verb ("happened" or "took"), and one doesn't.
- **Key Features in Surrounding Text:** The original version of the sentence creates a comma splice, which is unacceptable on the ACT English section, because the comma after "movement" comes between two groups of words that could each stand on their own as grammatical sentences.

Concepts in the question:

- **Comma Splice:** Choices and/or surrounding text use commas to join two groups of words that could each be sentences on their own. A comma can't be used in this way on the ACT English section. (See page 428)
- **Dependent and Independent Clauses:** Choices would create or join clauses. An independent clause has a main verb and can be a sentence by itself. A dependent clause can't, and starts with a conjunction or relative pronoun. (p. 426)
- **Intervening Phrase:** A phrase appears between two words that need to agree with each other grammatically. Remember to identify pairs of words that need to agree with each other, and ignore phrases that appear between those words. (See page 439)
- **Pronoun Ambiguity:** Choices include pronouns that could refer to more than one phrase in the surrounding text. We can't use a pronoun on the ACT when it isn't clear what that pronoun refers to. (See page 419)

- **Shorter is Better:** Choices include words or phrases that can be removed without impacting meaning or creating grammatical problems. The shortest grammatically acceptable choice that doesn't change the meaning is right. (p. 442)

ANSWER CHOICE ANALYSIS

A   **Incorrect:** As we noted above, this choice results in a comma splice, so it's wrong.

B   **Incorrect:** This choice has the same basic problem as (A), because "it took place in the 1950s and 1960s" can also stand on its own as a sentence.

C   **Incorrect:** This choice has the same problem as (A) and (B): "That happened in the 1950s and 1960s" can stand on its own as a sentence, with "that" as the subject and "happened" as the main verb.

D ✓   **Correct:** This is the only choice that avoids a comma splice, and it doesn't create any other issues, so we know it's right.

Answer choice patterns (page 442): shortest grammatically acceptable choice is correct

T3, Q30 (Form 16MC3 if you have 2020-2021 Red Book—see p. 23)TYPE:RC (usually has prompt; choices w/different meanings—see p. 413)

- **RC Question sub-type:** Effect of deletion. (The prompt asks what the effect would be if the author deleted a phrase or sentence. The right answer will be plainly and directly demonstrated by the text. See page 416)

Subjective Phrases to Ignore: "primarily"

ANSWER CHOICE ANALYSIS

F ✓   **Correct:** This is the only choice that's literally demonstrated by the previous sentence. The phrase "the flowers seem to celebrate…" is an "interpretation of the artwork," as (F) requires, which we know because the previous sentence tells us the flowers are in the artwork. The phrase "the women's accomplishments and…their shared vision" is a summary of the ideas in the essay, which mentions Truth, Tubman, Wells, Walker, Bethune, Hamer, Baker, and Parks, and the way they "strove…to support the cause of justice."

G   **Confused relationships:** The previous sentence doesn't even mention Ringgold. (The sentence *before* the previous sentence mentions Ringgold, but even that sentence doesn't *compare* the women to Ringgold.) (G) doesn't accurately describe the text, so it must be wrong.

H   **Barely relevant:** The sentence never says anything about the artist's "brushwork," as (H) would require. (Even if we weren't certain what "brushwork" meant, we could see that the sentence in question doesn't say anything at all about brushes or any technique, which means (H) couldn't possibly describe the text accurately.)

J   **Confused relationships:** The sentence doesn't even mention Ringgold, which (J) would require. The sentence does mention "beauty" and "accomplishments," but those words are related to the flowers and the women in the painting, not to Ringgold's talent. The sentence also doesn't say anything about Ringgold's place in history. This choice could attract some untrained test-takers who thought this whole paragraph was one sentence, and also didn't realize that it's praising the women in the painting, rather than the painter herself.

T3, Q31 (Form 16MC3 if you have 2020-2021 Red Book—see p. 23) TYPE: G/S/P (often no prompt; choices w/similar meanings—see p. 418)

- **Vertical Scan Results:** Some choices have different forms of the same base word.
- **Vertical Scan Notes:** Three of the choices involve singular verb forms ("has," "allows," and "was,"). One involves a plural verb form ("have").
- **Key Features in Surrounding Text:** The subject of the underlined verb—the word that's doing the "allow[ing]"—is the plural noun "times."

Concepts in the question:

- **Singular versus Plural:** Choices include singular and plural versions of the same base words that don't agree with other words in the surrounding text. Nouns, pronouns, and verbs must agree in number with the words they refer to or modify. (p. 423)
- **Verb Tense/Conjugation:** Choices include different forms of the same verb. Look at the surrounding text to find the verb's subject. Also look for other verbs that could indicate the proper tense or form for the verbs in the choices. (See p. 420-423)

ANSWER CHOICE ANALYSIS

A   **Incorrect:** As we noted above, this is a singular verb form, so it can't agree with the plural subject "times."

B ✓   **Correct:** This is the only choice with a plural verb form, which can agree with the plural subject "times."

C   **Incorrect:** This choice has the same basic problem as (A), because "allows" is a singular verb.

D   **Incorrect:** This choice has the same problem as (A) and (C), because "was" is singular.

Note   Many untrained test-takers will assume that the focus of this question is on the tense of the underlined verb, rather than on whether that verb is singular or plural. As trained test-takers, we should see right away that there's no definitive indication of the proper *tense* for the underlined verb—that is, no indication of whether the form of the verb should indicate that the "allow[ing]" happened in the past or the present. This means that the ACT English section can't be testing us on the verb's tense, because the ACT only does that when other verb phrases in the text make it clear which tense would be correct. Instead, this question focuses on whether the verb is singular or plural. We can tell it needs to be plural because we can see that it needs to agree with "times." Since only one answer choice is plural, we know that choice must be right. Keep this in mind on test day, when you run into a question that seems open-ended or unclear—there's a good chance you might be focusing on the wrong issue!

T3, Q32 (Form 16MC3 if you have 2020-2021 Red Book—see p. 23) TYPE: G/S/P (often no prompt; choices w/similar meanings—see p. 418)

- **Vertical Scan Results:** Similar phrases with different short words and/or punctuation.
- **Vertical Scan Notes:** We need to decide whether a comma should appear after "1902," and whether "when," "and when," "which," or "where" should appear at the end of the underlined phrase.
- **Key Features in Surrounding Text:** The underlined phrase is part of a sentence that describes when something happened.

Concepts in the question:

- **Changed Meaning:** Choices would change the meaning of the original text, or cause the relevant phrase/sentence not to make sense. The right answer must be grammatically acceptable and still preserve the original meaning. (See p. 438)
- **Commas:** Choices include commas. Commas can separate a list of 3 or more items, form sandwiches, separate interchangeable adjectives, or introduce an independent clause after a dependent clause. They can't appear for no reason. (p. 431)
- **Intervening Phrase:** A phrase appears between two words that need to agree with each other grammatically. Remember to identify pairs of words that need to agree with each other, and ignore phrases that appear between those words. (See page 439)
- **Pronoun Ambiguity:** Choices include pronouns that could refer to more than one phrase in the surrounding text. We can't use a pronoun on the ACT when it isn't clear what that pronoun refers to. (See page 419)
- **Punctuation Sandwich:** Choices involve phrases "sandwiched" between similar punctuation marks. When removed from the sentence, a proper sandwich leaves behind a grammatical sentence with the same original meaning. (See p. 432 and 433)

ANSWER CHOICE ANALYSIS

F ✓ **Correct:** This is the shortest option and it's grammatically acceptable, so, as trained test-takers, we know it has to be right. It avoids the issues in the other choices and uses the word "when" to refer back to the phrase "in 1902."

G **Incorrect:** This choice would arguably be grammatically acceptable in real life, because it could be read as a command to imagine two separate things: (1) "the excitement in 1902," and (2) the time "when audiences first saw" a particular movie. But, as trained test-takers, we can see that this choice must still be wrong on the ACT because (F) is shorter and grammatically acceptable, and because this choice would change the basic meaning of the sentence.

H **Incorrect:** Among other problems, this choice would cause the relative pronoun "which" not to refer to anything in particular, which isn't okay on the ACT English section. This choice would also have the problem that "which" should replace a noun phrase as the object of "saw" in this sentence, but the sentence already includes the object of "saw," which is *Le Voyage dans la lune.*" In other words, the word "saw" would have two objects with no logical connection in the text.

J **Incorrect:** Among other problems, this choice would make it sound like "1902" was the place "where" audiences saw the movie mentioned in the sentence, instead of being the time *when* that happened, as (F) would indicate.

Note Many untrained test-takers will focus on whether a comma should appear after "1902," but, as trained test-takers, we know that a comma isn't necessary in that position according to the ACT, which means it shouldn't be added. Instead, the key issue in this question is what should come after "1902:" should it be "when," "and when," "which," or "where?"

T3, Q33 (Form 16MC3 if you have 2020-2021 Red Book—see p. 23) TYPE: G/S/P (often no prompt; choices w/similar meanings—see p. 418)

- **Vertical Scan Results:** Some choices have different forms of the same base word.
- **Vertical Scan Notes:** Most of the choices are versions of possessive pronouns. "It's" is a contraction of "it is."
- **Key Features in Surrounding Text:** The underlined word is immediately followed by the phrase "spectacular magic productions." The previous sentence says Méliès was a "magician," and the sentence with the underlined word says "he" worked with "stage illusions." In this context, the "stage illusions" are the same as the "spectacular magic productions," so the underlined word must refers to Méliès himself, since Méliès was the person doing the magic.

Concepts in the question:

- **Plural/Possessive/Contraction:** Choices include nouns ending in "-s," with/without an apostrophe before or after the "-s." Recall the 3 rules for possessive forms (p. 424). Think of contractions in uncontracted forms ("you're" = "you are"). (p. 436)
- **Pronoun Ambiguity:** Choices include pronouns that could refer to more than one phrase in the surrounding text. We can't use a pronoun on the ACT when it isn't clear what that pronoun refers to. (See page 419)
- **Singular versus Plural:** Choices include singular and plural versions of the same base words that don't agree with other words in the surrounding text. Nouns, pronouns, and verbs must agree in number with the words they refer to or modify. (p. 423)

ANSWER CHOICE ANALYSIS

A Incorrect: As we noted above, the underlined word needs to refer to Méliès, who is a person, so we can't use any form of "it." This choice might tempt untrained test-takers who think the "spectacular stage productions" belong to the "camera."

B Incorrect: This is a plural possessive pronoun, which would be appropriate if the underlined word needed to refer to multiple people. This might attract some untrained test-takers who don't read carefully enough and assume that "Méliès" is plural because it ends in "-s," rather than being a singular noun.

C ✓ Correct: This is the singular masculine possessive pronoun "his," which is the only choice that can refer back to "Méliès" according to the ACT's grammar rules.

D Incorrect: This is a contraction of "it is," which some untrained test-takers might mistake for a possessive form—although, as we saw in the explanation for (A), the possessive form "its" would be wrong anyway.

▌ T3, Q34 (Form 16MC3 if you have 2020-2021 Red Book—see p. 23) TYPE: G/S/P (often no prompt; choices w/similar meanings—see p. 418)

- **Vertical Scan Results:** Some choices have the same words with different punctuation.
- **Vertical Scan Notes:** Should a comma appear after "out?" Should a comma, semicolon, or no punctuation appear after "however?"
- **Key Features in Surrounding Text:** The original version of the underlined phrase creates a comma sandwich around "however." This comma sandwich is acceptable under the ACT's rules because "however" can be removed from the sentence without fundamentally changing the meaning of the sentence, or causing it to break any grammar rules.

Concepts in the question:

- **Commas:** Choices include commas. Commas can separate a list of 3 or more items, form sandwiches, separate interchangeable adjectives, or introduce an independent clause after a dependent clause. They can't appear for no reason. (p. 431)
- **Dependent and Independent Clauses:** Choices would create or join clauses. An independent clause has a main verb and can be a sentence by itself. A dependent clause can't, and starts with a conjunction or relative pronoun. (p. 426)
- **Intervening Phrase:** A phrase appears between two words that need to agree with each other grammatically. Remember to identify pairs of words that need to agree with each other, and ignore phrases that appear between those words. (See page 439)
- **Punctuation Sandwich:** Choices involve phrases "sandwiched" between similar punctuation marks. When removed from the sentence, a proper sandwich leaves behind a grammatical sentence with the same original meaning. (See p. 432 and 433)
- **Semicolons:** Choices include one or more semicolons. Semicolons can be used to separate two sets of words that could each stand on their own as complete sentences. (See page 431.)

ANSWER CHOICE ANALYSIS

F ✓ Correct: As we noted above, the comma sandwich around "however" is acceptable on the ACT English section. Since this is the only choice that's grammatically acceptable according to the test's rules, we know it's right.

G Incorrect: There shouldn't be a semicolon after "however" because the part of the sentence after the semicolon couldn't stand on its own as a complete sentence, as the ACT English section requires.

H Incorrect: As trained test-takers, we know that none of the ACT's rules for comma placement will allow a single comma before "however" in this sentence. Among other things, the comma can't be part of a valid comma sandwich, because removing the words before or after the comma would fundamentally change the meaning of the sentence and/or cause it to be grammatically incomplete.

J Incorrect: This choice has issues similar to those in (H). This comma isn't used in a series, or in an acceptable sandwich, or to join a dependent clause to an independent one, etc., so it's unacceptable on the ACT English section.

Note The phrase "that the public preferred…" is an example of the use of "that" to transform a verb phrase into a noun phrase. In this case, the underlying verb phrase is the entire clause "the public preferred live magic acts to filmed versions," but adding the word "that" before this clause transforms the whole thing into a phrase that functions like a noun. In other words, the same way we could say, "He found out information," using the noun "information" as the object of "found out," we could say, "He found out that the public preferred live magic acts to filmed versions," using the entire phrase "that the public preferred live magic acts to filmed versions" as the object of "found out." You don't have to know this specifically to answer a question like this on test day, but we mention it here to clarify this issue for students who may wonder about the use of "that" in this sentence.

▌ T3, Q35 (Form 16MC3 if you have 2020-2021 Red Book—see p. 23) TYPE:RC (usually has prompt; choices w/different meanings—see p. 413)

- **RC Question sub-type:** Sentence or paragraph placement. (The prompt asks us where a sentence should go in a paragraph, or where a paragraph should go in the passage. The correct order will reflect a logical chronology, and/or will allow for pronouns to refer to nouns in a logical way, and/or will place related concepts near one another. See page 415)

ANSWER CHOICE ANALYSIS

A Causes text to refer to an idea that hasn't been mentioned yet: Sentence 1 describes Méliès as "undaunted," but at this stage in the paragraph there's no reason to think that he should be daunted by anything. Sentence 1 also includes the word "instead," but at this point in the paragraph we haven't seen any reason to use that word, either.

B   **Causes text to refer to an idea that hasn't been mentioned yet:** This choice has the same basic problem as (A): the words "undaunted" and "instead" don't make any sense, because Sentence 2 doesn't mention any reason why a reader would expect Méliès to be daunted, or what the alternative to "fantasy stories" is.

C   **Causes text to refer to an idea that hasn't been mentioned yet:** This choice has the same issue as (A) and (B).

D ✓   **Correct:** Sentence 5 says that the public liked live magic acts more than filmed magic acts. Since the paragraph discusses how Méliès hoped to film magic acts, the information in Sentence 5 would be daunting, which makes the word "Undaunted" at the beginning of Sentence 1 logical in this position. Further, the word "instead" in Sentence 1 makes logical sense if Sentence 1 is moved to the end of the paragraph, because that position allows "tell[ing] fantasy stories instead" to contrast logically with "filmed versions [of magic acts]" from Sentence 5. In other words, after Méliès found out that people didn't like filmed versions of magic acts, he decided "to tell fantasy stories instead."

Note   Many test-takers will be unfamiliar with the word "undaunted," but, as trained test-takers, we know that it's often possible to work around challenging vocabulary words on the ACT. Sure enough, we see that this question can be answered with total certainty if we ignore the word "undaunted" and focus only on the logical meaning of "instead," as we saw in the analysis above. On test day, remember not to give up on a question just because it has a term you're not familiar with—look for other indications of what the right answer must be!

T3, Q36 (Form 16MC3 if you have 2020-2021 Red Book—see p. 23)TYPE:RC (usually has prompt; choices w/different meanings—see p. 413)

- **RC Question sub-type:** Effect of deletion. (The prompt asks what the effect would be if the author deleted a phrase or sentence. The right answer will be plainly and directly demonstrated by the text. See page 416)

ANSWER CHOICE ANALYSIS

F   **Confused relationships:** The previous sentence does mention that Méliès has a "magician's eye," which is certainly relevant to the idea of his "ability as a magician"...but it never actually *describes* that ability, as (F) would require. In other words, the sentence doesn't tell us anything about the particular types of tricks that were Méliès's specialty, or whether he was particularly talented as a magician, etc.

G   **Pattern: Wrong part of the passage Incorrect:** The previous sentence mentions special effects but doesn't describe any trick photography techniques. It's true that the *following* sentence "begins" to mention specific "trick photography" techniques, as (G) would require. But the question asks about the *preceding* sentence, not the following one. This choice will attract a lot of untrained test-takers who don't pay attention to exactly which sentence is mentioned in the prompt.

H ✓   **Correct:** As (H) requires, the sentence serves as a bridge, or "transition," between the discussion of Méliès as a magician in the previous paragraph and Méliès as a filmmaker in this paragraph and the following paragraphs. The sentence mentions Méliès's "magician's eye," which refers to "Méliès the magician" as (H) requires; it also mentions Méliès "discover[ing] the basics of special effects," which is a reference to his work as a "filmmaker," as (H) also requires.

J   **Direct contradiction:** The sentence says that "Méliès's magician's eye led him to discover...special effects," which means that his interest and experience as a magician must have existed before his interest in trick photography, which is the opposite of what (J) says. This choice will attract a lot of untrained test-takers who read (J) or the sentence too quickly and mentally reverse the order described in one of them.

T3, Q37 (Form 16MC3 if you have 2020-2021 Red Book—see p. 23)TYPE:RC (usually has prompt; choices w/different meanings—see p. 413)

- **RC Question sub-type:** Best accomplishes X. (The prompt describes a goal of the author, and asks which choice achieves that goal. The right answer will be plainly demonstrated in the passage. See page 413)

     Subjective Phrases to Ignore: "best"

ANSWER CHOICE ANALYSIS

A   **Pattern: Same ballpark. Incorrect:** This choice mentions "interesting things," but doesn't specifically say *why* they were interesting—for all we know, they might have been interesting because of how embarrassing or clumsy they were, which is a possibility that the prompt doesn't allow for. Many untrained test-takers will pick this choice because they overlook the fact "interesting" doesn't necessarily mean the same thing as "skill[ful]" or "inventive[]," which is what the prompt requires.

B   **Pattern: Same ballpark. Incorrect:** Like (A), this choice doesn't specifically state that Méliès was "skill[ed]" and "inventive[]," which is what the prompt requires, because the text doesn't give us any way of knowing if the "effects...in his stage productions" required any "skill and inventiveness."

C   **Barely relevant:** This sentence tells us what "his actors" could do, which doesn't literally restate or demonstrate anything about Méliès's "skill" or "inventiveness," as (C) would require.

D ✓   **Correct:** The word "perfected" literally demonstrates that something was done with a high level of "skill," as the prompt requires, and the idea of staging "entrances and exits" using "pulleys and trapdoors" specifically demonstrates Méliès's "inventiveness," as the prompt also requires. Since this is the only choice that demonstrates skill and inventiveness in the literal-minded way required by the ACT, we know it must be right.

- **Vertical Scan Results:** Some choices have different forms of the same base word.
- **Vertical Scan Notes:** Two choices include the adverb "highly," while the other two include the adjective "high." Two choices include the adverb "excessively," while one includes the adverb "exceedingly" and the other includes the adjective "exceeding." Finally, three choices end with an adverb, and one choice ends with an adjective.
- **Key Features in Surrounding Text:** The underlined phrase describes the noun phrase "production costs of $4,000."

Concepts in the question:

- **Adjective/Adverb:** Choices involve a word in its adjective or adverb form. Remember that adverb forms often end in "-ly," but not always. Adjectives can modify nouns; adverbs can modify anything else (verbs, adjectives, other adverbs). (p. 423)

ANSWER CHOICE ANALYSIS

F   **Incorrect:** The ACT won't allow us to use an adverb (like "excessively") to modify a noun phrase (like "production costs of $4,000").

G   **Incorrect:** This choice has the same issue as (F), because "highly" is an adverb, which means it can't modify a noun phrase.

H   **Incorrect:** This choice has the same problem as (F) and (G), since it ends with an adverb.

J   ✓   **Correct:** This choice would cause the adjective "high" to modify the noun phrase "production costs of $4,000," and the adverb "exceedingly" to modify the adjective "high," all of which is acceptable according to the grammar rules of the ACT English section. Since this is the only choice that avoids using an adverb to describe a noun phrase—and also avoids any other issues—it's the only choice that's grammatically acceptable in the text, so it must be right.

Answer choice patterns (page 442): wrong answers try to imitate right answers

- **Vertical Scan Results:** Choices are long phrases/sentences.
- **Vertical Scan Notes:** All four choices include the word "fired." Three of the choices describe other, similar actions as well, using verbs like "launched," "projected," and "propelled."
- **Key Features in Surrounding Text:** The underlined phrase comes immediately before the phrase "from a cannon."

Concepts in the question:

- **Redundancy:** Choices and/or surrounding text could combine to repeat the same concept unnecessarily. On grammar/style/punctuation questions, we should avoid words that directly repeat ideas in the immediate surrounding text. (See p. 437)
- **Shorter is Better:** Choices include words or phrases that can be removed without impacting meaning or creating grammatical problems. The shortest grammatically acceptable choice that doesn't change the meaning is right. (p. 442)

ANSWER CHOICE ANALYSIS

A   **Incorrect:** "Fired," "launched," and "projected" all mean the same thing in this context, so two of these three words are redundant according to the ACT's rules.

B   ✓   **Correct:** This choice avoids the redundancy from the other choices, creating the acceptable phrase "fired from a cannon." Further, this is the shortest choice and it's grammatically correct, so, as trained test-takers, we know it must be right.

C   **Incorrect:** This choice has the same basic issue as (A), because it uses two words to repeat the same idea, which the ACT considers to be redundant, and therefore wrong.

D   **Incorrect:** This choice has the same issue as (A) and (C), except that the two redundant words are "fired" and "propelled."

Answer choice patterns (page 442): shortest grammatically acceptable choice is correct

- **Vertical Scan Results:** Choices are long phrases/sentences.
- **Vertical Scan Notes:** All four choices mention creatures, and three of the four choices make an additional statement (involving at least one comma) about the creatures.
- **Key Features in Surrounding Text:** The sentence containing the underlined phrase says that space travelers find creatures "in a strange terrain."

Concepts in the question:

- **Commas:** Choices include commas. Commas can separate a list of 3 or more items, form sandwiches, separate interchangeable adjectives, or introduce an independent clause after a dependent clause. They can't appear for no reason. (p. 431)
- **Intervening Phrase:** A phrase appears between two words that need to agree with each other grammatically. Remember to identify pairs of words that need to agree with each other, and ignore phrases that appear between those words. (See page 439)
- **Pronoun Ambiguity:** Choices include pronouns that could refer to more than one phrase in the surrounding text. We can't use a

pronoun on the ACT when it isn't clear what that pronoun refers to. (See page 419)

- **Punctuation Sandwich:** Choices involve phrases "sandwiched" between similar punctuation marks. When removed from the sentence, a proper sandwich leaves behind a grammatical sentence with the same original meaning. (See p. 432 and 433)
- **Redundancy:** Choices and/or surrounding text could combine to repeat the same concept unnecessarily. On grammar/style/punctuation questions, we should avoid words that directly repeat ideas in the immediate surrounding text. (See p. 437)
- **Shorter is Better:** Choices include words or phrases that can be removed without impacting meaning or creating grammatical problems. The shortest grammatically acceptable choice that doesn't change the meaning is right. (p. 442)
- **Who/Whom:** Choices involve "who" and "whom." "Who" is a subject pronoun (which does an action, like "he"). "Whom" is an object pronoun (which receives an action, like "him"). (See page 428)

ANSWER CHOICE ANALYSIS

F ✓ **Correct:** This choice avoids the ambiguity and redundancy from the other choices and doesn't create any other issues. Further, it's the shortest choice and it's grammatically acceptable, so we know it must be right according to the ACT.

G **Incorrect:** This choice uses the plural pronoun "they," which creates ambiguity in the sentence because there are two plural nouns in the sentence that "they" could refer to ("creatures" and "travelers"), and the ACT English section doesn't allow this kind of ambiguous pronoun use. (Some test-takers will think that the word "who" is also incorrect, but it actually isn't: without getting into too much detail, the pronoun "who" is the subject in the verb phrase "who...live there" before it's the object of the verb phrase "they now realize," so "who" is the appropriate form here, in case you were wondering.)

H **Incorrect:** This choice has a problem similar to the problem in (G), because it uses the plural pronoun "they" even though there are two plural nouns in the sentence.

J **Incorrect:** The phrase "who are found there" is redundant, since "there" would refer back to "the strange terrain," and the sentence already tells us the "creatures" are in the "strange terrain." Since the ACT English section doesn't allow redundant phrases in a sentence, we know (J) is wrong.

Answer choice patterns (page 442): shortest grammatically acceptable choice is correct

Note Once again, we see the importance of knowing the ACT's unwritten rules. While many untrained test-takers are trying to puzzle out which of these choices sounds better to them, we know right away that (F) must be right because it's the shortest choice and it doesn't pose any potential grammatical issues. Remember this kind of thing as you continue your training.

T3, Q41 (Form 16MC3 if you have 2020-2021 Red Book—see p. 23) TYPE: G/S/P (often no prompt; choices w/similar meanings—see p. 418)

- **Vertical Scan Results:** Similar phrases with different short words and/or punctuation.
- **Vertical Scan Notes:** Should there be a comma or a period after "moon," or no punctuation at all? Should "after" appear before "landing?"
- **Key Features in Surrounding Text:** The original version of the underlined phrase creates a comma splice, because "they escape…landing in the ocean" can stand alone as a sentence, and "they bob around…" can also stand alone as a sentence. (Note that this comma splice would still exist even if we considered "landing in the ocean" to be part of the second sentence, or if we treated it like a comma-sandwiched phrase that we could remove.)

Concepts in the question:

- **Comma Splice:** Choices and/or surrounding text use commas to join two groups of words that could each be sentences on their own. A comma can't be used in this way on the ACT English section. (See page 428)
- **Dependent and Independent Clauses:** Choices would create or join clauses. An independent clause has a main verb and can be a sentence by itself. A dependent clause can't, and starts with a conjunction or relative pronoun. (p. 426)

ANSWER CHOICE ANALYSIS

A **Incorrect:** As we discussed above, this choice results in a comma splice, which is unacceptable on the ACT English section.

B **Incorrect:** This choice has the same problem as (A), because it would still result in a comma splice—the only difference would be that the comma sandwich around "landing in the ocean" would be undone, but that doesn't affect the unacceptable comma splice.

C ✓ **Correct:** This choice correctly uses a period to separate two sets of words that can stand on their own as sentences.

D **Incorrect:** This choice has the same problem as (A) and (B), because everything up to and including "ocean" can stand alone as a sentence, and everything after and including "they" can stand alone as a separate sentence.

T3, Q42 (Form 16MC3 if you have 2020-2021 Red Book—see p. 23) TYPE: G/S/P (often no prompt; choices w/similar meanings—see p. 418)

- **Vertical Scan Results:** Some choices have different forms of the same base word.
- **Vertical Scan Notes:** Should the phrase include "had," "have," or "would of?" Should the phrase include "began" or "begun?"
- **Key Features in Surrounding Text:** The subject of the verb in the underlined phrase is the plural noun "explorations."

Concepts in the question:

- **Confused Homophones:** Choices include different homophone pairs (such as "their"/"they're" or "too"/"to"). Remember the correct formation of possessives. Remember to read contractions as their uncontracted forms (e.g. "it's" = "it is"). (p. 436)
- **Verb Tense/Conjugation:** Choices include different forms of the same verb. Look at the surrounding text to find the verb's subject. Also look for other verbs that could indicate the proper tense or form for the verbs in the choices. (See p. 420-423)

ANSWER CHOICE ANALYSIS

F   **Incorrect:** "Had began" is never an acceptable conjugation on the ACT English section, no matter what the context, because the past participle form of "to begin" is "begun," with a "u," and not "began," with an "a." (Acceptable conjugations would include "began" and "had begun.")

G   **Incorrect:** "Would of" can also never be part of an acceptable conjugation on the ACT English section, because "of" isn't a helping verb; instead, the phrase "would have" can be correct if the context calls for it.

H   **Incorrect:** This choice has the same problem as (F), because the form of "begin" that can be used with the helping verb "have" is "begun," with a "u."

J ✓   Correct: This is the only choice that uses the correct form of "begin" with a helping verb. As we noted for the other choices, "begun," with a "u," is the correct past participle of "to begin" on the ACT English section.

Note   In case you're wondering why "had begun" is correct, we wanted to provide a brief explanation of this type of verb. (Please bear in mind that you'll probably only see one question at most on test day that covers this topic.) "Begin" is a verb like "ring" or "sing," because it has a vowel that follows the "i"-"a"-"u" pattern for tenses. Just as we say, "I ring today, I rang yesterday, and I have rung before," or, "I sing today, I sang yesterday, and I have sung before," we say, "I begin today, I began yesterday, and I have begun before." But remember that this pattern doesn't apply to all verbs with an "i" in them. For example, there's no such thing as the form "*brang" or "*brung" to go with the verb "bring," and there's no such thing as "*thank" or "*thunk" to go with the verb "think." (Again, this isn't something you need to focus on for ACT purposes. It's just that students sometimes ask what's going on with this kind of verb, so we're explaining it here.)

T3, Q43 (Form 16MC3 if you have 2020-2021 Red Book—see p. 23)TYPE:RC (usually has prompt; choices w/different meanings—see p. 413)

- **RC Question sub-type:** Precision Vocabulary. (Choices include words or short phrases that either sound similar, or have vaguely similar but not identical meanings. Most or all of the choices will seem vaguely appropriate, but only one choice will be correct when we think very carefully and specifically about the word means and how it can be used. See page 415)

ANSWER CHOICE ANALYSIS

A   **Direct contradiction:** To "whet" someone's curiosity means the same thing as to "arouse" that person's curiosity—you may have heard the similar phrase "to whet your appetite." More literally, to "whet" something is to sharpen it, like a knife is sharpened. (See the note below for more.)

B   **Direct contradiction:** To "stimulate" someone's curiosity means the same thing as to "arouse" that person's curiosity, so (B) is also wrong.

C   **Direct contradiction:** This choice has the same issue as (A) and (B), because "awaken" is also a synonym for "arouse" in this context, just like "whet" and "stimulate" are.

D ✓   Correct: "Disturb[ing]" someone's curiosity has a negative connotation that the original version of the underlined phrase doesn't have, so (D) wouldn't be an acceptable alternative to "arouse," which makes this the only choice that satisfies the prompt.

Note   Don't be too worried if you weren't familiar with the word "whet" before answering this question. It's unlikely that you'll need to know the word "whet" to answer a question correctly on test day, since the ACT English section doesn't recycle challenging vocabulary words in that way. Still, you may see some other words on test day that you don't know. If that happens, your first instinct should be to see if you can work around the unknown word. In this case, for example, you might have been able to tell that "disturb" isn't acceptable in this context (as we saw in our discussion of (D)), so (D) must be right no matter what (A) means. On the other hand, you may not have felt very sure about any of the choices. If you find yourself in that situation, knowing that an obscure word is keeping you from answering with total confidence, then the best thing you can usually do is realize the situation quickly, mark down your best guess at an answer, and go invest your time in other questions that you can answer with certainty because they don't have vocabulary issues that you can't overcome. For more on this, see "The General Game Plan for Attacking a Section of the ACT on Test Day" on page 37.

T3, Q44 (Form 16MC3 if you have 2020-2021 Red Book—see p. 23)TYPE:RC (usually has prompt; choices w/different meanings—see p. 413)

- **RC Question sub-type:** Best accomplishes X. (The prompt describes a goal of the author, and asks which choice achieves that goal. The right answer will be plainly demonstrated in the passage. See page 413)

   Subjective Phrases to Ignore: "most effectively"

ANSWER CHOICE ANALYSIS

F **Barely relevant:** This choice doesn't refer to Méliès or his films in any way, so it can't literally demonstrate the author's view of "Méliès's role in science fiction filmmaking," as the prompt requires.

G ✓ **Correct:** This choice literally demonstrates the author's opinion of Méliès's "role in science fiction filmmaking," as the prompt requires. The phrase "this first space odyssey" refers to Méliès's work, which is described in the rest of the passage, and we know the author considers "space odyssey" to be an example of "science fiction filmmaking" because the first paragraph refers to Méliès's film as a "science fiction film[]." The phrase "provided the genesis for a genre" demonstrates the role of Méliès's work (the "space odyssey" mentioned in (G)) in science fiction filmmaking. Since this is the only choice that literally demonstrates what the prompt requires, we know it's right.

H **Pattern:** Same ballpark. **Incorrect:** This choice doesn't specifically refer to science fiction filmmaking, which is what the prompt requires. It will attract some untrained test-takers who don't read the prompt carefully enough to note the phrase "science fiction," or who don't realize that this choice doesn't mention science fiction.

J **Barely relevant:** This detail about Méliès's crew doesn't include any information about Méliès's "role in science fiction filmmaking," as the prompt requires.

T3, Q45 (Form 16MC3 if you have 2020-2021 Red Book—see p. 23) TYPE:RC (usually has prompt; choices w/different meanings—see p. 413)

- **RC Question sub-type:** Would essay fulfill goal? (The question describes a goal that the author had in writing the passage, and asks whether the author achieved that goal. The right answer choice will be directly restated or demonstrated by the passage, and logically answer the question in the prompt. See page 417)

ANSWER CHOICE ANALYSIS

A **Barely relevant:** The description in this choice isn't demonstrated in the text at all, because the passage never says anything about the "contributions" of other "artists" besides Méliès, and never even talks about whether "Méliès's work as a magician succeeded," as this choice would require.

B ✓ **Correct:** This choice is the only one whose description is literally demonstrated in the text, so, as trained test-takers, we know it must be right. Paragraph 2 tells us Méliès was a magician, as (B) requires. Paragraph 2 also tells us he was "fascinated by the...new...camera," which demonstrates the "curiosity" required in (B). Paragraph 3 tells us that his "magician's eye" played a key role in his "discover[ing] the basics of special effects," which demonstrates how he "use[d] his talents...to explore" the possibilities of film, as (B) also requires. Finally, Paragraph 5 literally demonstrates that Méliès "excel[led] in the film world" when it tells us that his movie created a genre that still attracts audiences.

C **Direct contradiction:** The essay *does* focus on a single artist's work: only Méliès's work is mentioned in the text, so the description in this choice is contradicted by the passage.

D **Barely relevant:** As we saw in our discussions of (A) and (C), the text never mentions other artists working with Méliès, so this choice doesn't accurately describe the passage.

T3, Q46 (Form 16MC3 if you have 2020-2021 Red Book—see p. 23) TYPE: G/S/P (often no prompt; choices w/similar meanings—see p. 418)

- **Vertical Scan Results:** Similar phrases with different short words and/or punctuation.
- **Vertical Scan Notes:** We need to choose between "went" and "gone," and between "out of" and "from."
- **Key Features in Surrounding Text:** The original version of the underlined phrase includes an incorrect conjugation on the ACT English section. The phrase needs to work grammatically with the helping verb "had" and the noun "style."

Concepts in the question:

- **Prepositional Idioms:** Choices typically include prepositional phrases with no other recognizable similarities. If you can't tell which choice contains an acceptable prepositional idiom in American English, guess and invest your time elsewhere. (p. 435)
- **Verb Tense/Conjugation:** Choices include different forms of the same verb. Look at the surrounding text to find the verb's subject. Also look for other verbs that could indicate the proper tense or form for the verbs in the choices. (See p. 420-423)

ANSWER CHOICE ANALYSIS

F **Incorrect:** The correctly formed past participle of "to go" is "had gone," not "*had went."

G ✓ **Correct:** As we noted for (F), "had gone" is the correctly formed past participle of "to go." Further, "out of" completes the idiomatic phrase "out of style," which is acceptable in conventional American English (see the note below).

H **Incorrect:** This choice has the same problem as (F). It also uses the wrong preposition, because the acceptable idiomatic phrase is "to go out of style," not "*to go from style."

J **Incorrect:** As we noted for (H), the acceptable idiomatic phrase is "to go out of style," not "*to go from style," so (J) is wrong.

Answer choice patterns (page 442): wrong answers try to imitate right answers

Note Many test-takers won't be able to answer this question with certainty, whether because they don't know how to conjugate "to go" appropriately, or because they aren't familiar with the prepositional idiom "out of style." As we've stressed for other questions about conjugating irregular verbs and correctly identifying prepositional idioms, the best thing you can do if you're not certain about the answer to a question like this is to recognize the situation quickly, make the best guess you can about the right answer, and then move on and invest your time in questions that don't rely on knowledge of prepositional idioms.

T3, Q47 (Form 16MC3 if you have 2020-2021 Red Book—see p. 23) TYPE: G/S/P (often no prompt; choices w/similar meanings—see p. 418)

- **Vertical Scan Results:** Some choices have different forms of the same base word.
- **Vertical Scan Notes:** Should "would" be followed by "of" or by "have?" Should "been" appear? Should the whole phrase be deleted?
- **Key Features in Surrounding Text:** The original version of the underlined phrase involves an incorrectly conjugated verb phrase, because "would of" can never be right on the ACT English section. The subject of the underlined verb phrase is the noun "sleuth," and the main verb phrase after the underlined phrase is "retired." The underlined verb occurs in the same sentence with the verb phrase "would have," this sentence says the author "was sure that" something was the case, and the sentence after the underlined phrase says the author was wrong, which means that the verbs in the underlined phrase didn't actually happen. (If that didn't make sense, rereading the first paragraph of the passage should help clear it up.)

Concepts in the question:

- **Parallelism:** Choices include options that would ignore a parallel structure in the surrounding text. The right answer should match the phrasing and grammatical structures in the surrounding text when possible. (See p. 440)
- **Verb Tense/Conjugation:** Choices include different forms of the same verb. Look at the surrounding text to find the verb's subject. Also look for other verbs that could indicate the proper tense or form for the verbs in the choices. (See p. 420-423)

ANSWER CHOICE ANALYSIS

A   **Incorrect:** As trained test-takers, we know that "would of" is never an acceptable part of a verb conjugation on the ACT English section, because "of" isn't a helping verb.

B ✓ **Correct:** This choice correctly uses "have" as a verb, instead of "of." It also uses the verb "would," which parallels the use of "would" earlier in the sentence, and makes it clear that "girls…would have" and "sleuth would have been retired" are two things the author "was sure [about]." This choice also shows that the action in the sentence didn't actually happen, as the passage requires for reasons we noted above. Since this is the only grammatically acceptable choice, we know it's right.

C   **Incorrect:** This choice has the same problem as (A), because "of" isn't a verb.

D   **Incorrect:** This choice fails to create the parallel verb structure with the phrase "would have" that appears earlier in this sentence, as we saw in our discussion of (B).

Note   This is a great example of the importance of reading the entire sentence before committing to an answer choice! Many untrained test-takers would assume that (D) was correct because they would only look at the surrounding text on the same line as the underlined phrase, which seems to say "sleuth retired" if we remove the underlined phrase. But when we read the whole sentence, we see that the verb "would" is part of the verb phrase with "have," and we know we need to pick the parallel verb structure in (B).

T3, Q48 (Form 16MC3 if you have 2020-2021 Red Book—see p. 23) TYPE: G/S/P (often no prompt; choices w/similar meanings—see p. 418)

- **Vertical Scan Results:** Some choices have different forms of the same base word; some choices have the same words with different punctuation.
- **Vertical Scan Notes:** Should "library" end in "-ies," or an apostrophe and an "s?" Should there be a comma after "dusty?"
- **Key Features in Surrounding Text:** The original version of the underlined phrase correctly uses an apostrophe and an "s" to show that the "rooms" belong to the "library[]," and the comma would indicate that the rooms are both "dusty" and "back."

Concepts in the question:

- **Commas:** Choices include commas. Commas can separate a list of 3 or more items, form sandwiches, separate interchangeable adjectives, or introduce an independent clause after a dependent clause. They can't appear for no reason. (p. 431)
- **Plural/Possessive/Contraction:** Choices include nouns ending in "-s," with/without an apostrophe before or after the "-s." Recall the 3 rules for possessive forms (p. 424). Think of contractions in uncontracted forms ("you're" = "you are"). (p. 436)

ANSWER CHOICE ANALYSIS

F   **Incorrect:** A comma isn't appropriate between the adjective "dusty" and the phrase "back rooms." Placing the comma here would mean that both adjectives describe the word "rooms" in the same way. In other words, this comma placement would indicate that the "rooms" were "dusty," and the rooms were also "back," rather than being "back rooms" that were "dusty."

G   **Incorrect:** This choice has the same comma problem as (F). It also uses the plural word "libraries," instead of the possessive form "library's." Either issue by itself would be enough to make (G) wrong.

H   **Incorrect:** As we saw for (G), the plural noun "libraries" should be the possessive form "library's" instead, to show that the "back rooms" belong to the library.

J ✓ **Correct:** This choice uses the possessive form "library's," and avoids the comma problem we saw in our discussion of (F).

- **RC Question sub-type:** Best accomplishes X. (The prompt describes a goal of the author, and asks which choice achieves that goal. The right answer will be plainly demonstrated in the passage. See page 413)

ANSWER CHOICE ANALYSIS

A **Pattern: Same ballpark. Incorrect:** The word "heaps" isn't specific, as the prompt requires, because a "heap" can be almost any size. A "heaping teaspoon" is one size, a "heaping helping" of mashed potatoes is (hopefully) larger, and a trash heap is larger still. So (A) doesn't indicate the scale of the number of novels in the sentence, which means it's less specific than (C).

B **Pattern: Same ballpark. Incorrect:** This choice has the same basic problem as (A): the phrase "a high number" could be taken a lot of ways. 1 can be a high number in statistics but a low number when it comes to legs on a table, while 5,000 is a low number of words in a dictionary but a high number of bugs in your socks, and so on.

C ✓ **Correct:** This choice tells us that Nancy Drew was in "hundreds" of novels, which provides more specificity than any other choice: it tells us she was in some number of novels that was more than a hundred and less than a thousand, while the other choices could conceivably refer to almost any number of books.

D **Pattern: Same ballpark. Incorrect:** This choice has the same problem as (A) or (B): whether a number can be called "plenty" depends entirely on the context, so almost any amount could be called "plenty." For instance, some people might think 5 silly examples of numerical subjectivity are plenty, while other people would require 6 examples before feeling like they had learned this concept.

- **Vertical Scan Results:** Some choices have the same words with different punctuation.
- **Vertical Scan Notes:** Should "novels" have a comma after it? Should "alive" have a comma after it?
- **Key Features in Surrounding Text:** The original version of the phrase creates an acceptable comma sandwich around the phrase "the teenaged heroine…novels," because the phrase can be removed from the original sentence without fundamentally changing the meaning of the sentence or causing any grammatical issues.

Concepts in the question:

- **Commas:** Choices include commas. Commas can separate a list of 3 or more items, form sandwiches, separate interchangeable adjectives, or introduce an independent clause after a dependent clause. They can't appear for no reason. (p. 431)
- **Intervening Phrase:** A phrase appears between two words that need to agree with each other grammatically. Remember to identify pairs of words that need to agree with each other, and ignore phrases that appear between those words. (See page 439)
- **Parallelism:** Choices include options that would ignore a parallel structure in the surrounding text. The right answer should match the phrasing and grammatical structures in the surrounding text when possible. (See p. 440)
- **Punctuation Sandwich:** Choices involve phrases "sandwiched" between similar punctuation marks. When removed from the sentence, a proper sandwich leaves behind a grammatical sentence with the same original meaning. (See p. 432 and 433)

ANSWER CHOICE ANALYSIS

F ✓ **Correct:** As we noted above, this choice creates an acceptable punctuation sandwich around the phrase "the teenaged heroine of heaps of young adult mystery novels."

G **Incorrect:** This choice creates the same acceptable punctuation sandwich that we discussed for (F), but it adds an unacceptable comma after "alive." There are a variety of ways to know that the comma after "alive" isn't okay on the ACT, but the easiest is probably to notice the parallelism in the phrase "alive and well and still…;" inserting a comma before only one of the "and"s would undo this parallelism. (Another issue is the use of a comma and the word "and" to separate the first two things in a list of three things, which we know the ACT doesn't allow from the training on page 431 of this book.)

H **Incorrect:** (H) would create an unacceptable punctuation sandwich around "the teenaged…is alive," because removing that sandwiched phrase would leave behind the ungrammatical sentence "*Nancy Drew and well and still on the job."

J **Incorrect:** This choice would cause the sentence to become a direct statement from the author to Nancy Drew herself, informing her that some other teenaged heroine was still on the job, which changes the meaning of the sentence and also makes no logical sense in the paragraph.

- **Vertical Scan Results:** Some choices are short phrases with no obvious similarity.
- **Vertical Scan Notes:** Two of the choices include the word "that." Two choices include at least one preposition (either "over" or "up on"). Only one choice is plural.
- **Key Features in Surrounding Text:** The original version of the underlined phrase is a singular pronoun that doesn't have a noun phrase on the page that it clearly refers to.

Concepts in the question:

- **Prepositional Idioms:** Choices typically include prepositional phrases with no other recognizable similarities. If you can't tell which choice contains an acceptable prepositional idiom in American English, guess and invest your time elsewhere. (p. 435)
- **Pronoun Ambiguity:** Choices include pronouns that could refer to more than one phrase in the surrounding text. We can't use a pronoun on the ACT when it isn't clear what that pronoun refers to. (See page 419)
- **Singular versus Plural:** Choices include singular and plural versions of the same base words that don't agree with other words in the surrounding text. Nouns, pronouns, and verbs must agree in number with the words they refer to or modify. (p. 423)

ANSWER CHOICE ANALYSIS

A   **Incorrect:** As we noted above, this choice is unacceptable on the ACT English section because there's no specific singular noun phrase on the page that could replace the singular pronoun "that."

B ✓   **Correct:** This choice avoids the ambiguity in the other choices by causing the phrase "the mysteries" to be the things that the "niece…and…friends" were reading. This phrase refers back to "young adult mystery novels" in the previous sentence.

C   **Incorrect:** This choice has the same basic problem as (A): it uses the singular pronoun "that" even though the text doesn't specify a singular noun that the pronoun could be replacing.

D   **Incorrect:** Like (A) and (C), this choice must be wrong because it uses a singular pronoun ("it") that doesn't clearly refer to any singular noun in context.

Note   Many untrained test-takers will assume that it's fine to refer to the whole body of Nancy Drew books as "that" or "it," because native speakers of American English might do that in everyday speech. But, as trained test-takers, we know that the ACT English section only allows us to use a pronoun when that pronoun agrees grammatically with a specific noun somewhere on the page, which doesn't happen here. (The phrase "Nancy Drew" is used in the passage only as the name of a character, not as a generic term for all Nancy Drew material, the way someone might say, "Did you read all of the Shakespeare for the literature final?".) This is one more example of the importance of understanding the differences between normal spoken English and the unwritten rules of the ACT English section!

T3, Q52 (Form 16MC3 if you have 2020-2021 Red Book—see p. 23) TYPE: G/S/P (often no prompt; choices w/similar meanings—see p. 418)

- **Vertical Scan Results:** Similar phrases with different short words and/or punctuation.
- **Vertical Scan Notes:** Should there be a comma after "school?" Should "and" be included? Should "she" be included? Should "had" or "having" be included?
- **Key Features in Surrounding Text:** The original version of the underlined phrase makes the "sentence" into one long dependent clause that never actually gets around to saying what happened "by the time Liana went back." Further, we know from the phrase "and had explored" that the form of the verb "to follow" must be parallel to the verb "had explored," in order for "and" to make logical and grammatical sense there. The phrase "by the time…" indicates that the underlined verb needs to show an action happening *before* the past tense verb "Liana went," because "by the time" indicates that something else has already been completed.

Concepts in the question:

- **Commas:** Choices include commas. Commas can separate a list of 3 or more items, form sandwiches, separate interchangeable adjectives, or introduce an independent clause after a dependent clause. They can't appear for no reason. (p. 431)
- **Dependent and Independent Clauses:** Choices would create or join clauses. An independent clause has a main verb and can be a sentence by itself. A dependent clause can't, and starts with a conjunction or relative pronoun. (p. 426)
- **Intervening Phrase:** A phrase appears between two words that need to agree with each other grammatically. Remember to identify pairs of words that need to agree with each other, and ignore phrases that appear between those words. (See page 439)
- **Parallelism:** Choices include options that would ignore a parallel structure in the surrounding text. The right answer should match the phrasing and grammatical structures in the surrounding text when possible. (See p. 440)
- **Punctuation Sandwich:** Choices involve phrases "sandwiched" between similar punctuation marks. When removed from the sentence, a proper sandwich leaves behind a grammatical sentence with the same original meaning. (See p. 432 and 433)
- **Verb Tense/Conjugation:** Choices include different forms of the same verb. Look at the surrounding text to find the verb's subject. Also look for other verbs that could indicate the proper tense or form for the verbs in the choices. (See p. 420-423)

ANSWER CHOICE ANALYSIS

F   **Incorrect:** This choice creates a non-sentence that's just one long dependent clause, as we noted above, so it must be wrong.

G ✓   **Correct:** This choice uses the phrase "had followed," which is parallel to the phrase "had explored" and creates the independent clause "she had followed…and had explored… *Cipher*." Since it's the only choice that creates a grammatically acceptable sentence, we know it's right.

H   **Incorrect:** This choice has a variety of issues. One of the clearest ones is that it doesn't provide a subject for the verb phrase "had explored," since there's no subject and no main verb in this version of the sentence, which basically turns this into a non-sentence composed of two dependent clauses: "by the time…school" and "having followed…*Cipher*."

J   Incorrect: The biggest problem with this choice is that it doesn't satisfy the ACT's requirements for verb forms to be parallel when they describe events in the same timeframe, because this causes the sentence to say, "by the time Liana went back, she followed Nancy...and had explored...." This choice will attract some untrained test-takers who apply their knowledge of spoken American English and don't bother to read the entire sentence, so that they never notice the phrase "and had explored." It could also attract some test-takers who mistakenly assume that the underlined verb needs to be parallel with the phrase "Liana went," instead of showing an action that happened *before* "Liana went," which is what the phrase "by the time" requires, as we discussed above.

T3, Q53 (Form 16MC3 if you have 2020-2021 Red Book—see p. 23) TYPE: G/S/P (often no prompt; choices w/similar meanings—see p. 418)

- **Vertical Scan Results:** Some choices have the same words with different punctuation.
- **Vertical Scan Notes:** We need to decide whether there should be a colon, semicolon, comma, or no punctuation after "solve."
- **Key Features in Surrounding Text:** The underlined phrase is a verb, and the object of that verb (*"The Spider Sapphire Mystery"*) immediately follows the underlined phrase.

Concepts in the question:

- **Colons:** Choices include colons. A colon can only be placed after a set of words that could be a sentence on their own, and only before a demonstration or example of the idea before the colon. No more than one colon per sentence. (p. 430)
- **Commas:** Choices include commas. Commas can separate a list of 3 or more items, form sandwiches, separate interchangeable adjectives, or introduce an independent clause after a dependent clause. They can't appear for no reason. (p. 431)
- **Semicolons:** Choices include one or more semicolons. Semicolons can be used to separate two sets of words that could each stand on their own as complete sentences. (See page 431.)

ANSWER CHOICE ANALYSIS

A ✓   Correct: For the reasons noted below, no punctuation is appropriate between the verb "solve" and its object, *"The Spider Sapphire Mystery."*

B   Incorrect: According to the rules of the ACT English section, there shouldn't be a colon after "solve," because the part of the sentence before the colon can't stand alone as a sentence, and the part after the colon isn't an example or explanation of what comes before the colon.

C   Incorrect: There shouldn't be a semicolon after "solve" because the groups of words before and after the semicolon can't each stand on their own as a complete sentence.

D   Incorrect: As trained test-takers, we see that this situation doesn't fit any of the times when a comma is acceptable on the ACT English section, because it would come immediately between the verb action "solve" and its object, *"The Spider Sapphire Mystery."*

T3, Q54 (Form 16MC3 if you have 2020-2021 Red Book—see p. 23) TYPE:RC (usually has prompt; choices w/different meanings—see p. 413)

- **RC Question sub-type:** Best accomplishes X. (The prompt describes a goal of the author, and asks which choice achieves that goal. The right answer will be plainly demonstrated in the passage. See page 413)

Subjective Phrases to Ignore: "best"

ANSWER CHOICE ANALYSIS

F   Pattern: Same ballpark. **Incorrect:** The phrases "different places" and "various cultures" don't actually give examples of what those places or cultures are, so they don't "illustrate[] the variety of settings," as the prompt requires.

G   Pattern: Same ballpark. **Incorrect:** The phrases "breathtaking adventures" and "colorful characters" don't actually tell us anything about the "settings" referred to in the prompt, because they don't mention settings at all—so (G) can't be right.

H ✓   Correct: This choice is the only one that literally demonstrates an "illustrat[ion]" of a "variety of settings," as the prompt requires, since Arizona, Argentina, Nairobi, and New York are all actual examples of different settings. The choice also demonstrates "Liana's interest" when it says that she "had chased suspects" with "Nancy in the lead," because Liana must be "interest[ed]," as the prompt requires, if she's actively "chas[ing] suspects."

J   Pattern: Same ballpark. **Incorrect:** This choice has a similar problem to the one in (F): the phrase "many new places around the world" doesn't actually provide any examples of the "variety of settings." Further, this choice doesn't demonstrate that Liana was really "interest[ed]" in the books, as the prompt requires, because it only says that "exposure" to them caused Liana to "learn[]" something, rather than saying that Liana was actively engaged in the books. Either issue is enough to make this choice wrong.

T3, Q55 (Form 16MC3 if you have 2020-2021 Red Book—see p. 23) TYPE:RC (usually has prompt; choices w/different meanings—see p. 413)

- **RC Question sub-type:** Including/excluding a phrase/sentence. (The question asks whether a given sentence or phrase should be included in the passage. The correct choice will include a comment that plainly describes the role of the phrase or sentence in the passage. Sentences that should be included will follow broad ACT standards for ideal sentences and paragraphs, while sentences that shouldn't be included will not follow those standards. See p. 416)

ANSWER CHOICE ANALYSIS

A   Pattern: Wrong part of the passage. **Incorrect:** This choice might be tempting to untrained test-takers who think that a series "begun in 1930" that includes "173 books" demonstrates "longevity," but the given sentence doesn't actually say anything about the *popularity* of the books, as this choice would require. In other words, it's possible for an author to write 173 books in a series and not have a single person read the books, or only have a small group of people ever read them or like them. So this choice doesn't accurately describe the provided sentence, and it must be wrong. (This choice might tempt test-takers who try to answer based on the previous sentence in the passage, which demonstrates the book's popularity with the author and her friends, but, as trained test-takers, we know that (A) requires *the sentence in the prompt* to "support[] statements about the…popularity" of the series, and that sentence doesn't restate or demonstrate the idea of "popularity.")

B   **Barely relevant:** The description in (B) isn't literally demonstrated by the text, because the sentence in the prompt doesn't say anything that would "explain" anyone's love for Nancy Drew—it just says that 173 books were written, but this doesn't tell us *why* the author loved those books, as (B) would require. (B) might attract some test-takers who get confused about what the prompt actually asked them about, and end up picking (B) because the rest of the paragraph explains the author's love of Nancy Drew (even though the sentence in the prompt doesn't explain that, which is what (B) would require).

C ✓ **Correct:** The rest of the paragraph discusses things that the narrator loved about Nancy Drew, such as her "companions" and "bravado," and how "confident" and "successful" she was. But the sentence from the prompt provides unrelated information about when the Nancy Drew Mystery Story series began, and how many total books were in the series, so (C) accurately describes the text: the sentence in the prompt isn't related to an explanation of why the author loved Nancy Drew. Excluding sentences that "distract[] from the main focus" of a paragraph follows the ACT's broader rules for ideal sentences and paragraphs, so we know (C) is right. (As we'll see below, the description in (D) is also literally demonstrated by the text, but the reasoning in (D) doesn't follow the ACT's unwritten rules about adding sentences to paragraphs.)

D   **Barely relevant:** It's true that the sentence in the prompt doesn't "include relevant information about the author of the series," just as (D) describes. But, as trained test-takers, we have to remember that the right answer to a question about including or excluding a phrase or sentence on the ACT English section must satisfy two requirements: first, it must accurately describe the text, and then its reasoning must follow the ACT's unwritten rules for ideal sentences and paragraphs. This choice fails to meet the second requirement because the sentence from the prompt would still be irrelevant even if it provided information about the author of the series, since the paragraph is about why someone loved Nancy Drew, not about the author of the Nancy Drew series.

T3, Q56 (Form 16MC3 if you have 2020-2021 Red Book—see p. 23) TYPE: G/S/P (often no prompt; choices w/similar meanings—see p. 418)

- **Vertical Scan Results:** Similar phrases with different short words and/or punctuation.
- **Vertical Scan Notes:** Three choices include the phrase "to do what she wanted," while one has the phrase "to do as one wants." The choices all mention the idea of freedom in different ways.
- **Key Features in Surrounding Text:** The underlined phrase is the third thing in a comma-separated list that includes "her loyal companions" and "her bravado." According to the ACT's rules, the right answer should have a structure that's parallel to the structure of the other two list items.

Concepts in the question:

- **Commas:** Choices include commas. Commas can separate a list of 3 or more items, form sandwiches, separate interchangeable adjectives, or introduce an independent clause after a dependent clause. They can't appear for no reason. (p. 431)
- **Parallelism:** Choices include options that would ignore a parallel structure in the surrounding text. The right answer should match the phrasing and grammatical structures in the surrounding text when possible. (See p. 440)
- **Pronoun Ambiguity:** Choices include pronouns that could refer to more than one phrase in the surrounding text. We can't use a pronoun on the ACT when it isn't clear what that pronoun refers to. (See page 419)
- **Verb Tense/Conjugation:** Choices include different forms of the same verb. Look at the surrounding text to find the verb's subject. Also look for other verbs that could indicate the proper tense or form for the verbs in the choices. (See p. 420-423)

ANSWER CHOICE ANALYSIS

F   **Incorrect:** This choice isn't parallel to the phrases "her loyal companions" and "her bravado," because it starts with the phrase "there was" instead of the word "her."

G   **Incorrect:** This choice has the same basic problem as (F): it doesn't start with "her," so it can't be parallel to "her loyal companions" and "her bravado."

H ✓ **Correct:** This choice is the only one that has a structure parallel to "her loyal companions" and "her bravado," because it puts the phrase "her freedom" right after the word "and." So we know it's the right answer.

J   **Incorrect:** Like (F) and (G), this choice isn't parallel to "her loyal companions" and "her bravado." It also switches the pronoun "she" to "one," and changes the verb tense from the past (which is parallel to "loved" earlier in the sentence) to the present. Any of these issues would be enough to make (H) wrong. This choice may attract untrained test-takers who think that "one" sounds more formal than "she," and assume that the ACT will reward a more formal phrase.

- **RC Question sub-type:** Transition Phrase. (The choices reflect different kinds of transitions between two concepts, with words or phrases like "however," "instead of," or "for example." The right answer must reflect the relationship between the previous concept in the passage and the following concept in the passage. See p. 416)

ANSWER CHOICE ANALYSIS

A   **Direct contradiction:** The previous sentence describes something "we loved," and this sentence also describes something else "we…loved." So the meaning of the word "furthermore" is literally demonstrated by the relationship among the ideas in the text, because this sentence provides further information that's similar to the information in the previous sentence.

B ✓ **Correct:** "Therefore" would indicate some kind of causal relationship. It would only be acceptable if the narrator and her friends "loved how smart she was and how pretty, how confident and successful" *because* they loved "her loyal companions, her bravado, and her freedom to do what she wanted," but the text never indicates that one kind of love was the reason for the other, so (B) is the only choice that isn't acceptable.

C   **Direct contradiction:** "Likewise" means something similar to "furthermore" from (A), so (C) has the same issue (A) has.

D   **Direct contradiction:** Removing the phrase still causes the second of the two consecutive sentences to talk about more things the narrator and her friend loved, so it wouldn't cause any kind of contradiction or other issue in the text.

Answer choice patterns (page 442): functionally equivalent answer choices

- **Vertical Scan Results:** Some choices have different forms of the same base word.
- **Vertical Scan Notes:** One choice has "solve," while two have "solving" and one has "solved." One choice has "was able to," while one has "was capable of" and another has "was good at."
- **Key Features in Surrounding Text:** The underlined phrase is part of a comma-separated list that includes "win golf tournaments," "kick bad guys in the shins," and "impress her father's distinguished clients."

Concepts in the question:

- **Commas:** Choices include commas. Commas can separate a list of 3 or more items, form sandwiches, separate interchangeable adjectives, or introduce an independent clause after a dependent clause. They can't appear for no reason. (p. 431)
- **Parallelism:** Choices include options that would ignore a parallel structure in the surrounding text. The right answer should match the phrasing and grammatical structures in the surrounding text when possible. (See p. 440)
- **Verb Tense/Conjugation:** Choices include different forms of the same verb. Look at the surrounding text to find the verb's subject. Also look for other verbs that could indicate the proper tense or form for the verbs in the choices. (See p. 420-423)

ANSWER CHOICE ANALYSIS

F ✓ **Correct:** The word "solve" is parallel to the other verbs in the comma-separated list: "win," "kick," and "impress." Since this is the only choice that follows the ACT's grammar rules, we know it's right.

G   **Incorrect:** The word "solving" isn't parallel to the other verbs in the comma-separated list, since they don't end in "-ing."

H   **Incorrect:** This choice also uses "solving," so it has the same basic problem as (G).

J   **Incorrect:** As we saw for (F), the other verbs in the comma-separated list don't end in "-ed," so "solved" can't be part of the right answer.

- **Vertical Scan Results:** Similar phrases with different short words and/or punctuation.
- **Vertical Scan Notes:** Should there be a semicolon or comma after "successful," or no punctuation at all? Should "they" appear? Should "already" appear? Should "know" be in the "-ing" form?
- **Key Features in Surrounding Text:** The original version of the underlined phrase creates a run-on sentence, because two independent clauses ("they…successful" and "they know that") are placed next to each other without a punctuation mark or conjunction between them. This is unacceptable on the ACT English section.

Concepts in the question:

- **Changed Meaning:** Choices would change the meaning of the original text, or cause the relevant phrase/sentence not to make sense. The right answer must be grammatically acceptable and still preserve the original meaning. (See p. 438)
- **Comma Splice:** Choices and/or surrounding text use commas to join two groups of words that could each be sentences on their own. A comma can't be used in this way on the ACT English section. (See page 428)
- **Dangling Participle:** When a phrase is joined to the main sentence by a comma and the phrase starts with an -ing/-ed/-en word, the first noun phrase in the independent clause is performing the action of the -ing/-ed/-en word. (See page 434.)
- **Dependent and Independent Clauses:** Choices would create or join clauses. An independent clause has a main verb and can be a

sentence by itself. A dependent clause can't, and starts with a conjunction or relative pronoun. (p. 426)

- **Parallelism:** Choices include options that would ignore a parallel structure in the surrounding text. The right answer should match the phrasing and grammatical structures in the surrounding text when possible. (See p. 440)
- **Proximity:** Answer choice(s) would place descriptive phrases next to ideas they don't describe. (See page 434)
- **Run-on Sentence:** Choices and/or surrounding text include consecutive sentences not separated by any punctuation. If two consecutive sets of words can stand on their own as sentences, they need to be separated by a period or a semicolon. (p. 428)
- **Semicolons:** Choices include one or more semicolons. Semicolons can be used to separate two sets of words that could each stand on their own as complete sentences. (See page 431.)
- **Shorter is Better:** Choices include words or phrases that can be removed without impacting meaning or creating grammatical problems. The shortest grammatically acceptable choice that doesn't change the meaning is right. (p. 442)
- **Verb Tense/Conjugation:** Choices include different forms of the same verb. Look at the surrounding text to find the verb's subject. Also look for other verbs that could indicate the proper tense or form for the verbs in the choices. (See p. 420-423)

ANSWER CHOICE ANALYSIS

A   **Incorrect:** As we noted above, this choice would cause two independent clauses ("they don't need…successful" and "they know that") to appear with no punctuation or conjunction between them, which the ACT English section doesn't allow.

B   **Incorrect:** This choice would have the same problem as (A): it causes two independent clauses ("they…successful" and "they already know that") to appear with nothing between them. The fact that one clause would have the word "already" doesn't fix the problem from the original version of the phrase.

C ✓ **Correct:** This choice places a semicolon between the two independent clauses we noted above ("they…successful" and "they know that"), which follows the ACT's rules for semicolon use, and uses parallelism to make it clear that "they" in both clauses refers to the same group, and "that" in both clauses refers to the same idea. Also, the verbs "need" and "know" are in the same form and tense, which reflects the logical connection between knowing something and not needing to be reminded of that thing. Since this is the only choice that follows all of the ACT's rules, we know it's right.

D   **Incorrect:** Among other issues, (D) would make it unclear what "that" in the phrase "knowing that" referred to. One possible meaning for "that" would be "Nancy Drew [is] a successful girl detective," and another possible meaning would be that the narrator is "overly optimistic," and still another possible meaning for "that" would be "girls can be successful." Since this choice causes the sentence to be ambiguous and not to reflect the clear meaning of the surrounding text, we know it's wrong.

Answer choice patterns (page 442): wrong answers try to imitate right answers

T3, Q60 (Form 16MC3 if you have 2020-2021 Red Book—see p. 23) TYPE:RC (usually has prompt; choices w/different meanings—see p. 413)

- **RC Question sub-type:** Best accomplishes X. (The prompt describes a goal of the author, and asks which choice achieves that goal. The right answer will be plainly demonstrated in the passage. See page 413)

Subjective Phrases to Ignore: "most effectively"

ANSWER CHOICE ANALYSIS

F ✓ **Correct:** The prompt tells us to pick the choice that "supports…the first part of [the] sentence" that includes the question. As trained test-takers, we know that the right answer to an ACT question based on reading comprehension like this one will have to be literally restated or demonstrated in the relevant text, which is the first part of the sentence in this case. We can see that the first part of the sentence mentions "the stories themselves;" (F) is the only choice that includes a restatement of the phrase "the stories," which occurs in the phrase "those exciting adventure tales." Since this is the only choice that involves literal restatement of the "first part of the sentence" as the prompt requires, it's right.

G   **Reasonable statement not in the text:** As we saw in our discussion of (F), the right answer needs to be restated or demonstrated in the first part of the sentence, which talks about "stories." But (G) doesn't even mention stories. In fact, nothing in this choice literally restates an idea from earlier in the sentence, as the prompt requires, so (G) is wrong. This choice will attract some untrained test-takers who think it sounds prettier or more literary than the other choices, but, as trained test-takers, we know that the ACT doesn't care if a phrase sounds more literary than another phrase.

H   **Barely relevant:** This choice has the same basic problem as (G): it doesn't even refer to "stories," so it can't support the statement about the "stories" from the first half of the sentence, according to the ACT's rules.

J   **Barely relevant:** This choice has the same issue as (G) and (H).

T3, Q61 (Form 16MC3 if you have 2020-2021 Red Book—see p. 23) TYPE: G/S/P (often no prompt; choices w/similar meanings—see p. 418)

- **Vertical Scan Results:** Some choices are short phrases with no obvious similarity.
- **Vertical Scan Notes:** One choice has two words, while the rest are each one word. There's no obvious similarity among the words in the choices, apart from the fact that they're all short words.
- **Key Features in Surrounding Text:** The sentence with the underlined phrase includes multiple commas. The next phrase after the first comma begins with "to." The original version of the underlined phrase causes the sentence to include two independent clauses

("there were…Negral" and "this planet…danger") with a comma-sandwiched prepositional phrase ("to…best-sellers") between them. This isn't acceptable on the ACT English section because, among other things, removing the sandwiched phrase would cause the sentence to consist of two consecutive independent clauses without a semicolon, period, colon, or conjunction between them. The sandwiched phrase also has no clear connection to the clause before or after it, and makes no sense in the context of the rest of the original version of the sentence, because it's not clear what's going "to" the "writers."

Concepts in the question:

- **Comma Splice:** Choices and/or surrounding text use commas to join two groups of words that could each be sentences on their own. A comma can't be used in this way on the ACT English section. (See page 428)
- **Commas:** Choices include commas. Commas can separate a list of 3 or more items, form sandwiches, separate interchangeable adjectives, or introduce an independent clause after a dependent clause. They can't appear for no reason. (p. 431)
- **Dependent and Independent Clauses:** Choices would create or join clauses. An independent clause has a main verb and can be a sentence by itself. A dependent clause can't, and starts with a conjunction or relative pronoun. (p. 426)
- **Intervening Phrase:** A phrase appears between two words that need to agree with each other grammatically. Remember to identify pairs of words that need to agree with each other, and ignore phrases that appear between those words. (See page 439)
- **Prepositional Idioms:** Choices typically include prepositional phrases with no other recognizable similarities. If you can't tell which choice contains an acceptable prepositional idiom in American English, guess and invest your time elsewhere. (p. 435)
- **Punctuation Sandwich:** Choices involve phrases "sandwiched" between similar punctuation marks. When removed from the sentence, a proper sandwich leaves behind a grammatical sentence with the same original meaning. (See p. 432 and 433)

ANSWER CHOICE ANALYSIS

A   **Incorrect:** As we noted above, this choice creates an unacceptable comma sandwich between two independent clauses. This choice might attract untrained test-takers who don't read carefully enough, and think the comma after "Negral" is a period.

B   **Incorrect:** This choice does avoid the problem of having two independent clauses that we saw in (A), but it creates other problems. One of those problems, simply put, is that it creates the phrase "When…astronomers who associated Mars…," but it never tells us what else those astronomers did in the timeframe that corresponds to the word "when." Another issue, as we'll see in our discussion of (C), is that it doesn't change the fact that the phrase "to…best-sellers" doesn't make any sense and isn't connected to any idea in the rest of this non-sentence.

C ✓   **Correct:** This is the only choice that causes "to…best-sellers" to make any sense, because it now corresponds to the phrase "from…Negral," allowing the sentence to demonstrate a range of time (basically "from…ancient [times]…to [the] twentieth century.") This choice also causes the sentence to have only one independent clause ("this planet…danger"), which is now preceded by two prepositional phrases describing a time period over which the independent clause is true.

D   **Incorrect:** This choice has a problem similar to (B): it causes the sentence to start out seeming like it's going to tell us what else the "astronomers" did, but then the sentence never does that. This choice also has the same issue with "to…best-sellers" that we noted in the other wrong answers. This choice might attract untrained test-takers who overlook the word "who" and think the comma after "Negral" is a period.

T3, Q62 (Form 16MC3 if you have 2020-2021 Red Book—see p. 23)TYPE:RC (usually has prompt; choices w/different meanings—see p. 413)

- **RC Question sub-type:** Best accomplishes X. (The prompt describes a goal of the author, and asks which choice achieves that goal. The right answer will be plainly demonstrated in the passage. See page 413)

Subjective Phrases to Ignore: "most"

ANSWER CHOICE ANALYSIS

F   **Barely relevant:** The next statement in the sentence says that Mars "has often been a symbol of ill will and danger," but (F) doesn't have anything to do with the idea of ill will or danger, as the prompt requires, so it's wrong.

G   **Barely relevant:** This choice has the same basic problem as (F), because a "wild imagination[]" about "outer space" doesn't have any necessary connection to "ill will" or "danger."

H ✓   **Correct:** The phrase "spine-tingling" describes something scary, which is relevant to the idea of "danger" from the text. Since this is the only choice that satisfies the requirement from the prompt, we know it must be right.

J   **Barely relevant:** This choice has the same problem as (F) and (G): it doesn't have any direct connection to the idea of "ill will" or "danger," so it can't be right.

T3, Q63 (Form 16MC3 if you have 2020-2021 Red Book—see p. 23)TYPE:RC (usually has prompt; choices w/different meanings—see p. 413)

- **RC Question sub-type:** Best accomplishes X. (The prompt describes a goal of the author, and asks which choice achieves that goal. The right answer will be plainly demonstrated in the passage. See page 413)

Subjective Phrases to Ignore: "best"

ANSWER CHOICE ANALYSIS

A   **Barely relevant:** When the ACT talks about leading from one paragraph to another, it wants us to find a sentence that restates elements of both paragraphs. The preceding paragraph is about how Mars has been "a symbol of ill will and danger," but this choice doesn't refer to that idea at all. This choice also doesn't refer to concepts from the rest of this paragraph, because this paragraph doesn't mention other countries, or competition.

B ✓   **Correct:** The phrase "such negative associations" refers to the phrases "ill will" and "danger" from the previous sentence. The idea that those "negative associations" are "dissipating" is then demonstrated by the rest of this paragraph, which talks about people being "excit[ed]" by the idea of a "mission to Mars." Since this choice is the only one that mentions ideas from the preceding text and the following text—as the prompt requires—it must be the right answer.

C   **Confused relationships:** This choice discusses concepts that are related to the following sentence, which mentions NASA…but it doesn't restate anything from the previous paragraph, as the prompt requires it to do. This choice might attract untrained test-takers who think the prompt is only asking them for a sentence that leads into the next sentence in the paragraph, without thinking about the previous paragraph.

D   **Barely relevant:** This choice might tempt some test-takers, because it does mention Mars, and both relevant paragraphs in the passage mention Mars as well. But, according to the ACT's rules, we can't "lead[]" from "one paragraph to the subject of [another] paragraph" by talking about just one concept that appears in both paragraphs—and this choice also mentions two other concepts ("Earth" and "the inner solar system") that don't appear in either paragraph!

T3, Q64 (Form 16MC3 if you have 2020-2021 Red Book—see p. 23) TYPE: G/S/P (often no prompt; choices w/similar meanings—see p. 418)

- **Vertical Scan Results:** Some choices have different forms of the same base word.
- **Vertical Scan Notes:** We need to pick the appropriate version of the verb "to send."
- **Key Features in Surrounding Text:** The subject of the verb in the underlined phrase is the singular noun "National Aeronautics and Space Administration."

Concepts in the question:

- **Confused Homophones:** Choices include different homophone pairs (such as "their"/"they're" or "too"/"to"). Remember the correct formation of possessives. Remember to read contractions as their uncontracted forms (e.g. "it's" = "it is"). (p. 436)
- **Intervening Phrase:** A phrase appears between two words that need to agree with each other grammatically. Remember to identify pairs of words that need to agree with each other, and ignore phrases that appear between those words. (See page 439)
- **Singular versus Plural:** Choices include singular and plural versions of the same base words that don't agree with other words in the surrounding text. Nouns, pronouns, and verbs must agree in number with the words they refer to or modify. (p. 423)
- **Verb Tense/Conjugation:** Choices include different forms of the same verb. Look at the surrounding text to find the verb's subject. Also look for other verbs that could indicate the proper tense or form for the verbs in the choices. (See p. 420-423)

ANSWER CHOICE ANALYSIS

F   **Incorrect:** This choice includes the ungrammatical phrase "would of," which is never acceptable on the ACT because "of" isn't a helping verb.

G ✓   **Correct:** This is the only choice with a properly formed singular verb form, which can agree grammatically with the singular subject of the sentence, as we noted above.

H   **Incorrect:** "Send" is a plural verb form, so it doesn't agree with the singular subject of this sentence. This choice might attract some untrained test-takers who misread it as "sent."

J   **Incorrect:** "Have sent" is a plural verb form, like the one in (H), so it doesn't agree with the singular subject of this sentence. This choice might appeal to test-takers who incorrectly think the plural noun "Aeronautics" is the subject of the verb, instead of the singular noun "National Aeronautics and Space Administration."

Note   Some untrained test-takers will assume that the focus of this question is on whether the verb should be in the simple past ("sent") or the past participle ("had sent"). But, as it turns out, the deciding issue in the question is that the verb should be singular, and there's only one singular verb form in the choices. Remember this kind of thing on test day—evaluate the choices that the test provides, instead of assuming beforehand that you know what a question is asking!

T3, Q65 (Form 16MC3 if you have 2020-2021 Red Book—see p. 23) TYPE: G/S/P (often no prompt; choices w/similar meanings—see p. 418)

- **Vertical Scan Results:** Similar phrases with different short words and/or punctuation.
- **Vertical Scan Notes:** Two choices have "prompted," while one has "prompting" and one doesn't have a form of "prompt." Two choices have "which." One choices has "has been," one has "is," and the other two don't have any form of "to be."
- **Key Features in Surrounding Text:** The original version of the sentence uses a comma to join two sets of words that could each stand on their own as a complete sentence ("by 2003…planet" and "speculation has been…fiction"). This is a comma splice, and the ACT English section doesn't allow us to use commas this way.

Concepts in the question:

- **Comma Splice:** Choices and/or surrounding text use commas to join two groups of words that could each be sentences on their own. A comma can't be used in this way on the ACT English section. (See page 428)
- **Dependent and Independent Clauses:** Choices would create or join clauses. An independent clause has a main verb and can be a sentence by itself. A dependent clause can't, and starts with a conjunction or relative pronoun. (p. 426)
- **Prepositional Idioms:** Choices typically include prepositional phrases with no other recognizable similarities. If you can't tell which choice contains an acceptable prepositional idiom in American English, guess and invest your time elsewhere. (p. 435)
- **Pronoun Ambiguity:** Choices include pronouns that could refer to more than one phrase in the surrounding text. We can't use a pronoun on the ACT when it isn't clear what that pronoun refers to. (See page 419)
- **Verb Tense/Conjugation:** Choices include different forms of the same verb. Look at the surrounding text to find the verb's subject. Also look for other verbs that could indicate the proper tense or form for the verbs in the choices. (See p. 420-423)

ANSWER CHOICE ANALYSIS

A Incorrect: As we noted above, this choice would create a comma splice.

B Incorrect: This choice makes it sound like "speculation has prompted to the red planet," which isn't an idiomatically acceptable use of the pronoun "to:" in American English, we can't say that something "*prompts speculation to" something else. Luckily, though, you don't have to know that prepositional idiom—as a trained test-taker, you could simply notice that (C) is grammatically acceptable and shorter than (B), which means (B) can't be the right answer.

C ✓ Correct: This choice avoids the issues from the other choices, causing the noun phrase "National Aeronautics and Space Administration (NASA)" to be the thing that's doing the "prompting" of the speculation, and joining the "-ing" phrase to the independent clause with a comma, which is acceptable on the ACT English section.

D Incorrect: The word "is" in this choice makes it sound like one of the ideas in the independent clause (such as "NASA" or "spacecraft" or "planet") is literally equivalent to the "speculation," which doesn't make any logical or grammatical sense.

T3, Q66 (Form 16MC3 if you have 2020-2021 Red Book—see p. 23) TYPE: G/S/P (often no prompt; choices w/similar meanings—see p. 418)

- **Vertical Scan Results:** Similar phrases with different short words and/or punctuation.
- **Vertical Scan Notes:** Should "maybe," "although," or "if any" be added to "few?"
- **Key Features in Surrounding Text:** The original version of the underlined phrase results in a comma splice, which is unacceptable on the ACT, because "few...exciting" and "who...expedition" can each stand on their own as separate sentences.

Concepts in the question:

- **Comma Splice:** Choices and/or surrounding text use commas to join two groups of words that could each be sentences on their own. A comma can't be used in this way on the ACT English section. (See page 428)
- **Commas:** Choices include commas. Commas can separate a list of 3 or more items, form sandwiches, separate interchangeable adjectives, or introduce an independent clause after a dependent clause. They can't appear for no reason. (p. 431)
- **Dependent and Independent Clauses:** Choices would create or join clauses. An independent clause has a main verb and can be a sentence by itself. A dependent clause can't, and starts with a conjunction or relative pronoun. (p. 426)
- **Punctuation Sandwich:** Choices involve phrases "sandwiched" between similar punctuation marks. When removed from the sentence, a proper sandwich leaves behind a grammatical sentence with the same original meaning. (See p. 432 and 433)

ANSWER CHOICE ANALYSIS

F Incorrect: As we noted above, this choice creates a comma splice, so it can't be right.

G Incorrect: (G) has the same problem as (F), because "Maybe a few....exciting" can still stand on its own as a sentence.

H ✓ Correct: The conjunction "although" turns the first half of the sentence into a dependent clause, which can be joined to an independent clause with a comma. This solves the problems from the other answer choices, and doesn't create any new problems, so it's the only choice that's grammatically acceptable.

J Incorrect: This choice has the same problem as (F) and (G), because the sandwiched phrase "if any" doesn't change the fact that "few, if any, would deny...exciting" can still stand on its own as a sentence.

T3, Q67 (Form 16MC3 if you have 2020-2021 Red Book—see p. 23) TYPE: G/S/P (often no prompt; choices w/similar meanings—see p. 418)

- **Vertical Scan Results:** Some choices have the same words with different punctuation.
- **Vertical Scan Notes:** Should a comma, colon, dash, or no punctuation appear after "yet?"
- **Key Features in Surrounding Text:** The original version of the sentence creates a comma sandwich around the phrase "the most ambitious NASA project yet," which is used to describe "the International Space Station." Since the sandwiched phrase can be removed from the sentence without fundamentally changing its meaning or causing it to break the ACT's grammar rules, we know the original comma sandwich is acceptable on the ACT.

Concepts in the question:

- **Colons:** Choices include colons. A colon can only be placed after a set of words that could be a sentence on their own, and only before a demonstration or example of the idea before the colon. No more than one colon per sentence. (p. 430)
- **Commas:** Choices include commas. Commas can separate a list of 3 or more items, form sandwiches, separate interchangeable adjectives, or introduce an independent clause after a dependent clause. They can't appear for no reason. (p. 431)
- **Dependent and Independent Clauses:** Choices would create or join clauses. An independent clause has a main verb and can be a sentence by itself. A dependent clause can't, and starts with a conjunction or relative pronoun. (p. 426)
- **Intervening Phrase:** A phrase appears between two words that need to agree with each other grammatically. Remember to identify pairs of words that need to agree with each other, and ignore phrases that appear between those words. (See page 439)
- **Punctuation Sandwich:** Choices involve phrases "sandwiched" between similar punctuation marks. When removed from the sentence, a proper sandwich leaves behind a grammatical sentence with the same original meaning. (See p. 432 and 433)

ANSWER CHOICE ANALYSIS

A ✓ **Correct:** As we discussed above, (A) creates an acceptable punctuation sandwich around the phrase "the most ambitious NASA project yet." Since this is the only choice that results in a grammatically acceptable sentence on the ACT, it's right.

B **Incorrect:** This choice essentially "unsandwiches" the phrase we discussed in (A), which causes a few problems in the sentence. Among other things, this choice turns the entire phrase "the most ambitious...billion dollars" into a side comment on the International Space Station, so that the sentence never gets around to telling us what "the fact" about the International Space Station actually is. (Another issue is that it causes "yet" not to make any logical or grammatical sense—it can't mean "up until now" because then it would need a comma after it, and it can't mean "however" because then the verb "carried" would be missing a subject.)

C **Incorrect:** The ACT English section won't allow a colon after "yet" because the part of the sentence before the colon can't stand on its own as a complete sentence, and because the part of the sentence after the colon isn't an explanation or example of the idea before the colon.

D **Incorrect:** This choice would almost create something like the acceptable punctuation sandwich in (A), but a punctuation sandwich must have the same punctuation on both sides of the sandwich (unless it occurs at the very beginning or end of a sentence, in which case one of the punctuation marks will be missing). Since the beginning of this punctuation sandwich uses a comma that we can't change, the end of the sandwich must also use a comma.

Answer choice patterns (page 442): wrong answers try to imitate right answers

T3, Q68 (Form 16MC3 if you have 2020-2021 Red Book—see p. 23) TYPE:RC (usually has prompt; choices w/different meanings—see p. 413)

- **RC Question sub-type:** Including/excluding a phrase/sentence. (The question asks whether a given sentence or phrase should be included in the passage. The correct choice will include a comment that plainly describes the role of the phrase or sentence in the passage. Sentences that should be included will follow broad ACT standards for ideal sentences and paragraphs, while sentences that shouldn't be included will not follow those standards. See p. 416)

ANSWER CHOICE ANALYSIS

F ✓ **Correct:** The description in this choice is literally demonstrated on the page, because the "assertion in the sentence" is that "NASA overspent," and we know from the previous sentence that the expected price tag was $17 billion. The "explicit detail" from the prompt that "strengthens" the assertion about overspending is that NASA paid $30 billion, which is over the projected price tag. Since this is the only choice that accurately describes the text, we know it must be right.

G **Barely relevant:** The given phrase doesn't make any statement related to the cost of spaceflight "in the future," as (G) would require, so (G) can't be right. (Some test-takers might try to do some kind of financial analysis of the numbers that appear in the passage to answer this question, but, if anything, the paragraph says that the future flight to Mars could cost $100 billion, which is *more* expensive than the $30 billion mentioned in the prompt, contradicting the idea that space flight will be "more affordable" in the future. Again, though, (G) only makes a statement about the sentence in the prompt, so we shouldn't consider other parts of the passage anyway when determining the right answer.)

H **Barely relevant:** The phrase in the prompt doesn't "weaken" any point in the paragraph, as (H) would require, because the paragraph says the cost would be "startling," and the idea of the International Space Station costing "30 billion dollars" doesn't contradict the idea of a flight to Mars costing a lot of money. Since the description in this choice isn't literally restated or demonstrated in the text, we know the choice is wrong.

J **Barely relevant:** This choice doesn't accurately describe the text, because the essay never discusses "the human experience" of a trip to Mars, as (J) would require. Instead, it talks about the cost of that kind of mission, and the ways that robotic systems can do "as much as any crew of scientists" for "a fraction of the cost." (The essay does mention "the idea of a human mission to Mars" in the paragraph before this question, but it never talks about—and certainly doesn't "focus on"—the "human *experience*" (emphasis added) of that mission, as (J) would require. There's no discussion of the physical effects of spaceflight, the emotional impact of landing on another planet, etc.) Since the description in this choice isn't reflected in the text, we know the choice is wrong.

- **Vertical Scan Results:** Some choices are short phrases with no obvious similarity.
- **Vertical Scan Notes:** Three of the choices are short words, and one choice involves deleting the underlined word.
- **Key Features in Surrounding Text:** The original version of the underlined phrase is a grammatically incomplete non-sentence, because nothing appears after the word "be" to state what would be equivalent to the final price.

Concepts in the question:

- **Dependent and Independent Clauses:** Choices would create or join clauses. An independent clause has a main verb and can be a sentence by itself. A dependent clause can't, and starts with a conjunction or relative pronoun. (p. 426)
- **Intervening Phrase:** A phrase appears between two words that need to agree with each other grammatically. Remember to identify pairs of words that need to agree with each other, and ignore phrases that appear between those words. (See page 439)

ANSWER CHOICE ANALYSIS

A   **Incorrect:** As we noted above, (A) causes the sentence not to finish getting around to saying what the price would be.

B   ✓   **Correct:** For most test-takers, (B) will be the only choice that sounds natural and grammatical if they read the entire sentence through carefully. On a technical level, (B) uses the relative pronoun "what" to link the phrase "the final price…would be" to the independent clause "one can only imagine;" in other words, "what" is the pronoun that's equivalent to "the final price" because of the word "be." Another way to think about this is that, because a person ("one") doesn't know what "the final price…would be," that person "can only imagine what the final price…would be." Again, if that wasn't clear, but you can still read the sentence through with each choice and see that this is the only one that makes any sense, then you don't need to worry about the more technical explanation.

C   **Incorrect:** This choice would be correct if the sentence were talking about something qualitative, instead of something quantitative, as we might say, "I can only imagine how my new neighbors will be." This choice would also be correct if the word "high" or "large" were included in the sentence, like this: "One can only imagine *how high* the final price of a human voyage to Mars would be." But none of this is the case, so (C) is wrong.

D   **Incorrect:** This choice might attract some untrained test-takers who misread the sentence and think it ends with the word "Mars," or who assume the word "high" appears after "be," because either of these would be acceptable sentences: "One can only imagine the final price of a human voyage to Mars," or "One can only imagine the final price of a human voyage to Mars would be high." But if we read the sentence carefully we see that only (B) is grammatically possible.

- **RC Question sub-type:** Best accomplishes X. (The prompt describes a goal of the author, and asks which choice achieves that goal. The right answer will be plainly demonstrated in the passage. See page 413)

Subjective Phrases to Ignore: "most effectively"

ANSWER CHOICE ANALYSIS

F   ✓   **Correct:** Only (F) literally demonstrates what the Rovers are, as the prompt requires: "robotic spacecraft."

G   **Barely relevant:** This doesn't provide any information about what the Rovers actually are, because "captur[ing]… imagination" is something the Rovers *did*, but it doesn't say what they *are*. So (G) doesn't "describe[]" the Rovers at all.

H   **Confused relationships:** (H) does say the Rovers were "described at length" *somewhere else*, but the prompt requires an answer choice that, itself, describes the Rovers, instead of referring to some other description of them.

J   **Confused relationships:** (J) is somewhat similar to (H): it relies on the "familiar[ity]" that people may have with the Rovers from another source, but it doesn't actually describe the Rovers in any way, as the prompt requires.

- **Vertical Scan Results:** Similar phrases with different short words and/or punctuation.
- **Vertical Scan Notes:** All four choices include the word "capacity," and three of the choices include another idea as well.
- **Key Features in Surrounding Text:** The underlined phrase describes something the Rovers have.

Concepts in the question:

- **Redundancy:** Choices and/or surrounding text could combine to repeat the same concept unnecessarily. On grammar/style/punctuation questions, we should avoid words that directly repeat ideas in the immediate surrounding text. (See p. 437)
- **Shorter is Better:** Choices include words or phrases that can be removed without impacting meaning or creating grammatical problems. The shortest grammatically acceptable choice that doesn't change the meaning is right. (p. 442)

ANSWER CHOICE ANALYSIS

A   **Incorrect:** In this context, "capacity" and "ability" mean the same thing, so one of them is redundant according to the rules of the ACT English section.

B   **Incorrect:** A lot of trained test-takers will be able to eliminate (A) and (C) fairly quickly, for the reasons we see in the discussions of those choices. Then, those test-takers will need to choose between (B) and (D). We know that the ACT prefers shorter answer choices over longer ones as a general rule, so we also know that we can't pick (B) unless there is some specific reason in the text that would require the addition of the word "genuine" to the sentence. But the idea of whether information about the Rovers is genuine or not—or "credible," or "reliable," or "believable," or anything else along those lines—doesn't appear anywhere in the passage, so there's no ACT-specific reason to include the word "genuine." That means (B) must be wrong, and (D) must be right.

C   **Incorrect:** The word "potential" in this choice would basically mean that the Rovers *could* have the mentioned ability some time in the future, but they don't right now. But words in the immediately surrounding text, like "are" and "answer," make it clear that these Rovers do exist, and these abilities currently exist as well. In other words, nothing restates or demonstrates the idea that these are "potential" abilities, so (C) can't be right.

D ✓   **Correct:** This choice avoids the problems we saw in our discussions of the other choices—without creating any problems of its own—so it's right.

Answer choice patterns (page 442): shortest grammatically acceptable choice is correct

T3, Q72 (Form 16MC3 if you have 2020-2021 Red Book—see p. 23)TYPE:RC (usually has prompt; choices w/different meanings—see p. 413)

- **RC Question sub-type:** Precision Vocabulary. (Choices include words or short phrases that either sound similar, or have vaguely similar but not identical meanings. Most or all of the choices will seem vaguely appropriate, but only one choice will be correct when we think very carefully and specifically about the word means and how it can be used. See page 415)

ANSWER CHOICE ANALYSIS

F   **Barely relevant:** This choice has one of two problems. If we take "older" to mean something like "pretty old"—which means basically the same thing as "aging"—then this choice is wrong because it uses two words to express the same idea, which is redundant and not acceptable on the ACT. If we think of "older" as a comparative form, then this choice would make the sentence say that the "visions" are either "aging" or "older [than aging]." It doesn't really make any sense to say that something is older than "aging," and nothing in the surrounding text explains what this could mean or justifies this usage of the "older." For either of these reasons, (F) must be wrong.

G   **Barely relevant:** "Old age" describes the period of time at the end of a person's natural life span. (G) would make the sentence say something about "visions of space travel" that either involved elderly people traveling, or that belong to elderly people or are related to elderly people, or something else along those lines. The meaning of this phrase would be unclear, and the phrase wouldn't restate, demonstrate, or relate to any ideas in context. For any of these reasons, (G) can't be right.

H   **Barely relevant:** (H) would describe the "visions of space travel" as "aging old." If something were "aging old," then that would mean it was already old, and then somehow continue to age even more. That text doesn't restate or demonstrate the idea of anything becoming old and then further aging beyond the state of being old, so (H) can't be right.

J ✓   **Correct:** The phrase "age-old" basically means that something has been around for a very long period of time. The phrase of "age-old visions of space travel" restates the idea from the first sentence in the passage that says, "the planet Mars has fascinated humans for thousands of years," and the idea in the second and third paragraphs of sending humans to Mars. This choice is the only one that reflects ideas already present in the passage without adding ideas that don't make any sense in context, so (J) is right.)

T3, Q73 (Form 16MC3 if you have 2020-2021 Red Book—see p. 23)TYPE:RC (usually has prompt; choices w/different meanings—see p. 413)

- **RC Question sub-type:** Transition Phrase. (The choices reflect different kinds of transitions between two concepts, with words or phrases like "however," "instead of," or "for example." The right answer must reflect the relationship between the previous concept in the passage and the following concept in the passage. See p. 416)

ANSWER CHOICE ANALYSIS

A   **Confused relationships:** (A) would be right if "keep[ing] in mind that the right equipment can accomplish as much as... scientists" restated the previous sentence's idea that "sending machines...drain[s] some...romance," but that's not the case.

B   **Direct contradiction:** There's no cause-effect relationship between the idea that "sending machines...drain[s] some of the romance," and the idea of "need[ing] to keep in mind that the right equipment" can do more than scientists, as (B) would require. In other words, the idea in the previous sentence isn't the reason for the rest of this sentence. In fact, as we'll see for (D), the sentence with the underlined phrase actually presents a conclusion *in spite of* the idea in the previous sentence.

C   **Barely relevant:** This choice would be appropriate if the previous sentence referred to a specific period of time, and the sentence with the underlined phrase described something happening in that time, but that's not what we have here. The previous sentence describes something as "old," but doesn't mention a timeframe.

D ✓   **Correct:** This choice correctly indicates that the sentence with the underlined phrase tells us something that's true *in spite of* what was mentioned in the previous sentence: "we need to keep in mind...the cost," even though "sending machines...drain[s] some of the romance." Since only (D) reflects the relationship in the text, we know it's right.

T3, Q74 (Form 16MC3 if you have 2020-2021 Red Book—see p. 23) TYPE: G/S/P (often no prompt; choices w/similar meanings—see p. 418)

- **Vertical Scan Results:** Similar phrases with different short words and/or punctuation.

- **Vertical Scan Notes:** Three choices are phrases with unrelated short words. One involves deleting the underlined phrase.
- **Key Features in Surrounding Text:** The underlined phrase comes right before the phrase "a fraction of the cost."

Concepts in the question:

- **Prepositional Idioms:** Choices typically include prepositional phrases with no other recognizable similarities. If you can't tell which choice contains an acceptable prepositional idiom in American English, guess and invest your time elsewhere. (p. 435)
- **Proximity:** Answer choice(s) would place descriptive phrases next to ideas they don't describe. (See page 434)

ANSWER CHOICE ANALYSIS

F   **Incorrect:** "Such as" would indicate that "a fraction of the cost" was an example of something mentioned earlier in the sentence, but that isn't the case.

G ✓ **Correct:** "At" completes the idiomatic phrase "at a fraction of the cost," which is acceptable in conventional American English. See the note below for more.

H   **Incorrect:** This choice indicates that something mentioned earlier in the sentence is "only a fraction of the cost," but that doesn't make any logical or grammatical sense in the sentence. This choice might attract people who thought it said "but at" or "but at only," instead of just "but only."

J   **Incorrect:** If we remove the underlined phrase, then "a fraction of the cost" becomes a modifier joined to the rest of the sentence by a dash—but that modifier isn't acceptable here, since neither "more" nor the "crew of scientists" is "a fraction of the cost"—so this choice isn't acceptable on the ACT English section.

Note   Most prepositional idiom questions on the ACT more or less require you to know the idiom from personal experience in order to answer with total certainty, but this question is different: since (F), (H), and (J) must be wrong for grammatical reasons, and can be eliminated, the question allows us to realize that "at a fraction of the cost" must be the correct answer even if we've never heard it before. This is one more example of why it's so important to consider what the answer choices are offering you before committing to an answer on a question.

T3, Q75 (Form 16MC3 if you have 2020-2021 Red Book—see p. 23) TYPE: RC (usually has prompt; choices w/different meanings—see p. 413)

- **RC Question sub-type:** Including/excluding a phrase/sentence. (The question asks whether a given sentence or phrase should be included in the passage. The correct choice will include a comment that plainly describes the role of the phrase or sentence in the passage. Sentences that should be included will follow broad ACT standards for ideal sentences and paragraphs, while sentences that shouldn't be included will not follow those standards. See p. 416)

ANSWER CHOICE ANALYSIS

A   **Barely relevant:** This choice is wrong for two main reasons. First, the sentence in the prompt describes a sense of "awe" related to the "heavenly skies." But the only "space exploration described in the essay" is the idea of sending people and/or equipment to Mars, and the only emotion connected to exploring Mars in the essay is the "excit[ement]" mentioned at the end of the second paragraph. The passage never says anything about "gaz[ing]" at the "sky" in "awe," or that such "awe" is the basis for "space exploration," as (A) would require. So (A) doesn't describe the sentence in the prompt accurately, which means (A) must be wrong. The other problem is that the rules of the ACT English section won't allow us to conclude this essay (which focuses primarily on the cost of a mission to Mars) with a statement about how the skies are inspirational and mysterious, because that idea doesn't appear anywhere else in the passage. So, again, (A) must be wrong.

B   **Barely relevant:** The sentence in the prompt doesn't mention money at all, and certainly doesn't compare the importance of money to the importance of "mystery," as the description in (B) would require. (B) might attract some untrained test-takers because they think it sounds literary and profound, but, as trained test-takers, we know the ACT doesn't care about that.

C   **Barely relevant:** This choice doesn't accurately describe the text, because the essay doesn't include a "chronological history of people who traveled in space," as (C) would require—in fact, no specific mention is ever made of any person actually having traveled to space, let alone multiple people. Since (C) doesn't accurately describe the text, it must be wrong.

D ✓ **Correct:** The essay clearly demonstrates a "focus on Mars and the cost of sending humans there," as (D) requires: the second paragraph talks about a "human voyage" to the "red planet" and who would "pay for such an expedition," while the third paragraph mentions "the final price of a human voyage to Mars," and the fifth paragraph says that the "staggering expense" of a "mission" to send an "astronaut" to "that distant planet" should be "carefully considered." We can also see that the sentence in the prompt doesn't mention anything specifically about Mars or the cost of a mission there, as the phrase "strays too far from the focus" in (D) requires. Since (D) is the only choice that's demonstrated by the text, it's right.

Part 10: Writing Test Training (The ACT Essay)

Before you begin training for the ACT Essay, you should make sure that your target schools actually want you to take it—many schools, including some of the most competitive, have decided that the ACT Essay doesn't reflect the type of educated, reflective writing that they want to see from their students. If your target schools do want you to submit an ACT Essay score, you'll find that the current version of the essay rewards a formulaic, shallow approach that's relatively easy to learn, and to implement on test day.

In this part, you'll learn the following:

- how ACT, Inc. has designed the ACT Essay
- the unwritten rules of the ACT Essay
- how little time the graders will spend on your essay, and the implications of those time restrictions for your writing
- why factual accuracy in your essay can't matter
- the true impact of spelling and grammar errors on your score
- how to address the provided perspectives in your essay
- whether the length of your essay is important
- why the 5-paragraph format is probably best (even if your essay doesn't end up with exactly 5 paragraphs)
- a step-by-step approach for generating a high-scoring ACT Essay consistently and efficiently
- why note-taking and essay-planning are generally bad ideas on test day, and how to avoid them
- an analysis of the high-scoring sample essays that appear in the Red Book and on ACT.org
- and more . . .

ACT Writing Test (The ACT Essay)

Have something to say, and say it as clearly as you can. That is the only secret of style.
Matthew Arnold

Important Notes!

Before we start talking about how to beat the ACT Writing Test, there are three important concepts that we need to clear up:

1. You might not need to do this test at all
2. How we'll talk about scores
3. We're not teaching you our idea of good writing!

You might not need to do this test at all

Before you spend your valuable time preparing to write an essay for the ACT, you should make sure the schools you're applying to will require you to submit an ACT Writing score (the ACT Writing score is the essay score)!

The ACT Writing test is an optional part of the ACT:

- some schools don't require or recommend that you submit an ACT Writing score
- some schools recommend you submit, but don't require it
- some schools require it

If you're not sure whether your target schools will require you to submit an ACT Writing score, contact them directly to find out. There's no reason to prepare for (or take) the ACT Essay if you aren't going to submit the ACT Writing score to anybody.

How we'll talk about scores

ACT, Inc., has tinkered with its scoring for the essay in the last few years, probably in an effort to hide the weaknesses of the essay test. At the time of this writing, your ACT Writing score is reported as a single number from 2 to 12. But the two people who read your essay will each score it in four separate domains, according to ACT, Inc.:

1. Ideas & Analysis
2. Development & Support
3. Organization
4. Language Use & Conventions

In each of these domains, each reader will give you a score from 1 to 6. Those scores will be added together to produce a "domain score" from 2 to 12, and then your four domain scores will be averaged and rounded to the nearest whole number to produce your final ACT Writing score.

The scores of sample ACT Essays are often reported as four-digit numbers, with each digit representing a score from 1-6 on one of the four domains above. For example, an essay that scores a perfect ACT Writing score of 12 might have received scores of 6666 from both graders; an essay that receives an ACT Writing score of 11 might have been scored a 5555 by one reader and a 6666 by the other.

This domain-based system was probably implemented because the old grading process for the ACT Essay simply involved two graders each assigning a single, holistic score on the 1-6 scale, and some critics of the process said that this holistic approach didn't provide enough information about a writer's ability. The domain-based approach is part of an effort by ACT, Inc., to make people feel that

> this enhancement allows for a finer-grain evaluation of a piece of writing than is possible with holistic scoring.[2]

But it's important to point out that the implementation of the domain-based scoring has had no apparent impact on the type of writing that scores well on the ACT Writing section, even though this type of scoring was implemented along with a minor redesign of the section that also involved changing the type of prompt and the amount of time provided for the essay task. The likely meaninglessness of this new domain-based scoring system is further supported by ACT, Inc., itself:

> All findings from the research studies and the first two administrations of the ACT writing test indicate that the new writing test has similar reliability, precision, and difficulty as [sic] the previous writing test. Subgroup differences in terms of reported score and variance did not change.[3]

(In fact, I wouldn't be surprised at all if many readers of the ACT Essay proceed by mentally assigning a single holistic score to an essay from 1-6, just as they did under the old system, and then simply filling in that score for each of the four domains. Whether readers do this or not, the fact remains that the type of writing that succeeds on the ACT Essay is basically the same as it always was, even though the scores are reported differently now.)

---

[2] *Linking the Current and Former ACT Writing Tests.* ACT, Inc. 2015. Page 1.
[3] *ACT Research Explains New ACT Test Writing Scores.* ACT, Inc. 2016. Page 9.

For our purposes in this section, we'll refer to scores on the ACT Essay section using a simple scale from 1 to 6, since that accurately reflects how they're graded without getting bogged down in domain scores that don't add anything useful.

We're not teaching you our idea of good writing!

It's worth pointing out that the goal of this section is to teach you how to write an essay that will get you a high score on the ACT Writing section . . . and nothing else. This means we're going to teach you to write something that's formulaic and pretty bland.

We mention this for two reasons:

1. We hope that in "real life"—or the part of real life that happens outside of your test booklet, anyway—you'll try to write things that are interesting and insightful. But the easiest and most reliable way to score well on the ACT Writing section is to produce an essay that isn't particularly interesting or insightful, so that's what we'll teach you to do.

2. We don't want you to worry if you feel like you're writing an essay that's not very good. As with everything else on the ACT, we'll find that the test rewards habits and thought processes that aren't rewarded in school.

Again, just so we're clear: the kind of writing we'll teach you now is specifically for the ACT Writing section! We recommend that you follow the training in this section when you write your ACT essay—but not when you write for any other purpose.

Overview and Important Reminders for the ACT Essay

By now, you probably won't be shocked to learn that the ACT Essay has very little in common with the essays you normally write in school—after all, pretty much nothing else on the ACT is the same as what we do in school. So let's take a minute to understand why the ACT Essay is so different from a school essay, and figure out how to structure our approach to the ACT Essay.

One of the most important differences between a school essay and the ACT Essay is that the people who grade your ACT Essay must do it in a way that reflects the ACT's standards (we'll see what those standards actually are in the next few pages). If every grader tried to use his own subjective judgment for each essay, then there would be no meaningful correlation among 6-scoring essays across different graders; an essay that seemed like a perfect 6 to one grader might only score a 4 if it were given to a more demanding grader instead, and there would be no objective way to resolve those differences, which would make ACT Essay scores pretty unreliable.

So we know that there must be standards for grading ACT Essays.

And, at this point, we know from our training that the best way to find out what those standards really are is to reverse-engineer top-scoring sample essays provided by ACT, Inc., instead of just trusting the writing advice that appears in the Red Book. At the time of this writing, there are two batches of sample essays provided to the public by ACT, Inc., each with one example of a 5-scoring essay and one example of a 6-scoring essay:

1. One batch appears in the Red Book, in the section about improving your score on the Writing Test.

2. The other batch appears on the ACT.org web site. You can find it by searching online for the sample ACT essays that talk about intelligent machines.

(My strategies for the ACT Essay are also informed by the experiences and results of tutoring clients, of course, but their essays aren't available to the public.)

As it turns out, the actual characteristics of top-scoring ACT Essays don't really reflect the Red Book's rubric for the ACT essay. This makes sense when we consider the practical realities of trying to grade a large number of essays in a standardized way.

For one thing, ACT Essay-scorers spend far less time on each essay than your teachers spend on your school essays. There are two main reasons for this:

1. ACT Essay-scorers have to score a much larger number of essays in a given period of time, and

2. scoring essays quickly actually allows the scorers to do a better job of working in a standardized, repetitive, reliable way, because it keeps them from getting bogged down in details, allowing them to concentrate on applying the same few key standards to each essay.

These facts have several implications for your essay-writing. Here are two of the most surprising implications, for many test-takers:

- Factual accuracy doesn't matter
- Creativity and reader engagement don't matter

Factual accuracy doesn't matter

Graders can't spend any time researching or confirming any factual claims you make in your essay! Since it isn't possible to evaluate all the factual claims in the hundreds of thousands of ACT essays written each year, and since all the essays have to be held to the same standard, the ACT graders can't evaluate ANY of the factual claims made in ANY of the essays they grade. This policy is the only way to treat all factual claims equally in the grading process.

That means you don't have to worry about being penalized for saying something that's factually wrong on your ACT essay, even though a teacher in high school or college would lower your grade if you submitted an essay to them with factual errors. On the ACT, your essay can be full of factual errors, and the grader wouldn't be allowed to lower your score as a result.

The only thing that matters about the statements you make in your essay is that they *would* support your thesis *if they were true.* In other words, it's okay to make a factually inaccurate statement if that statement would make sense in the context of your essay and support whatever conclusion you come to. But it will hurt your score if you make any statement—factually accurate or not—that doesn't logically support your thesis. (We'll talk more about this in "ACT Essay Rule 2: The grader doesn't care what kind of evidence or reasoning you cite, as long as it's relevant to your thesis" on page 558 of this Black Book.)

This means that you shouldn't spend any time at all on test day trying to remember accurate details about the examples you decide to cite. Invest that time in writing, instead—we'll talk about why that's so important in "ACT Essay Rule 4: Write more than two pages" on page 559 of this Black Book.

Creativity and reader engagement don't matter

For similar reasons, you shouldn't try to amuse or inform the reader of your ACT Essay, or do anything else creative, because your essay graders won't invest the time in reading your essay to pick up on those things.

Your essay-graders won't be sitting in a café, having a leisurely look over your paper for an afternoon while drinking a latte and contemplating life.

Instead, they'll spend roughly a minute or so on your work, with the goal of identifying key features of your essay that indicate which score it should receive. So you don't really want to try to make your ACT Essay stand out from the crowd, as you might try to do with an admissions essay or a scholarship essay.

On the contrary, you want your essay to blend in with all the other top-scoring essays by imitating the characteristics that most of those essays share (which is what you'll learn about in this section of this Black Book, of course).

Conclusion

ACT, Inc., doesn't just come out and say, "Gosh, we've sure got a lot of essays to grade, so yours probably won't be looked at for more than a few minutes. A couple of overworked essay-graders are going to read it once each, really quickly, and then assign it a score based on a few key things that we won't really discuss with you explicitly, and then move on to the next essay. So just make your essay more than two pages long and do a couple of other things, and you should score pretty high."

Instead, the Red Book says things like, "the writing test . . . measures . . . those writing skills emphasized in high school English classes and in entry-level college composition courses," which is obviously, laughably not true. (For example, as we saw above, the ACT Essay doesn't reward factual accuracy or creativity, which are both rewarded in most educational settings.)

On the next page, we'll discuss the unwritten rules for this part of the test, and later you'll see them in action.

Unwritten Test Design Rules of ACT Writing (The ACT Essay)

You're probably not used to thinking of essay tests as having "rules." But, as trained test-takers, we know that every part of a standardized test like the ACT must follow predictable guidelines, or else the results from different days' tests wouldn't be comparable to each other, and the test would have no purpose. That means there are unwritten rules that affect essay-grading on test day, which is why high-scoring ACT essays generally have so many attributes in common, even though those attributes don't appear in ACT, Inc.'s official scoring rubric for essays.

In this section, we'll learn the unwritten rules of the ACT Essay.

ACT Essay Rule 1: Relatable prompts

Every ACT Essay prompt will discuss some aspect of modern life that's relatable for high-school students in one way or another. In many cases, the prompts will ask your opinion on some topic related to education or technology, as we can see in the following examples:

- The prompt for the essay portion of practice test 1 in the Red Book (test 2 in the 2020-2021 Red Book) discusses whether free digital music has impacted our perception of the value of music.
- The prompt for the essay portion of practice test 2 in the Red Book (test 3 in the 2020-2021 Red Book) discusses attendance rates at public events, and whether technology makes physical presence at an event unnecessary.
- The prompt for the essay portion of practice test 3 in the Red Book (form 16MC3 online if you have the 2020-2021 Red Book) discusses whether schools should offer vocational training, like auto repair and office skills, in addition to academic subjects, like math and history.

This means you don't have to worry that the prompt might be on some obscure topic you don't know anything about. It's specifically designed to be something that you can easily form some kind of opinion on.

ACT Essay Rule 2: The grader doesn't care what kind of evidence or reasoning you cite, as long as it's relevant to your thesis

If we were writing an essay for a particular teacher in school, or for a scholarship or a college application, then we'd want to consider the personal biases and preferences of the people who were likely to read those essays, because those readers would make decisions about our work based on their personal feelings.

But the people who read the ACT Essay aren't allowed to lower our scores because we say something they find boring or disagreeable. ACT Essay graders are only allowed to lower your score if you use examples and reasoning that aren't actually relevant to your thesis.

For example, let's imagine you were trying to support the opinion that schools should *only* teach vocational skills without offering any academic subjects, and part of your argument was that vocational skills can help students find jobs, while academic subjects had no value in the real world, and were a waste of time for most people. This could be a pretty offensive thing for an ACT grader to read, because a lot of those graders are high-school teachers themselves, and they spend a lot of time and energy teaching academic subjects. But the grader wouldn't be able to lower your score for using this argument, even if they found it insulting, because it's directly relevant to the prompt: you were asked about the value of vocational training in education, and this part of the argument would be discussing your position that vocational training is actually *more* valuable than learning academic material. (Remember that we're discussing a hypothetical thesis in an essay, not your actual feelings or my actual feelings.)

The reason that graders for the ACT Essay aren't allowed to consider their personal feelings when grading your essay is the same reason we've seen for most of what the ACT does: standardization. Since different readers will have different feelings about different subjects, readers must ignore their personal feelings and only consider whether each part of an argument is relevant to its thesis, or else the essay-grading process will be much less standardized.

Similarly, the grader isn't allowed to consider whether your essay cites examples from history, literature, science, current events, or made-up stories about things that happened to you and your friends. Since there's no way to account for the wide variety in types of evidence that might be cited by hundreds of thousands of test-takers on test-day, the ACT's readers are forced to ignore the *type* of examples you cite, and only consider whether those examples provide evidence that supports your argument.

And, as we discussed in "Overview and Important Reminders for the ACT Essay" on page 556 of this Black Book, the ACT's essay-readers aren't even allowed to care if the examples we cite in our essays are *true*. So you can make up examples for your ACT Essay if you want—you can even make up the titles and contents of books and other works. You can also be wrong about the details of things that actually did happen. For example, you wouldn't be penalized for saying that the American Civil War happened in the 1200s, as long as whatever you were saying about the war supported your thesis.

(For the record, I wouldn't recommend going out of your way to make false statements in your essay, because at a certain point it could become distracting for the graders and make it harder for them to see whether your essay follows the standards for this section of the test. But you definitely don't need to worry about whether any statement you make in your essay is factual, as long as that statement is relevant to your thesis.)

****

So let's summarize all of this stuff about supporting examples and reasons:

1. Your ACT Essay needs to include supporting paragraphs that use reasoning and/or examples to back up your thesis

---

statement.

2. Your examples don't have to be academic. They only have to support the thesis.

3. Your examples don't have to be true. They only have to be statements that would support your thesis if they were true.

You shouldn't spend any time trying to guess what kinds of examples the essay-grader wants to hear! You aren't trying to interest your reader, nor do you need to worry about offending her, or saying something that's factually wrong.

ACT Essay Rule 3: There's no required essay format (but you should probably use a version of the 5-paragraph format anyway)

In theory, you can use any type of essay format to write a top-scoring ACT Essay, and we'll occasionally see top-scoring essays that don't use some version of the 5-paragraph format. In my experience, though, the top-scoring essays tend to use a structure similar to the standard 5-paragraph format:

- 1 introductory paragraph
- 2-4 body paragraphs, with each body paragraph usually dedicated to an individual reason or example that supports the thesis (the standard number of body paragraphs is 3, which is where the name "5-paragraph essay format" comes from)
- 1 closing paragraph

There are probably two reasons for this, and they're closely related to each other:

1. Many American high school students are taught the 5-paragraph format in literature and history classes.

2. ACT essay-graders are very used to seeing some version of the 5-paragraph format, which makes this format easy and familiar for them to analyze.

As we've said repeatedly, your main goal in writing your ACT Essay is to create an essay that looks just like all the other top-scoring essays, so your essay-graders can feel okay giving you 6's and moving on to the next essay they have to grade.

ACT Essay Rule 4: Write more than two pages

The single most important factor affecting the score of your ACT Essay is its length: the longer it is, the higher it can potentially score. If you want to be assured of having the possibility of scoring a perfect 12, I recommend you try to fill up at least two pages of writing space provided on the test. (In other words, your goal should be for your response to make it to part of the third page. Taking up any more space than that doesn't seem to have any further correlation with your score.)

Don't get me wrong: it's certainly *possible* to write a high-scoring essay and not make it onto the third page. For example, the highest-scoring essay in the Red Book doesn't quite make it onto the third page. But many top-scoring essays will be long enough to make it to the third page, and pretty much all of them will at least come very close to that.

If your essay is long enough to take up more than two full pages, then a grader can glance at your work, see that it looks like the other high-scoring essays in terms of length, and feel more comfortable giving you a good score. (Remember that the grader isn't going to spend much more than a minute evaluating your essay, and may even spend less time than that.)

Of course, this doesn't mean you can just write two-and-a-half pages of gibberish and expect to get a good score! You still need to articulate a clear position, discuss that position in relation to two or more of the provided perspectives, and support that position with relevant examples and reasoning, as we'll discuss in a few pages.

But this length guideline *does* mean that if you write a shorter essay (say, less than a page-and-a-half), then you have very little chance of getting out of the middle score range, no matter how splendid your writing is otherwise. So be prepared to write more than two pages in the 40 minutes that the ACT provides on the Writing test.

ACT Essay Rule 5: State your thesis clearly (preferably in the first paragraph)

After the length of your essay, the second-largest factor affecting your ACT Essay score is the degree to which your reasoning and examples support your thesis.

This means that your thesis needs to be clearly stated in a conspicuous way, so the reader can locate it quickly and easily. After all, if the reader can't identify your thesis statement, then he has no way of knowing whether the rest of your essay supports that thesis statement; if he can't tell whether the rest of the essay supports your thesis, then he can't give you a good score. This is probably why most high-scoring ACT Essays contain clear and conspicuous thesis statements.

Most top-scoring ACT Essays place the thesis statement in the first paragraph, often as the very last sentence of that paragraph. That's sort of the classic position for the thesis statement that's taught in most high-school English classes, so it makes sense that lots of test-takers are comfortable placing the thesis there, and that most graders are conditioned to expect the thesis to appear there. We'll see examples of thesis placement in top-scoring essays starting on page 566 of this Black Book.

ACT Essay Rule 6: You don't have to mention every perspective directly, and you don't have to agree with any of them

The high-scoring sample essays in the Red Book and on the ACT's website —the ones that received a 5 or 6 out of 6—address either 2 or 3 of the three provided perspectives, so that's what you should plan to do on test day.

Notice that "addressing a perspective" can mean that you talk about one idea mentioned in that perspective while bringing up an idea of your own, or that you explain why you agree with that perspective in its entirety, or you specifically contradict that perspective, among other things. We'll explore these ideas more in "Analysis of High-Scoring Sample Essays Provided by ACT, Inc." on page 566 of this Black Book.

You can just plan to address each of the three provided perspectives if you want to, but you shouldn't feel obligated to do that, because it's clearly possible to write a perfect-scoring ACT Essay while only addressing two perspectives.

ACT Essay Rule 7: A little imperfect grammar and spelling is okay

The high-scoring sample essays in *The Official ACT Prep Guide* contain a few grammatical and spelling mistakes, so we know that an ACT essay can make a perfect score even if its grammar isn't perfect. That doesn't mean you should go out of your way to make mistakes, or that you shouldn't try to use proper grammar. But it does mean that grammar shouldn't be your main concern when you write your ACT Essay. (When we analyze top-scoring ACT Essays on page 566 of this Black Book, we'll specifically mention their grammatical and spelling issues, so you can get a good sense of what the ACT's readers tolerate.)

So don't waste time trying to proof your essay thoroughly to catch and fix every grammatical error—just write your ideas down in a clear and direct way. As we've discussed, it's much more important to focus on length, supporting your thesis, and addressing other perspectives with relevant examples.

ACT Essay Rule 8: Vocabulary isn't a big deal

Untrained test-takers often hope to impress their graders by using big words in their ACT Essays. Please don't do this on test day. Your ACT Essay graders won't reward you for using a big word—but they might penalize you if they notice you using words incorrectly, which often happens when test-takers try to incorporate words they're not actually familiar with.

When we look at the sample essays from the Red Book on page 566 of this Black Book, we'll see that top-scoring essays don't make any particular effort to incorporate impressive vocabulary words. You shouldn't, either.

Recommended Step-By-Step Approach to the ACT Essay

The whole challenge of the ACT Essay is to write an essay in 40 minutes that includes the features that tend to appear in top-scoring ACT Essays. Because essay-writing is such an open-ended activity (as opposed to picking answer choices from multiple choice questions), there are many different ways you could choose to write an ACT essay that would be likely to score high, but I find the following approach to be the easiest and most straightforward. After we go over this process, I'll write a sample essay using these guidelines in the next section.

1. Watch the clock.

You only have 40 minutes, so losing focus for just a few minutes could really harm your score. Do your best to stay focused and keep writing until your response has made it onto the third page and you've finished your essay—for most people, that will take up practically all of your 40 minutes. (See "ACT Essay Rule 4: Write more than two pages" on page 559 of this Black Book for more.)

I recommend that you avoid doing extensive planning or pre-writing on test day, for two reasons:

1. Length is a very important factor if you want to score high. You'll probably need to spend as much time as possible on writing your actual essay, so your essay will make it onto the third page.

2. The ACT Essay task is pretty formulaic, so there's not much need for planning. We already know the prompt will talk about a fairly common issue and provide us with three example perspectives to work from if we want, and we already know we're going to write a version of the classic 5-paragraph essay. We also know we can make up any supporting facts we want, because the reader isn't allowed to consider whether our supporting statements are true, academic, or interesting. So what is there to plan, really?

I also recommend you complete Step 2 and Step 3 as quickly as possible, to give yourself more time for writing.

2. Read the prompt and take a position on it.

The prompt will address some issue related to modern life, often involving education and/or technology. You'll also be given three different perspectives to consider as you decide what you think about the provided topic. So it shouldn't be too hard for you to take a position on it.

If you don't have any strong feelings on the ideas in the prompt, you can try one of a few options to get your mental wheels turning:

1. You can choose one of the provided perspectives, and make that your position. (If you do this, be prepared to elaborate on *why* this is your position; don't just restate the exact perspective with no further information.)

2. You can decide that your position is the exact *opposite* of one of the provided perspectives.

3. You can also pick an idea from one of the provided perspectives and modify it slightly by adding the word "but" to the end of it, and then completing that thought as you see fit. You can use the result as your thesis, or use it to inspire your thesis.

Of course, there's no right or wrong answer to the prompt, and the grader isn't allowed to penalize you or reward you based on whether she agrees with your position.

Just remember that, whatever you choose, you can't simply repeat ideas directly from the prompt as your own position. You should mention and discuss those ideas, but you'll also need to add your own examples, reasoning, and so on—and you'll need to make sure your examples and reasoning directly support your position!

See our example essay process starting on page 563 of this Black Book for a demonstration of this step in action.

3. Come up with 3 or 4 reasons and/or examples to support your perspective. At least 2 of them should be closely related to ideas in the provided perspectives from the prompt.

Remember that one of the most important things about your essay is that your reasons or examples must clearly support your position! (I know I just said that—I'm saying it again because it's very important :))

Also remember that the reasons and examples don't have to be true or academic—they *can* be true or academic (or both, if you want)—but the graders aren't allowed to care either way. The only thing that matters is that your reasoning and examples would support your thesis if they were true. In identifying your supporting reasons and examples, consider each of the three provided perspectives. Your reasons or examples should relate strongly to at least two of those perspectives.

Some high-scoring test-takers will be able to use 2 reasons or examples, write a paragraph on each, and produce a long enough essay to make it to the third page; others will have the time to use four reason or example paragraphs and still finish the essay. But most will use three example paragraphs. As long you as observe the other relevant rules and standards discussed in this section—including making it onto the third page with your writing!—any number of example paragraphs can potentially result in a top-scoring essay.

For an example of this step in action, see page 563 of this Black Book.

4. Write your introduction paragraph, including your thesis statement.

Now that you've picked a perspective and thought of some supporting reasons and examples, it's time to start writing.

Remember that this is a 40-minute essay test, and you need to complete a pretty long essay that matches the standards described in this section of the Black Book. You don't want to waste time. The sooner you can start working on your opening paragraph, the better.

The introduction paragraph for most high-scoring ACT essays will start with a few opening sentences, building up to the final sentence in that paragraph, which will be the thesis. Those opening sentences will usually make some broad statements that are related to the topic and your thesis. They might refer to the supporting examples and reasoning that you'll use in the body paragraphs of the essay, but they don't have to.

(See the analysis of high-scoring example essays that starts on page 566 of this Black Book to understand how other test-takers have approached their opening paragraphs, and see page 563 for an example of an introductory paragraph inspired by a real ACT prompt.)

5. Write your first body paragraph, using examples and/or reasoning.

Once you've finished your introduction, you're ready to write your first supporting body paragraph.

Each support paragraph should more or less follow this structure:

- A sentence describing your reason or example that directly supports your thesis. Ideally, this sentence will start with a word or phrase that transitions from the idea mentioned in the previous sentence, like "one example of this would be," or "furthermore," or "we can see this idea at work when we consider," etc. Remember that this reason or example doesn't have to be entertaining, academic, or true (but it can be any or all of those things if you want).
- 2-4 sentences clearly explaining how this reason or example demonstrates that your thesis is valid.

Remember that at least two of your body paragraphs should incorporate concepts from the provided perspectives in the prompt. But don't quote one of those perspectives directly! Top-scoring essays generally don't include quotations.

Also remember that your goal is for your writing to make it to the third page, so your body paragraphs need to be long enough to allow that to happen.

(See page 564 for an example of a first body paragraph inspired by a real ACT prompt.)

6. Write your remaining body paragraphs, using examples and/or reasoning.

Repeat Step 5 for each of your other body paragraphs.

I recommend three body paragraphs in general, but, as we can see in the perfect-scoring sample essay in the Red Book, it's possible to get a good score without using exactly three supporting paragraphs. The overall length of the essay is more important than the number of paragraphs: use a number of body paragraphs that lets you reach the third page in the essay booklet by the time you conclude your essay, which we'll discuss in the next step.

(See page 564 of this Black Book for a demonstration of the process of writing the remaining body paragraphs in our example essay for a real ACT prompt.)

7. Conclude the essay.

At this point, you should be near the bottom of page 2, or even starting on page 3. It's time to write your conclusion and finish your essay.

Start with a couple of sentences rephrasing the thesis you wrote in the introduction of the essay. Then, in another couple of sentences, re-summarize your reasons and examples, and wrap up your thoughts. If necessary, you can draw this summary out to get to the third page.

(See page 564 of this Black Book for an example of a concluding paragraph in our sample ACT essay.)

Conclusion

Now that we've discussed this process in the abstract, let's take a look at some examples! Starting on the next page, you'll see me construct a sample ACT Essay using this process. After that, we'll analyze the exemplar essays in the Red Book to see how the top-scoring ones follow the principles we've been talking about.

Facebook.com/TestingIsEasy Youtube.com/TestingIsEasy

Example ACT Essay

In this exercise, I'll walk you through the process of writing a sample ACT Essay for the official prompt from the essay portion of practice test 2 in the Red Book (test 3 in the 2020-2021 Red Book). You'll see that the top-scoring official sample essays (available in the Red Book and on ACT.org) demonstrate the same key features you'll find in this sample.

So here we go! I'll include the steps from the recommended process we just discussed on page 561 of this Black Book, so you can follow along with my thought process.

1. Watch the clock.

We'll need to remember that we only have 40 minutes to write more than two pages of material by hand. So we'll start our writing as soon as we can, and we won't do any planning or pre-writing, for the reasons we discussed on page 561 of this Black Book.

2. Read the prompt and take a position on it.

The prompt from practice test 2 in the Red Book (test 3 in the 2020-2021 Red Book) is about attending public events, which isn't a topic that immediately fills me with a burning desire to opine.

But that's okay! Rather than get nervous about how little I feel like discussing this topic, I'm going to stay focused on coming up with a thesis as quickly as possible so I can get started with my writing.

I know that one option I have is to put my own twist on one of the provided perspectives by modifying it with the word "but," and then adding my own idea. I'll do this with an idea from the first perspective, which says this:

> People these days value convenience over community. It's easier to watch a game from home than to attend in person, so we do it, even though it keeps us isolated from each other.

I'll use the phrase "It's easier to watch a game from home than to attend in person, so we do it," and then I'm going to add "but" to the end of that phrase and finish it off with my own idea:

> It's easier to watch a game from home than to attend in person, so we do it, but we often watch from home surrounded by friends and loved ones, so we aren't necessarily losing the chance to socialize when we choose not to attend an event.

This is starting to look like a thesis expressing my perspective on the issues in the prompt—but part of it still quotes the original prompt directly, so I'll just modify the phrasing a little to make it my own:

> In the age of television, attending an event in person isn't necessarily more social than watching the event on TV: people can watch events from home while surrounded by friends and loved ones, and attendees of an event may not always have positive interactions with other attendees.

Okay, that looks pretty decent now, for ACT Writing purposes. (Remember that the ACT Writing section doesn't reward us for writing concisely, so it's fine that this perspective might seem a bit long.)

3. Come up with 3 or 4 reasons and/or examples to support your perspective. At least 2 of them should be closely related to ideas in the provided perspectives from the prompt.

My perspective is about people watching events from home while still being social, so my examples will reflect this kind of scenario.

For one example, I'll talk about the time my family watched our favorite football team win a Super Bowl on TV, and how we still view that as a bonding experience. This example is connected to ideas related to Perspectives One and Two.

Another example will be the way my brother watches international soccer matches on TV, which he wouldn't be able to experience otherwise. This example touches on ideas from Perspectives Two and Three.

And, as a third piece of support, I'll mention the time that I attended a sporting event and saw some rival fans get into a fight with each other, because that also popped into my mind just now—and I'll use this to make the counterpoint that people who attend events in person aren't guaranteed to have good experiences with the members of the public they encounter at the event. This is a counterexample to the idea in each perspective that attending an event will be a positive social experience.

Now I have three examples that are directly relevant to my perspective on the prompt.

Notice that my examples are connected to all three provided perspectives. Be sure to keep the provided perspectives in mind when you come up with your examples!

If your position is at all related to the ideas in the prompt and the perspectives—which of course it should be—then it shouldn't be difficult to come up with examples that can be connected to at least two of the perspectives.

It may seem like I've spent a while working out my perspective and my examples, but this process would play out much faster in my head than it does when I explain it all in writing. On test day, your goal is to come up with a perspective and some solid ideas for supporting paragraphs as quickly as you can, so you can get into the next step as early as possible, which will ultimately make it easier to come up with a written response that follows the standards in this section and is longer than two pages.

4. Write your introduction paragraph, including your thesis statement.

As we noted on page 561 of this Black Book, top-scoring ACT Essays often include introductory paragraphs with sentences that are broadly related to the concepts in the prompt, possibly mentioning the topics that will be used in the body paragraphs. My intro paragraph will follow that pattern.

Here it is. Notice that my thesis is the very last sentence in this paragraph, which is where most high-scoring ACT Essays will have it. Also notice that I've tweaked my thesis a little bit at this point, just because I like this wording a bit better:

> The days when a whole town or city would gather to watch a public event—like a political debate or a concert—are over. Television and the Internet have made it possible for audiences to watch events even though the members of the audience are in different places. As a result, we no longer have to interact with the public when we want to witness an event. We can choose to attend an event and be surrounded by strangers who share an interest in it, or we can watch the event on our televisions or phones. In the age of television, attending an event in person isn't necessarily more social than watching the event on TV: people can watch events from home while surrounded by friends and loved ones, and attendees of an event may not always have positive interactions with other attendees.

5. Write your first body paragraph, using examples and/or reasoning.

I already mentioned that my first example is going to be about a time when my family watched the Super Bowl together. As we noted on page 562 of this Black Book, this paragraph will start with a description of the example, and end with an explanation of how the example demonstrates the thesis. Here goes:

> This point was driven home for me a few years ago, when my family was excited about the New York Giants playing in the Super Bowl. Unfortunately, we knew that we would never be able to attend in person, because the tickets were expensive and hard to find. But this doesn't mean that we were unable to enjoy the event! In fact, for most fans, it's a tradition to spend Super Bowl Sunday with friends and family. As it turned out, our favorite team won the game in a dramatic last-minute play that had us all on our feet, cheering and hugging each other. We bonded as much over that game as we would have if we had attended it. In fact, we might have bonded even more at home, since we could easily talk with each other, without the noise and assigned seating of a stadium.

(By the way, some parts of what I wrote above are basically true, and some parts aren't. None of that really matters for the ACT; all that matters is that I've provided a solid example in support of my thesis statement, and I took up a good amount of space doing it.)

6. Write your remaining body paragraphs, using examples and/or reasoning.

Now I'll write the next two paragraphs, using the examples I came up with in Step 3 and the same basic paragraph structure we just used in Step 5:

> In addition to facilitating social gatherings around events in our own homes, television and the Internet make it possible to connect with communities in other parts of the world. For example, my brother loves to watch international soccer matches. He has become a fan of several teams, and even when he watches their games alone, he feels connected to other fans all over the world. He can wear his team jerseys and discuss his favorite teams and players on the internet between matches. In this case, TV and the Internet make it possible for my brother to be a part of an international community he otherwise wouldn't even know about!
>
> Further, it's no longer true that attending a public event in person will result in positive social experiences that strengthen a sense of community. Many people who attend political demonstrations or sporting events find themselves in confrontations that would have been avoided in the privacy and safety of home, sharing the social experience of watching the event with like-minded people. This shows that attendance at a public event doesn't necessarily go hand-in-hand with increasing a sense of community and social belonging.

These paragraphs—like all the paragraphs in this example essay—are certainly not perfect, and contain many phrases that we wouldn't want to include in a polished essay in real life. My goal here is to give a realistic presentation of the thought process that a trained test-taker might work through while generating an essay with a good chance to make a perfect score.

7. Conclude the essay.

We'll follow the basic structure laid out on page 562 of this Black Book for this:

> Even though event attendance may have decreased, we shouldn't assume that this indicates declining interest in socializing or building community. Instead, it reflects a trend of people taking advantage of the convenience of television and the Internet, which allow them to watch events from home, while still engaging socially with people in their homes—or even connecting to new communities in other parts of the world. This also makes it possible to avoid potentially negative, socially destructive interactions that can happen when strangers with different views confront each other at emotionally charged public events. Public events still have significant cultural and social value, but that value is no longer tied to in-person attendance.

Our whole sample essay in one place

Here's the entire sample essay without steps and commentary to break it up:

The days when a whole town or city would gather to watch a public event—like a political debate or a concert—are over. Television and the Internet have made it possible for audiences to watch events even though the members of the audience are in different places. As a result, we no longer have to interact with the public when we want to witness an event. We can choose to attend an event and be surrounded by strangers who share an interest in it, or we can watch the event on our televisions or phones.

This point was driven home for me a few years ago, when my family was excited about the New York Giants playing in the Super Bowl. Unfortunately, we knew that we would never be able to attend in person, because the tickets were expensive and hard to find. But this doesn't mean that we were unable to enjoy the event! In fact, for most fans, it's a tradition to spend Super Bowl Sunday with friends and family. As it turned out, our favorite team won the game in a dramatic last-minute play that had us all on our feet, cheering and hugging each other. We bonded as much over that game as we would have if we had attended it. In fact, we might have bonded even more at home, since we could easily talk with each other, without the noise and assigned seating of a stadium.

In addition to facilitating social gatherings around events in our own homes, television and the Internet make it possible to connect with communities in other parts of the world. For example, my brother loves to watch international soccer matches. He has become a fan of several teams, and even when he watches their games alone, he feels connected to other fans all over the world. He can wear his team jerseys and discuss his favorite teams and players on the internet between matches. In this case, TV and the Internet make it possible for my brother to be a part of an international community he otherwise wouldn't even know about!

Further, it's no longer true that attending a public event in person will result in positive social experiences that strengthen a sense of community. Many people who attend political demonstrations or sporting events find themselves in confrontations that would have been avoided in the privacy and safety of home, sharing the social experience of watching the event with like-minded people. This shows that attendance at a public event doesn't necessarily go hand-in-hand with increasing a sense of community and social belonging.

Even though event attendance may have decreased, we shouldn't assume that this indicates declining interest in socializing or building community. Instead, it reflects a trend of people taking advantage of the convenience of television and the Internet, which allow them to watch events from home, while still engaging socially with people in their homes—or even connecting to new communities in other parts of the world. This also makes it possible to avoid potentially negative, socially destructive interactions that can happen when strangers with different views confront each other at emotionally charged public events. Public events still have significant cultural and social value, but that value is no longer tied to in-person attendance.

Thoughts on this Sample Essay

The essay above follows the standards discussed in this section, which means it imitates the characteristics we consistently see in real, high-scoring sample ACT essays. The thought process described in pages 563-564 is a good example of what a trained test-taker might think about on test day.

It also has the following important attributes:

- It's long enough to reach onto the third page if we wrote it by hand. (If I were writing it out by hand on test day and I realized that I had already taken up a lot of space by the time I got ready to start my third example paragraph, I could always choose to skip it and go right into my conclusion paragraph if I was feeling tight on time.)
- The thesis is clearly stated at the end of the intro paragraph.
- The body paragraphs provide examples that clearly support the thesis in distinct ways. It doesn't matter that the examples are personal (as opposed to academic, historical, hypothetical, etc.) and it doesn't matter if any of them are factually accurate. All that matters is that they would each support the thesis for their own reasons if they were true statements.
- It routinely refers to concepts that appear throughout the given prompt.

Analysis of High-Scoring Sample Essays Provided by ACT, Inc.

In this section, we'll discuss the four high-scoring exemplar essays provided by ACT, Inc. This will help you develop your understanding of what the ACT Writing test rewards, so you can continue to see the ideas we've talked about in action. But first, we need to talk about the length of these sample essays as it pertains to the advice we gave in "ACT Essay Rule 4: Write more than two pages" on page 559 of this Black Book.

A Quick Note on the Length of the Sample Essays

You may have noticed that we talked about basing our approach to the ACT Writing test on the attributes of the high-scoring sample essays provided by the ACT, and the experience of personal clients. We said that one of the most important attributes of a high-scoring ACT essay was length—more specifically, that you should aim to write an essay that's at least two pages long. You may also notice that each of the 6-scoring sample essays we're about to look at is actually a little shorter than the corresponding 5-scoring essay for the same prompt.

There's a very likely explanation for this apparent discrepancy: when the SAT and ACT first introduced essay tests more than a decade ago, they took an absolute hammering in the media when it became clear that the length of an essay correlated very highly with its score, and writing quality (whatever that is) seemed to matter very little.

So the clever people at ACT, Inc., seem to have come up with a way to downplay this aspect of their essay scores in the Red Book. They seem to have decided to provide sample essays with a clear trend in increasing length as the scores increases . . . but with a highest-scoring sample essay that's actually a little shorter than the second-highest-scoring sample essay. They followed this pattern in the 3rd edition of the Red Book (the first one to include the ACT Writing test), and they've done it in the current edition of the Red Book, as well as on their website. Still, the experiences of individual test-takers strongly support the idea that length of your essay still correlates very highly with your ACT Writing score.

This is a good reminder that the approach we teach in this section isn't the only way to score high on the ACT Writing test. It's technically *possible* to get a 6 while writing less than two pages, or not using the 5-paragraph format, etc. But the odds would be against you if you chose not to do those things. The approach we teach in this section is the easiest, most reliable way to get a high score on the ACT Writing Test.

Essays in *The Official ACT Prep Guide* and on ACT.org

Now let's take a look at the four high-scoring sample essays provided in the Red Book and on ACT.org. We'll talk briefly about the most important aspects of these essays and what you can learn from them to make sure you write your best essay on test day.

The 5555 Sample Essay in the Red Book

Score: 5555, which works out to a 10 on the final ACT Writing scale

Length: roughly 2.2 pages

Thesis: The last sentence of the first paragraph says,

> The value of music in our society in [sic] not decreasing, [sic] we still view music as a vital aspect in [sic] our lives.

Support: The author cites the following supporting ideas and examples:

- The pop star Psy released music for free and became internationally famous.
- Other kinds of entertainment (like movies and TV shows) incorporate music.
- The author discovered a band because that band made its music available for free.

Incorporating ideas from multiple perspectives: The essay includes the following quotes, which are heavily inspired by ideas from the provided prompt:

- "Digital technologies have caused music to become cheaper."
- "…there are also many other inexpensive forms of entertainment."
- "The ubiquitous…nature of music…has…allowed the discovery of many new musicians."

These quotes from the essay reflect central ideas in the first, second, and third perspectives provided in the prompt, respectively, but the author uses the ideas in slightly different ways in the essay.

Selected grammatical errors:

- As we noted above, the thesis statement incorrectly uses a comma instead of a semicolon to join two independent clauses.
- The thesis statement also uses the preposition "in" instead of the verb "is."
- "aspect in our lives" should be "aspect of our lives"
- The last comma in the first sentence of the second paragraph shouldn't be there.
- The phrase "to more easily to allow [sic]" is some combination of a split infinitive and a mental hiccup.

Selected spelling errors:

- "recieve" instead of "receive"
- "techonologies" instead of "technologies"

- "rythme" instead of "rhythm"

Vocabulary: The fourth paragraph uses the word "ubiquitous," which is arguably the only somewhat exotic word in the essay.

Overview: This essay is a good example of how a long, mostly competent essay can score high without being particularly memorable. There are a few grammatical and spelling errors, but the writer's meaning is clear. This essay is one more piece of evidence to support the idea that ACT Essay readers don't pay very close attention to the content of the essays they grade—instead, they read over an essay quickly, noting things like its length and its thesis and the general style of writing, and then they give it a score and move on to the next essay.

This particular essay was probably a 5 and not a 6 because the fourth paragraph doesn't really add any new information. The second paragraph describes how a musician was able to connect with fans by offering free music on the internet, and the fourth paragraph describes how the author was able to become a fan of a band who offered free music on the internet, without offering any explanation as to why the situation in the fourth paragraph differs from the one described in the second paragraph.

The 6666 Sample Essay in the Red Book

Score: 6666, which works out to a 12 on the final ACT Writing scale

Length: roughly 1.6 pages

Thesis: The last sentence of the first paragraph says,

> In the modern technological environment, the value of music in our culture only increases.

Support: The author cites the following supporting ideas and examples:

- A preference for free music might make it seem like we don't like music as much, but its role in our culture shows that we value it as much as ever.
- We still have personal music libraries and attend concerts, and people use music for a variety of other reasons.

Incorporating ideas from multiple perspectives: The essay includes the following quotes, which are heavily inspired by ideas from the provided prompt:

- "Today, digital technology is the driving force behind free music. Various online sources offer music to anyone with internet access. There are many people who are unwilling to pay for music since they can get it for free from these sources."
- "The prevelance [sic] of music has not diminished; if anything it has increased. Even the fact that we take advantage of all the free music available demonstrats [sic] how much we value music!"

The first quote above reflects the view in Perspective One. The second quote reflects Perspective Three.

Selected grammatical errors:
The essay doesn't have any notable grammatical errors.

Selected spelling errors:
- "prevelance" instead of "prevalence"
- "throuh" instead of "through"
- "demonstrats" instead of "demonstrates"

Vocabulary: The most sophisticated word in the essay is probably "prevelance [sic]."

Overview: This is the highest-scoring essay in the Red Book, and it follows the standards we discussed for high-scoring essays:

- The examples are directly related to the thesis, and each one supports that thesis in a different way.
- The essay discusses ideas related to two of the perspectives from the prompt, which meets the requirement we discussed in our training.

Note that this essay is about a half-page shorter than most top-scoring essays, and we recommend that you write much more than this on test day—see "A Quick Note on the Length of the Sample Essays" on page 566 for more on that.

The 5555-Scoring Essay about Intelligent Machines on act.org

Score: 5555, which works out to a 10 on the final ACT Writing scale

Length: 563 words (roughly 2.5 handwritten pages)

Thesis: The last two sentences of the first paragraph say,

> …some people are more wary of this popular trend of automating the workforce and question whether this progress is truely [sic] positive. Their concerns, though, are outweighed by the benefits these machines offer.

Support: The author cites the following supporting ideas and examples:

- The automotive industry uses machines to build cars with greater speed, precision, and efficiency than people could achieve.
- As the invention of human flight shows, some technological developments can open up unforeseen possibilities for humanity, and intelligent machines may be this kind of development.
- We may become less polite, but that small cost is outweighed by the efficiency of things like automated checkout.

Incorporating ideas from multiple perspectives: The essay includes the following quotes, which are heavily inspired by ideas from the prompt (which appears near the top of the relevant page on act.org):

- "…today's workforce no longer consists entirely of people."
- "…in the automotive industry, most of a car's individual components are manufactured by pre-programmed robots…"
- "Innovation and invention of new more intelligent machines can push us as humans toward new, unimagined possibilities."
- "[some people] argue that by not having to interact with fellow humans, we no longer are required to be courteous and have tolerance for others."

The first two quotes from the essay reflect ideas taken directly from the opening paragraph of the prompt, reflecting Perspective Two. The third idea above is from Perspective Three in the prompt, and the last idea is from Perspective One.

Selected grammatical errors:

- The writer repeatedly uses "which" in places where "that" is correct.
- "future for the human race" should be "future of the human race"

Selected spelling errors:

- "truely" instead of "truly"

Vocabulary: The most advanced word in the essay is probably "cumulative," which is a word many students will know because teachers use it to describe exams. None of the other words in the essay is particularly long or complicated.

Overview: This essay is straightforward and direct. Its examples mostly support the idea in the thesis. If it were handwritten, it would probably be around two-and-a-half pages, which makes it ideal in terms of length for the ACT Writing test. It borrows ideas heavily from the information provided in the prompt, including specific examples like the idea of robots building cars or the idea of automated checkout at a grocery store.

Once again, we see that a formulaic essay with sufficient length can earn a score in the top 2% or 3% of all essays. This essay was probably a 5 and not a 6 because the third paragraph isn't obviously connected to the thesis: it's not clear why the existence of the airline industry is evidence that the benefits of intelligent machines outweigh their drawbacks. (Note that this example *could* possibly have been part of a 6-scoring essay if the author had made a clearer connection between the birth of the airline industry and the advent of intelligent machines, maybe by pointing out similarities between the problems, difficulties, or benefits related to the airline industry and the problems, difficulties, or benefits related to intelligent machines! But the essay doesn't contain any such analysis, which means the third paragraph isn't obviously connected to the thesis, which, again, is probably why this essay got a 5 and not a 6.)

The 6666-Scoring Essay about Intelligent Machines on act.org

Score: 6666, which works out to a 12 on the final ACT Writing scale

Length: 513 words (a little over 2 handwritten pages)

Thesis: The last sentence of the first paragraph says,

> Without caution and deliberation, replacing the natural with the mechanical would undoubtedly be disasterous [sic].

Support: The author cites the following supporting ideas and examples:

- Replacing humans with robots will leave the humans without jobs, ultimately making it impossible for them to buy things.
- Interacting with machines instead of people causes people to become rude and uncultured.
- Innovations in computing come too quickly for people to prepare for them.

Incorporating ideas from multiple perspectives: The essay includes the following quotes, which are heavily inspired by ideas from the prompt (which appears near the top of the relevant page on act.org):

- "…humans would surely be replaced…"
- "In a culture saturated with automation, we get used to treating machines rudely, and we begin to treat each other rudely."
- "We must figure out how to handle negative societal and cultural consequences…"

The first quote above is part of the first body paragraph in the essay, which contrasts with Perspective Two. The second quote is from the second body paragraph, which comes from Perspective One. The third quote is from the last body paragraph, which contradicts Perspective Three.

Selected grammatical errors:

- The phrase "to seriously degrade [sic]" is a split infinitive.

Selected spelling errors:

- "disasterous" should be "disastrous"
- "intolerence" should be "intolerance"

Vocabulary: None of the words in the essay are extremely advanced; the most advanced word is probably "incivility."

Overview: This essay is a great example to follow on test day:

- It's long enough to take up more than two handwritten pages.

- The thesis is clearly stated, and each of the examples clearly demonstrates in its own way that the thesis is true.
- Many of the key ideas are taken from the prompt, and each of the perspectives is addressed.
- The writing is solid and direct, without trying to be flashy or use exotic vocabulary for its own sake.

Notice that, like the other 6-scoring example essay we analyzed on page 567 of this Black Book, this essay is slightly shorter than the 5-scoring essay for the same prompt. See "A Quick Note on the Length of the Sample Essays" on page 566 for more on that.

ACT Writing Test (The ACT Essay) Quick Summary

This is a one-page summary of the major concepts you'll need to keep in mind when addressing the ACT Essay. Use it to evaluate your comprehension or jog your memory. For a more in-depth treatment of these ideas, see the rest of this section.

The Big Secret: The ACT Essay is just as standardized as the rest of the ACT, and if we can imitate other high-scoring essays, we can get a high score, too. It's all about giving the graders exactly what they're trained to look for in a high-scoring essay.

The prompt will be something relatively relatable, and will often deal with some aspect of new technology and/or education. Keep this in mind on test day so you're ready to come up with related material to support your position.

You need to make it to the third page. High-scoring essays are almost always longer essays. If you can make it onto the third page, you greatly increase the likelihood of scoring a 5 or 6 out of 6 on the essay.

Your thesis must be stated clearly, usually as the last sentence in the first paragraph. One of the most important factors in your score is how well your examples and reasons support your thesis. If your thesis isn't stated clearly, it's difficult for the grader to tell if you did a good job supporting it.

Support your position with reasons or examples (even made-up ones) that address at least two of the three provided perspectives. Your reasons or examples can be personal, academic, historical, etc.—all that matters is that they would support your position *if they were true*. So you can use examples and reasons that actually *are* true, or you can just make them up. You can address a perspective by agreeing with it, disagreeing with it, or offering your own take on some idea mentioned in the perspective.

Some imperfect grammar is okay. Don't waste time on thorough proofreading. You'll probably need to spend almost all of the allotted time on writing in order to make it to the third page.

Don't go out of your way to use obscure vocabulary words. Stick with words you feel comfortable using; if you try to inject a big word you're not comfortable with, you run the risk of sounding awkward, which can hurt your score if the grader notices it. Remember that the top-scoring example essays from the Red Book don't tend to use advanced vocabulary words.

There's no required format, but you should probably follow the 5-paragraph format we talked about.

Don't worry about being interesting or funny. The grader has to read your essay no matter how boring it is, and top-scoring ACT Essays are rarely interesting. Instead, focus on including the key features we've discussed in this Black Book: length, a clear thesis, relevant reasoning and examples that address at least two of the three perspectives, and so on.

Here's the general ACT Essay process that I recommend:

1. Watch the clock.
2. Read the prompt and take a position.
3. Come up with roughly 3 reasons or examples to support your thesis.
4. Write your introduction (including your thesis).
5. Write your three supporting paragraphs, using appropriate examples/reasoning for each.
6. Write your conclusion.

Go back through this section of the Black Book to see demonstrations of these ideas, especially in my analyses of the sample essays from the Red Book and ACT.org, and in my sample ACT Essay.

Part 11: Closing Thoughts

By now, we've covered everything you need to know for test day. You've seen how the ACT is designed, you know how to exploit that design to maximize your score, and you've seen these ideas applied to three official ACT Practice Tests from ACT, Inc. Now we'll close out this Black Book with some thoughts and observations that may be helpful for some readers . . . including guidance on how you can follow us for more advice on test-taking, admissions, lifestyle design, and other challenges facing high school and college students.

In this part of the Black Book, you'll learn the following:

- answers to frequently asked questions relating to the ACT and the process of training for it
- the critical importance of practicing the skills you learn in this book
- what to do when things go wrong in your approach to a real ACT question
- how to shoot for an elite score, or even a perfect score
- what to do if American English isn't your first language
- why every question I've ever been asked about the ACT has basically the same answer

Frequently Asked Questions

I thought it would be a good idea to address questions I often hear from clients and readers.

General Questions

How much time do I need to prepare for the ACT?

There's no universal answer to this question—some students will feel comfortable after studying for only a couple of days, while others will practice for a couple of months before they feel they've got the hang of it. Ideally, you should probably start at least a couple of months out from the test date to give yourself some extra time, but if you have less time than that you can still see great improvement. Try to think less about "putting in the time," and think more about developing a better understanding of the test with each practice session. See "Figuring out your Schedule" on page 32 of this Black Book for more.

What's the best way to get started?

The best way to get started is just to read the material in this Black Book in the order it's presented. You'll start out with some general information about the test, then you'll learn the strategies for a given section in the abstract, then you'll see them in action against real ACT practice questions (be sure to follow along in your copy of the Red Book).

Of course, after that, it's incredibly important that you try these techniques yourself on real practice ACT questions, and then carefully review your practice. For more on that, see the section called "How to Train for the ACT—Mastering the Ideas in this Book" on page 29 of this Black Book.

How did you learn these strategies?

I developed these strategies through careful analysis of the ACT over the course of many years. I've been teaching them now for decades through a variety of media, and in that time I've worked to refine the techniques—as well as the way I teach them—to make the whole process as effective and efficient as possible. To learn more about my background, see www.TestingIsEasy.com.

Do these strategies work on the SAT?

The SAT and the ACT are fundamentally similar: they're both internationally administered standardized tests that primarily evaluate basic reading and math skills in ways that differ from those used by "normal" classroom tests. In fact, many of the questions that appear on either test could also appear on the other one, because many of the rules on the two tests allow the same types of questions in many situations. (There are exceptions to this, of course—each test also has question types that don't even appear on the other test, for one thing. But the principles underlying the design of individual questions on both tests are largely similar.)

Still, it's important to realize that specific question types that might seem to be common to both tests are not perfectly identical! Each test has its own spin on reading, writing, math, and science (the SAT doesn't have a dedicated Science section, but it incorporates science-based passages into its other sections). So while all the underlying principles that you'll learn in this Black Book apply to both tests—the idea of testing simple concepts in unusual ways, the highly standardized structure, and so on—the specific strategies for specific question types aren't completely identical. If you're familiar with my SAT preparation materials, you may find that some of the more general information in this book is similar to the general information in my SAT Prep Black Book, though the specific details related to the question types may vary quite a bit.

Some students are able to take the fundamentals of my approach to the ACT and modify them appropriately to be used on the SAT. If you'd like to test that out, simply try to attack some real SAT practice questions from the College Board after you've become comfortable with the strategies in this Black Book. If you find you can apply them effectively, great. If not, then you'll probably want to use some SAT-specific training materials. I recommend my *SAT Prep Black Book, Second Edition* for that—but, of course, I'm biased :)

What if I want to score a 36? (Or a 22? Or 33? Or a 28? Or . . . ?)

There's a common misconception that a student who wants to achieve a certain score should follow a certain set of strategies, while a student with a different target score should use different strategies. In reality, the test's design is constant, so you should use the same set of strategies, and the same basic approach, no matter what your target score may be. The only difference is that you'll need to be more accurate in your execution if you want to reach a higher target score.

For more, see "How Well can I do on the ACT?" on page 27 of this Black Book, and "Shooting for a 36" on page 577.

What if I can't get a strategy to work?

At some point, almost everybody—myself included—runs into an official ACT question that they just can't seem to solve with the normal strategies. Although this sort of thing is always aggravating, it can be a very beneficial experience if you approach it in the right way. When you run into a problem like this, the very first thing you should do is confirm that you're working with a real ACT question written by ACT, Inc. It's very important to work only with real practice questions from the test-maker, not from some third-party company. If the question isn't written by the test-maker, then the strategies from this Black Book might not work against it, since fake tests usually don't follow the rules that the real test does.

After that, go back and make sure that you've read the answer key correctly. Many times I've talked to students who were completely baffled by a question they got wrong that they were sure they had solved correctly, only to have them realize afterwards that they *had* solved it correctly in the first place and had only misread the answer key.

If you know you're working with a real ACT question, and you know you've read the answer key correctly, and you're sure you can't figure out the question, then you're in a frustrating situation—but it's also potentially a very helpful situation.

Let me explain why.

When you find yourself facing a question that seems to break all the rules, you have to make sure you don't get frustrated and assume that the rules must not work, or that the ACT must have messed up on this question, or that something else out of your control is going on. If you let yourself get frustrated, you'll probably give up, and ultimately your score will suffer. Instead, take the time to understand each question that frustrates you. Figure out what's going on with it, where you went wrong in your initial approach, and *what you can do to avoid getting stuck like that in the future.*

The more you do this, the more you'll begin to understand how the test really works and how it's written, which will make it harder and harder for the test-maker to trick you in the future. That's why getting stuck on a hard question can actually be a huge opportunity for improvement: since the test is standardized, every time you get unstuck from a difficult situation is a time that helps you avoid those kinds of situations on test day.

See "Understand Your Mistakes" on page 34 of this Black Book and "When Things Go Wrong" on page 576 for more.

I got a question wrong, but my answer is better than the choice the ACT says is right—now what?

One big mistake that untrained test-takers make when they approach tests like the ACT is going through all the questions and just looking for the answer choices that seem best *to them.*

But it's very important for us test-takers to understand that the ACT doesn't care what we think. At all.

The ACT has its own system for deciding which answer choices satisfy its requirements, and which ones don't. For that reason, we have to stop looking at answer choices and thinking, "Which one do I like best?" Instead, we should think, "Which of these choices fulfills the ACT's requirements for a correct answer to this type of question?"

If you frequently find yourself feeling like your favorite answer choices are better than the ones the ACT says are right, take some time to review the advice in this Black Book and get a refresher on exactly what the ACT wants to see in correct answers to that type of question.

Which practice books should I buy?

This book was written so that the only other ACT book you'd need would be the "Red Book"—*The Official ACT Prep Guide.* See "Using the Official ACT Prep Guide (the "Red Book")" on page 21 of this Black Book for more.

English Questions

I found a correct answer that doesn't follow the rules of grammar I learned in school. How can that be?

Remember that the only thing that matters on the ACT is what the people who make the ACT say is right. In the context of ACT English, there are some grammar rules that the ACT likes to follow that may be different from the rules you're used to, particularly where punctuation is concerned.

Don't worry! The grammar rules used in the ACT English section must be standardized, just like every other aspect of the test, so we can learn these rules and answer the questions accordingly. Don't be shocked if you come across a correct answer on the ACT that seems to break the grammar rules you're used to, or an incorrect answer that seems to follow them. Always learn what the ACT rewards and punishes, and answer questions accordingly. For more on this, check out "Part 9: English Test Training and Walkthroughs" which begins on page 410 of this Black Book.

Math Questions

Which math formulas are most important for the ACT?

If I had to pick a single most important formula, it would probably be the Pythagorean Theorem, just because it shows up a lot in one form or another on the ACT. Beyond that, basic geometric formulas and rules (like the ones related to triangles, rectangles, circles, complementary and supplementary angles, and so on) also seem very common.

Still, you need to keep a few things in mind:

1. No matter what, you'll still need to be familiar with everything in the ACT Math Toolbox (pages 113-143 of this Black Book) if you want to be ready for anything you might encounter in an ACT Math question.

2. Frequently, just knowing a formula isn't going to be enough to get you the right answer to an ACT Math problem—you'll also need to be familiar with the special characteristics of ACT Math questions, and you may have to get a little "creative" in your approach to a question.

For further ACT Math training, take a look at "Part 7: Math Test Training and Walkthroughs" on page 110 of this Black Book.

Which type of calculator should I use?

This is a common question with a simple answer: use the type of calculator that you feel most comfortable with (assuming it's allowed, of course; most calculators are, but you should check to be sure). Remember that the most difficult part of finding the correct answer to an ACT Math question often lies in figuring out how to set up the problem, which is something a calculator can't do. The bottom line is that the most important part of your approach to this section is your own training, not your calculator.

For more on specific ways to use calculators on the ACT Math section, see "Using a Calculator" on page 158 of this Black Book, as well as the walkthroughs in the Math section of this Black Book, on pages 162-328.

I tried to find the answer based solely on patterns in the choices, and it didn't work. Why not?

Always remember that patterns in the answer choices are simply hints at the issues we can expect to be important to the solution for that question. They'll *often* point to a likely correct answer, *but not always*. For that reason, you should never rely completely on answer-choice patterns in determining the correct answer to any question, unless you've given up trying to answer the question with math and you just want to guess (as we discussed in "The General Game Plan for Attacking a Section of the ACT on Test Day" on page 37 of this Black Book).

The best way to use these answer-choice patterns is to let them guide your analysis if you're not sure what the best approach to a question might be, and/or to check your answer once you've finished the problem to make sure you didn't make a mistake. Read more on that on page 148 of this Black Book.

Reading Questions

You say the correct answer to each question is always spelled out on the page, but I found a question where it isn't. What does that mean?

You may remember that earlier we talked about how the ACT tries to be tricky, and to make questions seem less straightforward than they actually are. I definitely know what it feels like to look at a question and think you're certain that the answer isn't right there on the page, but this issue is always the result of an error made by the test-taker (that's you or me) and not an error made by the test-maker. (Of course, as always, this only applies if you're using real ACT practice questions made by the test-maker. If you're using questions written by some other company, then those aren't real ACT questions, and they can't be expected to work the same way as the real thing.)

The first thing you need to do is step back and accept that the error must be on your part, and realize that the answer to your problem must be somewhere in the passage, question, or answer choice. Then, try to clear your mind of anything you've thought about the question so far, and take a fresh look at it. Read the passage carefully, read the question carefully, and read all the answer choices carefully, and do your best to find the place in the text that spells out the answer choice—it's in there.

See "Understand Your Mistakes" on page 34 of this Black Book and "When Things Go Wrong" on page 576 for more.

Science Questions

How am I supposed to get a good score on the ACT Science section, if I've never studied most of the scientific topics that appear on the section?

The ACT is often not what it seems to be—and the ACT Science section is a prime example of this. Although we normally think of a science test as something that rewards us for knowing scientific concepts beforehand, we'll see that almost every ACT Science question will ask about information that's provided by the test itself, right there on the page in front of you, in one form or another. On the rare occasions when you do need outside scientific knowledge, that knowledge will be basic—usually the sort of thing you might learn in elementary school or middle school. For more on this, see ""Science" on the ACT Science Section: What You Need to Know, and What You Don't" on page 331 of this Black Book.

You Have to Practice

> *Constant practice devoted to one subject often prevails over both ability and skill.*
> Cicero

This is an idea that's come up a few times already, but now that you've actually read through all the training material, we need to talk about it one more time:

You've got to practice.

By now, you've learned my approach to every part of the ACT. Hopefully you feel like you've got a much better handle on the whole thing, and hopefully you're less worried than you were when you started, and hopefully you're going to get the score you need.

But before that happens, you've got to practice.

I always like to say that getting better at the ACT is a lot more like training for a sport or learning to play a musical instrument than like preparing for a "normal" high school test.

You're not just memorizing a list of facts or concepts that you have to spit back out on test day. You're developing a skill, and that means you actually have to sit down and do it for a while before you can expect to execute properly when it counts.

Would you feel comfortable suiting up for a football game, or walking out on stage for a piano recital, just because you read a book about football, or about playing the piano? Of course not! You wouldn't do either of those things unless you'd spent some time honing your skills. The ACT is the exact same way.

Most people who are getting ready to take a standardized test have at least a few important misconceptions about the test. Often, when I work with people, and I explain what's wrong with those misconceptions, and then we talk about how the test really works, it's like a light bulb turning on in their heads—things that didn't make any sense before suddenly do make sense.

That's great, but it can create a false sense of confidence. It's easy to look at a couple of examples from real ACT questions and feel like you understand what's going on, but that doesn't necessarily mean you'll automatically answer every future ACT question correctly without practicing.

In fact, the first practice questions you look at after you read this book might seem *more* challenging than you expect, because you'll have to work them out on your own, instead of just reading and understanding my analysis. You're probably going to get frustrated. But you simply have to stick with it. Just keep at your practice, analyze your mistakes until you understand them, and re-read parts of this Black Book (or even the whole thing) as necessary. You have to put in the time so you can learn to recognize the patterns we've talked about without me pointing them out to you for each new question, because I won't be able to do that for you on test day :)

Of course, learning the approach in this Black Book will take a lot less time and cause much less aggravation than following the typical approach to the ACT, and your results should also be better if you apply the methods correctly—but you'll still need to spend *some* time practicing.

You are now armed with the knowledge you need to beat the ACT. So make sure you invest the time to apply that knowledge to the real ACT practice questions in your copy of the Red Book, so you'll be able to give your best possible performance on test day.

When Things Go Wrong

If things go wrong, don't go with them.
Roger Babson

Everyone makes mistakes on the ACT at some point, because the test is long and repetitive, and we're only human.

Of course, one major goal of your training should be to minimize those mistakes in the first place as much as possible. But another major goal should be to develop the habit of looking out for mistakes *after* you've made them, so you can correct them.

When your training tells you something about a question just doesn't feel quite right, it's important not to ignore that instinct. Instead, you should re-evaluate your approach to the question until you understand how it follows the rules and patterns of the ACT's design that you've learned in this Black Book. Of course, this is what you should do during your practice—if it's test day, you should skip the question, work on the rest of the section, and come back to it later.

Here are some guidelines to help remind you what you might have overlooked when you can't figure out the answer to a question. I've broken them up by section. (If you'd like more a detailed refresher on the best ways to approach a given section of the ACT, you should refer back to that part of this Black Book for instructions and examples.)

Reading

- Are you reading the wrong part of the passage? (For more, see "ACT Reading Answer-Choice Pattern 6: Wrong Part of the Passage" on page 54 of this Black Book, and "How to Read Passages on The ACT Reading Section" on page 55.)
- Have you misunderstood, misread, or overlooked a word or phrase in the question, answer choice, or passage? (See "ACT Reading Answer-Choice Pattern 5: Off by One or Two Words" on page 54 of this Black Book.)
- Have you made an assumption that isn't actually restated or demonstrated by the text? (See "The Big Secret of ACT Reading" on page 49 of this Black Book for more.)

Math

- Did you misread the question, answer choice, or diagram? (See "The Big Secret of ACT Math" on page 111 of this Black Book for more.)
- Did you make any calculation mistakes? (Remember that it's still possible to make a mistake when you use a calculator! See "Using a Calculator" on page 158 of this Black Book for more, and "Hidden Pattern 5: Easy Calculation Mistake" on page 151 as well.)
- Could the question involve a math concept you haven't considered? (Remember that the question might involve concepts that are directly related to the concepts in the question and the answer choices, but the question can't require you to know calculus or advanced trigonometry or statistics—see "ACT Math Rule 4: Limited Subject Matter" on page 146 of this Black Book, and the ACT Math Toolbox on pages 113-143.)

Science

- Did you misread the question, answer choice, or data? (See "The Big Secret of ACT Science" on page 329 of this Black Book for more.)
- Did you overlook a label on an axis or column heading? (See "ACT Science Rule 2: Labels are Important" on page 340 of this Black Book.)
- Have you tried to rely on your own advanced scientific knowledge, rather than drawing your answers from the data? (Remember that a only small number of questions on the ACT Science section might require relatively basic knowledge of science, but nothing too sophisticated—see ""Science" on the ACT Science Section: What You Need to Know, and What You Don't" on page 331 of this Black Book for more.)

English

- Is it possible that a sentence before or after the underlined part of the passage might contain a parallel phrase that indicates which answer choice is correct? (See "Special Technique: Considering Parallelism when Answering ACT English Questions" on page 440 of this Black Book for more.)
- Is this one of the ACT English questions that involves reading comprehension rules? (See "ACT English Question Groups" on page 413 of this Black Book for more.)

Shooting for a 36

Trifles make perfection, and perfection is no trifle.
Michelangelo Buonarroti

If you've read the whole Black Book up to this point, you've already seen all the material you'll need to master in order to score a 36 on the ACT. In other words, as I've said before, there are no special, "secret" techniques or strategies for a perfect score: getting a perfect score is just a matter of perfecting the ACT strategies we've already discussed until you execute them almost flawlessly.

Still, there are a few topics we can discuss that can help you to have the right attitude in your preparation if you hope to get a perfect score on the ACT. Let's talk about them now.

Confront Problem Areas

Imagine you're looking at a list of 100 ACT questions, and you have to answer any one question on the list correctly. Almost anyone could do that—if you only had to answer one question correctly, you could just look through them until you found the one you were most comfortable with, and then answer that one.

Even if you had to answer any 10 ACT questions from the list correctly, you could probably do that without much difficulty, because you'd have the freedom to choose the 10 questions you found easiest.

But what if you'd already answered 90 out of those 100 ACT questions? At that point, you probably would have picked all the easy ones already. That means that answering each of the remaining 10 questions correctly would become increasingly hard, because the questions that are left will be the more challenging ones for you—the ones you chose to avoid earlier.

The bottom line here is that answering every single ACT question (or nearly every question) correctly will require you to confront every single weakness and problem area you have when it comes to the ACT. Even those who only want to score well above average can still miss a handful of challenging questions and do quite well—but you won't have that option if you want a perfect score.

As I said earlier, there's no special way to approach this issue except to use the same strategies we've already discussed. It's just useful to be aware of this challenge ahead of time—most people have to work harder to improve from a 33 to a 36 than they do to improve from a 23 to a 26.

Practice Intelligently

If you're serious about getting a 36, you're probably a pretty good student. Often, being a good student involves long hours and an ability to keep working when your assignments get tedious.

When you train for the ACT, though, you need to keep in mind that just putting in long hours won't cut it (in fact, for some students, long hours of ACT preparation are neither necessary nor helpful). Instead, you need to focus on making your practice time count. That means paying careful attention to your mistakes, and trying to figure out why they happen, so you can avoid them in the future. Look out for the issues that give you trouble, and think about ways to improve in those areas.

There are some academic situations where large quantities of mindless work can be beneficial. The ACT isn't one of them. Make sure you're engaged in your ACT practice (especially when you *review* your practice), or else you'll probably be wasting time.

Review Your Practice

This concept of review is so critical that it still deserves its own separate heading, even though it just came up in the previous sentence. You simply must review your practice work if you want to get a perfect score. Otherwise, your practice won't help much.

Have the Right Attitude

If you want a perfect score on the ACT, you've got to have the right mindset. Decide ahead of time to keep your frustration to a minimum, and not to blame other people when you run into difficulty. If you really are committed to this challenge, then you also need to accept full responsibility for the results. Don't make excuses—even if they're valid, they don't change anything.

Summary

Getting a perfect score on the ACT is hard. Executing flawlessly on the test doesn't really require any advanced knowledge or extreme intelligence, but it does require you to go through several hours of tedious test-taking without letting more than maybe a couple of mistakes get past you.

In this Black Book, you have all the information you need to get any score you want on the ACT, if you'll pay enough attention to detail and apply yourself diligently enough. All that's left is for you to train and practice with real ACT practice questions until you can apply these strategies consistently and without error. Commit to your goal and maintain a good attitude.

Good luck!

If American English isn't Your First Language . . .

The conquest of learning is achieved through the knowledge of languages.

Roger Bacon

Here are my general recommendations for foreign clients if their English isn't perfect.

1. Start with the questions you can already answer.

If you're able to read this book, and you're planning to take the ACT, you obviously have some English ability already. Start by using that existing ability to answer as many questions as possible without focusing specifically on improving your American English skills. These questions could potentially be on any section of the ACT, so just try out some different kinds of practice questions and figure out where you can already succeed with your current level of English. It's not going to be worthwhile for you to put significant effort into improving your English until you're getting the most out of what you already know, so do your best to learn the strategies from this Black Book and apply them as best you can before you start focusing on your language skills.

2. Next, learn "testing" vocabulary.

When you're ready to focus on your American English, try to learn the words the ACT uses to frame the actual questions you have to answer, because you're likely to see those words come up frequently on the test in the future. For example, the "testing" vocabulary words on the Reading and English sections could include things like "characterize" or "conclusion." On the Math and Science sections, "testing" vocabulary could include words like "experiment" or "variable." To figure out which words to study, just work with a lot of real ACT practice questions from the Red Book and make a note of the words you don't know that frequently appear in the prompts of ACT questions. These are the words you need to learn, because you're more likely to see them on test day.

3. Don't worry—nobody else knows all the science vocabulary either.

As you prepare for the ACT Science section, you'll probably notice a lot of large words and unusual phrases that you're not familiar with. But the odds are good that native speakers of American English don't know them, either.

As we discussed in "Dealing with strange terms and units" on page 330 of this Black Book, the ACT loves to include scientific-sounding terms like "vermicompost" and "baryon" that are either explained in the text, or irrelevant to the question. In either situation, you can answer the question correctly without knowing the phrase beforehand. Other than that, handle the Science section like any other part of the ACT, and just take note of the words that come up over and over again from section to section. Don't focus on learning the specialized words that only come up in a particular passage and then never get repeated in other passages. (Of course, if you want to learn them to enrich your English, you should feel free to do that—I'm just saying that you shouldn't waste time on those words if your only goal is to improve on the ACT, because your time would be better spent elsewhere.)

4. Take a look at ACT style and ACT grammar.

Once you've improved your ACT-taking skills and learned the ACT-specific vocabulary you need, you should learn the ACT's standards for style, grammar, and punctuation on the English section, which are laid out on pages 418-438 of this Black Book.

(It's important to make a distinction between the rules of modern American English and the things that are rewarded on the ACT English section, because the rules that sentences need to follow on the ACT aren't necessarily the rules that today's students learn when they study English.)

5. Find out if you need to take the ACT Writing test.

A lot of colleges don't care about the ACT Writing Test (also known as the ACT Essay), so you'll want to find out if your target schools require you to submit an ACT Writing score. If they do, then you'll need to write the best essay you can, of course.

If you need to write the ACT Essay, stick with sentence structures that you feel comfortable with, and use words whose meanings you're sure of. A lot of people try to impress the ACT Essay graders with big words or fancy sentences, but that doesn't work, as we discussed in "Creativity and reader engagement don't matter" on page 557 of this Black Book. It's much more important to stick with what you know and write in a way that sounds as natural and native as possible.

Conclusion

I know it's frustrating to look at an ACT question and feel like the language barrier is the only reason you can't answer it. But you have to remember that the ACT isn't like other tests, which means you can't prepare for it the same way you'd prepare for other tests. If your goal is to get the highest score you possibly can—and that really should be your goal, of course—then you'll probably have the easiest time picking up extra points by prioritizing things the way I've laid out here. Try to follow the advice in this section, and the strategies in this Black Book, to make the most of the English you know. Good luck!

Parting Advice

There is nothing impossible to one who will try.

Alexander The Great

By now you know everything you need to know to be able to get a great score on the ACT. You just need to practice these techniques and get comfortable using them against real ACT questions from the Red Book.

Let me offer you an important piece of advice to keep in mind as you do that practice.

The ACT is a highly detail-oriented test. It's much more detail-oriented than other aspects of your educational experience, and that's why so many people struggle with it. Paying careful attention to repetitive, detailed questions for hours at a time just isn't something most test-takers are used to doing.

Because of this, even trained test-takers will have lapses sometimes. I even do it myself, occasionally. When my students make these kinds of mistakes, I often hear something like this:

I found a question that doesn't follow the ACT rules you told me about. What should I do?

The first thing you need to check is that you're working with an actual ACT question written by ACT, Inc. Of course, what we've learned in this Black Book can only be reliably applied to real ACT questions, not fake questions written by other test-prep companies. Fake questions you get from other companies may not follow the same rules as official ACT questions.

But if you are indeed looking at a real ACT question, and if you are indeed familiar with the concepts in this Black Book, then the explanation for your difficulty is that you've overlooked or misunderstood some detail from the question, or the answer choice, and that's the reason the question doesn't seem to follow the normal ACT rules.

I know it can be frustrating to hear this, and it can be even more frustrating to spend a lot of time trying to hunt down your mistake on a question, but it's important not to forget the ACT's rules when you feel stuck. Don't give up!

Of course, it's also important to remember that you may be better off temporarily skipping a question if you're stuck on it, so you can focus on other questions in the section that are easier for you. Then you can come back for the troublesome questions later and see if you can figure out which detail you've missed, as we discussed in "The General Game Plan for Attacking a Section of the ACT on Test Day" on page 37 of this Black Book.

So please, when you're practicing these methods on real ACT practice questions, and you see something that makes you doubt the training I've given you, don't worry. It happens to everybody once in a while. The important thing—and it's very, very important—is that you take the time to figure out what's going on in that question, so you can choose an answer that correctly follows the ACT's rules.

On the ACT, as with most things in life, you tend to make the best progress when you're faced with the biggest challenges, and you overcome them.

You can do it.

Thanks for Reading!

I hope you've enjoyed learning my strategies for beating the ACT, and that you feel much better prepared for test day. Please be sure to spend some time practicing what you've learned in this Black Book on real ACT practice questions from the Red Book!

I know that preparing for a test like the ACT is a huge deal, and it means a lot to me that tens of thousands of students over the years have trusted me at such an important and stressful time in their lives.

If this book has helped you, I would really appreciate it if you could tell your friends about it, or even go on Amazon and leave an honest review, if you'd like to do that.

Thanks again for reading, and I wish you the best of luck—with your preparation, and with everything else in your life.

Made in the USA
Columbia, SC
11 September 2021